HORNGREN'S
Accounting
THE FINANCIAL CHAPTERS

THIRTEENTH EDITION

Tracie Miller-Nobles
Austin Community College

Brenda Mattison
Tri-County Technical College

Please contact https://support.pearson.com/getsupport/s/ with any queries on this content.
Cover Image by anttoniart/Shutterstock; suns07butterfly/Shutterstock vovan/Shutterstock

Microsoft and/or its respective suppliers make no representations about the suitability of the information contained in the documents and related graphics published as part of the services for any purpose. All such documents and related graphics are provided "as is" without warranty of any kind. Microsoft and/or its respective suppliers hereby disclaim all warranties and conditions with regard to this information, including all warranties and conditions of merchantability, whether express, implied or statutory, fitness for a particular purpose, title and non-infringement. In no event shall Microsoft and/or its respective suppliers be liable for any special, indirect or consequential damages or any damages whatsoever resulting from loss of use, data or profits, whether in an action of contract, negligence or other tortious action, arising out of or in connection with the use or performance of information available from the services.

The documents and related graphics contained herein could include technical inaccuracies or typographical errors. Changes are periodically added to the information herein. Microsoft and/or its respective suppliers may make improvements and/or changes in the product(s) and/or the program(s) described herein at any time. Partial screen shots may be viewed in full within the software version specified.

Microsoft® and Windows® are registered trademarks of the Microsoft Corporation in the U.S.A. and other countries. This book is not sponsored or endorsed by or affiliated with the Microsoft Corporation.

Copyright © 2021, 2018, 2016 by Pearson Education, Inc. or its affiliates, 221 River Street, Hoboken, NJ 07030. All Rights Reserved. Manufactured in the United States of America. This publication is protected by copyright, and permission should be obtained from the publisher prior to any prohibited reproduction, storage in a retrieval system, or transmission in any form or by any means, electronic, mechanical, photocopying, recording, or otherwise. For information regarding permissions, request forms, and the appropriate contacts within the Pearson Education Global Rights and Permissions department, please visit www.pearsoned.com/permissions/.

Acknowledgments of third-party content appear on the appropriate page within the text -OR- on pages P-1 and P-2, which constitutes an extension of this copyright page.

PEARSON, ALWAYS LEARNING, and MYLAB are exclusive trademarks owned by Pearson Education, Inc. or its affiliates in the U.S. and/or other countries.

Unless otherwise indicated herein, any third-party trademarks, logos, or icons that may appear in this work are the property of their respective owners, and any references to third-party trademarks, logos, icons, or other trade dress are for demonstrative or descriptive purposes only. Such references are not intended to imply any sponsorship, endorsement, authorization, or promotion of Pearson's products by the owners of such marks, or any relationship between the owner and Pearson Education, Inc., or its affiliates, authors, licensees, or distributors.

Cataloging-in-Publication Data is on file at the Library of Congress

Access Code Card
ISBN-10:   0-13-616175-8
ISBN-13: 978-0-13-616175-2

Rental
ISBN-10:   0-13-616218-5
ISBN-13: 978-0-13-616218-6

Instructor's Review Copy
ISBN-10:   0-13-662852-4
ISBN-13: 978-0-13-662852-1

12 2022

About the Authors

Tracie L. Miller-Nobles, CPA, is an associate professor at Austin Community College. She has teaching experience at the community college and university level. Prof. Miller-Nobles received her master's degree in accounting from Texas A&M University and is working on her doctoral degree in Adult Education also from Texas A&M University. Her research interest includes financial literacy education, adult learning theories, and online learning. She has public accounting experience with Deloitte Tax LLP.

Prof. Miller-Nobles is on the Board of Directors for the American Accounting Association (AAA) as Director-Focusing on Members. She has served in leadership roles for AAA's Teaching, Learning, and Curriculum section and AAA's Two Year College section and was a member of the Pathway's Commission on Accounting Higher Education. Prof. Miller-Nobles is also on the Board of Directors for Teachers of Accounting at Two Year Colleges (TACTYC) as Secretary/Webmaster. She is an active member of the American Institute of Certified Public Accountants (AICPA) Consumer Financial Education Advocates committee. At the state level, she serves on the Relations with Educational Institutes for the Texas Society of Certified Public Accountants (TXCPA).

Tracie has received several teaching and professional awards including the AAA J. Michael and Mary Anne Cook Prize, TXCPA Outstanding Accounting Educator, TXCPA Rising Star, and the TXCPA Austin Chapter CPA of the Year. In her spare time, Tracie enjoys spending time with her husband, Kevin, his three kids, Caleb, Josh, and Meggie, her parents, Kipp and Sylvia, and sister, Michelle. She believes that camping and hiking is restorative and calming and that life was meant for good friends and great adventures. Tracie has been mentored by many wonderful colleagues and inspired by her students.

Brenda L. Mattison, CMA, has a bachelor's degree in education and a master's degree in accounting, both from Clemson University. She is currently an Accounting Instructor at Tri-County Technical College in Pendleton, South Carolina. Brenda previously served as Accounting Program Coordinator at TCTC and has prior experience teaching accounting at Robeson Community College, Lumberton, North Carolina; University of South Carolina Upstate, Spartanburg, South Carolina; and Rasmussen Business College, Eagan, Minnesota. She also has accounting work experience in retail and manufacturing businesses and is a Certified Management Accountant.

Brenda is a member of the American Accounting Association, Institute of Management Accountants, South Carolina Technical Education Association, and Teachers of Accounting at Two Year Colleges. She is currently serving on the Board of Directors as Vice President of Conference Administration of Teachers of Accounting at Two Year Colleges.

Brenda previously served as Faculty Fellow at Tri-County Technical College. She has presented at state, regional, and national conferences on topics including active learning, course development, and student engagement.

In her spare time, Brenda enjoys reading and spending time with her family. She is also an active volunteer in the community, serving her church and other organizations.

Brief Contents

Chapter 1	Accounting and the Business Environment	1-1
Chapter 2	Recording Business Transactions	2-1
Chapter 3	The Adjusting Process	3-1
Chapter 4	Completing the Accounting Cycle	4-1
Chapter 5	Merchandising Operations	5-1
Chapter 6	Merchandise Inventory	6-1
Chapter 7	Accounting Information Systems	7-1
Chapter 8	Internal Control and Cash	8-1
Chapter 9	Receivables	9-1
Chapter 10	Plant Assets, Natural Resources, and Intangibles	10-1
Chapter 11	Current Liabilities and Payroll	11-1
Chapter 12	Partnerships	12-1
Chapter 13	Corporations	13-1
Chapter 14	Long-Term Liabilities	14-1
Chapter 15	Investments	15-1
Chapter 16	The Statement of Cash Flows	16-1
Chapter 17	Financial Statement Analysis	17-1

APPENDIX A—Present Value Tables and Future Value Tables — A-1
GLOSSARY — G-1
INDEX — I-1
PHOTO CREDITS — P-1

Contents

CHAPTER 1
Accounting and the Business Environment 1-1

Why Is Accounting Important? 1-2
- Decision Makers: The Users of Accounting Information 1-3
- Accounting Matters 1-4

What Are the Organizations and Rules That Govern Accounting? 1-6
- Governing Organizations 1-6
- Generally Accepted Accounting Principles 1-6
- The Economic Entity Assumption 1-7
- The Cost Principle 1-8
- The Going Concern Assumption 1-8
- The Monetary Unit Assumption 1-8
- International Financial Reporting Standards 1-8
- Ethics in Accounting and Business 1-9

What Is the Accounting Equation? 1-10
- Assets 1-10
- Liabilities 1-10
- Equity 1-10

How Do You Analyze a Transaction? 1-11
- Transaction Analysis for Smart Touch Learning 1-12

How Do You Prepare Financial Statements? 1-17
- Income Statement 1-18
- Statement of Owner's Equity 1-18
- Balance Sheet 1-19
- Statement of Cash Flows 1-20

How Do You Use Financial Statements to Evaluate Business Performance? 1-22
- Kohl's Corporation 1-22
- Return on Assets (ROA) 1-22

■ Review 1-24
■ Assess Your Progress 1-30
■ Critical Thinking 1-50

CHAPTER 2
Recording Business Transactions 2-1

What Is an Account? 2-2
- Assets 2-2
- Liabilities 2-2
- Equity 2-4
- Chart of Accounts 2-4
- Ledger 2-5

What Is Double-Entry Accounting? 2-6
- The T-Account 2-6
- Increases and Decreases in the Accounts 2-6
- Expanding the Rules of Debit and Credit 2-7
- The Normal Balance of an Account 2-7
- Determining the Balance of a T-Account 2-9

How Do You Record Transactions? 2-9
- Source Documents—The Origin of the Transactions 2-9
- Journalizing and Posting Transactions 2-10
- The Ledger Accounts After Posting 2-20
- The Four-Column Account: An Alternative to the T-Account 2-22

What Is the Trial Balance? 2-24
- Preparing Financial Statements from the Trial Balance 2-24
- Correcting Trial Balance Errors 2-25

How Do You Use the Debt Ratio to Evaluate Business Performance? 2-26

■ Review 2-28
■ Assess Your Progress 2-35
■ Critical Thinking 2-58

CHAPTER 3
The Adjusting Process 3-1

What Is the Difference Between Cash Basis Accounting and Accrual Basis Accounting? 3-2

What Concepts and Principles Apply to Accrual Basis Accounting? 3-4
- The Time Period Concept 3-4
- The Revenue Recognition Principle 3-4
- The Matching Principle 3-5

What Are Adjusting Entries, and How Do We Record Them? 3-6
- Deferred Expenses 3-7
- Deferred Revenues 3-13
- Accrued Expenses 3-14
- Accrued Revenues 3-18

What Is the Purpose of the Adjusted Trial Balance, and How Do We Prepare It? 3-22

What Is the Impact of Adjusting Entries on the Financial Statements? 3-24

How Could a Worksheet Help in Preparing Adjusting Entries and the Adjusted Trial Balance? 3-26

APPENDIX 3A: *Alternative Treatment of Recording Deferred Expenses and Deferred Revenues* 3-28

What Is an Alternative Treatment of Recording Deferred Expenses and Deferred Revenues? 3-28
- Deferred Expenses 3-28
- Deferred Revenues 3-30

■ Review 3-31
■ Assess Your Progress 3-38
■ Critical Thinking 3-61

CHAPTER 4
Completing the Accounting Cycle 4-1

How Do We Prepare Financial Statements? 4-2
- Relationships Among the Financial Statements 4-3
- Classified Balance Sheet 4-4

How Could a Worksheet Help in Preparing Financial Statements? 4-7
- Section 5—Income Statement 4-7
- Section 6—Balance Sheet 4-7
- Section 7—Determine Net Income or Net Loss 4-8

What Is the Closing Process, and How Do We Close the Accounts? 4-9
- Closing Temporary Accounts—Net Income for the Period 4-10
- Closing Temporary Accounts—Net Loss for the Period 4-13
- Closing Temporary Accounts—Summary 4-13

How Do We Prepare a Post-Closing Trial Balance? 4-16
What Is the Accounting Cycle? 4-17
How Do We Use the Current Ratio to Evaluate Business Performance? 4-19

APPENDIX 4A: *Reversing Entries: An Optional Step* 4-21

What Are Reversing Entries? 4-21
- Accounting for Accrued Expenses 4-21
- Accounting Without a Reversing Entry 4-22
- Accounting with a Reversing Entry 4-22

- Review 4-24
- Assess Your Progress 4-32
- Critical Thinking 4-57
- Comprehensive Problem F:4-1 for Chapters F:1–F:4 4-58
- Comprehensive Problem F:4-2 for Chapters F:1–F:4 4-60

CHAPTER 5

Merchandising Operations 5-1

What Are Merchandising Operations? 5-2
- The Operating Cycle of a Merchandising Business 5-2
- Merchandise Inventory Systems: Perpetual and Periodic Inventory Systems 5-4

How Are Purchases of Merchandise Inventory Recorded in a Perpetual Inventory System? 5-5
- Purchase of Merchandise Inventory 5-6
- Purchase Returns and Allowances 5-7
- Purchase Discounts 5-8
- Transportation Costs 5-10
- Net Cost of Inventory Purchased 5-11

How Are Sales of Merchandise Inventory Recorded in a Perpetual Inventory System? 5-12
- Cash and Credit Card Sales 5-12
- Sales on Account, No Discount 5-13
- Sales Returns and Allowances 5-14
- Sales on Account, with Discount 5-16
- Transportation Costs—Freight Out 5-18

What Are the Adjusting and Closing Entries for a Merchandiser? 5-18
- Adjusting Merchandise Inventory for Inventory Shrinkage 5-19
- Adjusting Sales Revenue and Merchandise Inventory for Estimated Sales Returns 5-19
- Closing the Accounts of a Merchandiser 5-20

How Are a Merchandiser's Financial Statements Prepared? 5-23
- Income Statement 5-23
- Multi-Step Income Statement 5-24
- Statement of Owner's Equity and the Balance Sheet 5-26

How Do We Use the Gross Profit Percentage to Evaluate Business Performance? 5-27

APPENDIX 5A: *Accounting for Multiple Performance Obligations* 5-28

How Are Multiple Performance Obligations Recorded in a Perpetual Inventory System? 5-28

APPENDIX 5B: *Accounting for Merchandise Inventory in a Periodic Inventory System* 5-30

How Are Merchandise Inventory Transactions Recorded in a Periodic Inventory System? 5-30
- Purchases of Merchandise Inventory—Periodic Inventory System 5-30
- Purchase Returns and Allowances—Periodic Inventory System 5-30
- Purchase Discounts—Periodic Inventory System 5-31
- Transportation Costs—Periodic Inventory System 5-32
- Net Cost of Inventory Purchased 5-32
- Sale of Merchandise Inventory—Periodic Inventory System 5-32
- Preparing Financial Statements—Periodic Inventory System 5-33
- Adjusting and Closing Entries—Periodic Inventory System 5-33

- Review 5-37
- Assess Your Progress 5-50
- Critical Thinking 5-75

CHAPTER 6

Merchandise Inventory 6-1

What Are the Accounting Principles and Controls That Relate to Merchandise Inventory? 6-2
- Accounting Principles 6-2
- Control Over Merchandise Inventory 6-3

How Are Merchandise Inventory Costs Determined Under a Perpetual Inventory System? 6-5
- Specific Identification Method 6-6
- First-In, First-Out (FIFO) Method 6-7
- Last-In, First-Out (LIFO) Method 6-9
- Weighted-Average Method 6-11

How Are Financial Statements Affected by Using Different Inventory Costing Methods? 6-14
- Income Statement 6-14
- Balance Sheet 6-15

How Is Merchandise Inventory Valued When Using the Lower-of-Cost-or-Market Rule? 6-17
- Computing the Lower-of-Cost-or-Market 6-17
- Recording the Adjusting Journal Entry to Adjust Merchandise Inventory 6-17

What Are the Effects of Merchandise Inventory Errors on the Financial Statements? 6-19

How Do We Use Inventory Turnover and Days' Sales in Inventory to Evaluate Business Performance? 6-21
- Inventory Turnover 6-22
- Days' Sales in Inventory 6-22
- Evaluating Kohl's Corporation 6-22

APPENDIX 6A: *Merchandise Inventory Costs Under a Periodic Inventory System* 6-23

How Are Merchandise Inventory Costs Determined Under a Periodic Inventory System? 6-23
- First-In, First Out (FIFO) Method 6-25
- Last-In, First-Out (LIFO) Method 6-26
- Weighted-Average Method 6-26

- Review 6-27
- Assess Your Progress 6-34
- Critical Thinking 6-49
- Comprehensive Problem for Chapters F:5 and F:6 6-51

CHAPTER 7

Accounting Information Systems 7-1

What Is an Accounting Information System? 7-2
Effective Accounting Information Systems 7-2
Components of an Accounting Information System 7-3

How Are Sales and Cash Receipts Recorded in a Manual Accounting Information System? 7-5
Special Journals 7-5
Subsidiary Ledgers 7-6
The Sales Journal 7-7
The Cash Receipts Journal 7-10

How Are Purchases, Cash Payments, and Other Transactions Recorded in a Manual Accounting Information System? 7-14
The Purchases Journal 7-14
The Cash Payments Journal 7-16
The General Journal 7-19

How Are Transactions Recorded in a Computerized Accounting Information System? 7-21
Accounting Software for Small Businesses 7-21
Enterprise Resource Planning (ERP) Systems 7-21
QuickBooks 7-22

■ Review 7-25
■ Assess Your Progress 7-30
■ Critical Thinking 7-49
■ Comprehensive Problem for Chapter F:7 7-51

CHAPTER 8

Internal Control and Cash 8-1

What Is Internal Control, and How Can It Be Used to Protect a Company's Assets? 8-2
Internal Control and the Sarbanes-Oxley Act 8-2
The Components of Internal Control 8-3
Internal Control Procedures 8-4
The Limitations of Internal Control—Costs and Benefits 8-6

What Are the Internal Control Procedures with Respect to Cash Receipts? 8-7
Cash Receipts Over the Counter 8-8
Cash Receipts by Mail 8-8

What Are the Internal Control Procedures with Respect to Cash Payments? 8-9
Controls Over Payment by Check 8-9

What Are the Internal Control Procedures Needed for Petty Cash and How Are Petty Cash Transactions Recorded? 8-11
Setting Up the Petty Cash Fund 8-12
Replenishing the Petty Cash Fund 8-12
Changing the Amount of the Petty Cash Fund 8-14

What Are the Internal Controls Needed with Debit and Credit Card Sales and How Are These Types of Sales Recorded? 8-14

How Can the Bank Account Be Used as a Control Device? 8-17
Signature Card 8-17
Deposit Ticket 8-17
Check 8-17
Bank Statement 8-18
Electronic Funds Transfers 8-18
Bank Reconciliation 8-19
Examining a Bank Reconciliation 8-22
Journalizing Transactions from the Bank Reconciliation 8-23

How Can the Cash Ratio Be Used to Evaluate Business Performance? 8-24

■ Review 8-25
■ Assess Your Progress 8-33
■ Critical Thinking 8-49

CHAPTER 9

Receivables 9-1

What Are Common Types of Receivables, and How Are Credit Sales Recorded? 9-2
Types of Receivables 9-2
Exercising Internal Control Over Receivables 9-3
Recording Sales on Credit 9-3
Decreasing Collection Time and Credit Risk 9-4

How Are Uncollectibles Accounted for When Using the Direct Write-Off Method? 9-6
Recording and Writing Off Uncollectible Accounts—Direct Write-off Method 9-6
Recovery of Accounts Previously Written Off—Direct Write-off Method 9-6
Limitations of the Direct Write-off Method 9-7

How Are Uncollectibles Accounted for When Using the Allowance Method? 9-8
Recording Bad Debts Expense—Allowance Method 9-8
Writing Off Uncollectible Accounts—Allowance Method 9-9
Recovery of Accounts Previously Written Off—Allowance Method 9-10
Comparison of Recording Transactions for Uncollectibles Using the Direct Write-Off Method Versus the Allowance Method 9-11
Estimating and Recording Bad Debts Expense—Allowance Method 9-12
Comparison of Income Statement Approach Versus Balance Sheet Approach 9-17

How Are Notes Receivable Accounted For? 9-18
Identifying Maturity Date 9-19
Computing Interest on a Note 9-20
Accruing Interest Revenue and Recording Honored Notes Receivable 9-21
Recording Dishonored Notes Receivable 9-23

How Do We Use the Acid-Test Ratio, Accounts Receivable Turnover Ratio, and Days' Sales in Receivables to Evaluate Business Performance? 9-24
Acid-Test (or Quick) Ratio 9-25
Accounts Receivable Turnover Ratio 9-26
Days' Sales in Receivables 9-26

■ Review 9-27
■ Assess Your Progress 9-34
■ Critical Thinking 9-52

CHAPTER 10

Plant Assets, Natural Resources, and Intangibles 10-1

How Does a Business Measure the Cost of Property, Plant, and Equipment? 10-2
Land and Land Improvements 10-3
Buildings 10-4
Machinery and Equipment 10-4
Furniture and Fixtures 10-5
Lump-Sum Purchase 10-5
Capital and Revenue Expenditures 10-6

What Is Depreciation, and How Is It Computed? 10-8
Factors in Computing Depreciation 10-8
Depreciation Methods 10-9
Partial-Year Depreciation 10-14
Changing Estimates of a Depreciable Asset 10-14
Reporting Property, Plant, and Equipment 10-15

How Are Disposals of Plant Assets Recorded? 10-16
Discarding Plant Assets 10-17
Selling Plant Assets 10-19

How Are Natural Resources Accounted For? 10-24

How Are Intangible Assets Accounted For? 10-25
Accounting for Intangibles 10-25
Specific Intangibles 10-25
Reporting of Intangible Assets 10-28

How Do We Use the Asset Turnover Ratio to Evaluate Business Performance? 10-29

APPENDIX 10A: Exchanging Plant Assets 10-30

How Are Exchanges of Plant Assets Accounted For? 10-30
Exchange of Plant Assets–Gain Situation 10-30
Exchange of Plant Assets–Loss Situation 10-31

■ Review 10-32
■ Assess Your Progress 10-38
■ Critical Thinking 10-51
■ Comprehensive Problem for Chapters F:8, F:9, and F:10 10-52

CHAPTER 11

Current Liabilities and Payroll 11-1

How Are Current Liabilities of Known Amounts Accounted For? 11-2
Accounts Payable 11-2
Sales Tax Payable 11-3
Unearned Revenue 11-3
Short-term Notes Payable 11-4
Current Portion of Long-term Notes Payable 11-5

How Do Companies Account for and Record Payroll? 11-6
Gross Pay and Net (Take-Home) Pay 11-7
Employee Payroll Withholding Deductions 11-7
Payroll Register 11-9
Journalizing Employee Payroll 11-10
Employer Payroll Taxes 11-11
Payment of Employer Payroll Taxes and Employees' Withholdings 11-13
Internal Control Over Payroll 11-13

How Are Current Liabilities That Must Be Estimated Accounted For? 11-14
Bonus Plans 11-14
Vacation, Health, and Pension Benefits 11-15
Warranties 11-15

How Are Contingent Liabilities Accounted For? 11-17
Remote Contingent Liability 11-17
Reasonably Possible Contingent Liability 11-17
Probable Contingent Liability 11-17

How Do We Use the Times-Interest-Earned Ratio to Evaluate Business Performance? 11-19

■ Review 11-20
■ Assess Your Progress 11-26
■ Critical Thinking 11-39

CHAPTER 12

Partnerships 12-1

What Are the Characteristics and Types of Partnerships? 12-2
Partnership Characteristics 12-2
Types of Partnerships 12-4
Other Forms of Business 12-5

How Are Partnerships Organized? 12-7
The Start-up of a Partnership 12-7
Partnership Financial Statements 12-8

How Are Partnership Profits and Losses Allocated? 12-8
Allocation Based on a Stated Ratio 12-9
Allocation Based on Capital Balances 12-10
Allocation Based on Services, Capital Balances, and Stated Ratios 12-10
Partner Withdrawal of Cash and Other Assets 12-12
Statement of Partners' Equity 12-13

How Is the Admission of a Partner Accounted For? 12-14
Admission by Purchasing an Existing Partner's Interest 12-14
Admission by Contributing to the Partnership 12-15

How Is the Withdrawal of a Partner Accounted For? 12-17
Withdrawal from the Partnership at Book Value—No Bonus to Any Partner 12-18
Withdrawal from the Partnership—Bonus to the Existing Partners 12-18
Withdrawal from the Partnership—Bonus to the Withdrawing Partner 12-19
Death of a Partner 12-19

How Is the Liquidation of a Partnership Accounted For? 12-20
Sale of Assets at a Gain 12-20
Sale of Assets at a Loss with Capital Deficiency 12-23

■ Review 12-26
■ Assess Your Progress 12-33
■ Critical Thinking 12-50

CHAPTER 13

Corporations 13-1

What Is a Corporation? 13-2
Characteristics of Corporations 13-2
Stockholders' Equity Basics 13-3

How Is the Issuance of Stock Accounted For? 13-6
Issuing Common Stock at Par Value 13-7
Issuing Common Stock at a Premium 13-7
Issuing No-Par Common Stock 13-8
Issuing Stated Value Common Stock 13-9
Issuing Common Stock for Assets Other Than Cash 13-9
Issuing Preferred Stock 13-10

How Is Treasury Stock Accounted For? 13-11
Treasury Stock Basics 13-11
Purchase of Treasury Stock 13-11
Sale of Treasury Stock 13-11
Retirement of Stock 13-15

How Are Dividends and Stock Splits Accounted For? 13-15
Cash Dividends 13-15
Stock Dividends 13-18
Stock Splits 13-22
Cash Dividends, Stock Dividends, and Stock Splits Compared 13-22

How Is the Complete Corporate Income Statement Prepared? 13-23
Continuing Operations 13-24
Discontinued Operations 13-24
Earnings per Share 13-24

How Is Equity Reported for a Corporation? 13-25
Statement of Retained Earnings 13-25
Statement of Stockholders' Equity 13-26

How Do We Use Stockholders' Equity Ratios to Evaluate Business Performance? 13-27
Earnings per Share 13-27
Price/Earnings Ratio 13-28
Rate of Return on Common Stockholders' Equity 13-28

- Review 13-29
- Assess Your Progress 13-37
- Critical Thinking 13-55

CHAPTER 14

Long-Term Liabilities 14-1

How Are Long-term Notes Payable and Mortgages Payable Accounted For? 14-2
Long-term Notes Payable 14-2
Mortgages Payable 14-3

What Are Bonds? 14-5
Types of Bonds 14-6
Bond Prices 14-7
Present Value and Future Value 14-7
Bond Interest Rates 14-8
Issuing Bonds Versus Issuing Stock 14-9

How Are Bonds Payable Accounted for Using the Straight-Line Amortization Method? 14-10
Issuing Bonds Payable at Face Value 14-10
Issuing Bonds Payable at a Discount 14-11
Issuing Bonds Payable at a Premium 14-14

How Is the Retirement of Bonds Payable Accounted For? 14-16
Retirement of Bonds at Maturity 14-16
Retirement of Bonds Before Maturity 14-17

How Are Liabilities Reported on the Balance Sheet? 14-18

How Do We Use the Debt to Equity Ratio to Evaluate Business Performance? 14-20

APPENDIX 14A: *The Time Value of Money* 14-21

What Is the Time Value of Money, and How Are Present Value and Future Value Calculated? 14-21
Time Value of Money Concepts 14-22
Present Value of a Lump Sum 14-24
Present Value of an Annuity 14-24
Present Value of Bonds Payable 14-25
Future Value of a Lump Sum 14-26
Future Value of an Annuity 14-27

APPENDIX 14B: *Effective-Interest Method of Amortization* 14-28

How Are Bonds Payable Accounted for Using the Effective-Interest Amortization Method? 14-28
Effective-Interest Amortization for a Bond Discount 14-28
Effective-Interest Amortization of a Bond Premium 14-29

- Review 14-31
- Assess Your Progress 14-36
- Critical Thinking 14-50
- Comprehensive Problem for Chapters F:11, F:13, and F:14 14-51

CHAPTER 15

Investments 15-1

Why Do Companies Invest? 15-2
Debt Securities Versus Equity Securities 15-2
Reasons to Invest 15-2
Classification and Reporting of Investments 15-3

How Are Investments in Debt Securities Accounted For? 15-5
Purchase of Debt Securities 15-5
Interest Revenue 15-6
Disposition at Maturity 15-6
Other Accounting Issues for Debt Investments 15-6

How Are Investments in Equity Securities Accounted For? 15-7
Equity Securities with No Significant Influence (Fair Value Method) 15-7
Equity Securities with Significant Influence (Equity Method) 15-8
Equity Securities with Controlling Interest (Consolidation Method) 15-10

How Are Debt and Equity Securities Reported? 15-10
Trading Debt Investments (Fair Value Method) 15-10
Available-for-Sale Debt Investments (Fair Value Method) 15-12
Held-to-Maturity Debt Investments (Amortized Cost) 15-14
Equity Investments with No Significant Influence (Fair Value Method) 15-14

How Do We Use the Rate of Return on Total Assets to Evaluate Business Performance?   15-16
- Review   15-17
- Assess Your Progress   15-22
- Critical Thinking   15-30

CHAPTER 16
The Statement of Cash Flows   16-1

What Is the Statement of Cash Flows?   16-2
Purpose of the Statement of Cash Flows   16-2
Classification of Cash Flows   16-3
Two Formats for Operating Activities   16-5

How Is the Statement of Cash Flows Prepared Using the Indirect Method?   16-5
Cash Flows from Operating Activities   16-8
Cash Flows from Investing Activities   16-12
Cash Flows from Financing Activities   16-14
Net Change in Cash and Cash Balances   16-18
Non-cash Investing and Financing Activities   16-18

How Do We Use Free Cash Flow to Evaluate Business Performance?   16-20

APPENDIX 16A: *Preparing the Statement of Cash Flows by the Direct Method*   16-21

How Is the Statement of Cash Flows Prepared Using the Direct Method?   16-21
Cash Flows from Operating Activities   16-22

APPENDIX 16B: *Preparing the Statement of Cash Flows Using the Indirect Method and a Spreadsheet*   16-28

How Is the Statement of Cash Flows Prepared Using the Indirect Method and a Spreadsheet?   16-28
- Review   16-32
- Assess Your Progress   16-38
- Critical Thinking   16-64

CHAPTER 17
Financial Statement Analysis   17-1

How Are Financial Statements Used to Analyze a Business?   17-2
Purpose of Analysis   17-2
Tools of Analysis   17-2
Corporate Financial Reports   17-2

How Do We Use Horizontal Analysis to Analyze a Business?   17-4
Horizontal Analysis of the Income Statement   17-5
Horizontal Analysis of the Balance Sheet   17-6
Trend Analysis   17-7

How Do We Use Vertical Analysis to Analyze a Business?   17-8
Vertical Analysis of the Income Statement   17-9
Vertical Analysis of the Balance Sheet   17-10
Common-Size Statements   17-11
Benchmarking   17-12

How Do We Use Ratios to Analyze a Business?   17-13
Evaluating the Ability to Pay Current Liabilities   17-14
Evaluating the Ability to Sell Merchandise Inventory and Collect Receivables   17-17
Evaluating the Ability to Pay Long-term Debt   17-19
Evaluating Profitability   17-21
Evaluating Stock as an Investment   17-24
Red Flags in Financial Statement Analyses   17-26

- Review   17-28
- Assess Your Progress   17-36
- Critical Thinking   17-55

APPENDIX A—Present Value Tables and Future Value Tables   A-1
GLOSSARY   G-1
INDEX   I-1
PHOTO CREDITS   P-1

Horngren's Accounting... Expanding on Proven Success

What's New to the Edition

UPDATED! End of Chapter exercises and problems have been updated with new years and company financial information.

UPDATED! Chapter openers, Tying It All Together features, and financial statement analysis companies (Kohl's and Target) have been updated with current company financial information.

NEW FEATURE ON DATA ANALYTICS! Data Analytics is becoming critically important in business—specifically in accounting. A new feature called Data Analytics in Accounting has been integrated throughout the narrative. In an increasingly competitive environment, having the ability to harness information to make sound business decisions is becoming crucial. Throughout the chapters, this feature highlights how real companies use Data Analytics to track inventory, monitor cash flow, forecast sales, and maximize profits. This feature also discusses emerging technologies, such as robotic process automation and artificial intelligence, and how they relate to businesses.

NEW DATA ANALYTICS PROJECTS! Each project contains a list of requirements, a dataset, a tutorial video, and instructions for using software such as Excel, Power BI, or Tableau to offer students hands-on practice in analyzing and reporting data. Using these tools, students learn how to extract and examine key information about a company related to its products, operations, and consumer buying habits. With this experience and knowledge, students are able to make smarter business decisions and are better prepared for the workforce.

NEW COVERAGE ON EMPLOYABILITY! The first courses in accounting are a great place to discuss the importance of accounting credentials in today's job market. Throughout the narrative, we highlight the role of accounting in businesses including the most relevant accounting credentials, as well as some new ones for students beginning their study of accounting. When discussing accounting in the business environment, in addition to the traditional career path (CPA), we also provide information about additional certifications available to accounting majors including Certified Management Accounting (CMA), Chartered Global Management Accountant (CGMA), and Certified Financial Planner (CFP).

Chapter 1: Accounting and the Business Environment
- Added discussion on additional certifications available to accounting majors including Chartered Global Management Accountant and Certified Financial Planner.
- Added discussion on the need for technology skills and knowledge for accountants.
- Clarified the equity discussion to help students better understand the changes in equity based on customer feedback/requests.

Chapter 2: Recording Business Transactions
- Added Data Analytics in Accounting feature about the chart of accounts.

Chapter 5: Merchandising Operations
- Realigned the order of the purchase section to better explain how a company records purchase returns and corresponding payment.
- Realigned the order of sales section to better explain how a company records sales returns and corresponding receipt.
- Added T-accounts to help students understand the journal entries.
- Added customer and vendor names for Accounts Receivable and Accounts Payable.
- Moved adjusting sales revenue and merchandise inventory for estimated sales returns to LO4 which covers adjusting and closing entries for merchandisers.
- Realigned Appendix 5B purchases and sales sections to better explain how a company records these transactions.
- Clarified discussion of how a periodic inventory system records estimated sales returns.
- Modified Check Your Understanding F:5-2 to include the new accounts introduced under Revenue Recognition Standard.
- Reviewed EOC to ensure that all new accounts (Estimated Returns Inventory, Refunds Payable, and Sales Discounts Forfeited) were adequately covered in problems.

- Adjusted EOC to give options for professors who do not want to cover Sales Returns and Allowances (Estimated Returns Inventory and Refunds Payable).
- Optional online appendix (and associated End of Chapter exercises) available for faculty who would like to cover the gross method of recording accounting receivables.

Chapter 6: Merchandise Inventory
- Added Data Analytics in Accounting feature discussing how companies track inventory.
- Added more explanation for how to calculate inventory cost flow for FIFO, LIFO, and weighted average under perpetual method.

Chapter 8: Internal Control and Cash
- Added Data Analytics in Accounting feature on cryptocurrencies and blockchain.
- Added internal control procedures for accepting debit and credit card sales.
- Changed company used in Tying It All Together feature to Chipotle Mexican Grill and discussed the unauthorized malware activity that occurred in April 2017.

Chapter 9: Receivables
- Changed company used in Tying It All Together feature from Sears to Amazon.com, Inc.

Chapter 10: Plant Assets, Natural Resources, and Intangibles
- Added Data Analytics in Accounting feature on water and energy consumption.

Chapter 11: Current Liabilities and Payroll
- Updated payroll tax amounts for 2019 (current at time of printing).

Chapter 16: The Statement of Cash Flows
- Added Data Analytics in Accounting feature on monitoring cash flow.

Solving Learning and Teaching Challenges

Accounting Cycle Tutorial

This interactive tutorial helps students master the Accounting Cycle for early and continued success in the Introduction to Accounting course. The tutorial, accessed by computer, smartphone, or tablet, provides students with brief explanations of each concept of the Accounting Cycle through engaging, interactive activities. Students are immediately assessed on their understanding and their performance is recorded. A built-in comprehensive problem can be assigned to reinforce the lessons learned in the accounting cycle tutorial. Whether the Accounting Cycle Tutorial is used as a remediation self-study tool or course assignment, students have yet another resource to help them be successful with the accounting cycle.

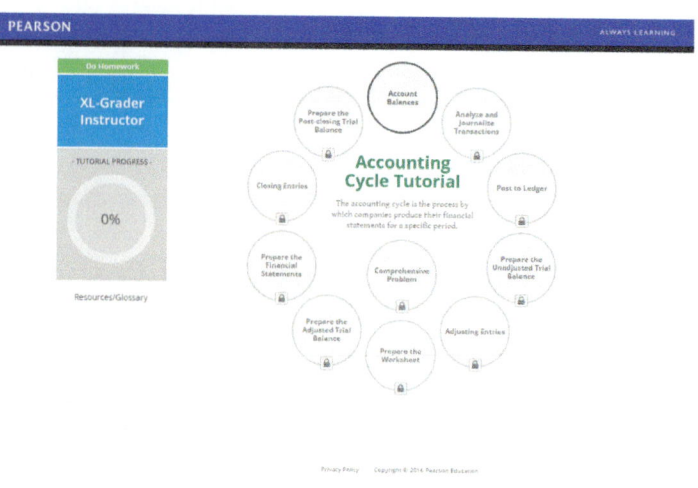

Chapter Openers

Chapter openers set up the concepts to be covered in the chapter using stories students can relate to. The implications of those concepts on a company's reporting and decision making processes are then discussed.

Tying It All Together

This feature ties together key concepts from the chapter using the company highlighted in the chapter opener. The in-chapter box feature presents scenarios and questions that the company could face and focuses on the decision-making process. The End of Chapter business case helps students synthesize the concepts of the chapter and reinforce critical thinking.

TYING IT ALL TOGETHER

Hyatt Hotels Corporation was founded in 1957 when Jay Pritzker purchased the first Hyatt hotel next to the Los Angeles International Airport. Today, Hyatt Hotels owns and operates hotels in 60 countries around the world. For the year ended December 31, 2018, the company reported revenues totaling $4.5 billion with net income of $769 million. (You can find Hyatt Hotels Corporation's annual report at https://www.sec.gov/Archives/edgar/data/1468174/000146817419000009/h10-k123118.htm).

Would Hyatt Hotels Corporation record closing entries and why?

Hyatt Hotels would record closing entries in order to get the accounts ready for next year. All companies record closing entries in order to zero out all revenue and expense accounts. In addition, the closing process updates the equity account balance for net income or loss during the period and any payments made to owners (stockholders).

Why are temporary accounts important in the closing process? What type of temporary accounts would Hyatt Hotels Corporation have?

Temporary accounts are important in the closing process because these accounts relate to a particular accounting period and are closed at the end of the period. Revenues, expenses, and withdrawals (called dividends for corporations) are all temporary accounts. Some examples of temporary accounts that Hyatt Hotels might have include Owned and Leased Hotels Revenue; Selling, General, and Administrative Expense; and Interest Expense.

When would Hyatt Hotels Corporation prepare its post-closing trial balance? What type of accounts would be reported on this trial balance?

A post-closing trial balance is a list of all permanent accounts and their balances at the end of the accounting period and is prepared after the closing process. Hyatt Hotels would report only permanent accounts on its post-closing trial balance. Some examples of permanent accounts that Hyatt Hotels might have include assets, such as Cash and Property; liabilities, such as Accounts Payable; and equity.

> Tying It All Together F:4-1

Before you begin this assignment, review the Tying It All Together feature in the chapter. It will also be helpful if you review Hyatt Hotels Corporation's 2018 annual report (https://www.sec.gov/Archives/edgar/data/1468174/000146817419000009/h10-k123118.htm#sE3993A8AD84040710041937D19B26344).

Hyatt Hotels Corporation is headquartered in Chicago and is a leading global hospitality company. The company develops, owns, and operates hotels, resorts, and vacation ownership properties in 60 different countries.

Requirements

1. Review Hyatt Hotels Corporation's income statement for year ended December 31, 2018. What does the income statement report? What was the amount of net income or loss for the year ending December 31, 2018?
2. Review the accounts that are listed on Hyatt Hotels Corporation's income statement and balance sheet. What are some examples of accounts that would be closed during the closing process?
3. Review the Hyatt Hotels Corporation's balance sheet. What does the balance sheet tell an investor? Did Hyatt Hotels Corporation present an unclassified or classified balance sheet? Explain.

Effect on the Accounting Equation

Next to every journal entry in both financial and managerial chapters, these illustrations help reinforce the connections between recording transactions and the effect those transactions have on the accounting equation.

On November 8, Smart Touch Learning collected cash of $5,500 for service revenue that the business earned by providing e-learning services for clients.

The asset Cash increased, so we debit Cash. Revenue increased, so we credit Service Revenue.

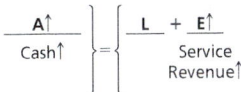

Date	Accounts and Explanation	Debit	Credit
Nov. 8	Cash	5,500	
	Service Revenue		5,500
	Performed services and received cash.		

Instructor Tips & Tricks

Found throughout the text, these handwritten notes mimic the experience of having an experienced teacher walk a student through concepts on the "board." Many include mnemonic devices or examples to help students remember the rules of accounting.

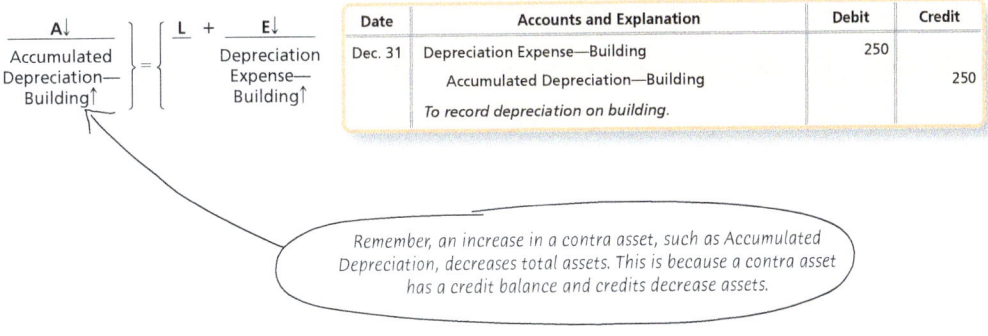

Common Questions, Answered

Our authors have spent years in the classroom answering students' questions and have found patterns in the concepts or rules that consistently confuse students. These commonly asked questions are located in the margin of the text next to where the answer or clarification can be found highlighted in purple text.

Why was the account Patent credited instead of Accumulated Amortization— Patent?

Notice that Smart Touch Learning credited the amortization directly to the intangible asset, Patent, instead of using an Accumulated Amortization account. A company may credit an intangible asset directly when recording amortization expense, or it may use the account Accumulated Amortization. **Companies frequently choose to credit the asset account directly because the residual value is generally zero and there is no physical asset to dispose of at the end of its useful life, so the asset essentially removes itself from the books through the process of amortization.**

At the end of the first year, Smart Touch Learning will report this patent at $160,000 ($200,000 cost minus first-year amortization of $40,000), the next year at $120,000, and so forth. Each year for five years the value of the patent will be reduced until the end of its five-year life, at which point its book value will be $0.

xv

Decision Boxes

This feature provides common questions and potential solutions business owners face. Students are asked to determine the course of action they would take based on concepts covered in the chapter and are then given potential solutions.

DECISIONS

What e-commerce internal controls should be put into place?

Jason Kane works as an information technology auditor for Netproducts, a retailer that sells merchandise over the Internet. Jason has been assigned the responsibility of reviewing the existing procedures and suggesting internal controls that could best protect the company. Netproducts sells all its merchandise over the Internet and accepts only credit card payments. Netproducts tracks trend information about its sales and maintains all customer, product, and pricing information on the company's intranet. In addition, Netproducts keeps employee information such as annual leave, payroll deposits, and Social Security numbers on its intranet. What e-commerce controls should Jason suggest?

Solution

Jason should suggest that specific controls be put into place, such as using encryption technology and firewalls, to protect customer and employee information. He should recommend that customers be required to create an online account with a password for the site and that the company only use secured Internet networks. In addition, Netproducts should ensure that the customer and employee data are physically secured and that access to the data can be obtained only by authorized individuals.

Things You Should Know

Provides students with a brief review of each learning objective presented in a question and answer format.

> **Things You Should Know**

1. **How do we prepare financial statements?**
   - Financial statements are prepared from the adjusted trial balance in the following order:
     1. Income statement—reports revenues and expenses and calculates net income or net loss during the period
     2. Statement of owner's equity—shows how capital changed during the period due to net income or net loss, owner contributions, and owner withdrawals
     3. Balance sheet—reports assets, liabilities, and owner's equity as of the last day of the period
   - A classified balance sheet classifies each asset and each liability into specific categories.

2. **How could a worksheet help in preparing financial statements?**
   - The columns of a worksheet can be extended to help in preparing the financial statements.
   - The income statement section will include only revenue and expense accounts.
   - The balance sheet section will include asset and liability accounts and all equity accounts except revenues and expenses.

Using Excel Problems

This End-of-Chapter problem introduces students to Excel to solve common accounting problems as they would in the business environment. Students will work from a template that will aid them in solving the problem related to accounting concepts taught in the chapter. Each chapter focuses on different Excel skills.

End-of-Chapter Continuing and Comprehensive Problems

> **Continuing Problem**

P-F:1-55 is the first problem in a continuing problem that will be used throughout the chapters to reinforce the concepts learned.

P-F:1-55 Using the accounting equation for transaction analysis, preparing financial statements, and calculating return on assets (ROA)

Canyon Canoe Company is a service-based company that rents canoes for use on local lakes and rivers. Amber Wilson graduated from college about 10 years ago. She worked for one of the "Big Four" accounting firms and became a CPA. Because she loves the outdoors, she decided to begin a new business that will combine her love of outdoor activities with her business knowledge. Amber decides that she will create a new sole proprietorship, Canyon Canoe Company, or CCC for short. The business began operations on November 1, 2024.

Nov.	1	Received $16,000 cash to begin the company and gave capital to Amber.
	2	Signed a lease for a building and paid $1,200 for the first month's rent.
	3	Purchased canoes for $4,800 on account.
	4	Purchased office supplies on account, $750.
	7	Earned $1,400 cash for rental of canoes.

Continuing Problem—Starts in Chapter F:1 and runs through the financial chapters, exposing students to recording entries for a service company and then moving into recording transactions for a merchandiser later in the text.

Practice Set—Starts in Chapter F:2 and goes through the financial chapters and provides another opportunity for students to practice the entire accounting cycle. The Practice Set uses the same company in each chapter, but is often not as extensive as the continuing problem.

> **Practice Set**

P-F:4-42 Completing the accounting cycle from adjusted trial balance to post-closing trial balance with an optional worksheet

Refer to the Practice Set data provided in Chapters F:2 and F:3 for Crystal Clear Cleaning.

Requirements

1. Prepare a worksheet (optional) at November 30, 2024. Use the unadjusted trial balance from Chapter F:2 and the adjusting entries from Chapter F:3.
2. Prepare an income statement and statement of owner's equity for the month ended November 30, 2024. Also prepare a classified balance sheet at November 30, 2024, using the report format. Assume the Notes Payable is long-term. Use the worksheet prepared in Requirement 1 or the adjusted trial balance from Chapter F:3.
3. Prepare closing entries at November 30, 2024, and post to the accounts. Open T-accounts for Income Summary and Hideaway, Capital. Determine the ending balance in each account. Denote each closing amount as *Clos.* and each account balance as *Balance*.
4. Prepare a post-closing trial balance at November 30, 2024.

Comprehensive Problem 1 for Chapters F:1–F:4—Covers the entire accounting cycle for a service company.

Comprehensive Problem 2 for Chapters F:1–F:4—A continuation of Comprehensive Problem 1. It requires the student to record transactions for the month after the closing process.

Comprehensive Problem for Chapters F:5 and F:6—Covers the entire accounting cycle for a merchandising company, including analysis.

Comprehensive Problem for Chapter F:7—Uses special journals and subsidiary ledgers and covers the entire accounting cycle for a merchandising company. Students can complete this comprehensive problem using the MyAccountingLab General Ledger or Quickbooks® software.

Comprehensive Problem for Chapters F:8, F:9, and F:10—Covers cash, receivables, and long-term assets transactions and analysis.

Comprehensive Problem for Chapters F:11, F:13, and F:14—Covers payroll, other current liabilities, long-term liabilities, and stockholders' equity transactions and analysis.

COMPREHENSIVE PROBLEMS

> **Comprehensive Problem F:4-1 for Chapters F:1–F:4**

Murphy Delivery Service completed the following transactions during December 2024:

Dec.		
1	Murphy Delivery Service began operations by receiving $13,000 cash and a truck with a fair value of $9,000 from Russ Murphy. The business issued Murphy capital in exchange for this contribution.
1	Paid $600 cash for a six-month insurance policy. The policy begins December 1.
4	Paid $750 cash for office supplies.
12	Performed delivery services for a customer and received $2,200 cash.
15	Completed a large delivery job, billed the customer $3,300, and received a promise to collect the $3,300 within one week.
18	Paid employee salary, $800.
20	Received $7,000 cash for performing delivery services.
22	Collected $2,200 in advance for delivery service to be performed later.
25	Collected $3,300 cash from customer on account.
27	Purchased fuel for the truck, paying $150 on account. (Credit Accounts Payable)
28	Performed delivery services on account, $1,400.
29	Paid office rent, $1,400, for the month of December.
30	Paid $150 on account.
31	Murphy withdrew cash of $2,500.

Dear Colleague,

Thank you for taking the time to review *Horngren's Accounting*. We are excited to share our most recent changes and innovations with you as we expand on the proven success of the Horngren family of textbooks. Using what we learned from market feedback, our colleagues, and our students, we've designed this edition to focus on several goals.

This edition we again focus on ensuring that we produce a textbook that provides students with the content and resources they need to be successful. We continually update our pedagogy and content to represent the leading methods and topics necessary for student success. As authors, we reviewed each and every component to ensure the textbook, student resources, and instructor supplements are clear, consistent, and accurate. We value our ongoing conversations with our colleagues and our time engaged at professional conferences to confirm that our textbook is up-to-date and we are providing resources for professors to create an active and engaging classroom.

We are excited to share with you some new features and changes in this latest edition. First, we have added a new Data Analytics in Accounting feature that highlights how companies used data analytics in the business environment. We also offer accompanying Data Analytics projects in MyLab Accounting for your students to learn how to apply data analytics to accounting problems. Financial Chapter 5 (Merchandising Operations) has been updated to provide better clarity and understanding based on the revised revenue recognition standard. All chapters went through a significant review with a focus of clarifying current coverage and expanding on content areas that needed more explanation.

We look forward to hearing from you and welcome your feedback and comments. Please do not hesitate to contact us at HorngrensAccounting@pearson.com or through our editor, Michael Trinchetto, Michael.Trinchetto@pearson.com.

Tracie L. Miller-Nobles, CPA   *Brenda Mattison, CMA*

Acknowledgments

Acknowledgments for This Edition:

Tracie Miller-Nobles would like to thank her husband, Kevin, her parents, Kipp and Sylvia, and her sister, Michelle, for their love and support. She would also like to dedicate this book to the many colleagues who have shaped her teaching, mentored her, and helped her grow as a professor.

Brenda Mattison appreciates the loving support of her family, especially from her husband, Grant. She also appreciates the support she receives from so many colleagues who share their experiences and encouragement. This book is dedicated to her students, who work hard to achieve their dreams, are a constant reminder of what's really important in our lives, and inspire her to continuously seek ways to improve her craft of teaching.

The authors would like to sincerely thank all of the Pearson team, specifically Michael Trinchetto, Christopher DeJohn, Lacey Vitetta, Ellen Geary, Sara Eilert, Ashley DePace, Nayke Heine, Carolyn Philips, Diane Bulpett, Mary Kate Murray, Martha LaChance, Melissa Feimer, and Roberta Sherman for their unwavering support of this edition. They express their extreme pleasure in working with each team member and are appreciative of their guidance, patience, and belief in the success of this project.

Advisory Panels, Focus Group Participants, and Reviewers:

Samad Adams, *Bristol Community College*
Sharon Agee, *Rollins College*
Markus Ahrens, *St. Louis Community College*
Janice Akao, *Butler County Community College*
Anna Alexander, *Caldwell Community College and Technical Institute*
Sheila Ammons, *Austin Community College*
Rai Lynn Anderson, *Northeast State Community College*
Sidney Askew, *Borough of Manhattan Community College*
John Babich, *Kankakee Community College*
Michael Barendse, *Grossmont College*
Robert Beatty, *Anne Arundel Community College*
Lana Becker, *East Tennessee State University*
Vikki Bentz, *Yavapai College*
Jeff Brennan, *Austin Community College*
Lisa Busto, *William Rainey Harper College*
Jennifer Cainas, *University of South Florida*
Anne Cardozo, *Broward College*
Elizabeth Carlson, *University of South Florida Sarasota-Manatee*
Martha Cavalaris, *Miami Dade College*
Donna Chadwick, *Sinclair Community College*
Matilda Channel-Ward, *University of Maryland, Baltimore County*
Colleen Chung, *Miami Dade College*
Tony Cioffi, *Lorain County Community College*
Tom Clement, *University of North Dakota*
Alan Czyzewski, *Indiana State University*
Geoffrey Danzig, *Miami Dade College-North*
Judy Daulton, *Piedmont Technical College*
Michelle Davidowitz, *Kingsborough Community College*
Annette Fisher Davis, *Glendale Community College*
Anthony Dellarte, *Luzerne County Community College*
Crystal Drum, *Guilford Technical Community College*
Mary Ewanechko, *Monroe Community College*
Elisa Fernandez, *Miami Dade College*
Julie Gilbert, *Triton College*
Lori Grady, *Bucks County Community College*
Marina Grau, *Houston Community College*
Gloria Grayless, *Sam Houston State University*

Becky Hancock, *El Paso Community College*
Dawn D. Hart, *Darton State College*
Lori Hatchell, *Aims Community College*
Shauna Hatfield, *Salt Lake Community College*
Sueann Hely, *West Kentucky Community & Technical College*
Neil Hesketh, *Saint Leo University*
Patricia Holmes, *Des Moines Area Community College*
Kay Jackson, *Tarrant County College*
Cynthia Johnson, *University of Arkansas, Little Rock*
Gina Jones, *Aims Community College*
Jeffrey Jones, *The College of Southern Nevada*
Thomas K. Y. Kam, *Hawaii Pacific University*
Naomi Karolinski, *Monroe Community College*
Anne Kenner, *Eastern Florida State College*
Stephanie (Sam) King, *Edison State College*
Emil Koren, *Saint Leo University*
Paul Koulakov, *Nashville State Community College*
Christy Land, *Catawba Valley Community College*
Suzanne Lay, *Colorado Mesa University*
Gary Laycock, *Ivy Tech Community College*
Cynthia Lewis, *Harford Community College*
Wayne Lewis, *Hudson Valley Community College*
Debbie Luna, *El Paso Community College*
Mabel Machin, *Valencia College*
Mostafa Maksy, *Kutztown University*
Richard Mandau, *Piedmont Technical College*
Christina Manzo, *Queensborough Community College*
Maria C. Mari, *Miami Dade College*
Cynthia J. Miller, *University of Kentucky*
Andrea Murowski, *Brookdale Community College*
Micki Nickla, *Ivy Tech Community College*
Joanne Orabone, *Community College of Rhode Island*
Robert Pacheco, *Massasoit Community College*
Kimberly Perkins, *Austin Community College*
Dorris Perryman, *Bristol Community College*
Denel Pierre, *Saint Leo University*
William Quilliam, *Florida Southern College*

Marcela Raphael, *Chippewa Valley Technical College*
Ryan Rees, *Salt Lake Community College*
Katheryn Reynolds, *Front Range Community College Larimer*
Alice Rivera, *Golden West College*
Cecile Robert, *Community College of Rhode Island*
Shani Nicole Robinson, *Sam Houston State University*
Eric Rothenburg, *Kingsborough Community College*
Carol Rowey, *Community College of Rhode Island*
Amanda J. Salinas, *Alto College*
Sayan Sarkar, *University of Texas, El Paso*
Maurice Savard, *East Stroudsburg University*
Constance Schwass, *West Shore Community College*
Perry Sellers, *Lone Star College*
Dennis Shea, *Southern New Hampshire University*
Jaye Simpson, *Tarrant County*
John Stancil, *Florida Southern*
Diana Sullivan, *Portland Community College*

Annette Taggart, *Texas A&M University–Commerce*
Linda Tarrago, *Hillsborough Community College*
Teresa Thompson, *Chaffey College*
Judy Toland, *Bucks County Community College*
Daniel Tschoop, *Saint Leo University*
Robin D. Turner, *Rowan-Cabarrus Community College*
William Van Glabek, *Edison State College*
Stanley Walker, *Georgia Northwestern Tech*
Christine Wayne, *William Rainey Harper College*
Deb Weber, *Hawkeye Community College*
Denise A. White, *Austin Community College*
Donald R. Wilke, *Northwest Florida State College*
Timothy Wiseman, *Saint Leo University*
Wanda Wong, *Chabot College*
Angela Woodland, *Montana State University*
Raymond Kurt Yann, *Saint Leo University*
Judy Zander, *Grossmont College*

Accuracy Checkers:
James L. Baker, *Harford Community College*

Connie Belden, *Butler Community College*

Supplements Authors and Reviewers:
Dave Alldredge, *Salt Lake Community College*
Sheila Ammons, *Austin Community College*
Sidney Askew, *Borough of Manhattan Community College, CUNY*
James L. Baker, *Harford Community College*
Connie Belden, *Butler Community College*
Alisa Brink, *Virginia Commonwealth University*
Helen Brubeck, *Saint Mary-of-the-Woods College*

Kate Demarest, *Carroll Community College*
Lori Hatchell, *Aims Community College*
Carol Hughes, *Asheville-Buncombe Technical Community College*
Brett Killion, *Lakeland College*
Diane O'Neill, *Seattle University*
Teresa Stephenson, *The University of South Dakota*
Stephanie Swaim, *North Lake College*

The authors would like to express their gratitude for the diligent and exemplary work of all of our contributors, reviewers, accuracy checkers, and supplement authors. Each of you played a part in making this book successful! Thank you!

Accounting and the Business Environment 1

Coffee, Anyone?

Aiden Jackson stared at the list the banker had given him during their meeting. *Business plan, cash flow projections, financial statements, tax returns.* Aiden had visited with the banker because he had a dream of opening a coffee shop near campus. He knew there was a need; students were always looking for a place to study and visit with their friends. He also had the experience. He had worked for the past three years as a manager of a coffee shop in a neighboring town. Aiden needed one thing, though—money. He had saved a small amount of money from his job and received several contributions from family and friends, but he still didn't have enough to open the business. He had decided the best option was to get a loan from his bank. After the meeting, Aiden felt overwhelmed and unsure of the future of his business.

You might think that Aiden was facing an impossible situation, but you'd be wrong. Almost every new business faces a similar situation. The owner starts with an inspiration, and then he or she needs to provide enough continuous cash flow to build the business. In addition, the owner has to make decisions such as: *Should we expand to another location? Do we have enough money to purchase a new coffee roaster? How do I know if the business made a profit?*

So how does Aiden get started? Keep reading. That's what accounting teaches you.

Why Study Accounting?

The situation that Aiden faced is similar to the situations faced in the founding of most businesses. **Starbucks Corporation**, for example, first opened its doors in Seattle, Washington, in 1971. Three partners, Jerry Baldwin, Zev Siegl, and Gordon Bowker, were inspired by a dream of selling high-quality coffee. We know their dream was successful because Starbucks currently has more than 22,000 stores in 67 countries. How did Starbucks grow from a small one-store shop to what it is today? The partners understood accounting—the language of business. They understood how to measure the activities of the business, process that information into reports (financial statements), and then use those reports to make business decisions. Your knowledge of accounting will help you better understand businesses. It will make you a better business owner, employee, or investor.

1-2 Financial chapter 1

Chapter 1 Learning Objectives

1. Explain why accounting is important and list the users of accounting information
2. Describe the organizations and rules that govern accounting
3. Describe the accounting equation and define assets, liabilities, and equity
4. Use the accounting equation to analyze transactions
5. Prepare financial statements
6. Use financial statements and return on assets (ROA) to evaluate business performance

WHY IS ACCOUNTING IMPORTANT?

Learning Objective 1
Explain why accounting is important and list the users of accounting information

Accounting
The information system that measures business activities, processes the information into reports, and communicates the results to decision makers.

You've heard the term *accounting*, but what exactly is it? **Accounting** is the information system that measures business activities, processes the information into reports, and communicates the results to decision makers. Accounting is the language of business. The better you understand the language of business, the better you can manage your own business, be a valuable employee, or make wise investments.

We tend to think of accountants as boring and dry. However, accounting is much more than simple recordkeeping or bookkeeping. Today's accountants participate in a broad range of activities such as the investigation of financial evidence, the development of computer programs to process accounting information, and the communication of financial results to interested parties. The knowledge of accounting is used every day to help make business decisions.

The Pathways Vision Model (see Exhibit F:1-1), created by the Pathways Commission, provides a visual interpretation of what accountants really do. Accounting starts with

Exhibit F:1-1 | Pathways Vision Model

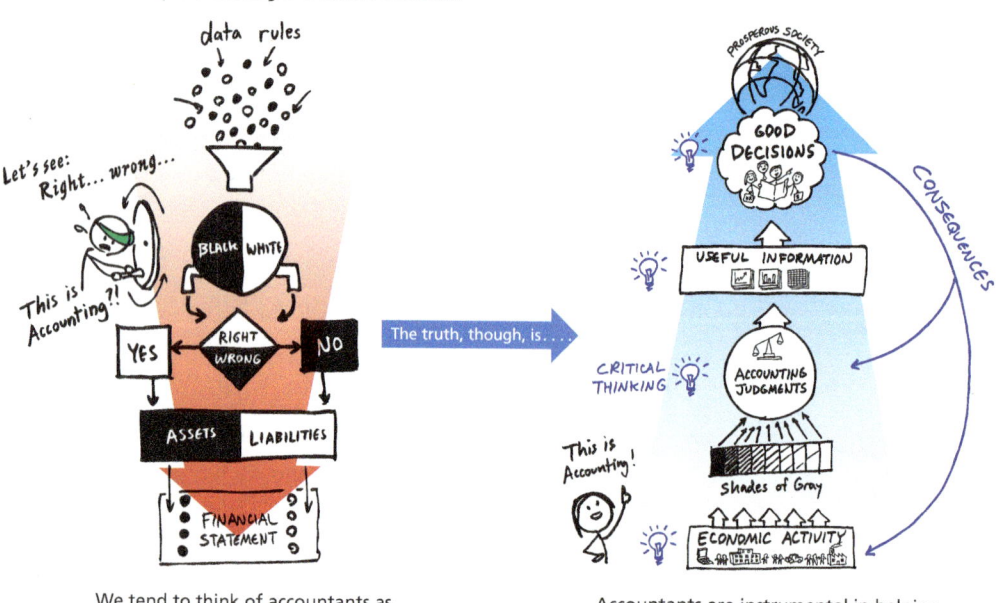

We tend to think of accountants as boring and dry.

Accountants are instrumental in helping to create a prosperous society.

This work is by The Pathways Commission. The Pathways Vision Model: AI artwork: AAA Commons. American Accounting Association.

economic activities that accountants review and evaluate using critical thinking and judgment to create useful information that helps individuals make good decisions. The model emphasizes that good decisions have an impact on accounting judgments and economic activity, thus creating a circular flow of cause and effect. Accountants are more than boring, tedious number crunchers. Instead, accountants play a critical role in supporting a prosperous society.

Decision Makers: The Users of Accounting Information

We can divide accounting into two major fields: financial accounting and managerial accounting. **Financial accounting** provides information for external decision makers, such as outside investors, lenders, customers, and the federal government. **Managerial accounting** focuses on information for internal decision makers, such as the company's managers and employees.

Exhibit F:1-2 illustrates the difference between financial accounting and managerial accounting. Regardless of whether they are external or internal to the company, all decision makers need information to make the best choices. The bigger the decision, the more information decision makers need. Let's look at some ways in which various people use accounting information to make important decisions.

Financial Accounting
The field of accounting that focuses on providing information for external decision makers.

Managerial Accounting
The field of accounting that focuses on providing information for internal decision makers.

Exhibit F:1-2 | Decision Making: Financial Versus Managerial Accounting

Financial Accounting

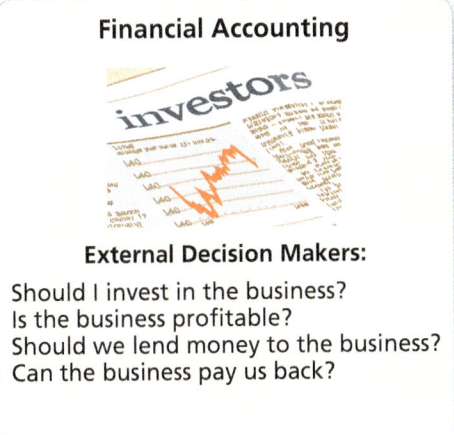

External Decision Makers:
Should I invest in the business?
Is the business profitable?
Should we lend money to the business?
Can the business pay us back?

Managerial Accounting

Internal Decision Makers:
How much money should the business budget for production?
Should the business expand to a new location?
How do actual costs compare to budgeted costs?

IFRS
Accounting is alive! As businesses evolve and the types of business transactions change, so must the language of business. The most significant changes in the business world in the last decade have been the huge increases in international commerce. Because more business is conducted internationally, decision makers are looking for an international accounting language.
Look for more information about International Financial Reporting Standards (IFRS) anywhere you see the IFRS heading.

Individuals

How much cash do you have? How much do you need to save each month to retire at a certain age or pay for your children's college education? Accounting can help you answer questions like these. By using accounting information, you can manage your money, evaluate a new job, and better decide whether you can afford to buy a new computer. Businesses need accounting information to make similar decisions.

Businesses

Business owners use accounting information to set goals, measure progress toward those goals, and make adjustments when needed. The financial statements give owners the information they need to help make those decisions. Financial statements are helpful when, for example, a business owner wants to know whether his or her business has enough cash to purchase another computer.

Investors

Outside investors who have some ownership interest often provide the money to get a business going. Suppose you're considering investing in a business. How would you decide whether it is a good investment? In making this decision, you might try to predict the amount of income you would earn on the investment. Also, after making an investment, investors can use a company's financial statements to analyze how their investment is performing.

You might have the opportunity to invest in the stock market through your company's retirement plan. Which investments should you pick? Understanding a company's financial statements will help you decide. You can view the financial statements of large companies that report to the Securities and Exchange Commission (SEC) by logging on to **http://www.finance.yahoo.com**, **http://www.google.com/finance**, or the SEC's EDGAR database (**http://www.sec.gov/edgar.shtml**).

Creditors

Creditor
Any person or business to whom a business owes money.

Any person or business to whom a business owes money is a **creditor**. Before extending credit to a business, a creditor evaluates the company's ability to make the payments by reviewing its financial statements. Creditors follow the same process when you need to borrow money for a new car or a house. The creditor reviews accounting data to determine your ability to make the loan payments. What does your financial position tell the creditor about your ability to repay the loan? Are you a good risk for the bank?

Taxing Authorities

Local, state, and federal governments levy taxes. Income tax is calculated using accounting information. Good accounting records can help individuals and businesses take advantage of lawful deductions. Without good records, the Internal Revenue Service (IRS) can disallow tax deductions, resulting in a higher tax bill plus interest and penalties.

Accounting Matters

Certified Public Accountants (CPAs)
Licensed professional accountants who serve the general public.

Chartered Global Management Accountant (CGMA)
Professional accountant with advanced knowledge in finance, operations, strategy, and management.

What if I want more information about becoming a CPA or CMA?

Certified Management Accountants (CMAs)
Professional accountants who specialize in accounting and financial management knowledge.

What do businesses such as Amazon.com, Walmart, or even your local sandwich shop across from campus have in common? They all rely upon accounting information to make business decisions. Even if you don't plan on majoring in accounting, the knowledge of accounting helps all businesses plan for the future and evaluate past performance. The skills you learn in this class will help you be a better business professional. Businesses can't function, though, without accountants. That is why a degree in accounting opens so many doors upon graduation. A bachelor's degree in accounting could lead you to several different accounting careers.

You've probably heard of a CPA before. **Certified Public Accountants**, or **CPAs**, are licensed professional accountants who serve the general public. CPAs work for public accounting firms, businesses, government entities, or educational institutions. What does it take to be a CPA? Although requirements vary between states, to be certified in a profession, one must meet the educational and/or experience requirements *and* pass a qualifying exam. Accountants can also obtain a **Chartered Global Management Accountant (CGMA)** designation. This distinguishes accountants who have advanced knowledge in finance, operations, strategy, and management. **The American Institute of Certified Public Accountants (AICPA) Web site (http://www.thiswaytocpa.com) contains a wealth of information about becoming a CPA or CGMA, career opportunities, and exam requirements.**

Certified Management Accountants, or **CMAs**, are certified professionals who specialize in accounting and financial management knowledge. Generally, CMAs work for a single company. **You can find information about becoming a CMA, how a CMA differs from a CPA, and why employers are recognizing the CMA certification on the Institute of Management Accountants (IMA) Web site (http://www.imanet.org).**

Another specialization in accounting is a **Certified Financial Planner**, or **CFP**. CFPs work with individuals to help them budget, plan for retirement, save for education, and manage their finances. Individuals who want to obtain their CFP must have the four E's: education, examination, experience, and ethics. You can find out more about becoming a CFP on the following Web site: **https://www.cfp.net/home**.

> **Certified Financial Planner (CFP)**
> Certified professional who specializes in budgeting, planning for retirement, and managing finances.

Studying accounting and becoming certified professionally can lead to a financially secure job. It's worth it for an accountant to spend the time and energy to get certified—certified accountants generally make 10–15% more than their noncertified colleagues when they enter the workforce. According to Robert Half's *2019 Salary Guide*, the top in-demand positions that rely on accounting skills are controllers, financial analysts, tax accountants, auditors, cost accountants, accounting clerks/bookkeepers, and business systems analysts. How much do these types of accountants make? Exhibit F:1-3 provides a snapshot of the earning potential for key positions.

Exhibit F:1-3 | Comparison of Accounting Positions

Position	Job Description	Salary Range
Controllers	Compile financial statements, interact with auditors, and oversee regulatory reporting.	$92,000–$207,750
Financial analysts	Review financial data and help to explain the story behind the numbers.	$42,500–$201,250
Business systems analysts	Use accounting knowledge to create computer systems.	$42,500–$185,000
Tax accountants	Help companies navigate tax laws.	$39,500–$212,250
Auditors	Perform reviews of companies to ensure compliance to rules and regulations.	$39,500–$208,750
Cost accountants	Typically work in a manufacturing business. Help analyze accounting data.	$42,000–$143,750
Accounting clerks/Bookkeepers	Record financial transactions and help prepare financial records.	$28,250–$65,750

Based on Robert Half's 2019 Salary Guide https://www.roberthalf.com/salary-guide

Accountants generally work either in corporate or industry accounting, public accounting, financial services, or governmental accounting. Corporate or industry accounting professionals are in demand in every sector of the business community, including manufacturing, construction, and healthcare. As the population of the world continues to age, accountants are in high demand in healthcare organizations to address billing and collections, data and business analysis, and changing revenue models. Corporate/industry accountants typically work for a single company, such as Amazon.com, Walmart, Dell, or UnitedHealthcare. Public accounting involves services such as auditing, tax preparation, and consulting. Well-known public accounting firms include Ernst & Young, Deloitte, PricewaterhouseCoopers (PwC), and KPMG. Accountants also work in financial services organizations such as banks. Other accountants work for federal, state, or local governments. Sought-after skills of accountants include being licensed or certified (e.g., CPA or CMA), data analytics, Excel, a strong work ethic, effective verbal and written communication, and leadership. Wherever accountants work, demand for their services is high. According to the U.S. Bureau of Labor Statistics, employment of accountants and auditors is expected to grow 10% (faster than average) from 2016–2026.

1-6 Financial  chapter 1

Data Analytics in Accounting

Today's accountants need to know more than just accounting knowledge. They also need to have an understanding of how technology is used to process financial information. Accounting and finance individuals actively work with information technology teams to develop accounting systems. Artificial intelligence, cloud-based systems, and robotic process automation are all changing the way companies handle financial information. Ideal accounting employees have knowledge in both accounting and technology.

Match the accounting terminology to the definitions.

1. Certified management accountants	a. information system that measures business activities, processes that information into reports, and communicates the results to decision makers
2. Accounting	b. professional accountants who serve the general public
3. Managerial accounting	c. person or business to whom a business owes money
4. Certified public accountants	d. field of accounting that focuses on providing information for internal decision makers
5. Financial accounting	e. professionals who work for a single company
6. Creditor	f. field of accounting that focuses on providing information for external decision makers

Check your answers online in MyLab Accounting or at http://www.pearsonhighered.com/Horngren.

For more practice, see Short Exercise S-F:1-1.   **MyLab Accounting**

WHAT ARE THE ORGANIZATIONS AND RULES THAT GOVERN ACCOUNTING?

Learning Objective 2
Describe the organizations and rules that govern accounting

All professions have regulations. Let's look at the organizations and rules that govern the accounting profession.

Governing Organizations

Financial Accounting Standards Board (FASB)
The private organization that oversees the creation and governance of accounting standards in the United States.

In the United States, the **Financial Accounting Standards Board (FASB)**, a privately funded organization, oversees the creation and governance of accounting standards. The FASB works with governmental regulatory agencies like the **Securities and Exchange Commission (SEC)**. The SEC is the U.S. governmental agency that oversees the U.S. financial markets. It also oversees those organizations that set standards (like the FASB). The FASB also works with congressionally created groups like the Public Company Accounting Oversight Board (PCAOB) and private groups like the American Institute of CPAs (AICPA), Institute of Management Accountants (IMA), and International Accounting Standards Board (IASB).

Securities and Exchange Commission (SEC)
U.S. governmental agency that oversees the U.S. financial markets.

Generally Accepted Accounting Principles

Generally Accepted Accounting Principles (GAAP)
Accounting guidelines, currently formulated by the Financial Accounting Standards Board (FASB); the main U.S. accounting rule book.

The guidelines for accounting information are called **Generally Accepted Accounting Principles (GAAP)**. GAAP is the main U.S. accounting rule book and is currently created and governed by the FASB. In order to use and prepare financial statements, it's important that we understand GAAP. GAAP rests on a conceptual framework that identifies the objectives, characteristics, elements, and implementation of financial statements and creates the acceptable accounting practices. The primary objective of financial reporting is to provide information useful for making investment and lending decisions. To be useful, information must be relevant and have *faithful representation*.[1] Relevant information allows users of the information to make a decision. Information that is faithfully representative is complete, neutral, and free from material error. These basic accounting assumptions and principles are part of the foundation for the financial reports that companies present.

Faithful Representation
Providing information that is complete, neutral, and free from error.

The Economic Entity Assumption

The most basic concept in accounting is that of the *economic entity assumption*. An economic (business) entity is an organization that stands apart as a separate economic unit. We draw boundaries around each entity to keep its affairs distinct from those of other entities. An entity refers to one business, separate from its owners.

A business can be organized as a sole proprietorship, partnership, corporation, or limited-liability company (LLC). Exhibit F:1-4 summarizes the similarities and differences among the four types of business organizations.

In order to demonstrate the economic entity assumption and several other concepts in this chapter, we will use a fictitious business—Smart Touch Learning—an e-learning business that specializes in providing online courses in accounting, economics, marketing, and management. This fictitious business will be used often throughout the book.

Economic Entity Assumption
An organization that stands apart as a separate economic unit.

Sole Proprietorship
A business with a single owner.

Partnership
A business with two or more owners and not organized as a corporation.

Corporation
A business organized under state law that is a separate legal entity.

Limited-Liability Company (LLC)
A company in which each member is only liable for his or her own actions.

Exhibit F:1-4 | Business Organizations

	Sole Proprietorship	Partnership	Corporation	Limited-Liability Company (LLC)
Definition	A business with a single owner	A business with two or more owners and not organized as a corporation	A business organized under state law that is a separate legal entity	A company in which each member is only liable for his or her own actions
Number of owners	One (called the *proprietor*)	Two or more (called *partners*)	One or more (called *stockholders*)	One or more (called *members* or *partners*)
Life of the organization	Terminates at owner's choice or death	Terminates at a partner's choice or death	Indefinite	Indefinite
Personal liability of the owner(s) for the business's debts	The owner is personally liable.	The partners are personally liable.	Stockholders are not personally liable.	Members are not personally liable.
Taxation	Not separate taxable entities. The owner pays tax on the proprietorship's earnings.	Partnership is not taxed. Instead partners pay tax on their share of the earnings.	Separate taxable entity. Corporation pays tax.	LLC is not taxed. Instead members pay tax on their share of earnings.
Type of business	Small businesses	Professional organizations of physicians, attorneys, and accountants	From small business to large multinational businesses	An alternative to the partnership

---

[1] This wording was changed from relevant and reliable by the *Statement of Financial Accounting Concepts No. 8*.

Assume Sheena Bright started the business by contributing cash of $30,000 (called *capital*). Following the economic entity assumption, the $30,000 is recorded separately from Sheena's personal assets, such as her clothing and car. To mix the $30,000 of business cash with Sheena's personal assets would make it difficult to measure the success or failure of Smart Touch Learning. The economic entity assumption requires that each entity be separate from other businesses and from the owners.

The Cost Principle

Cost Principle
A principle that states that acquired assets and services should be recorded at their actual cost.

The cost principle states that acquired assets and services should be recorded at their actual cost (also called *historical cost*). The cost principle means we record a transaction at the amount shown on the receipt—the actual amount paid. Even though the purchaser may believe the price is a bargain, the item is recorded at the price actually paid and not at the "expected" cost. For example, assume our fictitious company Smart Touch Learning purchased land for $20,000. The business might believe the land is instead worth $25,000. The cost principle requires that Smart Touch Learning record the land at $20,000, not $25,000.

IFRS
Under international reporting standards, the company would be allowed to restate and report the land at $30,000. The ability to report some assets and liabilities at their current fair value each year under international standards is a significant difference from U.S. rules.

The cost principle also holds that the accounting records should continue reporting the historical cost of an asset over its useful life. Why? Because cost is a reliable measure. Suppose Smart Touch Learning holds the land for six months. During that time land prices rise, and the land could be sold for $30,000. Should its accounting value—the figure on the books—be the actual cost of $20,000 or the current market value of $30,000? According to the cost principle, the accounting value of the land would remain at the actual cost of $20,000.

The Going Concern Assumption

Going Concern Assumption
Assumes that the entity will remain in operation for the foreseeable future.

Another reason for measuring assets at historical cost is the going concern assumption. This assumes that the entity will remain in operation for the foreseeable future. Under the going concern assumption, accountants assume that the business will remain in operation long enough to use existing resources for their intended purpose.

The Monetary Unit Assumption

In the United States, we record transactions in dollars because the dollar is the medium of exchange. The value of a dollar changes over time, and a rise in the price level is called *inflation*. During periods of inflation, a dollar will purchase less. But accountants assume that the dollar's purchasing power is stable. This is the basis of the monetary unit assumption, which requires that the items on the financial statements be measured in terms of a monetary unit.

Monetary Unit Assumption
The assumption that requires the items on the financial statements to be measured in terms of a monetary unit.

International Financial Reporting Standards

International Financial Reporting Standards (IFRS)
A set of global accounting guidelines, formulated by the International Accounting Standards Board (IASB).

International Accounting Standards Board (IASB)
The private organization that oversees the creation and governance of International Financial Reporting Standards (IFRS).

The concepts and principles that we have discussed so far apply to businesses that follow U.S. GAAP and are traded on a U.S. stock exchange, such as the New York Stock Exchange. The SEC requires that U.S. businesses follow U.S. GAAP. Companies who are incorporated in or do significant business in another country might be required to publish financial statements using International Financial Reporting Standards (IFRS), which are published by the International Accounting Standards Board (IASB). IFRS is a set of global accounting standards that are used by more than 166 nations/jurisdictions. They are generally less specific and based more on principle than U.S. GAAP. IFRS leaves more room for professional judgment. For example, unlike U.S. GAAP, IFRS allows periodic revaluation of certain assets and liabilities to restate them to market value, rather than keeping them at historical cost. At one point in time it was thought that the SEC would endorse IFRS. However, the SEC has backed away from this strategy and is currently considering whether a single set of global accounting standards is achievable.

Ethics in Accounting and Business

Ethical considerations affect accounting. Investors and creditors need relevant and faithfully representative information about a company that they are investing in or lending money to. Companies want to be profitable and financially strong to attract investors and attempt to present their financial statements in a manner that portrays the business in the best possible way. Sometimes these two opposing viewpoints can cause conflicts of interest. For example, imagine a company that is facing a potential million-dollar lawsuit due to a defective product. The company might not want to share this information with investors because it would potentially hurt the business's profitability. On the other hand, investors would want to know about the pending lawsuit so that they could make an informed decision about investing in the business. To handle these conflicts of interest and to provide reliable information, the SEC requires publicly held companies to have their financial statements audited by independent accountants. An **audit** is an examination of a company's financial statements and records. The independent accountants then issue an opinion that states whether the financial statements give a fair picture of the company's financial situation.

Audit
An examination of a company's financial statements and records.

The vast majority of accountants do their jobs professionally and ethically, but we often don't hear about them. Unfortunately, only those who cheat make the headlines. In recent years, we have seen many accounting scandals.

In response to the Enron and WorldCom reporting scandals, the U.S. government took swift action. It passed the **Sarbanes-Oxley Act (SOX)**, intended to curb financial scandals. SOX requires management to review internal control and take responsibility for the accuracy and completeness of their financial reports. In addition, SOX made it a criminal offense to falsify financial statements. The Sarbanes-Oxley Act also created a new watchdog agency, the **Public Company Accounting Oversight Board (PCAOB)**, to monitor the work of independent accountants who audit public companies. More recent scandals, such as the Bernie Madoff scandal in which Mr. Madoff pleaded guilty to defrauding thousands of investors by filing falsified trading reports, have further undermined the public's faith in financial reporting. This may result in more legislation that will influence future reporting.

Sarbanes-Oxley Act (SOX)
Requires management to review internal control and take responsibility for the accuracy and completeness of their financial reports.

Public Company Accounting Oversight Board (PCAOB)
Monitors the work of independent accountants who audit public companies.

Try It!

Match the accounting terminology to the definitions.

7. Cost principle — a. oversees the creation and governance of accounting standards in the United States
8. GAAP — b. requires an organization to be a separate economic unit
9. Faithful representation — c. oversees U.S. financial markets
10. SEC — d. states that acquired assets and services should be recorded at their actual cost
11. FASB — e. creates International Financial Reporting Standards
12. Monetary unit assumption — f. the main U.S. accounting rule book
13. Economic entity assumption — g. assumes that an entity will remain in operation for the foreseeable future
14. Going concern assumption — h. assumes that items on the financial statements are recorded in a monetary unit
15. IASB — i. requires information to be complete, neutral, and free from material error

Check your answers online in MyLab Accounting or at http://www.pearsonhighered.com/Horngren.

For more practice, see Short Exercises S-F:1-2 through S-F:1-5. **MyLab Accounting**

WHAT IS THE ACCOUNTING EQUATION?

Learning Objective 3
Describe the accounting equation and define assets, liabilities, and equity

Accounting Equation
The basic tool of accounting, measuring the resources of the business (what the business owns or has control of) and the claims to those resources (what the business owes to creditors and to the owners): Assets = Liabilities + Equity.

The basic tool of accounting is the **accounting equation**. It measures the resources of a business (what the business owns or has control of) and the claims to those resources (what the business owes to creditors and to the owners). The accounting equation is made up of three parts—assets, liabilities, and equity—and shows how these three parts are related. Assets appear on the left side of the equation, and the liabilities and equity appear on the right side.

Assets = Liabilities + Equity

Remember, the accounting equation is an equation—so the left side of the equation always equals the right side of the equation.

Example: If a business has assets of $230,000 and liabilities of $120,000, its equity must be $110,000 ($230,000 − $120,000).

Assets = Liabilities + Equity
$230,000 = $120,000 + ?
$230,000 = $120,000 + $110,000

Assets

Assets
Economic resources that are expected to benefit the business in the future and something the business owns or has control of.

An **asset** is an economic resource that is expected to benefit the business in the future. Assets are something of value that the business owns or has control of. Cash, Merchandise Inventory, Furniture, and Land are examples of assets.

Liabilities

Liabilities
Debts that are owed to creditors.

Claims to those assets come from two sources: liabilities and equity. **Liabilities** are debts that are owed to creditors. Liabilities are something the business owes and represent the creditors' claims on the business's assets. For example, a creditor who has loaned money to a business has a claim to some of the business's assets until the business pays the debt. Many liabilities have the word *payable* in their titles. Examples include Accounts Payable, Notes Payable, and Salaries Payable.

Equity

Equity
The owners' claims to the assets of the business.

Owner's Capital
Owner contributions to a business.

Revenues
Amounts earned from delivering goods or services to customers.

The owners' claims to the assets of the business are called **equity** (also called *owner's equity*). Equity represents the amount of assets that are left over after the company has paid its liabilities. It is the company's net worth.

Equity increases with owner contributions and revenues. Owner contributions to a business are referred to as **owner's capital**. An owner can contribute cash or other assets (such as equipment) to the business and receive capital. Equity is also increased by revenues. **Revenues** are earnings that result from delivering goods or services to customers. Examples of revenues are Sales Revenue, Service Revenue, and Rent Revenue.

Equity decreases with owner withdrawals and expenses. **Owner's withdrawals** or *drawings* are payments of equity (usually of cash) to the owner. An owner may or may not make withdrawals from the business. Owner withdrawals are the opposite of owner contributions and, therefore, decrease equity. Withdrawals are not expenses. **Expenses** are the costs of selling goods or services. Expenses are the opposite of revenues and, therefore, decrease equity. Examples of expenses are Rent Expense, Salaries Expense, Advertising Expense, and Utilities Expense.

Equity can be broken out into four components shown in the expanded accounting equation:

Owner's Withdrawals
Payments of equity to the owner.

Expenses
The costs of selling goods or services.

$$\text{ASSETS} = \text{LIABILITIES} + \underbrace{\text{Owner's Capital} - \text{Owner's Withdrawals} + \text{Revenues} - \text{Expenses}}_{\text{EQUITY}}$$

The difference between revenue and expenses is net income or net loss. Businesses strive for net income or profit. **Net income** occurs when revenues are greater than expenses. A **net loss** occurs when expenses are greater than revenues.

Net Income
The result of operations that occurs when total revenues are greater than total expenses.

Net Loss
The result of operations that occurs when total expenses are greater than total revenues.

16. Using the expanded accounting equation, solve for the missing amount.

Assets	$ 71,288
Liabilities	2,260
Owner's Capital	?
Owner's Withdrawal	14,420
Revenues	53,085
Expenses	28,675

Check your answer online in MyLab Accounting or at http://www.pearsonhighered.com/Horngren.

For more practice, see Short Exercises S-F:1-6 through S-F:1-8. MyLab Accounting

HOW DO YOU ANALYZE A TRANSACTION?

Accounting is based on actual transactions. A **transaction** is any event that affects the financial position of the business *and* can be measured with faithful representation. Transactions affect what the company has (assets), owes (liabilities), and/or its net worth (equity). Many

Learning Objective 4
Use the accounting equation to analyze transactions

Transaction
An event that affects the financial position of the business and can be measured with faithful representation.

events affect a company, including economic booms and recessions. Accountants, however, do not record the effects of those events. An accountant records only those events that have dollar amounts that can be measured reliably, such as the purchase of a building, a sale of merchandise, and the payment of rent.

Transaction Analysis for Smart Touch Learning

To illustrate accounting for a business, we'll use Smart Touch Learning, the business introduced earlier. We'll account for the transactions of Smart Touch Learning during November 2024 and show how each transaction affects the accounting equation.

Transaction 1—Owner Contribution

Assume Sheena Bright starts the new business, Smart Touch Learning, as a sole proprietorship. The e-learning business receives $30,000 cash from the owner, Sheena Bright, and in return the business gave capital to her. The effect of this transaction on the accounting equation of the business is as follows:

	ASSETS	=	LIABILITIES +	EQUITY
	Cash			Bright, Capital
(1)	+30,000			+30,000

Let's take a close look at the transaction above following these steps:

Step 1: Identify the accounts and the account type. Each transaction must affect at least two accounts but could affect more than two. The two accounts involved in this transaction are *Cash (Asset)* and *Bright, Capital (Equity)*.

Step 2: Decide if each account increases or decreases. Remember to always view this from the *business's* perspective, not from the owner's or customers' perspective. *Cash increases.* The business has more cash than it had before. *Bright, Capital increases.* The business received a $30,000 contribution which increases owner's capital.

Step 3: Determine if the accounting equation is in balance. For each transaction, the amount on the left side of the equation must equal the amount on the right side. $30,000 = $30,000

Transaction 2—Purchase of Land for Cash

The business purchases land for an office location, paying cash of $20,000. This transaction affects the accounting equation of Smart Touch Learning as follows:

	ASSETS		=	LIABILITIES	+	EQUITY
	Cash +	Land				Bright, Capital
Bal.	$30,000					$30,000
(2)	−20,000	+20,000				
Bal.	$10,000 +	$20,000				$30,000

Let's review the transaction using the steps we learned:

Step 1: Identify the accounts and the account type. The two accounts involved are *Cash (Asset)* and *Land (Asset)*.

Step 2: Decide if each account increases or decreases. *Cash decreases.* The business paid cash and therefore has less cash. *Land increases.* The business now has land.

Step 3: Determine if the accounting equation is in balance. *$10,000 + $20,000 = $30,000*

Transaction 3—Purchase of Office Supplies on Account

Smart Touch Learning buys office supplies on account (also called *buying on credit*), agreeing to pay $500 within 30 days. This transaction increases both the assets and the liabilities of the business as follows:

	ASSETS					=	LIABILITIES	+	EQUITY
	Cash	+	Office Supplies	+	Land		Accounts Payable	+	Bright, Capital
Bal.	$10,000			+	$20,000				$30,000
(3)			+500				+500		
Bal.	$10,000	+	$500	+	$20,000		$500	+	$30,000

Step 1: Identify the accounts and the account type. The two accounts involved are *Office Supplies (Asset)* and *Accounts Payable (Liability)*. Office Supplies is an asset, not an expense, because the supplies are something of value that the company has. The office supplies aren't used up yet but will be in the future. The liability created by purchasing "on account" is an **Accounts Payable**, which is a short-term liability that will be paid in the future. A payable is always a liability.

Accounts Payable
A short-term liability that will be paid in the future.

Step 2: Decide if each account increases or decreases. *Office Supplies increases.* The business now has more office supplies than it had before. *Accounts Payable increases.* The business now owes more debt than it did before.

Step 3: Determine if the accounting equation is in balance. *$10,000 + $500 + $20,000 = $500 + $30,000*

> Notice how the steps help when analyzing transactions. It's important that, as you are learning, you use the steps to complete the transactions. Moving forward, try writing the steps out yourself before looking at the transaction analysis.

Transaction 4—Earning of Service Revenue for Cash

Smart Touch Learning earns service revenue by providing training services for clients. The business earns $5,500 of revenue and collects this amount in cash. The effect on the accounting equation is an increase in Cash and an increase in Service Revenue as follows:

	ASSETS					=	LIABILITIES	+	EQUITY		
	Cash	+	Office Supplies	+	Land		Accounts Payable	+	Bright, Capital	+	Service Revenue
Bal.	$10,000	+	$500	+	$20,000		$500	+	$30,000		
(4)	+5,500										+5,500
Bal.	$15,500	+	$500	+	$20,000		$500	+	$30,000	+	$5,500

1-14 Financial  chapter 1

A revenue transaction grows the business, as shown by the increases in assets and equity.

Transaction 5—Earning of Service Revenue on Account

Smart Touch Learning performs a service for clients who do not pay immediately. The business receives the clients' promise to pay $3,000 within one month. This promise is an asset, an **Accounts Receivable**, because the business expects to receive the cash in the future. In accounting, we say that Smart Touch Learning performed this service *on account*. It is in performing the service (doing the work), not collecting the cash, that the company *earns* the revenue. As in Transaction 4, increasing revenue increases equity. Smart Touch Learning records the earning of $3,000 of revenue on account as follows:

> **Accounts Receivable**
> The right to receive cash in the future from customers for goods sold or for services performed.

	ASSETS				=	LIABILITIES +		EQUITY	
	Cash	+ Accounts Receivable	+ Office Supplies	+ Land		Accounts Payable	+	Bright, Capital	+ Service Revenue
Bal.	$15,500		+ $500	+ $20,000		$500	+	$30,000	+ $5,500
(5)		+3,000							+3,000
Bal.	$15,500 +	$3,000	+ $500	+ $20,000		$500	+	$30,000	+ $8,500

> The term *on account* can be used to represent either Accounts Receivable or Accounts Payable. If the business will be <u>receiving</u> cash in the future, the company will record an Accounts <u>Receivable</u>. If the business will be <u>paying</u> cash in the future, the company will record an Accounts <u>Payable</u>.

Transaction 6—Payment of Expenses with Cash

The business pays $3,200 in cash expenses: $2,000 for office rent and $1,200 for employee salaries. The effects on the accounting equation are as follows:

	ASSETS				=	LIABILITIES +		EQUITY			
	Cash	+ Accounts Receivable	+ Office Supplies	+ Land		Accounts Payable	+	Bright, Capital	+ Service Revenue	− Rent Expense	− Salaries Expense
Bal.	$15,500 +	$3,000	+ $500	+ $20,000		$500	+	$30,000	+ $8,500		
(6)	−3,200									−2,000	−1,200
Bal.	$12,300 +	$3,000	+ $500	+ $20,000		$500	+	$30,000	+ $8,500	− $2,000	− $1,200

Expenses have the opposite effect of revenues. Expenses shrink the business, as shown by the decreased balances of assets and equity. Each expense is recorded separately. We record the cash payment in a single amount for the sum of the expenses: $3,200 ($2,000 + $1,200). Notice that the accounting equation remains in balance ($12,300 + $3,000 + $500 + $20,000 = $500 + $30,000 + $8,500 − $2,000 − $1,200).

Accounting and the Business Environment  Financial 1-15

Transaction 7—Payment on Account (Accounts Payable)

The business pays $300 to the store from which it purchased office supplies in Transaction 3. In accounting, we say that the business pays $300 *on account*. The effect on the accounting equation is a decrease in Cash and a decrease in Accounts Payable as shown here:

	ASSETS				=	LIABILITIES +		EQUITY			
	Cash	+ Accounts Receivable	+ Office Supplies	+ Land		Accounts Payable	+	Bright, Capital	+ Service Revenue	− Rent Expense	− Salaries Expense
Bal.	$12,300	+ $3,000	+ $500	+ $20,000		$500	+	$30,000	+ $8,500	− $2,000	− $1,200
(7)	−300					−300					
Bal.	$12,000	+ $3,000	+ $500	+ $20,000		$200	+	$30,000	+ $8,500	− $2,000	− $1,200

The payment of cash on account has no effect on the amount of Office Supplies (Asset). Smart Touch Learning has not increased the amount of its office supplies; instead, it is paying off a liability (Accounts Payable decreased $300) with cash (Cash decreased $300). **To record an increase to Office Supplies, in this transaction, would be accounting for the purchase of office supplies twice.** We have already recorded the purchase of office supplies in Transaction 3; in this transaction, we are now ready to record only the payment on account.

Why didn't we record an increase to Office Supplies? We are making a payment for the supplies; wouldn't we increase Office Supplies and decrease Cash?

Transaction 8—Collection on Account (Accounts Receivable)

In Transaction 5, the business performed services for clients on account. Smart Touch Learning now collects $2,000 from a client. We say that Smart Touch Learning collects the cash *on account*. The business will record an increase in the asset Cash. Should it also record an increase in Service Revenue? No, because the business already recorded the revenue when it earned the revenue in Transaction 5. The phrase "collect cash on account" means to record an increase in Cash and a decrease in Accounts Receivable. Accounts Receivable is decreased because the $2,000 that the business was to collect at some point in the future is being collected today. The effect on the accounting equation is as follows:

	ASSETS				=	LIABILITIES +		EQUITY			
	Cash	+ Accounts Receivable	+ Office Supplies	+ Land		Accounts Payable	+	Bright, Capital	+ Service Revenue	− Rent Expense	− Salaries Expense
Bal.	$12,000	+ $3,000	+ $500	+ $20,000		$200	+	$30,000	+ $8,500	− $2,000	− $1,200
(8)	+2,000	−2,000									
Bal.	$14,000	+ $1,000	+ $500	+ $20,000		$200	+	$30,000	+ $8,500	− $2,000	− $1,200

This transaction is recorded as an increase in one asset (Cash) and a decrease in another asset (Accounts Receivable). Is the accounting equation still in balance? Yes. **As long as you record an increase and decrease of the same amount on one side of the accounting equation, the accounting equation remains in balance.** In other words, total Assets, Liabilities, and Equity are all unchanged from the preceding total. Why? Because Smart Touch Learning exchanged one asset (Cash) for another (Accounts Receivable), causing a zero effect on the total amount of assets in the accounting equation (+$2,000 − $2,000 = $0).

Don't I have to put an amount on the left side of the accounting equation and an amount on the right side of the accounting equation for the equation to balance?

1-16 Financial chapter 1

Transaction 9—Owner Withdrawal of Cash

Sheena Bright withdraws $5,000 cash from the business. The effect on the accounting equation is as follows:

	ASSETS				=	LIABILITIES +		EQUITY			
	Cash	+ Accounts Receivable	+ Office Supplies	+ Land		Accounts Payable	+ Bright, Capital	− Bright, Withdrawals	+ Service Revenue	− Rent Expense	− Salaries Expense
Bal.	$14,000	+ $1,000	+ $500	+ $20,000		$200	+ $30,000		+ $8,500	− $2,000	− $1,200
(9)	−5,000							−5,000			
Bal.	$ 9,000	+ $1,000	+ $500	+ $20,000		$200	+ $30,000	− $5,000	+ $8,500	− $2,000	− $1,200

The owner's withdrawal decreases the business's cash and equity. *Withdrawals do not represent an expense because they are not related to the earning of revenue. Therefore, owner's withdrawals do not affect the business's net income or net loss.*

A summary of all nine transactions for Smart Touch Learning is presented in Exhibit F:1-5.

Exhibit F:1-5 | Analysis of Transactions, Smart Touch Learning

1. Smart Touch Learning received $30,000 cash and gave capital to Sheena Bright, owner.
2. Paid $20,000 cash for land.
3. Bought $500 of office supplies on account.
4. Received $5,500 cash from clients for service revenue earned.
5. Performed services for clients on account, $3,000.
6. Paid cash expenses: office rent, $2,000; employee salaries, $1,200.
7. Paid $300 on the accounts payable created in Transaction 3.
8. Collected $2,000 on the accounts receivable created in Transaction 5.
9. Sheena Bright, owner, withdrew cash of $5,000.

	ASSETS				=	LIABILITIES +		EQUITY			
	Cash	+ Accounts Receivable	+ Office Supplies	+ Land		Accounts Payable	+ Bright, Capital	− Bright, Withdrawals	+ Service Revenue	− Rent Expense	− Salaries Expense
(1)	+30,000						+30,000				
(2)	−20,000			+20,000							
Bal.	$10,000			+ $20,000			$30,000				
(3)			+500			+500					
Bal.	$10,000		+ $500	+ $20,000		$500	+ $30,000				
(4)	+5,500								+5,500		
Bal.	$15,500		+ $500	+ $20,000		$500	+ $30,000		+ $5,500		
(5)		+3,000							+3,000		
Bal.	$15,500	+ $3,000	+ $500	+ $20,000		$500	+ $30,000		+ $8,500		
(6)	−3,200									−2,000	−1,200
Bal.	$12,300	+ $3,000	+ $500	+ $20,000		$500	+ $30,000		+ $8,500	− $2,000	− $1,200
(7)	−300					−300					
Bal.	$12,000	+ $3,000	+ $500	+ $20,000		$200	+ $30,000		+ $8,500	− $2,000	− $1,200
(8)	+2,000	−2,000									
Bal.	$14,000	+ $1,000	+ $500	+ $20,000		$200	+ $30,000		+ $8,500	− $2,000	− $1,200
(9)	−5,000							−5,000			
Bal.	$ 9,000	+ $1,000	+ $500	+ $20,000		$200	+ $30,000	− $5,000	+ $8,500	− $2,000	− $1,200

$30,500 = $30,500

17. Using the information provided, analyze the effects of Lawlor Lawn Service's transactions on the accounting equation.

May 1	Received $1,700 and gave capital to Eric Lawlor.
May 3	Purchased a mower on account, $1,440.
May 5	Performed lawn services for client on account, $200.
May 17	Paid $60 cash for gas used in mower.
May 28	Eric Lawlor withdrew cash of $300.

Check your answers online in MyLab Accounting or at http://www.pearsonhighered.com/Horngren.

For more practice, see Short Exercises S-F:1-9 and S-F:1-10.   MyLab Accounting

HOW DO YOU PREPARE FINANCIAL STATEMENTS?

We have now recorded Smart Touch Learning's transactions, and they are summarized in Exhibit F:1-5. Notice how total assets equal total liabilities plus equity ($30,500 = $30,500).

But a basic question remains: How will people actually use this information? The information in Exhibit F:1-5 does not tell a lender whether Smart Touch Learning can pay off a loan. The exhibit does not tell whether the business is profitable.

To address these important questions, we need financial statements. **Financial statements** are business documents that are used to communicate information needed to make business decisions. Four financial statements are prepared. These statements are prepared in the order listed in Exhibit F:1-6.

Because financial statements are used to communicate information, they always include a heading with important details about the reports. The standard three-line heading tells the reader of the statement who, what, and when—the name of the business, the title of the report, and the specific date or time period of the report.

Learning Objective 5
Prepare financial statements

Financial Statements
Business documents that are used to communicate information needed to make business decisions.

Exhibit F:1-6 | Financial Statements

Financial Statement	Information Provided and Purpose	How Is It Prepared?
Income statement	Provides information about profitability for a particular period for the company	Revenues − Expenses = Net Income or Net Loss
Statement of owner's equity	Shows the changes in the owner's capital account for a particular period	Owner, Capital, Beginning + Owner Contribution + Net Income or − Net Loss for the period − Owner withdrawal = Owner, Capital, Ending
Balance sheet	Provides valuable information to financial statement users about economic resources the company has (assets) as well as debts the company owes (liabilities), and allows decision makers to determine their opinion about the financial position of the company	Assets = Liabilities + Owner's Equity
Statement of cash flows	Reports on a business's cash receipts and cash payments for a period of time	Cash flows from operating activities Cash flows from investing activities Cash flows from financing activities

1-18 Financial      chapter 1

Income Statement

Income Statement
Reports the *net income* or *net loss* of the business for a specific period.

Let's start by reviewing the **income statement**. The income statement (also called the *statement of earnings*) presents a summary of a business entity's revenues and expenses for a period of time, such as a month, quarter, or year. The income statement tells us whether the business enjoyed net income or suffered a net loss. Remember:

- Net income means total revenues are greater than total expenses.
- Net loss means total expenses are greater than total revenues.

It's important to remember that the only two types of accounts that are reported on the income statement are revenues and expenses. Exhibit F:1-7 shows the income statement for Smart Touch Learning. Every income statement contains similar information.

Exhibit F:1-7 | Income Statement

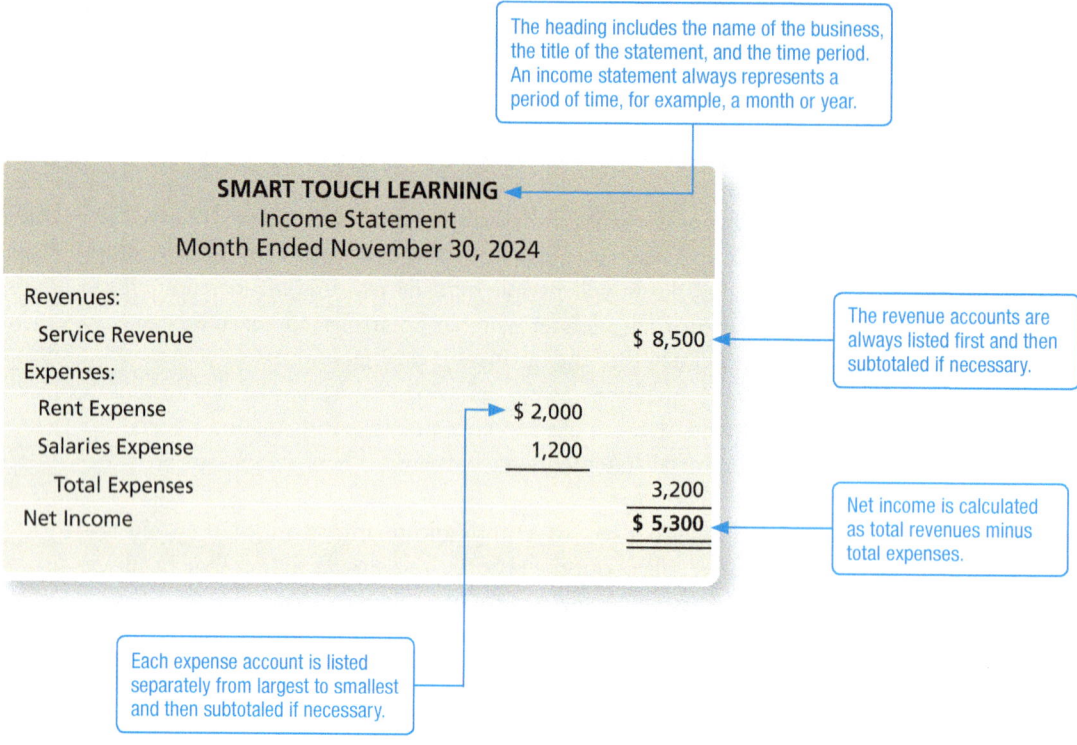

Statement of Owner's Equity

Statement of Owner's Equity
Shows the changes in the owner's capital account for a specific period.

The next statement prepared is the **statement of owner's equity**. The statement of owner's equity shows the changes in owner's capital for a business entity during a time period, such as a month, quarter, or year.

Review the statement of owner's equity for Smart Touch Learning in Exhibit F:1-8. Notice that the net income for the month is the net income that was calculated on the income statement. This is the main reason why the income statement is prepared before the statement of owner's equity. The net income (or net loss) must first be calculated on the income statement and then carried to the statement of owner's equity.

Exhibit F:1-8 | Statement of Owner's Equity

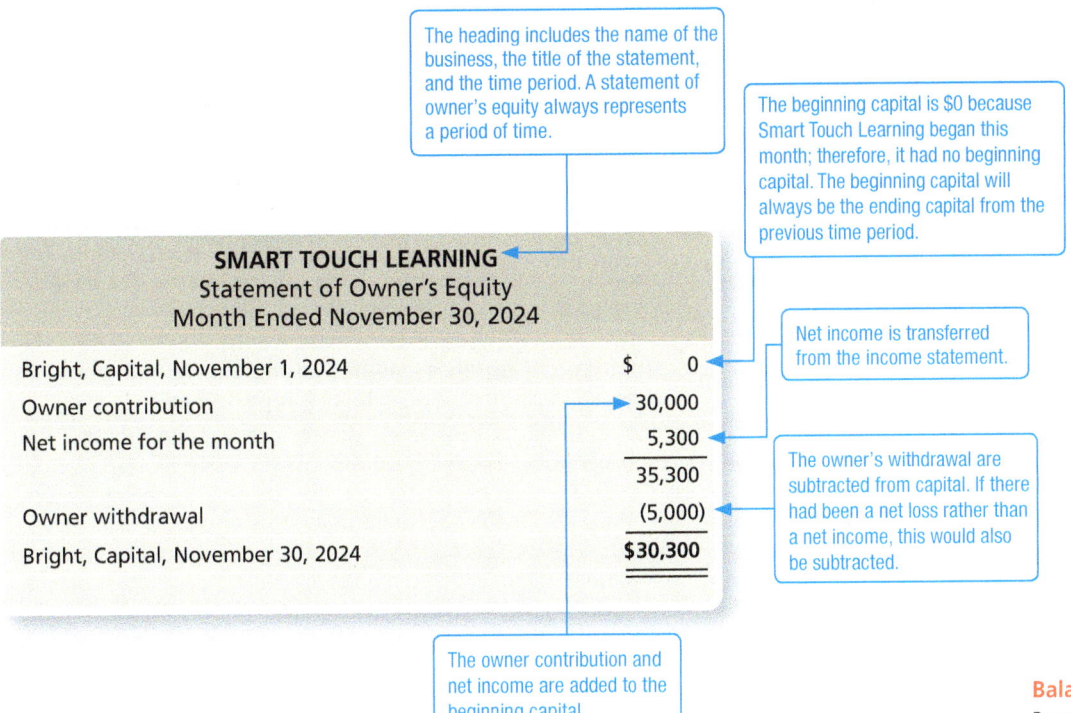

Balance Sheet

The **balance sheet** (also called the *statement of financial position*) lists a business entity's assets, liabilities, and owner's equity as of a specific date, usually the end of a month, quarter, or year. **The balance sheet is a snapshot of the entity. An investor or creditor can quickly assess the overall health of a business by viewing the balance sheet.**

Review the balance sheet for Smart Touch Learning in Exhibit F:1-9. Every balance sheet is prepared in a similar manner.

Balance Sheet
Reports on the assets, liabilities, and owner's equity of the business as of a specific date.

What does the balance sheet tell an investor or creditor?

Exhibit F:1-9 | Balance Sheet

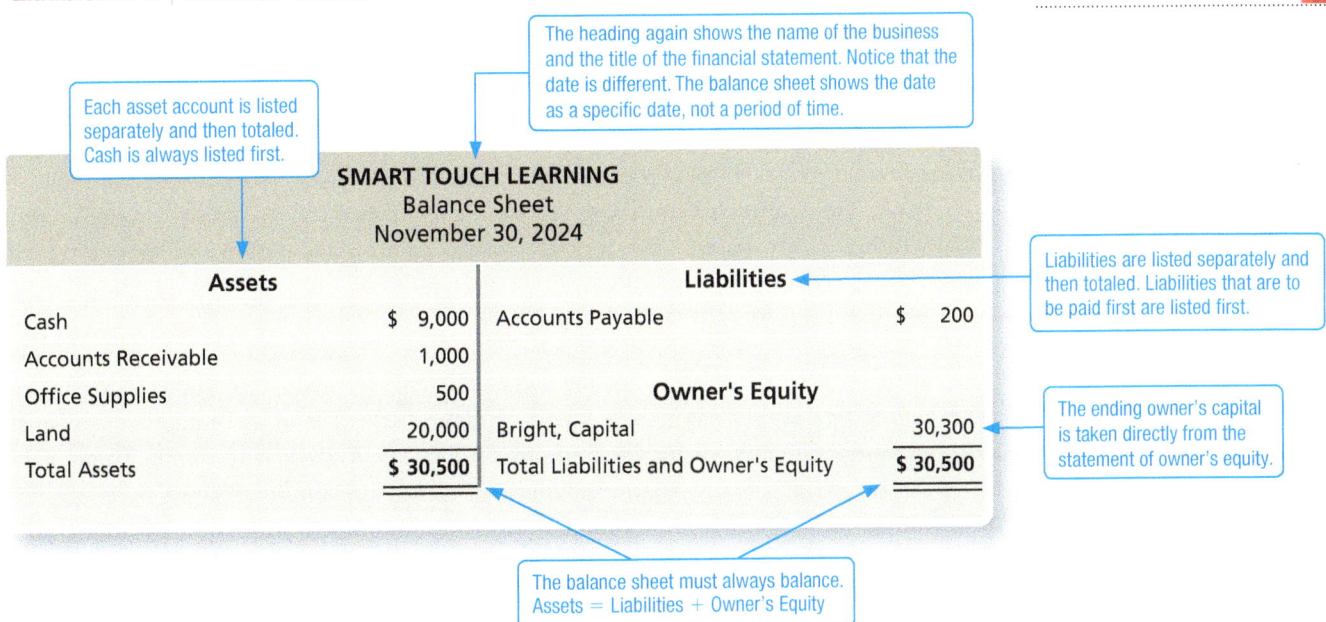

TYING IT ALL TOGETHER

At the beginning of the chapter, we introduced **Starbucks Corporation** as a leading retailer in the specialty coffee market. Starbucks purchases and roasts high-quality coffees and sells other beverages (such as tea). In addition, Starbucks sells a variety of fresh food items including snack offerings.

What type of asset accounts would Starbucks have and what financial statement would those assets be reported on?

Starbucks reports many assets on its balance sheet, including the following: Cash; Accounts Receivable; Inventories; and Property, Plant, and Equipment.

If Starbucks owed money to a vendor, how would this be reported on its financial statements?

Money owed to a vendor is reported on the balance sheet as Accounts Payable. As of October 1, 2017, Starbucks Corporation reported $782.5 million of Accounts Payable. This represents an increase in debt from the previous year of $730.6 million.

How does Starbucks earn revenue and where would this be reported on its financial statements?

Starbucks reports three main revenue sources on its income statement: revenue received from operating stores owned by the company, revenue received from stores licensed to sell Starbucks products, and revenue from consumer packaged goods such as packaged coffee and other beverages sold at grocery stores. The largest source of revenue for Starbucks comes from its company-operated stores and represents 79% of total revenue.

What type of expenses might Starbucks have and what financial statement would this be reported on?

Starbucks reports its expenses on the income statement. Its largest expense for the year ended October 1, 2017, is Cost of Sales at $9,038.2 million (i.e., the cost to purchase the items it sells). The income statement also includes store operating expenses of $6,493.3 million for costs (such as utilities, salaries, and benefits for employees). Starbucks also reports $553.8 million in other operating expenses for the year ending October 1, 2017. Other operating expenses might include items such as advertising expenses.

When you are preparing the financial statements, start by identifying which account goes on which statement. Each account will only go on one statement, except for Capital and Cash. For example, Service Revenue is only reported on the income statement. Liabilities, such as Accounts Payable, are only reported on the balance sheet. Cash and Capital appear on two statements. Cash is reported on the balance sheet and statement of cash flows, and Capital is reported on the statement of owner's equity and the balance sheet.

Statement of Cash Flows
Reports on a business's cash receipts and cash payments for a specific period.

Would the purchase of supplies on account be reported on the statement of cash flows?

Statement of Cash Flows

The **statement of cash flows** reports the cash coming in (positive amounts) and the cash going out (negative amounts) during a period. It only reports transactions that involve cash because it reports the net increase or decrease in *cash* during the period and the ending *cash* balance. **If a transaction does not involve cash, such as the purchase of supplies on account, it will not be reported on the statement of cash flows.**

The statement of cash flows is divided into three distinct sections: operating, investing, and financing. *Operating activities* involve cash receipts for services and cash payments for expenses. *Investing activities* include the purchase and sale of land and equipment for cash. *Financing activities* include cash contributions by the owner, cash withdrawals paid to the owner, cash received from borrowing, and cash paid when loans are repaid.

Take a look at the statement of cash flows for Smart Touch Learning (Exhibit F:1-10). Notice the important items that the statement of cash flows contains.

Accounting and the Business Environment Financial 1-21

Exhibit F:1-10 | **Statement of Cash Flows**

SMART TOUCH LEARNING
Statement of Cash Flows
Month Ended November 30, 2024

Cash flows from operating activities:		
Receipts:		
Collections from customers		$ 7,500
Payments:		
To suppliers	$ (2,300)	
To employees	(1,200)	(3,500)
Net cash provided by operating activities		4,000
Cash flows from investing activities:		
Acquisition of land	(20,000)	
Net cash used by investing activities		(20,000)
Cash flows from financing activities:		
Owner contribution	30,000	
Owner withdrawal	(5,000)	
Net cash provided by financing activities		25,000
Net increase in cash		9,000
Cash balance, November 1, 2024		0
Cash balance, November 30, 2024		$ 9,000

Annotations:
- The heading includes the name of the business, the title of the statement, and the time period. A statement of cash flows always represents a period of time.
- Each dollar amount is calculated by evaluating the cash column on Exhibit 1-5. For example, collections from customers is calculated by adding the cash received from customers in Transaction 4 ($5,500) plus Transaction 8 ($2,000).
- Operating activities involve cash receipts for services provided and cash payments for expenses paid.
- Investing activities include the purchase and sale of land and equipment for cash.
- Financing activities include cash contributions by the owner and owner withdrawals of cash.
- The ending cash balance must match the cash balance on the balance sheet.

18. Using the following information, complete the income statement, statement of owner's equity, and balance sheet for DR Painting for the month of March 2024. The business began operations on March 1, 2024.

Accounts Receivable	$ 1,400	Salaries Expense	$ 800
Accounts Payable	1,000	Service Revenue	7,000
Cash	22,300	Office Supplies	1,800
Owner contribution during March	40,000	Truck	20,000
Owner withdrawal during March	1,500	Utilities Expense	200
Richardson, Capital, March 1, 2024	0	Utilities Expense	200

Check your answers online in MyLab Accounting or at http://www.pearsonhighered.com/Horngren.

For more practice, see Short Exercises S-F:1-11 through S-F:1-15. MyLab Accounting

HOW DO YOU USE FINANCIAL STATEMENTS TO EVALUATE BUSINESS PERFORMANCE?

Learning Objective 6
Use financial statements and return on assets (ROA) to evaluate business performance

Each of the financial statements provides different information about the company to the users of the financial statements. Review Exhibit F:1-6 for the information provided and the purpose of each financial statement.

Kohl's Corporation

In this chapter, we have reviewed the transactions and financial statements of Smart Touch Learning, a fictitious company. Now it's time to apply what we have learned to a real-world company. In each chapter, we will review the financial statements of **Kohl's Corporation** to learn how to apply the concepts presented in the chapter to evaluate its business performance. Kohl's Corporation is a moderately priced retailer of apparel, footwear, accessories, beauty, and home products with more than 1,159 department stores, a website, 12 FILA outlets, and four Off-Aisle clearance centers. Kohl's has a merchandise mix that includes both national brands (61% of total sales in 2018) and private and exclusive brands (39% of total sales in 2018). Its private brands include Apt. 9, Croft & Barrow, Jumping Beans, SO, and Sonoma Goods for Life.

Take a moment to review the 2018 financial statements for Kohl's Corporation. Visit **http://www.pearsonhighered.com/Horngren** for a link to Kohl's Corporation's annual report. Let's start by identifying the financial statements that we've discussed in this chapter. The income statement is presented on page 37 of the annual report and is called the *Consolidated Statements of Income*. Notice that the income statement calculates net income (revenue minus expenses). Kohl's net income for the year ending February 2, 2019, was $801 (in millions) or $801,000,000.

The balance sheet is presented on page 36 of the annual report. Can you find assets, liabilities, and equity? As we have learned in this chapter, Kohl's assets of $12,469 million are equal to its liabilities and equity, $12,469 million.

Return on Assets (ROA)

Return on Assets (ROA)
Measures how profitably a company uses its assets. Net income / Average total assets.

One of the many tools that users of financial statements can use to determine how well a company is performing is the company's **return on assets (ROA)**. Return on assets measures how profitably a company uses its assets. Return on assets is calculated by dividing net income by average total assets. Average total assets is calculated by adding the beginning and ending total assets for the time period and then dividing by two.

DECISIONS

How can individuals make decisions about investing in the stock market?

Lori Cummings just inherited $10,000 from her grandmother. She has decided that she will invest the money in the stock market. She is thinking about investing in one of her favorite clothing stores. The problem is she can't decide between Kohl's or Target.
How should Lori decide between the companies? What resources should she use?

Solution

Lori should begin by reviewing the financial statements of each business. She can locate them on the companies' Web sites or on the Securities and Exchange Commission's Web site (**http://www.sec.gov/edgar.shtml**). She should review the income statements and compare net income. Which business was more profitable? She should look at the balance sheets, carefully reviewing each part of the accounting equation. What was the dollar amount of assets? How much debt does the business have? In addition, she could go online and research the individual companies using a Web site such as Yahoo! Finance. These Web sites provide news and information about the company, such as current headlines, key statistics, and industry comparisons.
Lori should also consider diversifying her investment. Diversifying involves investing in more than one company and in a variety of industries and companies of different sizes. Diversification reduces the risk of an investment. Lori should consider investing half of the $10,000 in a company in a different industry, such as her favorite restaurant or food manufacturer.

> Return on assets = Net income / Average total assets
> Average total assets = (Beginning total assets + Ending total assets) / 2

Let's take a moment to calculate Kohl's return on assets and measure how profitably it uses its assets. On its 2018 income statement, Kohl's reported net income of $801 million. The corporation reported beginning total assets (found on the balance sheet) of $13,389 million and ending total assets of $12,469 million. Kohl's return on assets for 2018 is (all amounts in millions):

> Return on assets = $801 / (($13,389 + $12,469) / 2)
> = $801 / $12,929
> = 0.0620 = 6.2%

How do we as an investor know if 6.2% is good or bad? We have to compare the return on assets of competing companies such as **Target Corporation** and J.C. Penney Corporation, Inc. What if we told you that Target Corporation's return on assets was 7.2% and J.C. Penney Corporation's return on assets was (3.2%)? Due to Kohl's and Target's higher ROAs, we now know that both of these companies have a stronger return on assets than does J.C. Penney Corporation. What does this mean? It means that Kohl's and Target produce more profit per every dollar of assets than J.C. Penney does. In fact, J.C. Penney did not earn a profit in 2018, but instead had a net loss as indicated by its negative ROA.

As you learn more about accounting, you will explore more financial tools that are available to help investors evaluate a company's performance. Only after an investor looks at the big picture of a company will he or she have a good sense of the company's investment potential.

Try It!

19. Using the following information, calculate the return on assets.

Net income for November, 2024	$ 5,000
Total assets, November 1, 2024	76,000
Total assets, November 30, 2024	80,250

Check your answer online in MyLab Accounting or at http://www.pearsonhighered.com/Horngren.

For more practice, see Short Exercise S-F:1-16. MyLab Accounting

REVIEW

> Things You Should Know

1. **Why is accounting important?**

   - Accounting is the language of business.
   - Accounting is used by decision makers including individuals, businesses, investors, creditors, and taxing authorities.
   - Accounting can be divided into two major fields: financial accounting and managerial accounting.
   - Financial accounting is used by external decision makers, and managerial accounting is used by internal decision makers.
   - All businesses need accountants. Accountants work in corporate or industry accounting, public accounting, financial services, and governmental accounting.
   - Accountants can be licensed or certified as a Certified Public Accountant (CPA), Chartered Global Management Accountant (CGMA), Certified Management Accountant (CMA), or Certified Financial Planner (CFP).

2. **What are the organizations and rules that govern accounting?**

   - Generally Accepted Accounting Principles (GAAP) are the rules that govern accounting in the United States.
   - The Financial Accounting Standards Board (FASB) is responsible for the creation and governance of accounting standards.
   - Economic entity assumption: Requires an organization to be a separate economic unit such as a sole proprietorship, partnership, corporation, or limited-liability company.
   - Cost principle: Acquired assets and services should be recorded at their actual cost.
   - Going concern assumption: Assumes that an entity will remain in operation for the foreseeable future.
   - Monetary unit assumption: Assumes financial transactions are recorded in a monetary unit.

3. **What is the accounting equation?**

   - Assets = Liabilities + Equity
     - Assets: Items the business owns or controls (examples: cash, furniture, land)
     - Liabilities: Items the business owes (examples: accounts payable, notes payable, salaries payable)
     - Equity: Owner's claims to the assets (examples: owner's capital, owner's withdrawal, revenues, expenses)

4. **How do you analyze a transaction?**

   - A transaction affects the financial position of a business and can be measured with faithful representation.
   - Transactions are analyzed using three steps:
     - **Step 1:** Identify the accounts and account type (Asset, Liability, or Equity).
     - **Step 2:** Decide whether each account increases or decreases.
     - **Step 3:** Determine whether the accounting equation is in balance.

5. **How do you prepare financial statements?**

    - Financial statements are prepared in the following order:
        1. Income statement:
            - Reports the net income or net loss of a business for a specific period.
            - Revenues − Expenses = Net Income or Net Loss
        2. Statement of owner's equity:
            - Reports on the changes in owner's capital for a specific period.
            - Capital, Beginning + Owner Contribution + Net Income (or − Net Loss) − Owner Withdrawal = Capital, Ending
        3. Balance sheet:
            - Reports on an entity's assets, liabilities, and owner's equity as of a specific date.
            - Assets = Liabilities + Owner's Equity
        4. Statement of cash flows:
            - Reports on a business's cash receipts and cash payments for a specific period.
            - Includes three sections:
                - Cash flows from operating activities: Involves cash receipts for services and cash payments for expenses.
                - Cash flows from investing activities: Includes the purchase and sale of land and equipment for cash.
                - Cash flows from financing activities: Includes cash contributions by owner, cash withdrawals paid to the owner, cash received from borrowing, and cash paid to repay loans.

6. **How do you use financial statements to evaluate business performance?**

    - Income statement evaluates profitability.
    - Statement of owner's equity shows the changes in the owner's capital account for a period of time.
    - Balance sheet details the economic resources the company has, the debts the company owes, and the company's net worth.
    - Statement of cash flows shows the change in cash.
    - Return on assets (ROA) = Net income / Average total assets.

> Check Your Understanding

Check your understanding of the chapter by completing this problem and then looking at the solution. Use this practice to help identify which sections of the chapter you need to study more.

Ron Smith opens an apartment-locator business near a college campus. The company will be named Campus Apartment Locators. During the first month of operations, July 2024, the business completes the following transactions:

a. Smith contributes $35,000 to the business. The business gives capital to Smith.

b. Purchases $350 of office supplies on account.

c. Pays cash of $30,000 to acquire a lot next to campus.

d. Locates apartments for clients and receives cash of $1,900.

e. Pays $100 on the accounts payable the business created in Transaction (b).

f. Pays cash expenses for office rent, $400, and utilities, $100.

g. Smith withdrew cash of $1,200.

Requirements

1. Analyze the preceding transactions in terms of their effects on the accounting equation of Campus Apartment Locators. Use Exhibit F:1-5 as a guide. (See Learning Objective 4)
2. Prepare the income statement, statement of owner's equity, balance sheet, and statement of cash flows of the business after recording the transactions. (See Learning Objective 5)
3. Calculate the return on assets (ROA). (See Learning Objective 6)

> Solution

Requirement 1

	ASSETS				=	LIABILITIES +		EQUITY				
	Cash +	Office Supplies +	Land			Accounts Payable +	Smith, Capital −	Smith, Withdrawals +	Service Revenue −	Rent Expense −	Utilities Expense
(a)	+35,000						+35,000				
(b)		+350				+350					
Bal.	$35,000 +	$350				$350 +	$35,000				
(c)	−30,000		+30,000								
Bal.	$5,000 +	$350 +	$30,000			$350 +	$35,000				
(d)	+1,900								+1,900		
Bal.	$6,900 +	$350 +	$30,000			$350 +	$35,000		+ $1,900		
(e)	−100					−100					
Bal.	$6,800 +	$350 +	$30,000			$250 +	$35,000		+ $1,900		
(f)	−500									−400	−100
Bal.	$6,300 +	$350 +	$30,000			$250 +	$35,000		+ $1,900 −	$400 −	$100
(g)	−1,200							−1,200			
Bal.	$5,100 +	$350 +	$30,000			$250 +	$35,000 −	$1,200 +	$1,900 −	$400 −	$100

$35,450 = $35,450

Requirement 2

CAMPUS APARTMENT LOCATORS
Income Statement
Month Ended July 31, 2024

Revenues:		
Service Revenue		$ 1,900
Expenses:		
Rent Expense	$ 400	
Utilities Expense	100	
Total Expenses		500
Net Income		$ 1,400

CAMPUS APARTMENT LOCATORS
Statement of Owner's Equity
Month Ended July 31, 2024

Smith, Capital, July 1, 2024	$ 0
Owner contribution	35,000
Net income for the month	1,400
	36,400
Owner withdrawal	(1,200)
Smith, Capital, July 31, 2024	$ 35,200

CAMPUS APARTMENT LOCATORS
Balance Sheet
July 31, 2024

Assets		Liabilities	
Cash	$ 5,100	Accounts Payable	$ 250
Office Supplies	350	**Owner's Equity**	
Land	30,000	Smith, Capital	35,200
Total Assets	$ 35,450	Total Liabilities and Owner's Equity	$ 35,450

CAMPUS APARTMENT LOCATORS
Statement of Cash Flows
Month Ended July 31, 2024

Cash flows from operating activities:		
Receipts:		
Collections from customers		$ 1,900
Payments:		
To suppliers		(600)
Net cash provided by operating activities		1,300
Cash flows from investing activities:		
Acquisition of land	$ (30,000)	
Net cash used by investing activities		(30,000)
Cash flows from financing activities:		
Owner contribution	35,000	
Owner withdrawal	(1,200)	
Net cash provided by financing activities		33,800
Net increase in cash		5,100
Cash balance, July 1, 2024		0
Cash balance, July 31, 2024		$ 5,100

Requirement 3

> Return on assets = Net income / Average total assets
> Average total assets = (Beginning total assets + Ending total assets) / 2
> Average total assets = ($0 + $35,450) / 2 = $17,725
> Return on assets = $1,400 / $17,725 = 0.079 = 7.9%

> Key Terms

Accounting (p. 1-2)
Accounting Equation (p. 1-10)
Accounts Payable (p. 1-13)
Accounts Receivable (p. 1-14)
Assets (p. 1-10)
Audit (p. 1-9)
Balance Sheet (p. 1-19)
Certified Financial Planner (CFP) (p. 1-5)
Certified Management Accountants (CMAs) (p. 1-4)
Certified Public Accountants (CPAs) (p. 1-4)
Chartered Global Management Accountant (CGMA) (p. 1-4)
Corporation (p. 1-7)
Cost Principle (p. 1-8)
Creditor (p. 1-4)
Economic Entity Assumption (p. 1-7)

Equity (p. 1-10)
Expenses (p. 1-11)
Faithful Representation (p. 1-7)
Financial Accounting (p. 1-3)
Financial Accounting Standards Board (FASB) (p. 1-6)
Financial Statements (p. 1-17)
Generally Accepted Accounting Principles (GAAP) (p. 1-6)
Going Concern Assumption (p. 1-8)
Income Statement (p. 1-18)
International Accounting Standards Board (IASB) (p. 1-8)
International Financial Reporting Standards (IFRS) (p. 1-8)
Liabilities (p. 1-10)
Limited-Liability Company (LLC) (p. 1-7)
Managerial Accounting (p. 1-3)
Monetary Unit Assumption (p. 1-8)

Net Income (p. 1-11)
Net Loss (p. 1-11)
Owner's Capital (p. 1-10)
Owner's Withdrawals (p. 1-11)
Partnership (p. 1-7)
Public Company Accounting Oversight Board (PCAOB) (p. 1-9)
Return on Assets (ROA) (p. 1-22)
Revenues (p. 1-10)
Sarbanes-Oxley Act (SOX) (p. 1-9)
Securities and Exchange Commission (SEC) (p. 1-6)
Sole Proprietorship (p. 1-7)
Statement of Cash Flows (p. 1-20)
Statement of Owner's Equity (p. 1-18)
Transaction (p. 1-11)

> Quick Check

Learning Objective 1

1. Accounting is the information system that
    a. measures business activities.
    b. communicates the results to decision makers.
    c. processes information into reports.
    d. All of the above

Learning Objective 1

2. Which of the following is not an external user of a business's financial information?
    a. Taxing authorities
    b. Customers
    c. Employees
    d. Investors

Learning Objective 2

3. Generally Accepted Accounting Principles (GAAP) are currently formulated by the
    a. Financial Accounting Standards Board (FASB).
    b. Securities and Exchange Commission (SEC).

c. Institute of Management Accountants (IMA).
d. American Institute of Certified Public Accountants (AICPA).

4. Which type of business organization is owned by only one owner? **Learning Objective 2**
   a. Corporation
   b. Partnership
   c. Sole proprietorship
   d. Items a, b, and c are all correct.

5. Which of the following characteristics best describes a corporation? **Learning Objective 2**
   a. A business with a single owner
   b. Is not taxed
   c. Stockholders not personally liable for entity's debts
   d. Not a separate taxable entity

6. Which of the following requires accounting information to be complete, neutral, and free from material error? **Learning Objective 2**
   a. Faithful representation concept
   b. Cost principle
   c. Economic entity assumption
   d. Going concern assumption

7. At the end of a recent year, Global Cleaning Service, a full-service house and office cleaning service, had total assets of $3,630 and equity of $2,280. How much were Global Cleaning Service's liabilities? **Learning Objective 3**
   a. $5,910
   b. $3,630
   c. $1,350
   d. $2,280

8. Consider the overall effects on Global Cleaning Service from selling and performing services on account for $6,400 and paying expenses totaling $2,500. What is Global Cleaning Service's net income or net loss? **Learning Objective 3**
   a. Net income of $3,900
   b. Net loss of $3,900
   c. Net income of $6,400
   d. Net income of $8,900

9. Assume that Global Cleaning Service performed cleaning services for a department store on account for $180. How would this transaction affect Global Cleaning Service's accounting equation? **Learning Objective 4**
   a. Increase both assets and liabilities by $180
   b. Increase both assets and equity by $180
   c. Increase both liabilities and equity by $180
   d. Decrease liabilities by $180, and increase equity by $180

10. The balance sheet reports the **Learning Objective 5**
    a. financial position on a specific date.
    b. results of operations on a specific date.
    c. financial position for a specific period.
    d. results of operations for a specific period.

11. Assume Global Cleaning Service had net income of $570 for the year. Global Cleaning Service's beginning and ending total assets were $4,520 and $4,180, respectively. Calculate Global Cleaning Service's return on assets for the year. **Learning Objective 6**
    a. 12.6%
    b. 13.6%
    c. 13.1%
    d. 7.63%

Check your answers at the end of the chapter.

ASSESS YOUR PROGRESS

> Review Questions

1. What is accounting?
2. Briefly describe the two major fields of accounting.
3. Describe the various types of individuals who use accounting information and how they use that information to make important decisions.
4. What are various certifications available for accountants? Briefly explain each certification.
5. What is the role of the Financial Accounting Standards Board (FASB)?
6. Explain the purpose of Generally Accepted Accounting Principles (GAAP), including the organization currently responsible for the creation and governance of these standards.
7. Describe the similarities and differences among the four different types of business entities discussed in the chapter.
8. A business purchases an acre of land for $5,000. The current market value is $5,550, and the land was assessed for property tax purposes at $5,250. What value should the land be recorded at, and which accounting principle supports your answer?
9. What does the going concern assumption mean for a business?
10. Which concept states that accounting information should be complete, neutral, and free from material error?
11. Financial statements in the United States are reported in U.S. dollars. What assumption supports this statement?
12. Explain the role of the International Accounting Standards Board (IASB) in relation to International Financial Reporting Standards (IFRS).
13. What is the accounting equation? Briefly explain each of the three parts.
14. What are two ways that equity increases? What are the two ways that equity decreases?
15. How is net income calculated? Define *revenues* and *expenses*.
16. What are the steps used when analyzing a business transaction?
17. List the four financial statements. Briefly describe each statement.
18. What is the calculation for ROA? Explain what ROA measures.

Short Exercises

Learning Objective 1

S-F:1-1 Identifying users of accounting information

For each user of accounting information, identify if the user would use financial accounting or managerial accounting.

a. investor
b. banker
c. IRS
d. manager of the business
e. controller
f. stockholder
g. human resources director
h. creditor

S-F:1-2 Determining organizations that govern accounting   **Learning Objective 2**

Suppose you are starting a business, Wholly Shirts, to imprint logos on T-shirts. In organizing the business and setting up its accounting records, you take your information to a CPA to prepare financial statements for the bank. Name the organization that governs the majority of the guidelines that the CPA will use to prepare financial statements for Wholly Shirts. What are those guidelines called?

S-F:1-3 Identifying types of business organizations   **Learning Objective 2**

Chloe Michaels plans on opening Chloe Michaels Floral Designs. She is considering the various types of business organizations and wishes to organize her business with unlimited life and wants owners of the business to not be held personally liable for the business's debts. Additionally, Chloe wants the business to be a separate taxable entity. Which type of business organization will meet Chloe's needs best?

S-F:1-4 Identifying types of business organizations   **Learning Objective 2**

You would like to start a cellular telephone equipment service business. You are considering organizing the business as a sole proprietorship. Identify the advantages and disadvantages of owning a sole proprietorship.

S-F:1-5 Applying accounting assumptions and principles   **Learning Objective 2**

Michael McNamee is the proprietor of a property management company, Apartment Exchange, near the campus of Pensacola State College. The business has cash of $8,000 and furniture that cost $9,000 and has a market value of $13,000. The business debts include accounts payable of $6,000. Michael's personal home is valued at $400,000, and his personal bank account has a balance of $1,200. Consider the accounting principles and assumptions discussed in the chapter, and identify the principle or assumption that best matches the situation:

a. Michael's personal assets are not recorded on the Apartment Exchange's balance sheet.

b. The Apartment Exchange records furniture at its cost of $9,000, not its market value of $13,000.

c. The Apartment Exchange reports its financial statements in U.S. dollars.

d. Michael expects the Apartment Exchange to remain in operation for the foreseeable future.

S-F:1-6 Using the accounting equation   **Learning Objective 3**

Thompson Handyman Services has total assets for the year of $18,400 and total liabilities of $9,050.

Requirements

1. Use the accounting equation to solve for equity.

2. If next year's assets increased by $4,300 and equity decreased by $3,850, what would be the amount of total liabilities for Thompson Handyman Services?

Learning Objective 3   S-F:1-7 Using the accounting equation

Roland's Overhead Doors reports the following financial information:

Assets	$ 45,800
Liabilities	17,220
Roland, Capital	27,460
Roland, Withdrawals	6,500
Revenues	8,850
Expenses	?

Requirements

1. Use the accounting equation to solve for the missing information.
2. Did Roland's Overhead Doors report net income or net loss?

Learning Objective 3   S-F:1-8 Identifying accounts

Consider the following accounts:

a. Accounts Payable
b. Cash
c. Owner, Capital
d. Accounts Receivable
e. Rent Expense
f. Service Revenue
g. Office Supplies
h. Owner, Withdrawals
i. Land
j. Salaries Expense

Identify each account as Asset, Liability, or Equity.

Learning Objective 4   S-F:1-9 Using the accounting equation to analyze transactions

Tiny Town Kennel earns service revenue by caring for the pets of customers. Tiny Town Kennel is organized as a sole proprietorship and owned by Earle Martin. During the past month, Tiny Town Kennel has the following transactions:

a. Received $520 cash for service revenue earned.
b. Paid $325 cash for salaries expense.
c. Martin contributed $1,000 to the business in exchange for capital.
d. Earned $640 for service revenue, but the customer has not paid Tiny Town Kennel yet.
e. Received utility bill of $85, which will be paid next month.
f. Martin withdrew $100 cash.

Indicate the effects of the business transactions on the accounting equation for Tiny Town Kennel. Transaction (a) is answered as a guide. Use the following accounts: Cash; Accounts Receivable; Accounts Payable; Martin, Capital; Martin, Withdrawals; Service Revenue; Salaries Expense; and Utilities Expense.

a. Increase asset (Cash); Increase equity (Service Revenue)

Learning Objective 4   S-F:1-10 Using the accounting equation to analyze transactions

Elaine's Inflatables earns service revenue by providing party planning services and inflatable playscapes. Elaine's Inflatables is organized as a sole proprietorship and owned by Elaine Gibson. During the past month, Elaine's Inflatables had the following transactions:

a. Gibson contributed $10,000 to the business in exchange for capital.
b. Purchased equipment for $5,000 on account.

c. Paid $400 for office supplies.

d. Earned and received $2,500 cash for service revenue.

e. Paid $400 for wages to employees.

f. Gibson withdrew $1,000 cash.

g. Earned $1,000 for services provided. Customer has not yet paid.

h. Paid $1,000 for rent.

i. Received a bill for $250 for the monthly utilities. The bill has not yet been paid.

Indicate the effects of the business transactions on the accounting equation for Elaine's Inflatables. Transaction (a) is answered as a guide. Use the following accounts: Cash; Accounts Receivable; Supplies; Equipment; Accounts Payable; Gibson, Capital; Gibson, Withdrawals; Service Revenue; Wages Expense; Rent Expense; and Utilities Expense.

a. Increase asset (Cash); Increase equity (Gibson, Capital)

S-F:1-11 Identifying accounts on the financial statements   *Learning Objective 5*

Consider the following accounts:

a. Accounts Payable
b. Cash
c. Owner, Capital
d. Accounts Receivable
e. Rent Expense
f. Service Revenue
g. Office Supplies
h. Owner, Withdrawals
i. Land
j. Salaries Expense

Identify the financial statement (or statements) that each account would appear on. Use I for Income Statement, OE for Statement of Owner's Equity, B for Balance Sheet, and C for Statement of Cash Flows.

Use the following information to answer Short Exercises S-F:1-12 through S-F:1-14.

Centerpiece Arrangements has just completed operations for the year ended December 31, 2024. This is the third year of operations for the company. The following data have been assembled for the business:

Insurance Expense	$ 4,500	Salaries Expense	$ 46,000
Service Revenue	70,000	Accounts Payable	17,600
Utilities Expense	1,400	Office Supplies	1,700
Rent Expense	16,000	Right, Withdrawals	4,800
Right, Capital, Jan. 1, 2024	9,000	Accounts Receivable	8,000
Cash	7,200	Equipment	12,100
Owner contribution during the year	5,100		

S-F:1-12 Preparing the income statement   *Learning Objective 5*

Prepare the income statement of Centerpiece Arrangements for the year ended December 31, 2024.

S-F:1-13 Preparing the statement of owner's equity   *Learning Objective 5*

Prepare the statement of owner's equity of Centerpiece Arrangements for the year ended December 31, 2024.

S-F:1-14 Preparing the balance sheet   *Learning Objective 5*

Prepare the balance sheet of Centerpiece Arrangements as of December 31, 2024.

Learning Objective 5

S-F:1-15 Preparing the statement of cash flows

Polk Street Homes had the following cash transactions for the month ended July 31, 2024.

Cash receipts:	
Collections from customers	$ 25,000
Owner contribution	13,000
Cash payments:	
Rent	500
Utilities	2,000
Salaries	1,500
Purchase of equipment	25,000
Owner withdrawal	4,000
Cash balance, July 1, 2024	14,000
Cash balance, July 31, 2024	19,000

Prepare the statement of cash flows for Polk Street Homes for the month ended July 31, 2024.

Learning Objective 6

S-F:1-16 Calculating ROA

Matured Water Services had net income for the month of October of $50,880. Assets as of the beginning and end of the month totaled $362,000 and $486,000, respectively. Calculate Matured Water Services' ROA for the month of October.

> Exercises

Learning Objective 1

E-F:1-17 Identifying users of accounting information

For each of the users of accounting information, identify whether the user is an external decision maker (E) or an internal decision maker (I):

a. customer
b. company manager
c. Internal Revenue Service
d. lender
e. investor
f. controller
g. cost accountant
h. SEC

Learning Objective 2

E-F:1-18 Using accounting vocabulary

Consider the following accounting terms and definitions and match each term to the definition:

1. Sole proprietorship
2. Faithful representation
3. Partnership
4. IFRS
5. Corporation
6. Audit

a. Set of global accounting guidelines, formulated by the IASB
b. Holds that fair market value should not be used over actual costs
c. Stands for Financial Accounting Standards Board
d. Owner is referred to as a proprietor
e. Asserts that accounting information should be complete, neutral, and free from material error

7. Cost principle

8. FASB

9. Creditors

10. SEC

f. An examination of a company's financial statements and records

g. Has two or more owners (called partners)

h. U.S. governmental agency that oversees the U.S. financial markets

i. Type of entity that is designed to limit personal liability exposure of owners to the entity's debts

j. Person or business lending money

E-F:1-19 Using accounting vocabulary

Learning Objectives 3, 5

Consider the following accounting terms and definitions and match each term to the definition:

1. Accounting equation
2. Asset
3. Balance sheet
4. Expense
5. Income statement
6. Liability
7. Net income
8. Net loss
9. Revenue
10. Statement of cash flows
11. Statement of owner's equity

a. An economic resource that is expected to be of benefit in the future

b. Debts that are owed to creditors

c. Excess of total expenses over total revenues

d. Excess of total revenues over total expenses

e. The basic tool of accounting, stated as Assets = Liabilities + Equity

f. Decreases in equity that occur in the course of selling goods or services

g. Increases in equity that occur in the course of selling goods or services

h. Reports on a business's cash receipts and cash payments during a period

i. Reports on an entity's assets, liabilities, and owner's equity as of a specific date

j. Reports on an entity's revenues, expenses, and net income or loss for the period

k. Reports how the owner's capital balance changed from the beginning to the end of the period

E-F:1-20 Using the accounting equation

Learning Objective 3

Compute the missing amount in the accounting equation for each entity from the financial information presented:

	Assets	Liabilities	Equity
Hair Styles	$?	$ 36,000	$ 36,000
Style Cuts	90,000	?	48,000
Your Basket	101,000	68,000	?

Learning Objective 3

E-F:1-21 Using the accounting equation

Wizco Advertising's balance sheet data at May 31, 2024, and June 30, 2024, follow:

	May 31, 2024	June 30, 2024
Total Assets	$ 122,000	$ 287,000
Total Liabilities	66,000	144,000

For each of the following situations that occurred in June 2024 with regard to owner contributions and owner withdrawals, compute the amount of net income or net loss during June 2024.

a. The owner contributed $10,000 to the business and made no withdrawals.

b. The owner made no contributions. The owner withdrew cash of $3,000.

c. The owner made contributions of $12,500 and withdrew cash of $30,000.

Learning Objective 3

E-F:1-22 Using the accounting equation

Mountain Drycleaners started 2024 with total assets of $19,000 and total liabilities of $14,000. At the end of 2024, Mountain's total assets stood at $12,000 and total liabilities were $9,000.

Requirements

1. Did the owner's equity of Mountain Drycleaners increase or decrease during 2024? By how much?
2. Identify the four possible reasons that owner's equity can change.

Learning Objective 3

E-F:1-23 Using the accounting equation

During 2024, Flowing Rivers Spa reported revenue of $30,000. Total expenses for the year were $15,000. Flowing Rivers Spa ended the year with total assets of $43,000, and it owed debts totaling $14,000. At year-end 2023, the business reported total assets of $28,000 and total liabilities of $14,000.

Requirements

1. Compute Flowing Rivers Spa's net income for 2024.
2. Did Flowing Rivers Spa's owner's equity increase or decrease during 2024? By how much?

Learning Objective 3

E-F:1-24 Using the accounting equation

The records of Felix Company show the following at December 31, 2024:

Assets & Liabilities:		Equity:	
Beginning:		Owner contribution	$ 11,000
Assets	$ 67,000	Owner withdrawal	8,000
Liabilities	11,000	Revenues	205,000
Ending:		Expenses	?
Assets	$ 46,000		
Liabilities	34,000		

Requirements

1. Compute the missing amount for Felix Company. You will need to work through owner's equity.
2. Did Felix earn a net income or suffer a net loss for the year? Compute the amount.

E-F:1-25 Using the accounting equation to analyze transactions
Learning Objective 4

As the manager of a Papa Sean's restaurant, you must deal with a variety of business transactions. Give an example of a transaction that has each of the following effects on the accounting equation:

a. Increase one asset and decrease another asset.
b. Decrease an asset and decrease equity.
c. Decrease an asset and decrease a liability.
d. Increase an asset and increase equity.
e. Increase an asset and increase a liability.

E-F:1-26 Using the accounting equation to analyze business transactions
Learning Objective 4

Indicate the effects of the following business transactions on the accounting equation of Vivian's Online Video store. Use the following accounts: Cash; Accounts Receivable; Office Supplies; Office Furniture; Accounts Payable; Vivian, Capital; Vivian, Withdrawals; Rental Revenue; and Rent Expense. Transaction (a) is answered as a guide.

a. Received cash of $10,000 from the owner and gave capital.

Answer: Increase asset (Cash); Increase equity (Vivian, Capital)

b. Earned video rental revenue on account, $2,800.
c. Purchased office furniture on account, $300.
d. Received cash on account, $400.
e. Paid cash on account, $100.
f. Rented videos and received cash of $200.
g. Paid monthly office rent of $1,000.
h. Paid $100 cash to purchase office supplies.

E-F:1-27 Using the accounting equation to analyze business transactions
Learning Objective 4

Indicate the effects of the following business transactions on the accounting equation for Sam's Snack Foods, a supplier of snack foods. Transaction (a) is answered as a guide.

a. Sam's Snack Foods received cash from the owner and gave capital.

Answer: Increase asset (Cash); Increase equity (Sam, Capital)

b. Cash purchase of land for a building site.
c. Paid cash on accounts payable.
d. Purchased equipment; signed a note payable.
e. Performed service for a customer on account.
f. Employees worked for the week but will be paid next Tuesday.
g. Received cash from a customer on accounts receivable.

1-38 Financial chapter 1

h. Borrowed money from the bank.
i. Owner withdrew cash.
j. Incurred utilities expense on account.

Learning Objective 4   **E-F:1-28 Using the accounting equation to analyze business transactions**

The analysis of the first eight transactions of Advanced Accounting Service follows. Describe each transaction.

	ASSETS				LIABILITIES +		EQUITY			
	Cash	+ Accounts Receivable	+ Equipment		Accounts Payable	+	Wei, Capital	− Wei, Withdrawals	+ Service Revenue	− Salaries Expense
1	+31,000						+31,000			
2		+3,800							+3,800	
Bal.	$31,000 +	$3,800					$31,000		+ $3,800	
3			+13,400		+13,400					
Bal.	$31,000 +	$3,800 +	$13,400		$13,400 +		$31,000		+ $3,800	
4	+190	−190								
Bal.	$31,190 +	$3,610 +	$13,400	=	$13,400 +		$31,000		+ $3,800	
5	−410		+410							
Bal.	$30,780 +	$3,610 +	$13,810		$13,400 +		$31,000		+ $3,800	
6	−8,000				−8,000					
Bal.	$22,780 +	$3,610 +	$13,810		$5,400 +		$31,000		+ $3,800	
7	+790								+790	
Bal.	$23,570 +	$3,610 +	$13,810		$5,400 +		$31,000		+ $4,590	
8	−1,500									−1,500
Bal.	$22,070 +	$3,610 +	$13,810		$5,400 +		$31,000		+ $4,590 −	$1,500

Learning Objective 4   **E-F:1-29 Using the accounting equation to analyze business transactions**

Ashley Stamper opened a medical practice. During July, the first month of operation, the business, titled Ashley Stamper, MD, experienced the following events:

Jul. 6	Stamper contributed $68,000 in the business by opening a bank account in the name of A. Stamper, MD. The business gave capital to Stamper.
9	Paid $56,000 cash for land.
12	Purchased medical supplies for $1,500 on account.
15	Officially opened for business.
20	Paid cash expenses: employees' salaries, $1,300; office rent, $1,500; utilities, $100.
31	Earned service revenue for the month, $13,000, receiving cash.
31	Paid $1,050 on account.

Analyze the effects of these events on the accounting equation of the medical practice of Ashley Stamper, MD, using the following format:

ASSETS			=	LIABILITIES +		EQUITY					
Cash +	Medical Supplies +	Land		Accounts Payable	+ Stamper, Capital	− Stamper, Withdrawals	+ Service Revenue	− Salaries Expense	− Rent Expense	− Utilities Expense

E-F:1-30 Preparing the financial statements

Learning Objective 5

Estella Osage publishes an online travel magazine. In need of cash, the business applies for a loan with National Bank. The bank requires borrowers to submit financial statements. With little knowledge of accounting, Estella Osage, the owner, does not know how to proceed.

Requirements

1. What are the four financial statements that the business will need to prepare?
2. Is there a specific order in which the financial statements must be prepared?
3. Explain how to prepare each statement.

Use the following information to answer Exercises E-F:1-31 through E-F:1-33.

The account balances of Wilson Towing Service at June 30, 2024, follow:

Equipment	$ 25,850	Service Revenue	$ 15,000
Office Supplies	1,000	Accounts Receivable	9,000
Notes Payable	6,800	Accounts Payable	8,000
Rent Expense	900	Wilson, Capital, June 1, 2024	3,250
Cash	1,400	Salaries Expense	2,400
Wilson, Withdrawals	3,500		

E-F:1-31 Preparing the income statement

Learning Objective 5

Requirements

Net Income $11,700

1. Prepare the income statement for Wilson Towing Service for the month ending June 30, 2024.
2. What does the income statement report?

E-F:1-32 Preparing the statement of owner's equity

Learning Objective 5

Requirements

Ending Capital $22,450

1. Prepare the statement of owner's equity for Wilson Towing Service for the month ending June 30, 2024. Assume Wilson contributed $11,000 during June.
2. What does the statement of owner's equity report?

E-F:1-33 Preparing the balance sheet

Learning Objective 5

Requirements

Total Assets $37,250

1. Prepare the balance sheet for Wilson Towing Service as of June 30, 2024.
2. What does the balance sheet report?

Use the following information to answer Exercises E-F:1-34 through E-F:1-36.

The assets, liabilities, and equities of Damon Design Studio have the following balances at December 31, 2024. The owner, Eric Damon, began the year with a $39,000 capital balance, contributed $13,000, and withdrew $57,000 during the year.

Notes Payable	$ 14,000	Office Furniture	$ 48,400
Rent Expense	23,000	Utilities Expense	7,200
Cash	3,200	Accounts Payable	3,600
Office Supplies	5,100	Service Revenue	154,600
Salaries Expense	65,000	Accounts Receivable	9,300
Property Tax Expense	2,200	Miscellaneous Expense	3,800

Learning Objective 5

Net Income $53,400

E-F:1-34 Preparing the income statement

Prepare the income statement for Damon Design Studio for the year ending December 31, 2024.

Learning Objective 5

Ending Capital $48,400

E-F:1-35 Preparing the statement of owner's equity

Prepare the statement of owner's equity for Damon Design Studio for the year ending December 31, 2024.

Learning Objective 5

Total Assets $66,000

E-F:1-36 Preparing the balance sheet

Prepare the balance sheet for Damon Design Studio as of December 31, 2024.

Learning Objective 5

E-F:1-37 Preparing the statement of cash flows

For each transaction, identify the appropriate section on the statement of cash flows to report the transaction. Choose from: Cash flows from operating activities (O), Cash flows from investing activities (I), Cash flows from financing activities (F), or Is not reported on the statement of cash flows (X). If reported on the statement, decide whether the transaction should be shown as a positive cash flow (+) or a negative cash flow (−):

a. The business received cash from the owner in exchange for capital.

b. Paid cash on accounts payable for office supplies purchased.

c. Performed services for a customer on account.

d. The owner withdrew cash.

e. Received cash from a customer for services performed.

f. Purchased equipment with cash.

g. Paid rent for the month.

h. Purchased land; signed a note payable.

i. Paid employees wages for the week.

j. Incurred utility expense on account.

Accounting and the Business Environment   Financial   1-41

E-F:1-38 Preparing the statement of cash flows

Learning Objective 5

Morning Bean Food Equipment Company had the following transactions for the month ending January 31, 2024. Morning Bean's cash balance on January 1, 2024, was $11,800.

Decrease in cash $9,350

Jan. 1	The owner contributed an additional $5,000 cash to the business in exchange for capital.
7	Purchased equipment for $2,400 on account.
14	Paid $19,000 cash for land.
17	Paid cash expenses: employees' salaries, $1,300; office rent, $1,600; utilities, $450.
23	The owner withdrew $500.
26	Earned service revenue for the month, $8,500, receiving cash.

Prepare the statement of cash flows of Morning Bean Food Equipment Company for the month ended January 31, 2024.

E-F:1-39 Calculating return on assets

Learning Objective 6

Alice Appliance Service had net income for the year of $58,500. In addition, the balance sheet reports the following balances:

	Jan. 1, 2024	Dec. 31, 2024
Notes Payable	$ 32,000	$ 58,000
Cash	34,000	134,200
Office Furniture	23,000	44,000
Building	160,000	160,000
Accounts Payable	11,500	11,000
Total Owner's Equity	204,500	333,000
Accounts Receivable	2,200	19,800
Equipment	24,000	42,000
Office Supplies	4,800	2,000

Calculate the return on assets for Alice Appliance Service for the year ending December 31, 2024.

E-F:1-40 Using the accounting equation for transaction analysis and calculating return on assets

Learning Objectives 4, 6

Vivian's Online Video currently has a return on assets of 10%. Indicate the effects of the following business transactions on the Vivian's Online Video return on assets. Consider each transaction independently of the others. Identify if the return on assets increases, decreases, or does not change. Explain your answer. Transaction (a) is answered as a guide.

a. Purchased office furniture on account, $300.

Answer: Decreases. The increase in assets (office furniture) increases the denominator in the equation and therefore decreases the ratio.

b. Earned video rental revenue on account, $2,800.

c. Paid $100 cash to purchase office supplies.

d. Received cash of $10,000 from owner in exchange for capital.

e. Paid cash on account, $100.

f. Received cash on account, $400.

> Problems Group A

Learning Objective 4

P-F:1-41A Using the accounting equation for transaction analysis

Cash $13,600

Meg McKinney opened a public relations firm called Solid Gold on August 1, 2024. The following amounts summarize her business on August 31, 2024:

ASSETS	=	LIABILITIES +	EQUITY
Cash + Accounts + Office + Land Receivable Supplies	=	Accounts Payable	+ McKinney, − McKinney, + Service − Rent − Advertising Capital Withdrawals Revenue Expense Expense
Bal. $1,900 + $3,200 + $0 + $15,000	=	$5,000	+ $11,900 + $3,200

During September 2024, the business completed the following transactions:

a. Meg McKinney contributed $17,000 cash in exchange for capital.
b. Performed service for a client and received cash of $800.
c. Paid off the beginning balance of accounts payable.
d. Purchased office supplies from OfficeMax on account, $1,200.
e. Collected cash from a customer on account, $2,000.
f. McKinney withdrew $1,600.
g. Consulted for a new band and billed the client for services rendered, $4,500.
h. Recorded the following business expenses for the month:
 Paid office rent: $1,000.
 Paid advertising: $500.

Analyze the effects of the transactions on the accounting equation of Solid Gold using the format presented in Exhibit F:1-5.

Learning Objective 4

P-F:1-42A Using the accounting equation for transaction analysis

Cash $21,500

Conner Thomas started a new business, Thomas Gymnastics, and completed the following transactions during December:

Dec. 1	Thomas contributed $19,000 cash in exchange for capital.
2	Received $3,800 cash from customers for services performed.
5	Paid $200 cash for office supplies.
9	Performed services for a customer and billed the customer for services rendered, $4,500.
10	Received $200 invoice for utilities due in two weeks.
15	Paid for advertising in the local paper, $250.
20	Paid utility invoice received on December 10.
25	Collected cash in full from customer billed on December 9.
28	Paid rent for the month, $1,600.
28	Paid $1,450 to assistant for wages.
30	Received $1,400 cash from customers for services performed.
31	Thomas withdrew $3,500.

Analyze the effects of the transactions on the accounting equation of Thomas Gymnastics using a format similar to Exhibit F:1-5. Use the following accounts: Cash; Accounts Receivable; Office Supplies; Accounts Payable; Thomas, Capital; Thomas, Withdrawals; Service Revenue; Rent Expense; Utilities Expense; Wages Expense; and Advertising Expense.

P-F:1-43A Preparing financial statements

Learning Objective 5

Presented here are the accounts of Hometown Décor Company for the year ended December 31, 2024.

1. Net Income $115,700

Land	$ 13,000	Owner contribution, 2024	$ 28,000
Notes Payable	33,000	Accounts Payable	14,000
Property Tax Expense	2,800	Accounts Receivable	800
Hunt, Withdrawals	36,000	Advertising Expense	17,000
Rent Expense	14,000	Building	170,400
Salaries Expense	67,000	Cash	2,800
Salaries Payable	1,300	Equipment	17,000
Service Revenue	225,000	Insurance Expense	1,700
Office Supplies	8,000	Interest Expense	6,800
Hunt, Capital, Dec. 31, 2023	56,000		

Requirements

1. Prepare Hometown Décor Company's income statement for the year ended December 31, 2024.
2. Prepare the statement of owner's equity for the year ended December 31, 2024.
3. Prepare the balance sheet as of December 31, 2024.

P-F:1-44A Preparing financial statements

Learning Objective 5

Picture Perfect Photography works weddings and prom-type parties. The balance of Williamson, Capital was $16,000 at December 31, 2023. At December 31, 2024, the business's accounting records show these balances:

b. Ending Capital $76,000

Insurance Expense	$ 6,000	Accounts Receivable	$ 13,000
Cash	42,000	Notes Payable	14,000
Accounts Payable	11,000	Williamson, Capital, Dec. 31, 2024	?
Advertising Expense	4,000	Salaries Expense	25,000
Service Revenue	75,000	Equipment	46,000
Williamson, Withdrawals	8,000	Owner contribution	28,000

Prepare the following financial statements for Picture Perfect Photography:

a. Income statement for the year ended December 31, 2024.

b. Statement of owner's equity for the year ended December 31, 2024.

c. Balance sheet as of December 31, 2024.

P-F:1-45A Preparing financial statements

Learning Objective 5

The bookkeeper of Outdoor Life Landscaping prepared the company's balance sheet while the accountant was ill. The balance sheet, shown on the next page, contains numerous errors. In particular, the bookkeeper knew that the balance sheet should balance, so he plugged in the owner's equity amount needed to achieve this balance.

Total Assets $47,100

The owner's equity is incorrect. All other amounts are correct, but some are out of place or should not be included in this statement. Prepare a corrected balance sheet.

OUTDOOR LIFE LANDSCAPING
Balance Sheet
Month Ended November 30, 2024

Assets		Liabilities	
Cash	$ 4,600	Accounts Receivable	$ 2,000
Office Supplies	600	Tarrant, Withdrawals	11,000
Land	34,100	Service Revenue	35,000
Salaries Expense	2,700	Property Tax Expense	3,000
Office Furniture	5,800	Accounts Payable	2,700
Notes Payable	24,600	**Owner's Equity**	
Rent Expense	450	Tarrant, Capital	19,150
Total Assets	$ 72,850	Total Liabilities	$ 72,850

Learning Objectives 4, 5

2b. Ending Capital $94,560

P-F:1-46A Using the accounting equation for transaction analysis and preparing financial statements

Allen Shonton recently opened his own accounting firm on April 1, which he operates as a sole proprietorship. The name of the new entity is Allen Shonton, CPA. Shonton experienced the following events during the organizing phase of the new business and its first month of operations in 2024:

Apr. 5	Shonton deposited $75,000 in a new business bank account titled Allen Shonton, CPA. The business gave capital to Shonton.
6	Paid $300 cash for letterhead stationery for new office.
7	Purchased office furniture for the office on account, $9,500.
10	Consulted with tax client and received $4,000 for services rendered.
11	Paid utilities, $190.
12	Finished tax hearings on behalf of a client and submitted a bill for accounting services, $20,000.
18	Paid office rent, $750.
25	Received amount due from client that was billed on April 12.
27	Paid full amount of accounts payable created on April 7.
30	Shonton withdrew cash of $3,500.

Requirements

1. Analyze the effects of the events on the accounting equation of Allen Shonton, CPA. Use a format similar to Exhibit F:1-5. Use the following accounts: Cash; Accounts Receivable; Office Supplies; Furniture; Accounts Payable; Shonton, Capital; Shonton, Withdrawals; Service Revenue; Rent Expense; and Utilities Expense.

2. Prepare the following financial statements:

   a. Income statement for the month ended April 30, 2024.

   b. Statement of owner's equity for the month ended April 30, 2024.

   c. Balance sheet as of April 30, 2024.

Accounting and the Business Environment Financial 1-45

P-F:1-47A Using the accounting equation for transaction analysis, preparing financial statements, and calculating return on assets

Learning Objectives 4, 5, 6

Annette Pachelo recently opened her own law office on March 1, which she operates as a sole proprietorship. The name of the new entity is Annette Pachelo, Attorney. Pachelo experienced the following events during the organizing phase of the new business and its first month of operation, March 2024. Some of the events were personal and did not affect the law practice. Others were business transactions and should be accounted for by the business.

2c. Total Assets $83,700

Mar.		
1	Sold personal investment in Amazon stock, which she had owned for several years, receiving $35,000 cash.
2	Deposited the $35,000 cash from the sale of the Amazon stock in her personal bank account.
3	Deposited $73,000 cash in a new business bank account titled Annette Pachelo, Attorney. The business gave capital to Pachelo.
5	Paid $700 cash for ink cartridges for the printer.
7	Purchased computer for the law office, agreeing to pay the account, $5,000, within three months.
9	Received $2,800 cash from customers for services rendered.
15	Received bill from *The Lawyer* for magazine subscription, $400. (Use Miscellaneous Expense account.)
23	Finished court hearings on behalf of a client and submitted a bill for legal services, $10,000, on account.
28	Paid bill from *The Lawyer*.
30	Paid utilities, $1,200.
31	Received $3,300 cash from clients billed on March 23.
31	Pachelo withdrew cash of $5,500.

Requirements

1. Analyze the effects of the preceding events on the accounting equation of Annette Pachelo, Attorney. Use a format similar to Exhibit F:1-5.
2. Prepare the following financial statements:
    a. Income statement for the month ended March 31, 2024.
    b. Statement of owner's equity for the month ended March 31, 2024.
    c. Balance sheet as of March 31, 2024.
    d. Statement of cash flows for the month ended March 31, 2024.
3. Calculate Annette Pachelo, Attorney's return on assets. Round to the nearest whole percent.

> Problems Group B

P-F:1-48B Using the accounting equation for transaction analysis

Learning Objective 4

Meg McIntyre opened a public relations firm called Pop Chart on August 1, 2024. The following amounts summarize her business on August 31, 2024:

Cash $12,650

ASSETS					LIABILITIES +			EQUITY			
Cash	+ Accounts Receivable	+ Office Supplies	+ Land	=	Accounts Payable	+ McIntyre, Capital	− McIntyre, Withdrawals	+ Service Revenue	− Rent Expense	− Advertising Expense
Bal. $2,600	+ $2,500	+ $0	+ $16,000		$5,000	+ $13,600		+ $2,500		

During September 2024, the business completed the following transactions:

a. Meg McIntyre contributed $14,000 cash in exchange for capital.
b. Performed service for a client and received cash of $1,600.
c. Paid off the beginning balance of accounts payable.
d. Purchased office supplies from OfficeMax on account, $1,200.
e. Collected cash from a customer on account, $2,300.
f. McIntyre withdrew $1,500.
g. Consulted for a new band and billed the client for services rendered, $4,000.
h. Recorded the following business expenses for the month:

Paid office rent: $900.

Paid advertising: $450.

Analyze the effects of the transactions on the accounting equation of Pop Chart using the format presented above.

Learning Objective 4

Cash $21,300

P-F:1-49B Using the accounting equation for transaction analysis

Cosmo Thomas started a new business, Thomas Gymnastics, and completed the following transactions during December:

Dec. 1	Thomas contributed $19,000 cash in exchange for capital.
2	Received $3,800 cash from customers for services performed.
5	Paid $300 cash for office supplies.
9	Performed services for a customer and billed the customer for services rendered, $4,500.
10	Received $150 invoice for utilities due in two weeks.
15	Paid for advertising in the local paper, $350.
20	Paid utility invoice received on Dec. 10.
25	Collected cash in full from customer billed on Dec. 9.
28	Paid rent for the month, $2,600.
28	Paid $1,200 to assistant for wages.
30	Received $1,600 cash from customers for services performed.
31	Thomas withdrew $3,000 cash from the business.

Analyze the effects of the transactions on the accounting equation of Thomas Gymnastics using a format similar to Exhibit F:1-5. Use the following accounts: Cash; Accounts Receivable; Office Supplies; Accounts Payable; Thomas, Capital; Thomas, Withdrawals; Service Revenue; Rent Expense; Utilities Expense; Salaries Expense; and Advertising Expense.

P-F:1-50B Preparing financial statements

Presented here are the accounts of Pembroke Bookkeeping Company for the year ended December 31, 2024:

Land	$ 10,000	Owner contribution, 2024	$ 29,000
Notes Payable	31,000	Accounts Payable	7,000
Property Tax Expense	3,100	Accounts Receivable	1,200
Pembroke, Withdrawals	28,000	Advertising Expense	12,000
Rent Expense	7,000	Building	147,400
Salaries Expense	64,000	Cash	2,800
Salaries Payable	800	Equipment	15,000
Service Revenue	192,000	Insurance Expense	1,700
Office Supplies	12,000	Interest Expense	6,600
Pembroke, Capital, Dec. 31, 2023	51,000		

Learning Objective 5

1. Net Income $97,600

Requirements

1. Prepare Pembroke Bookkeeping Company's income statement for the year ended December 31, 2024.
2. Prepare the statement of owner's equity for the year ended December 31, 2024.
3. Prepare the balance sheet as of December 31, 2024.

P-F:1-51B Preparing financial statements

Pretty Pictures works weddings and prom-type parties. The balance of Lemon, Capital was $20,000 at December 31, 2023. At December 31, 2024, the business's accounting records show these balances:

Insurance Expense	$ 6,000	Accounts Receivable	$ 5,000
Cash	42,000	Notes Payable	10,000
Accounts Payable	13,000	Lemon, Capital, Dec. 31, 2024	?
Advertising Expense	4,500	Salaries Expense	30,000
Service Revenue	115,000	Equipment	85,500
Lemon, Withdrawals	13,000	Owner contribution	28,000

Learning Objective 5

b. Ending Capital $109,500

Prepare the following financial statements for Pretty Pictures:

a. Income statement for the year ended December 31, 2024.
b. Statement of owner's equity for the year ended December 31, 2024.
c. Balance sheet as of December 31, 2024.

P-F:1-52B Preparing financial statements

The bookkeeper of Juniper Landscaping prepared the company's balance sheet while the accountant was ill. The balance sheet, shown on the next page, contains numerous errors. In particular, the bookkeeper knew that the balance sheet should balance, so he plugged in the owner's equity amount needed to achieve this balance. The owner's equity is incorrect. All other amounts are correct, but some are out of place or should not be included on this statement. Prepare a corrected balance sheet.

Learning Objective 5

Total Assets $48,700

JUNIPER LANDSCAPING
Balance Sheet
Month Ended July 31, 2024

Assets		Liabilities	
Cash	$ 5,300	Accounts Receivable	$ 1,800
Office Supplies	800	Simmon, Withdrawals	14,000
Land	34,500	Service Revenue	38,000
Salaries Expense	3,200	Property Tax Expense	3,300
Office Furniture	6,300	Accounts Payable	2,700
Notes Payable	24,700	**Owner's Equity**	
Rent Expense	300	Simmon, Capital	15,300
Total Assets	$ 75,100	Total Liabilities	$ 75,100

Learning Objective 5

2c. Total Assets $58,360

P-F:1-53B Using the accounting equation for transaction analysis and preparing financial statements

Amos Sharp recently opened his own accounting firm on October 1, which he operates as a sole proprietorship. The name of the new entity is Amos Sharp, CPA. Sharp experienced the following events during the organizing phase of the new business and its first month of operations in 2024:

Oct. 5	Sharp deposited $45,000 in a new business bank account titled Amos Sharp, CPA. The business gave capital to Sharp.
6	Paid $300 cash for letterhead stationery for new office.
7	Purchased office furniture for the office on account, $6,500.
10	Consulted with tax client and received $3,300 for services rendered.
11	Paid utilities, $340.
12	Finished tax hearings on behalf of a client and submitted a bill for accounting services, $16,000.
18	Paid office rent, $1,800.
25	Received amount due from client that was billed on October 12.
27	Paid full amount of Accounts Payable created on October 7.
31	Sharp withdrew cash of $3,800.

Requirements

1. Analyze the effects of the events on the accounting equation of Amos Sharp, CPA. Use a format similar to Exhibit F:1-5. Use the following accounts: Cash; Accounts Receivable; Office Supplies; Furniture; Accounts Payable; Sharp, Capital; Sharp, Withdrawals; Service Revenue; Rent Expense; and Utilities Expense.
2. Prepare the following financial statements:
   a. Income statement for the month ended October 31, 2024.
   b. Statement of owner's equity for the month ended October 31, 2024.
   c. Balance sheet as of October 31, 2024.

P-F:1-54B Using the accounting equation for transaction analysis, preparing financial statements, and calculating return on assets

Learning Objectives 4, 5, 6

2c. Total Assets $103,700

Abby Perry recently opened her own law office on December 1, which she operates as a sole proprietorship. The name of the new entity is Abby Perry, Attorney. Perry experienced the following events during the organizing phase of the new business and its first month of operation, December 2024. Some of the events were personal and did not affect the law practice. Others were business transactions and should be accounted for by the business.

Dec. 1	Sold personal investment in Nike stock, which she had owned for several years, receiving $30,000 cash.
2	Deposited the $30,000 cash from the sale of the Nike stock in her personal bank account.
3	Deposited $89,000 cash in a new business bank account titled Abby Perry, Attorney. The business gave capital to Perry.
5	Paid $600 cash for ink cartridges for the printer.
7	Purchased computer for the law office, agreeing to pay the account, $8,000, within three months.
9	Received $2,900 cash from customers for services rendered.
15	Received bill from *The Lawyer* for magazine subscription, $300. (Use Miscellaneous Expense account.)
23	Finished court hearings on behalf of a client and submitted a bill for legal services, $8,000, on account.
28	Paid bill from *The Lawyer*.
30	Paid utilities, $900.
31	Received $2,800 cash from clients billed on Dec. 23.
31	Perry withdrew cash of $3,000.

Requirements

1. Analyze the effects of the preceding events on the accounting equation of Abby Perry, Attorney. Use a format similar to Exhibit F:1-5.

2. Prepare the following financial statements:

   a. Income statement for the month ended December 31, 2024.

   b. Statement of owner's equity for the month ended December 31, 2024.

   c. Balance sheet as of December 31, 2024.

   d. Statement of cash flows for the month ended December 31, 2024.

3. Calculate Abby Perry, Attorney's return on assets. Round to the nearest whole percent.

1-50　Financial　chapter 1

CRITICAL THINKING

> Using Excel

Download Excel problems for this chapter online in MyLab Accounting or at **http://www.pearsonhighered.com/Horngren**.

> Continuing Problem

P-F:1-55 is the first problem in a continuing problem that will be used throughout the chapters to reinforce the concepts learned.

P-F:1-55 Using the accounting equation for transaction analysis, preparing financial statements, and calculating return on assets (ROA)

Canyon Canoe Company is a service-based company that rents canoes for use on local lakes and rivers. Amber Wilson graduated from college about 10 years ago. She worked for one of the "Big Four" accounting firms and became a CPA. Because she loves the outdoors, she decided to begin a new business that will combine her love of outdoor activities with her business knowledge. Amber decides that she will create a new sole proprietorship, Canyon Canoe Company, or CCC for short. The business began operations on November 1, 2024.

Nov. 1	Received $16,000 cash to begin the company and gave capital to Amber.
2	Signed a lease for a building and paid $1,200 for the first month's rent.
3	Purchased canoes for $4,800 on account.
4	Purchased office supplies on account, $750.
7	Earned $1,400 cash for rental of canoes.
13	Paid $1,500 cash for wages.
15	Wilson withdrew $50 cash from the business.
16	Received a bill for $150 for utilities. (Use separate payable account.)
20	Received a bill for $175 for cell phone expenses. (Use separate payable account.)
22	Rented canoes to Early Start Daycare on account, $3,000.
26	Paid $1,000 on account related to the November 3, 2024, purchase.
28	Received $750 from Early Start Daycare for canoe rental on November 22, 2024.
30	Wilson withdrew $100 cash from the business.

Requirements

1. Analyze the effects of Canyon Canoe Company's transactions on the accounting equation. Use the format of Exhibit F:1-5 and include these headings: Cash; Accounts Receivable; Office Supplies; Canoes; Accounts Payable; Utilities Payable; Telephone Payable; Wilson, Capital; Wilson, Withdrawals; Canoe Rental Revenue; Rent Expense; Utilities Expense; Wages Expense; and Telephone Expense.

2. Prepare the income statement of Canyon Canoe Company for the month ended November 30, 2024.

3. Prepare the statement of owner's equity for the month ended November 30, 2024.
4. Prepare the balance sheet as of November 30, 2024.
5. Calculate the return on assets for Canyon Canoe Company for November 2024.

> Tying It All Together Case F:1-1

Before you begin this assignment, review the Tying It All Together feature in the chapter.

Starbucks Corporation is the premier roaster, marketer, and retailer of specialty coffee in the world, operating in 78 countries. Starbucks generates revenues through company-operated stores, licensed stores, and consumer packaged goods. In fiscal 2018, revenues from company-operated stores accounted for 52% of total revenues, while the other 48% of total revenues was earned from the company's licensed stores. Starbucks states that its retail objective is to be the leading retailer and brand of coffee and tea by selling the finest quality coffee, tea, and related products. In addition, the company strives to provide the *Starbucks Experience* by exemplifying superior customer service and providing clean and well-maintained stores. Part of this experience involves providing free internet service to customers while they are enjoying their food and beverages.

Requirements

1. How would the cost of internet service be reported by Starbucks and on which financial statement?
2. Suppose Starbucks receives a bill from its internet service provider but has not yet paid the bill. What would be the effect on assets, liabilities, and equity when Starbucks receives this bill?
3. What would be the effect on assets, liabilities, and equity when Starbucks pays its internet service bill?
4. Suppose Starbucks expects that the cost of internet service will increase by 4% in the coming year. What would be the impact on Starbucks' net income? How might Starbucks overcome this impact?

> Decision Case F:1-1

Let's examine a case using Greg's Tunes and Sal's Silly Songs. It is now the end of the first year of operations, and both owners want to know how well each business came out at the end of the year. Neither business kept complete accounting records, and neither owner made any withdrawals. The businesses throw together the data shown below at year-end:

Sal's Silly Songs:	
Total Assets	$ 23,000
Owner contribution	8,000
Total Revenues	35,000
Total Expenses	22,000
Greg's Tunes:	
Total Liabilities	$ 10,000
Owner contribution	6,000
Total Expenses	44,000
Net Income	9,000

To gain information for evaluating the businesses, the owners ask you several questions. For each answer, you must show your work to convince the owners that you know what you are talking about.

Requirements

1. Which business has more assets?
2. Which business owes more to creditors?
3. Which business has more owner's equity at the end of the year?
4. Which business brought in more revenue?
5. Which business is more profitable?
6. Which of the foregoing questions do you think is most important for evaluating these two businesses? Why?
7. Which business looks better from a financial standpoint?

Ethical Issue F:1-1

The tobacco companies have paid billions because of smoking-related illnesses. In particular, Philip Morris, a leading cigarette manufacturer, paid more than $3,000,000,000 in settlement payments in one year.

Requirements

1. Suppose you are the chief financial officer (CFO) responsible for the financial statements of Philip Morris. What ethical issue would you face as you consider what to report in your company's annual report about the cash payments? What is the ethical course of action for you to take in this situation?
2. What are some of the negative consequences to Philip Morris for not telling the truth? What are some of the negative consequences to Philip Morris for telling the truth?

> Fraud Case F:1-1

Exeter is a building contractor on the Gulf Coast. After losing a number of big lawsuits, it was facing its first annual net loss as the end of the year approached. The owner, Hank Snow, was under intense pressure from the company's creditors to report positive net income for the year. However, he knew that the controller, Alice Li, had arranged a short-term bank loan of $10,000 to cover a temporary shortfall of cash. He told Li to record the incoming cash as "construction revenue" instead of a loan. That would nudge the company's income into positive territory for the year, and then, he said, the entry could be corrected in January when the loan was repaid.

Requirements

1. How would this action affect the year-end income statement? How would it affect the year-end balance sheet?
2. If you were one of the company's creditors, how would this fraudulent action affect you?

> Financial Statement Case F:1-1

This and similar cases in later chapters focus on the financial statements of a real company—**Target Corporation**, a discount merchandiser that sells a wide assortment of general merchandise and food. Target sells both national and private and exclusive brands, with approximately one-third of its 2018 sales related to private and exclusive brands. As you work each case, you will gain confidence in your ability to use the financial statements of real companies.

Visit **http://www.pearsonhighered.com/Horngren** to view a link to Target Corporation's Fiscal 2018 Annual Report.

Requirements

1. How much in cash (including cash equivalents) did Target Corporation have on February 2, 2019?

2. What were the company's total assets at February 2, 2019? At February 3, 2018 (as adjusted)?

3. Why were the financial statements for year ending on February 3, 2018 adjusted? Review Note 2 of the accompanying Notes to Consolidated Financial Statements.

4. Write the company's accounting equation at February 2, 2019, by filling in the dollar amounts:

$$\text{Assets} = \text{Liabilities} + \text{Equity}$$

5. Identify total sales (revenues) for the year ended February 2, 2019. How much did total revenue increase or decrease from fiscal year 2017 to fiscal year 2018? (Because Target's fiscal year end of February 2, 2019 ends at the beginning of 2019, the majority of Target's financial results were obtained in the calendar year of 2018. As a result, Target calls the fiscal year 2018 even though the year reported on the annual report ends on February 2, 2019.)

6. How much net income (net earnings) or net loss did Target earn for 2018 and for 2017? Based on net income, was 2018 better or worse than 2017?

7. Calculate Target Corporation's return on assets for the year ending February 2, 2019. Round to one decimal place.

8. How did Target Corporation's return on assets compare to Kohl's Corporation's return on assets?

> Quick Check Answers

1. d 2. c 3. a 4. c 5. c 6. a 7. c 8. a 9. b 10. a 11. c

Recording Business Transactions

2

Where's the Money?

Rachel Long scoured through the stacks of printouts. She had been hired to work on an embezzlement (stealing cash or assets of an entity) case for a local school district. The chief financial officer had called her because he suspected one of his employees was stealing money from the Parent Teacher Association (PTA). Rachel loved working on embezzlement cases. She enjoyed searching through the financial statements, identifying a problem, and then finding the transactions that documented the embezzlement. Rachel knew that if she looked deeply enough she would find the evidence that money was stolen. She always treated these cases as a puzzle that needed to be solved.

Sometimes businesses are unfortunate enough to have employees steal from them, and they need help in identifying the thief and providing enough evidence to turn the matter over to a law enforcement agency. Businesses often turn to an accountant, such as Rachel, who specializes in fraud, often called a *certified fraud examiner (CFE)*. In addition, businesses hire accountants to help protect their assets by identifying potential problems in their recordkeeping and control of cash and assets.

Where will Rachel start looking when she begins searching for the stolen money? She'll start at the source, by reviewing documents such as invoices, sales receipts, and bank deposit slips. She will then review the transactions that were recorded (or not recorded) from those documents. These two pieces will help Rachel determine whether money was stolen from the school district and how the embezzlement occurred. It's important to Rachel that she not only catches the thief, but also helps the school district prevent losses in the future. She will use her knowledge and experience in accounting to help her.

Why Is Recording Business Transactions Important?

Accounting is based on transactions. The recording of those transactions is based on source documents that provide the proof of the financial position of the business. The lack of that proof can lead to discoveries of stolen money and fictitious financial statements. As an example, in 2011, a former Fry's Electronics executive pleaded guilty, was sentenced to six years in federal prison, and ordered to pay $65 million dollars in restitution. The executive's fraud was discovered when another employee saw confidential source documents on the employee's desk that had been falsified. This discovery led to uncovering a dummy company that had received over $80 million dollars of payments without any evidence to support it. The recording of transactions from source documents is the first step in the accounting process—and one of the most important. In this chapter, you learn about source documents and how to record transactions.

Chapter 2 Learning Objectives

1. Explain accounts as they relate to the accounting equation and describe common accounts
2. Define debits, credits, and normal account balances using double-entry accounting and T-accounts
3. Record transactions in a journal and post journal entries to the ledger
4. Prepare the trial balance and illustrate how to use the trial balance to prepare financial statements
5. Use the debt ratio to evaluate business performance

Smart Touch Learning started out by recording the company's business transactions in terms of the accounting equation. That procedure works well when learning how to analyze transactions, but it's not a method in which a real-world business actually records transactions. In this chapter, you learn a more efficient way to capture business transactions. First, we need to start with a review of the accounting equation.

WHAT IS AN ACCOUNT?

Learning Objective 1
Explain accounts as they relate to the accounting equation and describe common accounts

Recall that the basic tool of accounting is the accounting equation:

$$\text{Assets} = \text{Liabilities} + \text{Equity}$$

Account
A detailed record of all increases and decreases that have occurred in an individual asset, liability, or equity during a specific period.

The accounting equation is made up of three parts or categories: assets, liabilities, and equity. Each category contains accounts. An **account** is the detailed record of all increases and decreases that have occurred in an individual asset, liability, or equity during a specified period.

Assets

Assets are economic resources that are expected to benefit the business in the future—something the business owns or has control of that has value. Exhibit F:2-1 contains a list of asset accounts that most businesses use.

Liabilities

I get confused by the difference between Accounts Receivable and Accounts Payable. Is there an easy way to remember these two accounts?

Recall that a *liability* is a debt—that is, something the business owes. A business generally has fewer liability accounts than asset accounts. Exhibit F:2-2 contains examples of common liability accounts.

You might be confused by the difference between the asset account, Accounts Receivable, and the liability account, Accounts Payable. An easy way to remember the distinction between these two accounts involves the words *Receivable* and *Payable*. A *receivable* involves a future *receipt* of cash. A *payable* involves a future *payment* of cash.

Recording Business Transactions  Financial 2-3

Exhibit F:2-1 | Asset Accounts

Account Name	Explanation
Cash	A business's money. Includes bank balances, bills, coins, and checks.
Accounts Receivable	A customer's promise to pay in the future for services or goods sold. Often described as "On Account."
Notes Receivable	A *written* promise that a customer will pay a fixed amount of money (principal) and *interest* by a certain date in the future. Usually more formal than an Accounts Receivable.
Prepaid Expense	A payment of an expense in advance. It is considered an asset because the prepayment provides a benefit in the future. Examples of prepaid expenses are *Prepaid Rent*, *Prepaid Insurance*, and *Office Supplies*.
Land	The cost of land a business uses in operations.
Building	The cost of an office building, a store, or a warehouse.
Equipment, Furniture, and Fixtures	The cost of equipment, furniture, and fixtures (such as light fixtures and shelving). A business has a separate asset account for each type.

Notes Receivable
A written promise that a customer will pay a fixed amount of principal plus interest by a certain date in the future.

Prepaid Expense
A payment of an expense in advance.

Exhibit F:2-2 | Liability Accounts

Account Name	Explanation
Accounts Payable	A promise made by the business to pay a debt in the future. Arises from a credit purchase.
Notes Payable	A *written* promise made by the business to pay a debt, usually involving *interest*, in the future.
Accrued Liability	An amount owed but not paid. A specific type of payable such as *Taxes Payable*, *Rent Payable*, and *Salaries Payable*.
Unearned Revenue	Occurs when a company receives cash from a customer but has not provided the product or service. The promise to provide services or deliver goods in the future.

Notes Payable
A *written* promise made by the business to pay a debt, usually involving *interest*, in the future.

Accrued Liability
A liability for which the business knows the amount owed, but the bill has not been paid.

Unearned Revenue
A liability created when a business collects cash from customers in advance of providing services or delivering goods.

Equity

The owner's claim to the assets of the business is called *equity* or *owner's equity*. As shown in Exhibit F:2-3, a company has separate accounts for each element of equity.

Exhibit F:2-3 | Equity Accounts

Account Name	Explanation
Owner, Capital	Represents the net contributions of the owner in the business. Increases equity.
Owner, Withdrawals	Distributions of cash or other assets to the owner. Decreases equity.
Revenues	Earnings that result from delivering goods or services to customers. Increases equity. Examples include *Service Revenue* and *Rent Revenue*.
Expenses	The cost of selling goods or services. Decreases equity. Examples include *Rent Expense*, *Salaries Expense*, and *Utilities Expense*.

Chart of Accounts

Chart of Accounts
A list of all of a company's accounts with their account numbers.

Companies need a way to organize their accounts. They use a **chart of accounts** to do this. A chart of accounts lists all company accounts along with the account numbers. The chart of accounts for Smart Touch Learning appears in Exhibit F:2-4. Account numbers are just shorthand versions of the account names. One account number equals one account name—just like your Social Security number is unique to you.

Exhibit F:2-4 | Chart of Accounts—Smart Touch Learning

Balance Sheet and Statement of Owner's Equity Accounts

Assets	Liabilities	Equity
101 Cash	201 Accounts Payable	301 Owner, Capital
111 Accounts Receivable	211 Salaries Payable	311 Owner, Withdrawals
121 Notes Receivable	221 Interest Payable	
141 Office Supplies	231 Unearned Revenue	
151 Land	241 Notes Payable	
171 Building		
191 Furniture		

Income Statement Accounts (Part of Equity)

Revenues	Expenses
401 Service Revenue	501 Rent Expense
411 Interest Revenue	511 Salaries Expense
	521 Utilities Expense
	531 Advertising Expense

Recording Business Transactions  Financial 2-5

> It can be confusing to choose the correct account to use when there are multiple accounts that sound similar. As an example, let's think about rent. There are four types of rent accounts: Prepaid Rent (asset), Rent Payable (liability), Rent Revenue (equity), and Rent Expense (equity). It is important that we understand the definition of each type of account so that we can use the account correctly. Prepaid Rent represents a _prepayment_ of cash for renting a building _in the future._ Rent Payable represents a _debt owed_ for renting a building _currently_, and Rent Expense represents the _cost_ of renting a building _currently_. Rent Revenue, on the other hand, relates to the _earning_ of revenue related to renting the building to a tenant _currently._

Account numbers usually have two or more digits. Assets are often numbered beginning with 1, liabilities with 2, owner's equity with 3, revenues with 4, and expenses with 5. The second and third digits in an account number indicate where the account fits within the category. For example, if Smart Touch Learning is using three-digit account numbers, Cash may be account number 101, the first asset account. Accounts Receivable may be account number 111, the second asset. Accounts Payable may be account number 201, the first liability. When numbers are used, all accounts are numbered by this system. However, each company chooses its own account numbering system.

Notice in Exhibit F:2-4 the gap in account numbers between 121 and 141. Smart Touch Learning may need to add another asset account in the future. For example, the business may start selling some type of inventory and want to use account number 131 for Merchandise Inventory. So, the chart of accounts will change as the business evolves.

The chart of accounts varies from business to business, though many account names are common to all companies. For example, you will find Cash on every company's chart of accounts. The chart of accounts contains the list of account names you will use to record a transaction.

IFRS
Worldwide, accounting systems are based on the same equation: Assets = Liabilities + Equity. Or, in Spanish: Activos = Pasivos + Patrimonio Neto. Accounts are the building blocks for all accounting systems.

Data Analytics in Accounting

How many accounts should a company have in its chart of accounts? The answer is it depends on the company's size, complexity, number of locations, and activities. The chart of accounts is a key tool for processing transactions and business activities and can also help companies analyze accounting data. It can be used to compare prior period amounts to current year, identify errors, and track changes in accounts. Companies should strive to have as small of a chart of accounts as possible because the more accounts a company has the more potential problems that can occur, including difficulty in reconciliations and reporting errors. A recent survey from the APQC (American Productivity & Quality Center) showed that on average companies have 450 different accounts in their chart of accounts.

Ledger
The record holding all the accounts of a business, the changes in those accounts, and their balances.

Ledger

In addition to a chart of accounts, companies need a way to show all of the increases and decreases in each account along with their balances. Companies use a **ledger** to fulfill this task. A ledger is a collection of all the accounts, the changes in those accounts, and their balances. **A chart of accounts and a ledger are similar in that they both list the account names and account numbers of the business. A ledger, though, provides more detail. It includes the increases and decreases of each account for a specific period and the balance of each account at a specific point in time.**

What are the similarities and differences between a chart of accounts and a ledger?

Try It!

Consider the following accounts and identify each as an asset (A), liability (L), or equity (E).

1. Rent Expense
2. Brock, Capital
3. Furniture
4. Service Revenue
5. Prepaid Insurance
6. Accounts Payable
7. Unearned Revenue
8. Notes Receivable
9. Brock, Withdrawals
10. Insurance Expense

Check your answers online in MyLab Accounting or at http://www.pearsonhighered.com/Horngren.

For more practice, see Short Exercise S-F:2-1. **MyLab Accounting**

WHAT IS DOUBLE-ENTRY ACCOUNTING?

Learning Objective 2
Define debits, credits, and normal account balances using double-entry accounting and T-accounts

Previously, you learned that every transaction must be recorded into at least two accounts. For example, when an owner contributes money in exchange for capital, the two accounts involved are Cash and Owner, Capital. Accounting uses this **double-entry system** to record the dual effects of each transaction. A transaction would be incomplete if only one side were recorded.

Consider a cash purchase of office supplies. What are the dual effects? A cash purchase of office supplies:

1. Increases the account Office Supplies (the business received office supplies).
2. Decreases Cash (the business paid cash).

Double-Entry System
A system of accounting in which every transaction affects at least two accounts.

The T-Account

T-Account
A summary device that is shaped like a capital *T* with debits posted on the left side of the vertical line and credits on the right side of the vertical line.

A shortened form of an account in the ledger is called the **T-account** because it takes the form of the capital letter *T*. The vertical line divides the account into its left and right sides, with the account name at the top. For example, the Cash T-account appears as follows:

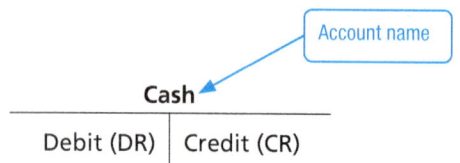

Debit
The left side of a T-account.

Credit
The right side of a T-account.

The left side of the T-account is called the **debit** side, and the right side is called the **credit** side. To become comfortable using these terms, remember the following: Debits go on the left; credits go on the right. Debit is abbreviated as DR, and Credit is abbreviated as CR.

Increases and Decreases in the Accounts

How we record increases and decreases to an account is determined by the account type (asset, liability, or equity). For any given account, increases are recorded on one side and decreases are recorded on the opposite side. The following T-accounts provide a summary:

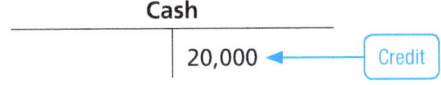

In other words, assets are always increased with a *debit* and decreased with a *credit*. Liabilities and equity are always increased with a *credit* and decreased with a *debit*. Whether an account is increased or decreased by a debit or a credit depends on the type of account. Debits are not "good" or "bad." Neither are credits. Debits are not always increases or always decreases—neither are credits. **The only thing a designation as a debit or credit means is where the item is placed—on the left or right side of the T-account.**

In a computerized accounting information system, the computer interprets debits and credits as increases or decreases, based on the account type. For example, a computer reads a debit to Cash as an increase because it is an asset account. The computer reads a debit to Accounts Payable as a decrease because it is a liability account.

Example: Assume a business wants to record an increase of $30,000 to the Cash account. The business would record a debit to Cash as follows:

Cash
Debit → 30,000

I always thought that a debit meant decrease and a credit meant increase. Am I wrong?

Cash is an asset account and, remember, asset accounts are increased with debits.

Example: What if the business, instead, wanted to record a decrease of $20,000 to the Cash account? The business would record a credit to Cash because Cash is an asset account and asset accounts are decreased with credits:

Cash
20,000 ← Credit

Expanding the Rules of Debit and Credit

As we have noted, equity contains four account types: Owner, Capital; Owner, Withdrawals; Revenues; and Expenses. Owner, Capital and Revenues increase equity, whereas Owner, Withdrawals and Expenses decrease equity. We must now expand the accounting equation and the rules of debits and credits to include all elements of equity:

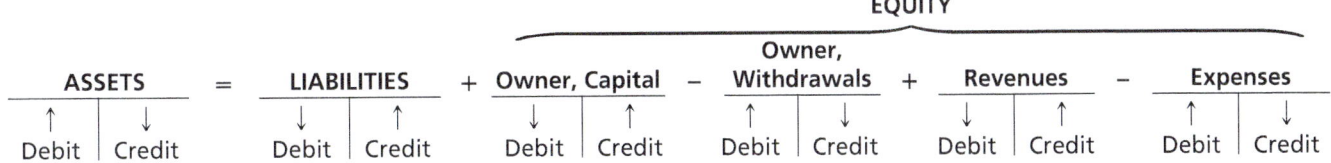

Notice in the expanded accounting equation that Owner, Withdrawals and Expenses record increases and decreases opposite of Owner, Capital and Revenues. This is because increases in Owner, Withdrawals and Expenses decrease equity.

The Normal Balance of an Account

All accounts have a normal balance. An account's **normal balance** appears on the side—either debit or credit—where we record an *increase* (↑) in the account's balance. For example, assets are increased with a debit, so the normal balance is a debit. Liabilities are

Normal Balance
The balance that appears on the increase side of an account.

increased with a credit, so the normal balance is a credit. Expenses and Owner, Withdrawals are equity accounts that have normal debit balances—unlike the other equity accounts. They have debit balances because they decrease equity. Owner, Capital and Revenues have a normal balance of credit. Let's look again at the accounting equation, this time with the normal balances marked:

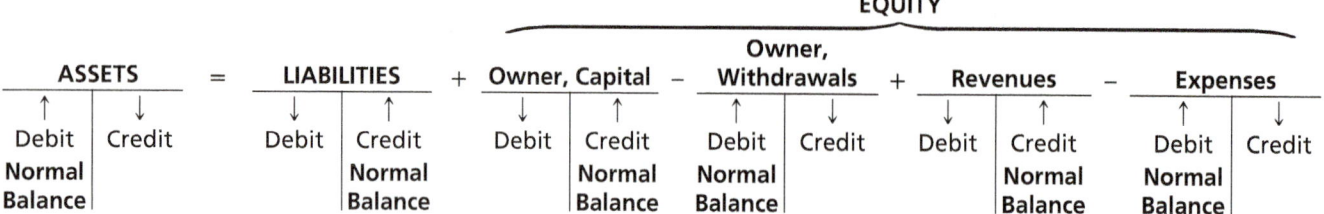

An account with a normal debit balance may occasionally have a credit balance. That indicates a negative amount in the account. For example, Cash will have a credit balance if the business overdraws its bank account. Also, the liability, Accounts Payable—a normal credit balance account—could have a debit balance if the company overpays its accounts payable. In other cases, a non-normal account balance indicates an error. For example, a credit balance in Office Supplies, Furniture, or Buildings is an error because negative amounts of these assets make no sense.

Exhibit F:2-5 summarizes the rules of debits and credits and the normal balances for each account type.

Exhibit F:2-5 | **Rules of Debits and Credits and Normal Balances for Each Account Type**

Account Type	Increases	Decreases	Normal Balance
Assets	Debit	Credit	Debit
Expenses	Debit	Credit	Debit
Owner, Withdrawals	Debit	Credit	Debit
Liabilities	Credit	Debit	Credit
Revenues	Credit	Debit	Credit
Owner, Capital	Credit	Debit	Credit

An easy way to remember the rules of debits and credits is to memorize this helpful sentence. All elephants will love rowdy children. The first three words in the sentence will help you remember that assets, expenses, and withdrawals all have normal debit balances. The last three words in the sentence will remind you that liabilities, revenues, and capital all have normal credit balances.

Determining the Balance of a T-Account

T-accounts can be used to determine the amount remaining in an account or the *balance* of the account. To illustrate, let's look at the following Cash T-Account:

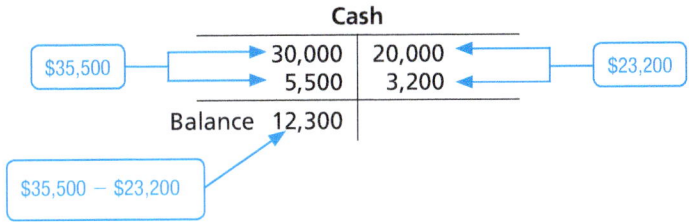

The balance of this Cash account is $12,300. This is calculated by adding each side of the account separately ($35,500 and $23,200) and then subtracting the smaller number from the larger number ($35,500 − $23,200). The balance ($12,300) is always reported on the side with the larger number.

For each account, identify if the change would be recorded as a debit (DR) or credit (CR).

11. Increase to Cash
12. Decrease to Accounts Payable
13. Increase to Owner, Capital
14. Increase to Unearned Revenue
15. Decrease to Accounts Receivable
16. Increase to Interest Revenue
17. Increase to Rent Expense
18. Decrease to Office Supplies
19. Increase to Prepaid Rent
20. Increase to Notes Payable

Check your answers online in MyLab Accounting or at http://www.pearsonhighered.com/Horngren.

For more practice, see Short Exercises S-F:2-2 through S-F:2-4.   MyLab Accounting

HOW DO YOU RECORD TRANSACTIONS?

When we reviewed the activity for Smart Touch Learning, we provided you with the transactions. In a real-world business, because of the faithful representation concept, accountants would need to provide evidence for those transactions.

Learning Objective 3
Record transactions in a journal and post journal entries to the ledger

Source Documents—The Origin of the Transactions

Accountants use **source documents** to provide the evidence and data for recording transactions. For example, consider Sheena Bright's contribution of $30,000 to the business. Exhibit F:2-6 (on the next page) illustrates the transaction. In that exhibit, Smart Touch Learning received $30,000 and deposited it in the bank. The business then gave capital to Sheena Bright. The check received and the bank deposit slip are the source documents that show the amount of cash received by the business and the equity contribution of the owner, Sheena Bright. Based on these documents, the business can determine how to record this transaction.

Source Document
Provides the evidence and data for accounting transactions.

Exhibit F:2-6 | **Flow of Accounting Data**

ETHICS

Are receipts really important?

Elijah Morris, assistant manager for Red's American Burger Restaurant, is responsible for purchasing equipment and supplies for the restaurant. Elijah recently purchased a $4,000 commercial-grade refrigerator for the restaurant, but he can't find the receipt. Elijah purchased the refrigerator with personal funds and is asking to be reimbursed by the restaurant. Hannah, the restaurant's accountant, has said that she is unsure if the business can reimburse Elijah without a receipt. Elijah suggests, "Hannah, it won't really matter if I have a receipt or not. You've seen the refrigerator in the restaurant, so you know I purchased it. What difference is a little receipt going to make?"

What should Hannah do? What would you do?

Solution

Hannah should not reimburse Elijah until she receives the receipt—the source document. Elijah could have purchased the refrigerator for less than the amount he is asking in reimbursement. Source documents provide the evidence of the amount of the transaction. If either an auditor or the owner of the restaurant investigated the $4,000 purchase, he or she would need to see the source document to verify the transaction. If Elijah truly cannot find the receipt, Hannah should ask for an alternative source document such as a credit card or bank statement that shows evidence of the purchase. In addition, Elijah should be warned about using personal funds to purchase equipment for the business.

Other source documents that businesses use include the following:

- **Purchase invoices.** Documents that tell the business how much and when to pay a vendor for purchases on account, such as office supplies.
- **Bank checks.** Documents that illustrate the amount and date of cash payments.
- **Sales invoices.** Documents provided to clients when a business sells services or goods; tells the business how much revenue to record.

Journalizing and Posting Transactions

After accountants review the source documents, they are then ready to record the transactions. Transactions are first recorded in a **journal**, which is the record of transactions in date order.

> **Journal**
> A record of transactions in date order.

Journalizing a transaction records the data only in the journal—not in the ledger (the record holding all of the accounts of a business). The data must also be transferred to the ledger. The process of transferring data from the journal to the ledger is called **posting**. We post from the journal to the ledger. Debits in the journal are posted as debits in the ledger and credits as credits—no exceptions.

> **Posting**
> Transferring data from the journal to the ledger.

Recording Business Transactions  Financial 2-11

The following diagram shows this process:

Date	Debit	Credit
Nov. 1 Cash	30,000	
Bright, Capital		30,000
Owner contribution.		

Transactions are recorded in a journal.

Cash	
30,000	

Bright, Capital	
	30,000

Data is posted (transferred) to the ledger.

You have learned steps to use when analyzing accounting transactions. Use a modified version of those steps to help when recording transactions in the journal and then posting the journal entries to the ledger. The journalizing and posting process has five steps:

Step 1: Identify the accounts and the account type (asset, liability, or equity).

Step 2: Decide whether each account increases or decreases, then apply the rules of debits and credits.

Step 3: Record the transaction in the journal.

Step 4: Post the journal entry to the ledger.

Step 5: Determine whether the accounting equation is in balance.

Let's begin by journalizing the first transaction of Smart Touch Learning.

Transaction 1—Owner Contribution

On November 1, the e-learning company received $30,000 cash from Sheena Bright and the business issued capital to her.

Step 1: Identify the accounts and the account type. The two accounts involved are Cash (Asset) and Bright, Capital (Equity).

Step 2: Decide whether each account increases or decreases, then apply the rules of debits and credits. Both accounts increase by $30,000. Reviewing the rules of debits and credits, we use the accounting equation to help determine debits and credits for each account. Cash is an asset account and is increasing, so we will record a debit to Cash. Bright, Capital is an equity account and is increasing, so we will record a credit to Bright, Capital.

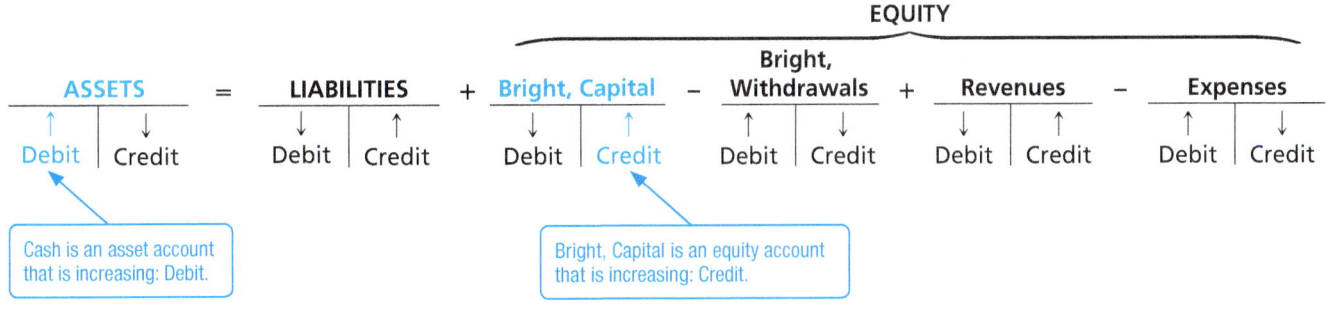

2-12 Financial chapter 2

Step 3: **Record the transaction in the journal.** The recording of a transaction in the journal creates a journal entry. The journal entry for Transaction 1 is illustrated below. Notice that each journal entry contains four parts.

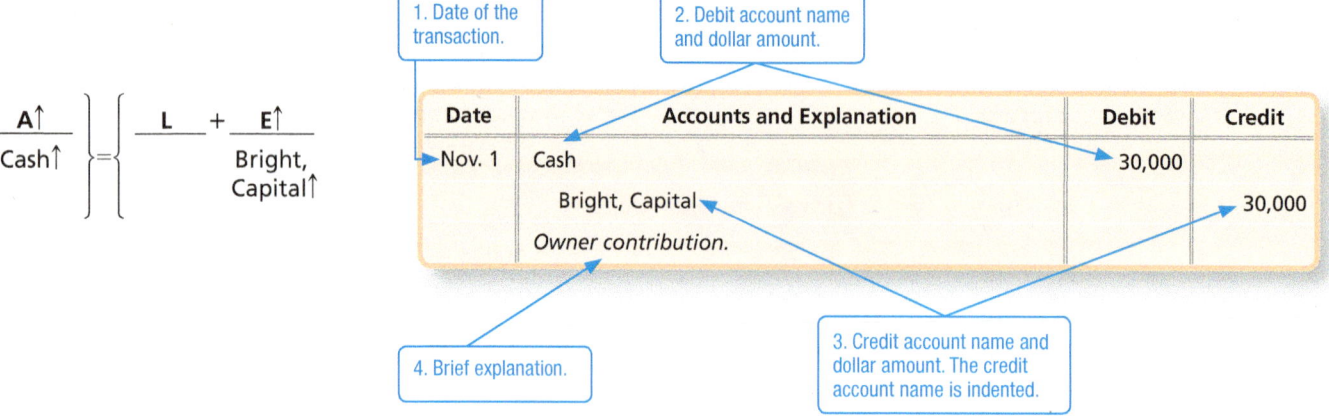

Step 4: **Post the journal entry to the ledger.** When transactions are posted from the journal to the ledger, the dollar amount is transferred from the debit and credit columns to the specific account. The date of the journal entry is also transferred to the T-accounts in the ledger. In a computerized system, this step is completed automatically when the transaction is recorded in the journal.

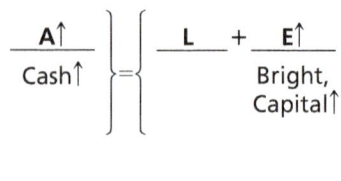

Date	Accounts and Explanation	Debit	Credit
Nov. 1	Cash	30,000	
	Bright, Capital		30,000
	Owner contribution.		

```
         Cash                    Bright, Capital
  Nov. 1  30,000                    30,000  Nov. 1
```

Step 5: **Determine if the accounting equation is in balance.**

```
    ASSETS           LIABILITIES  +  EQUITY
     Cash          =                  Bright,
                                      Capital
(1)  + 30,000                        + 30,000
```

To help reinforce your learning of the account types, we will illustrate the transaction in the margin. We will indicate the accounts and account type (Step 1) and whether each account is increasing or decreasing (Step 2). These notations would not normally show up in a journal, but we have included them here to reinforce the rules of debits and credits.

Let's look at Transaction 2 for Smart Touch Learning and apply the steps we just learned.

Transaction 2—Purchase of Land for Cash

On November 2, Smart Touch Learning paid $20,000 cash for land.

Step 1: Identify the accounts and the account type. The two accounts involved are Cash (Asset) and Land (Asset).

Step 2: Decide whether each account increases or decreases, then apply the rules of debits and credits. Cash decreases. The business paid cash. Therefore, we credit Cash. The land increased, so we debit the Land account.

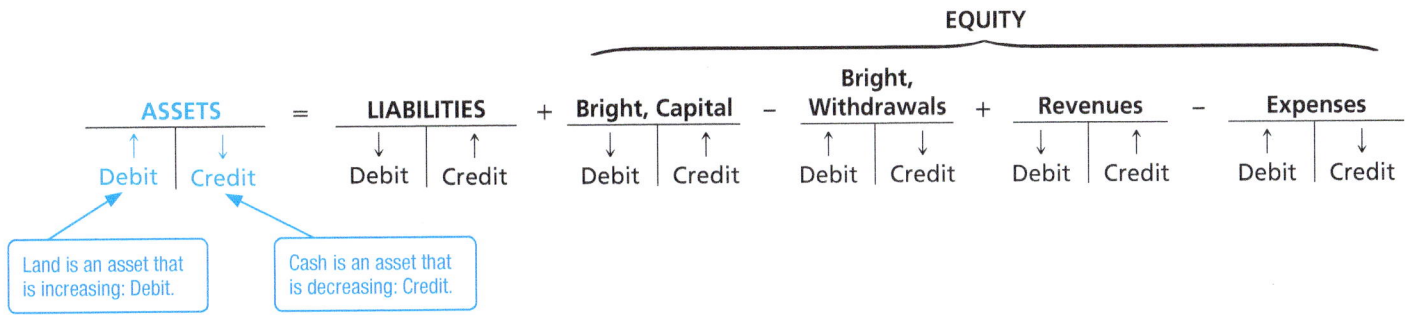

Step 3: Record the transaction in the journal.

Date	Accounts and Explanation	Debit	Credit
Nov. 2	Land	20,000	
	Cash		20,000
	Paid cash for land.		

$$A\updownarrow \begin{Bmatrix} Land\uparrow \\ Cash\downarrow \end{Bmatrix} = \begin{Bmatrix} L + E \end{Bmatrix}$$

Step 4: Post the journal entry to the ledger.

```
        Cash                    Land
Nov. 1  30,000 | 20,000 Nov. 2  Nov. 2  20,000
```

Step 5: Determine whether the accounting equation is in balance.

	ASSETS				LIABILITIES	+	EQUITY
	Cash	+	Land			+	Bright, Capital
Bal.	$30,000			=			$30,000
(2)	−20,000		+20,000				
Bal.	$10,000	+	$20,000				$30,000

We will now record journal entries for several more transactions for Smart Touch Learning. Now that you understand the steps, try to write the steps yourself before looking at the journal entry. Remember, if you need help, we'll provide the effect on the accounting equation in the margin.

Transaction 3—Purchase of Office Supplies on Account

Smart Touch Learning buys $500 of office supplies on account on November 3.

2-14 Financial  chapter 2

The supplies will benefit Smart Touch Learning in future periods, so they are an asset to the company until they are used. The asset Office Supplies increased, so we debit Office Supplies. The liability Accounts Payable increased, so we credit Accounts Payable.

$$\frac{A\uparrow}{\text{Office Supplies}\uparrow} \bigg\} = \bigg\{ \frac{L\uparrow}{\text{Accounts Payable}\uparrow} + \underline{}$$

Date	Accounts and Explanation	Debit	Credit
Nov. 3	Office Supplies	500	
	Accounts Payable		500
	Purchased office supplies on account.		

Office Supplies		Accounts Payable	
Nov. 3 500		500	Nov. 3

Transaction 4—Earning of Service Revenue for Cash

On November 8, Smart Touch Learning collected cash of $5,500 for service revenue that the business earned by providing e-learning services for clients.

The asset Cash increased, so we debit Cash. Revenue increased, so we credit Service Revenue.

$$\frac{A\uparrow}{\text{Cash}\uparrow} \bigg\} = \bigg\{ \underline{} + \frac{E\uparrow}{\text{Service Revenue}\uparrow}$$

Date	Accounts and Explanation	Debit	Credit
Nov. 8	Cash	5,500	
	Service Revenue		5,500
	Performed services and received cash.		

Cash				Service Revenue	
Nov. 1 30,000	20,000 Nov. 2				5,500 Nov. 8
Nov. 8 5,500					

Transaction 5—Earning of Service Revenue on Account

On November 10, Smart Touch Learning performed services for clients, for which the clients will pay the company later. The business earned $3,000 of service revenue on account.

This transaction increased Accounts Receivable, so we debit this asset. Service Revenue is increased with a credit.

$$\frac{A\uparrow}{\text{Accounts Receivable}\uparrow} \bigg\} = \bigg\{ \underline{} + \frac{E\uparrow}{\text{Service Revenue}\uparrow}$$

Date	Accounts and Explanation	Debit	Credit
Nov. 10	Accounts Receivable	3,000	
	Service Revenue		3,000
	Performed services on account.		

Accounts Receivable		Service Revenue	
Nov. 10 3,000		5,500	Nov. 8
		3,000	Nov. 10

Notice the differences and the similarities between Transactions 4 and 5. In both transactions, Service Revenue was increased (credited) because in both cases the company had earned revenue. However, in Transaction 4, the company was paid at the time of service. In Transaction 5, on the other hand, the company will receive cash later (Accounts

Receivable). This difference is key because the amount of revenue is not determined by when the company *receives* cash. Revenues are recorded when the company *does* the work or provides the service.

Transaction 6—Payment of Expenses with Cash

Smart Touch Learning paid the following cash expenses on November 15: office rent, $2,000, and employee salaries, $1,200. We need to debit each expense account to record its increase and credit Cash, an asset, for the total decrease.

Date	Accounts and Explanation	Debit	Credit
Nov. 15	Rent Expense	2,000	
	Salaries Expense	1,200	
	Cash		3,200
	Paid cash expenses.		

A↓ = L + E↓
Cash↓   Rent Expense↑
        Salaries Expense↑

```
        Cash                    Rent Expense
Nov. 1  30,000 | 20,000 Nov. 2  Nov. 15  2,000
Nov. 8   5,500 |  3,200 Nov. 15

                Salaries Expense
                Nov. 15  1,200
```

Notice that the journal entry has three accounts involved—two debits and one credit. This is a compound journal entry. A **compound journal entry** has more than two accounts, but the total dollar value of the debits still must equal the total dollar value of the credits.

Before we move to the next transaction, let's take a moment to carefully look at expenses. In Transaction 6, we recorded a debit to each expense account. The accounting equation and the rules of debits and credits state that a debit to an expense account increases the account.

We are recording an increase to the expense account because the business has more expenses now than it had before. But, remember, the overall effect on the accounting equation is that increases in expenses decrease equity. An easy way to think about it is that we are increasing a negative account.

Compound Journal Entry
A journal entry that is characterized by having multiple debits and/or multiple credits.

I thought expenses decreased equity, but we are debiting the expense, which records an increase to the account.

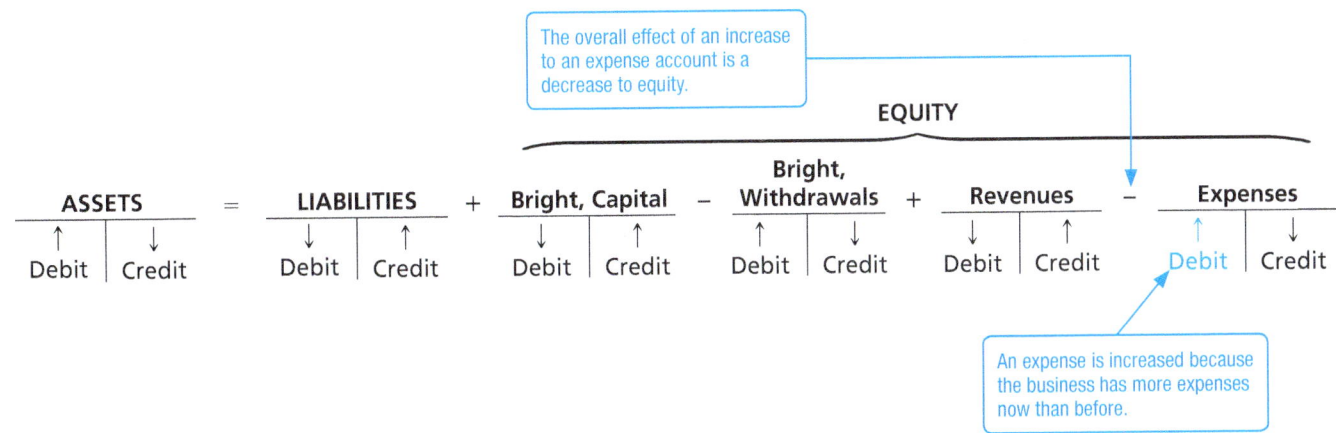

The overall effect of an increase to an expense account is a decrease to equity.

An expense is increased because the business has more expenses now than before.

Transaction 7—Payment on Account (Accounts Payable)

On November 21, Smart Touch Learning paid $300 on the accounts payable created in Transaction 3. The payment decreased cash, an asset, so we credit Cash. The payment decreased Accounts Payable, so we debit that liability.

$\dfrac{A\downarrow}{\text{Cash}\downarrow} \Big\} = \Big\{ \dfrac{L\downarrow}{\text{Accounts Payable}\downarrow} + E$

Date	Accounts and Explanation	Debit	Credit
Nov. 21	Accounts Payable	300	
	Cash		300
	Paid cash on account.		

Cash				Accounts Payable			
Nov. 1	30,000	20,000	Nov. 2	Nov. 21	300	500	Nov. 3
Nov. 8	5,500	3,200	Nov. 15				
		300	Nov. 21				

Notice that after recording this transaction and posting to the Accounts Payable account, the balance of Accounts Payable is $200 ($500 − $300). This is the new balance that the business owes to its creditor.

Transaction 8—Collection on Account (Accounts Receivable)

On November 22, Smart Touch Learning collected $2,000 cash from a client in Transaction 5. Cash is increased, so we debit the asset Cash. Accounts Receivable, also an asset, is decreased, so we credit Accounts Receivable. *Note:* This transaction has no effect on revenue; the related revenue was recorded in Transaction 5.

$\dfrac{A\uparrow\downarrow}{\substack{\text{Cash}\uparrow \\ \text{Accounts} \\ \text{Receivable}\downarrow}} \Big\} = \Big\{ \dfrac{L}{} + E$

Date	Accounts and Explanation	Debit	Credit
Nov. 22	Cash	2,000	
	Accounts Receivable		2,000
	Received cash on account.		

Cash				Accounts Receivable			
Nov. 1	30,000	20,000	Nov. 2	Nov. 10	3,000	2,000	Nov. 22
Nov. 8	5,500	3,200	Nov. 15				
Nov. 22	2,000	300	Nov. 21				

Transaction 9—Owner Withdrawal of Cash

On November 25, Sheena Bright withdrew cash of $5,000. The withdrawal decreased the entity's cash, so we credit Cash. The withdrawal also decreased equity. Decreases in equity that result from withdrawals are debited to the owner's withdrawal account, Bright, Withdrawals.

$\dfrac{A\downarrow}{\text{Cash}\downarrow} \Big\} = \Big\{ \dfrac{L}{} + \dfrac{E\downarrow}{\text{Bright, Withdrawals}\uparrow}$

Date	Accounts and Explanation	Debit	Credit
Nov. 25	Bright, Withdrawals	5,000	
	Cash		5,000
	Owner withdrawal.		

Cash				Bright, Withdrawals	
Nov. 1	30,000	20,000	Nov. 2	Nov. 25 5,000	
Nov. 8	5,500	3,200	Nov. 15		
Nov. 22	2,000	300	Nov. 21		
		5,000	Nov. 25		

Transaction 10—Prepaid Expenses

On December 1, Smart Touch Learning prepays three months' office rent of $3,000 ($1,000 per month × 3 months). The prepayment of the rent is recorded to the Prepaid Rent account (Asset). It is recorded as an asset because Smart Touch Learning will receive a benefit in the future. The asset, Prepaid Rent, is increasing, so we will need to debit it. Cash is decreasing and will be recorded as a credit.

Date	Accounts and Explanation	Debit	Credit
Dec. 1	Prepaid Rent	3,000	
	Cash		3,000
	Paid rent in advance.		

A↑↓ = L + E
Prepaid Rent↑
Cash↓

Cash				Prepaid Rent	
Nov. 1	30,000	20,000	Nov. 2	Dec. 1 3,000	
Nov. 8	5,500	3,200	Nov. 15		
Nov. 22	2,000	300	Nov. 21		
		5,000	Nov. 25		
		3,000	Dec. 1		

Transaction 11—Payment of Expense with Cash

On December 1, Smart Touch Learning paid employee salaries of $1,200. Salaries Expense will be debited to record its increase, and Cash will be credited for the decrease.

Date	Accounts and Explanation	Debit	Credit
Dec. 1	Salaries Expense	1,200	
	Cash		1,200
	Paid salaries.		

A↓ = L + E↓
Cash↓   Salaries Expense↑

Cash				Salaries Expense	
Nov. 1	30,000	20,000	Nov. 2	Nov. 15	1,200
Nov. 8	5,500	3,200	Nov. 15	Dec. 1	1,200
Nov. 22	2,000	300	Nov. 21		
		5,000	Nov. 25		
		3,000	Dec. 1		
		1,200	Dec. 1		

Transaction 12—Purchase of Building with Notes Payable

On December 1, Smart Touch Learning purchased a $60,000 building in exchange for a note payable. The building will benefit the business in the future, so it is recorded as an asset to the company. The asset Building is increased, so we debit Building. The liability Notes Payable increased, so we credit Notes Payable.

2-18 Financial chapter 2

$\dfrac{A\uparrow}{Building\uparrow} \Big\} = \Big\{ \dfrac{L\uparrow}{\substack{Notes \\ Payable\uparrow}} + \dfrac{E}{}$

Date	Accounts and Explanation	Debit	Credit
Dec. 1	Building	60,000	
	Notes Payable		60,000
	Purchased building with note.		

Building		Notes Payable	
Dec. 1 60,000		60,000 Dec. 1	

Transaction 13—Owner Contribution

On December 2, Smart Touch Learning received a contribution of furniture with a fair market value of $18,000 from Sheena Bright. In exchange, Smart Touch Learning issued capital. The furniture will benefit the company in the future, so it is recorded as an asset. The asset Furniture is increasing, so we debit it. Bright, Capital, an equity account, is also increasing and is recorded as a credit.

$\dfrac{A\uparrow}{Furniture\uparrow} \Big\} = \Big\{ \dfrac{L}{} + \dfrac{E\uparrow}{\substack{Bright, \\ Capital\uparrow}}$

Date	Accounts and Explanation	Debit	Credit
Dec. 2	Furniture	18,000	
	Bright, Capital		18,000
	Owner contribution of furniture.		

Furniture		Bright, Capital	
Dec. 2 18,000		30,000 Nov. 1	
		18,000 Dec. 2	

Transaction 14—Accrued Liability

On December 15, Smart Touch Learning received a telephone bill for $100 and will pay this expense next month. There is no cash payment now. This is an accrued liability. Remember, an accrued liability is a liability for which the business knows the amount owed, but the bill has not been paid. The Utilities Expense increased, so we debit this expense. The liability (Utilities Payable) increased, so we credit Utilities Payable. Alternatively, we could credit Accounts Payable instead of Utilities Payable.

$\dfrac{A}{} \Big\} = \Big\{ \dfrac{L\uparrow}{\substack{Utilities \\ Payable\uparrow}} + \dfrac{E\downarrow}{\substack{Utilities \\ Expense\uparrow}}$

Date	Accounts and Explanation	Debit	Credit
Dec. 15	Utilities Expense	100	
	Utilities Payable		100
	Accrued utility liability.		

Utilities Payable		Utilities Expense	
	100 Dec. 15	Dec. 15 100	

Transaction 15—Payment of Expense with Cash

On December 15, Smart Touch Learning paid employee salaries of $1,200. Salaries Expense will be debited to record its increase, and Cash will be credited for the decrease.

Date	Accounts and Explanation	Debit	Credit
Dec. 15	Salaries Expense	1,200	
	Cash		1,200
	Paid salaries.		

$A\downarrow$ Cash$\downarrow$ $\}= \{$ L + E$\downarrow$ Salaries Expense$\uparrow$

```
          Cash                    Salaries Expense
Nov. 1  30,000 | 20,000  Nov. 2   Nov. 15  1,200
Nov. 8   5,500 |  3,200  Nov. 15  Dec. 1   1,200
Nov. 22  2,000 |    300  Nov. 21  Dec. 15  1,200
               |  5,000  Nov. 25
               |  3,000  Dec. 1
               |  1,200  Dec. 1
               |  1,200  Dec. 15
```

Transaction 16—Unearned Revenue

On December 21, a law firm engages Smart Touch Learning to provide e-learning services and agrees to pay $600 in advance. Smart Touch Learning received cash but has not yet performed the services. Cash increased, so we debit Cash. The promise to perform services in the future will be recorded as Unearned Revenue, a liability account. Unearned Revenue is increasing, so we credit it. Notice that we did not record revenue. Revenue is not recorded until Smart Touch Learning provides the services.

Date	Accounts and Explanation	Debit	Credit
Dec. 21	Cash	600	
	Unearned Revenue		600
	Collected cash for future services.		

$A\uparrow$ Cash$\uparrow$ $\}= \{$ L$\uparrow$ Unearned Revenue$\uparrow$ + E

```
          Cash                    Unearned Revenue
Nov. 1  30,000 | 20,000  Nov. 2          600  Dec. 21
Nov. 8   5,500 |  3,200  Nov. 15
Nov. 22  2,000 |    300  Nov. 21
Dec. 21    600 |  5,000  Nov. 25
               |  3,000  Dec. 1
               |  1,200  Dec. 1
               |  1,200  Dec. 15
```

TYING IT ALL TOGETHER

Fry's Electronics, Inc. was founded in 1985 in Sunnyvale, California, and has grown to 34 stores in nine different states. The majority of its stores can be found in California and Texas. Fry's sells more than 50,000 electronic items, such as computers, tablets, mobile devices, and car electronics. Fry's Electronics also provides technical services, such as in-home installation of security systems, home theaters, and home networks. In addition, Fry's provides technical support for its customers.

Suppose Fry's Electronics rents the retail space where one of its stores is located. Due to an excess of cash, Fry's decides to prepay the next six months' rent, totaling $24,000. How would this transaction be recorded by Fry's?

The prepayment of rent expense would be recorded as Prepaid Rent. Prepaid Rent is an asset account that represents payment of an expense in advance. Fry's would record a journal entry as follows:

Date	Accounts and Explanation	Debit	Credit
	Prepaid Rent	24,000	
	Cash		24,000

Why is the prepayment of expenses considered an asset? On what financial statement would the account, Prepaid Rent, be reported?

The prepayment of expenses is considered an asset because the prepayment provides a benefit in the future. The rent expense will not be recorded until the monthly rental occurs. Prepaid Rent is reported on the Balance Sheet in the asset section.

Suppose Fry's Electronics rents the retail space from HDK Investments. How would HDK Investments record the receipt of cash for prepaid rent?

HDK Investments would record the receipt of cash as Unearned Revenue. The prepayment of rent would be recorded as unearned revenue because the rental service has not yet been provided. HDK Investments cannot record the prepayment as revenue until the monthly rent has been provided. HDK Investments would record a journal entry as follows:

Date	Accounts and Explanation	Debit	Credit
	Cash	24,000	
	Unearned Revenue		24,000

Notice that when Fry's Electronics recorded the payment of cash, it was a decrease to the asset, which is a credit to Cash. However, when HDK Investments recorded the receipt of cash, it was an increase to the asset, which is a debit to Cash. A payment of Cash by one business is a receipt of Cash by another.

Instead of prepaying expenses, what else could Fry's Electronics do with its excess cash?

If a company has excess cash, there are several options they could consider. First, the company could keep the cash in a high-interest savings account and earn interest on the cash. The company could also consider investing the money in financial investments such as stocks or bonds. Another option the company should consider is paying down debt.

Transaction 17—Earning of Service Revenue for Cash

On December 28, Smart Touch Learning collected cash of $8,000 for Service Revenue that the business earned by providing e-learning services for clients.

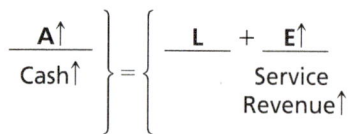

Date	Accounts and Explanation	Debit	Credit
Dec. 28	Cash	8,000	
	Service Revenue		8,000
	Performed services and received cash.		

Cash				Service Revenue	
Nov. 1	30,000	20,000	Nov. 2	5,500	Nov. 8
Nov. 8	5,500	3,200	Nov. 15	3,000	Nov. 10
Nov. 22	2,000	300	Nov. 21	8,000	Dec. 28
Dec. 21	600	5,000	Nov. 25		
Dec. 28	8,000	3,000	Dec. 1		
		1,200	Dec. 1		
		1,200	Dec. 15		

The Ledger Accounts After Posting

Exhibit F:2-7 shows the T-accounts of Smart Touch Learning after posting the journal entries from the journal to the ledger. The accounts are grouped under

Exhibit F:2-7 | Smart Touch Learning's Accounts After Posting Journal Entries in November and December

ASSETS = LIABILITIES + EQUITY

Cash

Nov. 1	30,000	20,000	Nov. 2
Nov. 8	5,500	3,200	Nov. 15
Nov. 22	2,000	300	Nov. 21
Dec. 21	600	5,000	Nov. 25
Dec. 28	8,000	3,000	Dec. 1
		1,200	Dec. 1
		1,200	Dec. 15
Bal.	12,200		

Accounts Receivable

Nov. 10	3,000	2,000	Nov. 22
Bal.	1,000		

Office Supplies

Nov. 3	500		
Bal.	500		

Prepaid Rent

Dec. 1	3,000		
Bal.	3,000		

Land

Nov. 2	20,000		
Bal.	20,000		

Building

Dec. 1	60,000		
Bal.	60,000		

Furniture

Dec. 2	18,000		
Bal.	18,000		

$114,700

Accounts Payable

Nov. 21	300	500	Nov. 3
		200	Bal.

Utilities Payable

		100	Dec. 15
		100	Bal.

Unearned Revenue

		600	Dec. 21
		600	Bal.

Notes Payable

		60,000	Dec. 1
		60,000	Bal.

$60,900

Bright, Capital

		30,000	Nov. 1
		18,000	Dec. 2
		48,000	Bal.

Bright, Withdrawals

Nov. 25	5,000		
Bal.	5,000		

Service Revenue

		5,500	Nov. 8
		3,000	Nov. 10
		8,000	Dec. 28
		16,500	Bal.

Rent Expense

Nov. 15	2,000		
Bal.	2,000		

Salaries Expense

Nov. 15	1,200		
Dec. 1	1,200		
Dec. 15	1,200		
Bal.	3,600		

Utilities Expense

Dec. 15	100		
Bal.	100		

$53,800

their headings. Notice that at December 31, Smart Touch Learning has assets of $114,700 ($12,200 + $1,000 + $500 + $3,000 + $18,000 + $60,000 + $20,000), liabilities of $60,900 ($200 + $100 + $600 + $60,000), and equity of $53,800 ($48,000 − $5,000 + $16,500 − $2,000 − $3,600 − $100). The accounting equation is in balance ($114,700 = $60,900 + $53,800).

The Four-Column Account: An Alternative to the T-Account

The ledger accounts illustrated thus far appear as T-accounts, with the debits on the left and the credits on the right. The T-account clearly separates debits from credits and is used for teaching. An alternative to using the T-account is the four-column account. The four-column account still has debit and credit columns, but it also adds two additional columns that are used to determine a running balance. Exhibit F:2-8 shows the Cash T-account and the Cash four-column account for Smart Touch Learning.

Exhibit F:2-8 | T-Account Versus Four-Column Account

Cash

	Debit		Credit	
Nov. 1	30,000	20,000	Nov. 2	
Nov. 8	5,500	3,200	Nov. 15	
Nov. 22	2,000	300	Nov. 21	
Dec. 21	600	5,000	Nov. 25	
Dec. 28	8,000	3,000	Dec. 1	
		1,200	Dec. 1	
		1,200	Dec. 15	
Bal.	12,200			

CASH   Account No. 101

Date	Item	Post Ref.	Debit	Credit	Balance Debit	Balance Credit
2024						
Nov. 1		J1	30,000		30,000	
Nov. 2		J1		20,000	10,000	
Nov. 8		J1	5,500		15,500	
Nov. 15		J1		3,200	12,300	
Nov. 21		J1		300	12,000	
Nov. 22		J1	2,000		14,000	
Nov. 25		J1		5,000	9,000	
Dec. 1		J2		3,000	6,000	
Dec. 1		J2		1,200	4,800	
Dec. 15		J2		1,200	3,600	
Dec. 21		J2	600		4,200	
Dec. 28		J2	8,000		12,200	

The first pair of Debit/Credit columns in the four-column account is for transaction amounts posted to the account from the journal, such as the $30,000 debit. The second pair of Debit/Credit columns shows the balance of the account as of each date. Because the four-column format provides more information, it is used more often in practice than the T-account. Notice that the balance after the last transaction on December 28 is $12,200, which is the same balance calculated in the T-account.

Recording Business Transactions  Financial 2-23

Do you notice the column labeled *Post Ref.* in the four-column account in Exhibit F:2-8? This column is used in the posting process. When the information is transferred from the journal to the ledger, a posting reference (Post Ref.) is added. This allows a user of the financial data to trace the amount in the ledger back to the journal. In a computerized system, the user would be able to click on the posting reference to view the related journal entry. Exhibit F:2-9 shows the posting and associated posting references for Transaction 1 of Smart Touch Learning. Remember, in a computerized environment, this process is completed automatically when the user enters the journal entry.

Exhibit F:2-9 | Posting References

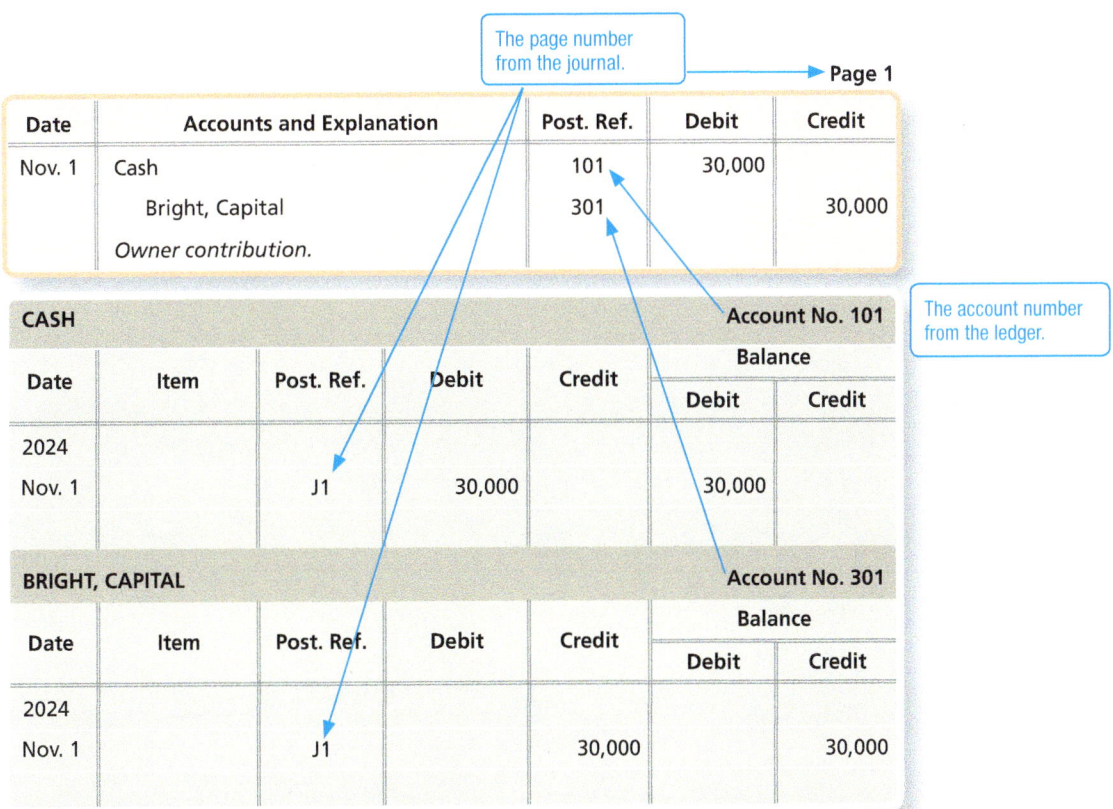

21. EMB Consulting Services had the following transactions for the month of November. Journalize the transactions and include an explanation with each entry.

Nov. 1	The business received $10,000 cash and gave capital to Eloise Martinez, the owner.
15	Purchased office supplies on account, $400.
18	Paid advertising bill, $150.
20	Received $1,000 from customers for services rendered.
28	Martinez withdrew $500 from the business.

Check your answers online in MyLab Accounting or at http://www.pearsonhighered.com/Horngren.

For more practice, see Short Exercises S-F:2-5 through S-F:2-7. **MyLab Accounting**

WHAT IS THE TRIAL BALANCE?

Learning Objective 4
Prepare the trial balance and illustrate how to use the trial balance to prepare financial statements

Trial Balance
A list of all ledger accounts with their balances at a point in time.

After the transactions are recorded in the journal and then posted to the ledger, a **trial balance** can be prepared. The trial balance summarizes the ledger by listing all the accounts with their balances—assets first, followed by liabilities, and then equity. In a manual accounting system, the trial balance provides an accuracy check by showing whether total debits equal total credits. In all types of systems, the trial balance is a useful summary of the accounts and their balances because it shows the balances on a specific date for all accounts in a company's accounting system. Exhibit F:2-10 is the trial balance of Smart Touch Learning at December 31, 2024.

Exhibit F:2-10 | Trial Balance

SMART TOUCH LEARNING
Trial Balance
December 31, 2024

Account Title	Debit	Credit
Cash	$ 12,200	
Accounts Receivable	1,000	
Office Supplies	500	
Prepaid Rent	3,000	
Land	20,000	
Building	60,000	
Furniture	18,000	
Accounts Payable		$ 200
Utilities Payable		100
Unearned Revenue		600
Notes Payable		60,000
Bright, Capital		48,000
Bright, Withdrawals	5,000	
Service Revenue		16,500
Rent Expense	2,000	
Salaries Expense	3,600	
Utilities Expense	100	
Total	$ 125,400	$ 125,400

The trial balance and the balance sheet are not the same. Make sure you understand the differences between these two documents. A trial balance verifies the equality of debits and credits and is an internal document used only by employees of the company. The balance sheet, on the other hand, presents the business's accounting equation and is a financial statement that can be used by both internal and external users.

Preparing Financial Statements from the Trial Balance

In addition to proving the equality of debits and credits, the trial balance is also used to prepare the financial statements. The account balances are taken directly from the trial balance and are used to prepare the income statement, statement of owner's equity, and balance sheet. In Exhibit F:2-11 we present the financial statements for the two months ended December 31, 2024, for Smart Touch Learning.

Recording Business Transactions  Financial 2-25

Exhibit F:2-11 | Smart Touch Learning's Financial Statements

SMART TOUCH LEARNING
Income Statement
Two Months Ended December 31, 2024

Revenues:		
Service Revenue		$ 16,500
Expenses:		
Salaries Expense	$ 3,600	
Rent Expense	2,000	
Utilities Expense	100	
Total Expenses		5,700
Net Income		$ 10,800

SMART TOUCH LEARNING
Statement of Owner's Equity
Two Months Ended December 31, 2024

Bright, Capital, November 1, 2024		$ 0
Owner contribution		48,000
Net income for the two months		10,800
		58,800
Owner withdrawal		(5,000)
Bright, Capital, December 31, 2018		$ 53,800

SMART TOUCH LEARNING
Balance Sheet
December 31, 2024

Assets		Liabilities	
Cash	$ 12,200	Accounts Payable	$ 200
Accounts Receivable	1,000	Utilities Payable	100
Office Supplies	500	Unearned Revenue	600
Prepaid Rent	3,000	Notes Payable	60,000
Land	20,000	Total Liabilities	60,900
Building	60,000		
Furniture	18,000	**Owner's Equity**	
		Bright, Capital	53,800
Total Assets	$ 114,700	Total Liabilities and Owner's Equity	$ 114,700

Correcting Trial Balance Errors

Throughout the accounting process, total debits should always equal total credits. If they do not, there is an error. Computerized accounting systems eliminate many errors because most software will not let you make a journal entry that does not balance. But computers cannot eliminate *all errors* because humans can input the wrong data.

Balancing errors can be detected by computing the difference between total debits and total credits on the trial balance. Then perform one or more of the following actions:

1. **Search the trial balance for a missing account.** For example, suppose the accountant omitted the Bright, Withdrawals account from the trial balance in Exhibit F:2-10. Total debits would then be $120,400 ($125,400 − $5,000). Trace each account from the ledger to the trial balance, and you will locate the missing account.
2. **Divide the difference between total debits and total credits by 2.** A debit treated as a credit, or vice versa, doubles the amount of the error. Suppose the accountant posted a $500 credit as a debit. Total debits contain the $500, and total credits omit the $500. The out-of-balance amount is $1,000. Dividing the difference by 2 identifies the

$500 amount of the transaction. Then search the journal or ledger for a $500 transaction and trace it to the account affected.

3. **Divide the out-of-balance amount by 9.** If the result is evenly divisible by 9, the error may be a *slide error* (example: writing $1,000 as $100 or writing $100 as $1,000) or a *transposition* (example: listing $1,200 as $2,100). Suppose, for example, that the accountant entered the $5,000 Bright, Withdrawals as $50,000 on the trial balance. This is a slide error. Total debits would differ from total credits by $45,000 ($50,000 − $5,000 = $45,000). Dividing $45,000 by 9 yields $5,000, the correct amount of the withdrawals. Look for an account in the ledger with a $5,000 balance until you reach the Bright, Withdrawals account. You have then found the error.

Total debits can equal total credits on the trial balance; however, there still could be errors in individual account balances because an incorrect account might have been selected in an individual journal entry.

Try It!

22. Using the following accounts and their balances, prepare the trial balance for Cooper Furniture Repair as of December 31, 2024. All accounts have normal balances.

Cash	$ 7,000	Advertising Expense	$ 1,200
Unearned Revenue	4,500	Utilities Expense	800
Equipment	10,000	Rent Expense	5,000
Service Revenue	8,000	Accounts Payable	2,300
Cooper, Capital	12,200	Cooper, Withdrawals	3,000

Check your answers online in MyLab Accounting or at http://www.pearsonhighered.com/Horngren.

For more practice, see Short Exercise S-F:2-8. MyLab Accounting

HOW DO YOU USE THE DEBT RATIO TO EVALUATE BUSINESS PERFORMANCE?

Learning Objective 5
Use the debt ratio to evaluate business performance

Debt Ratio
Shows the proportion of assets financed with debt. Total liabilities / Total assets.

Previously you learned that evaluating a company's return on assets (Net income / Average total assets) can help in determining how well a company is performing. In this chapter, you learn about another tool that can be used when reviewing financial statements. The **debt ratio** shows the proportion of assets financed with debt and is calculated by dividing total liabilities by total assets. It can be used to evaluate a business's ability to pay its debts.

Debt ratio = Total liabilities / Total assets

Think about the accounting equation (Assets = Liabilities + Equity). The equation shows who can claim the assets. The liabilities represent the claims of the creditors, and the equity represents the claims of the owner. Companies that have a high percentage of liabilities are at greater risk of default. If they are unable to pay their creditors as the amounts become due, the creditors have the right to claim the assets. The debt ratio calculates the percentage of assets that are financed with liabilities.

Let's look at **Kohl's Corporation** and evaluate its ability to pay its debts. On its February 2, 2019, balance sheet (a link is located online at **http://www.pearsonhighered.com/Horngren**), Kohl's reported (in millions) total liabilities of $6,942 ($2,730 + $1,861 + $1,523 + $184 + $644) and total assets of $12,469. The debt ratio for Kohl's as of February 2, 2019, follows:

$$\text{Debt ratio} = \text{Total liabilities} / \text{Total assets}$$
$$= \$6,942 / \$12,469$$
$$= 0.557 = 55.7\%$$

A debt ratio of 55.7% means that more than half, approximately 56%, of the assets of Kohl's Corporation are financed with debt. The other 44.3% (100% − 55.7%) are financed by stockholders (owners) of the corporation. The debt ratio indicates the risk of a company. The higher the debt ratio, the higher the risk. All liabilities must eventually be paid, and the debt ratio is one indication of the ability of the company to fulfill these obligations.

DECISIONS

Would you purchase equipment with debt?

Jackson Russell works as a district sales manager for a large pharmaceutical sales company. Jackson would like to purchase a new high-tech marketing display that he will be able to use at upcoming medical conferences. The marketing display will allow his customers to access up-to-date information and research statistics on the pharmaceuticals that his company sells by using multiple touch screen computers. He believes that the marketing display will significantly increase the sales revenue of the products he sells. The only problem is that the marketing display will cost $50,000, and he does not have the cash in his budget to purchase the display. Jackson will need to purchase the display using debt, which will increase the district's debt ratio from 20% to 58%. Jackson is aware that his company closely monitors the district's debt ratio and has a policy that the district must maintain a ratio below 55%. Should Jackson purchase the equipment?

Solution

If the company has a policy that the district's debt ratio must remain below 55%, then Jackson should not purchase the equipment. However, there might be a way to structure the purchase so that the district's debt ratio would stay below 55%. Jackson either needs to incur less debt or increase his total assets. He could do this in several possible ways. One alternative might be for Jackson to pay for part of the display equipment with cash and only finance part of it with debt. Even putting as little as $10,000 cash down on the equipment would keep the debt ratio below 55%. Another alternative might be for his district to recognize revenue. If there are open sales opportunities that his employees could close, they might be able to increase total assets (and revenue) and, thereby, decrease the debt ratio.

23. Using the following accounts and their balances, calculate the debt ratio for Cooper Furniture Repair as of December 31.

Cash	$ 7,000	Advertising Expense	$ 1,200
Unearned Revenue	4,500	Utilities Expense	800
Equipment	10,000	Rent Expense	5,000
Service Revenue	8,000	Accounts Payable	2,300
Cooper, Capital	12,200	Cooper, Withdrawals	3,000

Check your answer online in MyLab Accounting or at http://www.pearsonhighered.com/Horngren.

For more practice, see Short Exercise S-F:2-9. MyLab Accounting

REVIEW

> Things You Should Know

1. What is an account?

- An account is a detailed record of all increases and decreases that have occurred in an individual asset, liability, or equity during a specific period.
- Common asset accounts: Cash, Accounts Receivable, Notes Receivable, Prepaid Expenses, Land, Building, Furniture
- Common liability accounts: Accounts Payable, Notes Payable, Taxes Payable, Salaries Payable, Unearned Revenue
- Common equity accounts: Owner, Capital; Owner, Withdrawals; Revenues; Expenses
- A chart of accounts lists a company's accounts along with account numbers.
- A ledger shows the increases and decreases in each account along with their balances.

2. What is double-entry accounting?

- Double-entry accounting requires transactions to be recorded into at least two accounts.
- The T-account is shaped like a capital *T* with debits posted to the left side of the vertical line and credits posted to the right side of the vertical line.
- Debit = Left
- Credit = Right
- Assets; Owner, Withdrawals; and Expenses are increased with a debit and decreased with a credit.
- Liabilities; Owner, Capital; and Revenues are increased with a credit and decreased with a debit.
- The normal balance of an account is the increase side of an account.

3. How do you record transactions?

- Source documents provide the evidence and data for transactions.
- Transactions are recorded in a journal, and then the journal entries are posted (transferred) to the ledger.
- Transactions are journalized and posted using five steps:

   Step 1: Identify the accounts and the account type.
   Step 2: Decide whether each account increases or decreases, then apply the rules of debits and credits.
   Step 3: Record the transaction in the journal.
   Step 4: Post the journal entry to the ledger.
   Step 5: Determine whether the accounting equation is in balance.

4. **What is the trial balance?**
   - The trial balance summarizes the ledger by listing all the accounts with their balances.
   - Assets are listed first, followed by liabilities, and then equity.
   - The trial balance ensures that debits equal credits and is used to prepare the financial statements.

5. **How do you use the debt ratio to evaluate business performance?**
   - The debt ratio can be used to evaluate a business's ability to pay its debts.
   - Debt ratio = Total liabilities / Total assets.

> Check Your Understanding

Check your understanding of the chapter by completing this problem and then looking at the solution. Use this practice to help identify which sections of the chapter you need to study more.

The trial balance of Harper Service Center as of March 31, 2024, follows:

HARPER SERVICE CENTER
Trial Balance
March 31, 2024

Account Title	Debit	Credit
Cash	$ 23,900	
Accounts Receivable	4,500	
Office Supplies	0	
Land	0	
Accounts Payable		$ 2,000
Utilities Payable		0
Unearned Revenue		0
Notes Payable		0
Harper, Capital		18,500
Harper, Withdrawals	0	
Service Revenue		10,000
Salaries Expense	800	
Rent Expense	1,000	
Interest Expense	0	
Utilities Expense	300	
Total	$ 30,500	$ 30,500

During April, the business engaged in the following transactions:

Apr. 2	Borrowed $45,000 from the bank and signed a note payable in the name of the business.
4	Paid cash of $40,000 to acquire land.
9	Performed services for a customer and received cash of $5,000.
13	Purchased office supplies on account, $300.
15	Performed services for a customer on account, $2,600.
18	Paid $1,200 on account.
21	Paid the following cash expenses: salaries, $3,000; rent, $1,500; and interest, $400.
25	Received $3,100 from a customer on account.
27	Received a $200 utility bill that will be paid next month.
29	Received $1,500 for services to be performed next month.
30	Harper withdrew cash of $1,800.

Requirements

1. Open the accounts listed in the trial balance using the balances indicated. Use the T-account format. (See Learning Objective 2)
2. Journalize each transaction including explanations. (See Learning Objective 3)
3. Post the journal entries to the ledger (use T-account format). (See Learning Objective 3)
4. Prepare the trial balance of Harper Service Center as of April 30, 2024. (See Learning Objective 4)

> Solution

Requirement 1

ASSETS = LIABILITIES + EQUITY

Cash	Accounts Payable	Harper, Capital	Harper, Withdrawals	Service Revenue	Salaries Expense
Bal. 23,900	2,000 Bal.	18,500 Bal.	Bal. 0	10,000 Bal.	Bal. 800

Accounts Receivable	Utilities Payable				Rent Expense
Bal. 4,500	0 Bal.				Bal. 1,000

Office Supplies	Unearned Revenue				Interest Expense
Bal. 0	0 Bal.				Bal. 0

Land	Notes Payable				Utilities Expense
Bal. 0	0 Bal.				Bal. 300

Requirement 2

Date	Accounts and Explanation	Debit	Credit
Apr. 2	Cash	45,000	
	Notes Payable		45,000
	Borrowed cash on notes payable.		
4	Land	40,000	
	Cash		40,000
	Purchased land with cash.		
9	Cash	5,000	
	Service Revenue		5,000
	Performed services and received cash.		
13	Office Supplies	300	
	Accounts Payable		300
	Purchased office supplies on account.		
15	Accounts Receivable	2,600	
	Service Revenue		2,600
	Performed services on account.		
18	Accounts Payable	1,200	
	Cash		1,200
	Paid cash on account.		
21	Salaries Expense	3,000	
	Rent Expense	1,500	
	Interest Expense	400	
	Cash		4,900
	Paid cash expenses.		
25	Cash	3,100	
	Accounts Receivable		3,100
	Received cash on account.		
27	Utilities Expense	200	
	Utilities Payable		200
	Received utility bill.		
29	Cash	1,500	
	Unearned Revenue		1,500
	Collected cash for future services.		
30	Harper, Withdrawals	1,800	
	Cash		1,800
	Owner withdrawal.		

Requirement 3

```
           ASSETS              =        LIABILITIES           +                              EQUITY
            Cash               =      Accounts Payable        +   Harper, Capital  −  Harper, Withdrawals  +    Service Revenue          Salaries Expense
Bal.    23,900 | 40,000  Apr. 4    Apr.18 1,200 | 2,000  Bal.            18,500  Bal.   Bal.      0 |                      10,000  Bal.   Bal.      800 |
Apr. 2  45,000 |  1,200  Apr.18                   300   Apr. 13          18,500  Bal.   Apr. 30 1,800 |                     5,000  Apr. 9  Apr. 21 3,000 |
Apr. 9   5,000 |  4,900  Apr. 21                1,100   Bal.                            Bal.  1,800 |                       2,600  Apr. 15 Bal.    3,800 |
Apr. 25  3,100 |  1,800  Apr. 30        Utilities Payable                                                                   17,600  Bal.      Rent Expense
Apr. 29  1,500 |                                   0    Bal.                                                                             Bal.    1,000 |
Bal.    30,600 |                                  200   Apr. 27                                                                          Apr. 21 1,500 |
      Accounts Receivable                         200   Bal.                                                                             Bal.    2,500 |
Bal.     4,500 |  3,100  Apr. 25        Unearned Revenue                                                                                   Interest Expense
Apr. 15  2,600 |                                   0    Bal.                                                                             Bal.        0 |
Bal.     4,000 |                                1,500   Apr. 29                                                                          Apr. 21   400 |
       Office Supplies                          1,500   Bal.                                                                             Bal.      400 |
Bal.         0 |                          Notes Payable                                                                                    Utilities Expense
Apr. 13    300 |                                   0    Bal.                                                                             Bal.      300 |
Bal.       300 |                               45,000   Apr. 2                                                                           Apr. 27   200 |
            Land                               45,000   Bal.                                                                             Bal.      500 |
Bal.         0 |
Apr. 4  40,000 |
Bal.    40,000 |
```

Requirement 4

HARPER SERVICE CENTER
Trial Balance
April 30, 2024

Account Title	Debit	Credit
	Balance	
Cash	$ 30,600	
Accounts Receivable	4,000	
Office Supplies	300	
Land	40,000	
Accounts Payable		$ 1,100
Utilities Payable		200
Unearned Revenue		1,500
Notes Payable		45,000
Harper, Capital		18,500
Harper, Withdrawals	1,800	
Service Revenue		17,600
Salaries Expense	3,800	
Rent Expense	2,500	
Interest Expense	400	
Utilities Expense	500	
Total	$ 83,900	$ 83,900

> Key Terms

Account (p. 2-2)
Accrued Liability (p. 2-3)
Chart of Accounts (p. 2-4)
Compound Journal Entry (p. 2-15)
Credit (p. 2-6)
Debit (p. 2-6)
Debt Ratio (p. 2-26)

Double-Entry System (p. 2-6)
Journal (p. 2-10)
Ledger (p. 2-5)
Normal Balance (p. 2-7)
Notes Payable (p. 2-3)
Notes Receivable (p. 2-3)
Posting (p. 2-10)

Prepaid Expense (p. 2-3)
Source Document (p. 2-9)
T-Account (p. 2-6)
Trial Balance (p. 2-24)
Unearned Revenue (p. 2-3)

> Quick Check

1. The detailed record of the changes in a particular asset, liability, or owner's equity is called
   a. an account.
   b. a journal.
   c. a ledger.
   d. a trial balance.

   Learning Objective 1

2. Which of the following accounts is a liability?
   a. Accounts Receivable
   b. Service Revenue
   c. Unearned Revenue
   d. Prepaid Rent Expense

   Learning Objective 1

3. The left side of an account is used to record which of the following?
   a. Debit or credit, depending on the type of account
   b. Increases
   c. Credits
   d. Debits

   Learning Objective 2

4. Which of the following statements is correct?
   a. Prepaid Expenses are decreased with a debit.
   b. Unearned Revenue is increased with a debit.
   c. Rent Expense is increased with a credit.
   d. Accounts Payable is increased with a credit.

   Learning Objective 2

5. Your business purchased office supplies of $2,500 on account. The journal entry to record this transaction is as follows:

   Learning Objective 3

Date	Accounts and Explanation	Debit	Credit
a.	Office Supplies	2,500	
	Accounts Receivable		2,500
b.	Office Supplies	2,500	
	Accounts Payable		2,500
c.	Accounts Payable	2,500	
	Office Supplies		2,500
d.	Cash	2,500	
	Accounts Payable		2,500

Learning Objective 3

6. Sedlor Properties purchased office supplies on account for $800. Which journal entry records the payment on account of those office supplies?

Date	Accounts and Explanation	Debit	Credit
a.	Accounts Payable	800	
	Accounts Receivable		800
b.	Accounts Payable	800	
	Cash		800
c.	Cash	800	
	Accounts Payable		800
d.	Office Supplies	800	
	Cash		800

Learning Objective 3

7. Posting a $2,500 purchase of office supplies on account appears as follows:

a.
Cash		Office Supplies	
	2,500	2,500	

b.
Office Supplies		Accounts Payable	
	2,500		2,500

c.
Office Supplies		Accounts Receivable	
2,500			2,500

d.
Office Supplies		Accounts Payable	
2,500			2,500

Learning Objective 4

8. Pixel Copies recorded a cash collection on account by debiting Cash and crediting Accounts Payable. What will the trial balance show for this error?

a. Cash is overstated.
b. Liabilities are overstated.
c. Expenses are overstated.
d. The trial balance will not balance.

Learning Objectives 3, 4

9. Which sequence correctly summarizes the accounting process?

a. Journalize transactions, post to the accounts, prepare a trial balance.
b. Journalize transactions, prepare a trial balance, post to the accounts.
c. Post to the accounts, journalize transactions, prepare a trial balance.
d. Prepare a trial balance, journalize transactions, post to the accounts.

Learning Objective 5

10. Nathville Laundry reported assets of $800 and equity of $480. What is Nathville's debt ratio?

a. 60%
b. 40%
c. 67%
d. Not enough information is provided.

Check your answers at the end of the chapter.

ASSESS YOUR PROGRESS

> Review Questions

1. Identify the three categories of the accounting equation, and list at least four accounts associated with each category.
2. What is the purpose of the chart of accounts? Explain the numbering typically associated with the accounts.
3. What does a ledger show? What's the difference between a ledger and the chart of accounts?
4. Accounting uses a double-entry system. Explain what this sentence means.
5. What is a T-account? On which side is the debit? On which side is the credit? Where does the account name go on a T-account?
6. When are debits increases? When are debits decreases?
7. When are credits increases? When are credits decreases?
8. Identify which types of accounts have a normal debit balance and which types of accounts have a normal credit balance.
9. What are source documents? Provide examples of source documents that a business might use.
10. Where are transactions initially recorded?
11. Explain the five steps in journalizing and posting transactions.
12. What are the four parts of a journal entry?
13. What is involved in the posting process?
14. What is the purpose of the trial balance?
15. What is the difference between the trial balance and the balance sheet?
16. If total debits equal total credits on the trial balance, is the trial balance error-free? Explain your answer.
17. What is the calculation for the debt ratio? Explain what the debt ratio evaluates.

> Short Exercises

S-F:2-1 Identifying accounts

Consider the following accounts and identify each account as an asset (A), liability (L), or equity (E).

a. Notes Receivable
b. Nunez, Capital
c. Prepaid Insurance
d. Notes Payable
e. Rent Revenue
f. Taxes Payable
g. Rent Expense
h. Furniture
i. Nunez, Withdrawals
j. Unearned Revenue

Learning Objective 1

Learning Objective 2 — S-F:2-2 Identifying increases and decreases in accounts

For each account, identify whether the changes would be recorded as a debit (DR) or credit (CR).

a. Increase to Accounts Receivable
b. Decrease to Unearned Revenue
c. Decrease to Cash
d. Increase to Interest Expense
e. Increase to Salaries Payable
f. Decrease to Prepaid Rent
g. Increase to Proudfoot, Capital
h. Increase to Notes Receivable
i. Decrease to Accounts Payable
j. Increase to Interest Revenue

Learning Objective 2 — S-F:2-3 Identifying normal balances

For each account, identify whether the normal balance is a debit (DR) or credit (CR).

a. Notes Payable
b. Herman, Withdrawals
c. Service Revenue
d. Land
e. Unearned Revenue
f. Herman, Capital
g. Utilities Expense
h. Office Supplies
i. Advertising Expense
j. Interest Payable

Learning Objective 2 — S-F:2-4 Calculating the balance of a T-account

Calculate the Accounts Payable balance.

Accounts Payable			
May 2	6,000	21,000	May 1
May 22	11,500	500	May 5
		8,500	May 15
		500	May 23

Learning Objective 3 — S-F:2-5 Journalizing transactions

John Daniel opened a medical practice in Sacramento, California, and had the following transactions during the month of January:

Jan. 1	The business received $34,000 cash and gave capital to Daniel.
2	Purchased medical supplies on account, $17,000.
4	Performed services for patients receiving $1,600.
12	Paid monthly office rent of $3,000.
15	Recorded $7,000 revenue for services rendered to patients on account.

Journalize the transactions of John Daniel, M.D. Include an explanation with each entry.

S-F:2-6 Journalizing transactions

Harper Sales Consultants completed the following transactions during the latter part of January:

Jan. 22	Performed services for customers on account, $7,500.
30	Received cash on account from customers, $8,000.
31	Received a utility bill, $220, which will be paid during February.
31	Paid monthly salary to salesman, $2,500.
31	Received $2,310 for three months of consulting service to be performed starting in February.
31	The owner, Damon Harper, withdrew $950 from the business.

Journalize the transactions of Harper Sales Consultants. Include an explanation with each journal entry.

S-F:2-7 Journalizing transactions and posting to T-accounts

Roland Foster Optical Dispensary completed the following transactions during the latter part of March:

Mar. 15	Purchased office supplies on account, $3,400.
28	Paid $1,800 on account.

Requirements

1. Journalize the transactions of Roland Foster Optical Dispensary. Include an explanation with each journal entry.
2. Open the following accounts (use T-account format): Cash (Beginning Balance of $21,000), Office Supplies, and Accounts Payable. Post the journal entries from Requirement 1 to the accounts, and compute the balance in each account.

S-F:2-8 Preparing a trial balance

Smithson Floor Coverings reported the following summarized data at December 31, 2024. Accounts appear in no particular order, and all have normal balances.

Service Revenue	$ 26,000	Salaries Payable	$ 25,000
Equipment	36,000	Salaries Expense	1,600
Rent Expense	17,000	Cash	7,000
Smithson, Capital	24,000	Accounts Receivable	3,600
Accounts Payable	2,200	Interest Payable	6,000
Smithson, Withdrawals	16,100	Utilities Expense	1,900

Prepare the trial balance of Smithson Floor Coverings at December 31, 2024.

S-F:2-9 Calculating debt ratio

Aladdin Carpet Care had the following total assets, liabilities, and equity as of October 31:

Assets	$ 200,000
Liabilities	30,000
Equity	170,000

What is Aladdin Carpet Care's debt ratio as of October 31?

> Exercises

Learning Objectives 1, 2, 3, 4

E-F:2-10 Using accounting vocabulary

Match the accounting terms with the corresponding definitions.

1. Posting
2. Account
3. Debit
4. Journal
5. Chart of accounts
6. Trial balance
7. Normal balance
8. Ledger
9. Credit
10. Compound journal entry

a. A detailed record of all increases and decreases that have occurred in a particular asset, liability, or equity during a period
b. The record holding all the accounts of a business, the changes in those accounts, and their balances
c. A journal entry that is characterized by having multiple debits and/or multiple credits
d. A record of transactions in date order
e. Left side of a T-account
f. Side of an account where increases are recorded
g. Transferring amounts from the journal to the ledger
h. Right side of a T-account
i. A list of all accounts with their balances at a point in time
j. A list of all accounts with their account numbers

Learning Objective 1

E-F:2-11 Creating a chart of accounts

Raymond Autobody Shop has the following accounts:

Accounts Payable	Service Revenue
Cash	Equipment
Utilities Expense	Raymond, Capital
Automotive Supplies	Advertising Expense
Raymond, Withdrawals	Unearned Revenue

Create a chart of accounts for Raymond Autobody Shop using the standard numbering system. Each account is separated by a factor of 10. For example, the first asset account will be 100 and the next asset account will be 110.

Learning Objectives 1, 2

E-F:2-12 Identifying accounts, increases in accounts, and normal balances

a. Interest Revenue
b. Accounts Payable
c. Calhoun, Capital
d. Office Supplies
e. Advertising Expense
f. Unearned Revenue
g. Prepaid Rent
h. Utilities Expense
i. Calhoun, Withdrawals
j. Service Revenue

Requirements

1. Identify each account as asset (A), liability (L), or equity (E).
2. Identify whether the account is increased with a debit (DR) or credit (CR).
3. Identify whether the normal balance is a debit (DR) or credit (CR).

E-F:2-13 Identifying increases and decreases in accounts and normal balances **Learning Objective 2**

Insert the missing information into the accounting equation. Signify increases as Incr. and decreases as Decr.

(a)	=	LIABILITIES	+	(b)

ASSETS	=	(c)	+	Owner, Capital	−	(d)	+	Revenues	−	Expenses
(e) Debit / Decr. (n)		Decr. (o) / (f) Credit		(g) (p) / (h) Credit		(i) (q) / (j) Credit		(k) Debit / (l) Credit		Incr. (r) / (m) Credit

E-F:2-14 Identifying source documents **Learning Objective 3**

For each transaction, identify a possible source document.

a. The business received $20,000 cash and gave capital to owner.

b. Purchased office supplies on account, $500.

c. Recorded $1,000 revenue for services rendered to customers.

E-F:2-15 Analyzing and journalizing transactions **Learning Objective 3**

As the manager of Margarita Mexican Restaurant, you must deal with a variety of business transactions. Provide an explanation for the following transactions:

a. Debit Equipment and credit Cash.

b. Debit Garcia, Withdrawals and credit Cash.

c. Debit Wages Payable and credit Cash.

d. Debit Equipment and credit Garcia, Capital.

e. Debit Cash and credit Unearned Revenue.

f. Debit Advertising Expense and credit Cash.

g. Debit Cash and credit Service Revenue.

Use the following information to answer Exercises E-F:2-16 and E-F:2-17.

The following transactions occurred for Lawrence Engineering:

Jul. 2	Received $14,000 contribution from Brett Lawrence, owner, in exchange for capital.
4	Paid utilities expense of $370.
5	Purchased equipment on account, $1,600.
10	Performed services for a client on account, $2,900.
12	Borrowed $7,100 cash, signing a notes payable.
19	The owner, Brett Lawrence, withdrew $200 cash from the business.
21	Purchased office supplies for $840 and paid cash.
27	Paid the liability from July 5.

Learning Objective 3

E-F:2-16 Analyzing and journalizing transactions

Journalize the transactions of Lawrence Engineering. Include an explanation with each journal entry. Use the following accounts: Cash; Accounts Receivable; Office Supplies; Equipment; Accounts Payable; Notes Payable; Lawrence, Capital; Lawrence, Withdrawals; Service Revenue; and Utilities Expense.

Learning Objective 3

3. Cash Balance $18,090

E-F:2-17 Posting journal entries to T-accounts

Requirements

1. Open the following T-accounts for Lawrence Engineering: Cash; Accounts Receivable; Office Supplies; Equipment; Accounts Payable; Notes Payable; Lawrence, Capital; Lawrence, Withdrawals; Service Revenue; and Utilities Expense.

2. Post the journal entries to the T-accounts. Also transfer the dates to the T-accounts.

3. Compute the July 31 balance for each account.

Use the following information to answer Exercises E-F:2-18 and E-F:2-19.

The following transactions occurred for Wilke Technology Solutions:

May 1	The business received cash of $105,000 and gave capital to Zoe Wilke.
2	Purchased office supplies on account, $550.
4	Paid $57,000 cash for building and land. The building had a fair market value of $45,000.
6	Performed services for customers and received cash, $3,600.
9	Paid $350 on accounts payable.
17	Performed services for customers on account, $3,500.
19	Paid rent expense for the month, $1,200.
20	Received $1,500 from customers for services to be performed next month.
21	Paid $900 for advertising in next month's *IT Technology* magazine.
23	Received $3,100 cash on account from a customer.
31	Incurred and paid salaries, $1,700.

Learning Objective 3

E-F:2-18 Analyzing and journalizing transactions

Journalize the transactions of Wilke Technology Solutions. Include an explanation with each journal entry. Use the following accounts: Cash; Accounts Receivable; Office Supplies; Prepaid Advertising; Land; Building; Accounts Payable; Unearned Revenue; Wilke, Capital; Service Revenue; Rent Expense; and Salaries Expense.

Learning Objective 3

2. Cash Balance $52,050

E-F:2-19 Posting journal entries to four-column accounts

Requirements

1. Open four-column accounts using the following account numbers: Cash, 110; Accounts Receivable, 120; Office Supplies, 130; Prepaid Advertising, 140; Land, 150; Building, 160; Accounts Payable, 210; Unearned Revenue, 220; Wilke, Capital, 310; Service Revenue, 410; Rent Expense, 510; and Salaries Expense, 520.

2. Post the journal entries to the four-column accounts and determine the balance in the account after each transaction. Assume that the journal entries were recorded on page 10 of the journal. Make sure to complete the Post. Ref. columns in the journal and ledger.

E-F:2-20 Analyzing transactions from T-accounts

Learning Objective 3

The first nine transactions of North-West Airplane Repair have been posted to the T-accounts. Provide an explanation for each of the nine transactions.

```
           ASSETS              =        LIABILITIES        +                              EQUITY

            Cash               =     Accounts Payable      +   Early, Capital  -  Early, Withdrawals  +  Service Revenue  -   Rent Expense
(1)  370,000 | 360,000  (2)   (5)    1,200 |  1,500  (4)       370,000 (1) (8) | 7,000                    21,000  (9)  (7)   1,400
(3)  260,000 |   1,200  (5)          Notes Payable
(9)   21,000 |   1,500  (6)                                                                                                Salaries Expense
             |   3,900  (7)                 | 260,000  (3)                                                            (7)   2,500
             |   7,000  (8)
                                                                                                                      Property Tax Expense
        Office Supplies                                                                                               (6)   1,500
(4)    1,500 |

           Building
(2)  360,000 |
```

E-F:2-21 Journalizing transactions from T-accounts

Learning Objective 3

In December, the first five transactions of Abling's Lawn Care Company have been posted to the T-accounts. Prepare the journal entries that served as the sources for the five transactions. Include an explanation for each entry.

```
           Cash                    Office Supplies              Building                Equipment
(1) 57,000 | 40,000  (3)       (2)   800 |              (3)  40,000 |              (5)  3,800 |
(4) 46,000 |  3,800  (5)

     Accounts Payable              Notes Payable             Abling, Capital
             |   800  (2)                |  46,000  (4)              |  57,000  (1)
```

E-F:2-22 Preparing a trial balance

Learning Objective 4

The accounts of Anderson Moving Company follow with their normal balances as of August 31, 2024. The accounts are listed in no particular order.

Total Debits $191,800

Anderson, Capital	$ 49,800	Trucks	$ 123,000
Insurance Expense	600	Fuel Expense	1,000
Accounts Payable	4,000	Anderson, Withdrawals	5,600
Service Revenue	82,000	Utilities Expense	300
Building	41,000	Accounts Receivable	10,000
Advertising Expense	200	Notes Payable	56,000
Salaries Expense	6,000	Office Supplies	100
Cash	4,000		

Prepare Anderson's trial balance as of August 31, 2024.

Learning Objective 4

Total Debits $80,700

E-F:2-23 Preparing a trial balance from T-accounts

The T-accounts of McMahon Farm Equipment Repair follow as of May 31, 2024.

ASSETS	=	LIABILITIES	+	EQUITY

Cash
31,000 | 14,000
1,800 | 800
400 | 4,000
      | 2,000
      | 3,380

Accounts Receivable
3,500 | 400

Land
14,000

Building
29,000

Equipment
16,000

Salaries Payable
800 | 4,200

Notes Payable
4,000 | 29,000

McMahon, Capital
    | 31,000
    | 16,000

McMahon, Withdrawals
2,000 |

Service Revenue
    | 3,500
    | 1,800

Salaries Expense
2,100 |
4,200 |

Property Tax Expense
1,000 |

Advertising Expense
280 |

Prepare McMahon Farm Equipment Repair's trial balance as of May 31, 2024.

Learning Objectives 3, 4

3. Total Debits $24,670

E-F:2-24 Journalizing transactions, posting journal entries to four-column accounts, and preparing a trial balance

The following transactions occurred during the month for Teresa Parker, CPA:

Jun. 1	Parker opened an accounting firm by contributing $13,200 cash and office furniture with a fair market value of $5,300 in exchange for capital.
5	Paid monthly rent of $1,300.
9	Purchased office supplies on account, $600.
14	Paid employee's salary, $1,900.
18	Received a bill for utilities to be paid next month, $370.
21	Paid $500 of the accounts payable created on June 9.
25	Performed accounting services on account, $5,700.
28	Parker withdrew cash of $6,700.

Requirements

1. Open the following four-column accounts of Teresa Parker, CPA: Cash, 110; Accounts Receivable, 120; Office Supplies, 130; Office Furniture, 140; Accounts Payable, 210; Utilities Payable, 220; Parker, Capital, 310; Parker, Withdrawals, 320; Service Revenue, 410; Salaries Expense, 510; Rent Expense, 520; and Utilities Expense, 530.

2. Journalize the transactions and then post the journal entries to the four-column accounts. Explanations are not required for the journal entries. Keep a running balance in each account. Assume the journal entries are recorded on page 10 of the journal.

3. Prepare the trial balance as of June 30, 2024.

E-F:2-25 Analyzing accounting errors

Learning Objective 4

Courtney Meehan has trouble keeping her debits and credits equal. During a recent month, Courtney made the following accounting errors:

a. In preparing the trial balance, Courtney omitted a $5,000 Notes Payable. The debit to Cash was correct.

b. Courtney posted a $1,000 Utilities Expense as $100. The credit to Cash was correct.

c. In recording a $600 payment on account, Courtney debited Furniture instead of Accounts Payable.

d. In journalizing a receipt of cash for service revenue, Courtney debited Cash for $50 instead of the correct amount of $500. The credit was correct.

e. Courtney recorded a $210 purchase of office supplies on account by debiting Office Supplies for $120 and crediting Accounts Payable for $120.

Requirements

1. For each of these errors, state whether total debits equal total credits on the trial balance.

2. Identify each account that has an incorrect balance and the amount and direction of the error (e.g., "Accounts Receivable $500 too high").

E-F:2-26 Correcting errors in a trial balance

Learning Objective 4

The accountant for Countryside Painting Specialists is having a hard time preparing the trial balance as of November 30, 2024:

Total Debits $35,600

COUNTRYSIDE PAINTING SPECIALISTS
Trial Balance
November 30, 2024

Account Title	Debit	Credit
Painting Equipment	$ 13,500	
Cash	12,100	
Accounts Receivable	1,300	
Advertising Expense	550	
Watts, Withdrawals		$ 3,500
Accounts Payable		3,300
Rent Expense	1,800	
Watts, Capital	15,000	
Service Revenue		15,600
Unearned Revenue	1,700	
Salaries Expense	2,400	
Office Supplies		200
Utilities Expense	250	
Total	$ 48,600	$ 22,600

Prepare the corrected trial balance as of November 30, 2024. Assume all amounts are correct and all accounts have normal balances.

Learning Objective 4

Total Debits $35,300

E-F:2-27 Correcting errors in a trial balance

The following trial balance of Joy McDowell Tutoring Service as of May 31, 2024, does not balance.

JOY MCDOWELL TUTORING SERVICE
Trial Balance
May 31, 2024

Account Title	Balance Debit	Balance Credit
Cash	$ 2,800	
Accounts Receivable	2,000	
Office Supplies	600	
Computer Equipment	15,800	
Accounts Payable		$ 11,100
Utilities Payable		800
McDowell, Capital		11,600
McDowell, Withdrawals	10,400	
Service Revenue		9,600
Salaries Expense	1,900	
Rent Expense	800	
Utilities Expense	700	
Total	$ 35,000	$ 33,100

Investigation of the accounting records reveals that the bookkeeper:

a. Recorded a $400 cash revenue transaction by debiting Accounts Receivable. The credit entry was correct.

b. Posted a $2,000 credit to Accounts Payable as $200.

c. Did not record Utilities Expense or the related Utilities Payable in the amount of $300.

d. Understated McDowell, Capital by $100.

Prepare the corrected trial balance as of May 31, 2024, complete with a heading; journal entries are not required.

E-F:2-28 Calculating the debt ratio

John Hart, M.D., reported the following trial balance as of September 30, 2024:

JOHN HART, M.D.
Trial Balance
September 30, 2024

Account Title	Debit	Credit
Cash	$ 30,000	
Accounts Receivable	7,900	
Office Supplies	3,000	
Land	29,000	
Building	75,000	
Office Equipment	30,000	
Accounts Payable		$ 1,600
Utilities Payable		800
Unearned Revenue		24,795
Notes Payable		69,000
Hart, Capital		110,000
Hart, Withdrawals	57,000	
Service Revenue		50,505
Salaries Expense	23,500	
Utilities Expense	1,100	
Advertising Expense	200	
Total	$ 256,700	$ 256,700

Calculate the debt ratio for John Hart, M.D.

> Problems Group A

Learning Objectives 3, 4

2. Cash Balance $56,050

P-F:2-29A Journalizing transactions, posting journal entries to T-accounts, and preparing a trial balance

Vince York practices medicine under the business title Vince York, M.D. During July, the medical practice completed the following transactions:

Jul. 1	York contributed $63,000 cash to the business in exchange for capital.
5	Paid monthly rent on medical equipment, $510.
9	Paid $23,000 cash to purchase land to be used in operations.
10	Purchased office supplies on account, $1,600.
19	Borrowed $22,000 from the bank for business use.
22	Paid $1,100 on account.
28	The business received a bill for advertising in the daily newspaper to be paid in August, $240.
31	Revenues earned during the month included $6,400 cash and $6,000 on account.
31	Paid employees' salaries $2,200, office rent $1,900, and utilities $560. Record as a compound entry.
31	The business received $1,120 for medical screening services to be performed next month.
31	York withdrew cash of $7,200.

The business uses the following accounts: Cash; Accounts Receivable; Office Supplies; Land; Accounts Payable; Advertising Payable; Unearned Revenue; Notes Payable; York, Capital; York, Withdrawals; Service Revenue; Salaries Expense; Rent Expense; Utilities Expense; and Advertising Expense.

Requirements

1. Journalize each transaction. Explanations are not required.
2. Post the journal entries to the T-accounts, using transaction dates as posting references in the ledger accounts. Label the balance of each account *Bal.*
3. Prepare the trial balance of Vince York, M.D., as of July 31, 2024.

P-F:2-30A Journalizing transactions, posting journal entries to T-accounts, and preparing a trial balance

Learning Objectives 3, 4

Ann Simpson started her practice as a design consultant on September 1, 2024. During the first month of operations, the business completed the following transactions:

4. Total Debits $58,300

Sep. 1	Received $48,000 cash and gave capital to Simpson.
4	Purchased office supplies, $1,200, and furniture, $1,300, on account.
6	Performed services for a law firm and received $1,900 cash.
7	Paid $18,000 cash to acquire land to be used in operations.
10	Performed services for a hotel and received its promise to pay the $1,200 within one week.
14	Paid for the furniture purchased on September 4 on account.
15	Paid assistant's semimonthly salary, $1,500.
17	Received cash on account, $1,000.
20	Prepared a design for a school on account, $650.
25	Received $2,100 cash for design services to be performed in October.
28	Received $2,900 cash for consulting with Plummer & Gordon.
29	Paid $600 cash for a 12-month insurance policy starting on October 1.
30	Paid assistant's semimonthly salary, $1,500.
30	Paid monthly rent expense, $600.
30	Received a bill for utilities, $350. The bill will be paid next month.
30	Simpson withdrew cash of $3,700.

Requirements

1. Record each transaction in the journal using the following account titles: Cash; Accounts Receivable; Office Supplies; Prepaid Insurance; Land; Furniture; Accounts Payable; Utilities Payable; Unearned Revenue; Simpson, Capital; Simpson, Withdrawals; Service Revenue; Salaries Expense; Rent Expense; and Utilities Expense. Explanations are not required.
2. Open a T-account for each of the accounts.
3. Post the journal entries to the T-accounts, using transaction dates as posting references in the ledger accounts. Label the balance of each account *Bal.*
4. Prepare the trial balance of Ann Simpson, Designer, as of September 30, 2024.

Learning Objectives 3, 4

3. Cash Balance $50,160

P-F:2-31A Journalizing transactions, posting journal entries to four-column accounts, and preparing a trial balance

Terrence Murphy opened a law office on January 1, 2024. During the first month of operations, the business completed the following transactions:

Jan. 1	Murphy contributed $78,000 cash to the business, Terrence Murphy, Attorney. The business issued capital to Murphy.
3	Purchased office supplies, $600, and furniture, $1,700, on account.
4	Performed legal services for a client and received $1,000 cash.
7	Purchased a building with a market value of $130,000, and land with a market value of $25,000. The business paid $25,000 cash and signed a note payable to the bank for the remaining amount.
11	Prepared legal documents for a client on account, $400.
15	Paid assistant's semimonthly salary, $1,120.
16	Paid for the office supplies purchased on January 3 on account.
18	Received $2,700 cash for helping a client sell real estate.
19	Defended a client in court and billed the client for $1,800.
25	Received a bill for utilities, $600. The bill will be paid next month.
29	Received cash on account, $1,500.
30	Paid $1,200 cash for a 12-month insurance policy starting on February 1.
30	Paid assistant's semimonthly salary, $1,120.
31	Paid monthly rent expense, $1,800.
31	Murphy withdrew cash of $2,200.

Requirements

1. Record each transaction in the journal, using the following account titles: Cash; Accounts Receivable; Office Supplies; Prepaid Insurance; Land; Building; Furniture; Accounts Payable; Utilities Payable; Notes Payable; Murphy, Capital; Murphy, Withdrawals; Service Revenue; Salaries Expense; Rent Expense; and Utilities Expense. Explanations are not required.

2. Open the following four-column accounts including account numbers: Cash, 101; Accounts Receivable, 111; Office Supplies, 121; Prepaid Insurance, 131; Land, 141; Building, 151; Furniture, 161; Accounts Payable, 201; Utilities Payable, 211; Notes Payable, 221; Murphy, Capital, 301; Murphy, Withdrawals, 311; Service Revenue, 411; Salaries Expense, 511; Rent Expense, 521; and Utilities Expense, 531.

3. Post the journal entries to four-column accounts in the ledger, using dates, account numbers, journal references, and posting references. Assume the journal entries were recorded on page 1 of the journal.

4. Prepare the trial balance of Terrence Murphy, Attorney, at January 31, 2024.

P-F:2-32A Journalizing transactions, posting journal entries to four-column accounts, and preparing a trial balance

The trial balance of Shawn Merry, CPA, is dated March 31, 2024:

SHAWN MERRY, CPA
Trial Balance
March 31, 2024

Account Title	Debit	Credit
Cash	$ 11,000	
Accounts Receivable	16,500	
Office Supplies	400	
Land	30,000	
Furniture	0	
Automobile	0	
Accounts Payable		$ 3,800
Unearned Revenue		0
Merry, Capital		52,300
Merry, Withdrawals	0	
Service Revenue		8,200
Salaries Expense	5,600	
Rent Expense	800	
Total	$ 64,300	$ 64,300

Learning Objectives 3, 4

3. Cash Balance $12,500

During April, the business completed the following transactions:

Apr. 4	Collected $2,500 cash from a client on account.
8	Performed tax services for a client on account, $5,400.
13	Paid $3,000 on account.
14	Purchased furniture on account, $3,600.
15	Merry contributed his personal automobile to the business in exchange for capital. The automobile had a market value of $9,500.
18	Purchased office supplies on account, $900.
19	Received $2,700 for tax services performed on April 8.
20	Merry withdrew cash of $6,500.
21	Received $5,700 cash for consulting work completed.
24	Received $2,400 cash for accounting services to be completed next month.
27	Paid office rent, $600.
28	Paid employee salary, $1,700.

Requirements

1. Record the April transactions in the journal. Use the following accounts: Cash; Accounts Receivable; Office Supplies; Land; Furniture; Automobile; Accounts Payable; Unearned Revenue; Merry, Capital; Merry, Withdrawals; Service Revenue; Salaries Expense; and Rent Expense. Include an explanation for each entry.

2. Open the four-column ledger accounts listed in the trial balance, together with their balances as of March 31. Use the following account numbers: Cash, 11; Accounts Receivable, 12; Office Supplies, 13; Land, 14; Furniture, 15; Automobile, 16; Accounts Payable, 21; Unearned Revenue, 22; Merry, Capital, 31; Merry, Withdrawals, 33; Service Revenue, 41; Salaries Expense, 51; and Rent Expense, 52.

3. Post the journal entries to four-column accounts in the ledger, using dates, account numbers, journal references, and posting references. Assume the journal entries were recorded on page 5 of the journal.

4. Prepare the trial balance of Shawn Merry, CPA, at April 30, 2024.

Learning Objective 4

P-F:2-33A Correcting errors in a trial balance

Total Debits $123,250

The trial balance of Beautiful Tots Child Care does not balance.

BEAUTIFUL TOTS CHILD CARE
Trial Balance
August 31, 2024

Account Title	Debit	Credit
Cash	$ 7,900	
Accounts Receivable	6,700	
Office Supplies	1,000	
Prepaid Insurance	300	
Equipment	91,500	
Accounts Payable		$ 3,400
Notes Payable		45,000
Trumball, Capital		57,000
Trumball, Withdrawals	5,000	
Service Revenue		12,350
Salaries Expense	4,400	
Rent Expense	750	
Total	$ 117,550	$ 117,750

The following errors are detected:

a. Cash is understated by $1,500.

b. A $4,100 debit to Accounts Receivable was posted as a credit.

c. A $1,400 purchase of office supplies on account was neither journalized nor posted.

d. Equipment was incorrectly transferred from the ledger as $91,500. It should have been transferred as $83,000.

e. Salaries Expense is overstated by $700.

f. A $300 cash payment for advertising expense was neither journalized nor posted.

g. A $200 owner's withdrawal was incorrectly journalized as $2,000.

h. Service Revenue was understated by $4,100.

i. A 12-month insurance policy was posted as a $1,900 credit to Prepaid Insurance. Cash was posted correctly.

Prepare the corrected trial balance as of August 31, 2024. Journal entries are not required.

P-F:2-34A Preparing financial statements from the trial balance and calculating the debt ratio

Learning Objectives 4, 5

The trial balance as of July 31, 2024, for Sara Simon, Registered Dietician, is presented below:

2. Ending Capital $29,788

SARA SIMON, REGISTERED DIETICIAN
Trial Balance
July 31, 2024

Account Title	Debit	Credit
Cash	$ 38,000	
Accounts Receivable	9,000	
Office Supplies	2,300	
Prepaid Insurance	2,400	
Equipment	16,000	
Accounts Payable		$ 3,000
Unearned Revenue		3,912
Notes Payable		31,000
Simon, Capital		18,000
Simon, Withdrawals	2,800	
Service Revenue		17,888
Salaries Expense	1,700	
Rent Expense	1,100	
Utilities Expense	500	
Total	$ 73,800	$ 73,800

Requirements

1. Prepare the income statement for the month ended July 31, 2024.
2. Prepare the statement of owner's equity for the month ended July 31, 2024. The beginning balance of Simon, Capital was $0 and the owner contributed $18,000 during the month.
3. Prepare the balance sheet as of July 31, 2024.
4. Calculate the debt ratio as of July 31, 2024.

> Problems Group B

Learning Objectives 3, 4

2. Cash Balance $69,680

P-F:2-35B Journalizing transactions, posting journal entries to T-accounts, and preparing a trial balance

Victor Yang practices medicine under the business title Victor Yang, M.D. During March, the medical practice completed the following transactions:

Mar. 1	Yang contributed $62,000 cash to the business in exchange for capital.
5	Paid monthly rent on medical equipment, $570.
9	Paid $14,000 cash to purchase land to be used in operations.
10	Purchased office supplies on account, $1,500.
19	Borrowed $27,000 from the bank for business use.
22	Paid $1,400 on account.
28	The business received a bill for advertising in the daily newspaper to be paid in April, $220.
31	Revenues earned during the month included $6,700 cash and $5,800 on account.
31	Paid employees' salaries $2,100, office rent $1,500, and utilities $350. Record as a compound entry.
31	The business received $1,000 for medical screening services to be performed next month.
31	Yang withdrew cash of $7,100.

The business uses the following accounts: Cash; Accounts Receivable; Office Supplies; Land; Accounts Payable; Advertising Payable; Unearned Revenue; Notes Payable; Yang, Capital; Yang, Withdrawals; Service Revenue; Salaries Expense; Rent Expense; Utilities Expense; and Advertising Expense.

Requirements

1. Journalize each transaction. Explanations are not required.
2. Post the journal entries to the T-accounts, using transaction dates as posting references in the ledger accounts. Label the balance of each account *Bal.*
3. Prepare the trial balance of Victor Yang, M.D., as of March 31, 2024.

P-F:2-36B Journalizing transactions, posting journal entries to T-accounts, and preparing a trial balance

Learning Objectives 3, 4

4. Total Debits $51,430

Beth Stewart started her practice as a design consultant on November 1, 2024. During the first month of operations, the business completed the following transactions:

Nov. 1	Received $41,000 cash and gave capital to Stewart.
4	Purchased office supplies, $1,200, and furniture, $2,300, on account.
6	Performed services for a law firm and received $2,100 cash.
7	Paid $27,000 cash to acquire land to be used in operations.
10	Performed services for a hotel and received its promise to pay the $800 within one week.
14	Paid for the furniture purchased on November 4 on account.
15	Paid assistant's semimonthly salary, $1,470.
17	Received cash on account, $500.
20	Prepared a design for a school on account, $680.
25	Received $1,900 cash for design services to be performed in December.
28	Received $3,100 cash for consulting with Plummer & Gordon.
29	Paid $840 cash for a 12-month insurance policy starting on December 1.
30	Paid assistant's semimonthly salary, $1,470.
30	Paid monthly rent expense, $650.
30	Received a bill for utilities, $650. The bill will be paid next month.
30	Stewart withdrew cash of $2,800.

Requirements

1. Record each transaction in the journal using the following account titles: Cash; Accounts Receivable; Office Supplies; Prepaid Insurance; Land; Furniture; Accounts Payable; Utilities Payable; Unearned Revenue; Stewart, Capital; Stewart, Withdrawals; Service Revenue; Salaries Expense; Rent Expense; and Utilities Expense. Explanations are not required.
2. Open a T-account for each of the accounts.
3. Post the journal entries to the T-accounts, using transaction dates as posting references in the ledger accounts. Label the balance of each account *Bal.*
4. Prepare the trial balance of Beth Stewart, Designer, as of November 30, 2024.

Learning Objectives 3, 4

3. Service Revenue Balance $6,800

P-F:2-37B Journalizing transactions, posting journal entries to four-column accounts, and preparing a trial balance

Theodore McMahon opened a law office on April 1, 2024. During the first month of operations, the business completed the following transactions:

Apr. 1	McMahon contributed $70,000 cash to the business, Theodore McMahon, Attorney. The business gave capital to McMahon.
3	Purchased office supplies, $1,100, and furniture, $1,300, on account.
4	Performed legal services for a client and received $2,000 cash.
7	Purchased a building with a market value of $150,000, and land with a market value of $30,000. The business paid $40,000 cash and signed a note payable to the bank for the remaining amount.
11	Prepared legal documents for a client on account, $400.
15	Paid assistant's semimonthly salary, $1,200.
16	Paid for the office supplies purchased on April 3 on account.
18	Received $2,700 cash for helping a client sell real estate.
19	Defended a client in court and billed the client for $1,700.
25	Received a bill for utilities, $650. The bill will be paid next month.
28	Received cash on account, $1,100.
29	Paid $3,600 cash for a 12-month insurance policy starting on May 1.
29	Paid assistant's semimonthly salary, $1,200.
30	Paid monthly rent expense, $2,100.
30	McMahon withdrew cash of $3,200.

Requirements

1. Record each transaction in the journal, using the following account titles: Cash; Accounts Receivable; Office Supplies; Prepaid Insurance; Land; Building; Furniture; Accounts Payable; Utilities Payable; Notes Payable; McMahon, Capital; McMahon, Withdrawals; Service Revenue; Salaries Expense; Rent Expense; and Utilities Expense. Explanations are not required.

2. Open the following four-column accounts including account numbers: Cash, 101; Accounts Receivable, 111; Office Supplies, 121; Prepaid Insurance, 131; Land, 141; Building, 151; Furniture, 161; Accounts Payable, 201; Utilities Payable, 211; Notes Payable, 221; McMahon, Capital, 301; McMahon, Withdrawals, 311; Service Revenue, 411; Salaries Expense, 511; Rent Expense, 521; and Utilities Expense, 531.

3. Post the journal entries to four-column accounts in the ledger, using dates, account numbers, journal references, and posting references. Assume the journal entries were recorded on page 1 of the journal.

4. Prepare the trial balance of Theodore McMahon, Attorney, at April 30, 2024.

P-F:2-38B Journalizing transactions, posting journal entries to four-column accounts, and preparing a trial balance

Learning Objectives 3, 4

3. Cash Balance $20,250

The trial balance of John Menning, CPA, is dated March 31, 2024:

JOHN MENNING, CPA
Trial Balance
March 31, 2024

Account Title	Debit	Credit
Cash	$ 17,000	
Accounts Receivable	10,500	
Office Supplies	1,200	
Land	29,000	
Furniture	0	
Automobile	0	
Accounts Payable		$ 3,800
Unearned Revenue		0
Menning, Capital		46,200
Menning, Withdrawals	0	
Service Revenue		11,200
Salaries Expense	2,500	
Rent Expense	1,000	
Total	$ 61,200	$ 61,200

During April, the business completed the following transactions:

Apr. 4	Collected $6,000 cash from a client on account.
8	Performed tax services for a client on account, $5,500.
13	Paid $3,300 on account.
14	Purchased furniture on account, $4,000.
15	Menning contributed his personal automobile to the business in exchange for capital. The automobile had a market value of $11,500.
18	Purchased office supplies on account, $1,600.
19	Received $2,750 for tax services performed on April 8.
20	Menning withdrew cash of $7,500.
21	Received $4,900 cash for consulting work completed.
24	Received $2,500 cash for accounting services to be completed next month.
27	Paid office rent, $900.
28	Paid employee salary, $1,200.

Requirements

1. Record the April transactions in the journal using the following accounts: Cash; Accounts Receivable; Office Supplies; Land; Furniture; Automobile; Accounts Payable; Unearned Revenue; Menning, Capital; Menning, Withdrawals; Service Revenue; Salaries Expense; and Rent Expense. Include an explanation for each entry.

2. Open the four-column ledger accounts listed in the trial balance, together with their balances as of March 31. Use the following account numbers: Cash, 11; Accounts Receivable, 12; Office Supplies, 13; Land, 14; Furniture, 15; Automobile, 16; Accounts Payable, 21; Unearned Revenue, 22; Menning, Capital, 31; Menning, Withdrawals, 33; Service Revenue, 41; Salaries Expense, 51; and Rent Expense, 52.

3. Post the journal entries to four-column accounts in the ledger, using dates, account numbers, journal references, and posting references. Assume the journal entries were recorded on page 5 of the journal.

4. Prepare the trial balance of John Menning, CPA, at April 30, 2024.

Learning Objective 4

P-F:2-39B Correcting errors in a trial balance

Total Debits $123,300

The trial balance of Love to Learn Child Care does not balance.

LOVE TO LEARN CHILD CARE
Trial Balance
May 31, 2024

Account Title	Debit	Credit
Cash	$ 8,060	
Accounts Receivable	8,700	
Office Supplies	1,000	
Prepaid Insurance	1,700	
Equipment	90,400	
Accounts Payable		$ 3,000
Notes Payable		45,000
Ebony, Capital		54,000
Ebony, Withdrawals	3,740	
Service Revenue		16,300
Salaries Expense	4,350	
Rent Expense	400	
Total	$ 118,350	$ 118,300

The following errors are detected:

a. Cash is understated by $1,800.

b. A $3,800 debit to Accounts Receivable was posted as a credit.

c. A $1,000 purchase of office supplies on account was neither journalized nor posted.

d. Equipment was incorrectly transferred from the ledger as $90,400. It should have been transferred as $82,500.

e. Salaries Expense is overstated by $350.

f. A $300 cash payment for advertising expense was neither journalized nor posted.

g. A $160 owner's withdrawal was incorrectly journalized as $1,600.

h. Service Revenue was understated by $4,000.

i. A 12-month insurance policy was posted as a $1,400 credit to Prepaid Insurance. Cash was posted correctly.

Prepare the corrected trial balance as of May 31, 2024. Journal entries are not required.

P-F:2-40B Preparing financial statements from the trial balance and calculating the debt ratio

Learning Objectives 4, 5

The trial balance as of July 31, 2024, for Sheila Sanchez, Registered Dietician, is presented below:

1. Net Income $13,404

SHEILA SANCHEZ, REGISTERED DIETICIAN
Trial Balance
July 31, 2024

Account Title	Debit	Credit
Cash	$ 32,000	
Accounts Receivable	9,100	
Office Supplies	1,400	
Prepaid Insurance	2,600	
Equipment	24,000	
Accounts Payable		$ 3,400
Unearned Revenue		1,296
Notes Payable		34,000
Sanchez, Capital		20,000
Sanchez, Withdrawals	3,000	
Service Revenue		15,804
Salaries Expense	1,600	
Rent Expense	700	
Utilities Expense	100	
Total	$ 74,500	$ 74,500

Requirements

1. Prepare the income statement for the month ended July 31, 2024.
2. Prepare the statement of owner's equity for the month ended July 31, 2024. The beginning balance of Sanchez, Capital was $0 and the owner contributed $20,000 during the month.
3. Prepare the balance sheet as of July 31, 2024.
4. Calculate the debt ratio as of July 31, 2024.

CRITICAL THINKING

> Using Excel

Download Excel problems for this chapter online in MyLab Accounting or at **http://www.pearsonhighered.com/Horngren**.

> Continuing Problem

P-F:2-41 Journalizing transactions, posting to T-accounts, and preparing a trial balance

Problem P-F:2-41 continues with the company introduced in Chapter F:1, Canyon Canoe Company. Here you will account for Canyon Canoe Company's transactions as it is actually done in practice. Begin by reviewing the transactions from Chapter F:1. The transactions have been reprinted below.

Nov. 1	Received $16,000 cash to begin the company and gave capital to Amber Wilson.
2	Signed a lease for a building and paid $1,200 for the first month's rent.
3	Purchased canoes for $4,800 on account.
4	Purchased office supplies on account, $750.
7	Earned $1,400 cash for rental of canoes.
13	Paid $1,500 cash for wages.
15	Wilson withdrew $50 cash from the business.
16	Received a bill for $150 for utilities. (Use separate payable account.)
20	Received a bill for $175 for cell phone expenses. (Use separate payable account.)
22	Rented canoes to Early Start Daycare on account, $3,000.
26	Paid $1,000 on account related to the November 3 purchase.
28	Received $750 from Early Start Daycare for canoe rental on November 22.
30	Wilson withdrew cash of $100 from the business.

In addition, Canyon Canoe Company completed the following transactions for December.

Dec. 1	Amber contributed land on the river (worth $85,000) and a small building to use as a rental office (worth $35,000) in exchange for capital.
1	Prepaid $3,000 for three months' rent on the warehouse where the company stores the canoes.
2	Purchased canoes, signing a note payable for $7,200.
4	Purchased office supplies on account for $500.
9	Received $4,500 cash for canoe rentals to customers.
15	Rented canoes to customers for $3,500, but will be paid next month.
16	Received a $750 deposit from a canoe rental group that will use the canoes next month.
18	Paid the utilities and telephone bills from last month.
19	Paid various accounts payable, $2,000.
20	Received bills for the telephone ($325) and utilities ($295) which will be paid later.
31	Paid wages of $1,800.
31	Wilson withdrew cash of $300 from the business.

Requirements

1. Journalize the transactions for both November and December, using the following accounts: Cash; Accounts Receivable; Office Supplies; Prepaid Rent; Land; Building; Canoes; Accounts Payable; Utilities Payable; Telephone Payable; Unearned Revenue; Notes Payable; Wilson, Capital; Wilson, Withdrawals; Canoe Rental Revenue; Rent Expense; Utilities Expense; Wages Expense; and Telephone Expense. Explanations are not required. (Hint: For November transactions, refer to your answer for Chapter F:1.)
2. Open a T-account for each of the accounts.
3. Post the journal entries to the T-accounts and calculate account balances. Formal posting references are not required.
4. Prepare a trial balance as of December 31, 2024.
5. Prepare the income statement of Canyon Canoe Company for the two months ended December 31, 2024.
6. Prepare the statement of owner's equity for the two months ended December 31, 2024.
7. Prepare the balance sheet as of December 31, 2024.
8. Calculate the debt ratio for Canyon Canoe Company at December 31, 2024.

> Practice Set

P-F:2-42 Journalizing transactions, posting to T-accounts, and preparing a trial balance

Consider the following transactional data for the first month of operations for Crystal Clear Cleaning.

Nov. 1	Aaron Hideaway contributed $15,000 and a truck, with a market value of $3,000, to the business in exchange for capital.
2	The business paid $4,000 to Pleasant Properties for November through February rent. (Debit Prepaid Rent)
3	Paid $4,800 for a business insurance policy for the term November 1, 2024 through October 31, 2019. (Debit Prepaid Insurance)
4	Purchased cleaning supplies on account, $320.
5	Purchased on account an industrial vacuum cleaner costing $1,500. The invoice is payable November 25.
7	Paid $3,900 for a computer and printer.
9	Performed cleaning services on account in the amount of $4,700.
10	Received $200 for services rendered on November 9.
15	Paid employees, $400.
16	Received $15,000 for a 1-year contract beginning November 16 for cleaning services to be provided. Contract begins November 16, 2024, and ends November 15, 2019. (Credit Unearned Revenue)
17	Provided cleaning services and received $400 cash.
18	Received a utility bill for $175 with a due date of December 4, 2024. (Use Accounts Payable)
20	Borrowed $36,000 from bank with interest rate of 6% per year.
21	Received $500 on account for services performed on November 9.
25	Paid $750 on account for vacuum cleaner purchased on November 5.
29	Paid $200 for advertising.
30	Hideaway withdrew cash of $1,400 from the business.

Requirements

1. Journalize the transactions, using the following accounts: Cash; Accounts Receivable; Cleaning Supplies; Prepaid Rent; Prepaid Insurance; Equipment; Truck; Accounts Payable; Unearned Revenue; Notes Payable; Hideaway, Capital; Hideaway, Withdrawals; Service Revenue; Salaries Expense; Advertising Expense; and Utilities Expense. Explanations are not required.
2. Open a T-account for each account.
3. Post the journal entries to the T-accounts, and calculate account balances.
4. Prepare a trial balance as of November 30, 2024.

> Tying It All Together Case F:2-1

Before you begin this assignment, review the Tying It All Together feature in the chapter.

Part of the **Fry's Electronics, Inc.**'s experience involves providing technical support to its customers. This includes in-home installations of electronics and also computer support at their retail store locations.

Requirements

1. Suppose Fry's Electronics, Inc. provides $10,500 of computer support at the Dallas-Fort Worth store during the month of November. How would Fry's Electronics record this transaction? Assume all customers paid in cash. What financial statement(s) would this transaction affect?
2. Assume Fry's Electronics, Inc.'s Modesto, California, location received $24,000 for an annual contract to provide computer support to the local city government. How would Fry's Electronics record this transaction? What financial statement(s) would this transaction affect?
3. What is the difference in how revenue is recorded in requirements 1 and 2? Clearly state when revenue is recorded in each requirement.

> Decision Case F:2-1

Your friend, Dean McChesney, requested that you advise him on the effects that certain transactions will have on his business, A-Plus Travel Planners. Time is short, so you cannot journalize the transactions. Instead, you must analyze the transactions without a journal. McChesney will continue the business only if he can expect to earn a monthly net income of $6,000. The business completed the following transactions during June:

a. McChesney deposited $10,000 cash in a business bank account to start the company. The company gave capital to McChesney.
b. Paid $300 cash for office supplies.
c. Incurred advertising expense on account, $700.
d. Paid the following cash expenses: administrative assistant's salary, $1,400; office rent, $1,000.
e. Earned service revenue on account, $8,800.
f. Collected cash from customers on account, $1,200.

Requirements

1. Open the following T-accounts: Cash; Accounts Receivable; Office Supplies; Accounts Payable; McChesney, Capital; Service Revenue; Salaries Expense; Rent Expense; and Advertising Expense.
2. Post the transactions directly to the accounts without using a journal. Record each transaction by letter. Calculate account balances.
3. Prepare a trial balance at June 30, 2024.
4. Compute the amount of net income or net loss for this first month of operations. Would you recommend that McChesney continue in business?

> Ethical Issue F:2-1

Better Days Ahead, a charitable organization, has a standing agreement with First National Bank. The agreement allows Better Days Ahead to overdraw its cash balance at the bank when donations are running low. In the past, Better Days Ahead managed funds wisely and rarely used this privilege. Jacob Henson has recently become the president of Better Days Ahead. To expand operations, Henson acquired office equipment and spent large amounts on fundraising. During Henson's presidency, Better Days Ahead has maintained a negative bank balance of approximately $10,000.

What is the ethical issue in this situation, if any? State why you approve or disapprove of Henson's management of Better Days Ahead's funds.

> Fraud Case F:2-1

Roy Akins was the accounting manager at Zelco, a tire manufacturer, and he played golf with Hugh Stallings, the CEO, who was something of a celebrity in the community. The CEO stood to earn a substantial bonus if Zelco increased net income by year-end. Roy was eager to get into Hugh's elite social circle; he boasted to Hugh that he knew some accounting tricks that could increase company income by simply revising a few journal entries for rental payments on storage units. At the end of the year, Roy changed the debits from "rent expense" to "prepaid rent" on several entries. Later, Hugh got his bonus, and the deviations were never discovered.

Requirements

1. How did the change in the journal entries affect the net income of the company at year-end?
2. Who gained and who lost as a result of these actions?

> Financial Statement Case F:2-1

Refer to **http://www.pearsonhighered.com/Horngren** to view a link to **Target Corporation's** Fiscal 2018 Annual Report.

Requirements

1. Calculate the debt ratio for Target Corporation as of February 2, 2019.
2. How did the debt ratio for Target Corporation compare to the debt ratio for **Kohl's Corporation**? Discuss.

> Communication Activity F:2-1

In 35 words or fewer, explain the difference between a debit and a credit and explain what the normal balance of the six account types is.

> Quick Check Answers

1. a **2.** c **3.** d **4.** d **5.** b **6.** b **7.** d **8.** b **9.** a **10.** b

The Adjusting Process 3

Where's My Bonus?

Liam Mills was surprised when he opened his mail. He had just received his most recent quarterly bonus check from his employer, Custom Marketing, and the check was smaller than he expected. Liam worked as a sales manager and was responsible for product marketing and implementation in the southwest region of the United States. He was paid a monthly salary but also received a 3% bonus for all revenue generated from advertising services provided to customers in his geographical area. He was counting on his fourth quarter (October–December) bonus check to be large enough to pay off the credit card debt he had accumulated over the holiday break. It had been a great year-end for Liam. He had closed several open accounts, successfully signing several annual advertising contracts. In addition, because of his negotiating skills, he was able to collect half of the payments for services up front instead of waiting for his customers to pay every month. Liam expected that his bonus check would be huge because of this new business, but it wasn't.

The next day, Liam stopped by the accounting office to discuss his bonus check. He was surprised to learn that his bonus was calculated by the revenue earned by his company through December 31. Although Liam had negotiated to receive half of the payments up front, the business had not yet earned the revenue from those payments. Custom Marketing will not record revenue earned until the advertising services have been performed. Eventually Liam will see the new business reflected in his bonus check, but he'll have to wait until the revenue has been earned.

How Was Revenue Earned Calculated?

At the end of a time period (often December 31), companies are required to accurately report revenues earned and expenses incurred during that time period. In order to do this, the company reviews the account balances as of the end of the time period and determines whether any adjustments are needed. For example, **iHeartMedia, Inc.,** a company that has three distinct business segments: iHeartMedia, Americas Outdoor Advertising, and International Outdoor Advertising, must determine the amount of revenue earned from open advertising contracts. These contracts can cover only a few weeks or as long as several years. Only the amount earned in the current time period is reported as revenue on the income statement. *Adjusting the books* is the process of reviewing and adjusting the account balances so that amounts on the financial statements are reported accurately. This is what we will learn in this chapter.

3-2 Financial chapter 3

Chapter 3 Learning Objectives

1. Differentiate between cash basis accounting and accrual basis accounting
2. Define and apply the time period concept, revenue recognition, and matching principles
3. Explain the purpose of and journalize and post adjusting entries
4. Explain the purpose of and prepare an adjusted trial balance
5. Identify the impact of adjusting entries on the financial statements
6. Explain the purpose of a worksheet and use it to prepare adjusting entries and the adjusted trial balance
7. Understand the alternative treatment of recording deferred expenses and deferred revenues (Appendix 3A)

In Chapter F:1, we introduced you to the accounting equation and the financial statements. In Chapter F:2, you learned about T-accounts, debits, credits, and the trial balance. But have you captured all the transactions for a particular period? Not yet.

In this chapter, we continue our exploration of the accounting cycle by learning how to update the accounts at the end of the period. This process is called adjusting the books, and it requires special journal entries called *adjusting entries*. For example, you learn how, at the end of a particular period, you must determine how many office supplies you have used and how much you owe your employees—and make adjusting entries to account for these amounts. These are just some of the adjusting entries you need to make before you can see the complete picture of how well your company performed during a period of time.

Learning Objective 1
Differentiate between cash basis accounting and accrual basis accounting

Cash Basis Accounting
Accounting method that records revenues only when cash is received and expenses only when cash is paid.

Accrual Basis Accounting
Accounting method that records revenues when earned and expenses when incurred.

If cash basis accounting is not allowed by GAAP, why would a business choose to use this method?

WHAT IS THE DIFFERENCE BETWEEN CASH BASIS ACCOUNTING AND ACCRUAL BASIS ACCOUNTING?

There are two ways to record transactions—cash basis accounting or accrual basis accounting.

- **Cash basis accounting** records only transactions with cash: cash receipts and cash payments. When cash is received, revenues are recorded. When cash is paid, expenses are recorded. As a result, revenues are recorded only when cash is received and expenses are recorded only when cash is paid. The cash basis of accounting is not allowed under Generally Accepted Accounting Principles (GAAP); however, small businesses will sometimes use this method. **The cash method is an easier accounting method to follow because it generally requires less knowledge of accounting concepts and principles. The cash basis accounting method also does a good job of tracking a business's cash flows.**

- **Accrual basis accounting** records the effect of each transaction as it occurs—that is, revenues are recorded when earned and expenses are recorded when incurred. Revenues are considered to be earned when the services or goods are provided to the customers. Most businesses use the accrual basis as covered in this book. The accrual basis of accounting provides a better picture of a business's revenues and expenses. It records revenue only when it has been earned and expenses only when they have been incurred. Under accrual basis accounting, it is irrelevant when cash is received or paid.

Example: Suppose on May 1, Smart Touch Learning paid $1,200 for insurance for the next six months ($200 per month). This prepayment represents insurance coverage for May through October. Under the cash basis method, Smart Touch Learning would record Insurance Expense of $1,200 on May 1. This is because the cash basis method records an expense when cash is paid. Alternatively, accrual basis accounting requires the company to prorate the expense. Smart Touch Learning would record a $200 expense every month from May through October. This is illustrated as follows:

	Cash basis		Accrual basis	
Cash Payment Made	May 1:	$ 1,200	May 1:	$ 1,200
Expense Recorded	May 1:	$ 1,200	May 31:	$ 200
			June 30:	200
			July 31:	200
			August 31:	200
			September 30:	200
			October 31:	200
Total Expense Recorded		$ 1,200		$ 1,200

Now let's see how the cash basis and the accrual basis methods account for revenues.

Example: Suppose on April 30, Smart Touch Learning received $600 for services to be performed for the next six months (May through October). Under the cash basis method, Smart Touch Learning would record $600 of revenue when the cash is received on April 30. The accrual basis method, though, requires the revenue to be recorded only when it is earned. Smart Touch Learning would record $100 of revenue each month for the next six months beginning in May.

	Cash basis		Accrual basis	
Cash Received	April 30:	$ 600	April 30:	$ 600
Revenue Recorded	April 30:	$ 600	May 31:	$ 100
			June 30:	100
			July 31:	100
			August 31:	100
			September 30:	100
			October 31:	100
Total Revenue Recorded		$ 600		$ 600

Notice that under both methods, cash basis and accrual basis, the total amount of revenues and expenses recorded by October 31 was the same. The major difference between a cash basis accounting system and an accrual basis accounting system is the timing of recording the revenue or expense.

Total Pool Services earned $130,000 of service revenue during 2024. Of the $130,000 earned, the business received $105,000 in cash. The remaining amount, $25,000, was still owed by customers as of December 31. In addition, Total Pool Services incurred $85,000 of expenses during the year. As of December 31, $10,000 of the expenses still needed to be paid. In addition, Total Pool Services prepaid $5,000 cash in December 2024 for expenses incurred during the next year.

1. Determine the amount of service revenue and expenses for 2024 using a cash basis accounting system.
2. Determine the amount of service revenue and expenses for 2024 using an accrual basis accounting system.

Check your answers online in MyLab Accounting or at http://www.pearsonhighered.com/Horngren.

For more practice, see Short Exercises S-F:3-1 and S-F:3-2. **MyLab Accounting**

WHAT CONCEPTS AND PRINCIPLES APPLY TO ACCRUAL BASIS ACCOUNTING?

Learning Objective 2
Define and apply the time period concept, revenue recognition, and matching principles

As we have seen, the timing and recognition of revenues and expenses are the key differences between the cash basis and accrual basis methods of accounting. These differences can be explained by understanding the time period concept and the revenue recognition and matching principles.

The Time Period Concept

Smart Touch Learning will know with 100% certainty how well it has operated only if the company sells all of its assets, pays all of its liabilities, and gives any leftover cash to its owner. For obvious reasons, it is not practical to measure income this way. Because businesses need periodic reports on their affairs, the **time period concept** assumes that a business's activities can be sliced into small time segments and that financial statements can be prepared for specific periods, such as a month, quarter, or year.

Time Period Concept
Assumes that a business's activities can be sliced into small time segments and that financial statements can be prepared for specific periods, such as a month, quarter, or year.

The basic accounting period is one year, and most businesses prepare annual financial statements. The 12-month accounting period used for the annual financial statements is called a **fiscal year**. For most companies, the annual accounting period is the calendar year, from January 1 through December 31. Other companies use a fiscal year that ends on a date other than December 31. The year-end date is usually the low point in business activity for the year. Retailers are a notable example. For instance, Wal-Mart Stores, Inc. and J. C. Penney Company, Inc. use a fiscal year that ends around January 31 because the low point of their business activity comes about a month after the holidays.

Fiscal Year
An accounting year of any 12 consecutive months that may or may not coincide with the calendar year.

The Revenue Recognition Principle

Revenue Recognition Principle
Requires companies to record revenue when (or as) the entity satisfies each performance obligation.

The **revenue recognition principle**[1] tells accountants when to record revenue and requires companies follow a five-step process:

Step 1: Identify the contract with the customer. A contract is an agreement between two or more parties that creates enforceable rights and obligations.

Step 2: Identify the performance obligations in the contract. A performance obligation is a contractual promise with a customer to transfer a distinct good or service. A contract

---
[1] On May 28, 2014, the FASB and IASB issued new guidance on accounting for revenue recognition, *Revenue from Contracts with Customers (Topic 606)*. This new standard became effective for public business entities with annual reporting periods beginning after December 15, 2017.

might have multiple performance obligations.[2] For example, AT&T, Inc. often provides a new phone to customers who sign a two-year cellular service agreement. This represents two distinct performance obligations: the cellular service agreement and the new phone.

Step 3: Determine the transaction price. The transaction price is the amount that the entity expects to be entitled to as a result of transferring goods or services to the customer.

Step 4: Allocate the transaction price to the performance obligations in the contract. If the transaction has multiple performance obligations, the transaction price will need to be allocated among the different performance obligations.

Step 5: Recognize revenue when (or as) the entity satisfies each performance obligation. The business will recognize revenue when (or as) it satisfies each performance obligation by transferring a good or service to a customer. A good or service is considered transferred when the customer obtains control of the good or service. The amount of revenue recognized is the amount allocated to the satisfied performance obligation.

The Matching Principle

The **matching principle** (sometimes called the *expense recognition principle*) guides accounting for expenses and ensures the following:

- All expenses are recorded when they are incurred during the period.
- Expenses are matched against the revenues of the period.

> **Matching Principle**
> Guides accounting for expenses, ensures that all expenses are recorded when they are incurred during the period, and matches those expenses against the revenues of the period.

To match expenses against revenues means to subtract expenses incurred during one month from revenues earned during that same month. The goal is to compute an accurate net income or net loss for the time period.

There is a natural link between some expenses and revenues. For example, Smart Touch Learning pays a commission to the employee who sells the e-learning company's services. The commission expense is directly related to the e-learning company's revenue earned. Other expenses are not so easy to link to revenues. For example, Smart Touch Learning's monthly rent expense occurs regardless of the revenues earned that month. The matching principle tells us to identify those expenses with a particular period, such as a month or a year, when the related revenue occurred. The business will record rent expense each month based on the rental agreement.

Match the accounting terminology to the definitions.

3. Time period concept	**a.** Requires companies to record revenue when it satisfies each performance obligation.
4. Revenue recognition principle	**b.** Assumes that a business's activities can be sliced into small time segments and that financial statements can be prepared for specific periods.
5. Matching principle	**c.** Guides accounting for expenses, ensures that all expenses are recorded when they are incurred during the period, and matches those expenses against the revenues of the period.

Check your answers online in MyLab Accounting or at http://www.pearsonhighered.com/Horngren.

For more practice, see Short Exercises S-F:3-3 and S-F:3-4. **MyLab Accounting**

---

[2] Revenue recognition for multiple performance obligations will be discussed in Chapter F:5, Appendix 5B.

WHAT ARE ADJUSTING ENTRIES, AND HOW DO WE RECORD THEM?

Learning Objective 3
Explain the purpose of and journalize and post adjusting entries

The end-of-period process begins with the trial balance, which you learned how to prepare in the previous chapter. Exhibit F:3-1 is the unadjusted trial balance of Smart Touch Learning at December 31, 2024.

Exhibit F:3-1 | **Unadjusted Trial Balance**

SMART TOUCH LEARNING
Unadjusted Trial Balance
December 31, 2024

Account Title	Debit	Credit
Cash	$ 12,200	
Accounts Receivable	1,000	
Office Supplies	500	
Prepaid Rent	3,000	
Land	20,000	
Building	60,000	
Furniture	18,000	
Accounts Payable		$ 200
Utilities Payable		100
Unearned Revenue		600
Notes Payable		60,000
Bright, Capital		48,000
Bright, Withdrawals	5,000	
Service Revenue		16,500
Rent Expense	2,000	
Salaries Expense	3,600	
Utilities Expense	100	
Total	$ 125,400	$ 125,400

This *unadjusted trial balance* lists the revenues and expenses of the e-learning company for November and December. But these amounts are incomplete because they omit various revenue and expense transactions. Accrual basis accounting requires the business to review the unadjusted trial balance and determine whether any additional revenues and expenses need to be recorded. Are there revenues that Smart Touch Learning has earned that haven't been recorded yet? Are there expenses that have occurred that haven't been journalized?

For example, consider the Office Supplies account in Exhibit F:3-1. Smart Touch Learning uses office supplies during the two months. This reduces the office supplies on hand (an asset) and creates an expense (Supplies Expense). It is a waste of time to record Supplies Expense every time office supplies are used. But by December 31, enough of the $500 of Office Supplies on the unadjusted trial balance (Exhibit F:3-1) have probably been used that we need to adjust the Office Supplies account. This is an example of why we need to adjust some accounts at the end of the accounting period.

An **adjusting entry** is completed at the end of the accounting period and records revenues to the period in which they are earned and expenses to the period in which they occur. Adjusting entries also update the asset and liability accounts. Adjustments are needed to properly measure several items such as:

1. Net income (loss) on the income statement
2. Assets and liabilities on the balance sheet

> **Adjusting Entry**
> An entry made at the end of the accounting period that is used to record revenues to the period in which they are earned and expenses to the period in which they occur.

There are two basic categories of adjusting entries: *deferrals* and *accruals*. In a deferral adjustment, the cash payment occurs before an expense is incurred or the cash receipt occurs before the revenue is earned. Deferrals defer the recognition of revenue or expense to a date after the cash is received or paid. Accrual adjustments are the opposite. An accrual records an expense before the cash is paid, or it records the revenue before the cash is received.

The two basic categories of adjusting entries can be further separated into four types:

1. Deferred expenses (deferral)
2. Deferred revenues (deferral)
3. Accrued expenses (accrual)
4. Accrued revenues (accrual)

The focus of this chapter is on learning how to account for these four types of adjusting entries.

Deferred Expenses

Deferred expenses, also called *prepaid expenses*, are advance payments of future expenses. They are deferrals because the expense is not recognized at the time of payment but deferred until they are used up. Such payments are considered assets rather than expenses until they are used up. When the prepayment is used up, the used portion of the asset becomes an expense via an adjusting entry.

> **Deferred Expense**
> An asset created when a business makes advance payments of future expenses.

Prepaid Rent

Remember Transaction 10 in Chapter F:2? Smart Touch Learning prepaid three months' office rent of $3,000 ($1,000 per month × 3 months) on December 1, 2024. The entry to record the payment was as follows:

Date	Accounts and Explanation	Debit	Credit
Dec. 1	Prepaid Rent	3,000	
	Cash		3,000
	Paid rent in advance.		

$$\frac{A\uparrow\downarrow}{\text{Prepaid Rent}\uparrow} \bigg\} = \bigg\{ \frac{L}{} + \frac{E}{}$$
Cash↓

After posting, Prepaid Rent has a $3,000 debit balance.

Prepaid Rent

Dec. 1   3,000

Throughout December, Prepaid Rent maintains this balance. But $3,000 is *not* the amount of Prepaid Rent for the balance sheet at December 31. Why?

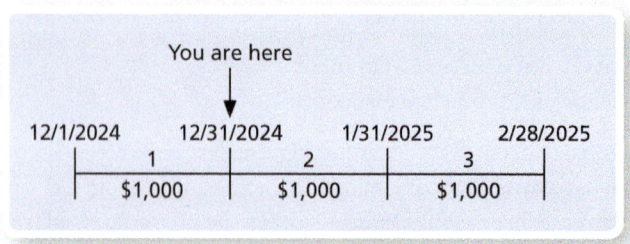

As of December 31, Prepaid Rent should be decreased for the amount that has been used up. The used-up portion is one month of the three months prepaid, or one-third of the prepayment. Recall that an asset that has expired is an *expense*. The adjusting entry transfers $1,000 ($3,000 × 1/3) from Prepaid Rent to Rent Expense. The adjusting entry is as follows:

$$\frac{A\downarrow}{\text{Prepaid Rent}\downarrow} \bigg\} = \bigg\{ \frac{L\ +\ E\downarrow}{\text{Rent Expense}\uparrow}$$

Date	Accounts and Explanation	Debit	Credit
Dec. 31	Rent Expense	1,000	
	Prepaid Rent		1,000
	To record rent expense.		

After posting, Prepaid Rent and Rent Expense show correct ending balances:

```
       Prepaid Rent                    Rent Expense
Dec. 1   3,000 | 1,000  Dec. 31-    Nov. 15  2,000
                                 ↳  Dec. 31  1,000

Bal.     2,000                      Bal.     3,000
```

Prepaid Rent is an example of an asset that was overstated prior to journalizing and posting the adjusting entry. Notice that the ending balance in Prepaid Rent is now $2,000. Because Prepaid Rent is an asset account for Smart Touch Learning, it should contain only two more months of rent on December 31 (for January and February). So we have $1,000 rent per month times two months equals the $2,000 Prepaid Rent balance.

If Smart Touch Learning had prepaid insurance, the same type of analysis would apply to the prepayment of three months of insurance. The only difference is in the account titles. Prepaid Insurance would be used instead of Prepaid Rent, and Insurance Expense would be used instead of Rent Expense.

Office Supplies

Office supplies are also accounted for as prepaid expenses. Let's look at another example. On November 3, Smart Touch Learning purchased $500 of office supplies on account.

The December 31 unadjusted trial balance, therefore, still lists Office Supplies with a $500 debit balance. But Smart Touch Learning's December 31 balance sheet should *not* report office supplies of $500. Why not?

During November and December, the e-learning company used office supplies to conduct business. The cost of the supplies used becomes *Supplies Expense*. To measure Supplies Expense, the business first counts the office supplies on hand at the end of

December. This is the amount of the asset still owned by the business. Assume that office supplies costing $100 remain on December 31. Then the business uses the Office Supplies T-account to determine the value of the supplies that were used:

Office Supplies		
Nov. 3	500	?
Bal.	100	

Amount of office supplies remaining ← Bal. 100

Amount of office supplies used = Supplies Expense → ?

So, we can solve for the office supplies used as follows:

Office Supplies balance before adjustment − Office supplies used = Office supplies on hand
$500 − Office supplies used = $100
Office supplies used = $400

The December 31 adjusting entry updates Office Supplies and records Supplies Expense for November and December as follows:

Date	Accounts and Explanation	Debit	Credit
Dec. 31	Supplies Expense	400	
	Office Supplies		400
	To record office supplies used.		

A↓ = L + E↓
Office Supplies↓ = Supplies Expense↑

After posting the adjusting entry, the December 31 balance of Office Supplies is correctly reflected as $100, and the Supplies Expense is correctly reflected as $400.

Office Supplies			
Nov. 3	500	400	Dec. 31
Bal.	100		

Supplies Expense	
Dec. 31	400
Bal.	400

The Office Supplies account then enters January with a $100 balance. If the adjusting entry for Office Supplies had not been recorded, the asset would have been overstated and Supplies Expense would have been understated. In making the adjusting entry, the correct balance of Office Supplies, $100, is now reported on the balance sheet as of December 31, and the income statement is correctly reporting an expense of $400.

Depreciation

Property, plant, and equipment (also called *plant assets*) are long-lived, tangible assets used in the operation of a business. Examples include land, buildings, equipment, furniture, and automobiles. As a business uses these assets, their value and usefulness decline. The decline in usefulness of a plant asset is an expense, and accountants systematically spread the asset's cost over its useful life. The allocation of a plant asset's cost over its useful life is called **depreciation**. For example, a business might pay cash for an automobile when purchased, but the automobile will last for years, so depreciation allocates the cost spent on the car over the time the business uses the car. All plant assets are depreciated, with the exception of land. We record no depreciation for land because, unlike buildings and equipment, it does not have a definitive or clearly estimable useful life, so it is difficult to allocate the cost of land.

Property, Plant, and Equipment
Long-lived, tangible assets, such as land, buildings, and equipment, used in the operation of a business.

Depreciation
The process by which businesses spread the allocation of a plant asset's cost over its useful life.

3-10 Financial chapter 3

Similarity to Prepaid Expenses The concept of accounting for plant assets is similar to that of prepaid expenses. The major difference is the length of time it takes for the asset to be used up. Prepaid expenses usually expire within a year, but plant assets remain useful for several years. As a business uses its plant assets, an adjusting entry is required to allocate the assets' costs. The adjusting entry records the cost allocation to an expense account called Depreciation Expense.

Let's review an example for Smart Touch Learning. On December 2, the business received a contribution of furniture with a market value of $18,000 from Sheena Bright. In exchange, Smart Touch Learning gave capital to Bright and made the following journal entry:

$$\frac{A\uparrow}{\text{Furniture}\uparrow} = \left\{ \frac{L}{} + \frac{E\uparrow}{\text{Bright, Capital}\uparrow} \right.$$

Date	Accounts and Explanation	Debit	Credit
Dec. 2	Furniture	18,000	
	Bright, Capital		18,000
	Owner contribution of furniture.		

After posting, the Furniture account has an $18,000 balance:

Furniture
Dec. 2 18,000

Residual Value
The expected value of a depreciable asset at the end of its useful life.

Straight-Line Method
A depreciation method that allocates an equal amount of depreciation each year. (Cost − Residual value) / Useful life.

Smart Touch Learning believes the furniture will remain useful for five years, and at the end of five years, Smart Touch Learning believes the furniture will be worthless. The expected value of a depreciable asset at the end of its useful life is called the **residual value**. Smart Touch Learning will use the straight-line method to compute the amount of depreciation. The **straight-line method** allocates an equal amount of depreciation each year and is calculated as:

$$\text{Straight-line depreciation} = (\text{Cost} - \text{Residual value}) / \text{Useful life}$$

Smart Touch Learning will calculate the depreciation of the furniture for the month of December as:

$$\begin{aligned}\text{Straight-line depreciation} &= (\text{Cost} - \text{Residual value}) / \text{Useful life} \\ &= (\$18{,}000 - \$0) / 5 \text{ years} \\ &= \$3{,}600 \text{ per year} / 12 \text{ months} \\ &= \$300 \text{ per month}\end{aligned}$$

Depreciation expense for December is recorded by the following adjusting entry:

$$\frac{A\downarrow}{\text{Accumulated Depreciation—Furniture}\uparrow} = \left\{ \frac{L}{} + \frac{E\downarrow}{\text{Depreciation Expense—Furniture}\uparrow} \right.$$

Date	Accounts and Explanation	Debit	Credit
Dec. 31	Depreciation Expense—Furniture	300	
	Accumulated Depreciation—Furniture		300
	To record depreciation on furniture.		

The Accumulated Depreciation Account Notice that in the preceding adjusting entry for depreciation, we credited Accumulated Depreciation—Furniture and not the asset account Furniture. Why? **We need to keep the original cost of the furniture separate from the accumulated depreciation because of the cost principle. Managers can then refer to the Furniture account to see how much the asset originally cost.** This information may help decide how much to sell the asset for in the future or how much to pay for new furniture. The **Accumulated Depreciation** account is the sum of all depreciation expense recorded for the depreciable asset to date. Accumulated Depreciation will increase (accumulate) over time.

Accumulated Depreciation is a contra asset, which means that it is an asset account with a normal credit balance. Contra means opposite. A **contra account** has two main characteristics:

- A contra account is paired with and is listed immediately after its related account in the chart of accounts and associated financial statement.
- A contra account's normal balance (debit or credit) is the opposite of the normal balance of the related account.

For example, Accumulated Depreciation—Furniture is the contra account that follows the Furniture account on the balance sheet. The Furniture account has a normal debit balance, so Accumulated Depreciation—Furniture, a contra asset, has a normal credit balance.

When recording depreciation, why don't we record a credit to the Furniture account?

Accumulated Depreciation
The sum of all the depreciation expense recorded to date for a depreciable asset.

Contra Account
An account that is paired with, and is listed immediately after, its related account in the chart of accounts and associated financial statement and whose normal balance is the opposite of the normal balance of the related account.

A business may have a separate Accumulated Depreciation account for each depreciable asset. Because Smart Touch Learning has both a Building and a Furniture account, it also has these two accounts: Accumulated Depreciation—Building and Accumulated Depreciation—Furniture. However, small companies often have only one Accumulated Depreciation account for all of their depreciable assets.

After posting the depreciation, the accounts appear as follows:

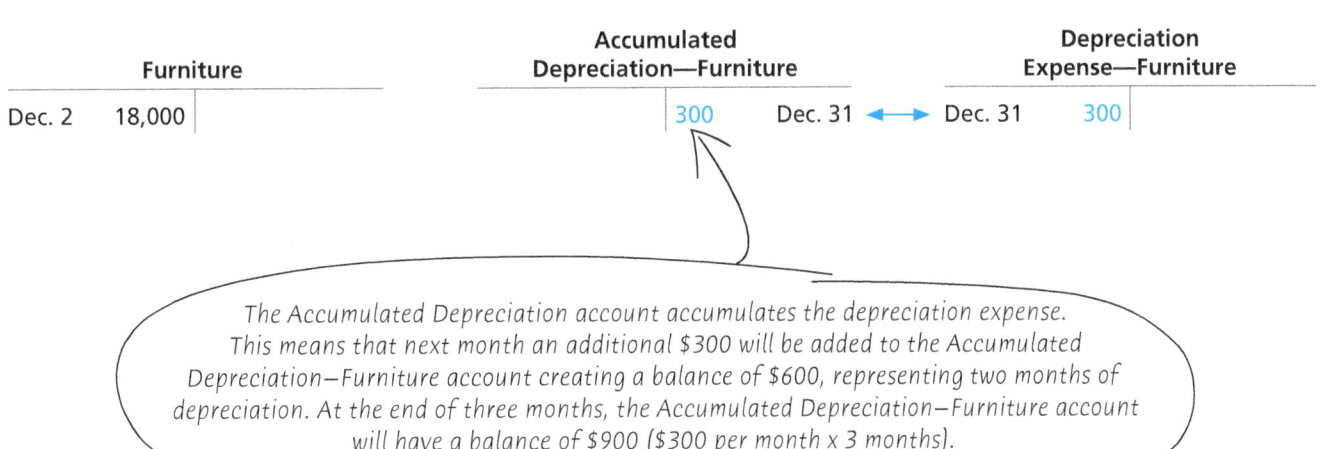

The Accumulated Depreciation account accumulates the depreciation expense. This means that next month an additional $300 will be added to the Accumulated Depreciation—Furniture account creating a balance of $600, representing two months of depreciation. At the end of three months, the Accumulated Depreciation—Furniture account will have a balance of $900 ($300 per month x 3 months).

Book Value The balance sheet reports both Furniture and Accumulated Depreciation—Furniture. Because it is a contra account, Accumulated Depreciation—Furniture is subtracted from Furniture. The resulting net amount (cost minus accumulated depreciation) of a plant asset is called its **book value**. The book value represents the cost invested in the asset that the business has not yet expensed. For Smart Touch Learning's furniture, the book value on December 31 is as follows:

Book Value
A depreciable asset's cost minus accumulated depreciation.

Book value of furniture:	
Furniture	$ 18,000
Less: Accumulated Depreciation—Furniture	(300)
Book value of furniture	$ 17,700

Depreciation on the building purchased on December 1 would be recorded in a similar manner. Suppose that the monthly depreciation is $250. The following adjusting entry would record depreciation for December:

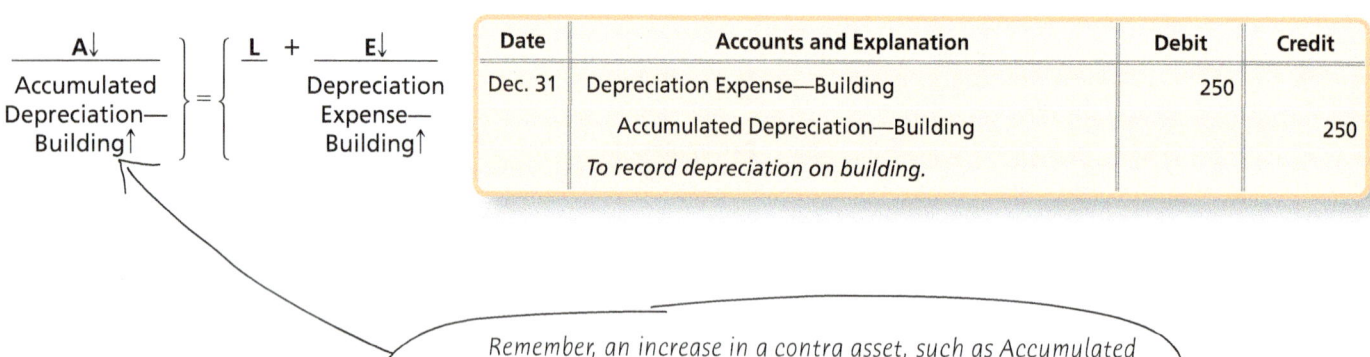

Had Smart Touch Learning not recorded the adjusting entries for depreciation on the furniture and building, plant assets would have been overstated and expenses would have been understated. After recording the adjusting entries, property, plant, and equipment (plant assets) are reported at the correct net amount, as shown on the December 31 partial balance sheet in Exhibit F:3-2.

The Adjusting Process Financial 3-13

Exhibit F:3-2 | Property, Plant, and Equipment on the Balance Sheet of Smart Touch Learning

SMART TOUCH LEARNING
Balance Sheet (Partial)
December 31, 2024

Property, Plant, and Equipment		
Land		$ 20,000
Building	$ 60,000	
Less: Accumulated Depreciation—Building	(250)	59,750
Furniture	18,000	
Less: Accumulated Depreciation—Furniture	(300)	17,700
Property, Plant, and Equipment, Net		$ 97,450

Deferred Revenues

Remember, deferred (or unearned) revenues occur when the company receives cash before it does the work or delivers a product to earn that cash. The company owes a product or a service to the customer, or it owes the customer his or her money back. Only after completing the job or delivering the product does the business *earn* the revenue. Because of this delay, unearned revenue is a liability and is also called **deferred revenue**. The revenue associated with the work or product is not recognized when the cash is received but is instead deferred until it is earned.

Deferred Revenue
A liability created when a business collects cash from customers in advance of completing a service or delivering a product.

Unearned Revenue

Suppose, for example, a law firm engages Smart Touch Learning to provide e-learning services for the next 30 days, agreeing to pay $600 in advance. Smart Touch Learning collected the amount on December 21 and recorded the following entry:

Date	Accounts and Explanation	Debit	Credit
Dec. 21	Cash	600	
	Unearned Revenue		600
	Collected cash for future services.		

$$\left.\begin{array}{c}A\uparrow\\ \text{Cash}\uparrow\end{array}\right\} = \left\{\begin{array}{c}L\uparrow\\ \text{Unearned}\\ \text{Revenue}\uparrow\end{array}\right. + \underline{\quad E \quad}$$

The liability account, Unearned Revenue, now shows that Smart Touch Learning owes $600 in services.

Unearned Revenue

600	Dec. 21

3-14 Financial chapter 3

During the last 10 days of the month—December 22 through December 31—Smart Touch Learning will *earn* approximately one-third (10 days divided by 30 days) of the $600, or $200. Therefore, Smart Touch Learning makes the following adjusting entry to record earning $200 of revenue:

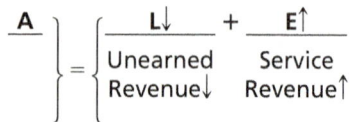

Date	Accounts and Explanation	Debit	Credit
Dec. 31	Unearned Revenue	200	
	Service Revenue		200
	To record service revenue earned that was collected in advance.		

This adjusting entry shifts $200 from the liability account to the revenue account. Service Revenue increases by $200, and Unearned Revenue decreases by $200. Now both accounts are up to date at December 31:

Unearned Revenue		Service Revenue	
Dec. 31 200	600 Dec. 21		5,500 Nov. 8
	400 Bal.		3,000 Nov. 10
			8,000 Dec. 28
			200 Dec. 31
			16,700 Bal.

Had the adjusting entry not been made, the liability, Unearned Revenue, would be overstated and Service Revenue would be understated.

Accrued Expenses

Accrued Expense
An expense that the business has incurred but has not yet paid.

Businesses often incur expenses before paying for them. The term **accrued expense** refers to an expense of this type. An accrued expense hasn't been paid for yet. Consider an employee's salary. Salaries Expense grows as the employee works, so the expense is said to *accrue*. Another accrued expense is interest expense on a note payable. Interest accrues as time passes on the note. An accrued expense always creates an accrued liability.

Businesses do not make daily or weekly journal entries to accrue expenses. Instead, they wait until the end of the accounting period. They make an adjusting entry to bring each expense (and the related liability) up to date for the financial statements.

Accrued Salaries Expense

Smart Touch Learning pays its employee a monthly salary of $2,400—half on the 15th and half on the first day of the next month. Notice on the calendar that the pay days are on December 15 and January 1.

The Adjusting Process Financial 3-15

December 2024						
Sunday	Monday	Tuesday	Wednesday	Thursday	Friday	Saturday
Dec 1	2	3	4	5	6	7
8	9	10	11	12	13	14
15 Pay Day	16	17	18	19	20	21
22	23	24	25	26	27	28
29	30	31	**Jan 1** Pay Day	2	3	4

During December, the company paid the first half-month salary on December 15, and made this entry:

Date	Accounts and Explanation	Debit	Credit
Dec. 15	Salaries Expense	1,200	
	Cash		1,200
	Paid salaries.		

$A\downarrow$ Cash$\downarrow$ = L + E$\downarrow$ Salaries Expense$\uparrow$

The December 15 entry records only the first half of December's salaries expense. The second payment of $1,200 will occur on January 1; however, the expense was incurred in December, so the expense must be recorded in December in order to follow the matching principle that states all expenses are recorded in the period when they are incurred. On December 31, Smart Touch Learning makes the following adjusting entry:

Date	Accounts and Explanation	Debit	Credit
Dec. 31	Salaries Expense	1,200	
	Salaries Payable		1,200
	To accrue salaries expense.		

A = L$\uparrow$ Salaries Payable$\uparrow$ + E$\downarrow$ Salaries Expense$\uparrow$

After posting, both Salaries Expense and Salaries Payable are up to date:

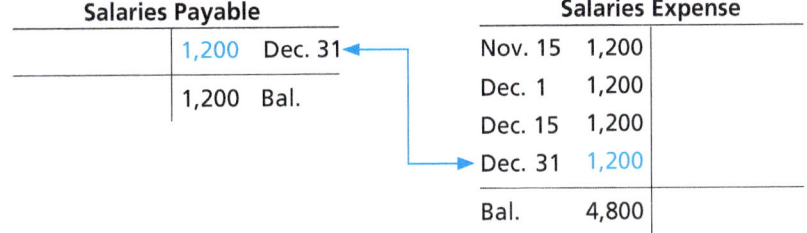

Salaries Expense shows a full two months' salary, and Salaries Payable shows the liability owed at December 31. This is an example of a liability that was understated before the adjusting entry was made. It also is an example of the matching principle. We are recording December's Salaries Expense in December so it will be reported on the same income statement as December's revenues.

Future Payment of Accrued Salaries Expense The adjusting entry at December 31 creates a liability that will eventually be paid. In this case, Smart Touch Learning will pay its employee the second half of December's wages on January 1. Because the expense has already been recorded, Smart Touch Learning will not record the expense again. To do so would record the expense twice, thus overstating the expense account. Instead, the business will decrease the amount of the liability, Salaries Payable, with a debit and record the cash payment. On January 1, Smart Touch Learning would record the following journal entry:

$\dfrac{A\downarrow}{\text{Cash}\downarrow} \Big\} = \Big\{ \dfrac{L\downarrow}{\text{Salaries Payable}\downarrow} + E$

Date	Accounts and Explanation	Debit	Credit
Jan. 1	Salaries Payable	1,200	
	Cash		1,200
	To record payment of accrued expense.		

Don't confuse this entry with an adjusting entry. Adjusting entries are recorded only at the end of the accounting period and are used to record either revenue earned or expenses incurred. This entry is a journal entry. It is simply recording an everyday business transaction—the payment of salaries previously accrued. In this example, the amount paid for salaries was equal to the amount of the liability in the adjusting entry. Sometimes, however, the amount paid might be different than the liability in the adjusting entry. For example, assume that instead of making a payment for salaries on January 1, Smart Touch Learning doesn't make the payment until January 15 and pays a full month's salary. By delaying the payment, Smart Touch Learning incurs additional days of salaries expense. The journal entry to record the payment on January 15 will not only decrease the payable recorded in the adjusting entry but will also record any additional expense incurred.

Accrued Interest Expense

Borrowing money creates an additional liability for a Note Payable. Remember the purchase of the building on December 1, 2024? Smart Touch Learning purchased a $60,000 building in exchange for a loan. Smart Touch Learning signed a one-year loan and recorded the following entry using the Notes Payable account:

$\dfrac{A\uparrow}{\text{Building}\uparrow} \Big\} = \Big\{ \dfrac{L\uparrow}{\text{Notes Payable}\uparrow} + E$

Date	Accounts and Explanation	Debit	Credit
Dec. 1	Building	60,000	
	Notes Payable		60,000
	Purchase of building with note.		

ETHICS

When should accrued expenses be recorded?

Evan is in the process of recording the adjusting entries for Green Landscaping Services. Bob Green, owner and manager, has asked Evan to record all of the adjusting entries except for accrued expenses. Bob has a meeting with the banker on Monday to apply for a business loan. Bob knows that the banker will review his balance sheet and income statement. Bob is concerned that by recording the accrued expenses, the business's liabilities will be significantly higher on the balance sheet and a net loss will be reported on the income statement (due to higher expenses). Bob has instructed Evan to delay recording the accrued expenses until after his meeting with the banker. What should Evan do?

Solution

Failing to record the adjusting entries for accrued expenses violates the matching principle. Recording the expenses now (before Monday) accurately matches the occurrence of the expenses with the revenues that were created during that period. If Evan does not record the adjusting entries, the financial statements will not accurately represent the financial position or operating performance of the business. The banker could be tricked into lending the company money. Then, if the business could not repay the loan, the bank would lose—all because the banker relied on incorrect accounting information supplied by the company.

Interest on this note is payable one year later, on December 1, 2025. Although the company won't make the interest payment for a year, the company must record the amount of interest expense that has been incurred by December 31, 2024. The company will make an adjusting entry to record interest expense for one month (December 1–December 31).

The formula for computing the interest is as follows:

> Amount of interest = Principal × Interest rate × Time

In the formula, time (period) represents the portion of a year that interest has accrued on the note. It may be expressed as a fraction of a year in months (number of months/12) or a fraction of a year in days (number of days/365). This keeps the units for interest and time the same. The note payable has an interest rate of 2% *per year* so the time accrued is expressed as 1/12 of a *year*. Smart Touch Learning computes interest expense for the month as follows:

> Amount of interest = Principal × Interest rate × Time
> = $60,000 × 0.02 × 1/12
> = $100

The December 31 adjusting entry to accrue interest expense is as follows:

Date	Accounts and Explanation	Debit	Credit
Dec. 31	Interest Expense	100	
	Interest Payable		100
	To accrue interest expense.		

$$A = \begin{cases} L\uparrow & + & E\downarrow \\ \text{Interest} & & \text{Interest} \\ \text{Payable}\uparrow & & \text{Expense}\uparrow \end{cases}$$

Notice that the adjusting entry records a credit to the liability, Interest Payable. This is because the interest payment will not be made until next year; therefore, Smart Touch Learning owes interest to the bank. Had the adjusting entry not been recorded, liabilities and expenses would have been understated, and the company would not have followed the matching principle. After posting, Interest Expense and Interest Payable now have the following correct balances:

Interest Payable		Interest Expense	
	100 Dec. 31	Dec. 31 100	
	100 Bal.	Bal. 100	

3-18 Financial chapter 3

Accrued Revenues

Accrued Revenue
A revenue that has been earned but for which the cash has not yet been collected.

As we have just seen, expenses can occur before a company makes a cash payment for them, which creates an accrued expense. Similarly, businesses can earn revenue before they receive the cash. This creates an **accrued revenue**, which is a revenue that has been earned but for which the cash has not yet been collected. The revenue recognition principle states a business will recognize revenue when (or as) it satisfies each performance obligation by transferring a good or service to a customer, not when the cash is collected.

Assume that Smart Touch Learning is hired on December 15 to perform e-learning services, beginning on December 16. Under this agreement, the business will earn $1,600 monthly and receive payment on January 15. At the date of hiring, Smart Touch Learning does not record a journal entry because revenue has not yet been earned. During December, it will earn half a month's fee, $800, for work December 16 through December 31. On December 31, Smart Touch Learning makes the following adjusting entry to record the revenue earned December 16 through December 31:

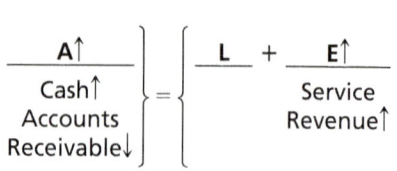

Date	Accounts and Explanation	Debit	Credit
Dec. 31	Accounts Receivable	800	
	Service Revenue		800
	To accrue service revenue.		

The adjusting entry records the earned revenue and brings the balance of the Service Revenue account to $17,500. In addition, the adjusting entry records an additional $800 account receivable. Smart Touch Learning did not record cash because the business has not yet received payment on the services provided. The cash will not be received until January 15. Smart Touch Learning's account balances after posting the adjusting entry are:

Accounts Receivable				Service Revenue	
Nov. 10	3,000	2,000	Nov. 22	5,500	Nov. 8
Dec. 31	800			3,000	Nov. 10
				8,000	Dec. 28
Bal.	1,800			200	Dec. 31
				800	Dec. 31
				17,500	Bal.

Without the adjustment, Smart Touch Learning's financial statements would understate both an asset, Accounts Receivable, and a revenue, Service Revenue.

Future Receipt of Accrued Revenues The adjusting entry on December 31 records revenue earned for half a month and also creates an accounts receivable. When Smart Touch Learning receives the payment on January 15, the business will record the following entry:

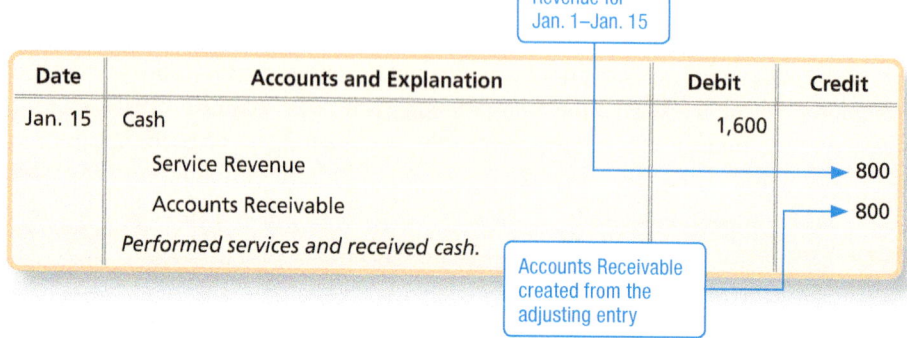

The Adjusting Process

Notice that on January 15, Smart Touch Learning records revenue only for the remaining half of the month (January 1–January 15). Smart Touch Learning recognizes that $800 of revenue was already recorded in December. The entry on January 15 removes the accounts receivable and records the remaining revenue. If the business had incorrectly recorded $1,600 of Service Revenue on January 15, the revenue would have been overstated in January.

Exhibit F:3-3 summarizes the adjusting entries for deferrals and accruals.

Exhibit F:3-3 | Summary of Deferral and Accrual Adjustments

	ORIGINAL ENTRY	ADJUSTING ENTRY
DEFERRALS—Cash receipt or Cash payment occurs first.		

Prepaid Expenses	Prepaid Rent XXX
	    Cash XXX
	Pay for rent in advance and record an asset first.
		Rent Expense XXX
		    Prepaid Rent XXX
		Adjust for rent used later.

Depreciation	Furniture XXX
	    Cash XXX
	Pay for furniture in advance and record an asset first.
		Depreciation Expense—Furniture XXX
		    Accumulated Depreciation—Furniture XXX
		Adjust for depreciation (use) of asset later.

Unearned Revenues	Cash XXX
	    Unearned Revenue XXX
	Receive cash in advance and record a liability first.
		Unearned Revenue XXX
		    Service Revenue XXX
		Adjust for revenue earned later.

ACCRUALS—Cash receipt or Cash payment occurs later.		
Accrued Expenses		Salaries Expense XXX Salaries Payable XXX *Accrual for expense incurred first.*
Accrued Revenues		Accounts Receivable XXX Service Revenue XXX *Accrual for revenue earned first.*

Two rules to remember about adjusting entries:
1. Adjusting entries *never* involve the Cash account.
2. Adjusting entries either
    a. Increase a revenue account (credit revenue) or
    b. Increase an expense account (debit expense).

The adjusting entries and account balances after posting for Smart Touch Learning at December 31 are shown in Exhibit F:3-4.

- Panel A gives the data for each adjustment.
- Panel B shows the adjusting entries.
- Panel C shows the T-accounts and balances after posting.

Exhibit F:3-4 | Journalizing and Posting the Adjusting Entries of Smart Touch Learning

Panel A: Information for Adjustments

a. Prepaid rent expired, $1,000.
b. Supplies used, $400.
c. Depreciation on furniture, $300.
d. Depreciation on building, $250.
e. Service revenue that was collected in advance and now has been earned, $200.
f. Accrued salaries expense, $1,200.
g. Accrued interest on note, $100.
h. Accrued service revenue, $800.

Panel B: Adjusting Entries

Date	Accounts and Explanation	Debit	Credit
(a) Dec. 31	Rent Expense	1,000	
	Prepaid Rent		1,000
	To record rent expense.		
(b) 31	Supplies Expense	400	
	Office Supplies		400
	To record office supplies used.		
(c) 31	Depreciation Expense—Furniture	300	
	Accumulated Depreciation—Furniture		300
	To record depreciation on furniture.		
(d) 31	Depreciation Expense—Building	250	
	Accumulated Depreciation—Building		250
	To record depreciation on building.		
(e) 31	Unearned Revenue	200	
	Service Revenue		200
	To record service revenue earned that was collected in advance.		
(f) 31	Salaries Expense	1,200	
	Salaries Payable		1,200
	To accrue salaries expense.		
(g) 31	Interest Expense	100	
	Interest Payable		100
	To accrue interest expense.		
(h) 31	Accounts Receivable	800	
	Service Revenue		800
	To accrue service revenue.		

Panel C: Account Balances After Posting

ASSETS = LIABILITIES + EQUITY

Cash

Nov. 1	30,000	20,000	Nov. 2
Nov. 8	5,500	3,200	Nov. 15
Nov. 22	2,000	300	Nov. 21
Dec. 21	600	5,000	Nov. 25
Dec. 28	8,000	3,000	Dec. 1
		1,200	Dec. 1
		1,200	Dec. 15
Bal.	12,200		

Accounts Receivable

Nov. 10	3,000	2,000	Nov. 22
Dec. 31	800		
Bal.	1,800		

Office Supplies

Nov. 3	500	400	Dec. 31
Bal.	100		

Prepaid Rent

Dec. 1	3,000	1,000	Dec. 31
Bal.	2,000		

Land

Nov. 2	20,000		
Bal.	20,000		

Building

Dec. 1	60,000		
Bal.	60,000		

Accumulated Depreciation— Building

		250	Dec. 31
		250	Bal.

Furniture

Dec. 2	18,000		
Bal.	18,000		

Accumulated Depreciation— Furniture

		300	Dec. 31
		300	Bal.

$113,550

Accounts Payable

Nov. 21	300	500	Nov. 3
		200	Bal.

Utilities Payable

		100	Dec. 15
		100	Bal.

Salaries Payable

		1,200	Dec. 31
		1,200	Bal.

Interest Payable

		100	Dec. 31
		100	Bal.

Unearned Revenue

Dec. 31	200	600	Dec. 21
		400	Bal.

Notes Payable

		60,000	Dec. 1
		60,000	Bal.

$62,000

Bright, Capital

		30,000	Nov. 1
		18,000	Dec. 2
		48,000	Bal.

Bright, Withdrawals

Nov. 25	5,000		
Bal.	5,000		

Service Revenue

		5,500	Nov. 8
		3,000	Nov. 10
		8,000	Dec. 28
		200	Dec. 31
		800	Dec. 31
		17,500	Bal.

Rent Expense

Nov. 15	2,000		
Dec. 31	1,000		
Bal.	3,000		

Salaries Expense

Nov. 15	1,200		
Dec. 1	1,200		
Dec. 15	1,200		
Dec. 31	1,200		
Bal.	4,800		

Supplies Expense

Dec. 31	400		
Bal.	400		

Utilities Expense

Dec. 15	100		
Bal.	100		

Depreciation Expense— Building

Dec. 31	250		
Bal.	250		

Depreciation Expense— Furniture

Dec. 31	300		
Bal.	300		

Interest Expense

Dec. 31	100		
Bal.	100		

$51,550

Startech Surveillance Services had the following adjustments as of the end of the year:

a. Equipment depreciation was $1,500.
b. $700 of advertising expense was incurred but not paid. (Use Advertising Payable.)
c. Office Supplies on hand at the end of the year totaled $250. The beginning balance of Office Supplies was $600.
d. $1,200 of rent revenue was earned but not recorded or received.
e. Unearned revenue of $3,000 had been earned.

6. For each situation, indicate which category of adjustment (deferral or accrual) is described.
7. Journalize the adjusting entry needed.

Check your answers online in MyLab Accounting or at http://www.pearsonhighered.com/Horngren.

For more practice, see Short Exercises S-F:3-5 through S-F:3-12. **MyLab Accounting**

WHAT IS THE PURPOSE OF THE ADJUSTED TRIAL BALANCE, AND HOW DO WE PREPARE IT?

Learning Objective 4
Explain the purpose of and prepare an adjusted trial balance

Adjusted Trial Balance
A list of all the accounts with their adjusted balances.

This chapter began with the *unadjusted* trial balance. After the adjustments have been journalized and posted, the account balances are updated, and an **adjusted trial balance** can be prepared by listing all the accounts with their adjusted balances. Remember, the purpose of a trial balance is to ensure that total debits equal total credits. Even if the trial balance balances, it does not guarantee that a mistake has not been made. For example, an adjusting entry could have been recorded for the incorrect amount or could have been omitted entirely. The equality of the trial balance ensures only that each posted transaction had an equal debit and credit amount.

The adjusted trial balance for Smart Touch Learning is shown in Exhibit F:3-5.

Exhibit F:3-5 | **Adjusted Trial Balance**

SMART TOUCH LEARNING
Adjusted Trial Balance
December 31, 2024

Account Title	Debit	Credit
Cash	$ 12,200	
Accounts Receivable	1,800	
Office Supplies	100	
Prepaid Rent	2,000	
Land	20,000	
Building	60,000	
Accumulated Depreciation—Building		$ 250
Furniture	18,000	
Accumulated Depreciation—Furniture		300
Accounts Payable		200
Utilities Payable		100
Salaries Payable		1,200
Interest Payable		100
Unearned Revenue		400
Notes Payable		60,000
Bright, Capital		48,000
Bright, Withdrawals	5,000	
Service Revenue		17,500
Rent Expense	3,000	
Salaries Expense	4,800	
Supplies Expense	400	
Utilities Expense	100	
Depreciation Expense—Building	250	
Depreciation Expense—Furniture	300	
Interest Expense	100	
Total	$ 128,050	$ 128,050

Try It!

8. Hooten Carpentry had the following accounts and account balances after adjusting entries. Assume all accounts have normal balances. Prepare the adjusted trial balance for Hooten Carpentry as of December 31, 2024.

Cash	$ 4,025	Hooten, Capital	$?
Land	5,000	Accounts Receivable	660
Utilities Expense	400	Office Supplies	120
Accounts Payable	225	Utilities Payable	210
Accumulated Depreciation—Equipment	1,000	Service Revenue	12,000
Salaries Expense	550	Unearned Revenue	300
Supplies Expense	80	Depreciation Expense—Equipment	800
Equipment	10,000	Hooten, Withdrawals	500

Check your answers online in MyLab Accounting or at http://www.pearsonhighered.com/Horngren.

For more practice, see Short Exercise S-F:3-13. MyLab Accounting

WHAT IS THE IMPACT OF ADJUSTING ENTRIES ON THE FINANCIAL STATEMENTS?

Learning Objective 5
Identify the impact of adjusting entries on the financial statements

The adjusted trial balance is used to prepare the financial statements. If adjusting entries are not recorded, the ledger accounts will not reflect the correct balances, and the adjusted trial balance will be incorrect. Remember, adjusting entries are completed to ensure that all revenues and expenses for the accounting period examined have been recorded. In addition, adjusting entries update the balance sheet accounts so that all accounts are properly valued. Exhibit F:3-6 summarizes the impact on the financial statements had the adjusting entries not been recorded.

The Adjusting Process

Exhibit F:3-6 | Impact of Adjusting Entries on Financial Statements

Type of Adjusting Entry	Description	Adjusting Entry	Impact on Financial Statements if Adjusting Entries Are Not Made
Deferred Expenses	Advance cash payments of future expenses.	Expense DR Asset* CR	Income Statement: expenses understated 　　　　　　　　 net income overstated Balance Sheet: assets overstated 　　　　　　　 equity overstated
Deferred Revenues	Advance cash receipts of future revenues.	Liability DR Revenue CR	Income Statement: revenues understated 　　　　　　　　 net income understated Balance Sheet: liabilities overstated 　　　　　　　 equity understated
Accrued Expenses	An expense that has been incurred but not paid.	Expense DR Liability CR	Income Statement: expenses understated 　　　　　　　　 net income overstated Balance Sheet: liabilities understated 　　　　　　　 equity overstated
Accrued Revenues	A revenue that has been earned but cash has not yet been collected.	Asset DR Revenue CR	Income Statement: revenues understated 　　　　　　　　 net income understated Balance Sheet: assets understated 　　　　　　　 equity understated

*If recording depreciation: the contra asset, Accumulated Depreciation, is credited.

Remember: Net income increases Owner, Capital, an equity account. Therefore, if net income is overstated, then equity will also be overstated. And if net income is understated, then equity will also be understated.

TYING IT ALL TOGETHER

iHeartMedia, Inc. is a company that has three distinct business segments: iHeartMedia (media and entertainment company), Americas Outdoor Advertising, and International Outdoor Advertising. iHeartMedia, Inc. currently operates more than 840 radio stations, and its mobile application is available on more than 2,000 devices, including smart speakers, tablets, smartphones, and more. It operates both traditional radio broadcasting and online and mobile radio stations. In addition, the company also produces nationally recognized events for their listeners such as the iHeartRadio Music Festival. The primary source of revenue for iHeartMedia, Inc. is the sale of commercials on its radio stations.

Suppose on March 1, iHeartMedia, Inc. signs an advertising contract with a local restaurant, Margaritas, to provide 12 months of commercials for $9,000. How would iHeartMedia report the advance payment from Margaritas?

The receipt of cash from Margaritas would represent unearned revenue because iHeartMedia has not satisfied the performance obligation to provide the commercials. iHeartMedia would record a journal entry as follows:

Cash	9,000	
Unearned Revenue		9,000

On December 31, would iHeartMedia, Inc. need to record an adjusting entry related to the advertising contract? If so, what would the adjusting entry be?

At the end of the year, iHeartMedia has provided 10 months (March through December) of advertising or $7,500 ($9,000 / 12 months = $750 per month × 10 months = $7,500) for Margaritas. iHeartMedia would need to record an adjusting entry showing that the Unearned Revenue has now been earned as follows:

Unearned Revenue	7,500	
Advertising Revenue		7,500

Suppose iHeartMedia, Inc. fails to record the adjusting entry related to the advertising contract, what would be the impact on the financial statements? Why is it important for companies to record adjusting entries?

Had iHeartMedia, Inc. failed to record the adjusting entry, its financial statements would be incorrect. The liability account, Unearned Revenue, would be overstated and Advertising Revenue would be understated. This would cause net income to be understated on the income statement. It is important for companies to follow the revenue recognition and matching principles when recording adjusting entries so that the correct balances of accounts are reported to users of the financial statements and an accurate picture of the company's financial health is represented.

Try It!

9. Identify the impact on the income statement and balance sheet if adjusting entries for the following situations were not recorded.
   a. Office Supplies used, $800.
   b. Accrued service revenue, $4,000.
   c. Depreciation on building, $3,500.
   d. Prepaid Insurance expired, $650.
   e. Accrued salaries expense, $2,750.
   f. Service revenue that was collected in advance has now been earned, $130.

Check your answers online in MyLab Accounting or at http://www.pearsonhighered.com/Horngren.

For more practice, see Short Exercise S-F:3-14.   **MyLab Accounting**

HOW COULD A WORKSHEET HELP IN PREPARING ADJUSTING ENTRIES AND THE ADJUSTED TRIAL BALANCE?

Learning Objective 6

Explain the purpose of a worksheet and use it to prepare adjusting entries and the adjusted trial balance

Worksheet

An internal document that helps summarize data for the preparation of financial statements.

A useful step in preparing adjusting entries and the adjusted trial balance is to create a worksheet. A **worksheet** is an internal document that helps summarize data for the preparation of the financial statements. The worksheet is not a journal, a ledger, or a financial statement. It is merely a summary device that helps identify the accounts that need adjustments. Most worksheets are completed using Microsoft Excel.

Exhibit F:3-7 shows the partially completed worksheet for Smart Touch Learning.

In this chapter, we complete a part of the worksheet. For now, we will concern ourselves with the first four sections.

Section 1: Account names. The account names are taken from and listed in the same order as the chart of accounts. (Cash first, Accounts Receivable second, and so on.)

Section 2: Unadjusted trial balance. The account balances are copied directly from the ledger before any adjustments. Total debits must equal total credits.

The Adjusting Process Financial 3-27

Exhibit F:3-7 | Partially Completed Worksheet

SMART TOUCH LEARNING
Worksheet
December 31, 2024

Account Names	Unadjusted Trial Balance Debit	Unadjusted Trial Balance Credit	Adjustments Debit	Adjustments Credit	Adjusted Trial Balance Debit	Adjusted Trial Balance Credit	Income Statement Debit	Income Statement Credit	Balance Sheet Debit	Balance Sheet Credit
Cash	$ 12,200				$ 12,200					
Accounts Receivable	1,000		(h) $ 800		1,800					
Office Supplies	500			$ 400 (b)	100					
Prepaid Rent	3,000			1,000 (a)	2,000					
Land	20,000				20,000					
Building	60,000				60,000					
Accumulated Depreciation—Building				250 (d)		$ 250				
Furniture	18,000				18,000					
Accumulated Depreciation—Furniture				300 (c)		300				
Accounts Payable		$ 200				200				
Utilities Payable		100				100				
Salaries Payable				1,200 (f)		1,200				
Interest Payable				100 (g)		100				
Unearned Revenue		600	(e) 200			400				
Notes Payable		60,000				60,000				
Bright, Capital		48,000				48,000				
Bright, Withdrawals	5,000				5,000					
Service Revenue		16,500		1,000 (e,h)		17,500				
Rent Expense	2,000		(a) 1,000		3,000					
Salaries Expense	3,600		(f) 1,200		4,800					
Supplies Expense			(b) 400		400					
Utilities Expense	100				100					
Depreciation Expense—Building			(d) 250		250					
Depreciation Expense—Furniture			(c) 300		300					
Interest Expense			(g) 100		100					
Total	$ 125,400	$ 125,400	$ 4,250	$ 4,250	$ 128,050	$ 128,050				

Section 3: Adjustments. Enter the adjusting journal entries that were made on December 31.

Section 4: Adjusted trial balance. Gives the account balances after adjustments. Each amount in these columns is computed by combining the unadjusted trial balance amounts plus or minus the adjustments. For example, Accounts Receivable starts with a debit balance of $1,000. Adding the $800 debit from the adjustment gives Accounts Receivable an adjusted balance of $1,800. Service Revenue starts with a $16,500 credit balance. Adding the $1,000 credit from the adjustments gives Service Revenue an adjusted balance of $17,500. As with the unadjusted trial balance, total debits must equal total credits.

> Note that the worksheet does not eliminate the need for recording the adjusting entries in the journal or posting them to the ledger. It is simply a tool to assist in evaluating the accounts and determining which accounts need adjustment.

The income statement and balance sheet sections of the worksheet remain to be completed. These will be covered in the next chapter.

3-28 Financial chapter 3

10. The partial worksheet for Sam's Delivery Service follows. Complete the adjusted trial balance columns.

SAM'S DELIVERY SERVICE
Worksheet
December 31, 2024

Account Names	Unadjusted Trial Balance Debit	Unadjusted Trial Balance Credit	Adjustments Debit	Adjustments Credit	Adjusted Trial Balance Debit	Adjusted Trial Balance Credit	Income Statement Debit	Income Statement Credit	Balance Sheet Debit	Balance Sheet Credit
Cash	$ 6,500									
Accounts Receivable	800		(g) $ 225							
Office Supplies	250			$ 80 (b)						
Prepaid Rent	1,000			800 (a)						
Delivery Van	23,000									
Accumulated Depreciation—Delivery Van				750 (c)						
Equipment	15,000									
Accumulated Depreciation—Equipment				300 (d)						
Accounts Payable		$ 800								
Utilities Payable		230								
Salaries Payable				875 (f)						
Unearned Revenue		400	(e) 130							
Sam, Capital		37,800								
Sam, Withdrawals	8,000									
Delivery Revenue		23,000		355 (e,g)						
Rent Expense	3,000		(a) 800							
Salaries Expense	4,500		(f) 875							
Supplies Expense			(b) 80							
Utilities Expense	180									
Depreciation Expense—Delivery Van			(c) 750							
Depreciation Expense—Equipment			(d) 300							
Total	$ 62,230	$ 62,230	$ 3,160	$ 3,160						

Check your answers online in MyLab Accounting or at http://www.pearsonhighered.com/Horngren.

For more practice, see Short Exercise S-F:3-15. **MyLab Accounting**

APPENDIX 3A: Alternative Treatment of Recording Deferred Expenses and Deferred Revenues

Chapters F:1–F:3 illustrate the most popular way to account for deferred expenses and deferred revenues. This appendix illustrates an alternative approach.

WHAT IS AN ALTERNATIVE TREATMENT OF RECORDING DEFERRED EXPENSES AND DEFERRED REVENUES?

Deferred Expenses

Learning Objective 7

Understand the alternative treatment of recording deferred expenses and deferred revenues

Recall that deferred expenses, also called *prepaid expenses*, are advance payments of future expenses, such as insurance, rent, and advertising. Office supplies are also accounted for as deferred expenses.

The Adjusting Process Financial 3-29

When a business prepays an expense—rent, for example—it can debit an *asset* account (Prepaid Rent) and defer the recognition of the expense. For example, Smart Touch Learning prepaid three months of office rent totaling $3,000 on December 1, 2024. The journal entry can be recorded as:

Date	Accounts and Explanation	Debit	Credit
Dec. 1	Prepaid Rent	3,000	
	Cash		3,000
	Paid rent in advance.		

$A\updownarrow$ | $L\ +\ E$
Prepaid Rent ↑
Cash ↓

Deferred Expense Recorded Initially as an Expense

Deferring an expense creates an asset. However, the asset may be so short lived that it will expire in the current accounting period—within one year or less. Thus, the accountant may decide to debit the prepayment to an expense account at the time of payment. The entry could, alternatively, be recorded as follows:

Date	Accounts and Explanation	Debit	Credit
Dec. 1	Rent Expense	3,000	
	Cash		3,000
	Paid rent in advance.		

$A\downarrow$ | $L\ +\ E\downarrow$
Cash↓ | Rent Expense↑

As of December 31, 2024, only one month's prepayment has expired, leaving two months of rent still prepaid. In this case, the accountant must transfer two-thirds of the original prepayment of $3,000, or $2,000, to the asset account Prepaid Rent to follow the matching principle. At December 31, 2024, the business still has the benefit of prepayment for January 1 through February 28, 2025. The adjusting entry at December 31 is as follows:

Date	Accounts and Explanation	Debit	Credit
Dec. 31	Prepaid Rent	2,000	
	Rent Expense		2,000
	To record prepaid rent.		

$A\uparrow$ | $L\ +\ E\uparrow$
Prepaid Rent↑ | Rent Expense↓

After posting, the two accounts appear as follows:

```
         Prepaid Rent                    Rent Expense
  Dec. 31   2,000                 Dec. 1   3,000 | 2,000  Dec. 31
  Bal.      2,000                 Bal.     1,000
```

At December 31, the $3,000 prepayment is correctly divided as $2,000 of Prepaid Rent and $1,000 of Rent Expense, regardless of whether the business initially debits the prepayment to an asset or to an expense account.

Deferred Revenues

Deferred revenues, also called unearned revenues, arise when a business collects cash before earning the revenue. Deferred revenues are liabilities because the business that receives the cash owes the customer goods or services to be delivered later.

When a business receives cash in advance of providing services, a *liability* can be created. As an example, a law firm engages Smart Touch Learning to provide monthly e-learning services, agreeing to pay $600 in advance. Smart Touch Learning received the $600 on December 21 for services to be provided in the next 30 days. Smart Touch Learning records the following entry, recognizing the liability and deferring the recognition of the revenue.

A↑ = L↑ + E
Cash↑   Unearned
        Revenue↑

Date	Accounts and Explanation	Debit	Credit
Dec. 21	Cash	600	
	Unearned Revenue		600
	Collected cash for future services.		

Deferred Revenues Recorded Initially as a Revenue

Another way to account for the receipt of cash is to credit a *revenue* account when the business receives cash.

A↑ = L + E↑
Cash↑   Service
            Revenue↑

Date	Accounts and Explanation	Debit	Credit
Dec. 21	Cash	600	
	Service Revenue		600
	Collected cash for future services.		

If the business then earns all the revenue within the same accounting period, no adjusting entry is needed at the end. However, if the business earns only part of the revenue in that period, it must make an adjusting entry to follow the revenue recognition principle. In our example, Smart Touch Learning has earned only one-third of the $600, or $200, by December 31, 2024. Accordingly, Smart Touch Learning must make an adjusting entry to transfer the unearned portion (2/3 of $600, or $400) from the revenue account to a liability, as follows:

A = L↑ + E↓
    Unearned Service
    Revenue↑ Revenue↓

Date	Accounts and Explanation	Debit	Credit
Dec. 31	Service Revenue	400	
	Unearned Revenue		400
	To record unearned revenue.		

The adjusting entry transfers the unearned portion of service revenue to the liability account because Smart Touch Learning still owes e-learning services next year. After posting, the total amount, $600, is properly divided between the liability account—$400, and the revenue account—$200, as follows:

```
        Unearned Revenue              Service Revenue
                 |  400    Dec. 31  ← Dec. 31  400 | 600   Dec. 21
                 |  400    Bal.                    | 200   Bal.
```

At December 31, the $600 cash receipt is correctly divided: $400 of Unearned Revenue and $200 of Service Revenue, regardless of whether the business initially credits the cash receipt to a liability or to a revenue account.

11A. Iron Horse Printing Services purchased $1,000 of printing supplies for cash, recording the transaction using the alternative treatment for deferred expenses. At the end of the year, Iron Horse had $300 of printing supplies remaining. Record the journal entry for the purchase of printing supplies and the adjusting entry for printing supplies not used.

Check your answer online in MyLab Accounting or at http://www.pearsonhighered.com/Horngren.

For more practice, see Short Exercises S-F:3A-16 and S-F:3A-17. **MyLab Accounting**

REVIEW

> Things You Should Know

1. **What is the difference between cash basis accounting and accrual basis accounting?**

   - Cash basis accounting: Revenue is recorded only when cash is received, and expenses are recorded only when cash is paid.
     - Does not follow GAAP
     - Often used by small businesses
   - Accrual basis accounting: Revenue is recorded when earned, and expenses are recorded when incurred.

2. **What concepts and principles apply to accrual basis accounting?**

   - The time period concept assumes that a business's activities can be sliced into small time segments and that financial statements can be prepared for specific periods, such as a month, quarter, or year.
   - The revenue recognition principle requires companies to record revenue when it has satisfied each performance obligation.
   - The matching principle guides accounting for expenses and ensures that all expenses are recorded when they are incurred during the period. It then matches those expenses against the revenues of the period.

3. **What are adjusting entries, and how do we record them?**

   - Adjusting entries are completed at the end of the accounting period and record revenues to the period in which they are earned and expenses to the period in which they occur.
   - Adjusting entries also update the asset and liability accounts.

- Four types of adjusting entries:
  - Deferred expenses (or *prepaid expenses*): advance payment of future expenses adjusted for amount used

Date	Accounts and Explanation	Debit	Credit
	Expense	XXX	
	Asset		XXX

  - Deferred revenues (or *unearned revenues*): advance receipts of future revenues adjusted for amount earned

Date	Accounts and Explanation	Debit	Credit
	Liability	XXX	
	Revenue		XXX

  - Accrued expenses: expenses that have been incurred but not paid

Date	Accounts and Explanation	Debit	Credit
	Expense	XXX	
	Liability		XXX

  - Accrued revenues: revenues that have been earned but not collected

Date	Accounts and Explanation	Debit	Credit
	Asset	XXX	
	Revenue		XXX

4. **What is the purpose of the adjusted trial balance, and how do we prepare it?**
   - An adjusted trial balance is a list of all the accounts with their adjusted balances.
   - It ensures that total debits equal total credits.

5. **What is the impact of adjusting entries on the financial statements?**
   - If adjusting entries are not recorded, the balance sheet and income statement accounts will either be overstated or understated.
   - Overstating or understating accounts causes the financial statements to be incorrect.

6. **How could a worksheet help in preparing adjusting entries and the adjusted trial balance?**
   - A worksheet is an internal document that helps identify the accounts that need adjustments.
   - In addition, a worksheet helps summarize data for the preparation of the financial statements.

7. **What is the alternative treatment of recording deferred expenses and deferred revenues? (Appendix 3A)**

   - Deferred expenses can be recorded to an expense account at the time of payment. The adjusting entry would transfer any remaining prepayment to the asset account, Prepaid Expenses.
   - Deferred revenues can be recorded to a revenue account at the time of cash receipt. The adjusting entry would transfer any remaining liability to the liability account, Unearned Revenue.

> Check Your Understanding

Check your understanding of the chapter by completing this problem and then looking at the solution. Use this practice to help identify which sections of the chapter you need to study more.

The unadjusted trial balance as of December 31, 2024, the end of the annual accounting period for Super Employment Services, follows:

SUPER EMPLOYMENT SERVICES
Unadjusted Trial Balance
December 31, 2024

Account Title	Debit	Credit
Cash	$ 6,000	
Accounts Receivable	5,000	
Office Supplies	1,000	
Land	10,000	
Building	40,000	
Accumulated Depreciation—Building		$ 30,000
Furniture	10,000	
Accumulated Depreciation—Furniture		4,000
Accounts Payable		2,000
Salaries Payable		
Unearned Revenue		8,000
Mudge, Capital		12,000
Mudge, Withdrawals	25,000	
Service Revenue		60,000
Salaries Expense	16,000	
Supplies Expense		
Depreciation Expense—Building		
Depreciation Expense—Furniture		
Advertising Expense	3,000	
Total	$ 116,000	$ 116,000

Data needed for the adjusting entries include the following:

a. Office Supplies on hand at year-end, $200.
b. Depreciation on furniture, $2,000.
c. Depreciation on building, $1,000.
d. Salaries owed but not yet paid, $500.
e. Accrued service revenue, $1,300.
f. $3,000 of the unearned revenue has been earned.

Requirements

1. Open the ledger accounts in T-account form with their unadjusted balances as shown on the unadjusted trial balance. (See Learning Objective 3)
2. Journalize Super's adjusting entries at December 31, 2024. Use the letter (*a*, *b*, and so on) as the date. (See Learning Objective 3)
3. Post the adjusting entries to T-accounts. Determine the ending balances in the T-accounts on December 31, 2024. (See Learning Objective 3)
4. Prepare an adjusted trial balance. (See Learning Objective 4)
5. Prepare a partial worksheet including the account names, unadjusted trial balance, adjustments, and adjusted trial balance. (See Learning Objective 6)

> Solution

Requirement 1 See next page

Requirement 2

Date	Accounts and Explanations	Debit	Credit
2024			
(a) Dec. 31	Supplies Expense ($1,000 − $200)	800	
	Office Supplies		800
	To record office supplies used.		
(b) 31	Depreciation Expense—Furniture	2,000	
	Accumulated Depreciation—Furniture		2,000
	To record depreciation expense on furniture.		
(c) 31	Depreciation Expense—Building	1,000	
	Accumulated Depreciation—Building		1,000
	To record depreciation expense on building.		
(d) 31	Salaries Expense	500	
	Salaries Payable		500
	To accrue salaries expense.		
(e) 31	Accounts Receivable	1,300	
	Service Revenue		1,300
	To accrue service revenue.		
(f) 31	Unearned Revenue	3,000	
	Service Revenue		3,000
	To record service revenue earned that was collected in advance.		

Requirements 1 and 3

ASSETS

Cash
Bal. 6,000	

Accounts Receivable
Bal. 5,000	
(e) 1,300	
Bal. 6,300	

Office Supplies
Bal. 1,000	800 (a)
Bal. 200	

Land
Bal. 10,000	

Building
Bal. 40,000	

Accumulated Depreciation—Building
	30,000 Bal.
	1,000 (c)
	31,000 Bal.

Furniture
Bal. 10,000	

Accumulated Depreciation—Furniture
	4,000 Bal.
	2,000 (b)
	6,000 Bal.

LIABILITIES

Accounts Payable
	2,000 Bal.

Salaries Payable
	500 (d)
	500 Bal.

Unearned Revenue
(f) 3,000	8,000 Bal.
	5,000 Bal.

EQUITY

Mudge, Capital
	12,000 Bal.

Mudge, Withdrawals
Bal. 25,000	

Service Revenue
	60,000 Bal.
	1,300 (e)
	3,000 (f)
	64,300 Bal.

Salaries Expense
Bal. 16,000	
(d) 500	
Bal. 16,500	

Supplies Expense
(a) 800	
Bal. 800	

Depreciation Expense—Building
(c) 1,000	
Bal. 1,000	

Depreciation Expense—Furniture
(b) 2,000	
Bal. 2,000	

Advertising Expense
Bal. 3,000	

Requirement 4

SUPER EMPLOYMENT SERVICES
Adjusted Trial Balance
December 31, 2024

Account Title	Debit	Credit
Cash	$ 6,000	
Accounts Receivable	6,300	
Office Supplies	200	
Land	10,000	
Building	40,000	
Accumulated Depreciation—Building		$ 31,000
Furniture	10,000	
Accumulated Depreciation—Furniture		6,000
Accounts Payable		2,000
Salaries Payable		500
Unearned Revenue		5,000
Mudge, Capital		12,000
Mudge, Withdrawals	25,000	
Service Revenue		64,300
Salaries Expense	16,500	
Supplies Expense	800	
Depreciation Expense—Building	1,000	
Depreciation Expense—Furniture	2,000	
Advertising Expense	3,000	
Total	$ 120,800	$ 120,800

Requirement 5

SUPER EMPLOYMENT SERVICES
Worksheet
December 31, 2024

Account Names	Unadjusted Trial Balance Debit	Unadjusted Trial Balance Credit	Adjustments Debit	Adjustments Credit	Adjusted Trial Balance Debit	Adjusted Trial Balance Credit
Cash	$ 6,000				$ 6,000	
Accounts Receivable	5,000		(e) $ 1,300		6,300	
Office Supplies	1,000			(a) $ 800	200	
Land	10,000				10,000	
Building	40,000				40,000	
Accumulated Depreciation—Building		$ 30,000		(c) 1,000		$ 31,000
Furniture	10,000				10,000	
Accumulated Depreciation—Furniture		4,000		(b) 2,000		6,000
Accounts Payable		2,000				2,000
Salaries Payable				(d) 500		500
Unearned Revenue		8,000	(f) 3,000			5,000
Mudge, Capital		12,000				12,000
Mudge, Withdrawals	25,000				25,000	
Service Revenue		60,000		(e) 1,300		
				(f) 3,000		64,300
Salaries Expense	16,000		(d) 500		16,500	
Supplies Expense			(a) 800		800	
Depreciation Expense—Building			(c) 1,000		1,000	
Depreciation Expense—Furniture			(b) 2,000		2,000	
Advertising Expense	3,000				3,000	
Total	$ 116,000	$ 116,000	$ 8,600	$ 8,600	$ 120,800	$ 120,800

> Key Terms

Accrual Basis Accounting (p. 3-2)
Accrued Expense (p. 3-14)
Accrued Revenue (p. 3-18)
Accumulated Depreciation (p. 3-11)
Adjusted Trial Balance (p. 3-22)
Adjusting Entry (p. 3-7)
Book Value (p. 3-12)
Cash Basis Accounting (p. 3-2)

Contra Account (p. 3-11)
Deferred Expense (p. 3-7)
Deferred Revenue (p. 3-13)
Depreciation (p. 3-9)
Fiscal Year (p. 3-4)
Matching Principle (p. 3-5)
Property, Plant, and Equipment (p. 3-9)

Residual Value (p. 3-10)
Revenue Recognition Principle (p. 3-4)
Straight-Line Method (p. 3-10)
Time Period Concept (p. 3-4)
Worksheet (p. 3-26)

> Quick Check

Learning Objective 1

1. Which of the following is true of accrual basis accounting and cash basis accounting?
    a. Accrual accounting records revenue only when it is earned.
    b. Accrual accounting is not allowed under GAAP.
    c. Cash basis accounting records all transactions.
    d. All of the above are true.

2. Get Fit Now gains a client who prepays $540 for a package of six physical training sessions. Get Fit Now collects the $540 in advance and will provide the training later. After four training sessions, what should Get Fit Now report on its income statement assuming it uses the accrual basis accounting method?

    a. Service revenue of $360
    b. Service revenue of $540
    c. Unearned service revenue of $360
    d. Cash of $180

    Learning Objective 1

3. The revenue recognition principle requires

    a. time to be divided into annual periods to measure revenue properly.
    b. revenue to be recorded only after the business has satisfied its performance obligation.
    c. expenses to be matched with revenue of the period.
    d. revenue to be recorded only after the cash is received.

    Learning Objective 2

4. Adjusting the accounts is the process of

    a. subtracting expenses from revenues to measure net income.
    b. recording transactions as they occur during the period.
    c. updating the accounts at the end of the period.
    d. zeroing out account balances to prepare for the next period.

    Learning Objective 3

5. Which of the following is an example of a deferral (or prepaid) adjusting entry?

    a. Recording the usage of office supplies during the period.
    b. Recording salaries expense for employees not yet paid.
    c. Recording revenue that has been earned but not yet received.
    d. Recording interest expense incurred on a notes payable not due until next year.

    Learning Objective 3

6. Assume that the weekly payroll of In the Woods Camping Supplies is $300. December 31, end of the year, falls on Tuesday, and In the Woods will pay its employee on Friday for the full week. What adjusting entry will In the Woods make on Tuesday, December 31? (Use five days as a full workweek.)

    Learning Objective 3

Date	Accounts and Explanation	Debit	Credit
a.	Salaries Expense	120	
	Salaries Payable		120
b.	Salaries Payable	300	
	Salaries Expense		300
c.	Salaries Expense	120	
	Cash		120
d.	No adjustment is needed because the company will pay the payroll on Friday.		

7. The adjusted trial balance shows

    a. amounts that may be out of balance.
    b. account balances after adjustments.
    c. assets and liabilities only.
    d. revenues and expenses only.

    Learning Objective 4

Learning Objective 5

8. A & D Window Cleaning performed $450 of services but has not yet billed customers for the month. If A & D fails to record the adjusting entry, what is the impact on the financial statements?

   a. balance sheet: assets understated; equity overstated
      income statement: expense understated
   b. balance sheet: liabilities overstated; equity understated
      income statement: revenues understated
   c. balance sheet: assets overstated; equity understated
      income statement: expenses understated
   d. balance sheet: assets understated; equity understated
      income statement: revenues understated

Learning Objective 6

9. A worksheet

   a. is a journal used to record transactions.
   b. is a financial statement that reports net income during the period.
   c. is an internal document that helps summarize data for the preparation of financial statements.
   d. is a ledger listing the account balances and changes in those accounts.

Learning Objective 7
Appendix 3A

10A. On February 1, Clovis Wilson Law Firm contracted to provide $3,000 of legal services for the next three months and received $3,000 cash from the client. Assuming Wilson records deferred revenues using the alternative treatment, what would be the adjusting entry recorded on February 28?

Date	Accounts and Explanation	Debit	Credit
a.	Cash	3,000	
	Unearned Revenue		3,000
b.	Service Revenue	2,000	
	Unearned Revenue		2,000
c.	Unearned Revenue	1,000	
	Service Revenue		1,000
d.	Cash	3,000	
	Service Revenue		3,000

Check your answers at the end of the chapter.

ASSESS YOUR PROGRESS

> Review Questions

1. What is the difference between cash basis accounting and accrual basis accounting?
2. Which method of accounting (cash or accrual basis) is consistent with Generally Accepted Accounting Principles?
3. Which accounting concept or principle requires companies to divide their activities into small time segments such as months, quarters, or years?
4. What is a fiscal year? Why might companies choose to use a fiscal year that is not a calendar year?

5. Under the revenue recognition principle, when is revenue recorded?
6. Under the matching principle, when are expenses recorded?
7. When are adjusting entries completed, and what is their purpose?
8. What are the two basic categories of adjusting entries? Provide two examples of each.
9. What is a deferred expense? Provide an example.
10. What is the process of allocating the cost of a plant asset over its useful life called?
11. What is a contra account?
12. In the recording of depreciation expense, which account is credited?
13. What does accumulated depreciation represent?
14. How is book value calculated, and what does it represent?
15. What is a deferred revenue? Provide an example.
16. What is an accrued expense? Provide an example.
17. What is an accrued revenue? Provide an example.
18. What are the two rules to remember about adjusting entries?
19. When is an adjusted trial balance prepared, and what is its purpose?
20. If an accrued expense is not recorded at the end of the year, what is the impact on the financial statements?
21. What is a worksheet, and how is it used to help prepare an adjusted trial balance?
22A. If a payment of a deferred expense was recorded under the alternative treatment, what account would be debited at the time of payment?
23A. If a payment of a deferred expense was recorded under the alternative treatment, what account would be debited in the adjusting entry?

> Short Exercises

S-F:3-1 Comparing cash and accrual basis accounting for expenses

Learning Objective 1

The Pink Peonies Law Firm prepays for advertising in the local newspaper. On January 1, the law firm paid $3,000 for 10 months of advertising.

How much advertising expense should Pink Peonies Law Firm record for the two months ending February 28 under the

a. cash basis?   b. accrual basis?

S-F:3-2 Comparing cash and accrual basis accounting for revenues

Learning Objective 1

Protection Home provides house-sitting for people while they are away on vacation. Some of its customers pay immediately after the job is finished. Some customers ask that the business send them a bill. As of the end of the year, Protection Home has collected $900 from cash-paying customers. Protection Home's remaining customers owe the business $1,300.

How much service revenue would Protection Home have for the year under the

a. cash basis?   b. accrual basis?

Learning Objective 2   **S-F:3-3 Applying the revenue recognition principle**

Movies Online sells subscriptions for $36 for 18 months. The company collects cash in advance and then subscribers have access to unlimited movies each month.

Apply the revenue recognition principle to determine

a. when *Movies Online* should record revenue for this situation.

b. the amount of revenue *Movies Online* should record for eight months.

Learning Objective 2   **S-F:3-4 Applying the matching principle**

Suppose on January 1, Andrew's Tavern prepaid rent of $16,800 for the full year.

At November 30, how much rent expense should be recorded for the period January 1 through November 30?

Learning Objective 3   **S-F:3-5 Identifying types of adjusting entries**

A select list of transactions for Anuradha's Goals follows:

Apr. 1	Paid six months of rent, $4,800.
10	Received $1,200 from customer for six-month service contract that began April 1.
15	Purchased a computer for $1,000.
18	Purchased $300 of office supplies on account.
30	Work performed but not yet billed to customer, $500.
30	Employees earned $600 in salaries that will be paid May 2.

For each transaction, identify what type of adjusting entry would be needed. Select from the following four types of adjusting entries: deferred expense, deferred revenue, accrued expense, and accrued revenue.

Learning Objective 3   **S-F:3-6 Journalizing and posting adjusting entries for prepaid rent**

On September 1, Big Fan of Toledo prepaid six months of rent, $3,300.

Requirements

1. Record the journal entry for the September 1 payment.
2. Record the adjusting entry required at September 30.
3. Using T-accounts, post the journal entry and adjusting entry to the accounts involved and show their balances at September 30. (Ignore the Cash account.)

Learning Objective 3   **S-F:3-7 Journalizing and posting an adjusting entry for office supplies**

On November 1, Carlisle Equipment had a beginning balance in the Office Supplies account of $600. During the month, Carlisle purchased $2,300 of office supplies. At November 30, Carlisle Equipment had $500 of office supplies on hand.

Requirements

1. Open the Office Supplies T-account and enter the beginning balance and purchase of office supplies.
2. Record the adjusting entry required at November 30.
3. Post the adjusting entry to the two accounts involved and show their balances at November 30.

S-F:3-8 Journalizing and posting an adjusting entry for depreciation and determining book value

On October 1, Orlando Gold Exchange paid cash of $57,600 for computers that are expected to remain useful for three years. At the end of three years, the value of the computers is expected to be zero.

Requirements

1. Calculate the amount of depreciation for the month of October using the straight-line depreciation method.
2. Record the adjusting entry for depreciation on October 31.
3. Post the purchase of October 1 and the depreciation on October 31 to T-accounts for the following accounts: Computer Equipment, Accumulated Depreciation—Computer Equipment, and Depreciation Expense—Computer Equipment. Show their balances at October 31.
4. What is the computer equipment's book value on October 31?

S-F:3-9 Journalizing and posting an adjusting entry for unearned revenue

Online Gaming collects cash from subscribers in advance and then provides online games to subscribers over a one-year period.

Requirements

1. Record the journal entry to record the original receipt of $180,000 cash.
2. Record the adjusting entry that *Online Gaming* makes to record earning $8,000 in subscription revenue that was collected in advance.
3. Using T-accounts, post the journal entry and adjusting entry to the accounts involved and show their balances after adjustments. (Ignore the Cash account.)

S-F:3-10 Journalizing and posting an adjusting entry for accrued salaries expense

Birch Park Senior Center has a weekly payroll of $12,500. December 31 falls on Wednesday, and Birch Park Senior Center will pay its employees the following Monday (January 5) for the previous full week. Assume Birch Park Senior Center has a five-day workweek and has an unadjusted balance in Salaries Expense of $620,000.

Requirements

1. Record the adjusting entry for accrued salaries on December 31.
2. Post the adjusting entry to the accounts involved and show their balances after adjustments.
3. Record the journal entry for payment of salaries made on January 5.

S-F:3-11 Journalizing and posting an adjusting entry for accrued interest expense

Resort Travel borrowed $33,000 on September 1, 2024, by signing a one-year, 6% note payable to State One Bank.

Requirements

1. Calculate the amount of interest expense to accrue at December 31, 2024. Round to the nearest dollar.
2. Record the adjusting entry to accrue interest expense at December 31, 2024.
3. Post the adjusting entry to the T-accounts of the two accounts affected by the adjustment.

Learning Objective 3

S-F:3-12 Journalizing an adjusting entry for accrued revenue

At the end of June, Gerber Dental had performed $9,000 of dental services but has not yet billed customers.

Record the adjusting entry for accrued revenue.

Learning Objective 4

S-F:3-13 Preparing an adjusted trial balance

Walker's Tax Services had the following accounts and account balances after adjusting entries. Assume all accounts have normal balances.

Cash	$?	Equipment	$ 11,000
Land	26,000	Accounts Receivable	4,950
Utilities Payable	150	Office Supplies	700
Accounts Payable	3,700	Walker, Capital	22,600
Accumulated Depreciation—Equipment	1,800	Utilities Expense	1,650
Service Revenue	75,000	Unearned Revenue	900
Supplies Expense	1,100	Depreciation Expense—Equipment	1,900
Walker, Withdrawals	14,000	Salaries Expense	5,600

Prepare the adjusted trial balance for Walker's Tax Services as of December 31, 2024.

Learning Objective 5

S-F:3-14 Determining the effects on financial statements

In recording adjusting entries, Reagan Financial Advisors failed to record the adjusting entries for the following situations:

a. Office supplies on hand, $100.

b. Accrued revenues, $5,000.

c. Accrued interest expense, $250.

d. Depreciation, $800.

e. Unearned revenue that has been earned, $550.

Determine the effects on the income statement and balance sheet by identifying whether assets, liabilities, equity, revenue, and expenses are either overstated or understated. Use the following table. Adjustment *a* has been provided as an example.

Adjustment Not Recorded	Balance Sheet			Income Statement	
	Assets	Liabilities	Equity	Revenue	Expenses
(a)	Overstated		Overstated		Understated

S-F:3-15 Preparing a partial worksheet

Learning Objective 6

Just Right Hair Stylists has begun the preparation of its worksheet as follows:

	A	B	C	D	E	F	G
1			JUST RIGHT HAIR STYLISTS				
2			Worksheet				
3			December 31, 2024				
4							
5	Account Names	Unadjusted Trial Balance		Adjustments		Adjusted Trial Balance	
6		Debit	Credit	Debit	Credit	Debit	Credit
7	Cash	$ 300					
8	Office Supplies	900					
9	Equipment	20,600					
10	Accumulated Depreciation—Equipment		$ 700				
11	Accounts Payable		500				
12	Interest Payable						
13	Note Payable		2,800				
14	Benoit, Capital		4,200				
15	Service Revenue		17,500				
16	Rent Expense	3,200					
17	Supplies Expense						
18	Depreciation Expense—Equipment						
19	Interest Expense	700					
20	Total	$ 25,700	$ 25,700				
21							

Year-end data include the following:

a. Office supplies on hand, $300.

b. Depreciation, $700.

c. Accrued interest expense, $800.

Complete Just Right's worksheet through the adjusted trial balance section. In the adjustments section, mark each adjustment by letter.

S-F:3A-16 Journalizing the alternative treatment of deferred expenses

Learning Objective 7
Appendix 3A

On October 1, 2024, Kitchen Design paid $15,000 for store rent covering the six-month period ending March 31, 2025.

Requirements

1. Journalize the entry on October 1 by using the alternative treatment of deferred expenses.

2. Record the December 31, 2024 adjusting entry.

S-F:3A-17 Journalizing the alternative treatment of deferred revenues

Learning Objective 7
Appendix 3A

On September 1, 2024, Salem Landscaping collected $24,000 in advance from customers for landscaping services. The service revenue will be earned monthly over the 12-month period ending August 31, 2025.

Requirements

1. Journalize the entry on September 1 by using the alternative treatment of deferred revenues.

2. Record the December 31, 2024 adjusting entry.

> Exercises

Learning Objectives 1, 2

E-F:3-18 Comparing cash and accrual basis accounting and applying the revenue recognition principle

Momentous Occasions is a photography business that shoots videos at college parties. The freshman class pays $1,000 in advance on March 3 to guarantee services for its party to be held on April 2. The sophomore class promises a minimum of $2,800 for filming its formal dance and actually pays cash of $4,100 on February 28 at the dance.

Answer the following questions about the correct way to account for revenue under the accrual basis:

a. Considering the $1,000 paid by the freshman class, on what date was revenue recognized? Did the recognition occur on the same date cash was received?

b. Considering the $4,100 paid by the sophomore class, on what date was revenue recognized? Did the recognition occur on the same date cash was received?

Learning Objectives 1, 2

E-F:3-19 Comparing cash and accrual basis accounting and applying the revenue recognition principle and the matching principle

Chef's Catering completed the following selected transactions during May 2024:

May 1	Prepaid rent for three months, $2,400.
5	Received and paid electricity bill, $700.
9	Received cash for meals served to customers, $2,600.
14	Paid cash for kitchen equipment, $3,000.
23	Served a banquet on account, $2,800.
31	Made the adjusting entry for rent (from May 1).
31	Accrued salary expense, $1,600.
31	Recorded depreciation for May on kitchen equipment, $50.

Requirements

1. Show whether each transaction would be handled as a revenue or an expense using both the cash basis and accrual basis accounting systems by completing the following table. (Expenses should be shown in parentheses.) Also, indicate the dollar amount of the revenue or expense. The May 1 transaction has been completed as an example.

	Amount of Revenue (Expense) for May	
Date	Cash Basis Amount of Revenue (Expense)	Accrual Basis Amount of Revenue (Expense)
May 1	$(2,400)	$0

2. After completing the table, calculate the amount of net income or net loss for Chef's Catering under the accrual basis and cash basis accounting systems for May.

3. Considering your results from Requirement 2, which method gives the best picture of the true earnings of Chef's Catering? Why?

E-F:3-20 Determining the amount of deferred expenses

Consider the following independent situations for Tropical View:

a. Tropical View had a January 1, 2024 beginning balance in its Prepaid Rent account of $1,400. During the year the company made payments for prepaid rent of $700. At the end of the year, December 31, 2024, the balance in the Prepaid Rent account was $800. What was the amount of rent expense for the year?

b. Tropical View had a January 1, 2024 beginning balance in its Prepaid Rent account of $1,000. During the year the company made payments for prepaid rent of $600. Tropical View recorded rent expense for the year of $900. What is the company's ending balance in its Prepaid Rent account as of December 31, 2024?

c. Tropical View had a December 31, 2024 ending balance in its prepaid rent account of $1,000. During the year the company made payments for prepaid rent of $900 and recorded rent expense for the year of $600. What is the company's beginning balance in its Prepaid Rent account as of January 1, 2024?

E-F:3-21 Journalizing adjusting entries

Consider the following situations:

a. Business receives $3,200 on January 1 for 10-month service contract for the period January 1 through October 31.

b. Total salaries for all employees is $3,600 per month. Employees are paid on the 1st and 15th of the month.

c. Work performed but not yet billed to customers for the month is $1,600.

d. The company pays interest on its $16,000, 4% note payable of $53 on the first day of each month.

Assume the company records adjusting entries monthly. Journalize the adjusting entries needed as of January 31.

E-F:3-22 Journalizing adjusting entries

Consider the following independent situations at December 31:

a. On October 1, a business collected $3,000 rent in advance, debiting Cash and crediting Unearned Revenue. The tenant was paying one year's rent in advance. On December 31, the business must account for the amount of rent it has earned.

b. Salaries expense is $1,800 per day—Monday through Friday—and the business pays employees each Friday. This year, December 31 falls on a Thursday.

c. The unadjusted balance of the Office Supplies account is $3,000. Office supplies on hand total $1,900.

d. Equipment depreciation was $500.

e. On April 1, when the business prepaid $4,320 for a two-year insurance policy, the business debited Prepaid Insurance and credited Cash.

Journalize the adjusting entry needed on December 31 for each situation. Use the letters to label the journal entries.

Learning Objective 3

E-F:3-23 Journalizing adjusting entries

Consider the following situations for Betterton Welding Services:

a. Depreciation for the current year includes equipment, $2,100.

b. Each Monday, Betterton pays employees for the previous week's work. The amount of weekly payroll is $1,400 for a seven-day workweek (Monday to Sunday). This year, December 31 falls on Thursday.

c. The beginning balance of Office Supplies was $2,300. During the year, Betterton purchased office supplies for $3,000, and at December 31 the office supplies on hand totaled $1,000.

d. Betterton prepaid a two full years' insurance on July 1 of the current year, $6,000. Record insurance expense for the year ended December 31.

e. Betterton had earned $2,800 of unearned revenue.

f. Betterton had incurred (but not recorded) $200 of interest expense on a note payable. The interest will not be paid until February 28.

g. Betterton billed customers $3,000 for welding services performed.

Journalize the adjusting entry needed on December 31 for each situation. Use the letters to label the journal entries.

Learning Objective 3

E-F:3-24 Journalizing adjusting entries and posting to T-accounts

3. Unearned Revenue bal. $800 CR

The accounting records of Mackay Architects include the following selected, unadjusted balances at March 31: Accounts Receivable, $1,500; Office Supplies, $700; Prepaid Rent, $2,240; Equipment, $8,000; Accumulated Depreciation—Equipment, $0; Salaries Payable, $0; Unearned Revenue, $900; Service Revenue, $4,100; Salaries Expense, $800; Supplies Expense, $0; Rent Expense, $0; Depreciation Expense—Equipment, $0. The data developed for the March 31 adjusting entries are as follows:

a. Service revenue accrued, $700.

b. Unearned revenue that has been earned, $100.

c. Office Supplies on hand, $300.

d. Salaries owed to employees, $200.

e. One month of prepaid rent has expired, $560.

f. Depreciation on equipment, $120.

Requirements

1. Open a T-account for each account using the unadjusted balances given.

2. Journalize the adjusting entries using the letter and March 31 date in the date column.

3. Post the adjustments to the T-accounts, entering each adjustment by letter. Show each account's adjusted balance.

E-F:3-25 Journalizing adjusting entries and posting to T-accounts

Learning Objective 3

The unadjusted trial balance for All Mopped Up Company, a cleaning service, is as follows:

3. Office Supplies bal. $300 DR

ALL MOPPED UP COMPANY
Unadjusted Trial Balance
December 31, 2024

Account Title	Debit	Credit
Cash	$ 800	
Office Supplies	2,000	
Prepaid Insurance	600	
Equipment	30,000	
Accumulated Depreciation—Equipment		$ 2,000
Accounts Payable		2,400
Salaries Payable		
Unearned Revenue		700
Jane, Capital		15,300
Jane, Withdrawals	5,000	
Service Revenue		25,000
Salaries Expense	7,000	
Supplies Expense		
Depreciation Expense—Equipment		
Insurance Expense		
Total	$ 45,400	$ 45,400

During the 12 months ended December 31, 2024, All Mopped Up:

a. Used office supplies of $1,700.

b. Used prepaid insurance of $580.

c. Depreciated equipment, $500.

d. Accrued salaries expense of $310 that hasn't been paid yet.

e. Earned $400 of unearned revenue.

Requirements

1. Open a T-account for each account using the unadjusted balances.

2. Journalize the adjusting entries using the letter and December 31 date in the date column.

3. Post the adjustments to the T-accounts, entering each adjustment by letter. Show each account's adjusted balance.

Learning Objective 4

Adj. trial balance $46,210 total

Note: Exercise E-F:3-26 should be used only in conjunction with Exercise E-F:3-25.

E-F:3-26 Preparing an adjusted trial balance

Refer to the data in Exercise E-F:3-25, and prepare an adjusted trial balance.

Learning Objectives 3, 5

E-F:3-27 Identifying the impact of adjusting entries on the financial statements

Austin Acoustics recorded the following transactions during October:

a. Received $2,500 cash from customer for three months of service beginning October 1 and ending December 31. The company recorded a $2,500 debit to Cash and a $2,500 credit to Unearned Revenue.

b. Employees are paid $3,000 on Monday following the five-day workweek. October 31 is on Friday.

c. The company pays $440 on October 1 for its six-month auto insurance policy. The company recorded a $440 debit to Prepaid Insurance and a $440 credit to Cash.

d. The company purchased office furniture for $8,300 on January 2. The company recorded an $8,300 debit to Office Furniture and an $8,300 credit to Accounts Payable. Annual depreciation for the furniture is $1,000.

e. The company began October with $50 of office supplies on hand. On October 10, the company purchased office supplies on account of $100. The company recorded a $100 debit to Office Supplies and a $100 credit to Accounts Payable. The company used $120 of office supplies during October.

f. The company received its electric bill on October 31 for $325 but did not pay it until November 10.

g. The company paid November's rent of $2,500 on October 30. On October 30, the company recorded a $2,500 debit to Rent Expense and a $2,500 credit to Cash.

Indicate if an adjusting entry is needed for each item on October 31 for the month of October. Assuming the adjusting entry is not made, indicate which specific category or categories of accounts on the financial statements are misstated and if they are overstated or understated. Use the following table as a guide. Item *a* is completed as an example:

Item	Adjusting Entry Needed?	Specific Category of Accounts on the Balance Sheet	Over / Understated	Specific Category of Accounts on the Income Statement	Over / Understated
(a)	Yes	Liability Equity	Over Under	Revenue	Under

Learning Objectives 3, 5

E-F:3-28 Journalizing adjusting entries and analyzing their effect on the income statement

The following data at July 31, 2024, are given for RCO:

a. Depreciation, $600.

b. Prepaid rent expires, $200.

c. Interest expense accrued, $700.

d. Employee salaries owed for Monday through Thursday of a five-day workweek; weekly payroll, $8,000.

e. Unearned revenue earned, $1,000.

f. Office supplies used, $150.

Requirements

1. Journalize the adjusting entries needed on July 31, 2024.

2. Suppose the adjustments made in Requirement 1 were not made. Compute the overall overstatement or understatement of net income as a result of the omission of these adjustments.

E-F:3-29 Using the worksheet to record the adjusting journal entries

The worksheet of Best Jobs Employment Service follows but is incomplete.

Learning Objective 6

1. Adjustments $3,700 total

	A	B	C	D	E	F	G
1		BEST JOBS EMPLOYMENT SERVICE					
2		Worksheet					
3		April 30, 2024					
4							
5	Account Names	Unadjusted Trial Balance		Adjustments		Adjusted Trial Balance	
6		Debit	Credit	Debit	Credit	Debit	Credit
7	Cash	$ 1,100					
8	Accounts Receivable	4,100					
9	Office Supplies	1,200					
10	Equipment	32,700					
11	Accumulated Depreciation—Equipment		$ 13,900				
12	Salaries Payable						
13	Kubota, Capital		25,200				
14	Kubota, Withdrawals	5,300					
15	Service Revenue		9,000				
16	Salaries Expense	2,200					
17	Rent Expense	1,500					
18	Depreciation Expense—Equipment						
19	Supplies Expense						
20	Total	$ 48,100	$ 48,100				
21							

The following data at April 30, 2024, are given for Best Jobs Employment Service:

a. Service revenue accrued, $700.

b. Office supplies used, $300.

c. Depreciation on equipment, $1,300.

d. Salaries owed to employees, $1,400.

Requirements

1. Calculate and enter the adjustment amounts directly in the Adjustments columns. Use letters *a* through *d* to label the four adjustments.

2. Calculate and enter the adjusted account balances in the Adjusted Trial Balance columns.

3. Prepare each adjusting journal entry calculated in Requirement 1. Date the entries, and include explanations.

Learning Objective 6   **E-F:3-30 Using the worksheet to prepare the adjusted trial balance**

The worksheet of Macey's Landscaping Services follows but is incomplete.

Adj. trial balance $273,700 total

MACEY'S LANDSCAPING SERVICES
Worksheet
December 31, 2024

Account Names	Unadjusted Trial Balance Debit	Unadjusted Trial Balance Credit	Adjustments Debit	Adjustments Credit	Adjusted Trial Balance Debit	Adjusted Trial Balance Credit
Cash	$ 27,400					
Accounts Receivable	6,700		(h) $ 3,500			
Office Supplies	500			(b) $ 350		
Prepaid Rent	2,300			(a) 1,150		
Equipment	50,000					
Accumulated Depreciation—Equipment				(c) 1,300		
Trucks	114,000					
Accumulated Depreciation—Trucks				(d) 1,900		
Accounts Payable		$ 3,800				
Utilities Payable		300				
Salaries Payable				(f) 7,200		
Interest Payable				(g) 300		
Unearned Revenue		4,500	(e) 3,200			
Notes Payable		25,000				
Macey, Capital		141,900				
Macey, Withdrawals	21,000					
Service Revenue		84,000		(e, h) 6,700		
Rent Expense	9,200		(a) 1,150			
Salaries Expense	23,800		(f) 7,200			
Supplies Expense			(b) 350			
Utilities Expense	4,600					
Depreciation Expense—Equipment			(c) 1,300			
Depreciation Expense—Trucks			(d) 1,900			
Interest Expense			(g) 300			
Total	$ 259,500	$ 259,500	$ 18,900	$ 18,900		

Requirements

1. Calculate and enter the adjusted account balances in the Adjusted Trial Balance columns.
2. Describe each adjusting entry. For example, a. Prepaid rent expires, $1,150.

E-F:3A-31 Understanding the alternative treatment of prepaid expenses

At the beginning of the year, office supplies of $1,200 were on hand. During the year, Tempo Air Conditioning Service paid $4,000 for more office supplies. At the end of the year, Tempo has $800 of office supplies on hand.

Requirements

1. Record the adjusting entry assuming that Tempo records the purchase of office supplies by initially debiting an asset account. Post the adjusting entry to the Office Supplies and Supplies Expense T-accounts. Make sure to include the beginning balance and purchase of office supplies in the Office Supplies T-account.
2. Record the adjusting entry assuming that Tempo records the purchase of office supplies by initially debiting an expense account. Post the adjusting entry to the Office Supplies and Supplies Expense T-accounts. Make sure to include the beginning balance in the Office Supplies T-account and the purchase of office supplies in the Supplies Expense T-account.
3. Compare the ending balances of the T-accounts under both approaches. Are they the same?

E-F:3A-32 Understanding the alternative treatment of unearned revenues

At the beginning of the year, Modish Advertising owed customers $2,100 for unearned revenue collected in advance. During the year, Modish received advance cash receipts of $6,100 and earned $20,000 of service revenue (exclusive of any amount earned from advance payments). At year-end, the liability for unearned revenue is $3,100 and unadjusted service revenue is $20,000.

Requirements

1. Record the adjusting entry assuming that Modish records the cash receipt of unearned revenue by initially crediting a liability account. Post the adjusting entry to the Unearned Revenue and Service Revenue T-accounts. Make sure to include the beginning balance and additional unearned revenue in the Unearned Revenue T-account.
2. Record the adjusting entry assuming that Modish records the cash receipt of unearned revenue by initially crediting a revenue account. Post the adjusting entry to the Unearned Revenue and Service Revenue T-accounts. Make sure to include the beginning balance in the Unearned Revenue T-account and the additional unearned revenue in the Service Revenue T-account.
3. Compare the ending balances of the T-accounts under both approaches. Are they the same?

> Problems Group A

P-F:3-33A Journalizing adjusting entries and subsequent journal entries

Laughter Landscaping has collected the following data for the December 31 adjusting entries:

a. Each Friday, Laughter pays employees for the current week's work. The amount of the weekly payroll is $8,000 for a five-day workweek. This year, December 31 falls on a Tuesday. Laughter will pay its employees on January 3.

b. On January 1 of the current year, Laughter purchases an insurance policy that covers two years, $8,000.

c. The beginning balance of Office Supplies was $4,300. During the year, Laughter purchased office supplies for $5,600, and at December 31 the office supplies on hand total $1,500.

d. During December, Laughter designed a landscape plan and the client prepaid $6,500. Laughter recorded this amount as Unearned Revenue. The job will take several months to complete, and Laughter estimates that the company has earned 40% of the total revenue during the current year.

e. At December 31, Laughter had earned $3,000 for landscape services completed for Turnkey Appliances. Turnkey has stated that it will pay Laughter on January 10.

f. Depreciation for the current year includes Equipment, $3,000; and Trucks, $2,200.

g. Laughter has incurred $250 of interest expense on a $550 interest payment due on January 15.

Requirements

1. Journalize the adjusting entry needed on December 31 for each of the previous items affecting Laughter Landscaping. Assume Laughter records adjusting entries only at the end of the year.

2. Journalize the subsequent journal entries for adjusting entries a, d, and g.

Learning Objectives 3, 5 **P-F:3-34A Journalizing adjusting entries and identifying the impact on financial statements**

Griffin Fishing Charters has collected the following data for the December 31 adjusting entries:

a. The company received its electric bill on December 31 for $375 but will not pay it until January 5. (Use the Utilities Payable account.)

b. Griffin purchased a three-month boat insurance policy on November 1 for $1,200. Griffin recorded a debit to Prepaid Insurance.

c. As of December 31, Griffin had earned $3,000 of charter revenue that has not been recorded or received.

d. Griffin's fishing boat was purchased on January 1 at a cost of $33,500. Griffin expects to use the boat for 10 years and that it will have a residual value of $3,500. Determine annual depreciation assuming the straight-line depreciation method is used.

e. On October 1, Griffin received $9,000 prepayment for a deep-sea fishing charter to take place in December. As of December 31, Griffin has completed the charter.

Requirements

1. Journalize the adjusting entries needed on December 31 for Griffin Fishing Charters. Assume Griffin records adjusting entries only at the end of the year.

2. If Griffin had not recorded the adjusting entries, indicate which specific category of accounts on the financial statements would be misstated and if the misstatement is overstated or understated. Use the following table as a guide.

Adjusting Entry	Specific Category of Accounts on the Balance Sheet	Over / Understated	Specific Category of Accounts on the Income Statement	Over / Understated

P-F:3-35A Journalizing and posting adjustments to the T-accounts and preparing an adjusted trial balance

The unadjusted trial balance of Anniston Air Purification System at December 31, 2024, and the data needed for the adjustments follow.

Learning Objectives 3, 4

3. Adjusted trial balance total $75,600

ANNISTON AIR PURIFICATION SYSTEM
Unadjusted Trial Balance
December 31, 2024

Account Title	Debit	Credit
Cash	$ 7,600	
Accounts Receivable	19,700	
Prepaid Rent	2,900	
Office Supplies	1,800	
Equipment	22,000	
Accumulated Depreciation—Equipment		$ 3,900
Accounts Payable		2,900
Salaries Payable		
Unearned Revenue		3,100
Anniston, Capital		43,800
Anniston, Withdrawals	9,900	
Service Revenue		15,300
Salaries Expense	3,300	
Rent Expense		
Depreciation Expense—Equipment		
Advertising Expense	1,800	
Supplies Expense		
Total	$ 69,000	$ 69,000

Adjustment data at December 31 follow:

a. On December 15, Anniston contracted to perform services for a client receiving $3,100 in advance. Anniston recorded this receipt of cash as Unearned Revenue. As of December 31, Anniston has completed $2,100 of the services.

b. Anniston prepaid two months of rent on December 1. (Assume the Prepaid Rent balance as shown on the unadjusted trial balance represents the two months of rent prepaid on December 1.)

c. Anniston used $750 of office supplies.

d. Depreciation for the equipment is $850.

e. Anniston received a bill for December's online advertising, $1,100. Anniston will not pay the bill until January. (Use Accounts Payable.)

f. Anniston pays its employees on Monday for the previous week's wages. Its employees earn $5,250 for a five-day workweek. December 31 falls on Tuesday this year.

g. On October 1, Anniston agreed to provide a four-month air system check (beginning October 1) for a customer for $3,400. Anniston has completed the system check every month, but payment has not yet been received and no entries have been made.

Requirements

1. Journalize the adjusting entries on December 31.
2. Using the unadjusted trial balance, open the T-accounts with the unadjusted balances. Post the adjusting entries to the T-accounts.
3. Prepare the adjusted trial balance.
4. How will Anniston Air Purification System use the adjusted trial balance?

Learning Objectives 3, 4

3. Adjusted trial balance $572,040 total

P-F:3-36A Journalizing and posting adjustments to the four-column accounts and preparing an adjusted trial balance

The unadjusted trial balance of Guthrie Inn Company at December 31, 2024, and the data needed for the adjustments follow.

GUTHRIE INN COMPANY
Unadjusted Trial Balance
December 31, 2024

Account Title	Debit	Credit
Cash	$ 13,500	
Accounts Receivable	15,100	
Prepaid Insurance	4,600	
Office Supplies	800	
Building	530,000	
Accumulated Depreciation—Building		$ 260,000
Accounts Payable		1,710
Salaries Payable		
Unearned Revenue		3,600
Guthrie, Capital		288,950
Guthrie, Withdrawals	2,340	
Service Revenue		15,500
Salaries Expense	2,800	
Insurance Expense		
Depreciation Expense—Building		
Advertising Expense	620	
Supplies Expense		
Total	$ 569,760	$ 569,760

Adjustment data at December 31 follow:

a. As of December 31, Guthrie had $700 of Prepaid Insurance remaining.
b. At the end of the month, Guthrie had $500 of office supplies remaining.
c. Depreciation on the building is $1,200.
d. Guthrie pays its employees weekly on Friday. Its employees earn $2,700 for a five-day workweek. December 31 falls on Tuesday this year.
e. On November 20, Guthrie contracted to perform services for a client, receiving $3,600 in advance. Guthrie recorded this receipt of cash as Unearned Revenue. As of December 31, Guthrie has $1,600 still unearned.

Requirements

1. Journalize the adjusting entries on December 31.
2. Using the unadjusted trial balance, open the accounts (use a four-column ledger) with the unadjusted balances. Post the adjusting entries to the ledger accounts.
3. Prepare the adjusted trial balance.
4. Assuming the adjusted trial balance has total debits equal to total credits, does this mean that the adjusting entries have been recorded correctly? Explain.

P-F:3-37A Using the worksheet to record the adjusting journal entries Learning Objective 6

Greavy Theater Production Company's partially completed worksheet as of December 31, 2024, follows.

	A	B	C	D	E	F	G
1	GREAVY THEATER PRODUCTION COMPANY						
2	Worksheet						
3	December 31, 2024						
4							
5	Account Names	Unadjusted Trial Balance		Adjustments		Adjusted Trial Balance	
6		Debit	Credit	Debit	Credit	Debit	Credit
7	Cash	$ 4,300					
8	Accounts Receivable	5,900					
9	Office Supplies	1,900					
10	Prepaid Insurance	4,550					
11	Equipment	30,000					
12	Accumulated Depreciation—Equipment		$ 7,600				
13	Accounts Payable		3,600				
14	Salaries Payable						
15	Greavy, Capital		21,950				
16	Greavy, Withdrawals	30,500					
17	Service Revenue		77,000				
18	Depreciation Expense—Equipment						
19	Supplies Expense						
20	Utilities Expense	5,500					
21	Salaries Expense	27,500					
22	Insurance Expense						
23	Total	$ 110,150	$ 110,150				
24							

Adjustment data at December 31 follow:

a. As of December 31, Greavy had performed $500 of service revenue but has not yet billed customers.

b. At the end of the month, Greavy had $700 of office supplies remaining.

c. Prepaid Insurance of $3,900 remained.

d. Depreciation expense, $4,000.

e. Accrued salaries expense of $200 that hasn't been paid yet.

Requirements

1. Complete the worksheet. Use letters *a* through *e* to label the five adjustments.
2. Journalize the adjusting entries.

Learning Objectives 3, 7 Appendix 3A

P-F:3A-38A Understanding the alternative treatment of prepaid expenses and unearned revenues

Rapid Way Pack'n Mail completed the following transactions during 2024:

Nov. 1	Paid $9,600 store rent covering the six-month period ending April 30, 2025.
Nov. 1	Paid $6,000 insurance covering the five-month period ending March 31, 2025.
Dec. 1	Collected $9,000 cash in advance from customers. The service revenue will be earned $1,800 monthly over the five-month period ending April 30, 2025.
Dec. 1	Collected $7,200 cash in advance from customers. The service revenue will be earned $2,400 monthly over the three-month period ending February 28, 2025.

Requirements

1. Journalize the transactions assuming that Rapid Way debits an asset account for prepaid expenses and credits a liability account for unearned revenues.
2. Journalize the related adjusting entries at December 31, 2024.
3. Post the journal and adjusting entries to the T-accounts and show their balances at December 31, 2024. (Ignore the Cash account.)
4. Repeat Requirements 1–3. This time, debit an expense account for prepaid expenses and credit a revenue account for unearned revenues.
5. Compare the account balances in Requirements 3 and 4. They should be equal.

> Problems Group B

Learning Objective 3

P-F:3-39B Journalizing adjusting entries and subsequent journal entries

Lopez Landscaping has the following data for the December 31 adjusting entries:

a. Each Friday, Lopez pays employees for the current week's work. The amount of the weekly payroll is $6,500 for a five-day workweek. This year, December 31 falls on a Wednesday. Lopez will pay its employees on January 2.

b. On January 1 of the current year, Lopez purchases an insurance policy that covers two years, $7,500.

c. The beginning balance of Office Supplies was $3,700. During the year, Lopez purchased office supplies for $5,800, and at December 31 the office supplies on hand total $3,000.

d. During December, Lopez designed a landscape plan and the client prepaid $6,000. Lopez recorded this amount as Unearned Revenue. The job will take several months to complete, and Lopez estimates that the company has earned 70% of the total revenue during the current year.

e. At December 31, Lopez had earned $7,500 for landscape services completed for Tomball Appliances. Tomball has stated that it will pay Lopez on January 10.

f. Depreciation for the current year includes Equipment, $3,800; and Trucks, $1,400.

g. Lopez has incurred $250 of interest expense on a $350 interest payment due on January 15.

Requirements

1. Journalize the adjusting entry needed on December 31 for each of the previous items affecting Lopez Landscaping. Assume Lopez records adjusting entries only at the end of the year.
2. Journalize the subsequent journal entries for adjusting entries *a*, *d*, and *g*.

P-F:3-40B Journalizing adjusting entries and identifying the impact on financial statements

Learning Objectives 3, 5

Harrison Fishing Charters has collected the following data for the December 31 adjusting entries:

a. The company received its electric bill on December 31 for $375 but will not pay it until January 5. (Use the Utilities Payable account.)

b. Harrison purchased a three-month boat insurance policy on November 1 for $3,600. Harrison recorded a debit to Prepaid Insurance.

c. As of December 31, Harrison had earned $1,000 of charter revenue that has not been recorded or received.

d. Harrison's fishing boat was purchased on January 1 at a cost of $56,500. Harrison expects to use the boat for five years and that it will have a residual value of $6,500. Determine annual depreciation assuming the straight-line depreciation method is used.

e. On October 1, Harrison received $5,000 prepayment for a deep-sea fishing charter to take place in December. As of December 31, Harrison has completed the charter.

Requirements

1. Journalize the adjusting entries needed on December 31 for Harrison Fishing Charters. Assume Harrison records adjusting entries only at the end of the year.
2. If Harrison had not recorded the adjusting entries, indicate which specific category of accounts on the financial statements would be misstated and if the misstatement is overstated or understated. Use the following table as a guide:

Adjusting Entry	Specific Category of Accounts on the Balance Sheet	Over / Understated	Specific Category of Accounts on the Income Statement	Over / Understated

Learning Objectives 3, 4

3. Adjusted trial balance total $69,800

P-F:3-41B Journalizing and posting adjustments to the T-accounts and preparing an adjusted trial balance

The unadjusted trial balance of Avery Air Purification System at December 31, 2024, and the data needed for the adjustments follow.

AVERY AIR PURIFICATION SYSTEM
Unadjusted Trial Balance
December 31, 2024

Account Title	Debit	Credit
Cash	$ 7,100	
Accounts Receivable	19,100	
Prepaid Rent	2,400	
Office Supplies	1,400	
Equipment	20,000	
Accumulated Depreciation—Equipment		$ 3,800
Accounts Payable		3,500
Salaries Payable		
Unearned Revenue		2,700
Avery, Capital		39,300
Avery, Withdrawals	9,400	
Service Revenue		15,900
Salaries Expense	3,900	
Rent Expense		
Depreciation Expense—Equipment		
Advertising Expense	1,900	
Supplies Expense		
Total	$ 65,200	$ 65,200

Adjustment data at December 31 follow:

a. On December 15, Avery contracted to perform services for a client, receiving $2,700 in advance. Avery recorded this receipt of cash as Unearned Revenue. As of December 31, Avery has completed $2,100 of the services.

b. Avery prepaid two months of rent on December 1. (Assume the Prepaid Rent balance as shown on the unadjusted trial balance represents the two months of rent prepaid on December 1.)

c. Avery used $750 of office supplies during the month.

d. Depreciation for the equipment is $800.

e. Avery received a bill for December's online advertising, $500. Avery will not pay the bill until January. (Use Accounts Payable.)

f. Avery pays its employees weekly on Monday for the previous week's wages. Its employees earn $3,000 for a five-day workweek. December 31 falls on Tuesday this year.

g. On October 1, Avery agreed to provide a four-month air system check (beginning October 1) for a customer for $2,800. Avery has completed the system check every month, but payment has not yet been received and no entries have been made.

Requirements

1. Journalize the adjusting entries on December 31.
2. Using the unadjusted trial balance, open the T-accounts with the unadjusted balances. Post the adjusting entries to the T-accounts.
3. Prepare the adjusted trial balance.
4. How will Avery Air Purification System use the adjusted trial balance?

P-F:3-42B Journalizing and posting adjustments to the four-column accounts and preparing an adjusted trial balance

Learning Objectives 3, 4

The unadjusted trial balance of Midway Inn Company at December 31, 2024, and the data needed for the adjustments follow.

3. Adjusted trial balance total $557,750

MIDWAY INN COMPANY
Unadjusted Trial Balance
December 31, 2024

Account Title	Debit	Credit
Cash	$ 14,500	
Accounts Receivable	15,100	
Prepaid Insurance	1,400	
Office Supplies	700	
Building	518,000	
Accumulated Depreciation—Building		$ 310,000
Accounts Payable		4,210
Salaries Payable		
Unearned Revenue		1,600
Midway, Capital		222,160
Midway, Withdrawals	1,890	
Service Revenue		16,900
Salaries Expense	2,600	
Insurance Expense		
Depreciation Expense—Building		
Advertising Expense	680	
Supplies Expense		
Total	$ 554,870	$ 554,870

Adjustment data at December 31 follow:

a. As of December 31, Midway Inn had $800 of Prepaid Insurance remaining.
b. At the end of the month, Midway Inn had $500 of office supplies remaining.
c. Depreciation on the building is $2,100.
d. Midway Inn pays its employees on Friday for the weekly salaries. Its employees earn $1,950 for a five-day workweek. December 31 falls on Tuesday this year.
e. On November 20, Midway Inn contracted to perform services for a client, receiving $1,600 in advance. Midway Inn recorded this receipt of cash as Unearned Revenue. As of December 31, Midway Inn has $1,400 still unearned.

Requirements

1. Journalize the adjusting entries on December 31.
2. Using the unadjusted trial balance, open the accounts (use a four-column ledger) with the unadjusted balances. Post the adjusting entries to the ledger accounts.
3. Prepare the adjusted trial balance.
4. Assuming the adjusted trial balance has total debits equal to total credits, does this mean that the adjusting entries have been recorded correctly? Explain.

Learning Objective 6

P-F:3-43B Using the worksheet to record the adjusting journal entries

Galaxy Theater Production Company's partially completed worksheet as of December 31, 2024, follows.

GALAXY THEATER PRODUCTION COMPANY
Worksheet
December 31, 2024

Account Names	Unadjusted Trial Balance Debit	Unadjusted Trial Balance Credit	Adjustments Debit	Adjustments Credit	Adjusted Trial Balance Debit	Adjusted Trial Balance Credit
Cash	$ 3,600					
Accounts Receivable	5,700					
Office Supplies	1,500					
Prepaid Insurance	900					
Equipment	23,000					
Accumulated Depreciation—Equipment		$ 8,500				
Accounts Payable		4,600				
Salaries Payable						
Galaxy, Capital		9,900				
Galaxy, Withdrawals	26,000					
Service Revenue		72,000				
Depreciation Expense—Equipment						
Supplies Expense						
Utilities Expense	4,300					
Salaries Expense	30,000					
Insurance Expense						
Total	$ 95,000	$ 95,000				

Adjustment data at December 31 follow:

a. As of December 31, Galaxy had performed $900 of service revenue but has not yet billed customers.
b. At the end of the month, Galaxy had $500 of office supplies remaining.
c. Prepaid Insurance of $600 remained.
d. Depreciation expense, $4,200.
e. Accrued salaries expense of $150 that hasn't been paid yet.

Requirements

1. Complete the worksheet. Use letters *a* through *e* to label the five adjustments.
2. Journalize the adjusting entries.

P-F:3A-44B Understanding the alternative treatment of prepaid expenses and unearned revenues

Learning Objectives 3, 7
Appendix 3A

Sent It Pack'n Mail completed the following transactions during 2024:

Nov. 1		Paid $6,000 store rent covering the four-month period ending February 28, 2025.
	1	Paid $7,800 insurance covering the six-month period ending April 30, 2025.
Dec. 1		Collected $12,000 cash in advance from customers. The service revenue will be earned $2,400 monthly over the five-month period ending April 30, 2025.
	1	Collected $7,500 cash in advance from customers. The service revenue will be earned $1,500 monthly over the five-month period ending April 30, 2025.

Requirements

1. Journalize the transactions assuming that Sent It Pack'n Mail debits an asset account for prepaid expenses and credits a liability account for unearned revenues.
2. Journalize the related adjusting entries at December 31, 2024.
3. Post the journal and adjusting entries to the T-accounts and show their balances at December 31, 2024. (Ignore the Cash account.)
4. Repeat Requirements 1–3. This time debit an expense account for prepaid expenses and credit a revenue account for unearned revenues.
5. Compare the account balances in Requirements 3 and 4. They should be equal.

CRITICAL THINKING

> Using Excel

Download Excel problems for this chapter online in MyLab Accounting or at **http://www.pearsonhighered.com/Horngren**.

> Continuing Problem

P-F:3-45 Preparing adjusting entries and preparing an adjusted trial balance

This problem continues the Canyon Canoe Company situation from Chapter F:2. You will need to use the unadjusted trial balance and posted T-accounts that you prepared in Chapter F:2.

At December 31, the business gathers the following information for the adjusting entries:
a. Office supplies on hand, $165.
b. Rent of one month has been used. (Hint: See Dec. 1 transaction from Chapter F:2.)
c. Determine the depreciation on the building using straight-line depreciation. Assume the useful life of the building is five years and the residual value is $5,000. (Hint: The building was purchased on December 1.)
d. $400 of unearned revenue has now been earned.

e. The employee who has been working the rental booth has earned $1,250 in wages that will be paid January 15, 2025.

f. Canyon Canoes has earned $1,850 of canoe rental revenue that has not been recorded or received.

g. Determine the depreciation on the canoes purchased on November 3 using straight-line depreciation. Assume the useful life of the canoes is four years and the residual value is $0.

h. Determine the depreciation on the canoes purchased on December 2 using straight-line depreciation. Assume the useful life of the canoes is four years and the residual value is $0.

i. Interest expense accrued on the notes payable, $50.

Requirements

1. Journalize and post the adjusting entries using the T-accounts that you completed in Chapter F:2. In the T-accounts, denote each adjusting amount as *Adj.* and an account balance as *Balance*.

2. Prepare an adjusted trial balance as of December 31, 2024.

> Practice Set

P-F:3-46 Preparing adjusting entries and preparing an adjusted trial balance

This problem continues the Crystal Clear Cleaning situation from Chapter F:2. Start from the unadjusted trial balance that Crystal Clear Cleaning prepared at November 30, 2024:

CRYSTAL CLEAR CLEANING
Unadjusted Trial Balance
November 30, 2024

Account Title	Debit	Credit
Cash	$51,650	
Accounts Receivable	4,000	
Cleaning Supplies	320	
Prepaid Rent	4,000	
Prepaid Insurance	4,800	
Equipment	5,400	
Truck	3,000	
Accounts Payable		$ 1,245
Unearned Revenue		15,000
Notes Payable		36,000
Hideaway, Capital		18,000
Hideaway, Withdrawals	1,400	
Service Revenue		5,100
Salaries Expense	400	
Advertising Expense	200	
Utilities Expense	175	
Total	$75,345	$75,345

Consider the following adjustment data:
a. Cleaning supplies on hand at the end of November were $50.
b. One month's combined depreciation on all depreciable assets was estimated to be $150.
c. One month's interest expense is $59.

Requirements

1. Using the data provided from the trial balance, the previous adjustment information, and the information from Chapter F:2, prepare all required adjusting journal entries at November 30.
2. Prepare an adjusted trial balance as of November 30 for Crystal Clear Cleaning.

> Tying It All Together Case F:3-1

Before you begin this assignment, review the Tying It All Together feature in the chapter.

iHeartMedia, Inc. in their annual report for the year ending December 31, 2018, state that the plant assets reported on its balance sheet includes the following:

Plant Asset	Useful Life
Buildings and improvements	10 to 39 years
Structures	3 to 20 years
Towers, transmitters, and studio equipment	5 to 20 years
Furniture and other equipment	2 to 20 years

Depreciation is computed using the straight-line method.

Requirements

1. Suppose iHeartMedia, Inc. purchases a new advertising structure for $100,000 on August 1. The residual value of the structure is $4,000 and the useful life is 10 years. How would iHeartMedia record the depreciation expense on December 31 in the first year of use? What about the second year of use?
2. What would be the book value of the structure at the end of the first year? What would be the book value of the structure at the end of the second year?
3. What would be the impact on iHeartMedia, Inc. financial statements if they failed to record the adjusting entry related to the structure?

> Decision Case F:3-1

One year ago, Tyler Stasney founded Swift Classified Ads. Stasney remembers that you took an accounting course while in college and comes to you for advice. He wishes to know how much net income his business earned during the past year in order to decide whether to keep the company going. His accounting records consist of the T-accounts from his ledger, which were prepared by an accountant who moved to another city. The ledger at December 31 follows. The accounts have *not* been adjusted.

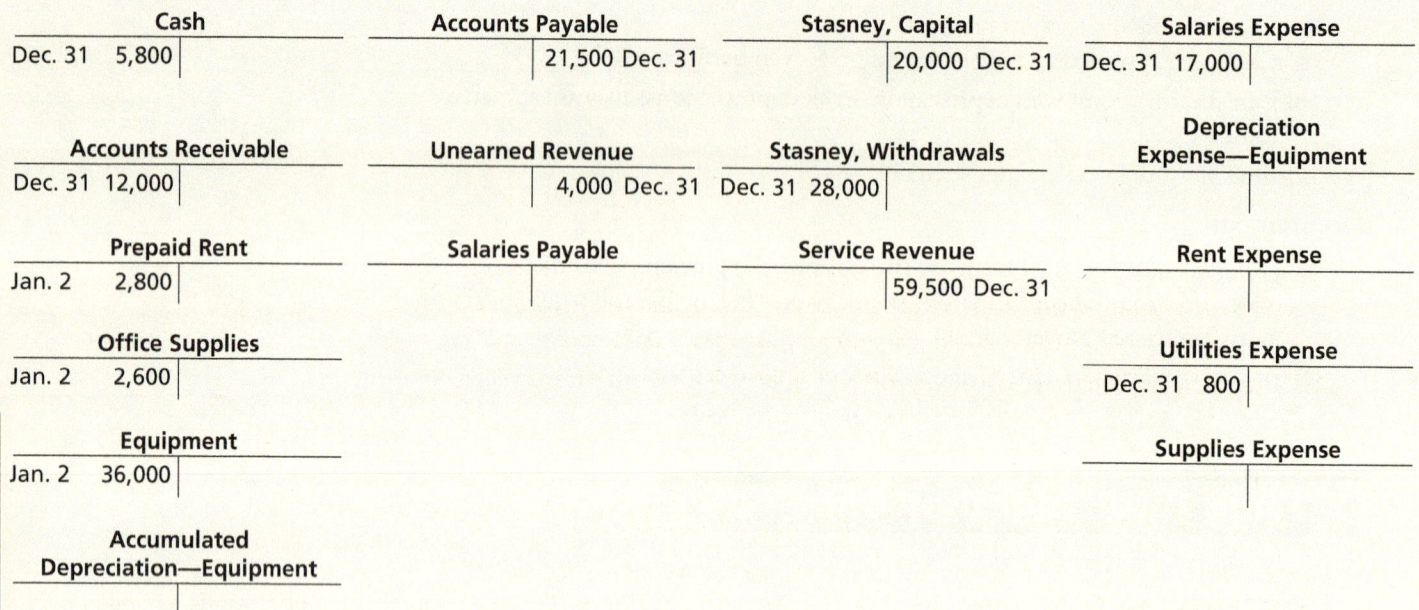

Stasney indicates that at year-end, customers owe the business $1,600 for accrued service revenue. These revenues have not been recorded. During the year, Swift Classified Ads collected $4,000 service revenue in advance from customers, but the business earned only $900 of that amount. Rent expense for the year was $2,400, and the business used up $1,700 of the supplies. Swift determines that depreciation on its equipment was $5,000 for the year. At December 31, the business owes an employee $1,200 accrued salary.

Help Swift Classified Ads compute its net income for the year. Advise Stasney whether to continue operating Swift Classified Ads.

> Ethical Issue F:3-1

The net income of Steinbach & Sons, a landscaping company, decreased sharply during 2024. Mort Steinbach, owner and manager of the company, anticipates the need for a bank loan in 2025. Late in 2024, Steinbach instructs the company's accountant to record $2,000 service revenue for landscape services for the Steinbach family, even though the services will not be performed until January 2025. Steinbach also tells the accountant *not* to make the following December 31, 2024, adjusting entries:

Salaries owed to employees	$ 900
Prepaid insurance that has expired	400

Requirements

1. Compute the overall effects of these transactions on the company's reported net income for 2024.
2. Why is Steinbach taking this action? Is his action ethical? Give your reason, identifying the parties helped and the parties harmed by Steinbach's action.
3. As a personal friend, what advice would you give the accountant?

> Fraud Case F:3-1

XM, Ltd. was a small engineering firm that built high-tech robotic devices for electronics manufacturers. One very complex device was partially completed at the end of 2024. Barb McLauren, owner and head engineer, knew the experimental technology was a failure and XM would not be able to complete the $20,000,000 contract next year. However, the business was getting ready to be sold in January. She told the controller that the device was 80% complete at year-end and on track for successful completion the following spring; the controller accrued 80% of the contract revenue at December 31, 2024. McLauren sold the company in January 2025 and retired. By mid-year, it became apparent that XM would not be able to complete the project successfully and the new owner would never recoup his investment.

Requirements

1. For complex, high-tech contracts, how does a company determine the percentage of completion and the amount of revenue to accrue?
2. What action do you think was taken by XM in 2025 with regard to the revenue that had been accrued the previous year?

> Financial Statement Case F:3-1

Target Corporation—like all other businesses—makes adjusting entries at year-end in order to measure assets, liabilities, revenues, and expenses properly. Examine Target Corporation's balance sheet and income statement in its Fiscal 2018 Annual Report. Visit **http://www.pearsonhighered.com/Horngren** to view a link to Target Corporation's annual report.

Requirements

1. Which asset accounts might Target record adjusting entries for?
2. Which liability accounts might Target record adjusting entries for?
3. Review Note 11 (Property and Equipment) in the Notes to Consolidated Financial Statements. How are property, plant, and equipment carried on the balance sheet? How is depreciation of these assets calculated? What is the range of useful lives used when depreciating these assets?

> Communication Activity F:3-1

In 75 words or fewer, explain adjusting journal entries.

> Quick Check Answers

1. a **2.** a **3.** b **4.** c **5.** a **6.** a **7.** b **8.** d **9.** c **10A.** b

Completing the Accounting Cycle

4

It's the End of the Year, Now What?

The Bear Paw Inn just celebrated its one-year anniversary. Christina Merthieu, owner, is excited that she has one year of owning a successful business. Although her previous job of working as a resort manager has helped her in dealing with customers, she has had to learn a lot about the accounting side of the business. Christina attributes her first-year success to always offering exceptional quality and personal service to her customers. In addition, Christina found a great accountant who has been helping her with the books.

From the beginning, Christina relied on her accountant to provide advice about recording transactions throughout the year. Now that the first year of business has been completed, she is ready to perform the final accounting tasks of the year. The business's accountant has told her that she can now prepare financial statements to help her evaluate the inn's profit for the year and its financial position. Bear Paw Inn will use those financial statements to assess the business's performance over the past year. The business is also ready to start the next year of business, and in order to do this, Christina must get the books ready for next year by recording closing entries.

What Happens at Year-End?

As we saw with Christina and the Bear Paw Inn, businesses have special tasks that have to be completed at the end of the accounting cycle. These tasks help the business in evaluating the past year's operations and also prepare the business to start a new year. For example, **Hyatt Hotels Corporation** must prepare annual financial statements that report on the business's profit or loss for the year and its financial position at the end of the year. In addition, Hyatt Hotels must prepare its books for next year—a process that is called *closing the books*, which consists of journalizing closing entries and updating the equity accounts for the year. These final tasks in the accounting cycle are what you learn about in this chapter.

Chapter 4 Learning Objectives

1. Prepare the financial statements including the classified balance sheet
2. Use the worksheet to prepare financial statements
3. Explain the purpose of, journalize, and post closing entries
4. Prepare the post-closing trial balance
5. Describe the accounting cycle
6. Use the current ratio to evaluate business performance
7. Explain the purpose of, journalize, and post reversing entries (Appendix 4A)

In Chapter F:3, our fictitious company, Smart Touch Learning, had completed the adjusting entries necessary to properly measure net income on the income statement and assets and liabilities on the balance sheet. Now that its accounts are up to date, Smart Touch Learning is ready to take the next step in the accounting cycle—preparing the financial statements. In this chapter, you review the financial statements that you have already learned about and learn how to prepare a more complete version of the balance sheet. In addition, you complete the accounting cycle by learning how to close the books.

HOW DO WE PREPARE FINANCIAL STATEMENTS?

Learning Objective 1
Prepare the financial statements including the classified balance sheet

The financial statements of Smart Touch Learning are prepared from the adjusted trial balance, which you learned in Chapter F:3. Exhibit F:4-1 shows the adjusted trial balance for Smart Touch Learning. In the right margin of the exhibit, we see how the accounts are distributed to the financial statements.

As always, the financial statements should be prepared in the following order:

IFRS
Following IFRS, companies must present a statement of profit or loss (income statement), statement of financial position (balance sheet), statement of changes in equity (similar to statement of owner's equity), and statement of cash flows—the same as U.S. companies. Yet the statements may look quite different. Revenue may be called *Turnover*, and Net Income may be called *Profit*. On the balance sheet, assets and liabilities are presented in a different order. Cash is often one of the last assets listed.

1. **Income statement**—reports revenues and expenses and calculates net income or net loss for the time period.
2. **Statement of owner's equity**—shows how capital changed during the period due to owner contributions, net income (or net loss), and owner withdrawals.
3. **Balance sheet**—reports assets, liabilities, and owner's equity as of the last day of the period.

Exhibit F:4-1 | Adjusted Trial Balance

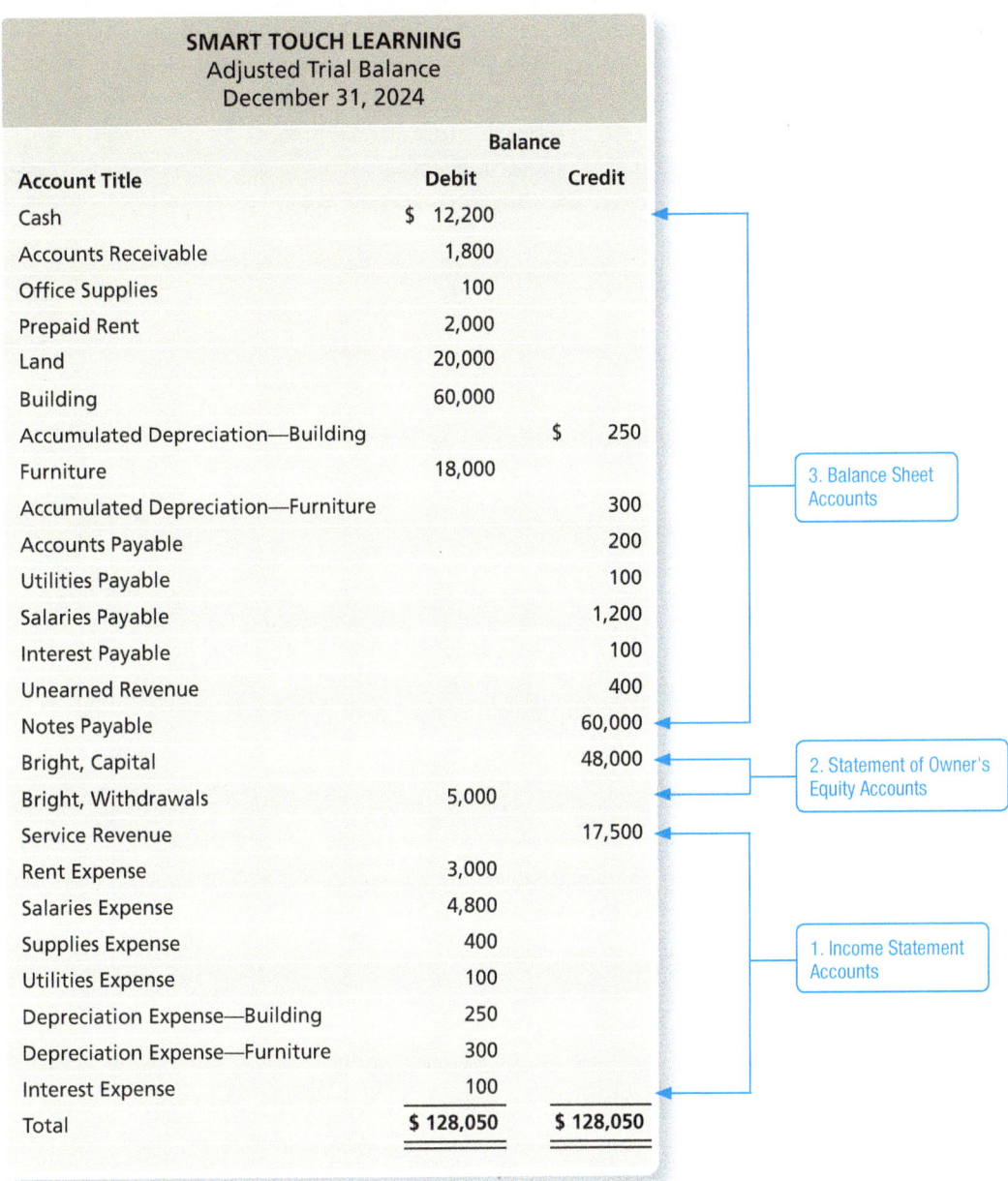

The financial statements for Smart Touch Learning are presented in Exhibit F:4-2 (on the next page).

Relationships Among the Financial Statements

The arrows in Exhibit F:4-2 (on the next page) show how the financial statements relate to each other.

1. Net income from the income statement increases owner's capital on the statement of owner's equity. A net loss decreases owner's capital.
2. Ending Owner, Capital from the statement of owner's equity goes to the balance sheet and makes total liabilities plus total owner's equity equal total assets, satisfying the accounting equation.

To solidify your understanding of these relationships, trace net income from the income statement to the statement of owner's equity. Then trace ending Owner, Capital to

4-4 Financial chapter 4

Exhibit F:4-2 | **Smart Touch Learning Financial Statements**

SMART TOUCH LEARNING
Income Statement
Two Months Ended December 31, 2024

Revenues:		
Service Revenue		$ 17,500
Expenses:		
Salaries Expense	$ 4,800	
Rent Expense	3,000	
Supplies Expense	400	
Depreciation Expense—Furniture	300	
Depreciation Expense—Building	250	
Utilities Expense	100	
Interest Expense	100	
Total Expenses		8,950
Net Income		$ 8,550

SMART TOUCH LEARNING
Statement of Owner's Equity
Two Months Ended December 31, 2024

Bright, Capital, November 1, 2024		$ 0
Owner contribution		48,000
Net income for the two months		8,550
		56,550
Owner withdrawal		(5,000)
Bright, Capital, December 31, 2024		$ 51,550

SMART TOUCH LEARNING
Balance Sheet
December 31, 2024

Assets			Liabilities		
Cash		$ 12,200	Accounts Payable		$ 200
Accounts Receivable		1,800	Utilities Payable		100
Office Supplies		100	Salaries Payable		1,200
Prepaid Rent		2,000	Interest Payable		100
Land		20,000	Unearned Revenue		400
Building	$ 60,000		Notes Payable		60,000
Less: Acc. Depr.—Building	(250)	59,750	Total Liabilities		62,000
Furniture	18,000		**Owner's Equity**		
Less: Acc. Depr.—Furniture	(300)	17,700	Bright, Capital		51,550
Total Assets		$ 113,550	Total Liabilities and Owner's Equity		$ 113,550

the balance sheet. Note that these are the three main financial statements you learned about in the first chapter. They are always prepared in the order described previously: income statement, then statement of owner's equity, and then balance sheet.

Classified Balance Sheet

Classified Balance Sheet
A balance sheet that places each asset and each liability into a specific category.

So far we have presented the *unclassified* balance sheet of Smart Touch Learning. We are now ready for the balance sheet that is actually used in practice, called a **classified balance sheet**. In a classified balance sheet, each asset and each liability are placed into a specific category or classification.

In a classified balance sheet, assets are shown in order of liquidity and liabilities are classified by the order in which they must be paid, either *current* (within one year) or *long-term* (more than one year). **Liquidity** measures how quickly and easily an account can be converted to cash (because cash is the most liquid asset). Accounts Receivable are relatively liquid because receivables are collected quickly. Office Supplies are less liquid, and Buildings and Furniture are even less so because they take longer to convert to cash or to be used up.

Assets

The balance sheet lists assets in the order of liquidity. A classified balance sheet reports two asset categories: *current assets* and *long-term assets*.

Current assets will be converted to cash, sold, or used up during the next 12 months or within the business's operating cycle if the cycle is longer than a year. The **operating cycle** is the time span when:

1. Cash is used to acquire goods and services.
2. These goods and services are sold to customers.
3. The business collects cash from customers.

For most businesses, the operating cycle is a few months. Cash, Accounts Receivable, Office Supplies, and Prepaid Expenses are examples of current assets.

Long-term assets are all the assets that will not be converted to cash or used up within the business's operating cycle or one year, whichever is greater. Long-term assets are typically made up of three categories: long-term investments; property, plant, and equipment; and intangible assets.

Long-term Investments Notes Receivable and other investments that are held long-term are considered **long-term investments** and include investments in bonds or stocks in which the company intends to hold for longer than one year.

Property, Plant, and Equipment Another category of long-term assets is **property, plant, and equipment** (also called *fixed assets* or *plant assets*). Land, Buildings, Furniture, and Equipment used in operations are plant assets. Property, plant, and equipment are presented in order of the category name, with Land (property) being presented first and then Buildings (plant) and Equipment, Furniture, and other accounts presented last.

Intangible Assets Assets with no physical form are **intangible assets**. Examples of intangible assets include patents, copyrights, and trademarks. Intangible assets are long-term assets that convey special rights, such as the exclusive right to produce or sell an invention (patent) or book (copyright), or the symbol or image of a distinctive brand (trademark).

Liabilities

The balance sheet lists liabilities in the order in which they must be paid. The two liability categories reported on the balance sheet are *current liabilities* and *long-term liabilities*.

Current liabilities must be paid with cash, or with goods and services, within one year or within the entity's operating cycle if the cycle is longer than a year. Accounts Payable, Notes Payable due within one year, Salaries Payable, Interest Payable, and Unearned Revenue are all current liabilities. Any portion of a long-term liability that is due within the next year is also reported as a current liability. Current liabilities are listed in the order that they are due.

Long-term liabilities are all liabilities that do not need to be paid within one year or within the entity's operating cycle, whichever is longer. Many Notes Payable are long-term, such as Smart Touch Learning's mortgage on its building.

Liquidity
A measure of how quickly an item can be converted to cash.

Current Asset
An asset that is expected to be converted to cash, sold, or used up during the next 12 months or within the business's normal operating cycle if the cycle is longer than a year.

Operating Cycle
The time span during which cash is paid for goods and services, which are then sold to customers and cash is collected.

Long-term Asset
An asset that will not be converted to cash or used up within the business's operating cycle or one year, whichever is greater.

Long-term Investment
Investments in bonds (debt securities) or stocks (equity securities) in which the company intends to hold the investment for longer than one year.

Property, Plant, and Equipment
Long-lived, tangible assets, such as land, buildings, and equipment, used in the operation of a business.

Intangible Asset
An asset with no physical form that is valuable because of the special rights it carries.

Current Liability
A liability that must be paid with cash, or with goods and services, within one year or within the entity's operating cycle if the cycle is longer than a year.

Long-term Liability
A liability that does not need to be paid within one year or within the entity's operating cycle, whichever is longer.

Owner's Equity

Owner's equity represents the owner's claims to the assets of the business. The owner's equity section reported on the balance sheet is transferred from the ending Owner, Capital balance on the statement of owner's equity. The ending equity balance reflects the owner's contributions, net income or net loss of the business, and owner's withdrawals. It represents the amount of assets that is left over after the business has paid its liabilities.

Exhibit F:4-3 presents Smart Touch Learning's classified balance sheet. Notice that the company classifies each asset and each liability into specific categories, and that the total assets of $113,550 is the same as the total assets on the unclassified balance sheet in Exhibit F:4-2.

Exhibit F:4-3 | Classified Balance Sheet

> This classified balance sheet contains both current assets and long-term assets, but there is only one category of long-term assets: Property, Plant, and Equipment. Other categories of long-term assets that could be included are Long-term Investments and Intangible Assets.

SMART TOUCH LEARNING
Balance Sheet
December 31, 2024

Assets

Current Assets:			
Cash		$ 12,200	
Accounts Receivable		1,800	
Office Supplies		100	
Prepaid Rent		2,000	
Total Current Assets			$ 16,100
Property, Plant, and Equipment:			
Land		20,000	
Building	$ 60,000		
Less: Accumulated Depreciation—Building	(250)	59,750	
Furniture	18,000		
Less: Accumulated Depreciation—Furniture	(300)	17,700	
Total Property, Plant, and Equipment			97,450
Total Assets			**$ 113,550**

Liabilities

Current Liabilities:		
Accounts Payable	$ 200	
Utilities Payable	100	
Salaries Payable	1,200	
Interest Payable	100	
Unearned Revenue	400	
Total Current Liabilities		$ 2,000
Long-term Liabilities:		
Notes Payable		60,000
Total Liabilities		62,000

Owner's Equity

Bright, Capital	51,550
Total Liabilities and Owner's Equity	**$ 113,550**

Completing the Accounting Cycle Financial 4-7

Compare the balance sheet in Exhibit F:4-3 with the balance sheet in Exhibit F:4-2. You'll notice two differences. Exhibit F:4-3 is a classified balance sheet, but it is also in a different format than Exhibit F:4-2. The balance sheet in Exhibit F:4-3 is being presented in the *report form*, which lists the assets at the top and liabilities and owner's equity below. Smart Touch Learning's balance sheet in Exhibit F:4-2 lists the assets on the left and the liabilities and the owner's equity on the right in an arrangement known as the *account form*. Although either form is acceptable, the *report form* is more popular.

Try It!

For each account listed, identify the category in which it would appear on a classified balance sheet.

1. Patents
2. Mortgage Payable (due in five years)
3. Land
4. Office Supplies
5. Unearned Revenue
6. Investments in stock of another company held long-term
7. Accumulated Depreciation—Furniture

Check your answers online in MyLab Accounting or at http://www.pearsonhighered.com/Horngren.

For more practice, see Short Exercises S-F:4-1 through S-F:4-5. MyLab Accounting

HOW COULD A WORKSHEET HELP IN PREPARING FINANCIAL STATEMENTS?

Previously you learned how a worksheet can be used to help prepare adjusting entries. Now you'll learn how the worksheet can be used to help in the preparation of financial statements. Exhibit F:4-4 (on the next page) shows the completed worksheet for Smart Touch Learning. Sections 1 through 4 of the worksheet, shown with a purple background, were completed in Chapter F:3. You are now ready to complete the remaining sections that will help in preparing the financial statements.

Learning Objective 2
Use the worksheet to prepare financial statements

Section 5—Income Statement

The income statement section includes only revenue and expense accounts. The revenues and expenses from the adjusted trial balance section will be transferred into the appropriate column in the income statement section. For example, the $17,500 credit balance for Service Revenue in the adjusted trial balance section will be carried over into the credit column in the income statement section. Each debit and credit column will then be totaled.

Section 6—Balance Sheet

The balance sheet section includes the asset and liability accounts and all equity accounts except revenues and expenses. The balance of each of these accounts will be transferred from the adjusted trial balance section of the worksheet to the appropriate column in the balance sheet section. For example, Accumulated Depreciation—Furniture, a contra-asset, has a $300 credit balance in the adjusted trial balance section. This amount will be reported as a credit of $300 in the balance sheet section. Each debit and credit column will then be totaled.

4-8 Financial chapter 4

Exhibit F:4-4 | Completed Worksheet

SMART TOUCH LEARNING
Worksheet
December 31, 2024

	Account Names	Unadjusted Trial Balance Debit	Unadjusted Trial Balance Credit	Adjustments Debit	Adjustments Credit	Adjusted Trial Balance Debit	Adjusted Trial Balance Credit	Income Statement Debit	Income Statement Credit	Balance Sheet Debit	Balance Sheet Credit
7	Cash	$ 12,200				$ 12,200				$ 12,200	
8	Accounts Receivable	1,000		(h) $ 800		1,800				1,800	
9	Office Supplies	500			$ 400 (b)	100				100	
10	Prepaid Rent	3,000			1,000 (a)	2,000				2,000	
11	Land	20,000				20,000				20,000	
12	Building	60,000				60,000				60,000	
13	Accumulated Depreciation—Building				250 (d)		$ 250				$ 250
14	Furniture	18,000				18,000				18,000	
15	Accumulated Depreciation—Furniture				300 (c)		300				300
16	Accounts Payable		$ 200				200				200
17	Utilities Payable		100				100				100
18	Salaries Payable				1,200 (f)		1,200				1,200
19	Interest Payable				100 (g)		100				100
20	Unearned Revenue		600	(e) 200			400				400
21	Notes Payable		60,000				60,000				60,000
22	Bright, Capital		48,000				48,000				48,000
23	Bright, Withdrawals	5,000				5,000				5,000	
24	Service Revenue		16,500		1,000 (e,h)		17,500		$ 17,500		
25	Rent Expense	2,000		(a) 1,000		3,000		$ 3,000			
26	Salaries Expense	3,600		(f) 1,200		4,800		4,800			
27	Supplies Expense			(b) 400		400		400			
28	Utilities Expense	100				100		100			
29	Depreciation Expense—Building			(d) 250		250		250			
30	Depreciation Expense—Furniture			(c) 300		300		300			
31	Interest Expense			(g) 100		100		100			
32	Total	$ 125,400	$ 125,400	$ 4,250	$ 4,250	$ 128,050	$ 128,050	$ 8,950	$ 17,500	$ 119,100	$ 110,550
33							Net Income	8,550			8,550
34	Total							$ 17,500	$ 17,500	$ 119,100	$ 119,100

Section 5 — Income Statement columns
Section 6 — Balance Sheet columns
Section 7 — Net Income row

Sections 1–4

Net Income = $17,500 − $8,950

What if Smart Touch Learning had a net loss instead of net income? Would the amount of net loss be entered in the debit column of the income statement section and the credit column of the balance sheet section?

Section 7—Determine Net Income or Net Loss

Compute net income or net loss as total revenues minus total expenses ($17,500 − $8,950). Enter net income (loss) as the balancing amount in the income statement and balance sheet sections. If net income exists, the balance will be entered in the *debit* column of the income statement section and the *credit* column of the balance sheet section. For example, Smart Touch Learning has net income of $8,550. This amount should be entered as a debit in the income statement section and a credit in the balance sheet section.

If expenses exceed revenues, the result is a net loss. In that event, print Net Loss on the worksheet next to the result. The net loss amount should be entered in the *credit* column of the income statement (to balance out) and in the *debit* column of the balance sheet (to balance out). The main thing to remember is that the net income or net loss is the balancing amount on the worksheet. It should always be entered on the side that makes the debit and credit columns balance.

Smart Touch Learning has now completed the worksheet as of December 31. Remember that the worksheet is an internal tool that can be used to help in recording adjusting entries and preparing financial statements. The adjusting entries still need to be recorded in the journal and posted to the ledger (as shown in Chapter F:3), and the financial statements must still be prepared (as shown in Exhibits F:4-2 and F:4-3).

Completing the Accounting Cycle Financial 4-9

For each account listed, identify whether the account would appear in either the income statement section or the balance sheet section of the worksheet. Assuming normal balances, identify if the account would be recorded in the debit (DR) or credit (CR) column.

8. Service Revenue
9. Accounts Payable
10. Cash
11. Depreciation Expense—Building
12. Sandy, Withdrawals
13. Accumulated Depreciation—Building

Check your answers online in MyLab Accounting or at http://www.pearsonhighered.com/Horngren.

For more practice, see Short Exercises S-F:4-6 through S-F:4-8. MyLab Accounting

WHAT IS THE CLOSING PROCESS, AND HOW DO WE CLOSE THE ACCOUNTS?

At the end of the accounting cycle, after the financial statements have been prepared, Smart Touch Learning is ready to close the books. Often referred to as the closing process, this consists of journalizing and posting the closing entries in order to get the accounts ready for the next period. The **closing process** zeroes out all revenue accounts and all expense accounts in order to measure each period's net income separately from all other periods. It also updates the Owner, Capital account balance for net income or loss during the period and any withdrawals made by the owner. The closing process prepares the accounts for the next time period by setting the balances of revenues, expenses, and withdrawals to zero. By completing the closing process, the business is following the time period concept in that it is slicing its activities into small time segments and preparing financial statements for only those specific periods.

Recall that the income statement reports net income for a specific period. For example, Smart Touch Learning's net income for the two months ended December 31, 2024, relates exclusively to November and December, 2024. At December 31, 2024, Smart Touch Learning closes its revenue and expense accounts for the last two months of the year. For this reason, revenues and expenses are called **temporary accounts** (also known as *nominal accounts*). For example, Smart Touch Learning's balance of Service Revenue at December 31, 2024, is $17,500. This balance relates exclusively to the last two months of 2024 and must be zeroed out before the company records revenue for the next year. Similarly, the various expense account balances are for the last two months of 2024 only and must also be zeroed out at the end of the year.

The Owner, Withdrawals account is also temporary and must be closed at the end of the period because it measures the payments to the owner for only that one period. All temporary accounts (revenues, expenses, and withdrawals) are closed (zeroed). The balances of temporary accounts do not carry forward into the next time period. Instead, the business starts the new time period with a zero beginning balance in the temporary accounts.

By contrast, the **permanent accounts** (also known as *real accounts*)—the assets, liabilities, and Owner, Capital—are not closed at the end of the period. Permanent account balances are carried forward into the next time period. All accounts on the balance sheet are permanent accounts.

Learning Objective 3
Explain the purpose of, journalize, and post closing entries

Closing Process
A step in the accounting cycle that occurs at the end of the period. The closing process consists of journalizing and posting the closing entries to set the balances of the revenues, expenses, Income Summary, and Owner, Withdrawals accounts to zero for the next period.

Temporary Account
An account that relates to a particular accounting period and is closed at the end of that period—the revenues, expenses, Income Summary, and Owner, Withdrawals accounts.

Permanent Account
An account that is *not* closed at the end of the period—the asset, liability, and Owner, Capital accounts.

Closing Entries
Entries that transfer the revenues, expenses, and Owner, Withdrawals balances to the Owner, Capital account to prepare the company's books for the next period.

Income Summary
A temporary account into which revenues and expenses are transferred prior to their final transfer into the Owner, Capital account. Summarizes net income (or net loss) for the period.

Closing entries transfer the revenues, expenses, and Owner, Withdrawals balances to the Owner, Capital account to prepare the company's books for the next period. This transfer to Owner, Capital also causes the Owner, Capital ledger account to now equal its balance reported on the balance sheet.

As an intermediate step, the revenues and the expenses may be transferred first to an account titled **Income Summary**. The Income Summary account *summarizes* the net income (or net loss) for the period by collecting the sum of all the expenses (a debit) and the sum of all the revenues (a credit). The Income Summary account is like a temporary "holding tank" that shows the amount of net income or net loss of the current period. Its ending balance—net income or net loss—is then transferred (closed) to the Owner, Capital account (the final account in the closing process). Exhibit F:4-5 summarizes the closing process.

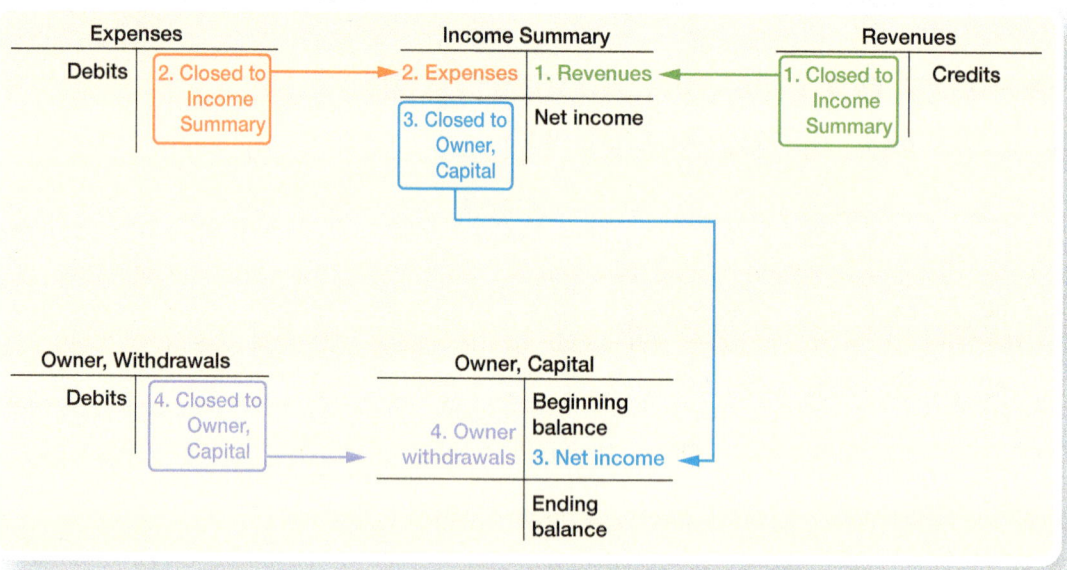

Exhibit F:4-5 | **The Closing Process**

When thinking about which accounts to close, consider your grades in this class as an example. If you made a failing grade on an exam in this class, would you want your exam grade for this class to carry forward to your next accounting class? Your answer would probably be no because your exam grade in this class does not necessarily represent your knowledge in your next class. In this example, your exam grades are temporary and should not carry forward to your next accounting class. In the same sense, a business's revenues, expenses, and withdrawals for a specific time period should not be carried forward to the next time period because doing so does not accurately reflect that future period.

Closing Temporary Accounts—Net Income for the Period

As stated previously, all temporary accounts are closed (zeroed out) during the closing process. Revenue, expenses, and Owner, Withdrawals accounts are not permanent. Only the balance sheet accounts are permanent. The four steps in closing the books follow (and are illustrated in Exhibit F:4-6).

Step 1: Make the revenue accounts equal zero via the Income Summary account. This closing entry transfers total revenues to the *credit* side of the Income Summary account.

For example, Smart Touch Learning has a $17,500 credit balance in Service Revenue. To close this account (make it zero), we *debit* Service Revenue and *credit* Income Summary.

```
      Service Revenue                  Income Summary
                  17,500  Adj. Bal.              17,500  Clos. 1
Clos. 1  17,500
                      0  Bal.
```

Date	Accounts and Explanation	Debit	Credit
Dec. 31	Service Revenue	17,500	
	Income Summary		17,500
	To close revenue.		

$$A = L + E\updownarrow$$
Service Revenue↓
Income Summary↑

Step 2: Make expense accounts equal zero via the Income Summary account. This closing entry transfers total expenses to the *debit* side of the Income Summary account.

As an example, we will review the Rent Expense account for Smart Touch Learning, which has a $3,000 debit balance. This account will be closed with a *credit* to Rent Expense.

```
           Rent Expense
Adj. Bal.  3,000
                    3,000  Clos. 2
Bal.           0
```

Smart Touch Learning will close all expense accounts in the same manner. This will most likely be done with a compound closing entry. Each individual expense account will be *credited* and the Income Summary account will be *debited* for the total amount of expenses.

Date	Accounts and Explanation	Debit	Credit
Dec. 31	Income Summary	8,950	
	Rent Expense		3,000
	Salaries Expense		4,800
	Supplies Expense		400
	Utilities Expense		100
	Depreciation Expense—Building		250
	Depreciation Expense—Furniture		300
	Interest Expense		100
	To close expenses.		

$$A = L + E\updownarrow$$
Income Summary↓
Expenses↓

The Income Summary account now holds the net income of $8,550 for the period. The Income Summary T-account after closing revenues and expenses is:

Income Summary	
Clos. 2 8,950	17,500 Clos. 1
	8,550 Bal.

Step 3: Make the Income Summary account equal zero via the Owner, Capital account. This closing entry transfers net income (or net loss) to the Owner, Capital account.

Smart Touch Learning has an $8,550 credit balance in the Income Summary account. This represents net income for the period. Net income will now be transferred to the Bright, Capital account. We will *debit* Income Summary and *credit* Bright, Capital. Notice that this closing entry, in effect, increases the Bright, Capital account for the net income of the period.

Income Summary		Bright, Capital	
Clos. 2 8,950	17,500 Clos. 1		0 Adj. Bal.
	8,550 Bal.		8,550 Clos. 3
Clos. 3 8,550			
	0 Bal.		

Net Income

A = L + E↑
Income Summary↓
Bright, Capital↑

Date	Accounts and Explanation	Debit	Credit
Dec. 31	Income Summary	8,550	
	Bright, Capital		8,550
	To close Income Summary.		

Step 4: Make the Owner, Withdrawals account equal zero via the Owner, Capital account. This entry transfers the withdrawals to the *debit* side of the Owner, Capital account.

Smart Touch Learning has a $5,000 debit balance in the Bright, Withdrawals account. This account will be closed with a *debit* to Bright, Capital and a *credit* to Bright, Withdrawals.

Bright, Capital		Bright, Withdrawals	
	0 Adj. Bal.	Adj. Bal. 5,000	
Clos. 4 5,000	8,550 Clos. 3		5,000 Clos. 4
	3,550 Bal.	Bal. 0	

Balance of Bright, Capital on the balance sheet

A = L + E↑
Bright, Capital↓
Bright, Withdrawals↓

Date	Accounts and Explanation	Debit	Credit
Dec. 31	Bright, Capital	5,000	
	Bright, Withdrawals		5,000
	To close withdrawals.		

Completing the Accounting Cycle Financial 4-13

Closing Temporary Accounts—Net Loss for the Period

If a business had a net loss for the period, closing entries 1, 2, and 4 would be similar to those completed for net income. However, the closing entry to close the Income Summary account would be different. Consider this example. Suppose a business had a net loss of $2,000. The Income Summary T-account would hold a *debit* balance instead of a *credit* balance. Therefore, the closing entry to close Income Summary would be a *debit* to Owner, Capital and a *credit* to Income Summary.

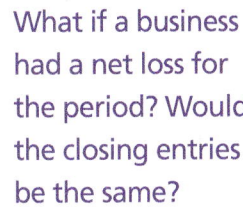

What if a business had a net loss for the period? Would the closing entries be the same?

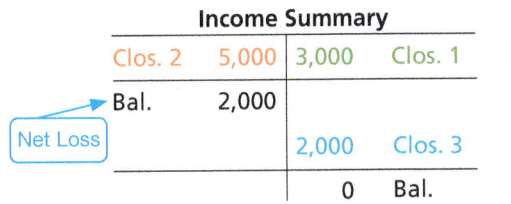

Date	Accounts and Explanation	Debit	Credit
Dec. 31	Owner, Capital	2,000	
	Income Summary		2,000
	To close Income Summary.		

$$A \;\;\Big\} = \Big\{\; L \;+\; E\updownarrow$$
Owner, Capital↓
Income Summary↑

Notice that the effect of this closing entry decreases Owner, Capital. This is because a net loss decreases the Owner, Capital account.

Closing Temporary Accounts—Summary

Exhibit F:4-6 (on the next page) shows the complete closing process for Smart Touch Learning. Panel A gives the closing entries, and Panel B shows the accounts after posting. After the closing entries, Bright, Capital ends with a balance of $3,550. Trace this balance to the statement of owner's equity and then to the balance sheet in Exhibit F:4-2.

Exhibit F:4-6 | Journalizing and Posting Closing Entries

Panel A: Journalizing

Date	Accounts and Explanation	Debit	Credit
Dec. 31	Service Revenue	17,500	
	Income Summary		17,500
	To close revenue.		
31	Income Summary	8,950	
	Rent Expense		3,000
	Salaries Expense		4,800
	Supplies Expense		400
	Utilities Expense		100
	Depreciation Expense—Building		250
	Depreciation Expense—Furniture		300
	Interest Expense		100
	To close expenses.		
31	Income Summary	8,550	
	Bright, Capital		8,550
	To close Income Summary.		
31	Bright, Capital	5,000	
	Bright, Withdrawals		5,000
	To close withdrawals.		

> When a business uses a computerized accounting system, the software automatically closes the books. The software identifies the temporary accounts, records the closing entries, and posts to the ledger accounts. The closing entries are completed in a matter of seconds.

Panel B: Posting

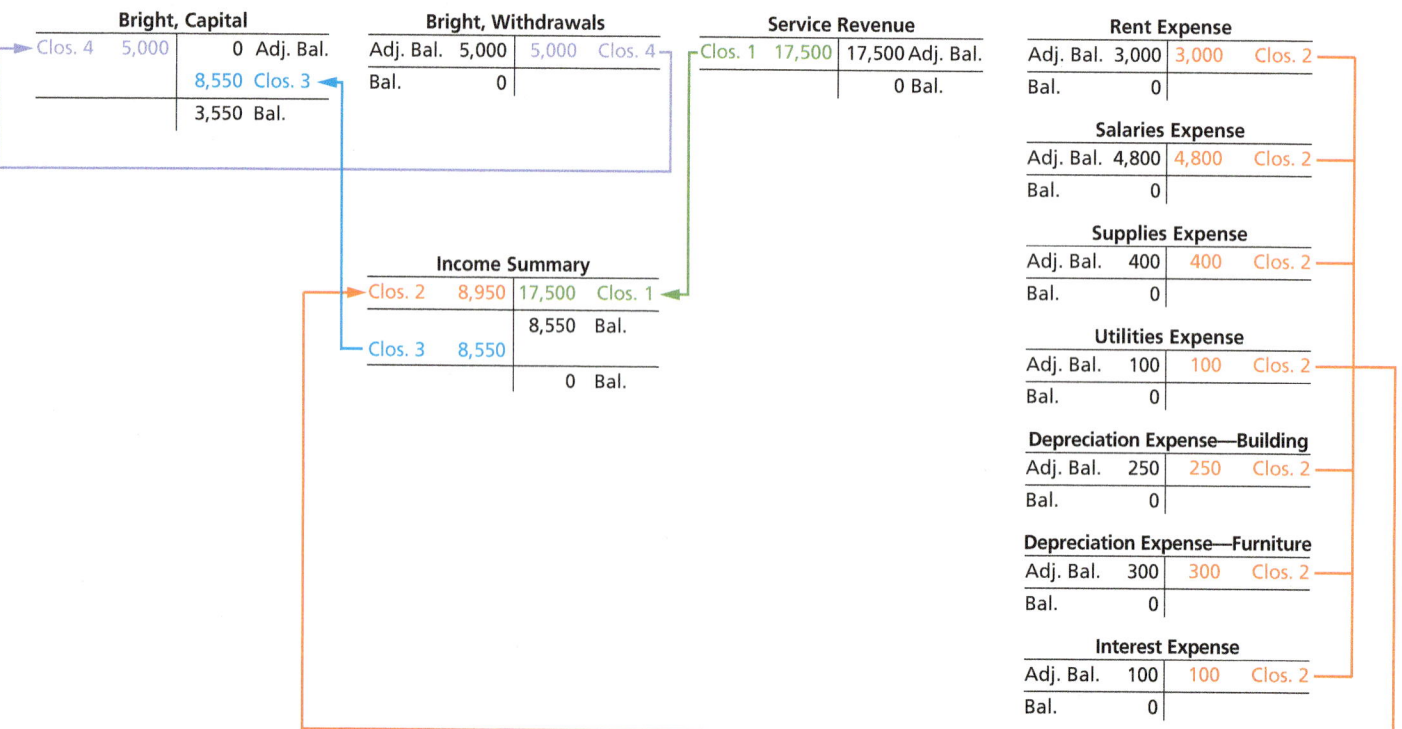

Completing the Accounting Cycle Financial 4-15

TYING IT ALL TOGETHER

Hyatt Hotels Corporation was founded in 1957 when Jay Pritzker purchased the first Hyatt hotel next to the Los Angeles International Airport. Today, Hyatt Hotels owns and operates hotels in 60 countries around the world. For the year ended December 31, 2018, the company reported revenues totaling $4.5 billion with net income of $769 million. (You can find Hyatt Hotels Corporation's annual report at **https://www.sec.gov/Archives/edgar/data/1468174/000146817419000009/h10-k123118.htm**)

Would Hyatt Hotels Corporation record closing entries and why?

Hyatt Hotels would record closing entries in order to get the accounts ready for next year. All companies record closing entries in order to zero out all revenue and expense accounts. In addition, the closing process updates the equity account balance for net income or loss during the period and any payments made to owners (stockholders).

Why are temporary accounts important in the closing process? What type of temporary accounts would Hyatt Hotels Corporation have?

Temporary accounts are important in the closing process because these accounts relate to a particular accounting period and are closed at the end of the period. Revenues, expenses, and withdrawals (called *dividends* for corporations) are all temporary accounts. Some examples of temporary accounts that Hyatt Hotels might have include Owned and Leased Hotels Revenue; Selling, General, and Administrative Expense; and Interest Expense.

When would Hyatt Hotels Corporation prepare its post-closing trial balance? What type of accounts would be reported on this trial balance?

A post-closing trial balance is a list of all permanent accounts and their balances at the end of the accounting period and is prepared after the closing process. Hyatt Hotels would report only permanent accounts on its post-closing trial balance. Some examples of permanent accounts that Hyatt Hotels might have include assets, such as Cash and Property; liabilities, such as Accounts Payable; and equity.

Benson Auto Repair had the following account balances after adjustments. Assume all accounts had normal balances.

Cash	$ 4,000	Benson, Capital	$ 35,700
Accounts Receivable	3,200	Benson, Withdrawals	2,100
Prepaid Rent	1,900	Service Revenue	1,600
Office Supplies	3,000	Depreciation Expense—Equipment	300
Equipment	34,800	Salaries Expense	800
Accumulated Depreciation—Equipment	1,600	Rent Expense	500
Accounts Payable	5,400	Utilities Expense	600
Notes Payable (long-term)	7,000	Supplies Expense	100

14. Prepare the closing entries for Benson at December 31.

15. What is the balance of Benson, Capital after closing entries have been recorded? (Use a T-account to determine the balance.)

Check your answers online in MyLab Accounting or at http://www.pearsonhighered.com/Horngren.

For more practice, see Short Exercises S-F:4-9 through S-F:4-12. MyLab Accounting

HOW DO WE PREPARE A POST-CLOSING TRIAL BALANCE?

Learning Objective 4
Prepare the post-closing trial balance

Post-Closing Trial Balance
A list of the accounts and their balances at the end of the period after journalizing and posting the closing entries. It should include only permanent accounts.

After closing entries are recorded and posted, the accounting cycle ends with a **post-closing trial balance** (see Exhibit F:4-7). This step lists the accounts and their balances after closing.

Only assets, liabilities, and Owner, Capital accounts (permanent accounts) appear on the post-closing trial balance. No temporary accounts—revenues, expenses, Income Summary, or Owner, Withdrawals—are included because they have been closed (their balances are zero). Also notice that the Owner, Capital account has been updated to reflect the period's net income (or net loss) and any owner withdrawals. The ledger is now up to date and ready for the next period.

> Notice that the Adjusted Trial Balance for Smart Touch Learning (Exhibit F:4-1) and the Post-Closing Trial Balance (Exhibit F:4-7) are similar. An easy way to make sure that you didn't make an error in the closing process is to compare the Adjusted Trial Balance to the Post-Closing Trial Balance to ensure that: (1) account balances above Owner, Capital are the same; (2) account balances below Owner, Capital are zero and, therefore, not included; and (3) the Owner, Capital account balance matches Owner, Capital on the balance sheet.

Exhibit F:4-7 | Post-Closing Trial Balance

SMART TOUCH LEARNING
Post-Closing Trial Balance
December 31, 2024

Account Title	Debit	Credit
Cash	$ 12,200	
Accounts Receivable	1,800	
Office Supplies	100	
Prepaid Rent	2,000	
Land	20,000	
Building	60,000	
Accumulated Depreciation—Building		$ 250
Furniture	18,000	
Accumulated Depreciation—Furniture		300
Accounts Payable		200
Utilities Payable		100
Salaries Payable		1,200
Interest Payable		100
Unearned Revenue		400
Notes Payable		60,000
Bright, Capital		51,550
Total	$ 114,100	$ 114,100

(Permanent Accounts)

For each account listed, identify whether the account would appear on the post-closing trial balance. Indicate either yes or no.

16. Evans, Withdrawals
17. Service Revenue
18. Cash
19. Advertising Expense
20. Evans, Capital

Check your answers online in MyLab Accounting or at http://www.pearsonhighered.com/Horngren.

For more practice, see Short Exercise S-F:4-13.   MyLab Accounting

WHAT IS THE ACCOUNTING CYCLE?

We have now completed the accounting cycle for Smart Touch Learning. The **accounting cycle** is the process by which companies produce their financial statements for a specific period. It is the steps that are followed throughout the time period. The accounting cycle starts with the beginning asset, liability, and owner's equity account balances left over from the preceding period. Exhibit F:4-8 (on the next page) outlines the complete accounting cycle of Smart Touch Learning and every other business. Start with Step 1 and move clockwise.

Accounting takes place at two different times:

- During the period (Steps 1 through 3)—Journalizing transactions and posting to the accounts
- End of the period (Steps 4 through 10)—Adjusting the accounts, preparing the financial statements, and closing the accounts

Learning Objective 5
Describe the accounting cycle

Accounting Cycle
The process by which companies produce their financial statements for a specific period.

Exhibit F:4-8 | The Accounting Cycle

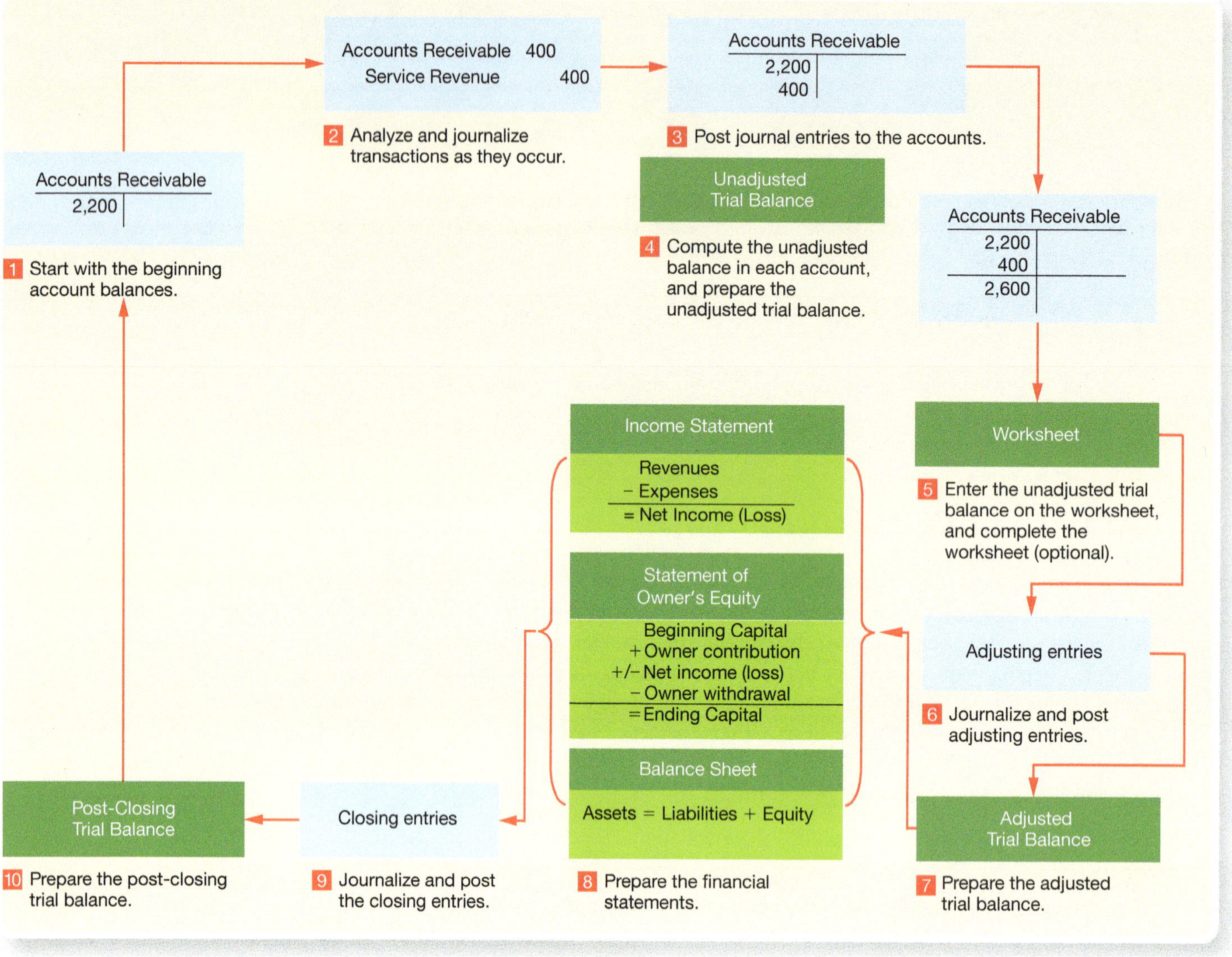

1 Start with the beginning account balances.

Accounts Receivable 2,200

2 Analyze and journalize transactions as they occur.

Accounts Receivable 400
Service Revenue 400

3 Post journal entries to the accounts.

Accounts Receivable
2,200
400

4 Compute the unadjusted balance in each account, and prepare the unadjusted trial balance.

Unadjusted Trial Balance

Accounts Receivable
2,200
400
2,600

5 Enter the unadjusted trial balance on the worksheet, and complete the worksheet (optional).

Worksheet

6 Journalize and post adjusting entries.

Adjusting entries

7 Prepare the adjusted trial balance.

Adjusted Trial Balance

8 Prepare the financial statements.

Income Statement
Revenues
− Expenses
= Net Income (Loss)

Statement of Owner's Equity
Beginning Capital
+ Owner contribution
+/− Net income (loss)
− Owner withdrawal
= Ending Capital

Balance Sheet
Assets = Liabilities + Equity

9 Journalize and post the closing entries.

Closing entries

10 Prepare the post-closing trial balance.

Post-Closing Trial Balance

Try It!

21. The steps of the accounting cycle are presented below. Identify the correct order of the steps.

   a. Journalize and post the closing entries.
   b. Start with the beginning account balances.
   c. Prepare the financial statements.
   d. Compute the unadjusted balance in each account and prepare the unadjusted trial balance.
   e. Journalize and post adjusting entries.
   f. Enter the unadjusted trial balance on the worksheet and complete the worksheet (optional).
   g. Prepare the adjusted trial balance.
   h. Analyze and journalize transactions as they occur.
   i. Post journal entries to the accounts.
   j. Prepare the post-closing trial balance.

Check your answers online in MyLab Accounting or at http://www.pearsonhighered.com/Horngren.

For more practice, see Short Exercise S-F:4-14.   **MyLab Accounting**

HOW DO WE USE THE CURRENT RATIO TO EVALUATE BUSINESS PERFORMANCE?

Accounting is designed to provide information that business owners, managers, and lenders can use to make decisions. A bank considering lending money to a business must predict whether that business can repay the loan. If a business already has a lot of debt, repayment is less certain than if it does not owe much money. In this chapter, we will introduce another ratio that can be used to measure the business's financial position, the current ratio.

The **current ratio** measures a company's ability to pay its current liabilities with its current assets. This ratio is computed as follows:

> Current ratio = Total current assets / Total current liabilities

Learning Objective 6
Use the current ratio to evaluate business performance

Current Ratio
Measures the company's ability to pay current liabilities from current assets. Total current assets / Total current liabilities.

A company prefers to have a high current ratio because that means it has plenty of current assets to pay its current liabilities. A current ratio that has increased from the prior period indicates improvement in a company's ability to pay its current debts. A current ratio that has decreased from the prior period signals deterioration in the company's ability to pay its current liabilities.

A rule of thumb: A strong current ratio is 1.50, which indicates that the business has $1.50 in current assets for every $1.00 in current liabilities. A current ratio of 1.00 is considered low and somewhat risky.

Returning to **Kohl's Corporation,** we can now evaluate Kohl's current ratio. Kohl's had the following total current assets and current liabilities, found on the balance sheet. Visit **http://www.pearsonhighered.com/Horngren** to view a link to Kohl's Corporation's annual report.

	As of Feb. 2, 2019	As of Feb. 3, 2018
Total current assets (in millions)	$ 4,835	$ 5,380
Total current liabilities (in millions)	2,730	2,709

The current ratio for Kohl's Corporation as of February 2, 2019, follows:

> Current ratio = $4,835 / $2,730 = 1.77

In comparison, the current ratio as of February 3, 2018, for Kohl's Corporation was:

> Current ratio = $5,380 / $2,709 = 1.99

The current ratio has decreased from 2018 to 2019. This indicates that Kohl's Corporation has deteriorated in its ability to pay its current debts. Given that the current ratio is above 1.5 for both years, Kohl's Corporation would be considered a less risky investment than another business with a lower current ratio. Similarly, creditors would be more willing to extend credit to Kohl's Corporation than another company with a lower current ratio.

4-20 Financial chapter 4

ETHICS

Should revenue be recorded early?

Carnival Custom Painting's owner, Kristi Seay, is hoping to get a loan from a local bank. The business's van engine has just died, and the business has no extra cash to replace the engine. It needs a short-term loan of $3,000. A teller at the bank has told Kristi that the bank will only approve the loan if the business has a current ratio that is above 1.2. Currently, Carnival's current ratio is 1.1. The business has just received a contract for painting a new commercial building. Kristi has told the teller that she expects revenue of $15,000 from the contract but won't receive payment until the job is completed. The business plans on starting the job next week but won't be finished for another two months, not soon enough to use the cash to replace the engine in the van. The teller has suggested to Kristi that she go ahead and record the revenue and cash receipt of the painting contract even though it hasn't been completed. This, he tells her, will increase the business's current assets and thereby increase the current ratio to 1.4, well above the bank minimum. What should Kristi do? What would you do?

Solution

Kristi should not record the revenue and cash receipt early. The revenue recognition principle requires that businesses record revenue only when it has been earned. Given that Carnival Custom Painting has not yet started the job, no revenue has been earned. Kristi should look for alternative sources of financing instead of trying to manipulate the current ratio to meet the minimum required by the bank. Another possibility would be for Kristi to renegotiate the contract with the new client to receive $3,000 in advance instead of after the completion of the job. This would allow Kristi to make the repairs on the van and not have to borrow the money from the bank.

Try It!

22. Benson Auto Repair has the following account balances at December 31, 2024, from its adjusted trial balance. Compute Benson Auto Repair's current ratio.

Cash	$ 4,000	Benson, Capital	$ 35,700
Accounts Receivable	3,200	Benson, Withdrawals	2,100
Prepaid Rent	1,900	Service Revenue	1,600
Office Supplies	3,000	Depreciation Expense—Equipment	300
Equipment	34,800	Salaries Expense	800
Accumulated Depreciation—Equipment	1,600	Rent Expense	500
Accounts Payable	5,400	Utilities Expense	600
Notes Payable (long-term)	7,000	Supplies Expense	100

Check your answer online in MyLab Accounting or at http://www.pearsonhighered.com/Horngren.

For more practice, see Short Exercise S-F:4-15. **MyLab Accounting**

APPENDIX 4A: Reversing Entries: An Optional Step

WHAT ARE REVERSING ENTRIES?

Reversing entries are special journal entries that ease the burden of accounting for transactions in a later period. Reversing entries are the exact opposite of certain adjusting entries. Reversing entries are used in conjunction with accrual-type adjustments, such as accrued salaries expense and accrued service revenue. Generally Accepted Accounting Principles (GAAP) do not require reversing entries. They are used only for convenience and to save time.

Learning Objective 7
Explain the purpose of, journalize, and post reversing entries

Accounting for Accrued Expenses

To see how reversing entries work, let's return to Smart Touch Learning. In the unadjusted trial balance, Salaries Expense has a debit balance of $3,600 for salaries paid during November and December. At December 31, the business still owes it employees an additional $1,200 for the last half of the month, so the business makes the following adjusting entry:

Date	Accounts and Explanation	Debit	Credit
Dec. 31	Salaries Expense	1,200	
	Salaries Payable		1,200
	To accrue salaries expense.		

$$A = \underbrace{L\uparrow}_{\text{Salaries Payable}\uparrow} + \underbrace{E\downarrow}_{\text{Salaries Expense}\uparrow}$$

After posting, the accounts are updated as of December 31:

Salaries Payable			Salaries Expense	
	1,200 Adj.	Nov. 15	1,200	
	1,200 Adj. Bal.	Dec. 1	1,200	
		Dec. 15	1,200	
		Adj.	1,200	
		Adj. Bal.	4,800	

After the adjusting entry, the following are noted:
- The income statement reports Salaries Expense of $4,800.
- The balance sheet reports Salaries Payable of $1,200.

The $4,800 debit balance of Salaries Expense is closed at December 31, 2024, with the following closing entry:

Date	Accounts and Explanation	Debit	Credit
Dec. 31	Income Summary	4,800	
	Salaries Expense		4,800
	To close expense.		

$$A = L + E\uparrow\downarrow \quad \text{Income Summary}\downarrow \quad \text{Salaries Expense}\downarrow$$

4-22 Financial chapter 4

After posting the closing entry, Salaries Expense has a zero balance as follows:

Salaries Expense			
Nov. 15	1,200		
Dec. 1	1,200		
Dec. 15	1,200		
Adj.	1,200		
Adj. Bal.	4,800		
		4,800	Clos.
Bal.	0		

Accounting Without a Reversing Entry

Assume that Smart Touch Learning will pay its employees the second half of December's salaries along with the first half of January on January 15, 2025. On January 15, the company would record the following journal entry:

$$\frac{A\downarrow}{Cash\downarrow} \Bigg\} = \Bigg\{ \frac{L\downarrow}{\substack{Salaries \\ Payable\downarrow}} + \frac{E\downarrow}{\substack{Salaries \\ Expense\uparrow}}$$

Date	Accounts and Explanation	Debit	Credit
2025			
Jan. 15	Salaries Payable	1,200	
	Salaries Expense	1,200	
	Cash		2,400
	To record payment of salaries.		

After posting the cash payment, the Salaries Payable and Salaries Expense accounts are as follows:

Salaries Payable				Salaries Expense		
		1,200	Bal. 1/1/25	Jan. 15	1,200	
Jan. 15	1,200					
		0 Bal.				

This method of recording the cash payment is correct. However, it wastes time because the business must refer back to the December 31 adjustments. Otherwise, the business does not know the amount of the debit to Salaries Payable (in this example $1,200). Searching December's adjusting entries wastes time and money. To save time, accountants can use reversing entries.

Reversing Entry
A special journal entry that eases the burden of accounting for transactions in the next period. Such entries are the exact opposite of a prior adjusting entry.

Accounting with a Reversing Entry

A **reversing entry** switches the debit and the credit of a previous entry. A reversing entry, then, is the exact opposite of a prior adjusting entry. The reversing entry is dated the first day of the new period.

To illustrate reversing entries, recall that on December 31 Smart Touch Learning made the following adjusting entry to accrue Salaries Expense:

Date	Accounts and Explanation	Debit	Credit
Dec. 31	Salaries Expense	1,200	
	Salaries Payable		1,200
	To accrue salaries expense.		

$$A = \begin{cases} L\uparrow & + & E\downarrow \\ \text{Salaries} & & \text{Salaries} \\ \text{Payable}\uparrow & & \text{Expense}\uparrow \end{cases}$$

The reversing entry just reverses the debit and the credit of the adjustment:

Date	Accounts and Explanation	Debit	Credit
2025			
Jan. 1	Salaries Payable	1,200	
	Salaries Expense		1,200
	To reverse the salaries adjusting entry.		

$$A = \begin{cases} L\downarrow & + & E\uparrow \\ \text{Salaries} & & \text{Salaries} \\ \text{Payable}\downarrow & & \text{Expense}\downarrow \end{cases}$$

Observe that the reversing entry is dated the first day of the new period. It is the exact opposite of the adjusting entry. Ordinarily, the accountant who makes the adjusting entries will also prepare reversing entries at the same time. Smart Touch Learning dates the reversing entry as of January 1 so that it affects only the new period. Note how the accounts appear after the accounting clerk posts the reversing entry:

```
         Salaries Payable                    Salaries Expense
                    | 1,200 Adj.         Bal. 1/1/25  0 |
                    | 1,200 Bal. 1/1/25               | 1,200 Rev. Jan. 1
    Rev. Jan. 1 1,200|
                    | 0 Bal.
```

The arrow between the T-accounts shows the transfer of the $1,200 from Salaries Payable to Salaries Expense. This credit in Salaries Expense does not mean that the entity has negative salaries expense, as you might think. Instead, the odd credit balance in the Salaries Expense account is merely a temporary result of the reversing entry. The credit balance is eliminated on January 15, when Smart Touch Learning pays the payroll and debits Salaries Expense:

Date	Accounts and Explanation	Debit	Credit
Jan. 15	Salaries Expense	2,400	
	Cash		2,400
	To record payment of salaries.		

$$\begin{matrix} A\downarrow \\ \text{Cash}\downarrow \end{matrix} = \begin{cases} L & + & E\downarrow \\ & & \text{Salaries} \\ & & \text{Expense}\uparrow \end{cases}$$

4-24 Financial chapter 4

This payment is posted to the Salaries Expense account as follows:

Salaries Expense			
Bal. 1/1/25	0		
Jan. 15	2,400	1,200	Rev. Jan. 1
Bal.	1,200		

Now Salaries Expense has a debit balance of $1,200, which is correct and represents only the January salaries. The payment of salaries covered two periods: $1,200 related to 2024 and $1,200 related to 2025. The Salaries Expense account should only contain the amount that relates to 2025.

Winters Landscape Services accrued $4,000 of Salaries Expense at December 31. Winters paid the next payroll at January 10 of $6,000. This payment included the accrued amount at December 31, plus $2,000 for the first few days of January.

23A. Record the adjusting entry to accrue Salaries Expense.
24A. Record the reversing entry.
25A. Journalize the cash payment.

Check your answers online in MyLab Accounting or at http://www.pearsonhighered.com/Horngren.

For more practice, see Short Exercise S-F:4A-16. **MyLab Accounting**

REVIEW

> Things You Should Know

1. **How do we prepare financial statements?**
   - Financial statements are prepared from the adjusted trial balance in the following order:
     1. Income statement—reports revenues and expenses and calculates net income or net loss during the period
     2. Statement of owner's equity—shows how capital changed during the period due to net income or net loss, owner contributions, and owner withdrawals
     3. Balance sheet—reports assets, liabilities, and owner's equity as of the last day of the period
   - A classified balance sheet classifies each asset and each liability into specific categories.

2. **How could a worksheet help in preparing financial statements?**
   - The columns of a worksheet can be extended to help in preparing the financial statements.
   - The income statement section will include only revenue and expense accounts.
   - The balance sheet section will include asset and liability accounts and all equity accounts except revenues and expenses.

3. What is the closing process, and how do we close the accounts?

- The closing process consists of zeroing out all temporary accounts (revenues, expenses, Income Summary, and Owner, Withdrawals) in order to get the accounts ready for the next period.
- The closing process also updates the Owner, Capital account balance for net income or net loss during the period and any withdrawals made by the owner.
- There are four steps in the closing process:
  1. Make the revenue accounts equal zero via the Income Summary account.
  2. Make the expense accounts equal zero via the Income Summary account.
  3. Make the Income Summary account equal zero via the Owner, Capital account.
  4. Make the Owner, Withdrawals account equal zero via the Owner, Capital account.

4. How do we prepare a post-closing trial balance?

- A post-closing trial balance is prepared after the closing entries are recorded and posted to the ledger.
- It contains only assets, liabilities, and Owner, Capital accounts (permanent accounts).

5. What is the accounting cycle?

- The accounting cycle is the process by which companies produce their financial statements for a specific period.
  1. Start with the beginning account balances.
  2. Analyze and journalize transactions as they occur.
  3. Post journal entries to the accounts.
  4. Compute the unadjusted balance in each account and prepare the unadjusted trial balance.
  5. Enter the unadjusted trial balance on the worksheet and complete the worksheet (optional).
  6. Journalize and post adjusting entries.
  7. Prepare the adjusted trial balance.
  8. Prepare the financial statements.
  9. Journalize and post the closing entries.
  10. Prepare the post-closing trial balance.

6. How do we use the current ratio to evaluate business performance?

- The current ratio measures a company's ability to pay its current liabilities with its current assets.
- Current ratio = Total current assets / Total current liabilities.

7. What are reversing entries? (Appendix 4A)

- Reversing entries are special journal entries that ease the burden of accounting for transactions in a later period.
- Reversing entries are the exact opposite of certain adjusting entries and are used only for accrual adjusting entries.

> Check Your Understanding

Check your understanding of the chapter by completing this problem and then looking at the solution. Use this practice to help identify which sections of the chapter you need to study more.

The adjusted trial balance of Martinez Advertising Services, at December 31, 2024, follows. This is the first year of operations.

MARTINEZ ADVERTISING SERVICES
Adjusted Trial Balance
December 31, 2024

Account Title	Debit	Credit
Cash	$ 6,000	
Accounts Receivable	6,300	
Office Supplies	200	
Land	10,000	
Building	42,000	
Accumulated Depreciation—Building		$ 24,000
Furniture	8,000	
Accumulated Depreciation—Furniture		6,000
Accounts Payable		2,000
Salaries Payable		500
Unearned Revenue		5,000
Notes Payable (long-term)		7,000
Martinez, Capital		12,000
Martinez, Withdrawals	25,000	
Service Revenue		64,300
Salaries Expense	16,500	
Supplies Expense	800	
Depreciation Expense—Building	1,000	
Depreciation Expense—Furniture	2,000	
Advertising Expense	3,000	
Total	$ 120,800	$ 120,800

Requirements

1. Prepare the income statement for the year ended December 31, 2024. (See Learning Objective 1)
2. Prepare the statement of owner's equity for the year ended December 31, 2024. (See Learning Objective 1)
3. Prepare the classified balance sheet at December 31, 2024. Use the report form. (See Learning Objective 1)

4. Calculate the current ratio at December 31, 2024. (See Learning Objective 6)
5. Journalize and post the closing entries. Indicate the balance of the Martinez, Capital account after the closing entries are posted. (See Learning Objective 3)
6. Prepare a post-closing trial balance at December 31, 2024. (See Learning Objective 4)

> Solution

Requirement 1

MARTINEZ ADVERTISING SERVICES
Income Statement
Year Ended December 31, 2024

Revenues:		
Service Revenue		$ 64,300
Expenses:		
Salaries Expense	$ 16,500	
Advertising Expense	3,000	
Depreciation Expense—Building	1,000	
Depreciation Expense—Furniture	2,000	
Supplies Expense	800	
Total Expenses		23,300
Net Income		$ 41,000

Requirement 2

MARTINEZ ADVERTISING SERVICES
Statement of Owner's Equity
Year Ended December 31, 2024

Martinez, Capital, January 1, 2024	$ 12,000
Owner contribution	0
Net income for the year	41,000
	53,000
Owner withdrawal	(25,000)
Martinez, Capital, December 31, 2024	$ 28,000

Requirement 3

MARTINEZ ADVERTISING SERVICES
Balance Sheet
December 31, 2024

Assets

Current Assets:		
Cash		$ 6,000
Accounts Receivable		6,300
Office Supplies		200
Total Current Assets		$ 12,500
Property, Plant, and Equipment:		
Land		10,000
Building	$ 42,000	
Less: Accumulated Depreciation—Building	(24,000)	18,000
Furniture	8,000	
Less: Accumulated Depreciation—Furniture	(6,000)	2,000
Total Property, Plant, and Equipment		30,000
Total Assets		**$ 42,500**

Liabilities

Current Liabilities:		
Accounts Payable	$ 2,000	
Salaries Payable	500	
Unearned Revenue	5,000	
Total Current Liabilities		$ 7,500
Long-term Liabilities:		
Notes Payable		7,000
Total Liabilities		14,500

Owner's Equity

Martinez, Capital	28,000
Total Liabilities and Owner's Equity	$ 42,500

Requirement 4

Current ratio = Total current assets / Total current liabilities = $12,500 / $7,500 = 1.67

Requirement 5

Date	Accounts and Explanation	Debit	Credit
Dec. 31	Service Revenue	64,300	
	Income Summary		64,300
	To close revenue.		
31	Income Summary	23,300	
	Salaries Expense		16,500
	Supplies Expense		800
	Depreciation Expense—Building		1,000
	Depreciation Expense—Furniture		2,000
	Advertising Expense		3,000
	To close expenses.		
31	Income Summary	41,000	
	Martinez, Capital		41,000
	To close Income Summary.		
31	Martinez, Capital	25,000	
	Martinez, Withdrawals		25,000
	To close withdrawals.		

Martinez, Capital
		0	Adj. Bal.
Dec. 31	25,000	41,000	Dec. 31
		16,000	Bal.

Martinez, Withdrawals
Adj. Bal.	25,000	25,000	Dec. 31
Bal.	0		

Service Revenue
Dec. 31	64,300	64,300	Adj. Bal.
		0	Bal.

Salaries Expense
Adj. Bal.	16,500	16,500	Dec. 31
Bal.	0		

Supplies Expense
Adj. Bal.	800	800	Dec. 31
Bal.	0		

Depreciation Expense—Building
Adj. Bal.	1,000	1,000	Dec. 31
Bal.	0		

Income Summary
Dec. 31	23,300	64,300	Dec. 31
		41,000	Bal.
Dec. 31	41,000		
		0	Bal.

Depreciation Expense—Furniture
Adj. Bal.	2,000	2,000	Dec. 31
Bal.	0		

Advertising Expense
Adj. Bal.	3,000	3,000	Dec. 31
Bal.	0		

Requirement 6

MARTINEZ ADVERTISING SERVICES
Post-Closing Trial Balance
December 31, 2024

Account Title	Balance Debit	Balance Credit
Cash	$ 6,000	
Accounts Receivable	6,300	
Office Supplies	200	
Land	10,000	
Building	42,000	
Accumulated Depreciation—Building		$ 24,000
Furniture	8,000	
Accumulated Depreciation—Furniture		6,000
Accounts Payable		2,000
Salaries Payable		500
Unearned Revenue		5,000
Notes Payable (long-term)		7,000
Martinez, Capital		28,000
Total	$ 72,500	$ 72,500

> Key Terms

Accounting Cycle (p. 4-17)
Classified Balance Sheet (p. 4-4)
Closing Entries (p. 4-10)
Closing Process (p. 4-9)
Current Asset (p. 4-5)
Current Liability (p. 4-5)
Current Ratio (p. 4-19)

Income Summary (p. 4-10)
Intangible Asset (p. 4-5)
Liquidity (p. 4-5)
Long-term Asset (p. 4-5)
Long-term Investment (p. 4-5)
Long-term Liability (p. 4-5)
Operating Cycle (p. 4-5)

Permanent Account (p. 4-9)
Property, Plant, and Equipment (p. 4-5)
Post-Closing Trial Balance (p. 4-16)
Reversing Entry (p. 4-22) (Appendix 4A)
Temporary Account (p. 4-9)

> Quick Check

Learning Objective 1

1. Assets are listed on the balance sheet in the order of their
   a. purchase date.
   b. adjustments.
   c. liquidity.
   d. balance.

Learning Objective 1

2. Which of the following accounts would be included in the property, plant, and equipment category of the classified balance sheet?
   a. Land (held for investment purposes)
   b. Accumulated Depreciation
   c. Office Supplies
   d. Mortgage Payable

3. Which situation indicates a net loss within the Income Statement section of the worksheet?   **Learning Objective 2**
   a. Total credits exceed total debits
   b. Total debits exceed total credits
   c. Total debits equal total credits
   d. None of the above

4. Which of the following accounts is *not* closed?   **Learning Objective 3**
   a. Depreciation Expense
   b. Owner, Withdrawals
   c. Service Revenue
   d. Accumulated Depreciation

5. What do closing entries accomplish?   **Learning Objective 3**
   a. Zero out the revenues, expenses, and Owner, Withdrawals
   b. Transfer revenues, expenses, and Owner, Withdrawals to the Owner, Capital account
   c. Bring the Owner, Capital account to its correct ending balance
   d. All of the above

6. Which of the following is *not* a closing entry?   **Learning Objective 3**

Date	Accounts and Explanation	Debit	Credit
a.	Owner, Capital	xxx	
	Owner, Withdrawals		xxx
b.	Service Revenue	xxx	
	Income Summary		xxx
c.	Salaries Payable	xxx	
	Income Summary		xxx
d.	Income Summary	xxx	
	Rent Expense		xxx

7. Which of the following accounts may appear on a post-closing trial balance?   **Learning Objective 4**
   a. Cash, Salaries Payable, and Owner, Capital
   b. Cash, Salaries Payable, and Service Revenue
   c. Cash, Service Revenue, and Salaries Expense
   d. Cash, Salaries Payable, and Salaries Expense

8. Which of the following steps of the accounting cycle is not completed at the end of the period?   **Learning Objective 5**
   a. Journalize transactions as they occur.
   b. Journalize and post the closing entries.
   c. Prepare the post-closing trial balance.
   d. Prepare the financial statements.

9. Clean Water Softener Systems has Cash of $600, Accounts Receivable of $900, and Office Supplies of $400. Clean owes $500 on Accounts Payable and has Salaries Payable of $200. Clean's current ratio is   **Learning Objective 6**
   a. 2.71
   b. 2.50
   c. 0.63
   d. 0.37

Learning Objective 7
Appendix 4A

10A. Which of the following statements concerning reversing entries is true?
   a. Reversing entries are required by Generally Accepted Accounting Principles (GAAP).
   b. Reversing entries are most often used with accrual-type adjustments.
   c. Reversing entries are dated December 31, the end of the fiscal year.
   d. Reversing entries are recorded before adjusting entries.

Check your answers at the end of the chapter.

ASSESS YOUR PROGRESS

> Review Questions

1. What document are financial statements prepared from?
2. What does the income statement report?
3. What does the statement of owner's equity show?
4. What does the balance sheet report?
5. Why are financial statements prepared in a specific order? What is that order?
6. What is a classified balance sheet?
7. Identify two asset categories on the classified balance sheet and give examples of each category.
8. Identify two liability categories on the classified balance sheet and give examples of each category.
9. What does liquidity mean?
10. How could a worksheet help in preparing financial statements?
11. If a business had a net loss for the year, where would the net loss be reported on the worksheet?
12. What is the closing process?
13. What are temporary accounts? Are temporary accounts closed in the closing process?
14. What are permanent accounts? Are permanent accounts closed in the closing process?
15. How is the Income Summary account used? Is it a temporary or permanent account?
16. What are the steps in the closing process?
17. If a business had a net loss for the year, what would be the closing entry to close Income Summary and transfer the net loss to the Owner, Capital account?
18. What types of accounts are listed on the post-closing trial balance?
19. List the steps of the accounting cycle.
20. What is the current ratio, and how is it calculated?
21A. What are reversing entries? Are they required by GAAP?

> Short Exercises

S-F:4-1 Preparing an income statement

Learning Objective 1

Dalton Hair Stylists' adjusted trial balance follows. Prepare Dalton's income statement for the year ended December 31, 2024.

DALTON HAIR STYLISTS
Adjusted Trial Balance
December 31, 2024

Account Title	Debit	Credit
Cash	$ 1,300	
Accounts Receivable	1,500	
Office Supplies	1,800	
Equipment	20,900	
Accumulated Depreciation—Equipment		$ 2,200
Accounts Payable		400
Interest Payable		500
Notes Payable		3,100
Dalton, Capital		16,150
Dalton, Withdrawals	1,400	
Service Revenue		13,800
Rent Expense	3,900	
Supplies Expense	850	
Depreciation Expense—Equipment	2,200	
Interest Expense	2,300	
Total	$ 36,150	$ 36,150

S-F:4-2 Preparing a statement of owner's equity

Learning Objective 1

Refer to the data in Short Exercise S-F:4-1. Prepare Dalton's statement of owner's equity for the year ended December 31, 2024. Assume the owner made no contributions during the year.

S-F:4-3 Preparing a balance sheet (unclassified, account form)

Learning Objective 1

Refer to the data in Short Exercise S-F:4-1. Prepare Dalton's *unclassified* balance sheet at December 31, 2024. Use the account form.

S-F:4-4 Preparing a balance sheet (classified, report form)

Learning Objective 1

Refer to the data in Short Exercise S-F:4-1. Prepare Dalton's classified balance sheet at December 31, 2024. Assume the Notes Payable is due on December 1, 2031. Use the report form.

Learning Objective 1   **S-F:4-5 Classifying balance sheet accounts**

For each account listed, identify the category in which it would appear on a classified balance sheet.

a. Office Supplies
b. Interest Payable
c. Golub, Capital
d. Copyrights
e. Land
f. Accumulated Depreciation—Furniture
g. Land (held for long-term investment purposes)
h. Unearned Revenue
i. Notes Payable (due in six years)

Learning Objective 2   **S-F:4-6 Using the worksheet to prepare financial statements**

Answer the following questions:

Requirements

1. What type of normal balance does the Owner, Capital account have—debit or credit?
2. Which type of income statement account has the same type of balance as the Owner, Capital account?
3. Which type of income statement account has the opposite type of balance as the Owner, Capital account?
4. What do we call the difference between total debits and total credits on the income statement section of the worksheet?

Learning Objective 2   **S-F:4-7 Determining net income using a worksheet**

A partial worksheet for Ramey Law Firm is presented below. Solve for the missing information.

	A	J	K	L	M
5		Income Statement		Balance Sheet	
6		Debit	Credit	Debit	Credit
32	Total	(a)	$ 24,850	$ 211,325	$ 202,950
33	Net (b)	8,375			(c)
34	Total	(d)	$ 24,850	(e)	(f)
35					

Learning Objective 2   **S-F:4-8 Determining net loss using a worksheet**

A partial worksheet for Aaron Adjusters is presented below. Solve for the missing information.

	A	J	K	L	M
5		Income Statement		Balance Sheet	
6		Debit	Credit	Debit	Credit
32	Total	$ 22,400	(a)	(b)	$ 61,400
33	Net (c)		5,300	(d)	
34	Total	(e)	(f)	(g)	$ 61,400
35					

S-F:4-9 Identifying temporary and permanent accounts

For each account listed, identify whether the account is a temporary account (T) or a permanent account (P).

a. Rent Expense
b. Prepaid Rent
c. Equipment
d. Morrison, Capital
e. Salaries Payable
f. Morrison, Withdrawals
g. Service Revenue
h. Supplies Expense
i. Office Supplies

S-F:4-10 Journalizing closing entries

Brett Teddy Enterprises had the following accounts and normal balances listed on its December 31 adjusted trial balance: Service Revenue, $21,900; Salaries Expense, $6,000; Rent Expense, $4,400; Advertising Expense, $3,100; and Teddy, Withdrawals, $6,900.

Journalize the closing entries for Teddy Enterprises.

S-F:4-11 Journalizing closing entries

Josh's Pool Service had the following selected accounts and normal balances listed on its December 31 adjusted trial balance:

Service Revenue	$ 65,000	Insurance Expense	$ 29,000
Accounts Payable	4,300	Supplies Expense	900
Salaries Expense	31,000	Equipment	47,000
Josh, Capital	236,000	Josh, Withdrawals	32,000
Utilities Expense	19,000	Office Supplies	950
Cash	19,000	Salaries Payable	3,100
Depreciation Expense—Equipment	6,500	Accumulated Depreciation—Equipment	21,000
Land	50,000		

Journalize the closing entries for Josh's Pool Service.

S-F:4-12 Posting closing entries directly to T-accounts

The following balances appear on the books of Sarah Simmons Enterprises: Simmons, Capital, $29,600; Simmons, Withdrawals, $10,500; Income Summary, $0; Service Revenue, $24,500; Salaries Expense, $6,200; Rent Expense, $3,500; and Advertising Expense, $2,000. All accounts have normal balances.

Requirements

1. Open a T-account for each account and insert its adjusted balance as given (denote as *Adj. Bal.*) at December 31.
2. Post the closing entries to the accounts, denoting posted amounts as *Clos.*
3. Compute the ending balance of Simmons, Capital.

Learning Objective 4

S-F:4-13 Identifying accounts included on a post-closing trial balance

For each account listed, identify whether the account would be included on a post-closing trial balance. Signify either Yes (Y) or No (N).

a. Office Supplies
b. Interest Expense
c. Grey, Capital
d. Grey, Withdrawals
e. Service Revenue
f. Accumulated Depreciation—Furniture
g. Rent Expense
h. Unearned Revenue
i. Accounts Payable

Learning Objective 5

S-F:4-14 Identifying steps in the accounting cycle

Review the steps in the accounting cycle and answer the following questions:

1. What is the first step?
2. Are any steps optional?
3. Which steps are completed throughout the period?
4. Which steps are completed only at the end of the period?
5. What is the last step in the accounting cycle?

Learning Objective 6

S-F:4-15 Calculating the current ratio

End of the Line Montana Refrigeration has these account balances at December 31, 2024:

Notes Payable, long-term	$ 9,200	Accounts Payable	$ 3,600
Prepaid Rent	2,500	Accounts Receivable	6,600
Salaries Payable	2,600	Cash	3,500
Service Revenue	15,600	Depreciation Expense—Equip.	400
Office Supplies	1,300	Equipment	24,000
Accumulated Depreciation—Equip.	4,000	Stapleton, Capital	6,000
Advertising Expense	900	Rent Expense	1,800

Requirements

1. Calculate End of the Line Montana Refrigeration's current ratio.
2. How much in *current* assets does End of the Line Montana Refrigeration have for every dollar of *current* liabilities that it owes?

Learning Objective 7
Appendix 4A

S-F:4A-16 Journalizing reversing entries

Ocean Breeze Associates accrued $8,500 of Service Revenue at December 31. Ocean Breeze Associates received $14,500 on January 15, including the accrued revenue recorded on December 31.

Requirements

1. Record the adjusting entry to accrue Service Revenue.
2. Record the reversing entry.
3. Journalize the cash receipt.

> Exercises

E-F:4-17 Preparing the financial statements

Learning Objective 1

The adjusted trial balance for Green Advertising Services is presented below:

2. Ending Green, Capital $38,200

GREEN ADVERTISING SERVICES
Adjusted Trial Balance
December 31, 2024

Account Title	Balance Debit	Balance Credit
Cash	$ 14,000	
Accounts Receivable	15,800	
Office Supplies	6,500	
Land	18,400	
Building	47,900	
Accumulated Depreciation—Building		$ 36,100
Furniture	19,600	
Accumulated Depreciation—Furniture		14,100
Accounts Payable		10,600
Salaries Payable		7,200
Unearned Revenue		16,000
Green, Capital		61,400
Green, Withdrawals	18,300	
Service Revenue		49,800
Salaries Expense	28,600	
Supplies Expense	8,400	
Depreciation Expense—Building	2,900	
Depreciation Expense—Furniture	1,300	
Advertising Expense	13,500	
Total	$ 195,200	$ 195,200

Requirements

1. Prepare the income statement for the year ending December 31, 2024.
2. Prepare the statement of owner's equity for the year ending December 31, 2024.
3. Prepare the classified balance sheet as of December 31, 2024. Use the report form.

E-F:4-18 Classifying balance sheet accounts

Learning Objective 1

For each account listed, identify the category in which it would appear on a classified balance sheet. Use the following categories: Current Assets; Long-term Investments; Property, Plant, and Equipment; Intangible Assets; Current Liabilities; Long-term Liabilities; and Owner's Equity. If the item does not belong on the classified balance sheet, put an X.

a. Land (used in operations)
b. Accumulated Depreciation—Equipment

c. Reed, Capital
d. Service Revenue
e. Investment in Starbucks Corporation (to be held long-term)
f. Accounts Receivable
g. Equipment
h. Buildings
i. Notes Payable (due in 10 years)
j. Unearned Revenue
k. Cash
l. Accounts Payable
m. Prepaid Rent
n. Reed, Withdrawals
o. Land (held for investment purposes)
p. Depreciation Expense

Learning Objectives 1, 6

1. Total Assets $62,600

E-F:4-19 Preparing a classified balance sheet and calculating the current ratio

The adjusted trial balance of Melanie O'Mallie Dance Studio Company follows:

MELANIE O'MALLIE DANCE STUDIO COMPANY
Trial Balance
August 31, 2024

Account Title	Debit	Credit
Cash	$ 16,000	
Office Supplies	1,800	
Prepaid Rent	1,500	
Equipment	49,000	
Accumulated Depreciation—Equipment		$ 5,700
Accounts Payable		4,800
Salaries Payable		100
Unearned Revenue		5,000
Notes Payable (long-term)		5,400
O'Mallie, Capital		37,000
O'Mallie, Withdrawals	1,100	
Service Revenue		18,100
Salaries Expense	3,600	
Rent Expense	1,100	
Depreciation Expense—Equipment	400	
Supplies Expense	500	
Utilities Expense	1,100	
Total	$ 76,100	$ 76,100

Requirements

1. Prepare the classified balance sheet of Melanie O'Mallie Dance Studio Company at August 31, 2024. Use the report form. You must compute the ending balance of O'Mallie, Capital.

2. Compute O'Mallie's current ratio at August 31, 2024. One year ago, the current ratio was 1.76. Indicate whether O'Mallie's ability to pay current debts has improved, deteriorated, or remained the same.

E-F:4-20 Preparing a worksheet

The unadjusted trial balance of Data Solution at November 30, 2024, follows:

DATA SOLUTION
Unadjusted Trial Balance
November 30, 2024

Account Title	Debit	Credit
Cash	$ 4,400	
Accounts Receivable	3,100	
Prepaid Rent	1,800	
Office Supplies	3,100	
Equipment	30,200	
Accumulated Depreciation—Equipment		$ 1,500
Accounts Payable		5,100
Salaries Payable		
Pryor, Capital		32,900
Pryor, Withdrawals	2,900	
Service Revenue		8,800
Depreciation Expense—Equipment		
Salaries Expense	2,100	
Rent Expense		
Utilities Expense	700	
Supplies Expense		
Total	$ 48,300	$ 48,300

Additional information at November 30, 2024:

a. Accrued Service Revenue, $800.

b. Depreciation, $350.

c. Accrued Salaries Expense, $650.

d. Prepaid Rent expired, $700.

e. Office Supplies used, $550.

Requirements

1. Complete Data Solution's worksheet for the month ended November 30, 2024.
2. How much was net income for November?

Learning Objectives 1, 2

2. Ending Pryor, Capital $34,550

Note: Exercise E-F:4-21 should be used only after completing Exercise E-F:4-20.

E-F:4-21 Preparing financial statements from the completed worksheet

Use your answer from Exercise E-F:4-20 to prepare Data Solution's financial statements.

Requirements

1. Complete the income statement for the month ended November 30, 2024.
2. Complete the statement of owner's equity for the month ended November 30, 2024. Assume beginning Pryor, Capital was $0.
3. Complete the classified balance sheet as of November 30, 2024. Use the report form.

Learning Objective 3

E-F:4-22 Preparing closing entries from an adjusted trial balance

The adjusted trial balance of Stone Sign Company follows:

STONE SIGN COMPANY
Adjusted Trial Balance
January 31, 2024

Account Title	Debit	Credit
Cash	$ 15,400	
Office Supplies	1,500	
Prepaid Rent	1,400	
Equipment	60,000	
Accumulated Depreciation—Equipment		$ 7,000
Accounts Payable		3,800
Salaries Payable		100
Unearned Revenue		4,200
Notes Payable (long-term)		4,300
Stone, Capital		48,800
Stone, Withdrawals	800	
Service Revenue		17,300
Salaries Expense	3,700	
Rent Expense	1,400	
Depreciation Expense—Equipment	400	
Supplies Expense	300	
Utilities Expense	600	
Total	$ 85,500	$ 85,500

Requirements

1. Assume Stone Sign Company has a January 31 year-end. Journalize Stone's closing entries at January 31.
2. How much net income or net loss did Stone Sign Company earn for the year ended January 31? How can you tell?

E-F:4-23 Preparing closing entries from T-accounts

Learning Objective 3

Selected accounts for Kebby Photography at December 31, 2024, follow:

Kebby, Capital
49,000

Kebby, Withdrawals	Service Revenue
14,000	33,000
	4,500

Salaries Expense	Supplies Expense
31,800	2,700
1,400	

Depreciation Expense—Building	Depreciation Expense—Furniture
7,000	1,500

Requirements

1. Journalize Kebby Photography's closing entries at December 31, 2024.
2. Determine Kebby Photography's ending Kebby, Capital balance at December 31, 2024.

E-F:4-24 Determining the effects of closing entries on the Owner, Capital account

Learning Objective 3

McGregor Insurance Agency started the year with a beginning McGregor, Capital balance of $27,500. During the year, McGregor Insurance Agency earned $34,000 of Service Revenue and incurred $23,500 of various expenses. McGregor withdrew $12,000 from the business. After the closing entries are recorded and posted, what will be the balance of McGregor, Capital?

Learning Objectives 3, 4, 6

E-F:4-25 Preparing closing entries from an adjusted trial balance; preparing a post-closing trial balance; and calculating the current ratio

Mark's Bowling Alley's adjusted trial balance as of December 31, 2024, is presented below:

MARK'S BOWLING ALLEY
Adjusted Trial Balance
December 31, 2024

Account Title	Debit	Credit
Cash	$ 20,000	
Accounts Receivable	2,900	
Office Supplies	1,150	
Prepaid Insurance	2,700	
Land	20,000	
Building	145,000	
Accumulated Depreciation—Building		$ 7,000
Equipment	43,000	
Accumulated Depreciation—Equipment		20,000
Accounts Payable		4,800
Utilities Payable		625
Salaries Payable		3,800
Unearned Revenue		1,900
Benoit, Capital		220,250
Benoit, Withdrawals	31,000	
Service Revenue		85,000
Insurance Expense	26,000	
Salaries Expense	28,000	
Supplies Expense	1,300	
Utilities Expense	15,000	
Depreciation Expense—Equipment	7,000	
Depreciation Expense—Building	325	
Total	$ 343,375	$ 343,375

Requirements

1. Prepare the closing entries for Mark's Bowling Alley.
2. Prepare a post-closing trial balance.
3. Compute the current ratio for Mark's Bowling Alley.

E-F:4-26 Preparing a worksheet, closing entries, and a post-closing trial balance

Learning Objectives 2, 3, 4

Houston Veterinary Hospital completed the following worksheet as of December 31, 2024.

1. Net Loss $(12,150)

	A	B	C	D	E	F	G	H	I	J	K	L	M
1		\multicolumn{12}{c}{HOUSTON VETERINARY HOSPITAL}
2		\multicolumn{12}{c}{Worksheet}
3		\multicolumn{12}{c}{December 31, 2024}
4													
5	Account Names	\multicolumn{2}{c}{Unadjusted Trial Balance}		\multicolumn{2}{c}{Adjustments}		\multicolumn{2}{c}{Adjusted Trial Balance}	\multicolumn{2}{c}{Income Statement}	\multicolumn{2}{c}{Balance Sheet}
6		Debit	Credit		Debit	Credit		Debit	Credit	Debit	Credit	Debit	Credit
7	Cash	$31,200						$31,200					
8	Accounts Receivable	8,700		(f)	$1,400			10,100					
9	Office Supplies	1,500				$275	(b)	1,225					
10	Prepaid Rent	6,000				600	(a)	5,400					
11	Equipment	27,000						27,000					
12	Accumulated Depreciation—Equipment					1,900	(c)		$1,900				
13	Accounts Payable		$3,400						3,400				
14	Utilities Payable		310						310				
15	Salaries Payable					1,075	(e)		1,075				
16	Unearned Revenue		13,000	(d)	1,300				11,700				
17	Houston, Capital		96,690						96,690				
18	Houston, Withdrawals	28,000						28,000					
19	Service Revenue		35,000			2,700	(d,f)		37,700				
20	Rent Expense	23,000		(a)	600			23,600					
21	Salaries Expense	12,000		(e)	1,075			13,075					
22	Supplies Expense			(b)	275			275					
23	Utilities Expense	11,000						11,000					
24	Depreciation Expense—Equipment			(c)	1,900			1,900					
25	Total	$148,400	$148,400		$6,550	$6,550		$152,775	$152,775				

Requirements

1. Complete the worksheet for Houston Veterinary Hospital.
2. Prepare the closing entries.
3. Prepare a post-closing trial balance.

E-F:4A-27 Journalizing reversing entries

Learning Objective 7
Appendix 4A

Lucas Architects recorded the following adjusting entries as of December 31:

a. Service Revenue accrued, $2,600.

b. Unearned Revenue that has been earned, $1,300.

c. Office Supplies on hand, $530. The balance of the Office Supplies account was $880.

d. Salaries owed to employees, $600.

e. One month of Prepaid Rent has expired, $3,100.

f. Depreciation on equipment, $1,075.

Journalize any necessary reversing entries for Lucas Architects.

**Learning Objective 7
Appendix 4A**

E-F:4A-28 Journalizing reversing entries

Mountain View Services had the following unadjusted balances at December 31, 2024: Salaries Payable, $0; and Salaries Expense, $1,900. The following transactions have taken place at the end of 2024 and beginning of 2025:

2024	
Dec. 31	Accrued Salaries Expense at December 31, $8,000.
31	Closed the Salaries Expense account.
2025	
Jan. 1	Reversed the accrued salaries. (Requirement 3 only)
4	Paid salaries of $8,500. This payment included the Salaries Payable amount, plus $500 for the first few days of January.

Requirements

1. Open T-accounts for Salaries Payable and Salaries Expense using their unadjusted balances at December 31, 2024.

2. Journalize the entries assuming Mountain View Services does not use reversing entries. **Do not record the reversing entry on Jan. 1.** Post to the accounts.

3. Open new T-accounts for Salaries Payable and Salaries Expense using their unadjusted balances at December 31, 2024. Journalize the entries assuming Mountain View Services uses reversing entries. **Don't forget to record the reversing entry on Jan. 1.** Post to the accounts. Compare the balances on January 4, 2025 with Requirement 2 balances on January 4, 2025.

> Problems Group A

P-F:4-29A Preparing financial statements including a classified balance sheet in report form, preparing and posting closing entries, and preparing a post-closing trial balance

Learning Objectives 1, 3, 4

1. Net Loss $(9,500)

The adjusted trial balance of Erickson Real Estate Appraisal at June 30, 2024, follows:

ERICKSON REAL ESTATE APPRAISAL
Adjusted Trial Balance
June 30, 2024

Account Title	Debit	Credit
Cash	$ 4,600	
Accounts Receivable	5,300	
Office Supplies	1,500	
Prepaid Insurance	1,700	
Land	13,000	
Building	82,000	
Accumulated Depreciation—Building		$ 25,200
Accounts Payable		18,700
Interest Payable		8,500
Salaries Payable		2,400
Unearned Revenue		7,600
Notes Payable (long-term)		40,000
Erickson, Capital		42,500
Erickson, Withdrawals	27,300	
Service Revenue		48,100
Insurance Expense	4,400	
Salaries Expense	33,500	
Supplies Expense	300	
Interest Expense	8,500	
Utilities Expense	2,700	
Depreciation Expense—Building	8,200	
Total	$ 193,000	$ 193,000

Requirements

1. Prepare the company's income statement for the year ended June 30, 2024.
2. Prepare the company's statement of owner's equity for the year ended June 30, 2024.
3. Prepare the company's classified balance sheet in report form at June 30, 2024.
4. Journalize the closing entries.
5. Open the T-accounts using the balances from the adjusted trial balance and post the closing entries to the T-accounts.
6. Prepare the company's post-closing trial balance at June 30, 2024.

Learning Objectives 1, 3, 6

2. Ending Boston, Capital $80,200

P-F:4-30A Preparing financial statements including a classified balance sheet in report form, preparing closing entries, and using the current ratio to evaluate a company

The adjusted trial balance of Boston Irrigation System at December 31, 2024, follows:

BOSTON IRRIGATION SYSTEM
Adjusted Trial Balance
December 31, 2024

Account Title	Debit	Credit
Cash	$ 11,800	
Accounts Receivable	46,000	
Office Supplies	29,500	
Prepaid Insurance	6,300	
Building	63,000	
Accumulated Depreciation—Building		$ 25,000
Equipment	28,000	
Accumulated Depreciation—Equipment		7,700
Accounts Payable		32,100
Interest Payable		2,200
Salaries Payable		2,600
Unearned Revenue		2,100
Notes Payable (long-term)		32,700
Boston, Capital		33,000
Boston, Withdrawals	2,200	
Service Revenue		74,500
Insurance Expense	1,100	
Salaries Expense	16,400	
Supplies Expense	1,100	
Interest Expense	2,200	
Depreciation Expense—Equipment	2,500	
Depreciation Expense—Building	1,800	
Total	$ 211,900	$ 211,900

Requirements

1. Prepare the company's income statement for the year ended December 31, 2024.
2. Prepare the company's statement of owner's equity for the year ended December 31, 2024.
3. Prepare the company's classified balance sheet in report form at December 31, 2024.
4. Journalize the closing entries for Boston Irrigation System.
5. Compute the company's current ratio at December 31, 2024. At December 31, 2023, the current ratio was 2.3. Did the company's ability to pay current debts improve or deteriorate, or did it remain the same?

P-F:4-31A Preparing a worksheet, financial statements, and closing entries

The *unadjusted* trial balance of Farish Investment Advisers at December 31, 2024, follows:

Learning Objectives 1, 2, 3

2. Total Assets $106,500

FARISH INVESTMENT ADVISERS
Unadjusted Trial Balance
December 31, 2024

Account Title	Debit	Credit
Cash	$ 30,000	
Accounts Receivable	51,000	
Office Supplies	7,000	
Equipment	28,000	
Accumulated Depreciation—Equipment		$ 9,000
Accounts Payable		13,000
Salaries Payable		
Unearned Revenue		5,500
Notes Payable (long-term)		21,000
Farish, Capital		56,500
Farish, Withdrawals	29,000	
Service Revenue		93,000
Insurance Expense	2,500	
Salaries Expense	40,000	
Supplies Expense		
Interest Expense	5,500	
Rent Expense	5,000	
Depreciation Expense—Equipment		
Total	$ 198,000	$ 198,000

Adjustment data at December 31, 2024:

a. Unearned Revenue earned during the year, $800.
b. Office Supplies on hand, $4,500.
c. Depreciation for the year, $4,500.
d. Accrued Salaries Expense, $5,000.
e. Accrued Service Revenue, $6,500.

Requirements

1. Prepare a worksheet for Farish Investment Advisers at December 31, 2024.
2. Prepare the income statement, the statement of owner's equity and the classified balance sheet in account format.
3. Prepare closing entries.

Learning Objectives 1, 2, 3, 4, 5, 6

5. Net Income $18,890

P-F:4-32A Completing the accounting cycle from adjusting entries to post-closing trial balance with an optional worksheet

The *unadjusted* trial balance of Walton Anvils at December 31, 2024, and the data for the adjustments follow:

WALTON ANVILS
Unadjusted Trial Balance
December 31, 2024

Account Title	Debit	Credit
Cash	$ 13,480	
Accounts Receivable	14,500	
Prepaid Rent	2,320	
Office Supplies	1,700	
Equipment	23,000	
Accumulated Depreciation—Equipment		$ 1,000
Accounts Payable		7,100
Salaries Payable		
Unearned Revenue		6,000
Walton, Capital		28,500
Walton, Withdrawals	4,600	
Service Revenue		19,500
Salaries Expense	2,500	
Rent Expense		
Depreciation Expense—Equipment		
Supplies Expense		
Total	$ 62,100	$ 62,100

Adjustment data:
a. Unearned Revenue still unearned at December 31, $1,800.
b. Prepaid Rent still in force at December 31, $2,100.
c. Office Supplies used, $1,500.
d. Depreciation, $390.
e. Accrued Salaries Expense at December 31, $200.

Requirements

1. Open the T-accounts using the balances in the unadjusted trial balance.
2. Complete the worksheet for the year ended December 31, 2024 (optional).
3. Prepare the adjusting entries and post to the accounts.
4. Prepare an adjusted trial balance.
5. Prepare the income statement, the statement of owner's equity, and the classified balance sheet in report form.

6. Prepare the closing entries and post to the accounts.
7. Prepare a post-closing trial balance.
8. Calculate the current ratio for the company.

P-F:4-33A Completing the accounting cycle from journal entries to post-closing trial balance with an optional worksheet

Learning Objectives 1, 2, 3, 4, 5

On December 1, Bob Waldo began an auto repair shop, Waldo's Quality Automotive. The following transactions occurred during December:

6. Ending Waldo, Capital $75,095

Dec. 1	Waldo contributed $70,000 cash to the business in exchange for capital.
1	Purchased $12,000 of equipment paying cash.
1	Paid $1,750 for a five-month insurance policy starting on December 1.
9	Paid $20,000 cash to purchase land to be used in operations.
10	Purchased office supplies on account, $2,800.
19	Borrowed $15,000 from the bank for business use. Waldo signed a note payable to the bank in the name of the business. The note is due in five years.
22	Paid $1,300 for advertising expenses.
26	Paid $900 on account.
28	The business received a bill for utilities to be paid in January, $280.
31	Revenues earned during the month included $16,000 cash and $3,600 on account.
31	Paid employees' salaries $3,800 and building rent $1,200. Record as a compound entry.
31	The business received $1,440 for auto screening services to be performed next month.
31	Waldo withdrew cash of $5,500.

The business uses the following accounts: Cash; Accounts Receivable; Office Supplies; Prepaid Insurance; Land; Equipment; Accumulated Depreciation—Equipment; Accounts Payable; Utilities Payable; Interest Payable; Unearned Revenue; Notes Payable; Waldo, Capital; Waldo, Withdrawals; Income Summary; Service Revenue; Salaries Expense; Rent Expense; Utilities Expense; Advertising Expense; Supplies Expense; Insurance Expense; Interest Expense; and Depreciation Expense—Equipment.

Adjustment data:

a. Office Supplies used during the month, $1,800.
b. Depreciation for the month, $200.
c. One month insurance has expired.
d. Accrued Interest Expense, $75.

Requirements

1. Prepare the journal entries and post to the T-accounts.
2. Prepare an unadjusted trial balance.
3. Complete the worksheet for the month ended December 31, 2024 (optional).
4. Prepare the adjusting entries and post to the T-accounts.
5. Prepare an adjusted trial balance.

6. Prepare the income statement, the statement of owner's equity, and the classified balance sheet in report form.
7. Prepare the closing entries and post to the T-accounts.
8. Prepare a post-closing trial balance.

Learning Objective 7
Appendix 4A

P-F:4A-34A Preparing adjusting entries and reversing entries

The unadjusted trial balance and adjustment data of Martha's Motors at December 31, 2024, follow:

MARTHA'S MOTORS
Unadjusted Trial Balance
December 31, 2024

Account Title	Debit	Credit
Cash	$ 4,200	
Accounts Receivable	27,200	
Office Supplies	1,000	
Prepaid Insurance	2,400	
Equipment	52,400	
Accumulated Depreciation—Equipment		$ 34,600
Accounts Payable		15,000
Wages Payable		
Unearned Revenue		7,900
Eaglin, Capital		18,500
Eaglin, Withdrawals	3,100	
Service Revenue		17,200
Depreciation Expense—Equipment		
Wages Expense	1,600	
Insurance Expense		
Utilities Expense	1,300	
Supplies Expense		
Total	$ 93,200	$ 93,200

Adjustment data at December 31, 2024:

a. Depreciation on equipment, $2,100.
b. Accrued Wages Expense, $1,100.
c. Office Supplies on hand, $500.
d. Prepaid Insurance expired during December, $600.
e. Unearned Revenue earned during December, $4,800.
f. Accrued Service Revenue, $1,300.

2025 transactions:

a. On January 4, Martha's Motors paid wages of $1,900. Of this, $1,100 related to the accrued wages recorded on December 31.
b. On January 10, Martha's Motors received $1,500 for Service Revenue. Of this, $1,300 is related to the accrued Service Revenue recorded on December 31.

Requirements

1. Journalize adjusting entries.
2. Journalize reversing entries for the appropriate adjusting entries.
3. Refer to the 2025 data. Journalize the cash payment and the cash receipt that occurred in 2025.

> Problems Group B

P-F:4-35B Preparing financial statements including a classified balance sheet in report form, preparing and posting closing entries, and preparing a post-closing trial balance

Learning Objectives 1, 3, 4

1. Net Loss $(6,600)

The adjusted trial balance of Rocket Real Estate Appraisal at June 30, 2024, follows:

ROCKET REAL ESTATE APPRAISAL
Adjusted Trial Balance
June 30, 2024

Account Title	Debit	Credit
Cash	$ 5,000	
Accounts Receivable	5,500	
Office Supplies	1,600	
Prepaid Insurance	1,700	
Land	12,800	
Building	71,000	
Accumulated Depreciation—Building		$ 25,200
Accounts Payable		18,700
Interest Payable		8,000
Salaries Payable		2,100
Unearned Revenue		1,000
Notes Payable (long-term)		37,000
Rocket, Capital		38,000
Rocket, Withdrawals	25,800	
Service Revenue		48,100
Insurance Expense	4,100	
Salaries Expense	32,000	
Supplies Expense	600	
Interest Expense	8,000	
Utilities Expense	2,900	
Depreciation Expense—Building	7,100	
Total	$ 178,100	$ 178,100

Requirements

1. Prepare the company's income statement for the year ended June 30, 2024.
2. Prepare the company's statement of owner's equity for the year ended June 30, 2024.
3. Prepare the company's classified balance sheet in report form at June 30, 2024.
4. Journalize the closing entries.
5. Open the T-accounts using the balances from the adjusted trial balance and post the closing entries to the T-accounts.
6. Prepare the company's post-closing trial balance at June 30, 2024.

Learning Objectives 1, 3, 6

2. Ending Bradley, Capital $73,200

P-F:4-36B Preparing financial statements including a classified balance sheet in report form, preparing closing entries, and using the current ratio to evaluate a company

The adjusted trial balance of Bradley Irrigation System at December 31, 2024, follows:

BRADLEY IRRIGATION SYSTEM
Adjusted Trial Balance
December 31, 2024

Account Title	Debit	Credit
Cash	$ 12,000	
Accounts Receivable	51,000	
Office Supplies	28,300	
Prepaid Insurance	4,700	
Building	57,300	
Accumulated Depreciation—Building		$ 25,300
Equipment	21,000	
Accumulated Depreciation—Equipment		6,800
Accounts Payable		40,700
Interest Payable		2,000
Salaries Payable		3,500
Unearned Revenue		1,800
Notes Payable (long-term)		21,000
Bradley, Capital		45,000
Bradley, Withdrawals	3,200	
Service Revenue		56,000
Insurance Expense	1,200	
Salaries Expense	16,200	
Supplies Expense	1,400	
Interest Expense	2,000	
Depreciation Expense—Building	1,200	
Depreciation Expense—Equipment	2,600	
Total	$ 202,100	$ 202,100

Requirements

1. Prepare the company's income statement for the year ended December 31, 2024.
2. Prepare the company's statement of owner's equity for the year ended December 31, 2024.
3. Prepare the company's classified balance sheet in report form at December 31, 2024.
4. Journalize the closing entries for Bradley Irrigation System.
5. Compute the company's current ratio at December 31, 2024. At December 31, 2023, the current ratio was 1.7. Did the company's ability to pay current debts improve or deteriorate, or did it remain the same?

P-F:4-37B Preparing a worksheet, financial statements, and closing entries

Learning Objectives 1, 2, 3

The *unadjusted* trial balance of Fleming Investment Advisers at December 31, 2024, follows:

2. Total Assets $92,000

FLEMING INVESTMENT ADVISERS
Unadjusted Trial Balance
December 31, 2024

Account Title	Balance Debit	Balance Credit
Cash	$ 25,000	
Accounts Receivable	51,000	
Office Supplies	7,500	
Equipment	26,000	
Accumulated Depreciation—Equipment		$ 19,000
Accounts Payable		14,000
Salaries Payable		
Unearned Revenue		4,500
Notes Payable (long-term)		26,000
Fleming, Capital		20,500
Fleming, Withdrawals	28,000	
Service Revenue		99,000
Insurance Expense	2,500	
Salaries Expense	33,000	
Supplies Expense		
Interest Expense	3,000	
Rent Expense	7,000	
Depreciation Expense—Equipment		
Total	$ 183,000	$ 183,000

Adjustment data at December 31, 2024:

a. Unearned Revenue earned during the year, $700.
b. Office Supplies on hand, $3,000.
c. Depreciation for the year, $3,000.
d. Accrued Salaries Expense, $4,500.
e. Accrued Service Revenue, $9,000.

Requirements

1. Prepare a worksheet for Fleming Investment Advisers at December 31, 2024.
2. Prepare the income statement, the statement of owner's equity, and the classified balance sheet in account format.
3. Prepare closing entries.

Learning Objectives 1, 2, 3, 4, 5, 6

5. Net Income $17,380

P-F:4-38B Completing the accounting cycle from adjusting entries to post-closing trial balance with an optional worksheet

The *unadjusted* trial balance of Watson Anvils at December 31, 2024, and the data for the adjustments follow:

WATSON ANVILS
Unadjusted Trial Balance
December 31, 2024

Account Title	Debit	Credit
Cash	$ 13,560	
Accounts Receivable	17,000	
Prepaid Rent	2,140	
Office Supplies	2,800	
Equipment	30,000	
Accumulated Depreciation—Equipment		$ 11,000
Accounts Payable		7,200
Salaries Payable		
Unearned Revenue		5,600
Watson, Capital		29,600
Watson, Withdrawals	4,600	
Service Revenue		19,000
Salaries Expense	2,300	
Rent Expense		
Depreciation Expense—Equipment		
Supplies Expense		
Total	$ 72,400	$ 72,400

Adjustment data:

a. Unearned Revenue still unearned at December 31, $3,600.
b. Prepaid Rent still in force at December 31, $2,000.
c. Office Supplies used, $600.
d. Depreciation, $400.
e. Accrued Salaries Expense at December 31, $180.

Requirements

1. Open the T-accounts using the balances in the unadjusted trial balance.
2. Complete the worksheet for the year ended December 31, 2024 (optional).
3. Prepare the adjusting entries and post to the accounts.
4. Prepare an adjusted trial balance.
5. Prepare the income statement, the statement of owner's equity, and the classified balance sheet in report form.
6. Prepare the closing entries and post to the accounts.
7. Prepare a post-closing trial balance.
8. Calculate the current ratio for the company.

P-F:4-39B Completing the accounting cycle from journal entries to post-closing trial balance with an optional worksheet

Learning Objectives 1, 2, 3, 4, 5

On December 1, Curt Wilson began an auto repair shop, Wilson's Quality Automotive. The following transactions occurred during December:

6. Ending Wilson, Capital $72,080

Dec. 1	Wilson contributed $63,000 cash to the business in exchange for capital.
1	Purchased $14,400 of equipment, paying cash.
1	Paid $3,600 for a twelve-month insurance policy starting on December 1.
9	Paid $15,000 cash to purchase land to be used in operations.
10	Purchased office supplies on account, $2,200.
19	Borrowed $24,000 from the bank for business use. Wilson signed a notes payable to the bank in the name of the business. The note is due in five years.
22	Paid $2,000 for advertising expenses.
26	Paid $1,000 on account.
28	The business received a bill for utilities to be paid in January, $260.
31	Revenues earned during the month included $18,500 cash and $3,800 on account.
31	Paid employees' salaries $3,900 and building rent $800. Record as a compound entry.
31	The business received $1,380 for auto screening services to be performed next month.
31	Wilson withdrew cash of $5,000.

The business uses the following accounts: Cash; Accounts Receivable; Office Supplies; Prepaid Insurance; Land; Equipment; Accumulated Depreciation—Equipment; Accounts Payable; Utilities Payable; Interest Payable; Unearned Revenue; Notes Payable; Wilson, Capital; Wilson, Withdrawals; Income Summary; Service Revenue; Salaries Expense; Rent Expense; Utilities Expense; Advertising Expense; Supplies Expense; Insurance Expense; Interest Expense; and Depreciation Expense—Equipment.

Adjustment data:

a. Office Supplies used during the month, $600.
b. Depreciation for the month, $240.
c. One month insurance has expired.
d. Accrued Interest Expense, $120.

Requirements

1. Prepare the journal entries and post to the T-accounts.
2. Prepare an unadjusted trial balance.
3. Complete the worksheet for the month ended December 31, 2024 (optional).
4. Prepare the adjusting entries and post to the T-accounts.
5. Prepare an adjusted trial balance.
6. Prepare the income statement, the statement of owner's equity, and the classified balance sheet in report form.
7. Prepare the closing entries and post to the T-accounts.
8. Prepare a post-closing trial balance.

Learning Objective 7
Appendix 4A

P-F:4A-40B Preparing adjusting entries and reversing entries

The unadjusted trial balance and adjustment data of Myla's Motors at December 31, 2024, follow:

MYLA'S MOTORS
Unadjusted Trial Balance
December 31, 2024

Account Title	Debit	Credit
Cash	$ 4,500	
Accounts Receivable	26,100	
Office Supplies	1,000	
Prepaid Insurance	1,500	
Equipment	50,500	
Accumulated Depreciation—Equipment		$ 35,000
Accounts Payable		13,700
Wages Payable		
Unearned Revenue		5,700
Withers, Capital		19,300
Withers, Withdrawals	4,300	
Service Revenue		17,200
Depreciation Expense—Equipment		
Wages Expense	1,200	
Insurance Expense		
Utilities Expense	1,800	
Supplies Expense		
Total	$ 90,900	$ 90,900

Adjustment data at December 31, 2024:

a. Depreciation on equipment, $1,700.
b. Accrued Wages Expense, $1,300.
c. Office Supplies on hand, $400.
d. Prepaid Insurance expired during December, $250.

e. Unearned Revenue earned during December, $4,200.

f. Accrued Service Revenue, $1,000.

2025 transactions:

a. On January 4, Myla's Motors paid wages of $1,900. Of this, $1,300 related to the accrued wages recorded on December 31.

b. On January 10, Myla's Motors received $1,700 for Service Revenue. Of this, $1,000 related to the accrued Service Revenue recorded on December 31.

Requirements

1. Journalize adjusting entries.
2. Journalize reversing entries for the appropriate adjusting entries.
3. Refer to the 2025 data. Journalize the cash payment and the cash receipt that occurred in 2025.

CRITICAL THINKING

> Using Excel

Download Excel problems for this chapter online in MyLab Accounting or at **http://www.pearsonhighered.com/Horngren**.

> Continuing Problem

P-F:4-41 Completing the accounting cycle from adjusted trial balance to post-closing trial balance with an optional worksheet

This problem continues the Canyon Canoe Company situation from Chapter F:3.

Requirements

1. Complete the worksheet at December 31, 2024 (optional). Use the unadjusted trial balance from Chapter F:2 and the adjusting entries from Chapter F:3.
2. Prepare an income statement for the two months ended December 31, 2024. Use the worksheet prepared in Requirement 1 or the adjusted trial balance from Chapter F:3.
3. Prepare a statement of owner's equity for the two months ended December 31, 2024.
4. Prepare a classified balance sheet (report form) at December 31, 2024. Assume the note payable is long-term.
5. Journalize and post the closing entries at December 31, 2024. Open T-accounts for Income Summary and Wilson, Capital. Determine the ending balance for each account. Denote each closing amount as *Clos.* and each account balance as *Balance*.
6. Prepare a post-closing trial balance at December 31, 2024.

> Practice Set

P-F:4-42 Completing the accounting cycle from adjusted trial balance to post-closing trial balance with an optional worksheet

Refer to the Practice Set data provided in Chapters F:2 and F:3 for Crystal Clear Cleaning.

Requirements

1. Prepare a worksheet (optional) at November 30, 2024. Use the unadjusted trial balance from Chapter F:2 and the adjusting entries from Chapter F:3.
2. Prepare an income statement and statement of owner's equity for the month ended November 30, 2024. Also prepare a classified balance sheet at November 30, 2024, using the report format. Assume the Notes Payable is long-term. Use the worksheet prepared in Requirement 1 or the adjusted trial balance from Chapter F:3.
3. Prepare closing entries at November 30, 2024, and post to the accounts. Open T-accounts for Income Summary and Hideaway, Capital. Determine the ending balance in each account. Denote each closing amount as *Clos.* and each account balance as *Balance*.
4. Prepare a post-closing trial balance at November 30, 2024.

COMPREHENSIVE PROBLEMS

> Comprehensive Problem F:4-1 for Chapters F:1–F:4

Murphy Delivery Service completed the following transactions during December 2024:

Dec. 1	Murphy Delivery Service began operations by receiving $13,000 cash and a truck with a fair value of $9,000 from Russ Murphy. The business issued Murphy capital in exchange for this contribution.
1	Paid $600 cash for a six-month insurance policy. The policy begins December 1.
4	Paid $750 cash for office supplies.
12	Performed delivery services for a customer and received $2,200 cash.
15	Completed a large delivery job, billed the customer $3,300, and received a promise to collect the $3,300 within one week.
18	Paid employee salary, $800.
20	Received $7,000 cash for performing delivery services.
22	Collected $2,200 in advance for delivery service to be performed later.
25	Collected $3,300 cash from customer on account.
27	Purchased fuel for the truck, paying $150 on account. (Credit Accounts Payable)
28	Performed delivery services on account, $1,400.
29	Paid office rent, $1,400, for the month of December.
30	Paid $150 on account.
31	Murphy withdrew cash of $2,500.

Requirements

1. Record each transaction in the journal using the following chart of accounts. Explanations are not required.

Cash	Murphy, Withdrawals
Accounts Receivable	Income Summary
Office Supplies	Service Revenue
Prepaid Insurance	Salaries Expense
Truck	Depreciation Expense—Truck
Accumulated Depreciation—Truck	Insurance Expense
Accounts Payable	Fuel Expense
Salaries Payable	Rent Expense
Unearned Revenue	Supplies Expense
Murphy, Capital	

2. Post the transactions in the T-accounts.
3. Prepare an unadjusted trial balance as of December 31, 2024.
4. Prepare a worksheet as of December 31, 2024 (optional).
5. Journalize the adjusting entries using the following adjustment data and also by reviewing the journal entries prepared in Requirement 1. Post adjusting entries to the T-accounts.

   Adjustment data:

   a. Accrued Salaries Expense, $800.
   b. Depreciation was recorded on the truck using the straight-line method. Assume a useful life of five years and a salvage value of $3,000.
   c. Prepaid Insurance for the month has expired.
   d. Office Supplies on hand, $450.
   e. Unearned Revenue earned during the month, $700.
   f. Accrued Service Revenue, $450.

6. Prepare an adjusted trial balance as of December 31, 2024.
7. Prepare Murphy Delivery Service's income statement and statement of owner's equity for the month ended December 31, 2024, and the classified balance sheet on that date. On the income statement, list expenses in decreasing order by amount—that is, the largest expense first, the smallest expense last.
8. Journalize the closing entries and post to the T-accounts.
9. Prepare a post-closing trial balance as of December 31, 2024.

> Comprehensive Problem F:4-2 for Chapters F:1–F:4

This comprehensive problem is a continuation of Comprehensive Problem 1. Murphy Delivery Service has completed closing entries and the accounting cycle for 2024. The business is now ready to record January 2025 transactions.

Jan.		
3	Collected $200 cash from customer on account.
5	Purchased office supplies on account, $1,000.
12	Performed delivery services for a customer and received $3,000 cash.
15	Paid employee salary, including the amount owed on December 31, $4,100.
18	Performed delivery services on account, $1,350.
20	Paid $300 on account.
24	Purchased fuel for the truck, paying $200 cash.
27	Completed the remaining work due for Unearned Revenue.
28	Paid office rent, $2,200, for the month of January.
30	Collected $3,000 in advance for delivery service to be performed later.
31	Murphy withdrew cash of $1,500.

Requirements

1. Record each January transaction in the journal. Explanations are not required.
2. Post the transactions in the T-accounts. Don't forget to use the December 31, 2024, ending balances as appropriate.
3. Prepare an unadjusted trial balance as of January 31, 2025.
4. Prepare a worksheet as of January 31, 2025 (optional).
5. Journalize the adjusting entries using the following adjustment data and also by reviewing the journal entries prepared in Requirement 1. Post adjusting entries to the T-accounts.

   Adjustment data:

   a. Office Supplies on hand, $600.
   b. Accrued Service Revenue, $1,800.
   c. Accrued Salaries Expense, $500.
   d. Prepaid Insurance for the month has expired.
   e. Depreciation was recorded on the truck for the month.

6. Prepare an adjusted trial balance as of January 31, 2025.
7. Prepare Murphy Delivery Service's income statement and statement of owner's equity for the month ended January 31, 2025, and the classified balance sheet on that date. On the income statement, list expenses in decreasing order by amount—that is, the largest expense first, the smallest expense last.
8. Calculate the following ratios as of January 31, 2025, for Murphy Delivery Service: return on assets, debt ratio, and current ratio.

> Tying It All Together F:4-1

Before you begin this assignment, review the Tying It All Together feature in the chapter. It will also be helpful if you review Hyatt Hotels Corporation's 2018 annual report (**https://www.sec.gov/Archives/edgar/data/1468174/000146817419000009/h10-k123118.htm#sE3993A8AD84040710041937D19B26344**).

Hyatt Hotels Corporation is headquartered in Chicago and is a leading global hospitality company. The company develops, owns, and operates hotels, resorts, and vacation ownership properties in 60 different countries.

Requirements

1. Review Hyatt Hotels Corporation's income statement for year ended December 31, 2018. What does the income statement report? What was the amount of net income or loss for the year ending December 31, 2018?
2. Review the accounts that are listed on Hyatt Hotels Corporation's income statement and balance sheet. What are some examples of accounts that would be closed during the closing process?
3. Review the Hyatt Hotels Corporation's balance sheet. What does the balance sheet tell an investor? Did Hyatt Hotels Corporation present an unclassified or classified balance sheet? Explain.

> Ethical Issue F:4-1

Grant Film Productions wishes to expand and has borrowed $100,000. As a condition for making this loan, the bank requires that the business maintain a current ratio of at least 1.50.

Business has been good but not great. Expansion costs have brought the current ratio down to 1.40 on December 15. Rita Grant, owner of the business, is considering what might happen if she reports a current ratio of 1.40 to the bank. One course of action for Grant is to record in December of this year $10,000 of revenue that the business will earn in January of next year. The contract for this job has been signed.

Requirements

1. Journalize the revenue transaction and indicate how recording this revenue in December would affect the current ratio.
2. Discuss whether it is ethical to record the revenue transaction in December. Identify the accounting principle relevant to this situation and give the reasons underlying your conclusion.

> Financial Statement Case F:4-1

This case, based on the balance sheet of **Target Corporation**, will familiarize you with some of the assets and liabilities of that company. Visit **http://www.pearsonhighered.com/Horngren** to view a link to Target Corporation's Fiscal 2018 Annual Report. Use the Target Corporation balance sheet to answer the following questions.

Requirements

1. Which balance sheet format does Target use?
2. Name the company's largest current asset and largest current liability at February 2, 2019.
3. Compute Target's current ratios at February 2, 2019, and February 3, 2018. Did the current ratio improve, worsen, or hold steady?
4. Under what category does Target report furniture, fixtures, and equipment?
5. What was the cost of the company's property, plant, and equipment at February 2, 2019? What was the amount of accumulated depreciation? What was the book value of the property, plant, and equipment?

> Team Project F:4-1

Kathy Wintz formed a lawn service business as a summer job. To start the business on May 1, 2024, she deposited $1,000 in a new bank account in the name of the business. The $1,000 consisted of a $600 loan from Bank One to her company, Wintz Lawn Service, and $400 of her own money. The company issued $400 of capital to Wintz. Wintz rented lawn equipment, purchased supplies, and hired other students to mow and trim customers' lawns.

At the end of each month, Wintz mailed bills to the customers. On August 31, she was ready to dissolve the business and return to college. Because she was so busy, she kept few records other than the checkbook and a list of receivables from customers.

At August 31, the business's checkbook shows a balance of $2,000, and customers still owe $750. During the summer, the business collected $5,500 from customers. The business checkbook lists payments for supplies totaling $400, and it still has gasoline, weed trimmer cord, and other supplies that cost a total of $50. The business paid employees $1,800 and still owes them $300 for the final week of the summer.

Wintz rented some equipment from Ludwig's Machine Shop. On May 1, the business signed a six-month rental agreement on mowers and paid $600 for the full rental period in advance. Ludwig's will refund the unused portion of the prepayment if the equipment is returned in good shape. In order to get the refund, Wintz has kept the mowers in excellent condition. In fact, the business had to pay $300 to repair a mower.

To transport employees and equipment to jobs, Wintz used a trailer that the business bought for $300. The business estimates that the summer's work used up one-third of the trailer's service potential. The business checkbook lists a payment of $500 for cash withdrawals paid during the summer. The business paid the loan back during August. (For simplicity, ignore any interest expense associated with the loan.)

Requirements

1. As a team, prepare the income statement and the statement of owner's equity of Wintz Lawn Service for the four months May 1 through August 31, 2024.
2. Prepare the classified balance sheet (report form) of Wintz Lawn Service at August 31, 2024.
3. Was Wintz's summer work successful? Give your team's reason for your answer.

> Quick Check Answers

1. c   **2.** b   **3.** b   **4.** d   **5.** d   **6.** c   **7.** a   **8.** a   **9.** a   **10A.** b

Merchandising Operations   5

Will They Buy It?

Julie Ryski studied the model on the catwalk who was wearing the latest spring fashion. As a retail buyer for a nationwide high-end department store, Julie is responsible for selecting merchandise that will be sold in stores across America. Not only must Julie have a keen eye for the latest fashion designs and seasonal variations, but she must also understand the needs of the department store's customers. Julie enjoys attending fashion shows and other fashion-oriented promotions, but she knows that there is more to her responsibilities than simply selecting the newest spring outfits.

As Julie contemplates the model and whether she should purchase this merchandise for the department store's spring line, she knows that she has to always keep the department store's gross profit in mind. She is responsible for ensuring that the merchandise she buys will be purchased by customers and that it is priced effectively to ensure the highest profit maximization possible. In addition, she must ensure that this merchandise can meet the department store's sales goals and ultimate financial objectives. In the long run, Julie is responsible for all aspects of the merchandise that is sold in the store. She must understand how merchandise is reported on the financial statements, how it is recorded in the accounting records, and how the department store determines gross profit (the difference between the original cost and the retail price). Julie's buying decisions and expertise play a major role in the company's profits. Her pricing decisions ultimately affect the net income of the department store and are a major component of the department store's bottom line.

How Do Businesses Account for Merchandise Inventory?

In this chapter, we begin our exploration of companies that sell goods (called *merchandise inventory*) to customers. Although many of the accounting concepts you have learned concerning service businesses apply, merchandisers (businesses that sell inventory) have some unique characteristics you must learn to account for. For example, **Macy's, Inc.,** a nationally known premier retailer of the Macy's, Bloomingdale's, and bluemercury brands with 867 stores in 43 states, must have a way of accurately tracking the purchase and sale of its inventory. In addition, Macy's needs to determine if it is selling its merchandise at the right sales prices in order to ensure maximum profit. This chapter explores merchandising operations and how these businesses account for merchandise inventory.

5-2 Financial chapter 5

Chapter 5 Learning Objectives

1. Describe merchandising operations and the two types of merchandise inventory systems
2. Account for the purchase of merchandise inventory using a perpetual inventory system
3. Account for the sale of merchandise inventory using a perpetual inventory system
4. Adjust and close the accounts of a merchandising business
5. Prepare a merchandiser's financial statements
6. Use the gross profit percentage to evaluate business performance
7. Account for multiple performance obligations using a perpetual inventory system (Appendix 5A)
8. Account for the purchase and sale of merchandise inventory using a periodic inventory system (Appendix 5B)

WHAT ARE MERCHANDISING OPERATIONS?

Learning Objective 1
Describe merchandising operations and the two types of merchandise inventory systems

In earlier chapters, you learned about accounting for Smart Touch Learning, an e-learning business that specializes in providing services: online courses in accounting, economics, marketing, and management. In this chapter, you learn about accounting for merchandisers. A **merchandiser** is a business that sells merchandise, or goods, to customers. The merchandise that this type of business sells is called **merchandise inventory**. Merchandisers are often identified as either wholesalers or retailers. A **wholesaler** is a merchandiser who buys goods from a manufacturer and then sells them to retailers. A **retailer** buys merchandise either from a manufacturer or a wholesaler and then sells those goods to consumers.

Merchandiser
A business that sells merchandise, or goods, to customers.

Merchandise Inventory
The merchandise that a business sells to customers.

Wholesaler
A type of merchandiser who buys goods from manufacturers and then sells them to retailers.

Retailer
A type of merchandiser who buys merchandise either from a manufacturer or a wholesaler and then sells those goods to consumers.

The Operating Cycle of a Merchandising Business

The operating cycle of a merchandiser is illustrated in Exhibit F:5-1.

Exhibit F:5-1 | **Operating Cycle of a Merchandiser**

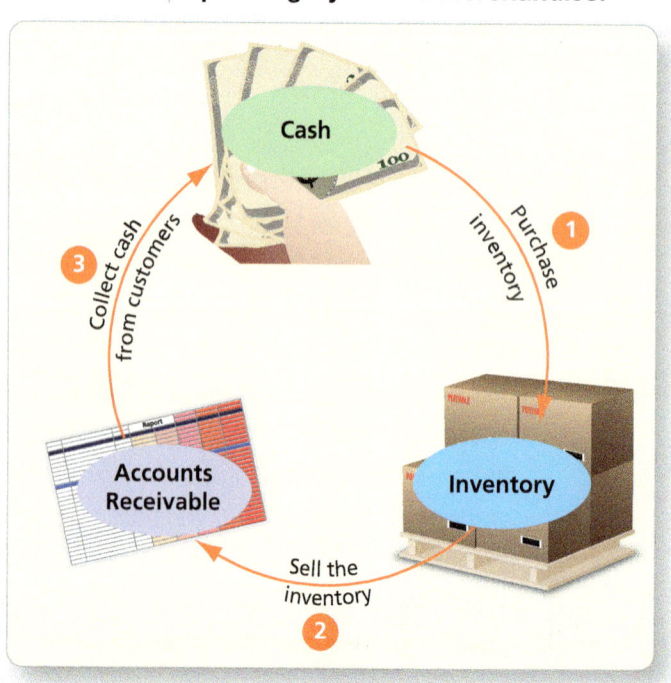

Merchandising Operations Financial 5-3

1. It begins when the company purchases inventory from an individual or business, called a **vendor**.
2. The company then sells the inventory to a customer.
3. Finally, the company collects cash from customers.

Vendor
The individual or business from whom a company purchases goods.

Because the operating cycle of a merchandiser is different than that of a service company, the financial statements differ. Exhibit F:5-2 shows how a service company's financial statements (on the left) differ from a merchandiser's financial statements (on the right). As you can see, merchandisers have some new balance sheet and income statement items.

On the income statement, a merchandising company reports revenues using an account called *Sales Revenue* rather than the account *Service Revenue* used by service companies. A merchandiser also reports the cost of merchandise inventory that has been sold to customers, or **Cost of Goods Sold (COGS)**. Cost of Goods Sold is also called *Cost of Sales*. Because COGS is usually a merchandiser's main expense, an intermediary calculation,

Cost of Goods Sold (COGS)
The cost of the merchandise inventory that the business has sold to customers.

Exhibit F:5-2 | Financial Statements of a Service Company and a Merchandising Company

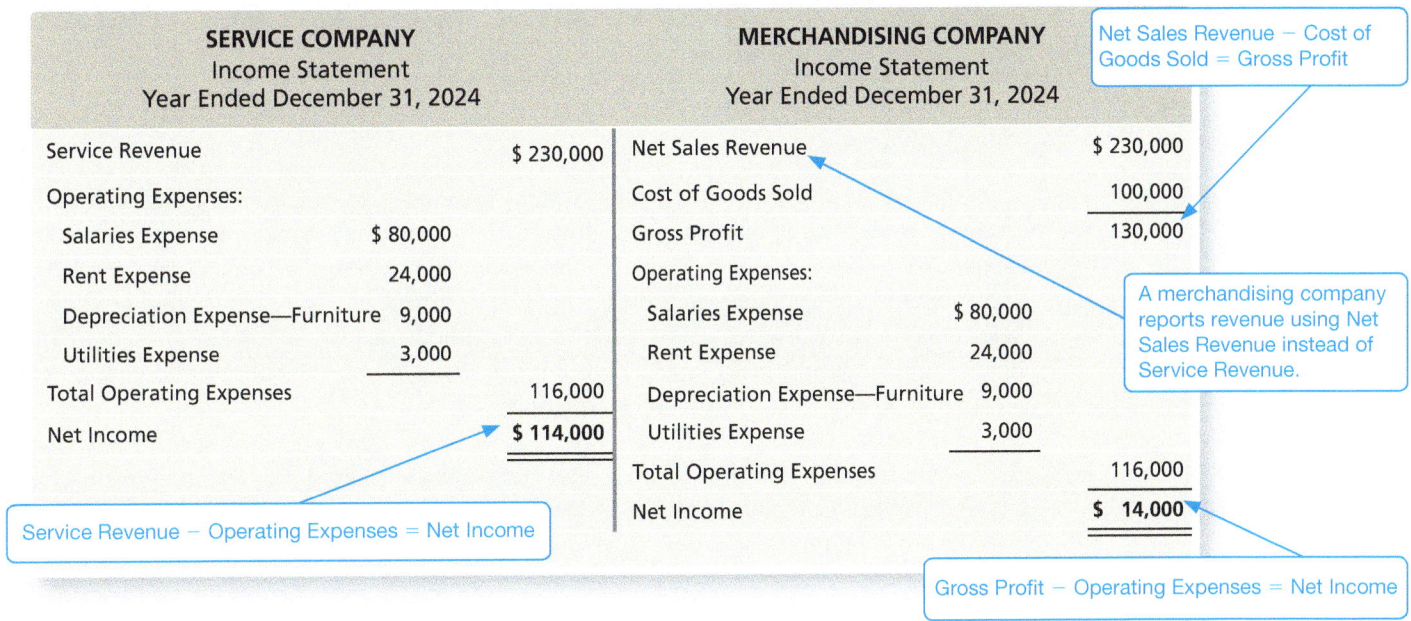

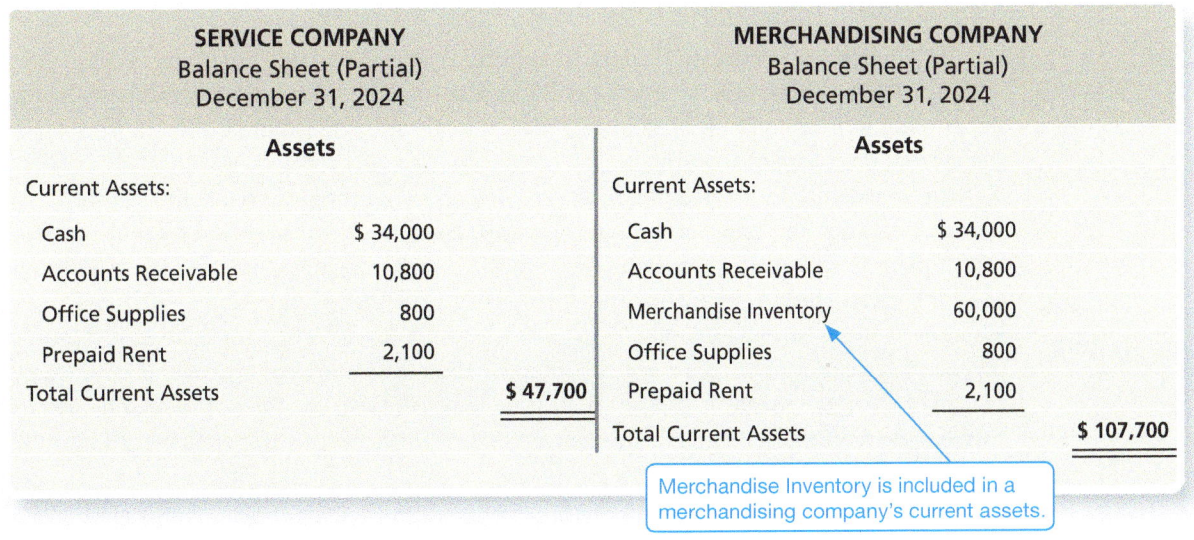

Gross Profit
Excess of Net Sales Revenue over Cost of Goods Sold.

gross profit, is determined before calculating net income. **Gross profit** (also called *gross margin*) is calculated as Net Sales Revenue minus Cost of Goods Sold and represents the markup on the merchandise inventory. Gross profit is the extra amount the company receives from the customer (for the merchandise sold) over what the company paid to the vendor. After calculating gross profit, operating expenses are then deducted to determine net income. **Operating expenses** are expenses, other than Cost of Goods Sold, that occur in the entity's major ongoing operations.

Operating Expenses
Expenses, other than Cost of Goods Sold, that are incurred in the entity's major ongoing operations.

On the balance sheet, a merchandiser includes Merchandise Inventory in the current assets section representing the value of inventory that the business has on hand to sell to customers. Remember that the assets in the current asset section are listed in the order of liquidity; therefore, Merchandise Inventory is usually listed below Accounts Receivable but before the prepaid assets, such as Office Supplies, Prepaid Rent, and Prepaid Insurance.

Merchandise Inventory Systems: Perpetual and Periodic Inventory Systems

Businesses must have a way to determine the value of merchandise inventory on hand and also the value of the merchandise inventory sold. There are two main types of inventory accounting systems that are used:

- Periodic inventory system
- Perpetual inventory system

Periodic Inventory System
An inventory system that requires businesses to obtain a physical count of inventory to determine quantities on hand.

The **periodic inventory system** requires businesses to obtain a physical count of inventory to determine the quantities on hand. The system is normally used for relatively inexpensive goods, such as in a small, local store without optical-scanning cash registers that does not keep a running record of every loaf of bread and every key chain that it sells. Restaurants and small retail stores often use the periodic inventory system. Appendix 5B covers the periodic inventory system, which is becoming less and less popular because most accounting is done using computerized methods.

Perpetual Inventory System
An inventory system that keeps a running computerized record of merchandise inventory.

The **perpetual inventory system** keeps a running computerized record of merchandise inventory—that is, the number of inventory units and the dollar amounts associated with the inventory are perpetually (constantly) updated. This system achieves better control over the inventory. A modern perpetual inventory system records the following:

- Units purchased and cost amounts.
- Units sold and sales and cost amounts.
- The quantity of merchandise inventory on hand and its cost.

In a perpetual inventory system, merchandise inventory and purchasing systems are integrated with the records for Accounts Receivable and Sales Revenue. For example, major department stores' computers use bar codes to keep up-to-the-minute records and show the current inventory at any time.

Are the bar codes I see on goods I purchase used to track inventory in the accounting system?

In a perpetual inventory system, the "cash register" at the store is a computer terminal that records sales and updates inventory records. **Bar codes are scanned by a laser. The bar coding is linked to merchandise inventory and cost data that are used to keep track of each unique inventory item.** However, note that even in a perpetual inventory system, the business must count inventory at least once a year. The physical count captures inventory transactions that are not recorded by the electronic system (such as misplaced, stolen, or damaged inventory). The count establishes the correct amount of ending inventory for the financial statements and also serves as a check on the perpetual records.

Merchandising Operations Financial 5-5

Match the accounting terminology to the definitions.

1. Cost of Goods Sold	a. An inventory system that requires businesses to obtain a physical count of inventory to determine quantities on hand.
2. Perpetual inventory system	
3. Vendor	b. Expenses, other than Cost of Goods Sold, that are incurred in the entity's major ongoing operations.
4. Periodic inventory system	c. Excess of Net Sales Revenue over Cost of Goods Sold.
5. Operating expenses	d. The cost of merchandise inventory that the business has sold to customers.
6. Gross profit	e. The individual or business from whom a company purchases goods.
	f. An inventory system that keeps a running computerized record of merchandise inventory.

Check your answers online in MyLab Accounting or at http://www.pearsonhighered.com/Horngren.

For more practice, see Short Exercise S-F:5-1.   **MyLab Accounting**

HOW ARE PURCHASES OF MERCHANDISE INVENTORY RECORDED IN A PERPETUAL INVENTORY SYSTEM?

As noted previously, the cycle of a merchandising entity begins with the purchase of merchandise inventory. We will continue to use our fictitious company, Smart Touch Learning, which has now decided to discontinue its service business and instead plans to sell touch screen tablet computers that are preloaded with its e-learning software programs. Smart Touch Learning will purchase these tablets from a vendor. We assume Smart Touch Learning uses a perpetual inventory system.

The vendor (Southwest Electronics Direct) ships the tablet computers to Smart Touch Learning and sends an invoice the same day. The **invoice** is the seller's (Southwest Electronics Direct) request for payment from the buyer (Smart Touch Learning). An invoice is also called a *bill*. Exhibit F:5-3 (on the next page) is the bill that Smart Touch Learning receives from Southwest Electronics Direct. After the merchandise inventory is received, Smart Touch Learning pays the vendor.

Learning Objective 2

Account for the purchase of merchandise inventory using a perpetual inventory system

Invoice

A seller's request for payment from the purchaser.

For Southwest Electronics Direct, the seller, the invoice is called a sales invoice. For Smart Touch Learning, the purchaser, the invoice is called a purchase invoice.

5-6 Financial 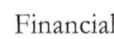 chapter 5

Exhibit F:5-3 | Purchase Invoice

1
Southwest Electronics Direct
P.O. BOX 101010
HOUSTON, TX 77212

Invoice	
Date	Number
3 6/1/25	410

2
Shipped To: SMART TOUCH LEARNING
227 LAKE STREET
POMPTON PLAINS, IL 07444

6 Pd. 6/15/25

4
Credit Terms
3/15, NET 30 DAYS

Description	Quantity Shipped	Unit Price	Total
Touch Screen Tablet Computers	100	$ 350	$35,000

Due Date & Due Amount	
06/16/25	07/01/2025
$33,950	$35,000
7	

Sub Total	$35,000
Ship. or Handl. Chg.	-
Tax (3%)	-
Total(s)	$35,000
	5

Explanations:

1. The seller is Southwest Electronics Direct.
2. The purchaser is Smart Touch Learning.
3. The invoice date is needed to determine whether the purchaser gets a discount for prompt payment (see 4).
4. Credit terms: If Smart Touch Learning pays within 15 days of the invoice date, it can deduct a 3% discount. Otherwise, the full amount—NET—is due in 30 days.
5. Total invoice amount is $35,000.
6. Smart Touch Learning's payment date. How much did Smart Touch Learning pay? (see 7).
7. Payment occurred 14 days after the invoice date—within the discount period—so Smart Touch Learning paid $33,950 ($35,000−3% discount).

Purchase of Merchandise Inventory

Here we use the actual invoice in Exhibit F:5-3 to illustrate the purchasing process. Suppose Smart Touch Learning receives the goods on June 3 and makes payment on that date (ignore the credit terms on the invoice at this point). Smart Touch Learning records this purchase as follows:

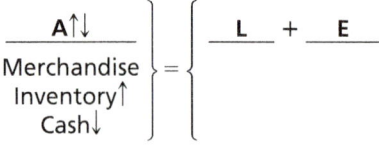

Date	Accounts and Explanation	Debit	Credit
Jun. 3	Merchandise Inventory	35,000	
	Cash		35,000
	Purchased inventory for cash.		

The Merchandise Inventory account, an asset, is used only for goods purchased that the business owns and intends to resell to customers. Office Supplies, Equipment, and other assets are recorded in their own accounts.

Assume that on June 3, instead of paying cash, Smart Touch Learning receives the merchandise inventory on account. The purchase of inventory on account is recorded as follows:

Date	Accounts and Explanation	Debit	Credit
Jun. 3	Merchandise Inventory	35,000	
	Accounts Payable—Southwest Electronics Direct		35,000
	Purchased inventory on account.		

A↑ = L↑ + E
Merchandise Inventory↑ = Accounts Payable↑

Notice that we have added the name of the vendor after the Accounts Payable account. This helps Smart Touch Learning keep track of the various companies it owes money to.

Purchase Returns and Allowances

Sellers allow purchasers to return merchandise that is defective, damaged, or otherwise unsuitable. This is called a **purchase return** from the purchaser's perspective. Alternatively, the seller may deduct an allowance from the amount the buyer owes. **Purchase allowances** are granted to the purchaser as an incentive to keep goods that are not "as ordered." Together, purchase returns and allowances decrease the buyer's cost of the merchandise inventory.

Refer back to the purchase invoice in Exhibit F:5-3. Suppose 20 of the tablets purchased on that invoice were damaged in shipment. On June 6, Smart Touch Learning returns the goods (tablets, in this case) valued at $7,000 to the vendor (Southwest Electronics Direct) and records the purchase return as follows:

Purchase Return
A situation in which sellers allow purchasers to return merchandise that is defective, damaged, or otherwise unsuitable.

Purchase Allowance
An amount granted to the purchaser as an incentive to keep goods that are not "as ordered."

Date	Accounts and Explanation	Debit	Credit
Jun. 6	Accounts Payable—Southwest Electronic Direct	7,000	
	Merchandise Inventory (20 tablets × $350 per tablet)		7,000
	Returned inventory to seller (vendor).		

A↓ = L↓ + E
Merchandise Inventory↓ = Accounts Payable↓

The purchase return reduces the amount Smart Touch Learning owes to Southwest Electronics Direct and also reduces the amount of merchandise inventory the company has in stock. The purchase return journal entry records a debit to Accounts Payable, reducing the liability; and a credit to Merchandise Inventory, reducing the asset, for the amount returned. The company's accounts now reflect the correct balance after the return.

Merchandise Inventory				Accounts Payable			
June 3	35,000	7,000	June 6	June 6	7,000	35,000	June 3
Bal.	28,000					28,000	Bal.

The exact same entry is made for a purchase allowance granted to the buyer from the seller (vendor) because the allowance also reduces the cost of the inventory. The only difference between a purchase return and a purchase allowance is that, in the case of the allowance, Smart Touch Learning keeps the inventory.

5-8 Financial   chapter 5

Purchase Discounts

Purchase Discount
A discount that businesses offer to purchasers as an incentive for early payment.

Credit Terms
The payment terms of purchase or sale as stated on the invoice.

Many businesses offer purchasers a discount for early payment called a **purchase discount**. Review the purchase invoice (Exhibit F:5-3) and notice in box 4 the **credit terms** (also called the *payment terms*) stated on the invoice. Southwest Electronics Direct's credit terms of "3/15, NET 30 DAYS" mean that Smart Touch Learning can deduct 3% from the total bill (excluding freight charges, if any) if the company pays within 15 days of the invoice date. Otherwise, the full amount—NET—is due in 30 days. These credit terms can also be expressed as "3/15, n/30."

Most credit terms express the discount, the discount time period, and the final due date. Other credit terms might be listed as n/30 or n/EOM. Terms of "n/30" mean that no discount is offered and payment is due 30 days after the invoice date. Occasionally, the credit terms are expressed as EOM, which means payment is due at the end of the current month, or 10 EOM, which means payment is due 10 days after the end of the month.

A purchase discount is applied on the amount owed. If a business returns merchandise inventory or receives a purchase allowance before payment is made, the purchase discount will be calculated net of the return or allowance. For example, if Smart Touch Learning pays on June 15, which is within the discount period, the company will receive a discount on the balance owed of $28,000 (not the original invoice price of $35,000). The discount amount will be $840 ($28,000 × 3%).

Merchandise Inventory				Accounts Payable			
June 3	35,000	7,000	June 6	June 6	7,000	35,000	June 3
Bal.	28,000					28,000	Bal.

> When calculating a purchase discount, make sure to always calculate the discount based on the amount owed. This would be the amount of the purchase invoice less any purchase returns or allowances.

Smart Touch Learning will record the following journal entry for the cash payment:

$$\left.\begin{array}{c}A\downarrow\\ \text{Cash}\downarrow\\ \text{Merchandise}\\ \text{Inventory}\downarrow\end{array}\right\} = \left\{\begin{array}{c}L\downarrow\\ \text{Accounts}\\ \text{Payable}\downarrow\end{array}\right. + E$$

Date	Accounts and Explanation	Debit	Credit
Jun. 15	Accounts Payable—Southwest Electronics Direct	28,000	
	Cash ($28,000 − $840)		27,160
	Merchandise Inventory ($28,000 × 0.03)		840
	Paid within discount period net of return.		

> When making payment within a discount period, always debit Accounts Payable for the amount of the invoice less any purchase returns or allowances; otherwise, there will be a balance remaining in the payable account even though the invoice has been paid in full.

Smart Touch Learning records a debit to Accounts Payable for the amount of the invoice less any purchase returns or allowances. This reduces the accounts payable by the amount owed. Cash is credited for the amount paid to the seller. The purchase discount is credited to the Merchandise Inventory account because the discount for early payment decreases the actual cost paid for Merchandise Inventory. After posting the entry to the

Merchandising Operations

accounts, the Merchandise Inventory account reflects a balance of exactly what the company paid for its merchandise, $27,160, and the Accounts Payable balance shows the invoice has been paid in full with no remaining balance:

Cash			Merchandise Inventory				Accounts Payable			
Bal.	60,500		June 3	35,000	7,000	June 6	June 6	7,000	35,000	June 3
		27,160 June 15	Bal.	28,000					28,000	Bal.
Bal.	33,340				840	June 15	June 15	28,000		
			Bal.	27,160					0	Bal.

What if, instead, Smart Touch Learning pays this invoice on June 24, after the discount period ends? Smart Touch Learning must pay the full $28,000, the amount of the invoice less the purchase return.

In that case, the payment entry is as follows. Notice, there is no reduction of the Merchandise Inventory account because the company did not receive the purchase discount.

What if a purchaser does not pay the invoice within the discount period?

Date	Accounts and Explanation	Debit	Credit
Jun. 24	Accounts Payable—Southwest Electronic Direct	28,000	
	Cash		28,000
	Paid after discount period net of return.		

$$\left.\begin{array}{c} A\downarrow \\ Cash\downarrow \end{array}\right\} = \left\{\begin{array}{c} L\downarrow \\ Accounts \\ Payable\downarrow \end{array}\right. + E$$

Cash			Merchandise Inventory				Accounts Payable			
Bal.	60,500		June 3	35,000	7,000	June 6	June 6	7,000	35,000	June 3
		28,000 June 24	Bal.	28,000					28,000	Bal.
Bal.	32,500						June 24	28,000		
									0	Bal.

ETHICS

How should you handle gifts from vendors?

Anthony Jackson works as a buyer for a large department store that has decided to expand into selling seasonal home decor. Anthony has been charged with the responsibility of selecting the vendor for the new inventory that the store will sell. His purchasing manager has provided him with two possible vendors to choose from. One vendor, Abbey's Wholesalers, has a long-standing relationship with the department store and can be counted on to provide high-quality goods on a timely basis. The other vendor, Zeta Wholesalers, is a new company that doesn't have much of a track record and is just getting established as a home decor wholesaler. Anthony has contacted both vendors to set up meetings to discuss the new inventory and possible credit terms available. The day before the meeting with the potential vendors, Anthony receives a pair of football tickets to a major NFL game in the mail from Abbey's Wholesalers thanking him for his continued relationship with the wholesaler. What should Anthony do?

Solution

Anthony should contact his purchasing manager and explain the situation to him or her. By accepting the football tickets, Anthony might unknowingly be violating the code of ethics of the business. Most businesses have a code of ethics that relates to inventory management and purchasing specifically discussing conflicts of interest. Conflicts of interest occur when a vendor is selected above another vendor because of possible personal financial gain, such as receiving gifts or entertainment from the selected vendor. Anthony should carefully discuss the situation with his manager before accepting the tickets.

TYING IT ALL TOGETHER

Macy's, Inc. was established in 1858 and sells an assortment of major brands such as Calvin Klein, Michael Kors, Ralph Lauren, and Tommy Hilfiger. Macy's purchases its inventory from third-party suppliers and for the year ending February 2, 2019, Macy's reported cost of sales of $15,215 million. Companies such as Macy's often have the opportunity to pay for their purchases within a discount period in order to receive a discount on the amount due.

How does a company decide if it should pay within the discount period?

Companies make decisions to pay within a discount period based on many factors. First, companies must evaluate if they have the excess cash flow to pay early or if the cash will be needed to pay other vendors. Second, the company should evaluate if the cash could be used for other more profitable purposes during the discount period. For example, some companies are able to invest the cash and earn more during the discount period than the available discount.

Should a company borrow money to make payment within the discount period?

Companies should borrow the money only if the amount of interest expense paid on the loan will be less than the discount received. It does not make sense for companies to borrow money to make an early payment if in the long run the company will end up paying more in interest expense than the discount received.

Transportation Costs

FOB Shipping Point
Situation in which the buyer takes ownership (title) to the goods when the goods leave the seller's place of business (shipping point) and the buyer typically pays the freight.

FOB Destination
Situation in which the buyer takes ownership (title) to the goods at the delivery destination point and the seller typically pays the freight.

Freight In
The transportation cost to ship goods to the purchaser's warehouse; therefore, it is freight on purchased goods.

Freight Out
The transportation cost to ship goods out of the seller's warehouse; therefore, it is freight on goods sold to a customer.

Either the seller or the buyer must pay the transportation cost of shipping merchandise inventory. The purchase agreement specifies FOB (free on board) terms to determine when title to the goods transfers to the purchaser and who pays the freight. Exhibit F:5-4 shows that:

- **FOB shipping point** means the buyer takes ownership (title) to the goods when the goods leave the seller's place of business (shipping point). In most cases, the buyer (owner of the goods while in transit) also pays the freight.

- **FOB destination** means the buyer takes ownership (title) to the goods at the delivery destination point. In most cases, the seller (owner of the goods while in transit) also pays the freight.

When merchandisers are required to pay for shipping costs, those costs are classified as either freight in or freight out as follows:

- **Freight in** is the transportation cost to ship goods to the purchaser's warehouse; thus, it is freight on purchased goods.

- **Freight out** is the transportation cost to ship goods out of the seller's warehouse and to the customer; thus, it is freight on goods sold to a customer.

Exhibit F:5-4 | FOB Terms Determine Who Pays the Freight

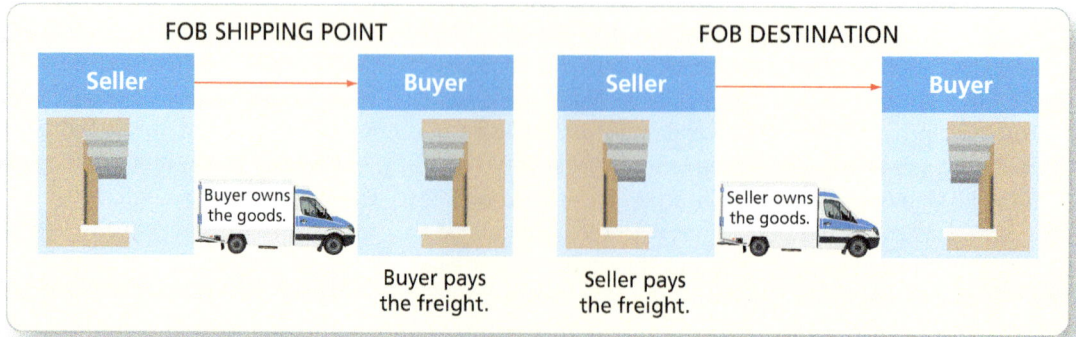

Freight In

With the terms FOB shipping point, the buyer owns the goods while they are in transit, so the buyer pays the freight. Because the freight is a cost that must be paid to acquire the inventory, freight in becomes part of the cost of merchandise inventory. As a result, freight in costs are debited to the Merchandise Inventory account. Suppose Smart Touch Learning pays a $60 freight charge on June 3 for a purchase with FOB shipping point, and makes the following entry:

Date	Accounts and Explanation	Debit	Credit
Jun. 3	Merchandise Inventory	60	
	Cash		60
	Paid a freight bill.		

A↑↓ = L + E
Merchandise Inventory↑
Cash↓

Freight In Within Discount Period

Discounts are computed only on the merchandise purchased from the seller. Discounts are not computed on the transportation costs because there is no discount on freight.

Under FOB shipping point, the seller sometimes prepays the transportation cost as a convenience and lists this cost on the invoice. Assume, for example, Smart Touch Learning makes a $5,000 purchase of goods from Klein Electronics, coupled with a related freight charge of $400, on June 20 on account with terms of 3/5, n/30. The terms of shipment are FOB shipping point. The seller prepays the freight charge. The purchase would be recorded as follows:

Date	Accounts and Explanation	Debit	Credit
Jun. 20	Merchandise Inventory ($5,000 + $400)	5,400	
	Accounts Payable—Klein Electronics		5,400
	Purchased inventory on account, including freight.		

A↑ = L↑ + E
Merchandise Inventory↑
Accounts Payable↑

If Smart Touch Learning pays within the discount period, the discount will be computed only on the $5,000 merchandise cost, not on the total invoice of $5,400. The $400 freight is not eligible for the discount. So, the 3% discount would be $150 ($5,000 × 0.03). The entry to record the early payment on June 25 follows:

Date	Accounts and Explanation	Debit	Credit
Jun. 25	Accounts Payable—Klein Electronics	5,400	
	Cash ($5,400 − $150)		5,250
	Merchandise Inventory ($5,000 × 0.03)		150
	Paid within discount period, including freight.		

A↓ = L↓ + E
Cash↓
Merchandise Inventory↓
Accounts Payable↓

Net Cost of Inventory Purchased

The net cost of merchandise inventory purchased includes the purchase cost of inventory, less purchase returns and allowances, less purchase discounts, plus freight in. Knowing the net cost of inventory allows a business to determine the actual cost of the merchandise purchased and is calculated as follows:

> Net Cost of Inventory Purchased = Purchase cost of inventory − Purchase returns and allowances − Purchase discounts + Freight in

5-12 Financial chapter 5

Suppose that during the year, Smart Touch Learning buys $697,710 of inventory, returns $150,000 of the goods, and takes a $9,510 early payment discount. The company also pays $36,400 of freight in. The following summary shows Smart Touch Learning's net cost of this merchandise inventory purchased.

Purchases	$ 697,710
Less: Purchase Returns and Allowances	150,000
Purchase Discounts	9,510
Plus: Freight In	36,400
Net Cost of Inventory Purchased	$ 574,600

Try It!

7. Sandy Electronics and Supply has the following transactions in July related to the purchase of merchandise inventory.

July 1	Purchase of $20,500 worth of computers on account, terms of 2/10, n/30, from Best Computers.
3	Return of $4,000 of the computers to Best Computers.
9	Payment made on account to Best Computers.

Journalize the purchase transactions for Sandy Electronics and Supply assuming the company uses the perpetual inventory system.

Check your answers online in MyLab Accounting or at http://www.pearsonhighered.com/Horngren.

For more practice, see Short Exercises S-F:5-2 and S-F:5-3. MyLab Accounting

HOW ARE SALES OF MERCHANDISE INVENTORY RECORDED IN A PERPETUAL INVENTORY SYSTEM?

Learning Objective 3
Account for the sale of merchandise inventory using a perpetual inventory system

After a company buys merchandise inventory, the next step is to sell the goods. We shift now to the selling side and follow Smart Touch Learning through a sequence of selling transactions using the perpetual inventory system.

Cash and Credit Card Sales

Sales Revenue
The amount that a merchandiser earns from selling its inventory.

The amount a business earns from selling merchandise inventory is called **Sales Revenue** (also called *Sales*). At the time of the sale, a company must record two entries in the perpetual inventory system: One entry records the sales revenue and the second entry records the cost of inventory sold (or Cost of Goods Sold). Remember, Cost of Goods Sold is an expense account and represents the cost of inventory that has been sold to customers.

Suppose Smart Touch Learning sold two tablets for cash on June 19 to a customer. The tablets had a sales price of $500 each and each tablet cost $350. Smart Touch Learning must record two journal entries:

1. A journal entry for the Sales Revenue and the Cash received, and
2. A journal entry for the expense (Cost of Goods Sold) and the reduction of Merchandise Inventory.

The first journal entry records the cash sale of $1,000 ($500 × 2) by debiting Cash and crediting Sales Revenue. The second journal entry records the expense, Cost of Goods Sold, of $700 ($350 × 2) and decrease of Merchandise Inventory.

Date	Accounts and Explanation	Debit	Credit
Jun. 19	Cash	1,000	
	Sales Revenue		1,000
	Cash sale.		
19	Cost of Goods Sold	700	
	Merchandise Inventory		700
	Recorded the cost of goods sold.		

This entry records the Sales Revenue.

This entry records the expense and the reduction of Merchandise Inventory.

$A\uparrow$ } = { L + $E\uparrow$
Cash↑   Sales Revenue↑

$A\downarrow$ } = { L + $E\downarrow$
Merchandise Inventory↓   Cost of Goods Sold↑

In a perpetual inventory system, the Cost of Goods Sold account keeps a running balance throughout the period of the cost of merchandise inventory sold. In this example, Cost of Goods Sold is $700 (the cost to Smart Touch Learning) rather than $1,000, the sales price (retail price) of the goods. Cost of Goods Sold is always based on the company's cost, not the retail price.

Merchandise Inventory				Cost of Goods Sold	
Bal. xx,xxx	700	June 19	→	June 19	700

Retailers, such as Smart Touch Learning, often sell merchandise inventory and receive payment in the form of a credit card. **Credit card sales are recorded in the same manner as cash sales because the payment is usually received via an electronic transfer from the credit card processor within a few days.** The retailer will also have to pay a fee associated with credit card sales, which we will discuss in a later chapter.

Sales on Account, No Discount

Many sales are made on account instead of with cash or a credit card. Let's assume that Smart Touch Learning sold five tablets to Pendleton Dentistry for $500 each, making a $2,500 (per tablet) sale on account on June 21. The goods cost $1,750. Smart Touch Learning issued the sales invoice shown in Exhibit F:5-5 (on the next page) to the customer. To the seller, a sales invoice is a bill showing what amount the customer must pay.

How do retailers record sales of merchandise inventory when a customer pays with a credit card instead of cash?

5-14 Financial chapter 5

Exhibit F:5-5 | **Sales Invoice**

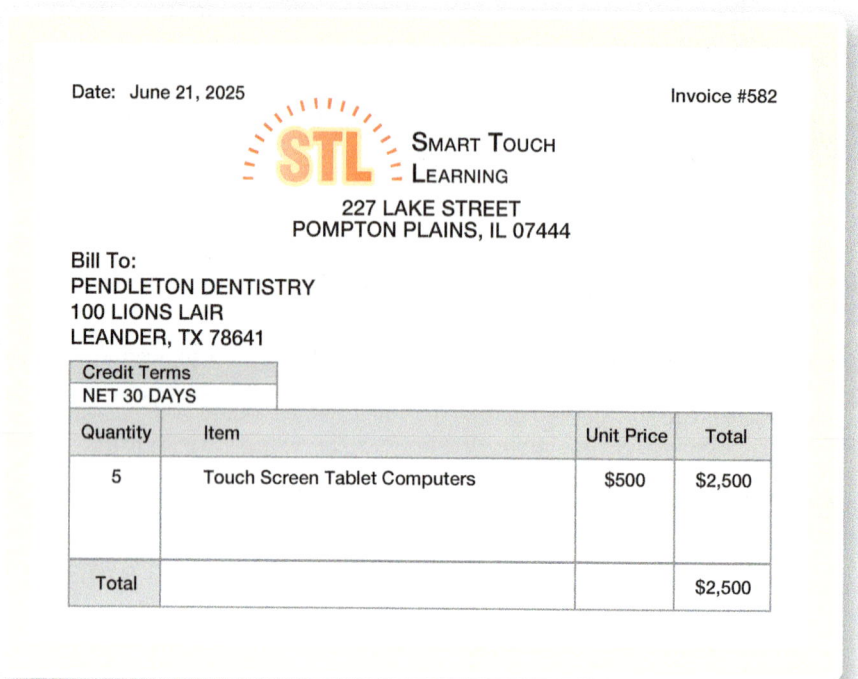

Smart Touch Learning would record the sale on account with two journal entries. First, the company would record the sales portion of the transaction. The company will debit Accounts Receivable and credit Sales Revenue for $2,500. Next, the company records the expense and merchandise inventory portion of the transaction by debiting the expense, Cost of Goods Sold, and crediting Merchandise Inventory for $1,750.

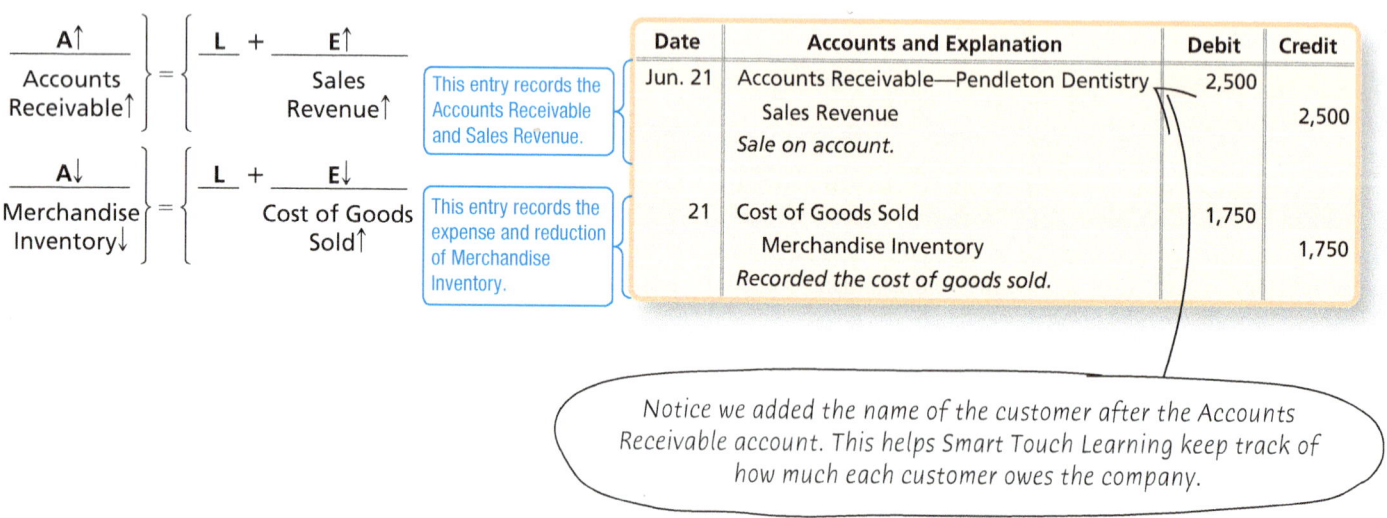

Sales Returns and Allowances

Sales Return
A reduction in the amount owed by a customer due to the return of merchandise.

After making a sale, Smart Touch Learning may have customers who return goods, asking for a refund or credit to the customer's account. The return of goods is called a **Sales Return**. Sales returns reduce the future cash collected from the customer or require a refund be made to the customer. Under the new revenue recognition standards, during the adjusting process, companies estimate the amount of sales returns from customers that will occur.

Merchandising Operations

For example, assume that during the adjusting process Smart Touch Learning estimates that approximately $10,000 of estimated refunds will be paid and merchandise inventory that cost $6,000 will be returned. The company sets up an asset account, **Estimated Returns Inventory**, to account for the cost of merchandise inventory the company believes it will receive in returns. Smart Touch Learning will also establish a liability account, **Refunds Payable**, for the amount of estimated refunds that will be paid to customers in the future. Smart Touch Learning's estimated accounts are as follows:

Estimated Returns Inventory
| 6,000 |

Refunds Payable
| | 10,000 |

> **Estimated Returns Inventory**
> An asset account used to estimate the cost of merchandise inventory a company will receive in returns.
>
> **Refunds Payable**
> A liability account used to estimate the amount of refunds that will be paid to customers in the future.

When a customer returns the merchandise inventory, the company will need to record a refund of cash to the customer or a credit to Accounts Receivable. The company must also record the return of merchandise inventory. Assume that on June 22, a customer returned merchandise purchased with cash with a sales price of $2,000. The cost of the goods was $800. Smart Touch Learning would need to record two journal entries for this transaction.

The first journal entry records the cash refund and the second entry records the return of the merchandise inventory. Smart Touch Learning's first journal entry would include a debit to Refunds Payable and a credit to Cash for $2,000. In this transaction we are debiting (or decreasing) Refunds Payable because the amount of the estimated refunds has decreased. (The company is expecting less estimated refunds in the future.) The second journal entry would include a debit to Merchandise Inventory to reflect the return of inventory and a credit to Estimated Returns Inventory. Estimated Returns Inventory is being credited (or decreased) because the amount of the estimated returns inventory has decreased.

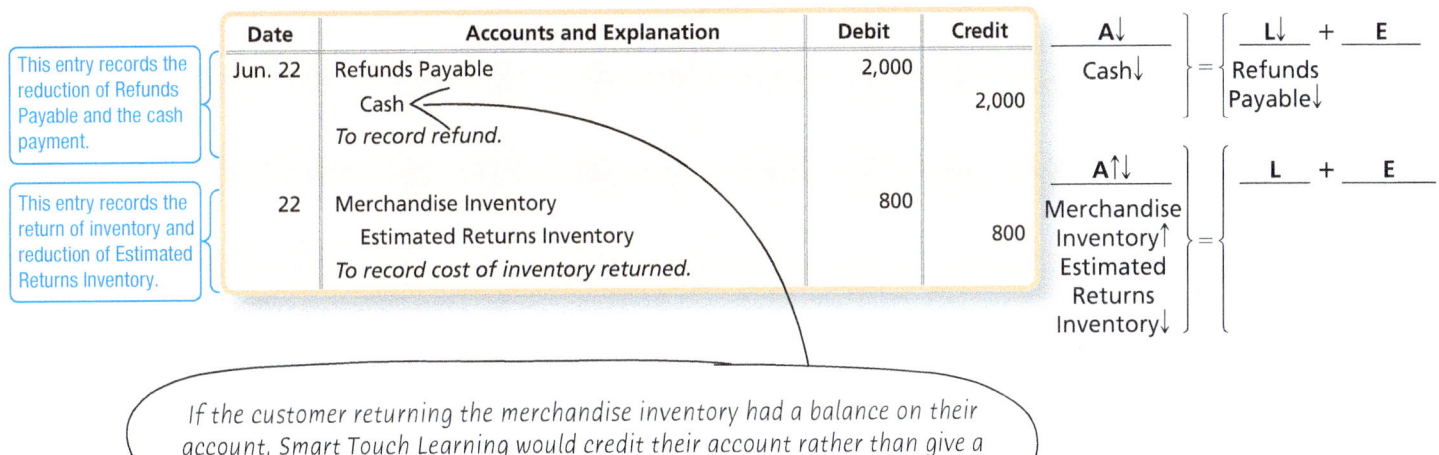

If the customer returning the merchandise inventory had a balance on their account, Smart Touch Learning would credit their account rather than give a cash refund. This would require a credit to Accounts Receivable instead of Cash.

After recording the sales return, Smart Touch Learning's Estimated Returns Inventory and Refunds Payable both reflect a decrease for the return made. Remember, this is because the estimated amount of total returns for the period has now decreased by the amount of the actual return.

Estimated Returns Inventory
Bal.	6,000		
		800	Jun. 22
Bal.	5,200		

Refunds Payable
		10,000	Bal.
Jun. 22	2,000		
		8,000	Bal.

Sales Allowance
A reduction in the amount owed by a customer that does not involve the return of merchandise inventory.

In some situations, the customer may request a refund of some portion owed but the customer does not return the inventory. This may occur when the inventory was slightly damaged or the wrong color but still usable. In this case, the seller grants the customer a **sales allowance** or a reduction in the amount owed by a customer that does not involve the return of merchandise inventory. When a seller grants a sales allowance, the company issues a credit memo indicating that the company will reduce the customer's Accounts Receivable or issue a cash refund. The company also reduces the estimated Refunds Payable account. Because there is no return of goods, the company does not need to record a second entry to adjust the Merchandise Inventory account. Suppose that on June 23, Smart Touch Learning grants a $100 sales allowance for goods damaged in transit to Pendleton Dentistry. The goods were sold on account and remain unpaid. A sales allowance is recorded as follows:

$\dfrac{A\downarrow}{\text{Accounts Receivable}\downarrow} = \dfrac{L\downarrow}{\text{Refunds Payable}\downarrow} + E$

Date	Accounts and Explanation	Debit	Credit
Jun. 23	Refunds Payable	100	
	Accounts Receivable—Pendleton Dentistry		100
	Granted a sales allowance for damaged goods.		

Before we record the cash receipt from Pendleton Dentistry, let's take a moment to review the Accounts Receivable account. Notice the Accounts Receivable account reflects the sale of inventory on June 21 and the sales allowance granted on June 23. The T-account shows the updated balance the customer owes Smart Touch Learning.

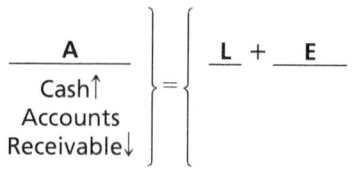

Accounts Receivable—Pendleton Dentistry
| June 21 | 2,500 | 100 | June 23 |
| Bal. | 2,400 | | |

When the customer, Pendleton Dentistry, pays the amount owed on June 30, Smart Touch Learning will record the receipt of cash and decrease the Accounts Receivable for $2,400 as follows:

$\dfrac{A}{\substack{\text{Cash}\uparrow \\ \text{Accounts Receivable}\downarrow}} = L + E$

Date	Accounts and Explanation	Debit	Credit
Jun. 30	Cash	2,400	
	Accounts Receivable—Pendleton Dentistry		2,400
	Cash collection.		

Sales on Account, with Discount

Sales Discounts
Reduction in the amount of revenue earned on sales for early payment.

Many merchandisers offer customers a discount for early payment. We saw that purchase discounts decrease the cost of inventory purchases. In the same way, **sales discounts** decrease the amount of revenue earned on sales. Under the new revenue recognition standards (introduced in Chapter F:3), sales are recorded at the net amount or the amount of the sale less any sales discounts.[1]

For example, assume that Smart Touch Learning sold 15 tablets for $500 each, making a $7,500 sale on account on June 23 to West High School. The goods cost $5,250. Smart Touch Learning offered West High School a sales discount of 2/10, n/30 for early payment. Smart Touch Learning would record the sale on account with two journal entries.

---

[1] This presentation is consistent with *Revenue from Contracts with Customers (Topic 606)*.

Merchandising Operations Financial 5-17

First, the company would record the sales portion of the transaction. The company will record the sale at the net amount of $7,350, which is the $7,500 less the 2% discount of $150 ($7,500 × 0.02), with a debit to Accounts Receivable and credit to Sales Revenue. Next, the company records the expense and merchandise inventory portion of the transaction by debiting the expense, Cost of Goods Sold, and crediting Merchandise Inventory for $5,250.

Date	Accounts and Explanation	Debit	Credit
Jun. 23	Accounts Receivable—West High School	7,350	
	Sales Revenue ($7,500 − ($7,500 × 0.02))		7,350
	Sale on account less discount.		
23	Cost of Goods Sold	5,250	
	Merchandise Inventory		5,250
	Recorded the cost of goods sold.		

This entry records the Accounts Receivable and Sales Revenue net of the discount.

A↑ Accounts Receivable↑ = L + E↑ Sales Revenue↑

This entry records the expense and reduction of Merchandise Inventory.

A↓ Merchandise Inventory↓ = L + E↓ Cost of Goods Sold↑

When the customer, West High School, makes payment within the discount period, Smart Touch Learning will record the receipt of cash and decrease the Accounts Receivable for $7,350 as follows:

Date	Accounts and Explanation	Debit	Credit
Jun. 30	Cash	7,350	
	Accounts Receivable—West High School		7,350
	Cash collection within the discount period.		

A↑↓ Cash↑ Accounts Receivable↓ = L + E

If for some reason West High School does not pay within the discount period, the customer will no longer receive the $150 discount ($7,500 × 0.02), and the customer must pay the full $7,500 amount. Smart Touch Learning would record the discount lost using the account Sales Discounts Forfeited. The account, Sales Discounts Forfeited, increases Other Income and Expenses on the income statement.

Date	Accounts and Explanation	Debit	Credit
Jul. 10	Cash	7,500	
	Accounts Receivable—West High School		7,350
	Sales Discounts Forfeited		150
	Cash collection outside the discount period.		

A↑↓ Cash↑ Accounts Receivable↓ = L + E↑ Sales Discounts Forfeited↑

Notice that in either scenario, if the customer paid within the discount period or outside of the discount period, Smart Touch Learning credited the Accounts Receivable for the net amount of the invoice. As shown in the following T-account, by doing this, Smart Touch Learning has shown that the invoice was paid in full with no remaining balance.

Accounts Receivable—West High School

June 23	7,350	7,350	Payment
	Bal.	0	

Transportation Costs—Freight Out

Remember that a freight out expense is one in which the seller pays freight charges to ship goods to customers. Freight out is a delivery expense to the seller. Delivery expense is an operating expense and is debited to the Delivery Expense account. For example, assume Smart Touch Learning paid $30 to ship goods to a customer on June 21. The entry to record that payment is as follows:

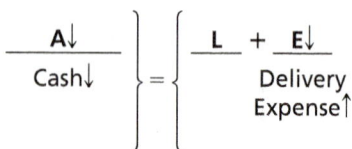

Date	Accounts and Explanation	Debit	Credit
Jun. 21	Delivery Expense	30	
	Cash		30
	Paid a freight bill.		

Try It!

8. Quick Computers has the following transactions in July related to the sale of merchandise inventory.

   July 3 Sold computers on account for $8,000 to South Auto Store, terms 3/15, n/30. The cost of the computers is $4,800.

   5 Sold two computers for $2,000 to Alex Harding. The cost of the computers is $1,200. Harding paid cash.

   12 Received full payment from South Auto Store on the balance due.

   15 Harding returned one computer from the July 5 sale. The computer sold for $1,000 and the cost was $600. Quick Computers issued a refund to the customer.

Journalize the sales transactions for Quick Computers assuming the company uses the perpetual inventory system.

Check your answers online in MyLab Accounting or at http://www.pearsonhighered.com/Horngren.

For more practice, see Short Exercises S-F:5-4 through S-F:5-8. MyLab Accounting

WHAT ARE THE ADJUSTING AND CLOSING ENTRIES FOR A MERCHANDISER?

Learning Objective 4
Adjust and close the accounts of a merchandising business

A merchandiser adjusts and closes accounts in a similar manner that a service entity does. If the optional worksheet is used, the unadjusted trial balance is entered, and the worksheet is completed to determine net income or net loss. In addition to adjusting for items covered in Chapter F:3, merchandisers must also adjust for inventory shrinkage and estimated sales returns.

Adjusting Merchandise Inventory for Inventory Shrinkage

The Merchandise Inventory account should stay current at all times in a perpetual inventory system. However, the actual amount of inventory on hand may differ from what the books show. This difference can occur because of theft and damage and is referred to as **inventory shrinkage**. For this reason, businesses take a physical count of inventory *at least* once a year. The most common time to count inventory is at the end of the fiscal year. The business then adjusts the Merchandise Inventory account based on the physical count. Smart Touch Learning must record an adjusting entry to account for this lost inventory.

Inventory Shrinkage
The loss of inventory that occurs because of theft and damage.

Suppose Smart Touch Learning's Merchandise Inventory account shows an unadjusted balance of $31,530. With no shrinkage—due to theft or damages—the business should have inventory costing $31,530. But on December 31, Smart Touch Learning counts the inventory on hand, and the total cost comes to only $30,000. Smart Touch Learning must reduce the Merchandise Inventory account by $1,530 to reflect the actual inventory on hand.

> Adjusting entry = Merchandise inventory balance before adjustment − Actual merchandise inventory on hand
> = $31,530 − $30,000
> = $1,530

Smart Touch Learning records this adjusting entry for inventory shrinkage:

Date	Accounts and Explanation	Debit	Credit
Dec. 31	Cost of Goods Sold	1,530	
	Merchandise Inventory		1,530
	Adjustment for inventory shrinkage.		

A↓   =   L + E↓
Merchandise Inventory↓   Cost of Goods Sold↑

This entry brings Merchandise Inventory to its correct balance and increases Cost of Goods Sold for the cost of the lost inventory.

```
           Merchandise Inventory
Unadj. Bal.   31,530 | 1,530   Adj. Dec. 31
      Bal.    30,000 |
```

Adjusting Sales Revenue and Merchandise Inventory for Estimated Sales Returns

As we discussed earlier, under the new revenue recognition standard, companies should only record sales revenue in the amount they expect to eventually realize. Therefore, at the end of the year, companies must estimate the amount of sales returns related to sales for that period and decrease sales revenue by the amount of expected sales returns. For example, assume that Smart Touch Learning estimates that approximately $4,000 of sales revenue and $1,600 of merchandise inventory will be returned. Smart Touch Learning will need to record two adjusting entries on December 31 to account for the estimated returns as follows:

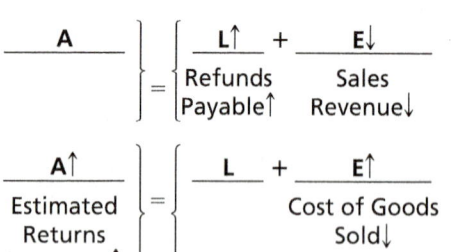

		This entry reduces the Sales Revenue by the amount of estimated refunds for the year.	Date	Accounts and Explanation	Debit	Credit
			Dec. 31	Sales Revenue	4,000	
				Refunds Payable		4,000
				To record estimated refunds for the year.		
		This entry records the cost of Estimated Returns Inventory for the year.	31	Estimated Returns Inventory	1,600	
				Cost of Goods Sold		1,600
				To record cost of estimated returns for the year.		

The first adjusting entry involves a debit to Sales Revenue that reduces sales for the year by the expected amount of the returns, thereby recording sales revenue at the net amount the company expects to eventually collect. Remember, Refunds Payable is a liability account and is reported on the balance sheet.

In the second adjusting entry, Smart Touch Learning debits an asset account, Estimated Returns Inventory, that represents the cost of the inventory the company believes it will receive in returns. The corresponding credit to Cost of Goods Sold decreases the expense. Estimated Returns Inventory is reported on the balance sheet as an asset.

Closing the Accounts of a Merchandiser

Exhibit F:5-6 presents Smart Touch Learning's adjusted trial balance and closing entries for the year, which are similar to those you have already learned, except for the new accounts (highlighted in blue). Closing still means to zero out all temporary accounts (accounts that aren't on the balance sheet).

The four-step closing process for a merchandising company follows:

Step 1: Make the revenue accounts equal zero via the Income Summary account.

Step 2: Make expense accounts equal zero via the Income Summary account.

Step 3: Make the Income Summary account equal zero via the Owner, Capital account. This closing entry transfers net income (or net loss) to Owner, Capital.

Step 4: Make the Owner, Withdrawals account equal zero via the Owner, Capital account.

Merchandising Operations

Exhibit F:5-6 | Adjusted Trial Balance and Closing Entries

SMART TOUCH LEARNING
Adjusted Trial Balance
December 31, 2025

Account Title	Debit	Credit
Cash	$ 88,500	
Accounts Receivable	4,400	
Merchandise Inventory	30,000	
Estimated Returns Inventory	1,600	
Office Supplies	100	
Prepaid Rent	4,000	
Land	20,000	
Building	60,000	
Accumulated Depreciation—Building		$ 1,750
Furniture	18,000	
Accumulated Depreciation—Furniture		2,100
Accounts Payable		6,800
Refunds Payable		4,000
Utilities Payable		2,500
Salaries Payable		5,280
Interest Payable		300
Unearned Revenue		900
Notes Payable		60,000
Bright, Capital		51,550
Bright, Withdrawals	10,000	
Sales Revenue		920,000
Sales Discounts Forfeited		2,000
Cost of Goods Sold	540,000	
Salaries Expense	92,580	
Rent Expense	63,800	
Utilities Expense	55,500	
Insurance Expense	31,900	
Depreciation Expense—Building	1,500	
Depreciation Expense—Furniture	1,800	
Advertising Expense	11,800	
Interest Expense	11,000	
Delivery Expense	7,800	
Supplies Expense	2,900	
Total	$ 1,057,180	$ 1,057,180

Temporary accounts that are closed.

5-22 Financial chapter 5

Exhibit F:5-6 | (Continued)

A = L + E↑↓
  Sales Revenue↓
  Sales Discounts Forfeited↓
  Income Summary↑

A = L + E↑↓
  Income Summary↓
  Expenses↓

Date	Accounts and Explanation	Debit	Credit
Dec. 31	Sales Revenue	920,000	
	Sales Discounts Forfeited	2,000	
	Income Summary		922,000
	To close revenue.		
31	Income Summary	820,580	
	Cost of Goods Sold		540,000
	Salaries Expense		92,580
	Rent Expense		63,800
	Utilities Expense		55,500
	Insurance Expense		31,900
	Depreciation Expense—Building		1,500
	Depreciation Expense—Furniture		1,800
	Advertising Expense		11,800
	Interest Expense		11,000
	Delivery Expense		7,800
	Supplies Expense		2,900
	To close expenses.		
31	Income Summary	101,420	
	Bright, Capital		101,420
	To close Income Summary.		
31	Bright, Capital	10,000	
	Bright, Withdrawals		10,000
	To close withdrawals.		

A = L + E↑↓
  Income Summary↓
  Bright, Capital↑

A = L + E↑↓
  Bright, Capital↓
  Bright, Withdrawals↓

Income Summary

Clos. 2	820,580	922,000	Clos. 1
		101,420	Bal.
Clos. 3	101,420		
		0	Bal.

Bright, Withdrawals

Adj. Bal.	10,000		
		10,000	Clos. 4
Bal.	0		

Bright, Capital

		51,550	Adj. Bal.
Clos. 4	10,000	101,420	Clos. 3
		142,970	Bal.

> 9. On December 31, Ace's Pharmacy's Merchandise Inventory account is showing a balance of $43,000. The physical count of inventory came up with $42,500. Journalize the adjusting entry needed to account for the inventory shrinkage. The company uses the perpetual inventory system.
> 10. On December 31, Ace's Pharmacy estimated that approximately $27,000 of merchandise sold during the past year will be returned with a cost of $8,100. Journalize the adjusting entry needed to account for the estimated returns.
>
> Check your answer online in MyLab Accounting or at http://www.pearsonhighered.com/Horngren.
>
> For more practice, see Short Exercises S-F:5-9 through S-F:5-11.   MyLab Accounting

HOW ARE A MERCHANDISER'S FINANCIAL STATEMENTS PREPARED?

The financial statements that you have learned for a service business are also used by a merchandiser. However, the merchandiser's financial statements will contain the new accounts that have been introduced in this chapter. Let's take a look at some of the differences for a merchandising business.

Learning Objective 5
Prepare a merchandiser's financial statements

Income Statement

In previous chapters, you learned how to prepare the income statement using what we now call the single-step format. In this chapter, we will introduce a new format: the multi-step format.

Single-Step Income Statement

The **single-step income statement** groups all revenues together and all expenses together without calculating other subtotals. Many companies use this format. The single-step format clearly distinguishes revenues from expenses and works well for service entities because they have no gross profit to report. Exhibit F:5-7 (on the next page) shows a single-step income statement for Smart Touch Learning.

Single-Step Income Statement
Income statement format that groups all revenues together and then lists and deducts all expenses together without calculating any subtotals.

Exhibit F:5-7 | Single-Step Income Statement

SMART TOUCH LEARNING
Income Statement
Year Ended December 31, 2025

Revenues:		
Net Sales Revenue		$ 920,000
Sales Discounts Forfeited		2,000
Total Revenues		922,000
Expenses:		
Cost of Goods Sold	$ 540,000	
Salaries Expense	92,580	
Rent Expense	63,800	
Utilities Expense	55,500	
Insurance Expense	31,900	
Depreciation Expense—Building	1,500	
Depreciation Expense—Furniture	1,800	
Advertising Expense	11,800	
Interest Expense	11,000	
Delivery Expense	7,800	
Supplies Expense	2,900	
Total Expenses		820,580
Net Income		$ 101,420

Sales Revenue is recorded net of sales discounts, so it is labeled Net Sales Revenue on the income statement.

Multi-Step Income Statement

Multi-Step Income Statement
Income statement format that contains subtotals to highlight significant relationships. In addition to net income, it reports gross profit and operating income.

A **multi-step income statement** is different than a single-step income statement because it lists several important subtotals. In addition to net income (the bottom line), it also reports subtotals for gross profit and operating income (also called *income from operations*). The multi-step income statement for Smart Touch Learning appears in Exhibit F:5-8.

Merchandising Operations Financial 5-25

Exhibit F:5-8 | Multi-Step Income Statement

SMART TOUCH LEARNING
Income Statement
Year Ended December 31, 2025

Net Sales Revenue		$ 920,000
Cost of Goods Sold		540,000
Gross Profit		380,000
Operating Expenses:		
Selling Expenses:		
Salaries Expense	$ 53,650	
Rent Expense	38,280	
Advertising Expense	11,800	
Depreciation Expense—Building	1,500	
Delivery Expense	7,800	
Total Selling Expenses	113,030	
Administrative Expenses:		
Utilities Expense	55,500	
Salaries Expense	38,930	
Insurance Expense	31,900	
Rent Expense	25,520	
Depreciation Expense—Furniture	1,800	
Supplies Expense	2,900	
Total Administrative Expenses	156,550	
Total Operating Expenses		269,580
Operating Income		110,420
Other Income and (Expenses):		
Sales Discounts Forfeited	2,000	
Interest Expense	(11,000)	
Total Other Income and (Expenses)		(9,000)
Net Income		**$ 101,420**

Gross Profit brackets: Net Sales Revenue, Cost of Goods Sold, Gross Profit
Operating Income brackets Operating Expenses through Operating Income
Other Income and (Expenses) and Net Income brackets the final section

    The income statement begins by calculating gross profit. Gross profit is the markup on the merchandise inventory and is calculated as net sales revenue minus cost of goods sold. Net sales revenue is sales revenue less discounts and estimated returns and allowances. Gross profit, along with net income, is a measure of a business's success. A sufficiently high gross profit is vital to a merchandiser. Next, the operating expenses, those expenses other than cost of goods sold that are related to the day-to-day operations of the business, are listed.
    Both merchandisers and service companies report operating expenses in two categories:

- **Selling expenses** are operating expenses related to marketing and selling the company's goods and services. These include sales salaries, sales commissions, advertising, depreciation on store buildings and equipment, store rent, utilities on store buildings, property taxes on store buildings, and delivery expense.

Selling Expenses
Operating expenses related to marketing and selling the company's goods and services.

Administrative Expenses
Operating expenses incurred that are not related to marketing the company's goods and services.

- **Administrative expenses** include operating expenses *not* related to marketing the company's goods and services. These include office expenses, such as the salaries of the executives and office employees; depreciation on office buildings and equipment; rent other than on stores (for example, rent on the administrative office); utilities other than on stores (for example, utilities on the administrative office); and property taxes on the administrative office building.

Operating Income
Measures the results of the entity's major ongoing activities. Gross profit minus operating expenses.

Gross profit minus operating expenses equals **operating income** (also called *income from operations*). Operating income measures the results of the entity's major ongoing activities (normal operations).

Other Income and Expenses
Revenues or expenses that are outside the normal, day-to-day operations of a business, such as a gain or loss on the sale of plant assets or interest expense.

The next section of the income statement is **other income and expenses**. This category reports revenues and expenses that fall outside the business's main, day-to-day, regular operations. Examples include interest revenue, sales discounts forfeited, interest expense, and gains and losses on the sale of plant assets. These examples have nothing to do with the business's "normal" operations but are related to investing or financing activities. As a result, they are classified as "other" items.

Statement of Owner's Equity and the Balance Sheet

A merchandiser's statement of owner's equity looks exactly like that of a service business. The balance sheet will also look the same as for a service business, except merchandisers have additional current asset accounts, Merchandise Inventory and Estimated Returns Inventory. In addition, merchandisers will have an additional current liability account, Refunds Payable, to represent the estimated amount of refunds that are due.

11. Capital City Motorcycle's selected accounts as of December 31, 2024, follow:

Selling Expenses	$ 10,500
Interest Revenue	1,000
Net Sales Revenue	113,000
Cost of Goods Sold	85,000
Administrative Expenses	8,000
Sales Discounts Forfeited	500

Prepare the multi-step income statement for the year ended December 31, 2024.

Check your answers online in MyLab Accounting or at http://www.pearsonhighered.com/Horngren.

For more practice, see Short Exercises S-F:5-12 and S-F:5-13. **MyLab Accounting**

HOW DO WE USE THE GROSS PROFIT PERCENTAGE TO EVALUATE BUSINESS PERFORMANCE?

Merchandisers use several ratios to evaluate their operations, and among them is the gross profit percentage. The **gross profit percentage** measures the profitability of each sales dollar above the cost of goods sold and is computed as follows:

> Gross profit percentage = Gross profit / Net sales revenue

Learning Objective 6
Use the gross profit percentage to evaluate business performance

Gross Profit Percentage
Measures the profitability of each sales dollar above the cost of goods sold. Gross profit / Net sales revenue.

The gross profit percentage is one of the most carefully watched measures of profitability. It reflects a business's ability to earn a profit on its merchandise inventory. The gross profit earned on merchandise inventory must be high enough to cover the remaining operating expenses and to earn net income. A small increase in the gross profit percentage from last year to this year may signal an important rise in income. Conversely, a small decrease from last year to this year may signal trouble. Gross profit percentages vary among industries, but in general, a high gross profit percentage is desired.

Returning to **Kohl's Corporation** we can now calculate the gross profit percentage. Kohl's Corporation had the following net sales and cost of merchandise sold (cost of goods sold), found on the income statement for the fiscal year ending February 2, 2019. Visit **http://www.pearsonhighered.com/Horngren** for a link to Kohl's Corporation's annual report.

	For year ended Feb. 2, 2019 (in millions)	For year ended February 3, 2018 (in millions)
Net sales	$ 19,167	$ 19,036
Cost of merchandise sold	12,199	12,176

Gross profit is calculated as net sales less cost of merchandise sold. To determine the gross profit percentage, the gross profit is then divided by net sales. The gross profit percentage for the year ending February 2, 2019, follows (amounts in millions):

> Gross profit percentage = ($19,167 − $12,199) / $19,167 = 0.364 = 36.4%

In comparison, the gross profit percentage for the year ending February 3, 2018, was:

> Gross profit percentage = ($19,036 − $12,176) / $19,036 = 0.360 = 36.0%

The gross profit percentage increased slightly from February 3, 2018 to February 2, 2019, signifying that the percentage of gross profit on sales is increasing. However, when compared with the industry average for gross profit percentage, 35%, Kohl's is slightly higher than average. Kohl's should monitor the amount of profit it is earning on its merchandise inventory and take action if the percentage begins to drop.

12. Six String Florist's selected accounts as of December 31, 2024, follow:

Selling Expenses	$ 8,500
Interest Revenue	2,000
Net Sales Revenue	150,500
Cost of Goods Sold	80,000
Administrative Expenses	10,000

Determine the gross profit percentage for the year ended December 31, 2024.

Check your answer online in MyLab Accounting or at http://www.pearsonhighered.com/Horngren.

For more practice, see Short Exercise S-F:5-14. MyLab Accounting

APPENDIX 5A: Accounting for Multiple Performance Obligations

HOW ARE MULTIPLE PERFORMANCE OBLIGATIONS RECORDED IN A PERPETUAL INVENTORY SYSTEM?

Learning Objective 7

Account for multiple performance obligations using a perpetual inventory system

Under the new revenue recognition standards, companies are required to identify the performance obligations associated with each contract. Remember, a performance obligation is a contractual promise with a customer to transfer a distinct good or service. Some contracts with customers might have multiple performance obligations. For example, assume that Smart Touch Learning often provides its customers with a two-year service contract when it sells its tablets. In this case, there are two distinct performance obligations: the two-year service contract and the tablet.

When contracts involve multiple performance obligations, the company is required to allocate the transaction price to each performance obligation separately. For example, assume on November 1 Smart Touch Learning sells one tablet (cost of $350) along with a two-year service contract to a customer for $620. The customer pays cash at the time of the sale. The $620 sales price must be allocated among each performance obligation. Smart Touch Learning allocates the sales price of $620 as follows: $500 for the tablet and $120 for the two-year service contract.

In recording the transaction, Smart Touch Learning should only recognize revenue when, or as, it satisfies each performance obligation. The $500 associated with the tablet would be recognized as Sales Revenue because the tablet has been delivered to the customer. The $120 for the two-year service contract would be recorded as Unearned Revenue because the company has not satisfied the obligation of servicing or fulfilling the service contract. Smart Touch Learning would record the transaction on November 1 as follows:

Merchandising Operations Financial 5-29

Date	Accounts and Explanation	Debit	Credit
Nov. 1	Cash	620	
	Sales Revenue		500
	Unearned Revenue		120
	Cash sale including two-year service contract.		
Nov. 1	Cost of Goods Sold	350	
	Merchandise Inventory		350
	Recorded the cost of goods sold.		

$$A\uparrow \atop Cash\uparrow \Bigg\} = \Bigg\{ {L\uparrow \atop Unearned\ Revenue\uparrow} + {E\uparrow \atop Sales\ Revenue\uparrow}$$

$$A\downarrow \atop Merchandise\ Inventory\downarrow \Bigg\} = \Bigg\{ L + {E\downarrow \atop Cost\ of\ Goods\ Sold\uparrow}$$

As Smart Touch Learning satisfies the service contract, the company would recognize the revenue. For example, at December 31, Smart Touch Learning has provided two months of service for the tablet. Smart Touch Learning would record $10 (($120 / 24 months) × 2 months) of Service Revenue when it prepares adjusting entries.

Date	Accounts and Explanation	Debit	Credit
Dec. 31	Unearned Revenue	10	
	Service Revenue (($120 / 24 months) x 2 months)		10
	Service revenue earned.		

$$A \quad \Bigg\} = \Bigg\{ {L\downarrow \atop Unearned\ Revenue\downarrow} + {E\uparrow \atop Service\ Revenue\uparrow}$$

13A. Click Computers has the following transactions related to the sale of merchandise inventory.

Mar. 1	Sold a computer (cost of $3,000) for $8,000 to a customer. The customer paid cash. The sales price included a one-year service contract valued at $168.
Dec. 31	Recorded the amount of service contract earned.

Journalize the transactions for Click Computers assuming that the company uses the perpetual inventory system.
Check your answers online in MyLab Accounting or at http://www.pearsonhighered.com/Horngren.

For more practice, see Short Exercise S-F:5A-15. MyLab Accounting

APPENDIX 5B: Accounting for Merchandise Inventory in a Periodic Inventory System

HOW ARE MERCHANDISE INVENTORY TRANSACTIONS RECORDED IN A PERIODIC INVENTORY SYSTEM?

Learning Objective 8
Account for the purchase and sale of merchandise inventory using a periodic inventory system

Some smaller businesses find it too expensive to invest in a perpetual inventory system. These businesses use a periodic inventory system. In a periodic inventory system, businesses must obtain a physical count of inventory to determine quantities on hand.

Purchases of Merchandise Inventory—Periodic Inventory System

All inventory systems use the Merchandise Inventory account. But in a periodic inventory system, purchases, purchase returns and allowances, purchase discounts, and freight in costs are recorded in separate accounts during the year and then the Merchandise Inventory account is updated in the closing process. Let's account for Smart Touch Learning's purchase of the tablet computers from Southwest Electronics Direct as shown in Exhibit F:5-3. Remember, Smart Touch Learning purchased $35,000 of inventory with terms 3/15, n/30.

Under the periodic inventory system, Smart Touch Learning will record the purchase of inventory using an account called Purchases (an expense account). Unlike in a perpetual inventory system, the purchase of inventory is not recorded directly into the Merchandise Inventory account.

$$\frac{A}{} \bigg| = \bigg\{ \frac{L\uparrow}{\text{Accounts}} + \frac{E\downarrow}{\text{Purchases}\uparrow}$$
Payable↑

Date	Accounts and Explanation	Debit	Credit
Jun. 3	Purchases	35,000	
	Accounts Payable—Southwest Electronics Direct		35,000
	Purchased inventory on account.		

Purchase Returns and Allowances—Periodic Inventory System

Suppose that, prior to payment, on June 6, Smart Touch Learning returned 20 tablets that cost $7,000 to Southwest Electronics Direct, the vendor. Smart Touch Learning would record this return as follows:

$$\frac{A}{} \bigg| = \bigg\{ \frac{L\downarrow}{\text{Accounts}} + \frac{E\uparrow}{\text{Purchase}}$$
Payable↓   Returns and
           Allowances↑

Date	Accounts and Explanation	Debit	Credit
Jun. 6	Accounts Payable—Southwest Electronics Direct	7,000	
	Purchase Returns and Allowances		7,000
	Returned inventory to seller (vendor).		

In the periodic inventory system, instead of recording the return to Merchandise Inventory, a separate account, Purchase Returns and Allowances, is used. Purchase Returns and Allowances is a contra expense account and decreases the Purchases account. The purchase return reduces the amount Smart Touch Learning owes to Southwest Electronics Direct. The purchase return journal entry records a debit to Accounts Payable, reducing the liability, and a credit to Purchase Returns and Allowances. The company's accounts now reflect the correct balance after the return.

Accounts Payable		Purchases		Purchase Returns and Allowances
June 6 7,000	35,000 June 3	June 3 35,000		7,000 June 6
	28,000 Bal.			

Purchase Discounts—Periodic Inventory System

When Smart Touch Learning makes payment for the merchandise, less the $7,000 return, it will need to apply the purchase discount, if paid within the discount period. Assume Smart Touch Learning makes payment to Southwest Electronics Direct on June 15, within the discount period. Smart Touch Learning will record the following journal entry for the cash payment:

Date	Accounts and Explanation	Debit	Credit
Jun. 15	Accounts Payable—Southwest Electronics Direct	28,000	
	Cash ($28,000 − $840)		27,160
	Purchase Discounts ($28,000 × 0.03)		840
	Paid within discount period net of return.		

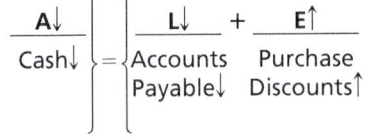

When using the periodic inventory system, the Merchandise Inventory account is not updated during the period. Therefore, it will never be used when recording purchases, discounts, returns, or sales of inventory.

Smart Touch Learning records a debit to Accounts Payable for the amount of the invoice less any purchase returns or allowances. This reduces the accounts payable by the amount owed. Cash is credited for the amount paid to the seller. The purchase discount is recorded in a separate account called Purchase Discounts (a contra expense account). After posting the entry to the accounts, the Accounts Payable balance shows the invoice has been paid in full with no remaining balance:

Cash		Accounts Payable		Purchase Discounts
Bal. 60,500		June 6 7,000	35,000 June 3	840 June 15
	27,160 June 15		28,000 Bal.	
Bal. 33,340		June 15 28,000		
			0 Bal.	

Transportation Costs—Periodic Inventory System

Under the periodic inventory system, freight in is debited to a separate Freight In account (an adjunct expense account) as opposed to debiting the Merchandise Inventory account. For example, suppose Smart Touch Learning pays a $60 freight charge on June 3. The company would make the following entry:

$$\frac{A\downarrow}{Cash\downarrow} \bigg\} = \bigg\{ \frac{L}{} + \frac{E\downarrow}{Freight\ In\uparrow}$$

Date	Accounts and Explanation	Debit	Credit
Jun. 3	Freight In	60	
	Cash		60
	Paid a freight bill.		

Net Cost of Inventory Purchased

Under the periodic inventory system, the net cost of merchandise inventory purchased must be calculated. This is because the balance of Purchases is a *gross* amount that does not include subtractions for purchase returns and allowances and purchase discounts or additions for freight in. Net cost of inventory purchased is the net cost of inventory after subtracting the contra accounts from Purchases and adding the adjunct account:

```
  Purchases
− Purchase Returns and Allowances
− Purchase Discounts
= Net Purchases
+ Freight In
= Net Cost of Inventory Purchased
```

Sale of Merchandise Inventory—Periodic Inventory System

Recording sales of merchandise inventory is streamlined in the periodic inventory system. With no running record of merchandise inventory to maintain, there is no need to record an entry to Merchandise Inventory and Cost of Goods Sold. Instead, a sale of inventory involves recording only the Sales Revenue portion. Suppose that on June 21, Smart Touch Learning sold 10 tablets to Lions Company for a total sale of $5,000 on account with terms of 2/10, n/30. The company would record the sale as follows:

$$\frac{A\uparrow}{Accounts\ Receivable\uparrow} \bigg\} = \bigg\{ \frac{L}{} + \frac{E\uparrow}{Sales\ Revenue\uparrow}$$

Date	Accounts and Explanation	Debit	Credit
Jun. 21	Accounts Receivable—Lions Company	4,900	
	Sales Revenue ($5,000 − ($5,000 × 0.02))		4,900
	Sale on account less discount.		

Accounting for sales discounts and sales returns and allowances is the same as in a perpetual inventory system, except that there are no entries for merchandise inventory.

Preparing Financial Statements—Periodic Inventory System

The financial statements under the perpetual and periodic inventory systems are similar. However, the periodic inventory system requires an additional calculation—the cost of goods sold. As we have seen under the perpetual inventory system, cost of goods sold is simply the sum of the amounts posted to that account. Cost of goods sold must be computed separately under the periodic inventory system. At the end of each period, the company combines a number of accounts to compute cost of goods sold for the period, and this calculation is shown on the income statement. Cost of goods sold is calculated as follows for Smart Touch Learning:

Beginning Merchandise Inventory		$ 0
Purchases	$ 695,310	
Less: Purchase Returns and Allowances	150,600	
Purchase Discounts	9,510	
Net Purchases	535,200	
Plus: Freight In	36,400	
Net Cost of Inventory Purchased		571,600
Cost of Goods Available for Sale		571,600
Less: Ending Inventory*		31,600
Cost of Goods Sold		$ 540,000

*(Includes $1,600 of Estimated Returns Inventory)

Adjusting and Closing Entries—Periodic Inventory System

When using the periodic inventory system, there is no need to record an adjusting entry for inventory shrinkage. This is because there is no perpetual running balance of the Merchandise Inventory account. Instead, the business determines the ending Merchandise Inventory amount by taking a physical count of inventory. The amount of the physical count is $30,000 and is recorded as ending Merchandise Inventory.

A company that uses the periodic inventory system will still need to record an adjusting entry for estimated refunds payable. The company will record an adjusting entry for only the refunds payable portion and not include the second entry to Merchandise Inventory required in a perpetual inventory system. The process of recording the Estimated Returns Inventory (and ending Merchandise Inventory) is completed through the closing entry process. Let's take a look at Smart Touch Learning's adjusted trial balance and closing entries for the year under the periodic inventory system shown in Exhibit F:5B-1 (on the next page). The accounts that are used in the periodic inventory system are highlighted in blue.

Exhibit F:5B-1 | Adjusted Trial Balance and Closing Entries

SMART TOUCH LEARNING
Adjusted Trial Balance
December 31, 2025

Account Title	Debit	Credit
Cash	$ 88,500	
Accounts Receivable	4,400	
Merchandise Inventory (beginning)	0	
Office Supplies	100	
Prepaid Rent	4,000	
Land	20,000	
Building	60,000	
Accumulated Depreciation—Building		$ 1,750
Furniture	18,000	
Accumulated Depreciation—Furniture		2,100
Accounts Payable		6,800
Refunds Payable		4,000
Utilities Payable		2,500
Salaries Payable		5,280
Interest Payable		300
Unearned Revenue		900
Notes Payable		60,000
Bright, Capital		51,550
Bright, Withdrawals	10,000	
Sales Revenue		920,000
Sales Discounts Forfeited		2,000
Purchases	695,310	
Purchase Returns and Allowances		150,600
Purchase Discounts		9,510
Freight In	36,400	
Salaries Expense	92,580	
Rent Expense	63,800	
Utilities Expense	55,500	
Insurance Expense	31,900	
Depreciation Expense—Building	1,500	
Depreciation Expense—Furniture	1,800	
Advertising Expense	11,800	
Interest Expense	11,000	
Delivery Expense	7,800	
Supplies Expense	2,900	
Total	$ 1,217,290	$ 1,217,290

Temporary accounts that are closed.

Exhibit F:5B-1 (Continued)

Date	Accounts and Explanation	Debit	Credit
Dec. 31	Sales Revenue	920,000	
	Sales Discounts Forfeited	2,000	
	Purchase Returns and Allowances	150,600	
	Purchase Discounts	9,510	
	Merchandise Inventory (ending)	30,000	
	Estimated Returns Inventory	1,600	
	Income Summary		1,113,710
	To close revenue and other credit accounts		
	and record ending merchandise inventory.		
31	Income Summary	1,012,290	
	Purchases		695,310
	Freight In		36,400
	Merchandise Inventory (beginning)		0
	Salaries Expense		92,580
	Rent Expense		63,800
	Utilities Expense		55,500
	Insurance Expense		31,900
	Depreciation Expense—Building		1,500
	Depreciation Expense—Furniture		1,800
	Advertising Expense		11,800
	Interest Expense		11,000
	Delivery Expense		7,800
	Supplies Expense		2,900
	To close expenses and other debit accounts		
	and remove beginning merchandise inventory.		
31	Income Summary	101,420	
	Bright, Capital		101,420
	To close Income Summary.		
31	Bright, Capital	10,000	
	Bright, Withdrawals		10,000
	To close withdrawals.		

Accounting equation effects:

A↑ Merchandise Inventory↑ Estimated Returns Inventory↑ = L + E↑ Sales Revenue↓ Sales Discounts Forfeited↓ Purchase Returns and Allowances↓ Purchase Discounts↓ Income Summary↑

A↓ Merchandise Inventory↓ = L + E↓ Income Summary↓ Expenses↓

A = L + E↑↓ Income Summary↓ Bright, Capital↑

A = L + E↑↓ Bright, Capital↓ Bright, Withdrawals↓

Income Summary

Clos. 2	1,012,290	1,113,710	Clos. 1
		101,420	Bal.
Clos. 3	101,420		
		0	Bal.

Bright, Capital

		51,550	Adj. Bal.
Clos. 4	10,000	101,420	Clos. 3
		142,970	**Bal.**

Bright, Withdrawals

Adj. Bal.	10,000		
		10,000	Clos. 4
Bal.	0		

The four-step closing process under the periodic inventory system is similar to the perpetual inventory system, but let's take a moment to highlight the differences:

Step 1: Using the periodic inventory system, Sales Revenue and Sales Discounts Forfeited are still closed with a debit via the Income Summary account, but in addition, all other temporary accounts with credit balances (Purchase Returns and Allowances and Purchase Discounts) are also closed. The ending Merchandise Inventory (determined from the physical count) and Estimated Returns Inventory are recorded as debits.

Step 2: Expense accounts and other temporary accounts with debit balances are still closed via the Income Summary account. In addition, the beginning Merchandise Inventory, Purchases, and Freight In are also closed via the Income Summary account. Notice in the Merchandise Inventory T-account shown below that the ending inventory is recorded with a debit entry and the beginning inventory is removed with a credit entry during the closing process.

Merchandise Inventory			
Adj. Bal.	0		
Clos. 1	30,000	0	Clos. 2
Bal.	30,000		

The key difference in the closing process under the periodic inventory system is how merchandise inventory is handled. In the periodic inventory system, the ending merchandise inventory balance must be recorded as a debit during closing and the beginning merchandise inventory balance must be recorded as a credit during closing. The additional Purchases and related contra and adjunct accounts must also be closed.

Step 3 and **Step 4:** These steps, closing the Income Summary and Owner, Withdrawals accounts, are the same under both methods.

14B. Schorr Electronics and Supply has the following transactions in July related to purchase and sale of merchandise inventory.

July 1 Purchase of $20,500 worth of computers on account, terms of 2/10, n/30, from Best Computers.
3 Return of $4,000 of the computers to Best Computers.
9 Payment made on account to Best Computers.
12 Sold computers on account for $8,000 to Morris Studios, terms 3/15, n/30.
26 Received payment from Morris Studios on balance due.

Journalize the transactions for Schorr Electronics and Supply assuming that the company uses the periodic inventory system.
Check your answers online in MyLab Accounting or at http://www.pearsonhighered.com/Horngren.

For more practice, see Short Exercises S-F:5B-16 through S-F:5B-19. MyLab Accounting

REVIEW

> Things You Should Know

1. **What are merchandising operations?**

   - A merchandiser is a business that sells merchandise, or goods, to customers.
   - There are two main types of inventory accounting systems that are used by merchandisers:
     - Periodic inventory system—requires businesses to obtain a physical count of inventory to determine quantities on hand
     - Perpetual inventory system—keeps a running computerized record of merchandise inventory

2. **How are purchases of merchandise inventory recorded in a perpetual inventory system?**

   - Purchase of merchandise inventory

Date	Accounts and Explanation	Debit	Credit
	Merchandise Inventory	XXX	
	Cash or Accounts Payable		XXX

   - Purchase return

Date	Accounts and Explanation	Debit	Credit
	Cash or Accounts Payable	XXX	
	Merchandise Inventory		XXX

   - Payment of freight in

Date	Accounts and Explanation	Debit	Credit
	Merchandise Inventory	XXX	
	Cash		XXX

   - Payment of merchandise inventory within discount period

Date	Accounts and Explanation	Debit	Credit
	Accounts Payable	XXX	
	Cash		XXX
	Merchandise Inventory		XXX

   - Payment of merchandise inventory after discount period

Date	Accounts and Explanation	Debit	Credit
	Accounts Payable	XXX	
	Cash		XXX

3. **How are sales of merchandise inventory recorded in a perpetual inventory system?**

- Sales of merchandise inventory are recorded at the net amount (sales price less any discount)

Date	Accounts and Explanation	Debit	Credit
	Cash or Accounts Receivable	XXX	
	Sales Revenue		XXX
	Cost of Goods Sold	XXX	
	Merchandise Inventory		XXX

- Sales return

Date	Accounts and Explanation	Debit	Credit
	Refunds Payable	XXX	
	Cash or Accounts Receivable		XXX
	Merchandise Inventory	XXX	
	Estimated Returns Inventory		XXX

- Sales allowance

Date	Accounts and Explanation	Debit	Credit
	Refunds Payable	XXX	
	Cash or Accounts Receivable		XXX

- Payment of freight out

Date	Accounts and Explanation	Debit	Credit
	Delivery Expense	XXX	
	Cash		XXX

- Collection of cash during discount period

Date	Accounts and Explanation	Debit	Credit
	Cash	XXX	
	Accounts Receivable		XXX

- Collection of cash after discount period

Date	Accounts and Explanation	Debit	Credit
	Cash	XXX	
	Accounts Receivable		XXX
	Sales Discounts Forfeited		XXX

4. What are the adjusting and closing entries for a merchandiser?

- An adjusting entry must be made for inventory shrinkage, the loss of inventory that occurs because of theft and damage.

Date	Accounts and Explanation	Debit	Credit
	Cost of Goods Sold	XXX	
	Merchandise Inventory		XXX
	Adjustment for inventory shrinkage.		

- Companies must also make an adjusting entry for the estimated amount of merchandise inventory that will be returned.

Date	Accounts and Explanation	Debit	Credit
	Sales Revenue	XXX	
	Refunds Payable		XXX
	Estimated Returns Inventory	XXX	
	Cost of Goods Sold		XXX

- The closing entries are similar to those already learned, except for including the new accounts (Sales Revenue, Sales Discounts Forfeited, Delivery Expense, and Cost of Goods Sold).

5. How are a merchandiser's financial statements prepared?

- There are two formats for the income statement:
  - Single-step income statement—groups all revenues together and all expenses together without calculating other subtotals
  - Multi-step income statement—lists several important subtotals including gross profit and operating income
- A merchandiser's statement of owner's equity looks exactly like that of a service business.
- The balance sheet will also look the same, except merchandisers have additional current asset accounts, such as Merchandise Inventory and Estimated Returns Inventory. In addition, a merchandiser's balance sheet also includes the current liability Refunds Payable.

6. How do we use the gross profit percentage to evaluate business performance?

- The gross profit percentage measures the profitability of each sales dollar above the cost of goods sold.
- Gross profit percentage = Gross profit / Net sales revenue.

7. How are multiple performance obligations recorded in a perpetual inventory system? (Appendix 5A)

- The sales price of contracts involving multiple performance obligations must be allocated among each distinct performance obligation.
- Revenue is recognized when, or as, the company satisfies each performance obligation.

8. **How are merchandise inventory transactions recorded in a periodic inventory system? (Appendix 5B)**

- The Merchandise Inventory account is not used when recording purchase transactions. Instead Purchases, Purchase Discounts, Purchase Returns and Allowances, and Freight In are used.

- Sales transactions only involve recording the Sales Revenue. The Merchandise Inventory account is not used.

- An adjustment for inventory shrinkage is not needed.

- Closing entries are similar to the perpetual inventory system with the addition of closing the new accounts discussed. Ending Merchandise Inventory must be recorded, and beginning Merchandise Inventory must be removed.

> Check Your Understanding F:5-1

Check your understanding of the chapter by completing this problem and then looking at the solution. Use this practice to help identify which sections of the chapter you need to study more.

Suppose Heat Miser Air Conditioner Company engaged in the following transactions during June of the current year:

Jun.	3	Purchased inventory on account with credit terms of 1/10, n/EOM, $1,600.
	9	Returned 40% of the inventory purchased on June 3. It was defective.
	12	Sold goods for cash, $920 (cost, $550).
	15	Purchased goods for $5,000 on account. Credit terms were 3/15, n/30.
	16	Paid a $260 freight bill on goods purchased.
	17	Sold inventory for $4,000 cash (cost, $2,360).
	18	Sold inventory for $2,000 on account with credit terms of 2/10, n/30 (cost, $1,180).
	22	Received returned goods from the customer of the June 17 sale, $800 (cost, $480).
	24	Paid supplier for goods purchased on June 15.
	28	Received cash in full settlement of the account from the customer who purchased inventory on June 18.
	29	Paid the amount owed on account from the purchase of June 3.
	30	The company estimated that $400 of merchandise sold will be returned with a cost of $240.

Requirement

Journalize the preceding transactions. Assume Heat Miser uses a perpetual inventory system. The company estimates sales returns at the end of each month. (See Learning Objectives 2, 3, and 4)

> Solution

Date	Accounts and Explanation	Debit	Credit
Jun. 3	Merchandise Inventory	1,600	
	Accounts Payable		1,600
	Purchased inventory on account.		
9	Accounts Payable ($1,600 × 0.40)	640	
	Merchandise Inventory		640
	Returned inventory to seller (vendor).		
12	Cash	920	
	Sales Revenue		920
	Cash sale.		
12	Cost of Goods Sold	550	
	Merchandise Inventory		550
	Recorded the cost of goods sold.		
15	Merchandise Inventory	5,000	
	Accounts Payable		5,000
	Purchased inventory on account.		
16	Merchandise Inventory	260	
	Cash		260
	Paid a freight bill.		
17	Cash	4,000	
	Sales Revenue		4,000
	Cash sale.		
17	Cost of Goods Sold	2,360	
	Merchandise Inventory		2,360
	Recorded the cost of goods sold.		

Date	Accounts and Explanation	Debit	Credit
Jun. 18	Accounts Receivable	1,960	
	Sales Revenue ($2,000 − ($2,000 × 0.02))		1,960
	Sale on account less discount.		
18	Cost of Goods Sold	1,180	
	Merchandise Inventory		1,180
	Recorded the cost of goods sold.		
22	Refunds Payable	800	
	Cash		800
	To record refund.		
22	Merchandise Inventory	480	
	Estimated Returns Inventory		480
	To record cost of inventory returned.		
24	Accounts Payable	5,000	
	Cash ($5,000 − $150)		4,850
	Merchandise Inventory ($5,000 × 0.03)		150
	Paid within discount period.		
28	Cash	1,960	
	Accounts Receivable		1,960
	Cash collection within discount period.		
29	Accounts Payable ($1,600 − $640)	960	
	Cash		960
	Paid after discount period net of return.		
30	Sales Revenue	400	
	Refunds Payable		400
	To record estimated refunds.		
30	Estimated Returns Inventory	240	
	Cost of Goods Sold		240
	To record cost of estimated returns.		

> Check Your Understanding F:5-2

Check your understanding of the chapter by completing this problem and then looking at the solution. Use this practice to help identify which sections of the chapter you need to study more.

King Cornelius Company uses a perpetual inventory system. The adjusted trial balance of King Cornelius Company follows:

KING CORNELIUS COMPANY
Adjusted Trial Balance
December 31, 2024

Account Title	Debit	Credit
Cash	$ 5,600	
Accounts Receivable	37,100	
Merchandise Inventory	20,000	
Estimated Returns Inventory	5,800	
Office Supplies	1,300	
Prepaid Rent	1,000	
Furniture	26,500	
Accumulated Depreciation—Furniture		$ 23,800
Accounts Payable		6,300
Refunds Payable		3,800
Salaries Payable		2,000
Interest Payable		600
Unearned Revenue		2,400
Notes Payable, long-term		31,200
Cornelius, Capital		22,200
Cornelius, Withdrawals	48,000	
Sales Revenue		226,000
Sales Discounts Forfeited		2,000
Cost of Goods Sold	81,000	
Salaries Expense	72,700	
Rent Expense	7,700	
Utilities Expense	5,800	
Depreciation Expense—Furniture	2,700	
Supplies Expense	2,200	
Interest Expense	2,900	
Total	$ 320,300	$ 320,300

Requirements

1. Prepare the company's multi-step income statement, statement of owner's equity, and balance sheet in report form for year ended December 31, 2024. Note: King Cornelius doesn't separate its operating expenses as either selling or administrative. (See Learning Objective 5)

2. Journalize the closing entries at December 31, 2024. Post to the Income Summary account as an accuracy check on net income. Recall that the credit balance closed out of Income Summary should equal net income as computed on the income statement. Also post to Cornelius, Capital, whose balance should agree with the amount reported on the balance sheet. (See Learning Objective 4)

3. Compute the gross profit percentage for 2024. (See Learning Objective 6)

> Solution

Requirement 1

KING CORNELIUS COMPANY
Income Statement
Year Ended December 31, 2024

Net Sales Revenue		$ 226,000
Cost of Goods Sold		81,000
Gross Profit		145,000
Operating Expenses:		
Salaries Expense	$ 72,700	
Rent Expense	7,700	
Utilities Expense	5,800	
Depreciation Expense—Furniture	2,700	
Supplies Expense	2,200	
Total Operating Expenses		91,100
Operating Income		53,900
Other Income and (Expenses):		
Sales Discounts Forfeited	2,000	
Interest Expense	(2,900)	
Total Other Income and (Expenses)		(900)
Net Income		$ 53,000

KING CORNELIUS COMPANY
Statement of Owner's Equity
Year Ended December 31, 2024

Cornelius, Capital, January 1, 2024	$ 22,200
Owner contribution	0
Net income for the year	53,000
	75,200
Owner withdrawal	(48,000)
Cornelius, Capital, December 31, 2024	$ 27,200

KING CORNELIUS COMPANY
Balance Sheet
December 31, 2024

Assets

Current Assets:		
Cash	$ 5,600	
Accounts Receivable	37,100	
Merchandise Inventory	20,000	
Estimated Returns Inventory	5,800	
Office Supplies	1,300	
Prepaid Rent	1,000	
Total Current Assets		$ 70,800
Property, Plant, and Equipment:		
Furniture	26,500	
Less: Accumulated Depreciation—Furniture	(23,800)	
Total Property, Plant, and Equipment		2,700
Total Assets		$ 73,500

Liabilities

Current Liabilities:		
Accounts Payable	$ 6,300	
Refunds Payable	3,800	
Salaries Payable	2,000	
Interest Payable	600	
Unearned Revenue	2,400	
Total Current Liabilities		$ 15,100
Long-term Liabilities:		
Notes Payable		31,200
Total Liabilities		46,300

Owner's Equity

Cornelius, Capital		27,200
Total Liabilities and Owner's Equity		$ 73,500

5-46 Financial chapter 5

Requirement 2

Date	Accounts and Explanation	Debit	Credit
Dec. 31	Sales Revenue	226,000	
	Sales Discounts Forfeited	2,000	
	Income Summary		228,000
	To close revenue accounts.		
31	Income Summary	175,000	
	Cost of Goods Sold		81,000
	Salaries Expense		72,700
	Rent Expense		7,700
	Utilities Expense		5,800
	Depreciation Expense—Furniture		2,700
	Supplies Expense		2,200
	Interest Expense		2,900
	To close expenses.		
31	Income Summary	53,000	
	Cornelius, Capital		53,000
	To close Income Summary.		
31	Cornelius, Capital	48,000	
	Cornelius, Withdrawals		48,000
	To close withdrawals.		

Income Summary

Clos. 2	175,000	228,000	Clos. 1
		53,000	Bal.
Clos. 3	53,000		
		0	Bal.

Cornelius, Capital

		22,200	Adj. Bal.
Clos. 4	48,000	53,000	Clos. 3
		27,200	Bal.

Cornelius, Withdrawals

Adj. Bal.	48,000		
		48,000	Clos. 4
Bal.	0		

Requirement 3

Gross profit percentage = Gross profit / Net sales revenue = $145,000 / $226,000 = 0.642 = 64.2%

> Key Terms

Administrative Expenses (p. 5-26)
Cost of Goods Sold (COGS) (p. 5-3)
Credit Terms (p. 5-8)
Estimated Returns Inventory (p. 5-15)
FOB Destination (p. 5-10)
FOB Shipping Point (p. 5-10)
Freight In (p. 5-10)
Freight Out (p. 5-10)
Gross Profit (p. 5-4)
Gross Profit Percentage (p. 5-27)
Inventory Shrinkage (p. 5-19)

Invoice (p. 5-5)
Merchandise Inventory (p. 5-2)
Merchandiser (p. 5-2)
Multi-Step Income Statement (p. 5-24)
Operating Expenses (p. 5-4)
Operating Income (p. 5-26)
Other Income and Expenses (p. 5-26)
Periodic Inventory System (p. 5-4)
Perpetual Inventory System (p. 5-4)
Purchase Allowance (p. 5-7)
Purchase Discount (p. 5-8)

Purchase Return (p. 5-7)
Refunds Payable (p. 5-15)
Retailer (p. 5-2)
Sales Discounts (p. 5-16)
Sales Allowance (p. 5-16)
Sales Return (p. 5-14)
Sales Revenue (p. 5-12)
Selling Expenses (p. 5-25)
Single-Step Income Statement (p. 5-23)
Vendor (p. 5-3)
Wholesaler (p. 5-2)

> Quick Check

1. Which account does a merchandiser use that a service company does not use?
   a. Cost of Goods Sold
   b. Merchandise Inventory
   c. Sales Revenue
   d. All of the above

   Learning Objective 1

2. The two main inventory accounting systems are the
   a. perpetual and periodic.
   b. purchase and sale.
   c. returns and allowances.
   d. cash and accrual.

   Learning Objective 1

3. The journal entry for the purchase of inventory on account using the perpetual inventory system is

   Learning Objective 2

Date	Accounts and Explanation	Debit	Credit
a.	Merchandise Inventory	XXX	
	Accounts Receivable		XXX
b.	Accounts Payable	XXX	
	Merchandise Inventory		XXX
c.	Merchandise Inventory	XXX	
	Accounts Payable		XXX
d.	Merchandise Inventory	XXX	
	Cash		XXX

4. JC Manufacturing purchased inventory for $5,300 and also paid a $260 freight bill. JC Manufacturing returned 45% of the goods to the seller and later took a 2% purchase discount. Assume JC Manufacturing uses a perpetual inventory system. What is JC Manufacturing's final cost of the inventory that it kept? (Round your answer to the nearest whole number.)

   a. $2,997
   b. $2,337
   c. $3,117
   d. $2,857

   Learning Objective 2

Learning Objective 3

5. Austin Sound sold inventory for $300,000, terms 2/10, n/30. Cost of goods sold was $152,000. How much sales revenue will Austin Sound report from the sale?

   a. $152,000
   b. $294,000
   c. $148,960
   d. $300,000

Learning Objective 4

6. Suppose Dave's Discount's Merchandise Inventory account showed a balance of $8,000 before the year-end adjustments. The physical count of goods on hand totaled $7,400. Dave uses a perpetual inventory system. To adjust the accounts, which entry would the company make?

Date	Accounts and Explanation	Debit	Credit
a.	Cost of Goods Sold	600	
	Merchandise Inventory		600
b.	Merchandise Inventory	600	
	Accounts Receivable		600
c.	Accounts Payable	600	
	Merchandise Inventory		600
d.	Merchandise Inventory	600	
	Cost of Goods Sold		600

Learning Objective 4

7. Which of the following accounts would be closed at the end of the year using the perpetual inventory system?

   a. Cost of Goods Sold
   b. Merchandise Inventory
   c. Accounts Receivable
   d. Accounts Payable

Learning Objective 5

8. What is the order of the subtotals that appear on a multi-step income statement?

   a. Gross Profit, Operating Income, Net Income, Total Other Income and Expenses
   b. Operating Income, Gross Profit, Net Income, Total Other Income and Expenses
   c. Total Other Income and Expenses, Operating Income, Gross Profit, Net Income
   d. Gross Profit, Operating Income, Total Other Income and Expenses, Net Income

Learning Objective 6

9. Assume Juniper Natural Dyes made Net Sales Revenue of $90,000 and Cost of Goods Sold totaled $58,000. What was Juniper Natural Dyes' gross profit percentage for this period? (Round your answer to the nearest whole percent.)

   a. 36%
   b. 3.4 times
   c. 64%
   d. 17%

10A. League Automobiles sold an automobile for $24,000 on account. The cost of the automobile was $13,440. The sale of the automobile came with one year of free oil changes valued at $360. What would be the journal entry to record the sale?

Learning Objective 7
Appendix 5A

Date	Accounts and Explanation	Debit	Credit
a.	Accounts Receivable	24,000	
	Sales Revenue		24,000
	Cost of Goods Sold	13,440	
	Merchandise Inventory		13,440
b.	Accounts Receivable	24,360	
	Sales Revenue		24,000
	Unearned Revenue		360
	Cost of Goods Sold	13,440	
	Merchandise Inventory		13,440
c.	Accounts Receivable	24,000	
	Sales Revenue		23,640
	Service Revenue		360
	Cost of Goods Sold	13,440	
	Merchandise Inventory		13,440
d.	Accounts Receivable	24,000	
	Sales Revenue		23,640
	Unearned Revenue		360
	Cost of Goods Sold	13,440	
	Merchandise Inventory		13,440

11B. The journal entry for the purchase of inventory on account using the periodic inventory system is

Learning Objective 8
Appendix 5B

Date	Accounts and Explanation	Debit	Credit
a.	Purchases	XXX	
	Accounts Receivable		XXX
b.	Accounts Payable	XXX	
	Merchandise Inventory		XXX
c.	Merchandise Inventory	XXX	
	Accounts Payable		XXX
d.	Purchases	XXX	
	Accounts Payable		XXX

Check your answers at the end of the chapter.

ASSESS YOUR PROGRESS

> Review Questions

1. What is a merchandiser, and what is the name of the merchandise that it sells?
2. What are the two types of merchandisers? How do they differ?
3. Describe the operating cycle of a merchandiser.
4. What is Cost of Goods Sold (COGS), and where is it reported?
5. How is gross profit calculated, and what does it represent?
6. What are the two types of inventory accounting systems? Briefly describe each.
7. What is an invoice?
8. What account is debited when recording a purchase of inventory when using the perpetual inventory system?
9. What would the credit terms of "2/10, n/EOM" mean?
10. What is a purchase return? How does a purchase allowance differ from a purchase return?
11. Describe FOB shipping point and FOB destination. When does the buyer take ownership of the goods, and who typically pays the freight?
12. How is the net cost of inventory calculated?
13. What are the two journal entries involved when recording the sale of inventory when using the perpetual inventory system?
14. Under the new revenue recognition standard, how is the sale of inventory recorded?
15. When granting a sales allowance, is there a return of merchandise inventory from the customer? Describe the journal entry(ies) that would be recorded.
16. What is freight out and how is it recorded by the seller?
17. What is inventory shrinkage? Describe the adjusting entry that would be recorded to account for inventory shrinkage.
18. Under the new revenue recognition standard, what must companies do at the end of the period related to sales returns? Describe the journal entries that would be recorded.
19. What are the four steps involved in the closing process for a merchandising company?
20. Describe the single-step income statement.
21. Describe the multi-step income statement.
22. What financial statement is merchandise inventory reported on, and in what section?
23. What does the gross profit percentage measure, and how is it calculated?
24A. When a company has a contract involving multiple performance obligations, how must the company recognize revenue?
25B. What account is debited when recording a purchase of inventory when using a periodic inventory system?
26B. When recording purchase returns and purchase allowances under the periodic inventory system, what account is used?

27B. What account is debited when recording the payment of freight in when using the periodic inventory system?

28B. Describe the journal entry(ies) when recording a sale of inventory using the periodic inventory system.

29B. Is an adjusting entry needed for inventory shrinkage when using the periodic inventory system? Explain.

30B. Highlight the differences in the closing process when using the periodic inventory system rather than the perpetual inventory system.

31B. Describe the calculation of cost of goods sold when using the periodic inventory system.

> Short Exercises

For all short exercises, assume the perpetual inventory system is used unless stated otherwise. Round all numbers to the nearest whole dollar unless stated otherwise.

S-F:5-1 Comparing periodic and perpetual inventory systems

Learning Objective 1

For each statement below, identify whether the statement applies to the periodic inventory system, the perpetual inventory system, or both.

a. Normally used for relatively inexpensive goods.

b. Keeps a running computerized record of merchandise inventory.

c. Achieves better control over merchandise inventory.

d. Requires a physical count of inventory to determine the quantities on hand.

e. Uses bar codes to keep up-to-the-minute records of inventory.

S-F:5-2 Journalizing purchase transactions

Learning Objective 2

Consider the following transactions for Toys and More:

May 8	Toys and More purchased $113,300 worth of MegoBlock toys on account with credit terms of 2/10, n/60.
12	Toys and More returned $11,250 of the merchandise to MegoBlock due to damage during shipment.
15	Toys and More paid the amount due, less the return and discount.

Requirements

1. Journalize the purchase transactions. Explanations are not required.
2. In the final analysis, how much did the inventory cost Toys and More?

S-F:5-3 Journalizing purchase transactions

Learning Objective 2

Consider the following transactions for Burlington Drug Store:

Feb. 2	Burlington purchased $23,800 worth of inventory on account with credit terms of 2/15, n/30, FOB shipping point from Green Medical Supplies.
4	Burlington paid a $50 freight charge.
9	Burlington returned $5,200 of the merchandise due to damage during shipment.
14	Burlington paid the amount due, less return and discount.

Requirements

1. Journalize the purchase transactions. Explanations are not required.
2. In the final analysis, how much did the inventory cost Burlington Drug Store?

Learning Objective 3

S-F:5-4 Journalizing sales transactions (with sales return)

Journalize the following sales transactions for Tomas Sportswear. Explanations are not required. The company estimates sales returns at the end of each month.

Jul. 1	Tomas sold $21,000 of men's sportswear for cash. Cost of goods sold is $10,000.
5	Tomas received a $6,000 sales return on damaged goods from the customer on July 1. Cost of goods damaged is $3,000.

Learning Objective 3

S-F:5-5 Journalizing sales transactions (with sales allowance)

Journalize the following sales transactions for Lucy's Boutique. Explanations are not required. The company estimates sales returns at the end of each month.

Mar. 3	Lucy sold $63,000 of women's clothes on account, credit terms are 3/10, n/30, to Maria's Dresses. Cost of goods is $35,000.
7	Lucy granted a sales allowance of $100 for the clothes sold on July 3. Maria's Dresses did not return the inventory.
10	Lucy received payment from Maria's Dresses on the amount due, less sales allowance and discount.

Learning Objective 3

S-F:5-6 Journalizing sales transactions (outside of sales discount period)

Journalize the following sales transactions for Henry's Craft Shop. Explanations are not required.

Feb. 3	Henry sold $4,000 of craft supplies on account, credit terms are 2/10, n/30, to Quick Quilts. Cost of goods is $1,200.
23	Henry received payment from Quick Quilts on the amount due.

Learning Objectives 2, 3

S-F:5-7 Journalizing purchase and sales transactions

Suppose Piranha.com sells 3,500 books on account for $17 each (cost of these books is $35,700) on October 10 to The Textbook Store. Several books were slightly damaged in shipment, so Piranha.com granted a sales allowance of $1,000 to The Textbook Store on October 13. On October 25, The Textbook Store paid the balance due.

Requirements

1. Journalize The Textbook Store's October transactions.
2. Journalize Piranha.com's October transactions. The company estimates sales returns at the end of each month.

Learning Objectives 2, 3

S-F:5-8 Journalizing purchase and sales transactions

On November 4, Cain Company sold merchandise inventory on account to Tarin Wholesalers, $12,000, that cost $4,800. Terms 3/10, n/30. On November 5, Tarin Wholesalers paid shipping of $30. Tarin Wholesalers paid the balance to Cain Company on November 13.

Requirements

1. Journalize Tarin Wholesaler's November transactions.
2. Journalize Cain Company's November transactions.

S-F:5-9 Adjusting for inventory shrinkage

Learning Objective 4

Jeana's Furniture's unadjusted Merchandise Inventory account at year-end is $69,000. The physical count of inventory came up with a total of $67,600. Journalize the adjusting entry needed to account for inventory shrinkage.

S-F:5-10 Estimating sales returns

Learning Objective 4

On December 31, John Photography Supplies estimated that $4,400 merchandise sold will be returned with a cost of $2,720. Journalize the adjusting entries needed to account for the estimated returns.

S-F:5-11 Journalizing closing entries

Learning Objective 4

Rocky RV Center's accounting records include the following accounts at December 31, 2024.

Cost of Goods Sold	$ 372,000	Cash	$ 47,000
Accounts Payable	12,000	Sales Revenue	636,500
Rent Expense	25,700	Depreciation Expense—Building	13,000
Building	113,000	Rocky, Withdrawals	58,000
Rocky, Capital	198,100	Interest Revenue	12,000
Merchandise Inventory	238,000	Refunds Payable	4,000
Estimated Returns Inventory	1,600	Sales Discounts Forfeited	2,000
Notes Receivable	34,000	Delivery Expense	300
Accumulated Depreciation—Building	38,000		

Requirements

1. Journalize the required closing entries for Rocky.
2. Determine the ending balance in the Rocky, Capital account.

Use the following information to answer Short Exercises S-F:5-12 and S-F:5-13.

Camilia Communications reported the following figures from its adjusted trial balance for its first year of business, which ended on July 31, 2024:

Cash	$ 2,900	Cost of Goods Sold	$ 18,700
Selling Expenses	1,400	Equipment, net	9,500
Accounts Payable	4,300	Salaries Payable	1,200
Camilia, Capital	4,365	Net Sales Revenue	28,450
Notes Payable, long-term	500	Accounts Receivable	3,200
Merchandise Inventory	1,000	Interest Expense	65
Administrative Expenses	3,300	Refunds Payable	600
Estimated Returns Inventory	100	Sales Discounts Forfeited	750

S-F:5-12 Preparing a merchandiser's income statement

Learning Objective 5

Prepare Camilia Communications' multi-step income statement for the year ended July 31, 2024.

Learning Objective 5

S-F:5-13 Preparing a merchandiser's statement of owner's equity and balance sheet

Requirements

1. Prepare Camilia Communications' statement of owner's equity for the year ended July 31, 2024. Assume that there were no contributions or withdrawals during the year and that the business began on August 1, 2023.
2. Prepare Camilia Communications' classified balance sheet at July 31, 2024. Use the report format.

Learning Objective 6

S-F:5-14 Computing the gross profit percentage

Macarthy Landscape Supply's selected accounts as of December 31, 2024, follow. Compute the gross profit percentage for 2024.

Selling Expenses	$ 12,900
Interest Revenue	900
Net Sales Revenue	134,700
Cost of Goods Sold	114,000
Administrative Expenses	10,200

Learning Objective 7
Appendix 5A

S-F:5A-15 Journalizing multiple performance obligations

Journalize the following sales transactions for King Company. Explanations are not required.

Apr. 1	King Company sold merchandise inventory for $150. The cost of the inventory was $90. The customer paid cash. King Company was running a promotion and the customer received a $20 award at the time of sale that can be used at a future date on any King Company merchandise.
May 15	The customer uses the $20 award when purchasing merchandise inventory for $30. The cost of the inventory was $18. The customer paid cash.

Learning Objective 8
Appendix 5B

S-F:5B-16 Journalizing purchase transactions—periodic inventory system

Consider the following transactions for Garman Packing Supplies:

Apr. 10	Garman Packing Supplies buys $175,000 worth of merchandise inventory on account with credit terms of 1/10, n/30 from WeHaul.
12	Garman returns $15,200 of the merchandise to WeHaul due to damage during shipment.
19	Garman paid the amount due, less the return and discount, to WeHaul.

Requirements

1. Journalize the purchase transactions assuming Garman Packing Supplies uses the periodic inventory system. Explanations are not required.
2. What is the net cost of inventory purchased?

Learning Objective 8
Appendix 5B

S-F:5B-17 Journalizing sales transactions—periodic inventory system

Journalize the following sales transactions for Sanborn Pool Supply Store using the periodic inventory system. Explanations are not required.

Dec. 3	Sanborn sold $41,900 of pool equipment on account, credit terms are 3/15, n/EOM, to Beautiful Pools.
17	Sanborn receives payment from Beautiful Pools on the amount due less the discount.

S-F:5B-18 Journalizing closing entries—periodic inventory system

Learning Objective 8
Appendix 5B

D & T Printing Supplies' accounting records include the following accounts at December 31, 2024.

Purchases	$ 187,900	Cash	$ 21,200
Accounts Payable	7,900	Sales Revenue	297,100
Rent Expense	8,000	Depreciation Expense—Building	4,800
Building	40,900	Treat, Withdrawals	27,200
Treat, Capital	50,100	Interest Expense	1,000
Merchandise Inventory, Beginning	117,000	Merchandise Inventory, Ending	103,500
Notes Payable	10,700	Purchase Returns and Allowances	21,900
Purchase Discounts	3,000	Freight In	700
Accumulated Depreciation—Building	18,000		

Requirements

1. Journalize the required closing entries for D & T Printing Supplies assuming that D & T uses the periodic inventory system.
2. Determine the ending balance in the Treat, Capital account.

S-F:5B-19 Computing cost of goods sold in a periodic inventory system

Learning Objective 8
Appendix 5B

M Wholesale Company began the year with merchandise inventory of $12,000. During the year, M purchased $92,000 of goods, had purchase discounts of $100, and returned $6,000 due to damage. M also paid freight charges of $1,600 on inventory purchases. At year-end, M's ending merchandise inventory balance stood at $16,900. Assume that M uses the periodic inventory system. Compute M's cost of goods sold for the year.

> Exercises

For all exercises, assume the perpetual inventory system is used unless stated otherwise. Round all numbers to the nearest whole dollar unless stated otherwise.

E-F:5-20 Using accounting vocabulary

Learning Objectives 1, 2, 3

Match the accounting terms with the corresponding definitions.

1. Credit Terms
2. FOB Destination
3. Invoice
4. Cost of Goods Sold
5. Purchase Allowance
6. FOB Shipping Point
7. Wholesaler
8. Purchase Discount
9. Retailer

a. The cost of the merchandise inventory that the business has sold to customers.
b. An amount granted to the purchaser as an incentive to keep goods that are not "as ordered."
c. A type of merchandiser that buys merchandise either from a manufacturer or a wholesaler and then sells those goods to consumers.
d. A situation in which the buyer takes ownership (title) at the delivery destination point.
e. A type of merchandiser that buys goods from manufacturers and then sells them to retailers.
f. A discount that businesses offer to purchasers as an incentive for early payment.
g. A situation in which the buyer takes title to the goods after the goods leave the seller's place of business.
h. The terms of purchase or sale as stated on the invoice.
i. A seller's request for cash from the purchaser.

Learning Objective 2

3. Oct. 1 Cash $769.35

E-F:5-21 Journalizing purchase transactions from an invoice

Kingston Tires received the following invoice from a supplier (Fields Distribution, Inc.):

 **FIELDS DISTRIBUTION, INC.**
7290 S. Prospect Street
Ravenna, OH 44266

Invoice date: September 23, 2024

Sold to: Kingston Tires
6678 Diamond Avenue
Ravenna, OH 44266

Payment terms: 1/10, n/30

Description	Quantity Shipped	Price	Amount
D39–X4 Radials	4	$38.12	$152.48
M223 Belted-bias	10	42.84	428.40
Q92 Truck tires	6	58.12	348.72
Total			$929.60

Due date:
  October 3, 2024
  October 4 through October 23, 2024

Amount:
$920.30
$929.60

Requirements

1. Journalize the transaction required by Kingston Tires on September 23, 2024. Do not round numbers to the nearest whole dollar. Assume tires are purchased on account.

2. Journalize the return on Kingston's books on September 28, 2024, of the D39–X4 Radials, which were ordered by mistake. Do not round numbers to the nearest whole dollar.

3. Journalize the payment on October 1, 2024, to Fields Distribution, Inc. Do not round numbers to the nearest whole dollar.

Learning Objective 2

July 24 Merch. Inv. $64 CR

E-F:5-22 Journalizing purchase transactions

Howie Jewelers had the following purchase transactions. Journalize all necessary transactions. Explanations are not required.

Jun. 20	Purchased inventory of $5,100 on account from Sanders Diamonds, a jewelry importer. Terms were 2/15, n/45, FOB shipping point.
20	Paid freight charges, $400.
Jul. 4	Returned $600 of inventory to Sanders.
14	Paid Sanders Diamonds, less return.
16	Purchased inventory of $3,500 on account from Southboro Diamonds, a jewelry importer. Terms were 2/10, n/EOM, FOB destination.
18	Received a $300 allowance from Southboro Diamonds for damaged but usable goods.
24	Paid Southboro Diamonds, less allowance and discount.

E-F:5-23 Journalizing sales transactions

Journalize the following sales transactions for Antique Mall. Explanations are not required. The company estimates sales returns at the end of each month.

Jan. 4	Sold $16,000 of antiques on account, credit terms are n/30, to Cavalli Designs. Cost of goods is $8,000.
8	Received a $300 sales return on damaged goods from Cavalli Designs. Cost of goods damaged is $150.
13	Antique Mall received payment from Cavalli Designs on the amount due from Jan. 4, less the return.
20	Sold $4,900 of antiques on account, credit terms are 1/10, n/45, FOB destination, to White Furniture. Cost of goods is $2,450.
20	Antique Mall paid $70 on freight out to White Furniture.
29	Received payment from White Furniture on the amount due from Jan. 20, less the discount.

E-F:5-24 Journalizing purchase and sales transactions

Journalize the following transactions for Soul Art Gift Shop. Explanations are not required.

Feb. 3	Purchased $3,300 of merchandise inventory on account under terms 3/10, n/EOM and FOB shipping point from Still Waters Herbs.
7	Returned $900 of defective merchandise purchased on February 3.
9	Paid freight bill of $400 on February 3 purchase.
10	Sold merchandise inventory on account for $4,700 to Trybe Yoga Studio. Payment terms were 2/15, n/30. These goods cost the company $2,350.
12	Paid amount owed on credit purchase of February 3, less the return and the discount.
28	Received cash from Trybe Yoga Studio in full settlement of their debt.

E-F:5-25 Journalizing adjusting entries including estimating sales returns

Emerson St. Book Shop's unadjusted Merchandise Inventory at June 30 was $5,200. The cost associated with the physical count of inventory on hand on June 30 was $4,900. In addition, Emerson St. Book Shop estimated approximately $1,000 of merchandise sold will be returned with a cost of $400.

Requirements

1. Journalize the adjustment for inventory shrinkage.
2. Journalize the adjustment for estimated sales returns.

Use the following information to answer Exercises E-F:5-26 through E-F:5-28.

The adjusted trial balance of Quality Office Systems at March 31, 2024, follows:

QUALITY OFFICE SYSTEMS
Adjusted Trial Balance
March 31, 2024

Account Title	Debit	Credit
Cash	$ 2,300	
Accounts Receivable	13,500	
Merchandise Inventory	30,200	
Estimated Returns Inventory	1,000	
Office Supplies	7,100	
Equipment	42,300	
Accumulated Depreciation—Equipment		$ 13,200
Accounts Payable		6,600
Refunds Payable		2,300
Salaries Payable		500
Notes Payable, long-term		7,700
Mumford, Capital		11,800
Mumford, Withdrawals	42,000	
Sales Revenue		235,500
Sales Discounts Forfeited		500
Cost of Goods Sold	94,400	
Selling Expense	27,300	
Administrative Expense	15,100	
Interest Expense	2,900	
Total	$ 278,100	$ 278,100

Learning Objective 4

2. Ending Mumford, Capital Balance $66,100

E-F:5-26 Journalizing closing entries

Requirements

1. Journalize the required closing entries at March 31, 2024.
2. Set up T-accounts for Income Summary; Mumford, Capital; and Mumford, Withdrawals. Post the closing entries to the T-accounts and calculate their ending balances.
3. How much was Quality Office's net income or net loss?

Learning Objective 5

Net Income $96,300

E-F:5-27 Preparing a single-step income statement

Prepare Quality Office's single-step income statement for the year ended March 31, 2024.

E-F:5-28 Preparing a multi-step income statement

Prepare Quality Office's multi-step income statement for the year ended March 31, 2024.

Learning Objective 5

Gross Profit $141,100

E-F:5-29 Computing the gross profit percentage

Crazy Cookies earned net sales revenue of $66,000,000 in 2024. Cost of goods sold was $39,600,000, and net income reached $7,000,000, the company's highest ever. Compute the company's gross profit percentage for 2024.

Learning Objective 6

E-F:5A-30 Journalizing multiple performance obligations and sales transactions

Journalize the following sales transactions for Morris Supply. Explanations are not required.

Learning Objectives 3, 7 Appendix 5A

Mar. 1	Morris Supply sold merchandise inventory for $3,000. The cost of the inventory was $1,800. The customer paid cash. Morris Supply was running a promotion and the customer received a $150 award at the time of sale that can be used at a future date on any Morris Supply merchandise.
3	Sold $6,000 of supplies on account. Credit terms are 2/10, n/45, FOB destination. Cost of goods is $3,600.
10	Received payment from the customer on the amount due from March 3, less the discount.
Apr. 15	The customer used the $150 award when purchasing merchandise inventory for $200, the cost of the inventory was $120. The customer paid cash.

E-F:5B-31 Journalizing purchase transactions—periodic inventory system

Lawrence Appliances had the following purchase transactions. Journalize all necessary transactions using the periodic inventory system. Explanations are not required.

Learning Objective 8 Appendix 5B

Sep. 4	Purchased inventory of $6,900 on account from Max Appliance Wholesale, an appliance wholesaler. Terms were 3/15, n/30, FOB shipping point.
4	Paid freight charges, $480.
10	Returned $300 of inventory to Max.
17	Paid Max Appliance Wholesale, less return and discount.
20	Purchased inventory of $3,900 on account from MY Appliance, an appliance wholesaler. Terms were 1/10, n/45, FOB destination.
22	Received a $400 allowance from MY Appliance for damaged but usable goods.
29	Paid MY Appliance, less allowance and discount.

**Learning Objective 8
Appendix 5B**

E-F:5B-32 Journalizing sales transactions—periodic inventory system

Journalize the following sales transactions for Straight Shot Archery using the periodic inventory system. Explanations are not required. The company estimates sales returns and allowances at the end of each month.

Aug. 1	Sold $6,500 of equipment on account to Brown Resort, credit terms are 1/10, n/30.
8	Straight Shot received payment from Brown Resort on the amount due from August 1, less the discount.
15	Sold $3,100 of equipment on account to Alaska Hunting Lodge, credit terms are n/45, FOB destination.
15	Straight Shot paid $90 on freight out to Alaska Hunting Lodge.
20	Straight Shot negotiated a sales allowance of $500 on the goods sold on August 15 to Alaska Hunting Lodge.
24	Received payment from Alaska Hunting Lodge on the amount due from August 15, less the allowance.

**Learning Objective 8
Appendix 5B**

E-F:5B-33 Journalizing purchase and sales transactions—periodic inventory system

Journalize the following transactions for Master Bicycles using the periodic inventory system. Explanations are not required.

Nov. 2	Purchased $3,400 of merchandise inventory on account under terms 2/10, n/EOM and FOB shipping point from Speedy Bikes.
6	Returned $800 of defective merchandise purchased on November 2.
8	Paid freight bill of $100 on November 2 purchase.
10	Sold merchandise inventory on account for $6,100 to Camillo Tours. Payment terms were 3/15, n/45.
11	Paid amount owed to Speedy Bikes on credit purchase of November 2, less the return and the discount.
22	Received cash from Camillo Tours on November 10 sale in full settlement of their debt, less the discount.

E-F:5B-34 Journalizing closing entries—periodic inventory system

Ocean Life Boat Supply uses the periodic inventory method. The adjusted trial balance of Ocean Life Boat Supply at December 31, 2024, follows:

Learning Objective 8
Appendix 5B

2. Ending Iver, Capital Balance $95,100

OCEAN LIFE BOAT SUPPLY
Adjusted Trial Balance
December 31, 2024

Account Title	Debit	Credit
Cash	$ 3,500	
Accounts Receivable	15,400	
Merchandise Inventory (beginning)	45,100	
Office Supplies	8,200	
Equipment	59,100	
Accumulated Depreciation—Equipment		$ 19,900
Accounts Payable		11,000
Refunds Payable		1,100
Salaries Payable		1,700
Notes Payable, long-term		11,300
Iver, Capital		37,700
Iver, Withdrawals	60,300	
Sales Revenue		334,250
Sales Discounts Forfeited		750
Interest Revenue		3,700
Purchases	274,800	
Purchase Returns and Allowances		95,100
Purchase Discounts		8,100
Selling Expense	38,100	
Administrative Expense	20,100	
Total	$ 524,600	$ 524,600

Requirements

1. Journalize the required closing entries at December 31, 2024. Assume ending Merchandise Inventory is $53,100 and Estimated Returns Inventory is $800.
2. Set up T-accounts for Income Summary; Iver, Capital; and Iver, Withdrawals. Post the closing entries to the T-accounts, and calculate their ending balances.
3. How much was Ocean Life's net income or net loss?

Learning Objective 8
Appendix 5B

E-F:5B-35 Computing cost of goods sold in a periodic inventory system

Clink Electric uses the periodic inventory system. Clink reported the following selected amounts at May 31, 2024:

Merchandise Inventory, June 1, 2023	$ 16,000	Freight In	$ 6,000
Merchandise Inventory, May 31, 2024	21,500	Net Sales Revenue	138,000
Purchases	81,000	Clink, Capital	49,000
Purchase Discounts	3,000		
Purchase Returns and Allowances	6,600		

Compute the following for Clink:

a. Cost of goods sold.

b. Gross profit.

> Problems Group A

For all problems, assume the perpetual inventory system is used unless stated otherwise. Round all numbers to the nearest whole dollar unless stated otherwise.

Learning Objectives 2, 3

P-F:5-36A Journalizing purchase and sale transactions

Journalize the following transactions that occurred in September for Water Works. No explanations are needed. Identify each accounts payable and accounts receivable with the vendor or customer name. Water Works estimates sales returns at the end of each month.

Sep. 3	Purchased merchandise inventory on account from Shallin Wholesalers, $5,000. Terms 3/15, n/EOM, FOB shipping point.
4	Paid freight bill of $70 on September 3 purchase.
4	Purchased merchandise inventory for cash of $2,400.
6	Returned $1,200 of inventory from September 3 purchase.
8	Sold merchandise inventory to Hilton Company, $6,200, on account. Terms 3/15, n/35. Cost of goods, $2,852.
9	Purchased merchandise inventory on account from Taylor Wholesalers, $7,000. Terms 2/10, n/30, FOB destination.
10	Made payment to Shallin Wholesalers for goods purchased on September 3, less return and discount.
12	Received payment from Hilton Company, less discount.
13	After negotiations, received a $250 allowance from Taylor Wholesalers.
15	Sold merchandise inventory to Julian Company, $3,300, on account. Terms n/EOM. Cost of goods, $1,485.
22	Made payment, less allowance, to Taylor Wholesalers for goods purchased on September 9.
25	Sold merchandise inventory to Shelton for $1,500 on account that cost $660. Terms of 3/10, n/30 was offered, FOB shipping point. As a courtesy to Shelton, $75 of freight was added to the invoice for which cash was paid by Water Works.
29	Received payment from Shelton, less discount.
30	Received payment from Julian Company.

P-F:5-37A Journalizing purchase and sale transactions (with returns)

Journalize the following transactions that occurred in November for May's Adventure Park. No explanations are needed. Identify each accounts payable and accounts receivable with the vendor or customer name. May's Adventure Park estimates sales returns at the end of each month and has a November 1 balance of $500 (debit) in Estimated Returns Inventory and $800 (credit) in Refunds Payable.

Learning Objectives 2, 3

Nov. 4	Purchased merchandise inventory on account from Valsad Company, $10,000. Terms 1/10, n/EOM, FOB shipping point.
6	Paid freight bill of $110 on November 4 purchase.
8	Returned half the inventory purchased on November 4 from Valsad Company.
10	Sold merchandise inventory for cash, $1,000. Cost of goods, $400. FOB destination.
11	Sold merchandise inventory to Garland Corporation, $10,000, on account, terms of 1/10, n/EOM. Cost of goods, $5,000. FOB shipping point.
12	Paid freight bill of $50 on November 10 sale.
13	Sold merchandise inventory to Cabot Company, $8,700, on account, terms of n/45. Cost of goods, $4,785. FOB shipping point.
14	Paid the amount owed on account from November 4, less return and discount.
17	Received defective inventory as a sales return from the November 13 sale, $300. Cost of goods, $165.
18	Purchased inventory of $4,000 on account from Rainer Corporation. Payment terms were 2/10, n/30, FOB destination.
20	Received cash from Garland Corporation, less discount.
26	Paid amount owed on account from November 18, less discount.
28	Received cash from Cabot Company, less return.
29	Purchased inventory from Swift Corporation for cash, $11,900, FOB shipping point. Freight in paid to shipping company, $200.

Learning Objectives 4, 5

2. Total Credits $463,945

P-F:5-38A Journalizing adjusting entries, preparing adjusted trial balance, and preparing multi-step income statement

The unadjusted trial balance for Tiger Electronics Company at March 31, 2024, follows:

TIGER ELECTRONICS COMPANY
Unadjusted Trial Balance
March 31, 2024

Account Title	Debit	Credit
Cash	$ 15,000	
Accounts Receivable	38,700	
Merchandise Inventory	46,250	
Office Supplies	5,700	
Equipment	129,500	
Accumulated Depreciation—Equipment		$ 36,500
Accounts Payable		15,900
Unearned Revenue		13,500
Notes Payable, long-term		43,000
Tiger, Capital		43,050
Tiger, Withdrawals	23,000	
Sales Revenue		305,750
Sales Discounts Forfeited		250
Cost of Goods Sold	141,000	
Salaries Expense (Selling)	28,000	
Rent Expense (Selling)	15,200	
Salaries Expense (Administrative)	5,600	
Utilities Expense (Administrative)	10,000	
Total	$ 457,950	$ 457,950

Requirements

1. Journalize the adjusting entries using the following data:
   a. Interest revenue accrued, $500.
   b. Salaries (Selling) accrued, $2,400.
   c. Depreciation Expense—Equipment (Administrative), $1,295.
   d. Interest expense accrued, $1,800.
   e. A physical count of inventory was completed. The ending Merchandise Inventory should have a balance of $46,000.
   f. Tiger estimates that approximately $4,500 of merchandise sold will be returned with a cost of $1,800.
2. Prepare Tiger Electronics' adjusted trial balance as of March 31, 2024.
3. Prepare Tiger Electronics' multi-step income statement for year ended March 31, 2024.

P-F:5-39A Preparing a multi-step income statement, journalizing closing entries, and preparing a post-closing trial balance

The adjusted trial balance of Sylvia's Music Company at June 30, 2024, follows:

Learning Objectives 4, 5

1. Operating Income $61,500

SYLVIA'S MUSIC COMPANY
Adjusted Trial Balance
June 30, 2024

Account Title	Debit	Credit
Cash	$ 3,700	
Accounts Receivable	38,500	
Merchandise Inventory	17,000	
Estimated Returns Inventory	400	
Office Supplies	800	
Furniture	39,800	
Accumulated Depreciation—Furniture		$ 8,300
Accounts Payable		13,000
Refunds Payable		600
Salaries Payable		700
Unearned Revenue		7,300
Notes Payable, long-term		13,500
Sylvia, Capital		35,800
Sylvia, Withdrawals	40,500	
Sales Revenue		179,900
Sales Discounts Forfeited		100
Cost of Goods Sold	81,000	
Selling Expense	19,100	
Administrative Expense	17,000	
Interest Expense	1,400	
Total	$ 259,200	$ 259,200

Requirements

1. Prepare Sylvia's multi-step income statement for the year ended June 30, 2024.
2. Journalize Sylvia's closing entries.
3. Prepare a post-closing trial balance as of June 30, 2024.

Learning Objectives 5, 6

2. Operating Income $93,120

P-F:5-40A Preparing a single-step income statement, preparing a multi-step income statement, and computing the gross profit percentage

The records of Farm Quality Steak Company list the following selected accounts for the quarter ended April 30, 2024:

Interest Revenue	$ 400	Accounts Payable	$ 17,700
Merchandise Inventory	45,000	Accounts Receivable	38,200
Notes Payable, long-term	54,000	Accumulated Depreciation—Equipment	37,700
Salaries Payable	2,800	Fisher, Capital	35,380
Net Sales Revenue	298,000	Fisher, Withdrawals	25,000
Rent Expense (Selling)	15,100	Cash	7,100
Salaries Expense (Administrative)	2,000	Cost of Goods Sold	154,960
Office Supplies	6,500	Equipment	132,000
Unearned Revenue	13,100	Interest Payable	1,700
Interest Expense	2,100	Rent Expense (Administrative)	7,100
Depreciation Expense—Equipment (Administrative)	1,320	Salaries Expense (Selling)	6,000
Utilities Expense (Administrative)	4,600	Utilities Expense (Selling)	10,000
Delivery Expense (Selling)	3,800		

Requirements

1. Prepare a single-step income statement.
2. Prepare a multi-step income statement.
3. M. Fisher, owner of the company, strives to earn a gross profit percentage of at least 50%. Did Farm Quality achieve this goal? Show your calculations.

Learning Objective 8
Appendix 5B

P-F:5B-41A Journalizing purchase and sale transactions—periodic inventory system

Journalize the following transactions that occurred in March for Double Company. Assume Double uses the periodic inventory system. No explanations are needed. Identify each accounts payable and accounts receivable with the vendor or customer name. Double estimates sales returns at the end of each month.

Mar. 3	Purchased merchandise inventory on account from Sidecki Wholesalers, $5,500. Terms 2/15, n/EOM, FOB shipping point.
4	Paid freight bill of $70 on March 3 purchase.
4	Purchased merchandise inventory for cash of $1,100.
6	Returned $900 of inventory from March 3 purchase.
8	Sold merchandise inventory to Herrick Company, $3,400, on account. Terms 1/15, n/35.
9	Purchased merchandise inventory on account from Tex Wholesalers, $5,600. Terms 2/10, n/30, FOB destination.
10	Made payment to Sidecki Wholesalers for goods purchased on March 3, less return and discount.
12	Received payment from Herrick Company, less discount.
13	After negotiations, received a $500 allowance from Tex Wholesalers.
15	Sold merchandise inventory to Jesper Company, $1,700, on account. Terms n/EOM.
22	Made payment, less allowance, to Tex Wholesalers for goods purchased on March 9.
23	Jesper Company returned $300 of the merchandise sold on March 15.
25	Sold merchandise inventory to Salter for $1,000 on account. Terms of 1/10, n/30 was offered, FOB shipping point.
29	Received payment from Salter, less discount.
30	Received payment from Jesper Company, less return.

P-F:5B-42A Preparing a multi-step income statement and journalizing closing entries

Learning Objective 8
Appendix 5B

Trudel Department Store uses a periodic inventory system. The adjusted trial balance of Trudel Department Store at December 31, 2024, follows:

1. Gross Profit $218,400

TRUDEL DEPARTMENT STORE
Adjusted Trial Balance
December 31, 2024

Account Title	Debit	Credit
Cash	$ 8,100	
Accounts Receivable	84,900	
Merchandise Inventory (beginning)	37,000	
Office Supplies	800	
Furniture	85,000	
Accumulated Depreciation—Furniture		$ 18,400
Accounts Payable		28,900
Salaries Payable		2,400
Unearned Revenue		14,800
Notes Payable, long-term		35,000
Trudel, Capital		58,900
Trudel, Withdrawals	90,500	
Sales Revenue		395,000
Purchases	292,000	
Purchase Returns and Allowances		110,000
Purchase Discounts		6,600
Freight In	400	
Selling Expense	41,800	
Administrative Expense	26,000	
Interest Expense	3,500	
Total	$ 670,000	$ 670,000

Requirements

1. Prepare Trudel Department Store's multi-step income statement for the year ended December 31, 2024. Assume ending Merchandise Inventory is $36,200.
2. Journalize Trudel Department Store's closing entries.
3. Prepare a post-closing trial balance as of December 31, 2024.

> Problems Group B

For all problems, assume the perpetual inventory system is used unless stated otherwise. Round all numbers to the nearest whole dollar unless stated otherwise.

Learning Objectives 2, 3

P-F:5-43B Journalizing purchase and sale transactions

Journalize the following transactions that occurred in February for Sea Green. No explanations are needed. Identify each accounts payable and accounts receivable with the vendor or customer name. Sea Green estimates sales returns at the end of each month.

Feb. 3	Purchased merchandise inventory on account from Sidecki Wholesalers, $6,000. Terms 1/15, n/EOM, FOB shipping point.
4	Paid freight bill of $70 on February 3 purchase.
4	Purchased merchandise inventory for cash of $1,500.
6	Returned $600 of inventory from February 3 purchase.
8	Sold merchandise inventory to Herrick Company, $5,400, on account. Terms 3/15, n/35. Cost of goods, $2,592.
9	Purchased merchandise inventory on account from Thomas Wholesalers, $7,500. Terms 2/10, n/30, FOB destination.
10	Made payment to Sidecki Wholesalers for goods purchased on February 3, less return and discount.
12	Received payment from Herrick Company, less discount.
13	After negotiations, received a $100 allowance from Thomas Wholesalers.
15	Sold merchandise inventory to Johnson Company, $3,300, on account. Terms n/EOM. Cost of goods, $1,584.
22	Made payment, less allowance, to Thomas Wholesalers for goods purchased on February 9.
25	Sold merchandise inventory to Smecker for $1,900 on account that cost $722. Terms of 2/10, n/30 were offered, FOB shipping point. As a courtesy to Smecker, $50 of freight was added to the invoice for which cash was paid by Sea Green.
27	Received payment from Smecker, less discount.
28	Received payment from Johnson Company.

P-F:5-44B Journalizing purchase and sale transactions (with returns)

Journalize the following transactions that occurred in January 2024 for Jill's Water World. No explanations are needed. Identify each accounts payable and accounts receivable with the vendor or customer name. Jill's Water World estimates sales returns at the end of each month and has a January 1 balance of $150 (debit) in Estimated Returns Inventory and $300 (credit) in Refunds Payable.

Learning Objectives 2, 3

Jan. 4	Purchased merchandise inventory on account from Vanderbilt Company, $6,000. Terms 3/10, n/EOM, FOB shipping point.
6	Paid freight bill of $180 on January 4 purchase.
8	Returned half the inventory purchased on January 4 from Vanderbilt Company.
10	Sold merchandise inventory for cash, $1,200. Cost of goods, $480. FOB destination.
11	Sold merchandise inventory to Gath Corporation, $10,100, on account, terms of 1/10, n/EOM. Cost of goods, $5,555. FOB shipping point.
12	Paid freight bill of $40 on January 10 sale.
13	Sold merchandise inventory to Cain Company, $9,400, on account, terms of n/45. Cost of goods, $4,700. FOB shipping point.
14	Paid the amount owed on account from January 4, less return and discount.
17	Received defective inventory as a sales return from the January 13 sale, $200. Cost of goods, $100.
18	Purchased inventory of $4,100 on account from Richmond Corporation. Payment terms were 2/10, n/30, FOB destination.
20	Received cash from Gath Corporation, less discount.
26	Paid amount owed on account from January 18, less discount.
28	Received cash from Cain Company, less return.
29	Purchased inventory from Sanders Corporation for cash, $12,400, FOB shipping point. Freight in paid to shipping company, $250.

Learning Objectives 4, 5

2. Total Credits $466,330

P-F:5-45B Journalizing adjusting entries, preparing adjusted trial balance, and preparing multi-step income statement

The unadjusted trial balance for Turtle Electronics Company follows:

TURTLE ELECTRONICS COMPANY
Unadjusted Trial Balance
October 31, 2024

Account Title	Debit	Credit
Cash	$ 14,000	
Accounts Receivable	38,400	
Merchandise Inventory	45,170	
Office Supplies	6,400	
Equipment	131,000	
Accumulated Depreciation—Equipment		$ 37,400
Accounts Payable		16,900
Unearned Revenue		13,500
Notes Payable, long-term		44,000
Turtle, Capital		59,670
Turtle, Withdrawals	24,000	
Sales Revenue		289,750
Sales Discounts Forfeited		250
Cost of Goods Sold	145,000	
Salaries Expense (Selling)	24,700	
Rent Expense (Selling)	15,500	
Salaries Expense (Administrative)	5,600	
Utilities Expense (Administrative)	10,700	
Total	$ 461,470	$ 461,470

Requirements

1. Journalize the adjusting entries using the following data:
   a. Interest revenue accrued, $350.
   b. Salaries (Selling) accrued, $2,200.
   c. Depreciation Expense—Equipment (Administrative), $1,310.
   d. Interest expense accrued, $1,000.
   e. A physical count of inventory was completed. The ending Merchandise Inventory should have a balance of $45,100.
   f. Turtle estimates that approximately $7,000 of merchandise sold will be returned with a cost of $4,200.

2. Prepare Turtle Electronics' adjusted trial balance as of October 31, 2024.

3. Prepare Turtle Electronics' multi-step income statement for year ended October 31, 2024.

P-F:5-46B Preparing a multi-step income statement, journalizing closing entries, and preparing a post-closing trial balance

Learning Objectives 4, 5

1. Operating Income $75,980

The adjusted trial balance of Pamela Potter Theater Company at April 30, 2024, follows:

PAMELA POTTER THEATER COMPANY
Adjusted Trial Balance
April 30, 2024

Account Title	Debit	Credit
Cash	$ 3,800	
Accounts Receivable	39,500	
Merchandise Inventory	17,000	
Estimated Returns Inventory	200	
Office Supplies	800	
Furniture	40,000	
Accumulated Depreciation—Furniture		$ 8,400
Accounts Payable		12,800
Refunds Payable		400
Salaries Payable		1,100
Unearned Revenue		7,100
Notes Payable, long-term		12,000
Potter, Capital		23,800
Potter, Withdrawals	39,000	
Sales Revenue		182,880
Sales Discounts Forfeited		120
Cost of Goods Sold	73,200	
Selling Expense	19,200	
Administrative Expense	14,500	
Interest Expense	1,400	
Total	$ 248,600	$ 248,600

Requirements

1. Prepare Pamela Potter's multi-step income statement for the year ended April 30, 2024.
2. Journalize Pamela Potter's closing entries.
3. Prepare a post-closing trial balance as of April 30, 2024.

Learning Objectives 5, 6

2. Operating Income $80,890

P-F:5-47B Preparing a single-step income statement, preparing a multi-step income statement, and computing the gross profit percentage

The records of Grade A Beef Company list the following selected accounts for the quarter ended September 30, 2024:

Interest Revenue	$ 900	Accounts Payable	$ 17,000
Merchandise Inventory	46,300	Accounts Receivable	33,500
Notes Payable, long-term	47,000	Accumulated Depreciation—Equipment	36,500
Salaries Payable	2,600	Douglas, Capital	41,610
Net Sales Revenue	294,000	Douglas, Withdrawals	15,000
Rent Expense (Selling)	16,700	Cash	7,300
Salaries Expense (Administrative)	2,500	Cost of Goods Sold	161,700
Office Supplies	5,800	Equipment	131,000
Unearned Revenue	13,800	Interest Payable	900
Interest Expense	2,300	Rent Expense (Administrative)	7,400
Depreciation Expense—Equipment (Administrative)	1,310	Salaries Expense (Selling)	5,000
Utilities Expense (Administrative)	4,500	Utilities Expense (Selling)	10,900
Delivery Expense (Selling)	3,100		

Requirements

1. Prepare a single-step income statement.
2. Prepare a multi-step income statement.
3. J. Douglas, owner of the company, strives to earn a gross profit percentage of at least 50%. Did Grade A Beef achieve this goal? Show your calculations.

P-F:5B-48B Journalizing purchase and sale transactions—periodic inventory system

Learning Objective 8
Appendix 5B

Journalize the following transactions that occurred in June for Daley Company. Assume Daley uses the periodic inventory system. No explanations are needed. Identify each accounts payable and accounts receivable with the vendor or customer name. Daley estimates sales returns at the end of each month.

Jun. 3	Purchased merchandise inventory on account from Sherry Wholesalers, $5,500. Terms 3/15, n/EOM, FOB shipping point.
4	Paid freight bill of $42 on June 3 purchase.
4	Purchased merchandise inventory for cash of $1,100.
6	Returned $200 of inventory from June 3 purchase.
8	Sold merchandise inventory to Henrich Company, $4,400, on account. Terms 2/15, n/35.
9	Purchased merchandise inventory on account from Tex Wholesalers, $4,600. Terms 1/10, n/30, FOB destination.
10	Made payment to Sherry Wholesalers for goods purchased on June 3, less return and discount.
12	Received payment from Henrich Company, less discount.
13	After negotiations, received a $300 allowance from Tex Wholesalers.
15	Sold merchandise inventory to Jarvis Company, $1,500, on account. Terms n/EOM.
22	Made payment, less allowance, to Tex Wholesalers for goods purchased on June 9.
23	Jarvis Company returned $100 of the merchandise sold on June 15.
25	Sold merchandise inventory to Smith for $700 on account. Terms of 3/10, n/30 was offered, FOB shipping point.
29	Received payment from Smith, less discount.
30	Received payment from Jarvis Company, less return.

**Learning Objective 8
Appendix 5B**

1. Gross Profit $209,400

P-F:5B-49B Preparing a multi-step income statement and journalizing closing entries

Travis Department Store uses a periodic inventory system. The adjusted trial balance of Travis Department Store at December 31, 2024, follows:

TRAVIS DEPARTMENT STORE
Adjusted Trial Balance
December 31, 2024

Account Title	Debit	Credit
Cash	$ 7,900	
Accounts Receivable	85,200	
Merchandise Inventory (beginning)	37,700	
Office Supplies	600	
Furniture	89,000	
Accumulated Depreciation—Furniture		$ 19,300
Accounts Payable		28,900
Salaries Payable		3,600
Unearned Revenue		14,600
Notes Payable, long-term		39,000
Travis, Capital		65,400
Travis, Withdrawals	88,900	
Sales Revenue		390,000
Purchases	297,000	
Purchase Returns and Allowances		112,000
Purchase Discounts		6,200
Freight In	600	
Selling Expense	42,600	
Administrative Expense	26,400	
Interest Expense	3,100	
Total	$ 679,000	$ 679,000

Requirements

1. Prepare Travis Department Store's multi-step income statement for the year ended December 31, 2024. Assume ending Merchandise Inventory is $36,500.
2. Journalize Travis Department Store's closing entries.
3. Prepare a post-closing trial balance as of December 31, 2024.

CRITICAL THINKING

> Using Excel

Download Excel problems for this chapter online in MyLab Accounting or at **http://www.pearsonhighered.com/Horngren**.

> Continuing Problem Part 1

P-F:5-50 Journalizing and posting purchase and sale transactions

This problem continues the Canyon Canoe Company situation from Chapter F:4. At the beginning of the new year, Canyon Canoe Company decided to carry and sell T-shirts with its logo printed on them. Canyon Canoe Company uses the perpetual inventory system to account for the inventory. During January 2025, Canyon Canoe Company completed the following merchandising transactions:

Jan. 1	Purchased 10 T-shirts at $4 each and paid cash.
2	Sold 6 T-shirts for $10 each, total cost of $24. Received cash.
3	Purchased 50 T-shirts on account at $5 each. Terms 2/10, n/30.
7	Paid the supplier for the T-shirts purchased on January 3, less discount.
8	Realized 4 T-shirts from the January 1 order were printed wrong and returned them for a cash refund.
10	Sold 40 T-shirts on account for $10 each, total cost of $200. Terms 3/15, n/45.
12	Received payment for the T-shirts sold on account on January 10, less discount.
14	Purchased 100 T-shirts on account at $4 each. Terms 4/15, n/30.
18	Canyon Company called the supplier from the January 14 purchase and told them that some of the T-shirts were the wrong color. The supplier offered a $50 purchase allowance.
20	Paid the supplier for the T-shirts purchased on January 14, less the allowance and discount.
21	Sold 60 T-shirts on account for $10 each, total cost of $220. Terms 2/20, n/30.
23	Received a payment on account for the T-shirts sold on January 21, less discount.
25	Purchased 320 T-shirts on account at $5 each. Terms 2/10, n/30, FOB shipping point.
27	Paid freight associated with the January 25 purchase, $48.
29	Paid for the January 25 purchase, less discount.
30	Sold 275 T-shirts on account for $10 each, total cost of $1,300. Terms 2/10, n/30.
31	Received payment for the T-shirts sold on January 30, less discount.

Requirements

1. Open the following T-accounts in the ledger, using the post-closing balances from Chapter F:4: Cash; Accounts Receivable; Merchandise Inventory; Estimated Returns Inventory; Office Supplies; Prepaid Rent; Land; Building; Accumulated Depreciation—Building; Canoes; Accumulated Depreciation—Canoes; Accounts Payable; Utilities Payable; Telephone Payable; Wages Payable; Refunds Payable; Interest Payable; Unearned Revenue; Notes Payable; Wilson, Capital; Income Summary; Sales Revenue; Canoe Rental Revenue; Cost of Goods Sold; Rent

Expense; Wages Expense; Utilities Expense; Telephone Expense; Supplies Expense; Depreciation Expense—Building; Depreciation Expense—Canoes; Interest Expense.

2. Journalize and post the transactions. Compute each account balance and denote the balance as *Balance*. Omit explanations.

> Continuing Problem Part 2

P-F:5-51 Making adjusting and closing entries, preparing financial statements, and computing the gross profit percentage

This problem continues the Canyon Canoe Company situation and focuses on non-merchandising transactions, adjusting and closing entries, and preparing financial statements. Canyon Canoe Company does not typically prepare adjusting and closing entries each month, but the company is surprised at how popular the shirts are and wishes to know the net income for January and would also like to understand how to prepare the closing entries for a merchandising company.

During January 2025, Canyon Canoe Company completed the following non-merchandising transactions:

Jan. 2	Collected $4,500 on account.
15	Paid the utilities and telephone bills from December.
15	Paid the wages accrued in December.
18	Rented canoes and received cash, $1,825.
20	Received bills for utilities ($360) and telephone ($275), which will be paid later.
23	Paid various accounts payable, $1,800.
30	Paid employee, $750.

Requirements

1. Journalize and post the January transactions. Omit explanations. Use the ledger from the previous problem for posting.
2. Journalize and post the adjusting entries for the month of January. Omit explanations. Denote each adjustment as *Adj*. Compute each account balance, and denote the balance as *Balance*. In addition to the adjusting entries from the data from previous chapters, Canyon Canoe Company provides this data:
   a. A physical count of the inventory at the end of the month revealed the cost was $470.
   b. The company estimated sales returns will be $30 with a cost of $15.
   c. Office supplies used, $55.
   d. The Unearned Revenue has now been earned.
   e. Interest expense accrued on the notes payable, $50.
3. Prepare the month ended January 31, 2025, single step income statement of Canyon Canoe Company.
4. Journalize and post the closing entries. Omit explanations. Denote each closing amount as *Clo.* and each balance as *Balance*. After posting all closing entries, prove the equality of debits and credits in the ledger by preparing a post-closing trial balance.
5. Compute the gross profit percentage for January for Canyon Canoe Company.

> Practice Set

P-F:5-52 Journalizing purchase and sale transactions, making closing entries, preparing financial statements, and computing the gross profit percentage

This problem continues the Crystal Clear Cleaning practice set begun in Chapter F:2 and continued through Chapters F:3 and F:4.

Crystal Clear Cleaning has decided that, in addition to providing cleaning services, it will sell cleaning products. Crystal Clear uses the perpetual inventory system. During December 2024, Crystal Clear completed the following transactions:

Dec. 2	Purchased 1,000 units of inventory for $4,000 on account from Sparkle Company on terms, 5/10, n/20.
5	Purchased 1,200 units of inventory from Borax on account with terms 4/10, n/30. The total invoice was for $6,000, which included a $300 freight charge.
7	Returned 300 units of inventory to Sparkle from the December 2 purchase (cost $1,200).
9	Paid Borax.
11	Sold 500 units of goods to Happy Maids for $5,500 on account with terms n/30. Crystal Clear's cost of the goods was $2,000.
12	Paid Sparkle.
15	Received 100 units with a retail price of $1,100 back from customer Happy Maids. The goods cost Crystal Clear $400.
21	Received payment from Happy Maids, settling the amount due in full.
28	Sold 500 units of goods to Bridget, Inc. on account for $6,500 (cost $2,022). Terms 1/15, n/30.
29	Paid cash for utilities of $550.
30	Paid cash for Sales Commission Expense of $214.
31	Received payment from Bridget, Inc., less discount.
31	Recorded the following adjusting entries: a. Physical count of inventory on December 31 showed 800 units of goods on hand, with a cost of $3,848. b. Depreciation, $150. c. Accrued salaries expense of $2,100. d. Estimated sales returns of $1,500, with cost of $540. e. Prepared all other adjustments necessary for December (Hint: You will need to review the adjustment information in Chapter F:3 to determine the remaining adjustments). Assume the cleaning supplies left at December 31 are $50.

Requirements

1. Open the following T-accounts in the ledger: Cash, $51,650; Accounts Receivable, $4,000; Merchandise Inventory, $0; Estimated Returns Inventory, $0; Cleaning Supplies, $50; Prepaid Rent, $3,000; Prepaid Insurance, $4,400; Equipment, $5,400; Truck, $3,000; Accumulated Depreciation, $150; Accounts Payable, $1,245; Salaries Payable, $0; Interest Payable, $59; Refunds Payable, $0; Unearned Revenue, $14,375; Notes Payable, $36,000; Hideaway, Capital, $19,671; Income Summary, $0; Hideaway, Withdrawals, $0; Service Revenue, $0; Sales Revenue, $0; Cost of Goods Sold, $0; Salaries Expense, $0; Sales Commission Expense, $0; Utilities Expense, $0; Depreciation Expense, $0; Rent Expense, $0; Insurance Expense, $0; Interest Expense, $0.

2. Journalize and post the December transactions. Omit explanations. Compute each account balance, and denote the balance as *Balance*. Identify each accounts payable and accounts receivable with the vendor or customer name.

3. Journalize and post the adjusting entries. Omit explanations. Denote each adjusting amount as *Adj*. Compute each account balance, and denote the balance as *Balance*. After posting all adjusting entries, prove the equality of debits and credits in the ledger by preparing an adjusted trial balance.

4. Prepare the single step income statement and statement of owner's equity for the month ended December 31, 2024. Also prepare a classified balance sheet at December 31, 2024. Assume the note payable is long-term.

5. Compute the gross profit percentage for December for the company.

> Tying It All Together Case F:5-1

Before you begin this assignment, review the Tying It All Together feature in the chapter. It will also be helpful if you review Macy's, Inc. 2018 annual report (**https://www.sec.gov/Archives/edgar/data/794367/000079436719000038/m-0202201910xk.htm**).

Macy's, Inc. is a premier retailer in the United States, operating nearly 867 stores in 43 states. Macy's, Bloomingdale's, and bluemercury are all brands that operate under Macy's, Inc. The company sells a wide range of merchandise including apparel and accessories, cosmetics, home furnishings, and other goods. Macy's, Inc. purchases its merchandise from many suppliers and also develops its own private label brands.

Requirements

1. Review the notes to the consolidated financial statements, specifically Recent Accounting Pronouncements. When did Macy's adopt the new revenue recognition standard (ASU No. 2014-09, Revenue from Contracts with Customers)? What impact and changes did the new revenue recognition standard have on Macy's?

2. Macy's, Inc. reported cost of sales of $15,215 million for the year ending February 2, 2019. Which financial statement is cost of sales (also known as cost of goods sold) reported on? What does cost of sales represent? What type of account is cost of sales?

3. Assume Macy's, Inc. purchases $100,000 of inventory from one of its vendors. The terms of the purchase are FOB shipping point. Who pays the freight and how does the cost of the freight get recorded? Assume Macy's uses the perpetual inventory system.

4. On which financial statement will Macy's report its merchandise inventory? How much is Macy's merchandise inventory as of February 2, 2019?

5. Assume Macy's, Inc. prepares a multi-step income statement. What would the format of that income statement look like? What is one benefit of preparing a multi-step income statement for merchandising companies such as Macy's, Inc.?

> Decision Case F:5-1

Party-Time T-Shirts sells T-shirts for parties at the local college. The company completed the first year of operations, and the shareholders are generally pleased with operating results as shown by the following income statement:

PARTY-TIME T-SHIRTS
Income Statement
Year Ended December 31, 2023

Net Sales Revenue	$ 350,000
Cost of Goods Sold	210,000
Gross Profit	140,000
Operating Expenses:	
Selling Expense	40,000
Administrative Expense	25,000
Net Income	$ 75,000

Bill Hildebrand, the controller, is considering how to expand the business. He proposes two ways to increase profits to $100,000 during 2024.

a. Hildebrand believes he should advertise more heavily. He believes additional advertising costing $20,000 will increase net sales by 30% and leave administrative expense unchanged. Assume that Cost of Goods Sold will remain at the same percentage of net sales as in 2023, so if net sales increase in 2024, Cost of Goods Sold will increase proportionately.

b. Hildebrand proposes selling higher-margin merchandise, such as party dresses, in addition to the existing product line. An importer can supply a minimum of 1,000 dresses for $40 each; Party-Time can mark these dresses up 100% and sell them for $80. Hildebrand realizes he will have to advertise the new merchandise, and this advertising will cost $5,000. Party-Time can expect to sell only 80% of these dresses during the coming year.

Help Hildebrand determine which plan to pursue. Prepare a multi-step income statement for 2024 to show the expected net income under each plan.

> Ethical Issue F:5-1

Dobbs Wholesale Antiques makes all sales under terms of FOB shipping point. The company usually ships inventory to customers approximately one week after receiving the order. For orders received late in December, Kathy Dobbs, the owner, decides when to ship the goods. If profits are already at an acceptable level, Dobbs delays shipment until January. If profits for the current year are lagging behind expectations, Dobbs ships the goods during December.

Requirements

1. Under Dobbs' FOB policy, when should the company record a sale?
2. Do you approve or disapprove of Dobbs' manner of deciding when to ship goods to customers and record the sales revenue? If you approve, give your reason. If you disapprove, identify a better way to decide when to ship goods. (There is no accounting rule against Dobbs' practice.)

> Fraud Case F:5-1

Rae Philippe was a warehouse manager for Atkins Oilfield Supply, a business that operated across eight Western states. She was an old pro and had known most of the other warehouse managers for many years. Around December each year, auditors would come to do a physical count of the inventory at each warehouse. Recently, Rae's brother started his own drilling company and persuaded Rae to "loan" him 80 joints of 5-inch drill pipe to use for his first well. He promised to have it back to Rae by December, but the well encountered problems and the pipe was still in the ground. Rae knew the auditors were on the way, so she called her friend Andy, who ran another Atkins warehouse. "Send me over 80 joints of 5-inch pipe tomorrow, and I'll get them back to you ASAP," said Rae. When the auditors came, all the pipe on the books was accounted for, and they filed a "no-exception" report.

Requirements

1. Is there anything the company or the auditors could do in the future to detect this kind of fraudulent practice?
2. How would this kind of action affect the financial performance of the company?

> Financial Statement Case F:5-1

This case uses both the income statement (consolidated statements of operations) and the balance sheet (consolidated statements of financial position) of **Target Corporation**. Visit **http://www.pearsonhighered.com/Horngren** to view a link to the Target Corporation Fiscal 2018 Annual Report, for the fiscal year ending on February 2, 2019.

Requirements

1. What was the value of the company's inventory at February 2, 2019, and February 3, 2018?
2. Review Note 9 (specifically Inventories) in the Notes to Consolidated Financial Statements. What does Target include in the cost of inventory?
3. What was the amount of Target's cost of goods sold (cost of sales) for the year ending February 2, 2019, and the year ending February 3, 2018?
4. What income statement format does Target use? Explain.
5. Compute Target's gross profit percentage for the year ending February 2, 2019, and the year ending February 3, 2018. Did the gross profit percentage improve, worsen, or hold steady? Assuming the industry average for gross profit percentage is 35%, how does Target compare in the industry?

> Quick Check Answers

1. d 2. a 3. c 4. c 5. b 6. a 7. a 8. d 9. a 10A. d 11B. d

Merchandise Inventory 6

What Is the Cost of This Merchandise Inventory?

Jorell was excited about the most recent shipment of merchandise inventory that he received today. As the controller of a successful sporting goods store, he has decided to expand the merchandise inventory line by offering outdoor cooking items, such as grills, cookers, and accessories. He believes that this new merchandise inventory will draw new customers to the store and eventually bring more profits to the business.

As Jorell prepares the merchandise inventory for sale, he must decide how the business will track the cost of each product sold. For example, if the business sells 500 identical outdoor grills that were purchased at different times and at different costs, how will the business determine the cost of each grill sold? Should the business keep detailed cost records for each specific grill sold? Or should the business use an inventory costing method that will approximate the flow of inventory costs? For example, the business might decide to assign the costs of the first grills purchased to the first grills sold rather than tracking the cost of each grill individually. Or it might decide, instead, to assign the costs of the last grills purchased to the first grills sold.

Jorell understands that he has several options when it comes to selecting an inventory costing method. He wants to select a method that will be relatively easy to implement and maintain. He knows that by selecting the best method for the business, he will be able to easily determine the cost of the goods sold and, ultimately, the gross profit.

What Is the Cost of Merchandise Inventory?

In this chapter, we expand our discussion on merchandise inventory by learning how to account for the cost of inventory. When **Dick's Sporting Goods, Inc.,** a retail chain that sells sporting goods, apparel, and footwear, purchases and sells inventory, the business must account for the inventory appropriately. Dick's must determine the cost of the inventory that is sold in order to calculate gross profit. If a business had only a small amount of inventory, identifying the cost of one particular item would be simple. However, large businesses, such as Dick's, have millions of items of inventory, which makes tracking costs very difficult. In this chapter, you learn that every business must select an inventory costing method that allows it to track costs and determine the cost of goods sold, gross profit, and value of ending merchandise inventory.

Chapter 6 Learning Objectives

1. Identify accounting principles and controls related to merchandise inventory
2. Account for merchandise inventory costs under a perpetual inventory system
3. Compare the effects on the financial statements when using the different inventory costing methods
4. Apply the lower-of-cost-or-market rule to merchandise inventory
5. Measure the effects of merchandise inventory errors on the financial statements
6. Use inventory turnover and days' sales in inventory to evaluate business performance
7. Account for merchandise inventory costs under a periodic inventory system (Appendix 6A)

WHAT ARE THE ACCOUNTING PRINCIPLES AND CONTROLS THAT RELATE TO MERCHANDISE INVENTORY?

Learning Objective 1
Identify accounting principles and controls related to merchandise inventory

Chapter F:5 introduced accounting for merchandise inventory. It showed how Smart Touch Learning, a fictitious merchandiser that sells tablet computers containing e-learning software programs, recorded the purchase and sale of its inventory. This chapter completes the accounting for merchandise inventory.

Accounting Principles

Let's begin by learning about several accounting principles that affect merchandise inventories. Among them are consistency, disclosure, materiality, and accounting conservatism.

Consistency Principle

Consistency Principle
A business should use the same accounting methods and procedures from period to period.

The **consistency principle** states that businesses should use the same accounting methods and procedures from period to period. Consistency helps investors and creditors compare a company's financial statements from one period to the next.

Suppose you are analyzing a company's net income over a two-year period in which there was an increase in net income from the first year to the second. Analysis of the income statement shows Net Sales Revenue was almost the same for both years, but Cost of Goods Sold decreased significantly, which resulted in increases in gross profit and operating income. Without further information, you might conclude that the company was able to purchase its inventory at a lower cost in the second year and that profits will continue to increase in future years. However, changing inventory costing methods could have caused this one-time change, in which case future profits will not be affected. Therefore, companies must be consistent in the accounting methods they use. If changes are made in accounting methods, these changes must be reported. Investors and creditors need this information to make wise decisions about the company.

Disclosure Principle

Disclosure Principle
A business's financial statements must report enough information for outsiders to make knowledgeable decisions about the company.

The **disclosure principle** holds that a company should report enough information for outsiders to make knowledgeable decisions about the company. In short, the company should report information that is relevant and has faithful representation. This includes disclosing the method used to account for merchandise inventories. All major accounting methods and procedures are described in the footnotes to the financial statements. Suppose a banker is comparing two companies—one using inventory costing method A and the other using inventory costing method B. The B company reports higher net income but only because of the inventory costing method it selected. Without knowledge of these accounting methods, the banker could lend money to the wrong business.

> Take a look at Kohl's Corporation's annual report, which can be reviewed by visiting **http://www.pearsonhighered.com/Horngren**. After the financial statements, you will find the notes to the financial statements. These footnotes contain important information summarizing the accounting policies that Kohl's Corporation uses and ensure that the company is providing full disclosure to its investors and creditors.

Materiality Concept

The materiality concept states that a company must perform strictly proper accounting *only* for significant items. Information is significant—or, in accounting terms, *material*—when it would cause someone to change a decision. The materiality concept frees accountants from having to report every last item in strict accordance with GAAP. For example, $10,000 is material to a small business with annual sales of $100,000. However, $10,000 isn't material to a large company with annual sales of $100,000,000. Therefore, the accounting principles followed for a $10,000 cost in a small company may be different from the accounting principles followed for a $10,000 cost in a large company.

Materiality Concept
A company must perform strictly proper accounting only for items that are significant to the business's financial situation.

Conservatism

Conservatism in accounting means exercising caution in reporting items in the financial statements. Conservatism espouses the following ideas:

- Anticipate no gains, but provide for all probable losses.
- If in doubt, record an asset at the lowest reasonable amount and a liability at the highest reasonable amount.
- When there's a question, record an expense rather than an asset.
- When you are faced with a decision between two possible options, you must choose the option that undervalues, rather than overvalues, your business.

Conservatism
A business should report the least favorable figures in the financial statements when two or more possible options are presented.

The goal of conservatism is to report realistic figures and never overstate assets or net income.

Control Over Merchandise Inventory

Maintaining good controls over merchandise inventory is very important for a merchandiser. Good controls ensure that inventory purchases and sales are properly authorized and accounted for by the accounting system. This can be accomplished by taking the following measures:

- Ensure merchandise inventory is not purchased without proper authorization, including purchasing only from approved vendors and within acceptable dollar ranges.
- After inventory is purchased, the order should be tracked and properly documented when received. At time of delivery, a count of inventory received should be completed and each item should be examined for damage.
- Damaged inventory should be properly recorded and then should either be used, disposed of, or returned to the vendor.

- A physical count of inventory should be completed at least once a year to track inventory shrinkage due to theft and damage.
- When sales are made, the inventory sold should be properly recorded and removed from the inventory count. This will prevent the company from running out of inventory, often called a *stockout*.

Data Analytics in Accounting

For merchandising and manufacturing companies, inventory is one of their most important assets as it is a business's main revenue source. Companies not only need to have control over their merchandise inventory, but they need to be able to understand how much inventory they have on hand. If they don't have enough inventory, they will have stockouts (not enough inventory for the demand from customers). If companies have too much inventory on hand, they could be left with inventory that they cannot sell.

Businesses can evaluate their inventory by using data analytics tools. For example, Airbnb, a company that operates an online marketplace for short-term rental properties, has collected information about its inventory (rental properties) since 2008. It has collected over 1.5 petabytes of data on the vacation habits and accommodation preferences of its customers. The company uses this information to help identify areas in cities that don't have enough listings (potential stockouts) and then recruits additional landlords to fill this need.

Dickey's Barbecue Pit provides another example of how companies can use data analytics to keep track of its inventory. Dickey's Barbecue Pit is a family-owned barbecue restaurant chain that specializes in quality beef brisket, pulled pork, and sausages with an array of homestyle sides. Information about Dickey's inventory at each of its 500 locations is examined every 20 minutes using data analysis software. This software provides real-time feedback on the amount of sales occurring and how much inventory (meat and sides) remain. If lower than expected sales occur, and the company has excess inventory, such as ribs, the company sends a text message to its loyal customers announcing a special discount on the inventory. Dickey's Barbecue Pit's ability to keep track of real-time data allows it to sell excess inventory on hand instead of being left with inventory that could spoil.

Source: Marr, B. (2016). *Big data in practice. How 45 successful companies use big data analytics to deliver extraordinary results*. West Sussex, United Kingdom: John Wiley and Sons Ltd.

Match the accounting terminology to the definitions.

1. Conservatism
2. Materiality concept
3. Disclosure principle
4. Consistency principle

a. A business should report the least favorable figures in the financial statements when two or more possible options are presented.

b. A business's financial statements must report enough information for outsiders to make knowledgeable decisions about the company.

c. A business should use the same accounting methods and procedures from period to period.

d. A company must perform strictly proper accounting only for items that are significant to the business's financial situation.

Check your answers online in MyLab Accounting or at http://www.pearsonhighered.com/Horngren.

For more practice, see Short Exercise S-F:6-1. **MyLab Accounting**

HOW ARE MERCHANDISE INVENTORY COSTS DETERMINED UNDER A PERPETUAL INVENTORY SYSTEM?

Previously you learned about merchandise inventory and cost of goods sold. Remember these key equations:

Learning Objective 2

Account for merchandise inventory costs under a perpetual inventory system

> Ending Merchandise Inventory = Number of units *on hand* × Unit cost
> Cost of Goods Sold = Number of units *sold* × Unit cost

Companies determine the number of units on hand from perpetual inventory records backed up by a physical count. Exhibit F:6-1 gives the inventory data for TAB0503, one model of tablets that Smart Touch Learning sells.

As shown in this exhibit, Smart Touch Learning began August with 2 TAB0503s in inventory. It purchased 4 more tablets on August 5, bringing the total quantity on hand to 6 (2 + 4). On August 15, it sold 4 tablets, leaving 2 remaining on hand (6 − 4). Smart Touch Learning then purchased 12 more on August 26 and sold 10 on August 31. It had 4 TAB0503s at the end of August (2 + 12 − 10). The company sold each tablet for $500 to its customers.

Exhibit F:6-1 | Perpetual Inventory Record

Item: TAB0503				
Date	Quantity Purchased	Quantity Sold	Cost per Unit	Quantity on Hand
Aug. 1			$350	2
5	4		$350	6 (2 + 4)
15		4		2 (6 − 4)
26	12		$350	14
31		10		4
Totals	16	14		4

Measuring inventory cost is easy when prices do not change. For example, looking at Exhibit F:6-1, you can see that Smart Touch Learning's cost per unit remained the same at $350. Therefore, ending inventory and cost of goods sold can be calculated easily.

> Ending Merchandise Inventory = Number of units *on hand* × Unit cost
> = 4 units × $350 per unit
> = $1,400
> Cost of Goods Sold = Number of units *sold* × Unit cost
> = 14 units × $350 per unit
> = $4,900

But what if unit cost does change? For example, what if the cost per unit increased to $360 on August 5 and $380 on August 26, as shown in Exhibit F:6-2? When inventory is sold on August 31, how many of the tablets sold cost $350? How many cost $360? And how many cost $380? To compute ending inventory and cost of goods sold, Smart Touch Learning must assign a unit cost to each inventory item. This is done by using one of four inventory costing methods:

1. Specific identification
2. First-in, first-out (FIFO)
3. Last-in, first-out (LIFO)
4. Weighted-average.

Exhibit F:6-2 | Perpetual Inventory Record—Changes in Cost per Unit

Item: TAB0503

Date	Quantity Purchased	Quantity Sold	Cost per Unit	Quantity on Hand
Aug. 1			$350	2
5	4		$360	6
15		4		2
26	12		$380	14
31		10		4
Totals	16	14		4

Inventory Costing Method
A method of approximating the flow of inventory costs in a business that is used to determine the amount of cost of goods sold and ending merchandise inventory.

Specific Identification Method
An inventory costing method based on the specific cost of particular units of inventory.

Each **inventory costing method** approximates the flow of inventory costs in a business (with the exception of the specific identification method) and is used to determine the amount of cost of goods sold and ending merchandise inventory.

Specific Identification Method

The **specific identification method** uses the specific cost of each unit of inventory to determine ending inventory and cost of goods sold. In the specific identification method, the company knows exactly which item was sold and exactly what the item cost. This costing method is best for businesses that sell unique, easily identified inventory items, such as automobiles (identified by the vehicle identification number [VIN]), jewels (a specific diamond ring), and real estate (identified by address). For instance, assume that of the 4 tablets sold on August 15, 1 had a cost of $350 and 3 had a cost of $360. As for the August 31 sale, 1 had a cost of $350 and 9 had a cost of $380. Cost of goods sold and ending merchandise inventory can be calculated as shown in Exhibit F:6-3.

Merchandise Inventory Financial 6-7

Exhibit F:6-3 | Perpetual Inventory Record: Specific Identification

	Purchases			Cost of Goods Sold			Inventory on Hand		
Date	Quantity	Unit Cost	Total Cost	Quantity	Unit Cost	Total Cost	Quantity	Unit Cost	Total Cost
Aug. 1							2 units	× $ 350	= $ 700 } $ 700
5	4 units	× $ 360	= $ 1,440				2 units 4 units	× $ 350 × $ 360	= $ 700 = $ 1,440 } $ 2,140
15				1 unit 3 units	× $ 350 × $ 360	= $ 350 = $ 1,080 } $ 1,430	1 unit 1 unit	× $ 350 × $ 360	= $ 350 = $ 360 } $ 710
26	12 units	× $ 380	= $ 4,560				1 unit 1 unit 12 units	× $ 350 × $ 360 × $ 380	= $ 350 = $ 360 = $ 4,560 } $ 5,270
31				1 unit 9 units	× $ 350 × $ 380	= $ 350 = $ 3,420 } $ 3,770	1 unit 3 units	× $ 360 × $ 380	= $ 360 = $ 1,140 } $ 1,500
Totals	16 units		**$ 6,000**	14 units		**$ 5,200**	4 units		**$ 1,500**

Notice that under the specific identification method, when inventory is sold, a specific cost is assigned to it. For example, on the August 15 sale, Smart Touch Learning knew that it had sold 1 unit costing $350 and 3 units costing $360. This left 1 unit (2 − 1) at $350 and 1 unit (4 − 3) at $360 in ending inventory. This method requires the business to keep detailed records of inventory purchases and sales and to also be able to carefully identify the inventory that is sold.

First-In, First-Out (FIFO) Method

Under the **first-in, first-out (FIFO) method**, the cost of goods sold is based on the oldest purchases—that is, the first units purchased are assumed to be the first units sold.

Inventory Calculations—FIFO

When companies use the FIFO method, the cost of goods sold is calculated based on the assumption that the units are sold in the order they were purchased—from oldest purchases to newest purchases. Because cost of goods sold is based on the oldest purchases, ending inventory (the units not sold and still on hand) is based on the most recent purchases. In Exhibit F:6-4 (on the next page), this is illustrated by the cost of goods sold calculation for the August 15 sale coming from the *first* goods purchased, which are from the August 1 beginning inventory (2 units) and then the next most recent purchase on August 5 (2 units). FIFO costing is consistent with the physical movement of inventory (for most companies). That is, under the FIFO inventory costing method, companies assume that they sell their oldest inventory first.

First-In, First-Out (FIFO) Method
An inventory costing method in which the first costs into inventory are the first costs out to cost of goods sold. Ending inventory is based on the costs of the most recent purchases.

6-8 Financial  chapter 6

Exhibit F:6-4 | **Perpetual Inventory Record: First-In, First-Out (FIFO)**

	Purchases			Cost of Goods Sold			Inventory on Hand			
Date	Quantity	Unit Cost	Total Cost	Quantity	Unit Cost	Total Cost	Quantity	Unit Cost	Total Cost	
Aug. 1							2 units	× $ 350	= $ 700	$ 700
5	4 units	× $ 360	= $ 1,440				2 units 4 units	× $ 350 × $ 360	= $ 700 = $ 1,440	$ 2,140
15				2 units 2 units	× $ 350 × $ 360	= $ 700 = $ 720 } $ 1,420	2 units	× $ 360	= $ 720	$ 720
26	12 units	× $ 380	= $ 4,560				2 units 12 units	× $ 360 × $ 380	= $ 720 = $ 4,560	$ 5,280
31				2 units 8 units	× $ 360 × $ 380	= $ 720 = $ 3,040 } $ 3,760	4 units	× $ 380	= $ 1,520	$ 1,520
Totals	16 units		$ 6,000	14 units		$ 5,180	4 units			$ 1,520

Take a moment to review the perpetual inventory card using the FIFO method in Exhibit F:6-4. Smart Touch Learning began August with 2 TAB0503s that cost $350 each for a total cost of $700. This is reported in the Inventory on Hand column. The August 5 purchase is recorded in the Purchases column and shows a total cost of $1,440 (4 units × $360). After the purchase, the Inventory on Hand column is updated to reflect the inventory on hand, which consists of 6 units (2 + 4) and has a cost of $2,140 (2 units @ $350 plus 4 units @ $360). Notice that we show the August 1 units and the units purchased on August 5 separately in the Inventory on Hand column. This will help us calculate the Cost of Goods Sold appropriately in the sales transaction on August 15.

On August 15, the company sold 4 units. Under FIFO, we will assume the units sold come first from the August 1 balance and then from the August 5 purchase. The first 2 units sold will come from the August 1 balance and had the oldest cost ($350 per unit). The next 2 units sold will come from the August 5 purchase with a cost of $360 each. The cost of goods sold for the August 15 sale will be a total of $1,420 (2 units @ $350 plus 2 units @ $360). After the August 15 sale, we will update the Inventory on Hand column. 2 units remain in inventory (6 units at August 5 less 4 units sold on August 15). The total cost of these 2 units is $720 (2 units @ $360).

The remainder of the inventory record follows the same pattern. Consider the sale on August 31 of 10 units. The oldest cost is from August 5 (2 units @ $360). The next oldest cost is from the August 26 purchase at $380 each (8 units @ $380). This leaves 4 units in inventory on August 31 at $380 each.

The FIFO monthly summary at August 31 is as follows:

- Cost of goods sold: 14 units that cost a total of $5,180 ($1,420 + $3,760).
- Ending inventory: 4 units that cost a total of $1,520 (4 units @ $380).

Cost of Goods Available for Sale
The total cost spent on inventory that was available to be sold during a period.

Notice the total cost of goods sold of $5,180 plus the total ending inventory of $1,520 equals the total **cost of goods available for sale** during August of $6,700 [(2 units @ $350) + (4 units @ $360) + (12 units @ $380)]. Cost of goods available for sale represents the total cost of merchandise inventory that is available for sale during the time period. At August 31, Smart Touch Learning will use the amount of cost of goods sold to determine gross profit on its income statement and to report ending merchandise inventory on its balance sheet.

Merchandise Inventory Financial 6-9

Journal Entries—FIFO

For each transaction reported on the FIFO perpetual inventory record (Exhibit F:6-4), the company will have to record a journal entry. The journal entries under FIFO are presented below. We assume all purchases and sales of inventory are on account. The amounts unique to FIFO are shown in blue for emphasis. All other amounts are the same for all four inventory methods.

Date	Accounts and Explanation	Debit	Credit
Aug. 5	Merchandise Inventory (4 × $360)	1,440	
	Accounts Payable		1,440
	Purchased inventory on account.		
15	Accounts Receivable (4 × $500)	2,000	
	Sales Revenue		2,000
	Sale on account.		
15	Cost of Goods Sold (2 × $350) + (2 × $360)	1,420	
	Merchandise Inventory		1,420
	Recorded the cost of goods sold.		
26	Merchandise Inventory (12 × $380)	4,560	
	Accounts Payable		4,560
	Purchased inventory on account.		
31	Accounts Receivable (10 × $500)	5,000	
	Sales Revenue		5,000
	Sale on account.		
31	Cost of Goods Sold (2 × $360) + (8 × $380)	3,760	
	Merchandise Inventory		3,760
	Recorded the cost of goods sold.		

Accounting equation effects (right column):
- A↑ Merchandise Inventory↑ = L↑ Accounts Payable↑ + E
- A↑ Accounts Receivable↑ = L + E↑ Sales Revenue↑
- A↓ Merchandise Inventory↓ = L + E↓ Cost of Goods Sold↑
- A↑ Merchandise Inventory↑ = L↑ Accounts Payable↑ + E
- A↑ Accounts Receivable↑ = L + E↑ Sales Revenue↑
- A↓ Merchandise Inventory↓ = L + E↓ Cost of Goods Sold↑

For example, on August 5, Smart Touch Learning purchased $1,440 of inventory and made the first journal entry. On August 15, the company sold 4 TAB0503s for the sales price of $500 each. Smart Touch Learning recorded the sale, $2,000, and the cost of goods sold, $1,420 (calculated in Exhibit F:6-4 as 2 units @ $350 plus 2 units @ $360). The remaining journal entries (August 26 and 31) follow the inventory data in Exhibit F:6-4.

Last-In, First-Out (LIFO) Method

Last-in, first-out (LIFO) is the opposite of FIFO. Under the **last-in, first-out (LIFO) method**, the cost of goods sold is based on the most recent purchases (newest costs)—that is, the last units purchased are assumed to be the first units sold.

Last-In, First-Out (LIFO) Method
An inventory costing method in which the last costs into inventory are the first costs out to cost of goods sold. The method leaves the oldest costs—those of beginning inventory and the earliest purchases of the period—in ending inventory.

6-10 Financial chapter 6

Inventory Calculations—LIFO

When companies use the LIFO method, the cost of goods sold is calculated based on the assumption that the units are sold from the most recent purchases. Because cost of goods sold is based on the most recent purchases, ending inventory (the units not sold and still on hand) is based on the oldest costs (beginning inventory and earliest purchases). In Exhibit F:6-5, this is illustrated by the cost of goods sold for the August 15 sale coming from the *last* goods in the warehouse—the August 5 purchase. Under the LIFO inventory costing method, companies are assumed to sell their newest inventory first.

Exhibit F:6-5 | **Perpetual Inventory Record: Last-In, First-Out (LIFO)**

	Purchases			Cost of Goods Sold			Inventory on Hand		
Date	Quantity	Unit Cost	Total Cost	Quantity	Unit Cost	Total Cost	Quantity	Unit Cost	Total Cost
Aug. 1							2 units	× $ 350 = $ 700	$ 700
5	4 units	× $ 360	= $ 1,440				2 units 4 units	× $ 350 = $ 700 × $ 360 = $ 1,440	$ 2,140
15				4 units	× $ 360	= $ 1,440 → $ 1,440	2 units	× $ 350 = $ 700	$ 700
26	12 units	× $ 380	= $ 4,560				2 units 12 units	× $ 350 = $ 700 × $ 380 = $ 4,560	$ 5,260
31				10 units	× $ 380	= $ 3,800 → $ 3,800	2 units 2 units	× $ 350 = $ 700 × $ 380 = $ 760	$ 1,460
Totals	16 units		$ 6,000	14 units		$ 5,240	4 units		$ 1,460

Exhibit F:6-5 shows the perpetual inventory card for Smart Touch Learning using the LIFO method. Again, Smart Touch Learning had 2 TAB0503s at the beginning. This is reported in the Inventory on Hand column (2 units @ $350). The purchase on August 5 is recorded in the Purchases column and then reflected in the Inventory on Hand balance. The company holds 6 units of inventory with a total cost of $2,140 (2 units @ $350 plus 4 units @ $360).

On August 15, Smart Touch Learning sells 4 units. Under LIFO, we will assume the units sold come from the most recent purchase on August 5. The cost of goods sold for August 15 will be $1,440 (4 units @ $360). After the August 15 sale, 2 units remain in inventory (all from the beginning inventory amount). The cost of these 2 units is $700 (2 units @ $350).

The purchase of 12 units on August 26 adds a new $380 layer to inventory on hand. Now inventory holds 14 units (2 units @ $350 plus 12 units @ $380). The sale of 10 units on August 31 will be assumed to come from the most recent purchase on August 26 or 10 units at $380 each. This leaves in Inventory on Hand 2 units from beginning inventory and 2 units at $380 from the August 26 purchase. The LIFO monthly summary at August 31 is as follows:

- Cost of goods sold: 14 units that cost a total of $5,240 ($1,440 + $3,800).
- Ending inventory: 4 units that cost a total of $1,460 (2 units @ $350 plus 2 units @ $380).

Journal Entries—LIFO

For each transaction shown on the LIFO perpetual inventory record (Exhibit F:6-5), the company will have to record journal entries. We assume all purchases and sales of inventory are on account. Amounts unique to LIFO are shown in blue. On August 5, Smart Touch

IFRS

LIFO is not permitted under International Financial Reporting Standards (IFRS). Under IFRS, companies may only use the specific identification, FIFO, and weighted-average methods to cost inventory. If LIFO were eliminated as an acceptable method under GAAP, those U.S. companies currently using the LIFO cost method would experience significant income statement and balance sheet effects. Approximately one-third of U.S. companies use the LIFO method to cost at least part of their inventory.

Learning purchased inventory of $1,440. The August 15 sale brought in sales revenue of $2,000 and cost of goods sold of $1,440. Remember, the cost of goods sold was calculated in Exhibit F:6-5. The August 26 and 31 entries also come from the data in Exhibit F:6-5.

Date	Accounts and Explanation	Debit	Credit
Aug. 5	Merchandise Inventory (4 × $360)	1,440	
	Accounts Payable		1,440
	Purchased inventory on account.		
15	Accounts Receivable (4 × $500)	2,000	
	Sales Revenue		2,000
	Sale on account.		
15	Cost of Goods Sold (4 × $360)	1,440	
	Merchandise Inventory		1,440
	Recorded the cost of goods sold.		
26	Merchandise Inventory (12 × $380)	4,560	
	Accounts Payable		4,560
	Purchased inventory on account.		
31	Accounts Receivable (10 × $500)	5,000	
	Sales Revenue		5,000
	Sale on account.		
31	Cost of Goods Sold (10 × $380)	3,800	
	Merchandise Inventory		3,800
	Recorded the cost of goods sold.		

A↑	=	L↑	+	E
Merchandise Inventory↑		Accounts Payable↑		

A↑	=	L	+	E↑
Accounts Receivable↑				Sales Revenue↑

A↓	=	L	+	E↓
Merchandise Inventory↓				Cost of Goods Sold↑

A↑	=	L↑	+	E
Merchandise Inventory↑		Accounts Payable↑		

A↑	=	L	+	E↑
Accounts Receivable↑				Sales Revenue↑

A↓	=	L	+	E↓
Merchandise Inventory↓				Cost of Goods Sold↑

> Think about going to the grocery store to buy a gallon of milk. Which gallon is in front of the milk cooler: the older milk or the newer milk? The older milk is in front. That's FIFO. Now visualize reaching all the way to the back of the cooler to get the newer milk. That's LIFO. It's important to understand that although this image represents the physical flow of goods, an inventory costing system may or may not match the physical flow. The costing system is only an assumption about how costs flow. The inventory does not have to actually be sold in the LIFO manner in order to record it as LIFO.

Weighted-Average Method

Under the **weighted-average method** (sometimes called *moving-average method*), the business computes a new weighted-average cost per unit after each purchase. Ending inventory and cost of goods sold are then based on the same weighted-average cost per unit.

Weighted-Average Method
An inventory costing method based on the weighted-average cost per unit of inventory that is calculated after each purchase. Weighted-average cost per unit is determined by dividing the cost of goods available for sale by the number of units available.

Inventory Calculations—Weighted-Average

The weighted-average cost per unit is calculated as follows:

> Weighted-average cost per unit = Cost of goods available for sale / Number of units available

Exhibit F:6-6 shows the perpetual inventory record using the weighted-average method for Smart Touch Learning. We round average unit cost to the nearest cent and total cost to the nearest dollar.

Exhibit F:6-6 | Perpetual Inventory Record: Weighted-Average

	Purchases			Cost of Goods Sold			Inventory on Hand			
Date	Quantity	Unit Cost	Total Cost	Quantity	Unit Cost	Total Cost	Quantity	Unit Cost	Total Cost	
Aug. 1							2 units	× $ 350.00	= $ 700	
5	4 units	× $ 360	= $ 1,440				6 units	× $ 356.67	= $ 2,140	$ 2,140 / 6 units = $ 356.67
15				4 units	× $ 356.67	= $ 1,427	2 units	× $ 356.67	= $ 713	
26	12 units	× $ 380	= $ 4,560				14 units	× $ 376.64	= $ 5,273	$ 5,273 / 14 units = $ 376.64
31				10 units	× $ 376.64	= $ 3,766	4 units	× $ 376.64	= $ 1,507	
Totals	16 units		$ 6,000	14 units		$ 5,193	4 units		$ 1,507	

As noted previously, after each purchase, Smart Touch Learning computes a new weighted-average cost per unit. For example, on August 5, the new weighted-average unit cost is as follows:

> Cost of goods available for sale / Number of units available = ($700 + $1,440) / (2 units + 4 units)
> = $2,140 / 6 units
> = $356.67

Under the weighted-average method, the cost per unit is a weighted average. You cannot take the average of the two unit costs ($350 and $360) to determine the new unit cost. Instead, you must use the total cost of goods available for sale ($2,140) divided by the number of units available (6 units).

The cost of goods sold on August 15 is calculated using the weighted-average cost of $356.67 per unit. On August 26 when the next purchase is made, the company will calculate a new weighted-average unit cost as follows:

> Cost of goods available for sale / Number of units available = ($713 + $4,560) / (2 units + 12 units)
> = $5,273 / 14 units
> = $376.64

Merchandise Inventory Financial 6-13

The weighted-average cost summary at August 31 is as follows:

- Cost of goods sold: 14 units that cost a total of $5,193 ($1,427 + $3,766).
- Ending inventory: 4 units that cost a total of $1,507 (4 units @ $376.64).

> With the weighted-average costing method, rounding errors can occur. However, this is not the case in this example. Notice that cost of goods sold and ending inventory total $6,700 ($5,193 + $1,507), which equals the total cost of goods available for sale.

Journal Entries—Weighted-Average

For each transaction shown on the weighted-average perpetual inventory record (Exhibit F:6-6), the company will record journal entries. We assume all purchases and sales of inventory are on account. Amounts unique to the weighted-average method are shown in blue.

On August 5, Smart Touch Learning purchased $1,440 of inventory and made the first journal entry. On August 15, Smart Touch Learning sold 4 TAB0503s for $500 each. The company recorded the sale ($2,000) and the cost of goods sold (4 units at $356.67). Remember, the amounts come from the weighted-average perpetual inventory record (Exhibit F:6-6). The remaining journal entries (August 26 and 31) follow the same procedure.

Date	Accounts and Explanation	Debit	Credit
Aug. 5	Merchandise Inventory (4 × $360)	1,440	
	Accounts Payable		1,440
	Purchased inventory on account.		
15	Accounts Receivable (4 × $500)	2,000	
	Sales Revenue		2,000
	Sale on account.		
15	Cost of Goods Sold (4 × $356.67)	1,427	
	Merchandise Inventory		1,427
	Recorded the cost of goods sold.		
26	Merchandise Inventory (12 × $380)	4,560	
	Accounts Payable		4,560
	Purchased inventory on account.		
31	Accounts Receivable (10 × $500)	5,000	
	Sales Revenue		5,000
	Sale on account.		
31	Cost of Goods Sold (10 × $376.64)	3,766	
	Merchandise Inventory		3,766
	Recorded the cost of goods sold.		

A↑ = L↑ + E   Merchandise Inventory↑ = Accounts Payable↑

A↑ = L + E↑   Accounts Receivable↑ = Sales Revenue↑

A↓ = L + E↓   Merchandise Inventory↓ = Cost of Goods Sold↑

A↑ = L↑ + E   Merchandise Inventory↑ = Accounts Payable↑

A↑ = L + E↑   Accounts Receivable↑ = Sales Revenue↑

A↓ = L + E↓   Merchandise Inventory↓ = Cost of Goods Sold↑

6-14 Financial chapter 6

Try It!

5. Serenity Books has the following transactions in August related to merchandise inventory.

Aug. 1	Beginning merchandise inventory, 10 books @ $15 each
3	Sold 3 books @ $20 each
12	Purchased 8 books @ $18 each
15	Sold 9 books @ $20 each
20	Purchased 4 books @ $20 each
28	Sold 5 books @ $25 each

a. Determine the cost of goods sold and ending merchandise inventory by preparing a perpetual inventory record using the specific identification method. Assume the following costing information for the books sold during the month:

August 3: 3 books costing $15 each
August 15: 4 books costing $15 each and 5 books costing $18 each
August 28: 2 books costing $18 each and 3 books costing $20 each

b. Determine the cost of goods sold and ending merchandise inventory by preparing a perpetual inventory record using the FIFO inventory costing method.

c. Determine the cost of goods sold and ending merchandise inventory by preparing a perpetual inventory record using the LIFO inventory costing method.

d. Determine the cost of goods sold and ending merchandise inventory by preparing a perpetual inventory record using the weighted-average inventory costing method. Round weighted-average unit cost to the nearest cent and total cost to the nearest dollar.

Check your answers online in MyLab Accounting or at http://www.pearsonhighered.com/Horngren.

For more practice, see Short Exercises S-F:6-2 through S-F:6-6. **MyLab Accounting**

HOW ARE FINANCIAL STATEMENTS AFFECTED BY USING DIFFERENT INVENTORY COSTING METHODS?

Learning Objective 3
Compare the effects on the financial statements when using the different inventory costing methods

What leads Smart Touch Learning to select the specific identification, FIFO, LIFO, or weighted-average inventory costing method? The different methods have different benefits.

Income Statement

Exhibit F:6-7 summarizes the results for the four inventory costing methods for Smart Touch Learning. It shows sales revenue, cost of goods sold, and gross profit for specific identification, FIFO, LIFO, and weighted-average.

Exhibit F:6-7 shows that FIFO produces the lowest cost of goods sold and the highest gross profit for Smart Touch Learning. Because operating expenses are the same, regardless

Exhibit F:6-7 | Comparative Results for Specific Identification, FIFO, LIFO, and Weighted-Average—Income Statement

	Specific Identification	FIFO	LIFO	Weighted-Average
Net Sales Revenue (14 units × $500)	$ 7,000	$ 7,000	$ 7,000	$ 7,000
Less: Cost of Goods Sold	5,200	5,180	5,240	5,193
Gross Profit	$ 1,800	$ 1,820	$ 1,760	$ 1,807

of which inventory method a company uses, net income is also the highest under FIFO when inventory costs are rising. **Many companies prefer high income in order to attract investors and borrow on favorable terms. FIFO offers this benefit in a period of rising costs.**

When inventory costs are rising, LIFO results in the highest cost of goods sold and the lowest gross profit. **Lower profits mean lower taxable income; thus, LIFO lets companies pay the lowest income taxes when inventory costs are rising.** Low tax payments conserve cash, and that is the main benefit of LIFO. The downside of LIFO is that the company reports lower net income.

The weighted-average method generates amounts that fall between the extremes of FIFO and LIFO. **Therefore, companies that seek a "middle-ground" solution use the weighted-average method for inventory.**

Balance Sheet

Consider again the beginning inventory and purchases made by Smart Touch Learning during August. The company had total inventory available for sale in August as follows:

Aug. 1	2 units × $350	$ 700
Aug. 5	4 units × $360	1,440
Aug. 26	12 units × $380	4,560
Cost of goods available for sale		$ 6,700

Only one of two things can happen to the tablets—either they remain in the warehouse (ending merchandise inventory) or they are sold (Cost of Goods Sold). Ending merchandise inventory can be calculated by determining first the cost of goods available for sale (beginning merchandise inventory plus inventory purchased) and then subtracting merchandise inventory sold (Cost of Goods Sold). Exhibit F:6-8 (on the next page) shows the results of Smart Touch Learning's ending merchandise inventory for each of the costing methods for August.

When using the FIFO inventory costing method, ending merchandise inventory will be the highest when costs are increasing. LIFO produces the lowest ending merchandise inventory with weighted-average again in the middle.

So far, we've ignored the effects on the income statement and balance sheet when using the specific identification method. This is because under specific identification, the results will vary depending on which costs are assigned to the inventory sold. Most companies will not choose to use the specific identification method unless they want to match each inventory item sold with its exact cost.

How do businesses decide which inventory costing method to use?

Exhibit F:6-8 | Comparative Results for Specific Identification, FIFO, LIFO, and Weighted-Average—Balance Sheet

	Specific Identification	FIFO	LIFO	Weighted-Average
Beginning Merchandise Inventory	$ 700	$ 700	$ 700	$ 700
Plus: Net Cost of Inventory Purchased	6,000	6,000	6,000	6,000
Cost of Goods Available for Sale	6,700	6,700	6,700	6,700
Less: Cost of Goods Sold	5,200	5,180	5,240	5,193
Ending Merchandise Inventory	$ 1,500	$ 1,520	$ 1,460	$ 1,507

The weighted-average ending merchandise inventory number shown in Exhibit F:6-6 may be slightly different than that found in Exhibit F:6-8. This is because of rounding. When completing your homework, always read carefully for directions on how to round when using the weighted-average method.

We have looked at the effects of different inventory costing methods on the financial statements when inventory costs are rising. When inventory costs are instead declining, the effects on the financial statements will be the opposite of those discussed above. Exhibit F:6-9 summarizes the effects of different inventory costing methods on the financial statements during periods of rising and declining inventory costs.

Exhibit F:6-9 | Effects on the Financial Statements During Periods of Rising and Declining Inventory Costs

Period of Rising Inventory Costs:

	Specific Identification	FIFO	LIFO	Weighted-Average
Income Statement:				
Cost of Goods Sold	Varies	Lowest	Highest	Middle
Net Income	Varies	Highest	Lowest	Middle
Balance Sheet:				
Ending Merchandise Inventory	Varies	Highest	Lowest	Middle

Period of Declining Inventory Costs:

	Specific Identification	FIFO	LIFO	Weighted-Average
Income Statement:				
Cost of Goods Sold	Varies	Highest	Lowest	Middle
Net Income	Varies	Lowest	Highest	Middle
Balance Sheet:				
Ending Merchandise Inventory	Varies	Lowest	Highest	Middle

6. Antelope Motors is considering which inventory costing method it should use. The business wants to maximize gross profits during a period of declining costs. Which inventory costing method should Antelope Motors select?

Check your answer online in MyLab Accounting or at http://www.pearsonhighered.com/Horngren.

For more practice, see Short Exercise S-F:6-7. **MyLab Accounting**

HOW IS MERCHANDISE INVENTORY VALUED WHEN USING THE LOWER-OF-COST-OR-MARKET RULE?

In addition to the specific identification, FIFO, LIFO, and weighted-average inventory costing methods, accountants face other inventory issues, such as the **lower-of-cost-or-market (LCM) rule**. LCM shows accounting conservatism in action and requires that merchandise inventory be reported in the financial statements at whichever is lower of the following:

- The historical cost of the inventory
- The market value of the inventory

Computing the Lower-of-Cost-or-Market

For inventories, market value generally means the current replacement cost (that is, the cost to replace the inventory on hand). If the replacement cost of inventory is less than its historical cost, the business must adjust the inventory value. By adjusting the inventory down (crediting Merchandise Inventory), the balance sheet value of the asset, Merchandise Inventory, is at its correct value (market) rather than its overstated value (cost). If the merchandise inventory's market value is greater than cost, then we don't adjust the Merchandise Inventory account because of the conservatism principle.

Recording the Adjusting Journal Entry to Adjust Merchandise Inventory

Suppose Smart Touch Learning paid $3,000 for its TAB0503 inventory. By December 31, the merchandise inventory can now be replaced for $2,200, and the decline in value appears permanent. Market value is below cost, and the entry to write down the inventory to LCM is as follows:

> **Learning Objective 4**
> Apply the lower-of-cost-or-market rule to merchandise inventory
>
> **Lower-of-Cost-or-Market (LCM) Rule**
> Rule that merchandise inventory should be reported in the financial statements at whichever is lower—its historical cost or its market value.
>
> **IFRS**
> Under International Financial Reporting Standards, inventory must be reported at the lower-of-cost-or-market value. However, "market" is defined differently. Under IFRS, the market value of inventory is defined as the "net realizable value," or essentially its sales price. If the historical cost is higher than the sales price, then inventory must be written down. The IFRS approach results in fewer write-downs on inventory.

Date	Accounts and Explanation	Debit	Credit
Dec. 31	Cost of Goods Sold	800	
	Merchandise Inventory ($3,000 − $2,200)		800
	To write merchandise inventory down to market value.		

$$\underline{\text{A}\downarrow}_{\text{Merchandise Inventory}\downarrow} = \underline{\text{L}} + \underline{\text{E}\downarrow}_{\text{Cost of Goods Sold}\uparrow}$$

In this case, Smart Touch Learning's balance sheet would report this inventory as follows:

SMART TOUCH LEARNING
Balance Sheet (Partial)
December 31, 2025

Current Assets:	
Merchandise Inventory	$ 2,200

Companies often disclose information about their merchandise inventory in the notes to their financial statements. Often this includes how merchandise inventories are valued. For example, Smart Touch Learning would record the following note:

> NOTE 1: STATEMENT OF SIGNIFICANT ACCOUNTING POLICIES
> *Merchandise Inventories.* Merchandise inventories are valued at the *lower-of-cost-or-market.* Cost is determined using the first-in, first-out (FIFO) method.

TYING IT ALL TOGETHER

Dick's Sporting Goods, Inc. is a leading sporting goods retailer that offers high-quality sports equipment, apparel, footwear, and other accessories. The company was founded in 1948 when Richard "Dick" Stack opened his original bait and tackle store in Binghamton, New York. Today, Dick's Sporting Goods operates over 800 stores in 47 states. The company sells a variety of sporting goods, active apparel, and footwear that appeals to the beginner, intermediate, and enthusiast sports consumer. (You can find Dick's Sporting Goods, Inc.'s annual report at **https://www.sec.gov/Archives/edgar/data/1089063/000108906319000017/dks-10k_20190202.htm**)

Would Dick's Sporting Goods most likely use a perpetual or periodic inventory system and why?
Dick's Sporting Goods would most likely use a perpetual inventory system. The company would be interested in keeping a running computerized record of its merchandise inventory in order to know the quantity of merchandise on hand and its costs. A perpetual inventory system also allows companies to have better control over their inventory. Companies such as Dick's Sporting Goods use bar codes that track the flow of inventory, enabling the company to easily know the types and amounts of inventory in each store and when the company needs to reorder.

What inventory costing method does Dick's Sporting Goods use?
According to the notes to the financial statements, Dick's Sporting Goods uses the weighted-average inventory costing method. This inventory costing method requires Dick's to compute a new weighted-average cost per unit after each purchase and records ending merchandise inventory somewhere between the lowest and highest cost. Use of the weighted-average method falls between the extremes of FIFO and LIFO.

Given that Dick's Sporting Goods uses a perpetual inventory system, would they still do a physical count of inventories? Why or why not?
Dick's Sporting Goods would still do a physical count of inventories. In the notes to the financial statements, the company states that it performs physical counts of inventories in its stores and distribution centers throughout the year. This physical count of inventory is necessary even though the company uses a perpetual inventory system in order to determine the amount of inventory shrinkage. Inventory shrinkage refers to the loss of inventory that occurs due to theft or damage. A company would want to know the amount of inventory shrinkage in order to report the correct amount of inventory on the company's balance sheet.

7. T. J. Jackson Supplies had merchandise inventory that cost $1,300. The market value of the merchandise inventory is $750. What value should Jackson Supplies show on the balance sheet for merchandise inventory? Record the adjusting entry, if one is needed.

Check your answer online in MyLab Accounting or at http://www.pearsonhighered.com/Horngren.

For more practice, see Short Exercise S-F:6-8. **MyLab Accounting**

WHAT ARE THE EFFECTS OF MERCHANDISE INVENTORY ERRORS ON THE FINANCIAL STATEMENTS?

Businesses perform a physical count of their merchandise inventory at the end of the accounting period. For the financial statements to be accurate, it is important to get a correct count. This can be difficult for a company with widespread operations.

An error in determining the cost of ending merchandise inventory creates a whole string of errors in other related accounts. To illustrate, suppose Smart Touch Learning accidentally reported $5,000 more ending merchandise inventory than it actually had. In that case, ending merchandise inventory would be overstated by $5,000 on the balance sheet. The following shows how an overstatement of ending inventory affects cost of goods sold, gross profit, and net income:

Learning Objective 5
Measure the effects of merchandise inventory errors on the financial statements

	Ending Merchandise Inventory Overstated $5,000
Net Sales Revenue	Correct
Cost of Goods Sold:	
Beginning Merchandise Inventory	Correct
Plus: Net Cost of Inventory Purchased	Correct
Cost of Goods Available for Sale	Correct
Less: Ending Merchandise Inventory	ERROR: Overstated $5,000
Cost of Goods Sold	Understated $5,000
Gross Profit	Overstated $5,000
Operating Expenses	Correct
Net Income	Overstated $5,000

Understating the ending inventory—reporting the inventory too low—has the opposite effect. If Smart Touch Learning understated the inventory by $1,200, the effect would be as shown here:

	Ending Merchandise Inventory Understated $1,200
Net Sales Revenue	Correct
Cost of Goods Sold:	
Beginning Merchandise Inventory	Correct
Plus: Net Cost of Inventory Purchased	Correct
Cost of Goods Available for Sale	Correct
Less: Ending Merchandise Inventory	ERROR: Understated $1,200
Cost of Goods Sold	Overstated $1,200
Gross Profit	Understated $1,200
Operating Expenses	Correct
Net Income	Understated $1,200

Recall that one period's ending merchandise inventory becomes the next period's beginning inventory. As a result, an error in ending merchandise inventory carries over into the next period. Exhibit F:6-10 (on the next page) illustrates the effect of an inventory error, assuming all other items on the income statement are unchanged for the three periods. Period 1's ending merchandise inventory is overstated by $5,000; Period 1's ending merchandise inventory should be $10,000. The error carries over to Period 2. Period 3 is correct. In fact, both Period 1 and Period 2 should look like Period 3.

Exhibit F:6-10 | Inventory Errors

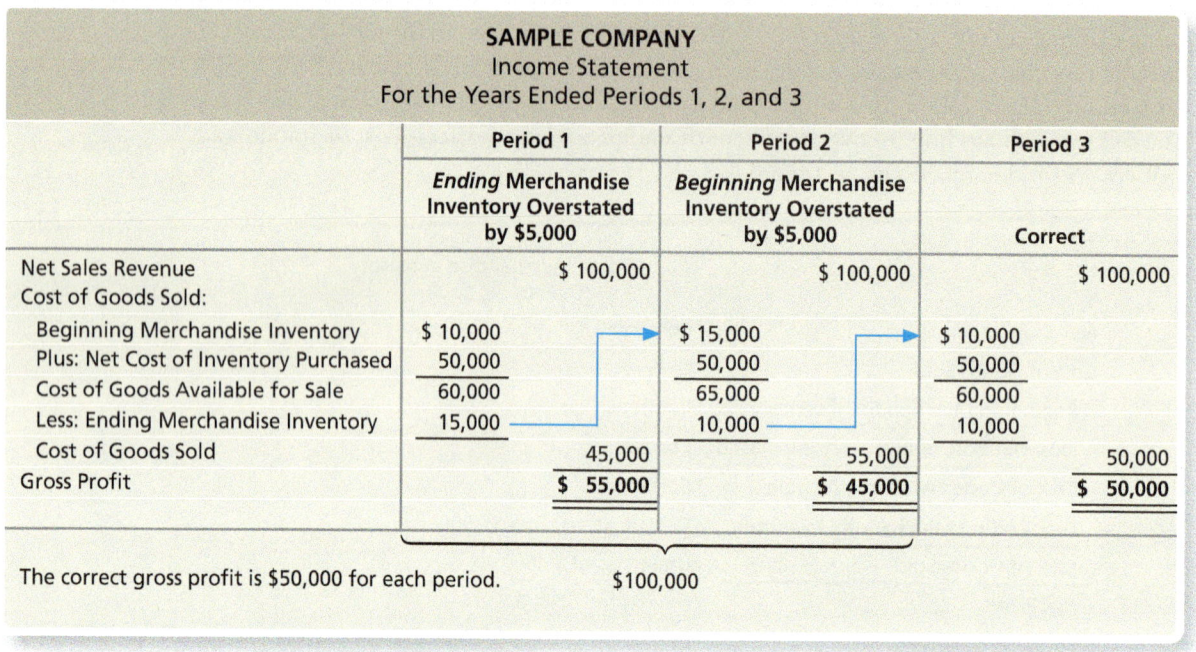

Ending merchandise inventory is *subtracted* to compute cost of goods sold in one period, and the same amount is *added* as beginning merchandise inventory in the next period. Therefore, an inventory error cancels out after two periods. The overstatement of cost of goods sold in Period 2 counterbalances the understatement for Period 1. Thus, total gross profit for the two periods combined is correct. The effects of inventory errors are summarized in Exhibit F:6-11.

Exhibit F:6-11 | Effects of Inventory Errors

SAMPLE COMPANY
Income Statement
For the Years Ended Periods 1 and 2

	Period 1 Cost of Goods Sold	Period 1 Gross Profit and Net Income	Period 2 Cost of Goods Sold	Period 2 Gross Profit and Net Income
Period 1 Ending Merchandise Inventory *overstated*	Understated	Overstated	Overstated	Understated
Period 1 Ending Merchandise Inventory *understated*	Overstated	Understated	Understated	Overstated

ETHICS

Should the inventory be included?

One of A'isha Sowell's main responsibilities at the end of the accounting period is to supervise the count of physical inventory for her employer. She knows that it is important that the business get an accurate count of inventory so that its financial statements are reported correctly. In reviewing the inventory count sheet, she realizes that a large crate of inventory that has already been sold but not yet delivered was included in the count of inventory. The crate has left her employer but is still in transit at fiscal year-end. A'isha does not believe that it should be included because the inventory was sold FOB shipping point. When A'isha went to her supervisor with this information, she was told that she shouldn't worry about it because the error would ultimately correct itself. What should A'isha do?

Solution

Companies whose profits are lagging can be tempted to increase reported income to make the business look more successful. One easy way to do this is to overstate ending inventory. A'isha is correct in her assumption that the inventory should not be included in the physical count of inventory. While this error will ultimately correct itself (in two years), in the current year, the business will be overstating gross profit and net income. This overstatement could cause investors to view the business more favorably than they should. A'isha should stand firm in her decision to not include the inventory in the count.

8. The Shirley's Gourmet Foods' merchandise inventory data for the year ended December 31, 2024, follow:

Net Sales Revenue		$ 48,000
Cost of Goods Sold:		
Beginning Merchandise Inventory	$ 3,360	
Plus: Net Cost of Inventory Purchased	21,280	
Cost of Goods Available for Sale	24,640	
Less: Ending Merchandise Inventory	4,960	
Cost of Goods Sold		19,680
Gross Profit		$ 28,320

Assume that the ending merchandise inventory was accidentally overstated by $1,920. What are the correct amounts for cost of goods sold and gross profit?

Check your answers online in MyLab Accounting or at http://www.pearsonhighered.com/Horngren.

For more practice, see Short Exercise S-F:6-9.   *MyLab Accounting*

HOW DO WE USE INVENTORY TURNOVER AND DAYS' SALES IN INVENTORY TO EVALUATE BUSINESS PERFORMANCE?

Learning Objective 6

Use inventory turnover and days' sales in inventory to evaluate business performance

Businesses strive to sell merchandise inventory quickly because the merchandise inventory generates no profit until it is sold. Further, fast-selling inventory is less likely to become obsolete (worthless) and does not require the business to pay for high storage and insurance costs often associated with keeping inventory on hand. There are two ratios that help businesses monitor their inventory levels: inventory turnover and days' sales in inventory.

Inventory Turnover

> **Inventory Turnover**
> Measures the number of times a company sells its average level of merchandise inventory during a period. Cost of goods sold / Average merchandise inventory.

Companies try to manage their inventory levels such that they will have just enough inventory to meet customer demand without investing large amounts of money in inventory sitting on the shelves gathering dust. **Inventory turnover** measures how rapidly merchandise inventory is sold. It is computed as follows:

> Inventory turnover = Cost of goods sold / Average merchandise inventory
> Average merchandise inventory = (Beginning merchandise inventory + Ending merchandise inventory) / 2

A high rate of turnover indicates ease in selling inventory; a low rate indicates difficulty. For example, an inventory turnover value of 4 means that the company sold its average level of inventory four times—once every three months—during the year. Inventory turnover varies widely with the nature of the business and should be evaluated against industry averages.

Days' Sales in Inventory

> **Days' Sales in Inventory**
> Measures the average number of days that inventory is held by a company. 365 days / Inventory turnover.

Another key measure is the **days' sales in inventory** ratio. This ratio measures the average number of days merchandise inventory is held by the company and is calculated as follows:

> Days' sales in inventory = 365 days / Inventory turnover

Days' sales in inventory also varies widely, depending on the business. A lower days' sales in inventory is preferable because it indicates that the company is able to sell its inventory quickly, thereby reducing its inventory storage and insurance costs, as well as reducing the risk of holding obsolete inventory.

Notice that inventory turnover and days' sales in inventory are expressing the same measure in two different units—times per year and number of days. If a company's inventory turnover is 4 times per year, then its day's sales in inventory is 91.25 days (365 days / 4 times per year). Therefore, companies seek to have a high inventory turnover, which translates into a low days' sales in inventory.

Evaluating Kohl's Corporation

Let's return to **Kohl's Corporation** and evaluate the company's inventory levels using the two ratios discussed. Visit http://www.pearsonhighered.com/Horngren to view a link to Kohl's Corporation's annual report. Presented below are the cost of goods sold and beginning and ending merchandise inventory figures (in millions) from Kohl's Corporation's income statement for the year ended February 2, 2019, and balance sheet on February 2, 2019.

Cost of goods sold (Cost of merchandise sold)	$ 12,199
Beginning merchandise inventory	3,542
Ending merchandise inventory	3,475

Kohl's inventory turnover is 3.48 times per year and is calculated as:

> Inventory turnover = Cost of goods sold / Average merchandise inventory
> = $12,199 / [($3,542 + $3,475) / 2]
> = 3.48 times per year

Its days' sales in inventory is 105 days and is calculated as:

Days sales in inventory = 365 days / Inventory turnover
= 365 days / 3.48
= 105 days

It appears that Kohl's sells its average inventory 3.48 times per year. A high turnover rate is desirable, and an increase in the turnover rate usually means higher profits. In addition, the days' sales in inventory of Kohl's indicates that the company, on average, takes 105 days to sell inventory. This seems a little high for a retail store, but it should be evaluated against the industry average.

9. Opa's Carving Shop had the following financial data for the year ended December 31, 2024:

Cost of Goods Sold	$ 484,000
Beginning Merchandise Inventory	88,800
Ending Merchandise Inventory	111,200

What are the inventory turnover and days' sales in inventory for the year?

Check your answers online in MyLab Accounting or at http://www.pearsonhighered.com/Horngren.

For more practice, see Short Exercise S-F:6-10.   MyLab Accounting

APPENDIX 6A: Merchandise Inventory Costs Under a Periodic Inventory System

HOW ARE MERCHANDISE INVENTORY COSTS DETERMINED UNDER A PERIODIC INVENTORY SYSTEM?

Learning Objective 7

Account for merchandise inventory costs under a periodic inventory system

We described the periodic inventory system briefly in the previous chapter. Accounting is simpler in a periodic inventory system because the company keeps no daily running record of inventory on hand. The only way to determine the ending merchandise inventory and cost of goods sold in a periodic inventory system is to take a physical inventory to count the goods left (on hand)—usually at the end of the fiscal year. The periodic inventory system works well for a small business in which the inventory can be controlled by visual inspection—that is, the inventory usually is not large in size or dollar amount.

To show how the periodic inventory system works, we use the same Smart Touch Learning data that we used for the perpetual inventory system (see Exhibit F:6A-1). We use these data to illustrate FIFO, LIFO, and weighted-average cost. We will not illustrate the specific identification inventory costing method because it is calculated the same way under both the perpetual and periodic inventory systems.

Exhibit F:6A-1 | **Perpetual Inventory Record—Changes in Cost per Unit**

Item: TAB0503

Date	Quantity Purchased	Quantity Sold	Cost per Unit	Quantity on Hand
Aug. 1			$350	2
5	4		$360	6
15		4		2
26	12		$380	14
31		10		4
Totals	16	14		4

Under the periodic method, for all four inventory costing methods, the company doesn't maintain a running balance of inventory; instead, the company will calculate ending merchandise inventory and cost of goods sold at the end of each time period using the cost of goods sold formula:

Beginning Merchandise Inventory
Plus: Net Cost of Inventory Purchased
Cost of Goods Available for Sale
Less: Ending Merchandise Inventory
Cost of Goods Sold

Cost of goods available for sale is always the sum of beginning inventory and net cost of inventory purchased:

Beginning Merchandise Inventory (2 units × $350)	$ 700
Plus: Net Cost of Inventory Purchased (4 units × $360) + (12 units × $380)	6,000
Cost of Goods Available for Sale (18 units)	**$ 6,700**

The different methods—specific identification, FIFO, LIFO, and weighted-average cost—compute different amounts for ending inventory and cost of goods sold. In other words, the $6,700 invested in cost of goods available for sale will be either on the balance sheet in Merchandise Inventory or expensed on the income statement as Cost of Goods Sold. The amount on the balance sheet will be the assumed cost of the four tablets that were not sold and are still on hand. The amount on the income statement will be the assumed cost of the 14 tablets sold.

First-In, First-Out (FIFO) Method

Under the First-In, First-Out (FIFO) method, the cost of goods sold is based on the oldest purchases—that is, the first units purchased are assumed to be the first units sold. The ending inventory comes from the newest—the most recent—purchases. During August, Smart Touch Learning sold 14 units; this leaves 4 units in ending inventory (18 units available for sale less 14 units sold). The ending inventory will be made up of the newest, most recent, purchase on August 26, which cost $380 per unit as illustrated below:

Beginning Merchandise Inventory (2 units × $350)	$ 700
Plus: Net Cost of Inventory Purchased (4 units × $360) + (12 units × $380)	6,000
Cost of Goods Available for Sale (28 units)	6,700
Less: Ending Merchandise Inventory (4 units × $380)	(1,520)
Cost of Goods Sold (2 units × $350) + (4 units × $360) + (8 units × $380)	**$ 5,180**

Notice that the FIFO periodic cost of goods sold is $5,180, exactly the same amount as we calculated using the FIFO perpetual inventory method. The amounts obtained for cost of goods sold and ending merchandise inventory are always the same for FIFO perpetual and FIFO periodic. This occurs because FIFO sells the oldest inventory acquisitions first. Therefore, it does not matter when FIFO is calculated; the earliest purchase will always be the same whether we calculate cost of goods sold on the sale date (perpetual) or at the end of the period (periodic).

The Cost of Goods Sold is made up of the beginning inventory (2 units @ $350) and the earliest costs (4 units @ $360 and 8 units @ $380).

Last-In, First-Out (LIFO) Method

Under the last-in, first-out (LIFO) method, the cost of goods sold is based on the most recent purchases (newest costs)—that is, the last units purchased are assumed to be the first units sold. Ending inventory comes from the oldest costs of the period—in this case, the beginning inventory of two units that cost $350 per unit, plus two from the first purchase on August 5 at $360. LIFO is calculated as follows:

Beginning Merchandise Inventory (2 units × $350)	$ 700
Plus: Net Cost of Inventory Purchased (4 units × $360) + (12 units × $380)	6,000
Cost of Goods Available for Sale (28 units)	6,700
Less: Ending Merchandise Inventory (2 units × $350) + (2 units × $360)	(1,420)
Cost of Goods Sold (12 units × $380) + (2 units × $360)	**$ 5,280**

The Cost of Goods Sold is made up of the most recent purchases (12 units @ $380 and 2 units @ $360).

Weighted-Average Method

In the weighted-average inventory costing method, when using the periodic inventory system, the business computes a single weighted-average cost per unit for the entire period:

> Cost of goods available for sale (entire period) / Number of units available = $6,700 / 18 units*
> = $372.22 per unit

*2 units from beginning inventory + 16 units purchased during August

The single weighted-average cost per unit will be applied to compute ending merchandise inventory and cost of goods sold, as shown:

Beginning Merchandise Inventory (2 units × $350)	$ 700
Plus: Net Cost of Inventory Purchased (4 units × $360) + (12 units × $380)	6,000
Cost of Goods Available for Sale (18 units)	6,700
Less: Ending Merchandise Inventory (4 units × $372.22)	(1,489)
Cost of Goods Sold (14 units × $372.22)	**$ 5,211**

Notice that when using the periodic system with the LIFO and weighted-average methods, the dollar amounts obtained for the ending merchandise inventory and cost of goods sold are different than those obtained with the perpetual inventory system. This is because the perpetual inventory system keeps a running balance of inventory, while the periodic inventory system does not. Under the periodic inventory system, the ending merchandise inventory is determined without regard to when the sales dates of inventory occurred.

10A. Serenity Books has the following transactions in August related to merchandise inventory.

Aug. 1	Beginning merchandise inventory, 10 books @ $15 each
3	Sold 3 books @ $20 each
12	Purchased 8 books @ $18 each
15	Sold 9 books @ $20 each
20	Purchased 4 books @ $20 each
28	Sold 5 books @ $25 each

a. Determine the cost of goods sold and ending merchandise inventory using the FIFO inventory costing method assuming Serenity Books uses the periodic inventory system.

b. Determine the cost of goods sold and ending merchandise inventory using the LIFO inventory costing method assuming Serenity Books uses the periodic inventory system.

c. Determine the cost of goods sold and ending merchandise inventory using the weighted-average inventory costing method assuming Serenity Books uses the periodic inventory system.

Check your answers online in MyLab Accounting or at http://www.pearsonhighered.com/Horngren.

For more practice, see Short Exercises S-F:6A-11 through S-F:6A-13.   **MyLab Accounting**

REVIEW

> Things You Should Know

1. **What are the accounting principles and controls that relate to merchandise inventory?**

   - Consistency principle: Businesses should use the same accounting methods and procedures from period to period.
   - Disclosure principle: A company's financial statements should report enough information for outsiders to make knowledgeable decisions about the company.
   - Materiality concept: A company must perform strictly proper accounting only for significant items.
   - Conservatism: A company should exercise caution in reporting items in the financial statements.
   - Controls over merchandise inventory ensure that inventory purchases and sales are properly authorized and accounted for by the accounting system.

2. **How are merchandise inventory costs determined under a perpetual inventory system?**

   - Four costing methods can be used to determine merchandise inventory costs:
     - Specific identification method—Uses the specific cost of each unit of inventory to determine ending inventory and cost of goods sold.

- **First-in, first-out (FIFO) method**—First costs into inventory are the first costs out to cost of goods sold; ending inventory is based on the costs of the most recent purchases.
- **Last-in, first-out (LIFO) method**—Last costs into inventory are the first costs out to cost of goods sold; ending inventory is based on the costs of the oldest inventory.
- **Weighted-average method**—Method based on the weighted-average cost per unit of inventory after each purchase. Weighted-average cost per unit = Cost of goods available for sale / Number of units available.

3. How are financial statements affected by using different inventory costing methods?

- The FIFO method results in the lowest cost of goods sold and the highest gross profit when costs are rising.
- The LIFO method results in the highest cost of goods sold and the lowest gross profit when costs are rising.
- The weighted-average method generates amounts for cost of goods sold and gross profit that fall between FIFO and LIFO if costs are consistently increasing or decreasing.

4. How is merchandise inventory valued when using the lower-of-cost-or-market rule?

- Lower-of-cost-or-market requires that merchandise be reported in the financial statements at whichever is lower of the following:
  - The historical cost of the inventory
  - The market value of the inventory
- An adjusting entry must be recorded to write down merchandise inventory if the market value is lower than the historical cost.

5. What are the effects of merchandise inventory errors on the financial statements?

- An error in ending merchandise inventory creates a whole string of errors in other related accounts.
- One period's ending merchandise inventory becomes the next period's beginning merchandise inventory.

6. How do we use inventory turnover and days' sales in inventory to evaluate business performance?

- Inventory turnover measures how rapidly merchandise inventory is sold and is calculated as:

  Cost of goods sold / Average merchandise inventory.

- Days' sales in inventory measures the average number of days merchandise inventory is held by the company and is calculated as:

  365 days / Inventory turnover.

7. **How are merchandise inventory costs determined under a periodic inventory system? (Appendix 6A)**
    - Specific identification, FIFO, LIFO, and weighted-average can be used in a periodic inventory system.
    - Specific identification and FIFO will produce the same amounts for ending merchandise inventory and cost of goods sold under both the perpetual and periodic inventory systems.
    - LIFO and weighted-average generally result in different amounts for ending merchandise inventory and cost of goods sold under the perpetual and periodic inventory systems.

> Check Your Understanding

Check your understanding of the chapter by completing this problem and then looking at the solution. Use this practice to help identify which sections of the chapter you need to study more.

Watches R Us specializes in designer watches and leather goods. Watches R Us uses the perpetual inventory system. Assume Watches R Us began June holding 10 wristwatches that cost $50 each. During June, Watches R Us bought and sold inventory as follows:

Jun. 3	Sold 8 units for $100 each.
16	Purchased 10 units at $56 each.
23	Sold 8 units for $100 each.

Requirements

1. Prepare a perpetual inventory record for Watches R Us using the FIFO, LIFO, and weighted-average inventory costing methods. (See Learning Objective 2)
2. Journalize all of Watches R Us's inventory transactions for June under all three costing methods. Assume all sales and purchases are on account. Explanations are not required. (See Learning Objective 2)
3. Show the computation of gross profit for each method. (See Learning Objective 2)
4. Which method maximizes net income? Which method minimizes income taxes? (See Learning Objective 3)

> Solution

1. Perpetual inventory records:

FIFO:

Date	Purchases Quantity	Purchases Unit Cost	Purchases Total Cost	COGS Quantity	COGS Unit Cost	COGS Total Cost	Inventory Quantity	Inventory Unit Cost	Inventory Total Cost
Jun. 1							10 units	× $50	= $500 } $500
3				8 units	× $50	= $400 } $400	2 units	× $50	= $100 } $100
16	10 units	× $56	= $560				2 units 10 units	× $50 × $56	= $100 = $560 } $660
23				2 units 6 units	× $50 × $56	= $100 = $336 } $436	4 units	× $56	= $224 } $224
Totals	10 units		$560	16 units		$836	4 units		$224

LIFO:

Date	Purchases Quantity	Purchases Unit Cost	Purchases Total Cost	COGS Quantity	COGS Unit Cost	COGS Total Cost	Inventory Quantity	Inventory Unit Cost	Inventory Total Cost
Jun. 1							10 units	× $50	= $500 } $500
3				8 units	× $50	= $400 } $400	2 units	× $50	= $100 } $100
16	10 units	× $56	= $560				2 units 10 units	× $50 × $56	= $100 = $560 } $660
23				8 units	× $56	= $448 } $448	2 units 2 units	× $50 × $56	= $100 = $112 } $212
Totals	10 units		$560	16 units		$848	4 units		$212

Weighted-Average:

Date	Purchases Quantity	Purchases Unit Cost	Purchases Total Cost	COGS Quantity	COGS Unit Cost	COGS Total Cost	Inventory Quantity	Inventory Unit Cost	Inventory Total Cost
Jun. 1							10 units	× $50	= $500
3				8 units	× $50	= $400	2 units	× $50	= $100
16	10 units	× $56	= $560				12 units	× $55	= $660 $660 / 12 units = $55
23				8 units	× $55	= $440	4 units	× $55	= $220
Totals	10 units		$560	16 units		$840	4 units		$220

2. Journal entries:

   FIFO:

Date	Accounts and Explanation	Debit	Credit
Jun. 3	Accounts Receivable (8 × $100)	800	
	Sales Revenue		800
3	Cost of Goods Sold (8 × $50)	400	
	Merchandise Inventory		400
16	Merchandise Inventory (10 × $56)	560	
	Accounts Payable		560
23	Accounts Receivable (8 × $100)	800	
	Sales Revenue		800
23	Cost of Goods Sold (2 × $50) + (6 × $56)	436	
	Merchandise Inventory		436

   LIFO:

Date	Accounts and Explanation	Debit	Credit
Jun. 3	Accounts Receivable (8 × $100)	800	
	Sales Revenue		800
3	Cost of Goods Sold (8 × $50)	400	
	Merchandise Inventory		400
16	Merchandise Inventory (10 × $56)	560	
	Accounts Payable		560
23	Accounts Receivable (8 × $100)	800	
	Sales Revenue		800
23	Cost of Goods Sold (8 × $56)	448	
	Merchandise Inventory		448

Weighted-average:

Date	Accounts and Explanation	Debit	Credit
Jun. 3	Accounts Receivable (8 × $100)	800	
	Sales Revenue		800
3	Cost of Goods Sold (8 × $50)	400	
	Merchandise Inventory		400
16	Merchandise Inventory (10 × $56)	560	
	Accounts Payable		560
23	Accounts Receivable (8 × $100)	800	
	Sales Revenue		800
23	Cost of Goods Sold (8 × $55)	440	
	Merchandise Inventory		440

3. Gross profit:

	FIFO	LIFO	Weighted-Average
Net Sales Revenue ($800 + $800)	$ 1,600	$ 1,600	$ 1,600
Less: Cost of Goods Sold ($400 + $436)	836		
($400 + $448)		848	
($400 + $440)			840
Gross Profit	$ 764	$ 752	$ 760

4. FIFO maximizes net income.

   LIFO minimizes income taxes.

> Key Terms

Conservatism (p. 6-3)
Consistency Principle (p. 6-2)
Cost of Goods Available for Sale (p. 6-8)
Days' Sales in Inventory (p. 6-22)
Disclosure Principle (p. 6-2)

First-In, First-Out (FIFO) Method (p. 6-7)
Inventory Costing Method (p. 6-6)
Inventory Turnover (p. 6-22)
Last-In, First-Out (LIFO) Method (p. 6-9)

Lower-of-Cost-or-Market (LCM) Rule (p. 6-17)
Materiality Concept (p. 6-3)
Specific Identification Method (p. 6-6)
Weighted-Average Method (p. 6-11)

> Quick Check

1. Which principle or concept states that businesses should use the same accounting methods and procedures from period to period? *(Learning Objective 1)*
   a. Disclosure
   b. Conservatism
   c. Consistency
   d. Materiality

2. Which inventory costing method assigns to ending merchandise inventory the newest—the most recent—costs incurred during the period? *(Learning Objective 2)*
   a. First-in, first-out (FIFO)
   b. Weighted-average
   c. Specific identification
   d. Last-in, first-out (LIFO)

3. Assume Nile.com began April with 14 units of inventory that cost a total of $266. During April, Nile.com purchased and sold goods as follows: *(Learning Objective 2)*

Apr. 8	Purchase	42 units @ $ 20
14	Sale	35 units @ $ 40
22	Purchase	28 units @ $ 22
27	Sale	42 units @ $ 40

   Under the FIFO inventory costing method and the perpetual inventory system, how much is Nile.com's cost of goods sold for the sale on April 14?
   a. $1,106
   b. $686
   c. $1,400
   d. $700

4. Suppose Nile.com used the weighted-average inventory costing method and the perpetual inventory system. Use the Nile.com data in Question 3 to compute the weighted-average unit cost of the company's inventory on hand at April 8. Round weighted-average unit cost to the nearest cent. *(Learning Objective 2)*
   a. $21.00
   b. $19.75
   c. $19.50
   d. Cannot be determined from the data given

5. Which inventory costing method results in the lowest net income during a period of rising inventory costs? *(Learning Objective 3)*
   a. Weighted-average
   b. Specific identification
   c. First-in, first-out (FIFO)
   d. Last-in, first-out (LIFO)

6. Which of the following is most closely linked to accounting conservatism? *(Learning Objective 4)*
   a. Lower-of-cost-or-market rule
   b. Materiality concept
   c. Disclosure principle
   d. Consistency principle

7. At December 31, 2024, Stevenson Company overstated ending inventory by $36,000. How does this error affect cost of goods sold and net income for 2024? *(Learning Objective 5)*
   a. Overstates cost of goods sold and understates net income
   b. Understates cost of goods sold and overstates net income
   c. Leaves both cost of goods sold and net income correct because the errors cancel each other
   d. Overstates both cost of goods sold and net income

Learning Objective 6

8. Suppose Maestro's had cost of goods sold during the year of $230,000. Beginning merchandise inventory was $35,000, and ending merchandise inventory was $45,000. Determine Maestro's inventory turnover for the year. Round to the nearest hundredth.

   a. 6.57 times per year
   b. 5.75 times per year
   c. 5.11 times per year
   d. 17.39 times per year

Learning Objective 7 Appendix 6A

9A. Suppose Nile.com used the LIFO inventory costing method and the periodic inventory system. Use the Nile.com data in Question 3 to determine Nile.com's cost of goods sold at the end of the month.

   a. $1,568
   b. $133
   c. $1,589
   d. $154

Check your answers at the end of the chapter.

ASSESS YOUR PROGRESS

> Review Questions

1. Which principle states that businesses should use the same accounting methods and procedures from period to period?
2. What does the disclosure principle require?
3. Discuss the materiality concept. Is the dollar amount that is material the same for a company that has annual sales of $10,000 compared with a company that has annual sales of $1,000,000?
4. What is the goal of conservatism?
5. Discuss some measures that should be taken to maintain control over merchandise inventory.
6. Under a perpetual inventory system, what are the four inventory costing methods and how does each method determine ending merchandise inventory and cost of goods sold?
7. When using a perpetual inventory system and the weighted-average inventory costing method, when does the business compute a new weighted-average cost per unit?
8. During periods of rising costs, which inventory costing method produces the highest gross profit?
9. What does the lower-of-cost-or-market (LCM) rule require?
10. What account is debited when recording the adjusting entry to write down merchandise inventory under the LCM rule?
11. What is the effect on cost of goods sold, gross profit, and net income if ending merchandise inventory is understated?
12. When does an inventory error cancel out, and why?
13. How is inventory turnover calculated, and what does it measure?
14. How is days' sales in inventory calculated, and what does it measure?
15A. When using the periodic inventory system, which inventory costing method(s) always produce(s) the same result as when using the perpetual inventory system?
16A. When using the periodic inventory system and weighted-average inventory costing method, when is the weighted-average cost per unit computed?

> Short Exercises

For all short exercises, assume the perpetual inventory system is used unless stated otherwise.

S-F:6-1 Determining inventory accounting principles

Learning Objective 1

Ward Hardware used the FIFO inventory costing method in 2024. Ward plans to continue using the FIFO method in future years. Which accounting principle is most relevant to Ward's decision?

S-F:6-2 Determining inventory costing methods

Learning Objective 2

Ward Hardware does not expect costs to change dramatically and wants to use an inventory costing method that averages cost changes.

Requirements

1. Which inventory costing method would best meet Ward's goal?
2. Assume Ward wanted to expense out the newer purchases of goods instead. Which inventory costing method would best meet that need?

Use the following information to answer Short Exercises S-F:6-3 through S-F:6-6.

Boston Cycles started October with 12 bicycles that cost $42 each. On October 16, Boston purchased 40 bicycles at $68 each. On October 31, Boston sold 34 bicycles for $100 each.

S-F:6-3 Preparing a perpetual inventory record and journal entries—Specific identification

Learning Objective 2

Requirements

1. Prepare Boston Cycle's perpetual inventory record assuming the company uses the specific identification inventory costing method. Assume that Boston sold 10 bicycles that cost $42 each and 24 bicycles that cost $68 each.
2. Journalize the October 16 purchase of merchandise inventory on account and the October 31 sale of merchandise inventory on account.

S-F:6-4 Preparing a perpetual inventory record and journal entries—FIFO

Learning Objective 2

Requirements

1. Prepare Boston Cycle's perpetual inventory record assuming the company uses the FIFO inventory costing method.
2. Journalize the October 16 purchase of merchandise inventory on account and the October 31 sale of merchandise inventory on account.

S-F:6-5 Preparing a perpetual inventory record and journal entries—LIFO

Learning Objective 2

Requirements

1. Prepare Boston Cycle's perpetual inventory record assuming the company uses the LIFO inventory costing method.
2. Journalize the October 16 purchase of merchandise inventory on account and the October 31 sale of merchandise inventory on account.

Learning Objective 2 — **S-F:6-6 Preparing a perpetual inventory record and journal entries—Weighted-average**

Requirements

1. Prepare Boston Cycle's perpetual inventory record assuming the company uses the weighted-average inventory costing method.
2. Journalize the October 16 purchase of merchandise inventory on account and the October 31 sale of merchandise inventory on account.

Note: Short Exercises S-F:6-4, S-F:6-5, and S-F:6-6 must be completed before attempting Short Exercise S-F:6-7.

Learning Objective 3 — **S-F:6-7 Comparing Cost of Goods Sold under FIFO, LIFO, and Weighted-average**

Refer to Short Exercises S-F:6-4 through S-F:6-6. After completing those exercises, answer the following questions:

Requirements

1. Which inventory costing method produced the lowest cost of goods sold?
2. Which inventory costing method produced the highest cost of goods sold?
3. If costs had been declining instead of rising, which inventory costing method would have produced the highest cost of goods sold?

Learning Objective 4 — **S-F:6-8 Applying the lower-of-cost-or-market rule**

Assume that a Best Burger restaurant has the following perpetual inventory record for hamburger patties:

Date	Purchases	Cost of Goods Sold	Merchandise Inventory on Hand
Jul. 9	$ 470		$ 470
22		$ 270	200
31	220		420

At July 31, the accountant for the restaurant determines that the current replacement cost of the ending merchandise inventory is $405. Make any adjusting entry needed to apply the lower-of-cost-or-market rule. Merchandise inventory would be reported on the balance sheet at what value on July 31?

Learning Objective 5 — **S-F:6-9 Determining the effect of an inventory error**

New York Pool Supplies' merchandise inventory data for the year ended December 31, 2025, follow:

Net Sales Revenue		$ 58,000
Cost of Goods Sold:		
Beginning Merchandise Inventory	$ 4,900	
Plus: Net Cost of Inventory Purchased	32,500	
Cost of Goods Available for Sale	37,400	
Less: Ending Merchandise Inventory	4,700	
Cost of Goods Sold		32,700
Gross Profit		$ 25,300

Requirements

1. Assume that the ending merchandise inventory was accidentally overstated by $1,800. What are the correct amounts for cost of goods sold and gross profit?
2. How would the inventory error affect New York Pool Supplies' cost of goods sold and gross profit for the year ended December 31, 2026, if the error is not corrected in 2025?

S-F:6-10 Computing the rate of inventory turnover and days' sales in inventory

Learning Objective 6

Broadway Communications reported the following figures in its annual financial statements:

Cost of Goods Sold	$ 18,400
Beginning Merchandise Inventory	560
Ending Merchandise Inventory	450

Compute the rate of inventory turnover and days' sales in inventory for Broadway Communications. (Round to two decimal places.)

Use the following information to answer Short Exercises S-F:6A-11 through S-F:6A-13.

The periodic inventory records of Flexon Prosthetics indicate the following for the month of July:

Jul. 1	Beginning merchandise inventory	6 units @ $ 60 each
8	Purchase	5 units @ $ 67 each
15	Purchase	10 units @ $ 70 each
26	Purchase	5 units @ $ 85 each

At July 31, Flexon counts four units of merchandise inventory on hand.

S-F:6A-11 Computing periodic inventory amounts—FIFO

Learning Objective 7
Appendix 6A

Compute ending merchandise inventory and cost of goods sold for Flexon using the FIFO inventory costing method.

S-F:6A-12 Computing periodic inventory amounts—LIFO

Learning Objective 7
Appendix 6A

Compute ending merchandise inventory and cost of goods sold for Flexon using the LIFO inventory costing method.

S-F:6A-13 Computing periodic inventory amounts—Weighted-average

Learning Objective 7
Appendix 6A

Compute ending merchandise inventory and cost of goods sold for Flexon using the weighted-average inventory costing method.

> # Exercises

For all exercises, assume the perpetual inventory system is used unless stated otherwise.

Learning Objectives 1, 2

E-F:6-14 Using accounting vocabulary

Match the accounting terms with the corresponding definitions.

1. Specific identification
2. Materiality concept
3. Last-in, first-out (LIFO)
4. Conservatism
5. Consistency principle
6. Weighted-average
7. Disclosure principle
8. First-in, first-out (FIFO)

a. Treats the oldest inventory purchases as the first units sold.
b. Requires that a company report enough information for outsiders to make knowledgeable decisions.
c. Identifies exactly which inventory item was sold. Usually used for higher cost inventory.
d. Calculates a weighted-average cost based on the cost of goods available for sale and the number of units available.
e. Principle whose foundation is to exercise caution in reporting financial statement items.
f. Treats the most recent/newest purchases as the first units sold.
g. Businesses should use the same accounting methods from period to period.
h. Principle that states significant items must conform to GAAP.

Learning Objective 2

1. Ending Merch. Inv. $16.30

E-F:6-15 Comparing inventory methods

Super Mart, a regional convenience store chain, maintains milk inventory by the gallon. The first month's milk purchases and sales at its Freeport, Florida, location follow:

Nov. 2	Purchased 11 gallons @ $2.15 each
6	Purchased 2 gallons @ $2.80 each
8	Sold 6 gallons of milk to a customer
13	Purchased 3 gallons @ $2.85 each
14	Sold 4 gallons of milk to a customer

Requirements

1. Determine the amount that would be reported in ending merchandise inventory on November 15 using the FIFO inventory costing method.
2. Determine the amount that would be reported in ending merchandise inventory on November 15 using the LIFO inventory costing method.
3. Determine the amount that would be reported in ending merchandise inventory on November 15 using the weighted-average inventory costing method. Round all amounts to the nearest cent.

Use the following information to answer Exercises E-F:6-16 through E-F:6-18.

Golf Unlimited carries an inventory of putters and other golf clubs. The sales price of each putter is $119. Company records indicate the following for a particular line of Golf Unlimited's putters:

Date	Item	Quantity	Unit Cost
Nov. 1	Balance	24	$ 53
6	Sale	20	
8	Purchase	30	70
17	Sale	30	
30	Sale	2	

E-F:6-16 Measuring and journalizing merchandise inventory and cost of goods sold—FIFO

Learning Objective 2

1. COGS $3,232

Requirements

1. Prepare a perpetual inventory record for the putters assuming Golf Unlimited uses the FIFO inventory costing method. Then identify the cost of ending inventory and cost of goods sold for the month.
2. Journalize Golf Unlimited's inventory transactions using the FIFO inventory costing method. (Assume purchases and sales are made on account.)

E-F:6-17 Measuring ending inventory and cost of goods sold in a perpetual inventory system—LIFO

Learning Objective 2

1. Ending Merch. Inv. $106

Requirements

1. Prepare Golf Unlimited's perpetual inventory record for the putters assuming Golf Unlimited uses the LIFO inventory costing method. Then identify the cost of ending inventory and cost of goods sold for the month.
2. Journalize Golf Unlimited's inventory transactions using the LIFO inventory costing method. (Assume purchases and sales are made on account.)

E-F:6-18 Measuring ending inventory and cost of goods sold in a perpetual inventory system—Weighted-average

Learning Objective 2

1. COGS $3,236

Requirements

1. Prepare Golf Unlimited's perpetual inventory record for the putters assuming Golf Unlimited uses the weighted-average inventory costing method. Round weighted-average cost per unit to the nearest cent and all other amounts to the nearest dollar. Then identify the cost of ending inventory and cost of goods sold for the month.
2. Journalize Golf Unlimited's inventory transactions using the weighted-average inventory costing method. (Assume purchases and sales are made on account.)

Learning Objectives 2, 3

2. Ending Merch. Inv. $73

E-F:6-19 Comparing amounts for cost of goods sold, ending inventory, and gross profit—FIFO and LIFO

Assume that the Toys Galore store purchased and sold a line of dolls during December as follows:

Dec. 1	Beginning merchandise inventory	13 units @ $ 9 each
8	Sale	8 units @ $ 22 each
14	Purchase	16 units @ $ 14 each
21	Sale	14 units @ $ 22 each

Requirements

1. Compute the cost of goods sold, cost of ending merchandise inventory, and gross profit using the FIFO inventory costing method.
2. Compute the cost of goods sold, cost of ending merchandise inventory, and gross profit using the LIFO inventory costing method.
3. Which method results in a higher cost of goods sold?
4. Which method results in a higher cost of ending merchandise inventory?
5. Which method results in a higher gross profit?

Learning Objectives 2, 3

1. COGS $2,140

E-F:6-20 Comparing cost of goods sold and gross profit—FIFO, LIFO, and weighted-average methods

Assume that AB Tire Store completed the following perpetual inventory transactions for a line of tires:

May 1	Beginning merchandise inventory	16 tires @ $ 65 each
11	Purchase	10 tires @ $ 78 each
23	Sale	12 tires @ $ 88 each
26	Purchase	14 tires @ $ 80 each
29	Sale	18 tires @ $ 88 each

Requirements

1. Compute cost of goods sold and gross profit using the FIFO inventory costing method.
2. Compute cost of goods sold and gross profit using the LIFO inventory costing method.
3. Compute cost of goods sold and gross profit using the weighted-average inventory costing method. (Round weighted-average cost per unit to the nearest cent and all other amounts to the nearest dollar.)
4. Which method results in the largest gross profit, and why?

E-F:6-21 Applying the lower-of-cost-or-market rule to merchandise inventories

Learning Objective 4

Clarmont Resources, which uses the FIFO inventory costing method, has the following account balances at May 31, 2025, prior to releasing the financial statements for the year:

Merchandise Inventory, ending	$ 13,500
Cost of Goods Sold	68,000
Net Sales Revenue	123,000

Clarmont has determined that the current replacement cost (current market value) of the May 31, 2025, ending merchandise inventory is $12,400.

Requirements

1. Prepare any adjusting journal entry required from the information given.
2. What value would Clarmont report on the balance sheet at May 31, 2025, for merchandise inventory?

E-F:6-22 Applying the lower-of-cost-or-market rule to inventories

Learning Objective 4

Nutriset Foods reports merchandise inventory at the lower-of-cost-or-market. Prior to releasing its financial statements for the year ended March 31, 2025, Nutriset's *preliminary* income statement, before the year-end adjustments, appears as follows:

2. GP $66,500

NUTRISET FOODS
Income Statement (Partial)
Year Ended March 31, 2025

Net Sales Revenue	$ 118,000
Cost of Goods Sold	47,000
Gross Profit	$ 71,000

Nutriset has determined that the current replacement cost of ending merchandise inventory is $19,500. Cost is $24,000.

Requirements

1. Journalize the adjusting entry for merchandise inventory, if any is required.
2. Prepare a revised partial income statement to show how Nutriset Foods should report sales, cost of goods sold, and gross profit.

E-F:6-23 Measuring the effect of an inventory error

Learning Objective 5

Hot Bread Bakery reported Net sales revenue of $44,000 and cost of goods sold of $33,000. Compute Hot Bread's correct gross profit if the company made either of the following independent accounting errors. Show your work.

b. Correct GP $19,000

a. Ending merchandise inventory is overstated by $8,000.
b. Ending merchandise inventory is understated by $8,000.

Learning Objective 5

1. 2025, NI $36,500

E-F:6-24 Correcting an inventory error—two years

Nature Foods Grocery reported the following comparative income statements for the years ended June 30, 2025 and 2024:

NATURE FOODS GROCERY
Income Statements
Years Ended June 30, 2025 and 2024

	2025		2024	
Net Sales Revenue		$ 134,000		$ 119,000
Cost of Goods Sold:				
Beginning Merchandise Inventory	$ 17,000		$ 14,000	
Plus: Net Cost of Inventory Purchased	78,000		67,000	
Cost of Goods Available for Sale	95,000		81,000	
Less: Ending Merchandise Inventory	18,000		17,000	
Cost of Goods Sold		77,000		64,000
Gross Profit		57,000		55,000
Operating Expenses		26,000		21,000
Net Income		$ 31,000		$ 34,000

During 2025, Nature Foods Grocery discovered that ending 2024 merchandise inventory was overstated by $5,500.

Requirements

1. Prepare corrected income statements for the two years.
2. State whether each year's net income—before your corrections—is understated or overstated, and indicate the amount of the understatement or overstatement.

Learning Objective 6

E-F:6-25 Computing inventory turnover and days' sales in inventory

Calm Day reported the following income statement for the year ended December 31, 2025:

CALM DAY
Income Statement
Year Ended December 31, 2025

Net Sales Revenue		$ 128,000
Cost of Goods Sold:		
Beginning Merchandise Inventory	$ 9,000	
Plus: Net Cost of Inventory Purchased	62,000	
Cost of Goods Available for Sale	71,000	
Less: Ending Merchandise Inventory	12,200	
Cost of Goods Sold		58,800
Gross Profit		69,200
Operating Expenses		41,600
Net Income		$ 27,600

Requirements

1. Compute Calm Day's inventory turnover rate for the year. (Round to two decimal places.)
2. Compute Calm Day's days' sales in inventory for the year. (Round to two decimal places.)

E-F:6A-26 Comparing ending merchandise inventory, cost of goods sold, and gross profit using the periodic inventory system—FIFO, LIFO, and weighted-average methods

Learning Objective 7
Appendix 6A

2. COGS $513

Assume that Jump Coffee Shop completed the following *periodic* inventory transactions for a line of merchandise inventory:

Jun. 1	Beginning merchandise inventory	17 units @ $ 15 each
12	Purchase	5 units @ $ 19 each
20	Sale	14 units @ $ 37 each
24	Purchase	11 units @ $ 23 each
29	Sale	13 units @ $ 37 each

Requirements

1. Compute ending merchandise inventory, cost of goods sold, and gross profit using the FIFO inventory costing method.
2. Compute ending merchandise inventory, cost of goods sold, and gross profit using the LIFO inventory costing method.
3. Compute ending merchandise inventory, cost of goods sold, and gross profit using the weighted-average inventory costing method. (Round weighted-average cost per unit to the nearest cent and all other amounts to the nearest dollar.)

E-F:6A-27 Computing periodic inventory amounts

Learning Objective 7
Appendix 6A

Consider the data of the following companies which use the periodic inventory system:

Company	Net Sales Revenue	Beginning Merchandise Inventory	Net Cost of Inventory Purchased	Ending Merchandise Inventory	Cost of Goods Sold	Gross Profit
Large	$ 105,000	$ 23,000	$ 59,000	$ 22,000	$ (a)	$ 45,000
Small	(b)	27,000	94,000	(c)	99,000	40,000
Medium	96,000	(d)	58,000	24,000	68,000	(e)
Petite	80,000	8,000	(f)	6,500	(g)	44,000

Requirements

1. Supply the missing amounts in the preceding table.
2. Prepare the income statement for the year ended December 31, 2025, for Large Company, which uses the periodic inventory system. Include a complete heading and show the full computation of cost of goods sold. Large's operating expenses for the year were $12,000.

Problems Group A

For all problems, assume the perpetual inventory system is used unless stated otherwise.

Learning Objectives 2, 3

2. Ending Merch. Inv. $990

P-F:6-28A Accounting for inventory using the perpetual inventory system—FIFO, LIFO, and weighted-average

Fit Gym began January with merchandise inventory of 78 crates of vitamins that cost a total of $4,290. During the month, Fit Gym purchased and sold merchandise on account as follows:

Jan. 5	Purchase	156 crates @ $ 64 each
13	Sale	180 crates @ $ 100 each
18	Purchase	114 crates @ $ 75 each
26	Sale	150 crates @ $ 116 each

Requirements

1. Prepare a perpetual inventory record, using the FIFO inventory costing method, and determine the company's cost of goods sold, ending merchandise inventory, and gross profit.
2. Prepare a perpetual inventory record, using the LIFO inventory costing method, and determine the company's cost of goods sold, ending merchandise inventory, and gross profit.
3. Prepare a perpetual inventory record, using the weighted-average inventory costing method, and determine the company's cost of goods sold, ending merchandise inventory, and gross profit. (Round weighted-average cost per unit to the nearest cent and all other amounts to the nearest dollar.)
4. If the business wanted to pay the least amount of income taxes possible, which method would it choose?

Learning Objectives 2, 3

5. FIFO GP $5,235

P-F:6-29A Accounting for inventory using the perpetual inventory system—FIFO, LIFO, and weighted-average, and comparing FIFO, LIFO, and weighted-average

Steel Mill began August with 50 units of iron inventory that cost $35 each. During August, the company completed the following inventory transactions:

		Units	Unit Cost	Unit Sales Price
Aug. 3	Sale	45		$ 85
8	Purchase	90	$ 54	
21	Sale	85		88
30	Purchase	15	58	

Requirements

1. Prepare a perpetual inventory record for the merchandise inventory using the FIFO inventory costing method.
2. Prepare a perpetual inventory record for the merchandise inventory using the LIFO inventory costing method.
3. Prepare a perpetual inventory record for the merchandise inventory using the weighted-average inventory costing method.

4. Determine the company's cost of goods sold for August using FIFO, LIFO, and weighted-average inventory costing methods.

5. Compute gross profit for August using FIFO, LIFO, and weighted-average inventory costing methods.

6. If the business wanted to maximize gross profit, which method would it select?

P-F:6-30A Accounting principles for inventory and applying the lower-of-cost-or-market rule   **Learning Objectives 1, 4**

Some of M and C Electronics' merchandise is gathering dust. It is now December 31, 2024, and the current replacement cost of the ending merchandise inventory is $24,000 below the business's cost of the goods, which was $97,000. Before any adjustments at the end of the period, the company's Cost of Goods Sold account has a balance of $380,000.

Requirements

1. Journalize any required entries.
2. At what amount should the company report merchandise inventory on the balance sheet?
3. At what amount should the company report cost of goods sold on the income statement?
4. Which accounting principle or concept is most relevant to this situation?

P-F:6-31A Correcting inventory errors over a three-year period and computing inventory turnover and days' sales in inventory   **Learning Objectives 5, 6**

Empire State Carpets' books show the following data. In early 2026, auditors found that the ending merchandise inventory for 2023 was understated by $8,000 and that the ending merchandise inventory for 2025 was overstated by $9,000. The ending merchandise inventory at December 31, 2024, was correct.

	2025		2024		2023	
Net Sales Revenue		$ 220,000		$ 162,000		$ 176,000
Cost of Goods Sold:						
Beginning Merchandise Inventory	$ 22,000		$ 29,000		$ 46,000	
Plus: Net Cost of Inventory Purchased	132,000		90,000		76,000	
Cost of Goods Available for Sale	154,000		119,000		122,000	
Less: Ending Merchandise Inventory	32,000		22,000		29,000	
Cost of Goods Sold		122,000		97,000		93,000
Gross Profit		98,000		65,000		83,000
Operating Expenses		72,000		38,000		48,000
Net Income		$ 26,000		$ 27,000		$ 35,000

Requirements

1. Prepare corrected income statements for the three years.
2. State whether each year's net income—before your corrections—is understated or overstated, and indicate the amount of the understatement or overstatement.
3. Compute the inventory turnover and days' sales in inventory using the corrected income statements for the three years. (Round all numbers to two decimals.)

Learning Objectives 2, 3, 7
Appendix 6A

1. LIFO Ending Merch. Inv. $6,680

P-F:6A-32A Accounting for inventory using the periodic inventory system—FIFO, LIFO, and weighted-average, and comparing FIFO, LIFO, and weighted-average

Futuristic Electronic Center began October with 65 units of merchandise inventory that cost $82 each. During October, the store made the following purchases:

Oct. 3	25 units @ $ 90 each
12	30 units @ $ 90 each
18	35 units @ $ 96 each

Futuristic uses the periodic inventory system, and the physical count at October 31 indicates that 80 units of merchandise inventory are on hand.

Requirements

1. Determine the ending merchandise inventory and cost of goods sold amounts for the October financial statements using the FIFO, LIFO, and weighted-average inventory costing methods.
2. Net sales revenue for October totaled $28,000. Compute Futuristic's gross profit for October using each method.
3. Which method will result in the lowest income taxes for Futuristic? Why? Which method will result in the highest net income for Futuristic? Why?

> Problems Group B

For all problems, assume the perpetual inventory system is used unless stated otherwise.

Learning Objectives 2, 3

2. Ending Merch. Inv. $4,550

P-F:6-33B Accounting for inventory using the perpetual inventory system—FIFO, LIFO, and weighted-average

Exercise World began January with merchandise inventory of 90 crates of vitamins that cost a total of $5,850. During the month, Exercise World purchased and sold merchandise on account as follows:

Jan. 2	Purchase	130 crates @ $ 76 each
5	Sale	140 crates @ $ 100 each
16	Purchase	170 crates @ $ 86 each
27	Sale	180 crates @ $ 104 each

Requirements

1. Prepare a perpetual inventory record, using the FIFO inventory costing method, and determine the company's cost of goods sold, ending merchandise inventory, and gross profit.
2. Prepare a perpetual inventory record, using the LIFO inventory costing method, and determine the company's cost of goods sold, ending merchandise inventory, and gross profit.

3. Prepare a perpetual inventory record, using the weighted-average inventory costing method, and determine the company's cost of goods sold, ending merchandise inventory, and gross profit. (Round weighted-average cost per unit to the nearest cent and all other amounts to the nearest dollar.)

4. If the business wanted to pay the least amount of income taxes possible, which method would it choose?

P-F:6-34B Accounting for inventory using the perpetual inventory system—FIFO, LIFO, and weighted-average, and comparing FIFO, LIFO, and weighted-average

Learning Objectives 2, 3

5. FIFO GP $4,640

Steel It began January with 55 units of iron inventory that cost $35 each. During January, the company completed the following inventory transactions:

		Units	Unit Cost	Unit Sales Price
Jan. 3	Sale	45		$ 83
8	Purchase	75	$ 52	
21	Sale	70		85
30	Purchase	10	55	

Requirements

1. Prepare a perpetual inventory record for the merchandise inventory using the FIFO inventory costing method.
2. Prepare a perpetual inventory record for the merchandise inventory using the LIFO inventory costing method.
3. Prepare a perpetual inventory record for the merchandise inventory using the weighted-average inventory costing method.
4. Determine the company's cost of goods sold for January using FIFO, LIFO, and weighted-average inventory costing methods.
5. Compute gross profit for January using FIFO, LIFO, and weighted-average inventory costing methods.
6. If the business wanted to maximize gross profit, which method would it select?

P-F:6-35B Accounting principles for inventory and applying the lower-of-cost-or-market rule

Learning Objectives 1, 4

Some of L and K Electronics' merchandise is gathering dust. It is now December 31, 2024, and the current replacement cost of the ending merchandise inventory is $32,000 below the business's cost of the goods, which was $98,000. Before any adjustments at the end of the period, the company's Cost of Goods Sold account has a balance of $410,000.

Requirements

1. Journalize any required entries.
2. At what amount should the company report merchandise inventory on the balance sheet?
3. At what amount should the company report cost of goods sold on the income statement?
4. Which accounting principle or concept is most relevant to this situation?

Learning Objectives 5, 6

P-F:6-36B Correcting inventory errors over a three-year period and computing inventory turnover and days' sales in inventory

Antique Carpets' books show the following data. In early 2026, auditors found that the ending merchandise inventory for 2023 was understated by $8,000 and that the ending merchandise inventory for 2025 was overstated by $9,000. The ending merchandise inventory at December 31, 2024, was correct.

	2025	2024	2023
Net Sales Revenue	$212,000	$161,000	$170,000
Cost of Goods Sold:			
Beginning Merchandise Inventory	$22,000	$28,000	$41,000
Plus: Net Cost of Inventory Purchased	131,000	100,000	86,000
Cost of Goods Available for Sale	153,000	128,000	127,000
Less: Ending Merchandise Inventory	34,000	22,000	28,000
Cost of Goods Sold	119,000	106,000	99,000
Gross Profit	93,000	55,000	71,000
Operating Expenses	63,000	28,000	39,000
Net Income	$30,000	$27,000	$32,000

Requirements

1. Prepare corrected income statements for the three years.
2. State whether each year's net income—before your corrections—is understated or overstated, and indicate the amount of the understatement or overstatement.
3. Compute the inventory turnover and days' sales in inventory using the corrected income statements for the three years. (Round all numbers to two decimals.)

Learning Objectives 2, 3, 7
Appendix 6A

P-F:6A-37B Accounting for inventory using the periodic inventory system—FIFO, LIFO, and weighted-average, and comparing FIFO, LIFO, and weighted-average

1. LIFO Ending Merch. Inv. $9,460

Right Now Electronic Center began October with 100 units of merchandise inventory that cost $70 each. During October, the store made the following purchases:

Oct. 3	35 units @ $82 each
12	45 units @ $84 each
18	75 units @ $90 each

Right Now uses the periodic inventory system, and the physical count at October 31 indicates that 130 units of merchandise inventory are on hand.

Requirements

1. Determine the ending merchandise inventory and cost of goods sold amounts for the October financial statements using the FIFO, LIFO, and weighted-average inventory costing methods.
2. Net sales revenue for October totaled $26,000. Compute Right Now's gross profit for October using each method.
3. Which method will result in the lowest income taxes for Right Now? Why? Which method will result in the highest net income for Right Now? Why?

CRITICAL THINKING

> Using Excel

Download Excel problems for this chapter online in MyLab Accounting or at **http://www.pearsonhighered.com/Horngren**.

> Continuing Problem

P-F:6-38 Accounting for inventory using the perpetual inventory system—FIFO

This problem continues the Canyon Canoe Company situation from Chapter F:5. At the beginning of January 2025, Canyon Canoe Company decided to carry and sell T-shirts with its logo printed on them. Canyon Canoe Company uses the perpetual inventory system to account for the inventory. During February 2025, Canyon Canoe Company completed the following merchandising transactions:

Feb. 2	Sold 60 T-shirts at $10 each.
5	Purchased 50 T-shirts at $6 each.
7	Sold 45 T-shirts for $10 each.
8	Sold 20 T-shirts for $10 each.
10	Canyon Canoe Company realized the inventory was running low, so it placed a rush order and purchased 20 T-shirts. The premium cost for these shirts was $7 each.
12	Placed a second rush order and purchased 40 T-shirts at $7 each.
13	Sold 20 T-shirts for $10 each.
15	Purchased 50 T-shirts for $6 each.
20	In order to avoid future rush orders, purchased 150 T-shirts. Due to the volume of the order, Canyon Canoe Company was able to negotiate a cost of $5 each.
21	Sold 40 T-shirts for $10 each.
22	Sold 35 T-shirts for $10 each.
24	Sold 20 T-shirts for $10 each.
25	Sold 45 T-shirts for $10 each.
27	Sold 40 T-shirts for $10 each.

Requirements

1. Assume Canyon Canoe Company began February with 94 T-shirts in inventory that cost $5 each. Prepare the perpetual inventory records for February using the FIFO inventory costing method.
2. Provide a summary for the month, in both units and dollars, of the change in inventory in the following format:

	Number of T-shirts	Dollar Amount
Beginning Balance		
Add: Purchases		
Less: Cost of Goods Sold		
Ending Balance		

> Practice Set

P-F:6-39 Accounting for inventory using the perpetual inventory system—FIFO

This problem continues the Crystal Clear Cleaning problem begun in Chapter F:2 and continued through Chapter F:5.

Consider the December transactions for Crystal Clear Cleaning that were presented in Chapter F:5. (Cost data have been removed from the sale transactions.) Crystal Clear uses the perpetual inventory system.

Dec. 2	Purchased 1,000 units of inventory for $4,000 on account from Sparkle Company on terms 5/10, n/20.
5	Purchased 1,200 units of inventory from Borax on account with terms 4/10, n/30. The total invoice was for $6,000, which included a $300 freight charge.
7	Returned 300 units of inventory to Sparkle from the December 2 purchase.
9	Paid Borax.
11	Sold 500 units of goods to Happy Maids for $5,500 on account with terms n/30.
12	Paid Sparkle.
15	Received 100 units with a sales price of $1,100 of goods back from customer Happy Maids.
21	Received payment from Happy Maids, settling the amount due in full.
28	Sold 500 units of goods to Bridget, Inc. on account for $6,500. Terms 1/15, n/30.
29	Paid cash for utilities of $550.
30	Paid cash for Sales Commission Expense of $214.
31	Received payment from Bridget, Inc., less discount.
31	Recorded the following adjusting entries:
	a. Physical count of inventory on December 31 showed 800 units of goods on hand.
	b. Depreciation, $150.
	c. Accrued salaries expense of $2,100.
	d. Estimated sales returns of $1,500, with cost of $540.
	e. Prepared all other adjustments necessary for December (Hint: You will need to review the adjustment information in Chapter F:3 to determine the remaining adjustments). Assume the cleaning supplies left at December 31 are $50.

Requirements

1. Prepare perpetual inventory records for December for Crystal Clear Cleaning using the FIFO inventory costing method. (Note: You must calculate the cost of goods sold on the 11th, 28th, and 31st (adjusting entry *a*).) Round per unit costs to two decimal places.

2. Journalize the transactions for December 11th, 28th, and 31st (adjusting entry *a* only) using the perpetual inventory record created in Requirement 1.

COMPREHENSIVE PROBLEM

> Comprehensive Problem for Chapters F:5 and F:6

The Davis Lamp Company (DLC), owned by Jenny Davis, is a wholesale company that purchases lamps from the manufacturer and resells them to retail stores. The company has three inventory items: desk lamps, table lamps, and floor lamps. DLC uses a perpetual inventory system—FIFO method. DCL owns land with a building, which is separated into two parts: office space and warehouse space. All expenses associated with the office are categorized as Administrative Expenses. All expenses associated with the warehouse, which is used for the shipping and receiving functions of the company, are categorized as Selling Expenses. In addition to the land and building, DLC also owns office furniture and equipment and warehouse fixtures. The company uses one accumulated depreciation account for all the depreciable assets.

The trial balance for DLC as of September 30, 2024 follows:

DAVIS LAMP COMPANY
Trial Balance
September 30, 2024

Account	Debit	Credit
Cash	$ 457,000	
Accounts Receivable	0	
Merchandise Inventory	126,000	
Office Supplies	275	
Warehouse Supplies	350	
Land	20,000	
Building	780,000	
Office Furniture and Equipment	125,000	
Warehouse Fixtures	260,000	
Accumulated Depreciation		$ 194,000
Accounts Payable		0
Davis, Capital		398,925
Davis, Withdrawals	0	
Sales Revenue		2,654,150
Cost of Goods Sold	1,061,450	
Salaries Expense—Selling	270,000	
Utilities Expense—Selling	32,000	
Supplies Expense—Selling	0	
Depreciation Expense—Selling	0	
Salaries Expense—Administrative	90,000	
Utilities Expense—Administrative	25,000	
Supplies Expense—Administrative	0	
Depreciation Expense—Administrative	0	
Total	$ 3,247,075	$ 3,247,075

Merchandise Inventory as of September 30 consists of the following lamps:

Item	Quantity	Unit Cost	Total Cost
Desk Lamp	2,500	$ 8	$ 20,000
Table Lamp	3,000	18	54,000
Floor Lamp	2,000	26	52,000
Total			**$ 126,000**

During the fourth quarter of 2024, DLC completed the following transactions:

Oct. 1   Purchased lamps on account from Blue Ridge Lights, terms n/30, FOB destination:

    5,000 desk lamps at $9 each
    7,500 table lamps at $19 each
    2,500 floor lamps at $25 each

12   Sold lamps on account to Atlas Home Furnishings, terms 2/10, n/30:

    4,000 table lamps at $45 each

15   Sold lamps on account to Hiawassee Office Supply, terms 2/10, n/30:

    1,000 desk lamps at $20 each

20   Received a check from Atlas Home Furnishings for full amount owed on Oct. 12 sale.

23   Received a check from Hiawassee Office Supply for full amount owed on Oct. 15 sale.

28   Sold lamps on account to Parkway Home Stores, terms 2/10, n/30:

    3,500 table lamps at $45 each
    1,500 floor lamps at $65 each

30   Paid amount due to Blue Ridge Lights from Oct. 1 purchase.

31   Paid salaries, $40,000 (75% selling, 25% administrative).

31   Paid utilities, $2,500 (60% selling, 40% administrative).

Nov. 1   Sold lamps on account to Hiawassee Office Supply, terms 2/10, n/30:

    3,000 desk lamps at $20 each

5   Purchased lamps on account from Blue Ridge Lights, terms n/30, FOB destination:

    5,000 desk lamps at $10 each
    10,000 table lamps at $21 each
    5,000 floor lamps at $27 each

5   Received a check from Parkway Home Stores for full amount owed on Oct. 28 sale.

8   Received a check from Hiawassee Office Supply for full amount owed on Nov. 1 sale.

10   Purchased and paid for supplies: $325 for the office; $675 for the warehouse.

15   Sold lamps on account to Anderson Office Supply, n/30:

    2,000 desk lamps at $20 each

18   Sold lamps on account to Go-Mart Discount Stores, terms 1/10, n/30:

    2,000 table lamps at $45 each
    2,000 floor lamps at $65 each

28   Received a check from Go-Mart Discount Stores for full amount owed on Nov. 18 sale.

30	Paid salaries, $40,000 (75% selling, 25% administrative).	
30	Paid utilities, $2,670 (60% selling, 40% administrative).	
Dec. 5	Paid amount due to Blue Ridge Lights from Nov. 5 purchase.	
15	Received a check from Anderson Office Supply for full amount owed on Nov. 15 sale.	
15	Davis withdrew $50,000 from the business.	

27	Sold lamps on account to Atlas Home Furnishings, terms 2/10, n/30:
	    4,500 desk lamps at $20 each
	    5,000 table lamps at $45 each	

31	Paid salaries, $40,000 (75% selling, 25% administrative).	
31	Paid utilities, $3,200 (60% selling, 40% administrative).	

Requirements

1. Open general ledger T-accounts and enter opening balances as of September 30, 2024.

2. Open inventory records for the three inventory items and enter opening balances as of September 30, 2024. Complete the inventory records using the following transactions: Oct. 1, 12, 15, 28; Nov. 1, 5, 15, 18, and Dec. 27.

3. Record the transactions in the general journal.

4. Post transactions to the general ledger.

5. Prepare adjusting entries for the year ended December 31, 2024, and post to the ledger:

   a. Depreciation, $48,500 (75% selling, 25% administrative).

   b. Supplies on hand: office, $200; and warehouse, $650.

   c. A physical inventory account resulted in the following counts: desk lamps, 1,990; table lamps, 5,995; and floor lamps, 6,000. Update the inventory records.

6. Prepare an adjusted trial balance.

7. Provide a summary for the month, in both units and dollars, of the change in inventory for each item in the following format:

	Desk Lamps		Table Lamps		Floor Lamps	
	Number of lamps	Dollar Amount	Number of lamps	Dollar Amount	Number of lamps	Dollar Amount
Beginning Balance						
Add: Purchases						
Less: COGS						
Ending Balance						

Does the sum of the ending balances in the inventory records match the balance in Merchandise Inventory in the general ledger? If not, review the transactions to find your error.

8. Prepare Davis Lamp Company's multi-step income statement and statement of owner's equity for the year ended December 31, 2024, and a classified balance sheet as of December 31, 2024.

9. Calculate the following ratios for DLC as of December 31, 2024: gross profit percentage, inventory turnover, and days' sales in inventory.
10. Record and post the closing entries.
11. Prepare a post-closing trial balance.

> Tying It All Together Case F:6-1

Before you begin this assignment, review the Tying It All Together feature in the chapter. It will also be helpful if you review Dick's Sporting Goods, Inc.'s 2018 annual report (**https://www.sec.gov/Archives/edgar/data/1089063/000108906319000017/dks-10k_20190202.htm**).

Dick's Sporting Goods, Inc. is headquartered in Pennsylvania and is a leading sporting goods retailer. Dick's offers a variety of high-quality sports equipment, apparel, footwear and accessories. The company sells inventory in their stores (Dick's Sporting Goods, Golf Galaxy, Field & Stream, and True Runner) and online through their Web site.

Requirements

1. On which financial statement would you find Merchandise Inventory? What was the amount of merchandise inventory as of February 2, 2019, and February 3, 2018?
2. On which financial statement would you find Cost of Goods Sold? What does Cost of Goods Sold represent? What was the amount of cost of goods sold for fiscal year ended February 2, 2019, and fiscal year ended February 3, 2018?
3. How could you determine the amount of profit that Dick's Sporting Goods earns when selling its merchandise inventory? What is this amount for the fiscal year ending February 2, 2019? Provide the calculation for gross profit.

> Decision Case F:6-1

Suppose you manage Campbell Appliance. The store's summarized financial statements for 2025, the most recent year, follow:

CAMPBELL APPLIANCE
Income Statement
Year Ended December 31, 2025

Net Sales Revenue	$ 800,000
Cost of Goods Sold	660,000
Gross Profit	140,000
Operating Expenses	100,000
Net Income	$ 40,000

CAMPBELL APPLIANCE
Balance Sheet
December 31, 2025

Assets		Liabilities and Owner's Equity	
Cash	$ 30,000	Accounts Payable	$ 35,000
Inventories	75,000	Note Payable	280,000
Land and Buildings, Net	360,000	Total Liabilities	315,000
		Campbell, Capital	150,000
Total Assets	$ 465,000	Total Liabilities and Owner's Equity	$ 465,000

Assume that you need to double net income. To accomplish your goal, it will be very difficult to raise the sales prices you charge because there is a discount appliance store nearby. Also, you have little control over your cost of goods sold because the appliance manufacturers set the amount you must pay.

Identify several strategies for doubling net income.

> Financial Statement Case F:6-1

The notes are an important part of a company's financial statements, giving valuable details that would clutter the tabular data presented in the statements. This case will help you learn to use a company's inventory notes. Visit **http://www.pearsonhighered .com/Horngren** to view a link to **Target Corporation's** fiscal year ended February 2, 2019, Annual Report. Access the financial statements and related notes, and answer the following questions:

Requirements

1. Which inventory costing method does Target use? How does Target value its inventories? See Note 9.

2. By using the cost of goods sold formula, you can compute net cost of inventory purchased, which is not reported in the Target financial statements. How much was Target's net cost of inventory purchased during the year ended February 2, 2019?

3. Determine Target's inventory turnover and days' sales in inventory for the year ended February 2, 2019. (Round each ratio to one decimal place.) How do Target's inventory turnover and days' sales in inventory compare with **Kohl's Corporation's** for the year ended February 2, 2019? Explain.

> Team Project F:6-1

Obtain the annual reports of as many companies as you have team members—one company per team member. Most companies post their financial statements on their Web sites.

Requirements

1. Identify the inventory costing method used by each company.

2. Compute each company's gross profit percentage, inventory turnover, and days' sales in inventory for the most recent two years.

3. For the industries of the companies you are analyzing, obtain the industry averages for gross profit percentage and inventory turnover from the Risk Management Association, *Annual Statement Studies*; Dun and Bradstreet, *Industry Norms and Key Business Ratios*; or Leo Troy, *Almanac of Business and Industrial Financial Ratios*.

4. How well does each of your companies compare with the average for its industry? What insight about your companies can you glean from these ratios?

> Quick Check Answers

1. c   2. a   3. b   4. b   5. d   6. a   7. b   8. b   9A. c

Accounting Information Systems 7

What Should I Do with All This Paperwork?

Sara Faraday stared at the stack of papers on her desk. It was early January, and her accountant had called to remind her that she needed to submit the business's accounting information so that the tax return could be prepared. Sara is the owner of a successful gourmet kitchen store that sells specialty food and kitchen products and also offers cooking classes and workshops. Sara loves interacting with her customers, whether she's helping them find the perfect kitchen product or teaching them a new technique. What she doesn't like about her business is the overwhelming amount of paperwork required to keep the business records. When she first started her business, she kept track of sales to customers and bills paid in a notebook. Now, though, her business has grown so much that it is no longer efficient to keep track of her accounting records in this manner.

Sara is considering asking her accountant to help her set up a more efficient accounting information system. She wants a system that will save her time and make the recordkeeping process easier. In addition, she would like to find a way to record all of her transactions on the computer so that her business's information is easily accessible. Sara also wants a system that will produce reports, such as financial statements, that can help her make business decisions. She knows that there has to be an easier way to record the transactions than what she is currently doing.

Is There a More Efficient Way?

Before the invention of computers, businesses had to handle all of their accounting transactions manually—that is, one journal entry at a time using paper and pencil. As computer technology progressed, more and more accounting information was processed using an automated system. Now, most businesses use some form of computerized accounting software. It might be a very basic system that handles only accounting information, or it might be a very advanced system that stores not only accounting information, but also information about human resources, production, and customer services. For example, **McCormick & Company, Incorporated** started with a desire to be the global leader in flavor. The company manufactures, markets, and distributes spices, seasoning mixes, condiments, and other flavorful products. In 1889, founder Willoughby M. McCormick sold flavors and extracts door to door. As the business has grown into a multinational company, McCormick & Company had to find a way to keep track of all of the business's accounting information. The company uses a specialized computerized system that integrates all of its lines of business. In this chapter, we explore how accounting information systems, such as the one that McCormick & Company uses, can help a business run more efficiently and effectively.

Chapter 7 Learning Objectives

1. Describe an effective accounting information system
2. Journalize and post sales and cash receipts in a manual accounting information system using special journals and subsidiary ledgers
3. Journalize and post purchases, cash payments, and other transactions in a manual accounting information system using special journals and subsidiary ledgers
4. Describe how transactions are recorded in a computerized accounting information system

WHAT IS AN ACCOUNTING INFORMATION SYSTEM?

Learning Objective 1
Describe an effective accounting information system

Accounting Information System (AIS)
A system that collects, records, stores, and processes accounting data to produce information that is useful for decision makers.

An **accounting information system (AIS)** collects, records, stores, and processes accounting data to produce information that is useful for decision makers. Businesses must have a way to collect and store data for a large number of transactions and then use that data to produce reports that owners, creditors, and managers can use to make decisions. Exhibit F:7-1 shows examples of business transactions and activities that are completed when using an accounting information system.

Exhibit F:7-1 | Business Transactions and AIS Activities

Business Transactions	AIS Activities
Sell merchandise inventory	Receipt of customer order Approval of credit sale Check availability of merchandise inventory Shipment of inventory to customer Processing of sales invoice Receipt of customer payment
Purchase of goods or services	Request for purchase of goods or services Approval of vendor Receipt of goods or services Processing of vendor invoice Payment for goods or services
Payroll	Approval of new employees Collection of time records Preparation and payment of payroll Preparation and payment of payroll taxes

Effective Accounting Information Systems

An effective accounting information system provides the following:

- Control
- Compatibility
- Flexibility
- Relevance
- Positive cost/benefit relationship

Control

An accounting information system must provide adequate controls of the business's assets and data. Internal controls can safeguard a business's assets and reduce the likelihood of fraud and errors. For example, a business needs procedures for making cash payments. An accounting information system creates the structure to encourage adherence to management's procedures.

Compatibility

A compatible system works smoothly with the business's employees and organizational structure. A small business doesn't need a big accounting information system. It could handle its accounting with a software package such as QuickBooks® or Sage® 50 Accounting (formerly called *Peachtree*). But a large company needs a different system—one that can manage multiple branches and track revenues and expenses in all divisions of the business.

Flexibility

An accounting information system must be flexible to accommodate changes in a business over time. Businesses might start selling some new products, or they might expand to new locations. This will require a more complicated accounting information system.

Relevance

An effective accounting information system provides information that is relevant. In other words, it improves decision making and reduces uncertainty. The information produced must be useful to the business in achieving its overall goals.

Positive Cost/Benefit Relationship

Control, compatibility, flexibility, and relevance can be expensive. A business needs a system that gives the most benefit for the least cost. A relatively inexpensive system, such as QuickBooks, may be the most economical way for a business to do its accounting. Or it may be necessary for a business to invest a large amount of cash in a more complicated system. In addition, the business must consider the cost of training employees to use the system and time spent on entering data into the system. The business must invest only in an accounting information system in which the benefits received outweigh the cost of the system.

An accounting information system can be either manual (completed using paper and pencil) or computerized. All the previously discussed features are needed whether the accounting information system is computerized or manual.

Components of an Accounting Information System

An accounting information system has three basic components:

- Source documents and input devices
- Processing and storage
- Outputs

Source Documents and Input Devices

All data must come from **source documents**, which provide the evidence for accounting transactions. Examples of source documents include purchase invoices, bank checks, and sales invoices. Many businesses have paper source documents that require employees to transfer data from the paper source document into the accounting information system. This can be done either by data entry procedures using a keyboard and computer or by using computerized scanning equipment.

Source Document
Provides the evidence and data for accounting transactions.

Most businesses now use computerized accounting information systems to create electronic source documents and capture the data in electronic format. Examples include an electronic invoice and an electronic receiving report.

Source documents also provide control and reliability in an accounting information system. Standardized source documents that require specific data to be input ensure that each transaction is recorded accurately and completely. In addition, prenumbered source documents provide necessary control in a system by automatically assigning a sequential number to each new transaction.

Processing and Storage

Once data has been input into the system, it must be processed. In a manual accounting information system, processing includes journalizing transactions and posting to the accounts. A computerized system, on the other hand, uses software to process transactions. This software reads and edits transaction data. It allows businesses to process transactions without actually requiring employees to journalize and post to the accounts.

A business's data must also be stored. In a manual system, data are contained in paper documents that are often stored in filing cabinets and off-site document warehouses. Computerized systems now allow businesses to keep data on a main computer, called a **server**, that often allows employees to access information from anywhere in the world. The protection and security of a business's data have become increasingly important. Businesses must be aware of threats to their data such as hacking (unauthorized access) and malware (viruses and spyware). Companies are spending increasingly large amounts of cash to ensure that their data and information are secure.

Server
The main computer where data are stored, which can be accessed from many different computers.

Outputs

Outputs are the reports used for decision making, including the financial statements. In a manual system, reports and financial statements must be created using Word documents, Excel spreadsheets, PowerPoint presentations, or other software applications. In a computerized system, the accounting software can generate reports instantaneously that can be easily formatted and used to make business decisions.

TYING IT ALL TOGETHER

McCormick & Company, Incorporated is a global leader in flavor that manufactures, markets, and distributes spices, seasoning mixes, condiments, and other flavorful products. The company's brands include McCormick, Lawry's, and Club House. In addition, the company also markets authentic ethnic brands, such as Zatarain's, Thai Kitchen, and Simply Asia. (You can find McCormick & Company's 2018 annual report at **https://www.sec.gov/Archives/edgar/data/63754/000006375419000017/mkc-11302018x10kxq42018.htm**.)

How do companies such as McCormick & Company rely on information technology systems?

In the annual report, McCormick & Company states that the company relies on its information technology systems to operate its business efficiently. Information technology systems allow companies to manage their business data, communications, supply chain, order entry and fulfillment, and other business processes.

What would happen if McCormick & Company's information technology systems fail to perform adequately?

McCormick & Company states, in its annual report, that a failure in its information technology system could disrupt its business and could result in transaction and reporting errors, processing inefficiencies, and the loss of sales and customers. Ultimately, the failure could cause McCormick & Company's business and results of operations to suffer.

Accounting Information Systems Financial 7-5

Match the benefit of an effective accounting information system with the definition.

Benefit	Definition
1. Control	a. Works smoothly with the business's employees and organization structure
2. Relevance	b. Can accommodate changes in the business over time
3. Flexibility	c. Provides safeguards for a business's assets and reduces the likelihood of fraud and errors
4. Compatibility	
5. Positive cost/benefit relationship	d. Benefits received outweigh the cost of the system
	e. Provides information that will improve decision making and reduce uncertainty

Check your answers online in MyLab Accounting or at http://www.pearsonhighered.com/Horngren.

For more practice, see Short Exercises S-F:7-1 and S-F:7-2. **MyLab Accounting**

HOW ARE SALES AND CASH RECEIPTS RECORDED IN A MANUAL ACCOUNTING INFORMATION SYSTEM?

We will begin by reviewing how transactions are recorded in a manual accounting information system. You may be wondering why we cover manual accounting information systems when many businesses have computerized systems. There are three main reasons:

1. Learning a manual system equips you to work with both manual and computerized systems. The accounting is the same regardless of the system.
2. Few small businesses have computerized all their accounting. Even companies that use QuickBooks or Sage 50 Accounting, two popular small business accounting information systems, keep some manual accounting records.
3. Learning a manual system helps you master accounting.

Learning Objective 2

Journalize and post sales and cash receipts in a manual accounting information system using special journals and subsidiary ledgers

Special Journals

In a manual system, transactions are classified by type. It is inefficient to record all transactions in the general journal, so businesses use special journals. A **special journal** is an accounting journal designed to record a specific type of transaction. Sales on account, cash receipts, purchases on account, and cash payments are treated as four separate categories and, therefore, create the four special journals. For example:

- Sales on account are recorded in a *sales journal*.
- Cash receipts are recorded in a *cash receipts journal*.
- Purchases of inventory and other assets on account are recorded in a *purchases journal*.
- Cash payments are recorded in a *cash payments journal*.
- Transactions that do not fit in any of the special journals, such as adjusting entries, are recorded in the *general journal*, which serves as the "journal of last resort."

Special Journal
An accounting journal designed to record one specific type of transaction.

The five types of transactions, the related journal, and the posting abbreviations used in a manual system are summarized in Exhibit F:7-2.

Exhibit F:7-2 | Manual Accounting Information System

Transaction	Journal	Posting Abbreviation
Sale on account	Sales journal	S
Cash receipt	Cash receipts journal	CR
Purchase on account	Purchases journal	P
Cash payment	Cash payments journal	CP
All others	General journal	J

Subsidiary Ledgers

Subsidiary Ledger
Record of accounts that provides supporting details on individual balances, the total of which appears in a general ledger account.

In addition to special journals, an accounting information system also uses subsidiary ledgers. A **subsidiary ledger** holds individual accounts that support a general ledger account. There are two common subsidiary ledgers: accounts receivable subsidiary ledger and accounts payable subsidiary ledger.

Accounts Receivable Subsidiary Ledger

Accounts Receivable Subsidiary Ledger
A subsidiary ledger that includes an accounts receivable account for each customer that contains detailed information such as the amount sold, received, and owed.

The **accounts receivable subsidiary ledger** includes a receivable account for each customer. The customer name and account balance are detailed in the subsidiary ledger. In addition, the subsidiary ledger contains detailed information such as the amount sold, received, and still due for each customer. The total of the accounts in the accounts receivable subsidiary ledger must equal the Accounts Receivable balance in the general ledger. This is demonstrated in Exhibit F:7-3. The Accounts Receivable balance of $4,319 in the general ledger equals the sum of the accounts in the accounts receivable subsidiary ledger ($935 + $907 + $694 + $1,783).

Exhibit F:7-3 | Accounts Receivable Subsidiary Ledger

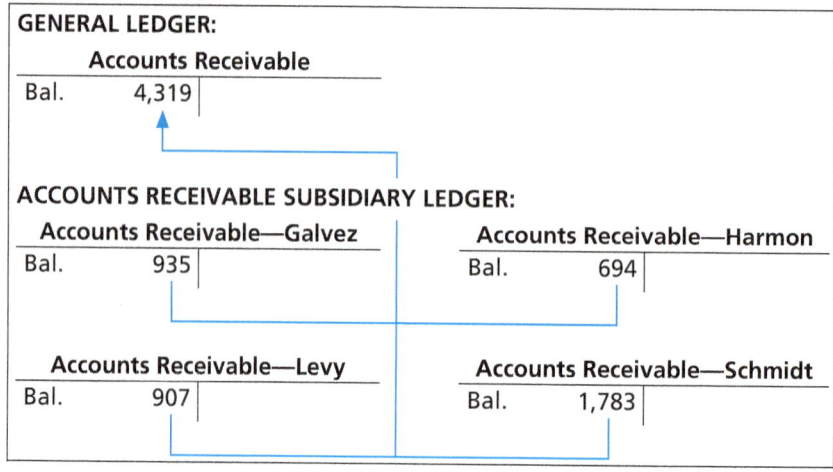

The Accounts Receivable account in the general ledger is called a **control account**. A control account's balance equals the sum of the balances of the accounts in a subsidiary ledger.

Accounts Payable Subsidiary Ledger

To pay debts on time, a company must know how much it owes each supplier. Accounts Payable in the general ledger shows only a single total for the amount owed on account. It does not indicate the amount owed to each vendor. Companies keep an accounts payable subsidiary ledger that is similar to the accounts receivable subsidiary ledger.

The **accounts payable subsidiary ledger** lists vendors in alphabetical order, along with amounts purchased from the vendors, amounts paid to the vendors, and the remaining amounts owed to them. The total of the individual balances in the subsidiary ledger equals the Accounts Payable (control account) balance in the general ledger.

> *Don't confuse the terms customers and vendors. Remember that a company sells to customers and purchases from vendors.*

Control Account
An account whose balance equals the sum of the balances in a group of related accounts in a subsidiary ledger.

Accounts Payable Subsidiary Ledger
A subsidiary ledger that includes an accounts payable account for each vendor that contains detailed information such as the amount purchased, paid, and owed.

The Sales Journal

Most merchandisers sell merchandise inventory on account. These credit sales are entered in the **sales journal**. The sales journal is used when recording the sale of merchandise inventory *on account*. The sale of merchandise inventory for cash is not recorded in the sales journal, but instead, it is recorded in the cash receipts journal. In addition, credit sales of assets other than merchandise inventory—for example, buildings—occur infrequently and are not recorded in the sales journal. They are, instead, recorded in the general journal.

Sales Journal
Special journal used to record credit sales.

Recording Sales on Account Transactions

Exhibit F:7-4 (on the next page) illustrates a sales journal (Panel A) and the related posting to the ledgers (Panel B). When a business completes a sale, the accountant enters the following information in the sales journal:

- Date
- Invoice number
- Customer name
- Transaction amount

Exhibit F:7-4 | Sales Journal with Posting

PANEL A—Sales Journal:

Sales Journal — Page 3

Date	Invoice No.	Customer Account Debited	Post. Ref.	Accounts Receivable DR Sales Revenue CR	Cost of Goods Sold DR Merchandise Inventory CR
2024					
Nov. 2	422	Maria Galvez	✓	935	505
13	423	Brent Harmon	✓	694	361
18	424	Susan Levy	✓	907	517
27	425	Clay Schmidt	✓	1,783	431
Nov. 30		Total		4,319	1,814
				(115/410)	(511/131)

- Individual accounts receivable are posted daily.
- Totals are posted at the end of the month.
- Totals are posted at the end of the month.

PANEL B—Posting to the Ledgers:

Accounts Receivable Subsidiary Ledger

Maria Galvez

Date	Post. Ref.	Debit	Credit	Balance Debit	Balance Credit
Nov. 2	S.3	935		935	

Brent Harmon

Date	Post. Ref.	Debit	Credit	Balance Debit	Balance Credit
Nov. 13	S.3	694		694	

Susan Levy

Date	Post. Ref.	Debit	Credit	Balance Debit	Balance Credit
Nov. 18	S.3	907		907	

Clay Schmidt

Date	Post. Ref.	Debit	Credit	Balance Debit	Balance Credit
Nov. 27	S.3	1,783		1,783	

General Ledger

Accounts Receivable — No. 115

Date	Post. Ref.	Debit	Credit	Balance Debit	Balance Credit
Nov. 30	S.3	4,319		4,319	

Merchandise Inventory — No. 131

Date	Post. Ref.	Debit	Credit	Balance Debit	Balance Credit
Nov. 1	Bal.			3,885	
30	S.3		1,814	2,071	

Sales Revenue — No. 410

Date	Post. Ref.	Debit	Credit	Balance Debit	Balance Credit
Nov. 30	S.3		4,319		4,319

Cost of Goods Sold — No. 511

Date	Post. Ref.	Debit	Credit	Balance Debit	Balance Credit
Nov. 30	S.3	1,814		1,814	

Consider the first transaction in Panel A. On November 2, the business sold merchandise inventory on account, terms 15/20, n/30, to Maria Galvez for $1,100 with a cost of $505. The invoice number is 422. In Chapter F:5, you learned that this transaction was recorded as follows when using the general journal:

Date	Accounts and Explanation	Debit	Credit
Nov. 2	Accounts Receivable	935	
	Sales Revenue ($1,100 − ($1,100 × 0.15))		935
	Sale on account less discount.		
2	Cost of Goods Sold	505	
	Merchandise Inventory		505
	Recorded the cost of goods sold.		

$\dfrac{A\uparrow}{\text{Accounts Receivable}\uparrow} \Big\} = \Big\{ \dfrac{L}{} + \dfrac{E\uparrow}{\text{Sales Revenue}\uparrow}$

$\dfrac{A\downarrow}{\text{Merchandise Inventory}\downarrow} \Big\} = \Big\{ \dfrac{L}{} + \dfrac{E\downarrow}{\text{Cost of Goods Sold}\uparrow}$

When using special journals, instead of recording this transaction in the general journal, the business records the transaction in the sales journal. All of the information related to the sale appears on a single line in the sales journal as follows:

Sales Journal — Page 3

Date	Invoice No.	Customer Account Debited	Post. Ref.	Accounts Receivable DR Sales Revenue CR	Cost of Goods Sold DR Merchandise Inventory CR
2024					
Nov. 2	422	Maria Galvez		935	505

- The Post. Ref. column is not used until the transaction is posted.
- This part of the journal records the sales revenue and associated receivable.
- This part of the journal records the expense and the reduction of merchandise inventory.

The entry records the sales revenue and associated accounts receivable by entering the net amount of the sale, $935, in the Accounts Receivable DR, Sales Revenue CR column. The entry also records the expense of the sale and the reduction of merchandise inventory by recording the cost of the sale, $505, in the Cost of Goods Sold DR, Merchandise Inventory CR column. By using a sales journal, the recording of sales is streamlined, thus saving a significant amount of time.

> *It's important to remember that a transaction is recorded in either the general journal or a special journal, but not in both. We are illustrating the general journal entry as a teaching tool to help you understand how the entry is recorded in the special journal. Transactions are not recorded in both journals. To do so would be to record the entry twice.*

This business, like most other companies, uses a perpetual inventory system. Throughout this chapter, we illustrate the perpetual inventory system. When recording a sale, the business must record the Cost of Goods Sold and the decrease in Merchandise Inventory. If the business instead used a periodic inventory system, the sales journal would not need the last column (Cost of Goods Sold DR, Merchandise Inventory CR) because there is no entry recorded to Cost of Goods Sold and Merchandise Inventory at the time of the sale.

In the sales journal that we are using in this example, there are only two columns used for dollar amounts. One column records the sales revenue and accounts receivable, and the other column records the expense of the sale. Businesses that collect sales tax would need to modify the sales journal shown to include an additional column for Sales Taxes Payable. The modified sales journal would have the following headings:

					Sales Journal			Page 3
Date	Invoice No.	Customer Account Debited	Post. Ref.	Accounts Receivable DR	Sales Taxes Payable CR	Sales Revenue CR	Cost of Goods Sold DR Merchandise Inventory CR	

Each business will modify its sales journal to fit the types of sales it makes. Remember, though, that only sales on account are recorded in the sales journal.

Posting from the Sales Journal

Entries in the sales journal are posted to both the accounts receivable subsidiary ledger and the general ledger.

Posting from the Sales Journal to the Accounts Receivable Subsidiary Ledger Individual accounts receivable are posted daily from the sales journal to the accounts receivable subsidiary ledger. For example, on November 2, the accountant posts the $935 receivable to the individual accounts receivable for Maria Galvez. Entries in the Accounts Receivable DR, Sales Revenue CR column in the sales journal are posted daily to the subsidiary ledger to keep a current record of the amount receivable from each customer.

After posting to the subsidiary ledger, the accountant enters a check mark in the posting reference column of the sales journal (see Exhibit F:7-4). That lets the business know that the transaction was posted to Galvez's account.

Posting from the Sales Journal to the General Ledger At the end of the month, the accountant totals (commonly called *footing*) the Accounts Receivable DR, Sales Revenue CR, and Cost of Goods Sold DR, Merchandise Inventory CR columns. The totals of these columns are posted from the sales journal to the general ledger.

In Exhibit F:7-4 (Panel A), November's credit sales total $4,319. The $4,319 is posted to the Accounts Receivable and Sales Revenue accounts in the general ledger. The account numbers of each account are then printed beneath the total in the sales journal. In Panel B of Exhibit F:7-4, the account number for Accounts Receivable is 115 and the account number for Sales Revenue is 410. Entering these account numbers in the sales journal shows that the $4,319 has been posted to the two accounts.

The debit to Cost of Goods Sold and the credit to Merchandise Inventory for the monthly total of $1,814 are also posted at the end of the month. After posting, these accounts' numbers are entered beneath the total to show that Cost of Goods Sold and Merchandise Inventory have been updated.

As the accountant posts to the ledgers, the journal page number and journal name abbreviation are entered in the ledger account to show the source of the data. All transaction data in Exhibit F:7-4 originated on page 3 of the sales journal, so all posting references are S.3. "S" indicates sales journal. After posting, the Accounts Receivable balance in the general ledger should equal the sum of the individual customer balances in the subsidiary ledger.

Trace all the postings in Exhibit F:7-4. The way to learn an accounting information system is to study the flow of data. The arrows indicate the direction of the information.

The Cash Receipts Journal

Cash Receipts Journal
Special journal used to record cash receipts.

All businesses have lots of cash transactions, and therefore a **cash receipts journal** comes in handy. The cash receipts journal is a special journal that is used to record cash receipts.

Exhibit F:7-5 illustrates the cash receipts journal. Every transaction recorded in this journal is a cash receipt.

Accounting Information Systems Financial 7-11

Exhibit F:7-5 | Cash Receipts Journal with Posting

PANEL A—Cash Receipts Journal:

Cash Receipts Journal — Page 5

Date	Account Credited	Post Ref.	Cash DR	Accounts Receivable CR	Sales Revenue CR	Sales Discounts Forfeited CR	Other Accounts CR	Cost of Goods Sold DR Merchandise Inventory CR
2024								
Nov. 6			517		517			290
11	Note Payable—First Bank	221	1,000				1,000	
14	Maria Galvez	✓	935	935				
19			853		853			426
22	Brent Harmon	✓	700	694		6		
25	Interest Revenue	460	762				762	
28			1,802		1,802			991
Nov. 30	Totals		6,569	1,629	3,172	6	1,762	1,707
			(101)	(115)	(410)	(420)	(X)	(511/131)

- Totals are posted at the end of the month.
- Individual accounts receivable are posted daily.
- Total is not posted.
- Total is posted at the end of the month.
- Individual amounts are posted at the end of the month.

PANEL B—Posting to the Ledgers:

Accounts Receivable Subsidiary Ledger

Maria Galvez

Date	Post. Ref.	Debit	Credit	Balance Debit	Balance Credit
Nov. 2	S.3	935		935	
14	CR.5		935	0	

Brent Harmon

Date	Post. Ref.	Debit	Credit	Balance Debit	Balance Credit
Nov. 13	S.3	694		694	
22	CR.5		694	0	

Susan Levy

Date	Post. Ref.	Debit	Credit	Balance Debit	Balance Credit
Nov. 18	S.3	907		907	

Clay Schmidt

Date	Post. Ref.	Debit	Credit	Balance Debit	Balance Credit
Nov. 27	S.3	1,783		1,783	

General Ledger

Cash — No. 101

Date	Post. Ref.	Debit	Credit	Balance Debit	Balance Credit
Nov. 30	CR.5	6,569		6,569	

Accounts Receivable — No. 115

Date	Post. Ref.	Debit	Credit	Balance Debit	Balance Credit
Nov. 30	S.3	4,319		4,319	
30	CR.5		1,629	2,690	

Merchandise Inventory — No. 131

Date	Post. Ref.	Debit	Credit	Balance Debit	Balance Credit
Nov. 1	Bal.			3,885	
30	S.3		1,814	2,071	
30	CR.5		1,707	364	

Note Payable—First Bank — No. 221

Date	Post. Ref.	Debit	Credit	Balance Debit	Balance Credit
Nov. 11	CR.5		1,000		1,000

Sales Revenue — No. 410

Date	Post. Ref.	Debit	Credit	Balance Debit	Balance Credit
Nov. 30	S.3		4,319		4,319
30	CR.5		3,172		7,491

Sales Discounts Forfeited — No. 420

Date	Post. Ref.	Debit	Credit	Balance Debit	Balance Credit
Nov. 30	CR.5		6		6

Interest Revenue — No. 460

Date	Post. Ref.	Debit	Credit	Balance Debit	Balance Credit
Nov. 25	CR.5		762		762

Cost of Goods Sold — No. 511

Date	Post. Ref.	Debit	Credit	Balance Debit	Balance Credit
Nov. 30	S.3	1,814		1,814	
30	CR.5	1,707		3,521	

The main sources of cash are collections on account and cash sales. Collections on account are recorded in the Accounts Receivable CR column and the Cash DR column. Cash sales are recorded in the Sales Revenue CR column, the Cash DR column, and Cost of Goods Sold DR, Merchandise Inventory CR column. The cash receipts journal also has an Other Accounts CR column that is used to record miscellaneous cash receipt transactions and a Sales Discounts Forfeited CR column used to record sales discounts forfeited.

Recording Cash Receipt Transactions

In Exhibit F:7-5, the first cash receipt occurred on November 6 and was a cash sale for $517 (cost of goods sold, $290). If the transaction had been recorded in the general journal, the following entries would have been recorded:

$\dfrac{A\uparrow}{\text{Cash}\uparrow} \Big\} = \Big\{ \dfrac{L}{} + \dfrac{E\uparrow}{\text{Sales Revenue}\uparrow}$

$\dfrac{A\downarrow}{\text{Merchandise Inventory}\downarrow} \Big\} = \Big\{ \dfrac{L}{} + \dfrac{E\downarrow}{\text{Cost of Goods Sold}\uparrow}$

Date	Accounts and Explanation	Debit	Credit
Nov. 6	Cash	517	
	Sales Revenue		517
	Cash sale.		
6	Cost of Goods Sold	290	
	Merchandise Inventory		290
	Recorded the cost of goods sold.		

By recording the transaction in the cash receipts journal instead, the entries can be recorded on one line. Observe the debit to Cash and the credit to Sales Revenue ($517) and the debit to Cost of Goods Sold and credit to Merchandise Inventory ($290) for the cost of the merchandise sold.

On November 11, the business borrowed $1,000 from First Bank. If the transaction had been recorded in the general journal, the following entry would have been made:

$\dfrac{A\uparrow}{\text{Cash}\uparrow} \Big\} = \Big\{ \dfrac{L\uparrow}{\text{Notes Payable}\uparrow} + \dfrac{E}{}$

Date	Accounts and Explanation	Debit	Credit
Nov. 11	Cash	1,000	
	Note Payable—First Bank		1,000
	Received cash in exchange for note.		

By recording it in the cash receipts journal instead, the accountant would record the $1,000 in the Cash DR column. The Other Accounts CR column is used for the Notes Payable credit because there is no specific credit column for borrowings. For this transaction, the account title, Note Payable—First Bank, is entered in the Account Credited column. The Other Accounts CR column is used when a transaction involves a credit entry that is not listed in the headings (columns) of the cash receipts journal. The entry on November 25 is another example. On November 25, the business received $762 cash of interest revenue. The cash receipts journal does not include a column for credits to interest revenue; therefore, the Other Accounts CR column must be used and the credit account must be written in the Account Credited column.

On November 14, the business collected $935 from Maria Galvez. Back on November 2, the business sold $1,100 of merchandise to Galvez, terms 15/20, n/30 and recorded the net sale in the sales journal. This credit sale allowed a $165 discount for prompt payment, and Galvez paid within the discount period. The business records this cash receipt in the cash receipts journal by debiting Cash for $935 and by crediting Accounts Receivable for $935. The customer's name appears in the Account Credited column.

The business does not have to deal with the sales discount associated with the Galvez sale because the sale was recorded net of discount at the time of sale. Only when a customer does not take advantage of the discount will the business use the Sales Discounts Forfeited CR column. Let's look at Brent Harmon as an example. On November 22, the business collected $700 from Brent Harmon representing the $694 he owed plus $6 sales discounts forfeited. Because Harmon did not pay within the discount period, he must pay more than the amount of the receivable. The transaction is recorded in the cash receipts journal as a $700 Cash DR, $694 Accounts Receivable CR, and $6 Sales Discounts Forfeited CR.

Posting from the Cash Receipts Journal

As with the sales journal, entries in the cash receipts journal are posted daily to the accounts receivable subsidiary ledger and monthly to the general ledger.

Posting from the Cash Receipts Journal to the Accounts Receivable Subsidiary Ledger
Amounts from the cash receipts journal are posted to the accounts receivable subsidiary ledger daily. The postings are credits. Trace the $935 credit to Maria Galvez's account. It reduces her balance to zero. The receipt from Brent Harmon reduces his balance to $0. After posting, the accountant enters a check mark in the posting reference column of the cash receipts journal and shows the CR.5 posting reference in the subsidiary ledger. CR.5 signifies that the posting is transferred from the cash receipts journal, page 5.

> The posting reference CR.5 should not be confused with the abbreviation for credit, CR. The posting reference for the cash receipts journal always includes a page reference while the abbreviation for credit does not.

Posting from the Cash Receipts Journal to the General Ledger At the end of the month, each column in the cash receipts journal is totaled. The equality of the debits and credits is verified by comparing the sum of all debit columns to the sum of all credit columns.

Debit Columns		Credit Columns	
Cash	$ 6,569	Accounts Receivable	$ 1,629
Cost of Goods Sold	1,707	Sales Revenue	3,172
		Sales Discounts Forfeited	6
		Other Accounts	1,762
		Merchandise Inventory	1,707
Total	$ 8,276		$ 8,276

All columns, except for the Other Accounts CR column, are posted in total to the general ledger. For example, the total for Cash ($6,569) is posted as a debit in the Cash account in the general ledger. After posting, the account number is printed below the column total in the cash receipts journal. The account number for Cash (101) appears below the column total, and likewise for the other column totals. The journal reference (CR) and page number (5) are shown in the general ledger as reference of the posting. Follow the arrows in Exhibit F:7-5, which track the posted amounts.

The column total for Other Accounts CR is *not* posted. Instead, these credits are posted individually. In Exhibit F:7-5, the November 11 transaction reads "Note Payable—First Bank." This $1,000 credit entry will need to be posted individually to the Note Payable—First Bank account in the general ledger. The account number (221) in the Post. Ref. column shows that the transaction amount was posted individually. The letter X below the column means that the column total was *not* posted.

7-14 Financial chapter 7

After posting, the sum of the individual ending balances in the accounts receivable subsidiary ledger equals the ending balance of Accounts Receivable in the general ledger, as follows:

GENERAL LEDGER	
Accounts Receivable debit balance	$ 2,690

SUBSIDIARY LEDGER: ACCOUNTS RECEIVABLE	
Customer	Balance
Maria Galvez	$ 0
Brent Harmon	0
Susan Levy	907
Clay Schmidt	1,783
Total Accounts Receivable	$ 2,690

These should be equal.

6. Evenson Co. sold merchandise inventory on account, terms n/30, to Brain Crain, $300. The cost of the goods sold was $240. What special journal should the transaction be recorded in, and what is the column used for the $300?

Check your answer online in MyLab Accounting or at http://www.pearsonhighered.com/Horngren.

For more practice, see Short Exercises S-F:7-3 through S-F:7-7. MyLab Accounting

HOW ARE PURCHASES, CASH PAYMENTS, AND OTHER TRANSACTIONS RECORDED IN A MANUAL ACCOUNTING INFORMATION SYSTEM?

Learning Objective 3

Journalize and post purchases, cash payments, and other transactions in a manual accounting information system using special journals and subsidiary ledgers

Purchases Journal

Special journal used to record all purchases of merchandise inventory, office supplies, and other assets on account.

In the previous section, you learned that when using a manual accounting information system, sales on account are recorded in the sales journal and cash receipts are recorded in the cash receipts journal. We now turn our attention to purchases and cash payments.

The Purchases Journal

A merchandising business purchases merchandise inventory and other items, such as office supplies, equipment, and furniture, on account. The **purchases journal** handles these transactions plus other purchases incurred *on account*. Cash purchases are not recorded in the purchases journal; instead, they are recorded in the cash payments journal.

Exhibit F:7-6 illustrates a purchases journal (Panel A) and posting to the ledgers (Panel B). The purchases journal has special columns for:

- Credits to Accounts Payable
- Debits to Merchandise Inventory, Office Supplies, and Other Accounts

The Other Accounts DR columns are used for purchases on account of items other than merchandise inventory and office supplies. This business uses a perpetual inventory system. In a periodic inventory system, the Merchandise Inventory DR column would be replaced with a column titled Purchases DR.

Accounting Information Systems Financial 7-15

Exhibit F:7-6 | Purchases Journal with Posting

PANEL A—Purchases Journal:

								Purchases Journal		Page 8
								Other Accounts DR		
Date	Vendor Account Credited	Terms	Post. Ref.	Accounts Payable CR	Merchandise Inventory DR	Office Supplies DR	Account Title	Post. Ref.	Amount	
2024										
Nov. 2	Hanes Textiles	3/15, n/30	✓	700	700					
5	Pioneer Plastics	n/30	✓	319	319					
9	City Office Supply	2/10, n/30	✓	440			Equipment	191	440	
12	Advanced Printing	n/30	✓	236	236					
13	Hanes Textiles	3/15, n/30	✓	451	451					
19	City Office Supply	2/10, n/30	✓	103		103				
23	O'Leary Furniture	n/60	✓	627			Furniture	181	627	
Nov. 30	Totals			2,876	1,706	103			1,067	
				(210)	(131)	(161)			(X)	

- Individual accounts payable are posted daily.
- Totals are posted at the end of the month.
- Total is not posted.
- Individual amounts are posted at the end of the month.

PANEL B—Posting to the Ledgers:

Accounts Payable Subsidiary Ledger

Advanced Printing

Date	Post. Ref.	Debit	Credit	Balance Debit	Balance Credit
Nov. 12	P.8		236		236

City Office Supply

Date	Post. Ref.	Debit	Credit	Balance Debit	Balance Credit
Nov. 9	P.8		440		440
19	P.8		103		543

Hanes Textiles

Date	Post. Ref.	Debit	Credit	Balance Debit	Balance Credit
Nov. 2	P.8		700		700
13	P.8		451		1,151

O'Leary Furniture

Date	Post. Ref.	Debit	Credit	Balance Debit	Balance Credit
Nov. 23	P.8		627		627

Pioneer Plastics

Date	Post. Ref.	Debit	Credit	Balance Debit	Balance Credit
Nov. 5	P.8		319		319

General Ledger

Merchandise Inventory No. 131

Date	Post. Ref.	Debit	Credit	Balance Debit	Balance Credit
Nov. 1	Bal.			3,885	
30	S.3		1,814	2,071	
30	CR.5		1,707	364	
30	P.8	1,706		2,070	

Office Supplies No. 161

Date	Post. Ref.	Debit	Credit	Balance Debit	Balance Credit
Nov. 30	P.8	103		103	

Furniture No. 181

Date	Post. Ref.	Debit	Credit	Balance Debit	Balance Credit
Nov. 23	P.8	627		627	

Equipment No. 191

Date	Post. Ref.	Debit	Credit	Balance Debit	Balance Credit
Nov. 9	P.8	440		440	

Accounts Payable No. 210

Date	Post. Ref.	Debit	Credit	Balance Debit	Balance Credit
Nov. 30	P.8		2,876		2,876

Recording Purchases on Account Transactions

Let's begin by looking at the first transaction. On November 2, the business purchased merchandise inventory costing $700 from Hanes Textiles on account. If the transaction had been recorded in the general journal, the following entry would have been recorded:

$$\dfrac{A\uparrow}{\text{Merchandise Inventory}\uparrow} \Bigg\} = \Bigg\{ \dfrac{L\uparrow}{\text{Accounts Payable}\uparrow} + E$$

Date	Accounts and Explanation	Debit	Credit
Nov. 2	Merchandise Inventory	700	
	Accounts Payable		700
	Purchased inventory on account.		

By recording the entry in the purchases journal, the transaction can be recorded on one line. The vendor's name (Hanes Textiles) is entered in the Vendor Account Credited column. The purchase terms of 3/15, n/30 are also entered to show the due date and the discount available. Accounts Payable is credited for the transaction amount, and Merchandise Inventory is debited.

Note the November 9 purchase of equipment on account from City Office Supply. The purchases journal holds no column for equipment, so the business uses the Other Accounts DR columns. Because this was a credit purchase, the accountant enters the vendor name (City Office Supply) in the Vendor Account Credited column and Equipment in the Account Title column.

Posting from the Purchases Journal

Entries from the purchases journal are posted daily to the accounts payable subsidiary ledger and monthly to the general ledger.

Posting from the Purchases Journal to the Accounts Payable Subsidiary Ledger Individual accounts payable are posted daily from the purchases journal to the accounts payable subsidiary ledger. This allows the business to always have a current record of the accounts payable for each vendor. For example, on November 2, the business would post the $700 accounts payable credit to the Hanes Textiles account in the accounts payable subsidiary ledger. After posting, the accountant enters a check mark in the posting reference column of the purchases journal to indicate that the amount was posted in the subsidiary ledger. In addition, the posting reference (P.8) is printed in the subsidiary ledger.

Posting from the Purchases Journal to the General Ledger Posting from the purchases journal is similar to posting from the other special journals. Exhibit F:7-6, Panel B, illustrates the posting process. At the end of each month, each column in the journal is totaled. All totals, except the Other Accounts DR Amount column, are posted to the general ledger. For example, the $2,876 Accounts Payable CR total is posted to the Accounts Payable account in the general ledger as a credit. After posting, the account number is listed in the purchases journal and the posting reference is listed in the general ledger. The column total for Other Accounts DR Amount is *not* posted. Instead, these debits are posted individually to the specific accounts, as done in the cash receipts journal. After all posting is complete, the Accounts Payable ending balance in the general ledger should equal the sum of the individual vendor ending balances in the subsidiary ledger.

The Cash Payments Journal

Cash Payments Journal
Special journal used to record cash payments by check and currency.

Businesses make most cash payments by check, and all checks (and payments of currency) are recorded in the **cash payments journal**. This special journal is also called the *check register* and the *cash disbursements journal*. Exhibit F:7-7 shows the cash payments journal, with the ledgers in Panel B.

Accounting Information Systems Financial 7-17

Exhibit F:7-7 | Cash Payments Journal with Posting

PANEL A–Cash Payments Journal:

Cash Payments Journal — Page 6

Date	Ck. No.	Account Debited	Post. Ref.	Other Accounts DR	Accounts Payable DR	Merchandise Inventory CR	Cash CR
2024							
Nov. 3	101	Rent Expense	541	1,200			1,200
8	102	Office Supplies	161	61			61
15	103	Hanes Textiles	✓		700	21	679
20	104	Pioneer Plastics	✓		119		119
26	105	Merchandise Inventory	131	2,200			2,200
Nov. 30		Totals		3,461	819	21	4,259
				(X)	(210)	(131)	(101)

Total is not posted.

Totals are posted at the end of the month.

Individual accounts payable are posted daily.

PANEL B–Posting to the Ledgers:

Accounts Payable Subsidiary Ledger

Advanced Printing

Date	Post. Ref.	Debit	Credit	Balance Debit	Balance Credit
Nov. 12	P.8		236		236

City Office Supply

Date	Post. Ref.	Debit	Credit	Balance Debit	Balance Credit
Nov. 9	P.8		440		440
19	P.8		103		543

Hanes Textiles

Date	Post. Ref.	Debit	Credit	Balance Debit	Balance Credit
Nov. 2	P.8		700		700
13	P.8		451		1,151
15	CP.6	700			451

O'Leary Furniture Co.

Date	Post. Ref.	Debit	Credit	Balance Debit	Balance Credit
Nov. 23	P.8		627		627

Pioneer Plastics

Date	Post. Ref.	Debit	Credit	Balance Debit	Balance Credit
Nov. 5	P.8		319		319
20	CP.6	119			200

Individual accounts are posted at the end of the month.

General Ledger

Cash — No. 101

Date	Post. Ref.	Debit	Credit	Balance Debit	Balance Credit
Nov. 30	CR. 5	6,569		6,569	
30	CP. 6		4,259	2,310	

Merchandise Inventory — No. 131

Date	Post. Ref.	Debit	Credit	Balance Debit	Balance Credit
Nov. 1	Bal.			3,885	
26	CP.6	2,200		6,085	
30	S.3		1,814	4,271	
30	CR.5		1,707	2,564	
30	P.8	1,706		4,270	
30	CP.6		21	4,249	

Office Supplies — No. 161

Date	Post. Ref.	Debit	Credit	Balance Debit	Balance Credit
Nov. 8	CP.6	61		61	
30	P.8	103		164	

Accounts Payable — No. 210

Date	Post. Ref.	Debit	Credit	Balance Debit	Balance Credit
Nov. 30	P.8		2,876		2,876
30	CP.6	819			2,057

Rent Expense — No. 541

Date	Post. Ref.	Debit	Credit	Balance Debit	Balance Credit
Nov. 3	CP.6	1,200		1,200	

The cash payments journal has two debit columns—one for Other Accounts and one for Accounts Payable. It has two credit columns—one for Merchandise Inventory (for purchase discounts) and one for Cash. This special journal also has columns for the date and check number of each cash payment and the account debited.

Recording Cash Payment Transactions

Let's review the first transaction listed in the cash payments journal. On November 3, the business paid cash of $1,200 for rent. This payment of cash is recorded in the cash payments journal by entering $1,200 in the Cash CR column and the Other Accounts DR column. The Other Accounts DR column is used to record debits to accounts for which no special column exists. The business enters the name of the other account used, Rent Expense, in the Account Debited column. The Other Accounts DR column was also used on November 8 for the purchase of office supplies for cash and on November 26 for the purchase of Merchandise Inventory with cash.

On November 15, the business paid the vendor, Hanes Textiles, on account, with credit terms of 3/15, n/30 (for details, see the first transaction in the purchases journal, Exhibit F:7-6). Paying within the discount period allowed a 3% discount ($21), and the business paid the remaining $679 ($700 less the $21 discount). If the business had recorded the transaction in the general journal, the following would have been recorded:

$$\left. \begin{array}{c} A\downarrow \\ \hline \text{Cash}\downarrow \\ \text{Merchandise} \\ \text{Inventory}\downarrow \end{array} \right\} = \left\{ \begin{array}{c} L\downarrow \\ \hline \text{Accounts} \\ \text{Payable}\downarrow \end{array} \right. + \quad E$$

Date	Accounts and Explanation	Debit	Credit
Nov. 15	Accounts Payable	700	
	Cash		679
	Merchandise Inventory		21
	Paid within discount period.		

Instead, the business will record the transaction in the cash payments journal. The entry will be recorded by entering the $679 in the Cash CR column. The Accounts Payable DR column will be recorded for $700, and the discount of $21 will be entered into the Merchandise Inventory CR column. All transactions involving cash payments are recorded in the cash payments journal.

Posting from the Cash Payments Journal

Entries in the cash payments journal are posted daily to the accounts payable subsidiary ledger and monthly to the general ledger.

Posting from the Cash Payments Journal to the Accounts Payable Subsidiary Ledger
Posting from the cash payments journal is similar to posting from the cash receipts journal. Individual vendor amounts (accounts payable) are posted daily to the accounts payable subsidiary ledger. The postings are debits and reduce the balance in the individual accounts payable account. Trace the $700 debit to Hanes Textiles' Accounts Payable. The $700 reduces the balance in the Hanes's subsidiary account to $451. After posting, a check mark is entered in the cash payments journal and the posting reference (CP.6) is printed in the subsidiary ledger.

Posting from the Cash Payments Journal to the General Ledger At the end of the month, each column is totaled. The totals, except for the Other Accounts DR column, are posted to the specific general ledger accounts. After posting, the account number is printed below the column total in the cash payments journal and the posting reference is printed in the general ledger.

Amounts in the Other Accounts DR column are posted individually (for example, Rent Expense—debit $1,200). When each Other Account DR is posted to the general ledger, the account number is printed in the Post. Ref. column. The letter X below the Other Accounts DR column signifies that the total is *not* posted.

To review accounts payable, companies list individual vendor ending balances in the accounts payable subsidiary ledger. The general ledger and subsidiary ledger totals should agree.

GENERAL LEDGER	
Accounts Payable credit balance	$ 2,057

SUBSIDIARY LEDGER: ACCOUNTS PAYABLE	
Vendor	Balance
Advanced Printing	$ 236
City Office Supply	543
Hanes Textiles	451
O'Leary Furniture Co.	627
Pioneer Plastics	200
Total Accounts Payable	$ 2,057

These should be equal.

The General Journal

Special journals save time recording repetitive transactions. But some transactions don't fit a special journal. Examples include the adjusting entries for depreciation, the expiration of prepaid insurance, and the accrual of salaries payable at the end of the period. Companies also use the general journal for sales returns and allowances and purchase returns and allowances not involving cash receipts or cash payments. All accounting information systems need a general journal. The adjusting entries and the closing entries are recorded in the general journal, along with other nonroutine transactions.

As we have seen, a manual accounting information system involves five journals: sales journal, cash receipts journal, purchases journal, cash payments journal, and the general journal. It's important to remember that transactions are recorded in either one of the special journals or in the general journal, but not both. Exhibit F:7-8 (on the next page) provides a summary of all five journals that will help you decide which journal to use when recording transactions in a manual system.

Exhibit F:7-8 | Recording Transactions in Special Journals

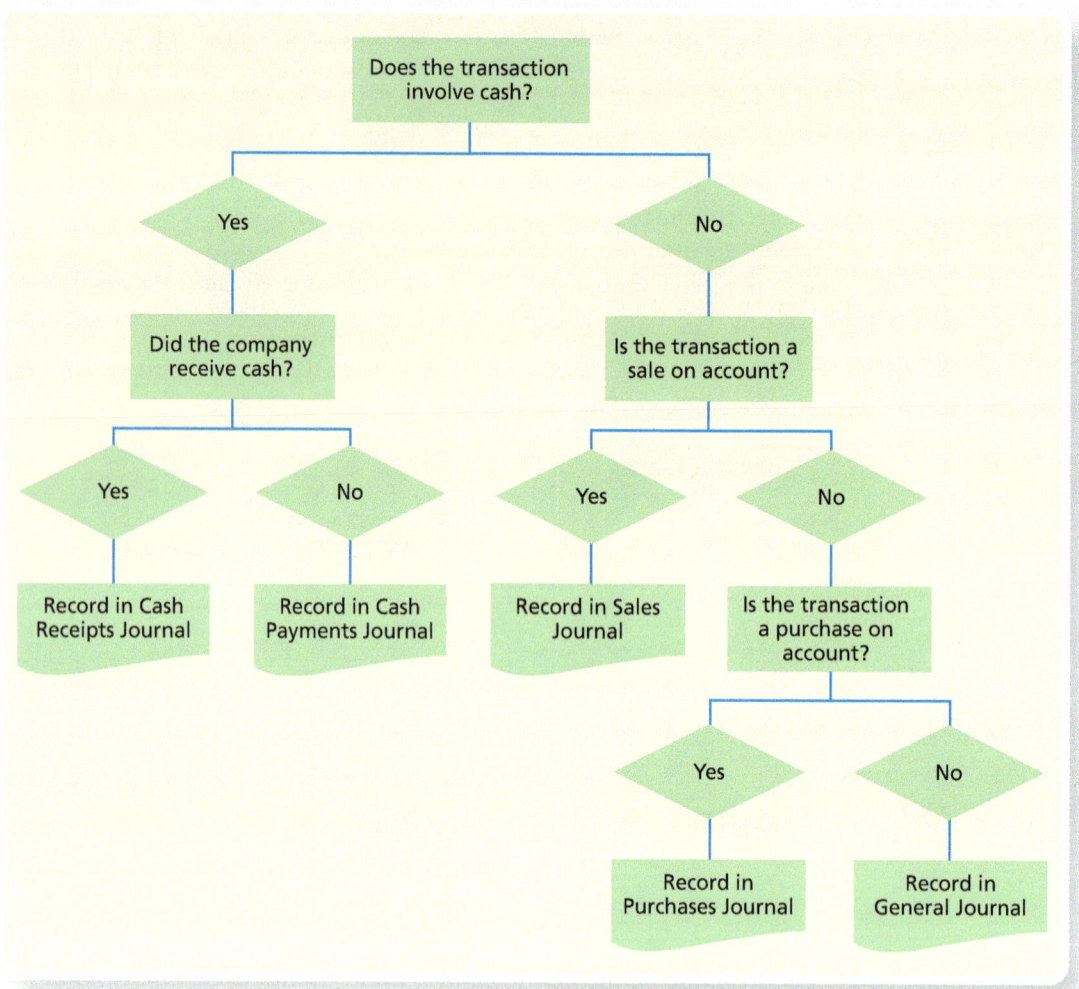

7. Fiscella Co. paid monthly rent of $2,000. What special journal should the transaction be recorded in? What columns will be used?

Check your answer online in MyLab Accounting or at http://www.pearsonhighered.com/Horngren.

For more practice, see Short Exercises S-F:7-8 through S-F:7-12. **MyLab Accounting**

HOW ARE TRANSACTIONS RECORDED IN A COMPUTERIZED ACCOUNTING INFORMATION SYSTEM?

A computerized accounting information system has two basic components:

- Hardware
- Software

Hardware is the electronic equipment: computers, monitors, printers, and the network that connects them. Most systems require a **network** to link computers. In a networked system, the server stores the program and the data.

Software is the set of programs that drives the computer. Accounting software reads, edits, and stores transaction data. It also generates the reports that businesses can use to make decisions. Many software packages are flexible. For example, a small cleaning business may be only partly computerized. This small business may use the computer for employee payrolls, but other parts of the accounting information system may be manual.

Accounting Software for Small Businesses

With increased availability of affordable computerized accounting information systems, more and more businesses are completing all of their accounting on the computer. Two popular software packages for small businesses are QuickBooks and Sage 50 Accounting. Both of these programs allow businesses to enter sales of services and merchandise inventory. In addition, these programs can record expenses and produce reports such as financial statements. These computerized accounting information systems are relatively easy to use, often requiring little knowledge of accounting or GAAP. Computerized accounting software allows businesses to organize finances, track sales and expenses, and complete record-keeping. QuickBooks and Sage 50 Accounting, though, work best for small businesses. As businesses grow and expand, they need a software system that can handle more advanced processes and transactions.

Enterprise Resource Planning (ERP) Systems

Larger companies will often use an **enterprise resource planning (ERP)** system to manage their data. ERP systems such as SAP® and Oracle® can integrate all company data into a single database. ERP feeds the data into software for all company activities—from purchasing to production and customer service.

Advantages of ERP systems include:

- Reduce operating costs.
- Help companies adjust to changes.
- Replace separate software systems, such as sales and payroll.

Disadvantages of ERP systems include:

- ERP is expensive. Major installations can cost millions of dollars.
- Implementation also requires a large commitment of time and people.

Many ERP systems and small business accounting systems can be offered in the "cloud." Cloud computing refers to purchasing software and data storage from a third party. In **cloud computing**, the software and data are stored on the third-party server instead of by the business. Employees access the software and data via the Internet by using a Web browser. Cloud computing can reduce costs by a significant amount for many businesses.

Learning Objective 4
Describe how transactions are recorded in a computerized accounting information system

Hardware
Electronic equipment that includes computers, monitors, printers, and the network that connects them.

Network
The system of electronic linkages that allows different computers to share the same information.

Software
Set of programs or instructions that drives the computer to perform the work desired.

Enterprise Resource Planning (ERP)
Software system that can integrate all of a company's functions, departments, and data into a single system.

Cloud Computing
Software and data are stored on a third-party server instead of by the business and can be accessed by employees via the Internet.

QuickBooks

One way to understand how computerized accounting software works is to view how transactions are handled in this type of system. We are now going to look at a common small business accounting system, QuickBooks. Although your instructor might not have you complete any assignments using QuickBooks, it will be helpful to view the way QuickBooks handles common accounting entries.

Most computerized accounting information systems are organized by function or task. A user can select a function, such as creating an invoice, from a menu. (A menu is a list of options for choosing computer functions.) QuickBooks uses a navigation panel located on the left-hand side of the screen that allows users to select from a menu of options such as Customers, Vendors, Employees, Transactions, and Reports. The tabs (Customers, Vendors, Employees, Transactions, and Reports) on the navigation panel handle all transactions that a company would use. Transactions involving customers, including invoices (accounts receivable), receipt of payments, and sales returns, would be recorded on the Customers tab. The Vendors tab handles transactions involving vendors, including entering bills (accounts payable), paying bills, and processing refunds. The financial reports of a business such as the income statement and balance sheet are also accessible from the navigation panel.

ETHICS

Should I change the transaction?

Girmanesh Landin is responsible for recording all of the transactions for Marshall's Home Care. This is Girmanesh's first job as a staff accountant, and she wants to do a good job. Last week, she recorded several cash payments for bills in the computerized accounting information system. She now realizes that she selected the incorrect cash account. She selected the savings account instead of the checking account. Girmanesh knows that she could go back into each transaction and make the correction without anyone knowing that she made the mistake, but she is unsure of what to do. Should Girmanesh make the correction?

Solution

Because Girmanesh is new to the job, she should find out the procedure for making corrections in the accounting information system before she changes each transaction. Attempting to hide her mistakes could cause her integrity to be questioned because it would appear that she was trying to cover up things rather than ask for clarification and help. Most businesses will prefer that Girmanesh make a separate correcting entry instead of going back in and changing the incorrect transaction. This procedure allows for businesses to have a record of the original transaction and then the correcting entry. It is generally never a good idea to change transactions that have already been recorded, and many software systems will not allow such actions as a method to prevent fraud.

Creating a Sales Invoice in QuickBooks

Suppose on June 23, Smart Touch Learning performed $3,000 of services for Richard Michura on account. To record this transaction in QuickBooks, Smart Touch Learning would need to create an invoice for Richard. Exhibit F:7-9 shows the invoice the company created. Notice that there are no debits and credits on the invoice. In a computerized accounting information system, the business does not have to record the transaction in debit and credit format. Instead, by creating the invoice, the software knows automatically to record a debit to Accounts Receivable—Michura and a credit to Service Revenue. After creating the invoice, the software posts the transaction to the appropriate general ledger accounts. There is no need for the business to manually post the transaction; the software takes care of the posting process.

Exhibit F:7-9 | QuickBooks Invoice

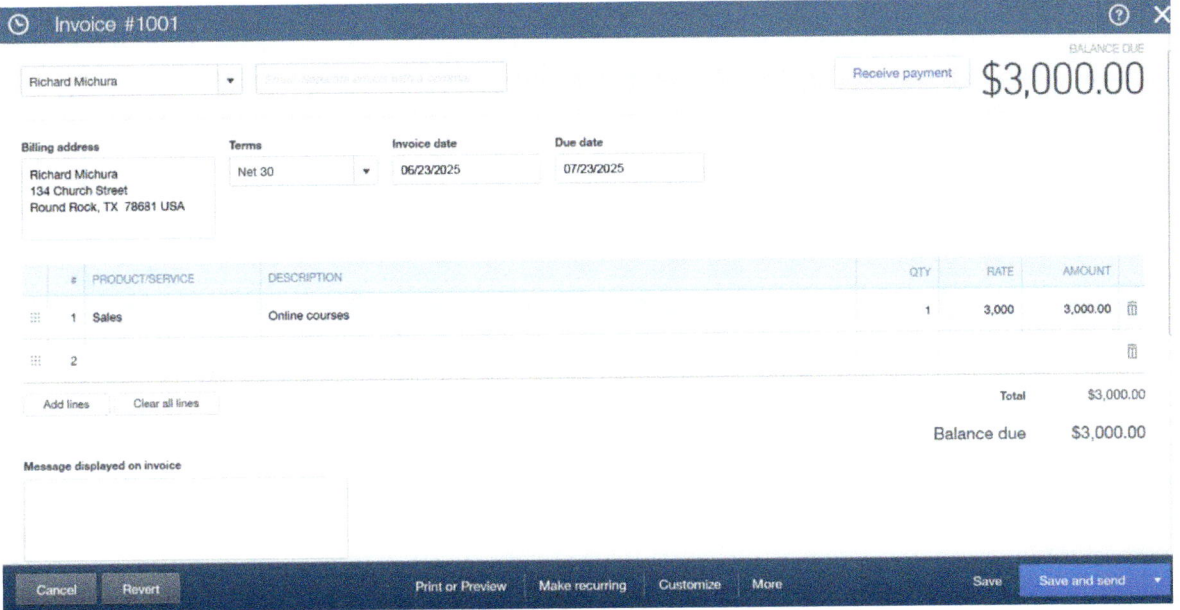

QuickBooks screenshot. Reprinted with permission © Quicken Inc. All rights reserved.

When Smart Touch Learning receives the $3,000 from the customer, the accounting clerk will enter the transaction in the Customers tab of QuickBooks by locating the customer's invoice and selecting the "Receive payment" action. By doing this, QuickBooks identifies that the invoice has been paid and that Richard Michura has no further outstanding balance.

Entering Bills in QuickBooks

When a business needs to record a bill received, it will use the Vendors tab of QuickBooks. Suppose that on June 25, Smart Touch Learning receives a $580 bill for utilities. Exhibit F:7-10 shows the bill that the company will record in QuickBooks. When Smart Touch Learning saves the bill, the software will automatically record a debit to Utilities Expense and credit to Accounts Payable—Smart Energy.

Exhibit F:7-10 | QuickBooks Bill

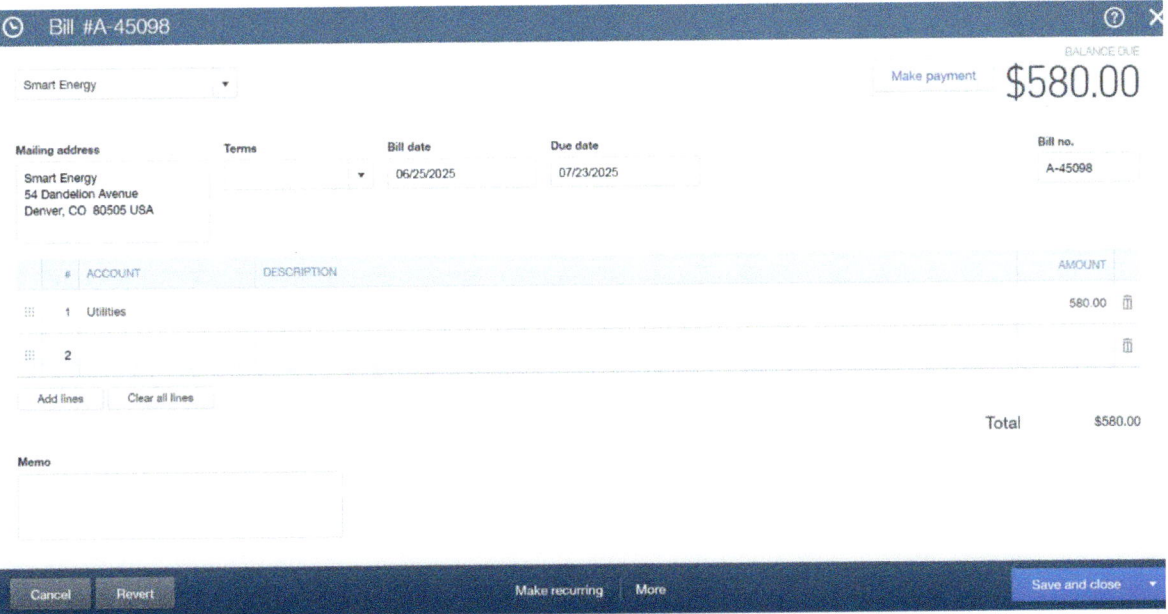

QuickBooks screenshot. Reprinted with permission © Quicken Inc. All rights reserved.

On July 5, when Smart Touch Learning makes payment on the bill, it will enter the payment in the Vendors tab of QuickBooks. The accounting clerk will select the bill to be paid and record the payment by selecting the "Make payment" action. Again, the software takes care of recording the journal entry and posting to the ledger accounts.

Viewing Financial Statements in QuickBooks

QuickBooks has the ability to produce numerous reports such as the income statement (called *Profit & Loss* in QuickBooks), balance sheet, and statement of cash flows. The software can also be used to create accounts receivable and accounts payable aging schedules. Exhibit F:7-11 shows an example of an income statement for Smart Touch Learning.

Exhibit F:7-11 | QuickBooks Income Statement

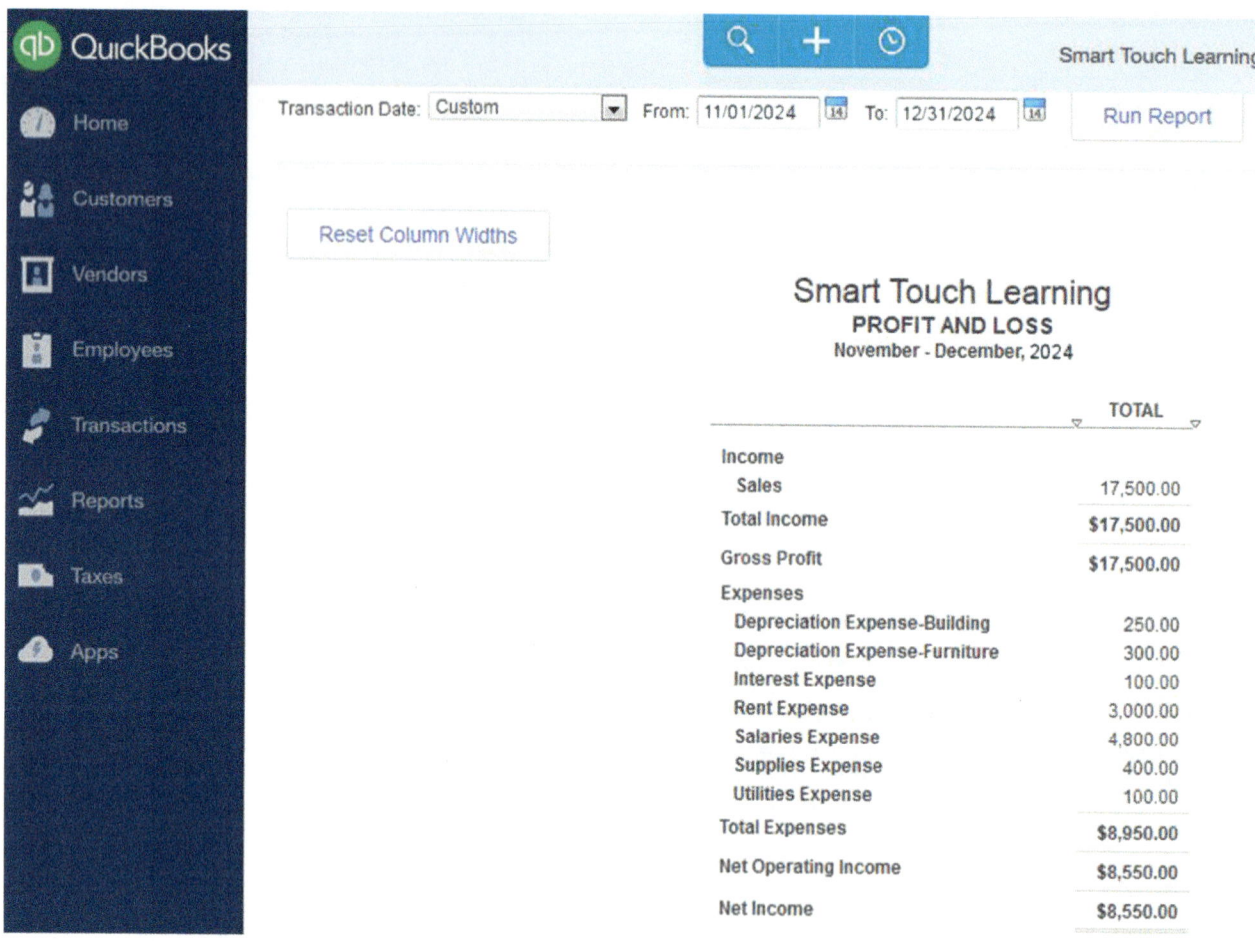

QuickBooks screenshot. Reprinted with permission © Quicken Inc. All rights reserved.

One of the many benefits of using a computerized accounting information system is the ease with which reports are created. For most reports needed, the software includes prebuilt templates that can be used. In addition, the software automatically transfers the amounts from the general ledger to the financial statements. The only thing the accountant needs to do is set the correct time period and review the financial statements for accuracy.

8. Fill in the missing information.
   a. _____ is the set of programs that drives the computer.
   b. Most systems require a(n) _____ to link computers.
   c. _____ is the electronic equipment used in a computerized accounting information system.

Check your answers online in MyLab Accounting or at http://www.pearsonhighered.com/Horngren.

For more practice, see Short Exercise S-F:7-13.   **MyLab Accounting**

REVIEW

> Things You Should Know

1. What is an accounting information system?

- An accounting information system (AIS) collects, records, stores, and processes accounting data to produce information that is useful for decision makers.
- An effective accounting information system provides control, compatibility, flexibility, relevance, and a positive cost/benefit relationship.
- An accounting information system has three basic components:
  - Source documents and input devices
  - Processing and storage
  - Outputs

2. How are sales and cash receipts recorded in a manual accounting information system?

- In a manual system, businesses use special journals that are designed to record a specific type of transaction. The four special journals and their uses are:
  - Sales journal—records sales on account
  - Cash receipts journal—records cash receipts
  - Purchases journal—records purchases on account
  - Cash payments journal—records cash payments
- Subsidiary ledgers are used to hold individual accounts that support a general ledger account. Two common subsidiary ledgers are the accounts receivable subsidiary ledger and accounts payable subsidiary ledger.
- Credit sales are recorded in the sales journal, which uses two columns—Accounts Receivable DR, Sales Revenue CR and Cost of Goods Sold DR, Merchandise Inventory CR.
- Cash receipts are recorded in the cash receipts journal, which includes a Cash DR column and various other debit and credit columns.

3. **How are purchases, cash payments, and other transactions recorded in a manual accounting information system?**

    - Purchases on account are recorded in the purchases journal, which includes an Accounts Payable CR column and various other debit columns.
    - Cash payments are recorded in the cash payments journal, which includes a Cash CR column and various other debit and credit columns.
    - The general journal is used for transactions that aren't recorded in one of the special journals, such as adjusting and closing entries.

4. **How are transactions recorded in a computerized accounting information system?**

    - A computerized accounting information system has two basic components:
      - Hardware—the electronic equipment
      - Software—the set of programs that drives the computer
    - Accounting software, such as QuickBooks and Sage 50 Accounting, is often used by small businesses.
    - Larger companies use an enterprise resource planning (ERP) system to manage their data.

> Check Your Understanding Problem

Check your understanding of the chapter by completing this problem and then looking at the solution. Use this practice to help identify which sections of the chapter you need to study more.

Houlihan Company completed the following selected transactions during March 2025:

Mar. 4	Received $500 for a cash sale of merchandise inventory to a customer (cost, $319).
6	Received $65 on account, terms n/30, from Brady Lee.
9	Received $1,080 on a note receivable from Beverly Mann. This amount includes the $1,000 note receivable plus interest revenue.
15	Received $800 for a cash sale of merchandise inventory to a customer (cost, $522).
24	Borrowed $2,200 by signing a note payable to Interstate Bank.
27	Received $1,200 on account from Lance Albert. Collection was received after the discount period and included $20 of sales discounts forfeited.

Requirements

The general ledger showed the following balances at February 28: Cash, $1,117; Accounts Receivable, $2,790; Note Receivable—Beverly Mann, $1,000; and Merchandise Inventory, $1,819. The accounts receivable subsidiary ledger at February 28 contained debit balances as follows: Lance Albert, $1,840; Melinda Fultz, $885; Brady Lee, $65.

1. Record the transactions in the cash receipts journal, page 7. (See Learning Objective 2)
2. Compute column totals at March 31. (See Learning Objective 2)
3. Post from the cash receipts journal to the general ledger and the accounts receivable subsidiary ledger. Use four-column accounts. Use complete posting references, including the following account numbers: Cash, 11; Accounts Receivable, 12; Note Receivable—Beverly Mann, 13; Merchandise Inventory, 14; Note Payable—Interstate Bank, 22;

Sales Revenue, 41; Sales Discounts Forfeited, 42; Interest Revenue, 46; and Cost of Goods Sold, 51. Insert a check mark (√) in the posting reference column for each February 28 account balance. (See Learning Objective 2)

4. Balance the Accounts Receivable subsidiary ledger with the Accounts Receivable account in the general ledger. (See Learning Objective 2)

> Solution

Requirements 1 and 2

Cash Receipts Journal — Page 7

Date	Account Credited	Post. Ref.	Cash DR	Accounts Receivable CR	Sales Revenue CR	Sales Discounts Forfeited CR	Other Accounts CR	Cost of Goods Sold DR Merchandise Inventory CR
2025								
Mar. 4			500		500			319
6	Brady Lee	√	65	65				
9	Note Receivable—Beverly Mann	13	1,080				1,000	
	Interest Revenue	46					80	
15			800		800			522
24	Note Payable—Interstate Bank	22	2,200				2,200	
27	Lance Albert	√	1,200	1,180		20		
31			5,845	1,245	1,300	20	3,280	841
			(11)	(12)	(41)	(42)	(X)	(51/14)

Requirement 3

ACCOUNTS RECEIVABLE SUBSIDIARY LEDGER

Lance Albert

Date	Post. Ref.	Debit	Credit	Balance Debit	Balance Credit
Feb. 28	√			1,840	
Mar. 27	CR.7		1,180	660	

Melinda Fultz

Date	Post. Ref.	Debit	Credit	Balance Debit	Balance Credit
Feb. 28	√			885	

Brady Lee

Date	Post. Ref.	Debit	Credit	Balance Debit	Balance Credit
Feb. 28	√			65	
Mar. 6	CR.7		65	0	

GENERAL LEDGER

Cash — No. 11

Date	Post. Ref.	Debit	Credit	Balance Debit	Balance Credit
Feb. 28	✓			1,117	
Mar. 31	CR.7	5,845		6,962	

Accounts Receivable — No. 12

Date	Post. Ref.	Debit	Credit	Balance Debit	Balance Credit
Feb. 28	✓			2,790	
Mar. 31	CR.7		1,245	1,545	

Note Receivable—Beverly Mann — No. 13

Date	Post. Ref.	Debit	Credit	Balance Debit	Balance Credit
Feb. 28	✓			1,000	
Mar. 9	CR.7		1,000	0	

Merchandise Inventory — No. 14

Date	Post. Ref.	Debit	Credit	Balance Debit	Balance Credit
Feb. 28	✓			1,819	
Mar. 31	CR.7		841	978	

Note Payable—Interstate Bank — No. 22

Date	Post. Ref.	Debit	Credit	Balance Debit	Balance Credit
Mar. 24	CR.7		2,200		2,200

Sales Revenue — No. 41

Date	Post. Ref.	Debit	Credit	Balance Debit	Balance Credit
Mar. 31	CR.7		1,300		1,300

Sales Discounts Forfeited — No. 42

Date	Post. Ref.	Debit	Credit	Balance Debit	Balance Credit
Mar. 31	CR.7		20		20

Interest Revenue — No. 46

Date	Post. Ref.	Debit	Credit	Balance Debit	Balance Credit
Mar. 9	CR.7		80		80

Cost of Goods Sold — No. 51

Date	Post. Ref.	Debit	Credit	Balance Debit	Balance Credit
Mar. 31	CR.7	841		841	

Requirement 4

GENERAL LEDGER	
Accounts Receivable debit balance	$ 1,545

SUBSIDIARY LEDGER: ACCOUNTS RECEIVABLE	
Customer	Balance
Lance Albert	$ 660
Melinda Fultz	885
Brady Lee	0
Total Accounts Receivable	$ 1,545

> Key Terms

Accounting Information System (AIS) (p. 7-2)
Accounts Payable Subsidiary Ledger (p. 7-7)
Accounts Receivable Subsidiary Ledger (p. 7-6)
Cash Payments Journal (p. 7-16)
Cash Receipts Journal (p. 7-10)
Cloud Computing (p. 7-21)
Control Account (p. 7-7)
Enterprise Resource Planning (ERP) (p. 7-21)
Hardware (p. 7-21)
Network (p. 7-21)
Purchases Journal (p. 7-14)
Sales Journal (p. 7-7)
Server (p. 7-4)
Software (p. 7-21)
Source Document (p. 7-3)
Special Journal (p. 7-5)
Subsidiary Ledger (p. 7-6)

> Quick Check

1. Which of the following benefits of an effective accounting information system provides safeguards for a business's assets and reduces the likelihood of fraud and errors? *(Learning Objective 1)*
   a. Flexibility
   b. Relevance
   c. Control
   d. Compatibility

2. The outputs of a computerized accounting information system are called *(Learning Objective 1)*
   a. reports.
   b. software.
   c. processing.
   d. purchase invoices.

3. Which of the following is not a special journal? *(Learning Objective 2)*
   a. Sales journal
   b. General journal
   c. Cash receipts journal
   d. Purchases journal

4. Mountain Day Spa sold merchandise inventory on credit, terms n/30, to Marvin Smith, $400. Cost of goods sold was $250. When using a manual accounting information system, where should Mountain record this transaction, and what is the appropriate column in which to record the $250? *(Learning Objective 2)*
   a. Sales journal; Accounts Receivable DR, Sales Revenue CR
   b. Cash receipts journal; Cash DR, Sales Revenue CR
   c. Sales journal; Cost of Goods Sold DR, Merchandise Inventory CR
   d. Cash receipts journal; Cash DR, Accounts Receivable CR

5. Which of the following correctly describes the posting of transactions from the sales journal? *(Learning Objective 2)*
   a. Individual accounts receivable are posted daily to the general ledger.
   b. At the end of the month, the totals of the columns are posted to the general ledger.
   c. Transactions are posted daily to the general ledger.
   d. The total of the Accounts Receivable DR, Sales Revenue CR column is posted to the accounts receivable subsidiary ledger.

Learning Objective 3

6. Centex Sound Systems purchased merchandise inventory costing $8,000 from Flower Co. on account. Where should Centex record this transaction, and what account is credited?
   a. Cash payments journal; credit Cash
   b. Sales journal; credit Sales Revenue
   c. Purchases journal; credit Accounts Payable
   d. General journal; credit Merchandise Inventory

Learning Objective 3

7. Every transaction recorded in the cash payments journal includes a
   a. credit to Cash.
   b. debit to Accounts Receivable.
   c. debit to Sales Discounts.
   d. debit to Cash.

Learning Objective 3

8. When using a manual accounting information system, which of the following transactions would be recorded in the general journal?
   a. Depreciation of office furniture
   b. Cash payment of rent
   c. Sale of merchandise inventory on account
   d. Purchase of merchandise inventory on account

Learning Objective 4

9. Which is a disadvantage of an enterprise resource planning (ERP) system?
   a. Helps companies adjust to changes
   b. Can replace separate software systems
   c. Can reduce operating costs
   d. Implementation requires a large commitment of time and people

Check your answers at the end of the chapter.

ASSESS YOUR PROGRESS

> Review Questions

1. What is an accounting information system (AIS)?
2. What does an effective accounting information system provide?
3. Explain the three basic components of an accounting information system.
4. What is a special journal?
5. What is the purpose of a subsidiary ledger?
6. What is a control account?
7. List the four special journals often used in a manual accounting information system. What types of transactions are recorded in each of the special journals?
8. Explain the posting process of the sales journal.
9. Provide some examples of transactions that would be recorded in the Other Accounts CR column of the cash receipts journal.
10. What are the columns that are typically used in the purchases journal?
11. Explain the posting process of the cash payments journal.

12. When is the general journal used in a manual accounting information system? Provide some examples of transactions that would be recorded in the general journal.
13. Explain the two components of a computerized accounting information system.
14. What are two common accounting software systems used by small businesses?
15. What is an enterprise resource planning (ERP) system? What are the advantages and disadvantages of using an ERP?
16. How is QuickBooks organized?
17. How would a business record a sale of services on account in QuickBooks?
18. How would a business record a bill received in QuickBooks?

> Short Exercises

S-F:7-1 Evaluating features of an effective accounting information system

Learning Objective 1

In Vogue, a T-shirt business, is growing fast and needs a better accounting information system. Consider the features of an effective system. Which features are most important? Why? Which feature must you consider if your financial resources are limited?

S-F:7-2 Defining components of an accounting information system

Learning Objective 1

Match each example with a component of a computerized accounting information system. Components may be used more than once.

Example	Component
1. Server	a. Source documents and input devices
2. Bank checks	b. Processing and storage
3. Reports	c. Outputs
4. Keyboard	
5. Software	
6. Financial statements	
7. Bar code scanner	

S-F:7-3 Identifying special journals

Learning Objective 2

Use the following abbreviations to indicate the journal in which you would record transactions *a* through *n*.

    J = General journal
    S = Sales journal
  CR = Cash receipts journal
    P = Purchases journal
  CP = Cash payments journal

Transactions:
    ___ a. Cash purchase of merchandise inventory
    ___ b. Collection of dividend revenue earned on an investment
    ___ c. Prepayment of insurance
    ___ d. Borrowing money on a long-term note payable
    ___ e. Purchase of equipment on account
    ___ f. Cost of goods sold along with a credit sale

___ g. Cash sale of merchandise inventory
___ h. Payment of rent
___ i. Depreciation of computer equipment
___ j. Purchase of merchandise inventory on account
___ k. Collection of accounts receivable
___ l. Expiration of prepaid insurance
___ m. Sale on account
___ n. Payment on account

Learning Objective 2

S-F:7-4 Recording transactions in a sales journal

Jun. 1	Sold merchandise inventory on account to Fran Jack, $1,220. Cost of goods, $980. Invoice no. 101.
8	Sold merchandise inventory on account to Ireland Frank, $2,025. Cost of goods, $1,640. Invoice no. 102.
13	Sold merchandise inventory on account to Jake Thompson, $420. Cost of goods, $210. Invoice no. 103.
28	Sold merchandise inventory on account to Gabe West, $820. Cost of goods, $620. Invoice no. 104.

Use the following sales journal to record the preceding transactions. All credit sales are terms of n/30.

Sales Journal — Page 1

Date	Invoice No.	Customer Account Debited	Post. Ref.	Accounts Receivable DR Sales Revenue CR	Cost of Goods Sold DR Merchandise Inventory CR
2024					

Note: Short Exercise S-F:7-4 must be completed before attempting Short Exercise S-F:7-5.

Learning Objective 2

S-F:7-5 Posting transactions from a sales journal to a subsidiary ledger and general ledger

Review your results from Short Exercise S-F:7-4.

Requirements

1. Total each column of the sales journal.
2. Open the following four-column accounts in the accounts receivable subsidiary ledger: Accounts Receivable—Frank; Accounts Receivable—Jack; Accounts Receivable—Thompson; Accounts Receivable—West. Post the transactions to the accounts receivable subsidiary ledger.

3. Open the following selected four-column accounts in the general ledger: Accounts Receivable (112); Merchandise Inventory (118), Bal. $5,000; Sales Revenue (411); Cost of Goods Sold (511). Post the total of each column to the general ledger.

4. Balance the total of the customer ending balances in the accounts receivable subsidiary ledger against Accounts Receivable in the general ledger.

S-F:7-6 Recording transactions in a cash receipts journal

Learning Objective 2

Jul. 5	Sold merchandise inventory for cash, $1,700. Cost of goods, $1,400.
12	Collected interest revenue of $2,050.
18	Received cash from Heidi Next, $1,200, on account. There was no discount.
29	Received $5,300 from Mitch Dylan in full settlement of his account receivable including sales discounts forfeited of $20.

Use the following cash receipts journal to record the preceding transactions.

									Cash Receipts Journal					Page 3
Date	Account Credited	Post. Ref.	Cash DR	Accounts Receivable CR	Sales Revenue CR	Sales Discounts Forfeited CR	Other Accounts CR	Cost of Goods Sold DR Merchandise Inventory CR
2024								

Note: Short Exercise S-F:7-6 must be completed before attempting Short Exercise S-F:7-7.

S-F:7-7 Posting transactions from a cash receipts journal to a subsidiary ledger and general ledger

Learning Objective 2

Review your results from Short Exercise S-F:7-6.

Requirements

1. Total each column of the cash receipts journal.

2. Open the following four-column accounts in the accounts receivable subsidiary ledger: Accounts Receivable—Dylan, Bal. $5,280; Accounts Receivable—Next, Bal. $2,250. Post the transactions to the accounts receivable subsidiary ledger.

3. Open the following selected four-column accounts in the general ledger: Cash (111), Bal. $4,550; Accounts Receivable (112), Bal. $7,530; Merchandise Inventory (118), Bal. $3,250; Sales Revenue (411), Bal. $25,000; Sales Discounts Forfeited (412); Interest Revenue (419); Cost of Goods Sold (511), Bal. $14,500. Post the total of each column to the general ledger. Also, post the Other Accounts column to the general ledger.

4. Balance the total of the customer ending balances in the accounts receivable subsidiary ledger against Accounts Receivable in the general ledger.

7-34 Financial chapter 7

Learning Objective 3

S-F:7-8 Recording transactions in a purchases journal

Oct. 1	Purchased merchandise inventory on account with credit terms of 4/10, n/30 from Mayer Co., $2,200.
11	Purchased office supplies on account from Bird Co., $600. Terms were n/EOM.
24	Purchased furniture on account with credit terms of 3/10, n/60 from Silly Co., $900.

Use the following purchases journal to record the preceding transactions.

Purchases Journal — Page 6

Date	Vendor Account Credited	Terms	Post. Ref.	Accounts Payable CR	Merchandise Inventory DR	Office Supplies DR	Other Accounts DR — Account Title	Post Ref.	Amount
2024									

Note: Short Exercise S-F:7-8 must be completed before attempting Short Exercise S-F:7-9.

Learning Objective 3

S-F:7-9 Posting transactions from a purchases journal to a subsidiary ledger and general ledger

Review your results from Short Exercise S-F:7-8.

Requirements

1. Total each column of the purchases journal.
2. Open the following four-column accounts in the accounts payable subsidiary ledger: Accounts Payable—Bird Co.; Accounts Payable—Mayer Co.; Accounts Payable—Silly Co. Post the transactions to the accounts payable subsidiary ledger.
3. Open the following selected four-column accounts in the general ledger: Merchandise Inventory (115); Office Supplies (116); Furniture (151); Accounts Payable (211). Post the total of each column to the general ledger. Also, post the Other Accounts column to the general ledger.
4. Balance the total of the vendor ending balances in the accounts payable subsidiary ledger against Accounts Payable in the general ledger.

Learning Objective 3

S-F:7-10 Recording transactions in a cash payments journal

Jan. 5	Issued check no. 430 to purchase equipment for cash, $1,700.
7	Purchased merchandise inventory for cash, $450, issuing check no. 431.
18	Paid Kat Co. amount owed, $775, less $100 discount. Issued check no. 432.
28	Issued check no. 433 to pay utilities, $260. The bill was just received, and there is no liability recorded.

Use the following cash payments journal to record the preceding transactions.

				Cash Payments Journal			Page 8
Date	Ck. No.	Account Debited	Post. Ref.	Other Accounts DR	Accounts Payable DR	Merchandise Inventory CR	Cash CR
2024							

Note: Short Exercise S-F:7-10 must be completed before attempting Short Exercise S-F:7-11.

S-F:7-11 Posting transactions from a cash payments journal to a subsidiary ledger and general ledger

Learning Objective 3

Review your results from Short Exercise S-F:7-10.

Requirements

1. Total each column of the cash payments journal.
2. Open the following four-column accounts in the accounts payable subsidiary ledger: Accounts Payable—Kat Co., Bal. $1,900. Post the transactions to the accounts payable subsidiary ledger.
3. Open the following selected four-column accounts in the general ledger: Cash (111), Bal. $5,000; Merchandise Inventory (118), $2,100; Equipment (150), $9,900; Accounts Payable (211), $1,900; Utilities Expense (541). Post the total of each column to the general ledger. Also, post the Other Accounts column to the general ledger.
4. Balance the total of the vendor ending balances in the accounts payable subsidiary ledger against Accounts Payable in the general ledger.

S-F:7-12 Recording transactions in a general journal

Learning Objective 3

Mar. 2	Sold merchandise inventory on account, terms n/30, to B. Kelp, issuing invoice no. 501 for $1,000 (cost, $680).
6	Issued credit memo to B. Kelp for $1,000 for merchandise returned to the business by the customer. Also accounted for receipt of the merchandise inventory at cost.
21	Purchased merchandise inventory on credit terms of 3/10, n/30 from Pond Co., $600.
28	Returned damaged merchandise inventory to Pond Co., issuing a debit memo for $600.

Journalize the above transactions that should be recorded in the general journal. If a transaction should not be recorded in the general journal, identify the special journal that should be used. Assume the company uses the perpetual inventory system.

Learning Objective 4

S-F:7-13 Understanding components of a computerized accounting information system

Ned Timmons, engineer, is considering using a computerized accounting system for his professional engineering business. Ned has asked that you help him understand the components of a computerized accounting information system by answering the following questions:

Requirements

1. What are the two basic components of a computerized accounting information system?
2. Provide examples of each component.
3. If Ned were interested in a software system for his small business, what software might you recommend?

> Exercises

Learning Objective 2

Accounts Receivable DR, Sales Revenue CR column total $1,550

E-F:7-14 Recording transactions—sales journal

Feb. 1	Sold merchandise inventory on account, terms n/30, to Cole Co., $1,050. Cost of goods, $860. Invoice no. 401.
6	Sold merchandise inventory for cash, $950 (cost, $750).
12	Collected interest revenue of $170.
15	Received cash from Cole Co. in full settlement of its account receivable.
20	Sold merchandise inventory on account, terms n/30, to Dump Co., issuing invoice no. 402 for $500 (cost, $325).
22	Sold merchandise inventory for cash, $600 (cost $530).
26	Sold office supplies to an employee for cash of $150.
28	Received $500 from Dump Co. in full settlement of its account receivable.

Requirements

1. Prepare headings for a sales journal. Journalize the transactions that should be recorded in the sales journal. Assume the company uses the perpetual inventory system.
2. Total each column of the sales journal.

Learning Objective 2

Accounts Receivable CR column total $1,550

E-F:7-15 Recording transactions—cash receipts journal

Refer to information in Exercise E-F:7-14.

Requirements

1. Prepare headings for a cash receipts journal. Journalize the transactions that should be recorded in the cash receipts journal.
2. Total each column of the cash receipts journal.

E-F:7-16 Using the sales and cash receipts journals

Learning Objective 2

The sales and cash receipts journals of Caverly Office Products include the following entries:

Sales Journal — Page 1

Date	Invoice No.	Customer Account Debited	Post. Ref.	Accounts Receivable DR Sales Revenue CR	Cost of Goods Sold DR Merchandise Inventory CR
2024					
May 7	601	L. Ebert	✓	110	63
10	602	T. Ross	✓	65	33
10	603	E. Loop	✓	95	37
12	604	B. Goebel	✓	120	76
May 31		Total		390	209

Cash Receipts Journal — Page 5

Date	Account Credited	Post. Ref.	Cash DR	Accounts Receivable CR	Sales Revenue CR	Sales Discounts Forfeited CR	Other Accounts CR	Cost of Goods Sold DR Merchandise Inventory CR
2024								
May 16	L. Ebert	✓						
19	E. Loop	✓						
24			320		320			250
30	T. Ross	✓						
May 31	Total							

Identify the missing information in the cash receipts journal for those transactions listed. All credit sales are terms n/30. Assume all the accounts are paid in full. Also, total the columns in the cash receipts journal and show that total debits equal total credits.

E-F:7-17 Analyzing postings from the cash receipts journal

Learning Objective 2

The cash receipts journal of Silver Plastics follows:

Cash Receipts Journal — Page 7

Date	Account Credited	Post. Ref.	Cash DR	Accounts Receivable CR	Sales Revenue CR	Sales Discounts Forfeited CR	Other Accounts CR	Cost of Goods Sold DR Merchandise Inventory CR
2024								
Jan. 2	Awesome Corp.	(g)	830	810		20		
9	King, Inc.	(h)	490	490				
19	Note Receivable	(i)	4,480				4,000	
	Interest Revenue	(j)					480	
30	J. T. Folk	(k)	330		320	10		
31			4,230		4,230			3,500
Jan. 31	Total		10,360	1,620	4,230	30	4,480	3,500
			(a)	(c)	(d)	(b)	(e)	(f)

Silver's general ledger includes the following selected accounts, along with their account numbers:

Number	Account
110	Cash
115	Accounts Receivable
118	Merchandise Inventory
125	Notes Receivable
510	Sales Revenue
512	Sales Discounts Forfeited
520	Interest Revenue
611	Cost of Goods Sold

Indicate whether each posting reference (a) through (k) should be a(n)

- Check mark (✓) for a posting to a customer account in the accounts receivable subsidiary ledger.
- Account number for a posting to an account in the general ledger. If so, give the account number.
- Letter (X) for an amount not posted.

Learning Objective 2

E-F:7-18 Identifying transactions in the accounts receivable subsidiary ledger

A customer account in the accounts receivable subsidiary ledger of Leger Old Company follows:

JOSH WILLOW

Date	Post. Ref.	Debit	Credit	Balance Debit	Balance Credit
Nov. 1				400	
9	S.5	1,180		1,580	
18	J.8		190	1,390	
30	CR.9		700	690	

Describe the three posted transactions.

Learning Objective 3

E-F:7-19 Recording transactions—purchases journal

Accounts Payable CR column total $4,800

Apr. 2	Purchased merchandise inventory on credit terms of 3/10, n/60 from Vanderbilt Co., $2,400.
5	Issued check no. 820 to purchase equipment for cash, $3,600.
11	Purchased merchandise inventory for cash, $750, issuing check no. 821.
12	Issued check no. 822 to pay Vanderbilt Co. net amount owed from Apr. 2.
19	Purchased office supplies on account from Downing Supplies, $500. Terms were n/EOM.
24	Purchased merchandise inventory on credit terms of net 30 from Wilmington Sales, $1,900.
28	Issued check no. 823 to pay for insurance coverage, debiting Prepaid Insurance for $1,000.
29	Issued check no. 824 to pay rent for the month, $1,250.

Requirements

1. Prepare headings for a purchases journal. Journalize the transactions that should be recorded in the purchases journal. The company uses the perpetual inventory system.
2. Total each column of the purchases journal.

E-F:7-20 Recording transactions—cash payments journal

Refer to information in Exercise E-F:7-19.

Learning Objective 3

Cash CR column total $8,928

Requirements

1. Prepare headings for a cash payments journal. Journalize the transactions that should be recorded in the cash payments journal.
2. Total each column of the cash payments journal.

E-F:7-21 Posting from the purchases journal; balancing the ledgers

The purchases journal of Southeastern Publishing Company follows:

Learning Objective 3

Merchandise Inventory DR column total $2,300

Purchases Journal — Page 7

Date	Vendor Account Credited	Terms	Post. Ref.	Accounts Payable CR	Merchandise Inventory DR	Office Supplies DR	Account Title	Post. Ref.	Amount
2024									
Sep. 2	Leap Tech	n/30		830	830				
5	Jell Supply	n/30		155		155			
13	Leap Tech	5/10, n/30		1,470	1,470				
26	Fallon Equipment	n/30		880			Equipment		880
Sep. 30	Total								

Other Accounts DR

Requirements

1. Total each column of the purchases journal.
2. Open four-column ledger accounts for Merchandise Inventory (118), Office Supplies (120), Equipment (150), and Accounts Payable (211). Post to these accounts from the purchases journal. Use dates and posting references in the accounts.
3. Open four-column accounts in the accounts payable subsidiary ledger for Fallon Equipment, Jell Supply, and Leap Tech. Post from the purchases journal. Use dates and posting references in the ledger accounts.
4. Balance the Accounts Payable control account in the general ledger with the total of the ending balances in the accounts payable subsidiary ledger.

Learning Objective 3

E-F:7-22 Identifying transactions in the accounts payable subsidiary ledger

A vendor account in the accounts payable subsidiary ledger of Frost Company follows.

LARRY CARPENTER					
				\multicolumn{2}{c}{Balance}
Date	Post. Ref.	Debit	Credit	Debit	Credit
Dec. 1					1,800
12	P.4		2,340		4,140
20	J.10	200			3,940
29	CP.6	1,500			2,440

Describe the three posted transactions.

Learning Objectives 2, 3

E-F:7-23 Identifying errors in special journals

Transaction	Recording
a. Henry Associates paid $490 on account for an earlier purchase of merchandise inventory.	Purchases journal
b. Recorded depreciation expense for the month.	Cash payments journal
c. Collected interest revenue.	Cash receipts journal
d. Sold merchandise inventory on account.	Cash receipts journal
e. Issued check no. 535 for purchase of merchandise inventory.	Purchases journal
f. Returned damaged inventory that was purchased on account.	Purchases journal
g. Sold merchandise inventory for cash.	Sales journal

For each transaction listed, identify the recording error and indicate the journal that should have been used.

> Problems Group A

All problems can be completed manually or by using either MyLab Accounting General Ledger or QuickBooks.

Learning Objectives 2, 3

Cash Receipts Journal, Accounts Receivable CR column total $11,600

P-F:7-24A Using the sales, cash receipts, and general journals

Assume Sparkling Springs Glass Company uses the perpetual inventory system. The general ledger of Sparkling Springs Glass Company includes the following selected accounts, along with their account numbers:

Number	Account	Number	Account
11	Cash	18	Equipment
12	Accounts Receivable	19	Land
13	Notes Receivable	41	Sales Revenue
15	Merchandise Inventory	51	Cost of Goods Sold
16	Office Supplies		

Sales and cash receipts transactions in July were as follows:

Jul. 2	Sold merchandise inventory on credit, terms n/30, to Intel, Inc., $1,500 (cost, $200).
3	Sold office supplies to an employee at cost, $80, receiving cash.
7	Cash sales for the week totaled $2,300 (cost, $1,500).
9	Sold merchandise inventory on account, terms n/30, to A. B. Miller, $7,700 (cost, $5,200).
10	Sold land that cost $10,000 for cash of the same amount.
11	Sold merchandise inventory on account, terms n/30, to Speedy Electric, $5,400 (cost, $3,350).
12	Received cash from Intel in full settlement of its account receivable from July 2.
14	Cash sales for the week were $2,600 (cost, $1,700).
15	Sold merchandise inventory on credit, terms n/30, to the partnership of William & Bill, $3,400 (cost, $2,400).
20	Sold merchandise inventory on account, terms n/30, to Speedy Electric, $500 (cost, $250).
21	Cash sales for the week were $980 (cost, $640).
22	Received $4,000 cash from A. B. Miller in partial settlement of his account receivable.
25	Received cash from William & Bill for its account receivable from July 15.
25	Sold merchandise inventory on account, terms n/30, to Oscar Co., $1,520 (cost, $1,000).
27	Collected $5,000 on a note receivable. There was no interest earned.
28	Cash sales for the week totaled $3,710 (cost, $2,450).
29	Sold merchandise inventory on account, terms n/30, to R. O. Bart, $200 (cost, $100).
31	Received $2,700 cash on account from A. B. Miller.

Requirements

1. Use the appropriate journal to record the preceding transactions in a sales journal (omit the Invoice No. column) and a cash receipts journal (omit the Sales Discounts Forfeited column).
2. Total each column of the sales journal and the cash receipts journal. Show that total debits equal total credits.
3. Show how postings would be made by writing the account numbers and check marks in the appropriate places in the journals.

Learning Objective 3

Purchases Journal, Accounts Payable CR column total $19,540

P-F:7-25A Using the purchases, cash payments, and general journals

The general ledger of Shiny Lake Golf Shop includes the following selected accounts, along with their account numbers:

Number	Account	Number	Account
111	Cash	181	Equipment
131	Merchandise Inventory	211	Accounts Payable
161	Prepaid Insurance	564	Rent Expense
171	Office Supplies	583	Utilities Expense

Transactions in December that affected purchases and cash payments follow:

Dec. 2	Purchased merchandise inventory on credit from Tomas, $4,500. Terms were 1/10, n/30.
3	Paid monthly rent, debiting Rent Expense for $2,300.
5	Purchased office supplies on credit terms of 1/10, n/30 from Right Supply, $440.
8	Received and paid electricity utility bill, $580.
9	Purchased equipment on account from Ace Equipment, $6,600. Payment terms were n/30.
10	Returned the equipment to Ace Equipment. It was damaged.
11	Paid Tomas the amount owed on the purchase of December 2.
12	Purchased merchandise inventory on account from Callahan Golf, $4,000. Terms were 3/10, n/30.
13	Purchased merchandise inventory for cash, $600.
14	Paid a semiannual insurance premium, debiting Prepaid Insurance, $1,400.
16	Paid its account payable to Right Supply from December 5.
18	Received and paid gas and water utility bills, $200.
21	Purchased merchandise inventory on credit terms of 2/10, n/45 from Dormer, Inc., $3,400.
21	Paid its account payable to Callahan Golf from December 12.
22	Purchased office supplies on account from Office World, Inc., $600. Terms were n/30.
26	Returned to Dormer, Inc. $1,000 of the merchandise inventory purchased on December 21.
31	Paid Dormer, Inc. the net amount owed from December 21 less the return on December 26.

Requirements

1. Shiny Lake Golf Shop records purchase returns in the general journal. Use the appropriate journal to record the transactions in a purchases journal, a cash payments journal (omit the Check No. column), and a general journal. The company uses the perpetual inventory system.
2. Total each column of the special journals. Show that total debits equal total credits in each special journal.
3. Show how postings would be made from the journals by writing the account numbers and check marks in the appropriate places in the journals.

P-F:7-26A Using all journals, posting, and balancing the ledgers

Tulsa Computer Security uses the perpetual inventory system and makes all credit sales on terms of n/30. Tulsa completed the following transactions during May:

Learning Objectives 2, 3

Trial balance, total debits $48,600

May 2	Issued invoice no. 913 for sale on account to K. D. King, $2,200 (cost, $1,500).
3	Purchased merchandise inventory on credit terms of 3/10, n/60 from Henderson Co., $2,900.
5	Sold merchandise inventory for cash, $1,800 (cost, $350).
5	Issued check no. 532 to purchase furniture for cash, $2,950.
8	Collected interest revenue of $1,350.
9	Issued invoice no. 914 for sale on account to Berkner Co., $5,700 (cost, $2,000).
10	Purchased merchandise inventory for cash, $1,000, issuing check no. 533.
12	Received cash from K. D. King in full settlement of her account receivable from the sale on May 2.
13	Issued check no. 534 to pay Henderson Co. the net amount owed from May 3. Round to the nearest dollar.
13	Purchased office supplies on account from Magyar, Inc., $500. Terms were n/EOM.
15	Sold merchandise inventory on account to M. O. Small, issuing invoice no. 915 for $850 (cost, $400).
18	Issued invoice no. 916 for credit sale to K. D. King, $300 (cost, $150).
19	Received cash from Berkner Co. in full settlement of its account receivable from May 9.
20	Purchased merchandise inventory on credit terms of n/30 from Silva Distributing, $2,100.
22	Purchased furniture on credit terms of 3/10, n/60 from Henderson Co., $500.
22	Issued check no. 535 to pay for insurance coverage, debiting Prepaid Insurance for $1,400.
24	Sold office supplies to an employee for cash of $125, which was Tulsa's cost.
25	Received bill and issued check no. 536 to pay utilities, $550.
28	Purchased merchandise inventory on credit terms of 2/10, n/30 from Magyar, Inc., $575.
29	Returned damaged merchandise inventory to Magyar, Inc., issuing a debit memo for $575.
29	Sold merchandise inventory on account to Berkner Co., issuing invoice no. 917 for $2,400 (cost, $1,400).
30	Issued check no. 537 to pay Magyar, Inc. in full for May 13 purchase.
31	Received cash in full from K. D. King on credit sale of May 18.
31	Issued check no. 538 to pay monthly salaries of $2,250.

Requirements

1. Open four-column general ledger accounts using Tulsa's account numbers and balances as of May 1, 2024, that follow. All accounts have normal balances.

Number	Account	Bal.
111	Cash	$ 15,000
112	Accounts Receivable	1,700
114	Merchandise Inventory	7,000
116	Office Supplies	600
117	Prepaid Insurance	0
151	Furniture	2,200
211	Accounts Payable	900
311	Osage, Capital	21,400
411	Sales Revenue	7,800
419	Interest Revenue	1,300
511	Cost of Goods Sold	2,800
531	Salaries Expense	1,900
541	Utilities Expense	200

2. Open four-column accounts in the subsidiary ledgers with beginning balances as of May 1, if any. Accounts receivable subsidiary ledger—Balakrishnan Co., $1,700; Berkner Co., $0; M. O. Small, $0; and K. D. King, $0. Accounts payable subsidiary ledger—Henderson Co., $0; Magyar, Inc., $0; Silva Distributing, $0; and White Co., $900.

3. Enter the transactions in a sales journal (page 7), a cash receipts journal (page 5, omit Sales Discounts Forfeited column), a purchases journal (page 10), a cash payments journal (page 8), and a general journal (page 6), as appropriate.

4. Post daily to the accounts receivable subsidiary ledger and to the accounts payable subsidiary ledger.

5. Total each column of the special journals. Show that total debits equal total credits in each special journal. On May 31, post to the general ledger.

6. Prepare a trial balance as of May 31, 2024, to verify the equality of the general ledger. Balance the total of the customer account ending balances in the accounts receivable subsidiary ledger against Accounts Receivable in the general ledger. Do the same for the accounts payable subsidiary ledger and Accounts Payable in the general ledger.

> Problems Group B

All problems can be completed manually or by using either MyLab Accounting General Ledger or QuickBooks.

P-F:7-27B Using the sales, cash receipts, and general journals

Assume Peaceful Springs Company uses the perpetual inventory system. The general ledger of Peaceful Springs Company includes the following selected accounts, along with their account numbers:

Learning Objectives 2, 3

Cash Receipts Journal, Accounts Receivable CR column total $11,800

Number	Account	Number	Account
11	Cash	18	Equipment
12	Accounts Receivable	19	Land
13	Notes Receivable	41	Sales Revenue
15	Merchandise Inventory	51	Cost of Goods Sold
16	Office Supplies		

Sales and cash receipts transactions in November were as follows:

Nov. 2 Sold merchandise inventory on credit, terms n/30, to Intelysis, Inc., $2,200 (cost, $400).

6 Sold office supplies to an employee at cost, $85, receiving cash.

6 Cash sales for the week totaled $2,400 (cost, $1,400).

8 Sold merchandise inventory on account, terms n/30, to A. Z. Morris, $7,500 (cost, $5,000).

9 Sold land that cost $9,000 for cash of the same amount.

11 Sold merchandise inventory on account, terms n/30, to Sloan Electric, $5,000 (cost, $3,450).

11 Received cash from Intelysis in full settlement of its account receivable from November 2.

13 Cash sales for the week were $2,200 (cost, $1,750).

15 Sold merchandise inventory on credit, terms n/30, to West and Michael, $3,000 (cost, $2,200).

19 Sold merchandise inventory on account, terms n/30, to Sloan Electric, $700 (cost, $200).

20 Cash sales for the week were $940 (cost, $640).

21 Received $4,400 cash from A. Z. Morris in partial settlement of its account receivable.

22 Received cash from West and Michael for its account receivable from November 15.

22 Sold merchandise inventory on account, terms n/30, to Olivia Co., $1,510 (cost, $980).

25 Collected $5,800 on a note receivable. There was no interest earned.

27 Cash sales for the week totaled $3,780 (cost, $2,430).

27 Sold merchandise inventory on account, terms n/30, to R. A. Brown, $230 (cost, $110).

30 Received $2,200 cash on account from A. Z. Morris.

Requirements

1. Use the appropriate journal to record the preceding transactions in a sales journal (omit the Invoice No. column) and a cash receipts journal (omit the Sales Discounts Forfeited column).
2. Total each column of the sales journal and the cash receipts journal. Determine that total debits equal total credits.
3. Show how postings would be made from the journals by writing the account numbers and check marks in the appropriate places in the journals.

Learning Objective 3

P-F:7-28B Using the purchases, cash payments, and general journals

Purchases Journal, Accounts Payable CR column total $19,470

The general ledger of Finnish Lake Golf Shop includes the following selected accounts, along with their account numbers:

Number	Account	Number	Account
111	Cash	181	Equipment
131	Merchandise Inventory	211	Accounts Payable
161	Prepaid Insurance	564	Rent Expense
171	Office Supplies	583	Utilities Expense

Transactions in December that affected purchases and cash payments were as follows:

Dec. 2	Purchased merchandise inventory on credit from Tighe, $4,100. Terms were 3/10, n/30.
3	Paid monthly rent, debiting Rent Expense for $2,200.
5	Purchased office supplies on credit terms of 3/10, n/30 from Rapid Supply, $470.
8	Received and paid electricity utility bill, $510.
9	Purchased equipment on account from A-1 Equipment, $6,900. Payment terms were net 30.
10	Returned the equipment to A-1 Equipment. It was damaged.
11	Paid Tighe the amount owed on the purchase of December 2.
12	Purchased merchandise inventory on account from Crystal Golf, $4,900. Terms were 1/10, n/30.
13	Purchased merchandise inventory for cash, $660.
14	Paid a semiannual insurance premium, debiting Prepaid Insurance, $1,200.
16	Paid its account payable to Rapid Supply from December 5.
18	Received and paid gas and water utility bills, $500.
21	Purchased merchandise inventory on credit terms of 1/10, n/45 from Devin, Inc., $3,000.
21	Paid its account payable to Crystal Golf from December 12.
22	Purchased office supplies on account from Office Stuff, Inc., $100. Terms were n/30.
26	Returned to Devin, Inc. $1,000 of the merchandise inventory purchased on December 21.
31	Paid Devin, Inc. the net amount owed from December 21 less the return on December 26.

Requirements

1. Use the appropriate journal to record the preceding transactions in a purchases journal, a cash payments journal (omit the Check No. column), and a general journal. Finnish Lake Golf Shop records purchase returns in the general journal. The company uses the perpetual inventory system.

2. Total each column of the special journals. Show that total debits equal total credits in each special journal.

3. Show how postings would be made from the journals by writing the account numbers and check marks in the appropriate places in the journals.

P-F:7-29B Using all journals, posting, and balancing the ledgers

Learning Objectives 2, 3

Atlanta Computer Security uses the perpetual inventory system and makes all credit sales on terms of n/30. During March, Atlanta completed these transactions:

Trial balance, total debits $47,950

Mar. 2	Issued invoice no. 191 for sale on account to L. E. Kingston, $3,000 (cost, $800).
3	Purchased merchandise inventory on credit terms of 3/10, n/60 from High, $2,500.
4	Sold merchandise inventory for cash, $1,100 (cost, $300).
5	Issued check no. 473 to purchase furniture for cash, $2,450.
8	Collected interest revenue of $1,150.
9	Issued invoice no. 192 for sale on account to Common Co., $5,700 (cost, $2,200).
10	Purchased merchandise inventory for cash, $1,400, issuing check no. 474.
12	Received cash from L. E. Kingston in full settlement of her account receivable from the sale of March 2.
13	Issued check no. 475 to pay High net amount owed from March 3. Round to the nearest dollar.
13	Purchased office supplies on account from Mann Corp., $350. Terms were n/EOM.
15	Sold merchandise inventory on account to Suarez Co., issuing invoice no. 193 for $700 (cost, $250).
18	Issued invoice no. 194 for credit sale to L. E. Kingston, $400 (cost, $200).
19	Received cash from Common Co. in full settlement of its account receivable from March 9.
20	Purchased merchandise inventory on credit terms of n/30 from James Swenson, $2,200.
22	Purchased furniture on credit terms of 3/10, n/60 from High, $400.
22	Issued check no. 476 to pay for insurance coverage, debiting Prepaid Insurance for $1,800.
24	Sold office supplies to an employee for cash of $100, which was Atlanta's cost.
25	Received bill and issued check no. 477 to pay utilities, $550.
28	Purchased merchandise inventory on credit terms of 2/10, n/30 from Mann Corp., $550.
29	Returned damaged merchandise inventory to Mann Corp., issuing a debit memo for $550.
29	Sold merchandise inventory on account to Common Co., issuing invoice no. 195 for $2,800 (cost, $1,400).
30	Issued check no. 478 to pay Mann Corp. in full for March 13 purchase.
31	Received cash in full from L. E. Kingston on credit sale of March 18.
31	Issued check no. 479 to pay monthly salaries of $1,550.

Requirements

1. Open four-column general ledger accounts using Atlanta Computer Security's account numbers and balances as of March 1, 2024, that follow. All accounts have normal balances.

Number	Account	Bal.
111	Cash	$ 15,800
112	Accounts Receivable	1,900
114	Merchandise Inventory	6,500
116	Office Supplies	600
117	Prepaid Insurance	0
151	Furniture	2,000
211	Accounts Payable	900
311	Diaz, Capital	20,600
411	Sales Revenue	7,600
419	Interest Revenue	1,400
511	Cost of Goods Sold	2,100
531	Salaries Expense	1,300
541	Utilities Expense	300

2. Open four-column accounts in the subsidiary ledgers with beginning balances as of March 1, if any. Accounts receivable subsidiary ledger: Arrundel Co., $1,900; Common Co., $0; L. E. Kingston, $0; and Suarez, $0. Accounts payable subsidiary ledger: High, $0; Mann Corp, $0; James Swenson, $0; and Young Co., $900.

3. Enter the transactions in a sales journal (page 8), a cash receipts journal (page 3, omit Sales Discounts Forfeited column), a purchases journal (page 6), a cash payments journal (page 9), and a general journal (page 4), as appropriate.

4. Post daily to the accounts receivable subsidiary ledger and to the accounts payable subsidiary ledger.

5. Total each column of the special journals. Show that total debits equal total credits in each special journal. On March 31, post to the general ledger.

6. Prepare a trial balance as of March 31, 2024, to verify the equality of the general ledger. Balance the total of the customer account ending balances in the accounts receivable subsidiary ledger against Accounts Receivable in the general ledger. Do the same for the accounts payable subsidiary ledger and Accounts Payable in the general ledger.

Accounting Information Systems   Financial   7-49

CRITICAL THINKING

> Continuing Problem

P-F:7-30 Using all journals

This problem continues the Canyon Canoe Company situation from Chapter F:6. At the beginning of the new year, Canyon Canoe Company decided to carry and sell T-shirts with its logo printed on them. Canyon Canoe Company uses the perpetual inventory system to account for the inventory. During January 2025, Canyon Canoe Company completed the following merchandising transactions:

Jan.	Transaction
1	Purchased 10 T-shirts at $4 each and paid cash.
2	Sold 6 T-shirts for $10 each, total cost of $24. Received cash.
3	Purchased 50 T-shirts on account at $5 each. Terms 2/10, n/30.
7	Paid the supplier for the T-shirts purchased on January 3, less discount.
8	Realized 4 T-shirts from the January 1 order were printed wrong and returned them for a cash refund.
10	Sold 40 T-shirts on account for $10 each, total cost of $200. Terms 3/15, n/45.
12	Received payment for the T-shirts sold on account on January 10, less discount.
14	Purchased 100 T-shirts on account at $4 each. Terms 4/15, n/30.
18	Canyon Company called the supplier from the January 14 purchase and told them that some of the T-shirts were the wrong color. The supplier offered a $50 purchase allowance.
20	Paid the supplier for the T-shirts purchased on January 14, less the allowance and discount.
21	Sold 60 T-shirts on account for $10 each, total cost of $220. Terms 2/20, n/30.
23	Received a payment on account for the T-shirts sold on January 21, less discount.
25	Purchased 320 T-shirts on account at $5 each. Terms 2/10, n/30, FOB shipping point.
27	Paid freight associated with the January 25 purchase, $48.
29	Paid for the January 25 purchase, less discount.
30	Sold 275 T-shirts on account for $10 each, total cost of $1,300. Terms 2/10, n/30.
31	Received payment for the T-shirts sold on January 30, less discount.

Requirements

1. Enter the transactions in a sales journal (page 2), a cash receipts journal (page 5, omit Sales Discounts Forfeited column), a purchases journal (page 7), a cash payments journal (page 6), and a general journal (page 4), as appropriate.
2. Total each column of the special journals. Show that total debits equal total credits in each special journal.

> Practice Set

P-F:7-31 Using all journals

This problem continues the Crystal Clear Cleaning practice set from Chapter F:6.

Crystal Clear Cleaning has decided that, in addition to providing cleaning services, it will sell cleaning products. Crystal Clear uses the perpetual inventory system. During December 2024, Crystal Clear completed the following transactions:

Dec.		
2	Purchased 1,000 units of inventory for $4,000 on account from Sparkle Company on terms, 5/10, n/20.
5	Purchased 1,200 units of inventory from Borax on account with terms 4/10, n/30. The total invoice was for $6,000, which included a $300 freight charge.
7	Returned 300 units of inventory to Sparkle from the December 2 purchase (cost $1,200).
9	Paid Borax.
11	Sold 500 units of goods to Happy Maids for $5,500 on account with terms n/30. Crystal Clear's cost of the goods was $2,000.
12	Paid Sparkle.
15	Received 100 units with a retail price of $1,100 back from customer Happy Maids. The goods cost Crystal Clear $400.
21	Received payment from Happy Maids, settling the amount due in full.
28	Sold 500 units of goods to Bridget, Inc. on account for $6,500 (cost $2,022). Terms 1/15, n/30.
29	Paid cash for utilities of $550.
30	Paid cash for Sales Commission Expense of $214.
31	Received payment from Bridget, Inc., less discount.

Requirements

1. Use the appropriate journal to record the preceding transactions in a sales journal (omit the Invoice No. column), a cash receipts journal (omit Sales Discounts Forfeited column), a purchases journal, a cash payments journal (omit the Check No. column), and a general journal.

2. Total each column of the special journals. Show that total debits equal total credits in each special journal.

COMPREHENSIVE PROBLEM

> Comprehensive Problem for Chapter 7

Completing the Accounting Cycle for a Merchandising Entity—Using Special Journals

Amherst Networking Systems adjusts and closes its books and then prepares financial statements monthly. Amherst uses the perpetual inventory system and all sales on credit have terms of n/30. The company completed the following transactions during August:

Aug. 1	Issued check no. 682 for August office rent of $1,300.
2	Issued check no. 683 to pay the salaries payable of $1,300 from July 31.
2	Issued invoice no. 503 for sale on account to R. T. Loeb, $700. Amherst's cost of this merchandise inventory was $210.
3	Purchased merchandise inventory on credit terms of 1/15, n/60 from Goldner, Inc., $1,400.
4	Received cash on account from Friend Company, $2,400.
4	Sold merchandise inventory for cash, $370 (cost, $111).
5	Issued check no. 684 to purchase office supplies for cash, $730.
7	Issued invoice no. 504 for sale on account to K. D. Sanders, $2,100 (cost, $630).
8	Issued check no. 685 to pay Filter Company $2,500 of the amount owed at July 31. This payment occurred after the end of the discount period.
11	Issued check no. 686 to pay Goldner, Inc. the net amount owed from August 3.
12	Received cash from R. T. Loeb in full settlement of her account receivable from August 2.
16	Issued check no. 687 to pay salaries expense of $1,290.
19	Purchased merchandise inventory for cash, $850, issuing check no. 688.
22	Purchased furniture on credit terms of 3/15, n/60 from Bradford Corporation, $510.
23	Sold merchandise inventory on account to Friend Company, issuing invoice no. 505 for $9,000 (cost, $2,700).
24	Received half the July 31 amount receivable from K. D. Sanders.
26	Purchased office supplies on credit terms of 2/10, n/30 from Filter Company, $240.
30	Returned damaged merchandise inventory to the company from whom Amherst made the cash purchase on August 19, receiving cash of $850.
31	Purchased merchandise inventory on credit terms of 1/10, n/30 from Seacrest Supply, $8,000.
31	Issued check no. 689 to Lenny Moore, owner of the business, for personal withdrawal, $600.

Requirements

1. Open these four-column accounts (on the next page) with their account numbers and July 31 balances in the various ledgers.

General Ledger

Nbr.	Account Name	Debit	Credit
101	Cash	$ 5,020	
102	Accounts Receivable	22,490	
105	Merchandise Inventory	41,300	
109	Office Supplies	1,680	
117	Prepaid Insurance	2,600	
160	Furniture	37,000	
161	Accumulated Depreciation—Furniture		$ 10,000
201	Accounts Payable		12,700
204	Salaries Payable		1,300
220	Note Payable, Long-term		25,000
301	Moore, Capital		61,090
310	Moore, Withdrawals		
400	Income Summary		
401	Sales Revenue		
501	Cost of Goods Sold		
510	Salaries Expense		
513	Rent Expense		
514	Depreciation Expense—Furniture		
516	Insurance Expense		
519	Supplies Expense		

Accounts Receivable Subsidiary Ledger: Friend Company, $2,400; R. T. Loeb, $0; Parker, Inc., $11,300; and K. D. Sanders, $8,790.

Accounts Payable Subsidiary Ledger: Bradford Corporation, $0; Filter Company, $12,700; Goldner, Inc., $0; and Seacrest Supply, $0.

2. Journalize the August transactions using a sales journal (page 4), a cash receipts journal (page 11, omit Sales Discounts Forfeited column), a purchases journal (page 8), a cash payments journal (page 5), and a general journal (page 9).

3. Post daily to the accounts receivable subsidiary ledger and the accounts payable subsidiary ledger. On August 31, post to the general ledger.

4. Prepare an unadjusted trial balance for the month ended August 31.

5. Journalize and post the following adjusting entries:
   a. Office supplies on hand, $1,000.
   b. Prepaid insurance expired, $350.
   c. Depreciation expense on furniture, $250.
   d. Accrued salaries expense, $1,060.

6. Prepare an adjusted trial balance.

7. Prepare a multistep income statement, statement of owner's equity, and classified balance sheet.

8. Journalize closing entries and post.

9. Prepare a post-closing trial balance.

> Tying It All Together Case

Before you begin this assignment, review the Tying It All Together feature in the chapter. It will also be helpful if you review McCormick & Company, Incorporated's 2018 annual report (**https://www.sec.gov/Archives/edgar/data/63754/000006375419000017/mkc-11302018x10kxq42018.htm**).

McCormick & Company, Incorporated, is a global leader in flavor that manufactures, markets, and distributes spices, seasoning mixes, condiments, and other flavorful products. The company's brands include McCormick, Lawry's, and Club House. In addition, the company also markets authentic ethnic brands such as Zatarain's, Thai Kitchen, and Simply Asia.

Requirements

1. Review Item 1A (Risk Factors) of the Notes to the Financial Statements. How does McCormick & Company, Incorporated minimize the risks associated with data breaches or cyber attacks?
2. Perform a Web search on ways businesses can prevent security breaches. What are some security solutions that McCormick & Company might use?

> Decision Case F:7-1

A fire destroyed certain accounting records of Green Books. The controller, Marilyn Green, asks your help in reconstructing the records. All of the sales are on account, with credit terms of n/30. The only accounting record preserved from the fire is the accounts receivable subsidiary ledger, which follows.

Requirements

1. Determine the beginning and ending balances of Accounts Receivable.
2. Determine the sales on account in the month of April.
3. Determine total cash receipts on account from customers during April.

Garcia Sales

Date	Post. Ref.	Debit	Credit	Balance Debit	Balance Credit
Apr. 1				450	
3	CR.8		450	0	
25	S.6	3,600		3,600	
29	S.6	1,100		4,700	

Leewright, Inc.

Date	Post. Ref.	Debit	Credit	Balance Debit	Balance Credit
Apr. 1				2,800	
15	S.6	2,600		5,400	
29	CR.8		1,500	3,900	

Sally Jones

Date	Post. Ref.	Debit	Credit	Balance Debit	Balance Credit
Apr. 1				1,100	
5	CR.8		1,100	0	
11	S.6	400		400	
21	CR.8		400	0	
24	S.6	2,000		2,000	

Jacques LeHavre

Date	Post. Ref.	Debit	Credit	Balance Debit	Balance Credit
Apr. 1				0	
8	S.6	2,400		2,400	
16	S.6	900		3,300	
18	CR.8		2,400	900	
19	J.5		200	700	
27	CR.8		700	0	

> Fraud Case F:7-1

Didrikson Rubin, the auditor of Red Barn Farm Equipment, was verifying cash payments to vendors for the past several months. She noticed that several checks had been paid to a specific vendor, but she couldn't find a record of the transactions in the computerized system. Didrikson suspects that an employee is issuing checks to a fictitious "vendor" and then deleting the transactions from the computerized system. How might Didrikson investigate the suspected fraud?

> Team Project F:7-1

Ace Moving is considering investing in a computerized accounting information system for their small business. Ace needs a system that can record customer invoices and cash receipts. In addition, it would like to track all of its bills and cash payments. As a team, investigate the two common small business accounting software products: QuickBooks and Sage 50 Accounting. Prepare a PowerPoint presentation that summarizes the similarities and differences between the two software systems.

> Communication Activity F:7-1

In 150 words or fewer, explain what an accounting information system is and describe an effective system.

> Quick Check Answers

1. c   2. a   3. b   4. c   5. b   6. c   7. a   8. a   9. d

Internal Control and Cash 8

Where Did the Cash Go?

Andrew Goard, chief financial officer of a sports-themed restaurant located in Brentwood, California, stared at the bank statement on his desk. The business recently experienced record-breaking revenue due to increased customer traffic and expanded menu and drink offerings. Andrew knew that the expenses of the business had also increased, but he had expected the cash in the business's checking account to increase, not decrease, as the bank statement was showing.

Andrew wondered if it was possible that one of his employees was stealing money from the cash register. He really liked all of his employees and didn't think that any of them would steal from the business. But the deposits on the bank statement from customer sales just didn't make sense. Given the increased sales, the cash deposits should have been much higher.

Andrew knew that it was his responsibility to ensure that procedures were put into place to be sure the cash and other assets of the business remained secure. He had thought that completing employee background checks was enough to prevent the theft of the business's assets, but he now suspected that further controls needed to be put into place. Andrew began by reviewing the bank statement and comparing it to the cash records on hand. In doing this, he identified that cash was indeed being stolen from the business by the employee who was responsible for making the daily cash deposits. Andrew realized, though, that it wasn't enough to fire the employee responsible; he needed to put security measures into place that would decrease the likelihood of employee theft happening again.

What Are Internal Controls?

Safeguarding and securing assets should be a concern of all businesses—no matter how small or large the business is. The procedures that businesses put into place to protect their assets are called *internal controls* and are a key management responsibility. For example, **Chipotle Mexican Grill, Inc.,** a company that owns and operates restaurants that feature burritos, burrito bowls, tacos, and salads, must assure its investors that proper controls have been put into place to protect its assets, promote operational efficiency, and ensure accurate and reliable accounting records. In this chapter, we look at the policies and procedures that companies such as Chipotle Mexican Grill use to fulfill this responsibility.

Chapter 8 Learning Objectives

1. Define internal control and describe the components of internal control and control procedures
2. Apply internal controls to cash receipts
3. Apply internal controls to cash payments
4. Explain the internal controls associated with and journalize petty cash transactions
5. Explain the internal controls associated with and journalize debit and credit card sales
6. Demonstrate the use of a bank account as a control device and prepare a bank reconciliation and related journal entries
7. Use the cash ratio to evaluate business performance

WHAT IS INTERNAL CONTROL, AND HOW CAN IT BE USED TO PROTECT A COMPANY'S ASSETS?

Learning Objective 1
Define internal control and describe the components of internal control and control procedures

Internal Control
The organizational plan and all the related measures adopted by an entity to safeguard assets, encourage employees to follow company policies, promote operational efficiency, and ensure accurate and reliable accounting records.

A key responsibility of a business manager is to control operations. Owners set goals, hire managers to lead the way, and hire employees to carry out the business plan. **Internal control** is the organizational plan and all the related measures designed to accomplish the following:

1. **Safeguard assets.** A company must protect its assets; otherwise it is throwing away resources. If you fail to safeguard cash, the most liquid of assets, it will quickly slip away.
2. **Encourage employees to follow company policies.** Everyone in an organization needs to work toward the same goals. It is important for a business to identify policies to help meet the company's goals. These policies are also important for the company to ensure that all customers are treated similarly and that results can be measured effectively.
3. **Promote operational efficiency.** Businesses cannot afford to waste resources. Businesses work hard to make sales and do not want to waste any of the benefits. Promoting operational efficiency reduces expenses and increases business profits.
4. **Ensure accurate, reliable accounting records.** Accurate, reliable accounting records are essential. Without reliable records, managers cannot tell which part of the business is profitable and which part needs improvement. A business could be losing money on every product sold and not realize it—unless it keeps accurate and reliable records.

Internal Control and the Sarbanes-Oxley Act

Committee of Sponsoring Organizations (COSO)
A committee that provides thought leadership related to enterprise risk management, internal control, and fraud deterrence.

Public Company
A company that sells its stock to the general public.

Internal controls are critical for all companies. Several organizations and laws have helped shape the way companies carry out internal controls. The **Committee of Sponsoring Organizations (COSO)**, for example, provides thought leadership related to enterprise risk management, internal control, and fraud deterrence. COSO's mission is to develop frameworks and guidance to help companies improve their internal controls and reduce fraud in organizations. **Public companies** sell their stock to the general public and are required by the U. S. Congress to maintain a system of internal controls.

The Enron Corporation and WorldCom accounting scandals rocked the United States in the early years of this millennium. Enron overstated profits and went out of business almost overnight. WorldCom reported expenses as assets and overstated both profits and assets. The same accounting firm, Arthur Andersen LLP, had audited both companies' financial statements. Arthur Andersen voluntarily closed its doors in 2002 after nearly 90 years in public accounting.

Internal Control and Cash  Financial 8-3

As the scandals unfolded, many people asked, "How could this happen? Where were the auditors?" To address public concern, Congress passed the **Sarbanes-Oxley Act**, abbreviated as **SOX**. This act requires companies to review internal control and take responsibility for the accuracy and completeness of their financial reports. SOX revamped corporate governance in the United States and affected the accounting profession. Here are some of the SOX provisions:

1. Public companies must issue an **internal control report**, which is a report by management describing its responsibility for and the adequacy of internal controls over financial reporting. Additionally, an outside auditor must evaluate the client's internal controls and report on the internal controls as part of the audit report.
2. A new body, the Public Company Accounting Oversight Board (PCAOB), oversees the work of auditors of public companies.
3. Accounting firms are not allowed to audit a public company and also provide certain consulting services for the same client.
4. Stiff penalties await violators—25 years in prison for securities fraud and 20 years for an executive making false sworn statements.

The Sarbanes-Oxley Act changed the rules for auditors, limiting what services they can perform in addition to the audit and requiring a report on the internal controls of each public company audited. How does a business achieve good internal control? The next section identifies the components of internal control.

The Components of Internal Control

A business can achieve its internal control objectives by addressing the five components listed below:

- **C**ontrol procedures
- **R**isk assessment
- **I**nformation system
- **M**onitoring of controls
- **E**nvironment

You can remember the five components of internal control by using the acronym CRIME.

Control Procedures
Control procedures are designed to ensure that the business's goals are achieved. The next section, "Internal Control Procedures," discusses the procedures in greater detail.

Risk Assessment
A company must identify its risks. For example, food manufacturers face the risk that their food products may harm people; airplane carrier businesses face the possibility that planes may crash; music companies face copyright infringement risks; and all companies face the risk of bankruptcy. Companies facing difficulties might be tempted to falsify their financial statements to make themselves look better than they really are. As part of the internal control system, the company's business risk, as well as the risk concerning individual accounts, must be assessed. The higher the risk, the more controls a company must put in place to safeguard its assets and accounting records.

Information System
As we have seen, the information system is critical. Controls must be in place within the information system to ensure that only authorized users have access to various parts of the accounting information system. Additionally, controls must be in place to ensure adequate

Sarbanes-Oxley Act (SOX)
Requires companies to review internal control and take responsibility for the accuracy and completeness of their financial reports.

Internal Control Report
A report by management describing its responsibility for and the adequacy of internal controls over financial reporting.

IFRS
To be IFRS compliant, foreign companies are not required to have their internal controls audited by outside auditors. While all companies have internal controls, foreign companies do not have the added expense of an audit of their internal controls. On the other hand, readers of the financial reports of foreign companies have no assurance that the controls are effective.

approvals for recorded transactions are required. The decision makers need accurate information to keep track of assets and measure profits and losses.

Monitoring of Controls

Internal Auditor
An employee of the business who ensures the company's employees are following company policies, that the company meets all legal requirements, and that operations are running efficiently.

External Auditor
An outside accountant, completely independent of the business, who evaluates the controls to ensure that the financial statements are presented fairly, in accordance with GAAP.

Companies hire auditors to monitor their controls. An **internal auditor** is an employee of the business who ensures that the company's employees are following company policies and that operations are running efficiently. Internal auditors also determine whether the company is following legal requirements for internal controls to safeguard assets. An **external auditor** is an outside accountant who is completely independent of the business. External auditors evaluate the controls to ensure that the financial statements are presented fairly, in accordance with Generally Accepted Accounting Principles (GAAP).

Environment

The environment is the "tone at the top" or the culture of the business. It starts with the CFO or CEO and the top managers. They must behave honorably to set a good example for company employees. Each must demonstrate the importance of internal controls if he or she expects the employees to take the controls seriously.

Internal Control Procedures

Whether the business is a small business that generates less than $10,000 in annual sales or a large business generating $10 billion in annual sales, all companies need the following internal control procedures:

Competent, Reliable, and Ethical Personnel

Employees should be competent, reliable, and ethical. Paying good salaries will attract high-quality employees. Employees should also be trained to do the job, and their work should be adequately supervised.

Assignment of Responsibilities

In a business with good internal controls, no duty is overlooked. Each employee has certain, carefully defined responsibilities. For example, in a large company, the person in charge of signing checks is called the *treasurer*. The chief accounting officer is called the *controller*. Even an entry-level bookkeeper, whose job includes recording accounting transactions accurately, has clear responsibilities. This assignment of responsibilities creates job accountability, thus ensuring all important tasks get done.

Separation of Duties

Separation of Duties
Dividing responsibilities between two or more people to limit fraud and promote the accuracy of accounting records.

Smart management policies divide responsibilities between two or more people. **Separation of duties** limits fraud and promotes the accuracy of the accounting records. Separation of duties can be divided into two parts:

1. **Separating operations from accounting.** Accounting should be completely separate from the operating departments, such as production and sales. What would happen if sales personnel recorded the company's revenue? Sales figures could be inflated, and then top managers would not know how much the company actually sold.
2. **Separating the custody of assets from accounting.** Accountants must not handle cash, and cashiers must not have access to the accounting records. If one employee has both duties, that employee could steal cash and conceal the theft in the accounting records. The treasurer of a company handles cash, and the controller accounts for the cash. Neither person has both responsibilities. This control applies to all assets, not just cash.

Audits

To assess the adequacy and accuracy of their accounting records, most companies perform both internal and external audits. Remember that an audit is an examination of a company's financial statements and accounting system by a trained accounting professional called an *auditor*. Internal audits are performed by employees of the company. External audits are performed by independent auditors who are not employees of the company.

To evaluate the accounting system, auditors must examine the internal controls and test them to ensure the controls are working properly. For example, a control might require authorization by a manager for payments more than $50. An auditor would check a sample of payments greater than $50 to determine whether all payments were properly authorized by a manager.

Documents

Documents provide the details of business transactions and include invoices and orders, which may be paper or electronic. Documents should be prenumbered to prevent theft and inefficiency. A gap in the numbered sequence draws attention.

For example, for Smart Touch Learning, a key document is the sales invoice. The manager can compare the total cash sales on the invoices with the amount of cash received and deposited into the bank account.

Electronic Devices

Accounting systems are relying less on paper documents and more on electronic documents and digital storage devices. For example, retailers control inventory by attaching an electronic sensor to merchandise. The cashier removes the sensor after a sale is made. If a customer tries to leave the store with the sensor attached, an alarm sounds. Devices such as these can significantly reduce theft.

E-Commerce

E-commerce creates its own unique types of risks. Hackers may gain access to confidential information, such as account numbers and passwords, or introduce computer viruses, Trojans, or phishing expeditions. To address the risks posed by e-commerce, companies have devised a number of security measures. One technique for protecting customer data is encryption. **Encryption** rearranges plain-text messages by a mathematical process. The encrypted message cannot be read by those who do not know the code. An accounting encryption example uses check-sum digits for account numbers. Each account number has its last digit equal to the sum of the previous digits. For example, consider customer number 2237, where 2 + 2 + 3 = 7. Any account number failing this test triggers an error message.

Another technique for protecting data is firewalls. **Firewalls** limit access into a local network. Members can access the network, but nonmembers cannot. Usually several firewalls are built into the system. At the point of entry, additional security measures, such as passwords, PINs (personal identification numbers), and signatures are used. For additional security, more sophisticated firewalls are used deeper in the network to protect more sensitive data.

Encryption
Rearranging plain-text messages by a mathematical process—the primary method of achieving security in e-commerce.

Firewall
A device that enables members of a local network to access the network, while keeping nonmembers out of the network.

Data Analytics in Accounting

In recent years, cryptocurrencies, such as Bitcoin, Ethereum, and Ripple, have been gaining use in online financial transactions. Cryptocurrency is a medium of exchange, such as the U.S. dollar. Cryptocurrency has no actual value, no physical form, is not legal tender, and is not backed by any government or legal entity. Cryptocurrencies haven't been around that long (since 2009) but companies such as Overstock.com and Microsoft are already accepting cryptocurrencies as a form of payment. As of August 2018, an estimated 5% of Americans hold cryptocurrencies and over 2.3 million people have used Bitcoin to make payments.

Why would a company choose to accept cryptocurrencies for retail purposes? It's because most cryptocurrency is more resistant to counterfeiting and provides faster, more secure transactions that protect a company's and individual's data. Cryptocurrencies work on a blockchain or list of all of a cryptocurrency's transactions. A blockchain allows companies and individuals to transfer financial resources across the Internet without using a third party (such as a bank) and without sharing company and personal data. Any identifying information, such as an individual's name and address, is encrypted and not shared with the merchant. While transactions are not completely anonymous because law enforcement can trace transactions to a person or company if illegal activity is suspected, cryptocurrencies create a "pseudo anonymity" that protects individuals' and companies' identity and data.

Sources: "Money is no object: Understanding the evolving cryptocurrency market," PWC, August 2015, www.pwc.com/fsi; "How many people use Bitcoin in 2019?," Bitcoin Market Journal, February 2019, https://www.bitcoinmarketjournal.com/how-many-people-use-bitcoin/

Other Controls

The types of other controls are as endless as the types of businesses that employ them. Some examples of other common controls include the following:

- Fireproof vaults to store important documents
- Burglar alarms, fire alarms, and security cameras
- Loss-prevention specialists who train company employees to spot suspicious activity
- Fidelity bonds to reimburse the company for any losses due to employee theft
- Mandatory vacations and job rotation

DECISIONS

What e-commerce internal controls should be put into place?

Jason Kane works as an information technology auditor for Netproducts, a retailer that sells merchandise over the Internet. Jason has been assigned the responsibility of reviewing the existing procedures and suggesting internal controls that could best protect the company. Netproducts sells all its merchandise over the Internet and accepts only credit card payments. Netproducts tracks trend information about its sales and maintains all customer, product, and pricing information on the company's intranet. In addition, Netproducts keeps employee information such as annual leave, payroll deposits, and Social Security numbers on its intranet. What e-commerce controls should Jason suggest?

Solution

Jason should suggest that specific controls be put into place, such as using encryption technology and firewalls, to protect customer and employee information. He should recommend that customers be required to create an online account with a password for the site and that the company only use secured Internet networks. In addition, Netproducts should ensure that the customer and employee data are physically secured and that access to the data can be obtained only by authorized individuals.

The Limitations of Internal Control—Costs and Benefits

Collusion
Two or more people working together to circumvent internal controls and defraud a company.

Unfortunately, most internal controls can be overcome. **Collusion**—two or more people working together—can beat internal controls. For example, consider the following scenario with Galaxy Theater. Ralph and Lana, employees of Galaxy Theater, can design a scheme in which Ralph, the ticket seller, sells tickets and pockets the cash from 10 customers. Lana, the ticket taker, admits 10 customers to the theater without taking their tickets. Ralph and Lana split the cash. Ralph and Lana have colluded to circumvent controls, resulting in Galaxy Theater losing revenues. To prevent this situation, the manager must take additional steps, such as matching the number of people in the theater against the number of ticket stubs retained, which takes time away from the manager's other duties. It is difficult and costly to plan controls that can prevent collusion.

The stricter the internal control system, the more it costs. A complex system of internal control can strangle the business with red tape. How tight should the controls be? Internal controls must always be judged in light of their costs versus their benefits. Following is an example of a positive cost–benefit relationship: A security guard at a retail store costs about $28,000 a year. On average, each guard prevents about $50,000 of theft each year. The net savings to the retail store is $22,000. An example of a negative cost–benefit relationship would be paying the same security guard $28,000 a year to guard a $1,000 cash drawer. The cost exceeds the benefit by $27,000.

So far we have discussed what internal control is and how it can be used to protect a company's assets. We will now spend the remainder of the chapter concentrating on cash because it is the asset most likely to be stolen. However, it is important to remember that internal controls should be applied to all assets, not just cash.

Match the accounting terminology to the definitions.

1. Sarbanes-Oxley Act
2. Internal control
3. Encryption
4. Separation of duties
5. Internal auditors

a. Organizational plan and all the related measures adopted by an entity to safeguard assets, encourage employees to follow company policies, promote operational efficiency, and ensure accurate and reliable accounting records.

b. Employees of the business who ensure that the company's employees are following company policies and meeting legal requirements and that operations are running efficiently.

c. Rearranging plain-text messages by a mathematical process—the primary method of achieving security in e-commerce.

d. Requires companies to review internal control and take responsibility for the accuracy and completeness of their financial reports.

e. Dividing responsibilities between two or more people.

Check your answers online in MyLab Accounting or at http://www.pearsonhighered.com/Horngren.

For more practice, see Short Exercise S-F:8-1.   MyLab Accounting

WHAT ARE THE INTERNAL CONTROL PROCEDURES WITH RESPECT TO CASH RECEIPTS?

Cash receipts occur primarily when a business sells merchandise or services. All cash receipts should be deposited in the bank for safekeeping shortly after the cash is received. Companies receive cash either over the counter, through the mail, or by electronic funds transfer. Each source of cash has its own security measures. We have already discussed internal control procedures for e-commerce, so this section focuses on over-the-counter and mailed cash receipts.

Learning Objective 2
Apply internal controls to cash receipts

Cash Receipts Over the Counter

A cash receipt over the counter in a store involves a point-of-sale terminal (cash register) that provides control over the cash receipts. Consider a retail store. For each transaction, the retail store issues a receipt to ensure that each sale is recorded. The cash drawer opens after the clerk enters a transaction, and the machine (cash register) records it. At the end of the day, a manager proves the cash by comparing the cash in the drawer against the machine's record of cash sales. This step helps prevent theft by the clerk.

At the end of the day—or several times a day if business is brisk—the manager deposits the cash in the bank. The machine tape then goes to the accounting department to record the journal entry for cash receipts and sales revenue. These measures, coupled with oversight by a manager, discourage theft.

Cash Receipts by Mail

Many companies receive checks by mail for payments of services or merchandise. Checks sent via mail are considered to be cash receipts. Exhibit F:8-1 shows how companies control cash received by mail.

Exhibit F:8-1 | Cash Receipts by Mail

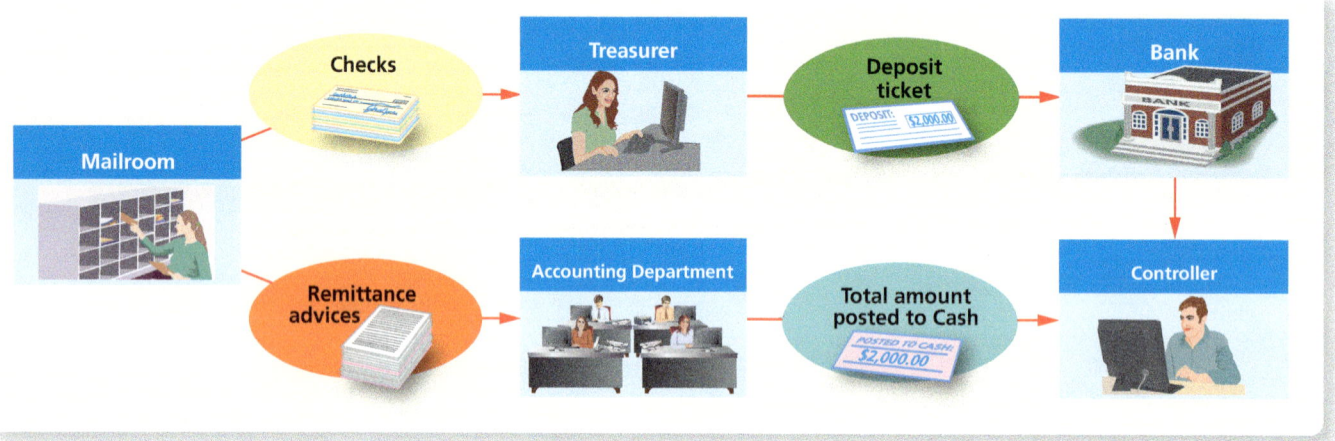

The process works like this:

Step 1: All incoming mail is opened by a mailroom employee. The mailroom then sends all customer checks to the treasurer and all remittance advices to the accounting department. A **remittance advice** is an optional attachment to a check that tells the business the reason for the payment.

Remittance Advice
An optional attachment to a check that tells the business the reason for the payment.

Step 2: The treasurer has the cashier deposit the checks in the bank. The cashier receives a deposit receipt.

Step 3: The accounting department (or bookkeeper) uses the remittance advices to record the journal entries to Cash and customer accounts.

Step 4: As a final control, the controller compares the following records for the day:

- Bank deposit amount from the treasurer
- Debit to Cash from the accounting department

The debit to Cash should equal the amount deposited in the bank. If it does, all cash receipts are safe in the bank, and the company's books are up to date.

Many companies use a **lock-box system** as an alternative to accepting cash or checks via the mail or over the counter. In a lock-box system, customers send their checks directly to a post office box that belongs to a bank. A bank employee empties the box daily and records the deposits into the company's bank account. Internal control is tight because company personnel never touch incoming cash. The lock-box system puts a business's cash into the company's bank account quickly.

Lock-Box System
A system in which customers send their checks to a post office box that belongs to a bank. A bank employee empties the box daily and records the deposits into the company's bank account.

Try It!

6. Fill in the missing information concerning how companies control cash received by mail.

    a. The _____ opens the mail and sends customer checks to the treasurer.
    b. The _____ deposits the customer checks in the bank.
    c. The _____ uses the remittance advices to record the journal entries for cash receipts.
    d. The _____ compares the bank deposit to the journal entry for cash receipts.

Check your answers online in MyLab Accounting or at http://www.pearsonhighered.com/Horngren.

For more practice, see Short Exercises S-F:8-2 and S-F:8-3. MyLab Accounting

WHAT ARE THE INTERNAL CONTROL PROCEDURES WITH RESPECT TO CASH PAYMENTS?

Companies make many payments by check. They also pay small amounts from a petty cash fund, which is discussed later in the chapter. Let's begin by discussing cash payments by check.

Learning Objective 3
Apply internal controls to cash payments

Controls Over Payment by Check

Companies need a good separation of duties between the operations of the business and writing checks for cash payments. Payment by check is an important internal control for the following reasons:

- The check provides a record of the payment.
- The check must be signed by an authorized official.
- Before signing the check, the official reviews the invoice or other evidence supporting the payment.

Controls Over Purchases and Payments

To illustrate the internal control over cash payments by check, suppose Smart Touch Learning buys its tablets from an electronics manufacturer. The purchasing and payment process follows these steps, as shown in Exhibit F:8-2 (on the next page).

Step 1: Smart Touch Learning sends a purchase order to the electronics manufacturer that contains the quantity and type of goods needed.

Step 2: The electronics manufacturer ships the inventory and sends an invoice back to Smart Touch Learning.

Step 3: Smart Touch Learning receives the inventory and prepares a receiving report.

Step 4: After approving all documents, Smart Touch Learning sends a check to the electronics manufacturer.

Exhibit F:8-2 | Cash Payments by Check

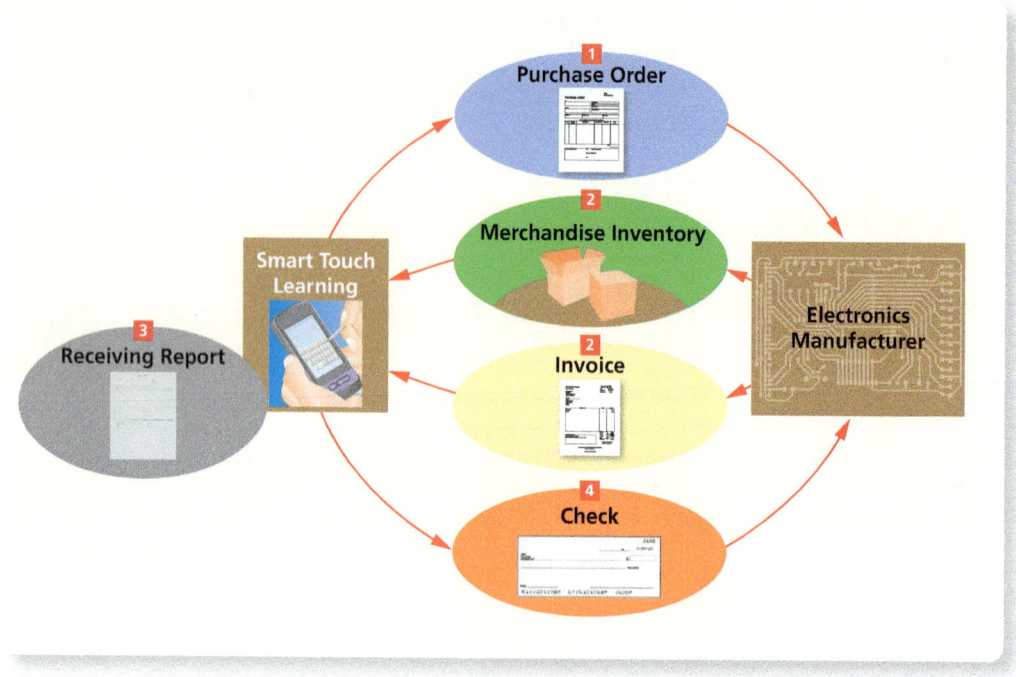

For good internal control, the purchasing agent (the employee who prepares the purchase order) should neither receive the goods nor approve the payment. If these duties are not separated, a purchasing agent could buy goods and have them shipped to his or her home. Or a purchasing agent could overpay for purchases, approve the payment, and split the excess with the supplier.

Exhibit F:8-3 shows Smart Touch Learning's payment packet of documents, which may be in either electronic or paper format. Before signing the check for payment of goods, the controller or the treasurer should examine the packet to prove that all the documents agree. Only then does the company know the following:

1. It received the goods ordered.
2. It is paying only for the goods received and authorized.
3. It is paying the correct amount.

Exhibit F:8-3 | Payment Packet

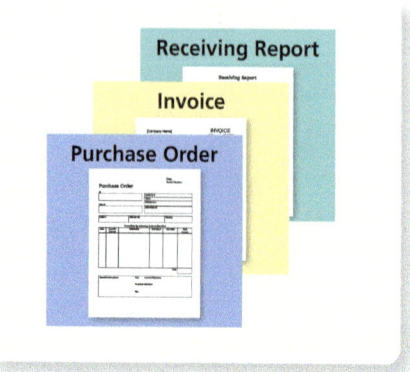

Internal Control and Cash  Financial 8-11

After payment, the payment packet is marked as paid to prevent the bill from being paid twice. Electronically paid invoices are automatically marked "paid" by most accounting systems.

Streamlined Procedures

Technology is streamlining payment procedures. **Evaluated receipts settlement (ERS)** compresses the payment approval process into a single step by comparing the receiving report to the purchase order. If those documents match, then Smart Touch Learning got the tablets it ordered and payment is made to the vendor.

An even more streamlined process bypasses paper documents altogether. In **electronic data interchange (EDI)**, a retailer's computers communicate directly with the computers of suppliers. When the retailer's inventory reaches a low level, the computer creates and sends an electronic purchase order to the supplier. The supplier then ships the inventory and electronically sends an invoice to the retailer. A manager approves the invoice, and then an electronic fund transfer (EFT) sends the retailer's payment to the supplier. These streamlined EDI procedures are used for both cash payments and cash receipts in many companies.

Evaluated Receipts Settlement (ERS)
A procedure that compresses the payment approval process into a single step by comparing the receiving report to the purchase order.

Electronic Data Interchange (EDI)
A streamlined process that bypasses paper documents altogether. Computers of customers communicate directly with the computers of suppliers to automate routine business transactions.

Try It!

7. Fill in the missing information.
   a. The vendor ships the inventory and sends a(n) _____ back to the purchaser.
   b. After approving all documents, the purchaser sends a(n) _____ to the vendor.
   c. When ordering merchandise inventory, the purchaser sends a(n) _____ to the vendor.
   d. The purchaser receives the inventory and prepares a(n) _____.

Check your answers online in MyLab Accounting or at http://www.pearsonhighered.com/Horngren.

For more practice, see Short Exercise S-F:8-4.   MyLab Accounting

WHAT ARE THE INTERNAL CONTROL PROCEDURES NEEDED FOR PETTY CASH AND HOW ARE PETTY CASH TRANSACTIONS RECORDED?

It is not cost effective for a business to write a check for parking or the delivery of a package across town. To meet these needs and to streamline record keeping for small cash transactions, companies keep cash on hand to pay small amounts. This fund is called **petty cash**.

We have already established that cash is the most liquid of assets. Petty cash is more liquid than cash in the bank because none of the bank controls are in place. Therefore, petty cash needs controls such as the following:

- Designate a custodian of the petty cash fund. The custodian is the individual assigned responsibility for the petty cash fund.
- Designate a specific amount of cash to be kept in the petty cash fund.
- Support all petty cash fund payments with a petty cash ticket. These tickets are sequentially numbered. The petty cash ticket serves as an authorization voucher and explanation.

Learning Objective 4
Explain the internal controls associated with and journalize petty cash transactions

Petty Cash
A fund containing a small amount of cash that is used to pay for minor expenditures.

8-12　Financial　　chapter 8

Setting Up the Petty Cash Fund

The petty cash fund is opened when the company writes a check for the designated amount. The company makes the check payable to Petty Cash. Suppose on August 1, Smart Touch Learning creates a petty cash fund of $200. The custodian cashes the $200 check and places the currency in the fund box. The journal entry is as follows:

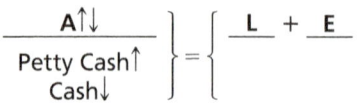

Date	Accounts and Explanation	Debit	Credit
Aug. 1	Petty Cash	200	
	Cash		200
	To open the petty cash fund.		

For each petty cash payment, the custodian prepares a petty cash ticket like the one in Exhibit F:8-4.

Exhibit F:8-4 | Petty Cash Ticket

```
              PETTY CASH TICKET              #101
Date  Aug 25, 2025
Amount  $60
For  Letterhead invoices
Debit  Office Supplies
Received by  Lewis Wright     Fund Custodian  MAR
```

Signatures (or initials) identify the recipient of the cash and the fund custodian. The custodian keeps the petty cash tickets in the fund box. The sum of the cash plus the total of the petty cash tickets should equal the fund balance, $200, at all times.

Maintaining the Petty Cash account at its designated balance is the nature of an **imprest system**. The imprest system requires that, at any point in time, the petty cash box contain cash and petty cash tickets that total the amount of the imprest balance. This clearly identifies the amount of cash for which the custodian is responsible, and it is the system's main internal control feature.

Imprest System
A way to account for petty cash by maintaining a constant balance in the petty cash account. At any time, cash plus petty cash tickets must total the amount allocated to the petty cash fund.

Replenishing the Petty Cash Fund

Payments decrease the fund, so periodically the fund must be replenished. Suppose that on August 31, the petty cash fund holds $118 in cash and $80 in petty cash tickets (ticket no. 101 for $60 for office supplies and ticket no. 102 for $20 for a delivery).

You can see $2 is missing:

Fund balance		$ 200
Cash on hand	$ 118	
Petty cash tickets	80	
Total accounted for		198
Amount of cash missing		$ 2

To replenish the petty cash fund, you need to bring the cash on hand up to $200. The company writes a check, payable to Petty Cash, for $82 ($200 imprest balance − $118 cash on hand). The fund custodian cashes this check and puts $82 back in the fund box. Now the fund box holds $200 cash as it should.

The petty cash tickets tell you what to debit and the check amount tells you what to credit, as shown in this entry to replenish the fund:

Date	Accounts and Explanation	Debit	Credit
Aug. 31	Office Supplies	60	
	Delivery Expense	20	
	Cash Short & Over	2	
	Cash		82
	To replenish the petty cash fund.		

$$\left. \begin{array}{c} A\downarrow \\ \text{Office} \\ \text{Supplies}\uparrow \\ \text{Cash}\downarrow \end{array} \right\} = \left\{ \begin{array}{c} L + E\downarrow \\ \text{Delivery} \\ \text{Expense}\uparrow \\ \text{Cash Short} \\ \text{\& Over}\uparrow \end{array} \right.$$

Missing petty cash funds are debited to a new account, Cash Short & Over. In this case, $2 was missing, so we debit Cash Short & Over for the missing petty cash. Another way to look at this is that we needed another $2 debit to make the journal entry balance.

The Petty Cash account keeps its $200 balance at all times. **The Petty Cash account is used in a journal entry only when the fund is started (see the August 1 entry) or when its amount is increased or decreased.** If the business increases the fund amount from $200 to $250, this would require a check to be cashed for $50 and the debit would be to Petty Cash. **When replenishing the fund, the company debits either the associated expense incurred or the asset purchased with the funds.**

At times the sum of cash in the petty cash fund plus the tickets may exceed the fund balance. Consider the previous example. Assume the petty cash ticket no. 102 for delivery was for $30 instead of $20. Because we know the amount of the petty cash tickets and the amount of cash on hand, we can find out the amount of cash shortage or overage.

Why wasn't Petty Cash debited when the fund was replenished?

Fund balance		$ 200
Cash on hand	$ 118	
Petty cash tickets	90	
Total accounted for		208
Amount of cash overage		$ 8

In this case, the cash on hand plus petty cash tickets ($208) is more than the fund balance ($200). A cash overage exists. The journal entry to replenish the fund would be:

Date	Accounts and Explanation	Debit	Credit
Aug. 31	Office Supplies	60	
	Delivery Expense	30	
	Cash Short & Over		8
	Cash		82
	To replenish the petty cash fund.		

$$\left. \begin{array}{c} A\downarrow \\ \text{Office} \\ \text{Supplies}\uparrow \\ \text{Cash}\downarrow \end{array} \right\} = \left\{ \begin{array}{c} L + E\downarrow \\ \text{Delivery} \\ \text{Expense}\uparrow \\ \text{Cash Short} \\ \text{\& Over}\downarrow \end{array} \right.$$

We know the total debits are $90 ($60 + $30). We know the check to replenish the fund was still $82 (credit to Cash) because the fund balance should total $200 and there was $118 in the petty cash box. For this situation, we need an $8 credit to make the journal entry balance, a gain, which is credited to Cash Short & Over.

The Cash Short & Over account is used for both shortages and overages. Therefore, it may have either a debit or credit balance. If at the end of the year, the account has a debit balance, then there were more shortages than overages, and it is considered an expense when preparing the income statement. However, if the end of year balance is a credit, then there were more overages than shortages, and the balance is considered revenue.

Changing the Amount of the Petty Cash Fund

Suppose that on September 1, Smart Touch Learning decides to increase the amount of the petty cash fund from $200 to $300. In order to increase the fund, Smart Touch Learning must write a check for the additional $100, cash the check, and place the additional currency in the petty cash box. Because the amount of the fund has changed, the company must record the following journal entry showing this change:

Date	Accounts and Explanation	Debit	Credit
Sep. 1	Petty Cash	100	
	Cash		100
	To increase the petty cash fund.		

A↑↓ = L + E
Petty Cash↑
Cash↓

Had the Petty Cash fund been decreased, the debit would've been to Cash and the credit to the Petty Cash account. Remember that the only time the Petty Cash account is used in the journal entry is when the account is established, increased, or decreased.

Try It!

8. The following petty cash transactions of Green Golf Equipment occurred in May:

May 1	Established a petty cash fund with a $200 balance.
31	The petty cash fund has $18 in cash and $180 in petty cash tickets that were issued to pay for Office Supplies ($81), Delivery Expense ($36), Postage Expense ($54), and Miscellaneous Expense ($9). The petty cash custodian replenished the fund and recorded the expenses.

Prepare the journal entries.

Check your answers online in MyLab Accounting or at http://www.pearsonhighered.com/Horngren.

For more practice, see Short Exercise S-F:8-5. **MyLab Accounting**

WHAT ARE THE INTERNAL CONTROLS NEEDED WITH DEBIT AND CREDIT CARD SALES AND HOW ARE THESE TYPES OF SALES RECORDED?

Learning Objective 5
Explain the internal controls associated with and journalize debit and credit card sales

In addition to receiving cash receipts from customers over the counter, most companies also accept credit cards and debit cards. By accepting credit cards and debit cards, such as Visa, MasterCard, and American Express, businesses are able to attract more customers.

Internal Control and Cash  Financial 8-15

Credit cards offer the customer the convenience of buying something without having to pay cash immediately. Debit cards, on the other hand, reduce the customer's bank account immediately but allow the customer to pay electronically instead of with currency or by writing a check.

Accepting payments by credit cards and debit cards can reduce a company's risk associated with sales. They don't have to worry about employees handling cash when processing customer sales, which reduces the risk associated with sales. When a customer uses a credit card, the business doesn't have to worry about collecting the cash from the customer because the card issuer (Visa, for example) has the responsibility of collection. Companies that choose to accept credit cards and debit cards from customers must establish internal control procedures to protect their customers' data. These internal control procedures should include the following:

- Use designated point-of-sale (POS) terminals to process card payments that are in accordance with the payment card industry data security standards (PCI DSS)
- Never print the full 16-digit card number on either the business or customer copy of the receipt
- Employees involved in processing transactions should be trained on appropriate procedures
- Refunds of credit/debit card payments should be made by an individual other than the person reconciling the transactions
- The storage and retention of credit/debit card information should be kept to a minimum
- Cardholder data should be maintained on a secure network behind a firewall and encrypted

Companies hire a third-party processor to process credit and debit card transactions. Transactions are usually entered into an electronic terminal (card scanner) that the company either purchases or rents from the processor. The fees the card processor charges the company for its processing services vary depending on the type of card and the specific agreement the company has with the card processor. The processor agreement specifies how fees are paid to the processor. The following are two common methods of handling the proceeds and processing fees:

- **Net**—The total sale less the processing fee assessed equals the net amount of cash deposited by the processor, usually within a few days of the sale date.
- **Gross**—The total sale is deposited daily within a few days of the actual sale date. The processing fees for all transactions processed for the month are deducted from the company's bank account by the processor, often on the last day of the month.

Proceeds from credit and debit card transactions are usually deposited within a few business days after the sale. Therefore, credit and debit card sales are journalized similar to cash sales. For example, Smart Touch Learning sells merchandise inventory (ignore Cost of Goods Sold) to a customer for $3,000 on August 15. The customer pays with a third-party credit card. Smart Touch Learning would record the entry, assuming the card processor assesses a 4% fee and deposits the net amount, as follows:

Date	Accounts and Explanation	Debit	Credit
Aug. 15	Cash	2,880	
	Credit Card Expense ($3,000 × 0.04)	120	
	Sales Revenue		3,000
	Recorded credit card sales, net of fee.		

$A\uparrow$ = $L +$ $E\uparrow$
Cash↑   Sales Revenue↑
         Credit Card Expense↑

The same entry, assuming the processor uses the gross method, on the sale date would be as follows:

Date	Accounts and Explanation	Debit	Credit
Aug. 15	Cash	3,000	
	Sales Revenue		3,000
	Recorded credit card sales.		

A↑ Cash↑ = L + E↑ Sales Revenue↑

At the end of August, the processor would collect the fees assessed for the month. (*Note:* We assume only the one credit card sale for this month.)

Date	Accounts and Explanation	Debit	Credit
Aug. 31	Credit Card Expense	120	
	Cash		120
	Paid fees assessed by credit card processor.		

A↓ Cash↓ = L + E↓ Credit Card Expense↑

TYING IT ALL TOGETHER

Chipotle Mexican Grill, Inc. owns and operates more than 2,452 restaurants throughout the United States, 37 international Chipotle restaurants, and two non-Chipotle restaurants. Steve Ells, founder, opened his first restaurant in 1993 in Denver, Colorado, to show that food served fast didn't have to be the typical "fast-food" experience. Chipotle uses high-quality ingredients, raised with respect for animals, farmers, and the environment. (You can find Chipotle Mexican Grill, Inc.'s annual report at **https://www.sec.gov/Archives/edgar/data/1058090/000105809019000007/cmg-20181231x10k.htm**)

In April 2017, Chipotle Mexican Grill detected unauthorized activity (malware) on its network that supports credit card payment processing. The malware was designed to access payment card data including cardholder name, card number, expiration date, and internal verification codes. What could Chipotle Mexican Grill do to ensure the security of its credit and debit card payments?

Chipotle Mexican Grill should use and regularly update antivirus software, implement strong access controls, regularly monitor and test networks, and maintain policies that address information security for employees.

Who is responsible for the internal controls and what could happen if the internal controls fail?

According to the notes in the financial statements, the management of Chipotle Mexican Grill is responsible for establishing and maintaining effective internal control. Internal controls are meant to provide reasonable assurance regarding the reliability of financial reporting. Failure to maintain internal controls could limit the ability of the company to report accurate financial results and detect and prevent fraud. If significant enough, a failure of internal controls could cause a loss of investor confidence and a decline in the market price of the company's stock.

Phoenix Restaurant accepts credit and debit cards as forms of payment. Assume Phoenix had $12,000 of credit and debit card sales on June 30, 2023.

9. Suppose Phoenix's processor charges a 2% fee and deposits sales net of the fee. Journalize the sales transaction for the restaurant.
10. Suppose Phoenix's processor charges a 2% fee and deposits sales using the gross method. Journalize the sales transaction for the restaurant.

Check your answers online in MyLab Accounting or at http://www.pearsonhighered.com/Horngren.

For more practice, see Short Exercise S-F:8-6. **MyLab Accounting**

Internal Control and Cash  Financial 8-17

HOW CAN THE BANK ACCOUNT BE USED AS A CONTROL DEVICE?

Cash is the most liquid asset reported on the balance sheet because it is the medium of exchange. Because cash is easy to conceal and relatively easy to steal, businesses keep their cash in a bank account. The bank has established practices for safeguarding the business's money. This section identifies the most common controls applied to a bank account.

> **Learning Objective 6**
> Demonstrate the use of a bank account as a control device and prepare a bank reconciliation and related journal entries

Signature Card

Banks require each person authorized to sign on an account to provide a **signature card**. This helps protect against forgery because the signature card should be checked frequently by bank personnel to authenticate written checks or deposits made by the business.

> **Signature Card**
> A card that shows each authorized person's signature for a bank account.

Deposit Ticket

Banks supply standard forms such as a deposit ticket. Completed by the customer, the **deposit ticket** shows the amount of each deposit. As proof of the transaction, the customer receives a deposit receipt from the bank.

> **Deposit Ticket**
> A bank form that is completed by the customer and shows the amount of each deposit.

Check

To pay cash, the depositor writes a **check,** which is a prenumbered document that tells the bank to pay the designated party a specified amount. Exhibit F:8-5 shows a check drawn by Smart Touch Learning. There are three parties to a check: the maker, payee, and bank. The **maker** is the issuer of the check, in this case, Smart Touch Learning. The **payee** (California Office Products) is the individual or business to whom the check is paid.

> **Check**
> A document that instructs a bank to pay the designated person or business a specified amount of money.
>
> **Maker**
> The party who issues the check.
>
> **Payee**
> The individual or business to whom the check is paid.

Exhibit F:8-5 | Check with Remittance Advice

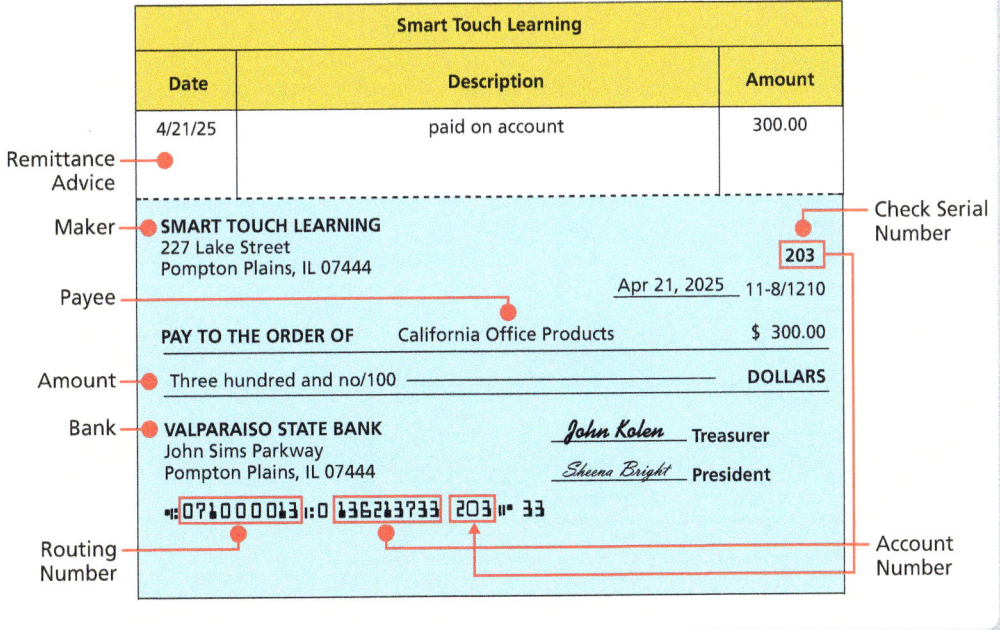

An easy way to remember the difference between the maker and the payee is the maker is the party who is making the promise that the cash is available in the bank to settle the check.

8-18 Financial  chapter 8

Routing Number
On a check, the 9-digit number that identifies the bank upon which the payment is drawn.

Account Number
On a check, the number that identifies the account upon which the payment is drawn.

Bank Statement
A document from the bank that reports the activity in the customer's account. It shows the bank account's beginning and ending balances and lists the month's cash transactions conducted through the bank account.

Canceled Checks
Physical or scanned copies of the maker's cashed (paid) checks.

Electronic Funds Transfer (EFT)
A system that transfers cash by electronic communication rather than by paper documents.

This check has two parts, the check itself and the remittance advice. In addition, the check includes the routing number and account number. The **routing number** is a 9-digit number that identifies the bank upon which the payment is drawn. The **account number** identifies the account upon which the payment is drawn.

Bank Statement

Banks send monthly statements to customers either electronically or in the mail. A **bank statement** reports the activity in the customer's account. The statement shows the account's beginning and ending balances, cash receipts, and cash payments. Included with the statement sometimes are physical or scanned copies of the maker's **canceled checks**, the checks written by the maker that have been cashed (paid) by the bank. Exhibit F:8-6 is the April 30, 2025, bank statement of Smart Touch Learning.

Electronic Funds Transfers

Electronic funds transfer (EFT) moves cash by electronic communication. Many bills and other payments, such as salaries, rent, utilities, and insurance, are now paid by EFT. It is much cheaper to pay these items by EFT without having to mail a check. Debit card transactions and direct deposits are also considered EFTs.

Exhibit F:8-6 | **Bank Statement**

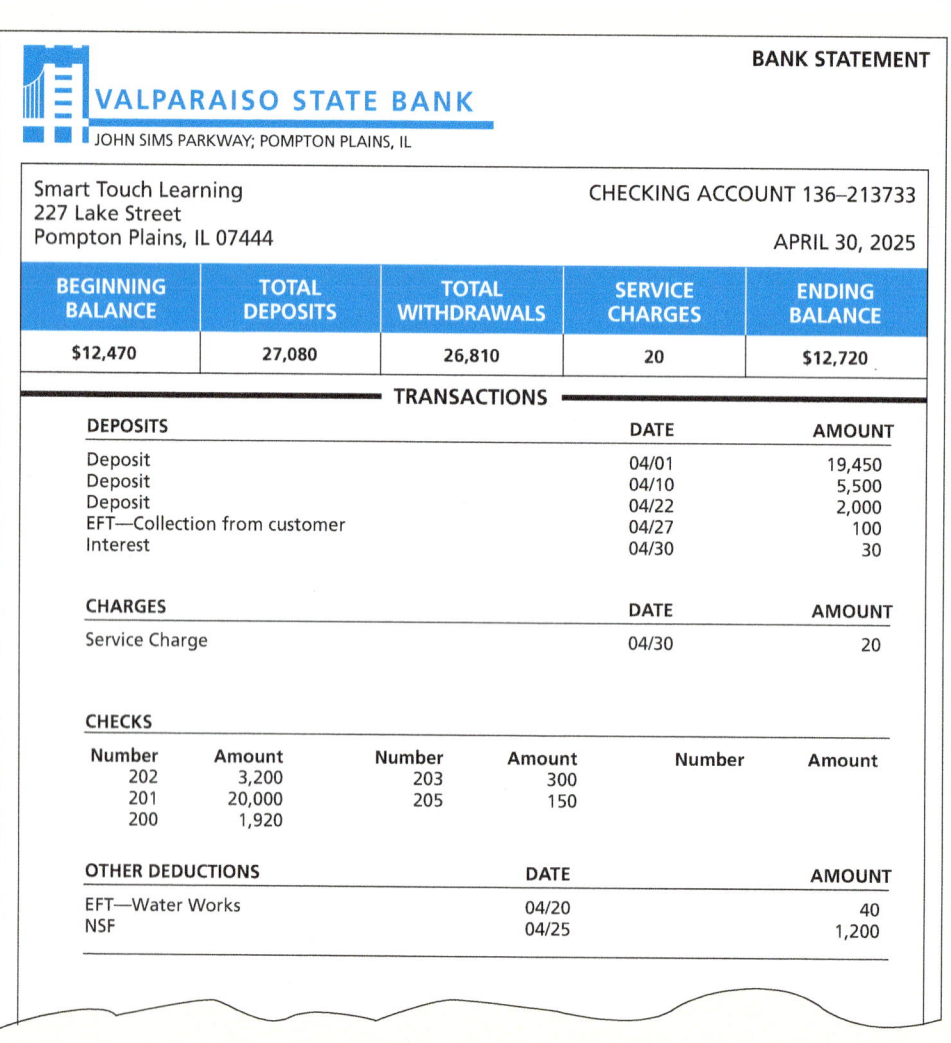

Internal Control and Cash  Financial 8-19

Bank Reconciliation

The **bank reconciliation** compares and explains the differences between cash on the company's books and cash according to the bank's records on a specific date. There are two records of a business's cash:

Bank Reconciliation
A document explaining the reasons for the difference between a depositor's cash records and the depositor's cash balance in its bank account.

1. The Cash account in the company's general ledger. April's Cash T-account for Smart Touch Learning is shown below.

Cash			
Beg. Bal.	10,550	20,000	Apr. 2
Apr. 1	19,450	3,200	Apr. 15
Apr. 8	5,500	300	Apr. 21
Apr. 22	2,000	2,000	Apr. 30
Apr. 30	9,000	150	Apr. 30
End. Bal.	20,850		

2. The bank statement, which shows the cash receipts and payments transacted through the bank. In Exhibit F:8-6, however, the bank shows an ending balance of $12,720 for Smart Touch Learning.

The books (the balance in the Cash account in the general ledger) and the bank statement usually show different cash balances. Differences may arise because of a time lag in recording transactions, called **timing differences**. Three examples of timing differences follow:

Timing Difference
Difference that arises between the balance on the bank statement and the balance on the company's books because of a time lag in recording transactions.

- When a business writes a check, it immediately deducts the amount in its checkbook and Cash account. The bank, however, does not subtract the check from the company's account until the bank pays the check a few days later.
- When a company deposits cash in its account, it immediately adds the cash receipt to the checkbook and Cash account. The bank, however, may take a day or two to add deposits to the company's balance.
- EFT cash payments and EFT cash receipts are often recorded by the bank before a company learns of them.

To obtain accurate cash records, a company must update its Cash account after the company receives its bank statement. A bank reconciliation is used to carry out the updating process. The bank reconciliation explains all differences between the company's cash records and the bank's records of the company's balance. The person who prepares the bank reconciliation should have no other cash duties. This means the reconciler should not be a person who has access to cash or duties that require journalizing cash transactions. Otherwise, he or she could steal cash and manipulate the reconciliation to conceal the theft.

Preparing the Bank Side of the Bank Reconciliation

Here are the items that appear on the bank side of the bank reconciliation. They all cause differences between the bank balance and the book balance.

The bank side contains items not yet recorded by the bank but recorded by the company, or errors made by the bank. These items include the following:

Deposits in Transit (Outstanding Deposits) A **deposit in transit** has been recorded and has already been added to the company's book balance, but the bank has not yet recorded it. These are shown as "Add: Deposits in transit" on the bank side because when the bank does record these deposits, it will increase the bank balance.

Deposit in Transit
A deposit recorded by the company but not yet by its bank.

Outstanding Checks An **outstanding check** is a check that has been recorded and has already been deducted from the company's book balance, but the bank has not yet

Outstanding Check
A check issued by a company and recorded on its books but not yet paid by its bank.

paid (deducted) it. Such checks are shown as "Less: Outstanding checks" on the bank side because when the bank does make payment for the checks, it will decrease the bank balance.

Bank Errors Bank errors are posting errors made by the bank that either incorrectly increase or decrease the bank balance. All bank errors are corrected on the bank side of the reconciliation by reversing the effect of the errors.

> *Errors are always recorded on the side of the reconciliation of the party that made the error. If the bank made the error, it is recorded on the bank side. If the business made the error, it is recorded on the book side.*

Preparing the Book Side of the Bank Reconciliation

The book side contains items not yet recorded by the company on its books but that have been recorded by the bank, or errors made by the company. Items to show on the book side include the following:

Bank Collections Bank collections are cash receipts the bank has received and recorded for a company's account but that the company has not recorded yet on its books. An example of a bank collection would occur when a business has its customers use a lock-box system. Another example is a bank collecting on a note receivable for a business. A bank collection is often referred to as a credit memorandum. A **credit memorandum** indicates that the customer's account has been increased. A bank collection (which increases the bank balance) that appears on the bank statement will show as "Add: Bank collections" on the book side of the reconciliation because it represents cash receipts not yet recorded by the company.

Credit Memorandum
An increase in a bank account.

Electronic Funds Transfers The bank may receive or pay cash on a company's behalf. An EFT may be a cash receipt or a cash payment. These will either show up on the book side of the reconciliation as "Add: EFT" for receipts not yet added to the company's books or "Less: EFT" for payments not yet deducted on the company's books.

Service Charge This cash payment is the bank's fee for processing a company's transactions. Service charges can also include the cost of printed checks and other bank fees such as ATM fees. Service charges could also include the fees charged by the bank for processing credit and debit card transactions if the company used the gross method for recording credit card sales. A service charge is often referred to as a **debit memorandum** and represents a decrease in the bank account. This will show as "Less: Service charges" on the book side of the reconciliation because it represents a cash payment not yet subtracted from the company's cash balance.

Debit Memorandum
A decrease in a bank account.

Interest Revenue on a Checking Account A business will sometimes earn interest if it keeps enough cash in its account. The bank statement tells the company of this cash receipt. This will show as "Add: Interest revenue" on the book side of the reconciliation because it represents cash receipts not yet added in the company's cash balance.

Nonsufficient Funds (NSF) Check
A check for which the maker's bank account has insufficient money to pay the check.

Nonsufficient Funds (NSF) Checks **Nonsufficient funds (NSF) checks** represent checks received from customers for payment of services rendered or merchandise sold that have turned out to be worthless. NSF checks (sometimes called *hot checks* or *bad checks*) are treated as subtractions on a company's bank reconciliation. NSF checks are customer checks the company has received and deposited for which the customer doesn't have enough money in his or her bank account to cover. NSF checks will show as "Less: NSF checks" on the book side of the reconciliation, as the company previously recorded this receipt as an increase in cash when they were deposited into the account, which now has to be deducted as the funds were not actually received.

Internal Control and Cash  Financial 8-21

Book Errors Book errors are errors made on the books of the company that either incorrectly increase or decrease the cash balance in the company's general ledger. All book errors are corrected on the book side of the reconciliation by reversing the effect of the errors.

Completing the Bank Reconciliation

The bank statement in Exhibit F:8-6 shows that the April 30 bank balance of Smart Touch Learning is $12,720 (upper-right corner). However, the company's Cash account has a balance of $20,850. This situation calls for a bank reconciliation to explain the difference. In completing the bank reconciliation, Smart Touch Learning will review the bank statement and the business's Cash account to determine the timing differences. Exhibit F:8-7, Panel A, lists the reconciling items for your easy reference, and Panel B shows the completed reconciliation.

Exhibit F:8-7 | Bank Reconciliation

PANEL A—Reconciling Items

Bank side:
1. Deposit in transit, Apr. 30, $9,000.
2. Outstanding check no. 204, $2,000.

Book side:
3. EFT receipt from customer, $100.
4. Interest revenue earned on bank balance, $30.
5. Bank service charge, $20.
6. EFT payment of water bill, $40.
7. NSF check, $1,200.

PANEL B—Bank Reconciliation

SMART TOUCH LEARNING
Bank Reconciliation
April 30, 2025

BANK			BOOK		
Balance, April 30, 2025		$ 12,720	Balance, April 30, 2025		$ 20,850
ADD:			ADD:		
1. Deposit in transit		9,000	3. EFT receipt from customer	$ 100	
		21,720	4. Interest revenue earned on bank balance	30	130
					20,980
LESS:			LESS:		
			5. Service charge	20	
2. Outstanding checks			6. EFT payment of water bill	40	
No. 204		2,000	7. NSF check	1,200	1,260
Adjusted bank balance, April 30, 2025		$ 19,720	Adjusted book balance, April 30, 2025		$ 19,720

These amounts must agree.

SUMMARY OF THE VARIOUS RECONCILING ITEMS:

BANK BALANCE—ALWAYS
- *Add* deposits in transit.
- *Subtract* outstanding checks.
- *Add* or *subtract* corrections of bank errors.

BOOK BALANCE—ALWAYS
- *Add* bank collections, interest revenue, and EFT receipts.
- *Subtract* service charges, NSF checks, and EFT payments.
- *Add* or *subtract* corrections of book errors.

Examining a Bank Reconciliation

Let's go through each side of the bank reconciliation for Smart Touch Learning.

Bank Side of the Reconciliation

Smart Touch Learning begins by recording the bank balance as of April 30, 2025, which is taken from the bank statement, $12,720. The business then identifies any additions or subtractions affecting the bank balance:

1. **Deposit in transit.** Smart Touch Learning reviews the bank statement and the Cash account to determine whether any cash deposits made by the business have not yet been recorded by the bank. Smart Touch Learning identifies that the deposit made on April 30 for $9,000 has not yet been recorded by the bank. This amount is added to the bank balance.
2. **Outstanding check.** The business reviews the canceled checks included with the statement to determine whether any checks written by the business have not yet cleared the bank. Smart Touch Learning identifies check number 204 for $2,000 as outstanding. This amount is subtracted from the bank balance.

After all items affecting the bank side have been identified, the adjusted bank balance is determined.

Book Side of the Reconciliation

The book side of the reconciliation begins by Smart Touch Learning listing the Cash account balance as of April 30, 2025. This amount—$20,850—is found in the general ledger. Next, Smart Touch Learning reviews the Cash account and bank statement for items that affect the company's Cash account balance but are not recorded by the company:

3. **Electronic funds transfer (EFT).** In reviewing the bank statement, Smart Touch Learning identifies an EFT receipt from a customer in the amount of $100. The company has not recorded this receipt in the Cash account; therefore, it will need to be added to the book balance.
4. **Interest revenue.** Smart Touch Learning identifies a $30 deposit on the bank statement for interest earned that has not yet been recorded in the Cash account. This deposit will be added to the book balance.
5. **Service charge.** The bank statement shows a $20 service charge. Smart Touch Learning has not recorded this charge in the company's Cash account and will, therefore, need to subtract this amount from the book balance.
6. **Electronic funds transfer (EFT).** Listed in the other deductions section on the bank statement, Smart Touch Learning identifies an EFT payment to Water Works for $40. This payment has not been recorded in the company's Cash account. Smart Touch Learning will subtract this amount from the book balance.
7. **Nonsufficient funds (NSF) check.** Smart Touch Learning identifies an NSF check from a customer on the bank statement. The company had recorded the receipt of this check as an increase to cash originally. The bank has now communicated that the customer's check did not clear and that the customer's payment was never deposited into the business's account. Smart Touch Learning must subtract this amount from the book balance.

After recording all of the items that affect the book balance, Smart Touch Learning determines the adjusted book balance and verifies that it equals the adjusted bank balance. This amount represents the correct cash balance as of April 30, 2025.

Journalizing Transactions from the Bank Reconciliation

The bank reconciliation is an accountant's tool separate from the journals and ledgers. It does *not* account for transactions in the journal. To get the transactions into the accounts, we must make journal entries and post to the ledger. All items on the book side of the bank reconciliation require journal entries. We make no journal entries from the items on the bank side because we have already recorded these items in the business's Cash account.

The bank reconciliation in Exhibit F:8-7 requires Smart Touch Learning to make journal entries to bring the Cash account up to date. Numbers in the journal entries correspond to the reconciling items listed in Exhibit F:8-7, Panel A, and to the book side of the reconciliation in Panel B. Note that we chose to list each item in a separate journal entry here, but one compound entry could be made instead of the five separate entries illustrated.

Date	Accounts and Explanation	Debit	Credit
3: Apr. 30	Cash	100	
	Accounts Receivable		100
	To record account receivable collected by bank.		
4: 30	Cash	30	
	Interest Revenue		30
	To record interest earned on bank balance.		
5: 30	Bank Expense	20	
	Cash		20
	To record bank service charges incurred.		
6: 30	Utilities Expense	40	
	Cash		40
	To record payment of water bill by EFT.		
7: 30	Accounts Receivable	1,200	
	Cash		1,200
	To record NSF check returned by bank.		

A↑↓ = L + E
Cash↑
Accounts Receivable↓

A↑ = L + E↑
Cash↑   Interest Revenue↑

A↓ = L + E↓
Cash↓   Bank Expense↑

A↓ = L + E↓
Cash↓   Utilities Expense↑

A↑↓ = L + E
Accounts Receivable↑
Cash↓

The above journal entries are posted to the Cash T-account to update the balance as shown below:

Cash			
Beg. Bal.	10,550	20,000	Apr. 2
Apr. 1	19,450	3,200	Apr. 15
Apr. 8	5,500	300	Apr. 21
Apr. 22	2,000	2,000	Apr. 30
Apr. 30	9,000	150	Apr. 30
Bal.	20,850		
Apr. 30	100	20	Apr. 30
Apr. 30	30	40	Apr. 30
		1,200	Apr. 30
End. Bal.	19,720		

8-24 Financial chapter 8

Notice that the ending balance in the Cash T-account equals the adjusted book balance and the adjusted bank balance on the bank reconciliation at April 30, 2025.

Try It!

For each of the following items, determine whether the item would be:

   a. added to the bank balance
   b. subtracted from the bank balance
   c. added to the book balance
   d. subtracted from the book balance

11. Interest revenue earned
12. NSF check
13. Deposit in transit
14. Service charge
15. Outstanding check

Check your answers online in MyLab Accounting or at http://www.pearsonhighered.com/Horngren.

For more practice, see Short Exercises S-F:8-7 through S-F:8-10. MyLab Accounting

HOW CAN THE CASH RATIO BE USED TO EVALUATE BUSINESS PERFORMANCE?

Learning Objective 7
Use the cash ratio to evaluate business performance

Cash Ratio
A measure of a company's ability to pay current liabilities from cash and cash equivalents: (Cash + Cash equivalents) / Total current liabilities.

Cash Equivalent
A highly liquid investment that can be converted into cash in three months or less.

Cash is an important part of every business. Without an adequate supply of available cash, businesses cannot continue to operate. Businesses, therefore, monitor cash very carefully. One measure that can be used to measure a company's liquidity is the cash ratio. The **cash ratio** helps to determine a company's ability to meet its short-term obligations. It is calculated as follows:

Cash ratio = (Cash + Cash equivalents) / Total current liabilities

Notice that the cash ratio includes cash and cash equivalents. **Cash equivalents** are highly liquid investments that can be converted into cash in three months or less. Examples of cash equivalents are money-market accounts and investments in U.S. government securities.

Returning to **Kohl's Corporation**, let's evaluate the company's liquidity using the cash ratio. Kohl's cash and cash equivalents and total current liabilities can be found on the balance sheet (visit http://www.pearsonhighered.com/Horngren to view a link to Kohl's Corporation's annual report) and are presented below (shown in millions):

	February 2, 2019	February 3, 2018
Cash and cash equivalents	$ 934	$ 1,308
Total current liabilities	2,730	2,709

Kohl's cash ratio as of February 2, 2019, follows:

Cash ratio = $934 / $2,730 = 0.34

In comparison, the cash ratio as of February 3, 2018, was:

Cash ratio = $1,308 / $2,709 = 0.48

Internal Control and Cash Financial 8-25

The cash ratio has decreased slightly from February 3, 2018 to February 2, 2019 due to a decrease in available cash and cash equivalents and an increase in its total current liabilities. This ratio is the most conservative valuation of liquidity because it looks at only cash and cash equivalents, leaving out other current assets such as merchandise inventory and accounts receivable. Notice that for both years the cash ratio was below 1.0. Having a cash ratio below 1.0 is a good thing. A cash ratio above 1.0 might signify that the company has an unnecessarily large amount of cash supply. This cash could be used to generate higher profits or be paid out in the form of withdrawals to the owner. However, a very low ratio doesn't send a strong message to creditors that the company has the ability to repay its short-term debt.

16. The Scott Sun & Shade Company had the following financial data at December 31, 2024:

Cash and cash equivalents	$ 60,000
Total current liabilities	75,000

What is the cash ratio as of December 31, 2024, for Scott Sun & Shade?

Check your answer online in MyLab Accounting or at http://www.pearsonhighered.com/Horngren.

For more practice, see Short Exercise S-F:8-11. MyLab Accounting

REVIEW

> Things You Should Know

1. **What is internal control, and how can it be used to protect a company's assets?**

   - Internal control is the organizational plan and all the related measures designed to safeguard assets, encourage employees to follow company policies, promote operational efficiency, and ensure accurate and reliable accounting records.
   - The Sarbanes-Oxley Act was passed by Congress to revamp corporate governance in the United States.
   - Internal control includes five components: control procedures, risk assessment, information system, monitoring of controls, and environment.

2. **What are the internal control procedures with respect to cash receipts?**

   - A point-of-sale terminal provides control over cash receipts over the counter.
   - Companies control cash by mail by ensuring appropriate separation of duties when handling cash and recording the transaction.

3. **What are the internal control procedures with respect to cash payments?**

   - Good separation of duties between operations of the business and writing checks for cash payments should exist.
   - Many companies use technology to make secure payments.

4. **What are the internal control procedures needed for petty cash and how are petty cash transactions recorded?**

    - A petty cash fund allows a business to keep cash on hand to pay for small miscellaneous items such as postage, office supplies, and parking.
    - An individual should be designated as the custodian of the petty cash fund and all petty cash payments should be supported by a petty cash ticket.
    - When the petty cash fund is established, the company records a debit to Petty Cash and a credit to Cash.
    - The petty cash fund is replenished by debiting the associated asset and expense accounts and crediting Cash.
    - Discrepancies in petty cash funds are either debited (for shortages) or credited (for overages) to the Cash Short & Over account.

5. **What are the internal control procedures needed for debit and credit card sales and how are these types of sales recorded?**

    - Credit and debit card sales require additional internal controls, including the use of point-of-sale terminals and storage of cardholder data on a secure and encrypted network.
    - Sales by credit cards and debit cards are treated as cash sales and typically include a fee (Credit Card Expense) that is paid by the business to the credit card processor.
    - Sales can be either recorded using the net or gross method. The net method records the amount of the sale less the processing fee at the time of sale. The gross method records the gross amount of the sale at the time of sale and the processing fees are recorded at a later time.

6. **How can the bank account be used as a control device?**

    - Bank accounts provide established practices that safeguard a business's money. These controls include use of signature cards, deposit tickets, checks, bank statements, and electronic funds transfers.
    - A bank reconciliation can also be used as a form of internal control. The bank reconciliation compares and explains the difference between cash on the company's books and cash according to the bank's records on a specific date.
    - After the bank reconciliation has been prepared, journal entries must be completed for all items on the book side of the bank reconciliation.

7. **How can the cash ratio be used to evaluate business performance?**

    - The cash ratio measures a company's ability to pay its current liabilities from cash and cash equivalents.
    - Cash ratio = (Cash + Cash equivalents) / Total current liabilities.

> Check Your Understanding F:8-1

Check your understanding of the chapter by completing this problem and then looking at the solution. Use this practice to help identify which sections of the chapter you need to study more.

Misler Company established a $300 petty cash fund on January 12, 2024. Karen Misler (KM) is the fund custodian. At the end of the month, the petty cash fund contains the following:

a. Cash: $163

b. Petty cash tickets, as follows:

No.	Amount	Issued to	Signed by	Account Debited
44	$ 14	B. Jarvis	B. Jarvis and KM	Office Supplies
45	39	S. Bell	S. Bell	Delivery Expense
47	43	R. Tate	R. Tate and KM	—
48	33	L. Blair	L. Blair and KM	Travel Expense

Requirements

1. Identify three internal control weaknesses revealed in the given data. (See Learning Objectives 1, 4)
2. Journalize the following transactions (See Learning Objective 4):
   a. Establishment of the petty cash fund on January 12, 2024.
   b. Replenishment of the fund on January 31, 2024. Assume petty cash ticket no. 47 was issued for the purchase of office supplies.
3. What is the balance in the Petty Cash account immediately before replenishment? Immediately after replenishment? (See Learning Objective 4)

> Solution

Requirement 1

The three internal control weaknesses are as follows:

1. Petty cash ticket no. 46 is missing. There is no indication of what happened to this ticket. The company should investigate.
2. The petty cash custodian (KM) did not sign petty cash ticket no. 45. This omission may have been an oversight on her part. However, it raises the question of whether she authorized the payment. Both the fund custodian and the recipient of the cash should sign the petty cash ticket.
3. Petty cash ticket no. 47 does not indicate which account to debit on the actual ticket. If Tate or Karen Misler do not remember where the $43 went, then the accountant will not know what account should be debited.

Requirement 2

Petty cash journal entries:

a. Entry to establish the petty cash fund:

Date	Accounts and Explanation	Debit	Credit
Jan. 12	Petty Cash	300	
	Cash		300
	To open the petty cash fund.		

b. Entry to replenish the fund:

Date	Accounts and Explanation	Debit	Credit
Jan. 31	Office Supplies	57	
	Delivery Expense	39	
	Travel Expense	33	
	Cash Short & Over	8	
	Cash		137
	To replenish the petty cash fund.		

Requirement 3

The balance in the Petty Cash account is *always* its imprest balance, in this case $300.

> Check Your Understanding F:8-2

Check your understanding of the chapter by completing this problem and then looking at the solution. Use this practice to help identify which sections of the chapter you need to study more.

The Cash account of Baylor Associates at February 28, 2025, follows:

Cash			
Beg. Bal.	3,995	400	Feb. 3
Feb. 6	800	3,100	Feb. 12
Feb. 15	1,800	1,100	Feb. 19
Feb. 23	1,100	500	Feb. 25
Feb. 28	2,400	900	Feb. 27
End. Bal.	4,095		

Baylor Associates received the following bank statement on February 28, 2025:

BANK STATEMENT

BANK OF TOMORROW
123 PETER PAN RD, KISSIMMEE, FL 34747

Baylor Associates
14 W Gadsden St
Pensacola, FL 32501

CHECKING ACCOUNT 136–213734

FEBRUARY 28, 2025

BEGINNING BALANCE	TOTAL DEPOSITS	TOTAL WITHDRAWALS	SERVICE CHARGES	ENDING BALANCE
$3,995	4,715	5,630	10	$3,070

TRANSACTIONS

DEPOSITS	DATE	AMOUNT
Deposit	02/07	800
Deposit	02/15	1,800
EFT—Collection of note	02/17	1,000
Deposit	02/24	1,100
Interest	02/28	15

CHARGES	DATE	AMOUNT
Service Charge	02/28	10

CHECKS

Number	Amount	Number	Amount	Number	Amount
102	400	103	1,100		
101	3,100				

OTHER DEDUCTIONS	DATE	AMOUNT
EFT—EZ Rent	02/01	330
NSF Check	02/13	700

Additional data:

Baylor deposits all cash receipts in the bank and makes all payments by check.

Requirements

1. Prepare the bank reconciliation of Baylor Associates at February 28, 2025. (See Learning Objective 6)
2. Journalize the entries based on the bank reconciliation. (See Learning Objective 6)

> Solution

Requirement 1

BAYLOR ASSOCIATES
Bank Reconciliation
February 28, 2025

Bank:		
Balance, February 28, 2025		$ 3,070
Add: Deposit of February 28 in transit		2,400
		5,470
Less: Outstanding checks issued on February 25		
($500) and February 27 ($900)		1,400
Adjusted bank balance, February 28, 2025		$ 4,070
Books:		
Balance, February 28, 2025		$ 4,095
Add: Bank collection of note receivable	$ 1,000	
Interest revenue earned on bank balance	15	1,015
		5,110
Less: Service charge	10	
NSF check	700	
EFT—Rent expense	330	1,040
Adjusted book balance, February 28, 2025		$ 4,070

Must be equal.

Requirement 2

Date	Accounts and Explanation	Debit	Credit
Feb. 28	Cash	1,000	
	Notes Receivable		1,000
	Note receivable collected by bank.		
28	Cash	15	
	Interest Revenue		15
	Interest earned on bank balance.		
28	Bank Expense	10	
	Cash		10
	Bank service charge.		
28	Accounts Receivable	700	
	Cash		700
	NSF check returned by bank.		
28	Rent Expense	330	
	Cash		330
	Monthly rent expense.		

> Key Terms

Account Number (p. 8-18)
Bank Reconciliation (p. 8-19)
Bank Statement (p. 8-18)
Canceled Checks (p. 8-18)
Cash Equivalent (p. 8-24)
Cash Ratio (p. 8-24)
Check (p. 8-17)
Collusion (p. 8-6)
Committee of Sponsoring Organizations (COSO) (p. 8-2)
Credit Memorandum (p. 8-20)
Debit Memorandum (p. 8-20)
Deposit in Transit (p. 8-19)
Deposit Ticket (p. 8-17)

Electronic Data Interchange (EDI) (p. 8-11)
Electronic Funds Transfer (EFT) (p. 8-18)
Encryption (p. 8-5)
Evaluated Receipts Settlement (ERS) (p. 8-11)
External Auditor (p. 8-4)
Firewall (p. 8-5)
Imprest System (p. 8-12)
Internal Auditor (p. 8-4)
Internal Control (p. 8-2)
Internal Control Report (p. 8-3)
Lock-Box System (p. 8-9)

Maker (p. 8-17)
Nonsufficient Funds (NSF) Check (p. 8-20)
Outstanding Check (p. 8-19)
Payee (p. 8-17)
Petty Cash (p. 8-11)
Public Company (p. 8-2)
Remittance Advice (p. 8-8)
Routing Number (p. 8-18)
Sarbanes-Oxley Act (SOX) (p. 8-3)
Separation of Duties (p. 8-4)
Signature Card (p. 8-17)
Timing Difference (p. 8-19)

> Quick Check

Learning Objective 1

1. Which of the following is *not* part of the definition of internal control?
   a. Separation of duties
   b. Safeguard assets
   c. Encourage employees to follow company policies
   d. Promote operational efficiency

Learning Objective 1

2. The Sarbanes-Oxley Act
   a. created the Private Company Accounting Board.
   b. allows accountants to audit and to perform any type of consulting work for a public company.
   c. stipulates that violators of the act may serve 20 years in prison for securities fraud.
   d. requires that an outside auditor must evaluate a public company's internal controls.

Learning Objective 1

3. Encryption
   a. avoids the need for separation of duties.
   b. creates firewalls to protect data.
   c. cannot be broken by hackers.
   d. rearranges messages by a special process.

Learning Objective 1

4. Separation of duties is important for internal control of
   a. cash receipts.
   b. cash payments.
   c. Neither of the above
   d. Both a and b

Learning Objective 2

5. Michelle Darby receives cash from customers. Her other assigned job is to post the collections to customer accounts receivable. Her company has weak
   a. assignment of responsibilities.
   b. ethics.
   c. computer controls.
   d. separation of duties.

Learning Objective 3

6. Payment by check is an important internal control over cash payments because
   a. the check must be signed by an authorized official.
   b. before signing the check, the official reviews the invoice supporting the payment.
   c. Both a and b
   d. None of the above

Learning Objective 4

7. The petty cash fund had an initial imprest balance of $100. It currently has $20 and petty cash tickets totaling $75 for office supplies. The entry to replenish the fund would contain
   a. a credit to Cash Short & Over for $5.
   b. a credit to Petty Cash for $80.
   c. a debit to Cash Short & Over for $5.
   d. a debit to Petty Cash for $80.

Learning Objective 5

8. When recording credit card or debit card sales using the net method,
   a. cash received equals sales.
   b. cash received equals sales minus the fee assessed by the card processing company.
   c. cash received equals sales plus the fee assessed by the card processing company.
   d. cash isn't received by the seller until the customer pays his or her credit card statement.

9. The document that explains all the differences between the company's cash records and the bank's figures is called a(n)

   a. bank collection.
   b. electronic fund transfer.
   c. bank statement.
   d. bank reconciliation.

Learning Objective 6

10. Sahara Company's Cash account shows an ending balance of $650. The bank statement shows a $29 service charge and an NSF check for $150. A $240 deposit is in transit and outstanding checks total $420. What is Sahara's adjusted cash balance?

    a. $291   b. $829   c. $471   d. $470

Learning Objective 6

11. Espinoza Air Conditioning & Heating had the following select financial data as of June 30, 2024.

Learning Objective 7

Cash	$ 10,000
Cash Equivalents	8,850
Accounts Receivable	3,700
Total current liabilities	29,000

What is Espinoza's cash ratio?

a. 0.34   b. 0.65   c. 0.78   d. 1.54

Check your answers at the end of the chapter.

ASSESS YOUR PROGRESS

> Review Questions

1. What is internal control?
2. How does the Sarbanes-Oxley Act relate to internal controls?
3. What are the five components of internal control? Briefly explain each component.
4. What is the difference between an internal auditor and external auditor?
5. What is separation of duties?
6. List internal control procedures related to e-commerce.
7. What are some limitations of internal controls?
8. How do businesses control cash receipts over the counter?
9. How do businesses control cash receipts by mail?
10. What are the steps taken to ensure control over purchases and payments by check?
11. What are the controls needed to secure the petty cash fund?
12. When are the only times the Petty Cash account is used in a journal entry?
13. What are two common methods used when accepting deposits for credit card and debit card transactions?
14. What are some common controls used with a bank account?
15. What is a bank reconciliation?

16. List some examples of timing differences, and for each difference, determine if it would affect the book side of the reconciliation or the bank side of the reconciliation.

17. Why is it necessary to record journal entries after the bank reconciliation has been prepared? Which side of the bank reconciliation requires journal entries?

18. What does the cash ratio help determine, and how is it calculated?

> Short Exercises

Learning Objective 1

S-F:8-1 Defining internal control

Internal controls are designed to safeguard assets, encourage employees to follow company policies, promote operational efficiency, and ensure accurate accounting records.

Requirements

1. Which objective do you think is most important?
2. Which objective do you think the internal controls must accomplish for the business to survive? Give your reason.

Learning Objective 2

S-F:8-2 Applying internal control over cash receipts

Sandra Kristof sells furniture for McKinney Furniture Company. Kristof is having financial problems and takes $650 that she received from a customer. She rang up the sale through the cash register. What will alert Megan McKinney, the controller, that something is wrong?

Learning Objective 2

S-F:8-3 Applying internal control over cash receipts by mail

Review the internal controls over cash receipts by mail presented in the chapter. Exactly what is accomplished by the final step in the process, performed by the controller?

Learning Objective 3

S-F:8-4 Applying internal control over cash payments by check

A purchasing agent for Franklin Office Supplies receives the goods that he purchases and also approves payment for the goods.

Requirements

1. How could this purchasing agent cheat his company?
2. How could Franklin avoid this internal control weakness?

Learning Objective 4

S-F:8-5 Journalizing petty cash

Prepare the journal entries for the following petty cash transactions of Everly Gaming Supplies:

Mar. 1		Established a petty cash fund with a $250 balance.
	31	The petty cash fund has $24 in cash and $235 in petty cash tickets that were issued to pay for Office Supplies ($35) and Entertainment Expense ($200). Replenished the fund and recorded the expenditures.
Apr. 15		Increased the balance of the petty cash fund to $300.

S-F:8-6 Recording credit card and debit card sales

Restaurants do a large volume of business by credit and debit cards. Suppose Summer, Sand, and Castles Resort restaurant had these transactions on January 28, 2024:

| National Express credit card sales | $ 10,800 |
| ValueCard debit card sales | 10,000 |

Requirements

1. Suppose Summer, Sand, and Castles Resort's processor charges a 2% fee and deposits sales net of the fee. Journalize these sales transactions for the restaurant.
2. Suppose Summer, Sand, and Castles Resort's processor charges a 2% fee and deposits sales using the gross method. Journalize these sales transactions for the restaurant.

S-F:8-7 Understanding bank account controls

Answer the following questions about the controls in bank accounts:

Requirements

1. Which bank control protects against forgery?
2. Which bank control reports the activity in the customer's account each period?
3. Which bank control confirms the amount of money put into the bank account?

S-F:8-8 Identifying timing differences related to a bank reconciliation

For each timing difference listed, identify whether the difference would be reported on the book side of the reconciliation or the bank side of the reconciliation. In addition, identify whether the difference would be an addition or subtraction.

a. Deposit in transit
b. Bank collection
c. Debit memorandum from bank
d. EFT cash receipt
e. Outstanding checks
f. $1,000 deposit erroneously recorded by the bank as $100
g. Service charges
h. Interest revenue
i. $2,500 cash payment for rent expense erroneously recorded by the business as $250
j. Credit memorandum from bank

S-F:8-9 Preparing a bank reconciliation

The Cash account of Guard Dog Security Systems reported a balance of $2,540 at December 31, 2024. There were outstanding checks totaling $400 and a December 31 deposit in transit of $100. The bank statement, which came from Park Cities Bank, listed the December 31 balance of $3,340. Included in the bank balance was a collection of $510 on account from Brendan Ballou, a Guard Dog customer who pays the bank directly. The bank statement also shows a $30 service charge and $20 of interest revenue that Guard Dog earned on its bank balance. Prepare Guard Dog's bank reconciliation at December 31.

Note: Short Exercise S-F:8-9 must be completed before attempting Short Exercise S-F:8-10.

Learning Objective 6

S-F:8-10 Recording transactions from a bank reconciliation

Review your results from preparing Guard Dog Security Systems' bank reconciliation in Short Exercise S-F:8-9. Journalize the company's transactions that arise from the bank reconciliation. Include an explanation with each entry.

Learning Objective 7

S-F:8-11 Computing the cash ratio

Smythe Banners reported the following figures in its financial statements:

Cash	$ 26,500
Cash Equivalents	5,000
Total Current Liabilities	30,000

Compute the cash ratio for Smythe Banners.

> Exercises

Learning Objective 1

E-F:8-12 Understanding the Sarbanes-Oxley Act and identifying internal control strengths and weaknesses

The following situations suggest a strength or a weakness in internal control.

a. Top managers delegate all internal control procedures to the accounting department.

b. Accounting department staff (or the bookkeeper) orders merchandise and approves invoices for payment.

c. Cash received over the counter is controlled by the sales clerk, who rings up the sale and places the cash in the register. The sales clerk matches the total recorded by the register to each day's cash sales.

d. The employee who signs checks need not examine the payment packet because he is confident the amounts are correct.

Requirements

1. Define *internal control*.
2. The system of internal control must be tested by external auditors. What law or rule requires this testing?
3. Identify each item in the list above as either a strength or a weakness in internal control, and give your reason for each answer.

Learning Objective 1

E-F:8-13 Identifying internal controls

Consider each situation separately. Identify the missing internal control procedure from these characteristics:

- Assignment of responsibilities
- Separation of duties
- Audits
- Electronic devices
- Other controls (specify)

a. While reviewing the records of Quality Pharmacy, you find that the same employee orders merchandise and approves invoices for payment.

b. Business is slow at Amazing Amusement Park on Tuesday, Wednesday, and Thursday nights. To reduce expenses, the business decides not to use a ticket taker on those nights. The ticket seller (cashier) is told to keep the tickets as a record of the number sold.

c. The same trusted employee has served as cashier for 12 years.

d. When business is brisk, Fast Mart deposits cash in the bank several times during the day. The manager at one store wants to reduce the time employees spend delivering cash to the bank, so he starts a new policy. Cash will build up over weekends, and the total will be deposited on Monday.

e. Grocery stores such as Convenience Market and Natural Foods purchase most merchandise from a few suppliers. At another grocery store, the manager decides to reduce paperwork. He eliminates the requirement that the receiving department prepare a receiving report listing the goods actually received from the supplier.

E-F:8-14 Evaluating internal control over cash receipts

Learning Objective 2

Dogtopia sells pet supplies and food and handles all sales with a cash register. The cash register displays the amount of the sale. It also shows the cash received and any change returned to the customer. The register also produces a customer receipt but keeps no internal record of the transactions. At the end of the day, the clerk counts the cash in the register and gives it to the cashier for deposit in the company bank account.

Requirements

1. Identify the internal control weakness over cash receipts.
2. What could you do to correct the weakness?

E-F:8-15 Evaluating internal control over cash payments

Learning Objective 3

Gary's Great Cars purchases high-performance auto parts from a Nebraska vendor. Dave Simon, the accountant for Gary's, verifies receipt of merchandise and then prepares, signs, and mails the check to the vendor.

Requirements

1. Identify the internal control weakness over cash payments.
2. What could the business do to correct the weakness?

Learning Objectives 1, 2, 3

E-F:8-16 Understanding internal control, components, procedures, and laws

Match the following terms with their definitions.

Terms	Definitions
1. Internal control	a. Two or more people working together to overcome internal controls.
2. Control procedures	b. Part of internal control that ensures resources are not wasted.
3. Firewalls	
4. Encryption	c. Requires companies to review internal control and take responsibility for the accuracy and completeness of their financial reports.
5. Environment	
6. Information system	d. Should be prenumbered to prevent theft and inefficiency.
7. Separation of duties	
8. Collusion	e. Limits access to a local network.
9. Documents	f. Example: The person who opens the bank statement should not also be the person who is reconciling cash.
10. Audits	g. Identification of uncertainties that may arise due to a company's products, services, or operations.
11. Operational efficiency	
12. Risk assessment	h. Examination of a company's financial statements and accounting system by a trained accounting professional.
13. Sarbanes-Oxley Act	
	i. Without a sufficient one of these, information cannot properly be gathered and summarized.
	j. The organizational plan and all the related measures that safeguard assets, encourage employees to follow company policies, promote operational efficiency, and ensure accurate and reliable accounting data.
	k. Component of internal control that helps ensure business goals are achieved.
	l. Rearranges data by a mathematical process.
	m. To establish an effective one, a company's CEO and top managers must behave honorably to set a good example for employees.

Learning Objective 4

2. Cash Short & Over $15

E-F:8-17 Accounting for petty cash

Jackie's Dance Studio created a $220 imprest petty cash fund. During the month, the fund custodian authorized and signed petty cash tickets as follows:

Petty Cash Ticket No.	Item	Account Debited	Amount
1	Delivery of programs to customers	Delivery Expense	$ 20
2	Mail package	Postage Expense	10
3	Newsletter	Printing Expense	25
4	Key to closet	Miscellaneous Expense	40
5	Copier paper	Office Supplies	70

Requirements

1. Make the general journal entry to create the petty cash fund. Include an explanation.
2. Make the general journal entry to record the petty cash fund replenishment. Cash in the fund totals $40. Include an explanation.
3. Assume that Jackie's Dance Studio decides to decrease the petty cash fund to $120. Make the general journal entry to record this decrease.

E-F:8-18 Controlling petty cash

Just Hangin' Night Club maintains an imprest petty cash fund of $150, which is under the control of Sandra Morgan. At March 31, the fund holds $14 cash and petty cash tickets for office supplies, $128, and delivery expense, $15.

Requirements

1. Explain how an imprest petty cash system works.
2. Journalize the establishment of the petty cash fund on March 1 and the replenishing of the fund on March 31.
3. Prepare a T-account for Petty Cash and post to the account. What is the balance of the Petty Cash account at all times?

Learning Objective 4

2. March 31, Cash CR $136

E-F:8-19 Journalizing credit card sales

Marathon Running Shoes reports the following:

2024	
Sep. 1	Recorded National Express credit card sales of $96,000, net of processor fee of 1%. Ignore Cost of Goods Sold.
15	Recorded ValueMax credit card sales of $80,000. Processor charges a 1.5% fee. ValueMax charges the fee at the end of the month; therefore, Marathon uses the gross method for these credit card sales. Ignore Cost of Goods Sold.
30	ValueMax collected the fees for the month of September. Assume the September 15 transaction is the only ValueMax credit card sale.

Journalize all entries required for Marathon Running Shoes.

Learning Objective 5

E-F:8-20 Classifying bank reconciliation items

The following items could appear on a bank reconciliation:

a. Outstanding checks, $670.
b. Deposits in transit, $1,500.
c. NSF check from customer, no. 548, for $175.
d. Bank collection of note receivable of $800, and interest of $80.
e. Interest earned on bank balance, $20.
f. Service charge, $10.
g. The business credited Cash for $200. The correct amount was $2,000.
h. The bank incorrectly decreased the business's account by $350 for a check written by another business.

Classify each item as (1) an addition to the book balance, (2) a subtraction from the book balance, (3) an addition to the bank balance, or (4) a subtraction from the bank balance.

Learning Objective 6

8-40 Financial chapter 8

Learning Objective 6

1. Adjusted Balance $1,137

E-F:8-21 Preparing a bank reconciliation

Hardy Photography's checkbook lists the following:

Date	Check No.	Item	Check	Deposit	Balance
Nov. 1					$ 500
4	622	Quick Mailing	$ 45		455
9		Service Revenue		$ 135	590
13	623	Photo Supplies	85		505
14	624	Utilities	45		460
18	625	Cash	50		410
26	626	Office Supplies	110		300
28	627	Upstate Realty Co.	290		10
30		Service Revenue		1,235	1,245

Hardy's November bank statement shows the following:

Balance			$ 500
Deposits			135
Checks:	No.	Amount	
	622	$ 45	
	623	85	
	624	105*	
	625	50	(285)
Other charges:			
Printed checks		23	
Service charge		25	(48)
Balance			$ 302

*This is the correct amount for check number 624.

Requirements

1. Prepare Hardy Photography's bank reconciliation at November 30, 2024.
2. How much cash does Hardy actually have on November 30, 2024?
3. Journalize any transactions required from the bank reconciliation.

Learning Objective 6

1. Book Deductions $314

E-F:8-22 Preparing a bank reconciliation

Jim Root Company operates four bowling alleys. The business just received the October 31, 2024, bank statement from City National Bank, and the statement shows an ending balance of $910. Listed on the statement are an EFT rent collection of $440, a service charge of $7, NSF checks totaling $50, and a $23 charge for printed checks. In reviewing the cash records, the business identified outstanding checks totaling $440 and a deposit in transit of $1,800. During October, the business recorded a $260 check by debiting Salaries Expense and crediting Cash for $26. The business's Cash account shows an October 31 balance of $2,144.

Requirements

1. Prepare the bank reconciliation at October 31.
2. Journalize any transactions required from the bank reconciliation.

E-F:8-23 Computing cash ratio

Learning Objective 7

Mountain Cabin Rentals reported the following selected amounts in its post-closing trial balance as of December 31, 2023 and December 31, 2024. All accounts have normal balances.

	2024	2023
Cash	$ 6,500	$ 5,250
Cash Equivalents	2,300	1,700
Accounts Receivable	800	1,200
Office Supplies	250	355
Merchandise Inventory	8,750	9,500
Prepaid Insurance	900	800
Equipment	15,000	15,000
Accumulated Depreciation—Equipment	2,000	1,500
Accounts Payable	800	1,200
Utilities Payable	230	250
Salaries Payable	1,200	1,100
Unearned Revenue	875	650
DePace, Capital	29,395	29,105

Requirements

1. Calculate the cash ratio for the two years. Round to two decimal places.
2. Did the company's position improve or weaken? Explain your answer.

> Problems Group A

P-F:8-24A Identifying internal control weakness in cash receipts

Learning Objective 2

Seawind Productions makes all sales on credit. Cash receipts arrive by mail. Justin Broadway, the mailroom clerk, opens envelopes and separates the checks from the accompanying remittance advices. Broadway forwards the checks to another employee, who makes the daily bank deposit but has no access to the accounting records. Broadway sends the remittance advices, which show cash received, to the accounting department for entry in the accounts. Broadway's only other duty is to grant sales allowances to customers. (A *sales allowance* decreases the customer's account receivable.) When Broadway receives a customer check for $600 less a $30 allowance, he records the sales allowance and forwards the document to the accounting department.

Requirements

1. Identify the internal control weakness in this situation.
2. Who should record sales allowances?
3. What is the amount that should be shown in the ledger for cash receipts?

Learning Objectives 1, 2, 3

P-F:8-25A Correcting internal control weaknesses

Each of the following situations has an internal control weakness.

a. Upside-Down Applications develops custom programs to customers' specifications. Recently, development of a new program stopped while the programmers redesigned Upside-Down's accounting system. Upside-Down's accountants could have performed this task.

b. Norma Rottler has been your trusted employee for 24 years. She performs all cash-handling and accounting duties. Norma just purchased a new luxury car and a new home in an expensive suburb. As owner of the company, you wonder how she can afford these luxuries because you pay her only $30,000 a year, and she has no source of outside income.

c. Izzie Hardwoods, a private company, falsified sales and inventory figures in order to get an important loan. The loan went through, but Izzie later went bankrupt and could not repay the bank.

d. The office supply company where Pet Grooming Goods purchases sales receipts recently notified Pet Grooming Goods that its documents were not prenumbered. Howard Mustro, the owner, replied that he never uses receipt numbers.

e. Discount stores such as Cusco make most of their sales in cash, with the remainder in credit card sales. To reduce expenses, one store manager ceases purchasing fidelity bonds on the cashiers.

f. Cornelius's Corndogs keeps all cash receipts in an empty box for a week because the owner likes to go to the bank on Tuesdays when Joann is working.

Requirements

1. Identify the missing internal control characteristics in each situation.
2. Identify the possible problem caused by each control weakness.
3. Propose a solution to each internal control problem.

Learning Objective 4

3. June 30, Cash CR $210

P-F:8-26A Accounting for petty cash transactions

On June 1, Fab Salad Dressings creates a petty cash fund with an imprest balance of $300. During June, Al Franklin, the fund custodian, signs the following petty cash tickets:

Petty Cash Ticket Number	Item	Amount
101	Office supplies	$ 30
102	Cab fare for executive	20
103	Delivery of package across town	50
104	Business dinner	40
105	Merchandise inventory	90

On June 30, prior to replenishment, the fund contains these tickets plus cash of $90. The accounts affected by petty cash payments are Office Supplies, Travel Expense, Delivery Expense, Entertainment Expense, and Merchandise Inventory.

Requirements

1. Explain the characteristics and the internal control features of an imprest fund.
2. On June 30, how much cash should the petty cash fund hold before it is replenished?
3. Journalize all required entries to create the fund and replenish it. Include explanations.
4. Make the July 1 entry to increase the fund balance to $375. Include an explanation and briefly describe what the custodian does.

P-F:8-27A Accounting for petty cash transactions

Learning Objective 4

Suppose that on June 1, Rockin' Gyrations, a disc jockey service, creates a petty cash fund with an imprest balance of $300. During June, Michael Martell, fund custodian, signs the following petty cash tickets:

2. June 30, Cash CR $160

Petty Cash Ticket Number	Item	Amount
1	Postage for package received	$ 30
2	Office party	25
3	Two boxes of stationery	20
4	Printer cartridges	15
5	Business dinner	65

On June 30, prior to replenishment, the fund contains these tickets plus cash of $140. The accounts affected by petty cash payments are Office Supplies, Entertainment Expense, and Postage Expense.

Requirements

1. On June 30, how much cash should this petty cash fund hold before it is replenished?
2. Journalize all required entries to (a) create the fund and (b) replenish it. Include explanations.
3. Make the entry on July 1 to increase the fund balance to $325. Include an explanation.

P-F:8-28A Preparing a bank reconciliation and journal entries

Learning Objective 6

The December cash records of Davidson Insurance follow:

1. Adjusted Balance $18,025

Cash Receipts		Cash Payments	
Date	Cash Debit	Check No.	Cash Credit
Dec. 4	$ 4,240	1416	$ 810
9	550	1417	180
14	600	1418	630
17	1,900	1419	1,390
31	1,860	1420	1,490
		1421	700
		1422	600

Learning Objectives 1, 2, 3

P-F:8-31B Correcting internal control weaknesses

Each of the following situations has an internal control weakness.

a. Jade Applications has decided that one way to cut costs in the upcoming year is to fire the external auditor. The business believes that the internal auditor should be able to efficiently monitor the company's internal controls.

b. In an effort to minimize the amount of paperwork, Ross Homes has decided that it will not keep copies of customer invoices related to sales revenue. Ross believes that this effort will minimize the amount of data storage the company will have to pay for.

c. Elle Bee, a trusted employee for many years, has never taken a vacation. The owner believes that he's lucky that she is so committed to her job.

d. The Medicine Chest Company keeps a small petty cash fund to handle small cash transactions. Because no one wants to volunteer to be the custodian, the business manager has decided that all employees should have access to the petty cash. She figures that as long as each employee fills out a petty cash ticket, then there are proper controls in place.

e. Due to the cost of maintaining the security cameras, Wings and More has decided that it will remove the cameras that monitor the cash register.

f. Bryan Miller, manager of Hardware Emporium, prides himself on hiring exceptionally skilled employees who need no training to do their jobs.

Requirements

1. Identify the missing internal control characteristics in each situation.
2. Identify the possible problem caused by each control weakness.
3. Propose a solution to each internal control problem.

Learning Objective 4

3. Cash Short & Over CR $15

P-F:8-32B Accounting for petty cash transactions

On September 1, Party Salad Dressings creates a petty cash fund with an imprest balance of $600. During September, Michael Martell, the fund custodian, signs the following petty cash tickets:

Petty Cash Ticket Number	Item	Amount
101	Office supplies	$ 60
102	Cab fare for executive	25
103	Delivery of package across town	45
104	Business dinner	55
105	Merchandise inventory	75

On September 30, prior to replenishment, the fund contains these tickets plus cash of $355. The accounts affected by petty cash payments are Office Supplies, Travel Expense, Delivery Expense, Entertainment Expense, and Merchandise Inventory.

Requirements

1. Explain the characteristics and the internal control features of an imprest fund.
2. On September 30, how much cash should the petty cash fund hold before it is replenished?

3. Journalize all required entries to create the fund and replenish it. Include explanations.

4. Make the October 1 entry to increase the fund balance to $800. Include an explanation and briefly describe what the custodian does.

P-F:8-33B Accounting for petty cash transactions

Learning Objective 4

Suppose that on September 1, Cool Gyrations, a disc jockey service, creates a petty cash fund with an imprest balance of $350. During September, Ruth Mangan, fund custodian, signs the following petty cash tickets:

2. Sep. 30, Cash CR $140

Petty Cash Ticket Number	Item	Amount
1	Postage for package received	$ 25
2	Office party	10
3	Two boxes of stationery	20
4	Printer cartridges	15
5	Business dinner	65

On September 30, prior to replenishment, the fund contains these tickets plus cash of $210. The accounts affected by petty cash payments are Office Supplies, Entertainment Expense, and Postage Expense.

Requirements

1. On September 30, how much cash should this petty cash fund hold before it is replenished?
2. Journalize all required entries to (a) create the fund and (b) replenish it. Include explanations.
3. Make the entry on October 1 to increase the fund balance to $425. Include an explanation.

P-F:8-34B Preparing a bank reconciliation and journal entries

Learning Objective 6

The May cash records of Donald Insurance follow:

1. Adjusted Balance $17,580

Cash Receipts		Cash Payments	
Date	Cash Debit	Check No.	Cash Credit
May 4	$ 4,230	1416	$ 890
9	520	1417	120
14	530	1418	630
17	1,950	1419	1,090
31	1,840	1420	1,420
		1421	900
		1422	670

Donald's Cash account shows a balance of $17,750 at May 31. On May 31, Donald Insurance received the following bank statement:

Bank Statement for May

Beginning Balance				$ 14,400
Deposits and other Credits:				
May	1	EFT	$ 450	
May	5		4,230	
May	10		520	
May	15		530	
May	18		1,950	
May	22	BC	1,700	9,380
Checks and other Debits:				
May	8	NSF	1,100	
May	11 (check no. 1416)		890	
May	19	EFT	375	
May	22 (check no. 1417)		120	
May	29 (check no. 1418)		630	
May	31 (check no. 1419)		1,900	
May	31	SC	35	(5,050)
Ending Balance				$ 18,730

Explanations: BC–bank collection; EFT–electronic funds transfer; NSF–nonsufficient funds checks; SC–service charge

Additional data for the bank reconciliation follow:

a. The EFT credit was a receipt of rent. The EFT debit was an insurance payment.

b. The NSF check was received from a customer.

c. The $1,700 bank collection was for a note receivable.

d. The correct amount of check 1419, for rent expense, is $1,900. Donald's controller mistakenly recorded the check for $1,090.

Requirements

1. Prepare the bank reconciliation of Donald Insurance at May 31, 2024.
2. Journalize any required entries from the bank reconciliation.

Learning Objective 6

1. Book Deductions $630

P-F:8-35B Preparing a bank reconciliation and journal entries

The October 31 bank statement of Wyndham's Healthcare has just arrived from State Bank. To prepare the bank reconciliation, you gather the following data:

a. The October 31 bank balance is $6,290.

b. The bank statement includes two charges for NSF checks from customers. One is for $370 (#1), and the other is for $180 (#2).

c. The following Wyndham's checks are outstanding at October 31:

Check No.	Amount
237	$ 120
288	140
291	570
294	570
295	30
296	110

d. Wyndham's collects from a few customers by EFT. The October bank statement lists a $2,200 EFT deposit for a collection on account.

e. The bank statement includes two special deposits that Wyndham's hasn't recorded yet: $900 for dividend revenue and $100 for the interest revenue Wyndham's earned on its bank balance during October.

f. The bank statement lists an $80 subtraction for the bank service charge.

g. On October 31, the Wyndham's treasurer deposited $270, but this deposit does not appear on the bank statement.

h. The bank statement includes a $750 deduction for a check drawn by Multi-State Freight Company. Wyndham's notified the bank of this bank error.

i. Wyndham's Cash account shows a balance of $3,200 on October 31.

Requirements

1. Prepare the bank reconciliation for Wyndham's Healthcare at October 31, 2024.
2. Journalize any required entries from the bank reconciliation. Include an explanation for each entry.

CRITICAL THINKING

> Using Excel

Download Excel problems for this chapter online in MyLab Accounting or at http://www.pearsonhighered.com/Horngren.

> Continuing Problem

P-F:8-36 Preparing a bank reconciliation and journal entries

This problem continues the Canyon Canoe Company situation from Chapter F:7. Canyon Canoe Company has decided to open a new checking account at River Nations Bank during March 2025. Canyon Canoe Company's March Cash T-account for the new cash account from its general ledger is as follows:

8-50 Financial chapter 8

Cash—River Nations Bank Checking Account						
Mar. 1	Balance	0				
2	Deposit	10,000	200	Mar. 2	Ck#101
13	Deposit	2,325	4,300	4	Ck#102
20	Deposit	2,750	750	9	Ck#103
27	Deposit	4,500	1,675	14	Ck#104
31	Deposit	3,490	1,500	21	Ck#105
			175	28	Ck#106
			300	30	Ck#107
Balance		14,165			

Canyon Canoe Company's bank statement dated March 31, 2025, follows:

Beginning Balance, March 1, 2025			$ 0
Deposits and other credits:			
Mar. 2		$10,000	
14		2,325	
21		2,750	
28		4,500	
29	EFT Sport Shirts[1]	500	
31	Interest Revenue	45	20,120
Checks and other debits:			
Mar. 2	EFT to Bank Checks[2]	55	
3	Ck#101	200	
6	Ck#102	4,300	
15	Ck#104	1,675	
16	Ck#103	750	
28	EFT to Rivers Energy[3]	270	
29	Ck#106	175	
31	Bank service charge	70	(7,495)
Ending balance, March 31, 2025			$ 12,625

[1] Sport Shirts is a customer making a payment on account.
[2] Bank Checks is a company that prints business checks (considered a bank expense) for Canyon Canoe Company.
[3] Rivers Energy is a utility provider.

Requirements

1. Prepare the bank reconciliation at March 31, 2025.
2. Journalize any transactions required from the bank reconciliation.
3. Compute the adjusted account balance for the Cash T-account and denote the balance as *End. Bal.* Does the adjusted balance of the Cash T-account match the adjusted book balance on the bank reconciliation?

> Practice Set

P-F:8-37 Preparing a bank reconciliation and journal entries

This problem continues the Crystal Clear Cleaning problem begun in Chapter F:2 and continued through Chapter F:7.

In March 2025, Crystal Clear Cleaning opened a new checking account at First Regional Bank. The bank statement dated March 31, 2025, for Crystal Clear Cleaning follows:

Beginning Balance, March 1, 2025			$	0
Deposits and other credits:				
Mar. 2		$33,000		
10		900		
18		19,000		
20		50,000		
23	EFT Peg's Restaurant[1]	350		
31	Interest Revenue	50		103,300
Checks and other debits:				
Mar. 2	EFT to Check Art[2]	10		
5	Ck#235	2,400		
9	Ck#237	1,500		
9	Ck#236	2,900		
26	Ck#239	2,000		
28	EFT to Texas Energy[3]	130		
29	Ck#240	300		
31	Bank service charge	25		(9,265)
Ending balance, March 31, 2025			$	94,035

[1] Peg's Restaurant is a customer making a payment on account.
[2] Check Art is a company that prints business checks (considered a bank expense) for Crystal Clear Cleaning.
[3] Texas Energy is a utility provider.

Crystal Clear Cleaning's Cash account in the general ledger shows the following transactions for March:

Cash—First Regional Bank Checking Account

Balance			0				
Mar. 2	Deposit	33,000		2,400	Mar. 2	Ck#235	
10	Deposit	900		2,900	4	Ck#236	
18	Deposit	19,000		1,500	5	Ck#237	
20	Deposit	50,000		400	10	Ck#238	
31	Deposit	1,770		2,000	21	Ck#239	
				300	23	Ck#240	
				300	29	Ck#241	
Balance		94,870					

Requirements

1. Prepare the bank reconciliation at March 31, 2025.
2. Journalize any required entries from the bank reconciliation. Post to the Cash T-account to verify the balance of the account matches the adjusted book balance from the bank reconciliation.

> Tying It All Together Case F:8-1

Before you begin this assignment, review the Tying It All Together feature in the chapter. It will also be helpful if you review Chipotle Mexican Grill, Inc.'s 2018 annual report (**https://www.sec.gov/Archives/edgar/data/1058090/000105809019000007/cmg-20181231x10k.htm**).

Chipotle Mexican Grill, Inc. owns and operates more than 2,452 restaurants throughout the United States, 37 international Chipotle restaurants, and two non-Chipotle restaurants. Steve Ells, founder, opened his first restaurant in 1993 in Denver, Colorado, to show that food served fast didn't have to be the typical "fast-food" experience. Chipotle uses high-quality ingredients, raised with respect for animals, farmers, and the environment.

Requirements

1. Review Item 9a (Controls and Procedures) of the Notes to the Financial Statements. What are the internal controls over financial reporting designed to do? Do internal controls prevent or detect all misstatements?
2. Review the auditor's report over internal controls (p. 67 of the annual report). What did the auditor have to say about the company's internal controls?
3. Review Item 13 (Commitments and Contingencies) of the Notes to the Financial Statements. What is the estimated amount of potential liabilities that Chipotle Mexican Grill expects to have associated with anticipated future claims in regards to the data security incident that occurred in April 2017?

> Decision Cases

Decision Case F:8-1

Conduct an Internet search for information on internal control and the Sarbanes-Oxley Act. Write a report of your findings. In your report, discuss some of the advantages and disadvantages of the Sarbanes-Oxley Act. Present it to your class (if required by your instructor).

Decision Case F:8-2

This case is based on an actual situation. Centennial Construction Company, headquartered in Dallas, Texas, built a Rodeway Motel 35 miles north of Dallas. The construction foreman, whose name was Slim Chance, hired the 40 workers needed to complete the project. Slim had the construction workers fill out the necessary tax forms, and he sent their documents to the home office.

Work on the motel began on April 1 and ended September 1. Each week, Slim filled out a time card of hours worked by each employee during the week. Slim faxed the time cards to the home office, which prepared the payroll checks on Friday morning. Slim drove to the home office on Friday, picked up the payroll checks, and returned to the construction site. At 5 p.m. on Friday, Slim distributed payroll checks to the workers.

Requirements

1. Describe in detail the main internal control weakness in this situation. Specify what negative result(s) could occur because of the internal control weakness.
2. Describe what you would do to correct the internal control weakness.

> Fraud Case F:8-1

Levon Helm was a kind of one-man mortgage broker. He would drive around Tennessee looking for homes that had second mortgages, and if the criteria were favorable, he would offer to buy the second mortgage for "cash on the barrelhead." Helm bought low and sold high, making sizable profits. Being a small operation, he employed one person, Cindy Patterson, who did all his bookkeeping. Patterson was an old family friend, and he trusted her so implicitly that he never checked up on the ledgers or the bank reconciliations. At some point, Patterson started "borrowing" from the business and concealing her transactions by booking phony expenses. She intended to pay it back someday, but she got used to the extra cash and couldn't stop. By the time the scam was discovered, she had drained the company of funds that it owed to many of its creditors. The company went bankrupt, Patterson did some jail time, and Helm lost everything.

Requirements

1. What was the key control weakness in this case?
2. Many small businesses cannot afford to hire enough people for adequate separation of duties. What can they do to compensate for this?

> Financial Statement Case F:8-1

Visit **http://www.pearsonhighered.com/Horngren** to view a link to **Target Corporation's** 2018 Fiscal Year Annual Report. Study the audit opinion (labeled Report of Independent Registered Public Accounting Firm) of Target Corporation and the Target Corporation financial statements. Answer the following questions about the company:

Requirements

1. What is the name of Target's outside auditing firm (independent registered public accounting firm)? What office of this firm signed the audit report?
2. Who bears primary responsibility for the financial statements? How can you tell?
3. Does it appear that Target's internal controls are adequate? How can you tell?
4. What standard of auditing did the outside auditors use in examining the Target financial statements?
5. By how much did Target's cash balance (including cash equivalents) change during the year ended February 2, 2019? What were the beginning and ending cash balances?
6. Review the notes to the consolidated financial statements, specifically Note 11 dealing with Cash Equivalents. What type of instruments does Target consider to be cash equivalents?
7. Determine Target's cash ratio as of February 2, 2019, and February 3, 2018. How do Target's cash ratios compare with **Kohl's Corporation** as illustrated in the chapter? Explain.

> Communication Activity F:8-1

In 100 words or fewer, explain why there may be a difference between the bank statement ending cash balance and the ending balance in the Cash account. Give at least two examples each of adjustments to the bank balance and to the book balance.

> Quick Check Answers

1. a   2. d   3. d   4. d   5. d   6. c   7. c   8. b   9. d   10. c   11. b

Receivables 9

Should Credit Be Extended?

James Hulsey works for a large department store as a credit manager. His main responsibility is managing all credit sales that generate accounts receivable. James must evaluate each customer's request for credit and determine which customers are allowed to purchase goods on credit. He does this by reviewing the customer's credit history and credit score. James has an important decision to make. He understands that granting credit increases the sales of the department store, but it also has its disadvantages.

One of those disadvantages is that the department store has to wait to receive cash. But, for James, the biggest disadvantage—and the most frustrating part of his job—is when customers don't pay. When this happens, the department store suffers a loss because it will never collect the cash associated with the sale. The department store must have a way to take the accounts of customers who will never make payment off the books; this is called a *write-off*. In addition, James must also help the department store estimate the amount of receivables that will be uncollectible. It's important that the department store have a good idea of the amount of cash that will actually be collected on its receivables so it can estimate future cash flows.

How Are Receivables Accounted For?

In this chapter, we determine how companies account for receivables. Receivables represent the right to receive cash in the future from a current transaction. We begin by looking at how companies such as **Amazon.com, Inc.** record accounts receivable, including when customers don't make the required payments. Then we review notes receivable, which usually extend over a longer term than accounts receivable and typically involve interest. We finish the chapter by looking at how companies can use financial ratios to evaluate a company's ability to collect cash on accounts receivable.

Chapter 9 Learning Objectives

1. Define and explain common types of receivables and journalize sales on credit
2. Apply the direct write-off method for uncollectibles
3. Apply the allowance method for uncollectibles and estimate bad debts expense based on the percent-of-sales, percent-of-receivables, and aging-of-receivables methods
4. Account for notes receivable including computing interest and recording honored and dishonored notes
5. Use the acid-test ratio, accounts receivable turnover ratio, and days' sales in receivables to evaluate business performance

WHAT ARE COMMON TYPES OF RECEIVABLES, AND HOW ARE CREDIT SALES RECORDED?

Learning Objective 1
Define and explain common types of receivables and journalize sales on credit

A **receivable** occurs when a business sells goods or services to another party on account (on credit). It is a monetary claim against a business or an individual. The receivable is the seller's claim for the amount of the transaction. Receivables also occur when a business loans money to another party. A receivable is the right to *receive* cash in the future from a current transaction. It is something the business owns; therefore, it is an asset. *Each* receivable transaction involves two parties:

Receivable
A monetary claim against a business or an individual.

- The creditor, who receives a receivable (an asset). The creditor will collect cash from the customer or borrower.

Debtor
The party to a credit transaction who takes on an obligation/payable.

- The **debtor**, the party to a credit transaction who takes on an obligation/payable (a liability). The debtor will pay cash later.

Types of Receivables

The three major types of receivables are:

- Accounts receivable
- Notes receivable
- Other receivables

Accounts Receivable

Accounts Receivable
The right to receive cash in the future from customers for goods sold or for services performed.

Accounts receivable, also called *trade receivables*, represent the right to receive cash in the future from customers for goods sold or for services performed. Accounts receivable are usually collected within a short period of time, such as 30 or 60 days, and are therefore reported as a current asset on the balance sheet.

Notes Receivable

Notes Receivable
A written promise that a customer will pay a fixed amount of principal plus interest by a certain date in the future.

Notes receivable usually have longer terms than accounts receivable. Notes receivable, sometimes called *promissory notes*, represent a written promise that a customer (or another individual or business) will pay a fixed amount of principal plus interest by a certain date in the future—called the **maturity date**. The maturity date is the date on which the notes receivable is due. A written document known as a promissory note serves as evidence of

Maturity Date
The date when a note is due.

the debt and is signed by the debtor. Notes receivable due within 12 months or within the normal operating cycle if the cycle is longer than a year are considered current assets. Notes receivable due beyond one year are long-term assets.

Other Receivables

Other receivables make up a miscellaneous category that includes any other type of receivable where there is a right to receive cash in the future. Common examples include dividends receivable and interest receivable. These other receivables may be either current or long-term assets, depending on whether they will be received within one year or the normal operating cycle if the cycle is longer than a year (current asset) or received more than a year in the future (long-term asset).

Exercising Internal Control Over Receivables

Businesses that sell goods or services on account receive cash by mail, usually in the form of a check, or online payments via electronic funds transfer (EFT), so internal control over collections is important. As we discussed in the previous chapter, a critical element of internal control is the separation of cash-handling and cash-accounting duties.

Most large companies also have a credit department to evaluate customers' credit applications to determine if they meet the company's credit approval standards. The extension of credit is a balancing act. The company does not want to lose sales to good customers, but it also wants to avoid receivables that will never be collected. For good internal control over cash collections from receivables, separation of duties must be maintained. The credit department should have no access to cash, and those who handle cash should not be in a position to grant credit to customers. If a credit department employee also handles cash, he or she could pocket money received from a customer. The employee could then label the customer's account as uncollectible, and the company would stop billing that customer. In this scenario, the employee may have covered his or her theft.

Recording Sales on Credit

As discussed earlier, selling on account (on credit) creates an account receivable. Businesses must maintain a separate accounts receivable account for each customer in order to account for payments received from the customer and amounts still owed.

For example, Smart Touch Learning provides $5,000 in services to customer Brown on account and sells $10,000 (sales price) of merchandise inventory to customer Smith on account on August 8. The revenue is recorded (ignore Cost of Goods Sold) as follows:

Date	Accounts and Explanation	Debit	Credit
Aug. 8	Accounts Receivable—Brown	5,000	
	Service Revenue		5,000
	Performed service on account.		
8	Accounts Receivable—Smith	10,000	
	Sales Revenue		10,000
	Sold goods on account.		

$A\uparrow \Big\} = \Big\{ L + E\uparrow$
Accounts Receivable↑ = Service Revenue↑

$A\uparrow \Big\} = \Big\{ L + E\uparrow$
Accounts Receivable↑ = Sales Revenue↑

9-4 Financial chapter 9

These separate customer accounts receivable (for example, Accounts Receivable—Brown) are called *subsidiary accounts*. The sum of all balances in subsidiary accounts receivable equals a control account balance. In this case, Accounts Receivable serves as the control account. This is illustrated as follows:

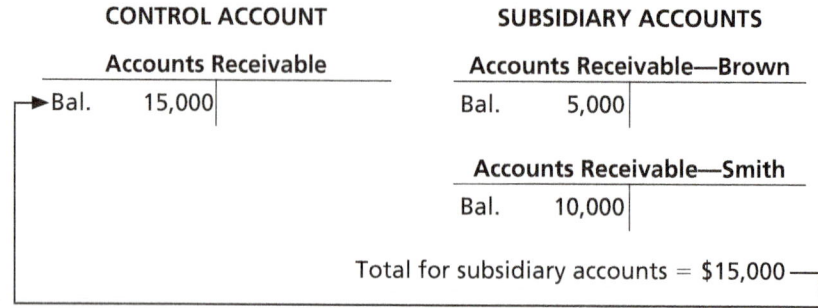

The control account, Accounts Receivable, shows a balance of $15,000. The individual customer accounts in the subsidiary ledger (Accounts Receivable—Brown $5,000 + Accounts Receivable—Smith $10,000) add up to a total of $15,000.

When the business collects cash from both customers on August 29—$4,000 from Brown and $8,000 from Smith—Smart Touch Learning makes the following entry and posts the entry to the T-accounts:

Date	Accounts and Explanation	Debit	Credit
Aug. 29	Cash	12,000	
	Accounts Receivable—Brown		4,000
	Accounts Receivable—Smith		8,000
	Collected cash on account.		

A↓↑
Cash↑
Accounts Receivable↓
= L + E

CONTROL ACCOUNT

Accounts Receivable
Bal. 15,000 | 12,000 Aug. 29
Bal. 3,000

SUBSIDIARY ACCOUNTS

Accounts Receivable—Brown
Bal. 5,000 | 4,000 Aug. 29
Bal. 1,000

Accounts Receivable—Smith
Bal. 10,000 | 8,000 Aug. 29
Bal. 2,000

Total for subsidiary accounts = $3,000

Decreasing Collection Time and Credit Risk

One of the many drawbacks of accepting sales on account is that the company must wait for the receipt of cash. Sometimes this time period could be delayed as much as 60 to 90 days. In addition, there is always the risk that the company will never collect on the receivable. Let's look at some options companies have to decrease the collection time in receiving cash while also transferring the risk of noncollection to a third party.

Credit Card and Debit Card Sales

In the previous chapter, we looked at accepting third-party credit cards and debit cards, such as American Express, MasterCard, and Visa, as a way to increase sales. By accepting credit cards and debit cards, businesses are able to attract more customers. Credit cards offer the customer the convenience of buying something without having to pay cash immediately. Debit cards, on the other hand, reduce the customer's bank account immediately but allow the customer to pay electronically instead of with currency or by writing a check.

Businesses also benefit from accepting payment by credit and debit cards. They do not have to check each customer's credit rating or worry about keeping accounts receivable records or even collecting from the customer because the card issuer has the responsibility of collecting from the customer. Thus, instead of collecting cash from the customer, the seller will receive cash from the card issuer. While there is almost always a fee to the seller to cover the processing costs charged by the card issuer, most businesses consider the benefits of transferring the risk of not being able to collect from the customer and avoiding the costs associated with credit customers are greater than the costs of the processing fees.

Factoring and Pledging Receivables

When a business factors its receivables, it sells its receivables to a finance company or bank (often called a *factor*). The business immediately receives cash less an applicable fee from the factor for the receivables. The factor, instead of the business, now collects the cash on the receivables. The business no longer has to deal with the collection of the receivable from the customer. The business receives cash associated with the receivable from the factor instead of the customer.

Pledging of receivables is another option for businesses that need cash immediately. In a pledging situation, a business uses its receivables as security for a loan. The business borrows money from a bank and offers its receivables as collateral. The business is still responsible for collecting on the receivables, but it uses this money to pay off the loan along with interest. In pledging, if the loan is not paid, the bank can collect on the receivables.

In both situations, the business has managed to receive cash immediately for the receivables instead of having to wait for collection.

Match the accounting terminology to the definitions.

1.	Factoring receivables	a. A monetary claim against a business or an individual.
2.	Debtor	b. The party to a transaction who takes on an obligation/payable.
3.	Accounts receivable	c. Using receivables as security (collateral) for a loan.
4.	Maturity date	d. The right to receive cash in the future from customers for goods sold or for services provided.
5.	Receivable	e. The date when a note is due.
6.	Pledging receivables	f. Selling receivables to a finance company or bank.

Check your answers online in MyLab Accounting or at http://www.pearsonhighered.com/Horngren.

For more practice, see Short Exercises S-F:9-1 and S-F:9-2. **MyLab Accounting**

9-6 Financial chapter 9

HOW ARE UNCOLLECTIBLES ACCOUNTED FOR WHEN USING THE DIRECT WRITE-OFF METHOD?

Learning Objective 2
Apply the direct write-off method for uncollectibles

Selling on account brings both a benefit and a cost:

- The benefit to a business is the potential increased revenues and profits by making sales to a wider range of customers.
- The cost, however, is that some customers do not pay, creating uncollectible receivables.

Customers' accounts receivable are an asset. Accounts receivable that are uncollectible must be written off, which means they must be removed from the books, because the company does not expect to receive cash in the future. Instead, the company must record an expense associated with the cost of the uncollectible account. This expense is called **bad debts expense**. Bad debts expense is sometimes called *doubtful accounts expense* or *uncollectible accounts expense*.

Bad Debts Expense
The cost to the seller of extending credit. It arises from the failure to collect from some credit customers.

There are two methods of accounting for uncollectible receivables and recording the related bad debts expense:

- Direct write-off method
- Allowance method

Recording and Writing Off Uncollectible Accounts—Direct Write-off Method

Direct Write-off Method
A method of accounting for uncollectible receivables in which the company records bad debts expense when a customer's account receivable is uncollectible.

The **direct write-off method** of accounting for uncollectible receivables is primarily used by small, nonpublic companies. Under the direct write-off method, accounts receivable are written off and bad debts expense is recorded when the business determines that it will never collect from a specific customer.

For example, let's assume that on August 9 Smart Touch Learning determines that it will not be able to collect $200 from customer Dan King for a sale of merchandise inventory made on May 5. The company would write off the customer's account receivable by debiting Bad Debts Expense and crediting the customer's Accounts Receivable as follows:

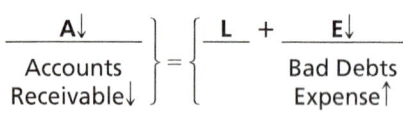

Date	Accounts and Explanation	Debit	Credit
Aug. 9	Bad Debts Expense	200	
	Accounts Receivable—King		200
	Wrote off an uncollectible account.		

Once an account receivable is written off, the company stops pursuing the collection. Some companies might turn delinquent receivables over to an attorney or other collection agency to recover some of the cash for the company, but generally companies do not expect to receive any future payment.

Recovery of Accounts Previously Written Off—Direct Write-off Method

Occasionally after a company writes off an account, the customer will decide to make payment. To account for this recovery, the company must reverse the earlier write-off. For example, on September 10, Smart Touch Learning unexpectedly receives $200 cash from

Receivables Financial 9-7

Dan King. The company will reverse the earlier write-off and then record the cash collection as follows:

Date	Accounts and Explanation	Debit	Credit
Sep. 10	Accounts Receivable—King	200	
	Bad Debts Expense		200
	Reinstated previously written off account.		
10	Cash	200	
	Accounts Receivable—King		200
	Collected cash on account.		

$$\left.\frac{A\uparrow}{\text{Accounts Receivable}\uparrow}\right\} = \left\{\frac{L\ +\ E\uparrow}{\text{Bad Debts Expense}\downarrow}\right.$$

$$\left.\frac{A\uparrow\downarrow}{\substack{\text{Cash}\uparrow \\ \text{Accounts Receivable}\downarrow}}\right\} = \left\{\frac{L\ +\ E}{}\right.$$

In order to keep accurate records about the collection of cash for a previously written off account, the business should reestablish the Accounts Receivable by debiting the receivable account. Then the business can record the receipt of cash for the receivable by debiting Cash and crediting Accounts Receivable. This helps restore the credit history of the customer by showing that the customer did fulfill the promise of payment.

Limitations of the Direct Write-off Method

The direct write-off method, as stated earlier, is often used only by small, nonpublic companies. This is because the direct write-off method violates the matching principle. The matching principle requires that the expense of uncollectible accounts be matched with the related revenue. For example, when using the direct write-off method, a company might record sales revenue in 2023 but not record the bad debts expense until 2024. By recording the bad debts expense in a different year than when the revenue was recorded, the company is overstating net income in 2023 and understating net income in 2024. In addition, on the balance sheet at December 31, 2023, Accounts Receivable will be overstated because the company will have some receivables that will be uncollectible but are not yet written off. This method is only acceptable for companies that have very few uncollectible receivables. Most companies must use a method that does a better job of matching expenses to the associated sales revenue. This method is called the *allowance method*, and it is the method required by GAAP.

Williams Company uses the direct write-off method to account for uncollectible receivables. On July 18, Williams wrote off a $6,800 account receivable from customer W. Jennings. On August 24, Williams unexpectedly received full payment from Jennings on the previously written off account.

7. Journalize Williams's write-off on the uncollectible receivable.
8. Journalize Williams's collection of the previously written off receivable.

Check your answers online in MyLab Accounting or at http://www.pearsonhighered.com/Horngren.

For more practice, see Short Exercises S-F:9-3 and S-F:9-4. **MyLab Accounting**

HOW ARE UNCOLLECTIBLES ACCOUNTED FOR WHEN USING THE ALLOWANCE METHOD?

Learning Objective 3
Apply the allowance method for uncollectibles and estimate bad debts expense based on the percent-of-sales, percent-of-receivables, and aging-of-receivables methods

Most companies use the allowance method to measure the amount of bad debts expense associated with the cost of uncollectible accounts. The **allowance method** is based on the matching principle; thus, the key concept is to record bad debts expense in the same period as the related sales revenue. The business does not wait to see which customers will not pay. Instead, it records a bad debts expense based on estimates developed from past experience. The offset to the Bad Debts Expense account is a contra asset account called **Allowance for Bad Debts** or *Allowance for Doubtful Accounts* or *Allowance for Uncollectible Accounts*. The Allowance for Bad Debts holds the estimated amount of "unknown" uncollectible accounts. As the Allowance for Bad Debts account is a contra asset, it is subtracted from the asset Accounts Receivable on the company's balance sheet.

Allowance Method
A method of accounting for uncollectible receivables in which the company estimates bad debts expense instead of waiting to see which customers the company will not collect from.

Allowance for Bad Debts
A contra asset account, related to accounts receivable, that holds the estimated amount of uncollectible accounts.

Recording Bad Debts Expense—Allowance Method

When using the allowance method, companies estimate bad debts expense at the end of the period and then record an adjusting entry. Suppose that as of December 31, 2025, Smart Touch Learning estimates that $80 of its $4,400 accounts receivable are uncollectible. The accounting clerk will record the following adjusting entry:

Date	Accounts and Explanation	Debit	Credit
2025			
Dec. 31	Bad Debts Expense	80	
	Allowance for Bad Debts		80
	Recorded bad debts expense for the period.		

$$\frac{A\downarrow}{\text{Allowance for Bad Debts}\uparrow} \Bigg\} = \Bigg\{ \frac{L}{} + \frac{E\downarrow}{\text{Bad Debts Expense}\uparrow}$$

After posting the adjusting entry, Smart Touch Learning has the following balances in its accounts:

Accounts Receivable		Allowance for Bad Debts		Bad Debts Expense	
Dec. 31 4,400			80 Dec. 31	Dec. 31 80	

Net Realizable Value
The net value a company expects to collect from its accounts receivable. Accounts Receivable less Allowance for Bad Debts.

Smart Touch Learning will report the Accounts Receivable on the balance sheet at the net realizable value. **Net realizable value** is the net value the company expects to collect from its accounts receivable or Accounts Receivable less Allowance for Bad Debts. Smart Touch Learning would report the following on its balance sheet:

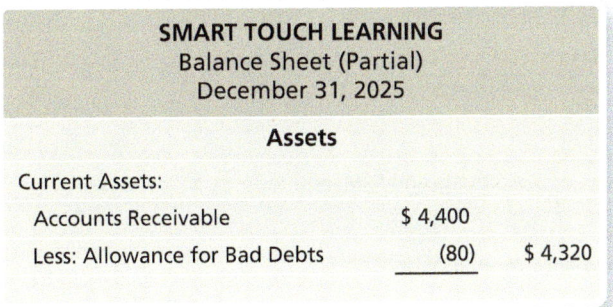

SMART TOUCH LEARNING
Balance Sheet (Partial)
December 31, 2025

Assets

Current Assets:		
Accounts Receivable	$ 4,400	
Less: Allowance for Bad Debts	(80)	$ 4,320

> **IFRS**
> Under IFRS, receivables are recognized and reported similarly to what is required by GAAP. Accounts Receivable must be reported at net realizable value. The allowance method is used to accomplish the matching of bad debt expense to the sales of the period and to report receivables at net realizable value. Under IFRS, the Allowance for Bad Debts may be called the *Provision for Bad Debts*. IFRS provides more detailed criteria than GAAP for determining when an account is uncollectible.

The balance sheet now reports the amount of accounts receivable that Smart Touch Learning expects to collect, $4,320. The contra account, Allowance for Bad Debts, is subtracted from Accounts Receivable showing that although $4,400 is owed to Smart Touch Learning, the company estimates that $80 of accounts receivable will be uncollectible.

ETHICS

Should the uncollectible accounts be underestimated?

Norah Wang is in the process of recording adjusting entries for her employer, Happy Kennels. She is evaluating the uncollectible accounts and determining the amount of bad debts expense to record for the year. Her manager, Gillian Tedesco, has asked that Norah underestimate the amount of uncollectible accounts for the year. Gillian is hoping to get a bank loan for an expansion of the kennel facility, and she is concerned that the net income of the company will be too low for a loan to be approved. What should Norah do?

Solution

It is important that accounts receivable be reported at the appropriate amount on the balance sheet. This involves determining an accurate estimate of uncollectible accounts and recognizing the associated bad debts expense. In understating the amount of uncollectible accounts, Norah would be misleading the bank on the amount of cash that Happy Kennels expects to collect in the future. Norah would also understate Bad Debts Expense and overstate net income on the income statement.

Writing Off Uncollectible Accounts—Allowance Method

When using the allowance method, companies still write off accounts receivable that are uncollectible. However, instead of recording a debit to Bad Debts Expense (as done when using the direct write-off method), the company will record a debit to Allowance for Bad Debts. **Bad Debts Expense is not debited when a company writes off an account receivable when using the allowance method because the company has already recorded the Bad Debts Expense as an adjusting entry.** The entry to write off an account under the allowance method has no effect on net income at the time of entry.

Why isn't Bad Debts Expense debited when writing off an account receivable when using the allowance method?

For example, on January 10, 2026, Smart Touch Learning determines that it cannot collect a total of $25 from its customer, Shawn Clark. The accounting clerk would record the following entry to write off the account:

Date	Accounts and Explanation	Debit	Credit
2026			
Jan. 10	Allowance for Bad Debts	25	
	Accounts Receivable—Clark		25
	Wrote off an uncollectible account.		

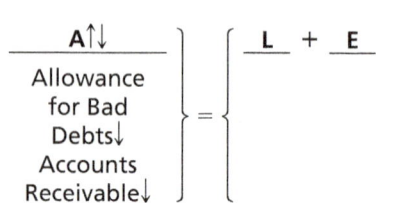

Smart Touch Learning's account balances after the write-off are:

Accounts Receivable				Allowance for Bad Debts			
Jan. 1, 2026	4,400					80	Jan. 1, 2026
		25	Jan. 10, 2026	Jan. 10, 2026	25		
Bal.	4,375					55	Bal.

The entry to write off a receivable reduces the amount of the Allowance for Bad Debts account and also the Accounts Receivable account, but it does not affect the net realizable value shown on the balance sheet. This is because both Allowance for Bad Debts (contra asset) and Accounts Receivable (asset) were reduced by the amount of the write-off. In addition, the write-off of a receivable does not affect net income because the entry does not involve revenue or expenses.

	Before Write-off	After Write-off
Accounts Receivable	$ 4,400	$ 4,375
Less: Allowance for Bad Debts	(80)	(55)
Net Realizable Value	$ 4,320	$ 4,320

Recovery of Accounts Previously Written Off—Allowance Method

After a company has previously written off an account, the company stops attempting to collect on the receivable. Customers will occasionally make payment on receivables that have already been written off. A business will need to reverse the write-off to the Allowance for Bad Debts account and then record the receipt of cash. In reversing the write-off, the business is reestablishing the receivable account and reversing the write-off from the Allowance for Bad Debts account.

Recall that Smart Touch Learning wrote off the $25 receivable from customer Shawn Clark on January 10, 2026. It is now March 4, 2026, and Smart Touch Learning unexpectedly receives $25 cash from Clark. The entries to reverse the write-off and record the receipt of cash are as follows:

Date	Accounts and Explanation	Debit	Credit
2026			
Mar. 4	Accounts Receivable—Clark	25	
	Allowance for Bad Debts		25
	Reinstated previously written off account.		
4	Cash	25	
	Accounts Receivable—Clark		25
	Collected cash on account.		

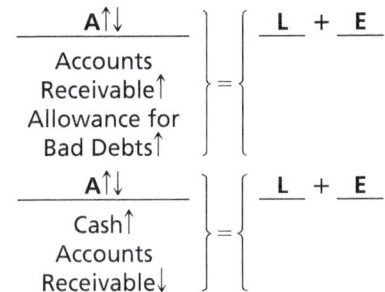

Comparison of Recording Transactions for Uncollectibles Using the Direct Write-Off Method versus the Allowance Method

Exhibit F:9-1 shows the journal entries that are recorded when using the direct write-off method versus the allowance method of accounting for uncollectibles. Take a moment to review the differences in these two methods. Remember that when using the direct write-off method, the business does not use an allowance account and that this method does not conform with GAAP.

Exhibit F:9-1 | Direct Write-off Method Versus Allowance Method

DIRECT WRITE-OFF METHOD	ALLOWANCE METHOD
Write-off of an uncollectible account:	

Bad Debts Expense 25
   Accounts Receivable—Customer Name 25
Wrote off an uncollectible account.
	Allowance for Bad Debts 25
	   Accounts Receivable—Customer Name 25
	Wrote off an uncollectible account.

Recovery of accounts previously written off:	

Accounts Receivable—Customer Name 25
   Bad Debts Expense 25
Reinstated previously written off account.
	Accounts Receivable—Customer Name 25
	   Allowance for Bad Debts 25
	Reinstated previously written off account.

Cash 25
   Accounts Receivable—Customer Name 25
Collected cash on account.
	Cash 25
	   Accounts Receivable—Customer Name 25
	Collected cash on account.

Adjusting entry to recognize bad debts:	
No adjusting entry recorded.	Bad Debts Expense 300 Allowance for Bad Debts 300 *Recorded bad debts expense for the period.*

TYING IT ALL TOGETHER

Amazon.com, Inc. opened its virtual doors in July 1995. The business serves customers through its retail Web sites and physical stores and focuses on selection, price, and convenience. The company sells hundreds of millions of unique products through its Web site. Amazon also manufactures and sells electronic devices, including Kindle e-readers, Fire tablets, and Echo devices. In addition, Amazon.com, Inc. offers Amazon Prime, a membership program that includes unlimited free shipping and instant streaming of thousands of movies and TV episodes. (You can find Amazon.com, Inc.'s annual report at **https://www.sec.gov/Archives/edgar/data/1018724/000101872419000004/0001018724-19-000004-index.htm**.)

Amazon.com, Inc. reported Accounts Receivable of $16,677 million as of December 31, 2018. What do these receivables represent?

In the notes to the financial statements, Amazon.com, Inc. states the accounts receivable relate primarily to customers, vendors, and sellers. As of December 31, 2018, customer receivables were $9.4 billion, vendor receivables were $3.2 billion, and seller receivables were $710 million. Seller receivables are amounts due from sellers related to a lending program that provides funding to sellers to help obtain inventory.

Which method, the direct write-off method or the allowance method, does Amazon.com, Inc. use to account for bad debts? Why?

The corporation uses the allowance method to account for bad debts. On the corporation's financial statements, the company states that accounts receivables are reported at net realizable value. Net realizable value is the amount the company expects to collect from its accounts receivable (Accounts Receivable less Allowance for Bad Debts). Amazon.com, Inc. uses the allowance method because this method provides a better matching of bad debts expense with the sales revenue. Additionally, as a publicly traded company, Amazon is required by GAAP to use the allowance method.

Estimating and Recording Bad Debts Expense—Allowance Method

How do companies determine the amount of bad debts expense when using the allowance method? When using the allowance method, companies must estimate the amount of bad debts expense at the end of the period and then record an adjusting entry. Companies use their past experience as well as consider the economy, the industry they operate in, and other variables in order to estimate the amount of uncollectible accounts. In short, they make an educated guess, called an *estimate*. Companies estimate bad debt expense using either an income statement approach, which focuses on the amount of Bad Debt Expense that is reported on the income statement, or a balance sheet approach, which focuses on the amount of Accounts Receivables that is reported on the balance sheet. There are three basic ways to estimate uncollectibles:

- Percent-of-sales (income statement approach)
- Percent-of-receivables (balance sheet approach)
- Aging-of-receivables (balance sheet approach)

Percent-of-Sales Method (Income Statement Approach)

Percent-of-Sales Method
A method of estimating uncollectible receivables that calculates bad debts expense based on a percentage of net credit sales.

The **percent-of-sales method** computes bad debts expense as a percentage of net credit sales. (Some companies will use all sales, not just credit sales.) This method is also called the *income-statement approach* because it focuses on the amount of expense that is reported on the income statement.

Let's return to Smart Touch Learning. Based on prior experience, the company's bad debts expense is normally 0.5% of net credit sales, which totaled $60,000 for the year. The accountant calculates bad debts expense using the percent-of-sales method as follows:

Percent-of-Sales Method:
Bad Debts Expense = Net credit sales × %
= $60,000 × 0.005
= $300

Receivables Financial 9-13

At December 31, Smart Touch Learning records the following adjusting entry to recognize bad debts expense for the year:

Date	Accounts and Explanation	Debit	Credit
2026			
Dec. 31	Bad Debts Expense	300	
	Allowance for Bad Debts		300
	Recorded bad debts expense for the period.		

$A\downarrow$ Allowance for Bad Debts $\uparrow$ = L + $E\downarrow$ Bad Debts Expense $\uparrow$

When using the allowance method, the only time Bad Debts Expense is recorded is as an adjusting entry.

After posting the adjusting entry, Smart Touch Learning has the following balances in its balance sheet and income statement accounts. Ignore the previously recorded reversal of the write-off and assume collections on account during the year are $58,000:

Balance sheet accounts:

Accounts Receivable			
Jan. 1, 2026, Bal.	4,400		
Net credit sales	60,000	25	Write-off
		58,000	Collections
Unadj. Bal.	6,375		
Dec. 31, 2026, Bal.	6,375		

Allowance for Bad Debts			
		80	Jan. 1, 2026, Bal.
Write-off	25		
		55	Unadj. Bal.
		300	Adj.
		355	Dec. 31, 2026, Bal.

Income statement account:

Bad Debts Expense	
Jan. 1, 2026, Bal.	0
Adj.	300
Dec. 31, 2026, Bal.	300

Percent-of-Receivables and Aging-of-Receivables Methods (Balance Sheet Approach)

The percent-of-receivables and aging-of-receivables methods are based on the balance of accounts receivable. These approaches are also called *balance-sheet approaches* because they focus on Accounts Receivable (a balance sheet account) and determine a target allowance balance based on a percentage of the receivable balance.

Percent-of-Receivables Method The first balance sheet approach is the **percent-of-receivables method**. In the percent-of-receivables method, the business once again determines a percentage of uncollectible accounts based on past experience. This method is different than the percent-of-sales method because it multiplies the percentage by the *ending* unadjusted balance in the Accounts Receivable account instead of by net credit sales.

Percent-of-Receivables Method
A method of estimating uncollectible receivables by determining the balance of the Allowance for Bad Debts account based on a percentage of accounts receivable.

The calculation for bad debts expense under the percent-of-receivables method is a two-step process. First, the company determines the target balance of Allowance for Bad Debts. Then, it uses the target balance to determine the amount of the bad debts expense.

> **Percent-of-Receivables Method:**
>
> **Step 1:** Determine the target balance of Allowance for Bad Debts.
>
> Target balance = Ending balance of accounts receivable × %
>
> **Step 2:** Determine the amount of bad debts expense by evaluating the allowance account.
>
> Bad debts expense = Target balance − Unadjusted credit balance of Allowance for Bad Debts
>
> OR
>
> Bad debts expense = Target balance + Unadjusted debit balance of Allowance for Bad Debts

Let's look at an example for Smart Touch Learning. Assume that at December 31, 2026, the company's unadjusted accounts receivable balance is $6,375. Smart Touch Learning estimates that 4% of its accounts receivable will be uncollectible. In Step 1, the company determines the target balance for the Allowance for Bad Debts account: $255 ($6,375 × 0.04). Next, its accountant determines the amount of the bad debts expense adjustment: $255 − $55 = $200.

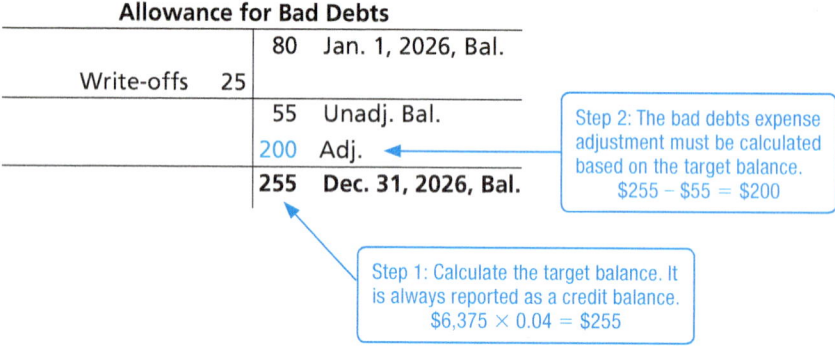

Smart Touch Learning records the following adjusting entry on December 31 to recognize bad debts expense for the year:

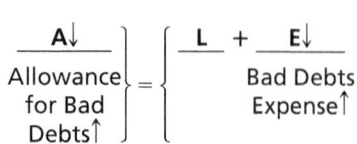

Date	Accounts and Explanation	Debit	Credit
2026			
Dec. 31	Bad Debts Expense	200	
	Allowance for Bad Debts		200
	Recorded bad debts expense for the period.		

Receivables Financial 9-15

After posting the adjusting entry, Smart Touch Learning has the following balances in its balance sheet and income statement accounts:

Balance sheet accounts:

Accounts Receivable			
Jan. 1, 2026, Bal.	4,400		
Net credit sales	60,000	25	Write-offs
		58,000	Collections
Unadj. Bal.	6,375		
Dec. 31, 2026, Bal.	6,375		

Allowance for Bad Debts			
		80	Jan. 1, 2026, Bal.
Write-offs	25		
		55	Unadj. Bal.
		200	Adj.
		255	Dec. 31, 2026, Bal.

Income statement account:

Bad Debts Expense		
Jan. 1, 2026, Bal.	0	
Adj.	200	
Dec. 31, 2026, Bal.	200	

The Allowance for Bad Debts has a credit unadjusted balance because the company overestimated the bad debt expense and has written off less accounts receivable than it expected during the year.

In the preceding example, Smart Touch Learning had an unadjusted *credit* balance in the allowance account. **If a company has a debit balance before the adjustment, the calculation for bad debts expense is a little different. Instead of subtracting the unadjusted balance of the Allowance for Bad Debts from the target balance, the unadjusted balance will be *added* to the target balance.**

Let's look at an example. Suppose that Martin's Music has a *debit* balance in its Allowance for Bad Debts account of $150. Assume that it estimates its percentage of uncollectible accounts will be 2% of $40,000 of Accounts Receivable. Martin's Music's bad debts expense adjustment would be calculated as follows:

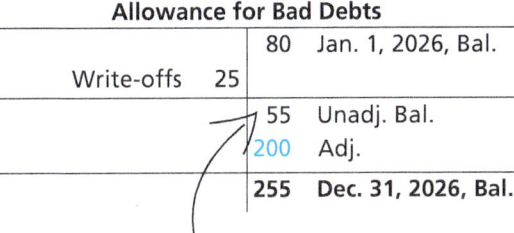

What if a business had a debit balance in the Allowance for Bad Debts account before the adjustment for bad debts expense?

Allowance for Bad Debts			
Unadj. Bal.	150		
		950	Adj.
		800	Bal.

Step 2: The bad debts expense adjustment must be calculated based on the target balance.
$800 + $150 = $950

Step 1: Calculate the target balance. It is always reported as a credit balance.
$40,000 × 0.02 = $800

A company will have a debit unadjusted balance in the Allowance for Bad Debts account if the company has underestimated the bad debt expense and written off more accounts receivable than it expected to during the year.

Notice that when the allowance account has an unadjusted debit balance, the target balance must be added to the unadjusted balance of the Allowance for Bad Debts to determine the bad debts expense adjustment. Martin's Music would record the following adjusting entry to recognize bad debts expense:

$$\left.\begin{array}{c} A\downarrow \\ \text{Allowance} \\ \text{for Bad} \\ \text{Debts}\uparrow \end{array}\right\} = \left\{\begin{array}{c} L + E\downarrow \\ \text{Bad Debts} \\ \text{Expense}\uparrow \end{array}\right.$$

Date	Accounts and Explanation	Debit	Credit
Dec. 31	Bad Debts Expense	950	
	Allowance for Bad Debts		950
	Recorded bad debts expense for the period.		

Aging-of-Receivables Method
A method of estimating uncollectible receivables by determining the balance of the Allowance for Bad Debts account based on the age of individual accounts receivable.

Aging-of-Receivables Method The **aging-of-receivables method** is similar to the percent-of-receivables method. However, in the aging method, businesses group individual accounts (Broxson, Andrews, and so on) according to how long the receivable has been outstanding. Then they apply a different percentage uncollectible to each aging category. Exhibit F:9-2 shows the aging schedule for Smart Touch Learning.

Exhibit F:9-2 | **Aging of Accounts Receivable**

	Age of Account as of December 31, 2026				
Customer Name	1–30 Days	31–60 Days	61–90 Days	Over 90 Days	Total Balance
Broxson	$ 800				$ 800
Phi Chi Fraternity	2,100				2,100
Andrews		$ 350			350
Jones		480			480
Perez	1,345				1,345
Thompson			$ 1,200		1,200
Clark				$ 100	100
Totals	$ 4,245	$ 830	$ 1,200	$ 100	$ 6,375
Estimated percentage uncollectible	× 1%	× 2%	× 3%	× 90%	
Estimated total uncollectible	$ 42	$ 17	$ 36	$ 90	$ 185 ← Target balance

At year-end, Smart Touch Learning will need to record the adjusting entry to recognize bad debts expense. The procedure is similar to the percent-of-receivables method.

Aging-of-Receivables Method:

Step 1: Determine the target balance of Allowance for Bad Debts by using the age of each account.

Step 2: Determine the amount of bad debts expense by evaluating the allowance account.

Bad debts expense = Target balance − Unadjusted credit balance of Allowance for Bad Debts

OR

Bad debts expense = Target balance + Unadjusted debit balance of Allowance for Bad Debts

Based on Exhibit F:9-2, Smart Touch Learning knows the target balance of the Allowance for Bad Debts account is $185. Smart Touch Learning will determine its bad debts expense by subtracting the $55 unadjusted credit balance in the allowance account from the target balance, $185.

Allowance for Bad Debts

		80	Jan. 1, 2026, Bal.
Write-offs	25		
		55	Unadj. Bal.
		130	Adj.
		185	Dec. 31, 2026, Bal.

Step 1: Calculate the target balance using the aging schedule. It is always reported as a credit balance.

Step 2: The bad debts expense adjustment must be calculated based on the target balance. $185 − $55 = $130

Smart Touch Learning will record the following adjusting entry on December 31 to recognize bad debts expense for the year:

Date	Accounts and Explanation	Debit	Credit
2026			
Dec. 31	Bad Debts Expense	130	
	Allowance for Bad Debts		130
	Recorded bad debts expense for the period.		

A↓
Allowance for Bad Debts↑
= L + E↓
Bad Debts Expense↑

After posting the adjusting entry, Smart Touch Learning has the following balances in its balance sheet and income statement accounts:

Balance sheet accounts:

Accounts Receivable

Jan. 1, 2026, Bal.	4,400		
Net credit sales	60,000	25	Write-offs
		58,000	Collections
Unadj. Bal.	6,375		
Dec. 31, 2026, Bal.	6,375		

Allowance for Bad Debts

		80	Jan. 1, 2026, Bal.
Write-offs	25		
		55	Unadj. Bal.
		130	Adj.
		185	Dec. 31, 2026, Bal.

Income statement account:

Bad Debts Expense

Jan. 1, 2026, Bal.	0
Adj.	130
Dec. 31, 2026, Bal.	130

Comparison of Income Statement Approach versus Balance Sheet Approach

Under the allowance method of accounting for uncollectibles, businesses must estimate the amount of the bad debts expense at the end of the accounting period. This is done using either an income statement approach (percent-of-sales) or a balance sheet approach (percent-of-receivables or aging-of-receivables). Exhibit F:9-3 (on the next page) summarizes the differences between the income statement approach and the balance sheet approach.

Exhibit F:9-3 | Comparison of Income Statement Approach versus Balance Sheet Approach

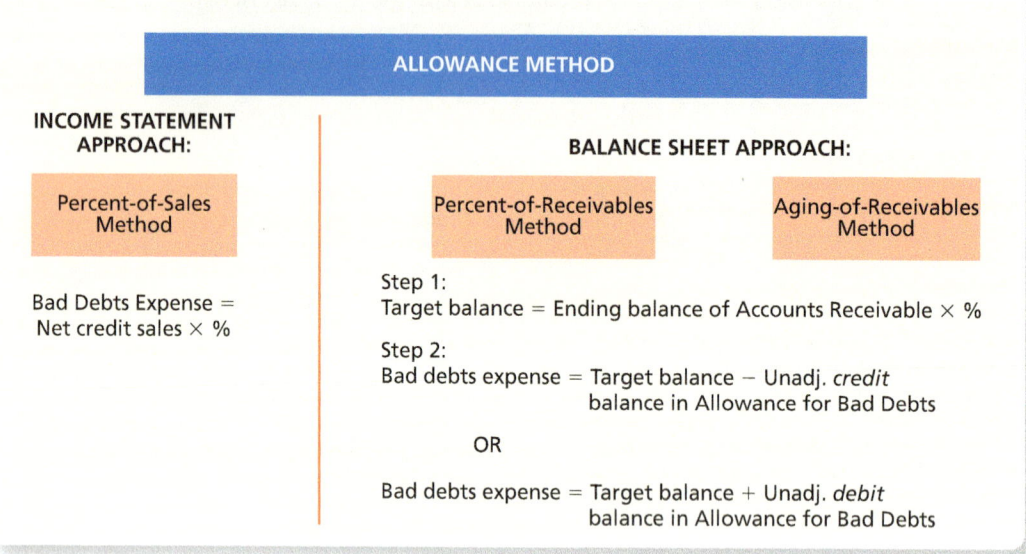

Johnson Company uses the allowance method to account for uncollectible receivables. On September 2, Johnson wrote off a $14,000 account receivable from customer J. Mraz. On December 12, Johnson unexpectedly received full payment from Mraz on the previously written off account. Johnson records an adjusting entry for bad debts expense of $800 on December 31.

9. Journalize Johnson's write-off of the uncollectible receivable.
10. Journalize Johnson's collection of the previously written off receivable.
11. Journalize Johnson's adjustment for bad debts expense.

Check your answers online in MyLab Accounting or at http://www.pearsonhighered.com/Horngren.

For more practice, see Short Exercises S-F:9-5 through S-F:9-8. MyLab Accounting

HOW ARE NOTES RECEIVABLE ACCOUNTED FOR?

Learning Objective 4
Account for notes receivable including computing interest and recording honored and dishonored notes

Notes receivable are more formal than accounts receivable. The debtor signs a promissory note as evidence of the transaction. Before launching into the accounting, let's define the special terms used for notes receivable:

- **Promissory note**—A written promise to pay a specified amount of money at a particular future date, usually with interest.
- **Maker of the note (debtor)**—The entity that signs the note and promises to pay the required amount; the maker of the note is the debtor.
- **Payee of the note (creditor)**—The entity to whom the maker promises future payment; the payee of the note is the creditor. The creditor is the company that loans the money.

Principal
The amount loaned by the payee and borrowed by the maker of the note.

- **Principal**—The amount loaned by the payee and borrowed by the maker of the note.

Interest
The revenue to the payee for loaning money—the expense to the debtor.

- **Interest**—The revenue to the payee for loaning money. Interest is an expense to the debtor and revenue to the creditor.

- **Interest period**—The period of time during which interest is computed. It extends from the original date of the note to the maturity date. Also called the *note term*.
- **Interest rate**—The percentage rate of interest specified by the note. Interest rates are almost always stated for a period of one year.
- **Maturity date**—As stated earlier, this is the date when final payment of the note is due. Also called the *due date*.
- **Maturity value**—The sum of the principal plus interest due at maturity. Maturity value is the total amount that will be paid back.

Exhibit F:9-4 illustrates a promissory note.

> **Interest Period**
> The period of time during which interest is computed. It extends from the original date of the note to the maturity date.
>
> **Interest Rate**
> The percentage rate of interest specified by the note.
>
> **Maturity Value**
> The sum of the principal plus interest due at maturity.

Exhibit F:9-4 | Promissory Note

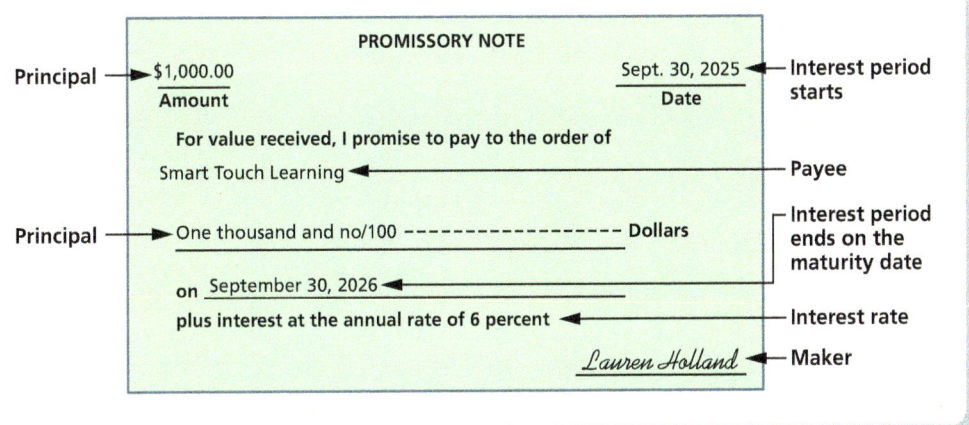

In Exhibit F:9-4, we can see Smart Touch Learning is lending Lauren Holland $1,000 on September 30, 2025, for one year at an annual interest rate of 6%. The accounting clerk for Smart Touch Learning would record the following journal entry:

Date	Accounts and Explanation	Debit	Credit
2025			
Sep. 30	Notes Receivable—Holland	1,000	
	Cash		1,000
	Accepted note in exchange for cash.		

$$\left.\begin{array}{c}A\uparrow\downarrow \\ \text{Notes} \\ \text{Receivable}\uparrow \\ \text{Cash}\downarrow\end{array}\right\} = \left\{\begin{array}{c}L + E\end{array}\right.$$

Identifying Maturity Date

Some notes specify the maturity date. For example, September 30, 2026, is the maturity date of the note shown in Exhibit F:9-4. Other notes state the period of the note in days or months. When the period is given in months, the note's maturity date falls on the same day of the month as the date the note was issued. For example, a six-month note dated February 16, 2025, would mature on August 16, 2025.

When the period is given in days, the maturity date is determined by counting the actual days from the date of issue. A 180-day note dated February 16, 2025, matures on August 15, 2025, as shown here:

Month	Number of Days	Cumulative Total
Feb. 2025	28 − 16 = 12	12
Mar. 2025	31	43
Apr. 2025	30	73
May 2025	31	104
Jun. 2025	30	134
Jul. 2025	31	165
Aug. 2025	15	180

In counting the number of days in a note term, remember to:

- Count the maturity date.
- Omit the date the note was issued.

Computing Interest on a Note

The formula for computing the interest is as follows:

> Amount of interest = Principal × Interest rate × Time

In the formula, time (period) represents the portion of a year that interest has accrued on the note. It may be expressed as a fraction of a year in months (number of months/12) or a fraction of a year in days (number of days/365). Using the data in Exhibit F:9-4, Smart Touch Learning computes interest revenue for one year as follows:

> Amount of interest = Principal × Interest rate × Time
> = $1,000 × 0.06 × 12/12
> = $60

The maturity value of the note is $1,060 ($1,000 principal + $60 interest). The time element is 12/12 or 1 because the note's term is one year.

When the term of a note is stated in months, we compute the interest based on the 12-month year. Interest on a $2,000 note at 10% for nine months is computed as follows:

> Amount of interest = Principal × Interest rate × Time
> = $2,000 × 0.10 × 9/12
> = $150

When the interest period is stated in days, we sometimes compute interest based on a 360-day year rather than on a 365-day year. A 360-day year eliminates some rounding and was used frequently in the past. However, with the use of computers to calculate interest, a 365-day year is much more common now. A 365-day year will be used for all calculations in this chapter. The interest on a $5,000 note at 12% for 60 days can be computed as follows:

$$\text{Amount of interest} = \text{Principal} \times \text{Interest rate} \times \text{Time}$$
$$= \$5,000 \times 0.12 \times 60/365$$
$$= \$98.63$$

Keep in mind that interest rates are stated as an annual rate. Therefore, the time in the interest formula should also be expressed in terms of a fraction of one year.

Accruing Interest Revenue and Recording Honored Notes Receivable

Some notes receivable may be outstanding at the end of an accounting period. The interest revenue earned on the note up to year-end is part of that year's earnings. Recall that interest revenue is earned over time, not just when cash is received. Because of the revenue recognition principle, we want to record the earnings from the note in the year in which they were earned.

Now, we continue analyzing Smart Touch Learning's note receivable from Exhibit F:9-4. Smart Touch Learning's accounting period ends December 31.

- How much of the total interest revenue does Smart Touch Learning earn in 2025 (from September 30 through December 31)? Smart Touch Learning earns three months (October, November, and December) of interest.

$$\$1,000 \times 0.06 \times 3/12 = \$15$$

The accounting clerk makes the following adjusting entry at December 31, 2025:

Date	Accounts and Explanation	Debit	Credit
2025			
Dec. 31	Interest Receivable	15	
	Interest Revenue		15
	Accrued interest revenue.		

$$\frac{A\uparrow}{\text{Interest Receivable}\uparrow} = \left\{ \frac{L}{} + \frac{E\uparrow}{\text{Interest Revenue}\uparrow} \right.$$

- How much interest revenue does Smart Touch Learning earn in 2026 (for January 1 through September 30)? Smart Touch Learning earns nine months (January through September) of interest.

$$\$1,000 \times 0.06 \times 9/12 = \$45$$

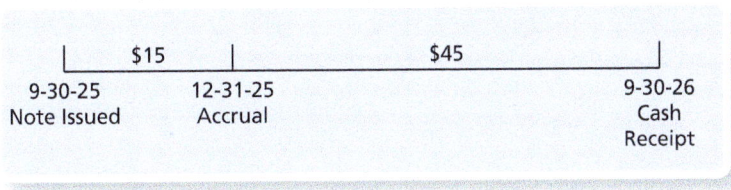

On the maturity date of the note, Smart Touch Learning will receive cash for the principal amount plus interest. The company considers the note honored and makes the following entry:

Date	Accounts and Explanation	Debit	Credit
2026			
Sep. 30	Cash ($1,000 + ($1,000 × 0.06 × 12/12))	1,060	
	Notes Receivable—Holland		1,000
	Interest Receivable		15
	Interest Revenue		45
	Collected note receivable plus interest.		

A↑ Cash↑ Notes Receivable↓ Interest Receivable↓ = L + E↑ Interest Revenue↑

Some companies sell merchandise in exchange for notes receivable. Assume that on July 1, 2025, Rosa Electric sells household appliances for $2,000 to Dorman Builders. Dorman signs a nine-month promissory note at 10% annual interest. Rosa's entries to record the sale (ignore Cost of Goods Sold), interest accrual, and collection from Dorman are as follows:

Date	Accounts and Explanation	Debit	Credit
2025			
Jul. 1	Notes Receivable—Dorman Builders	2,000	
	Sales Revenue		2,000
Dec. 31	Interest Receivable ($2,000 × 0.10 × 6/12)	100	
	Interest Revenue		100
2026			
Apr. 1	Cash ($2,000 + ($2,000 × 0.10 × 9/12))	2,150	
	Notes Receivable—Dorman Builders		2,000
	Interest Receivable		100
	Interest Revenue ($2,000 × 0.10 × 3/12)		50

A↑ Notes Receivable↑ = L + E↑ Sales Revenue↑

A↑ Interest Receivable↑ = L + E↑ Interest Revenue↑

A↑ Cash↑ Notes Receivable↓ Interest Receivable↓ = L + E↑ Interest Revenue↑

A company may accept a note receivable from a credit customer who fails to pay an account receivable. The customer signs a promissory note and gives it to the creditor. Suppose Sports Club cannot pay Blanding Services the amount due on accounts receivable of

$5,000. Blanding may accept a 60-day, $5,000 note receivable, with 12% interest, from Sports Club on November 19, 2025. Blanding's entries are as follows:

Date	Accounts and Explanation	Debit	Credit
2025			
Nov. 19	Notes Receivable—Sports Club	5,000	
	Accounts Receivable—Sports Club		5,000
Dec. 31	Interest Receivable ($5,000 × 0.12 × 42/365)	69	
	Interest Revenue		69
2026			
Jan. 18	Cash ($5,000 + ($5,000 × 0.12 × 60/365))	5,099	
	Notes Receivable—Sports Club		5,000
	Interest Receivable		69
	Interest Revenue ($5,000 × 0.12 × 18/365)		30

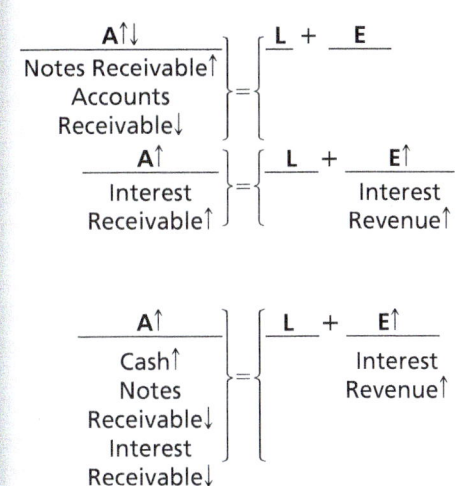

Recording Dishonored Notes Receivable

If the maker of a note does not pay at maturity, the maker **dishonors a note** (also called *defaulting on a note*). Because the note has expired, it is no longer in force. But the debtor still owes the payee. The payee can transfer the note receivable amount to Accounts Receivable. Suppose Rubinstein Jewelers has a six-month, 10% note receivable for $1,200 from Mark Adair that was signed on March 3, 2025, and Adair defaults. Rubinstein Jewelers will record the default on September 3, 2025, as follows:

Dishonor a Note
Failure of a note's maker to pay a note receivable at maturity.

Date	Accounts and Explanation	Debit	Credit
2025			
Sep. 3	Accounts Receivable—Adair	1,260	
	Notes Receivable—Adair		1,200
	Interest Revenue ($1,200 × 0.10 × 6/12)		60

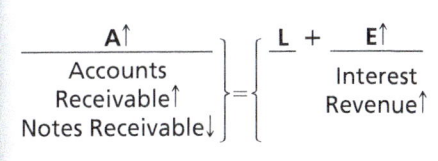

Rubinstein will then bill Adair for the account receivable. This also allows Rubinstein to eventually write off the receivable using either the direct write-off method or the allowance method if at a later date Rubinstein can still not collect the account receivable.

Try It!

On August 1, Taylor Company lent $80,000 to L. King on a 90-day, 5% note.

12. Journalize for Taylor Company the lending of the money on August 1.
13. Journalize the collection of the principal and interest at maturity. Specify the date. Round interest to the nearest dollar.

Check your answers online in MyLab Accounting or at http://www.pearsonhighered.com/Horngren.

For more practice, see Short Exercises S-F:9-9 through S-F:9-12. **MyLab Accounting**

HOW DO WE USE THE ACID-TEST RATIO, ACCOUNTS RECEIVABLE TURNOVER RATIO, AND DAYS' SALES IN RECEIVABLES TO EVALUATE BUSINESS PERFORMANCE?

Learning Objective 5

Use the acid-test ratio, accounts receivable turnover ratio, and days' sales in receivables to evaluate business performance

As discussed earlier in the text, the balance sheet lists assets in the order of liquidity (how quickly an asset can be converted to cash). We can evaluate a company's liquidity by analyzing the company's current assets. The partial balance sheet of **Kohl's Corporation**, shown in Exhibit F:9-5, lists only three current assets: cash and cash equivalents, merchandise inventories, and other current assets. Kohl's does not list any receivables on its balance sheet. While the company does promote and accept the private label Kohl's credit card, the card is issued by an unrelated third party. When the company accepts the private label Kohl's card, the sales are accounted for similar to other credit card sales, such as American Express, MasterCard, and Visa. Kohl's has transferred the risk of collecting cash from its customers to a third party.

Exhibit F:9-5 | Kohl's Corporation Partial Balance Sheet

KOHL'S CORPORATION
Balance Sheet (Partial)
February 2, 2019, and February 3, 2018
(in millions)

Assets	February 2, 2019	February 3, 2018
Current Assets:		
Cash and Cash Equivalents	$ 934	$ 1,308
Merchandise Inventories	3,475	3,542
Other Current Assets	426	530
Total Current Assets	$ 4,835	$ 5,380
Total Current Liabilities	$ 2,730	$ 2,709

Financial statement data is useful by showing the relationships among assets, liabilities, and revenues. Because Kohl's does not list receivables on its balance sheet, we will use one of its competitors, **Amazon.com, Inc.,** to examine three important ratios that include receivables in the calculations. Amazon.com, Inc. serves customers through its retail Web sites and physical stores and focuses on selection, price, and convenience. The company's accounts receivable, shown on its balance sheet, relate to amounts due from customers, vendors, and sellers. The following is a summary of financial information for Amazon.com, Inc. (with all amounts shown in millions):

(In millions)	Dec. 31, 2018	Dec. 31, 2017
Balance sheet—partial		
Current Assets:		
Cash and Cash Equivalents	$ 31,750	$ 20,522
Marketable Securities	9,500	10,464
Inventories	17,174	16,047
Accounts Receivable, Net	16,677	13,164
Total Current Assets	75,101	60,197
Total Current Liabilities	68,391	57,883
Income statement—partial		
Total Net Sales	232,887	177,866

Acid-Test (or Quick) Ratio

Previously we discussed the current ratio, which measures a company's ability to pay current liabilities with current assets, and the cash ratio, which measures a company's ability to meet its short-term obligations with cash and cash equivalents. We now introduce the **acid-test ratio**, also called the *quick ratio*, which is also used to measure a company's ability to pay its current liabilities. The acid-test ratio is a more stringent measure than the current ratio but it is not as stringent as the cash ratio. The acid-test ratio is a ratio of the sum of a company's quick assets to total current liabilities. Quick assets are defined as cash including cash equivalents, short-term investments (such as marketable securities), and net current receivables. The acid-test ratio reveals whether the entity could pay all its current liabilities if they were to become due immediately.

The higher the acid-test ratio, the more able the business is to pay its current liabilities. Amazon.com, Inc.'s acid-test ratio of 0.85 as of December 31, 2018, means that the business has $0.85 of quick assets to pay each $1.00 of current liabilities.

Acid-Test Ratio
The ratio of the sum of cash, cash equivalents, short-term investments, and net current receivables to total current liabilities. The ratio tells whether the entity could pay all its current liabilities if they came due immediately. (Cash including cash equivalents + Short-term investments + Net current receivables) / Total current liabilities.

Acid-test ratio = (Cash including cash equivalents + Short-term investments + Net current receivables) / Total current liabilities
= ($31,750 + $9,500 + $16,677) / $68,391
= 0.85

What is an acceptable acid-test ratio? That depends on the industry. In general, an acid-test ratio of 1.00 or higher is considered safe. It is not uncommon, though, for retail companies such as Amazon.com, Inc. to have acid-test ratios lower than 1.00. Remember, an acceptable acid-test ratio depends on the industry.

Accounts Receivable Turnover Ratio

Accounts Receivable Turnover Ratio
A ratio that measures the number of times the company collects the average accounts receivable balance in a year. Net credit sales / Average net accounts receivable.

The **accounts receivable turnover ratio** measures the number of times the company collects the average accounts receivable balance in a year. The higher the ratio, the faster the cash collections. Amazon.com, Inc.'s accounts receivable turnover ratio, presented below, indicates that the business turns over its receivables 15.61 times a year.

> Accounts receivable turnover ratio = Net credit sales / Average net accounts receivable
> = $232,877 / [($16,677 + $13,164) / 2]
> = 15.61 times

In calculating the accounts receivable turnover ratio for Amazon.com, Inc., we use total net sales instead of net credit sales. This is because most companies don't report the level of detail needed to determine net credit sales.

Days' Sales in Receivables

Days' Sales in Receivables
The ratio of average net accounts receivable to one day's sales. The ratio tells how many days it takes to collect the average level of accounts receivable. 365 days / Accounts receivable turnover ratio.

After making a credit sale, the next step is to collect the receivable. **Days' sales in receivables**, also called the *collection period*, indicates how many days it takes to collect the average level of accounts receivable. The number of days' sales in receivables should be close to the number of days customers are allowed to make payment when credit is extended. The shorter the collection period, the more quickly the organization can use its cash. The longer the collection period, the less cash is available for operations. Amazon.com, Inc.'s days' sales in receivables can be computed as follows:

> Days' sales in receivables = 365 days / Accounts receivable turnover ratio
> = 365 days / 15.61
> = 23 days

On average, it takes Amazon.com, Inc. 23 days to collect its accounts receivable. However, this figure is somewhat misleading. We used total net sales rather than net credit sales when calculating the accounts receivable turnover. Therefore, our calculation includes both cash and credit sales.

The length of the collection period depends on the credit terms of the sale. For example, sales on net 30 terms should be collected within approximately 30 days. When there is a discount, such as 2/10, net 30, the collection period may be shorter than 30 days. Credit terms of net 45 result in a longer collection period than 30 days.

Try It!

Lovett Company reported the following selected items at March 31, 2024 (last year's—2023—amounts also given as needed):

Accounts Payable	$ 128,000	Accounts Receivable, net:	
Cash	104,000	March 31, 2024	$ 108,000
Merchandise Inventory:		March 31, 2023	68,000
March 31, 2024	116,000	Cost of Goods Sold	460,000
March 31, 2023	80,000	Short-term Investments	56,000
Net Credit Sales Revenue	1,168,000	Other Current Assets	48,000
Long-term Assets	168,000	Other Current Liabilities	72,000
Long-term Liabilities	52,000		

14. Compute Lovett's (a) acid-test ratio, (b) accounts receivable turnover ratio, and (c) days' sales in receivables as of March 31, 2024.

Check your answers online in MyLab Accounting or at http://www.pearsonhighered.com/Horngren.

For more practice, see Short Exercise S-F:9-13. **MyLab Accounting**

REVIEW

> Things You Should Know

1. What are common types of receivables, and how are credit sales recorded?

- A receivable is a monetary claim against a business or an individual.
- There are three major types of receivables:
  - Accounts receivable—Represent the right to receive cash in the future from customers for goods sold or for services performed.
  - Notes receivable—Represent a written promise that the customer will pay a fixed amount of principal plus interest by a certain date in the future.
  - Other receivables—A miscellaneous category that includes any other type of receivables where there is a right to receive cash in the future.
- A critical component of internal control over receivables is the separation of cash-handling and cash-accounting duties.
- A separate accounts receivable account (called a subsidiary account) must be maintained for each customer in order to account for payments received from the customer and amounts still owed.
- The sum of all balances in the subsidiary accounts receivable will equal a control account balance, Accounts Receivable.
- As a way to receive cash quicker and reduce risk of uncollectibles, businesses can accept credit cards and debit cards and/or factor or pledge their receivables.

2. How are uncollectibles accounted for when using the direct write-off method?

- Writing off uncollectible accounts when using the direct write-off method involves a debit to Bad Debts Expense and a credit to Accounts Receivable.
- Recovery of accounts previously written off is recorded by reversing the write-off entry and then recording an entry to receive the cash.
- The direct write-off method violates the matching principle and is not the method required by GAAP.

3. How are uncollectibles accounted for when using the allowance method?

- When using the allowance method, companies estimate bad debts expense at the end of the period and record an adjusting entry that debits Bad Debts Expense and credits Allowance for Bad Debts.
- There are three ways to estimate bad debts expense:
    - Percent-of-sales method (income statement approach)—Computes bad debts expense as a percentage of net credit sales.
    - Percent-of-receivables method (balance sheet approach)—Determines the balance of the Allowance for Bad Debts account based on a percentage of accounts receivable.
    - Aging-of-receivables method (balance sheet approach)—Determines the balance of the Allowance for Bad Debts account based on the age of individual accounts receivable.
- Writing off uncollectible accounts involves a debit to Allowance for Bad Debts and a credit to Accounts Receivable.
- Recovery of accounts previously written off is recorded by reversing the write-off entry and then recording an entry to receive the cash.
- The allowance method follows the matching principle and is required by GAAP.

4. How are notes receivable accounted for?

- Notes receivable involve interest that is computed as principal times interest rate times time.
- Interest on notes must be accrued at the end of each period, and an adjusting entry must be recorded by debiting Interest Receivable and crediting Interest Revenue.
- The receipt of cash at a note's maturity includes the principal plus interest.
- When a customer dishonors a note, the business can transfer the note receivable (plus interest earned) to an accounts receivable.

5. How do we use the acid-test ratio, accounts receivable turnover ratio, and days' sales in receivables to evaluate business performance?

- The acid-test ratio reveals whether an entity could pay all its current liabilities if they were due immediately. (Cash including cash equivalents + Short-term investments + Net current receivables) / Total current liabilities.
- Accounts receivable turnover ratio measures the number of times the company collects the average accounts receivable balance in a year. Net credit sales / Average net accounts receivable.
- The days' sales in receivables indicates how many days it takes to collect the average level of accounts receivable. 365 days / Accounts receivable turnover ratio.

> Check Your Understanding F:9-1

Check your understanding of the chapter by completing this problem and then looking at the solution. Use this practice to help identify which sections of the chapter you need to study more.

Monarch Map Company's balance sheet at December 31, 2023, reported the following:

Accounts Receivable	$ 60,000
Less: Allowance for bad debts	2,000

Requirements

1. How much of the receivables did Monarch expect to collect? Stated differently, what was the net realizable value of these receivables? (See Learning Objective 3)
2. Journalize, without explanations, 2024 entries for Monarch and post to the Accounts Receivable and Allowance for Bad Debts T-accounts. (See Learning Objectives 1, 3)
   a. Total credit sales for 2024 were $80,000 (ignore Cost of Goods Sold).
   b. Monarch received cash payments on account during 2024 of $74,300.
   c. Accounts receivable identified to be uncollectible totaled $2,700.
3. Record the adjusting entry to recognize bad debts expense using the following independent situations, and then post to the Bad Debts Expense and Allowance for Bad Debts T-accounts. (See Learning Objective 3)
   a. 3% of credit sales were estimated to be uncollectible.
   b. An aging of receivables indicates that $2,200 of the receivables are estimated to be uncollectible.

> Solution

Requirement 1

Net realizable value of receivables = $60,000 − $2,000 = $58,000

Requirement 2

Date		Accounts and Explanation	Debit	Credit
2024				
(a)		Accounts Receivable	80,000	
		Sales Revenue		80,000
(b)		Cash	74,300	
		Accounts Receivable		74,300
(c)		Allowance for Bad Debts	2,700	
		Accounts Receivable		2,700

Accounts Receivable					Allowance for Bad Debts			
Jan. 1, 2024, Bal.	60,000						2,000	Jan. 1, 2024, Bal.
(a)	80,000	74,300	(b)		(c)	2,700		
		2,700	(c)					
							Unadj. Bal.	700
Unadj. Bal.	63,000							

Requirement 3a

Bad debts expense = Net credit sales × % = $80,000 × 0.03 = $2,400

Date	Accounts and Explanation	Debit	Credit
2024			
Dec. 31	Bad Debts Expense	2,400	
	Allowance for Bad Debts		2,400

Allowance for Bad Debts					Bad Debts Expense		
		2,000	Jan. 1, 2024, Bal.		Adj.	2,400	
(c)	2,700				Dec. 31, 2024, Bal.	2,400	
Unadj. Bal.	700						
		2,400	Adj.				
		1,700	Dec. 31, 2024, Bal.				

Requirement 3b

Bad debts expense = Target balance + Unadj. debit balance = $2,200 + $700 = $2,900

Date	Accounts and Explanation	Debit	Credit
2024			
Dec. 31	Bad Debts Expense	2,900	
	Allowance for Bad Debts		2,900

Allowance for Bad Debts					Bad Debts Expense		
		2,000	Jan. 1, 2024, Bal.		Adj.	2,900	
(c)	2,700				Dec. 31, 2024, Bal.	2,900	
Unadj. Bal.	700						
		2,900	Adj.				
		2,200	Dec. 31, 2024, Bal.				

> Check Your Understanding F:9-2

Check your understanding of the chapter by completing this problem and then looking at the solution. Use this practice to help identify which sections of the chapter you need to study more.

Suppose First Fidelity Bank engaged in the following transactions:

2024		
Apr. 1	Loaned $8,000 to Bland Co. Received a six-month, 10% note.	
Oct. 1	Collected the Bland note at maturity.	
Dec. 1	Loaned $6,000 to Flores, Inc. on a 180-day, 12% note.	
31	Accrued interest revenue on the Flores note.	
2025		
May 30	Collected the Flores note at maturity.	

Journalize the 2024 and 2025 transactions on First Fidelity's books. Explanations are not needed. Use a 365-day year to compute interest. Round interest calculations to the nearest dollar. First Fidelity's accounting period ends on December 31. (See Learning Objective 4)

> Solution

Date	Accounts and Explanation	Debit	Credit
2024			
Apr. 1	Notes Receivable—Bland Co.	8,000	
	Cash		8,000
Oct. 1	Cash ($8,000 + $400)	8,400	
	Notes Receivable—Bland Co.		8,000
	Interest Revenue ($8,000 × 0.10 × 6/12)		400
Dec. 1	Notes Receivable—Flores, Inc.	6,000	
	Cash		6,000
Dec. 31	Interest Receivable	59	
	Interest Revenue ($6,000 × 0.12 × 30/365)		59
2025			
May 30	Cash ($6,000 + ($6,000 × 0.12 × 180/365))	6,355	
	Notes Receivable—Flores, Inc.		6,000
	Interest Receivable		59
	Interest Revenue ($6,000 × 0.12 × 150/365)		296

> Key Terms

Accounts Receivable (p. 9-2)
Accounts Receivable Turnover Ratio (p. 9-26)
Acid-Test Ratio (p. 9-25)
Aging-of-Receivables Method (p. 9-16)
Allowance for Bad Debts (p. 9-8)
Allowance Method (p. 9-8)
Bad Debts Expense (p. 9-6)

Days' Sales in Receivables (p. 9-26)
Debtor (p. 9-2)
Direct Write-off Method (p. 9-6)
Dishonor a Note (p. 9-23)
Interest (p. 9-18)
Interest Period (p. 9-19)
Interest Rate (p. 9-19)
Maturity Date (p. 9-2)

Maturity Value (p. 9-19)
Net Realizable Value (p. 9-8)
Notes Receivable (p. 9-2)
Percent-of-Receivables Method (p. 9-13)
Percent-of-Sales Method (p. 9-12)
Principal (p. 9-18)
Receivable (p. 9-2)

> Quick Check

Learning Objective 1

1. With good internal controls, the person who handles cash can also
   a. account for cash payments.
   b. account for cash receipts from customers.
   c. issue credits to customers for sales returns.
   d. None of the above

Learning Objective 2

2. Which of the following is a limitation of the direct write-off method of accounting for uncollectibles?
   a. The direct write-off method overstates assets on the balance sheet.
   b. The direct write-off method does not match expenses against revenue very well.
   c. The direct write-off method does not set up an allowance for uncollectibles.
   d. All of the above

Learning Objective 2

3. The entry to record a write-off of an uncollectible account when using the direct write-off method involves a
   a. debit to Allowance for Bad Debts.
   b. credit to Cash.
   c. debit to Accounts Receivable.
   d. debit to Bad Debts Expense.

Learning Objective 3

4. Brickman Company uses the allowance method to account for uncollectible receivables. At the beginning of the year, Allowance for Bad Debts had a credit balance of $1,000. During the year Brickman wrote off uncollectible receivables of $2,100. Brickman recorded Bad Debts Expense of $2,700. What is Brickman's year-end balance in Allowance for Bad Debts?
   a. $1,600   b. $4,800   c. $3,700   d. $600

Learning Objective 3

5. Brickman's ending balance of Accounts Receivable is $19,500. Use the data in the preceding question to compute the net realizable value of Accounts Receivable at year-end.
   a. $16,800   b. $19,500   c. $17,400   d. $17,900

6. During the year, Bernard Company had net credit sales of $45,000. At the end of the year, before adjusting entries, the balance in Accounts Receivable was $12,500 (debit) and the balance in Allowance for Bad Debts was $650 (credit). If the company uses an income statement approach to estimate bad debts at 5%, what is the ending balance in the Allowance for Bad Debts account?

Learning Objective 3

   a. $1,275 b. $1,600 c. $2,250 d. $2,900

7. At December 31 year-end, Crain Company has an $8,400 note receivable from a customer. Interest of 10% has accrued for 10 months on the note. What will Crain's financial statements report for this situation at December 31?

Learning Objective 4

   a. The balance sheet will report the note receivable of $8,400.
   b. The balance sheet will report the note receivable of $8,400 and interest receivable of $700.
   c. Nothing because the business has not received the cash yet.
   d. The income statement will report a note receivable of $8,400.

8. Using the data in the preceding question, what will the income statement for the year ended December 31 report for this situation?

Learning Objective 4

   a. Nothing because the business has not received the cash yet
   b. Note receivable of $8,400
   c. Interest revenue of $700
   d. Both b and c

9. At year-end, Schultz Company has cash of $11,600, current accounts receivable of $48,900, merchandise inventory of $37,900, and prepaid expenses totaling $5,100. Liabilities of $55,900 must be paid next year. What is Schultz's acid-test ratio?

Learning Objective 5

   a. 1.08
   b. 0.21
   c. 1.76
   d. Cannot be determined from the data given

10. Using the data in the preceding question, assume accounts receivable had a beginning balance of $67,400 and net credit sales for the current year totaled $807,800. How many days did it take Schultz to collect its average level of receivables?

Learning Objective 5

   a. 49 b. 35 c. 29 d. 26

Check your answers at the end of the chapter.

ASSESS YOUR PROGRESS

> Review Questions

1. What is the difference between accounts receivable and notes receivable?
2. List some common examples of other receivables, besides accounts receivable and notes receivable.
3. What is a critical element of internal control in the handling of receivables by a business? Explain how this element is accomplished.
4. When dealing with receivables, give an example of a subsidiary account.
5. What type of account must the sum of all subsidiary accounts be equal to?
6. What are some benefits to a business in accepting credit cards and debit cards?
7. What occurs when a business factors its receivables?
8. What occurs when a business pledges its receivables?
9. What is the expense account associated with the cost of uncollectible receivables called?
10. When is bad debts expense recorded when using the direct write-off method?
11. What are some limitations of using the direct write-off method?
12. When is bad debts expense recorded when using the allowance method?
13. When using the allowance method, how are accounts receivable shown on the balance sheet?
14. When using the allowance method, what account is debited when writing off uncollectible accounts? How does this differ from the direct write-off method?
15. When a receivable is written off under the allowance method, how does it affect the net realizable value shown on the balance sheet?
16. How does the percent-of-sales method compute bad debts expense?
17. How do the percent-of-receivables and aging-of-receivables methods compute bad debts expense?
18. What is the difference between the percent-of-receivables and aging-of-receivables methods?
19. In accounting for bad debts, how do the income statement approach and the balance sheet approach differ?
20. What is the formula to compute interest on a note receivable?
21. Why must companies record accrued interest revenue at the end of the accounting period?
22. How is the acid-test ratio calculated, and what does it signify?
23. What does the accounts receivable turnover ratio measure, and how is it calculated?
24. What does the days' sales in receivables indicate, and how is it calculated?

> Short Exercises

S-F:9-1 Ensuring internal control over the collection of receivables
Learning Objective 1

Consider internal control over receivables collections. What job must be withheld from a company's credit department in order to safeguard its cash? If the credit department does perform this job, what can a credit department employee do to hurt the company?

S-F:9-2 Recording credit sales and collections
Learning Objective 1

Record the following transactions for Summer Consulting. Explanations are not required.

Apr. 15	Provided consulting services to Bob Jones and billed the customer $1,500.
18	Provided consulting services to Samantha Cruise and billed the customer $865.
25	Received $750 cash from Jones.
28	Provided consulting services to Regan Taylor and billed the customer $625.
28	Received $865 cash from Cruise.
30	Received $1,375 cash, $750 from Jones and $625 from Taylor.

S-F:9-3 Applying the direct write-off method to account for uncollectibles
Learning Objective 2

Shawna Valley is an attorney in Los Angeles. Valley uses the direct write-off method to account for uncollectible receivables.

At April 30, 2024, Valley's accounts receivable totaled $19,000. During May, she earned revenue of $22,000 on account and collected $15,000 on account. She also wrote off uncollectible receivables of $1,100 on May 31, 2024.

Requirements
1. Use the direct write-off method to journalize Valley's write-off of the uncollectible receivables.
2. What is Valley's balance of Accounts Receivable at May 31, 2024?

S-F:9-4 Collecting a receivable previously written off—direct write-off method
Learning Objective 2

Spring Garden Greenhouse had trouble collecting its account receivable from Steve Stone. On June 19, 2024, Spring Garden Greenhouse finally wrote off Stone's $600 account receivable. On December 31, Stone sent a $600 check to Spring Garden Greenhouse.

Journalize the entries required for Spring Garden Greenhouse, assuming Spring Garden Greenhouse uses the direct write-off method.

S-F:9-5 Applying the allowance method to account for uncollectibles
Learning Objective 3

The Accounts Receivable balance and Allowance for Bad Debts for Signature Lamp Company at December 31, 2023, were $10,800 and $2,000 (credit balance), respectively. During 2024, Signature Lamp Company completed the following transactions:

a. Sales revenue on account, $273,400 (ignore Cost of Goods Sold).
b. Collections on account, $223,000.
c. Write-offs of uncollectibles, $5,900.
d. Bad debts expense of $5,200 was recorded.

Requirements

1. Journalize Signature Lamp Company's transactions for 2024 assuming Signature Lamp Company uses the allowance method.
2. Post the transactions to the Accounts Receivable, Allowance for Bad Debts, and Bad Debts Expense T-accounts, and determine the ending balance of each account.
3. Show how accounts receivable would be reported on the balance sheet at December 31, 2024.

Learning Objective 3

S-F:9-6 Applying the allowance method (percent-of-sales) to account for uncollectibles

During its first year of operations, Fall Wine Tour earned net credit sales of $311,000. Industry experience suggests that bad debts will amount to 3% of net credit sales. At December 31, 2024, accounts receivable total $44,000. The company uses the allowance method to account for uncollectibles.

Requirements

1. Journalize Fall Wine Tour's Bad Debts Expense using the percent-of-sales method.
2. Show how to report accounts receivable on the balance sheet at December 31, 2024.

Learning Objective 3

S-F:9-7 Applying the allowance method (percent-of-receivables) to account for uncollectibles

The Accounts Receivable balance for Lake Company at December 31, 2023, was $20,000. During 2024, Lake earned revenue of $454,000 on account and collected $325,000 on account. Lake wrote off $5,600 receivables as uncollectible. Industry experience suggests that uncollectible accounts will amount to 5% of accounts receivable.

Requirements

1. Assume Lake had an unadjusted $2,700 credit balance in Allowance for Bad Debts at December 31, 2024. Journalize Lake's December 31, 2024, adjustment to record bad debts expense using the percent-of-receivables method.
2. Assume Lake had an unadjusted $2,400 debit balance in Allowance for Bad Debts at December 31, 2024. Journalize Lake's December 31, 2024, adjustment to record bad debts expense using the percent-of-receivables method.

Learning Objective 3

S-F:9-8 Applying the allowance method (aging-of-receivables) to account for uncollectibles

Surf and Sun had the following balances at December 31, 2024, before the year-end adjustments:

Accounts Receivable	Allowance for Bad Debts
81,000	2,063

The aging of accounts receivable yields the following data:

	Age of Accounts Receivable		
	0–60 Days	Over 60 Days	Total Receivables
Accounts Receivable	$ 78,000	$ 3,000	$ 81,000
Estimated percent uncollectible	× 2%	× 23%	

Requirements

1. Journalize Surf and Sun's entry to record bad debts expense for 2024 using the aging-of-receivables method.
2. Prepare a T-account to compute the ending balance of Allowance for Bad Debts.

S-F:9-9 Computing interest amounts on notes receivable

Learning Objective 4

A table of notes receivable for 2024 follows:

	Principal	Interest Rate	Interest Period During 2024
Note 1	$ 30,000	6%	6 months
Note 2	12,000	10%	270 days
Note 3	14,000	14%	75 days
Note 4	100,000	7%	10 months

For each of the notes receivable, compute the amount of interest revenue earned during 2024. Round to the nearest dollar.

S-F:9-10 Accounting for a note receivable

Learning Objective 4

On June 6, Lakeland Bank & Trust lent $80,000 to Stephan Stow on a 30-day, 9% note.

Requirements

1. Journalize for Lakeland the lending of the money on June 6.
2. Journalize the collection of the principal and interest at maturity. Specify the date. Round to the nearest dollar.

S-F:9-11 Accruing interest revenue and recording collection of a note

Learning Objective 4

On December 1, Kyle Company accepted a 60-day, 9%, $12,000 note receivable from J. Michael in exchange for his account receivable.

Requirements

1. Journalize the transaction on December 1.
2. Journalize the adjusting entry needed on December 31 to accrue interest revenue. Round to the nearest dollar.
3. Journalize the collection of the principal and interest at maturity. Specify the date. Round to the nearest dollar.

S-F:9-12 Recording a dishonored note receivable

Learning Objective 4

McKale Company has a three-month, $18,000, 9% note receivable from L. Peters that was signed on June 1, 2024. Peters defaults on the loan on September 1.

Journalize the entry for McKale to record the default of the loan.

Learning Objective 5

S-F:9-13 Using the acid-test ratio, accounts receivable turnover ratio, and days' sales in receivables to evaluate a company

Silver Clothiers reported the following selected items at April 30, 2024 (last year's—2023—amounts also given as needed):

Accounts Payable	$ 328,000	Accounts Receivable, net:	
Cash	573,720	April 30, 2024	$ 11,000
Merchandise Inventory:		April 30, 2023	165,000
April 30, 2024	250,000	Cost of Goods Sold	1,200,000
April 30, 2023	210,000	Short-term Investments	148,000
Net Credit Sales Revenue	3,212,000	Other Current Assets	100,000
Long-term Assets	350,000	Other Current Liabilities	188,000
Long-term Liabilities	130,000		

Compute Silver's (a) acid-test ratio, (b) accounts receivable turnover ratio, and (c) days' sales in receivables for the year ending April 30, 2024. Evaluate each ratio value as strong or weak. Silver sells on terms of net 30. (Round days' sales in receivables to a whole number.)

> Exercises

Learning Objective 1

E-F:9-14 Defining common receivables terms

Match the terms with their correct definition.

Terms	Definitions
1. Accounts receivable	a. The party to a credit transaction who takes on an obligation/payable.
2. Other receivables	
3. Debtor	b. The party who receives a receivable and will collect cash in the future.
4. Notes receivable	
5. Maturity date	c. A written promise to pay a specified amount of money at a particular future date.
6. Creditor	
	d. The date when the note receivable is due.
	e. A miscellaneous category that includes any other type of receivable where there is a right to receive cash in the future.
	f. The right to receive cash in the future from customers for goods sold or for services performed.

E-F:9-15 Identifying and correcting internal control weakness

Learning Objective 1

Suppose The Right Rig Dealership is opening a regional office in Omaha. Cary Regal, the office manager, is designing the internal control system. Regal proposes the following procedures for credit checks on new customers, sales on account, cash collections, and write-offs of uncollectible receivables:

- The credit department runs a credit check on all customers who apply for credit. When an account proves uncollectible, the credit department authorizes the write-off of the accounts receivable.
- Cash receipts come into the credit department, which separates the cash received from the customer remittance slips. The credit department lists all cash receipts by customer name and amount of cash received.
- The cash goes to the treasurer for deposit in the bank. The remittance slips go to the accounting department for posting to customer accounts.
- The controller compares the daily deposit slip to the total amount posted to customer accounts. Both amounts must agree.

Recall the components of internal control. Identify the internal control weakness in this situation, and propose a way to correct it.

E-F:9-16 Recording credit sales and collections

Learning Objective 1

Steller Company had the following transactions in June:

3. $695

Jun. 1	Sold merchandise inventory on account to Carter Company, $1,575.
6	Sold merchandise inventory for cash, $550.
12	Received cash from Carter Company in full settlement of its accounts receivable.
20	Sold merchandise inventory on account to Iris Company, $765.
22	Sold merchandise inventory on account to Driver Company, $230.
28	Received cash from Iris Company in partial settlement of its accounts receivable, $300.

Requirements

1. Journalize the transactions. Ignore Cost of Goods Sold. Omit explanations.
2. Post the transactions to the general ledger and the accounts receivable subsidiary ledger. Assume all beginning balances are $0.
3. Verify the ending balance in the control account, Accounts Receivable, equals the sum of the balances in the subsidiary ledger.

E-F:9-17 Journalizing transactions using the direct write-off method

Learning Objectives 1, 2

On June 1, 2024, Best Performance Cell Phones sold $21,000 of merchandise to Anthony Trucking Company on account. Anthony fell on hard times and on July 15 paid only $5,000 of the account receivable. After repeated attempts to collect, Best Performance finally wrote off its accounts receivable from Anthony on September 5. Six months later, March 5, 2025, Best Performance received Anthony's check for $16,000 with a note apologizing for the late payment.

Requirements

1. Journalize the transactions for Best Performance Cell Phones using the direct write-off method. Ignore Cost of Goods Sold.
2. What are some limitations that Best Performance will encounter when using the direct write-off method?

Learning Objectives 1, 3

E-F:9-18 Journalizing transactions using the allowance method

Desert Landscape Supply completed the following selected transactions during 2024:

2024	
Jan. 20	Sold merchandise inventory to Kathy Weiler, $1,600, on account. Ignore Cost of Goods Sold.
Mar. 21	Sold merchandise inventory to David Morris, $2,000, on account. Ignore Cost of Goods Sold.
Apr. 1	Received amount due from David Morris.
Jun. 14	Wrote off Kathy Weiler's account as uncollectible after repeated efforts to collect from her.
Sept. 30	Received $1,600 from Kathy Weiler along with a letter apologizing for being so late. Reinstated Weiler's account in full and recorded the cash receipt.
Oct. 13	Sold merchandise inventory to Alsalemi Landscape Installation, $800, on account. Ignore Cost of Goods Sold.
Nov. 4	Alsalemi Landscape Installation declared bankruptcy and Desert wrote off Alsalemi's account as uncollectible.
Dec. 1	Sold merchandise inventory to Eco Design and Landscape, $10,000, on account. Ignore Cost of Goods Sold.
Dec. 31	Estimated that bad debts expense for the year was $2,000.

Journalize the transactions for Desert Landscape Supply using the allowance method. Include the name of the customer with the Accounts Receivable account. Explanations are not required.

Use the following information to answer Exercises E-F:9-19 and E-F:9-20.

At January 1, 2024, Hilltop Flagpoles had Accounts Receivable of $28,000, and Allowance for Bad Debts had a credit balance of $3,000. During the year, Hilltop Flagpoles recorded the following transactions for January:

a. Sales of $185,000 ($164,000 on account; $21,000 for cash). Ignore Cost of Goods Sold.

b. Collections on account, $135,000.

c. Write-offs of uncollectible receivables, $2,300.

Learning Objectives 1, 3

2. AR, Dec. 31 $54,700

E-F:9-19 Accounting for uncollectible accounts using the allowance method (percent-of-sales) and reporting receivables on the balance sheet

Requirements

1. Journalize Hilltop's transactions that occurred during January. The company uses the allowance method.

2. Post Hilltop's transactions to the Accounts Receivable and Allowance for Bad Debts T-accounts.

3. Journalize Hilltop's adjustment to record bad debts expense assuming Hilltop estimates bad debts as 3% of credit sales on January 31, 2024. Post the adjustment to the appropriate T-accounts.

4. Show how Hilltop Flagpoles will report net accounts receivable on its January 31, 2024, balance sheet.

E-F:9-20 Accounting for uncollectible accounts using the allowance method (percent-of-receivables) and reporting receivables on the balance sheet

Learning Objectives 1, 3

3. Bad Debts Expense $4,770

Requirements

1. Journalize Hilltop's transactions that occurred during January. The company uses the allowance method.
2. Post Hilltop's transactions to the Accounts Receivable and Allowance for Bad Debts T-accounts.
3. Journalize Hilltop's adjustment to record bad debts expense assuming Hilltop estimates bad debts as 10% of accounts receivable on January 31, 2024. Post the adjustment to the appropriate T-accounts.
4. Show how Hilltop Flagpoles will report net accounts receivable on its January 31, 2024, balance sheet.

E-F:9-21 Accounting for uncollectible accounts using the allowance method (aging-of-receivables) and reporting receivables on the balance sheet

Learning Objective 3

2. Allowance CR Bal. $25,360

At December 31, 2024, the Accounts Receivable balance of GPS Technology is $200,000. The Allowance for Bad Debts account has a $24,110 debit balance. GPS Technology prepares the following aging schedule for its accounts receivable:

	Age of Accounts			
	1–30 Days	31–60 Days	61–90 Days	Over 90 Days
Accounts Receivable	$ 65,000	$ 50,000	$ 40,000	$ 45,000
Estimated percent uncollectible	0.4%	3.0%	5.0%	48.0%

Requirements

1. Journalize the year-end adjusting entry for bad debts on the basis of the aging schedule. Show the T-account for the Allowance for Bad Debts at December 31, 2024.
2. Show how GPS Technology will report its net accounts receivable on its December 31, 2024, balance sheet.

E-F:9-22 Journalizing transactions using the direct write-off method versus the allowance method

Learning Objectives 1, 2, 3

During August 2024, Lima Company recorded the following:

- Sales of $133,300 ($122,000 on account; $11,300 for cash). Ignore Cost of Goods Sold.
- Collections on account, $106,400.
- Write-offs of uncollectible receivables, $990.
- Recovery of receivable previously written off, $800.

Requirements

1. Journalize Lima's transactions during August 2024, assuming Lima uses the direct write-off method.
2. Journalize Lima's transactions during August 2024, assuming Lima uses the allowance method.

Learning Objectives 1, 4

E-F:9-23 Journalizing credit sales, note receivable transactions, and accruing interest

Endurance Running Shoes reports the following:

2024	
May 6	Recorded credit sales of $102,000. Ignore Cost of Goods Sold.
Jul. 1	Loaned $18,000 to Jerry Paul, an executive with the company, on a one-year, 7% note.
Dec. 31	Accrued interest revenue on the Paul note.
2025	
Jul. 1	Collected the maturity value of the Paul note.

Journalize all entries required for Endurance Running Shoes.

Learning Objective 4

E-F:9-24 Journalizing note receivable transactions including a dishonored note

On September 30, 2024, Team Bank loaned $94,000 to Kendall Warner on a one-year, 6% note. Team's fiscal year ends on December 31.

Requirements

1. Journalize all entries for Team Bank related to the note for 2024 and 2025.
2. Which party has a
   a. note receivable?
   b. note payable?
   c. interest revenue?
   d. interest expense?
3. Suppose that Kendall Warner defaulted on the note. What entry would Team record for the dishonored note?

Learning Objective 4

E-F:9-25 Journalizing note receivable transactions

Jul. 1, 2025 Cash DR $17,280

The following selected transactions occurred during 2024 and 2025 for Baltic Importers. The company ends its accounting year on September 30.

2024	
Jul. 1	Loaned $16,000 cash to Bud Shyne on a one-year, 8% note.
Sep. 6	Sold goods to Lawn Pro, receiving a 90-day, 6% note for $11,000. Ignore Cost of Goods Sold.
30	Made a single entry to accrue interest revenue on both notes.
?	Collected the maturity value of the Lawn Pro note.
2025	
Jul. 1	Collected the maturity value of the Shyne note.

Journalize all required entries. Make sure to determine the missing maturity date. Round to the nearest dollar.

E-F:9-26 Journalizing note receivable transactions

Learning Objective 4

Oct. 31 Cash DR $18,355

Professional Steam Cleaning performs services on account. When a customer account becomes four months old, Professional converts the account to a note receivable. During 2024, the company completed the following transactions:

Apr. 28	Performed service on account for Parkview Club, $18,000.
Sep. 1	Received an $18,000, 60-day, 12% note from Parkview Club in satisfaction of its past-due account receivable.
Oct. 31	Collected the Parkview Club note at maturity.

Record the transactions in Professional's journal. Round to the nearest dollar.

E-F:9-27 Evaluating ratio data

Learning Objective 5

Abanaki Carpets reported the following amounts in its 2024 financial statements. The 2023 figures are given for comparison.

	2024		2023	
Balance sheet—partial				
Current Assets:				
Cash		$ 5,000		$ 11,000
Short-term Investments		25,000		14,000
Accounts Receivable	$ 64,000		$ 77,000	
Less: Allowance for Bad Debts	(7,000)	57,000	(6,000)	71,000
Merchandise Inventory		194,000		190,000
Prepaid Insurance		2,000		2,000
Total Current Assets		283,000		288,000
Total Current Liabilities		105,000		107,000
Income statement—partial				
Net Sales (all on account)		742,400		730,000

Requirements

1. Calculate Abanaki's acid-test ratio for 2024. (Round to two decimals.) Determine whether Abanaki's acid-test ratio improved or deteriorated from 2023 to 2024. How does Abanaki's acid-test ratio compare with the industry average of 0.80?

2. Calculate Abanaki's accounts receivable turnover ratio for 2024. (Round to two decimals.) How does Abanaki's ratio compare to the industry average accounts receivable turnover of 10?

3. Calculate the days' sales in receivables for 2024. (Round to the nearest day.) How do the results compare with Abanaki's credit terms of net 30?

E-F:9-28 Computing the collection period for receivables

Learning Objective 5

Unique Media Sign sells on account. Recently, Unique reported the following figures:

	2024	2023
Net Credit Sales	$ 594,920	$ 602,000
Net Receivables at end of year	38,500	47,100

Requirements

1. Compute Unique's days' sales in receivables for 2024. (Round to the nearest day.)
2. Suppose Unique's normal credit terms for a sale on account are 2/10, net 30. How well does Unique's collection period compare to the company's credit terms? Is this good or bad for Unique?

> Problems Group A

Learning Objectives 1, 2, 3

1. Bad Debts Expense $11,000

P-F:9-29A Accounting for uncollectible accounts using the allowance (percent-of-sales) and direct write-off methods and reporting receivables on the balance sheet

On August 31, 2024, Bouquet Floral Supply had a $140,000 debit balance in Accounts Receivable and a $5,600 credit balance in Allowance for Bad Debts. During September, Bouquet made:

- Sales on account, $550,000. Ignore Cost of Goods Sold.
- Collections on account, $584,000.
- Write-offs of uncollectible receivables, $4,000.

Requirements

1. Journalize all September entries using the *allowance* method. Bad debts expense was estimated at 2% of credit sales. Show all September activity in Accounts Receivable, Allowance for Bad Debts, and Bad Debts Expense (post to these T-accounts).
2. Using the same facts, assume that Bouquet used the direct write-off method to account for uncollectible receivables. Journalize all September entries using the *direct write-off* method. Post to Accounts Receivable and Bad Debts Expense and show their balances at September 30, 2024.
3. What amount of Bad Debts Expense would Bouquet report on its September income statement under each of the two methods? Which amount better matches expense with revenue? Give your reason.
4. What amount of *net* accounts receivable would Bouquet report on its September 30, 2024, balance sheet under each of the two methods? Which amount is more realistic? Give your reason.

Learning Objectives 1, 3

2. Allowance CR Bal. $8,482 at Dec. 31, 2024

P-F:9-30A Accounting for uncollectible accounts using the allowance method (aging-of-receivables) and reporting receivables on the balance sheet

At September 30, 2024, the accounts of Green Terrace Medical Center (GTMC) include the following:

Accounts Receivable	$ 145,000
Allowance for Bad Debts (credit balance)	3,500

During the last quarter of 2024, GTMC completed the following selected transactions:

- Sales on account, $450,000. Ignore Cost of Goods Sold.
- Collections on account, $427,100.
- Wrote off accounts receivable as uncollectible: Regan Co., $1,400; Owen Reis, $800; and Patterson, Inc., $700.
- Recorded bad debts expense based on the aging of accounts receivable, as follows:

	Age of Accounts			
	1–30 Days	31–60 Days	61–90 Days	Over 90 Days
Accounts Receivable	$ 104,000	$ 39,000	$ 14,000	$ 8,000
Estimated percent uncollectible	0.3%	3%	30%	35%

Requirements

1. Open T-accounts for Accounts Receivable and Allowance for Bad Debts. Journalize the transactions (omit explanations) and post to the two accounts.
2. Show how Green Terrace Medical Center should report net accounts receivable on its December 31, 2024, balance sheet.

P-F:9-31A Accounting for uncollectible accounts using the allowance method (percent-of-sales) and reporting receivables on the balance sheet

Learning Objectives 1, 3

2. Net AR $119,800

Delta Watches completed the following selected transactions during 2024 and 2025:

2024	
Dec. 31	Estimated that bad debts expense for the year was 2% of credit sales of $450,000 and recorded that amount as expense. The company uses the allowance method.
31	Made the closing entry for bad debts expense.
2025	
Jan. 17	Sold merchandise inventory to Mack Smith, $400, on account. Ignore Cost of Goods Sold.
Jun. 29	Wrote off Mack Smith's account as uncollectible after repeated efforts to collect from him.
Aug. 6	Received $400 from Mack Smith, along with a letter apologizing for being so late. Reinstated Smith's account in full and recorded the cash receipt.
Dec. 31	Made a compound entry to write off the following accounts as uncollectible: Cam Carter, $1,400; Mike Venture, $1,200; and Russell Reeves, $400.
31	Estimated that bad debts expense for the year was 2% of credit sales of $510,000 and recorded the expense.
31	Made the closing entry for bad debts expense.

Requirements

1. Open T-accounts for Allowance for Bad Debts and Bad Debts Expense, assuming the accounts begin with a zero balance. Record the transactions in the general journal (omit explanations) and post to the two T-accounts.
2. Assume the December 31, 2025, balance of Accounts Receivable is $136,000. Show how net accounts receivable would be reported on the balance sheet at that date.

Learning Objectives 1, 3, 4

Dec. 31, 2024 Interest Receivable $1,640

P-F:9-32A Accounting for uncollectible accounts (aging-of-receivables method), notes receivable, and accrued interest revenue

Sleepy Recliner Chairs completed the following selected transactions:

2024

Jul. 1	Sold merchandise inventory to Stan-Mart, receiving a $41,000, nine-month, 8% note. Ignore Cost of Goods Sold.
Oct. 31	Recorded cash sales for the period of $24,000. Ignore Cost of Goods Sold.
Dec. 31	Made an adjusting entry to accrue interest on the Stan-Mart note.
31	Made an adjusting entry to record bad debts expense based on an aging of accounts receivable. The aging schedule shows that $13,800 of accounts receivable will not be collected. Prior to this adjustment, the credit balance in Allowance for Bad Debts is $11,800.

2025

Apr. 1	Collected the maturity value of the Stan-Mart note.
Jun. 23	Sold merchandise inventory to Appeal Corp., receiving a 60-day, 6% note for $7,000. Ignore Cost of Goods Sold.
Aug. 22	Appeal Corp. dishonored its note at maturity; the business converted the maturity value of the note to an account receivable.
Nov. 16	Loaned $17,000 cash to Crosby, Inc., receiving a 90-day, 16% note.
Dec. 5	Collected in full on account from Appeal Corp.
31	Accrued the interest on the Crosby, Inc. note.

Record the transactions in the journal of Sleepy Recliner Chairs. Explanations are not required. (Round to the nearest dollar.)

Learning Objective 4

1. Note 3 Dec. 18, 2024

P-F:9-33A Accounting for notes receivable and accruing interest

Carley Realty loaned money and received the following notes during 2024.

Note	Date	Principal Amount	Interest Rate	Term
(1)	Apr. 1	$ 6,000	7%	1 year
(2)	Sep. 30	12,000	6%	6 months
(3)	Sep. 19	18,000	8%	90 days

Requirements

1. Determine the maturity date and maturity value of each note.
2. Journalize the entries to establish each Note Receivable and to record collection of principal and interest at maturity. Include a single adjusting entry on December 31, 2024, the fiscal year-end, to record accrued interest revenue on any applicable note. Explanations are not required. Round to the nearest dollar.

P-F:9-34A Accounting for notes receivable, dishonored notes, and accrued interest revenue

Consider the following transactions for CC Publishing.

Learning Objective 4

Dec. 31, 2024 Income Summary CR $74

2024	
Dec. 6	Received a $18,000, 90-day, 6% note in settlement of an overdue accounts receivable from Go Go Publishing.
31	Made an adjusting entry to accrue interest on the Go Go Publishing note.
31	Made a closing entry for interest revenue.
2025	
Mar. 6	Collected the maturity value of the Go Go Publishing note.
Jun. 30	Loaned $11,000 cash to Lincoln Music, receiving a six-month, 20% note.
Oct. 2	Received a $2,400, 60-day, 20% note for a sale to Tusk Music. Ignore Cost of Goods Sold.
Dec. 1	Tusk Music dishonored its note at maturity.
1	Wrote off the receivable associated with Tusk Music. (Use the allowance method.)
30	Collected the maturity value of the Lincoln Music note.

Journalize all transactions for CC Publishing. Round all amounts to the nearest dollar.

P-F:9-35A Using ratio data to evaluate a company's financial position

The comparative financial statements of Norfolk Cosmetic Supply for 2024, 2023, and 2022 include the data shown here:

Learning Objective 5

	2024	2023	2022
Balance sheet—partial			
Current Assets:			
Cash	$ 70,000	$ 60,000	$ 50,000
Short-term investments	140,000	170,000	120,000
Accounts Receivable, Net	280,000	240,000	260,000
Merchandise Inventory	355,000	330,000	310,000
Prepaid Expenses	70,000	35,000	35,000
Total Current Assets	915,000	835,000	775,000
Total Current Liabilities	560,000	630,000	640,000
Income statement—partial			
Net Sales (all on account)	5,890,000	5,130,000	4,210,000

Requirements

1. Compute these ratios for 2024 and 2023:
   a. Acid-test ratio (Round to two decimals.)
   b. Accounts receivable turnover (Round to two decimals.)
   c. Days' sales in receivables (Round to the nearest whole day.)
2. Considering each ratio individually, which ratios improved from 2023 to 2024 and which ratios deteriorated? Is the trend favorable or unfavorable for the company?

> Problems Group B

Learning Objectives 1, 2, 3

1. Sep. 30 Bal. Accounts Receivable $91,000

P-F:9-36B Accounting for uncollectible accounts using the allowance (percent-of-sales) and direct write-off methods and reporting receivables on the balance sheet

On August 31, 2024, Forget-Me-Not Floral Supply had a $140,000 debit balance in Accounts Receivable and a $5,600 credit balance in Allowance for Bad Debts. During September, Forget-Me-Not made the following transactions:

- Sales on account, $530,000. Ignore Cost of Goods Sold.
- Collections on account, $573,000.
- Write-offs of uncollectible receivables, $6,000.

Requirements

1. Journalize all September entries using the *allowance* method. Bad debts expense was estimated at 2% of credit sales. Show all September activity in Accounts Receivable, Allowance for Bad Debts, and Bad Debts Expense (post to these T-accounts).
2. Using the same facts, assume that Forget-Me-Not used the direct write-off method to account for uncollectible receivables. Journalize all September entries using the *direct write-off* method. Post to Accounts Receivable and Bad Debts Expense, and show their balances at September 30, 2024.
3. What amount of Bad Debts Expense would Forget-Me-Not report on its September income statement under each of the two methods? Which amount better matches expense with revenue? Give your reason.
4. What amount of *net* accounts receivable would Forget-Me-Not report on its September 30, 2024, balance sheet under each of the two methods? Which amount is more realistic? Give your reason.

Learning Objectives 1, 3

2. Dec. 31, 2024 Allowance CR Bal. $11,401

P-F:9-37B Accounting for uncollectible accounts using the allowance method (aging-of-receivables) and reporting receivables on the balance sheet

At September 30, 2024, the accounts of Spring Mountain Medical Center (SMMC) include the following:

Accounts Receivable	$145,000
Allowance for Bad Debts (credit balance)	3,400

During the last quarter of 2024, SMMC completed the following selected transactions:

- Sales on account, $475,000. Ignore Cost of Goods Sold.
- Collections on account, $451,800.
- Wrote off accounts receivable as uncollectible: Randall Co., $1,800; Oliver Welch, $900; and Rain, Inc., $500
- Recorded bad debts expense based on the aging of accounts receivable, as follows:

	Age of Accounts			
	1–30 Days	31–60 Days	61–90 Days	Over 90 Days
Accounts Receivable	$ 97,000	$ 37,000	$ 17,000	$ 14,000
Estimated percent uncollectible	0.3%	3%	30%	35%

Requirements

1. Open T-accounts for Accounts Receivable and Allowance for Bad Debts. Journalize the transactions (omit explanations) and post to the two accounts.
2. Show how Spring Mountain Medical Center should report net accounts receivable on its December 31, 2024, balance sheet.

P-F:9-38B Accounting for uncollectible accounts using the allowance method (percent-of-sales) and reporting receivables on the balance sheet

Learning Objectives 1, 3

Dialex Watches completed the following selected transactions during 2024 and 2025:

1. Dec. 31, 2024, Allowance CR Bal. $12,300

2024		
Dec. 31		Estimated that bad debts expense for the year was 3% of credit sales of $410,000 and recorded that amount as expense. The company uses the allowance method.
31		Made the closing entry for bad debts expense.
2025		
Jan. 17		Sold merchandise inventory to Marty White, $400, on account. Ignore Cost of Goods Sold.
Jun. 29		Wrote off Marty White's account as uncollectible after repeated efforts to collect from him.
Aug. 6		Received $400 from Marty White, along with a letter apologizing for being so late. Reinstated White's account in full and recorded the cash receipt.
Dec. 31		Made a compound entry to write off the following accounts as uncollectible: Barry Krisp, $1,600; Maria Bryant, $1,100; and Richard Renik, $400.
31		Estimated that bad debts expense for the year was 3% of credit sales of $490,000 and recorded the expense.
31		Made the closing entry for bad debts expense.

Requirements

1. Open T-accounts for Allowance for Bad Debts and Bad Debts Expense, assuming the accounts begin with a zero balance. Record the transactions in the general journal (omit explanations) and post to the two T-accounts.
2. Assume the December 31, 2025, balance of Accounts Receivable is $136,000. Show how net accounts receivable would be reported on the balance sheet at that date.

Learning Objectives 1, 3, 4

Dec. 31, 2024 Bad Debts Expense $4,200

P-F:9-39B Accounting for uncollectible accounts (aging-of-receivables method), notes receivable, and accrued interest revenue

Relax Recliner Chairs completed the following selected transactions:

2024	
Jul. 1	Sold merchandise inventory to Go-Mart, receiving a $43,000, nine-month, 16% note. Ignore Cost of Goods Sold.
Oct. 31	Recorded cash sales for the period of $23,000. Ignore Cost of Goods Sold.
Dec. 31	Made an adjusting entry to accrue interest on the Go-Mart note.
31	Made an adjusting entry to record bad debts expense based on an aging of accounts receivable. The aging schedule shows that $14,900 of accounts receivable will not be collected. Prior to this adjustment, the credit balance in Allowance for Bad Debts is $10,700.
2025	
Apr. 1	Collected the maturity value of the Go-Mart note.
Jun. 23	Sold merchandise inventory to Allure Corp., receiving a 60-day, 6% note for $7,000. Ignore Cost of Goods Sold.
Aug. 22	Allure Corp. dishonored its note at maturity; the business converted the maturity value of the note to an account receivable.
Nov. 16	Loaned $20,000 cash to Tench, Inc., receiving a 90-day, 8% note.
Dec. 5	Collected in full on account from Allure Corp.
31	Accrued the interest on the Tench, Inc. note.

Record the transactions in the journal of Relax Recliner Chairs. Explanations are not required. (Round to the nearest dollar.)

Learning Objective 4

1. Note 2 Maturity Value $20,430

P-F:9-40B Accounting for notes receivable and accruing interest

Logan Realty loaned money and received the following notes during 2024.

Note	Date	Principal Amount	Interest Rate	Term
(1)	Oct. 1	$ 16,000	7%	1 year
(2)	Jun. 30	18,000	18%	9 months
(3)	Sep. 19	12,000	8%	90 days

Requirements

1. Determine the maturity date and maturity value of each note.
2. Journalize the entries to establish each Note Receivable and to record collection of principal and interest at maturity. Include a single adjusting entry on December 31, 2024, the fiscal year-end, to record accrued interest revenue on any applicable note. Explanations are not required. Round to the nearest dollar.

P-F:9-41B Accounting for notes receivable, dishonored notes, and accrued interest revenue

Consider the following transactions for TLC Company.

2024	
Dec. 6	Received a $8,000, 90-day, 9% note in settlement of an overdue accounts receivable from Forest Music.
31	Made an adjusting entry to accrue interest on the Forest Music note.
31	Made a closing entry for interest revenue.
2025	
Mar. 6	Collected the maturity value of the Forest Music note.
Jun. 30	Loaned $14,000 cash to Washington Music, receiving a six-month, 12% note.
Oct. 2	Received a $1,000, 60-day, 12% note for a sale to ZZZ Music. Ignore Cost of Goods Sold.
Dec. 1	ZZZ Music dishonored its note at maturity.
1	Wrote off the receivable associated with ZZZ Music. (Use the allowance method.)
30	Collected the maturity value of the Washington Music note.

Journalize all transactions for TLC Company. Round all amounts to the nearest dollar.

Learning Objective 4

March 6, 2025 Interest Revenue $128

P-F:9-42B Using ratio data to evaluate a company's financial position

The comparative financial statements of Newton Cosmetic Supply for 2024, 2023, and 2022 include the data shown here:

	2024	2023	2022
Balance sheet—partial			
Current Assets:			
Cash	$ 80,000	$ 50,000	$ 30,000
Short-term investment	150,000	170,000	125,000
Accounts Receivable, Net	310,000	260,000	220,000
Merchandise Inventory	360,000	335,000	330,000
Prepaid Expenses	50,000	30,000	35,000
Total Current Assets	950,000	845,000	740,000
Total Current Liabilities	530,000	630,000	670,000
Income statement—partial			
Net Sales (all on account)	5,850,000	5,110,000	425,000

Requirements

1. Compute these ratios for 2024 and 2023:
   a. Acid-test ratio (Round to two decimals.)
   b. Accounts receivable turnover (Round to two decimals.)
   c. Days' sales in receivables (Round to the nearest whole day.)
2. Considering each ratio individually, which ratios improved from 2023 to 2024 and which ratios deteriorated? Is the trend favorable or unfavorable for the company?

Learning Objective 5

1. Days' sales in receivables (2024) 18 days

CRITICAL THINKING

> **Using Excel**

Download Excel problems for this chapter online in MyLab Accounting or at **http://www.pearsonhighered.com/Horngren**.

> **Continuing Problem**

P-F:9-43 Accounting for uncollectible accounts using the allowance method

This problem continues the Canyon Canoe Company situation from Chapter F:8. Canyon Canoe Company has experienced rapid growth in its first few months of operations and has had a significant increase in customers renting canoes and purchasing T-shirts. Many of these customers are asking for credit terms. Amber Wilson, owner and company manager, has decided it is time to review the business transactions and update some of the business practices. Her first step is to make decisions about handling accounts receivable.

So far, year-to-date credit sales have been $15,500. A review of outstanding receivables resulted in the following aging schedule:

Age of Accounts as of June 30, 2025					
Customer Name	1–30 Days	31–60 Days	61–90 Days	Over 90 Days	Total Balance
Canyon Youth Club	$ 250				$ 250
Crazy Tees	200	$ 150			350
Early Start Daycare				$ 500	500
Lakefront Pavilion	575				575
Outdoor Center			$ 300		300
Rivers Canoe Club	350				350
Sport Shirts	450	120			570
Zack's Marina	75	75	75		225
Totals	$ 1,900	$ 345	$ 375	$ 500	$ 3,120

Requirements

1. The company wants to use the allowance method to estimate bad debts. Determine the estimated bad debts expense under the following methods at June 30, 2025. Assume a zero beginning balance for Allowance for Bad Debts. Round to the nearest dollar.

   a. Percent-of-sales method, assuming 4.5% of credit sales will not be collected.

   b. Percent-of-receivables method, assuming 22.5% of receivables will not be collected.

   c. Aging-of-receivables method, assuming 5% of invoices 1–30 days will not be collected, 20% of invoices 31–60 days, 40% of invoices 61–90 days, and 75% of invoices over 90 days.

2. Journalize the entry at June 30, 2025, to adjust for bad debts expense using the percent-of-sales method.

3. Journalize the entry at June 30, 2025, to record the write-off of the Early Start Daycare invoice.

4. At June 30, 2025, open T-accounts for Accounts Receivable and Allowance for Bad Debts before Requirements 2 and 3. Post entries from Requirements 2 and 3 to those accounts. Assume a zero beginning balance for Allowance for Bad Debts.

5. Show how Canyon Canoe Company will report net accounts receivable on the balance sheet on June 30, 2025.

> Practice Set

P-F:9-44 Accounting for uncollectible accounts using the allowance method and reporting net accounts receivable on the balance sheet

This problem continues the Crystal Clear Cleaning problem begun in Chapter F:2 and continued through Chapter F:8.

Crystal Clear Cleaning uses the allowance method to estimate bad debts. Consider the following April 2025 transactions for Crystal Clear Cleaning:

Apr. 1	Performed cleaning service for Debbie's D-list for $13,000 on account with terms n/20.
10	Borrowed money from First Regional Bank, $30,000, making a 180-day, 12% note.
12	After discussions with customer More Shine, Crystal Clear has determined that $230 of the receivable owed will not be collected. Wrote off this portion of the receivable.
15	Sold goods to Warner for $9,000 on account with terms n/30. Cost of Goods Sold was $4,500.
28	Sold goods to Lelaine, Inc. for cash of $2,800 (cost $840).
28	Collected from More Shine, $230 of receivable previously written off.
29	Paid cash for utilities of $150.
30	Created an aging schedule for Crystal Clear Cleaning for accounts receivable. Crystal Clear determined that $7,000 of receivables outstanding for 1–30 days were 3% uncollectible, $10,000 of receivables outstanding for 31–60 days were 20% uncollectible, and $5,870 of receivables outstanding for more than 60 days were 30% uncollectible. Crystal Clear Cleaning determined the total amount of estimated uncollectible receivables and adjusted the Allowance for Bad Debts. Assume the account had an unadjusted credit balance of $260. (Round to nearest whole dollar.)

Requirements

1. Prepare all required journal entries for Crystal Clear. Omit explanations.

2. Show how net accounts receivable would be reported on the balance sheet as of April 30, 2025.

> Tying It All Together Case F:9-1

Before you begin this assignment, review the Tying It All Together feature in the chapter. It will also be helpful if you review *Amazon.com, Inc.'s* 2018 annual report (**https://www.sec.gov/Archives/edgar/data/1018724/000101872419000004/0001018724-19-000004-index.htm**).

Amazon.com, Inc. opened its virtual doors in July 1995. The business serves customers through its retail Web sites and physical stores and focuses on selection, price, and convenience. The company sells hundreds of millions of unique products through its Web site. Amazon.com, Inc. also manufactures and sells electronic devices, including Kindle e-readers, Fire tablets, and Echo devices. In addition, Amazon.com, Inc. offers Amazon Prime, a membership program that includes unlimited free shipping and instant streaming of thousands of movies and TV episodes.

Requirements

1. What was the amount of net Accounts Receivable as of December 31, 2018? As of December 31, 2017?
2. Review the notes to the financial statements and read the note labeled Accounts Receivable, Net and Other in Note 1–Description of Business and Accounting Policies. How does Amazon.com, Inc. estimate losses on receivables? When are receivables written off?
3. Review the notes to the financial statements and read the note labeled Accounts Receivable, Net and Other in Note 1–Description of Business and Accounting Policies. What was the amount of Allowance for Doubtful Accounts as of December 31, 2018? As of December 31, 2017?
4. Using the information from requirements 2 and 3, determine the gross amount of Accounts Receivable as of December 31, 2018. As of December 31, 2017.
5. Review the notes to the financial statements and read the note labeled Accounts Receivable, Net and Other in Note 1–Description of Business and Accounting Policies. What was the amount of additions to the allowance for doubtful accounts for 2018? What was the amount of deductions to the allowance for doubtful accounts for 2018? Draw a T-account that details the changes in the Allowance for Doubtful Accounts account for 2018. What would additions charged to the allowance for doubtful accounts represent? What would deductions from the account represent?

> Decision Cases

Decision Case F:9-1

Weddings on Demand sells on account and manages its own receivables. Average experience for the past three years has been as follows:

Sales	$ 350,000
Cost of Goods Sold	210,000
Bad Debts Expense	4,000
Other Expenses	61,000

Unhappy with the amount of bad debts expense she has been experiencing, Aledia Sanchez, controller, is considering a major change in the business. Her plan would be to stop selling on account altogether but accept either cash, credit cards, or debit cards from her customers. Her market research indicates that if she does so, her sales will increase by 10% (i.e., from $350,000 to $385,000), of which $200,000 will be credit or debit card sales and the rest will be cash sales. With a 10% increase in sales, there will also be a 10% increase in Cost of Goods Sold. If she adopts this plan, she will no longer have bad debts expense, but she will have to pay a fee on debit/credit card transactions of 2% of applicable sales. She also believes this plan will allow her to save $5,000 per year in other operating expenses.

Should Sanchez start accepting credit cards and debit cards? Show the computations of net income under her present arrangement and under the plan.

Decision Case F:9-2

Pauline's Pottery has always used the direct write-off method to account for uncollectibles. The company's revenues, bad debt write-offs, and year-end receivables for the most recent year follow:

Year	Revenues	Write-offs	Receivables at Year-end
2024	$ 150,000	$ 3,900	$ 14,000

The business is applying for a bank loan, and the loan officer requires figures based on the allowance method of accounting for bad debts. In the past, bad debts have run about 4% of revenues.

Requirements

Pauline must give the banker the following information:

1. How much more or less would net income be for 2024 if Pauline's Pottery were to use the allowance method for bad debts? Assume Pauline uses the percent-of-sales method.
2. How much of the receivables balance at the end of 2024 does Pauline's Pottery actually expect to collect? (Disregard beginning account balances for the purpose of this question.)
3. Explain why net income is more or less using the allowance method versus the direct write-off method for uncollectibles.

> Fraud Case F:9-1

Dylan worked for a propane gas distributor as an accounting clerk in a small Midwestern town. Last winter, his brother Mike lost his job at the machine plant. By January, temperatures were sub-zero, and Mike had run out of money. Dylan saw that Mike's account was overdue, and he knew Mike needed another delivery to heat his home. He decided to credit Mike's account and debit the balance to the parts inventory because he knew the parts manager, the owner's son, was incompetent and would never notice the extra entry. Months went by, and Dylan repeated the process until an auditor ran across the charges by chance. When the owner fired Dylan, he said, "If you had only come to me and told me about Mike's situation, we could have worked something out."

Requirements

1. What can a business like this do to prevent employee fraud of this kind?
2. What effect would Dylan's actions have on the balance sheet? The income statement?
3. How much discretion does a business have with regard to accommodating hardship situations?

> Financial Statement Case F:9-1

Use **Target Corporation's** Fiscal 2018 Annual Report and Note 5 "Consideration Received from Vendors" and Note 10 "Other Current Assets" to answer the following questions. Visit **http://www.pearsonhighered.com/Horngren** to view a link to Target Corporation's annual report.

Requirements

1. How much accounts receivable did Target report on its balance sheet as of February 2, 2019? As of February 3, 2018?
2. Refer to Note 10, "Other Current Assets." What types of receivables are included in Target's other current assets on its balance sheet as of February 2, 2019 and February 3, 2018?
3. Refer to Note 5 "Consideration Received from Vendors." What does Vendor Income Receivable represent?
4. Compute Target's acid-test ratio as of February 2, 2019 and February 3, 2018. Did the ratio improve or deteriorate? For each date, if all the current liabilities came due immediately, could Target pay them?

> Quick Check Answers

1. d **2.** d **3.** d **4.** a **5.** d **6.** d **7.** b **8.** c **9.** a **10.** d

Plant Assets, Natural Resources, and Intangibles 10

What Do I Do with This Equipment?

Jerry Drake has been working hard at a new landscaping business for several months. Things are great—sales are increasing every month, and the customer base is increasing. So far, Jerry has been renting lawn equipment or borrowing equipment from his friends. Jerry is now considering buying several new lawn mowers, trimmers, and leaf blowers.

Jerry is trying to figure out how to record the purchase of these items on his books. Should he expense them all or set up asset accounts for each of the items? Jerry is also considering how long each item will last before he needs to purchase new equipment. He knows that his accountant will ask him about depreciation. She has told him there are several methods he should consider. Jerry knows he wants a depreciation method that will match the cost of the equipment with the revenue that the business earns.

In addition, Jerry plans on keeping the equipment as long as he can, which means that he will be making repairs and maintaining the equipment. He is wondering how the cost of the repairs should be recorded. And what happens when he finally sells the equipment? Jerry realizes there is a lot to consider when a business buys equipment. He knows that his accountant will help answer his many questions so he can properly record the cost of the equipment and any future associated costs.

How Are Plant Assets, Natural Resources, and Intangibles Accounted For?

Plant assets, natural resources, and intangibles are some of the most important assets on the balance sheet. These assets help create the revenue of the business. For example, TruGreen, a company that specializes in lawn and landscape services, wouldn't earn a profit without the lawn equipment it uses to service its customers' lawns. ExxonMobil Corporation wouldn't have made a $20.8 billion profit in 2018 without its natural resource of oil reserves. And we are all familiar with **McDonald's** trademark "golden arches." In this chapter, we discuss how to record the purchase, cost allocation, and disposal of these assets.

Chapter 10 Learning Objectives

1. Measure the cost of property, plant, and equipment
2. Account for depreciation using the straight-line, units-of-production, and double-declining-balance methods
3. Journalize entries for the disposal of plant assets
4. Account for natural resources
5. Account for intangible assets
6. Use the asset turnover ratio to evaluate business performance
7. Journalize entries for the exchange of plant assets (Appendix 10A)

HOW DOES A BUSINESS MEASURE THE COST OF PROPERTY, PLANT, AND EQUIPMENT?

Learning Objective 1
Measure the cost of property, plant, and equipment

Property, Plant, and Equipment (PP&E)
Long-lived, tangible assets, such as land, buildings, and equipment, used in the operation of a business.

Depreciation
The process by which businesses spread the allocation of a plant asset's cost over its useful life.

Property, plant, and equipment (PP&E) are long-lived, tangible assets used in the operations of a business. Examples include land, buildings, equipment, furniture, and automobiles. Often, property, plant, and equipment are referred to as *plant assets, operational assets,* or *fixed assets* in financial statements. Many businesses use the heading Property, Plant, and Equipment on their classified balance sheets when reporting on these assets. However, the term *plant assets* is commonly used in conversation. We will use the terms interchangeably.

Plant assets are unique from other assets, such as office supplies, because plant assets are long term (lasting several years). This requires a business to allocate the cost of the asset over the years that the asset is expected to be used. This allocation of a plant asset's cost over its useful life is called **depreciation** and follows the matching principle. The matching principle ensures that all expenses are matched against the revenues of the period. Because plant assets are used over several years, a business will record a portion of the cost of the asset as an expense in each of those years. All plant assets except land are depreciated. We record no depreciation for land because it does not have a definitive or clearly estimable life, so it is difficult to allocate the cost of land.

Plant assets are used in the operations of the business. This means that they are not specifically acquired for resale, but instead they are used to help create the business's revenue. For example, a business that has a vacant building that is not currently being used would classify this asset as a long-term investment instead of as a plant asset. This is because the vacant building is sitting idle and not currently being used in the operations of the business.

Exhibit F:10-1 summarizes the life cycle of a plant asset in a business. The business begins by acquiring the asset and recording the asset on its books. This involves determining

Exhibit F:10-1 | Life Cycle of a Plant Asset

1. Acquisition of asset

2. Usage of asset

3. Disposal of asset

the asset cost that is reported on the balance sheet. As the business uses the asset, it must record depreciation expense. In addition, the business also incurs additional expenses (such as repairs and maintenance) related to the asset. And lastly, when the asset has reached the end of its useful life, the business disposes of the asset. Each of these stages in the life of a plant asset must be recorded on the business's books.

Plant assets are recorded at historical cost—the amount paid for the asset. This follows the **cost principle**, which states that acquired assets (and services) should be recorded at their actual cost. The *actual cost of a plant asset* is its purchase price plus taxes, purchase commissions, and all other amounts paid to ready the asset for its intended use. Let's begin by reviewing the different categories of plant assets.

Cost Principle
A principle that states that acquired assets and services should be recorded at their actual cost.

Land and Land Improvements

The cost of land includes the following amounts paid by the purchaser:

- Purchase price
- Brokerage commission
- Survey and legal fees
- Delinquent property taxes
- Taxes assessed to transfer the ownership (title) on the land
- Cost of clearing the land and removing unwanted buildings

The cost of land does *not* include the following costs:

- Fencing
- Paving
- Sprinkler systems
- Lighting
- Signs

These separate plant assets (fencing, paving, and so on) are called **land improvements**. Unlike land, land improvements are subject to depreciation.

Suppose Smart Touch Learning needs property and purchases land on August 1, 2025, for $50,000 with a note payable for the same amount. The company also pays cash as follows: $4,000 in delinquent property taxes, $2,000 in transfer taxes, $5,000 to remove an old building, and a $1,000 survey fee. What is the company's cost of this land? Exhibit F:10-2 shows all the costs incurred to bring the land to its intended use.

Land Improvement
A depreciable improvement to land, such as fencing, sprinklers, paving, signs, and lighting.

Exhibit F:10-2 | **Measuring the Cost of Land**

Purchase price of land		$ 50,000
Add related costs:		
Property taxes	$ 4,000	
Transfer taxes	2,000	
Removal of building	5,000	
Survey fee	1,000	12,000
Total cost of land		$ 62,000

The entry to record the purchase of the land on August 1, 2025, follows:

$$\frac{A\uparrow}{\text{Land}\uparrow \atop \text{Cash}\downarrow} \Big\} = \Big\{ \frac{L\uparrow}{\text{Notes} \atop \text{Payable}\uparrow} + E$$

Date	Accounts and Explanation	Debit	Credit
Aug. 1	Land	62,000	
	Notes Payable		50,000
	Cash		12,000
	To record purchase of land with cash and note payable.		

Capitalize
Recording the acquisition of land, building, or other assets by debiting (increasing) an asset account.

We would say that Smart Touch Learning *capitalized* the cost of the land at $62,000. **Capitalized** means that an asset account was debited (increased) because the company acquired an asset. So, for our land example, Smart Touch Learning debited the Land account for $62,000, the capitalized cost of the asset.

Suppose Smart Touch Learning then pays $20,000 for fences, paving, lighting, and signs on August 15, 2025. The following entry records the cost of these land improvements:

$$\frac{A\uparrow\downarrow}{\text{Land} \atop \text{Improvements}\uparrow \atop \text{Cash}\downarrow} \Big\} = \Big\{ L + E$$

Date	Accounts and Explanation	Debit	Credit
Aug. 15	Land Improvements	20,000	
	Cash		20,000
	To record purchase of land improvements for cash.		

Land and land improvements are two entirely separate assets. Recall that land is not depreciated. However, the cost of land improvements *is* depreciated over that asset's useful life.

Buildings

The cost of a building depends on whether the company is constructing the building itself or is buying an existing one. These costs include the following:

Constructing a Building	Purchasing an Existing Building
• Architectural fees • Building permits • Contractor charges • Payments for materials, labor, and miscellaneous costs	• Purchase price • Costs to renovate the building to ready the building for use, which may include any of the charges listed under the "Constructing a Building" column

Machinery and Equipment

The cost of machinery and equipment includes the following:

- Purchase price (less any discounts)
- Transportation charges
- Insurance while in transit
- Sales tax and other taxes
- Purchase commission
- Installation costs
- Testing costs (prior to use of the asset)

After the asset is up and running, the company no longer capitalizes the cost of insurance, taxes, ordinary repairs, and maintenance to the Equipment account. From that point on, insurance, taxes, repairs, and maintenance costs are recorded as expenses.

Furniture and Fixtures

Furniture and fixtures include desks, chairs, file cabinets, display racks, shelving, and so forth. The cost of furniture and fixtures includes the basic cost of each asset (less any discounts), plus all other costs to ready the asset for its intended use. For example, for a desk, this may include the cost to ship the desk to the business and the cost paid to a laborer to assemble the desk.

Lump-Sum Purchase

A company may pay a single price for several assets as a group—a lump-sum purchase (sometimes called a *basket purchase*). For example, Smart Touch Learning may pay a single price for land and a building. For accounting purposes, the company must identify the cost of each asset purchased. The total cost paid (100%) is divided among the assets according to their relative market values. This is called the **relative-market-value method**.

Suppose Smart Touch Learning paid a combined purchase price of $100,000 on August 1, 2025, for the land and building. An appraisal indicates that the land's market value is $30,000 and the building's market value is $90,000. It is clear that the company got a good deal, paying less than fair market value, which is $120,000 for the combined assets. But how will the accountant allocate the $100,000 paid for both assets?

First, calculate the ratio of each asset's market value to the total market value for both assets. The total appraised value is $120,000.

> **Relative-Market-Value Method**
> A method of allocating the total cost (100%) of multiple assets purchased at one time. Total cost is divided among the assets according to their relative market values.

$$\text{Total market value} = \text{Land market value} + \text{Building market value}$$
$$= \$30,000 + \$90,000$$
$$= \$120,000$$

The land makes up 25% of the total market value and the building 75%, as follows:

$$\text{Percentage of total value} = \text{Land market value} / \text{Total market value}$$
$$= \$30,000 / \$120,000$$
$$= 25\%$$
$$\text{Percentage of total value} = \text{Building market value} / \text{Total market value}$$
$$= \$90,000 / \$120,000$$
$$= 75\%$$

For Smart Touch Learning, the land is assigned the cost of $25,000 and the building is assigned the cost of $75,000. The calculations follow:

Asset	Market Value	Percentage of Total Value	×	Total Purchase Price	=	Assigned Cost of Each Asset
Land	$ 30,000	$30,000 / $120,000 = 25%	×	$100,000	=	$ 25,000
Building	90,000	$90,000 / $120,000 = 75%	×	$100,000	=	75,000
Total	$ 120,000	100%				$ 100,000

Suppose the company purchased the assets by signing a note payable. The entry to record the purchase of the land and building is as follows:

$\dfrac{A\uparrow}{\text{Land}\uparrow \ \text{Building}\uparrow} \Big\} = \Big\{ \dfrac{L\uparrow}{\text{Notes Payable}\uparrow} + \dfrac{E}{\ }$

Date	Accounts and Explanation	Debit	Credit
Aug. 1	Land	25,000	
	Building	75,000	
	Notes Payable		100,000
	To record purchase of land and building in exchange for note payable.		

Capital and Revenue Expenditures

Accountants divide spending on plant assets after the acquisition into two categories:

- Capital expenditures
- Revenue expenditures

Capital Expenditure
An expenditure that increases the capacity or efficiency of a plant asset or extends its useful life. Capital expenditures are debited to an asset account.

A **capital expenditure** is debited to an asset account because it increases the asset's capacity or efficiency or extends the asset's useful life. A capital expenditure is also called a *balance sheet expenditure* because the cost of the expenditure is reported on the balance sheet as an asset.

Examples of capital expenditures include the purchase price plus all the other costs to bring an asset to its intended use, as discussed in the preceding sections. Also, an **extraordinary repair** is a capital expenditure because it extends the asset's capacity or useful life. An example of an extraordinary repair would be spending $3,000 to rebuild the engine on a five-year-old truck. This extraordinary repair would extend the asset's life past the normal expected life. As a result, its cost would be debited to the asset account for the truck as follows:

Extraordinary Repair
Repair work that generates a capital expenditure because it extends the asset's life past the normal expected life.

$\dfrac{A\uparrow\downarrow}{\text{Truck}\uparrow \ \text{Cash}\downarrow} \Big\} = \Big\{ \dfrac{L}{\ } + \dfrac{E}{\ }$

Date	Accounts and Explanation	Debit	Credit
	Truck	3,000	
	Cash		3,000
	To record cost of rebuilding engine on truck.		

Expenses incurred to maintain the asset in working order, such as repair or maintenance expense, are *not* debited to an asset account. Examples include the costs of maintaining equipment, such as repairing the air conditioner on a truck, changing the oil filter, and replacing its tires. These ordinary repairs are called **revenue expenditures** and are debited to an expense account, such as Repairs and Maintenance Expense. Revenue expenditures, often called *income statement expenditures*, do not increase the capacity or efficiency of an asset or extend its useful life and are reported on the income statement as an expense in the period incurred.

Revenue Expenditure
An expenditure that does not increase the capacity or efficiency of an asset or extend its useful life. Revenue expenditures are debited to an expense account.

Suppose that Smart Touch Learning paid $500 cash to replace tires on the truck. This expenditure does not extend the useful life of the truck or increase its efficiency. The company's accounting clerk records this transaction as a revenue expenditure as shown:

$\dfrac{A\downarrow}{\text{Cash}\downarrow} \Big\} = \Big\{ \dfrac{L}{\ } + \dfrac{E\downarrow}{\text{Repairs and Maintenance Expense}\uparrow}$

Date	Accounts and Explanation	Debit	Credit
	Repairs and Maintenance Expense	500	
	Cash		500
	To record repairs and maintenance costs incurred.		

Exhibit F:10-3 shows some capital expenditures and revenue expenditures for a delivery truck.

Exhibit F:10-3 | **Delivery Truck Expenditures—Capital Expenditure and Revenue Expenditure**

CAPITAL EXPENDITURE: Debit an Asset Account	REVENUE EXPENDITURE: Debit an Expense Account

Capital Expenditures:
  Major engine or transmission overhaul
  Modification for new use
  Addition to storage capacity
  Anything that increases the life of the asset
	Revenue Expenditures:
	  Repair of transmission or engine
	  Oil change, lubrication, and so on
	  Replacement of tires or windshield
	  Paint job

Treating a capital expenditure as an expense, or vice versa, creates an accounting error. Suppose a business replaces the engine in the truck. This would be an extraordinary repair because it increases the truck's life. If the company expenses the cost by debiting Repairs and Maintenance Expense rather than capitalizing it (debiting the asset), the company would be making an accounting error. This error has the following effects:

- Overstates Repairs and Maintenance Expense on the income statement
- Understates net income on the income statement
- Understates owner's equity on the statement of owner's equity and balance sheet due to understated net income
- Understates the Truck account (asset) on the balance sheet

Incorrectly capitalizing an expense creates the opposite error. Assume a minor repair, such as replacing the water pump on the truck, was incorrectly debited to the asset account. The error would result in expenses being understated and net income being overstated on the income statement. Additionally, the cost of the truck would be overstated and owner's equity overstated on the balance sheet by the amount of the repair bill.

Data Analytics in Accounting

Companies who own a large amount of properties, such as Greystar Real Estate Partners, a global leader in rental housing, can use data analytics to help maximize profits. Data about geographical information can help inform companies where they should purchase their next properties. It can help companies identify vacancy rate of potential new geographic areas and identify tenant mix in those areas. Weather data can help companies plan their maintenance ordering and scheduling. For example, if a certain time period generally has more rain than other months, the company can schedule inside maintenance during that time period and wait to do outside maintenance, such as roof repairs and painting, for the sunnier months.

Data analytics can also help companies understand the amount of water and energy consumption that occurs in its buildings. Information can be gathered on areas such as glass, energy consumption, lighting, and the usage of toilets and water consumption. Companies can use this information to provide an overall understanding of how much of each resource is consumed in comparison and seek out ways to save energy. Additionally, companies can be notified when higher than normal consumption occurs, such as when a faucet is running nonstop or a toilet is leaking, and maintenance technicians can be alerted to make needed repairs. Not only does this help conserve resources for the environment, but it also lowers the cost of expenses resulting in higher profits.

Sources: Littman, J. (2018, February 14). Data collection is the future of property management. *Bisnow*. Retrieved from https://www.bisnow.com/san-francisco/news/property-management/post-event-property-management-84890

Sumter, C. (2017, March 21). Property management with IBM Analytics: A month in the life. *Business Analytics Blog*. Retrieved from https://www.ibm.com/blogs/business-analytics/month-property-management-ibm-analytics/

Try It!

1. Budget Banners pays $200,000 cash for a group purchase of land, building, and equipment. At the time of acquisition, the land has a market value of $22,000, the building $187,000, and the equipment $11,000. Journalize the lump-sum purchase.

Check your answer online in MyLab Accounting or at http://www.pearsonhighered.com/Horngren.

For more practice, see Short Exercises S-F:10-1 and S-F:10-2.   **MyLab Accounting**

WHAT IS DEPRECIATION, AND HOW IS IT COMPUTED?

Learning Objective 2
Account for depreciation using the straight-line, units-of-production, and double-declining-balance methods

As we learned earlier, depreciation is the allocation of a plant asset's cost to expense over its useful life. Depreciation matches the expense against the revenue generated from using the asset to measure net income.

All assets, except land, wear out as they are used. For example, a business's delivery truck can only go so many miles before it is worn out. As the truck is driven, this use is part of what causes depreciation. Additionally, physical factors, like age and weather, can cause depreciation of assets.

Obsolete
An asset is considered obsolete when a newer asset can perform the job more efficiently.

Some assets, such as computers and software, may become *obsolete* before they wear out. An asset is **obsolete** when a newer asset can perform the job more efficiently. As a result, an asset's useful life may be shorter than its physical life. In all cases, the asset's cost is depreciated over its useful life.

Now that we have discussed causes of depreciation, let's discuss what depreciation is *not*.

1. *Depreciation is not a process of valuation.* Businesses do not record depreciation based on changes in the asset's market value.
2. *Depreciation does not mean that the business sets aside cash to replace an asset when it is used up.* Depreciation has nothing to do with cash.

Factors in Computing Depreciation

Depreciation of a plant asset is based on three main factors:

1. Capitalized cost
2. Estimated useful life
3. Estimated residual value

Capitalized cost is a known cost and, as mentioned earlier in this chapter, includes all items paid for the asset to perform its intended function. The other two factors are estimates.

Useful Life
Length of the service period expected from an asset. May be expressed in time or usage.

Estimated **useful life** is how long the company expects it will use the asset. Useful life may be expressed in time, such as months or years, or usage, such as units produced, hours used (for machinery), or miles driven (for a vehicle). A company's useful life estimate might be shorter than the actual life of the asset. For example, a business might estimate a useful life of five years for a delivery truck because it has a policy that after five years the truck will be traded in for a new vehicle. The business knows that the truck will last longer than five years, but the business uses a useful life of only five years because this is how long the company expects to use the asset.

Useful life is an estimate based on a company's experience and judgment. The goal is to define estimated useful life with the measure (years, units, and so on) that best matches the asset's decline or use. When determining useful life, a company considers how long it will use the asset and when the asset will become obsolete.

Plant Assets, Natural Resources, and Intangibles Financial 10-9

Estimated **residual value**, also called *salvage value*, is the asset's expected value at the end of its useful life. When a company decides to dispose of an asset, the company will sell or scrap it. The residual value is the amount the company expects to receive when the company disposes of the asset. Residual value can sometimes be zero if a company does not expect to receive anything when disposing of the asset. If a company plans on trading the asset in for a new asset, the residual value will be the expected trade-in value. Estimated residual value is *not* depreciated because the company expects to receive this amount at the end. Cost minus estimated residual value is called **depreciable cost**.

Residual Value
The expected value of a depreciable asset at the end of its useful life.

Depreciable Cost
The cost of a plant asset minus its estimated residual value.

> Depreciable cost = Cost − Estimated residual value

Depreciation Methods

There are many depreciation methods for plant assets, but three are used most commonly:

1. Straight-line method
2. Units-of-production method
3. Double-declining-balance method

These methods work differently in *how* they derive the yearly depreciation amount, but they all result in the same total depreciation over the total life of the asset. Exhibit F:10-4 gives the data we will use for a truck that Smart Touch Learning purchases and places in service on January 1, 2025.

Exhibit F:10-4 | **Data for Truck**

Data Item	Amount
Cost of truck	$ 41,000
Less: Estimated residual value	1,000
Depreciable cost	$ 40,000
Estimated useful life—Years	5 years
Estimated useful life—Units	100,000 miles

Straight-Line Method

The **straight-line method** allocates an equal amount of depreciation each year and is calculated as follows:

Straight-Line Method
A depreciation method that allocates an equal amount of depreciation each year. (Cost − Residual value) / Useful life.

> Straight-line depreciation = (Cost − Residual value) / Useful life
> = ($41,000 − $1,000) / 5 years
> = $8,000 per year

Because the asset was placed in service on the first day of the year, the adjusting entry to record each year's depreciation is as follows:

Date	Accounts and Explanation	Debit	Credit
Dec. 31	Depreciation Expense—Truck	8,000	
	Accumulated Depreciation—Truck		8,000
	To record depreciation on truck.		

A↓
Accumulated Depreciation—Truck↑
=
L + E↓
Depreciation Expense—Truck↑

Book Value
A depreciable asset's cost minus accumulated depreciation.

Depreciation Expense is reported on the income statement. Accumulated Depreciation is a contra asset that is reported on the balance sheet following the Truck account. The **book value** of the plant asset, cost minus accumulated depreciation, is reported on the balance sheet at December 31, 2025, as follows:

Property, Plant, and Equipment	
Truck	$ 41,000
Less: Accumulated Depreciation—Truck	(8,000)
Truck, Net	$ 33,000

A straight-line depreciation schedule for this truck is shown in Exhibit F:10-5. The final column on the right shows the asset's book value, which is cost less accumulated depreciation. Notice that the depreciation expense amount is the same every year and that the accumulated depreciation is the sum of all depreciation expense recorded to date for the depreciable asset.

Exhibit F:10-5 | Straight-Line Depreciation Schedule

Date	Asset Cost	Depreciable Cost	Useful Life		Depreciation Expense	Accumulated Depreciation	Book Value
1-1-2025	$ 41,000						$ 41,000
12-31-2025		($41,000 – $1,000)	/ 5 years	=	$ 8,000	$ 8,000	33,000
12-31-2026		($41,000 – $1,000)	/ 5 years	=	8,000	16,000	25,000
12-31-2027		($41,000 – $1,000)	/ 5 years	=	8,000	24,000	17,000
12-31-2028		($41,000 – $1,000)	/ 5 years	=	8,000	32,000	9,000
12-31-2029		($41,000 – $1,000)	/ 5 years	=	8,000	40,000	1,000 ← Residual value

As an asset is used, accumulated depreciation increases and book value decreases. (See the Accumulated Depreciation and Book Value columns in Exhibit F:10-5.) At the end of its estimated useful life, the asset is said to be fully depreciated. An asset's final book value is its residual value ($1,000 in this example).

Units-of-Production Method

Units-of-Production Method
A depreciation method that allocates a varying amount of depreciation each year based on an asset's usage.

The **units-of-production method** allocates a varying amount of depreciation each year based on an asset's usage. Units-of-production method depreciates by units rather than by years. As we noted earlier, a unit of output can be miles, units, hours, or output, depending on which unit type best defines the asset's use. When a plant asset's usage varies every year, the units-of-production method does a better of job of matching expenses with revenues.

The truck in our example is estimated to be driven 20,000 miles the first year, 30,000 the second, 25,000 the third, 15,000 the fourth, and 10,000 during the fifth (for a total useful life of 100,000 miles). The units-of-production depreciation for each period varies with the number of units (miles, in the case of the truck) the asset produces. Units-of-production depreciation is calculated as follows:

Step 1:

> Depreciation per unit = (Cost − Residual value) / Useful life in units
> = ($41,000 − $1,000) / 100,000 miles
> = $0.40 per mile

Step 2:

> Units-of-production depreciation = Depreciation per unit × Current year usage
> = $0.40 per mile × 20,000 miles
> = $8,000 (Year 1)

Units-of-production depreciation for the truck is illustrated in Exhibit F:10-6.

Exhibit F:10-6 | **Units-of-Production Depreciation Schedule**

		Depreciation for the Year				
Date	Asset Cost	Depreciation Per Unit	Number of Units	Depreciation Expense	Accumulated Depreciation	Book Value
1-1-2025	$41,000					$41,000
12-31-2025		$0.40 ×	20,000 =	$8,000	$8,000	33,000
12-31-2026		0.40 ×	30,000 =	12,000	20,000	21,000
12-31-2027		0.40 ×	25,000 =	10,000	30,000	11,000
12-31-2028		0.40 ×	15,000 =	6,000	36,000	5,000
12-31-2029		0.40 ×	10,000 =	4,000	40,000	1,000 ← Residual value

Double-Declining-Balance Method

An **accelerated depreciation method** expenses more of the asset's cost near the start of an asset's life and less at the end of its useful life. The main accelerated method of depreciation is the **double-declining-balance method**. The double-declining-balance method multiplies an asset's decreasing book value (the asset's cost less its accumulated depreciation) by a constant percentage that is twice the straight-line depreciation rate. The straight-line depreciation rate is calculated as 1 / Useful life. Therefore, the double-declining-balance method rate will be 2 × (1 / Useful life). Double-declining-balance amounts can be computed using the following formula:

> Double-declining-balance depreciation = (Cost − Accumulated depreciation) × 2 × (1 / Useful life)

For the first year of the truck, the calculation would be as shown:

> Double-declining-balance depreciation = (Cost − Accumulated depreciation) × 2 × (1 / Useful life)
> = ($41,000 − $0) × 2 × (1 / 5 years)
> = $16,400 (Year 1)

Accelerated Depreciation Method
A depreciation method that expenses more of the asset's cost near the start of its useful life and less at the end of its useful life.

Double-Declining-Balance Method
An accelerated depreciation method that computes annual depreciation by multiplying the depreciable asset's decreasing book value by a constant percent that is two times the straight-line depreciation rate.

In Year 2, the amount of depreciation would decline because the asset has accumulated some depreciation (the $16,400 for the first year). For the second year of the truck, therefore, the calculation would be as shown:

> Double-declining-balance depreciation = (Cost − Accumulated depreciation) × 2 × (1 / Useful life)
> = ($41,000 − $16,400) × 2 × (1 / 5 years)
> = $9,840 (Year 2)

Note that residual value is not included in the formula. Residual value is ignored until the depreciation expense takes the book value below the residual value. When this occurs, the final year depreciation is calculated as the amount needed to bring the asset to its residual value. In the case of the truck, residual value was given at $1,000. In the double-declining-balance schedule in Exhibit F:10-7, notice that, after Year 4 (December, 31, 2028), the truck's book value is $5,314. By definition, the truck is to last five years, which ends on December 31, 2029. At the end of the asset's life, its book value should equal the residual value. Therefore, in the final year, depreciation is book value, $5,314, less the $1,000 residual value, or $4,314 in depreciation expense.

Exhibit F:10-7 | Double-Declining-Balance Depreciation Schedule

Date	Asset Cost	Book Value	DDB Rate	Depreciation Expense	Accumulated Depreciation	Book Value
1-1-2025	$41,000					$41,000
12-31-2025		$41,000 × 2 × (1 / 5 years) =		$16,400	$16,400	24,600
12-31-2026		24,600 × 2 × (1 / 5 years) =		9,840	26,240	14,760
12-31-2027		14,760 × 2 × (1 / 5 years) =		5,904	32,144	8,856
12-31-2028		8,856 × 2 × (1 / 5 years) =		3,542	35,686	5,314
12-31-2029				4,314*	40,000	1,000 ← Residual value

*Last year depreciation is the "plug figure" needed to reduce book value to the residual amount ($5,314 − $1,000 = $4,314).

Comparing Depreciation Methods

Let's compare the depreciation methods. Annual depreciation expense amounts vary, but total accumulated depreciation is $40,000 for all three methods.

AMOUNT OF DEPRECIATION PER YEAR

Year	Straight-Line	Units-of-Production	Accelerated Method Double-Declining-Balance
1	$ 8,000	$ 8,000	$16,400
2	8,000	12,000	9,840
3	8,000	10,000	5,904
4	8,000	6,000	3,542
5	8,000	4,000	4,314
Total Accumulated Depreciation	$40,000	$40,000	$40,000

Deciding which method is best depends on the asset. A business should match an asset's expense against the revenue that the asset produces. The following are some guidelines for which method to use:

Method	Asset Characteristics	Effect on Depreciation	Example Assets
Straight-line	Generates revenue evenly over time	Equal amount each period	Building
Units-of-production	Depreciates due to wear and tear rather than obsolescence	More usage causes larger depreciation	Vehicles (miles) Machinery (machine hours)
Double-declining-balance	Produces more revenue in early years	Higher depreciation in early years, less later	Computers

Exhibit F:10-8 shows the three methods in one graph for additional comparison. Notice that the straight-line method produces a straight line on the graph because there is an equal amount of depreciation expense each year. The double-declining-balance method produces a line that is decreasing, and the units-of-production method's line varies based on usage.

Exhibit F:10-8 | Annual Depreciation by Method

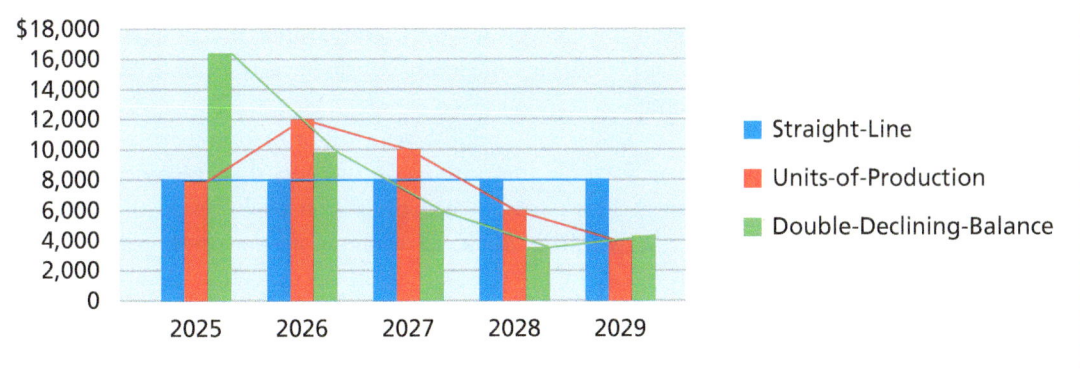

DECISIONS

Which depreciation method should be selected?

Three Junes Weaving has just purchased an automated weaving machine and is trying to figure out which depreciation method to use: straight-line, units-of-production, or double-declining-balance. Ira Glasier, the controller, is interested in using a depreciation method that approximates the usage of the weaving machine. He also expects that the weaving machine will have increasing repairs and maintenance as the asset ages. Which method should Ira choose?

Solution

If Ira is interested in using a depreciation method that approximates the usage of the weaving machine, he should use the units-of-production method to depreciate the asset. He could use number of machine hours as the unit of output. This method would best match the usage of the machine to the amount of expense recorded. Ira should be aware, though, that this method could produce varying amounts of depreciation expense each year. For example, if Three Junes Weaving does not use the weaving machine in one year, no depreciation expense would be recorded. This could cause net income to vary significantly from year to year. Because Ira expects the weaving machine to need more repairs as the asset ages, Ira might consider using the double-declining-balance method instead. The double-declining-balance method records a higher amount of depreciation in the early years and less later. This method works well for assets that are expected to have increasing repairs and maintenance in their later years because the total expense (depreciation, repairs, and maintenance) can be spread out equally over the life of the asset.

Depreciation for Tax Purposes

The Internal Revenue Service (IRS) requires that companies use a specific depreciation method for tax purposes. This method is the **Modified Accelerated Cost Recovery System (MACRS)**.

Modified Accelerated Cost Recovery System (MACRS)
A depreciation method that is used for tax purposes.

Under MACRS, assets are divided into specific classes, such as 3-year, 5-year, 7-year, and 39-year property. Businesses do not get to choose the useful life of the asset. Instead, the IRS specifies the useful life based on the specific classes. For example, office furniture has a 7-year life for tax purposes but might only be depreciated for five years for book purposes.

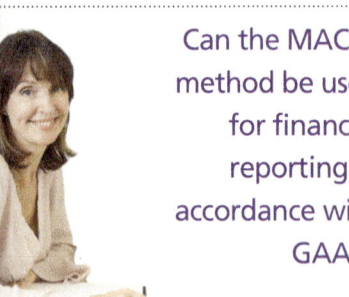

Can the MACRS method be used for financial reporting in accordance with GAAP?

In addition, the MACRS method ignores residual value. For tax purposes, an asset is fully depreciated to a book value of zero. **MACRS is not acceptable for financial reporting under Generally Accepted Accounting Principles (GAAP).** This requires that businesses record depreciation for plant assets under two methods—book method (straight-line, units-of-production, or double-declining-balance) and tax method (MACRS).

Partial-Year Depreciation

In the previous examples, we calculated depreciation for the entire year. What would happen if the business placed the truck in service on July 1, 2025, instead of January 1, 2025? Would the depreciation for any of the methods change? Yes, but only the methods that are calculated based on a time period, which means only straight-line and double-declining-balance would change. Units-of-production does not consider years in its formula; thus, that calculation remains the same.

When a business purchases an asset during the year (other than January 1), the business should record depreciation for only the portion of the year that the asset was used in the operations of the business. This partial-year depreciation could be calculated to the nearest day, but this is unnecessary. In this book, we will assume a method called *modified half-month convention*, which means if an asset is purchased on or before the 15th of the month, the asset will be depreciated for the whole month. If the asset is purchased after the 15th of the month, the asset will not be depreciated until the following month.

Returning to our example, assume that the truck was placed into service on July 1, 2025. Therefore, the truck was in service for six months in 2025, from July 1 through December 31. The revised straight-line calculation for 2025 under the altered in-service date is as follows:

$$\begin{aligned}\text{Straight-line depreciation} &= [(\text{Cost} - \text{Residual value}) / \text{Useful life}] \times (\text{Number of months} / 12 \text{ months}) \\ &= [(\$41{,}000 - \$1{,}000) / 5 \text{ years}] \times (6/12) \\ &= \$4{,}000\end{aligned}$$

Because the business used the asset for six months of the year, we only record 6/12 (6 out of 12 months) of straight-line depreciation expense, or $4,000, in 2025.

Partial-year depreciation also applies to disposals of assets (which we will cover later in this chapter). If an asset is disposed of during the year, the business must calculate depreciation for only the time period the asset was in service before the asset was disposed, not the entire year.

Changing Estimates of a Depreciable Asset

Estimating the useful life and residual value of a plant asset poses a challenge. As the asset is used, the business may change its estimated useful life or estimated residual value. If this happens, the business must recalculate depreciation expense. For example, the business may find that its truck lasts eight years instead of five. This is a change in estimated useful life. Accounting changes like this are common because useful life and residual value are estimates and, as a result, are not based on perfect foresight. When a company makes an accounting change, GAAP requires the business to recalculate the depreciation for the asset in the year of change and in future periods. They do not require that businesses restate prior years' financial statements for this change in estimate.

For a change in either estimated asset life or residual value, the asset's remaining depreciable book value is spread over the asset's remaining life. Suppose Smart Touch Learning used the truck purchased on January 1, 2025, for two full years. Under the straight-line method, accumulated depreciation would be $16,000. (Refer to Exhibit F:10-5.)

$$\begin{aligned}
\text{Straight-line depreciation} &= (\text{Cost} - \text{Residual value}) / \text{Useful life} \\
&= (\$41,000 - \$1,000) / 5 \text{ years} \\
&= \$8,000 \text{ per year} \times 2 \text{ years} \\
&= \$16,000
\end{aligned}$$

Remaining depreciable book value (cost *less* accumulated depreciation) is $25,000 ($41,000 − $16,000). Suppose Smart Touch Learning believes the truck will remain useful for six more years (for a total of eight years). Residual value is unchanged. At the start of 2027, the company would recompute depreciation as follows:

$$\begin{aligned}
\text{Revised depreciation} &= (\text{Book value} - \text{Revised residual value}) / \text{Revised useful life remaining} \\
&= (\$25,000 - \$1,000) / 6 \text{ years} \\
&= \$4,000 \text{ per year}
\end{aligned}$$

Make sure to use the useful life remaining as the denominator in the formula.

In years 2027 to 2032, the yearly depreciation entry based on the new useful life would be as follows:

Date	Accounts and Explanation	Debit	Credit
Dec. 31	Depreciation Expense—Truck	4,000	
	Accumulated Depreciation—Truck		4,000
	To record depreciation on truck.		

A↓ Accumulated Depreciation—Truck↑ = L + E↓ Depreciation Expense—Truck↑

Reporting Property, Plant, and Equipment

Property, plant, and equipment are reported at book value on the balance sheet. Companies may choose to report plant assets as a single amount, with a note to the financial statements that provides detailed information, or companies may provide detailed information on the face of the statement. The cost of the asset and the related accumulated depreciation should be disclosed. Exhibit F:10-9 (on the next page) shows the two alternative reporting treatments for plant assets.

IFRS
IFRS permits the presentation of plant assets at their fair market value because market value may be more relevant and thus more useful to readers of financial statements.

10-16 Financial chapter 10

Exhibit F:10-9 | Reporting Property, Plant, and Equipment

Treatment 1: Property, Plant, and Equipment on the Balance Sheet of Smart Touch Learning (December 31)		
Property, Plant, and Equipment:		
Land		$ 20,000
Building	$ 60,000	
Less: Accumulated Depreciation—Building	(250)	59,750
Furniture	18,000	
Less: Accumulated Depreciation—Furniture	(300)	17,700
Property, Plant, and Equipment, Net		**$ 97,450**

Treatment 2: Property, Plant, and Equipment on the Balance Sheet of Smart Touch Learning (December 31)	
Property, Plant, and Equipment, Net (See Note 8)	$ 97,450

> 2. On January 1, Alamo Cranes purchased a crane for $140,000. Alamo expects the crane to remain useful for six years (1,000,000 lifts) and to have a residual value of $2,000. The company expects the crane to be used for 80,000 lifts the first year.
>
> Compute the first-year depreciation expense on the crane using the following methods:
>
>   **a.** Straight-line
>   **b.** Units-of-production (Round *depreciation per unit* to two decimals. Round depreciation expense to the nearest whole dollar.)
>
> Compute the first-year and second-year depreciation expense on the crane using the following method:
>
>   **c.** Double-declining-balance (Round depreciation expense to the nearest whole dollar.)
>
> Check your answers online in MyLab Accounting or at http://www.pearsonhighered.com/Horngren.
>
> For more practice, see Short Exercises S-F:10-3 through S-F:10-6. **MyLab Accounting**

HOW ARE DISPOSALS OF PLANT ASSETS RECORDED?

Learning Objective 3
Journalize entries for the disposal of plant assets

Eventually, an asset wears out or becomes obsolete. The business then has several options regarding property, plant, and equipment:

- Discard the plant asset.
- Sell the plant asset.
- Exchange the plant asset for another plant asset.

In this section, we discuss the first two options. Exchanging a plant asset for another asset is covered in the appendix to this chapter (Appendix 10A).

Plant assets remain on the business's books until they are disposed of. For example, a fully depreciated asset, one that has reached the end of its estimated useful life and is still in service, will still be reported as an asset on the balance sheet. If the asset is still useful, the company may continue using it even though no additional depreciation is recorded. If the asset is no longer useful, it is disposed of. This requires the business to remove the asset and associated accumulated depreciation from the books. In addition, a gain or loss might be recognized by the company.

Regardless of the type of disposal, there are four steps:

1. Bring the depreciation up to date.
2. Remove the old, disposed-of asset and associated accumulated depreciation from the books.
3. Record the value of any cash received (or paid) in the disposal of the asset.
4. Finally, determine the amount of any gain or loss. Gain or loss is determined by comparing the cash received and the market value of any other assets received with the book value of the asset disposed of.

Discarding Plant Assets

Discarding of plant assets involves disposing of the asset for no cash. If an asset is disposed of when it is fully depreciated and has no residual value, then the business simply removes the asset and contra asset, Accumulated Depreciation, from the books (Step 2). There is no need to bring the depreciation up to date (Step 1) because the asset is already fully depreciated. In addition, no cash was received or paid and no gain or loss is recognized (Steps 3 and 4).

For example, assume that on July 1, Smart Touch Learning discards equipment with a cost of $10,000 and accumulated depreciation of $10,000. The asset and contra asset accounts are shown below before disposal.

Equipment	Accumulated Depreciation—Equipment
10,000	10,000

To dispose of the equipment, Smart Touch Learning will need to credit the asset account, Equipment, and debit Accumulated Depreciation—Equipment. The accounting clerk will record the transaction as follows:

Date	Accounts and Explanation	Debit	Credit
Jul. 1	Accumulated Depreciation—Equipment	10,000	
	Equipment		10,000
	Discarded fully depreciated equipment.		

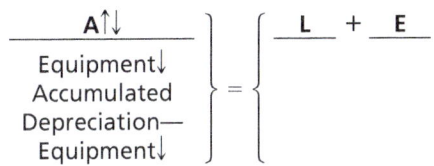

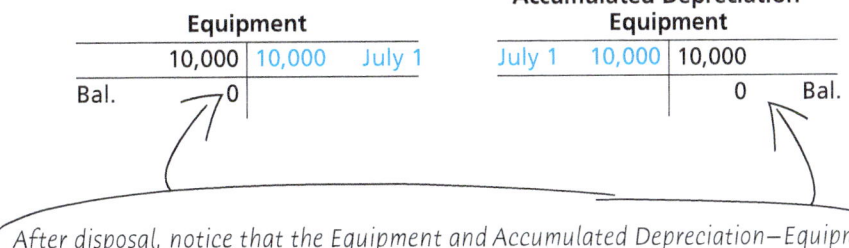

After disposal, notice that the Equipment and Accumulated Depreciation–Equipment accounts now have a zero balance. These accounts will no longer be reported on the financial statements because Smart Touch Learning no longer owns the equipment.

Suppose, instead, that on July 1, Smart Touch Learning discarded the equipment, which has a cost of $10,000 but it is not fully depreciated. As of December 31 of the previous year, accumulated depreciation was $8,000. Annual depreciation expense is $1,000 per year.

10-18 Financial chapter 10

The first step in recording the disposal is to bring the asset up to date on depreciation. Because Smart Touch Learning disposes of the asset on July 1 and the asset was in service from January 1 through July 1 since the last recording of depreciation, one-half of a year's depreciation will be recorded ($1,000 × 1/2 = $500) as follows:

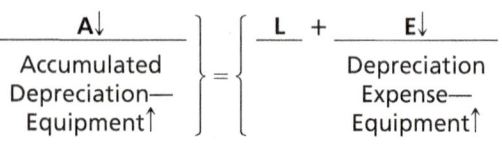

Date	Accounts and Explanation	Debit	Credit
Jul. 1	Depreciation Expense—Equipment	500	
	Accumulated Depreciation—Equipment		500
	To record depreciation on equipment.		

Steps 2 through 4 involve recording the disposal of the equipment and accumulated depreciation and calculating any gain or loss. In this situation, there is a $1,500 loss calculated as follows:

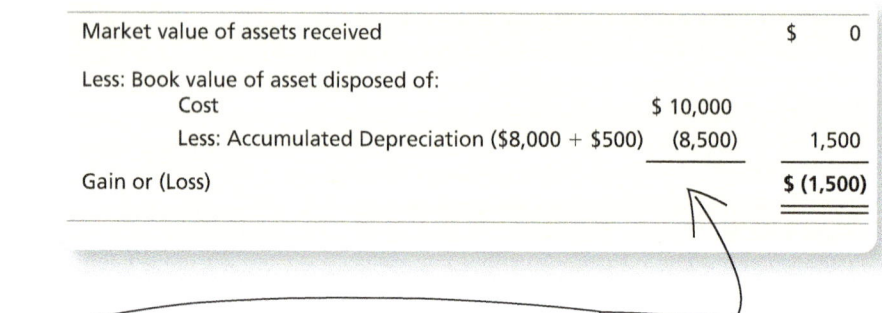

When calculating gain or loss, don't forget to update the Accumulated Depreciation account. In this example, before recording depreciation, the Accumulated Depreciation account was $8,000; $500 of additional depreciation was recorded at disposal, bringing the total accumulated depreciation to $8,500.

The account, Loss on Disposal, will be used. This account has a normal debit balance and is reported in the Other Income and (Expenses) section of the income statement that includes gains and losses on the sale of plant assets.

Smart Touch Learning records the following entry to dispose of the equipment:

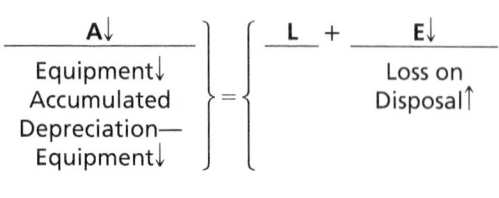

Date	Accounts and Explanation	Debit	Credit
Jul. 1	Accumulated Depreciation—Equipment	8,500	
	Loss on Disposal	1,500	
	Equipment		10,000
	Discarded equipment with a book value of $1,500.		

```
         Equipment                    Accumulated Depreciation—                 
                                              Equipment                  Loss on Disposal
     10,000 | 10,000  July 1                          | 8,000         July 1   1,500 |
Bal.      0 |                     July 1   8,500 |   500  July 1
                                                       |     0   Bal.
```

Selling Plant Assets

Companies will often sell a plant asset for cash. We will again use Smart Touch Learning as an example. On July 1, the company sells equipment with a historical cost of $10,000 and accumulated depreciation, as of December 31 of the previous year, of $8,000. Annual depreciation is $1,000. The first step is to bring the depreciation up to date for the six months from the last recording of depreciation through the date of disposal.

Date	Accounts and Explanation	Debit	Credit
Jul. 1	Depreciation Expense—Equipment	500	
	Accumulated Depreciation—Equipment		500
	To record depreciation on equipment.		

$$\frac{A\downarrow}{\text{Accumulated Depreciation—Equipment}\uparrow} = \left\{ \frac{L\ +\ E\downarrow}{\text{Depreciation Expense—Equipment}\uparrow} \right.$$

This entry brings the accumulated depreciation to $8,500 ($8,000 + $500). The equipment now has a book value of $1,500 ($10,000 − $8,500). Now that we have recorded Step 1, let's look at Steps 2 through 4 for several different scenarios.

Selling a Plant Asset at Book Value

Suppose that Smart Touch Learning sells the equipment for $1,500. Notice that the cash received is equal to the book value of the asset. When a business sells an asset for book value, no gain or loss is recorded. This is because the cash received is equal to the book value of the asset sold.

Market value of assets received		$ 1,500
Less: Book value of asset disposed of:		
Cost	$ 10,000	
Less: Accumulated Depreciation	(8,500)	1,500
Gain or (Loss)		$ 0

In recording the journal entry, Smart Touch Learning will debit cash for $1,500 and then take the equipment and accumulated depreciation off the books as follows:

Date	Accounts and Explanation	Debit	Credit
Jul. 1	Cash	1,500	
	Accumulated Depreciation—Equipment	8,500	
	Equipment		10,000
	Sold equipment for cash.		

$$\frac{A\updownarrow}{\substack{\text{Cash}\uparrow \\ \text{Equipment}\downarrow \\ \text{Accumulated Depreciation—Equipment}\downarrow}} = \left\{ L\ +\ E \right.$$

Cash
July 1 1,500	

Equipment
10,000	10,000 July 1
Bal. 0	

Accumulated Depreciation— Equipment
	8,000
July 1 8,500	500 July 1
	0 Bal.

Selling a Plant Asset Above Book Value

If Smart Touch Learning sells the equipment for $4,000, the company will record a gain on sale of the equipment. Notice that the cash received is more than the book value of the asset. When a business sells an asset for more than its book value, a gain is recorded.

Market value of assets received		$ 4,000
Less: Book value of asset disposed of:		
Cost	$ 10,000	
Less: Accumulated Depreciation	(8,500)	1,500
Gain or (Loss)		$ 2,500

The account, Gain on Disposal, will be used. This account has a normal credit balance and is reported in the Other Income and (Expenses) section of the income statement.

In recording the journal entry, Smart Touch Learning will remove the old equipment and accumulated depreciation from the books (Step 2), record a debit to Cash for $4,000 (Step 3), and then record a credit to Gain on Disposal (Step 4) as follows:

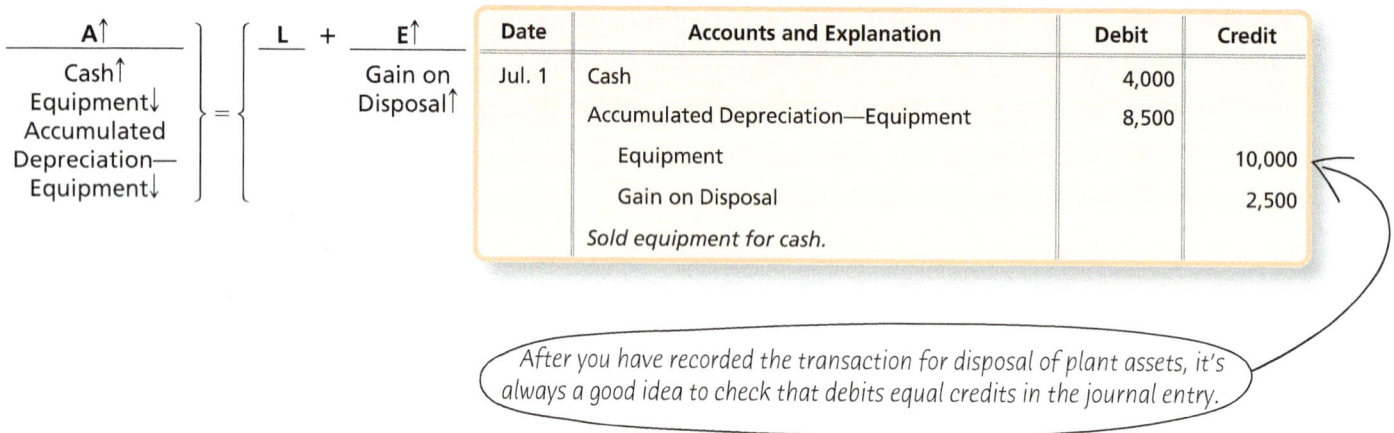

After you have recorded the transaction for disposal of plant assets, it's always a good idea to check that debits equal credits in the journal entry.

Selling a Plant Asset Below Book Value

If Smart Touch Learning sells the equipment for $500, the company will record a loss on the sale of the equipment. Notice that the cash received is less than the book value of the asset. When a business sells an asset for less than its book value, a loss is recorded.

Market value of assets received		$ 500
Less: Book value of asset disposed of:		
Cost	$ 10,000	
Less: Accumulated Depreciation	(8,500)	1,500
Gain or (Loss)		$ (1,000)

In recording the journal entry, Smart Touch Learning will remove the old equipment and accumulated depreciation from the books (Step 2), record a debit to Cash for $500 (Step 3), and then record a debit to Loss on Disposal (Step 4) as follows:

Date	Accounts and Explanation	Debit	Credit
Jul. 1	Cash	500	
	Accumulated Depreciation—Equipment	8,500	
	Loss on Disposal	1,000	
	Equipment		10,000
	Sold equipment for cash.		

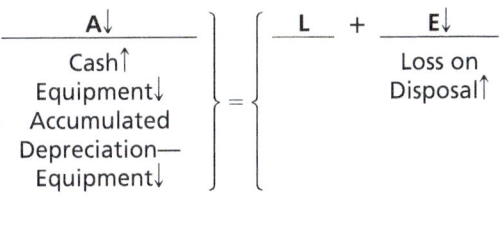

Cash	
July 1 500	

Equipment	
10,000	10,000 July 1
Bal. 0	

Accumulated Depreciation—Equipment	
	8,000
July 1 8,500	500 July 1
	0 Bal.

Loss on Disposal	
July 1 1,000	

Summary

In each disposal illustrated, the company has decreased net income over the life of the asset by recording depreciation expense each year prior to the disposal. When the company records the disposal, the company will record a gain, a loss, or neither. Gains recorded at disposal increase net income and losses recorded at disposal decrease net income. Over the life of the asset, the company records a net decrease in net income equal to the net cost of the asset. The net cost of the asset is the amount paid for the asset when it was purchased less the cash received at disposal. For each scenario, let's compare the effect on net income to the net cost, as shown in the table below:

	Asset Discarded		Asset Sold		
	Fully Depreciated	Not Fully Depreciated	At Book Value	Above Book Value	Below Book Value
Accumulated depreciation	$ 10,000	$ 8,500	$ 8,500	$ 8,500	$ 8,500
Plus: Loss on disposal	0	1,500	0	0	1,000
Less: Gain on disposal	0	0	0	2,500	0
Net decrease in net income	$ 10,000	$ 10,000	$ 8,500	$ 6,000	$ 9,500
Cost	$ 10,000	$ 10,000	$ 10,000	$ 10,000	$ 10,000
Less: Cash received at disposal	0	0	1,500	4,000	500
Net cost	$ 10,000	$ 10,000	$ 8,500	$ 6,000	$ 9,500

Notice in each case that the net decrease in net income is equal to the net cost of the asset. We have, in effect, expensed the net cost of the asset over its life.

In this section, we have also reviewed the journal entries for discarding and selling of plant assets. Exhibit F:10-10 summarizes what you have learned. Before moving on, take a moment to review the exhibit.

Plant Assets, Natural Resources, and Intangibles Financial 10-23

Exhibit F:10-10 | Disposals of Plant Assets

Discarding of a fully depreciated plant asset:

Date	Accounts and Explanation	Debit	Credit
	Accumulated Depreciation	10,000	
	Plant Asset		10,000

Discarding of a plant asset that is not fully depreciated:

Date	Accounts and Explanation	Debit	Credit
	Accumulated Depreciation	8,500	
	Loss on Disposal	1,500	
	Plant Asset		10,000

Selling a plant asset at book value:

Date	Accounts and Explanation	Debit	Credit
	Cash	1,500	
	Accumulated Depreciation	8,500	
	Plant Asset		10,000

Selling a plant asset above book value:

Date	Accounts and Explanation	Debit	Credit
	Cash	4,000	
	Accumulated Depreciation	8,500	
	Plant Asset		10,000
	Gain on Disposal		2,500

Selling a plant asset below book value:

Date	Accounts and Explanation	Debit	Credit
	Cash	500	
	Accumulated Depreciation	8,500	
	Loss on Disposal	1,000	
	Plant Asset		10,000

3. Counselors of Atlanta purchased equipment on January 1, 2023, for $20,000. Counselors of Atlanta expected the equipment to last for four years and have a residual value of $2,000. Suppose Counselors of Atlanta sold the equipment for $8,000 on December 31, 2025, after using the equipment for three full years. Assume depreciation for 2025 has been recorded. Journalize the sale of the equipment, assuming straight-line depreciation was used.

Check your answer online in MyLab Accounting or at http://www.pearsonhighered.com/Horngren.

For more practice, see Short Exercises S-F:10-7 through S-F:10-10. MyLab Accounting

HOW ARE NATURAL RESOURCES ACCOUNTED FOR?

Learning Objective 4
Account for natural resources

Natural Resource
An asset that comes from the earth and is consumed.

Depletion
The process by which businesses spread the allocation of a natural resource's cost over its usage.

Natural resources are assets that come from the earth that are consumed. Examples include iron ore, oil, natural gas, diamonds, gold, coal, and timber. Natural resources are expensed through depletion. **Depletion** is the process by which businesses spread the allocation of a natural resource's cost to expense over its usage. It's called depletion because the company is depleting (using up) a natural resource such that at some point in time, there is nothing left to extract. Depletion expense is computed by the units-of-production method.

For example, an oil well cost $700,000 and is estimated to hold 70,000 barrels of oil. There is no residual value. If 3,000 barrels are extracted and sold during the year, then depletion expense is calculated as follows:

Step 1:

Depletion per unit = (Cost − Residual value) / Estimated total units
= ($700,000 − $0) / 70,000 barrels
= $10 per barrel

Step 2:

Depletion expense = Depletion per unit × Number of units extracted
= $10 per barrel × 3,000 barrels
= $30,000 (Year 1)

The depletion entry for the year is as follows:

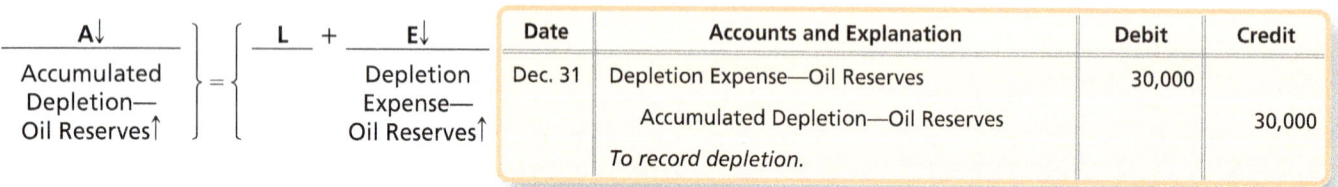

Accumulated Depletion is a contra asset account similar to Accumulated Depreciation. Natural resources can be reported on the balance sheet as shown for oil reserves in the following example:

Oil Reserves	$ 700,000	
Less: Accumulated Depletion—Oil Reserves	(30,000)	$ 670,000

Plant Assets, Natural Resources, and Intangibles Financial 10-25

4. Amplify Petroleum holds huge reserves of oil. Assume that at the end of 2023, Amplify Petroleum's cost of oil reserves totaled $80,000,000, representing 100,000,000 barrels of oil. Suppose Amplify Petroleum removed and sold 20,000,000 barrels of oil during 2024. Journalize depletion expense for 2024.

Check your answer online in MyLab Accounting or at http://www.pearsonhighered.com/Horngren.

For more practice, see Short Exercise S-F:10-11.   MyLab Accounting

HOW ARE INTANGIBLE ASSETS ACCOUNTED FOR?

Intangible assets are assets that have no physical form. Instead, these assets convey special rights from patents, copyrights, trademarks, and other creative works.

In our technology-driven economy, intangibles are very important. The intellectual property of a business is difficult to measure. However, when one company buys another, we get a glimpse of the value of the intellectual property of the acquired company. For example, in 2006, Google acquired YouTube. Google said it would pay $1.65 billion for YouTube even though YouTube had never had a profitable year. Why so much for so little? Because YouTube's intangible assets were extremely valuable. Intangibles can account for most of a company's market value, so companies must value their intangibles just as they value other assets, such as merchandise inventory and equipment.

Accounting for Intangibles

Intangible assets that are purchased are recorded at cost. If an intangible is not purchased, only some limited costs can be capitalized. Most purchased intangibles are expensed through amortization, the allocation of the cost of an intangible asset to expense over its useful life. Amortization applies to intangibles exactly as depreciation applies to equipment and depletion to oil and timber.

Intangibles either have a definite life or an indefinite life. Intangibles with an indefinite life have no factors (such as legal and contractual obligations) that limit the usage of the intangible asset. Only intangibles that have a definite life are amortized. Intangible assets with an indefinite life are tested for impairment annually. Impairment occurs when the fair value of an asset is less than the book value. In other words, there has been a permanent decline in the value of the asset. If an impairment occurs, the company records a loss in the period that the decline is identified.

Specific Intangibles

As noted earlier, patents, copyrights, and trademarks are intangible assets. The accounting for the purchase and amortization of each asset is similar.

Patents

A patent is an intangible asset that is a federal government grant conveying an exclusive 20-year right to produce and sell an invention. The invention may be a process, product, or formula—for example, the Dolby noise-reduction process or a prescription drug formula. The acquisition cost of a patent is debited to the Patent account.

Learning Objective 5
Account for intangible assets

Intangible Asset
An asset with no physical form that is valuable because of the special rights it carries.

Amortization
The process by which businesses spread the allocation of an intangible asset's cost over its useful life.

Impairment
A permanent decline in asset value.

Patent
An intangible asset that is a federal government grant conveying an exclusive 20-year right to produce and sell a process, product, or formula.

Like any other asset, a patent may be purchased. Suppose Smart Touch Learning pays $200,000 to acquire a patent on January 1. The accounting clerk records the following entry at acquisition:

Date	Accounts and Explanation	Debit	Credit
Jan. 1	Patent	200,000	
	Cash		200,000
	To record purchase of patent.		

Smart Touch Learning believes this patent's useful life is only five years because it is likely that a new, more efficient process will be developed within that time. Amortization expense is calculated using the straight-line method as follows:

Amortization expense = (Cost − Residual value) / Useful life
= ($200,000 − $0) / 5 years
= $40,000 per year

For most intangibles, the residual value will be zero.

The company's accounting clerk would record the following adjusting entry for amortization:

Date	Accounts and Explanation	Debit	Credit
Dec. 31	Amortization Expense—Patent	40,000	
	Patent		40,000
	To record amortization of patent.		

Notice that Smart Touch Learning credited the amortization directly to the intangible asset, Patent, instead of using an Accumulated Amortization account. A company may credit an intangible asset directly when recording amortization expense, or it may use the account Accumulated Amortization. **Companies frequently choose to credit the asset account directly because the residual value is generally zero and there is no physical asset to dispose of at the end of its useful life, so the asset essentially removes itself from the books through the process of amortization.**

At the end of the first year, Smart Touch Learning will report this patent at $160,000 ($200,000 cost minus first-year amortization of $40,000), the next year at $120,000, and so forth. Each year for five years the value of the patent will be reduced until the end of its five-year life, at which point its book value will be $0.

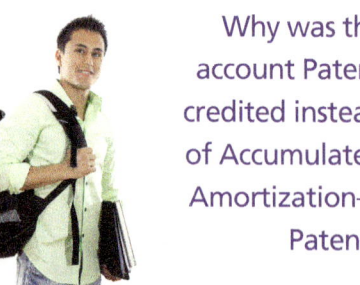

Why was the account Patent credited instead of Accumulated Amortization—Patent?

Copyrights and Trademarks

Copyright
Exclusive right to reproduce and sell a book, musical composition, film, other work of art, or intellectual property.

A **copyright** is the exclusive right to reproduce and sell a book, musical composition, film, other work of art, or intellectual property. Copyrights also protect computer software programs, such as Microsoft® Windows® and the Microsoft® Excel® spreadsheet software. Issued by the federal government, a copyright is granted for the life of the creator plus 70 years.

A company may pay a large sum to purchase an existing copyright. For example, the publisher Simon & Schuster may pay $1 million for the copyright on a popular novel because it thinks it will be able to profit from selling the novel. Even though copyrights have a long legal life (life of creator plus 70 years), most copyrights have short useful lives. Copyrights are amortized over their legal life or useful life, whichever is shorter.

A **trademark** (also called *trade name*) is an asset that represents distinctive identifications of products or services, such as the Nike "swoosh" or the McDonald's "golden arches." Legally protected slogans include Chevrolet's "Like a Rock" and De Beers' "A Diamond Is Forever." The cost of a trademark or trade name is amortized over its useful life.

> **Trademark**
> An asset that represents distinctive identifications of a product or service.

Franchises and Licenses

Franchises are privileges granted by a business to sell goods or services under specified conditions. The Dallas Cowboys football organization is a franchise granted by the National Football League. McDonald's and Subway are well-known business franchises. **Licenses** are privileges granted by a government to use public property in performing services. A radio station might be granted permission by the federal government to use the airwaves to broadcast its music. The acquisition cost of a franchise or license is amortized over its useful life.

> **Franchise**
> Privilege granted by a business to sell a product or service under specified conditions.
>
> **License**
> Privilege granted by a government to use public property in performing services.

Goodwill

In accounting, **goodwill** is the excess of the cost to purchase another company over the market value of its net assets (assets minus liabilities). Goodwill is the value paid above the net worth of the company's assets and liabilities.

Suppose White Company acquired Mocha Company on January 1, 2024. The sum of the market values of Mocha's assets was $9 million and its liabilities totaled $1 million, so Mocha's net assets totaled $8 million. Suppose White paid $10 million to purchase Mocha. In this case, White paid $2 million above the market value of Mocha's net assets. Therefore, that $2 million is considered goodwill and is computed as follows:

> **Goodwill**
> Excess of the cost of an acquired company over the sum of the market values of its net assets (assets minus liabilities).

Purchase price to acquire Mocha		$ 10,000,000
Market value of Mocha's assets	$ 9,000,000	
Less: Market value of Mocha's liabilities	(1,000,000)	
Less: Market value of Mocha's net assets		8,000,000
Goodwill		$ 2,000,000

White's entry to record the purchase of Mocha, including the goodwill that White purchased, would be as follows:

Date	Accounts and Explanation	Debit	Credit
Jan. 1	Assets	9,000,000	
	Goodwill	2,000,000	
	Liabilities		1,000,000
	Cash		10,000,000
	To record purchase of Mocha Company.		

$$\underline{A\uparrow} \Big\} = \Big\{ \underline{L\uparrow} + \underline{\quad E \quad}$$

Assets↑
Goodwill↑   Liabilities↑
Cash↓

Goodwill has some special features:

- Goodwill is recorded only by an acquiring company when it purchases another company and pays more for that company than the market value of the net assets acquired (as in our entry above where White purchased Mocha for $2 million more than the market value of Mocha's net assets). An outstanding reputation may create goodwill, but that company never records goodwill for its own business.

- According to GAAP, goodwill is *not* amortized. Instead, the acquiring company measures the fair value of its acquired goodwill each year. If the goodwill has increased in fair value, there is nothing to record. But if goodwill's fair value has decreased, then the company records an impairment loss and writes the goodwill down by debiting (increasing) the Impairment Loss on Goodwill account and crediting (decreasing) the Goodwill account.

Reporting of Intangible Assets

Intangible assets are reported on the balance sheet similarly to plant assets. If a company uses the contra account, Accumulated Amortization, this account is not typically shown on the balance sheet. Instead, intangible assets are shown only at their net book value. Amortization expense is reported on the income statement as part of operations.

Exhibit F:10-11 summarizes our coverage of plant assets, natural resources, and intangibles. Remember that plant assets are those assets that have physical characteristics and are used in operations. Natural resources are assets that come from the physical earth and can be ultimately used up, and intangible assets are assets whose value is not derived from their physical substance.

Exhibit F:10-11 | **Assets and Their Related Expenses**

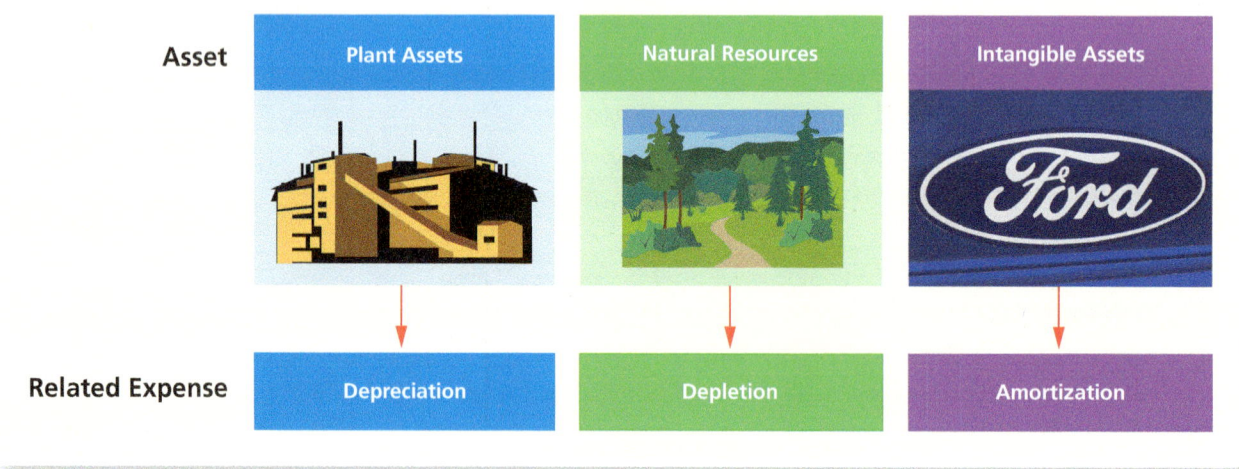

TYING IT ALL TOGETHER

Most of us, at one time or another, have visited a McDonald's. Widely known for its "golden arches," **McDonald's Corporation** is the world's leading global food service retailer with more than 37,000 locations worldwide in more than 120 countries. The corporation operates and franchises McDonald's restaurants, which serve menu items such as the Big Mac, Chicken McNuggets, and McFlurry desserts. In addition, McDonald's also serves McCafé beverages and pastries.

Would McDonald's Corporation report plant assets on its financial statements?

Yes, McDonald's Corporation reports plant assets including buildings, leasehold improvements, and equipment on its balance sheet. The corporation owns real estate in connection with its restaurants and in many cases owns the building. In addition, McDonald's owns the equipment inside restaurants such as the fryers, ovens, and tables.

How do franchises affect McDonald's Corporation?

In addition to owning McDonald's restaurants, the company also franchises restaurants. Approximately 93% of McDonald's restaurants are owned and operated by independent franchisees. When an individual franchises a McDonald's restaurant, the franchisee maintains control over personnel, purchasing, marketing, and pricing decisions while still benefiting from McDonald's global brand. Under a conventional franchise arrangement, McDonald's Corporation owns the land and building. The franchisee purchases the equipment, signs, seating, and décor.

5. On January 1, Orange Manufacturing paid $40,000 for a patent. Although it gives legal protection for 20 years, the patent is expected to provide a competitive advantage for only eight years. Assuming the straight-line method of amortization, record the journal entry for amortization for Year 1.

Check your answer online in MyLab Accounting or at http://www.pearsonhighered.com/Horngren.

For more practice, see Short Exercises S-F:10-12 and S-F:10-13. MyLab Accounting

HOW DO WE USE THE ASSET TURNOVER RATIO TO EVALUATE BUSINESS PERFORMANCE?

The **asset turnover ratio** measures the amount of net sales revenue generated for each average dollar of total assets invested. This ratio measures how well a company is using its assets to generate net sales revenue. To compute this ratio, we divide net sales revenue by average total assets. Using net sales revenue and total assets (in millions) from **Kohl's Corporation's** 2018 Annual Report for the fiscal year ended February 2, 2019 (see **http://www.pearsonhighered.com/Horngren** for a link to the 2018 Annual Report), we can calculate the asset turnover ratio.

Learning Objective 6
Use the asset turnover ratio to evaluate business performance

Asset Turnover Ratio
Measures how efficiently a business uses its average total assets to generate sales. Net sales revenue / Average total assets.

	February 2, 2019	February 3, 2018
Net sales revenue	$ 19,167	$ 19,036
Total assets	12,469	13,389

Asset turnover ratio = Net sales revenue / Average total assets
= $19,167 / [($12,469 + $13,389) / 2]
= 1.48 times

10-30 Financial chapter 10

Suppose that the asset turnover ratio for the industry is 1.90 times. Kohl's asset turnover ratio of 1.48 times is significantly lower than the industry average. This tells us that Kohl's is only producing $1.48 of net sales revenue for each dollar ($1.00) of assets invested while the average company in this industry is producing $1.90 in net sales revenue for every dollar invested in assets. Kohl's should evaluate ways to improve its efficiency and increase its asset turnover ratio, such as increasing net sales revenue or decreasing average total assets. A high asset turnover ratio is desirable.

6. Maxim Company reported beginning and ending total assets of $140,000 and $160,000, respectively. Its net sales revenue for the year was $240,000. What was Maxim's asset turnover ratio?

Check your answer online in MyLab Accounting or at http://www.pearsonhighered.com/Horngren.

For more practice, see Short Exercise S-F:10-14. **MyLab Accounting**

APPENDIX 10A: Exchanging Plant Assets

HOW ARE EXCHANGES OF PLANT ASSETS ACCOUNTED FOR?

Learning Objective 7
Journalize entries for the exchange of plant assets

Commercial Substance
A characteristic of a transaction that causes a change in future cash flows.

Earlier in the chapter, we discussed ways that businesses could dispose of plant assets. One way is for a business to exchange a plant asset for another plant asset. In this section, we evaluate how to account for exchanges that have *commercial substance*. An exchange has **commercial substance** if the future cash flows change as a result of the transaction. In other words, an exchange has commercial substance if, in the future, cash flows (receipts of revenue or payment of expenses) of the business will change because of the exchange. For example, exchanging an older asset for a new asset will increase productivity, thereby creating more revenue for the business. Therefore, this exchange has commercial substance.

Exchanges that have commercial substance require any gain or loss on the transaction to be recognized. The old asset will be removed from the books, and the new asset will be recorded at its market value. Exchanges that lack commercial substance ignore any gain or loss on the transaction, except in limited situations. The new asset is recorded at the old asset's book value plus cash paid and minus cash received instead of at market value.

Exchange of Plant Assets—Gain Situation

Suppose that on December 31, Smart Touch Learning exchanges used equipment for new equipment. The old equipment has a historical cost of $10,000 and accumulated depreciation of $9,000. Its current book value is $1,000 ($10,000 − $9,000). The company acquires the new equipment with a market value of $8,000 and pays cash of $2,000. Assuming this exchange has commercial substance, the gain will be calculated as follows:

Market value of assets received		$ 8,000
Less:		
Book value of asset exchanged	$ 1,000	
Cash paid	2,000	3,000
Gain or (Loss)		$ 5,000

The accounting clerk records the following entry:

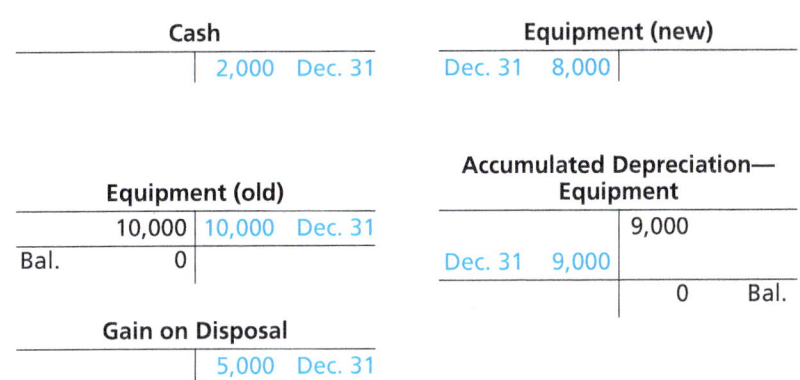

Exchange of Plant Assets—Loss Situation

Suppose instead that on December 31, Smart Touch Learning exchanges used equipment for new equipment. The old equipment has a historical cost of $10,000 and accumulated depreciation of $9,000. Its current book value is $1,000 ($10,000 − $9,000). The company acquires the new equipment with a market value of $3,000 and pays cash of $2,500. Assuming this exchange has commercial substance, the loss will be calculated as follows:

Market value of assets received		$ 3,000
Less:		
Book value of asset exchanged	$ 1,000	
Cash paid	2,500	3,500
Gain or (Loss)		$ (500)

10-32 Financial chapter 10

The accounting clerk records the following entry:

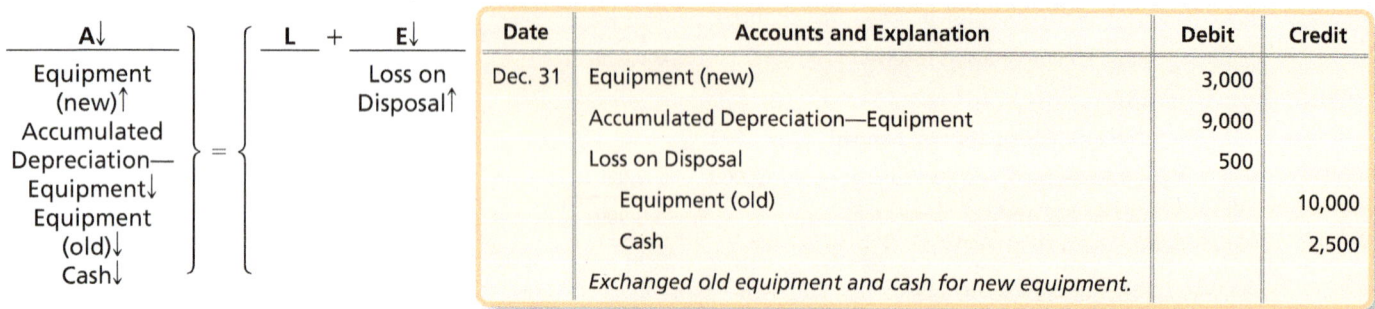

Try It!

7A. Arca Salvage purchased equipment for $10,000. Arca recorded total depreciation of $8,000 on the equipment. Assume that Arca exchanged the old equipment for new equipment, paying $4,000 cash. The fair market value of the new equipment is $5,000. Journalize Arca's exchange of equipment. Assume this exchange has commercial substance.

Check your answer online in MyLab Accounting or at http://www.pearsonhighered.com/Horngren.

For more practice, see Short Exercises S-F:10A-15 and S-F:10A-16.   MyLab Accounting

REVIEW

> Things You Should Know

1. **How does a business measure the cost of property, plant, and equipment?**
   - Property, plant, and equipment are long-lived, tangible assets used in the operations of a business. They are commonly referred to as plant assets.
   - Plant assets are recorded at historical cost—the amount paid for the asset. This includes the purchase price plus taxes, purchase commissions, and all other amounts paid to ready the asset for its intended use.

- A lump-sum purchase involves paying a single price for multiple assets. The cost of each asset purchased must be identified based on the relative-market-value method.
- Two additional types of expenditures are often incurred on plant assets:
  - Capital expenditures—debited to an asset account because they increase the asset's capacity or efficiency or extend the asset's useful life
  - Revenue expenditures—debited to an expense account, such as Repairs and Maintenance Expense, because they are incurred to maintain the asset in working order

2. What is depreciation, and how is it computed?

- Depreciation is the allocation of a plant asset's cost to expense over its useful life.
- Three common depreciation methods are:
  - Straight-line method—allocates an equal amount of depreciation to each year
  - Units-of-production method—allocates a varying amount of depreciation each year based on an asset's usage
  - Double-declining-balance method—an accelerated depreciation method that computes annual depreciation by multiplying the depreciable asset's book value by a constant percent that is two times the straight-line rate
- Modified Accelerated Cost Recovery System (MACRS) is used for tax purposes.
- Occasionally a business may change its estimated residual value or estimated useful life of a depreciable asset. This change requires depreciation to be recalculated in the year of change and moving forward.
- Plant assets are reported on the balance sheet in the Property, Plant, and Equipment section at book value (Cost − Accumulated depreciation).

3. How are disposals of plant assets recorded?

- There are four steps to recording disposals.
  - Step 1: Bring the depreciation up to date.
  - Step 2: Remove the old, disposed-of asset and associated accumulated depreciation from the books.
  - Step 3: Record the value of any cash received (or paid) in the disposal of the asset.
  - Step 4: Determine the amount of any gain or loss. (Market value of assets received compared to the book value of the asset disposed of.)
- Review Exhibit F:10-10 for a summary of disposal of plant assets journal entries.

4. How are natural resources accounted for?

- Natural resources are assets that come from the earth and are consumed. Examples include iron ore, oil, natural gas, diamonds, gold, and timber.
- Depletion is the process by which businesses spread the allocation of a natural resource's cost over its usage.
- Depletion expense is computed by the units-of-production method.

5. **How are intangible assets accounted for?**
   - Intangible assets are assets that have no physical form and are valuable because of special rights they carry. Examples include patents, copyrights, trademarks, franchises, licenses, and goodwill.
   - Amortization is the process by which businesses spread the allocation of an intangible asset's cost over its useful life.
   - Amortization expense is computed by the straight-line method.

6. **How do we use the asset turnover ratio to evaluate business performance?**
   - The asset turnover ratio measures the amount of net sales generated for each average dollar of total assets invested.
   - Net sales / Average total assets.

7. **How are exchanges of plant assets accounted for? (Appendix 10A)**
   - Exchanges that have commercial substance require the recording of any gain or loss on the transaction.
   - Exchanges that lack commercial substance ignore any gain or loss on the transaction, except in a few limited cases.

> Check Your Understanding

Check your understanding of the chapter by completing this problem and then looking at the solution. Use this practice to help identify which sections of the chapter you need to study more.

Latté On Demand purchased a coffee drink machine on January 1, 2024, for $44,000. Expected useful life is 10 years or 100,000 drinks. In 2024, 3,000 drinks were sold, and in 2025, 14,000 drinks were sold. Residual value is $4,000.

Requirements

1. Determine the depreciation expense for 2024 and 2025 using the following methods (See Learning Objective 2):
   a. Straight-line
   b. Units-of-production
   c. Double-declining-balance

2. Prepare a schedule that shows annual depreciation expense, accumulated depreciation, and book value for 2024 and 2025 using the following methods (See Learning Objective 2):
   a. Straight-line
   b. Units-of-production
   c. Double-declining-balance

3. Assume that Latté On Demand sold the equipment for $27,000 cash on July 1, 2026. Assume that management has depreciated the equipment by using the double-declining-balance method. Record Latté On Demand's depreciation for 2026 and the sale of the equipment on July 1, 2026. (See Learning Objective 3)

> Solution

Requirement 1

a.
> 2024: ($44,000 − $4,000) / 10 years = $4,000
> 2025: ($44,000 − $4,000) / 10 years = $4,000

b.
> Depreciation per unit = ($44,000 − $4,000) / 100,000 drinks = $0.40 per drink
> 2024: $0.40 per drink × 3,000 drinks = $1,200
> 2025: $0.40 per drink × 14,000 drinks = $5,600

c.
> 2024: ($44,000 − $0) × 2 × (1 / 10 years) = $8,800
> 2025: ($44,000 − $8,800) × 2 × (1 / 10 years) = $7,040

Requirement 2

a.

Year	Annual Depreciation Expense	Accumulated Depreciation	Book Value
1-1-2024			$ 44,000
12-31-2024	$ 4,000	$ 4,000	40,000
12-31-2025	4,000	8,000	36,000

b.

Year	Annual Depreciation Expense	Accumulated Depreciation	Book Value
1-1-2024			$ 44,000
12-31-2024	$ 1,200	$ 1,200	42,800
12-31-2025	5,600	6,800	37,200

c.

Year	Annual Depreciation Expense	Accumulated Depreciation	Book Value
1-1-2024			$ 44,000
12-31-2024	$ 8,800	$ 8,800	35,200
12-31-2025	7,040	15,840	28,160

Requirement 3

Depreciation expense for 2026:

$$(\$44{,}000 - \$15{,}840) \times 2 \times (1 / 10 \text{ years}) \times (6/12) = \$2{,}816$$

Date	Accounts and Explanation	Debit	Credit
2026			
Jul. 1	Depreciation Expense—Equipment	2,816	
	Accumulated Depreciation—Equipment		2,816
	To record depreciation on equipment.		
1	Cash	27,000	
	Accumulated Depreciation—Equipment ($15,840 + $2,816)	18,656	
	Gain on Disposal		1,656
	Equipment		44,000
	Sold equipment for cash.		

> Key Terms

Accelerated Depreciation Method (p. 10-11)
Amortization (p. 10-25)
Asset Turnover Ratio (p. 10-29)
Book Value (p. 10-10)
Capital Expenditure (p. 10-6)
Capitalize (p. 10-4)
Commercial Substance (p. 10-30) (Appendix 10A)
Copyright (p. 10-26)
Cost Principle (p. 10-3)
Depletion (p. 10-24)
Depreciable Cost (p. 10-9)

Depreciation (p. 10-2)
Double-Declining-Balance Method (p. 10-11)
Extraordinary Repair (p. 10-6)
Franchise (p. 10-27)
Goodwill (p. 10-27)
Impairment (p. 10-25)
Intangible Asset (p. 10-25)
Land Improvement (p. 10-3)
License (p. 10-27)
Modified Accelerated Cost Recovery System (MACRS) (p. 10-14)
Natural Resource (p. 10-24)

Obsolete (p. 10-8)
Patent (p. 10-25)
Property, Plant, and Equipment (PP&E) (p. 10-2)
Relative-Market-Value Method (p. 10-5)
Residual Value (p. 10-9)
Revenue Expenditure (p. 10-6)
Straight-Line Method (p. 10-9)
Trademark (p. 10-27)
Units-of-Production Method (p. 10-10)
Useful Life (p. 10-8)

> Quick Check

1. Which cost is *not* recorded as part of the cost of a building? **Learning Objective 1**
   a. Real estate commission paid to buy the building
   b. Construction materials and labor
   c. Concrete for the building's foundation
   d. Annual building maintenance

2. How should you record a capital expenditure? **Learning Objective 1**
   a. Debit a liability
   b. Debit capital
   c. Debit an expense
   d. Debit an asset

3. Which method almost always produces the most depreciation in the first year? **Learning Objective 2**
   a. Units-of-production
   b. Straight-line
   c. Double-declining-balance
   d. All produce the same depreciation in the first year.

4. A Celty Airline jet costs $28,000,000 and is expected to fly 200,000,000 miles during its 10-year life. Residual value is expected to be zero because the plane was used when acquired. If the plane travels 1,000,000 miles the first year, how much depreciation should Celty Airline record under the units-of-production method? **Learning Objective 2**
   a. $2,800,000
   b. $140,000
   c. $560,000
   d. Cannot be determined from the data given

5. A copy machine costs $45,000 when new and has accumulated depreciation of $44,000. Suppose Print and Photo Center discards this machine and receives nothing. What is the result of the disposal transaction? **Learning Objective 3**
   a. No gain or loss
   b. Gain of $1,000
   c. Loss of $1,000
   d. Loss of $45,000

6. Suppose Print and Photo Center in the preceding question sold the machine for $1,000. What is the result of this disposal transaction? **Learning Objective 3**
   a. Loss of $44,000
   b. Gain of $1,000
   c. Loss of $1,000
   d. No gain or loss

7. Which method is used to compute depletion? **Learning Objective 4**
   a. Double-declining-balance method
   b. Straight-line method
   c. Depletion method
   d. Units-of-production method

8. Which intangible asset is recorded only as part of the acquisition of another company? **Learning Objective 5**
   a. Patent
   b. Goodwill
   c. Copyright
   d. Franchise

Learning Objective 6

9. Liberty Company reported beginning and ending total assets of $25,000 and $22,000, respectively. Its net sales for the year were $18,800. What was Liberty's asset turnover ratio?

   a. 0.75   b. 0.85   c. 0.80   d. 1.25

Learning Objective 7
Appendix 10A

10A. A truck costs $50,000 when new and has accumulated depreciation of $35,000. Suppose Wilson Towing exchanges the truck for a new truck. The new truck has a market value of $60,000, and Wilson pays cash of $40,000. Assume the exchange has commercial substance. What is the result of this exchange?

   a. No gain or loss
   b. Gain of $5,000
   c. Loss of $5,000
   d. Gain of $45,000

Check your answers at the end of the chapter.

ASSESS YOUR PROGRESS

> Review Questions

1. Define property, plant, and equipment. Provide some examples.
2. Plant assets are recorded at historical cost. What does the historical cost of a plant asset include?
3. How do land improvements differ from land?
4. What does the word *capitalize* mean?
5. What is a lump-sum purchase, and how is it accounted for?
6. What is the difference between a capital expenditure and a revenue expenditure? Give an example of each.
7. What is depreciation? Define useful life, residual value, and depreciable cost.
8. Which depreciation method ignores residual value until the last year of depreciation? Why?
9. How does a business decide which depreciation method is best to use?
10. What is the depreciation method that is used for tax accounting purposes? How is it different than the methods that are required by GAAP to be used for financial accounting purposes?
11. If a business changes the estimated useful life or estimated residual value of a plant asset, what must the business do in regard to depreciation expense?
12. What financial statement are property, plant, and equipment reported on, and how?
13. How is discarding of a plant asset different from selling a plant asset?
14. How is gain or loss determined when disposing of plant assets? What situation constitutes a gain? What situation constitutes a loss?
15. What is a natural resource? What is the process by which businesses spread the allocation of a natural resource's cost over its usage?
16. What is an intangible asset? Provide some examples.

17. What is the process by which businesses spread the allocation of an intangible asset's cost over its useful life?

18. What is goodwill? Is goodwill amortized? What happens if the value of goodwill has decreased at the end of the year?

19. What does the asset turnover ratio measure, and how is it calculated?

20A. What does it mean if an exchange of plant assets has commercial substance? Are gains and losses recorded on the books because of the exchange?

> Short Exercises

S-F:10-1 Determining the cost of an asset
Learning Objective 1

Highland Clothing purchased land, paying $96,000 cash and signing a $300,000 note payable. In addition, Highland paid delinquent property tax of $1,100, title insurance costing $600, and $4,600 to level the land and remove an unwanted building. Record the journal entry for purchase of the land.

S-F:10-2 Making a lump-sum asset purchase
Learning Objective 1

Concord Pet Care Clinic paid $210,000 for a group purchase of land, building, and equipment. At the time of the acquisition, the land had a market value of $110,000, the building $88,000, and the equipment $22,000. Journalize the lump-sum purchase of the three assets for a total cost of $210,000, the amount for which the business signed a note payable.

S-F:10-3 Computing first-year depreciation and book value
Learning Objective 2

On January 1, 2024, Air Canadians purchased a used airplane for $37,000,000. Air Canadians expects the plane to remain useful for five years (4,000,000 miles) and to have a residual value of $5,000,000. The company expects the plane to be flown 1,400,000 miles during the first year.

Requirements

1. Compute Air Canadians' *first-year* depreciation expense on the plane using the following methods:
   a. Straight-line
   b. Units-of-production
   c. Double-declining-balance
2. Show the airplane's book value at the end of the first year for all three methods.

S-F:10-4 Computing second-year depreciation and accumulated depreciation
Learning Objective 2

On January 1, 2024, Advanced Airline purchased a used airplane at a cost of $60,500,000. Advanced Airline expects the plane to remain useful for eight years (5,000,000 miles) and to have a residual value of $5,500,000. Advanced Airline expects the plane to be flown 1,100,000 miles the first year and 1,200,000 miles the second year.

Requirements

1. Compute *second-year* (2025) depreciation expense on the plane using the following methods:
   a. Straight-line
   b. Units-of-production
   c. Double-declining-balance
2. Calculate the balance in Accumulated Depreciation at the end of the second year for all three methods.

Learning Objective 2

S-F:10-5 Calculating partial-year depreciation

On February 28, 2023, Rural Tech Support purchased a copy machine for $53,400. Rural Tech Support expects the machine to last for six years and have a residual value of $3,000. Compute depreciation expense on the machine for the year ended December 31, 2023, using the straight-line method.

Learning Objective 2

S-F:10-6 Changing the estimated life of an asset

Assume that Smith's Auto Sales paid $45,000 for equipment with a 15-year life and zero expected residual value. After using the equipment for six years, the company determines that the asset will remain useful for only five more years.

Requirements

1. Record depreciation expense on the equipment for Year 7 by the straight-line method.
2. What is accumulated depreciation at the end of Year 7?

Learning Objective 3

S-F:10-7 Discarding of a fully depreciated asset

On June 15, 2023, Family Furniture discarded equipment that had a cost of $27,000, a residual value of $0, and was fully depreciated. Journalize the disposal of the equipment.

Learning Objective 3

S-F:10-8 Discarding an asset

On October 31, 2024, Alternative Landscapes discarded equipment that had a cost of $26,920. Accumulated Depreciation as of December 31, 2023, was $25,000. Assume annual depreciation on the equipment is $1,920. Journalize the partial-year depreciation expense and disposal of the equipment.

Learning Objective 3

S-F:10-9 Selling an asset at gain or loss

Alpha Communication purchased equipment on January 1, 2024, for $27,500. Suppose Alpha Communication sold the equipment for $20,000 on December 31, 2026. Accumulated Depreciation as of December 31, 2026, was $10,000. Journalize the sale of the equipment, assuming straight-line depreciation was used.

Learning Objective 3

S-F:10-10 Selling an asset at gain or loss

Peter Company purchased equipment on January 1, 2024, for $28,000. Suppose Peter Company sold the equipment for $4,000 on December 31, 2025. Accumulated Depreciation as of December 31, 2025, was $11,000. Journalize the sale of the equipment, assuming straight-line depreciation was used.

S-F:10-11 Accounting for depletion of natural resources

Ajax Petroleum holds huge reserves of oil assets. Assume that at the end of 2024, Ajax Petroleum's cost of oil reserves totaled $27,000,000, representing 3,000,000 barrels of oil.

Requirements

1. Which method does Ajax Petroleum use to compute depletion?
2. Suppose Ajax Petroleum removed and sold 500,000 barrels of oil during 2025. Journalize depletion expense for 2025.

S-F:10-12 Accounting for an intangible asset

On October 1, 2024, Modern Company purchased a patent for $153,600 cash. Although the patent gives legal protection for 20 years, the patent is expected to be used for only eight years.

Requirements

1. Journalize the purchase of the patent.
2. Journalize the amortization expense for the year ended December 31, 2024. Assume straight-line amortization.

S-F:10-13 Accounting for goodwill

Decca Publishing paid $230,000 to acquire *Thrifty Nickel*, a weekly advertising paper. At the time of the acquisition, *Thrifty Nickel*'s balance sheet reported total assets of $130,000 and liabilities of $70,000. The fair market value of *Thrifty Nickel*'s assets was $100,000. The fair market value of *Thrifty Nickel*'s liabilities was $70,000.

Requirements

1. How much goodwill did Decca Publishing purchase as part of the acquisition of *Thrifty Nickel*?
2. Journalize Decca Publishing's acquisition of *Thrifty Nickel*.

S-F:10-14 Computing the asset turnover ratio

Biagas had net sales of $55,600,000 for the year ended May 31, 2024. Its beginning and ending total assets were $52,800,000 and $98,500,000, respectively. Determine Biagas's asset turnover ratio for the year ended May 31, 2024.

S-F:10A-15 Exchanging plant assets

Micron Precision purchased a computer for $2,500, debiting Computer Equipment. During 2022 and 2023, Micron Precision recorded total depreciation of $1,600 on the computer. On January 1, 2024, Micron Precision traded in the computer for a new one, paying $2,100 cash. The fair market value of the new computer is $3,900. Journalize Micron Precision's exchange of computers. Assume the exchange had commercial substance.

S-F:10A-16 Exchanging plant assets

White Company purchased equipment for $22,000. White recorded total depreciation of $19,000 on the equipment. On January 1, 2024, White traded in the equipment for new equipment, paying $23,200 cash. The fair market value of the new equipment is $25,100. Journalize White Company's exchange of equipment. Assume the exchange had commercial substance.

> Exercises

Learning Objective 1

1. Land $333,000

E-F:10-17 Determining the cost of assets

Lawson Furniture purchased land, paying $65,000 cash and signing a $250,000 note payable. In addition, Lawson paid delinquent property tax of $5,000, title insurance costing $4,000, and $9,000 to level the land and remove an unwanted building. The company then constructed an office building at a cost of $400,000. It also paid $54,000 for a fence around the property, $12,000 for a sign near the entrance, and $8,000 for special lighting of the grounds.

Requirements

1. Determine the cost of the land, land improvements, and building.
2. Which of these assets will Lawson depreciate?

Learning Objective 1

Lot 3 $177,500

E-F:10-18 Making a lump-sum purchase of assets

Maplewood Properties bought three lots in a subdivision for a lump-sum price. An independent appraiser valued the lots as follows:

Lot	Appraised Value
1	$ 144,000
2	96,000
3	240,000

Maplewood paid $355,000 in cash. Record the purchase in the journal, identifying each lot's cost in a separate Land account. Round decimals to two places, and use the computed percentages throughout.

Learning Objective 1

E-F:10-19 Distinguishing capital expenditures from revenue expenditures

Consider the following expenditures:

a. Purchase price.

b. Ordinary recurring repairs to keep the machinery in good working order.

c. Lubrication before machinery is placed in service.

d. Periodic lubrication after machinery is placed in service.

e. Major overhaul to extend useful life by three years.

f. Sales tax paid on the purchase price.

g. Transportation and insurance while machinery is in transit from seller to buyer.

h. Installation.

i. Training of personnel for initial operation of the machinery.

Classify each of the expenditures as a capital expenditure or a revenue expenditure related to machinery.

E-F:10-20 Computing depreciation—three methods

Crispy Fried Chicken bought equipment on January 2, 2024, for $33,000. The equipment was expected to remain in service for four years and to operate for 6,750 hours. At the end of the equipment's useful life, Crispy's estimates that its residual value will be $6,000. The equipment operated for 675 hours the first year, 2,025 hours the second year, 2,700 hours the third year, and 1,350 hours the fourth year.

Learning Objective 2

1. Double-declining-balance, 12/31/25, Dep. Exp. $8,250

Requirements

1. Prepare a schedule of *depreciation expense, accumulated depreciation,* and *book value* per year for the equipment under the three depreciation methods: straight-line, units-of-production, and double-declining-balance. Show your computations. *Note: Three depreciation schedules must be prepared.*
2. Which method tracks the wear and tear on the equipment most closely?

E-F:10-21 Changing an asset's useful life and residual value

Salem Hardware Consultants purchased a building for $540,000 and depreciated it on a straight-line basis over a 40-year period. The estimated residual value is $100,000. After using the building for 15 years, Salem realized that wear and tear on the building would wear it out before 40 years and that the estimated residual value should be $88,000. Starting with the 16th year, Salem began depreciating the building over a revised total life of 35 years using the new residual value. Journalize depreciation expense on the building for years 15 and 16.

Learning Objective 2

Yr. 16 $14,350

E-F:10-22 Recording partial-year depreciation and sale of an asset

On January 2, 2023, Comfy Clothing Consignments purchased showroom fixtures for $17,000 cash, expecting the fixtures to remain in service for five years. Comfy has depreciated the fixtures on a double-declining-balance basis, with zero residual value. On October 31, 2024, Comfy sold the fixtures for $7,600 cash. Record both depreciation expense for 2024 and sale of the fixtures on October 31, 2024.

Learning Objectives 2, 3

Depr. Exp. $3,400

E-F:10-23 Recording partial-year depreciation and sale of an asset

On January 2, 2022, Pet Spa purchased fixtures for $37,800 cash, expecting the fixtures to remain in service for six years. Pet Spa has depreciated the fixtures on a straight-line basis, with $9,000 residual value. On May 31, 2024, Pet Spa sold the fixtures for $24,200 cash. Record both depreciation expense for 2024 and sale of the fixtures on May 31, 2024.

Learning Objectives 2, 3

Loss $(2,000)

E-F:10-24 Journalizing natural resource depletion

Cannon Mountain Mining paid $462,300 for the right to extract mineral assets from a 400,000-ton deposit. In addition to the purchase price, Cannon also paid a $900 filing fee, a $1,800 license fee to the state of Nevada, and $55,000 for a geological survey of the property. Because Cannon purchased the rights to the minerals only and did not purchase the land, it expects the asset to have zero residual value. During the first year, Cannon removed and sold 50,000 tons of the minerals. Make journal entries to record (a) purchase of the minerals (debit Minerals), (b) payment of fees and other costs, and (c) depletion for the first year.

Learning Objective 4

Depletion per unit = $1.30 per ton

E-F:10-25 Handling acquisition of patent, amortization, and change in useful life

Melbourn Printers (MP) manufactures printers. Assume that MP recently paid $200,000 for a patent on a new laser printer. Although it gives legal protection for 20 years, the patent is expected to provide a competitive advantage for only eight years.

Learning Objectives 2, 5

2. Amort. Exp. $50,000

Requirements

1. Assuming the straight-line method of amortization, make journal entries to record (a) the purchase of the patent and (b) amortization for the first full year.
2. After using the patent for four years, MP learns at an industry trade show that another company is designing a more efficient printer. On the basis of this new information, MP decides, starting with Year 5, to amortize the remaining cost of the patent over two remaining years, giving the patent a total useful life of six years. Record amortization for Year 5.

Learning Objective 5

1. Goodwill $1,000,000

E-F:10-26 Measuring and recording goodwill

Princeton has acquired several other companies. Assume that Princeton purchased Kelleher for $9,000,000 cash. The book value of Kelleher's assets is $19,000,000 (market value, $20,000,000), and it has liabilities of $12,000,000 (market value, $12,000,000).

Requirements

1. Compute the cost of the goodwill purchased by Princeton.
2. Record the purchase of Kelleher by Princeton.

Learning Objective 6

E-F:10-27 Computing asset turnover ratio

Blackerby Photo reported the following figures on its December 31, 2024, income statement and balance sheet:

Net sales		$ 441,000	
		Dec. 31, 2024	Dec. 31, 2023
Cash		$ 31,000	$ 30,000
Accounts Receivable		68,000	65,000
Merchandise Inventory		80,000	79,000
Prepaid Expenses		16,000	5,000
Property, Plant, and Equipment, net		175,000	18,000

Compute the asset turnover ratio for 2024. Round to two decimal places.

Learning Objective 7
Appendix 10A

2. Loss $(7,000)

E-F:10A-28 Exchanging assets—two situations

Partner Bank recently traded in office fixtures. Here are the facts:

Old fixtures:	New fixtures:
Cost, $91,000	Cash paid, $110,000
Accumulated depreciation, $68,000	Market value, $133,000

Requirements

1. Record Partner Bank's trade-in of old fixtures for new ones. Assume the exchange had commercial substance.
2. Now let's change one fact. Partner Bank feels compelled to do business with Elm Furniture, a bank customer, even though the bank can get the fixtures elsewhere at a better price. Partner Bank is aware that the new fixtures' market value is only $126,000. Record the trade-in. Assume the exchange had commercial substance.

E-F:10A-29 Measuring asset cost, units-of-production depreciation, and asset trade

Learning Objectives 1, 2, 7
Appendix 10A

1. $11,880

Wimot Trucking Company uses the units-of-production depreciation method because units-of-production best measures wear and tear on the trucks. Consider these facts about one Mack truck in the company's fleet.

When acquired in 2021, the rig cost $360,000 and was expected to remain in service for 10 years or 1,000,000 miles. Estimated residual value was $90,000. The truck was driven 80,000 miles in 2021, 120,000 miles in 2022, and 160,000 miles in 2023. After 44,000 miles, on March 15, 2024, the company traded in the Mack truck for a less expensive Freightliner. Wimot also paid cash of $20,000. Fair market value of the Mack truck was equal to its net book value on the date of the trade.

Requirements

1. Record the journal entry for depreciation expense in 2024.
2. Determine Wimot's cost of the new truck.
3. Record the journal entry for the exchange of assets on March 15, 2024. Assume the exchange had commercial substance.

> Problems Group A

P-F:10-30A Determining asset cost and recording partial-year depreciation, straight-line

Learning Objectives 1, 2

1. Bldg. $461,100

Discount Parking, near an airport, incurred the following costs to acquire land, make land improvements, and construct and furnish a small building:

a. Purchase price of three acres of land	$ 80,000
b. Delinquent real estate taxes on the land to be paid by Discount Parking	6,300
c. Additional dirt and earthmoving	9,000
d. Title insurance on the land acquisition	3,200
e. Fence around the boundary of the property	9,600
f. Building permit for the building	1,000
g. Architect's fee for the design of the building	20,700
h. Signs near the front of the property	9,300
i. Materials used to construct the building	215,000
j. Labor to construct the building	175,000
k. Interest cost on construction loan for the building	9,400
l. Parking lots on the property	28,500
m. Lights for the parking lots	11,200
n. Salary of construction supervisor (80% to building; 20% to parking lot and concrete walks)	50,000
o. Furniture	11,200
p. Transportation of furniture from seller to the building	2,200
q. Additional fencing	6,600

Discount Parking depreciates land improvements over 15 years, buildings over 40 years, and furniture over 10 years, all on a straight-line basis with zero residual value.

Requirements

1. Set up columns for Land, Land Improvements, Building, and Furniture. Show how to account for each cost by listing the cost under the correct account. Determine the total cost of each asset.

2. All construction was complete and the assets were placed in service on October 1. Record partial-year depreciation expense for the year ended December 31. Round to the nearest dollar.

Learning Objectives 1, 2

1. Units-of-production, 12/31/24, Dep. Exp. $24,000

P-F:10-31A Determining asset cost, preparing depreciation schedules (three methods), and identifying depreciation results that meet management objectives

On January 3, 2024, Rapid Delivery Service purchased a truck at a cost of $100,000. Before placing the truck in service, Rapid spent $3,000 painting it, $600 replacing tires, and $10,400 overhauling the engine. The truck should remain in service for five years and have a residual value of $12,000. The truck's annual mileage is expected to be 32,000 miles in each of the first four years and 8,000 miles in the fifth year—136,000 miles in total. In deciding which depreciation method to use, Andy Sargeant, the general manager, requests a depreciation schedule for each of the depreciation methods (straight-line, units-of-production, and double-declining-balance).

Requirements

1. Prepare a depreciation schedule for each depreciation method, showing asset cost, depreciation expense, accumulated depreciation, and asset book value.

2. Rapid prepares financial statements using the depreciation method that reports the highest net income in the early years of asset use. Consider the first year that Rapid uses the truck. Identify the depreciation method that meets the company's objectives.

Learning Objectives 1, 2, 3

Sep. 1 Gain $193,250

P-F:10-32A Recording lump-sum asset purchases, depreciation, and disposals

Ellie Johnson Associates surveys American eating habits. The company's accounts include Land, Buildings, Office Equipment, and Communication Equipment, with a separate Accumulated Depreciation account for each depreciable asset. During 2024, Ellie Johnson Associates completed the following transactions:

Jan. 1	Purchased office equipment, $113,000. Paid $80,000 cash and financed the remainder with a note payable.
Apr. 1	Acquired land and communication equipment in a lump-sum purchase. Total cost was $310,000 paid in cash. An independent appraisal valued the land at $244,125 and the communication equipment at $81,375.
Sep. 1	Sold a building that cost $520,000 (accumulated depreciation of $285,000 through December 31 of the preceding year). Ellie Johnson Associates received $420,000 cash from the sale of the building. Depreciation is computed on a straight-line basis. The building has a 40-year useful life and a residual value of $25,000.
Dec. 31	Recorded depreciation as follows:
	Communication equipment is depreciated by the straight-line method over a five-year life with zero residual value.
	Office equipment is depreciated using the double-declining-balance method over five years with a $1,000 residual value.

Record the transactions in the journal of Ellie Johnson Associates.

P-F:10-33A Accounting for natural resources

Conseco Oil has an account titled Oil and Gas Properties. Conseco paid $6,600,000 for oil reserves holding an estimated 1,000,000 barrels of oil. Assume the company paid $570,000 for additional geological tests of the property and $450,000 to prepare for drilling. During the first year, Conseco removed and sold 72,000 barrels of oil. Record all of Conseco's transactions, including depletion for the first year.

Learning Objective 4

Depl. Exp. $548,640

P-F:10-34A Accounting for intangibles

Midtown Telecom, a communication service provider in Iowa, Nebraska, the Dakotas, and Montana had the following transactions related to its intangibles during the year:

Learning Objective 5

1. Goodwill $620,000

Feb. 13	Midtown Telecom purchased Samson Wireless Enterprises for $480,000 cash plus a $720,000 note payable. Samson's book value of assets was $700,000. Samson's market value of assets and liabilities was $1,100,000 and $520,000, respectively.
Apr. 1	Paid $400,000 to acquire a patent. Midtown believes the patent's useful life will be 10 years.
Oct. 1	Paid $820,000 for the trademark, "Fast as Lightning," with a useful life of 20 years.
Dec. 31	Recorded amortization expense (separately) for the patent and trademark.

Requirements

1. Journalize the entries to record Midtown Telecom's transactions during the year.
2. What special asset does Midtown Telecom's acquisition of Samson Wireless identify? How should Midtown Telecom account for this asset after acquiring Midtown Wireless? Explain in detail.

P-F:10A-35A Journalizing partial-year depreciation and asset disposals and exchanges

During 2024, Mora Company completed the following transactions:

Learning Objectives 2, 3, 7
Appendix 10A

Jan. 1 Gain $8,000

Jan. 1	Traded in old office equipment with book value of $55,000 (cost of $127,000 and accumulated depreciation of $72,000) for new equipment. Mora also paid $70,000 in cash. Fair value of new equipment is $133,000. Assume the exchange had commercial substance.
Apr. 1	Sold equipment that cost $18,000 (accumulated depreciation of $8,000 through December 31 of the preceding year). Mora received $6,100 cash from the sale of the equipment. Depreciation is computed on a straight-line basis. The equipment has a five-year useful life and a residual value of $0.
Dec. 31	Recorded depreciation as follows: Office equipment is depreciated using the double-declining-balance method over four years with a $9,000 residual value.

Record the transactions in the journal of Mora Company.

> Problems Group B

Learning Objectives 1, 2

1. Bldg. $483,500

P-F:10-36B Determining asset cost and recording partial-year depreciation

Safe Parking, near an airport, incurred the following costs to acquire land, make land improvements, and construct and furnish a small building:

a.	Purchase price of three acres of land	$ 86,000
b.	Delinquent real estate taxes on the land to be paid by Safe Parking	6,300
c.	Additional dirt and earthmoving	8,400
d.	Title insurance on the land acquisition	3,400
e.	Fence around the boundary of the property	9,600
f.	Building permit for the building	900
g.	Architect's fee for the design of the building	20,100
h.	Signs near the front of the property	9,000
i.	Materials used to construct the building	217,000
j.	Labor to construct the building	172,000
k.	Interest cost on construction loan for the building	9,500
l.	Parking lots on the property	29,400
m.	Lights for the parking lots	11,600
n.	Salary of construction supervisor (80% to building; 20% to parking lot and concrete walks)	80,000
o.	Furniture	11,700
p.	Transportation of furniture from seller to the building	1,900
q.	Additional fencing	6,900

Safe Parking depreciates land improvements over 15 years, buildings over 40 years, and furniture over 10 years, all on a straight-line basis with zero residual value.

Requirements

1. Set up columns for Land, Land Improvements, Building, and Furniture. Show how to account for each cost by listing the cost under the correct account. Determine the total cost of each asset.
2. All construction was complete and the assets were placed in service on September 1. Record partial-year depreciation expense for the year ended December 31. Round to the nearest dollar.

Learning Objectives 1, 2

1. Units-of-production, 12/31/24, Dep. Exp. $15,000

P-F:10-37B Determining asset cost, preparing depreciation schedules (three methods), and identifying depreciation results that meet management objectives

On January 3, 2024, Speedy Delivery Service purchased a truck at a cost of $67,000. Before placing the truck in service, Speedy spent $3,000 painting it, $1,200 replacing tires, and $3,500 overhauling the engine. The truck should remain in service for five years and have a residual value of $5,100. The truck's annual mileage is expected to be 20,000 miles in each of the first four years and 12,800 miles in the fifth year—92,800 miles in total. In deciding which depreciation method to use, Alec Rivera, the general manager, requests a depreciation schedule for each of the depreciation methods (straight-line, units-of-production, and double-declining-balance).

Requirements

1. Prepare a depreciation schedule for each depreciation method, showing asset cost, depreciation expense, accumulated depreciation, and asset book value.
2. Speedy prepares financial statements using the depreciation method that reports the highest net income in the early years of asset use. Consider the first year that Speedy uses the truck. Identify the depreciation method that meets the company's objectives.

P-F:10-38B Recording lump-sum asset purchases, depreciation, and disposals

Learning Objectives 1, 2, 3

Sep. 1 Gain $163,250

Whitney Plumb Associates surveys American eating habits. The company's accounts include Land, Buildings, Office Equipment, and Communication Equipment, with a separate Accumulated Depreciation account for each asset. During 2024, Whitney Plumb completed the following transactions:

Jan. 1	Purchased office equipment, $117,000. Paid $77,000 cash and financed the remainder with a note payable.
Apr. 1	Acquired land and communication equipment in a lump-sum purchase. Total cost was $350,000 paid in cash. An independent appraisal valued the land at $275,625 and the communication equipment at $91,875.
Sep. 1	Sold a building that cost $520,000 (accumulated depreciation of $285,000 through December 31 of the preceding year). Whitney Plumb received $390,000 cash from the sale of the building. Depreciation is computed on a straight-line basis. The building has a 40-year useful life and a residual value of $25,000.
Dec. 31	Recorded depreciation as follows:
	Communication equipment is depreciated by the straight-line method over a five-year life with zero residual value.
	Office equipment is depreciated using the double-declining-balance method over five years with a $2,000 residual value.

Record the transactions in the journal of Whitney Plumb Associates.

P-F:10-39B Accounting for natural resources

Learning Objective 4

Depl. Exp. $1,383,750

Donahue Oil has an account titled Oil and Gas Properties. Donahue paid $6,400,000 for oil reserves holding an estimated 400,000 barrels of oil. Assume the company paid $510,000 for additional geological tests of the property and $470,000 to prepare for drilling. During the first year, Donahue removed and sold 75,000 barrels of oil. Record all of Donahue's transactions, including depletion for the first year.

Learning Objective 5

1. Goodwill $10,000

P-F:10-40B Accounting for intangibles

Central States Telecom provides communication services in Iowa, Nebraska, the Dakotas, and Montana and had the following transactions during the year:

Mar. 28	Central States purchased Swift Wireless Company for $280,000 cash plus a $420,000 note payable. Swift's book value of assets was $700,000. Swift's market value of assets and liabilities was $1,200,000 and $510,000, respectively.
July 1	Paid $62,000 to acquire a patent. Central States believes the patent's useful life will be eight years.
Aug. 1	Paid $240,000 for the trademark, "Fast as Lightning," with a useful life of 16 years.
Dec. 31	Recorded amortization expense (separately) for the patent and trademark.

Requirements

1. Journalize the entry to record Central States' transactions during the year.
2. What special asset does Central States' acquisition of Swift Wireless identify? How should Central States Telecom account for this asset after acquiring Swift Wireless? Explain in detail.

Learning Objectives 2, 3, 7
Appendix 10A

Jan. 1 Gain $6,000

P-F:10A-41B Journalizing partial-year depreciation and asset disposals and exchanges

During 2024, Lora Company completed the following transactions:

Jan. 1	Traded in old office equipment with book value of $55,000 (cost of $129,000 and accumulated depreciation of $74,000) for new equipment. Lora also paid $55,000 in cash. Fair value of new equipment is $116,000. Assume the exchange had commercial substance.
Apr. 1	Sold equipment that cost $12,000 (accumulated depreciation of $1,000 through December 31 of the preceding year). Lora received $7,100 cash from the sale of the equipment. Depreciation is computed on a straight-line basis. The equipment has a five-year useful life and a residual value of $0.
Dec. 31	Recorded depreciation as follows: Office equipment is depreciated using the double-declining-balance method over four years with a $7,000 residual value.

Record the transactions in the journal of Lora Company.

CRITICAL THINKING

> Using Excel

Download Excel problems for this chapter online in MyLab Accounting or at **http://www.pearsonhighered.com/Horngren**.

> Continuing Problem

P-F:10-42 Calculating and journalizing partial-year depreciation

This problem continues the Canyon Canoe Company situation from Chapter F:9. Amber Wilson is continuing to review business practices. Currently, she is reviewing the company's property, plant, and equipment and has gathered the following information:

Asset	Acquisition Date	Cost	Estimated Life	Estimated Residual Value	Depreciation Method*	Monthly Depreciation Expense
Canoes	Nov. 3, 2024	$ 4,800	4 years	$ 0	SL	$ 100
Land	Dec. 1, 2024	85,000			n/a	
Building	Dec. 1, 2024	35,000	5 years	5,000	SL	500
Canoes	Dec. 2, 2024	7,200	4 years	0	SL	150
Computer	Mar. 2, 2025	3,600	3 years	300	DDB	
Office Furniture	Mar. 3, 2025	3,000	5 years	600	SL	

*SL = Straight-line; DDB = Double-declining-balance

Requirements

1. Calculate the amount of monthly depreciation expense for the computer and office furniture for 2025.

2. For each asset, determine the book value as of December 31, 2024. Then, calculate the depreciation expense for the first six months of 2025 and the book value as of June 30, 2025.

3. Prepare a partial balance sheet showing Property, Plant, and Equipment as of June 30, 2025.

COMPREHENSIVE PROBLEM

> Comprehensive Problem for Chapters F:8, F:9, and F:10

Top Quality Appliance—Long Beach has just purchased a franchise from Top Quality Appliance (TQA). TQA is a manufacturer of kitchen appliances. TQA markets its products via retail stores that are operated as franchises. As a TQA franchisee, Top Quality Appliance—Long Beach will receive many benefits, including having the exclusive right to sell TQA brand appliances in Long Beach. TQA appliances have an excellent reputation and the TQA name and logo are readily recognized by consumers. TQA also manages national television advertising campaigns that benefit the franchisees. In exchange for these benefits, Top Quality Appliance—Long Beach will pay an annual franchise fee to TQA based on a percentage of sales. The annual franchise fee is a separate cost and in addition to the purchase of the franchise.

In addition to purchasing the franchise, Top Quality Appliance—Long Beach will also purchase land with an existing building to use for its retail store, store fixtures, and office equipment. The business will purchase appliances from TQA and resell them in its store, primarily to local building contractors for installation in new homes.

Following is the chart of accounts for Top Quality Appliance—Long Beach. As a new business, all beginning balances are $0.

Top Quality Appliance—Long Beach
Chart of Accounts

Cash	Baker, Capital
Petty Cash	Baker, Withdrawals
Accounts Receivable	Sales Revenue
Allowance for Bad Debts	Interest Revenue
Merchandise Inventory	Cost of Goods Sold
Office Supplies	Franchise Fee Expense
Prepaid Insurance	Salaries Expense
Interest Receivable	Utilities Expense
Notes Receivable	Insurance Expense
Land	Supplies Expense
Building	Bad Debt Expense
Accumulated Depreciation—Building	Bank Expense
Store Fixtures	Credit Card Expense
Accumulated Depreciation—Store Fixtures	Depreciation Expense—Building
Office Equipment	Depreciation Expense—Store Fixtures
Accumulated Depreciation—Office Equipment	Depreciation Expense—Office Equipment
Franchise	Amortization Expense—Franchise
Accounts Payable	Interest Expense
Interest Payable	Cash Short and Over
Notes Payable	

Top Quality Appliance—Long Beach completed the following transactions during 2024, its first year of operations:

a.	Received $500,000 cash from owner, T. Baker, in exchange for capital. Opened a new checking account at Long Beach National Bank and deposited the cash received from the owner.
b.	Paid $50,000 cash for a TQA franchise.
c.	Paid $200,000 cash and issued a $400,000, 10-year, 5% notes payable for land with an existing building. The assets had the following market values: Land, $100,000; Building, $500,000.
d.	Paid $75,000 for store fixtures.
e.	Paid $45,000 for office equipment.
f.	Paid $600 for office supplies.
g.	Paid $3,600 for a two-year insurance policy.
h.	Purchased appliances from TQA (merchandise inventory) on account for $425,000.
i.	Established a petty cash fund for $150.
j.	Sold appliances on account to B&B Contractors for $215,000, terms n/30 (cost, $86,000).
k.	Sold appliances to Davis Contracting for $150,000 (cost, $65,000), receiving a 6-month, 8% note.
l.	Recorded credit card sales of $80,000 (cost, $35,000), net of processor fee of 2%.
m.	Received payment in full from B&B Contractors.
n.	Purchased appliances from TQA on account for $650,000.
o.	Made payment on account to TQA, $300,000.
p.	Sold appliances for cash to LB Home Builders for $350,000 (cost, $175,000).
q.	Received payment in full on the maturity date from Davis Contracting for the note.
r.	Sold appliances to Leard Contracting for $265,000 (cost, $130,000), receiving a 9-month, 8% note.
s.	Made payment on account to TQA, $500,000.
t.	Sold appliances on account to various businesses for $985,000, terms n/30 (cost, $395,000).
u.	Collected $715,000 cash on account.
v.	Paid cash for expenses: Salaries, $180,000; Utilities, $12,650.
w.	Replenished the petty cash fund when the fund had $62 in cash and petty cash tickets for $85 for office supplies.
x.	Baker withdrew $5,000.
y.	Paid the franchise fee to TQA of 5% of total sales of $2,045,000.

Requirements

1. Record the transactions in the general journal. Omit explanations.
2. Post to the general ledger.
3. It is a common business practice to reconcile the bank accounts on a monthly basis. However, in this problem, the reconciliation of the company's checking account will be done at the end of the year, based on an annual summary.

    Reconcile the bank account by comparing the following annual summary statement from Long Beach National Bank to the Cash account in the general ledger. Record journal entries as needed and post to the general ledger. Use transaction z as the posting reference.

Beginning Balance, January 1, 2024			$ 0
Deposits and other credits:			
		$ 500,000	
		78,400	
		215,000	
		350,000	
		715,000	
Interest Revenue		1,565	1,859,965
Checks and other debits:			
EFT to Bank Checks[1]		125	
Checks:		50,000	
		200,000	
		45,000	
		75,000	
		150	
		3,600	
		600	
		300,000	
		500,000	
		192,650	
Bank service charge		2,340	(1,369,465)
Ending balance, December 31, 2024			$ 490,500

[1] Bank Checks is a company that prints business checks (considered a bank expense) for Top Quality Appliance—Long Beach.

4. In preparation for preparing the adjusting entries, complete depreciation schedules for the first five years for the depreciable plant assets, assuming the assets were purchased on January 2, 2024:

   a. Building, straight-line, 30 years, $50,000 residual value.
   b. Store Fixtures, straight-line, 15 years, no residual value.
   c. Office Equipment, double-declining-balance, five years, $5,000 residual value.

5. Record adjusting entries for the year ended December 31, 2024:

   a. One year of the prepaid insurance has expired.
   b. Management estimates that 5% of Accounts Receivable will be uncollectible.
   c. An inventory of office supplies indicates $475 of supplies have been used.
   d. Calculate the interest earned on the outstanding Leard Contracting note receivable. Assume the note was received on October 31. Round to the nearest dollar.
   e. Record depreciation expense for the year.
   f. Record amortization expense for the year on the franchise, which has a 10-year life.
   g. Calculate the interest owed on the note payable. Assume the note was issued on January 1.

6. Post adjusting entries and prepare an adjusted trial balance.

7. Prepare a multi-step income statement and statement of owner's equity for the year ended December 31, 2024. Prepare a classified balance sheet as of December 31, 2024. Assume Interest Receivable is a current asset and Interest Payable is a current liability.

8. Evaluate the company's success for the first year of operations by calculating the following ratios. Round to two decimal places. Comment on the results.

   a. Liquidity:
      i. Current ratio
      ii. Acid-test ratio
      iii. Cash ratio

   b. Efficiency:
      i. Accounts receivable turnover
      ii. Day's sales in receivables
      iii. Asset turnover
      iv. Rate of return on total assets

> Tying It All Together Case F:10-1

Before you begin this assignment, review the Tying It All Together feature in the chapter. It will also be helpful if you review McDonald's Corporation 2018 annual report (**https://www.sec.gov/ix?doc=/Archives/edgar/data/63908/000006390819000010/mcd-12312018x10k.htm**).

McDonald's Corporation is the world's leading global food service retailer with more than 37,000 locations worldwide in more than 120 countries. The corporation operates and franchises McDonald's restaurants, which serve menu items such as the Big Mac, Chicken McNuggets, and McFlurry desserts. In addition, McDonald's also serves McCafé beverages and pastries.

Requirements

1. Where would McDonald's Corporation report plant assets on its financial statements? How are plant assets reported and what is the value as of December 31, 2018?
2. Does McDonald's Corporation depreciate its plant assets? How do you know? What is the depreciation method used and the useful lives?
3. How is the book value of plant assets calculated? What is the net book value of McDonald's plant assets as of December 31, 2018?
4. What type of intangibles would be included on McDonald's financial statements and where?
5. What is goodwill? Does McDonald's Corporation report goodwill? If so, how much goodwill is reported as of December 31, 2018? What does McDonald's goodwill primarily result from?

> Ethical Issue F:10-1

Western Bank & Trust purchased land and a building for the lump sum of $3,000,000. To get the maximum tax deduction, Western allocated 90% of the purchase price to the building and only 10% to the land. A more realistic allocation would have been 70% to the building and 30% to the land.

Requirements

1. Explain the tax advantage of allocating too much to the building and too little to the land.
2. Was Western's allocation ethical? If so, state why. If not, why not? Identify who was harmed.

> Fraud Case F:10-1

Jim Reed manages a fleet of utility trucks for a rural county government. He's been in his job for 30 years, and he knows where the angles are. He makes sure that when new trucks are purchased, the residual value is set as low as possible. Then, when they become fully depreciated, they are sold off by the county at residual value. Jim makes sure his buddies in the construction business are first in line for the bargain sales, and they make sure he gets a little something back. Recently, a new county commissioner was elected with vows to cut expenses for the taxpayers. Unlike other commissioners, this man has a business degree, and he is coming to visit Jim tomorrow.

Requirements

1. When a business sells a fully depreciated asset for its residual value, is a gain or loss recognized?
2. How do businesses determine what residual values to use for their various assets? Are there "hard and fast" rules for residual values?
3. How would an organization prevent the kind of fraud depicted here?

> Financial Statement Case F:10-1

View a link to **Target Corporation's** Fiscal 2018 annual report at **http://www.pearsonhighered.com/Horngren**. Refer to the Target Corporation financial statements, including Notes 11, 12, and 13. Answer the following questions.

Requirements

1. Which depreciation method does Target Corporation use for reporting in the financial statements?
2. What was the amount of depreciation and amortization expense for the year ending February 2, 2019?
3. The statement of cash flows reports the cash purchases of property, plant, and equipment. How much were Target's additions to property, plant, and equipment during the year ending February 2, 2019? Did Target record any proceeds from the sale of property, plant, and equipment?
4. What was the amount of accumulated depreciation at February 2, 2019? What was the net book value of property, plant, and equipment for Target as of February 2, 2019?
5. Compute Target's asset turnover ratio for year ending February 2, 2019. Round to two decimal places. How does Target's ratio compare with that of **Kohl's Corporation?**

> Communication Activity F:10-1

In 150 words or fewer, explain the different methods that can be used to calculate depreciation. Your explanation should include how to calculate depreciation expense using each method.

> Quick Check Answers

1. d **2.** d **3.** c **4.** b **5.** c **6.** d **7.** d **8.** b **9.** c **10A.** b

Current Liabilities and Payroll

11

How Much Does One Employee Cost?

Mary Green, MD, recently opened a health care clinic, Family Medicine, that serves low-income families and uninsured individuals. Family Medicine prides itself on keeping its costs low but still providing excellent health care to its patients. When Mary opened the clinic, she hired only one part-time nurse. Now, with the clinic growing, Mary is considering hiring several more nurses and another doctor.

Mary knows that having employees is expensive. Not only does the business have to pay their wages, but there are additional payroll taxes that must be paid. As Mary is deciding what salary to offer her new employees, she must consider these additional costs. She knows that if she offers the new doctor a salary of $100,000, the business will end up paying more than $100,000. This is because of additional payroll taxes such as Social Security and unemployment compensation. In addition, Family Medicine will need to offer health care and retirement benefits to each employee. All of these extra expenses cost money—money she could be saving. But Mary knows that in order to provide the quality of service her patients expect, she must pay the cost of having quality employees.

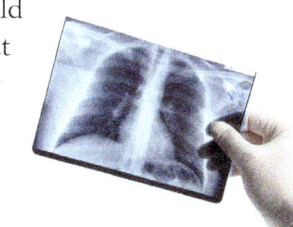

How Do Businesses Account for Current Liabilities and Payroll?

We now begin our focus on liabilities, or debts, a business owes. Payroll is one of those liabilities. Companies such as **UnitedHealth Group Incorporated,** a leading health care company that provides health care benefits, value hiring smart, committed, and talented people. Part of UnitedHealth's recruiting package is the salary it offers employees. In addition, UnitedHealth Group also offers benefits such as vacation, health care, and retirement to reward its employees. Payroll and employee benefits are reported as current liabilities on the balance sheet until the company makes payment. In this chapter, we look at how businesses, such as UnitedHealth Group, account for and record payroll and other current liabilities.

Chapter 11 Learning Objectives

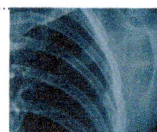

1. Account for current liabilities of known amount
2. Calculate and journalize basic payroll transactions
3. Account for current liabilities that must be estimated
4. Account for contingent liabilities
5. Use the times-interest-earned ratio to evaluate business performance

Up to this point, we've been focusing on all the assets a business owns. But what about the bills a business owes? A business needs to know what it owes (liabilities) and by what date they have to be paid. Why? To be sure the business has cash on hand to pay these bills. In this chapter, we focus on some common current liabilities a business may owe. As with other chapters, we'll continue to focus on Smart Touch Learning and see how it manages its current liabilities.

HOW ARE CURRENT LIABILITIES OF KNOWN AMOUNTS ACCOUNTED FOR?

Learning Objective 1
Account for current liabilities of known amount

Liabilities are debts that are owed to creditors. Liabilities have three main characteristics:

1. They occur because of a past transaction or event.
2. They create a present obligation for future payment of cash or services.
3. They are an unavoidable obligation.

Liabilities
Debts that are owed to creditors.

Current Liability
A liability that must be paid with cash or with goods and services within one year or within the entity's operating cycle, whichever is longer.

Liabilities can be split into two main categories: current and long-term. In this chapter, we discuss current liabilities. **Current liabilities** must be paid either with cash or with goods and services within one year or within the entity's operating cycle if the cycle is longer than a year.

Accounts Payable, Notes Payable due within one year, Salaries Payable, Interest Payable, and Unearned Revenue are all current liabilities. Any portion of a long-term liability that is due within the next year is also reported as a current liability. Current liabilities are listed on the balance sheet in the order in which they are due.

Long-term Liability
A liability that does not need to be paid within one year or within the entity's operating cycle, whichever is longer.

Long-term liabilities are liabilities that do not need to be paid within one year or within the entity's operating cycle, whichever is longer. Many Notes Payable are long-term, such as a mortgage on a building. We will explore more about long-term liabilities in the next chapter.

The amounts of most liabilities are known. For example, if a business receives a bill that is due in 30 days or a business takes out a 90-day loan from a bank, then the company knows how much it owes. We will begin our discussion with current liabilities of a known amount.

Accounts Payable

IFRS
IFRS defines current and long-term liabilities in the same manner as GAAP.

Amounts owed for products or services purchased on account are *accounts payable*. Because these are typically due in 30 days, they are current liabilities. We have seen many accounts payable illustrations in preceding chapters. Businesses can record accounts payable for the purchase of goods or for the receipt of services. Accounts payable occur because the business receives the goods or services before payment has been made.

Current Liabilities and Payroll Financial 11-3

Sales Tax Payable

Most states assess sales tax on retail sales. Retailers collect the sales tax in addition to the price of the item sold. Sales Tax Payable is a current liability because the retailer must pay the state in less than a year. Sales tax is usually calculated as a percentage of the amount of the sale.

For example, suppose December's taxable sales for Smart Touch Learning totaled $10,000. The company collected an additional 6% sales tax, which would equal $600 ($10,000 × 0.06). The accounting clerk would record that month's cash sales as follows:

Date	Accounts and Explanation	Debit	Credit
Dec. 31	Cash	10,600	
	Sales Revenue		10,000
	Sales Tax Payable ($10,000 × 0.06)		600
	To record cash sales and the related sales tax.		

$$\frac{A\uparrow}{Cash\uparrow} \Bigg\} = \Bigg\{ \frac{L\uparrow}{Sales\ Tax\ Payable\uparrow} + \frac{E\uparrow}{Sales\ Revenue\uparrow}$$

Sales tax is not an expense of the business. It is a current liability. Companies collect the sales tax and then forward it to the state at regular intervals. They normally submit it monthly, but they could file it at other intervals, depending on the state and the amount of the tax. To pay the tax, the company debits Sales Tax Payable and credits Cash.

Date	Accounts and Explanation	Debit	Credit
Jan. 20	Sales Tax Payable	600	
	Cash		600
	To record cash payment for sales tax payable.		

$$\frac{A\downarrow}{Cash\downarrow} \Bigg\} = \Bigg\{ \frac{L\downarrow}{Sales\ Tax\ Payable\downarrow} + \frac{E}{}$$

Unearned Revenue

Unearned revenue is also called *deferred revenue*. Unearned revenue arises when a business has received cash in advance of providing goods or performing work and, therefore, has an obligation to provide goods or services to the customer in the future. Unearned revenues are current liabilities until they are earned.

Suppose Smart Touch Learning received $900 in advance on May 21 for a month's work beginning on that date. On May 21, because it received cash before earning the revenue, the company has a liability to perform work for the client. The liability is called *Unearned Revenue*. The entry made by the accounting clerk on May 21 follows:

Date	Accounts and Explanation	Debit	Credit
May 21	Cash	900	
	Unearned Revenue		900
	Collected cash for future services.		

$$\frac{A\uparrow}{Cash\uparrow} \Bigg\} = \Bigg\{ \frac{L\uparrow}{Unearned\ Revenue\uparrow} + \frac{E}{}$$

11-4 Financial chapter 11

During May, Smart Touch Learning delivered one-third of the work and earned $300 ($900 × 1/3) of the revenue. On May 31, the accounting clerk would record the following adjusting entry to show that some work had been completed and some revenue had now been earned:

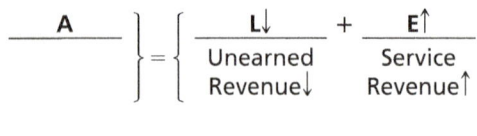

Date	Accounts and Explanation	Debit	Credit
May 31	Unearned Revenue	300	
	Service Revenue		300
	To record service revenue earned that was collected in advance.		

At this point, Smart Touch Learning has earned $300 of the revenue and still owes $600 of work to the customer as shown in the T-accounts:

Unearned Revenue				Service Revenue	
May 31	300	900	May 21		300 May 31
		600	Bal.		

Short-term Notes Payable

Short-term Note Payable
A written promise made by the business to pay a debt, usually involving interest, within one year or less.

Short-term notes payable are a common form of financing. Short-term notes payable represent a written promise by the business to pay a debt, usually involving interest, within one year or less. Assume on May 1, Smart Touch Learning purchased merchandise inventory with a 10%, 90-day note payable, for $8,000. The company uses the perpetual inventory system. The entry to record the note and purchase of inventory follows:

$$\frac{A\uparrow}{\text{Merchandise Inventory}\uparrow} \bigg\} = \bigg\{ \frac{L\uparrow}{\text{Notes Payable}\uparrow} + E$$

Date	Accounts and Explanation	Debit	Credit
May 1	Merchandise Inventory	8,000	
	Notes Payable		8,000
	Purchased merchandise inventory in exchange for 90-day, 10% note.		

On July 30, when the note is due, Smart Touch Learning will pay the note plus interest and record the following entry:

$$\frac{A\downarrow}{\text{Cash}\downarrow} \bigg\} = \bigg\{ \frac{L\downarrow}{\text{Notes Payable}\downarrow} + \frac{E\downarrow}{\text{Interest Expense}\uparrow}$$

Date	Accounts and Explanation	Debit	Credit
Jul. 30	Notes Payable	8,000	
	Interest Expense ($8,000 × 0.10 × 90/365)	197	
	Cash		8,197
	Paid note and interest at maturity.		

Remember that the calculation for interest is principal × interest rate × time. Both the interest rate and the time are expressed in the same units, which in this case is as an annual amount.

Businesses occasionally borrow cash from banks. The bank requires the business to sign a *promissory note* that states that the business will pay the *principal* plus *interest* at a specified *maturity date*. As an example, assume that on November 1, 2024, Smart Touch Learning borrows $10,000 from First Street Bank at 6% for five months. On November 1, the accounting clerk records the following entry:

Date	Accounts and Explanation	Debit	Credit
2024			
Nov. 1	Cash	10,000	
	Notes Payable		10,000
	Received cash in exchange for 5-month, 6% note.		

$$\frac{A\uparrow}{Cash\uparrow} \bigg\} = \bigg\{ \frac{L\uparrow}{Notes\ Payable\uparrow} + \frac{E}{}$$

At year-end, the matching principle requires the business to accrue interest expense for November and December as follows:

Date	Accounts and Explanation	Debit	Credit
2024			
Dec. 31	Interest Expense ($10,000 × 0.06 × 2/12)	100	
	Interest Payable		100
	Accrued interest expense at year-end.		

$$\frac{A}{} \bigg\} = \bigg\{ \frac{L\uparrow}{Interest\ Payable\uparrow} + \frac{E\downarrow}{Interest\ Expense\uparrow}$$

The interest accrual at December 31, 2024, allocated $100 of the interest on this note to 2024. During 2025, the interest on this note for the three remaining months is $150. When Smart Touch Learning records payment for the note, it will record the remaining interest expense and also remove the interest payable and note payable from the books as shown:

Date	Accounts and Explanation	Debit	Credit
2025			
Apr. 1	Notes Payable	10,000	
	Interest Expense ($10,000 × 0.06 × 3/12)	150	
	Interest Payable	100	
	Cash		10,250
	Paid note and interest at maturity.		

$$\frac{A\downarrow}{Cash\downarrow} \bigg\} = \bigg\{ \frac{L\downarrow}{\substack{Notes\ Payable\downarrow \\ Interest\ Payable\downarrow}} + \frac{E\downarrow}{Interest\ Expense\uparrow}$$

Current Portion of Long-term Notes Payable

Long-term notes payable are typically reported in the long-term liability section of the balance sheet. If, however, the long-term debt is paid in installments, the business will report the current portion of notes payable (also called *current maturity*) as a current liability. The **current portion of notes payable** is the principal amount that will be paid within one year of the balance sheet date. The remaining portion of the note will be classified as long-term.

Let's consider a $20,000 note payable that is paid in $5,000 installments over four years. The portion that must be paid within one year, $5,000, is current. The remaining $15,000 will be classified as long-term. No journal entry is needed to reclassify the current portion. It is, instead, only classified as current or long-term for reporting purposes on the balance sheet. Notice that the reclassification does not change the total amount of debt. It only reclassifies $5,000 of the total debt from long-term to current.

Current Portion of Notes Payable
The amount of the principal that is payable within one year of the balance sheet date.

11-6 Financial   chapter 11

On August 10, Swanson Company recorded sales of merchandise inventory on account, $4,000. The sales were subject to sales tax of 4%. The company uses the perpetual inventory system. On September 30, Swanson paid $500 of sales tax to the state.

1. Journalize the transaction to record the sale on August 10. Ignore cost of goods sold.
2. Journalize the transaction to record the payment of sales tax to the state.

Check your answers online in MyLab Accounting or at http://www.pearsonhighered.com/Horngren.

For more practice, see Short Exercises S-F:11-1 through S-F:11-5.   MyLab Accounting

HOW DO COMPANIES ACCOUNT FOR AND RECORD PAYROLL?

Learning Objective 2
Calculate and journalize basic payroll transactions

Payroll, also called *employee compensation*, also creates liabilities for a business. For service organizations—such as CPA firms and travel agencies—payroll is *the* major expense. Labor cost is so important that most businesses develop a special payroll system.

There are numerous ways to label an employee's pay:

- *Salary* is pay stated at an annual, monthly, or weekly rate, such as $62,400 per year, $5,200 per month, or $1,200 per week.
- *Wages* are pay amounts stated at an hourly rate, such as $15 per hour.
- *Commission* is pay stated as a percentage of a sale amount, such as a 5% commission on a sale. A realtor who earns 5% commission, for example, earns $5,000 on a $100,000 sale of real estate ($100,000 × 5%).
- *Bonus* is pay over and above base salary (or wage or commission). A bonus is usually paid for exceptional performance—in a single amount after year-end.
- *Benefits* are extra compensation—items that are not paid directly to the employee. Benefits cover health, life, and disability insurance. The employer pays the insurance company, which then provides coverage for the employee. Another type of benefit, retirement, sets aside money for the employee for his or her future retirement.

Businesses pay employees at a base rate for a set period—called *straight time*. For additional hours—*overtime*—the employee may get a higher pay rate, depending on the job classification and wage and hour laws.

Assume Ryan Park was hired to work for Smart Touch Learning. His pay is as follows:

- Ryan earns wages of $15 per hour for straight time (40 hours), so his weekly pay is $600 ($15 per hour × 40 hours).
- The company pays *time-and-a-half* for overtime. That rate is 150% (1.5 times) the straight-time pay rate. Thus, Ryan earns $22.50 per hour of overtime ($15.00 × 1.5).
- For working 42 hours during a week, he earns gross pay of $645, computed as follows:

Straight-time pay for 40 hours	$ 600
Overtime pay for 2 hours: 2 × $22.50	45
Gross Pay	**$ 645**

Gross Pay and Net (Take-Home) Pay

Two pay amounts are important for accounting purposes. **Gross pay** is the total amount of salary, wages, commissions, and bonuses earned by the employee during a pay period before taxes or any other deductions. Gross pay is an expense to the employer. In the preceding example, Ryan Park's gross pay was $645. **Net pay** is the amount the employee gets to keep. Net pay is also called *take-home pay*. Net pay equals gross pay minus all deductions such as income tax withheld. The employer either writes a paycheck to each employee for his or her take-home pay or directly deposits the employee's take-home pay into the employee's bank account.

> **Gross Pay**
> The total amount of salary, wages, commissions, and any other employee compensation before taxes and other deductions.
>
> **Net Pay**
> Gross pay minus all deductions. The amount of compensation that the employee actually takes home.

Employee Payroll Withholding Deductions

The federal government, most states, and many municipalities require employers to deduct taxes from employee paychecks. Insurance companies and investment companies may also get some of the employee's gross pay. Amounts withheld from paychecks are called *withholding deductions*. Payroll withholding deductions are the difference between gross pay and take-home pay. These deductions are withheld from paychecks and sent directly to the government, to insurance companies, or to other entities. Payroll withholding deductions fall into two categories:

- *Required deductions*, such as employee federal and state income tax, Social Security tax, and other deductions required by federal, state, or local laws. For example, employees pay their income tax and Social Security tax through payroll deductions.
- *Optional deductions*, including insurance premiums, retirement plan contributions, charitable contributions, and other amounts that are withheld at the employee's request.

After being withheld, payroll deductions become the liability of the employer, who then pays the outside parties—taxes to the government and contributions to charitable organizations, for example.

Withholding for Employee Income Tax

U.S. law and some states, cities, and counties require companies to withhold income tax from employee paychecks. The income tax deducted from gross pay is called **income tax withholding**. The amount withheld depends on the employee's gross pay and on the number of *withholding allowances* he or she claims.

For federal tax withholdings, an employee files Form W-4[1] with his or her employer to indicate the number of allowances claimed for income tax withholding. Each allowance lowers the amount of tax withheld:

- An unmarried taxpayer usually claims one allowance.
- A childless married couple usually claims two allowances.
- A married couple with one child usually claims three allowances, and so on.

Exhibit F:11-1 (on the next page) shows a W-4 for Ryan Park, who claims married with three allowances (lines 3 and 5).

> **Income Tax Withholding**
> Income tax deducted from an employee's gross pay.

---

[1] In 2020, the Internal Revenue Service (IRS) updated the Form W-4 to reflect the most recent tax changes. For an updated copy of the Form W-4, please refer to the IRS website: **www.irs.gov**.

Exhibit F:11-1 | W-4

Form W-4 — Employee's Withholding Allowance Certificate
Department of the Treasury, Internal Revenue Service
OMB No. 1545-0074
2019

► Whether you are entitled to claim a certain number of allowances or exemption from withholding is subject to review by the IRS. Your employer may be required to send a copy of this form to the IRS.

1 Your first name and middle initial	Last name	2 Your social security number
Ryan G.	Park	123-45-6789

Home address (number and street or rural route)
305 Lost Cove Drive

3 ☐ Single ☑ Married ☐ Married, but withhold at higher Single rate.
Note. If married, but legally separated, or spouse is a nonresident alien, check the "Single" box.

City or town, state, and ZIP code
Pompton Plains, IL 07444

4 If your last name differs from that shown on your social security card, check here. You must call 800-772-1213 for a replacement card. ► ☐

5	Total number of allowances you are claiming (from the applicable worksheet on the following pages)	5	3
6	Additional amount, if any, you want withheld from each paycheck	6	$

7 I claim exemption from withholding for 2019, and I certify that I meet **both** of the following conditions for exemption.
 • Last year I had a right to a refund of **all** federal income tax withheld because I had **no** tax liability, **and**
 • This year I expect a refund of **all** federal income tax withheld because I expect to have **no** tax liability.
If you meet both conditions, write "Exempt" here . . . . ► 7

Under penalties of perjury, I declare that I have examined this certificate and, to the best of my knowledge and belief, it is true, correct, and complete.

Employee's signature (This form is not valid unless you sign it.) ► *Ryan G. Park*   Date ► 11/15/2019

8 Employer's name and address (Employer: Complete lines 8 and 10 only if sending to the IRS and complete boxes 8, 9, and 10 if sending to State Directory of New Hires.)	9 First date of employment	10 Employer identification number (EIN)
Smart Touch Learning, 227 Lake Street, Pompton Plains, IL 07444		20-1234567

For Privacy Act and Paperwork Reduction Act Notice, see page 4.   Cat. No. 10220Q   Form **W-4** (2019)

Withholding for Employee Social Security Tax (FICA)

The **Federal Insurance Contributions Act (FICA)**, also known as the Social Security Act, created the Social Security tax. The Social Security program provides retirement, disability, and medical benefits. The law requires employers to withhold **Social Security (FICA) tax** from employees' paychecks. The FICA tax has two components:

1. OASDI (old age, survivors, and disability insurance)
2. Medicare (medical benefits)

OASDI provides retirement benefits to individuals based upon age, benefits to survivors of qualified individuals, and disability insurance to individuals who cannot work because of a medical condition. The amount of tax withheld varies from year to year because the wage base is subject to OASDI tax changes each year. For 2019, the OASDI tax applies to the first $132,900 of employee earnings in a year. The taxable amount of earnings is usually adjusted annually. The OASDI tax rate for employees for 2019 is 6.2%. Therefore, the maximum OASDI tax that an employee paid in 2019 was $8,239.80 ($132,900 × 0.062).

The Medicare portion of the FICA tax provides health insurance to individuals based on age or disability. Medicare applies to all employee earnings—that means there is no maximum tax. For 2019, this tax rate is 1.45% for earnings up to $200,000. Earnings over $200,000 are taxed an additional 0.9%, for a total of 2.35%. Therefore, an employee pays a combined FICA tax rate of 7.65% (6.2% + 1.45%) of the first $132,900 of annual earnings, plus 1.45% of earnings above $132,900 up to $200,000, and 2.35% on earnings above $200,000.

Federal Insurance Contributions Act (FICA)
The federal act that created the Social Security tax that provides retirement, disability, and medical benefits.

Social Security (FICA) Tax
Federal Insurance Contributions Act (FICA) tax, which is withheld from employees' pay and matched by the employer.

The percentage used and the wage base for payroll withholdings and taxes vary from year to year. We are using amounts that are current at the time of printing. You should use these numbers when you complete this chapter's assignments.

Assume that James Kolen, another employee of Smart Touch Learning, earned $128,600 prior to December. Kolen's salary for December is $10,000. Kolen's FICA tax withheld from his paycheck is calculated as follows:

	OASDI	Medicare
Employee earnings subject to tax	$132,900	No Max
Employee earnings prior to the current month	128,600	
Current pay subject to tax	$ 4,300	$ 10,000
Tax rate	× 0.062	× 0.0145
Tax to be withheld from paycheck	$ 267*	$ 145
Total FICA tax withheld ($267 + $145)	$ 412	

*Numbers in examples are rounded to nearest dollar for simplicity. Payroll amounts are usually rounded to the nearest cent.

Notice that only $4,300 of Kolen's $10,000 salary is subject to OASDI tax. This is because in December, Kolen reaches the maximum amount of earnings that is subject to OASDI. Once an employee has earned $132,900, no further earnings are taxed for OASDI in that year.

Medicare tax, on the other hand, has no maximum. All earnings are subject to the tax. Kolen pays Medicare tax on the entire $10,000 earned in December.

> Why did James Kolen only pay OASDI tax on $4,300 of earnings?

Optional Withholding Deductions

As a convenience to employees, some companies withhold payroll deductions and then pay designated organizations according to employee instructions. Insurance premiums, retirement savings, union dues, and gifts to charities are examples.

The table below summarizes James Kolen's final pay period on December 31 assuming he authorized a $180 payment for health insurance and a $20 contribution to United Way. Employee income tax is assumed to be 20% of gross pay.

Gross pay		$ 10,000
Withholding deductions:		
Employee income tax (20%)	$ 2,000	
Employee OASDI tax (calculated on prior page)	267	
Employee Medicare tax (1.45%)	145	
Employee health insurance	180	
Employee contribution to United Way	20	
Total withholdings		2,612
Net (take-home) pay		$ 7,388

Payroll Register

Many companies use a **payroll register** to help summarize the earnings, withholdings, and net pay for each employee. Exhibit F:11-2 (on the next page) shows the payroll register for Smart Touch Learning for the month of December.

> **Payroll Register**
> A schedule that summarizes the earnings, withholdings, and net pay for each employee.

11-10 Financial chapter 11

Exhibit F:11-2 | Payroll Register

Employee Name	Earnings — Beginning Cumulative Earnings	Earnings — Current Period Earnings	Earnings — Ending Cumulative Earnings	Withholdings — OASDI	Withholdings — Medicare	Withholdings — Income Tax	Withholdings — Health Insurance	Withholdings — Other	Total Withholdings	Net Pay	Check No.	Salaries and Wages Expense
James Kolen	$128,600	$10,000	$138,600	$267	$145	$2,000	$180	$20	$2,612	$7,388	530	$10,000
Benito Munez	62,100	5,500	67,600	341	80	825	110	0	1,356	4,144	531	5,500
Ryan Park	37,400	2,580	39,980	160	37	465	110	0	772	1,808	532	2,580
Lisa Smart	0	4,000	4,000	248	58	1,400	65	0	1,771	2,229	533	4,000
Sharon Zapato	71,500	6,500	78,000	403	94	1,625	180	40	2,342	4,158	534	6,500
Total	$299,600	$28,580	$328,180	$1,419	$414	$6,315	$645	$60	$8,853	$19,727		$28,580

A business's payroll register typically includes the following columns:

1. Employee Name.
2. Beginning cumulative earnings—the amount the employee has earned through the last pay period.
3. Current period earnings—earnings for the current period (includes regular and overtime earnings, commissions, and bonuses).
4. Ending cumulative earnings—beginning cumulative earnings plus current period earnings.
5. OASDI—6.2% tax on the first $132,900 earnings.
6. Medicare—1.45% tax on the first $200,000; 2.35% on earnings over $200,000.
7. Income Tax—includes federal, state, and any local government income tax withheld; varies depending on filing status and number of withholding allowances.
8. Health Insurance—withholdings made for employee-paid health care coverage.
9. Other—employees' voluntary withholdings, such as charitable contributions and union dues.
10. Total Withholdings—total of all withholdings.
11. Net Pay—current period earnings less total withholdings. This is the amount that is paid to each employee.
12. Check No.—the check number used to make payment for earnings.
13. Salaries and Wages Expense—the amount debited to Salaries and Wages Expense for the current pay period.

Journalizing Employee Payroll

The information from the payroll register is used to record the payroll journal entry. Payroll and payroll withholdings are recorded as liabilities until the amounts are paid. The totals from the payroll register will be used to create the journal entry for Smart Touch Learning.

$$\frac{A}{} = \begin{cases} \frac{L\uparrow}{\text{Various Payables}\uparrow \\ \text{Salaries and Wages Payable}\uparrow} + \frac{E\downarrow}{\text{Salaries and Wages Expense}\uparrow} \end{cases}$$

Date	Accounts and Explanation	Debit	Credit
Dec. 31	Salaries and Wages Expense	28,580	
	FICA—OASDI Taxes Payable		1,419
	FICA—Medicare Taxes Payable		414
	Employee Income Taxes Payable		6,315
	Employee Health Insurance Payable		645
	United Way Payable		60
	Salaries and Wages Payable		19,727
	To record salaries and wages expense and payroll withholdings.		

Current Liabilities and Payroll Financial 11-11

In the above journal entry, Salaries and Wages Expense ($28,580) represents the gross pay for all employees. Gross pay includes both the amount owed for salaries and wages ($19,727) and payroll withholdings ($1,419 + $414 + $6,315 + $645 + $60).

On payday, Smart Touch Learning will make payment of $19,727 to its employees and record the following journal entry:

Date	Accounts and Explanation	Debit	Credit
Jan. 5	Salaries and Wages Payable	19,727	
	Cash		19,727
	To record payment of salaries.		

A↓ = L↓ + E
Cash↓   Salaries and Wages Payable↓

The other payable accounts, FICA, Employee Income Taxes Payable, Health Insurance, and any charitable contributions, will be removed from the books when payments are made on those specific payables with debits to the liability accounts and a credit to Cash.

Employer Payroll Taxes

In addition to income tax and FICA tax, which are withheld from employee paychecks, *employers* must pay at least three payroll taxes. These taxes are not withheld from employees' gross earnings but instead are paid by the employer:

1. Employer FICA tax (OASDI and Medicare)
2. State unemployment compensation tax (SUTA)
3. Federal unemployment compensation tax (FUTA)

Employer FICA Tax

In addition to the FICA tax withheld from the employee's paycheck, the employer must also pay both OASDI and Medicare. The employer portion of OASDI is 6.2% on the first $132,900 of each employee's annual earnings. The employer's tax rate for Medicare is 1.45% on all earnings. (The employer does not pay the additional 0.9% Medicare tax on earnings above $200,000.) The Social Security system is funded by contributions from both the employer and employee.

State and Federal Unemployment Compensation Taxes

The Federal Unemployment Tax Act (FUTA) and the State Unemployment Tax Act (SUTA) finance workers' compensation for people laid off from work. These **unemployment compensation taxes** are paid by the employer; they are not deducted from employees' gross pay. (Some states require employees to contribute to SUTA. For our purposes, we will assume that unemployment compensation taxes are paid only by the employer.) In recent years, employers have paid a combined tax of 6.0% on the first $7,000 of each employee's annual earnings for unemployment tax. The proportion paid to the state depends on the individual state, but for many it is 5.4% to the state plus 0.6% to the federal government. For this payroll tax, the employer uses two liability accounts:

- Federal Unemployment Taxes Payable (FUTA Payable)
- State Unemployment Taxes Payable (SUTA Payable)

Exhibit F:11-3 (on the next page) shows the distribution of payroll for an employee who earns $1,000, assuming the employee has not reached the payroll tax limits.

Unemployment Compensation Taxes
Payroll tax paid by employers to the government, which uses the cash to pay unemployment benefits to people who are out of work.

Exhibit F:11-3 | Payroll Costs

Employee's net pay and withholdings					Employer's taxes			
Net (Take-Home) Pay	OASDI (6.2% on first $132,900)	Medicare (1.45% on first $200,000, then 2.35%)	Income Tax (20% assumed)	OASDI (6.2% on first $132,900)	Medicare (1.45% on all earnings)	FUTA (0.6% on first $7,000)	SUTA (5.4% on first $7,000)
$723 +	$62 +	$15 +	$200	$62 +	$15 +	$6 +	$54
= $1,000				= $137			
				Employer pays a total of $1,137.			

Journalizing Employer Payroll Taxes

Smart Touch Learning's employer payroll taxes for December will be calculated as follows:

	Earnings			Employer Payroll Taxes				
Employee Name	Beginning Cumulative Earnings	Current Period Earnings	Ending Cumulative Earnings	OASDI (6.2%)	Medicare (1.45%)	FUTA (0.6%)	SUTA (5.4%)	Total Taxes
James Kolen	$ 128,600	$ 10,000	$ 138,600	$ 267	$ 145	$ 0	$ 0	$ 412
Benito Munez	62,100	5,500	67,600	341	80	0	0	421
Ryan Park	37,400	2,580	39,980	160	37	0	0	197
Lisa Smart	0	4,000	4,000	248	58	24	216	546
Sharon Zapato	71,500	6,500	78,000	403	94	0	0	497
Total	$ 299,600	$ 28,580	$ 328,180	$ 1,419	$ 414	$ 24	$ 216	$ 2,073

As with employee contributions, the federal FICA—OASDI is determined as 6.2% on the first $132,900 earned by each employee. Smart Touch Learning must pay OASDI tax on all employees; however, the amount paid on James Kolen's earnings is limited to the first $132,900 [($132,900 − $128,600) × 6.2% = $267]. FICA—Medicare applies to all earnings at a rate of 1.45%.

FUTA (0.6%) and SUTA (5.4%) tax is only paid on the first $7,000 of each employee's earnings. Smart Touch Learning will only pay unemployment taxes on Lisa Smart because all other employees have earned more than $7,000 prior to the December pay period.

Smart Touch Learning records the employer's payroll tax expense as a debit to Payroll Tax Expense and a credit to the various payable accounts:

$$\frac{A}{=}\begin{cases} \frac{L\uparrow}{\text{Various Payables}\uparrow} + \frac{E\downarrow}{\text{Payroll Tax Expense}\uparrow} \end{cases}$$

Date	Accounts and Explanation	Debit	Credit
Dec. 31	Payroll Tax Expense	2,073	
	FICA—OASDI Taxes Payable		1,419
	FICA—Medicare Taxes Payable		414
	Federal Unemployment Taxes Payable		24
	State Unemployment Taxes Payable		216
	To record employer's payroll tax expense.		

Payment of Employer Payroll Taxes and Employees' Withholdings

On payday, or shortly thereafter, Smart Touch Learning will make payments to the various government agencies and other designated organizations for the employees' withholdings and Smart Touch Learning's tax obligations. The information for the payment comes from the journal entries to record employee payroll and employer payroll taxes. Notice that FICA—OASDI Taxes Payable and FICA—Medicare Taxes Payable are included in the journal entry to record employee payroll and the journal entry to record employer payroll taxes. That is because the FICA taxes are obligations of both the employee and the employer. Smart Touch Learning will combine those amounts when recording the payments. Assuming the payments are made on January 15, the journal entry is:

Date	Accounts and Explanation	Debit	Credit
Jan. 15	FICA—OASDI Taxes Payable ($1,419 + $1,419)	2,838	
	FICA—Medicare Taxes Payable ($414 + $414)	828	
	Employee Income Taxes Payable	6,315	
	Employee Health Insurance Payable	645	
	United Way Payable	60	
	Federal Unemployment Taxes Payable	24	
	State Unemployment Taxes Payable	216	
	Cash		10,926
	To record payment of payroll liabilities.		

$$\left. \begin{array}{c} A\downarrow \\ \text{Cash}\downarrow \end{array} \right\} = \left\{ \begin{array}{c} L\downarrow \\ \text{Various} \\ \text{Payables}\downarrow \end{array} \right. + \underline{\quad E \quad}$$

Internal Control Over Payroll

There are two main controls for payroll:

- Controls for efficiency
- Controls to safeguard payroll disbursements

Controls for Efficiency

Payroll transactions are ideal for computer processing. The payroll data are stored in a file, and the computer makes the calculations, prints paychecks, and updates all records electronically. In addition, companies may require direct deposits for employees' pay so that paper checks do not have to be written to each employee. Direct deposits also increase efficiency by reducing the amount of reconciling needed on outstanding checks.

Controls to Safeguard Payroll Disbursements

An owner of a small business can monitor his or her payroll by personal contact with employees. Large companies cannot. A particular risk is that a paycheck may be written to a fictitious person and cashed by a dishonest employee. To guard against this, large businesses adopt strict internal controls for payroll.

Hiring and firing employees should be separated from accounting and from passing out paychecks. Photo IDs ensure that only actual employees are paid. Employees clock in at the start and clock out at the end of the workday to prove their attendance and hours worked.

The foundation of internal control is the separation of duties. This is why all but the smallest companies have separate departments for the following activities:

- The Human Resources Department hires and fires workers.
- The Payroll Department maintains employee earnings records.
- The Accounting Department records all transactions.
- The Treasurer distributes paychecks to employees.

11-14 chapter 11

3. Theodore Simpson works for Blair Company all year and earns a monthly salary of $4,000. There is no overtime pay. Based on Theodore's W-4, Blair withholds income taxes at 15% of his gross pay. As of July 31, Theodore had $28,000 of cumulative earnings.

Journalize the accrual of salary expense for Blair Company related to the employment of Theodore Simpson for the month of August.

Check your answer online in MyLab Accounting or at http://www.pearsonhighered.com/Horngren.

For more practice, see Short Exercises S-F:11-6 through S-F:11-8. MyLab Accounting

HOW ARE CURRENT LIABILITIES THAT MUST BE ESTIMATED ACCOUNTED FOR?

Learning Objective 3
Account for current liabilities that must be estimated

A business may know that a liability exists but not know the exact amount. The business cannot simply ignore the liability. It must estimate the amount of the liability and report it on the balance sheet. Common examples of liabilities that are often estimated are bonus plans, vacation pay, health and pension benefits, and warranties.

Bonus Plans

Many companies give bonuses to their employees in addition to their regular wages. These bonuses are often based on meeting a specific goal, such as the employee meeting an expected sales goal or the business achieving a target profit. Usually a company does not know the amount of the year-end bonus at year-end; the company, instead, estimates the amount of the bonus based on a set percentage. For example, assume Smart Touch Learning estimates that it will pay a 5% bonus on annual net income after deducting the bonus. Assume the company reports net income of $315,000 before the calculation of the bonus. The accounting department will calculate the bonus as follows:

$$\text{Bonus} = (\text{Bonus \%} \times \text{Net income before bonus}) / (1 + \text{Bonus \%})$$
$$= (0.05 \times \$315{,}000) / (1 + 0.05)$$
$$= \$15{,}000$$

This formula allows you to back into the bonus amount. For example, net income minus the bonus is $300,000 ($315,000 − $15,000). The bonus of $15,000 is really 5% of net income after the bonus has been subtracted ($300,000 × 0.05 = $15,000).

Assuming Smart Touch Learning will not make payment until the next year, it must record a liability for the bonus due to its employees. The accounting clerk will record the following entry:

A = L↑ + E↓
Employee Bonus Payable↑
Employee Bonus Expense↑

Date	Accounts and Explanation	Debit	Credit
Dec. 31	Employee Bonus Expense	15,000	
	Employee Bonus Payable		15,000
	To record employee bonus expense.		

Current Liabilities and Payroll Financial   11-15

When Smart Touch Learning makes payment, it will debit Employee Bonus Payable and credit Cash.

Vacation, Health, and Pension Benefits

Businesses typically offer vacation, health, and pension benefits to its employees. A **pension plan** provides benefits to retired employees. Vacation, health, and pension benefits must be estimated and recorded as a liability. Suppose Smart Touch Learning employees earn two weeks of vacation throughout the year. The company estimates that the cost of providing vacation benefits is $1,000 per month. The accounting clerk will record the following journal entry monthly:

Pension Plan
A plan that provides benefits to retired employees.

Date	Accounts and Explanation	Debit	Credit
	Vacation Benefits Expense	1,000	
	Vacation Benefits Payable		1,000
	To record employee vacation benefits expense.		

$$\underline{A} = \begin{cases} \underline{L\uparrow} + \underline{E\downarrow} \\ \text{Vacation} \quad \text{Vacation} \\ \text{Benefits} \quad \text{Benefits} \\ \text{Payable}\uparrow \quad \text{Expense}\uparrow \end{cases}$$

When an employee takes paid vacation, Smart Touch Learning will reduce the liability, Vacation Benefits Payable, with a debit and credit Cash. Other benefits, such as health and pension benefits, are recorded in the same manner.

Warranties

Many businesses guarantee their products against defects under **warranty** agreements. The time period of warranty agreements varies. The matching principle requires businesses to record Warranty Expense in the same period that the company records the revenue related to that warranty. The expense, therefore, is incurred when the company makes a sale, not when the company pays the warranty claims. At the time of the sale, the company does not know the exact amount of warranty expense but can estimate it.

Warranty
An agreement that guarantees a company's product against defects.

Assume that Smart Touch Learning made sales on account of $50,000 (cost of merchandise inventory sold, $35,000) subject to product warranties on June 10 and estimates that warranty costs will be 3% of sales. The company would record the sales revenue, cost of goods sold, and estimated warranty expense as follows:

Date	Accounts and Explanation	Debit	Credit
Jun. 10	Accounts Receivable	50,000	
	Sales Revenue		50,000
	Recorded sale on account.		
10	Cost of Goods Sold	35,000	
	Merchandise Inventory		35,000
	Recorded the cost of goods sold.		
10	Warranty Expense ($50,000 × 0.03)	1,500	
	Estimated Warranty Payable		1,500
	To accrue warranty payable.		

$$\underline{A\uparrow} = \begin{cases} \underline{L} + \underline{E\uparrow} \\ \text{Accounts} \quad \text{Sales} \\ \text{Receivable}\uparrow \quad \text{Revenue}\uparrow \end{cases}$$

$$\underline{A\downarrow} = \begin{cases} \underline{L} + \underline{E\downarrow} \\ \text{Merchandise} \quad \text{Cost of} \\ \text{Inventory}\downarrow \quad \text{Goods Sold}\uparrow \end{cases}$$

$$\underline{A} = \begin{cases} \underline{L\uparrow} + \underline{E\downarrow} \\ \text{Estimated} \quad \text{Warranty} \\ \text{Warranty} \quad \text{Expense}\uparrow \\ \text{Payable}\uparrow \end{cases}$$

Assume that some of Smart Touch Learning's customers make claims that must be honored through the warranty offered by the company. The warranty costs total $800 and are made on June 27. The company replaces the defective goods and makes the following journal entry:

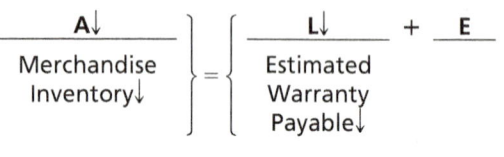

Date	Accounts and Explanation	Debit	Credit
Jun. 27	Estimated Warranty Payable	800	
	Merchandise Inventory		800
	To replace merchandise inventory under warranty.		

Smart Touch Learning replaced the defective goods, so the credit was to Merchandise Inventory. If the company had given the customer a refund instead of a replacement, the credit would be to Cash.

Smart Touch Learning's expense on the income statement is $1,500, the estimated amount, not the $800 actually honored. After honoring these warranties, the company's liability account has a credit balance of $700. This $700 balance represents warranty claims Smart Touch Learning expects to honor in the future based on its estimates; therefore, the $700 is a liability to Smart Touch Learning.

Estimated Warranty Payable

Jun. 27	800	1,500	Jun. 10
		700	Bal.

TYING IT ALL TOGETHER

UnitedHealth Group Incorporated is a health and well-being company dedicated to helping people live healthier lives. The company provides products and services under two distinct brands: UnitedHealthcare and Optum. UnitedHealthcare provides health care coverage and benefits for more than 30 million people. Optum provides information and technology-enabled health services. (You can find UnitedHealth Group Incorporated's 2018 annual report at https://www.sec.gov/Archives/edgar/data/731766/000073176619000005/unh2018123110-k.htm.)

On UnitedHealth Group Incorporated's balance sheet, the company lists several different types of current liabilities including medical costs payable. What does medical costs payable represent?

In the notes to the financial statements, UnitedHealth Group states medical costs payable include the company's obligations for medical care services that have been provided to insured consumers but that have not yet been paid. In addition, medical costs payable also includes physician, hospital, and other medical costs disputes.

How does UnitedHealth Group Incorporated estimate the amount of medical costs payable that is recorded on its balance sheet?

UnitedHealth Group estimates the amount of medical costs payable based on factors such as time from date of service to claim receipt, claim backlogs, and other medical cost trends. The estimated costs associated with medical disputes are based on an analysis of potential outcomes. The estimates are re-evaluated frequently and adjustments are made as needed.

Current Liabilities and Payroll Financial 11-17

4. O'Conner guarantees its vacuums for four years. Prior experience indicates that warranty costs will be approximately 6% of sales. Assume that O'Conner made sales totaling $200,000 during 2024. Record the warranty expense for the year.

Check your answer online in MyLab Accounting or at http://www.pearsonhighered.com/Horngren.

For more practice, see Short Exercises S-F:11-9 through S-F:11-11.   MyLab Accounting

HOW ARE CONTINGENT LIABILITIES ACCOUNTED FOR?

A **contingent liability** is a potential, rather than an actual, liability because it depends on a *future* event. For a contingent liability to be paid, some event (the contingency) must happen in the future. For example, suppose Smart Touch Learning is sued because of alleged patent infringement on one of its online learning videos. The company, therefore, faces a contingent liability, which may or may not become an actual liability. If the outcome of this lawsuit is unfavorable, it could hurt Smart Touch Learning by increasing its liabilities. Therefore, it would be unethical to withhold knowledge of the lawsuit from its creditors.

Another contingent liability arises when a company *co-signs a note payable* for another entity. The company co-signing has a contingent liability until the note comes due and is paid by the other entity. If the other company pays off the note, the contingent liability vanishes. If the other company doesn't pay off the note, the co-signing company must pay the debt for the other entity. How businesses record or don't record contingent liabilities is based on one of three likelihoods of the event occurring in the future:

- Remote
- Reasonably possible
- Probable

Remote Contingent Liability

A contingency that is remote has little chance of the event occurring in the future. If a contingency is remote, the company does not need to record a liability and does not need to disclose it in the notes to the financial statements. An example of a remote contingency would be a frivolous lawsuit.

Reasonably Possible Contingent Liability

Contingencies that are reasonably possible have a greater chance of occurring but are not likely. A reasonably possible contingency should be described in the notes to the financial statements. For example, consider a company that is the defendant in a significant lawsuit. If the company has been advised by legal counsel that it is reasonably possible that it will lose the lawsuit, then it should report the lawsuit in its notes to the financial statements.

Probable Contingent Liability

If a contingency is probable, it means that the future event is likely to occur. Only contingencies that are probable *and* can be estimated are recorded as a liability and an expense is accrued. An example of an estimable probable contingency is a warranty.

Learning Objective 4
Account for contingent liabilities

Contingent Liability
A potential liability that depends on some future event.

IFRS
Under IFRS, "probable" is defined more broadly as "more likely than not" that the future event will result in a liability. "More likely than not" means more than a 50% chance.

Contingencies that are probable but *cannot* be estimated are disclosed in the notes to the financial statements. A liability is not recorded because the amount of the contingency cannot be estimated. Exhibit F:11-4 summarizes the rules for contingent liabilities.

Exhibit F:11-4 | Contingent Liabilities

Likelihood of Future Event	How to Report the Contingency
Remote	Do not disclose.
Reasonably possible	Describe the situation in a note to the financial statements.
Probable and the amount of the expense or loss *cannot* be estimated	Describe the situation in a note to the financial statements.
Probable and the amount of the expense or loss *can* be estimated	Record an expense or loss and a liability based on estimated amounts.

DECISIONS

How should the contingency be reported?

Emily Gallagher is the independent auditor of Tate Manufacturing, a maker of handheld drills and other carpentry tools. Emily is evaluating current lawsuits for the company to determine whether any contingent liabilities should be disclosed. Tate Manufacturing is currently in litigation for a product liability case. The suit claims that a Tate handheld drill heated up quickly and caused a fire. Tate's attorney has told Emily that it is likely that the manufacturer will lose the case, but he does not want to estimate the amount of damages. The attorney is concerned that estimating the amount of damages would establish a dollar amount for settlement and could place their case in jeopardy. What should Emily do?

Solution

GAAP requires that businesses report a contingency if it is probable that the event will occur in the future. The issue here is where the reporting should be made. If the attorney cannot reasonably estimate the amount of the possible damage award, Tate should report the contingent liability in the notes to the financial statements. If an amount can be determined, Tate Manufacturing should record an expense or loss and a liability based on the estimated amount. Emily should determine whether the attorney *can* estimate the damages but just doesn't want to. If the damages can be estimated, Emily should require that the company record a contingent liability.

Alternative Solution

The attorney's concern is understandable. He feels that disclosing the amount of the contingent liability could hurt the determination of the case. If the jury were to find out about the disclosure, it might be more likely to award damages to the plaintiff, or the plaintiff might be able to negotiate a larger settlement with Tate. The attorney has a right to be concerned about the transparency of the financial reporting and potential damage to the outcome of the case. The attorney should provide an estimate only if he is reasonably confident with the amount of damages.

Match the likelihood of a future event with the reporting of the contingency. An answer may be selected more than once.

Likelihood of Future Event	How to Report the Contingency
5. Remote	a. Do not disclose.
6. Reasonably possible	b. Record an expense and a liability based on estimated amounts.
7. Probable and the amount of the loss *cannot* be estimated	c. Describe the situation in a note to the financial statements.
8. Probable and the amount of the loss *can* be estimated	

Check your answers online in MyLab Accounting or at http://www.pearsonhighered.com/Horngren.

For more practice, see Short Exercise S-F:11-12. **MyLab Accounting**

Current Liabilities and Payroll Financial 11-19

HOW DO WE USE THE TIMES-INTEREST-EARNED RATIO TO EVALUATE BUSINESS PERFORMANCE?

The **times-interest-earned ratio** can be used to evaluate a business's ability to pay interest expense. This ratio measures the number of times earnings before interest and taxes (EBIT) can cover (pay) interest expense. The times-interest-earned ratio is also called the *interest-coverage ratio*. A high interest-coverage ratio indicates a business's ease in paying interest expense; a low ratio suggests difficulty. The times-interest-earned ratio is calculated as EBIT (Net income + Income tax expense + Interest expense) divided by Interest expense.

Smart Touch Learning, which is organized as a sole proprietorship, is not a separate taxable entity. The owner, Sheena Bright, pays the income tax on the company's earnings instead of the business. Therefore, Smart Touch Learning (the business) will not have income tax expense. However, many businesses are organized as corporations, which are separate taxable entities. The corporation pays the income tax on the company's earnings and has an account, Income Tax Expense, to record the expense.

Let's evaluate **Kohl's Corporation's** ability to pay its interest expense. The following amounts (in millions) are taken from Kohl's income statement.

Learning Objective 5
Use the times-interest-earned ratio to evaluate business performance

Times-Interest-Earned Ratio
Evaluates a business's ability to pay interest expense. (Net income + Income tax expense + Interest expense) / Interest expense.

	Year Ended February 2, 2019	Year Ended February 3, 2018
Net income	$ 801	$ 859
Income tax expense	241	258
Interest expense	256	299

Kohl's times-interest-earned ratios for the years ended February 2, 2019 (2018 fiscal year), and February 3, 2018 (2017 fiscal year), are calculated as follows:

Times-interest-earned ratio = (Net income + Income tax expense + Interest expense) / Interest expense

2018
= ($801 + $241 + $256) / $256
= 5.07

2017
= ($859 + $258 + $299) / $299
= 4.74

Notice that from 2017 to 2018, Kohl's experienced a slight increase in its times-interest-earned ratio. This is because Kohl's incurred less interest expense in 2018. This decrease in interest expense increased Kohl's times-interest-earned ratio from 4.74 times to 5.07 times. It would appear that Kohl's can cover its interest expense.

11-20 Financial chapter 11

9. Fitzgerald Company reported the following amounts on its 2024 income statement:

	Year Ended December 31, 2024
Net income	$ 19,300
Income tax expense	5,800
Interest expense	900

What is Fitzgerald's times-interest-earned ratio for 2024? (Round your answer to two decimals.)

Check your answer online in MyLab Accounting or at http://www.pearsonhighered.com/Horngren.

For more practice, see Short Exercise S-F:11-13. **MyLab Accounting**

REVIEW

> Things You Should Know

1. How are current liabilities of known amounts accounted for?

- Current liabilities are liabilities that must be paid with cash or with goods and services within one year or within the entity's operating cycle if the cycle is longer than a year.
- Some examples of current liabilities are accounts payable, sales tax payable, unearned revenue, and short-term notes payable.
- Current liabilities also include any current portion of long-term notes payable.

2. How do companies account for and record payroll?

- Gross pay is the total amount of salary, wages, commissions, and other compensation earned by the employee. Net pay is the amount that each employee gets to keep (take-home pay).
- Payroll withholding deductions are the difference between gross pay and net pay. Examples of payroll deductions that *employees* pay include:
  - Income tax withholding: federal, state, and local income tax
  - Employee FICA tax (for 2019):
    - OASDI: 6.2% on the first $132,900 of annual earnings
    - Medicare: 1.45% on earnings up to $200,000, 2.35% on all earnings above $200,000
  - Optional withholdings: charitable contributions, union dues, and so on
- A payroll register can be used to help summarize the earnings, withholdings, and net pay for each employee.
- Businesses record a journal entry for payroll and payroll withholdings as a debit to Salaries and Wages Expense and a credit to various liabilities until the amounts are paid.

- *Employers* must pay at least three payroll taxes:
  - Employer FICA tax (for 2019):
    - OASDI: 6.2% on the first $132,900 of each employee's annual earnings
    - Medicare: 1.45% on all earnings
  - State unemployment compensation tax (SUTA): varies by state; we will use 5.4% on the first $7,000 of each employee's annual earnings
  - Federal unemployment compensation tax (FUTA): 0.6% on the first $7,000 of each employee's annual earnings
- Payroll taxes are recorded as a debit to Payroll Tax Expense and a credit to various liabilities until they are paid.
- Internal control over payroll involves efficiency and safeguarding of payroll disbursements.

3. How are current liabilities that must be estimated accounted for?

- Bonuses are based on meeting a specific goal and are considered liabilities (Employee Bonus Payable) until paid.
- Vacation, health, and pension benefits must be estimated and recorded as liabilities until paid.
- Warranty Expense (DR) and Estimated Warranty Payable (CR) must be recorded in the same period that the company records the revenue related to the warranty.
- As warranties are honored, the Estimated Warranty Payable account is reduced.

4. How are contingent liabilities accounted for?

- A contingent liability is a potential liability that depends on some future event.
- Accounting for contingent liabilities is based on the following likelihoods:
  - Remote: Do not disclose.
  - Reasonably possible: Describe the situation in a note to the financial statements.
  - Probable and the amount of the expense or loss *cannot* be estimated: Describe the situation in a note to the financial statements.
  - Probable and the amount of the expense or loss *can* be estimated: Record an expense or loss and a liability based on estimated amounts.

5. How do we use the times-interest-earned ratio to evaluate business performance?

- The times-interest-earned ratio is calculated as
(Net income + Income tax expense + Interest expense) / Interest expense.
- It measures the number of times earnings before interest and taxes (EBIT) can cover (pay) interest expense.

> Check Your Understanding F:11-1

Check your understanding of the chapter by completing this problem and then looking at the solution. Use this practice to help identify which sections of the chapter you need to study more.

Answer each question independently.

Requirements

1. A restaurant made cash sales of $4,000 subject to a 5% sales tax. Record the sales and the related sales tax. Also record the payment of the tax to the state. (See Learning Objective 1)
2. On October 1, 2024, Rhodes Company purchased equipment at a cost of $10,000, signing a nine-month, 8% note payable for that amount. Record the October 1 purchase. Also record the adjusting entry needed on December 31, 2024, and payment of the note plus interest at maturity on July 1, 2025. (See Learning Objective 1)
3. How does a contingent liability differ from a known liability? When would a contingent liability be journalized? (See Learning Objective 4)

> Solution

Requirement 1

Date	Accounts and Explanation	Debit	Credit
	Cash	4,200	
	Sales Revenue		4,000
	Sales Tax Payable ($4,000 × 0.05)		200
	To record cash sales and the related sales tax.		
	Sales Tax Payable	200	
	Cash		200
	To record cash payment for sales tax payable.		

Requirement 2

Date	Accounts and Explanation	Debit	Credit
2024			
Oct. 1	Equipment	10,000	
	Notes Payable		10,000
	Purchased equipment in exchange for nine-month, 8% note.		
Dec. 31	Interest Expense ($10,000 × 0.08 × 3/12)	200	
	Interest Payable		200
	Accrued interest expense at year-end.		
2025			
Jul. 1	Notes Payable	10,000	
	Interest Expense ($10,000 × 0.08 × 6/12)	400	
	Interest Payable	200	
	Cash		10,600
	Paid note and interest at maturity.		

Requirement 3

A contingent liability is a *potential*, rather than an actual, liability because it depends on a future event. Some event must happen (the contingency) for a contingent liability to have to be paid. Contingent liabilities are journalized when the likelihood of an actual loss is *probable* and the amount of the expense can be reasonably estimated.

> Check Your Understanding F:11-2

Check your understanding of the chapter by completing this problem and then looking at the solution. Use this practice to help identify which sections of the chapter you need to study more.

Rags-to-Riches, a clothing resale store, employs one salesperson, Dee Hunter. Hunter's straight-time wage is $10 per hour, with time-and-a-half pay for hours above 40. Rags-to-Riches withholds income tax (20%), FICA—OASDI (6.2%), and FICA—Medicare (1.45%) from Hunter's pay. Rags-to-Riches also pays payroll taxes for FICA—OASDI (6.2%), FICA—Medicare (1.45%), and state and federal unemployment (5.4% and 0.6%, respectively).

During the week ended December 26, Hunter worked 50 hours. Prior to this week, she had earned $2,000.

Requirements

(Round all amounts to the nearest dollar.)

1. Compute Hunter's gross pay and net (take-home) pay for the week. (See Learning Objective 2)
2. Record the payroll entries that Rags-to-Riches would make for each of the following (See Learning Objective 2):
   a. Accrual of salaries and wages expense and subsequent payment related to Hunter
   b. Employer payroll taxes accrual related to Hunter
   c. Payment of all payroll taxes (employee and employer related)
3. How much was Rags-to-Riches' total payroll expense for the week? (See Learning Objective 2)

> Solution

Requirement 1

Gross pay:		
Straight-time pay ($40 hours × $10 / hour)		$ 400
Overtime pay:		
Rate per hour ($10 × 1.5)	$ 15	
Hours (50 hours − 40 hours)	× 10	
		150
Gross pay		$ 550
Net pay:		
Gross pay		$ 550
Withholding deductions:		
Employee income tax ($550 × 0.20)	$ 110	
Employee OASDI ($550 × 0.062)	34	
Employee Medicare ($550 × 0.0145)	8	
Total withholdings		152
Net (take-home) pay		$ 398

Requirement 2

Date	Accounts and Explanation	Debit	Credit
a.	Salaries and Wages Expense	550	
	FICA—OASDI Taxes Payable		34
	FICA—Medicare Taxes Payable		8
	Employee Income Taxes Payable		110
	Salaries and Wages Payable		398
	To record salaries and wages expense and payroll withholdings.		
	Salaries and Wages Payable	398	
	Cash		398
	To record payment of salaries and wages.		
b.	Payroll Tax Expense	75	
	FICA—OASDI Taxes Payable ($550 × 0.062)		34
	FICA—Medicare Taxes Payable ($550 × 0.0145)		8
	Federal Unemployment Taxes Payable ($550 × 0.006)		3
	State Unemployment Taxes Payable ($550 × 0.054)		30
	To record employer's payroll tax expense.		
c.	FICA—OASDI Taxes Payable ($34 + $34)	68	
	FICA—Medicare Taxes Payable ($8 + $8)	16	
	Employee Income Taxes Payable	110	
	Federal Unemployment Taxes Payable	3	
	State Unemployment Taxes Payable	30	
	Cash		227
	To record payment of payroll tax liabilities.		

Requirement 3

Rags-to-Riches incurred *total payroll expense* of $625 (gross pay of $550 + payroll tax expense of $75).

> Key Terms

Contingent Liability (p. 11-17)
Current Liability (p. 11-2)
Current Portion of Notes Payable (p. 11-5)
Federal Insurance Contributions Act (FICA) (p. 11-8)
Gross Pay (p. 11-7)

Income Tax Withholding (p. 11-7)
Liabilities (p. 11-2)
Long-term Liability (p. 11-2)
Net Pay (p. 11-7)
Payroll Register (p. 11-9)
Pension Plan (p. 11-15)
Short-term Note Payable (p. 11-4)

Social Security (FICA) Tax (p. 11-8)
Times-Interest-Earned Ratio (p. 11-19)
Unemployment Compensation Taxes (p. 11-11)
Warranty (p. 11-15)

> Quick Check

1. On January 1, 2024, a business borrowed $18,000 on a five-year, 5% note payable. At December 31, 2024, the business should record

   a. interest payable of $900.
   b. note receivable of $18,000.
   c. cash payment of $18,000.
   d. nothing. (The note is already on the books.)

2. A company sells $180,000 (sales price) of goods and collects sales tax of 8%. What current liability does the sale create?

   a. Sales tax payable of $14,400
   b. Sales revenue of $194,400
   c. Unearned revenue of $14,400
   d. None; the company collected cash up front.

3. Jade Larson Antiques owes $20,000 on a truck purchased for use in the business. Assume the company makes timely principal payments of $5,000 each year at December 31 plus interest at 8%. Which of the following is true?

   a. After the first payment is made, the company owes $15,000 plus three years' interest.
   b. After the first payment, $15,000 would be shown as a long-term liability.
   c. After the first payment is made, $5,000 would be shown as the current portion due on the long-term note.
   d. Just before the last payment is made, $5,000 will appear as a long-term liability on the balance sheet.

4. An employee has year-to-date earnings of $129,800. The employee's gross pay for the next pay period is $5,000. If the FICA—OASDI is 6.2% and the wage base is $132,900, how much FICA—OASDI tax will be withheld from the employee's pay? (Answer is rounded to whole dollar.)

   a. $192   b. $210   c. $310   d. $73

5. The employer is responsible for which of the following payroll taxes?

   a. 6.2% FICA—OASDI tax
   b. 1.45% FICA—Medicare tax
   c. Federal and state unemployment taxes
   d. All of the above

6. Known liabilities of estimated amounts are

   a. ignored. (Record them when paid.)
   b. reported on the balance sheet.
   c. reported on the income statement.
   d. reported only in the notes to the financial statements.

7. Wells Electric (WE) owed Estimated Warranty Payable of $1,200 at the end of 2023. During 2024, WE made sales of $120,000 and expects product warranties to cost the company 3% of the sales. During 2024, WE paid $2,300 for warranties. What is WE's Estimated Warranty Payable at the end of 2024?

   a. $2,300   b. $2,500   c. $3,600   d. $4,800

Learning Objective 3

8. Vega Company expects to pay a 4% bonus on net income after deducting the bonus. Assume the company reports net income of $130,000 before the calculation of the bonus. The journal entry to record the accrued bonus includes

    a. a debit to Employee Bonus Payable, $5,000.
    b. a debit to Employee Bonus Expense, $5,200.
    c. a credit to Employee Bonus Payable, $5,000.
    d. a credit to Cash, $5,200.

Learning Objective 4

9. Swell Company has a lawsuit pending from a customer claiming damages of $100,000. Swell's attorney advises that the likelihood the customer will win is remote. GAAP requires at a minimum that this contingent liability be

    a. disclosed in the footnotes.
    b. disclosed in the footnotes, with ranges of potential loss.
    c. recorded as a journal entry, as well as disclosed in the footnotes.
    d. No disclosure is required.

Learning Objective 5

10. McDaniel and Associates, Inc. reported the following amounts on its 2024 income statement:

	Year Ended December 31, 2024
Net income	$ 60,500
Income tax expense	12,100
Interest expense	5,000

    What was McDaniel's times-interest-earned ratio for 2024?

    a. 12.10   b. 15.52   c. 13.10   d. 14.52

Check your answers at the end of the chapter.

ASSESS YOUR PROGRESS

> Review Questions

1. What are the three main characteristics of liabilities?
2. What is a current liability? Provide some examples of current liabilities.
3. How is sales tax recorded? Is it considered an expense of a business? Why or why not?
4. How do unearned revenues arise?
5. What do short-term notes payable represent?
6. Coltrane Company has a $5,000 note payable that is paid in $1,000 installments over five years. How would the portion that must be paid within the next year be reported on the balance sheet?
7. What is the difference between gross pay and net pay?
8. List the required employee payroll withholding deductions and provide the tax rate for each.

9. How might a business use a payroll register?
10. What payroll taxes is the employer responsible for paying?
11. What are the two main controls for payroll? Provide an example of each.
12. When do businesses record warranty expense, and why?
13. What is a contingent liability? Provide some examples of contingencies.
14. Curtis Company is facing a potential lawsuit. Curtis's lawyers think that it is reasonably possible that it will lose the lawsuit. How should Curtis report this lawsuit?
15. How is the times-interest-earned ratio calculated, and what does it evaluate?

> Short Exercises

For all payroll calculations, use the following tax rates and round amounts to the nearest cent.

Employee: OASDI: 6.2% on first $132,900 earned; Medicare: 1.45% up to $200,000, 2.35% on earnings above $200,000.

Employer: OASDI: 6.2% on first $132,900 earned; Medicare: 1.45%; FUTA: 0.6% on first $7,000 earned; SUTA: 5.4% on first $7,000 earned.

S-F:11-1 Determining current versus long-term liabilities

Learning Objective 1

Rios Raft Company had the following liabilities.

a. Accounts Payable
b. Note Payable due in three years
c. Salaries Payable
d. Note Payable due in six months
e. Sales Tax Payable
f. Unearned Revenue due in eight months

Determine whether each liability would be considered a current liability (CL) or a long-term liability (LTL).

S-F:11-2 Recording sales tax

Learning Objective 1

On July 5, Williams Company recorded sales of merchandise inventory on account, $55,000. The sales were subject to sales tax of 4%. On August 15, Williams Company paid the sales tax owed to the state from the July 5 transaction.

Requirements

1. Journalize the transaction to record the sale on July 5. Ignore cost of goods sold.
2. Journalize the transaction to record the payment of sales tax to the state on August 15.

S-F:11-3 Recording unearned revenue

Learning Objective 1

On June 1, *Movies Online* collected cash of $63,000 on future annual subscriptions starting on July 1.

Requirements

1. Journalize the transaction to record the collection of cash on June 1.
2. Journalize the transaction required at December 31, the company's year-end, assuming no revenue earned has been recorded. (Round adjustment to the nearest whole dollar.)

Learning Objective 1

S-F:11-4 Accounting for a note payable

On December 31, 2023, Franklin purchased $13,000 of merchandise inventory on a one-year, 9% note payable. Franklin uses a perpetual inventory system.

Requirements

1. Journalize the company's purchase of merchandise inventory on December 31, 2023.
2. Journalize the company's accrual of interest expense on June 30, 2024, its fiscal year-end.
3. Journalize the company's payment of the note plus interest on December 31, 2024.

Learning Objective 1

S-F:11-5 Determining current portion of long-term note payable

On January 1, Irving Company purchased equipment of $280,000 with a long-term note payable. The debt is payable in annual installments of $56,000 due on December 31 of each year. At the date of purchase, how will Irving Company report the note payable?

Learning Objective 2

S-F:11-6 Computing and journalizing an employee's total pay

Lucy Rose works at College of Fort Worth and is paid $12 per hour for a 40-hour workweek and time-and-a-half for hours above 40.

Requirements

1. Compute Rose's gross pay for working 60 hours during the first week of February.
2. Rose is single, and her income tax withholding is 15% of total pay. Rose's only payroll deductions are payroll taxes. Compute Rose's net (take-home) pay for the week. Assume Rose's earnings to date are less than the OASDI limit.
3. Journalize the accrual of wages expense and the payment related to the employment of Lucy Rose.

Learning Objective 2

S-F:11-7 Computing payroll amounts considering FICA tax limits

Lily Carter works for JDK all year and earns a monthly salary of $12,300. There is no overtime pay. Lily's income tax withholding rate is 15% of gross pay. In addition to payroll taxes, Lily elects to contribute 4% monthly to United Way. JDK also deducts $200 monthly for co-payment of the health insurance premium. As of September 30, Lily had $125,100 of cumulative earnings.

Requirements

1. Compute Lily's net pay for October.
2. Journalize the accrual of salaries expense and the payment related to the employment of Lily Carter.

Learning Objective 2

S-F:11-8 Computing and journalizing the payroll expense and payments

Macintosh Company has monthly salaries of $26,000. Assume Macintosh pays all the standard payroll taxes, no employees have reached the payroll tax limits, total income tax withheld is $2,000, and the only payroll deductions are payroll taxes. Journalize the accrual of salaries expense, accrual of employer payroll taxes, and payment of employee and employer payroll taxes for Macintosh Company.

Learning Objective 3

S-F:11-9 Computing bonus payable

On December 31, Weston Company estimates that it will pay its employees a 5% bonus on net income after deducting the bonus. The company reports net income of $64,000 before the calculation of the bonus. The bonus will be paid on January 15 of the next year.

Requirements

1. Journalize the December 31 transaction for Weston.
2. Journalize the payment of the bonus on January 15.

S-F:11-10 Journalizing vacation benefits

Samuel Industries has three employees. Each employee earns two vacation days a month. Samuel pays each employee a weekly salary of $1,250 for a five-day workweek.

Requirements

1. Determine the amount of vacation expense for one month.
2. Journalize the entry to accrue the vacation expense for the month.

S-F:11-11 Accounting for warranty expense and warranty payable

Trail Runner guarantees its snowmobiles for three years. Company experience indicates that warranty costs will be approximately 5% of sales.

Assume that the Trail Runner dealer in Colorado Springs made sales totaling $600,000 during 2024. The company received cash for 20% of the sales and notes receivable for the remainder. Warranty payments totaled $10,000 during 2024.

Requirements

1. Record the sales, warranty expense, and warranty payments for the company. Ignore cost of goods sold.
2. Assume the Estimated Warranty Payable is $0 on January 1, 2024. Post the 2024 transactions to the Estimated Warranty Payable T-account. At the end of 2024, how much in Estimated Warranty Payable does the company owe?

S-F:11-12 Accounting treatment for contingencies

Freeman Motors, a motorcycle manufacturer, had the following contingencies.

a. Freeman estimates that it is reasonably possible but not likely that it will lose a current lawsuit. Freeman's attorneys estimate the potential loss will be $4,500,000.

b. Freeman received notice that it was being sued. Freeman considers this lawsuit to be frivolous.

c. Freeman is currently the defendant in a lawsuit. Freeman believes it is likely that it will lose the lawsuit and estimates the damages to be paid will be $75,000.

Determine the appropriate accounting treatment for each of the situations Freeman is facing.

S-F:11-13 Computing times-interest-earned ratio

Abernathy Electronics, Inc. reported the following amounts on its 2024 income statement:

Year Ended December 31, 2024	
Net income	$ 45,000
Income tax expense	6,750
Interest expense	3,750

What is Abernathy's times-interest-earned ratio for 2024? (Round to two decimals.)

> Exercises

For all payroll calculations, use the following tax rates and round amounts to the nearest cent.

Employee: OASDI: 6.2% on first $132,900 earned; Medicare: 1.45% up to $200,000, 2.35% on earnings above $200,000.

Employer: OASDI: 6.2% on first $132,900 earned; Medicare: 1.45%; FUTA: 0.6% on first $7,000 earned; SUTA: 5.4% on first $7,000 earned.

Learning Objective 1

Sales Tax Payable $16,100

E-F:11-14 Recording sales tax

Consider the following transactions of Sapphire Software:

| Mar. 31 | Recorded cash sales of $230,000, plus sales tax of 7% collected for the state of New Jersey. |
| Apr. 6 | Sent March sales tax to the state. |

Journalize the transactions for the company. Ignore cost of goods sold.

Learning Objective 1

Aug. 1, 2024 Interest Expense $840

E-F:11-15 Recording note payable transactions

Consider the following note payable transactions of Creative Video Productions.

2023	
Aug. 1	Purchased equipment costing $16,000 by issuing a one-year, 9% note payable.
Dec. 31	Accrued interest on the note payable.
2024	
Aug. 1	Paid the note payable plus interest at maturity.

Journalize the transactions for the company.

Learning Objective 1

Dec. 31 Subscription Revenue $80

E-F:11-16 Recording and reporting current liabilities

Watson Publishing completed the following transactions during 2024:

Oct. 1	Sold a six-month subscription (starting on November 1), collecting cash of $240, plus sales tax of 8%.
Nov. 15	Remitted (paid) the sales tax to the state of Tennessee.
Dec. 31	Made the necessary adjustment at year-end to record the amount of subscription revenue earned during the year.

Journalize the transactions (explanations are not required). Round to the nearest dollar.

Learning Objectives 1, 2

Salaries Expense $3,400

E-F:11-17 Journalizing current liabilities

Erin O'Neil Associates reported short-term notes payable and salaries payable as follows:

	2024	2023
Current Liabilities—partial:		
Short-term Notes Payable	$ 16,900	$ 16,000
Salaries Payable	3,400	4,000

During 2024, O'Neil paid off both current liabilities that were left over from 2023, borrowed cash on short-term notes payable, and accrued salaries expense. Journalize all four of these transactions for O'Neil during 2024. Assume no interest on short-term notes payable of $16,000.

E-F:11-18 Computing and recording gross and net pay

Learning Objective 2

1. Net Pay $576.69

Hugh Stanley manages a Dairy House drive-in. His straight-time pay is $12 per hour, with time-and-a-half for hours in excess of 40 per week. Stanley's payroll deductions include withheld income tax of 20%, FICA tax, and a weekly deduction of $5 for a charitable contribution to United Way. Stanley worked 58 hours during the week.

Requirements

1. Compute Stanley's gross pay and net pay for the week. Assume earnings to date are $18,000.
2. Journalize Dairy House's wages expense accrual for Stanley's work. An explanation is not required.
3. Journalize the subsequent payment of wages to Stanley.

E-F:11-19 Recording employer payroll taxes and employee benefits

Learning Objective 2

1. Payroll Tax Expense $6,063.00

Ricardo's Mexican Restaurant incurred salaries expense of $62,000 for 2024. The payroll expense includes employer FICA tax, in addition to state unemployment tax and federal unemployment tax. Of the total salaries, $22,000 is subject to unemployment tax. Also, the company provides the following benefits for employees: health insurance (cost to the company, $3,000), life insurance (cost to the company, $330), and retirement benefits (cost to the company, 10% of salaries expense).

Requirements

1. Journalize Ricardo's expenses for employee benefits and for payroll taxes. Explanations are not required.
2. What was Ricardo's total expense for 2024 related to payroll?

E-F:11-20 Recording employee and employer payroll taxes

Learning Objective 2

2. Salaries & Wages Payable $12,462.10

Stream Company had the following partially completed payroll register:

Earnings			Withholdings								
Beginning Cumulative Earnings	Current Period Earnings	Ending Cumulative Earnings	OASDI	Medicare	Income Tax	Health Insurance	United Way	Total Withholdings	Net Pay	Check No.	Salaries and Wages Expense
$ 79,000	$ 4,200				$ 1,680	$ 84	$ 5			801	
126,000	7,200				1,800	144	40			802	
56,000	3,900				1,560	78	0			803	
61,500	4,700				1,175	94	20			804	
0	1,000				250	20	0			805	
$ 322,500	$ 21,000				$ 6,465	$ 420	$ 65				

11-32 Financial chapter 11

Requirements
1. Complete the payroll register. Round to two decimals.
2. Journalize Stream Company's salaries and wages expense accrual for the current pay period.
3. Journalize Stream Company's expenses for employer payroll taxes for the current pay period.
4. Journalize the payment to employees.
5. Journalize the payment for withholdings and employer payroll taxes.

Learning Objective 3

E-F:11-21 Accounting for warranty expense and warranty payable

The accounting records of Sculpted Ceramics included the following at January 1, 2024:

1. Warranty Expense $10,170

Estimated Warranty Payable	
	5,000 Beg. Bal.

In the past, Sculpted's warranty expense has been 9% of sales. During 2024, Sculpted made sales of $113,000 and paid $7,000 to satisfy warranty claims.

Requirements
1. Journalize Sculpted's warranty expense and warranty payments during 2024. Explanations are not required.
2. What balance of Estimated Warranty Payable will Sculpted report on its balance sheet at December 31, 2024?

Learning Objective 3

E-F:11-22 Accounting for warranties, vacation, and bonuses

McNight Industries completed the following transactions during 2024:

Nov. 1	Made sales of $52,000. McNight estimates that warranty expense is 6% of sales. (Record only the warranty expense.)
20	Paid $1,600 to satisfy warranty claims.
Dec. 31	Estimated vacation benefits expense to be $6,000.
31	McNight expected to pay its employees a 3% bonus on net income after deducting the bonus. Net income for the year is $52,000.

Journalize the transactions. Explanations are not required. Round to the nearest dollar.

Learning Objective 4

E-F:11-23 Accounting treatment for contingencies

Analyze the following independent situations.

a. Weaver Company is being sued by a former employee. Weaver believes that there is a remote chance that the employee will win. The employee is suing Weaver for damages of $40,000.

b. Gulf Oil Refinery had a gas explosion on one of its oil rigs. Gulf believes it is likely that it will have to pay environmental clean-up costs and damages in the future due to the gas explosion. Gulf cannot estimate the amount of the damages.

c. Lawson Enterprises estimates that it will have to pay $75,000 in warranty repairs next year.

Determine how each contingency should be treated.

E-F:11-24 Computing times-interest-earned ratio

Learning Objective 5

The following financial information was obtained from the year ended 2024 income statements for Cash Automotive, Inc. and Pennington Automotive, Inc.:

	Cash	Pennington
Net income	$ 26,070	$ 74,188
Income tax expense	9,270	27,080
Interest expense	300	2,900

Requirements

1. Compute the times-interest-earned ratio for each company. Round to two decimals.
2. Which company was better able to cover its interest expense?

> Problems Group A

For all payroll calculations, use the following tax rates and round amounts to the nearest cent.

Employee: OASDI: 6.2% on first $132,900 earned; Medicare: 1.45% up to $200,000, 2.35% on earnings above $200,000.

Employer: OASDI: 6.2% on first $132,900 earned; Medicare: 1.45%; FUTA: 0.6% on first $7,000 earned; SUTA: 5.4% on first $7,000 earned.

P-F:11-25A Journalizing and posting liabilities

Learning Objectives 1, 2

The general ledger of Seal-N-Ship at June 30, 2024, the end of the company's fiscal year, includes the following account balances before payroll and adjusting entries.

Accounts Payable	$ 114,000
Interest Payable	0
Salaries Payable	0
Employee Income Taxes Payable	0
FICA—OASDI Taxes Payable	0
FICA—Medicare Taxes Payable	0
Federal Unemployment Taxes Payable	0
State Unemployment Taxes Payable	0
Unearned Rent Revenue	7,200
Long-term Notes Payable	210,000

The additional data needed to develop the payroll and adjusting entries at June 30 are as follows:

a. The long-term debt is payable in annual installments of $42,000, with the next installment due on July 31. On that date, Seal-N-Ship will also pay one year's interest at 9%. Interest was paid on July 31 of the preceding year. Make the adjusting entry to accrue interest expense at year-end.

b. Gross unpaid salaries for the last payroll of the fiscal year were $4,700. Assume that employee income taxes withheld are $910 and that all earnings are subject to OASDI.

c. Record the associated employer taxes payable for the last payroll of the fiscal year, $4,700. Assume that the earnings are not subject to unemployment compensation taxes.

d. On February 1, the company collected one year's rent of $7,200 in advance.

Requirements

1. Using T-accounts, open the listed accounts and insert the unadjusted June 30 balances.
2. Journalize and post the June 30 payroll and adjusting entries to the accounts that you opened. Identify each adjusting entry by letter. Round to the nearest dollar.
3. Prepare the current liabilities section of the balance sheet at June 30, 2024.

Learning Objective 2

P-F:11-26A Computing and journalizing payroll amounts

1. Net Pay $146,935

Lenny Worthington is general manager of Countrywide Salons. During 2024, Worthington worked for the company all year at a $13,400 monthly salary. He also earned a year-end bonus equal to 10% of his annual salary.

Worthington's federal income tax withheld during 2024 was $938 per month, plus $3,216 on his bonus check. State income tax withheld came to $70 per month, plus $50 on the bonus. FICA tax was withheld on the annual earnings. Worthington authorized the following payroll deductions: Charity Fund contribution of 2% of total earnings and life insurance of $20 per month.

Countrywide incurred payroll tax expense on Worthington for FICA tax. The company also paid state unemployment tax and federal unemployment tax.

Requirements

1. Compute Worthington's gross pay, payroll deductions, and net pay for the full year 2024. Round all amounts to the nearest dollar.
2. Compute Countrywide's total 2024 payroll tax expense for Worthington.
3. Make the journal entry to record Countrywide's expense for Worthington's total earnings for the year, his payroll deductions, and net pay. Debit Salaries Expense and Bonus Expense as appropriate. Credit liability accounts for the payroll deductions and Cash for net pay. An explanation is not required.
4. Make the journal entry to record the accrual of Countrywide's payroll tax expense for Worthington's total earnings.
5. Make the journal entry for the payment of the payroll withholdings and taxes.

Learning Objectives 1, 3

P-F:11-27A Journalizing liability transactions

Jan. 29 Cash $16,695

The following transactions of Plymouth Pharmacies occurred during 2023 and 2024:

2023		
Jan.	9	Purchased computer equipment at a cost of $12,000, signing a six-month, 9% note payable for that amount.
	29	Recorded the week's sales of $63,000, three-fourths on credit and one-fourth for cash. Sales amounts are subject to a 6% state sales tax. Ignore cost of goods sold.
Feb.	5	Sent the last week's sales tax to the state.
Jul.	9	Paid the six-month, 9% note, plus interest, at maturity.
Aug.	31	Purchased merchandise inventory for $9,000, signing a six-month, 10% note payable. The company uses the perpetual inventory system.
Dec.	31	Accrued warranty expense, which is estimated at 4% of sales of $609,000.
	31	Accrued interest on all outstanding notes payable.
2024		
Feb.	28	Paid the six-month 10% note, plus interest, at maturity.

Journalize the transactions in Plymouth's general journal. Explanations are not required. Round to the nearest dollar.

P-F:11-28A Journalizing liability transactions

Learning Objectives 3, 4

The following transactions of Jasmine Reef occurred during 2024:

Apr. 30	Reef is party to a patent infringement lawsuit of $190,000. Reef's attorney is certain it is remote that Reef will lose this lawsuit.
Jun. 30	Estimated warranty expense at 2% of sales of $350,000.
Jul. 28	Warranty claims paid in the amount of $5,500.
Sep. 30	Reef is party to a lawsuit for copyright violation of $80,000. Reef's attorney advises that it is probable Reef will lose this lawsuit. The attorney estimates the loss at $80,000.
Dec. 31	Reef estimated warranty expense on sales for the second half of the year of $510,000 at 2%.

Requirements

1. Journalize required transactions, if any, in Reef's general journal. Explanations are not required.
2. What is the balance in Estimated Warranty Payable assuming a beginning balance of $0?

P-F:11-29A Computing times-interest-earned ratio

Learning Objective 5

The income statement for California Communications, Inc. follows. Assume California Communications, Inc. signed a three-month, 9%, $3,000 note on June 1, 2024, and that this was the only note payable for the company.

CALIFORNIA COMMUNICATIONS, INC.
Income Statement
Year Ended July 31, 2024

Net Sales Revenue		$ 21,800
Cost of Goods Sold		14,000
Gross Profit		7,800
Operating Expenses:		
Selling Expenses	$ 720	
Administrative Expenses	1,650	
Total Operating Expenses		2,370
Operating Income		5,430
Other Income and (Expenses):		
Interest Expense	?	
Total Other Income and (Expenses)		?
Net Income before Income Tax Expense		?
Income Tax Expense		1,080
Net Income		$?

Requirements

1. Fill in the missing information for California's year ended July 31, 2024, income statement. Round to the nearest dollar.
2. Compute the times-interest-earned ratio for the company. Round to two decimals.

> Problems Group B

Learning Objectives 1, 2

P-F:11-30B Journalizing and posting liabilities

The general ledger of Prompt Ship at June 30, 2024, the end of the company's fiscal year, includes the following account balances before payroll and adjusting entries.

Accounts Payable	$ 118,000
Interest Payable	0
Salaries Payable	0
Employee Income Taxes Payable	0
FICA—OASDI Taxes Payable	0
FICA—Medicare Taxes Payable	0
Federal Unemployment Taxes Payable	0
State Unemployment Taxes Payable	0
Unearned Rent Revenue	5,400
Long-term Notes Payable	198,000

The additional data needed to develop the payroll and adjusting entries at June 30 are as follows:

a. The long-term debt is payable in annual installments of $39,600, with the next installment due on July 31. On that date, Prompt Ship will also pay one year's interest at 10%. Interest was paid on July 31 of the preceding year. Make the adjusting entry to accrue interest expense at year-end.

b. Gross unpaid salaries for the last payroll of the fiscal year were $4,800. Assume that employee income taxes withheld are $920 and that all earnings are subject to OASDI.

c. Record the associated employer taxes payable for the last payroll of the fiscal year, $4,800. Assume that the earnings are not subject to unemployment compensation taxes.

d. On February 1, the company collected one year's rent of $5,400 in advance.

Requirements

1. Using T-accounts, open the listed accounts and insert the unadjusted June 30 balances.
2. Journalize and post the June 30 payroll and adjusting entries to the accounts that you opened. Identify each adjusting entry by letter. Round to the nearest dollar.
3. Prepare the current liabilities section of the balance sheet at June 30, 2024.

P-F:11-31B Computing and journalizing payroll amounts

Learning Objective 2

1. Net Pay $134,380

Lee Werner is general manager of Worldwide Salons. During 2024, Werner worked for the company all year at a $12,400 monthly salary. He also earned a year-end bonus equal to 20% of his annual salary.

Werner's federal income tax withheld during 2024 was $1,860 per month, plus $4,464 on his bonus check. State income tax withheld came to $90 per month, plus $70 on the bonus. FICA tax was withheld on the annual earnings. Werner authorized the following payroll deductions: Charity Fund contribution of 3% of total earnings and life insurance of $5 per month.

Worldwide incurred payroll tax expense on Werner for FICA tax. The company also paid state unemployment tax and federal unemployment tax.

Requirements

1. Compute Werner's gross pay, payroll deductions, and net pay for the full year 2024. Round all amounts to the nearest dollar.
2. Compute Worldwide's total 2024 payroll tax expense for Werner.
3. Make the journal entry to record Worldwide's expense for Werner's total earnings for the year, his payroll deductions, and net pay. Debit Salaries Expense and Bonus Expense as appropriate. Credit liability accounts for the payroll deductions and Cash for net pay. An explanation is not required.
4. Make the journal entry to record the accrual of Worldwide's payroll tax expense for Werner's total earnings.
5. Make the journal entry for the payment of the payroll withholdings and taxes.

P-F:11-32B Journalizing liability transactions

Learning Objectives 1, 3

Jan. 29 Cash $18,020

The following transactions of Philadelphia Pharmacies occurred during 2023 and 2024:

2023	
Jan. 9	Purchased computer equipment at a cost of $7,000, signing a six-month, 8% note payable for that amount.
29	Recorded the week's sales of $68,000, three-fourths on credit and one-fourth for cash. Sales amounts are subject to a 6% state sales tax. Ignore cost of goods sold.
Feb. 5	Sent the last week's sales tax to the state.
Jul. 9	Paid the six-month, 8% note, plus interest, at maturity.
Aug. 31	Purchased merchandise inventory for $3,000, signing a six-month, 10% note payable. The company uses a perpetual inventory system.
Dec. 31	Accrued warranty expense, which is estimated at 2% of sales of $609,000.
31	Accrued interest on all outstanding notes payable.
2024	
Feb. 28	Paid the six-month 10% note, plus interest, at maturity.

Journalize the transactions in Philadelphia's general journal. Explanations are not required.

Learning Objectives 3, 4

P-F:11-33B Journalizing liability transactions

The following transactions of Belkin Howe occurred during 2024:

Apr. 30	Howe is party to a patent infringement lawsuit of $230,000. Howe's attorney is certain it is remote that Howe will lose this lawsuit.
Jun. 30	Estimated warranty expense at 3% of sales of $390,000.
Jul. 28	Warranty claims paid in the amount of $6,300.
Sep. 30	Howe is party to a lawsuit for copyright violation of $90,000. Howe's attorney advises that it is probable Howe will lose this lawsuit. The attorney estimates the loss at $90,000.
Dec. 31	Howe estimated warranty expense on sales for the second half of the year of $520,000 at 3%.

Requirements

1. Journalize required transactions, if any, in Howe's general journal. Explanations are not required.
2. What is the balance in Estimated Warranty Payable assuming a beginning balance of $0?

Learning Objective 5

P-F:11-34B Computing times-interest-earned ratio

The income statement for Vermont Communications, Inc. follows. Assume Vermont Communications, Inc. signed a three-month, 3%, $6,000 note on June 1, 2024, and that this was the only note payable for the company.

VERMONT COMMUNICATIONS, INC.
Income Statement
Year Ended July 31, 2024

Net Sales Revenue		$ 26,500
Cost of Goods Sold		12,200
Gross Profit		14,300
Operating Expenses:		
Selling Expenses	$ 690	
Administrative Expenses	1,550	
Total Operating Expenses		2,240
Operating Income		12,060
Other Income and (Expenses):		
Interest Expense	?	
Total Other Income and (Expenses)		?
Net Income before Income Tax Expense		?
Income Tax Expense		2,410
Net Income		$?

Requirements

1. Fill in the missing information for Vermont's year ended July 31, 2024, income statement. Round to the nearest dollar.
2. Compute the times-interest-earned ratio for the company. Round to two decimals.

CRITICAL THINKING

> Using Excel

Download Excel problems for this chapter online in MyLab Accounting or at **http://www.pearsonhighered.com/Horngren**.

> Continuing Problem

P-F:11-35 Accounting for liabilities of a known amount

This problem continues the Canyon Canoe Company situation from Chapter F:10. Amber Wilson is continuing her analysis of the company's position and believes the company will need to borrow $15,000 in order to expand operations. She consults Rivers Nation Bank and secures a 6%, one-year note on September 1, 2025, with interest due at maturity. Additionally, the company hires an employee, John Vance, on September 1. John will receive a salary of $3,000 per month. Payroll deductions include federal income tax at 25%, OASDI at 6.2%, Medicare at 1.45%, and monthly health insurance premium of $250. The company will incur matching FICA taxes, FUTA tax at 0.6%, and SUTA tax at 5.4%. Round calculations to two decimals. Omit explanations on journal entries.

Requirements

1. Record the issuance of the $15,000 note payable on September 1, 2025.
2. Record the employee payroll and employer payroll tax entries on September 30, 2025.
3. Record all payments related to September's payroll. Payments are made on October 15, 2025.
4. Record the entry to accrue interest due on the note at December 31, 2025.
5. Record the entry Canyon Canoe Company would make to record the payment to the bank on September 1, 2026.

> Tying It All Together Case F:11-1

Before you begin this assignment, review the Tying It All Together feature in the chapter. It will also be helpful if you review UnitedHealth Group Incorporated's 2018 annual report (**https://www.sec.gov/Archives/edgar/data/731766/000073176619000005/unh2018123110-k.htm**).

UnitedHealth Group Incorporated is a diversified health and well-being company dedicated to helping people live healthier lives. The company operates under two distinct platforms: health benefits (UnitedHealthcare) and health services (Optum).

Requirements

1. What are contingent liabilities?
2. Review Note 12 (Commitments and Contingencies), specifically the section labeled Legal Matters. Does UnitedHealth Group Incorporated report any contingencies? If so, provide a summary.
3. How should a company handle contingent liabilities that are reasonably possible or probable but cannot be estimated?
4. Review Note 12 (Commitments and Contingencies), specifically the section labeled Department of Justice (DOJ). How did UnitedHealth Group Incorporated handle the recording of this contingent liability?

> Decision Cases

Decision Case F:11-1

Golden Bear Construction operates throughout California. The owner, Gaylan Beavers, employs 15 work crews. Construction supervisors report directly to Beavers, and the supervisors are trusted employees. The home office staff consists of an accountant and an office manager.

Because employee turnover is high in the construction industry, supervisors hire and fire their own crews. Supervisors notify the office of all personnel changes. Also, supervisors forward the employee W-4 forms to the home office. Each Thursday, the supervisors submit weekly time sheets for their crews, and the accountant prepares the payroll. At noon on Friday, the supervisors come to the office to get paychecks for distribution to the workers at 5 p.m.

The company accountant prepares the payroll, including the paychecks. Beavers signs all paychecks. To verify that each construction worker is a bona fide employee, the accountant matches the employee's endorsement signature on the back of the canceled paycheck with the signature on that employee's W-4 form.

Requirements

1. Identify one way that a supervisor can defraud Golden Bear Construction under the present system.

2. Discuss a control feature that the company can use to safeguard against the fraud you identified in Requirement 1.

Decision Case F:11-2

Sell-Soft is the defendant in numerous lawsuits claiming unfair trade practices. Sell-Soft has strong incentives not to disclose these contingent liabilities. However, GAAP requires that companies report their contingent liabilities.

Requirements

1. Why would a company prefer *not* to disclose its contingent liabilities?

2. Describe how a bank could be harmed if a company seeking a loan did not disclose its contingent liabilities.

3. What ethical tightrope must companies walk when they report contingent liabilities?

> Ethical Issue F:11-1

Many small businesses have to squeeze down costs any way they can just to survive. One way many businesses do this is by hiring workers as "independent contractors" rather than as regular employees. Unlike rules for regular employees, a business does not have to pay Social Security (FICA) taxes and unemployment insurance payments for independent contractors. Similarly, it does not have to withhold federal, state, or local income taxes or the employee's share of FICA taxes. The IRS has a "20 factor test" that determines whether a worker should be considered an employee or a contractor, but many businesses ignore those rules or interpret them loosely in their favor. When workers are treated as independent contractors, they do not get a W-2 form at tax time (they get a 1099 instead), they do not have any income taxes withheld, and they find themselves subject to "self-employment" taxes, by which they bear the brunt of both the employee's and the employer's shares of FICA taxes.

Requirements

1. When a business abuses this issue, how is the independent contractor hurt?
2. If a business takes an aggressive position—that is, interprets the law in a very slanted way—is there an ethical issue involved? Who is hurt?

> Financial Statement Case F:11-1

Details about a company's liabilities appear in a number of places in the annual report. Visit **http://www.pearsonhighered.com/Horngren** to view a link to **Target Corporation's** Annual Report. Use Target Corporation's fiscal 2018 financial statements to answer the following questions.

Requirements

1. Give the breakdown of Target's current liabilities at February 2, 2019.
2. Calculate Target's times-interest-earned ratio for the year ending February 2, 2019. How does Target's ratio compare to **Kohl's Corporation's** ratio?

> Communication Activity F:11-1

In 150 words or fewer, explain how contingent liabilities are accounted for.

> Quick Check Answers

1. a **2.** a **3.** c **4.** a **5.** d **6.** b **7.** b **8.** c **9.** d **10.** b

Partnerships   12

Should the Business Be Organized as a Partnership?

Christina White and Denise Cavalli are considering opening a miniature golf course in the small mountain community of Grand Park, Colorado. The golf course will have 18 holes with dinosaurs, windmills, water features, and more. Christina has been carefully evaluating the tourism industry in the town and believes that the golf course will be busy enough during the summer tourist season to close during the winter months, allowing Christina and Denise plenty of time to ski and snowboard in the off-season.

Christina and Denise are considering organizing the business as a partnership. Christina is willing to contribute a piece of property in the prime downtown area of Grand Park. She is also interested in managing the day-to-day operations of the business. Denise, with her degree in accounting, has agreed to handle the accounting and business aspects of the golf course.

Now all Christina and Denise need to decide is how the partnership will be organized. Some questions that they are considering include: What are the specific responsibilities of each partner? How should profits and losses be shared between the partners? What if one of the partners wants out of the partnership in the future? How does the partnership handle admitting new partners? Christina and Denise have asked their accountant and attorney to help answer all of these questions and more. They are ready to open the doors on their new business.

What Is a Partnership?

Many small businesses decide to operate as a partnership. Most partnerships are formed because that business structure allows individuals to pool their talents and resources to offer a better product or service to customers. In addition, partnerships are generally easy to organize and have substantial tax benefits. A partnership allows the business entity to pay out its earnings to its owners without incurring federal taxation at the entity level. Many partnerships are private organizations that are not open to public investors. However, some partnerships, such as **Cedar Fair, L.P.**, a regional amusement park operator that owns 11 amusement parks, two outdoor water parks, one indoor water park, and four hotels, are open to public investors. For the year ended December 31, 2018, Cedar Fair, L.P. had net income of $126,653,000 and paid a total of $203,199,000 in distributions to its partners. In this chapter, you learn about the characteristics and types of partnerships and how partnership earnings are allocated and distributions are accounted for.

Chapter 12 Learning Objectives

1. Identify the characteristics and types of partnerships
2. Account for the start-up of a partnership and prepare partnership financial statements
3. Allocate profits and losses to the partners
4. Account for the admission of a new partner
5. Account for a partner's withdrawal from the partnership
6. Account for the liquidation of a partnership

WHAT ARE THE CHARACTERISTICS AND TYPES OF PARTNERSHIPS?

Learning Objective 1
Identify the characteristics and types of partnerships

Partnership
A business with two or more owners and not organized as a corporation.

Sheena Bright, owner of Smart Touch Learning, is considering starting a new software business with her friend Martin Gonzalez. They have already talked about the product development, marketing, and sales goals. Now they just have to finalize how they will operate. They decide a **partnership**, a business with two or more owners that is not organized as a corporation, will work best for their needs and decide to draft a plan for the Bright & Gonzalez partnership.

Forming a partnership allows new opportunities to open up as Sheena Bright and Martin Gonzalez pool their talents and resources. Bright & Gonzalez can offer a fuller range of goods and services than either one of them can provide individually. Partnerships come in all sizes. Many have just two owners, but some are quite large.

You have learned how to account for sole proprietorships. However, partnership accounting is different. In this chapter, we address these differences using Bright and Gonzalez's new partnership.

Partnership Characteristics

Many businesses are organized as partnerships because of the characteristics that are common to this type of entity. These characteristics provide some unique advantages and disadvantages over the sole proprietorship and corporate organizational formats. Let's look at some characteristics of partnerships.

The Written Agreement

Partnership Agreement
The contract between partners that specifies such items as the name, location, and nature of the business; the name, capital contribution, and duties of each partner; and the method of sharing profits and losses among the partners.

A partnership is somewhat like a marriage. To be successful, the partners must cooperate. But the partners don't vow to remain together for life. To increase the partners' understanding of how the business is run, they should draw up a written **partnership agreement**, also called the *articles of partnership*. This agreement is a contract between the partners and is governed by contract law. The partnership agreement outlines the rules of the partnership. The articles of partnership should specify the following:

- Name, location, and nature of the business
- Name, capital contribution, and duties of each partner
- Procedures for admitting a new partner
- Method of sharing profits and losses among the partners
- Procedure for withdrawal of assets by the partners
- Procedures for withdrawal of a partner from the partnership
- Procedures for liquidating the partnership—selling the assets, paying the liabilities, and giving any remaining cash to the partners

Limited Life

A partnership has a limited life. Any change in the existing partners, whether someone withdraws or dies or a new partner is added, causes the old partnership to dissolve. **Dissolution** is the ending of a partnership. The addition of a new partner dissolves the old partnership but creates a new partnership.

Dissolution
Ending of a partnership.

Mutual Agency

Mutual agency means that every partner is a mutual agent of the firm. Any partner can bind the business to a contract within the scope of its regular business operations. If Sheena Bright, a partner in the firm of Bright & Gonzalez, contracts to borrow cash, then the firm of Bright & Gonzalez—not just Bright—owes the liability. If Bright signs a contract to buy her own personal car (not to be used in the partnership), however, the partnership is not liable because it is a personal matter for Bright.

Mutual Agency
Every partner can bind the business to a contract within the scope of the partnership's regular business operations.

Unlimited Liability

Each partner has **unlimited personal liability** for the debts of the business. When a partnership can't pay its debts, the partners must pay with their personal assets.

For example, suppose Bright & Gonzalez can't pay a $20,000 business debt. Then Sheena Bright and Martin Gonzalez each become personally liable for the $20,000 because each partner has *unlimited liability* for the business's debts. If either partner can't pay his or her part of the debt, the other partner must pay the total. For example, if Sheena Bright can pay only $5,000 of the liability, Martin Gonzalez must pay $15,000 ($20,000 – $5,000). If Sheena Bright can't pay anything, Martin Gonzalez must pay the full $20,000.

Unlimited Personal Liability
When a partnership (or a sole proprietorship) cannot pay its debts with business assets, the partners (or the proprietor) must use personal assets to meet the debt.

ETHICS

Should Erik buy the new equipment?

Erik Morales was very angry with his brother. He had just come from a partnership meeting concerning the purchase of new equipment for their recording studio. His brother, Juan, disagreed about purchasing the new equipment, stating that the business didn't have enough cash to purchase the equipment without incurring additional debt. After thinking about their conversation, Erik decided that he would secure a loan to purchase the equipment. Erik knew that if his brother could just see how well the new equipment worked, Juan would change his mind. Should Erik buy the new equipment? What would you do?

However, the fact that his partner, Juan, does not agree with incurring additional debt should discourage Erik from taking out the loan. Erik should consider that the partnership's debt becomes a personal liability not only to Erik, but also to Juan. If the partnership can't repay the debt, then Erik and Juan must use personal assets to meet the debt. Erik could not only endanger the liquidity of the partnership by taking out a loan, but he might also risk his relationship with his brother. Erik should not go behind his brother's back to purchase the equipment, even though he thinks it will be a good decision in the long run.

Solution

Mutual agency allows Erik to act as an agent of the partnership and secure debt for the purchase of new equipment.

Co-ownership of Property

Any asset—cash, merchandise inventory, computers, and so on—that a partner contributes to the partnership becomes the property of the partnership. The partner who contributed the asset is no longer its sole owner. In addition, any new assets purchased by the partnership are jointly owned by each partner.

No Partnership Income Tax

A partnership pays no business income tax. Instead, the net income of the business flows through and becomes the taxable income of the individual partners. Suppose the Bright & Gonzalez firm earned net income of $200,000, shared equally by the partners. The firm pays no income tax *as a business entity*. But Sheena Bright and Martin Gonzalez each pay personal income tax on $100,000 ($200,000 / 2) of partnership income.

Partners' Capital Accounts

Accounting for a partnership is much like accounting for a sole proprietorship. Because a partnership has more than one partner (owner), each partner needs a separate capital account. For example, the equity account for Sheena Bright is Bright, Capital. Similarly, each partner has a withdrawal account such as Bright, Withdrawals.

Exhibit F:12-1 lists the advantages and disadvantages of partnerships compared with sole proprietorships and corporations. (Corporations will be covered in the next chapter.) As you can see, most features of a sole proprietorship also apply to a partnership:

- Limited life
- Unlimited liability
- No business income tax

Exhibit F:12-1 | **Advantages and Disadvantages of Partnerships**

Partnership Advantages	Partnership Disadvantages
Versus Sole Proprietorships:	1. Partnership agreement may be difficult to formulate. Each time a new partner is admitted or a partner withdraws, the business needs a new partnership agreement.
1. Partnership can raise more capital.	
2. Partnership brings together the abilities of more than one person.	2. Relations among partners may be fragile.
3. Partners working well together can add more value than by working alone.	3. Mutual agency and unlimited liability create personal obligations for each partner.
Versus Corporations:	
1. Partnership is less expensive to organize than a corporation, which requires a charter from the state.	
2. There's no double taxation. Partnership income is taxed only to the partners as individuals.	

Types of Partnerships

There are two basic types of partnerships: general and limited.

General Partnership

General Partnership
A form of partnership in which each partner is a co-owner of the business, with all the privileges and risks of ownership.

A **general partnership** is the basic form. Each partner is a co-owner of the business, with all the privileges and risks of ownership. The profits and losses of the partnership pass through to the partners, who then pay personal income tax on their share of the income. All the other features we just covered apply to a general partnership.

Limited Partnership

Limited Partnership (LP)
A partnership with at least two classes of partners: one or more general partners and one or more limited partners.

General Partner
A partner who has unlimited personal liability in the partnership.

A **limited partnership (LP)** has at least two classes of partners. There must be at least one **general partner**, who takes primary responsibility and usually operates the business. The general partner has unlimited personal liability and therefore takes most of the risk if the partnership goes bankrupt. Usually, the general partner is the last owner to receive a share of profits and losses. But the general partner often gets all the excess profit after the limited partners get their share of the income.

A **limited partner** is usually an investor who does not participate in the day-to-day operations of the partnership and has limited personal liability for partnership debts. Limited partners have no personal liability for the debts of the partnership beyond their contribution in the business. They usually have first claim to profits and losses, but only up to a certain limit. In exchange for their limited liability, their potential for profits is also limited.

A variation of a limited partnership is the **limited liability partnership (LLP)**. This type of partnership is designed to protect partners from malpractice or negligence of another partner's actions. In an LLP, each partner is not personally liable for the malpractice committed by another partner. In most states, however, each partner is still personally liable for other business debts. LLPs must carry large insurance policies to protect the public in case the partnership is found guilty of malpractice. Medical, accounting, legal, and other professional firms are often organized as LLPs.

> **Limited Partner**
> A partner who has limited personal liability in the partnership.
>
> **Limited Liability Partnership (LLP)**
> A form of partnership in which each partner is protected from the malpractice or negligence of the other partners.

TYING IT ALL TOGETHER

Cedar Fair, L.P. is a Delaware limited partnership that began operations in 1983. The partnership is a regional amusement park operator that owns 11 amusement parks, two outdoor water parks, one indoor water park, and four hotels. The partnership is publicly traded and listed on The New York Stock Exchange under the symbol FUN. (You can find Cedar Fair's annual report at **https://www.sec.gov/Archives/edgar/data/811532/000081153219000037/cedarfair-10kx2018.htm**.)

What type of partners does Cedar Fair, L.P. have?
Cedar Fair, L.P. has both a general partner (Cedar Fair Management, Inc.) and limited partners. The partnership's general partner represents 0.001% interest in the partnership's income, losses, and cash distributions. In addition, the general partner has full responsibility for the management of the partnership.

Other Forms of Business

There are other forms of business that have some characteristics that are similar to a partnership. These entities are similar to partnerships but have unique characteristics that make them separate from partnerships.

Limited Liability Company (LLC)

A **limited liability company (LLC)** is its own form of business organization—neither a partnership nor a corporation. It combines the advantages of both. The LLC form is perhaps the most flexible way to organize a business because the owners, called *members*, have numerous choices.

The features of a limited liability company that parallel a *corporation* are as follows:

- The LLC is a legal entity that requires the business to file articles of organization with the state.
- The business name must include "LLC" or a similar designation to alert the public about the limited liability of the members.
- The members are *not* personally liable for the business's debts. This is one of the chief advantages of an LLC compared to a sole proprietorship or a partnership.

The features of an LLC that are similar to a *partnership* are as follows:

- The LLC can elect *not* to pay business income tax. The income of the LLC can be taxed to the members as though they were partners. This is the other big advantage of an LLC as compared to a corporation. Corporations pay a corporate income tax. Then the stockholders pay personal income tax on any dividends they receive from the corporation. This is why we say that corporations face *double taxation*.

> **Limited Liability Company (LLC)**
> A form of business organization that is neither a partnership nor a corporation but combines the advantages of both.

- The members (owners of the LLC) can participate actively in management of the business.
- The accounting for an LLC generally follows the pattern for a partnership.

S Corporation

S Corporation
A corporation with 100 or fewer stockholders that can elect to be taxed in the same way as a partnership.

An **S corporation** is a corporation with 100 or fewer stockholders that can elect to be taxed as a partnership. This form of business organization comes from Subchapter S of the U.S. Internal Revenue Code. An S corporation offers its owners (called *stockholders*) the benefits of a corporation—no personal liability for business debts—and of a partnership—no double taxation. An ordinary (Subchapter C) corporation is subject to double taxation.

An S corporation pays no corporate income tax. Instead, the corporation's income flows through to the stockholders, who pay personal income tax on their share of the S corporation's income. Exhibit F:12-2 summarizes the different types of business organizations.

Exhibit F:12-2 | Types of Business Organizations

Organization	Legal Entity	Personal Liability of the Owners	Pays Business Income Tax
Sole Proprietorship	No	Unlimited	No
Partnership	No		No
General partners		Unlimited	
Limited partners		Limited	
Limited Liability Company (LLC)	Yes	Limited	No*
S Corporation	Yes	Limited	No
C Corporation	Yes	Limited	Yes

*In some states, a limited liability company can elect to pay corporate income tax.

Match the accounting terminology to the definitions.

1. Limited liability company
2. Partnership
3. General partnership
4. Partnership agreement
5. Limited partnership
6. Dissolution

a. A form of partnership in which each partner is a co-owner of the business, with all the privileges and risks of ownership.
b. A form of business organization that is neither a partnership nor a corporation but combines the advantages of both.
c. The contract between partners.
d. The ending of a partnership.
e. A business with two or more owners that is not organized as a corporation.
f. A partnership with at least two classes of partners: one or more general partners and one or more limited partners.

Check your answers online in MyLab Accounting or at http://www.pearsonhighered.com/Horngren.

For more practice, see Short Exercise S-F:12-1. **MyLab Accounting**

Partnerships Financial 12-7

HOW ARE PARTNERSHIPS ORGANIZED?

Forming a partnership is easy. It requires no permission from the government and no outside legal assistance, though enlisting an attorney to draw up the partnership agreement is always a wise choice. A partnership combines the contributed assets and abilities of the partners. Let's look at how Sheena Bright and Martin Gonzalez organized the start-up of their partnership.

Learning Objective 2
Account for the start-up of a partnership and prepare partnership financial statements

The Start-up of a Partnership

When a partnership begins, partners may contribute both assets and liabilities. These contributions are journalized the same way as for a sole proprietorship—debit the assets and credit the liabilities. The excess—assets minus liabilities—measures each partner's capital contribution.

Suppose Sheena Bright and Martin Gonzalez form a partnership to sell computer software on June 1, 2025. The partners agree on the following values:

Bright's Contribution
- Cash, $15,000; Merchandise Inventory, $40,000; and Accounts Payable, $80,000 (The current market values for these items equal Bright's values.)
- Computer Equipment—cost, $80,000; Accumulated Depreciation, $20,000; *current market value, $55,000*

Gonzalez's Contribution
- Cash, $2,000
- Office Furniture—cost, $20,000; Accumulated Depreciation, $1,500; *current market value, $18,000*

The partnership records the partners' contributions at *current market value*. Why? Because the partnership is receiving the assets and assuming the liabilities at their current market values. The partnership journal entries are as follows:

Date	Accounts and Explanation	Debit	Credit
2025			
Jun. 1	Cash	15,000	
	Merchandise Inventory	40,000	
	Computer Equipment	55,000	
	Accounts Payable		80,000
	Bright, Capital ($15,000 + $40,000 + $55,000 − $80,000)		30,000
	To record Bright's contribution.		
1	Cash	2,000	
	Office Furniture	18,000	
	Gonzalez, Capital ($2,000 + $18,000)		20,000
	To record Gonzalez's contribution.		

A↑ Cash↑ Merchandise Inventory↑ Computer Equipment↑ = L↑ Accounts Payable↑ + E↑ Bright, Capital↑

A↑ Cash↑ Office Furniture↑ = L + E↑ Gonzalez, Capital↑

12-8 Financial chapter 12

Partnership Financial Statements

Partnership financial statements are similar to the statements of a sole proprietorship but with the following differences:

Statement of Partners' Equity
Summary of the changes in each partner's capital account for a specific period of time.

- A partnership equity statement is referred to as the **statement of partners' equity**, sometimes called the *statement of partners' capital*. The statement of partners' equity shows the changes in each partner's capital account for a specific period of time.
- A partnership balance sheet reports a separate capital account for each partner. The initial partnership balance sheet for Bright & Gonzalez as of June 1, 2025, appears in Exhibit F:12-3.

Exhibit F:12-3 | Balance Sheet

BRIGHT & GONZALEZ Balance Sheet June 1, 2025				
Assets			**Liabilities**	
Cash ($15,000 + $2,000)	$ 17,000		Accounts Payable	$ 80,000
Merchandise Inventory	40,000			
Computer Equipment	55,000		**Partners' Equity**	
Office Furniture	18,000		Bright, Capital	30,000
			Gonzalez, Capital	20,000
			Total Partners' Equity	50,000
Total Assets	$ 130,000		Total Liabilities and Partners' Equity	$ 130,000

Try It!

7. Stevie Lewis and Mack Young are forming a partnership to develop a golf course. Lewis contributes cash of $1,000,000 and land with a current market value of $10,000,000. When Lewis purchased the land in 2012, it cost $7,000,000. Young contributes cash of $3,000,000 and equipment with a current market value of $800,000. Journalize the partnership's receipt of assets from Lewis and Young.

Check your answer online in MyLab Accounting or at http://pearsonhighered.com/Horngren.

For more practice, see Short Exercises S-F:12-2 and S-F:12-3.   MyLab Accounting

HOW ARE PARTNERSHIP PROFITS AND LOSSES ALLOCATED?

Learning Objective 3
Allocate profits and losses to the partners

Allocating profits and losses among partners can be challenging. The partners can agree to any profit-and-loss-sharing method they desire. Typical arrangements include the following:

- Sharing of profits and losses based on a stated ratio for each partner, such as 50/50 for two partners or 4:3:3 for three partners (which means you first add the parts, 4 + 3 + 3 parts for 10 total parts, so 4/10 to Partner A, 3/10 to Partner B, and 3/10 to Partner C)
- Sharing based on each partner's capital balance
- Sharing based on each partner's service
- Sharing based on a combination of stated ratios, capital balances, and service

If the partners have no partnership agreement specifying how to divide profits and losses, then they share equally. If the partnership agreement specifies a method for sharing profits but not losses, then losses are shared the same way as profits. For example, a partner who gets 75% of the profits will absorb 75% of any losses.

Let's see how some of these profit-and-loss-sharing methods work.

Allocation Based on a Stated Ratio

The partnership agreement may state each partner's ratio of the profits and losses. Suppose Bright and Gonzalez allocate 2/3 of the profits and losses to Bright and 1/3 to Gonzalez. This sharing rule can also be expressed as 2:1 (2 + 1 = 3, so 2/3 to Bright and 1/3 to Gonzalez). If the partnership's net income for the year was $60,000, Bright and Gonzalez would share the net income as follows:

> Allocation of net income based on stated ratio = Net income × Stated ratio
> = $60,000 × 2/3
> = $40,000 (Bright)
>
> = $60,000 × 1/3
> = $20,000 (Gonzalez)

The entry to close net income, represented as a credit balance in Income Summary, to the partners' capital accounts would be as follows:

Date	Accounts and Explanation	Debit	Credit
Dec. 31	Income Summary	60,000	
	Bright, Capital		40,000
	Gonzalez, Capital		20,000
	To close Income Summary.		

A = L + E↕

Income Summary↓
Bright, Capital↑
Gonzalez, Capital↑

After posting, the accounts would look like this:

Income Summary				Bright, Capital				Gonzalez, Capital		
Clos. 3	60,000	60,000	Bal.			30,000	Jun. 1		20,000	Jun. 1
		0	Bal.			40,000	Clos. 3		20,000	Clos. 3
						70,000	Bal.		40,000	Bal.

If, instead, the partnership had a net loss of $18,000, the Income Summary account would have a debit balance of $18,000 as follows:

Income Summary		
Bal.	18,000	

In that case, the partners' capital accounts would be reduced by their ratio of the loss. The following closing entry would be recorded:

Date	Accounts and Explanation	Debit	Credit
Dec. 31	Bright, Capital ($18,000 × 2/3)	12,000	
	Gonzalez, Capital ($18,000 × 1/3)	6,000	
	Income Summary		18,000
	To close Income Summary.		

A = L + E↕

Income Summary↑
Bright, Capital↓
Gonzalez, Capital↓

After posting the loss, the account balances would take this form:

Income Summary				Bright, Capital				Gonzalez, Capital			
Bal.	18,000	18,000	Clos. 3			30,000	Jun. 1			20,000	Jun. 1
		0	Bal.	Clos. 3	12,000			Clos. 3	6,000		
						18,000	Bal.			14,000	Bal.

Allocation Based on Capital Balances

In a partnership, one partner may contribute more capital. Therefore, the profits and losses may be divided based on partner capital balances instead of on a stated ratio.

Let's reconsider Bright & Gonzalez's original partnership agreement. Bright contributed $30,000 in capital, whereas Gonzalez contributed only $20,000. Allocation based on capital balances uses the ratio of the partner's capital balance to the total capital.

Suppose Bright & Gonzalez has a net income of $60,000. The allocation of net income is calculated as follows. The journal entry to close the net income into each partner's capital account follows the format shown previously.

> Allocation of net income based on capital balances = Net income × (Capital balance / Total capital)
> = $60,000 × [$30,000 / ($30,000 + $20,000)]
> = $36,000 (Bright)
>
> = $60,000 × [$20,000 / ($30,000 + $20,000)]
> = $24,000 (Gonzalez)

Allocation Based on Services, Capital Balances, and Stated Ratios

As we have seen, allocation of net income can be based on stated ratios or on capital balances. It can also be based on a combination of services, capital balances, and stated ratios. A partnership might want to use this method if one partner contributes more capital but the other partner devotes more time to the business by managing the day-to-day operations or handling the accounting. One way to reward partners who provide services to the partnership is by offering a salary allowance in addition to an allocation based on capital. In this allocation method, the profits and losses may be divided based on a combination of partner capital balances, services, and stated ratios.

Suppose Bright and Gonzalez agree to share profits and losses as follows:

1. The first allocation is a salary allowance with Bright receiving $16,000 and Gonzalez $24,000.
2. The next allocation is based on 10% of the partners' capital balances.
3. Any remaining profit or loss is allocated equally.

Because the partnership agreement specifies three steps, all three steps must be performed whenever the partnership allocates profits or losses. The partnership's net income for the first year is still $60,000, but the partners share the profit in this way:

	Bright	Gonzalez	Total
Net income (loss)			$ 60,000
Salary allowances:			
Bright	$ 16,000		
Gonzalez		$ 24,000	
Capital allocation:			
Bright ($30,000 × 10%)	3,000		
Gonzalez ($20,000 × 10%)		2,000	
Total salary and capital allocation	19,000	26,000	(45,000)
Net income (loss) remaining for allocation			15,000
Remainder shared equally:			
Bright ($15,000 × 1/2)	7,500		
Gonzalez ($15,000 × 1/2)		7,500	
Total allocation			(15,000)
Net income (loss) remaining for allocation			$ 0
Net income (loss) allocated to each partner	$ 26,500	$ 33,500	

The net income (loss) allocated to each partner should always equal the total net income (loss). $26,500 + $33,500 = $60,000

For this allocation, the closing entry would now be as follows:

Date	Accounts and Explanation	Debit	Credit
Dec. 31	Income Summary	60,000	
	Bright, Capital		26,500
	Gonzalez, Capital		33,500
	To close Income Summary.		

A = L + E↕

Income Summary↓
Bright, Capital↑
Gonzalez, Capital↑

12-12 Financial chapter 12

What happens if this same income-sharing agreement were in place but Bright & Gonzalez incurred a total net loss of $18,000? Because the partnership sharing agreement has three steps, the allocation of the net loss also goes through all three steps as follows:

	Bright	Gonzalez	Total
Net income (loss)			$ (18,000)
Salary allowances:			
Bright	$ 16,000		
Gonzalez		$ 24,000	
Capital allocation:			
Bright ($30,000 × 10%)	3,000		
Gonzalez ($20,000 × 10%)		2,000	
Total salary and capital allocation	19,000	26,000	(45,000)
Net income (loss) remaining for allocation			(63,000)
Remainder shared equally:			
Bright ($63,000 × 1/2)	(31,500)		
Gonzalez ($63,000 × 1/2)		(31,500)	
Total allocation			63,000
Net income (loss) remaining for allocation			$ 0
Net income (loss) allocated to each partner	$ (12,500)	$ (5,500)	

The closing entry to allocate the $18,000 loss under this three-level sharing agreement is as follows:

A = L + E↑↓
Income Summary↑
Bright, Capital↓
Gonzalez, Capital↓

Date	Accounts and Explanation	Debit	Credit
Dec. 31	Bright, Capital	12,500	
	Gonzalez, Capital	5,500	
	Income Summary		18,000
	To close Income Summary.		

Partner Withdrawal of Cash and Other Assets

Partners can withdraw cash or other assets from the partnership based on what is allowed by the written partnership agreement. Withdrawals (also called *drawings*) from a partnership are recorded in a temporary equity account, such as Bright, Withdrawals. Assume that Sheena Bright and Martin Gonzalez each made withdrawals of $3,000. The partnership records the December 31 withdrawals with the following entry:

A↓ = L + E↓
Cash↓
Bright, Withdrawals↑
Gonzalez, Withdrawals↑

Date	Accounts and Explanation	Debit	Credit
Dec. 31	Bright, Withdrawals	3,000	
	Gonzalez, Withdrawals	3,000	
	Cash		6,000
	Partner withdrawals of cash.		

The withdrawal accounts are closed at the end of the period, exactly as they are for a sole proprietorship. Credit each partner's withdrawal account and debit his or her capital account:

Date	Accounts and Explanation	Debit	Credit
Dec. 31	Bright, Capital	3,000	
	Gonzalez, Capital	3,000	
	Bright, Withdrawals		3,000
	Gonzalez, Withdrawals		3,000
	To close withdrawals.		

A | L + E↕
Bright, Capital↓
Gonzalez, Capital↓
Bright, Withdrawals↓
Gonzalez, Withdrawals↓

Bright's and Gonzalez's capital accounts, assuming the $60,000 net income is allocated based on service, capital balances, and stated ratios, are as follows:

Bright, Capital

		30,000	Jun. 1
Clos. 4	3,000	26,500	Clos. 3
		53,500	Bal.

Gonzalez, Capital

		20,000	Jun. 1
Clos. 4	3,000	33,500	Clos. 3
		50,500	Bal.

Statement of Partners' Equity

Now that we have seen how partnership profits and losses are allocated, let's review Bright & Gonzalez's statement of partners' equity for the year. Remember that the statement of partners' equity shows the changes in each partner's capital account for a specific period of time. Unlike a sole proprietorship statement of owner's equity, the statement of partners' equity will show *each* partner's capital account separately, including partner contributions, net income allocation, and partner withdrawals. Exhibit F:12-4 shows Bright & Gonzalez's statement of partners' equity assuming the $60,000 net income is allocated based on service, capital balances, and stated ratios.

Exhibit F:12-4 | **Statement of Partners' Equity**

BRIGHT & GONZALEZ
Statement of Partners' Equity
Seven Months Ended December 31, 2025

	Bright	Gonzalez	Total
Capital, June 1, 2025	$ 0	$ 0	$ 0
Partner contributions	30,000	20,000	50,000
Net income for seven months	26,500	33,500	60,000
	56,500	53,500	110,000
Partner withdrawals	(3,000)	(3,000)	(6,000)
Capital, December 31, 2025	$ 53,500	$ 50,500	$ 104,000

The ending capital balances on the statement of partners' equity should match with the ending balances in the partners' capital accounts in the ledger.

8. Scott, Hill, and Carter have capital balances of $20,000, $40,000, and $80,000. The partners share profits 1:1:3, respectively. The partnership had net income of $100,000 for the year. Journalize the closing entry to allocate the net income.

Check your answer online in MyLab Accounting or at http://www.pearsonhighered.com/Horngren.

For more practice, see Short Exercises S-F:12-4 and S-F:12-5. **MyLab Accounting**

HOW IS THE ADMISSION OF A PARTNER ACCOUNTED FOR?

Learning Objective 4
Account for the admission of a new partner

Admitting a new partner dissolves the old partnership and begins a new one. Any time the partner mix changes, the old partnership ceases to exist and a new partnership begins. Often, outsiders do not notice the change—the business continues to operate in the same way, but with different owners. Let's look at the ways a new owner can be added to a partnership.

Admission by Purchasing an Existing Partner's Interest

A person can become a partner by purchasing an existing partner's interest. First, however, the new person must gain the approval of the other partners. The purchase of an existing partner's interest is a personal transaction between the two individuals and not the partnership.

For example, suppose Bright wants to sell Cheryl Kaska, an outside party, half of her partnership interest ($53,500 × 1/2 = $26,750) on January 1, 2026. Gonzalez accepts Kaska as a new partner, and Bright agrees to accept $30,000. The partnership records the transfer of capital interest with the following entry:

A = L + E↑
Bright, Capital↓
Kaska, Capital↑

Date	Accounts and Explanation	Debit	Credit
2026			
Jan. 1	Bright, Capital	26,750	
	Kaska, Capital		26,750
	To transfer one-half of Bright's capital to Kaska.		

Why does a purchase of another partner's interest not involve a debit to cash on the partnership's books?

The debit decreases Bright's capital account, and the credit sets up Kaska's capital account. The entry amount is half of Bright's capital balance of $26,750 and not the $30,000 that Kaska paid Bright. **The partnership receives no cash because the transaction was between Kaska and Bright, not between Kaska and the partnership. The full $30,000 went to Bright, not the partnership. The only entry the partnership records is the transfer of partner's capital.**

The old partnership of Bright & Gonzalez has dissolved. Bright, Gonzalez, and Kaska draw up a new partnership agreement with a new profit-and-loss-sharing method and continue in business. The capital accounts after admission of the new partner are as follows:

Bright, Capital		Gonzalez, Capital		Kaska, Capital	
	53,500 Bal.		50,500 Bal.		26,750 Jan. 1
Jan. 1 26,750					
	26,750 Bal.				

Admission of a partner by purchasing an existing partner's interest has two important characteristics:

- The only journal entry the partnership records is the transfer of partner's capital. It does not record the transfer of cash from the new partner to the existing partner.
- Admission of the partner does not affect *total* assets, liabilities, and equity. It simply transfers capital from one partner's account to another's.

Admission by Contributing to the Partnership

A person can enter a partnership by contributing directly to the business. (This is different than buying out an existing partner, as previously described.) In this situation, the new partner contributes assets—for example, cash or equipment—to the business. Let's consider several possible ways to add a new partner.

Admission by Contributing to the Partnership at Book Value—No Bonus to Any Partner

Cheryl Kaska wants to join the Bright & Gonzalez partnership on January 1, 2026. Kaska can contribute land with a market value of $52,000. Bright and Gonzalez agree to dissolve their partnership and start a new one, giving Kaska a 1/3 interest in the new partnership for her $52,000 contribution, as follows:

Partnership capital before admission of new partner ($53,500 + $50,500)	$ 104,000
Contribution of new partner	52,000
Partnership capital after admission of new partner	$ 156,000
Capital of new partner ($156,000 × 1/3)	$ 52,000

Notice that Kaska is buying into the partnership at book value because her contribution of $52,000 equals 1/3 of the new partnership's total capital of $156,000. The partnership's entry to record Kaska's contribution is as follows:

Date	Accounts and Explanation	Debit	Credit
2026			
Jan. 1	Land	52,000	
	Kaska, Capital		52,000
	To record Kaska's contribution.		

$$\left.\begin{array}{c} A\uparrow \\ Land\uparrow \end{array}\right\} = \left\{\begin{array}{c} L + E\uparrow \\ Kaska, \\ Capital\uparrow \end{array}\right.$$

After the admission of Kaska as a new partner, the partnership's assets and equity have increased by $52,000. Kaska's 1/3 interest in equity does not necessarily entitle her to 1/3 of the profits. Remember: The sharing of profits and losses is a separate element from the creation of the partnership.

Admission by Contributing to the Partnership—Bonus to the Existing Partners

A successful partnership may require a higher payment from a new partner. The existing partners may demand a bonus, which will increase their capital accounts, before admitting a new partner.

Assume, instead, that Bright and Gonzalez admit Cheryl Kaska to a 1/4 interest in the new partnership for Kaska's cash contribution of $100,000. Kaska's capital balance on the new partnership books would only be $51,000, computed as follows:

Partnership capital before admission of new partner ($53,500 + $50,500)	$ 104,000
Contribution of new partner	100,000
Partnership capital after admission of new partner	$ 204,000
Capital of new partner ($204,000 × 1/4)	$ 51,000

In effect, Kaska had to buy into the partnership at a contribution of $100,000, which is above the $51,000 book value of her 1/4 interest. Kaska's higher-than-book-value contribution creates a *bonus* for Bright and Gonzalez as shown below:

Contribution of new partner	$ 100,000
Capital of new partner	(51,000)
Bonus to *existing* partners	$ 49,000

Assuming Bright and Gonzalez's original partnership agreement had them sharing profits and losses equally, the partnership entry to record the receipt of Kaska's contribution is as follows:

$$\frac{A\uparrow}{Cash\uparrow} = \frac{L\ +\ E\uparrow}{\begin{array}{c}Kaska,\ Capital\uparrow\\ Bright,\ Capital\uparrow\\ Gonzalez,\ Capital\uparrow\end{array}}$$

Date	Accounts and Explanation	Debit	Credit
2026			
Jan. 1	Cash	100,000	
	Kaska, Capital		51,000
	Bright, Capital ($49,000 × 1/2)		24,500
	Gonzalez, Capital ($49,000 × 1/2)		24,500
	To record Kaska's contribution and bonus to existing partners.		

It's always a good idea to check that debits equal credits after you have recorded the journal entry.

Kaska's capital account was credited for her 1/4 interest in the new partnership, $51,000. The *bonus* was allocated to Bright and Gonzalez based on their original profit-and-loss-sharing ratio (equally).

Admission by Contributing to the Partnership—Bonus to the New Partner

A new partner may be so valuable that the existing partners offer a partnership share that includes a bonus to the new person.

Let's go back to our Kaska partner admission. On January 1, 2026, Kaska gives Bright and Gonzalez $98,000 but instead gets a 60% interest in the new partnership. The computation of Kaska's 60% equity in the new partnership is as shown on the next page:

Partnerships Financial 12-17

Partnership capital before admission of new partner ($53,500 + $50,500)	$ 104,000
Contribution of new partner	98,000
Partnership capital after admission of new partner	$ 202,000
Capital of new partner ($202,000 × 60%)	$ 121,200
Capital of new partner	$ 121,200
Contribution of new partner	(98,000)
Bonus to *new* partner	$ 23,200

In this case, Kaska entered the partnership at a price less than the book value of her equity of $121,200. The bonus of $23,200 went to Kaska from the other partners so their capital accounts are debited (reduced) for the bonus. The existing partners share this decrease in capital as though it were a loss, on the basis of their profit-and-loss-sharing ratio (equally). The entry to record Kaska's contribution is as follows:

Date	Accounts and Explanation	Debit	Credit
2026			
Jan. 1	Cash	98,000	
	Bright, Capital ($23,200 × 1/2)	11,600	
	Gonzalez, Capital ($23,200 × 1/2)	11,600	
	Kaska, Capital		121,200
	To record Kaska's contribution and bonus.		

$$A\uparrow \atop \text{Cash}\uparrow \Bigg\} = \Bigg\{ L + E\uparrow \atop \begin{array}{l}\text{Kaska,}\\ \text{Capital}\uparrow\\ \text{Bright,}\\ \text{Capital}\downarrow\\ \text{Gonzalez,}\\ \text{Capital}\downarrow\end{array}$$

Try It!

9. Parker has $40,000 capital and Flores has $20,000 capital in the Parker & Flores partnership. Parker and Flores share profits and losses equally. Ray Rivera contributes cash of $30,000 to acquire a 25% interest in the new partnership. Journalize the partnership's receipt of the $30,000 from Rivera.

Check your answer online in MyLab Accounting or at http://www.pearsonhighered.com/Horngren.

For more practice, see Short Exercises S-F:12-6 through S-F:12-8. MyLab Accounting

HOW IS THE WITHDRAWAL OF A PARTNER ACCOUNTED FOR?

Learning Objective 5
Account for a partner's withdrawal from the partnership

A partner may leave the business for many reasons, including retirement, death, or a dispute. The withdrawal of a partner dissolves the old partnership. The partnership agreement should specify the procedures to follow when a partner withdraws from the partnership. Any time the partner mix changes, the old partnership ceases to exist but a new partnership might begin.

In the simplest case, a partner may sell his or her interest to another party in a personal transaction. This is the same as admitting a new person who purchases an existing partner's interest, as we saw earlier. The journal entry simply debits the withdrawing partner's capital account and credits the new partner's capital. The dollar amount is the withdrawing partner's capital balance. Often, however, the withdrawal is more complex, as cash or other assets are withdrawn from the partnership in settlement of the partner's interest.

Withdrawal from the Partnership at Book Value—No Bonus to Any Partner

Assume the partnership of Bright, Gonzalez, & Kaska has the following capital balances and the partnership agreement allocates profit-and-loss-sharing 1/6 to Bright, 2/6 to Gonzalez, and 3/6 to Kaska (or 1:2:3):

BRIGHT, GONZALEZ, & KASKA Partners' Equity January 1, 2026	
Bright, Capital	$ 53,500
Gonzalez, Capital	50,500
Kaska, Capital	52,000
Total Partners' Equity	$ 156,000

If on January 2, 2026, Bright withdraws from the partnership by receiving cash for the book value of her capital account, the following entry would be recorded:

$$\frac{A\downarrow}{Cash\downarrow} \Bigg\} = \Bigg\{ \frac{L \;+\; E\downarrow}{Bright, Capital\downarrow}$$

Date	Accounts and Explanation	Debit	Credit
2026			
Jan. 2	Bright, Capital	53,500	
	Cash		53,500
	To record withdrawal of Bright from the partnership.		

Bright's capital account is now closed, and Gonzalez and Kaska may or may not continue in the new partnership of Gonzalez & Kaska. If they continue, they will need to draft a new partnership agreement and determine a new profit-and-loss-sharing ratio.

Withdrawal from the Partnership—Bonus to the Existing Partners

The withdrawing partner may be so eager to depart that he or she will take less than his or her full equity interest (capital balance). Assume that Bright withdraws from the business and agrees to receive cash of $47,200. This settlement is $6,300 less than Bright's $53,500 capital balance. The remaining partners share this $6,300 difference—a bonus to them—according to their existing profit-and-loss-sharing ratio. This means the former 1:2:3 ratio is now 2:3 (Gonzalez's and Kaska's parts only).

The entry to record Bright's withdrawal at less than her book value is as follows:

Date	Accounts and Explanation	Debit	Credit
2026			
Jan. 2	Bright, Capital	53,500	
	Cash		47,200
	Gonzalez, Capital ($6,300 × 2/5)		2,520
	Kaska, Capital ($6,300 × 3/5)		3,780
	To record withdrawal of Bright from the partnership.		

$$A\downarrow \atop Cash\downarrow \Big\} = \Big\{ L + E\downarrow \atop {Bright, Capital\downarrow \atop Gonzalez, Capital\uparrow \atop Kaska, Capital\uparrow}$$

Withdrawal from the Partnership—Bonus to the Withdrawing Partner

A withdrawing partner may receive assets worth more than the book value of his or her equity. This situation creates the following:

- A bonus to the withdrawing partner
- A decrease in the remaining partners' capital accounts, shared in their profit-and-loss-sharing ratio

Let's assume instead that Bright is given cash of $57,200, which is $3,700 ($57,200 − $53,500) more than Bright's capital account of $53,500. The remaining partners share this $3,700 difference—a capital reduction to them—according to their existing profit-and-loss-sharing ratio (2:3), Gonzalez's and Kaska's parts only.

The entry for Bright to withdraw under these new assumptions is as follows:

Date	Accounts and Explanation	Debit	Credit
2026			
Jan. 2	Bright, Capital	53,500	
	Gonzalez, Capital ($3,700 × 2/5)	1,480	
	Kaska, Capital ($3,700 × 3/5)	2,220	
	Cash		57,200
	To record withdrawal of Bright from the partnership.		

$$A\downarrow \atop Cash\downarrow \Big\} = \Big\{ L + E\downarrow \atop {Bright, Capital\downarrow \atop Gonzalez, Capital\downarrow \atop Kaska, Capital\downarrow}$$

Death of a Partner

The death of a partner dissolves the partnership. At the time of death, the partnership ceases to exist, and the deceased partner's estate will have ownership of the partner's equity in the partnership. The partnership agreement should state how the partner's equity will be paid out to the estate. This could involve selling the partnership interest to another individual or distributing partnership assets.

10. Cooper, Kelly, and Richardson each have a capital balance of $100,000. Kelly is retiring from the partnership. The profit-and-loss-sharing ratio is 1:2:1, respectively. Journalize the payment of $120,000 to Kelly upon retirement.

Check your answer online in MyLab Accounting or at http://www.pearsonhighered.com/Horngren.

For more practice, see Short Exercises S-F:12-9 and S-F:12-10. **MyLab Accounting**

HOW IS THE LIQUIDATION OF A PARTNERSHIP ACCOUNTED FOR?

Learning Objective 6
Account for the liquidation of a partnership

Liquidation
The process of going out of business by selling the entity's assets, paying its liabilities, and distributing any remaining cash to the partners based on their equity balances.

As we've seen, the admission or withdrawal of a partner dissolves the partnership. However, it may resume operating with no apparent change to outsiders. In contrast, **liquidation** shuts down the business by selling its assets and paying its liabilities. The final step in liquidation is to distribute any remaining cash to the partners based on their equity balances. Before a business is liquidated, its books should be adjusted and then closed. Liquidation in a partnership includes three steps:

Step 1: Sell the assets. Allocate the gain or loss to the partners' capital accounts *based on the profit-and-loss-sharing ratio.*

Step 2: Pay all partnership liabilities.

Step 3: Pay the remaining cash, if any, to the partners *based on their capital balances, not* their profit-and-loss-sharing agreement.

The key to liquidation is that all accounts of the company are closed (zeroed out). The liquidation of a business can stretch over weeks or months—a year or longer for a big company. To avoid excessive detail in our illustrations, we include only two asset categories—Cash and Non-cash Assets—and a single liability—Accounts Payable. Our examples assume that the business sells the assets in a single transaction and then pays the liabilities at once.

Sale of Assets at a Gain

Assume that Bright, Gonzalez, and Kaska decide to liquidate on November 30. Bright, Gonzalez, and Kaska have shared profits and losses in the ratio of 1:2:3. (This ratio is equal to 1/6, 2/6, 3/6, respectively.) Exhibit F:12-5 shows the balance sheet of the partnership after the books are adjusted and closed and before liquidation.

Exhibit F:12-5 | **Balance Sheet Before Liquidation**

BRIGHT, GONZALEZ & KASKA
Balance Sheet
November 30, 2026

Assets		Liabilities	
Cash	$ 10,000	Accounts Payable	$ 30,000
Non-cash Assets	90,000		
		Partners' Equity	
		Bright, Capital	40,000
		Gonzalez, Capital	20,000
		Kaska, Capital	10,000
		Total Partners' Equity	70,000
Total Assets	$ 100,000	Total Liabilities and Partners' Equity	$ 100,000

Step 1: The partnership sells the non-cash assets for $150,000 (book value, $90,000). The partnership realizes a gain of $60,000 ($150,000 − $90,000), allocated to the partners based on their profit-and-loss-sharing ratio. The entry to record this sale and allocate the gain is as shown on the next page:

Date	Accounts and Explanation	Debit	Credit
2026			
Nov. 30	Cash	150,000	
	Non-cash Assets		90,000
	Gain on Disposal		60,000
	Sale of non-cash assets at liquidation.		
30	Gain on Disposal	60,000	
	Bright, Capital ($60,000 × 1/6)		10,000
	Gonzalez, Capital ($60,000 × 2/6)		20,000
	Kaska, Capital ($60,000 × 3/6)		30,000
	To allocate gain on liquidation of assets.		

$A\uparrow$ { Cash$\uparrow$ / Non-cash Assets$\downarrow$ } = { L + E$\uparrow$ / Gain on Disposal$\uparrow$ }

A { } = { L + E$\uparrow\downarrow$ / Gain on Disposal$\downarrow$ / Bright, Capital$\uparrow$ / Gonzalez, Capital$\uparrow$ / Kaska, Capital$\uparrow$ }

Step 2: The partnership then pays off its liabilities:

Date	Accounts and Explanation	Debit	Credit
2026			
Nov. 30	Accounts Payable	30,000	
	Cash		30,000
	To pay liabilities.		

$A\downarrow$ { Cash$\downarrow$ } = { L$\downarrow$ + E / Accounts Payable$\downarrow$ }

Step 3: After paying the liabilities, the partnership has the following balances in its accounts:

	Cash	+ Non-cash Assets	= Accounts Payable	+ Bright, Capital	+ Gonzalez, Capital	+ Kaska, Capital
Balances before liquidation	$ 10,000	$ 90,000	$ 30,000	$ 40,000	$ 20,000	$ 10,000
Step 1: Sell assets and allocate gain or loss	150,000	(90,000)		10,000	20,000	30,000
Step 2: Pay all partnership liabilities	(30,000)		(30,000)			
Balances for distribution	$ 130,000	$ 0	$ 0	$ 50,000	$ 40,000	$ 40,000

Cash			
Nov. 30	10,000		
Liq. 1	150,000	30,000	Liq. 2
Bal.	130,000		

Non-cash Assets			
Nov. 30	90,000		
		90,000	Liq. 1
Bal.	0		

Accounts Payable			
		30,000	Nov. 30
Liq. 2	30,000		
		0	Bal.

Bright, Capital			
		40,000	Nov. 30
		10,000	Liq. 1
		50,000	Bal.

Gonzalez, Capital			
		20,000	Nov. 30
		20,000	Liq. 1
		40,000	Bal.

Kaska, Capital			
		10,000	Nov. 30
		30,000	Liq. 1
		40,000	Bal.

12-22 Financial chapter 12

Because there is cash left in the partnership, the final liquidation transaction pays all remaining cash to the partners *according to their capital balances* as follows:

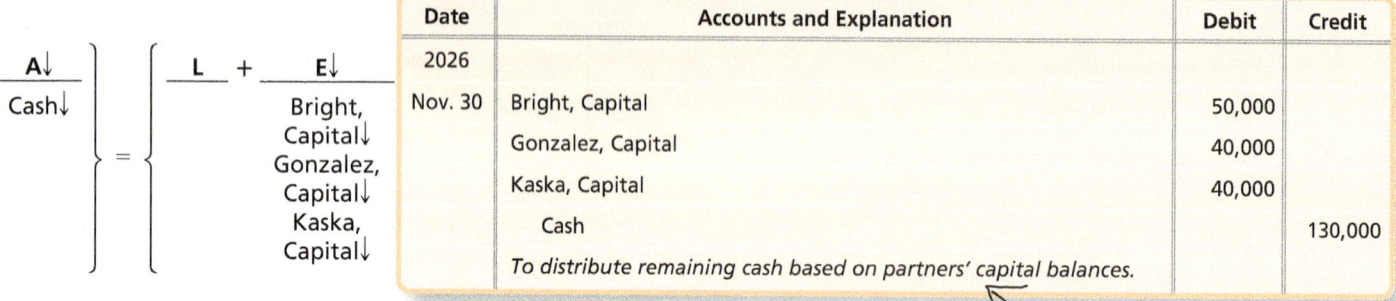

Date	Accounts and Explanation	Debit	Credit
2026			
Nov. 30	Bright, Capital	50,000	
	Gonzalez, Capital	40,000	
	Kaska, Capital	40,000	
	Cash		130,000
	To distribute remaining cash based on partners' capital balances.		

The remaining cash is paid out according to the partners' capital balances, not the profit-and-loss-sharing ratio.

The liquidation of the Bright, Gonzalez, & Kaska partnership is summarized below. It's important to remember that upon liquidation, gains and losses on the sale of assets are divided according to the *profit-and-loss-sharing ratio* and that the final cash payment is divided according to the *capital balances*.

	ASSETS		= LIABILITIES +	EQUITY		
	Cash	+ Non-cash Assets	= Accounts Payable	+ Bright, Capital	+ Gonzalez, Capital	+ Kaska, Capital
Balances before liquidation	$ 10,000	$ 90,000	$ 30,000	$ 40,000	$ 20,000	$ 10,000
Step 1:						
Sell assets and allocate gain or loss	150,000	(90,000)		10,000	20,000	30,000
Step 2:						
Pay all partnership liabilities	(30,000)		(30,000)			
Balances for distribution	130,000	0	0	50,000	40,000	40,000
Step 3:						
Pay the remaining cash	(130,000)			(50,000)	(40,000)	(40,000)
Balances after liquidation	$ 0	$ 0	$ 0	$ 0	$ 0	$ 0

Cash				Non-cash Assets				Accounts Payable		
Nov. 30	10,000			Nov. 30	90,000				30,000	Nov. 30
Liq. 1	150,000	30,000	Liq. 2			90,000	Liq. 1	Liq. 2	30,000	
Bal.	130,000			Bal.	0				0	Bal.
		130,000	Liq. 3							
Bal.	0									

Bright, Capital				Gonzalez, Capital				Kaska, Capital		
		40,000	Nov. 30			20,000	Nov. 30			10,000	Nov. 30
		10,000	Liq. 1			20,000	Liq. 1			30,000	Liq. 1
		50,000	Bal.			40,000	Bal.			40,000	Bal.
Liq. 3	50,000			Liq. 3	40,000			Liq. 3	40,000		
		0	Bal.			0	Bal.			0	Bal.

Sale of Assets at a Loss with Capital Deficiency

Liquidation of a business often includes the sale of assets at a loss. In this case, the loss must be allocated to the partners' capital accounts based on their profit-and-loss-sharing ratio.

Step 1: Assume Bright, Gonzalez, and Kaska decide to liquidate on November 30 and sell the non-cash assets for $60,000. The partnership realizes a loss of $30,000 ($60,000 − $90,000). This loss is allocated to the partners based on their profit-and-loss-sharing ratio as follows:

Date	Accounts and Explanation	Debit	Credit
2026			
Nov. 30	Cash	60,000	
	Loss on Disposal	30,000	
	Non-cash Assets		90,000
	Sale of assets at liquidation.		
30	Bright, Capital ($30,000 × 1/6)	5,000	
	Gonzalez, Capital ($30,000 × 2/6)	10,000	
	Kaska, Capital ($30,000 × 3/6)	15,000	
	Loss on Disposal		30,000
	To allocate loss on liquidation of assets.		

A↓ { Cash↑, Non-cash Assets↓ } = L + E↓ { Loss on Disposal↑ }

A { } = L + E↑↓ { Loss on Disposal↓, Bright, Capital↓, Gonzalez, Capital↓, Kaska, Capital↓ }

Step 2: Bright, Gonzalez, and Kaska then use the remaining cash of $70,000 ($10,000 + $60,000) to pay the liabilities. The partnership records the following entry:

Date	Accounts and Explanation	Debit	Credit
2026			
Nov. 30	Accounts Payable	30,000	
	Cash		30,000
	To pay liabilities.		

A↓ { Cash↓ } = L↓ { Accounts Payable↓ } + E

In this case, there is sufficient cash in the partnership to pay its liabilities. Had there not been, there would have been a shortfall in which each partner (with a debit balance in their capital account) would need to contribute cash according to his or her debit capital balance. Remember that partners are personally liable for the debts of the partnership.

Step 3: After the liabilities have been paid, each partners' capital account is as follows:

Bright, Capital			Gonzalez, Capital			Kaska, Capital		
	40,000	Nov. 30		20,000	Nov. 30		10,000	Nov. 30
Liq. 1 5,000			Liq. 1 10,000			Liq. 1 15,000		
	35,000	Bal.		10,000	Bal.	Bal. 5,000		

12-24 Financial chapter 12

Capital Deficiency
A partnership's claim against a partner. Occurs when a partner's capital account has a debit balance.

Notice that Kaska's capital account has a debit balance. This represents a **capital deficiency** and is the partnership's claim against the partner. Kaska must contribute cash in the amount of the deficiency as follows:

$$\frac{A\uparrow}{Cash\uparrow} \bigg\} = \bigg\{ L + \frac{E\uparrow}{Kaska, Capital\uparrow}$$

Date	Accounts and Explanation	Debit	Credit
2026			
Nov. 30	Cash	5,000	
	Kaska, Capital		5,000
	Receipt of cash for Kaska deficiency.		

The amount of cash left in the partnership and the partners' capital balances are as follows:

	ASSETS		= LIABILITIES +	EQUITY		
	Cash +	Non-cash Assets	= Accounts Payable +	Bright, Capital +	Gonzalez, Capital +	Kaska, Capital
Balances before liquidation	$ 10,000	$ 90,000	$ 30,000	$ 40,000	$ 20,000	$ 10,000
Step 1:						
Sell assets and allocate gain or loss	60,000	(90,000)		(5,000)	(10,000)	(15,000)
Step 2:						
Pay all partnership liabilities	(30,000)		(30,000)			
Balances for distribution	40,000	0	0	35,000	10,000	(5,000)
Step 3:						
Receipt of cash for deficiency	5,000					5,000
Balances for distribution	$ 45,000	$ 0	$ 0	$ 35,000	$ 10,000	$ 0

Cash		
Nov. 30	10,000	
Liq. 1	60,000	30,000 Liq. 2
Bal.	40,000	
Liq. 3	5,000	
Bal.	45,000	

Non-cash Assets		
Nov. 30	90,000	
		90,000 Liq. 1
Bal.	0	

Accounts Payable		
		30,000 Nov. 30
Liq. 2	30,000	
		0 Bal.

Bright, Capital		
		40,000 Nov. 30
Liq. 1	5,000	
		35,000 Bal.

Gonzalez, Capital		
		20,000 Nov. 30
Liq. 1	10,000	
		10,000 Bal.

Kaska, Capital		
		10,000 Nov. 30
Liq. 1	15,000	
Bal.	5,000	
		5,000 Liq. 3
		0 Bal.

The partners divide the remaining cash according to their capital balances. Notice that only Bright and Gonzalez receive a distribution of the cash because Kaska has no remaining capital in the partnership.

Date	Accounts and Explanation	Debit	Credit
2026			
Nov. 30	Bright, Capital	35,000	
	Gonzalez, Capital	10,000	
	Cash		45,000
	To distribute remaining cash based on partners' capital balances.		

$$\begin{array}{c} A\downarrow \\ Cash\downarrow \end{array} \Bigg\} = \Bigg\{ \begin{array}{c} L + E\downarrow \\ Bright, Capital\downarrow \\ Gonzalez, Capital\downarrow \end{array}$$

The liquidation of a partnership at a loss with a capital deficiency is summarized below:

	ASSETS		= LIABILITIES +		EQUITY	
	Cash	+ Non-cash Assets	= Accounts Payable	+ Bright, Capital	+ Gonzalez, Capital	+ Kaska, Capital
Balances before liquidation	$ 10,000	$ 90,000	$ 30,000	$ 40,000	$ 20,000	$ 10,000
Step 1:						
Sell assets and allocate gain or loss	60,000	(90,000)		(5,000)	(10,000)	(15,000)
Step 2:						
Pay all partnership liabilities	(30,000)		(30,000)			
Balances for distribution	40,000	0	0	35,000	10,000	(5,000)
Step 3:						
Receipt of cash for deficiency	5,000					5,000
Balances for distribution	45,000	0	0	35,000	10,000	0
Pay the remaining cash	(45,000)			(35,000)	(10,000)	
Balances after liquidation	$ 0	$ 0	$ 0	$ 0	$ 0	$ 0

Cash					Non-cash Assets				Accounts Payable			
Nov. 30	10,000				Nov. 30	90,000					30,000	Nov. 30
Liq. 1	60,000	30,000	Liq. 2				90,000	Liq. 1	Liq. 2	30,000		
Bal.	40,000				Bal.	0					0	Bal.
Liq. 3	5,000											
Bal.	45,000											
		45,000	Liq. 3									
Bal.	0											

Bright, Capital					Gonzalez, Capital				Kaska, Capital			
		40,000	Nov. 30				20,000	Nov. 30			10,000	Nov. 30
Liq. 1	5,000				Liq. 1	10,000			Liq. 1	15,000		
		35,000	Bal.				10,000	Bal.	Bal.	5,000		
Liq. 3	35,000				Liq. 3	10,000					5,000	Liq. 3
		0	Bal.				0	Bal.			0	Bal.

11. The Bennett and Cruz partnership has decided to liquidate. After selling its non-cash assets and paying off its liabilities, the partnership has cash of $50,000. Bennett and Cruz's capital accounts are $20,000 and $30,000, respectively. Bennett and Cruz share profits 1:5. Journalize the final distribution of cash to the partners.

Check your answer online in MyLab Accounting or at http://www.pearsonhighered.com/Horngren.

For more practice, see Short Exercises S-F:12-11 and S-F:12-12. **MyLab Accounting**

REVIEW

> Things You Should Know

1. **What are the characteristics and types of partnerships?**

   - Partnerships have the following characteristics:
     - Written agreement—called a partnership agreement
     - Limited life
     - Mutual agency
     - Unlimited personal liability
     - Co-ownership of property
     - No partnership income tax
     - Partners' capital accounts
   - There are two basic types of partnerships:
     - General partnership—each partner is a co-owner of the business with all privileges and risks of ownership.
     - Limited partnership—partnership with at least two classes of partners; one or more general partners and one or more limited partners.
   - Limited liability companies and S corporations have characteristics of both partnerships and corporations.

2. **How are partnerships organized?**

   - Partnerships record partners' contributions at current market value by debiting the assets and crediting the liabilities. The excess—assets minus liabilities—is recorded as a credit to each partner's capital account.
   - A partnership equity statement is referred to as the statement of partners' equity and summarizes the changes in each partner's capital account for a specific period of time.
   - A partnership balance sheet reports a separate capital account for each partner.

3. How are partnership profits and losses allocated?

- Partnership profits and losses can be shared based on a stated ratio, each partner's capital balance, each partner's services, or some combination of services, capital balances, and stated ratios.
- Allocation of net income is journalized by debiting the Income Summary account and crediting each partner's capital account based on the arrangement in the partnership agreement.
- Allocation of net loss is journalized by debiting each partner's capital account based on the arrangement in the partnership agreement and crediting the Income Summary account.
- Withdrawals of cash and other assets by a partner in a partnership are recorded by using the account, Partner Name, Withdrawals.

4. How is the admission of a partner accounted for?

- The purchase of an existing partner's interest involves transferring the capital interest from one partner to the new partner.
- An individual can contribute to a partnership at book value. The partnership would record a debit for the assets contributed and a credit to the new partner's capital account.
- Existing partners might receive a bonus upon the admission of a new partner. This bonus increases the capital account of each of the existing partners on the basis of their profit-and-loss-sharing ratios.
- Admission of a new partner might involve a bonus to the new partner. This bonus decreases the capital account of each of the existing partners on the basis of their profit-and-loss-sharing ratios.

5. How is the withdrawal of a partner accounted for?

- A withdrawal of a partner at book value involves debiting the withdrawing partner's capital account and crediting cash or other assets withdrawn.
- When a partner withdraws, a bonus may be allocated to the existing partners. This bonus increases the capital account of each of the existing partners on the basis of their profit-and-loss-sharing ratios.
- Withdrawal of a partner might involve a bonus to the withdrawing partner. This bonus decreases the capital account of each of the existing partners on the basis of their profit-and-loss-sharing ratios.

6. How is the liquidation of a partnership accounted for?

- Liquidation of a partnership involves three steps:
  - Selling the assets and allocating the gain or loss to the partners' capital accounts based on the profit-and-loss-sharing ratio
  - Paying all partnership liabilities
  - Distributing remaining cash, if any, based on the partners' capital account balances
- A capital deficiency, representing the partnership's claim against the partner, could exist if a partner's capital account has a debit balance during the liquidation process.

> Check Your Understanding

Check your understanding of the chapter by completing this problem and then looking at the solution. Use this practice to help identify which sections of the chapter you need to study more.

The partnership of Red & White admits Blue as a partner on January 1, 2024. The partnership has these balances on December 31, 2023:

RED & WHITE Balance Sheet December 31, 2023				
Assets			**Liabilities**	
Cash		$ 9,000	Accounts Payable	$ 50,000
Non-cash Assets		110,000		
			Partners' Equity	
			Red, Capital	45,000
			White, Capital	24,000
			Total Partners' Equity	69,000
Total Assets		$ 119,000	Total Liabilities and Partners' Equity	$ 119,000

Red's share of profits and losses is 60% and White receives 40%.

Requirements

(Requirements 1, 2, and 3 are independent situations.)

1. Suppose Blue pays White $30,000 to buy out White. Red approves Blue as a partner. (See Learning Objective 4)
    a. Record the transfer of equity on the partnership books on January 1, 2024.
    b. Prepare the partnership balance sheet immediately after Blue is admitted as a partner.
2. Suppose Blue becomes a partner by contributing $31,000 cash on January 1, 2024, to acquire a one-fourth interest in the business. (See Learning Objective 4)
    a. Compute Blue's capital balance, and determine whether there's any bonus. If so, who gets the bonus?
    b. Journalize Blue's contribution in the business.
    c. Prepare the partnership balance sheet immediately after Blue is admitted as a partner. Include the heading.
3. Assume the Red & White partnership liquidates by selling its non-cash assets for $100,000. Prepare the entries to liquidate the partnership on January 1, 2024. (See Learning Objective 6)

> Solution

Requirement 1

a.

Date	Accounts and Explanation	Debit	Credit
Jan. 1	White, Capital	24,000	
	Blue, Capital		24,000
	To transfer White's capital to Blue.		

b. The balance sheet for the partnership of Red & Blue is almost identical to the balance sheet given for Red & White in the problem, except that Blue replaces White in the title and in the listing of capital accounts, and the date of the balance sheet is January 1, 2024:

RED & BLUE
Balance Sheet
January 1, 2024

Assets			Liabilities	
Cash	$ 9,000		Accounts Payable	$ 50,000
Non-cash Assets	110,000			
			Partners' Equity	
			Red, Capital	45,000
			Blue, Capital	24,000
			Total Partners' Equity	69,000
Total Assets	$ 119,000		Total Liabilities and Partners' Equity	$ 119,000

Requirement 2

a. Computation of Blue's capital balance.

Partnership capital before admission of new partner ($45,000 + $24,000)	$ 69,000
Contribution of new partner	31,000
Partnership capital after admission of new partner	$ 100,000
Capital of new partner ($100,000 × 1/4)	$ 25,000
Contribution of new partner	$ 31,000
Capital of new partner	(25,000)
Bonus to *existing* partners	$ 6,000

b. Journal entry to record Blue's contribution:

Date	Accounts and Explanation	Debit	Credit
Jan. 1	Cash	31,000	
	Blue, Capital		25,000
	Red, Capital ($6,000 × 60%)		3,600
	White, Capital ($6,000 × 40%)		2,400
	To record Blue's contribution and bonus to existing partners.		

c. New partnership balance sheet:

RED, WHITE & BLUE
Balance Sheet
January 1, 2024

Assets		Liabilities	
Cash ($9,000 + $31,000)	$ 40,000	Accounts Payable	$ 50,000
Non-cash Assets	110,000		
		Partners' Equity	
		Red, Capital ($45,000 + $3,600)	48,600
		White, Capital ($24,000 + $2,400)	26,400
		Blue, Capital	25,000
		Total Partners' Equity	100,000
Total Assets	$ 150,000	Total Liabilities and Partners' Equity	$ 150,000

Requirement 3

Date	Accounts and Explanation	Debit	Credit
2024			
Jan. 1	Cash	100,000	
	Loss on Disposal	10,000	
	Non-cash Assets		110,000
	Sale of assets at liquidation.		
1	Red, Capital ($10,000 × 60%)	6,000	
	White, Capital ($10,000 × 40%)	4,000	
	Loss on Disposal		10,000
	To allocate loss on liquidation of assets.		
1	Accounts Payable	50,000	
	Cash		50,000
	To pay liabilities.		
1	Red, Capital ($45,000 − $6,000)	39,000	
	White, Capital ($24,000 − $4,000)	20,000	
	Cash ($9,000 + $100,000 − $50,000)		59,000
	To distribute remaining cash based on partners' capital balances.		

> Key Terms

Capital Deficiency (p. 12-24)
Dissolution (p. 12-3)
General Partner (p. 12-4)
General Partnership (p. 12-4)
Limited Liability Company (LLC) (p. 12-5)
Limited Liability Partnership (LLP) (p. 12-5)
Limited Partner (p. 12-5)
Limited Partnership (LP) (p. 12-4)
Liquidation (p. 12-20)
Mutual Agency (p. 12-3)
Partnership (p. 12-2)
Partnership Agreement (p. 12-2)
S Corporation (p. 12-6)
Statement of Partners' Equity (p. 12-8)
Unlimited Personal Liability (p. 12-3)

> Quick Check

1. Which characteristic identifies a general partnership? *Learning Objective 1*
   a. Limited personal liability
   b. Unlimited life
   c. No business income tax
   d. All of the above

2. Which characteristic identifies a limited liability company? *Learning Objective 1*
   a. Members have limited personal liability.
   b. Members can actively participate in the management of the business.
   c. The LLC can elect not to pay business income tax.
   d. All of the above

3. Abbott and Brown form a partnership. Abbott contributes $10,000 cash and merchandise inventory with a current market value of $40,000. Brown contributes $5,000 in cash and land with a current market value of $30,000 (cost of $15,000). Which of the following is correct? *Learning Objective 2*
   a. Brown, Capital is credited for $20,000.
   b. Brown, Capital is credited for $35,000.
   c. Brown, Capital is debited for $20,000.
   d. Brown receives a bonus of $30,000 from Abbott.

4. Which financial statement shows the changes in each partner's capital account for a specific period of time? *Learning Objective 2*
   a. Balance Sheet
   b. Income Statement
   c. Statement of Partners' Equity
   d. Statement of Owner's Equity

5. The partnership of Abbott and Brown splits profits 1/4 to Abbott and 3/4 to Brown. There is no provision for losses. The partnership has a net loss of $200,000. What is Brown's share of the loss? *Learning Objective 3*
   a. $50,000
   b. $200,000
   c. $150,000
   d. Cannot be determined because the loss-sharing ratio is not given.

6. Partner withdrawals *Learning Objective 3*
   a. decrease partnership capital.
   b. increase partnership liabilities.
   c. decrease partnership net income.
   d. increase partnership capital.

Learning Objective 4

7. Charles pays $30,000 to Steven to acquire Steven's $15,000 interest in a partnership. The journal entry to record this transaction is

Date	Accounts and Explanation	Debit	Credit
a.	Charles, Capital	15,000	
	Steven, Capital		15,000
b.	Steven, Capital	15,000	
	Charles, Capital		15,000
c.	Steven, Capital	30,000	
	Charles, Capital		30,000
d.	Charles, Capital	30,000	
	Steven, Capital		30,000

Learning Objective 4

8. Peter and Steve admit Meredith to their partnership, with Meredith paying $70,000 more than the book value of her equity in the new business. Peter and Steve have no formal profit-and-loss-sharing agreement. What effect does admitting Meredith to the partnership have on the capital balances of Peter and Steve?

   a. Credit the Peter and Steve capital accounts for $35,000 each.
   b. Cannot be determined because there's no profit-and-loss-sharing ratio.
   c. Debit the Peter and Steve capital accounts for $35,000 each.
   d. Credit the Peter and Steve capital accounts for $70,000 each.

Learning Objective 5

9. Wright retires from the partnership of Edwards, Lee, and Wright. The partners share profits and losses in the ratio of 3:2:5, respectively. Wright's capital balance is $32,000, and he receives $37,000 in final settlement. What is the effect on the capital accounts of Edwards and Lee?

   a. Edwards' capital decreases by $3,000.
   b. Edwards' capital decreases by $5,000.
   c. Edwards' capital increases by $3,000.
   d. Lee's capital decreases by $5,000.

Learning Objective 6

10. The book value of the non-cash assets of the MLW partnership is $150,000. In liquidation, the partnership sells the non-cash assets for $174,000. Partners M, L, and W split profits equally. How should the partnership account for the sale of the non-cash assets?

    a. Debit cash for $174,000
    b. Increase each of the partners' capital accounts by $8,000
    c. Credit the non-cash assets for $150,000
    d. All of the above

Check your answers at the end of the chapter.

ASSESS YOUR PROGRESS

> Review Questions

1. What is the purpose of a partnership agreement, and what should it include?
2. What causes a partnership to dissolve?
3. What does mutual agency mean in respect to partnership debt?
4. Is the net income of a partnership taxed? Who pays the tax?
5. How does a limited partnership differ from a general partnership?
6. Describe a limited liability partnership (LLP).
7. Describe a limited liability company (LLC).
8. Describe an S corporation.
9. At what value does a partnership record partners' contributions?
10. What does the statement of partners' equity show?
11. How can partnership profits and losses be allocated?
12. What is the effect on total assets, liabilities, and equity of a partnership when a partner is admitted by purchasing an existing partner's interest? Why?
13. What is the effect on the existing partners' capital accounts if a bonus is paid to a new partner upon admission into the partnership?
14. What happens to the partnership at the death of a partner?
15. How does liquidation of a partnership differ from dissolution?
16. What are the three steps involved in liquidation of a partnership?
17. When does a capital deficiency occur?

> Short Exercises

S-F:12-1 Determining the characteristics of a partnership

Learning Objective 1

Study the characteristics of a partnership.

Requirements

1. List five *advantages* of a partnership over a sole proprietorship and a corporation.
2. List three *disadvantages* of a partnership compared to a sole proprietorship and a corporation.

S-F:12-2 Accounting for partner contributions

Learning Objective 2

On January 1, 2024, Mackus contributes land in a partnership with Williams. Mackus purchased the land in 2019 for $275,000. A real estate appraiser now values the land at $700,000. Mackus wants $700,000 capital in the new partnership, but Williams objects. Williams believes that Makus's capital contribution should be measured by the book value of his land. Williams and Makus seek your advice.

Requirements

1. Which value of the land is appropriate for measuring Makus's capital—book value or current market value?
2. Give the partnership's journal entry to record Makus's contribution in the business.

Learning Objective 2

S-F:12-3 Accounting for partner contributions

Kurt and Wyatt are forming a partnership to develop a theme park near Carlson City, Florida. Kurt contributes cash of $3,000,000 and land with a current market value of $10,500,000. When Kurt purchased the land in 2021, its cost was $5,500,000. The partnership will assume Kurt's $3,500,000 note payable on the land. Wyatt contributes cash of $5,000,000 and equipment with a current market value of $5,500,000.

Requirements

1. Journalize the partnership's receipt of assets and liabilities from Kurt and from Wyatt.
2. Compute the partnership's total assets, total liabilities, and total partners' equity immediately after organizing.

Learning Objective 3

S-F:12-4 Allocating profits and losses to the partners

Stone and Smith had beginning capital balances of $18,000 and $13,000, respectively. The two partners fail to agree on a profit-and-loss-sharing ratio. For the first month (June 2024), the partnership has a net loss of $9,000.

Requirements

1. How much of this loss goes to Stone? How much goes to Smith?
2. The partners withdrew no assets during June. What is each partner's capital balance at June 30? Prepare a T-account for each partner's capital account.

Learning Objective 3

S-F:12-5 Allocating profits and losses to the partners

Anderson, Macer, and Bell have capital balances of $22,000, $33,000, and $55,000, respectively. The partners share profits and losses as follows:

a. The first $50,000 is divided based on the partners' capital balances.
b. The next $50,000 is based on services, shared equally by Anderson and Bell. Macer does not receive a salary allowance.
c. The remainder is divided equally.

Requirements

1. Compute each partner's share of the $112,000 net income for the year.
2. Journalize the closing entry to allocate net income for the year.

Learning Objective 4

S-F:12-6 Accounting for the admission of a new partner

Sweet has a capital balance of $25,000; Scott's balance is $21,000. Hamlet pays $100,000 to purchase Scott's interest in the Sweet & Scott partnership. Scott receives the full $100,000.

Requirements

1. Journalize the partnership's transaction to admit Hamlet to the partnership.
2. Must Sweet accept Hamlet as a full partner? What rights does Hamlet have after purchasing Scott's interest in the partnership?

Learning Objective 4

S-F:12-7 Accounting for the admission of a new partner

Penn has $90,500 capital and Hammet has $68,500 capital in the Penn & Hammet partnership. Penn and Hammet share profits and losses equally. Judy Pilard contributes cash of $53,000 to acquire a 1/4 interest in the new partnership.

Requirements

1. Calculate Pilard's capital in the new partnership.
2. Journalize the partnership's receipt of the $53,000 from Pilard.

S-F:12-8 Accounting for the admission of a new partner

Learning Objective 4

Eddie and Hagar have partner capital balances of $297,000 and $243,000, respectively. Eddie receives 60% of profits and losses, and Hagar receives 40%. Assume Parker contributes $135,000 to acquire a 25% interest in the new partnership of Eddie, Hagar, and Parker.

Requirements

1. Calculate Parker's capital in the new partnership.
2. Journalize the partnership's receipt of cash from Parker.

S-F:12-9 Accounting for withdrawal of a partner

Learning Objective 5

Jaden, Sophia, and Clement each have a $350,000 capital balance. They share profits and losses as follows: 1:1:2 to Jaden, Sophia, and Clement, respectively. Suppose Clement is withdrawing from the business.

Requirements

1. Journalize the withdrawal of Clement if the partnership agrees to pay Clement $350,000 cash.
2. Journalize the withdrawal of Clement if the partnership agrees to pay Clement $200,000 cash.

S-F:12-10 Accounting for withdrawal of a partner

Learning Objective 5

Jonas, Jeffrey, and Jude each have a $90,000 capital balance. Jonas is retiring from the business. The profit-and-loss-sharing ratio for Jonas, Jeffrey, and Jude is 1:2:3, respectively. Journalize the payment of $97,000 to Jonas upon his retirement on July 31.

S-F:12-11 Accounting for the liquidation of a partnership

Learning Objective 6

The Murphy & Kent partnership has the following balances on June 30, 2024:

MURPHY & KENT Balance Sheet June 30, 2024			
Assets		**Liabilities**	
Cash	$ 10,000	Accounts Payable	$ 15,000
Non-cash Assets	22,000		
		Partners' Equity	
		Murphy, Capital	9,000
		Kent, Capital	8,000
		Total Partners' Equity	17,000
Total Assets	$ 32,000	Total Liabilities and Partners' Equity	$ 32,000

Murphy and Kent share profits 3:2, respectively. Murphy and Kent decide to liquidate the partnership. Journalize the sale of the non-cash assets for $15,000, the payment of the liabilities, and the payment to the partners.

Learning Objective 6

S-F:12-12 Accounting for the liquidation of a partnership

The Jarrin & Martin partnership has the following balances on December 31, 2024:

JARRIN & MARTIN
Balance Sheet
December 31, 2024

Assets		Liabilities	
Cash	$ 38,000	Accounts Payable	$ 72,000
Non-cash Assets	94,000		
		Partners' Equity	
		Jarrin, Capital	38,000
		Martin, Capital	22,000
		Total Partners' Equity	60,000
Total Assets	$ 132,000	Total Liabilities and Partners' Equity	$ 132,000

Jarrin and Martin share profits 1:3, respectively. Jarrin and Martin decide to liquidate the partnership. Journalize the sale of the non-cash assets for $58,000, the payment of the liabilities, and the payment to the partners. Assume Martin contributes cash equal to the capital deficiency.

> Exercises

Learning Objective 1

E-F:12-13 Describing characteristics of a partnership

Cameron Blair, a friend from college, asks you to form a partnership to import fragrances. Since graduating, Blair has worked for the Spanish Embassy, developing important contacts among government officials. Blair believes she is in a unique position to capitalize on an important market. With expertise in accounting, you would have responsibility for the partnership's accounting and finance. List the seven items that would need to be incorporated into the written partnership agreement.

E-F:12-14 Accounting for partner contributions and preparing partnership financial statements

Learning Objective 2

1. Demetrius, Capital $92,000 CR

On December 31, 2024, Demetrius and Garnett agree to combine their sole proprietorships into a partnership. Their balance sheets on December 31 are shown as follows:

	Demetrius's Business Book Value	Demetrius's Business Current Market Value	Garnett's Business Book Value	Garnett's Business Current Market Value
Assets				
Cash	$ 9,000	$ 9,000	$ 3,000	$ 3,000
Accounts Receivable	23,000	21,000	16,000	14,000
Merchandise Inventory	49,000	43,000	40,000	40,000
Plant Assets, Net	126,000	108,000	54,000	58,000
Total Assets	$ 207,000	$ 181,000	$ 113,000	$ 115,000
Liabilities and Owner's Equity				
Accounts Payable	$ 23,000	$ 23,000	$ 12,000	$ 12,000
Other Accrued Payables	13,000	13,000		
Notes Payable	53,000	53,000		
Demetrius, Capital	118,000	?		
Garnett, Capital			101,000	?
Total Liabilities and Owner's Equity	$ 207,000	$ 181,000	$ 113,000	$ 115,000

Requirements

1. Journalize the contributions of Demetrius and Garnett to the partnership.
2. Prepare the partnership balance sheet at December 31, 2024.

E-F:12-15 Accounting for partner contributions

Learning Objective 2

1. Building $92,000 DR

Nancy Fernando has been operating an apartment-locator service as a sole proprietorship. She and Melissa Morris have decided to form a partnership. Fernando's contribution consists of Cash, $10,000; Accounts Receivable, $11,000; Furniture, $18,000; Building (net), $51,000; and Notes Payable, $22,000.

To determine Fernando's equity in the partnership, she and Morris hire an independent appraiser. The appraiser values all the assets and liabilities at their book value except the building, which has a current market value of $92,000. Also, there are additional Accounts Payable of $3,000 that Fernando will contribute. Morris will contribute cash equal to Fernando's equity in the partnership.

Requirements

1. Journalize the entry on the partnership books to record Fernando's contribution.
2. Journalize the entry on the partnership books to record Morris's contribution.

Learning Objective 3

2. Polacco, Capital $100,320 CR

E-F:12-16 Allocating profits and losses to the partners

Polacco and Walsh have formed a partnership. During their first year of operations, the partnership earned $140,000. Their profit-and-loss-sharing agreement states that, first, each partner will receive 10% of their capital balances. The second level is based on services, with $25,000 to Polacco and $15,000 to Walsh. The remainder then will be shared 4:1 between Polacco and Walsh, respectively.

Requirements

1. Calculate the amount of income each partner will receive under their profit-and-loss-sharing agreement assuming Polacco's capital balance is $78,000 and Walsh's capital balance is $78,000.
2. Journalize the entry to close the Income Summary account for the year.

Learning Objective 3

E-F:12-17 Allocating profits and losses to the partners

Finnegan and Healey form a partnership, contributing $35,000 and $105,000, respectively.

Determine their shares of net income or net loss for each of the following independent situations:

a. Net loss is $90,000 and the partners have no written partnership agreement.

b. Net income is $110,000 and the partnership agreement states that the partners share profits and losses on the basis of their capital balances.

c. Net income is $180,000. The first $108,000 is shared on the basis of capital balances. The next $54,000 is based on partner service, with Finnegan receiving 70% and Healey 30%. The remainder is shared equally.

Learning Objective 3

3. Hunter, Capital $44,000

E-F:12-18 Journalizing withdrawal of cash from partnership

Fultz and Hunter form a partnership on January 1, 2024, contributing $59,000 and $20,000, respectively. The partnership had net income of $164,000. Based on the partnership agreement, Fultz's share of net income was $95,000 and Hunter's share was $69,000. Fultz and Hunter each withdrew cash of $45,000 for personal use during the year.

Requirements

1. Journalize the entry to close net income to the partners.
2. Journalize closing the partners' withdrawal accounts. Explanations are not required.
3. Calculate the balances in each partner's capital account after allocation of net income and partners' withdrawals of cash. (Assume the partnership's accounting year began on January 1, 2024, and ended on December 31, 2024.)

Learning Objective 4

2.c. Nole, Capital $16,875 CR

E-F:12-19 Accounting for the admission of a new partner

Hylands is admitted to the partnership of Reddick & Nole. Prior to her admission, the partnership books show Reddick's capital balance at $180,000 and Nole's at $90,000. Assume Reddick and Nole share profits and losses equally.

Requirements

1. Compute each partner's equity on the books of the new partnership under the following plans:

    a. Hylands pays $100,000 for Nole's equity. Hylands pays Nole directly.

    b. Hylands contributes $90,000 to acquire a 1/4 interest in the partnership.

c. Hylands contributes $135,000 to acquire a 1/4 interest in the partnership.

2. Journalize the entries for admitting the new partner under plans a, b, and c.

E-F:12-20 Accounting for withdrawal of a partner

Learning Objective 5

The O'Hara, Parness, and Lincoln partnership balance sheet reports capital of $50,000 for O'Hara, $125,000 for Parness, and $25,000 for Lincoln. O'Hara is withdrawing from the firm. The partners have shared profits and losses in the ratio of 1/2 to O'Hara, 1/4 to Parness, and 1/4 to Lincoln. The partnership agreement states that a withdrawing partner will receive cash equal to the book value of his or her partners' equity. Journalize the withdrawal of O'Hara.

E-F:12-21 Accounting for withdrawal of a partner

Learning Objective 5

On March 31, Sara retires from the partnership of Sara, Brenden, and Tim. The partner capital balances are Sara, $48,000; Brenden, $48,000; and Tim, $21,000. The profit-and-loss-sharing ratio has been 5:3:2 for Sara, Brenden, and Tim, respectively.

1. Tim, Capital $4,800 DR

Requirements

1. Journalize the withdrawal of Sara assuming she receives $60,000 cash.
2. Journalize the withdrawal of Sara assuming she receives $30,000 cash.

E-F:12-22 Accounting for the liquidation of a partnership

Learning Objective 6

Dallas, Valdez, and Wagman are liquidating their partnership. Before selling the assets and paying the liabilities, the capital balances are Dallas $41,000; Valdez, $32,000; and Wagman, $22,000. The profit-and-loss-sharing ratio has been 2:2:1 for Dallas, Valdez, and Wagman, respectively. The partnership has $73,000 cash, $48,000 non-cash assets, and $26,000 accounts payable.

Requirements

1. Assuming the partnership sells the non-cash assets for $57,000, record the journal entries for the sale of non-cash assets, allocation of gain or loss on liquidation, the payment of the outstanding liabilities, and the distribution of remaining cash to partners.
2. Assuming the partnership sells the non-cash assets for $18,000, record the journal entries for the sale of non-cash assets, allocation of gain or loss on liquidation, the payment of the outstanding liabilities, and the distribution of remaining cash to partners.

> Problems Group A

P-F:12-23A Determining characteristics of a partnership and accounting for partner contributions

Learning Objectives 1, 2

3. Accounts Payable $25,000 CR

Stone and Thombs are forming a partnership, Salem Leather Goods, to import merchandise from Spain. Stone is especially artistic and will travel to Spain to buy the merchandise. Thombs is a super salesman and has already lined up several department stores to sell the leather goods.

Requirements

1. What is the purpose of the partnership agreement?
2. If the partnership agreement does not state the profit-and-loss-sharing ratios, how will profits or losses be shared?
3. Stone is contributing $175,000 in cash and accounts payable of $25,000. Thombs is contributing a building that cost Thombs $65,000. The building's current market value is $90,000. Journalize the contribution of the two partners.

Learning Objectives 2, 3

P-F:12-24A Accounting for partner contributions, allocating profits and losses to the partners, preparing partnership financial statements

2. Loiselle, Capital $43,100

Loiselle and Randall formed a partnership on March 15, 2024. The partners agreed to contribute equal amounts of capital. Loiselle contributed her sole proprietorship's assets and liabilities (credit balances in parentheses) as follows:

	Loiselle's Business	
	Book Value	Current Market Value
Accounts Receivable	$ 12,700	$ 10,400
Merchandise Inventory	44,000	30,000
Prepaid Expenses	3,200	2,700
Store Equipment, Net	44,000	24,000
Accounts Payable	(24,000)	(24,000)

On March 15, Randall contributed cash in an amount equal to the current market value of Loiselle's partnership capital. The partners decided that Loiselle will earn 60% of partnership profits because she will manage the business. Randall agreed to accept 40% of the profits. During the period ended December 31, the partnership earned net income of $79,000. Loiselle's withdrawals were $41,000, and Randall's withdrawals totaled $29,000.

Requirements

1. Journalize the partners' initial contributions.
2. Prepare the partnership balance sheet immediately after its formation on March 15, 2024.
3. Journalize the closing of the Income Summary and partner Withdrawal accounts on December 31, 2024.

Learning Objectives 2, 3

P-F:12-25A Allocating profits and losses to the partners, preparing partnership financial statements

2. Chad, Capital $70,800

On October 1, 2024, Art, Bryce, and Chad formed the A, B, and C partnership. Art contributed $20,000; Bryce, $32,000; and Chad, $48,000. Art will manage the store; Bryce will work in the store three-quarters of the time; and Chad will not work in the business.

Requirements

1. Compute the partners' shares of profits and losses under each of the following plans:
   a. Net loss for the year ended September 30, 2025, is $45,000, and the partnership agreement allocates 50% of profits to Art, 40% to Bryce, and 10% to Chad. The agreement does not discuss sharing of losses.

b. Net income for the year ended September 30, 2025, is $98,000. The first $35,000 is allocated on the basis of relative partner capital balances. The next $27,000 is based on services, with $17,000 going to Art and $10,000 going to Bryce. Any remainder is shared equally.

2. Using plan b, prepare the partnership statement of partners' equity for the year ended September 30, 2025. Assume Art, Bryce, and Chad each withdrew $6,000 from the partnership during the year.

P-F:12-26A Accounting for the admission of a new partner

George, Murphy, and Lincoln, a partnership, is considering admitting Thorton as a new partner. On July 31, 2024, the capital accounts of the three existing partners and their profit-and-loss-sharing ratio are as follows:

Learning Objective 4

4. Lincoln, Capital $15,950 DR

	Capital	Profit-and-Loss-Sharing %
George	$ 43,500	20%
Murphy	87,000	25%
Lincoln	130,500	55%

Requirements

Journalize the admission of Thorton as a partner on July 31 for each of the following independent situations:

1. Thorton pays Lincoln $174,000 cash to purchase Lincoln's interest.
2. Thorton contributes $87,000 to the partnership, acquiring a 1/4 interest in the business.
3. Thorton contributes $87,000 to the partnership, acquiring a 1/6 interest in the business.
4. Thorton contributes $87,000 to the partnership, acquiring a 1/3 interest in the business.

P-F:12-27A Accounting for withdrawal of a partner

Ho-Kim-Ling Design Company is a partnership owned by three individuals. The partners share profits and losses in the ratio of 30% to Ho, 40% to Kim, and 30% to Ling. At December 31, 2024, the firm has the following balance sheet. On December 31, Ho withdraws from the partnership.

Learning Objective 5

2. Notes Payable $25,000 CR

HO-KIM-LING DESIGN COMPANY
Balance Sheet
December 31, 2024

Assets		Liabilities	
Cash	$ 10,000	Accounts Payable	$ 87,000
Accounts Receivable, Net	12,000		
Merchandise Inventory	94,000	**Partners' Equity**	
Equipment, Net	95,000	Ho, Capital	35,000
		Kim, Capital	47,000
		Ling, Capital	42,000
		Total Partners' Equity	124,000
Total Assets	$ 211,000	Total Liabilities and Partners' Equity	$ 211,000

Requirements

Record Ho's withdrawal from the partnership under the following independent plans:

1. In a personal transaction, Ho sells her equity to Wei, who pays Ho $120,000 for her interest. Kim and Ling agree to accept Wei as a partner.
2. The partnership pays Ho cash of $10,000 and gives her a note payable for the remainder of her book equity in settlement of her partnership interest.
3. The partnership pays Ho $65,000 for her book equity.
4. The partnership pays Ho $25,000 for her book equity.

Learning Objective 6

P-F:12-28A Accounting for the liquidation of a partnership

2. Loss on Disposal $20,000

The partnership of Seymour, Packard, & Malone has experienced operating losses for three consecutive years. The partners—who have shared profits and losses in the ratio of Seymour, 15%; Packard, 60%; and Malone, 25%—are liquidating the business. They ask you to analyze the effects of liquidation. They present the following condensed partnership balance sheet at December 31, 2024:

SEYMOUR, PACKARD, & MALONE
Balance Sheet
December 31, 2024

Assets		Liabilities	
Cash	$ 28,000	Accounts Payable	$ 59,000
Non-cash Assets	120,000		
		Partners' Equity	
		Seymour, Capital	25,000
		Packard, Capital	41,000
		Malone, Capital	23,000
		Total Partners' Equity	89,000
Total Assets	$ 148,000	Total Liabilities and Partners' Equity	$ 148,000

Requirements

1. Assume the non-cash assets are sold for $150,000. Journalize the liquidation transactions.
2. Assume the non-cash assets are sold for $100,000. Journalize the liquidation transactions.

P-F:12-29A Allocating profits and losses to the partners, accounting for the liquidation of a partnership

ABC is a partnership owned by Angus, Black, and Campini, who share profits and losses in the ratio of 2:1:1, respectively. The account balances of the partnership at June 30, 2024, follow:

Learning Objectives 3, 6

2. Black, Capital Bal. $33,500

ABC
Adjusted Trial Balance
June 30, 2024

Account Title	Debit	Credit
Cash	$ 35,000	
Non-cash Assets	110,000	
Notes Payable		$ 32,000
Angus, Capital		23,000
Black, Capital		44,000
Campini, Capital		50,000
Angus, Withdrawals	9,000	
Black, Withdrawals	31,000	
Campini, Withdrawals	46,000	
Service Revenue		166,000
Salaries Expense	69,000	
Rent Expense	15,000	
Total	$ 315,000	$ 315,000

Requirements

1. Prepare the June 30 entries to close the revenue, expense, income summary, and withdrawal accounts.
2. Open each partner's capital T-account with the adjusted balance, post the closing entries to their accounts, and determine each partner's ending capital balance.
3. Prepare the June 30 entries to liquidate the partnership assuming the non-cash assets are sold for $111,000.

Learning Objectives 2, 3, 5, 6

1. End. Bal. Oliver, Capital $28,200

P-F:12-30A Allocating profits and losses to the partners, accounting for withdrawal of a partner, accounting for the liquidation of a partnership, and preparing partnership financial statements

LOT is a partnership owned by Long, Oliver, and Taker. The partners' profit-and-loss-sharing ratio is 2:2:1, respectively. The adjusted trial balance of the partnership at November 30, 2024, follows:

LOT
Adjusted Trial Balance
November 30, 2024

Account Title	Debit	Credit
Cash	$ 10,000	
Merchandise Inventory	8,000	
Building	225,000	
Accumulated Depreciation—Building		$ 45,000
Accounts Payable		13,000
Mortgage Payable		60,000
Long, Capital		65,000
Oliver, Capital		45,000
Taker, Capital		60,000
Long, Withdrawals	10,000	
Oliver, Withdrawals	10,000	
Taker, Withdrawals	8,000	
Sales Revenue		68,000
Cost of Goods Sold	48,000	
Salaries Expense	27,000	
Rent Expense	10,000	
Total	$ 356,000	$ 356,000

Requirements

1. Prepare statement of partners' equity for the month ended November 30, 2024. Use a separate column for each partner in the statement of partners' equity. Assume no new capital contributions during November.

2. Prepare the four closing entries for the month ended November 30, 2024.

3. Taker decides to withdraw from the partnership on December 1, 2024. Her settlement includes all the Merchandise Inventory and all of the Cash in exchange for her equity interest in the partnership.

4. Immediately after Taker's withdrawal, Long and Oliver decide to liquidate the partnership. They sell the building for $150,000. Then they pay the liabilities and distribute the cash to complete the liquidation. Journalize these liquidation entries. Assume the profit-and-loss-sharing ratios remain the same.

> Problems Group B

P-F:12-31B Determining characteristics of a partnership and accounting for partner contributions

Learning Objectives 1, 2

3. Accounts Payable $15,000 CR

Spade and Thress are forming a partnership, Vintage Leather Goods, to import merchandise from Ireland. Spade is especially artistic and will travel to Ireland to buy the merchandise. Thress is a super salesman and has already lined up several department stores to sell the leather goods.

Requirements

1. What is the purpose of the partnership agreement?
2. If the partnership agreement does not state the profit-and-loss-sharing ratios, how will profits or losses be shared?
3. Spade is contributing $195,000 in cash and accounts payable of $15,000. Thress is contributing a building that cost Thress $100,000. The building's current market value is $130,000. Journalize the contribution of the two partners.

P-F:12-32B Accounting for partner contributions, allocating profits and losses to the partners, preparing partnership financial statements

Learning Objectives 2, 3

2. Lincoln, Capital $45,300

Lincoln and Rafferty formed a partnership on March 15, 2024. The partners agreed to contribute equal amounts of capital. Lincoln contributed her sole proprietorship's assets and liabilities (credit balances in parentheses) as follows:

	Lincoln's Business	
	Book Value	Current Market Value
Accounts Receivable	$ 12,200	$ 10,500
Merchandise Inventory	42,000	35,000
Prepaid Expenses	3,500	2,800
Store Equipment, Net	42,000	23,000
Accounts Payable	(26,000)	(26,000)

On March 15, Rafferty contributed cash in an amount equal to the current market value of Lincoln's partnership capital. The partners decided that Lincoln will earn 60% of partnership profits because she will manage the business. Rafferty agreed to accept 40% of the profits. During the period ended December 31, the partnership earned net income of $72,000. Lincoln's withdrawals were $36,000, and Rafferty's withdrawals totaled $26,000.

Requirements

1. Journalize the partners' initial contributions.
2. Prepare the partnership balance sheet immediately after its formation on March 15, 2024.
3. Journalize the closing of the Income Summary and partner Withdrawal accounts on December 31, 2024.

Learning Objectives 2, 3

2. Caden, Capital $70,400

P-F:12-33B Allocating profits and losses to the partners, preparing partnership financial statements

On October 1, 2024, Andy, Brian, and Caden formed the A, B, and C partnership. Andy contributed $27,300; Brian, $45,500; and Caden, $57,200. Andy will manage the store; Brian will work in the store three-quarters of the time; and Caden will not work in the business.

Requirements

1. Compute the partners' shares of profits and losses under each of the following plans:
    a. Net loss for the year ended September 30, 2025, is $45,000, and the partnership agreement allocates 60% of profits to Andy, 30% to Brian, and 10% to Caden. The agreement does not discuss sharing of losses.
    b. Net income for the year ended September 30, 2025, is $93,000. The first $30,000 is allocated on the basis of relative partner capital balances. The next $24,000 is based on service, with $14,000 going to Andy and $10,000 going to Brian. Any remainder is shared equally.
2. Using plan b, prepare the partnership statement of partners' equity for the year ended September 30, 2025. Assume Andy, Brian, and Caden each withdrew $13,000 from the partnership during the year.

Learning Objective 4

4. Loiselle, Capital $14,850 DR

P-F:12-34B Accounting for the admission of a new partner

Hudson, Meehan, and Loiselle, a partnership, is considering admitting Thompson as a new partner. On July 31, 2024, the capital accounts of the three existing partners and their profit-and-loss-sharing ratio are as follows:

	Capital	Profit-and-Loss-Sharing %
Hudson	$ 40,500	20%
Meehan	81,000	25%
Loiselle	121,500	55%

Requirements

Journalize the admission of Thompson as a partner on July 31 for each of the following independent situations:

1. Thompson pays Loiselle $162,000 cash to purchase Loiselle's interest.
2. Thompson contributes $81,000 to the partnership, acquiring a 1/4 interest in the business.
3. Thompson contributes $81,000 to the partnership, acquiring a 1/6 interest in the business.
4. Thompson contributes $81,000 to the partnership, acquiring a 1/3 interest in the business.

Learning Objective 5

2. Notes Payable $27,000 CR

P-F:12-35B Accounting for withdrawal of a partner

Huang-Kong-Lung Design Company is a partnership owned by three individuals. The partners share profits and losses in the ratio of 30% to Huang, 40% to Kong, and 30% to Lung. At December 31, 2024, the firm has the following balance sheet. On December 31, Huang withdraws from the partnership.

HUANG-KONG-LUNG DESIGN COMPANY
Balance Sheet
December 31, 2024

Assets		Liabilities	
Cash	$ 13,000	Accounts Payable	$ 66,000
Accounts Receivable, Net	19,000		
Merchandise Inventory	89,000	**Partners' Equity**	
Equipment, Net	70,000	Huang, Capital	32,000
		Kong, Capital	46,000
		Lung, Capital	47,000
		Total Partners' Equity	125,000
Total Assets	$ 191,000	Total Liabilities and Partners' Equity	$ 191,000

Requirements

Record Huang's withdrawal from the partnership under the following independent plans:

1. In a personal transaction, Huang sells her equity to Wo, who pays Huang $145,000 for her interest. Kong and Lung agree to accept Wo as a partner.
2. The partnership pays Huang cash of $5,000 and gives her a note payable for the remainder of her book equity in settlement of her partnership interest.
3. The partnership pays Huang $80,000 for her book equity.
4. The partnership pays Huang $27,000 for her book equity.

P-F:12-36B **Accounting for the liquidation of a partnership**

The partnership of Saxton, Parkerson, & Murray has experienced operating losses for three consecutive years. The partners—who have shared profits and losses in the ratio of Saxton, 10%; Parkerson, 65%; and Murray, 25%—are liquidating the business. They ask you to analyze the effects of liquidation. They present the following condensed partnership balance sheet at December 31, 2024:

Learning Objective 6

2. Loss on Disposal $55,000

SAXTON, PARKERSON, & MURRAY
Balance Sheet
December 31, 2024

Assets		Liabilities	
Cash	$ 30,000	Accounts Payable	$ 58,000
Non-cash Assets	125,000		
		Partners' Equity	
		Saxton, Capital	17,000
		Parkerson, Capital	48,000
		Murray, Capital	32,000
		Total Partners' Equity	97,000
Total Assets	$ 155,000	Total Liabilities and Partners' Equity	$ 155,000

Requirements

1. Assume the non-cash assets are sold for $170,000. Journalize the liquidation transactions.
2. Assume the non-cash assets are sold for $70,000. Journalize the liquidation transactions.

Learning Objectives 3, 6

2. Buxton, Capital Bal. $25,625

P-F:12-37B Allocating profits and losses to the partners, accounting for the liquidation of a partnership

ABC is a partnership owned by Adams, Buxton, and Carlson, who share profits and losses in the ratio of 3:1:4, respectively. The account balances of the partnership at June 30 follow:

ABC
Adjusted Trial Balance
June 30, 2024

Account Title	Debit	Credit
Cash	$ 25,000	
Non-cash Assets	114,000	
Notes Payable		$ 30,000
Adams, Capital		25,000
Buxton, Capital		45,000
Carlson, Capital		55,000
Adams, Withdrawals	12,000	
Buxton, Withdrawals	29,000	
Carlson, Withdrawals	52,000	
Service Revenue		163,000
Salaries Expense	68,000	
Rent Expense	18,000	
Total	$ 318,000	$ 318,000

Requirements

1. Prepare the June 30 entries to close the revenue, expense, income summary, and withdrawal accounts.
2. Open each partner's capital T-account with the adjusted balance, post the closing entries to their accounts, and determine each partner's ending capital balance.
3. Prepare the June 30 entries to liquidate the partnership assuming the non-cash assets are sold for $116,000.

P-F:12-38B Allocating profits and losses to the partners, accounting for withdrawal of a partner, accounting for the liquidation of a partnership, and preparing partnership financial statements

Learning Objectives 2, 3, 5, 6

1. End. Bal. Noon, Capital $45,000

JNW is a partnership owned by Johnson, Noon, and West. The partners' profit-and-loss-sharing ratio is 1:1:2, respectively. The adjusted trial balance of the partnership at April 30, 2024, follows:

JNW
Adjusted Trial Balance
April 30, 2024

Account Title	Debit	Credit
Cash	$ 32,000	
Merchandise Inventory	8,000	
Building	240,000	
Accumulated Depreciation—Building		$ 40,000
Accounts Payable		16,000
Mortgage Payable		70,000
Johnson, Capital		85,000
Noon, Capital		55,000
West, Capital		65,000
Johnson, Withdrawals	12,000	
Noon, Withdrawals	4,000	
West, Withdrawals	11,000	
Sales Revenue		73,000
Cost of Goods Sold	55,000	
Salaries Expense	32,000	
Rent Expense	10,000	
Total	$ 404,000	$ 404,000

Requirements

1. Prepare statement of partners' equity for the month ended April 30, 2024. Use a separate column for each partner in the statement of partners' equity. Assume no new capital contributions during April.
2. Prepare the four closing entries for the month ended April 30, 2024.
3. West decides to withdraw from the partnership on May 1, 2024. Her settlement includes all the Merchandise Inventory and all the Cash in exchange for her equity interest in the partnership.
4. Immediately after West's withdrawal, Johnson and Noon decide to liquidate the partnership. They sell the building for $164,000. Then they pay the liabilities and distribute the cash to complete the liquidation. Journalize these liquidation entries. Assume the profit-and-loss-sharing ratios are the same.

CRITICAL THINKING

> Using Excel

Download Excel problems for this chapter online in MyLab Accounting or at **http://www.pearsonhighered.com/Horngren**.

> Continuing Problem

P-F:12-39 Accounting for partner contributions, allocating profits and losses to the partners, accounting for withdrawal of a partner

This problem is related to the Canyon Canoe Company situation started in Chapter F:1. Wilson, Turner, and White decide to form a T-shirt design partnership. Amber Wilson figures this T-shirt design business will help her other company, Canyon Canoe Company, with any T-shirt design needs. Additionally, Turner and White have connections with many companies and can expand and grow this new partnership. Each of the three partners contributes $12,000 cash to start up the WTW partnership. They agree to share profits in two steps. First, Turner will receive $11,000 and White will receive $16,000 because they will do most of the graphic design work. Any remaining profits or losses will be shared 1:2:3, respectively for Wilson, Turner, and White. The business starts on January 1, 2025. On December 31, 2025, the business posted a loss of $12,000. Wilson decides to withdraw from the partnership on December 31, 2025. Turner and White agree to give Wilson $4,000 for her equity interest.

Requirements

1. Journalize the contribution of the partners in the partnership on January 1, 2025.
2. Journalize the allocation of the loss from the Income Summary account.
3. Journalize the withdrawal of Wilson as a partner on December 31, 2025.
4. Calculate the ending balances in Turner and White's capital accounts.

> Tying It All Together Case F:12-1

Before you begin this assignment, review the Tying It All Together feature in the chapter.

Cedar Fair, L.P. is a Delaware limited partnership that began operations in 1983. The partnership is a regional amusement park operator that owns 11 amusement parks, two outdoor water parks, one indoor water park, and four hotels. The partnership is publicly traded and listed on The New York Stock Exchange under the symbol FUN. (You can find Cedar Fair's annual report for 2018 at **https://www.sec.gov/Archives/edgar/data/811532/000081153219000037/cedarfair-10kx2018.htm#sECCAE91D24C05DCDB12C98C6ED624739**)

Requirements

1. What is the name of the CPA firm that audited Cedar Fair, L.P. in 2018?
2. Give a reason why you think the partners may have chosen the limited partnership form of business.
3. Could you be a stakeholder in Cedar Fair? How? What would your stake be called?
4. How much did Cedar Fair earn for each limited partner unit for the year ended December 31, 2018?

> Decision Cases

Decision Case F:12-1

The following questions relate to issues faced by partnerships.

Requirements

1. The text states that a written partnership agreement should be drawn up between the partners. One benefit of a partnership agreement is that it provides a mechanism for resolving disputes between the partners. List five areas of dispute that might be resolved by a partnership agreement.
2. Loomis & Nelson is a law partnership. Don Loomis is planning to retire from the partnership and move to Canada. What options are available to Loomis to enable him to convert his share of the partnership assets to cash?

Decision Case F:12-2

Jana Bell originally contributed $20,000 and Matt Fischer originally contributed $10,000 in a public relations firm that has operated for 10 years. Bell and Fischer have shared profits and losses in a 2:1 ratio of their capital balances in the business. Bell manages the office, supervises employees, and does the accounting. Fischer, the moderator of a television talk show, is responsible for marketing. His high-profile status generates important revenue for the business. During the year ended December 31, 2024, the partnership earned net income of $220,000, shared in the 2:1 ratio. On December 31, 2024, Bell's capital balance was $150,000, and Fischer's capital balance was $100,000.

Requirements

Respond to each of the following independent situations.

1. During January 2025, Bell learned that revenues of $60,000 were omitted from the reported 2024 income. She brings this omission to Fischer's attention, pointing out that Bell's share of this added income is 2/3, or $40,000, and Fischer's share is 1/3, or $20,000. Fischer believes they should share this added income on the basis of their capital balances—60%, or $36,000, to Bell and 40%, or $24,000, to himself. Which partner is correct? Why?
2. Assume that the 2024 omission of $60,000 was for an operating expense. On what basis would the partners share this amount?

> Ethical Issue F:12-1

Hart Nance and Jason Symington operate gift boutiques in shopping malls. The partners split profits and losses equally, and each takes an annual withdrawal of $80,000. To even out the workload, Nance travels around the country inspecting their properties. Symington manages the business and serves as the accountant. From time to time, they use small amounts of store merchandise for personal use. In preparing for his daughter's wedding, Symington took inventory that cost $10,000. He recorded the transaction as follows:

Date	Accounts and Explanation	Debit	Credit
	Cost of Goods Sold	10,000	
	Merchandise Inventory		10,000

Requirements
1. How should Symington have recorded this transaction?
2. Discuss the ethical aspects of Symington's action.

> Financial Statement Case F:12-1

The 2018 10K for Magellan Midstream Partners, L.P., a publicly traded partnership, is located at **https://www.sec.gov/Archives/edgar/data/1126975/ 000112697519000059/mmp12311810-k.htm**. Review the financial statements.

Requirements
1. What is the name of the CPA firm that audited Magellan Midstream Partners, L.P.?
2. In what industry is Magellan? What form of business is Magellan? Give a reason why you think the partners may have chosen this form of business.
3. Could you be a stakeholder in Magellan? How? What would your stake be called?
4. How much did Magellan earn for each limited partner unit for the year ended December 31, 2018?

> Quick Check Answers

1. c 2. d 3. b 4. c 5. c 6. a 7. b 8. a 9. a 10. d

# Corporations 13

How Do We Raise More Cash?

Lacey Snyder and Alison Mason, stockholders of Sharemymovie.com, were reviewing the latest financial statements of their business. Sharemymovie.com, a video-sharing Web site in which users can upload, share, and view videos, started five years ago with a cash contribution from each owner and a small bank loan. In the past five years, the site has grown rapidly with more than one million video views each day. Lacey and Alison are excited about the success of the business, but the business has recently been experiencing growing pains.

With the increase in the number of users visiting the site and uploading new videos daily, Lacey and Alison know they need to invest in a new Web site design and purchase updated software. But these expansions will take cash, and they are reluctant to borrow more money from the bank. Lacey and Alison considered asking friends and family to invest in the business. They realized that in order to gain enough cash to meet the growing needs of the business, they would need a large influx of money. After talking to their accountant, they are considering expanding their corporation and taking their business public. In other words, the business will offer ownership (through stock) for anyone who is willing to invest.

By offering the opportunity to own a share in the business, Sharemymovie.com can quickly raise the necessary cash to meet its expansion needs. In addition, the corporate form of business offers liability protection for the stockholders. But there are also some disadvantages to the corporate form, such as double taxation and increased government regulation. As Lacey and Alison move forward with their decision, they need to understand the pros and cons of corporations and carefully evaluate the impact of this decision.

How Much Is the Business Worth?

On February 1, 2012, **Facebook, Inc.**, the popular social media Web site, announced that it planned to issue shares of stock on the stock market under the ticker symbol FB. On May 18, Mark Zuckerberg, the mastermind behind Facebook, rang the opening bell of the stock exchange and shares of Facebook stock began selling at $42.05 per share. On that day, more than 500 million shares were sold and exchanged with an estimated market capitalization of more than $104 billion, one of the largest initial public offerings (IPO) to date. It's interesting to note that in less than a month after its IPO, Facebook stock lost more than a quarter of its value and continues to fluctuate.

Why did Facebook decide to issue stock? What are the advantages and disadvantages of a corporation? How is stock reported on the financial statements? What does the drop in market price of the stock mean to Facebook? In this chapter, we explore the answers to these questions and many more. You learn why businesses decide to organize as a corporation and how to account for transactions unique to a corporation.

Chapter 13 Learning Objectives

1. Identify the characteristics of a corporation
2. Journalize the issuance of stock
3. Account for the purchase and sale of treasury stock
4. Account for cash dividends, stock dividends, and stock splits
5. Prepare a corporate income statement including earnings per share
6. Explain how equity is reported for a corporation
7. Use earnings per share, rate of return on common stockholders' equity, and the price/earnings ratio to evaluate business performance

WHAT IS A CORPORATION?

Learning Objective 1
Identify the characteristics of a corporation

A **corporation** is a business organized under state law that is a separate legal entity. Corporations dominate business activity in the United States. Most well-known companies are corporations and tend to be large multinational businesses.

Corporation
A business organized under state law that is a separate legal entity.

Characteristics of Corporations

A corporation has many unique characteristics:

- **Separate legal entity**—A corporation is a separate legal entity. It is organized independently of its owners.
- **Number of owners**—Corporations have one or more owners (called *stockholders*). A *public* corporation is a corporation whose stock can be purchased on an organized stock exchange, such as the New York Stock Exchange (NYSE) or the NASDAQ Stock Market. Public corporations often have thousands of owners. Some corporations are *privately held*, which means that the stock cannot be purchased on a stock exchange. These corporations often have only a few stockholders.
- **No personal liability of the owner(s) for business's debts**—Stockholders are not personally liable for the debts of the corporation.
- **Lack of mutual agency**—Unlike owners of a sole proprietorship and partnership, stockholders of the corporation are not mutual agents of the business. Stockholders cannot bind the business to a contract.
- **Indefinite life**—Corporations have an indefinite life. They can exist until the business decides to terminate. Withdrawal or death of an owner does not cause termination of the business.
- **Taxation**—Corporations are separate taxable entities. The corporation pays the income tax on the business earnings and is also responsible for paying payroll taxes on employee salaries and wages. Corporations also experience double taxation. Double taxation occurs when corporations make cash payments (called *dividends*) to stockholders. These payments are taxed once as earnings of the corporation and then again when the stockholder receives the dividend. The tax is first paid by the corporation on its corporate income tax return, and then the dividends received by the stockholder are reported on the stockholder's personal income tax return.

- **Double taxation**—Corporations also experience double taxation which occurs when corporations make cash payments (called *dividends*) to stockholders. These payments are taxed once as earnings of the corporation and then again when the stockholder receives the dividend. The tax is first paid by the corporation on its corporate income tax return, and then the dividends received by the stockholder are reported on the stockholder's personal income tax return.
- **Capital accumulation**—Corporations can raise more money than sole proprietorships and partnerships. This is completed through an initial public offering (IPO) and represents the initial offering of corporate shares of stock to the public.

Exhibit F:13-1 summarizes the advantages and disadvantages of a corporation.

Exhibit F:13-1 | Corporations: Advantages and Disadvantages

Advantages	Disadvantages
1. Corporations can raise more money than a proprietorship or partnership.	1. Ownership and management are often separated.
2. A corporation has a continuous life.	2. The earnings of a corporation may be subject to double taxation.
3. The transfer of corporate ownership is easy.	3. Government regulation is expensive.
4. There is no mutual agency among the stockholders and the corporation.	4. Start-up costs are higher than other business forms.
5. Stockholders have limited liability.	

Stockholders' Equity Basics

A corporation is created by filing a certificate of formation with a state. The state authorizes the business to be organized as a corporation and grants the entity a charter or articles of incorporation. The corporation then prepares a set of bylaws, which provide the rules and procedures that the corporation will follow.

The corporate charter of a corporation identifies the maximum number of shares of stock the corporation may issue, called **authorized stock**. The charter provides a state's permission for the corporation to operate. Authorized stock can be issued or unissued. **Issued stock** has been issued by the corporation but may or may not be held by stockholders. A corporation issues **stock certificates** to the stockholders when they buy the stock. The stock certificate represents the individual's ownership of the corporation's capital, so it is called **capital stock**. The basic unit of stock is a share. A corporation may issue a physical stock certificate for any number of shares. Today, many corporations issue the stocks electronically rather than printing a paper certificate. Exhibit F:13-2 (on the next page) shows a stock certificate for 288 shares of Smart Touch Learning common stock owned by Courtney Edwards.

Authorized Stock
The maximum number of shares of stock that the corporate charter allows the corporation to issue.

Issued Stock
Stock that has been issued but may or may not be held by stockholders.

Stock Certificate
Paper evidence of ownership in a corporation.

Capital Stock
Represents the individual's ownership of the corporation's capital.

13-4　Financial 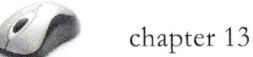 chapter 13

Exhibit F:13-2 | Stock Certificate

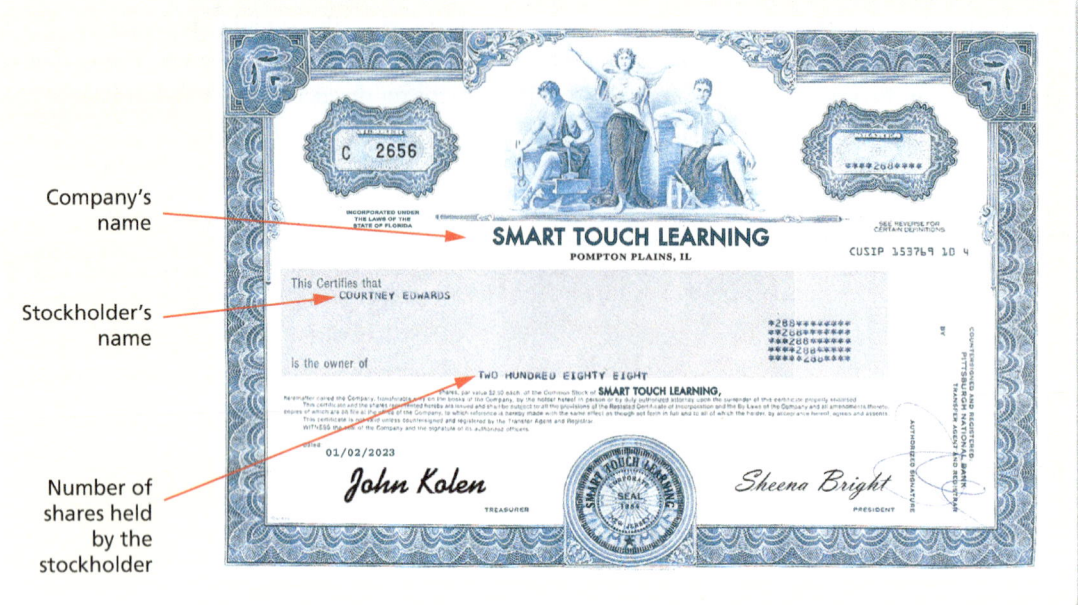

The stock certificate shows the following:

- Company name
- Stockholder name
- Number of shares owned by the stockholder

Outstanding Stock
Issued stock in the hands of stockholders.

Stock that is held by the stockholders is said to be **outstanding stock**. The outstanding stock of a corporation represents 100% of its ownership. The numbers of shares of authorized stock, issued stock, and outstanding stock are most likely going to be different amounts. Exhibit F:13-3 explains the differences between these categories of stock.

Exhibit F:13-3 | Categories of Stock

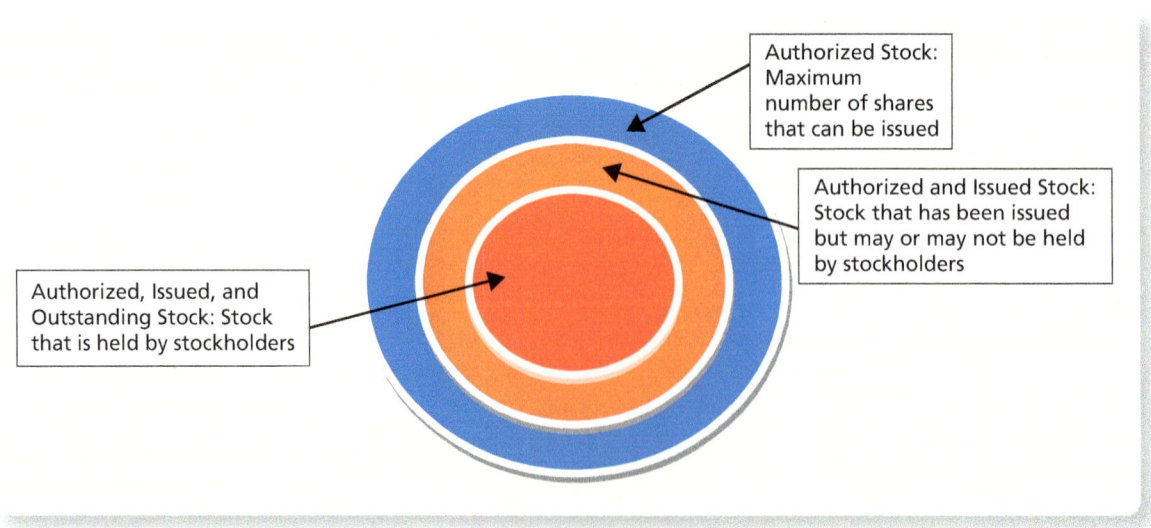

Stockholders' Rights

A stockholder has four basic rights, unless a right is withheld by contract:

1. **Vote.** Stockholders participate in management indirectly by voting on corporate matters at stockholders' meetings (or sometimes through the mail or electronic voting). This is

Corporations  Financial 13-5

the only way in which a stockholder can help to manage the corporation. Normally, each share of basic ownership in the corporation carries one vote.

2. **Dividends.** Stockholders receive a proportionate part of any **dividend** that is declared and paid. A dividend is a distribution of a corporation's earnings to stockholders. Each share of stock receives an equal dividend so, for example, a shareholder who owns 1% of the total shares in the company receives 1% of any total dividend.

3. **Liquidation.** Stockholders receive their proportionate share of any assets remaining after the corporation pays its debts and liquidates (goes out of business).

4. **Preemptive right.** Stockholders have a **preemptive right** to maintain their proportionate ownership in the corporation. For example, suppose a stockholder owns 5% of a corporation's stock. If the corporation issues 100,000 new shares of stock, it must offer the stockholder the opportunity to buy 5% (5,000) of the new shares. This right, however, is usually withheld by contract for most corporations.

Dividend
A distribution of a corporation's earnings to stockholders.

Preemptive Right
Stockholder's right to maintain his or her proportionate ownership in the corporation.

Capital Stock

Corporations can issue different classes of stock. The stock of a corporation may be either common or preferred. Every corporation issues **common stock**, which represents the basic ownership of the corporation. Some companies issue Class A common stock, which carries the right to vote. They may also issue Class B common stock, which may be nonvoting. There must be at least one voting class of stock. However, there is no limit as to the number or types of classes of stock that a corporation may issue. Each class of stock has a separate account in the company's ledger.

Preferred stock gives its owners certain advantages over common stock. Most notably, preferred stockholders receive a dividend preference over common stockholders. This ensures that if a corporation pays dividends, the preferred stockholders receive their dividends first. They also receive assets before common stockholders if the corporation liquidates. When dividends are declared, corporations pay a fixed dividend on preferred stock. The amount of the preferred dividend is printed on the face of the preferred stock certificate. Investors usually buy preferred stock to earn those fixed dividends. With these advantages, preferred stockholders take less investment risk than common stockholders.

Owners of preferred stock also have the four basic stockholder rights, unless a right is withheld. The right to vote, for example, is usually withheld from preferred stock. Companies may issue different series of preferred stock (Series A and Series B, for example). Each series is recorded in a separate account. Preferred stock is rarer than you might think. Many corporations have the authorization to issue preferred stock, but few actually issue the preferred shares.

Stock may carry a par value or it may be no-par stock. **Par value is an amount assigned by a company to a share of its stock. Most companies set par value low to avoid issuing their stock below par. The par value of a stock has no relation to the market value, which is the price at which the stock is bought and sold.**

The par value of preferred stock may be higher per share than common stock par values. Par value is arbitrary and is assigned when the organizers file the corporate charter with the state. There is no real reason for why par values vary. It is a choice made by the organizers of the corporation.

Some states allow the issuance of no-par stock. **No-par stock** does not have par value. No-par value stock has an advantage because there is no confusion between the par value and market value of the stock. **Stated value stock** is no-par stock that has been assigned an amount similar to par value. Stated value represents the minimum amount that the corporation can issue the stock for. Usually the state the company incorporates in will determine whether a stock may be par or stated value stock. For accounting purposes, par value stock is treated the same as stated value stock except for the account names.

Common Stock
Represents the basic ownership of a corporation.

Preferred Stock
Stock that gives its owners certain advantages over common stockholders, such as the right to receive dividends before the common stockholders and the right to receive assets before the common stockholders if the corporation liquidates.

Par Value
An amount assigned by a company to a share of its stock.

Is the par value of a stock the price at which the stock is bought and sold?

No-Par Stock
Stock that has no amount (par) assigned to it.

Stated Value Stock
No-par stock that has been assigned an amount similar to par value.

13-6 Financial chapter 13

Stockholders' Equity
A corporation's equity that includes paid-in capital and retained earnings.

Paid-In Capital
Represents amounts received from the stockholders of a corporation in exchange for stock.

Retained Earnings
Equity earned by profitable operations of a corporation that is not distributed to stockholders.

Stockholders' Equity

A corporation's equity is called **stockholders' equity**. State laws require corporations to report their sources of owners' capital because some of the capital must be maintained by the company. The two basic sources of stockholders' equity are as follows:

- **Paid-in capital** (also called *contributed capital*) represents amounts received from the stockholders in exchange for stock. Common stock is the main source of paid-in capital. Paid-in capital is *externally* generated capital and results from transactions with outsiders.

- **Retained earnings** is equity earned by profitable operations that is not distributed to stockholders. Retained earnings is *internally* generated equity because it results from corporate decisions to retain net income to use in future operations or for expansion.

TYING IT ALL TOGETHER

Facebook, Inc. is a mobile application and Web site that enables people to connect, share, discover, and communicate with each other. On average in December 2018, Facebook had 1.52 billion daily active users. Facebook also owns Instagram, Messenger, WhatsApp, and Oculus. Facebook incorporated in Delaware in July 2004 and completed an initial public offering in May 2012. The company's Class A common stock is listed on the NASDAQ under the symbol "FB." (You can find Facebook's annual report at **https://www.sec.gov/Archives/edgar/data/1326801/000132680119000009/fb-12312018x10k.htm.**)

What types of stock does Facebook have?
Facebook has Class A common stock that is listed on the NASDAQ. The company also has Class B common stock that is not listed nor traded on any stock exchange.

How many stockholders were of record as of December 31, 2018?
As of December 31, 2018, there were 3,780 stockholders of record of the Class A common stock. There were 41 stockholders of record of the company's Class B common stock. As of December 31, 2018, the closing price of Facebook's Class A common stock was $131.09 per share.

Match the key term to the definition.

1. Stock certificate	a.	The maximum number of shares of stock that the corporate charter allows the corporation to issue.
2. Preemptive right	b.	Stock that gives its owners certain advantages over common stockholders.
3. Authorized stock	c.	Stockholders' right to maintain their proportionate ownership in the corporation.
4. Preferred stock	d.	Represents amounts received from stockholders of a corporation in exchange for stock.
5. Paid-in capital	e.	Paper evidence of ownership in a corporation.

Check your answers online in MyLab Accounting or at http://www.pearsonhighered.com/Horngren.

For more practice, see Short Exercise S-F:13-1. **MyLab Accounting**

HOW IS THE ISSUANCE OF STOCK ACCOUNTED FOR?

Learning Objective 2
Journalize the issuance of stock

Large corporations such as Intel Corporation and Nike, Inc. need huge quantities of money. They cannot finance all their operations through borrowing, so they raise capital by issuing stock. A company can sell its stock directly to stockholders, or it can use the services of an

Corporations Financial 13-7

underwriter, such as the brokerage firms of Merrill Lynch & Co., Inc., Morgan Stanley, and JPMorgan Chase & Co. An underwriter usually assumes some of the risk of issuing stock by agreeing to buy all the stock the firm cannot sell to its clients. Stocks of public companies are bought and sold on a stock exchange, such as the New York Stock Exchange (NYSE) or NASDAQ Stock Market.

The amount that the corporation receives from issuing stock is called the issue price. Usually, the issue price exceeds par value because par value is normally set quite low.

Underwriter
A firm that handles the issuance of a company's stock to the public, usually assuming some of the risk by agreeing to buy the stock if the firm cannot sell all of the stock to its clients.

Issue Price
The amount that the corporation receives from issuing stock.

Issuing Common Stock at Par Value

In this chapter, we will continue using Smart Touch Learning; however, we will now assume that Smart Touch Learning's common stock carries a par value of $1 per share and that the charter authorizes 20,000,000 shares of common stock. The journal entry for the issue of 15,000 shares at par value would be as follows:

Date	Accounts and Explanation	Debit	Credit
	Cash	15,000	
	Common Stock—$1 Par Value ($1 per share × 15,000 shares)		15,000
	Issued common stock at par.		

$\dfrac{A\uparrow}{Cash\uparrow} = \left\{\dfrac{L}{} + \dfrac{E\uparrow}{Common\ Stock\uparrow}\right.$

Issuing Common Stock at a Premium

As stated previously, most corporations set par value low and issue common stock for a price above par. The amount above par is called a premium. Assume Smart Touch Learning issues an additional 3,000 shares for $5 per share. The $4 difference between the issue price ($5) and par value ($1) is a premium.

Premium
The amount above par at which a stock is issued.

A premium on the issue of stock is not a gain, income, or profit for the corporation because the company is dealing with its own stock. This situation illustrates one of the fundamentals of accounting in that a company cannot report a profit or loss when buying or selling its own stock. So, the premium is another type of paid-in capital account known as **Paid-In Capital in Excess of Par**. It is also called *additional paid-in capital*. The Paid-In Capital in Excess of Par account is an equity account that is reported on the balance sheet.

Paid-In Capital in Excess of Par
Represents amounts received from stockholders in excess of par value.

With a par value of $1, Smart Touch Learning's entry to record the issuance of 3,000 shares of its common stock at $5 per share is as follows:

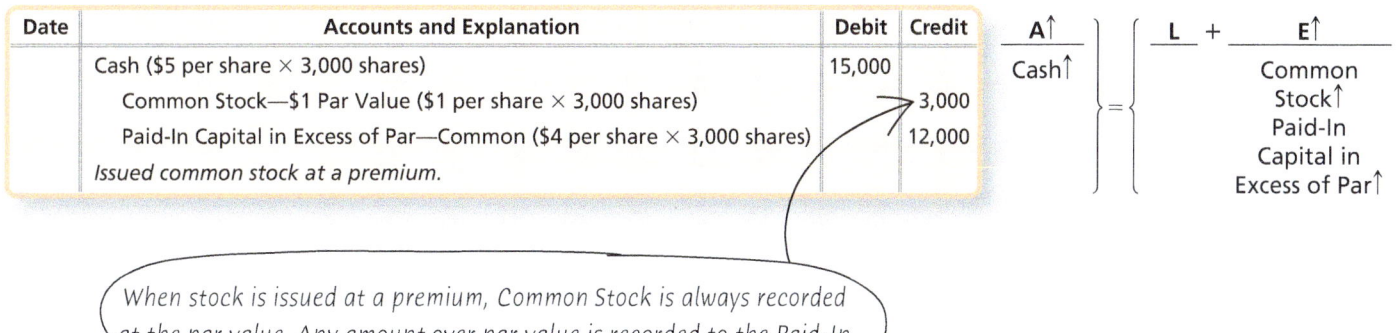

When stock is issued at a premium, Common Stock is always recorded at the par value. Any amount over par value is recorded to the Paid-In Capital in Excess of Par account.

Exhibit F:13-4 (on the next page) shows how Smart Touch Learning would report stockholders' equity on its balance sheet after the stock issuances, assuming that the balance of Retained Earnings is $3,550.

Exhibit F:13-4 | Stockholders' Equity

SMART TOUCH LEARNING, INC.
Balance Sheet (Partial)
December 31, 2024

Stockholders' Equity

Paid-In Capital:

Common Stock—$1 Par Value; 20,000,000 shares authorized, 18,000 shares issued and outstanding	$ 18,000
Paid-In Capital in Excess of Par—Common	12,000
Total Paid-In Capital	30,000
Retained Earnings	3,550
Total Stockholders' Equity	$ 33,550

Issuing No-Par Common Stock

When a company issues no-par stock, it debits the asset received and credits the stock account. For no-par stock, there can be no Paid-In Capital in Excess of Par because there is no par to be in excess of.

Assume that, instead of $1 par value, Smart Touch Learning's common stock is no-par. How would that change the recording of the issuance of 15,000 shares for $1 and 3,000 shares for $5? The stock-issuance entries would be as follows:

Date	Accounts and Explanation	Debit	Credit
	Cash ($1 per share × 15,000 shares)	15,000	
	Common Stock—No-Par Value		15,000
	Issued no-par common stock.		
	Cash ($5 per share × 3,000 shares)	15,000	
	Common Stock— No-Par Value		15,000
	Issued no-par common stock.		

A↑ Cash↑ = L + E↑ Common Stock↑

A↑ Cash↑ = L + E↑ Common Stock↑

Regardless of the stock's issue price, Cash is debited and Common Stock is credited for the cash received. So, although the total paid-in capital of $30,000 remains the same, the Common Stock account differs from $18,000 (par stock) to $30,000 (no-par stock).

Exhibit F:13-5 shows how the stockholders' equity section of the balance sheet would change.

Exhibit F:13-5 | Stockholders' Equity—No-Par Stock

SMART TOUCH LEARNING, INC.
Balance Sheet (Partial)
December 31, 2024

Stockholders' Equity

Paid-In Capital:

Common Stock—No-Par Value; 20,000,000 shares authorized, 18,000 shares issued and outstanding	$ 30,000
Retained Earnings	3,550
Total Stockholders' Equity	$ 33,550

Issuing Stated Value Common Stock

Accounting for stated value common stock is almost identical to accounting for par value stock. The only difference is that stated value stock uses an account titled Paid-In Capital in Excess of *Stated* to record amounts received above the stated value.

For example, assume that instead of issuing 3,000 shares of $1 par value stock for $5 per share, Smart Touch Learning issues 3,000 shares of $1 *stated* value stock for $5 per share. Smart Touch Learning would record the following journal entry:

Date	Accounts and Explanation	Debit	Credit
	Cash ($5 per share × 3,000 shares)	15,000	
	Common Stock—$1 Stated Value ($1 per share × 3,000 shares)		3,000
	Paid-In Capital in Excess of Stated—Common ($4 per share × 3,000 shares)		12,000
	Issued common stock at a premium.		

A↑ = L + E↑
Cash↑ = Common Stock↑
Paid-In Capital in Excess of Stated↑

Issuing Common Stock for Assets Other Than Cash

A corporation may issue stock for assets other than cash. It records the transaction at the market value of the stock issued or the market value of the assets received, whichever is more clearly determinable. Now let's consider that Smart Touch Learning receives an additional contribution of furniture with a market value of $18,000 in exchange for 5,000 shares of its $1 par common stock. How would the entry be recorded?

Date	Accounts and Explanation	Debit	Credit
	Furniture	18,000	
	Common Stock—$1 Par Value ($1 par value × 5,000 shares)		5,000
	Paid-In Capital in Excess of Par—Common ($18,000 − $5,000)		13,000
	Issued common stock in exchange for furniture.		

A↑ = L + E↑
Furniture↑ = Common Stock↑
Paid-In Capital in Excess of Par↑

As you can see, the common stock is still recorded at its $1 par value, and the difference between the market value of the furniture and the par value is recorded to the Paid-In Capital in Excess of Par account. The contributed asset is recorded at its current market value.

ETHICS

What should the building be valued at?

Reed Hiller, the accountant for Snyder Corporation, is trying to decide how to record the company's most recent issuance of stock. Jack Chavez, a majority stockholder, has contributed a building in exchange for common stock. Jack believes that the building should be valued at $4 million, his evaluation of the building's market value. Jack argues that by recording the asset at such a large amount, the business will look more prosperous to investors. Reed is concerned that Jack is overvaluing the asset. What should Reed do?

Solution

Issuance of stock for cash poses no ethical challenge because the value of the asset received (cash) is clearly understood. Issuing stock for assets other than cash can pose a challenge, though. A company should record an asset received at its current market value or the market value of the stock issued, whichever is more clearly determinable. One person's evaluation of a building's market value can differ from another's. Reed should encourage the company to hire an independent appraiser to determine the current market value of the building and then record the building at that value. Alternatively, the company can use the market value of the stock issued to determine the value of the building. This would be appropriate if the stock is traded on an organized exchange.

13-10 Financial chapter 13

Issuing Preferred Stock

Accounting for preferred stock follows the pattern illustrated for issuing common stock. Assume that Smart Touch Learning has authorization from the state to issue 2,000 shares of preferred stock. Smart Touch Learning decides to issue 1,000 shares of its $50 par, 6% preferred stock on January 3, 2025, at $55 per share. (The 6% in the description of the preferred stock refers to the stated dividend associated with the stock and is explained later in the chapter.) The issuance entry would be as follows:

A↑ Cash↑ = L + E↑ Preferred Stock↑ Paid-In Capital in Excess of Par↑

Date	Accounts and Explanation	Debit	Credit
Jan. 3	Cash ($55 per share × 1,000 shares)	55,000	
	Preferred Stock—$50 Par Value ($50 per share × 1,000 shares)		50,000
	Paid-In Capital in Excess of Par—Preferred ($5 per share × 1,000 shares)		5,000
	Issued preferred stock at a premium.		

Preferred Stock is included in the stockholders' equity section of the balance sheet and is often listed first. Any Paid-In Capital in Excess of Par—Preferred is listed next, followed by Common Stock and Paid-In Capital in Excess of Par—Common. Exhibit F:13-6 shows the stockholders' equity section of Smart Touch Learning's balance sheet, assuming both stocks were par value stocks.

Exhibit F:13-6 | Stockholders' Equity

SMART TOUCH LEARNING, INC.
Balance Sheet (Partial)
January 3, 2025

Stockholders' Equity

Paid-In Capital:

Preferred Stock—$50 Par Value; 2,000 shares authorized, 1,000 shares issued and outstanding	$ 50,000
Paid-In Capital in Excess of Par—Preferred	5,000
Common Stock—$1 Par Value; 20,000,000 shares authorized, 23,000 shares issued and outstanding	23,000
Paid-In Capital in Excess of Par—Common	25,000
Total Paid-In Capital	103,000
Retained Earnings	3,550
Total Stockholders' Equity	$ 106,550

6. London Corporation has two classes of stock: Common, $1 par value; and Preferred, $4 par value. Journalize the issuance of 10,000 shares of common stock for $8 per share.

Check your answer online in MyLab Accounting or at http://www.pearsonhighered.com/Horngren.

For more practice, see Short Exercises S-F:13-2 through S-F:13-5. MyLab Accounting

Corporations  Financial 13-11

HOW IS TREASURY STOCK ACCOUNTED FOR?

A company's own stock that it has previously issued and later reacquired is called **treasury stock**. In effect, the corporation holds the stock in its treasury. A corporation, such as Smart Touch Learning, may purchase treasury stock for several reasons:

1. Management wants to increase net assets by buying low and selling high.
2. Management wants to support the company's stock price.
3. Management wants to avoid a takeover by an outside party by reducing the number of outstanding shares that have voting rights.
4. Management wants to reward valued employees with stock.

Learning Objective 3
Account for the purchase and sale of treasury stock

Treasury Stock
A corporation's own stock that it has previously issued and later reacquired.

Treasury Stock Basics

Here are the basics of accounting for treasury stock:

- The Treasury Stock account has a normal debit balance, which is the opposite of the other stockholders' equity accounts. Therefore, *Treasury Stock is a contra equity account*.
- Treasury stock is recorded at cost (what the company paid to reacquire the shares), without reference to par value. (We illustrate the *cost* method of accounting for treasury stock because it is used most widely. Intermediate accounting courses also cover an alternative method.)
- The Treasury Stock account is reported beneath Retained Earnings on the balance sheet as a reduction to total stockholders' equity.

Treasury stock decreases the company's stock that is outstanding—held by outsiders (the stockholders). Therefore, outstanding stock is issued stock less treasury stock. Only outstanding shares have voting rights and receive cash or stock dividends. Treasury stock does not carry a vote, and it receives no cash or stock dividends. Now we illustrate how to account for treasury stock, continuing with Smart Touch Learning.

Purchase of Treasury Stock

Review Smart Touch Learning's stockholders' equity before purchasing treasury stock as shown in Exhibit F:13-6.

Assume that on March 31, Smart Touch Learning purchased 1,000 shares of previously issued common stock, paying $5 per share. To record the purchase, the company debits Treasury Stock—Common and credits Cash:

Date	Accounts and Explanation	Debit	Credit
Mar. 31	Treasury Stock—Common ($5 per share × 1,000 shares)	5,000	
	Cash		5,000
	Purchased treasury stock.		

A↓ } = { L + E↓
Cash↓   Treasury Stock↑

Sale of Treasury Stock

Companies buy their treasury stock and eventually sell or retire it. A company may sell treasury stock at, above, or below its cost (what the company paid for the shares).

Sale at Cost

If treasury stock is sold for cost—the same price the corporation paid for it—there is no difference between the cost per share and the sale price per share to journalize. Assume Smart Touch Learning sells 100 of the treasury shares on April 1 for $5 each. The entry follows:

A↑ = L + E↑
Cash↑   Treasury Stock↓

Date	Accounts and Explanation	Debit	Credit
Apr. 1	Cash	500	
	Treasury Stock—Common ($5 per share × 100 shares)		500
	Sold treasury stock at cost.		

Treasury Stock—Common
Mar. 31	5,000		
		500	Apr. 1
Bal.	4,500		

Sale Above Cost

If treasury stock is sold for more than cost, the difference is credited to a new stockholders' equity account, Paid-In Capital from Treasury Stock Transactions. This excess is additional paid-in capital because it came from the company's stockholders. It has no effect on net income. Suppose Smart Touch Learning sold 200 of its treasury shares for $6 per share on April 2 (recall that cost was $5 per share). The entry to sell treasury stock for an amount above cost is as follows:

A↑ = L + E↑
Cash↑   Treasury Stock↓
         Paid-In Capital from Treasury Stock Transactions↑

Date	Accounts and Explanation	Debit	Credit
Apr. 2	Cash ($6 per share × 200 shares)	1,200	
	Treasury Stock—Common ($5 per share × 200 shares)		1,000
	Paid-In Capital from Treasury Stock Transactions ($1 per share × 200 shares)		200
	Sold treasury stock above cost.		

Treasury Stock—Common
Mar. 31	5,000		
		500	Apr. 1
		1,000	Apr. 2
Bal.	3,500		

Paid-In Capital from Treasury Stock Transactions
		200	Apr. 2

Paid-In Capital from Treasury Stock Transactions is reported with the other paid-in capital accounts on the balance sheet, beneath Common Stock and Paid-In Capital in Excess of Par.

Sale Below Cost

The sales price of treasury stock can be less than cost. The shortfall is debited first to Paid-In Capital from Treasury Stock Transactions. However, this account can only be debited for an amount that brings it to $0 (it cannot have a debit balance). If this account's balance is too small, Retained Earnings is debited for the remaining amount. To illustrate, assume Smart Touch Learning had two additional treasury stock sales. First, on April 3, Smart Touch Learning sold 200 treasury shares for $4.30 each. The entry to record the sale is as follows:

Date	Accounts and Explanation	Debit	Credit
Apr. 3	Cash ($4.30 per share × 200 shares)	860	
	Paid-In Capital from Treasury Stock Transactions ($0.70 per share × 200 shares)	140	
	Treasury Stock—Common ($5 per share × 200 shares)		1,000
	Sold treasury stock below cost.		

A↑ Cash↑ = L + E↑ Paid-In Capital from Treasury Stock Transactions↓ Treasury Stock↓

Treasury Stock—Common

Mar. 31	5,000		
		500	Apr. 1
		1,000	Apr. 2
		1,000	Apr. 3
Bal.	2,500		

Paid-In Capital from Treasury Stock Transactions

Apr. 3	140	200	Apr. 2
		60	Bal.

The treasury shares were sold for $140 less than their cost. Smart Touch Learning had previously sold treasury shares for $200 more than their cost, so the $200 credit balance in Paid-In Capital from Treasury Stock Transactions is large enough to cover the $140 debit.

Now, what happens if Smart Touch Learning sells an additional 200 treasury shares for $4.50 each on April 4? Smart Touch Learning records the following entry:

Date	Accounts and Explanation	Debit	Credit
Apr. 4	Cash ($4.50 per share × 200 shares)	900	
	Paid-In Capital from Treasury Stock Transactions	60	
	Retained Earnings ($1,000 − $900 − $60)	40	
	Treasury Stock—Common ($5 per share × 200 shares)		1,000
	Sold treasury stock below cost.		

A↑ Cash↑ = L + E↑ Paid-In Capital from Treasury Stock Transactions↓ Retained Earnings↓ Treasury Stock↓

Treasury Stock—Common

Mar. 31	5,000		
		500	Apr. 1
		1,000	Apr. 2
		1,000	Apr. 3
		1,000	Apr. 4
Bal.	1,500		

Paid-In Capital from Treasury Stock Transactions

Apr. 3	140	200	Apr. 2
Apr. 4	60		
		0	Bal.

Retained Earnings

		3,550	Bal.
Apr. 4	40		
		3,510	Bal.

The 200 treasury shares are sold for $100 less than their cost [($4.50 sales price per share − $5 cost per share) × 200 shares]. However, only $60 remains in Paid-In Capital from Treasury Stock Transactions. The difference of $40 ($100 − $60) is debited to Retained Earnings because the paid-in capital accounts cannot have debit balances.

Now we can show the revised stockholders' equity for Smart Touch Learning as shown in Exhibit F:13-7.

Exhibit F:13-7 | Stockholders' Equity After Treasury Stock Transactions

SMART TOUCH LEARNING, INC.
Balance Sheet (Partial)
April 4, 2025

Stockholders' Equity

Paid-In Capital:	
Preferred Stock—$50 Par Value; 2,000 shares authorized, 1,000 shares issued and outstanding	$ 50,000
Paid-In Capital in Excess of Par—Preferred	5,000
Common Stock—$1 Par Value; 20,000,000 shares authorized, 23,000 shares issued, 22,700 shares outstanding	23,000
Paid-In Capital in Excess of Par—Common	25,000
Total Paid-In Capital	103,000
Retained Earnings	3,510
Treasury Stock—Common; 300 shares at cost	(1,500)
Total Stockholders' Equity	$ 105,010

So, how many common shares are outstanding on April 4? The 23,000 common shares previously issued minus 300 treasury shares equals 22,700 outstanding common shares.

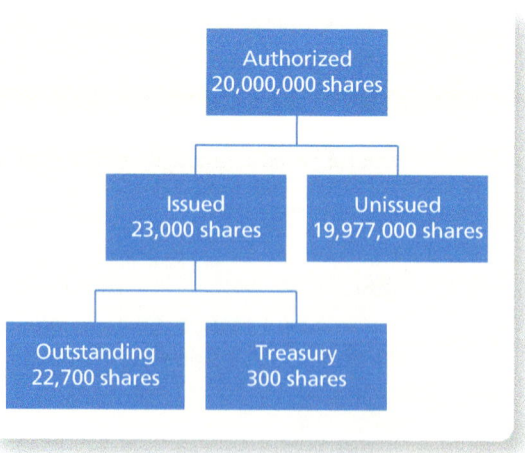

Retirement of Stock

Not all companies repurchase their previously issued stock to hold it in the treasury. A corporation may retire its stock by canceling the stock certificates. Retired stock cannot be reissued.

Retirements of preferred stock are common as companies seek to avoid paying the preferred dividends. To repurchase previously issued stock for retirement, we debit the stock accounts—for example, Preferred Stock and Paid-In Capital in Excess of Par—Preferred—and credit Cash. That removes the retired stock from the company's books, which reduces total assets and total stockholders' equity.

7. On January 3, Halsall Corporation purchased 2,000 shares of the company's $2 par value common stock as treasury stock, paying cash of $8 per share. On January 30, Halsall sold 1,200 shares of the treasury stock for cash of $10 per share. Journalize these transactions.

Check your answers online in MyLab Accounting or at http://www.pearsonhighered.com/Horngren.

For more practice, see Short Exercise S-F:13-6. **MyLab Accounting**

HOW ARE DIVIDENDS AND STOCK SPLITS ACCOUNTED FOR?

A profitable corporation may make distributions to stockholders in the form of *dividends*. Dividends can be paid in the form of cash, stock, or other property.

Learning Objective 4
Account for cash dividends, stock dividends, and stock splits

Cash Dividends

Cash dividends cause a decrease in both assets (Cash) and equity (Retained Earnings). Most states prohibit using paid-in capital for dividends. Accountants, therefore, use the term **legal capital** to refer to the portion of stockholders' equity that cannot be used for dividends.

Legal Capital
The portion of stockholders' equity that cannot be used for dividends.

A corporation declares a dividend before paying it. Three dividend dates are relevant:

1. **Declaration date.** On the declaration date—say, May 1—the board of directors announces the intention to pay the dividend. The declaration of a cash dividend creates an obligation (liability) for the corporation.
2. **Date of record** (or *record date*). Those stockholders holding the stock at the end of business on the date of record—a week or two after declaration, say, May 15—will receive the dividend check. Date of record is the date the corporation records the stockholders who receive dividend checks.
3. **Payment date.** Payment of the dividend usually follows the record date by a week or two—say, May 30.

13-16 Financial   chapter 13

Declaring and Paying Dividends—Common Stock

Suppose on May 1, Smart Touch Learning declares a $0.05 per share cash dividend on 22,700 outstanding shares of common stock (23,000 shares issued less 300 shares of treasury stock). On the date of declaration, Smart Touch Learning records a debit to Cash Dividends and a credit to Dividends Payable—Common (a current liability) as follows:

Date	Accounts and Explanation	Debit	Credit
May 1	Cash Dividends ($0.05 per share × 22,700 shares)	1,135	
	Dividends Payable—Common		1,135
	Declared a cash dividend.		

$\dfrac{A}{=}\begin{cases} \dfrac{L\uparrow}{\text{Dividends Payable}\uparrow} + \dfrac{E\downarrow}{\text{Cash Dividends}\uparrow} \end{cases}$

Dividends are only paid on outstanding shares. Remember that outstanding stock is issued stock less treasury stock. A corporation will never pay dividends on treasury stock.

On May 15, the date of record, no journal entry is recorded. This is simply the cutoff point to determine who owns the stock and will, therefore, receive the cash payment.

To pay the dividend on the payment date, May 30, Smart Touch Learning debits Dividends Payable—Common and credits Cash:

Date	Accounts and Explanation	Debit	Credit
May 30	Dividends Payable—Common	1,135	
	Cash		1,135
	Payment of cash dividend.		

$\dfrac{A\downarrow}{\text{Cash}\downarrow} = \begin{cases} \dfrac{L\downarrow}{\text{Dividends Payable}\downarrow} + \dfrac{E}{} \end{cases}$

At the end of the accounting period, Smart Touch Learning will close the Cash Dividends account to Retained Earnings as follows:

Date	Accounts and Explanation	Debit	Credit
Dec. 31	Retained Earnings	1,135	
	Cash Dividends		1,135
	To close Cash Dividends.		

$\dfrac{A}{=} \begin{cases} \dfrac{L}{} + \dfrac{E\uparrow\downarrow}{\text{Retained Earnings}\downarrow\ \text{Cash Dividends}\downarrow} \end{cases}$

Declaring and Paying Dividends—Preferred Stock

The cash dividend rate on preferred stock is often expressed as a percentage of the preferred stock par value, such as 6%. Sometimes, however, cash dividends on preferred stock are expressed as a flat dollar amount per share, such as $3 per share. Therefore, preferred dividends are computed two ways, depending on how the preferred stock cash dividend rate is stated on the preferred stock certificate. To illustrate, assume a fictitious company, Greg's

Games, Inc., has 1,000 outstanding shares of 6%, $50 par value preferred stock. The dividend is computed as follows:

> Preferred dividend = Outstanding shares × Par value × Preferred dividend rate
> = 1,000 shares × $50 par value per share × 6%
> = $3,000

The journal entries to account for the declaration and payment of a cash dividend on preferred stock are similar to those of common stock. The only difference is that Dividends Payable—Preferred is used instead of Dividends Payable—Common.

Earlier in the chapter, we discussed the dividend preference that preferred stockholders receive. When a company has issued both preferred and common stock, the preferred stockholders receive their dividends first. The common stockholders receive dividends only if the total dividend is large enough to satisfy the preferred requirement. In other words, the common stockholders receive the residual—the amount remaining after the preferred dividends are paid.

For example, if Greg's Games has 1,000 shares of $50 par, 6% preferred stock outstanding and 2,000,000 shares of $1 par common stock outstanding, preferred stockholders will receive $3,000 of any cash dividend declared. So, total declared dividends must exceed $3,000 for the common stockholders to receive a dividend.

If the year's dividend is equal to or less than the annual preferred amount, the preferred stockholders will receive the entire dividend, and the common stockholders will not receive a dividend that year. But, if Greg's Games' dividend is large enough to cover the preferred dividend, the preferred stockholders get their regular dividend of $3,000, and the common stockholders receive any amount remaining.

Remember that a dividend preference on preferred stock does not guarantee that a corporation will pay a dividend equal to the preferred amount. A corporation may fail to pay the preferred dividend if, for example, it does not have cash to fund the dividend. This is called *passing the dividend*, and the dividend is said to be a **dividend in arrears**. In other words, a preferred stock dividend is in arrears if the dividend has not been paid for the year.

Preferred stock can be either cumulative or noncumulative. Most preferred stock is cumulative. As a result, preferred stock is assumed to be cumulative unless it is specifically designated as noncumulative. **Cumulative preferred stock** shareholders must receive all dividends in arrears plus the current year dividends before the common stockholders receive a dividend. If the preferred stock is **noncumulative preferred stock**, the corporation will not have any dividends in arrears because the corporation is not required to pay passed dividends.

Suppose Greg's Games' preferred stock is cumulative and in 2024 the business did not pay any cash dividends. Before paying any common dividend in 2025, Greg's Games must first pay preferred dividends of $3,000 for 2024 and $3,000 for 2025, a total of $6,000. Assume that on September 6, 2025, Greg's Games declares a $50,000 total dividend. How much of this dividend goes to the preferred stockholders? How much goes to the common stockholders? The allocation of this $50,000 dividend is as follows:

Dividend in Arrears
A preferred stock dividend is in arrears if the dividend has not been paid for the year and the preferred stock is cumulative.

Cumulative Preferred Stock
Preferred stock whose owners must receive all dividends in arrears plus the current year dividend before the corporation pays dividends to the common stockholders.

Noncumulative Preferred Stock
Preferred stock whose owners do not receive passed dividends.

Total Dividend		$ 50,000
Dividend to Preferred Stockholders:		
Dividend in Arrears (2024)	$ 3,000	
Current Year Dividend (2025)	3,000	
Total Dividend to Preferred Stockholders		(6,000)
Dividend to Common Stockholders		**$ 44,000**

13-18　Financial chapter 13

Greg's Games' entry to record the declaration of this dividend on September 6, 2025, is as follows:

$$A \Bigg\} = \Bigg\{ \underbrace{L\uparrow}_{\text{Dividends Payable}\uparrow} + \underbrace{E\downarrow}_{\text{Cash Dividends}\uparrow}$$

Date	Accounts and Explanation	Debit	Credit
2025			
Sep. 6	Cash Dividends	50,000	
	Dividends Payable—Common		44,000
	Dividends Payable—Preferred		6,000
	Declared a cash dividend.		

Dividends in arrears are *not* a liability. A liability for dividends arises only after the board of directors *declares* the dividend. But a corporation reports cumulative preferred dividends in arrears in notes to the financial statements. This shows the common stockholders how big the declared dividend will need to be for them to receive any dividends.

Remember that if the preferred stock is noncumulative preferred stock, the corporation is not required to pay any passed dividends. Keep in mind that this is a risk that the investor bears when investing in noncumulative preferred stock. Suppose Greg's Games' preferred stock is noncumulative and the company passed the 2024 dividend. The preferred stockholders would lose the 2024 dividend of $3,000 forever. Then, before paying any common dividends in 2025, Greg's Games would have to pay only the 2025 preferred dividend of $3,000, which would leave $47,000 for the common stockholders as follows:

Total Dividend		$ 50,000
Dividend to Preferred Stockholders:		
Current Year Dividend (2025)	$ 3,000	
Total Dividend to Preferred Stockholders		(3,000)
Dividend to Common Stockholders		$ 47,000

Stock Dividends

Stock Dividend
A distribution by a corporation of its own stock to its stockholders.

A **stock dividend** is a distribution of a corporation's own stock to its stockholders. Unlike cash dividends, stock dividends do not give any of the corporation's assets, like cash, to the stockholders. Stock dividends have the following characteristics:

- They affect *only* stockholders' equity accounts (including Retained Earnings, Stock Dividends, Common Stock, and Paid-In Capital in Excess of Par).
- They have *no* effect on total stockholders' equity.
- They have *no* effect on assets or liabilities.

The corporation distributes stock dividends to stockholders in proportion to the number of shares the stockholders already own. Suppose a stockholder owns 1,000 shares of Greg's Games' common stock. If Greg's Games distributes a 10% stock dividend, the stockholder would receive 100 additional shares (1,000 shares × 0.10). The stockholder now owns 1,100 shares of the stock. All other Greg's Games' stockholders also receive additional shares equal to 10% of their stock holdings, so all stockholders are in the same relative position after the stock dividend as they were before. With a stock dividend, the total number of shares issued and outstanding increases, but the percentage of total ownership of individual stockholders stays the same.

Why Issue Stock Dividends?

A company issues stock dividends for several reasons:

- **To continue dividends but conserve cash.** A company may wish to continue the distribution of dividends to keep stockholders happy but may need to keep its cash for operations. A stock dividend is a way to do so without using corporate cash.
- **To reduce the market price per share of its stock.** Depending on its size, a stock dividend may cause the company's market price per share to fall because of the increased supply of the stock. Suppose that a share of Greg's Games' stock was traded at $50 recently. Doubling the shares issued and outstanding by issuing a stock dividend would likely cause Greg's Games' stock market price per share to drop closer to $25 per share. One objective behind a stock dividend might be to make the stock less expensive and, therefore, more available and attractive to investors.
- **To reward investors.** Investors often feel like they have received something of value when they get a stock dividend.

Recording Stock Dividends

As with a cash dividend, there are three dates for a stock dividend:

- Declaration date
- Date of record
- Distribution date

The board of directors announces the stock dividend on the declaration date. The date of record and the distribution date then follow. The declaration of a stock dividend does *not* create a liability because the corporation is not obligated to pay assets. (Recall that a liability is a claim on *assets*.) With a stock dividend, the corporation has declared its intention to distribute its stock. The distribution date is similar to the payment date for a cash dividend. With stock dividends, however, there is no payment of cash—only a distribution of shares of stock.

The entry to record a stock dividend depends on the size of the dividend. Generally Accepted Accounting Principles (GAAP) distinguish between small and large stock dividends in the following manner:

- **Small stock dividend**—less than 20% to 25% of issued and outstanding stock
- **Large stock dividend**—greater than 20% to 25% of issued and outstanding stock

Small Stock Dividend
A stock dividend of less than 20% to 25% of the issued and outstanding stock.

Large Stock Dividend
A stock dividend greater than 20% to 25% of the issued and outstanding stock.

Small Stock Dividends—Less than 20% to 25% Small stock dividends are accounted for at the stock's market value. Here is how the various accounts are affected at the date of declaration:

- Stock Dividends is debited for the *market value* of the dividend shares.
- Common Stock Dividend Distributable is credited for the dividend stock's *par value*.
- Paid-In Capital in Excess of Par is credited for the excess.

Assume, for example, that Greg's Games distributes a 5% common stock dividend on 2,000,000 shares issued and outstanding when the market value of Greg's Games' common stock is $50 per share and par value is $1 per share. Greg's Games will issue 100,000 (2,000,000 shares × 0.05) shares to its stockholders. The entry on the next page illustrates the accounting for this 5% stock dividend on the declaration date of February 1.

A = L + E↕

Stock Dividends↑
Common Stock Dividend Distributable↑
Paid-In Capital in Excess of Par↑

Date	Accounts and Explanation	Debit	Credit
Feb. 1	Stock Dividends ($50 per share × 2,000,000 shares × 0.05)	5,000,000	
	Common Stock Dividend Distributable ($1 per share × 2,000,000 shares × 0.05)		100,000
	Paid-In Capital in Excess of Par—Common ($5,000,000 − $100,000)		4,900,000
	Declared a 5% stock dividend.		

Similar to Cash Dividends, Stock Dividends is closed to Retained Earnings at the end of the accounting period.

Notice that Common Stock Dividend Distributable is credited for the par value of the common stock. Common Stock Dividend Distributable is an *equity* account, not a liability. It is reported as an addition to paid-in capital in stockholders' equity until the stock is distributed. On February 25, when Greg's Games distributes the common stock, it would record the following entry:

A = L + E↕

Common Stock Dividend Distributable↓
Common Stock↑

Date	Accounts and Explanation	Debit	Credit
Feb. 25	Common Stock Dividend Distributable	100,000	
	Common Stock—$1 Par Value		100,000
	Issued 5% stock dividend.		

After the journal entry for the declaration and issuance of the common stock dividend and the closing entry to close Stock Dividends to Retained Earnings, Greg's Games' accounts are as follows:

Common Stock—$1 Par Value

	2,000,000	Bal.
	100,000	Feb. 25
	2,100,000	Bal.

Paid-In Capital in Excess of Par—Common

	19,000,000	Bal.
	4,900,000	Feb. 1
	23,900,000	Bal.

Common Stock Dividend Distributable

		100,000	Feb. 1
Feb. 25	100,000		
		0	Bal.

Retained Earnings

		9,000,000	Bal.
Dec. 31	5,000,000		
		4,000,000	Bal.

The Stock Dividends account is closed with a credit, and the corresponding debit to Retained Earnings decreases the equity account.

Remember that a stock dividend does not affect assets, liabilities, or *total* stockholders' equity. A stock dividend merely rearranges the balances in the stockholders' equity accounts, leaving total stockholders' equity unchanged. Exhibit F:13-8 shows what Greg's Games' stockholders' equity looks like before and after the 5% common stock dividend.

Corporations   Financial 13-21

Exhibit F:13-8 | Stockholders' Equity—Small Stock Dividend

GREG'S GAMES, INC.
Balance Sheet (Partial)
February 25, 2025

Before Small Stock Dividend:

Stockholders' Equity

Paid-In Capital:

Preferred Stock—$50 Par Value; 2,000 shares authorized, 1,000 shares issued and outstanding	$ 50,000
Paid-In Capital in Excess of Par—Preferred	5,000
Common Stock—$1 Par Value; 20,000,000 shares authorized, 2,000,000 shares issued and outstanding	2,000,000
Paid-In Capital in Excess of Par—Common	19,000,000
Total Paid-In Capital	21,055,000
Retained Earnings	9,000,000
Total Stockholders' Equity	$ 30,055,000

After Small Stock Dividend:

Stockholders' Equity

Paid-In Capital:

Preferred Stock—$50 Par Value; 2,000 shares authorized, 1,000 shares issued and outstanding	$ 50,000
Paid-In Capital in Excess of Par—Preferred	5,000
Common Stock—$1 Par Value; 20,000,000 shares authorized, 2,100,000 shares issued and outstanding	2,100,000
Paid-In Capital in Excess of Par—Common	23,900,000
Total Paid-In Capital	26,055,000
Retained Earnings	4,000,000
Total Stockholders' Equity	$ 30,055,000

Note that total stockholders' equity stays at $30,055,000. Total paid-in capital increased $5,000,000, and retained earnings decreased $5,000,000.

Large Stock Dividends—Greater than 20% to 25% Large stock dividends are rare, but when they are declared, they are normally accounted for at the stock's par value instead of the stock's market value. Par value is used because the larger number of issued and outstanding shares will reduce market price per share, making market price per share an invalid measurement of the stock dividend value. Assume, for example, on March 2 that Greg's Games declares a second common stock dividend of 50% when the market value of Greg's Games' common stock is $50 per share. The entries to record the large stock dividend on the declaration date (March 2) and distribution date (March 30) are as follows:

Date	Accounts and Explanation	Debit	Credit
Mar. 2	Stock Dividends ($1 per share × 2,100,000 shares × 0.50)	1,050,000	
	Common Stock Dividend Distributable		1,050,000
	($1 per share × 2,100,000 shares × 0.50)		
	Declared a 50% stock dividend.		
30	Common Stock Dividend Distributable	1,050,000	
	Common Stock—$1 Par Value		1,050,000
	Issued 50% stock dividend.		

A = L + E↓
Stock Dividends↑
Common Stock Dividend Distributable↑

A = L + E↕
Common Stock Dividend Distributable↓
Common Stock↑

Cash dividends and stock dividends are always declared based on the number of shares issued and outstanding. It's important to keep a running balance of the amount of shares outstanding in order to determine the correct amount of dividends to record. In this case, Greg's Games started with 2,000,000 common shares outstanding and then issued a stock dividend of 100,000 common shares for a total of 2,100,000 common shares issued and outstanding.

Notice that the large stock dividend also does not change total stockholders' equity. Total paid-in capital increased $1,050,000 and retained earnings decreased $1,050,000 after closing Stock Dividends to Retained Earnings.

Stock Splits

Stock Split
An increase in the number of issued and outstanding shares of stock coupled with a proportionate reduction in the par value of the stock.

A stock split is fundamentally different from a stock dividend. A **stock split** increases the number of issued and outstanding shares of stock. A stock split also decreases par value per share, whereas stock dividends do not affect par value per share. For example, if Greg's Games splits its common stock 2-for-1, the number of issued and outstanding shares is doubled and par value per share is cut in half. A stock split also decreases the market price per share of the stock. A 2-for-1 stock split of a $2 par stock with a $20 market value per share will result in two shares of $1 par value with approximately $10 market value per share.

> A stock split, just like any other stock issuance, cannot involve issuing more shares of stock than authorized in the corporate charter.

The market value of a share of Greg's Games' common stock has been approximately $50 per share. Assume that Greg's Games wishes to decrease the market price to approximately $25 per share. The company can make the market price drop to around $25 by effecting a 2-for-1 split of its common stock. A 2-for-1 stock split means that Greg's Games will have twice as many shares of stock issued and outstanding after the split as it did before, and each share's par value is cut in half. Assume Greg's Games has 3,150,000 shares issued and outstanding of $1 par common stock before the split. After the stock split, Greg's Games will have 6,300,000 shares (3,150,000 shares × 2) issued and outstanding of $0.50 par value stock ($1 par value / 2) as follows:

Common Stock Before Stock Split		Common Stock After Stock Split	
Common Stock—$1 Par Value; 3,150,000 shares issued and outstanding	$ 3,150,000	Common Stock—$0.50 Par Value; 6,300,000 shares issued and outstanding	$ 3,150,000

Memorandum Entry
An entry in the journal that notes a significant event, but has no debit or credit amount.

Because the stock split does not affect any account balances, no formal journal entry is needed. Instead, the split is recorded in a **memorandum entry**, an entry in the journal that notes a significant event but has no debit or credit amount.

Cash Dividends, Stock Dividends, and Stock Splits Compared

Cash dividends, stock dividends, and stock splits have some similarities and some differences. Exhibit F:13-9 summarizes their effects on the accounting equation.

Exhibit F:13-9 | **Effects of Dividends and Stock Splits on the Accounting Equation**

Effect On	Cash Dividend	Small Stock Dividend	Large Stock Dividend	Stock Split
Total Assets	Decrease	No effect	No effect	No effect
Total Liabilities	No effect	No effect	No effect	No effect
Common Stock	No effect	Increase	Increase	No effect
Paid-In Capital in Excess of Par	No effect	Increase	No effect	No effect
Retained Earnings	Decrease	Decrease	Decrease	No effect
Total Stockholders' Equity	Decrease	No effect	No effect	No effect

Corporations   Financial   13-23

8. On August 1, Hagino Corporation declared a $1.50 per share cash dividend on its common stock (20,000 shares) for stockholders on record as of August 15. Hagino paid the dividend on August 31. Journalize the entries declaring the cash dividend and paying the dividend.

Check your answers online in MyLab Accounting or at http://www.pearsonhighered.com/Horngren.

For more practice, see Short Exercises S-F:13-7 through S-F:13-11. MyLab Accounting

HOW IS THE COMPLETE CORPORATE INCOME STATEMENT PREPARED?

A corporation's income statement includes some unique items that do not often apply to sole proprietorships and partnerships. One of the major differences is that corporations are required to pay **income tax expense**. Therefore, a corporate income statement includes a separate section that reports the federal and state income taxes that are incurred by the corporation. The calculation of income tax expense is complicated and will be covered in later accounting courses and is only presented here for informational purposes. We will review the fictitious company Kevin's Vintage Guitars, Inc.'s income statement for year ended December 31, 2024, shown in Exhibit F:13-10, to illustrate these items.

Learning Objective 5
Prepare a corporate income statement including earnings per share

Income Tax Expense
Expense incurred by a corporation related to federal and state income taxes.

Exhibit F:13-10 | Kevin's Vintage Guitars, Inc.—Income Statement

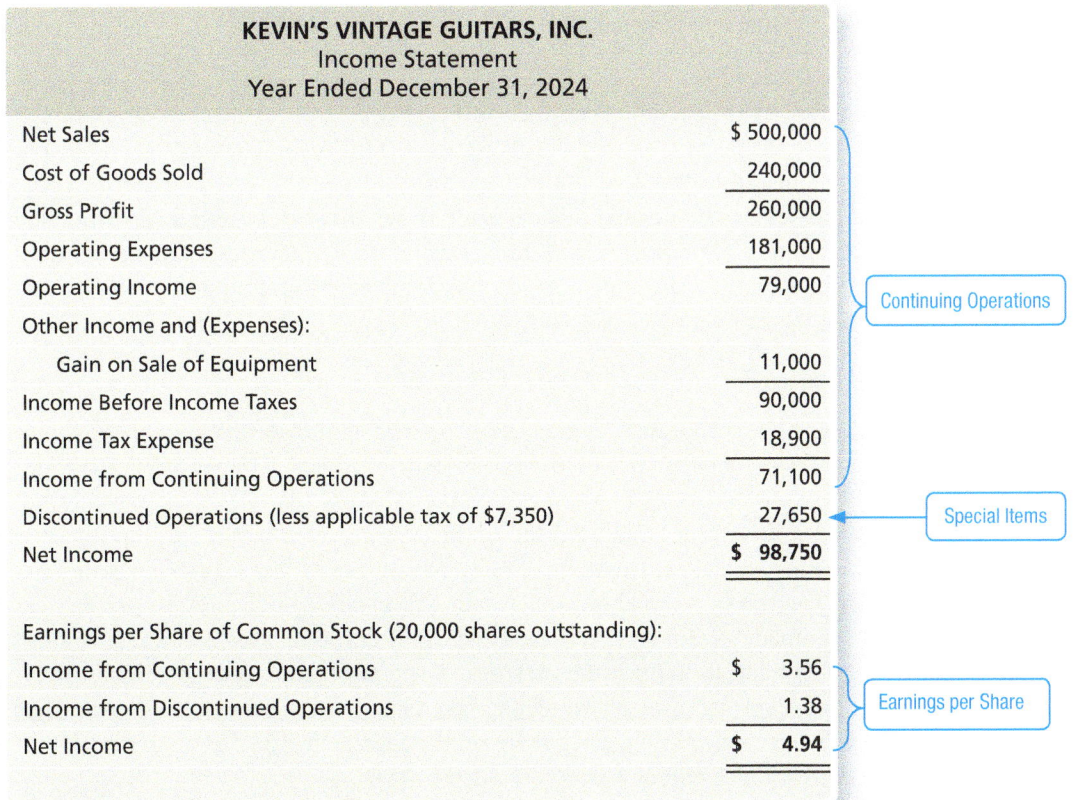

Continuing Operations

In Exhibit F:13-10, the first section reports continuing operations. This part of the business should continue from period to period. Income from continuing operations, therefore, helps investors make predictions about future earnings. We may use this information to predict that Kevin's Vintage Guitars, Inc. may earn approximately $71,100 next year.

The continuing operations of Kevin's Vintage Guitars, Inc. include two items that warrant explanation:

- Kevin's Vintage Guitars had a gain on the sale of equipment, which is outside the company's core business of selling vintage guitars. This is why the gain is reported in the "other" category—separately from Kevin's Vintage Guitars' operating income. Interest revenue and interest expense are examples of other items which are included in this section.

- Income tax expense of $18,900 is subtracted to arrive at income from continuing operations. Kevin's Vintage Guitars' income tax rate is 21% ($90,000 × 0.21 = $18,900).

Discontinued Operations

After continuing operations, an income statement may include gains and losses from discontinued operations. These gains and losses occur when a company sells or disposes of an identifiable division (sometimes called a *segment of the business*). The gain or loss on discontinued operations is reported separately from continued operations because this type of disposal does not occur frequently. A company would report information on the segments that have been sold under the heading Discontinued Operations. In our example, income from discontinued operations of $35,000 is taxed at 21% and is reported net of its income tax effect as shown below.

Income from discontinued operations	$ 35,000
Less: Income tax expense (21%)	(7,350)
Discontinued operations	**$ 27,650**

Trace this item to the income statement in Exhibit F:13-10. A loss on discontinued operations is reported similarly, but with a subtraction for the income tax *savings* on the loss (the tax savings reduces the loss).

Gains and losses on the normal sale of plant assets are *not* reported as discontinued operations. Instead, they are reported as "Other Income and (Expenses)" among continuing operations because companies dispose of old plant assets and equipment more frequently than business segments.

Earnings per Share

Earnings per Share (EPS)
Amount of a company's net income (loss) for each share of its outstanding common stock. (Net income − Preferred dividends) / Weighted average number of common shares outstanding.

The final segment of a corporate income statement reports the company's **earnings per share (EPS)**. EPS is the most widely used of all business statistics. EPS reports the amount of net income (loss) for each share of the company's *outstanding common stock*. Earnings per share is calculated as net income minus preferred dividends divided by the weighted average number of common shares outstanding. Preferred dividends are subtracted from net income because the preferred stockholders have the first claim to dividends. Therefore, that portion of the company's earnings is not available to the common stockholders and is not included in the EPS calculation on common stock. The computation for the weighted average number of common shares outstanding is covered in advanced accounting courses. For simplicity, we will determine earnings per share on the average number of shares outstanding (beginning balance plus ending balance, divided by two).

Corporations Financial 13-25

A company that reports discontinued operations must report earnings per share for discontinued operations, either on the face of the income statement (as shown in Exhibit F:13-10) or in the notes to the financial statements. Earnings per share for continuing operations must be reported on the face of the income statement.

9. Rocky Corporation's accounting records include the following items, listed in no particular order, at December 31, 2024:

Other Income and (Expenses)	$ (6,000)	Cost of Goods Sold	$ 29,200
Net Sales Revenue	70,800	Operating Expenses	22,000
Gain on Discontinued Operations	4,800		

The income tax rate for Rocky Corporation is 30%. Prepare Rocky's income statement for the year ended December 31, 2024. Omit earnings per share. Use a multi-step format.

Check your answers online in MyLab Accounting or at http://www.pearsonhighered.com/Horngren.

For more practice, see Short Exercises S-F:13-12 and S-F:13-13. MyLab Accounting

HOW IS EQUITY REPORTED FOR A CORPORATION?

Earlier, you learned that a corporation's equity contains two basic sources: paid-in capital and retained earnings. Let's explore how stockholders' equity is reported.

Learning Objective 6
Explain how equity is reported for a corporation

Statement of Retained Earnings

The statement of retained earnings reports how the company's retained earnings balance changed from the beginning of the period to the end of the period. Remember that retained earnings is the equity earned by profitable operations that is not distributed to stockholders. Exhibit F:13-11 shows the statement of retained earnings of Smart Touch Learning for 2024.

Exhibit F:13-11 | Statement of Retained Earnings

SMART TOUCH LEARNING, INC. Statement of Retained Earnings Two Months Ended December 31, 2024	
Retained Earnings, November 1, 2024	$ 0
Net income for two months	8,550
	8,550
Dividends declared	(5,000)
Retained Earnings, December 31, 2024	$ 3,550

Companies can report a negative amount in retained earnings. This is called a **deficit** and is reflected by a debit balance in the Retained Earnings account. A deficit occurs when a company has recurring losses and/or declares dividends in excess of retained earnings. Most states prohibit corporations from paying a dividend if a deficit will occur.

Deficit
Debit balance in the Retained Earnings account.

Appropriations of Retained Earnings

Cash dividends and treasury stock purchases require a cash payment. These cash outlays leave fewer resources to pay liabilities. For example, a bank may agree to loan $500,000 to a company only if the company maintains a minimum level of stockholders' equity by limiting both its declaration of dividends and its purchases of treasury stock. The restriction often focuses on the balance of retained earnings. Companies usually report their retained earnings restrictions in notes to the financial statements.

Appropriation of Retained Earnings
Restriction of a portion of retained earnings that is recorded by a journal entry.

Appropriations of retained earnings are retained earnings restrictions recorded by journal entries. A corporation may *appropriate*—that is, segregate in a separate account—a portion of retained earnings for a specific use. For example, the board of directors may appropriate part of retained earnings for expansion or contingencies (such as a potential liability associated with a lawsuit).

Prior-Period Adjustments

Occasionally a company may make an accounting error as a result of mathematical mistakes, misapplying accounting principles, or oversight that is not discovered until the following period. Once discovered, these errors must be corrected because the Retained Earnings account balance is wrong. The error is corrected by adjusting the beginning balance in the Retained Earnings account in the period the error is discovered. Corrections to Retained Earnings for errors of an earlier period are called **prior-period adjustments**. The prior-period adjustment either increases or decreases the beginning balance of the Retained Earnings account and appears on the statement of retained earnings.

Prior-Period Adjustment
A correction to Retained Earnings for an error of an earlier period.

To illustrate, assume a fictitious company, Mountain Home, Inc., recorded $30,000 of salaries expense for 2024. The correct amount of salaries expense was $40,000. This error had the following effect:

- Understated Salaries Expense by $10,000
- Overstated net income by $10,000

In 2025, Mountain Home paid the extra $10,000 in salaries owed for the prior year. Mountain Home's prior-period adjustment decreased Retained Earnings as shown in Exhibit F:13-12.

Exhibit F:13-12 | **Statement of Retained Earnings—Prior-period Adjustment**

MOUNTAIN HOME, INC. Statement of Retained Earnings Year Ended December 31, 2025	
Retained Earnings, January 1, 2025 as originally reported	$ 140,000
Prior-period adjustment	(10,000)
Retained Earnings, January 1, 2025 as adjusted	130,000
Net income for the year	63,000
	193,000
Dividends declared	(23,000)
Retained Earnings, December 31, 2025	$ 170,000

Statement of Stockholders' Equity

The statement of stockholders' equity is another option for reporting the changes in stockholders' equity of a corporation. This statement has more information than the statement of retained earnings in that it reports the changes in all stockholders' equity accounts, not just Retained Earnings. The statement of stockholders' equity shows the beginning balance, any additions or subtractions, and the ending balance for all equity accounts. In addition, the statement of stockholders' equity also reports the number of shares and any changes during the year in preferred, common, and treasury stock. Exhibit F:13-13 shows a statement of stockholders' equity for Mountain Home, Inc.

IFRS
IFRS requires a Statement of Stockholders' Equity, reporting the changes in all of the equity accounts.

Exhibit F:13-13 | Statement of Stockholders' Equity

MOUNTAIN HOME, INC.
Statement of Stockholders' Equity
Year Ended December 31, 2025

	Common Stock Shares	Common Stock Amount	Paid-In Capital in Excess of Par	Retained Earnings	Total Stockholders' Equity
Balances, January 1, 2025, as originally reported	20,000	$ 20,000	$ 80,000	$ 140,000	$ 240,000
Prior-period adjustment				(10,000)	(10,000)
Balances, January 1, 2025, as adjusted	20,000	$ 20,000	$ 80,000	$ 130,000	$ 230,000
Net income for the year				63,000	63,000
Dividends declared				(23,000)	(23,000)
Balances, December 31, 2025	20,000	$ 20,000	$ 80,000	$ 170,000	$ 270,000

10. Sjostrom, Inc. had beginning retained earnings of $300,000 on January 1, 2024. During the year, Sjostrom declared and paid $140,000 of cash dividends and earned $200,000 of net income. Prepare a statement of retained earnings for Sjostrom, Inc. for the year ended December 31, 2024.

Check your answer online in MyLab Accounting or at http://www.pearsonhighered.com/Horngren.

For more practice, see Short Exercises S-F:13-14 and S-F:13-15. MyLab Accounting

HOW DO WE USE STOCKHOLDERS' EQUITY RATIOS TO EVALUATE BUSINESS PERFORMANCE?

Investors are constantly comparing companies' profits. To compare companies of different sizes, we need some standard profitability measures. Three important ratios to use for comparison are earnings per share, price/earnings ratio, and rate of return on common stockholders' equity.

Learning Objective 7
Use earnings per share, rate of return on common stockholders' equity, and the price/earnings ratio to evaluate business performance

Earnings per Share

As discussed earlier in the chapter, the final segment of a corporate income statement reports the company's earnings per share. Earnings per share (EPS) reports the amount of net income (loss) for each share of the company's *outstanding common stock*. Earnings per share is calculated as net income minus preferred dividends divided by the weighted average number of common shares outstanding. The computation for the weighted average number of common shares outstanding is covered in advanced accounting courses. For simplicity, we will determine earnings per share on the average number of shares outstanding (beginning balance plus ending balance, divided by two).

For example, the **Kohl's Corporation** Fiscal 2018 Annual Report reports the following amounts:

(In millions)	February 2, 2019 (Fiscal year 2018)	February 3, 2018 (Fiscal year 2017)
Net Income (for the year ended)	$ 801	$ 859
Preferred Dividends	0	0
Total Stockholders' Equity	5,527	5,419
Stockholders' Equity attributable to Preferred Stock	0	0
Number of Common Shares Outstanding	163 shares	168 shares

Kohl's earnings per share for fiscal year 2018 is computed as follows:

> Earnings per share = (Net income − Preferred dividends) / Average number of common shares outstanding
> = ($801 − $0) / [(163 shares + 168 shares) / 2]
> = $4.84 per share

FASB requires that earnings per share be reported on the income statement.

Price/Earnings Ratio

Price/Earnings Ratio
The ratio of the market price of a share of common stock to the company's earnings per share. Measures the value that the stock market places on $1 of a company's earnings. Market price per share of common stock / Earnings per share.

The **price/earnings ratio** is the ratio of the market price of a share of common stock to the company's earnings per share. The price/earnings ratio shows the market price of $1 of earnings. Assuming Kohl's Corporation has a market price of $65.00 per share of common stock, Kohl's price/earnings ratio for fiscal year 2018 is calculated as follows:

> Price/earnings ratio = Market price per share of common stock / Earnings per share
> = $65.00 per share / $4.84 per share
> = 13.43

The price/earnings ratio implies that Kohl's stock is selling at 13.43 times one year's earnings per share. This ratio is commonly used by investors to evaluate their ability to earn a return on their investment. It tells investors how much they should be willing to pay for $1 of a company's earnings. A higher price/earnings ratio signifies a higher return on investment. As with other ratios, the price/earnings ratio is most useful when comparing one company to another.

Rate of Return on Common Stockholders' Equity

Rate of Return on Common Stockholders' Equity
Shows the relationship between net income available to common stockholders and their average common equity invested in the company. (Net income − Preferred dividends) / Average common stockholders' equity.

Rate of return on common stockholders' equity, often shortened to *return on equity*, shows the relationship between net income available to common stockholders and their average common equity invested in the company. The numerator is net income minus preferred dividends. Preferred dividends are subtracted because the preferred stockholders have first claim to any dividends. The denominator is average common stockholders' equity—total equity minus preferred equity.

Corporations Financial 13-29

Returning to Kohl's Corporation, the rate of return on common stockholders' equity for fiscal year 2018 is calculated as follows:

> Rate of return on common stockholders' equity = (Net income − Preferred dividends) / Average common stockholders' equity
> = ($801 − $0) / [($5,527 + $5,419) / 2]
> = 0.15 = 15%

Kohl's has returned $0.15 for each $1 of the average amount invested by common stockholders. A rate of return on common stockholders' equity of 15% to 20% is considered good in most industries. At 15%, Kohl's has a return on equity that is considered good, but it should still be compared with companies in the same industry.

Vollmer, Inc. had reported the following balances:

	December 31, 2025	December 31, 2024
Net Income	$ 80,000	$ 60,000
Preferred Dividends	2,000	5,000
Total Stockholders' Equity	340,000	310,000
Stockholders' Equity attributable to Preferred Stock	20,000	20,000
Number of Common Shares Outstanding	10,000	14,000

11. Compute Vollmer's earnings per share for 2025.
12. Compute Vollmer's price/earnings ratio for 2025, assuming the market price is $40 per share.
13. Compute Vollmer's rate of return on common stockholders' equity for 2025.

Check your answers online in MyLab Accounting or at http://www.pearsonhighered.com/Horngren.

For more practice, see Short Exercises S-F:13-16 through S-F:13-18.   MyLab Accounting

REVIEW

> Things You Should Know

1. What is a corporation?

- A business organized under state law that is a separate legal entity.
- Corporations have capital stock that represents shares of ownership.
  - Authorized stock is the maximum number of shares of stock that the corporate charter allows the corporation to issue.
  - Outstanding stock is stock that has been issued and is in the hands of stockholders.
- Corporations can have different classes of stock:
  - Common stock represents the basic ownership of a corporation.
  - Preferred stock gives its owners certain advantages, such as the right to receive preferential dividends.

- A corporation's equity is called *stockholders' equity*. Stockholders' equity consists of two basic sources:
  - Paid-in capital—amounts received from stockholders in exchange for stock.
  - Retained earnings—equity earned by profitable operations that is not distributed to stockholders.

2. **How is the issuance of stock accounted for?**

   - Issuance of common stock (and preferred stock) at par value

Date	Accounts and Explanation	Debit	Credit
	Cash	Par Value	
	Common Stock—$1 Par Value		Par Value
	Issued common stock at par.		

   - Issuance of common stock (and preferred stock) at a premium

Date	Accounts and Explanation	Debit	Credit
	Cash	Issuance Price	
	Common Stock—$1 Par Value		Par Value
	Paid-In Capital in Excess of Par—Common		Difference
	Issued common stock at a premium.		

   - Issuing stated value stock is almost identical to accounting for par value stock. The only difference is the use of the Paid-In Capital in Excess of *Stated* account.
   - Stock can be issued for assets other than cash. The transaction should be recorded at the market value of the stock issued or the market value of the assets received, whichever is more clearly determinable.

3. **How is treasury stock accounted for?**

   - Treasury stock is a corporation's own stock that it has previously issued and later reacquired.
   - When treasury stock is purchased, it is recorded at cost, not par value.

Date	Accounts and Explanation	Debit	Credit
	Treasury Stock—Common	Cost	
	Cash		Cost
	Purchased treasury stock.		

   - Treasury Stock is a contra equity account, has a normal debit balance, and is a reduction to total stockholders' equity.
   - Treasury stock can be sold at cost, below cost, or above cost.
   - As an alternative to treasury stock, corporations can retire stock, which removes the stock from the company's books.

4. How are dividends and stock splits accounted for?

- Cash dividends cause a decrease in both assets (Cash) and equity (Retained Earnings).
- Preferred stockholders receive a dividend preference that ensures that the preferred stockholders will receive dividends first. There are two categories of preferred stock:
  - Cumulative preferred stock—owners must receive all dividends in arrears (passed dividends) and current year dividends before the corporation pays dividends to the common stockholders.
  - Noncumulative preferred stock—owners do not receive any passed dividends.
- Stock dividends are distributions of a corporation's stock and have no effect on total stockholders' equity, assets, or liabilities.
  - Small stock dividends (less than 20% to 25%) are recorded at the stock's market value.
  - Large stock dividends (greater than 20% to 25%) are recorded at the stock's par value.
- Stock splits increase the number of issued and outstanding shares of stock coupled with a proportionate reduction in the par value of the stock.
- Stock splits do not affect any account balances, and no journal entry is needed.

5. How is the complete corporate income statement prepared?

- A corporation's income statement includes the following unique items:
  - Income from Continuing Operations.
  - Discontinued Operations.
- Earnings per share for income from continuing operations must be reported on the face of the income statement.

6. How is equity reported for a corporation?

- The statement of retained earnings reports how the company's retained earnings balance changed from the beginning of the period to the end of the period.
- Retained earnings can be appropriated (set aside) for a specific use.
- Prior-period adjustments must be made to beginning retained earnings for mathematical mistakes, misapplied accounting principles, or oversight.
- The statement of stockholders' equity reports the changes in all stockholders' equity accounts.

7. How do we use stockholders' equity ratios to evaluate business performance?

- Earnings per share calculates the amount of a company's net income (loss) for each share of its outstanding common stock. (Net income − Preferred dividends) / Weighted average number of common shares outstanding.
- The price/earnings ratio measures the value that the stock market places on $1 of a company's earnings. Market price per share of common stock / Earnings per share.
- Rate of return on common stockholders' equity shows the relationship between net income available to common stockholders and their average common equity invested in the company. (Net income − Preferred dividends) / Average common stockholders' equity.

> Check Your Understanding

Check your understanding of the chapter by completing this problem and then looking at the solution. Use this practice to help identify which sections of the chapter you need to study more.

Delphian Corporation's balance sheet as of December 31, 2024, follows:

DELPHIAN CORPORATION
Balance Sheet (Partial)
December 31, 2024

Stockholders' Equity

Paid-In Capital:	
Common Stock—$1 Par Value; 11,000,000 shares authorized, 8,000,000 shares issued and outstanding	$ 8,000,000
Paid-In Capital in Excess of Par—Common	200,000
Total Paid-In Capital	8,200,000
Retained Earnings	800,000,000
Total Stockholders' Equity	$ 808,200,000

During 2025, Delphian Corporation had the following transactions:

Jan. 1	Issued 10,000 shares of common stock for $10 per share.
Feb. 15	Issued 2,000 shares of common stock for $8 per share.
Mar. 1	Declared a $0.20 per share cash dividend on its common stock to be paid on March 30. Date of record: March 15.
30	Paid the cash dividend to stockholders.
Nov. 1	Declared a 1% common stock dividend on all common stock outstanding. Current market price of the stock was $8. Date of record: Nov. 15.
30	Distributed stock to stockholders.
Dec. 1	Purchased 5,000 shares of treasury stock—common at $12 per share.
20	Sold 3,000 shares of treasury stock—common at $14 per share.

Requirements

1. Journalize Delphian's transactions for 2025. (See Learning Objectives 2, 3, and 4)
2. Prepare the stockholders' equity section of the balance sheet as of December 31, 2025. Assume Delphian had net income of $20,000,000 during 2025 and that Cash Dividends and Stock Dividends have been closed to the Retained Earnings account. (See Learning Objectives 2, 3, 4, and 6)
3. Determine Delphian's earnings per share for 2025. (See Learning Objectives 5 and 7)
4. Assuming Delphian's market value per common share as of December 31, 2025, was $15, calculate Delphian's price/earnings ratio for 2025. (See Learning Objective 7)

> Solution

1.

Date	Accounts and Explanation	Debit	Credit
Jan. 1	Cash ($10 per share × 10,000 shares)	100,000	
	Common Stock—$1 Par Value ($1 per share × 10,000 shares)		10,000
	Paid-In Capital in Excess of Par—Common ($9 per share × 10,000 shares)		90,000
	Issued common stock at a premium.		
Feb. 15	Cash ($8 per share × 2,000 shares)	16,000	
	Common Stock—$1 Par Value ($1 per share × 2,000 shares)		2,000
	Paid-In Capital in Excess of Par—Common ($7 per share × 2,000 shares)		14,000
	Issued common stock at a premium.		
Mar. 1	Cash Dividends ($0.20 per share × (8,000,000 shares + 10,000 shares + 2,000 shares))	1,602,400	
	Dividends Payable—Common		1,602,400
	Declared a cash dividend.		
15	No entry recorded.		
30	Dividends Payable—Common	1,602,400	
	Cash		1,602,400
	Payment of cash dividend.		
Nov. 1	Stock Dividends ($8 per share × 8,012,000 shares × 0.01)	640,960	
	Common Stock Dividend Distributable ($1 per share × 8,012,000 shares × 0.01)		80,120
	Paid-In Capital in Excess of Par—Common ($640,960 − $80,120)		560,840
	Declared a 1% stock dividend.		
15	No entry recorded.		
30	Common Stock Dividend Distributable	80,120	
	Common Stock—$1 Par Value		80,120
	Issued 1% stock dividend.		
Dec. 1	Treasury Stock—Common ($12 per share × 5,000 shares)	60,000	
	Cash		60,000
	Purchased treasury stock.		
20	Cash ($14 per share × 3,000 shares)	42,000	
	Treasury Stock—Common ($12 per share × 3,000 shares)		36,000
	Paid-In Capital from Treasury Stock Transactions ($2 per share × 3,000 shares)		6,000
	Sold treasury stock above cost.		

2.

DELPHIAN CORPORATION
Balance Sheet (Partial)
December 31, 2025

Stockholders' Equity

Paid-In Capital:		
Common Stock—$1 Par Value; 11,000,000 shares authorized, 8,092,120 shares issued, 8,090,120 outstanding	$	8,092,120
Paid-In Capital in Excess of Par—Common		864,840
Paid-In Capital in from Treasury Stock Transactions		6,000
Total Paid-In Capital		8,962,960
Retained Earnings		817,756,640
Treasury Stock at Cost		(24,000)
Total Stockholders' Equity		$ 826,695,600

Calculations:

Common stock—number of shares issued and outstanding:

Beginning balance, Jan. 1	8,000,000 shares
Stock issuance on Jan. 1	10,000
Stock issuance on Feb. 15	2,000
Shares outstanding before dividend	8,012,000
Stock dividend on Nov. 30 (8,012,000 × 0.01)	80,120
Common stock issued	8,092,120
Purchase of treasury stock on Dec. 1	(5,000)
Sale of treasury stock on Dec. 20	3,000
Common stock outstanding	8,090,120 shares

Paid-In Capital in Excess of Par:

Beginning balance, Jan. 1	$ 200,000
Stock issuance on Jan. 1	90,000
Stock issuance on Feb. 15	14,000
Stock dividend on Nov. 1	560,840
Total Paid-In Capital in Excess of Par	$ 864,840

Retained Earnings:

Beginning balance, Jan. 1	$ 800,000,000
Cash dividend on Mar. 1	(1,602,400)
Stock dividend on Nov. 1	(640,960)
Net income for the year	20,000,000
Ending balance, Dec. 31	$ 817,756,640

3. Earnings per share = (Net income − Preferred dividends) / Average number of common shares outstanding = ($20,000,000 − $0) / [(8,000,000 shares + 8,090,120 shares) / 2] = $2.49 per share

4. Price/earnings ratio = Market price per share of common stock / Earnings per share = $15 per share / $2.49 per share = 6.02

> Key Terms

Appropriation of Retained Earnings (p. 13-26)
Authorized Stock (p. 13-3)
Capital Stock (p. 13-3)
Common Stock (p. 13-5)
Corporation (p. 13-2)
Cumulative Preferred Stock (p. 13-17)
Deficit (p. 13-25)
Dividend (p. 13-5)
Dividend in Arrears (p. 13-17)
Earnings per Share (EPS) (p. 13-24)
Income Tax Expense (p. 13-23)
Issue Price (p. 13-7)
Issued Stock (p. 13-3)
Large Stock Dividend (p. 13-19)
Legal Capital (p. 13-15)
Memorandum Entry (p. 13-22)
No-Par Stock (p. 13-5)
Noncumulative Preferred Stock (p. 13-17)
Outstanding Stock (p. 13-4)
Paid-In Capital (p. 13-6)
Paid-In Capital in Excess of Par (p. 13-7)
Par Value (p. 13-5)
Preemptive Right (p. 13-5)
Preferred Stock (p. 13-5)
Premium (p. 13-7)
Price/Earnings Ratio (p. 13-28)
Prior-Period Adjustment (p. 13-26)
Rate of Return on Common Stockholders' Equity (p. 13-28)
Retained Earnings (p. 13-6)
Small Stock Dividend (p. 13-19)
Stated Value Stock (p. 13-5)
Stock Certificate (p. 13-3)
Stock Dividend (p. 13-18)
Stock Split (p. 13-22)
Stockholders' Equity (p. 13-6)
Treasury Stock (p. 13-11)
Underwriter (p. 13-7)

> Quick Check

1. Which characteristic of a corporation is a disadvantage?
   a. Mutual agency
   b. Double taxation
   c. Limited liability
   d. None are disadvantages.

2. The two basic sources of stockholders' equity are
   a. assets and equity.
   b. preferred and common.
   c. retained earnings and dividends.
   d. paid-in capital and retained earnings.

3. Suppose Value Home and Garden Imports issued 400,000 shares of $0.10 par common stock at $4 per share. Which journal entry correctly records the issuance of this stock?

Date	Accounts and Explanation	Debit	Credit
a.	Common Stock—$0.10 Par Value	1,600,000	
	Cash		40,000
	Paid-In Capital in Excess of Par—Common		1,560,000
b.	Common Stock—$0.10 Par Value	1,600,000	
	Cash		1,600,000
c.	Cash	1,600,000	
	Common Stock—$0.10 Par Value		40,000
	Paid-In Capital in Excess of Par—Common		1,560,000
d.	Cash	1,600,000	
	Common Stock—$0.10 Par Value		1,600,000

4. Suppose Yummy Treats Bakery issues common stock in exchange for a building. Yummy Treats Bakery should record the building at
   a. the par value of the stock given.
   b. its book value.
   c. its market value.
   d. a value assigned by the board of directors.

Learning Objective 3

5. A company's own stock that it has issued and repurchased is called
   a. outstanding stock.
   b. dividend stock.
   c. issued stock.
   d. treasury stock.

Learning Objective 3

6. Assume that a company paid $6 per share to purchase 1,100 shares of its $3 par common stock as treasury stock. The purchase of treasury stock
   a. increased total equity by $3,300.
   b. decreased total equity by $3,300.
   c. decreased total equity by $6,600.
   d. increased total equity by $6,600.

Learning Objective 4

7. Winston Corporation has 9,000 shares of 4%, $10 par cumulative preferred stock and 47,000 shares of common stock outstanding. Winston declared no dividends in 2023 and had no dividends in arrears prior to 2023. In 2024, Winston declares a total dividend of $54,000. How much of the dividends go to the common stockholders?
   a. $54,000
   b. $50,400
   c. $46,800
   d. None; it all goes to preferred stockholders.

Learning Objective 4

8. A small stock dividend
   a. decreases common stock.
   b. has no effect on total equity.
   c. increases Retained Earnings.
   d. Items a, b, and c are correct.

Learning Objective 5

9. Which of the following is not included in continuing operations?
   a. Loss on the sale of equipment
   b. Gain on the sale on a segment of a business that has been discontinued
   c. Salaries expense
   d. Interest revenue

Learning Objective 6

10. Jackson Health Foods has 8,000 shares of $2 par common stock outstanding, which were issued at $15 per share. Jackson also has a deficit balance in Retained Earnings of $86,000. How much is Jackson's total stockholders' equity?
    a. $16,000
    b. $120,000
    c. $206,000
    d. $34,000

Learning Objective 7

11. Dale Corporation has the following data:

Net income	$ 24,000
Preferred dividends	12,000
Average common stockholders' equity	100,000

    Dale's rate of return on common stockholders' equity is
    a. 24%
    b. 50%
    c. 12%
    d. 36%

Check your answers at the end of the chapter.

ASSESS YOUR PROGRESS

> ## Review Questions

1. What is a corporation?
2. List three characteristics of a corporation.
3. How does authorized stock differ from outstanding stock?
4. What are the four basic rights of stockholders?
5. How does preferred stock differ from common stock?
6. What is par value?
7. What are the two basic sources of stockholders' equity? Describe each source.
8. What account is used to record the premium when issuing common stock? What type of account is this?
9. If stock is issued for assets other than cash, describe the recording of this transaction.
10. What is treasury stock? What type of account is Treasury Stock, and what is the account's normal balance?
11. Where and how is treasury stock reported on the balance sheet?
12. What is the effect on the accounting equation when cash dividends are declared? What is the effect on the accounting equation when cash dividends are paid?
13. What are the three relevant dates involving cash dividends? Describe each.
14. How does cumulative preferred stock differ from noncumulative preferred stock?
15. What is a stock dividend?
16. What is the effect on the accounting equation when a stock dividend is declared? What is the effect on the accounting equation when a stock dividend is distributed?
17. What are some reasons corporations issue stock dividends?
18. What is a stock split?
19. What is reported in the discontinued operations section of the income statement?
20. What does the statement of retained earnings report?
21. What is a prior-period adjustment?
22. What does the statement of stockholders' equity report? How does the statement of stockholders' equity differ from the statement of retained earnings?
23. What does earnings per share report, and how is it calculated?
24. What is the price/earnings ratio, and how is it calculated?
25. What does the rate of return on common stock show, and how is it calculated?

> ## Short Exercises

S-F:13-1 Describing corporation characteristics

Learning Objective 1

Due to recent beef recalls, Southwest Steakhouse is considering incorporating. Bob, the owner, wants to protect his personal assets in the event the restaurant is sued.

Requirements

1. Which advantage of incorporating is most applicable? What are other advantages of organizing as a corporate entity?
2. What are some disadvantages of organizing as a corporation?

Learning Objective 2

S-F:13-2 Journalizing issuance of stock—at par and at a premium

Colorado Corporation has two classes of stock: common, $3 par value; and preferred, $30 par value.

Requirements

1. Journalize Colorado's issuance of 4,500 shares of common stock for $6 per share.
2. Journalize Colorado's issuance of 4,500 shares of preferred stock for a total of $135,000.

Learning Objective 2

S-F:13-3 Journalizing issuance of stock—no-par

Wolcott Corporation issued 5,000 shares of no-par common stock for $2 per share on January 13. Record the stock issuance.

Learning Objective 2

S-F:13-4 Journalizing issuance of stock—stated value

Nelson Corporation issued 9,000 shares of $3 stated value common stock for $11 per share on July 7. Record the stock issuance.

Learning Objective 2

S-F:13-5 Journalizing issuance of stock for assets other than cash

Cedar Corporation issued 36,000 shares of $1 par value common stock in exchange for a building with a market value of $160,000. Record the stock issuance.

Learning Objective 3

S-F:13-6 Accounting for the purchase and sale of treasury stock

Discount Furniture, Inc. completed the following treasury stock transactions in 2024:

Dec. 1	Purchased 1,900 shares of the company's $1 par value common stock as treasury stock, paying cash of $5 per share.
15	Sold 200 shares of the treasury stock for cash of $8 per share.
20	Sold 1,000 shares of the treasury stock for cash of $1 per share. (Assume the balance in Paid-In Capital from Treasury Stock Transactions on December 20 is $2,400.)

Requirements

1. Journalize these transactions. Explanations are not required.
2. How will Discount Furniture, Inc. report treasury stock on its balance sheet as of December 31, 2024?

Learning Objective 4

S-F:13-7 Accounting for cash dividends

Java Company earned net income of $85,000 during the year ended December 31, 2024. On December 15, Java declared the annual cash dividend on its 4% preferred stock (par value, $120,000) and a $0.25 per share cash dividend on its common stock (50,000 shares). Java then paid the dividends on January 4, 2025.

Requirements

1. Journalize for Java the entry declaring the cash dividends on December 15, 2024.
2. Journalize for Java the entry paying the cash dividends on January 4, 2025.

S-F:13-8 Dividing cash dividends between preferred and common stock

Learning Objective 4

Copperhead Trust has the following classes of stock:

Preferred Stock—6%, $12 par value; 8,500 shares authorized, 7,000 shares issued and outstanding
Common Stock—$0.10 par value; 2,100,000 shares authorized, 1,400,000 shares issued and outstanding

Requirements

1. Copperhead declares cash dividends of $44,000 for 2024. How much of the dividend goes to preferred stockholders? How much goes to common stockholders?
2. Assume the preferred stock is cumulative and Copperhead passed the preferred dividend in 2022 and 2023. In 2024, the company declares cash dividends of $46,000. How much of the dividend goes to preferred stockholders? How much goes to common stockholders?
3. Assume the preferred stock is noncumulative and Copperhead passed the preferred dividend in 2022 and 2023. In 2024, the company declares cash dividends of $46,000. How much of the dividend goes to preferred stockholders? How much goes to common stockholders?

S-F:13-9 Journalizing a small stock dividend

Learning Objective 4

Element Water Sports has 13,000 shares of $1 par value common stock outstanding. Element distributes a 5% stock dividend when the market value of its stock is $15 per share.

Requirements

1. Journalize Element's declaration of the stock dividend on August 15 and distribution on August 31.
2. What is the overall effect of the stock dividend on Element's total assets?
3. What is the overall effect on total stockholders' equity?

S-F:13-10 Journalizing a large stock dividend

Learning Objective 4

Nelly, Inc. had 320,000 shares of $2 par value common stock issued and outstanding as of December 15, 2024. The company is authorized to issue 1,300,000 common shares. On December 15, 2024, Nelly declared a 40% stock dividend when the market value for Nelly's common stock was $7 per share. The stock was issued on Dec. 30.

Requirements

1. Journalize the declaration and distribution of the stock dividend.
2. How many shares of common stock are outstanding after the dividend?

Learning Objective 4   **S-F:13-11 Accounting for a stock split**

Decor and More Imports recently reported the following stockholders' equity:

Stockholders' Equity	
Paid-In Capital:	
Common Stock—$1 Par Value; 490,000,000 shares authorized, 119,000,000 shares issued and outstanding	$ 119,000,000
Paid-In Capital in Excess of Par—Common	148,000,000
Total Paid-In Capital	267,000,000
Retained Earnings	654,000,000
Total Stockholders' Equity	$ 921,000,000

Suppose Decor and More split its common stock 2-for-1 in order to decrease the market price per share of its stock. The company's stock was trading at $17 per share immediately before the split.

Requirements

1. Prepare the stockholders' equity section of the Decor and More Imports balance sheet after the stock split.
2. Were the account balances changed or unchanged after the stock split?

Learning Objective 5   **S-F:13-12 Preparing a corporate income statement**

ABC Corporation's accounting records include the following items, listed in no particular order, at December 31, 2024:

Other Income and (Expenses)	$ (7,200)	Cost of Goods Sold	$ 30,000
Net Sales	81,000	Operating Expenses	25,000
Gain on Discontinued Operations	3,600		

The income tax rate for ABC Corporation is 21%.

Prepare ABC's income statement for the year ended December 31, 2024. Omit earnings per share. Use the multi-step format.

Learning Objective 5   **S-F:13-13 Reporting earnings per share**

Return to the ABC data in Short Exercise S-F:13-12. ABC had 8,000 shares of common stock outstanding during 2024. ABC declared and paid preferred dividends of $4,000 during 2024.

Show how ABC reports EPS data on its 2024 income statement.

Learning Objective 6   **S-F:13-14 Preparing a statement of retained earnings**

Kingston, Inc. had beginning retained earnings of $135,000 on January 1, 2024. During the year, Kingston declared and paid $85,000 of cash dividends and earned $75,000 of net income. Prepare a statement of retained earnings for Kingston, Inc. for the year ending December 31, 2024.

Learning Objective 6   **S-F:13-15 Analyzing the effect of prior-period adjustments**

Taylor Corporation discovered in 2025 that it had incorrectly recorded in 2024 a cash payment of $70,000 for utilities expense. The correct amount of the utilities expense was $35,000.

Requirements

1. Determine the effect of the error on the accounting equation in 2024.
2. How should this error be reported in the 2025 financial statements?

S-F:13-16 Computing earnings per share

Learning Objective 7

HEB Corporation had net income for 2024 of $60,450. HEB had 15,500 shares of common stock outstanding at the beginning of the year and 20,100 shares of common stock outstanding as of December 31, 2024. During the year, HEB declared and paid preferred dividends of $2,600. Compute HEB's earnings per share.

Note: Short Exercise S-F:13-16 must be completed before attempting Short Exercise S-F:13-17.

S-F:13-17 Computing price/earnings ratio

Learning Objective 7

Refer to the HEB data in Short Exercise S-F:13-16. Assume the market price of HEB's common stock is $19.50 per share. Compute HEB's price/earnings ratio.

S-F:13-18 Computing rate of return on common stockholders' equity

Learning Objective 7

Wyler, Inc.'s 2024 balance sheet reported the following items—with 2023 figures given for comparison:

WYLER, INC.
Balance Sheet
As of December 31, 2024 and December 31, 2023

	December 31, 2024	December 31, 2023
Total Assets	$ 39,600	$ 33,462
Total Liabilities	17,100	14,962
Total Stockholders' Equity (all common)	22,500	18,500
Total Liabilities and Stockholders' Equity	$ 39,600	$ 33,462

Net income for 2024 was $3,690. Compute Wyler's rate of return on common stockholders' equity for 2024.

> Exercises

E-F:13-19 Identifying advantages and disadvantages of a corporation

Learning Objective 1

Following is a list of advantages and disadvantages of the corporate form of business. Identify each quality as either an advantage or a disadvantage.

a. Ownership and management are separated.
b. Entity has continuous life.
c. Transfer of ownership is easy.
d. Stockholders' liability is limited.
e. Exposure to double taxation is evident.
f. Entity can raise more money than a partnership or sole proprietorship.
g. Government regulation is expensive.

13-42 Financial chapter 13

Learning Objective 2

E-F:13-20 Determining paid-in capital for a corporation

Aruba Corporation recently organized. The company issued common stock to an inventor in exchange for a patent with a market value of $57,000. In addition, Aruba received cash for 6,000 shares of its $10 par preferred stock at par value and 6,500 shares of its no-par common stock at $20 per share. Without making journal entries, determine the total *paid-in capital* created by these transactions.

Learning Objective 2

E-F:13-21 Journalizing issuance of stock

Steller Systems completed the following stock issuance transactions:

May 19	Issued 1,700 shares of $3 par value common stock for cash of $10.50 per share.
Jun. 3	Issued 300 shares of $9, no-par preferred stock for $15,000 cash.
11	Received equipment with a market value of $68,000 in exchange for 5,000 shares of the $3 par value common stock.

Requirements

1. Journalize the transactions. Explanations are not required.
2. How much paid-in capital did these transactions generate for Steller Systems?

Learning Objective 2

1. a. Cash $104,000

E-F:13-22 Journalizing issuance of no-par stock

Eates Corp. issued 8,000 shares of no-par common stock for $13 per share.

Requirements

1. Record issuance of the stock if the stock:
   a. is true no-par stock.
   b. has stated value of $3 per share.
2. Which type of stock results in more total paid-in capital?

Learning Objective 2

2. Total Stockholders' Equity $94,500

E-F:13-23 Journalizing issuance of stock and preparing the stockholders' equity section of the balance sheet

The charter for ASAP-TV, Inc. authorizes the company to issue 100,000 shares of $5, no-par preferred stock and 500,000 shares of common stock with $1 par value. During its start-up phase, ASAP-TV completed the following transactions:

Sep. 6	Issued 550 shares of common stock to the promoters who organized the corporation, receiving cash of $16,500.
12	Issued 400 shares of preferred stock for cash of $23,000.
14	Issued 1,500 shares of common stock in exchange for land with a market value of $17,000.

Requirements

1. Record the transactions in the general journal.
2. Prepare the stockholders' equity section of the ASAP-TV balance sheet at September 30, 2024, assuming ASAP-TV, Inc. had net income of $38,000 for the month.

E-F:13-24 Journalizing issuance of stock and preparing the stockholders' equity section of the balance sheet

The charter of Evergreen Corporation authorizes the issuance of 900 shares of preferred stock and 1,400 shares of common stock. During a two-month period, Evergreen completed these stock-issuance transactions:

Mar. 23	Issued 230 shares of $3 par value common stock for cash of $15 per share.
Apr. 12	Received inventory with a market value of $27,000 and equipment with a market value of $19,000 for 320 shares of the $3 par value common stock.
17	Issued 900 shares of 5%, $20 par value preferred stock for $20 per share.

Learning Objective 2

March 23 Common Stock $690

Requirements

1. Record the transactions in the general journal.
2. Prepare the stockholders' equity section of the Evergreen balance sheet as of April 30, 2024, for the transactions given in this exercise. Retained Earnings has a balance of $73,000 at April 30, 2024.

E-F:13-25 Journalizing treasury stock transactions and reporting stockholders' equity

Southern Amusements Corporation had the following stockholders' equity on November 30:

On December 30, Southern purchased 200 shares of treasury stock at $15 per share.

Learning Objective 3

2. Total Stockholders' Equity $52,000

Stockholders' Equity	
Paid-In Capital:	
Common Stock—$5 Par Value; 1,300 shares authorized, 250 shares issued and outstanding	$ 1,250
Paid-In Capital in Excess of Par—Common	3,750
Total Paid-In Capital	5,000
Retained Earnings	50,000
Total Stockholders' Equity	$ 55,000

Requirements

1. Journalize the purchase of the treasury stock.
2. Prepare the stockholders' equity section of the balance sheet at December 31, 2024. Assume the balance in retained earnings is unchanged from November 30.
3. How many shares of common stock are outstanding after the purchase of treasury stock?

E-F:13-26 Journalizing issuance of stock and treasury stock transactions

Stock transactions for Careful Driving School, Inc. follow:

Mar. 4	Issued 27,000 shares of $1 par value common stock at $10 per share.
May 22	Purchased 1,300 shares of treasury stock—common at $13 per share.
Sep. 22	Sold 500 shares of treasury stock—common at $23 per share.
Oct. 14	Sold 800 shares of treasury stock—common at $9 per share.

Journalize the transactions.

Learning Objectives 2, 3

May 22 Treasury Stock $16,900

Learning Objective 4

1. Preferred Dividend 2024 $9,000

E-F:13-27 Computing dividends on preferred and common stock and journalizing

Northern Communications has the following stockholders' equity on December 31, 2024:

Stockholders' Equity	
Paid-In Capital:	
Preferred Stock—5%, $11 Par Value; 150,000 shares authorized, 20,000 shares issued and outstanding	$ 220,000
Common Stock—$2 Par Value; 575,000 shares authorized, 380,000 shares issued and outstanding	760,000
Paid-In Capital in Excess of Par—Common	680,000
Total Paid-In Capital	1,660,000
Retained Earnings	200,000
Total Stockholders' Equity	$ 1,860,000

Requirements

1. Assuming the preferred stock is cumulative, compute the amount of dividends to preferred stockholders and to common stockholders for 2024 and 2025 if total dividends are $9,000 in 2024 and $45,000 in 2025. Assume no changes in preferred stock and common stock in 2025.

2. Record the journal entries for 2024, assuming that Northern Communications declared the dividend on December 1 for stockholders of record on December 10. Northern Communications paid the dividend on December 20.

Learning Objective 4

2. July 1 Cash Dividends $185,000

E-F:13-28 Computing dividends on preferred and common stock and journalizing

The following elements of stockholders' equity are from the balance sheet of Sneed Marketing Corp. at December 31, 2023:

Stockholders' Equity	
Paid-In Capital:	
Preferred Stock—4%, $2 Par Value; 80,000 shares authorized, 55,000 shares issued and outstanding	$ 110,000
Common Stock—$0.10 Par Value; 8,750,000 shares authorized, 8,000,000 shares issued and outstanding	800,000

Sneed paid no preferred dividends in 2023.

Requirements

1. Compute the dividends to the preferred and common shareholders for 2024 if total dividends are $185,000 and assuming the preferred stock is noncumulative. Assume no changes in preferred and common stock in 2024.

2. Record the journal entries for 2024 assuming that Sneed Marketing Corp. declared the dividends on July 1 for stockholders of record on July 15. Sneed paid the dividends on July 31.

E-F:13-29 Journalizing a stock dividend and reporting stockholders' equity

Learning Objective 4

The stockholders' equity of Lakeside Occupational Therapy, Inc. on December 31, 2023, follows:

2. Total Stockholders' Equity $122,000

Stockholders' Equity	
Paid-In Capital:	
Common Stock—$1 Par Value; 1,200 shares authorized, 400 shares issued and outstanding	$ 400
Paid-In Capital in Excess of Par—Common	1,600
Total Paid-In Capital	2,000
Retained Earnings	120,000
Total Stockholders' Equity	$ 122,000

On April 30, 2024, the market price of Lakeside's common stock was $16 per share and the company declared a 13% stock dividend. The stock was distributed on May 15.

Requirements

1. Journalize the declaration and distribution of the stock dividend.
2. Prepare the stockholders' equity section of the balance sheet as of May 31, 2024. Assume Retained Earnings are $120,000 on April 30, 2024, before the stock dividend, and the only change made to Retained Earnings before preparing the balance sheet was closing the Stock Dividends account.

E-F:13-30 Journalizing cash and stock dividends

Learning Objective 4

Self-Defense Schools, Inc. is authorized to issue 200,000 shares of $2 par common stock. The company issued 73,000 shares at $5 per share. When the market price of common stock was $7 per share, Self-Defense Schools declared and distributed a 14% stock dividend. Later, Self-Defense Schools declared and paid a $0.70 per share cash dividend.

1. Common Stock $20,440

Requirements

1. Journalize the declaration and the distribution of the stock dividend.
2. Journalize the declaration and the payment of the cash dividend.

E-F:13-31 Reporting stockholders' equity after a stock split

Learning Objective 4

Wood Golf Club Corp. had the following stockholders' equity at December 31, 2023:

Total Stockholders' Equity $3,410

Stockholders' Equity	
Paid-In Capital:	
Common Stock—$1 Par Value; 650 shares authorized, 270 shares issued and outstanding	$ 270
Paid-In Capital in Excess of Par—Common	540
Total Paid-In Capital	810
Retained Earnings	2,600
Total Stockholders' Equity	$ 3,410

On June 30, 2024, Wood Golf Club split its common stock 2-for-1. Prepare the stockholders' equity section of the balance sheet immediately after the split. Assume the balance in Retained Earnings is unchanged from December 31, 2023.

Learning Objective 4

E-F:13-32 Determining the effects of cash dividends, stock dividends, and stock splits

Complete the following chart by inserting a check mark (√) for each statement that is true.

	Cash dividend	Stock dividend	Stock split
Decreases retained earnings			
Has no effect on a liability			
Increases paid-in capital by the same amount that it decreases retained earnings			
Decreases both total assets and total stockholders' equity			
Has no effect on total stockholders' equity			

Learning Objectives 3, 4

E-F:13-33 Determining the effect of stock dividends, stock splits, and treasury stock transactions

Many types of transactions may affect stockholders' equity. Identify the effects of the following transactions on total stockholders' equity. Each transaction is independent.

a. A 10% stock dividend. Before the dividend, 540,000 shares of $1 par value common stock were outstanding; market value was $9 per share at the time of the dividend.

b. A 2-for-1 stock split. Prior to the split, 66,000 shares of $5 par value common stock were outstanding.

c. Purchase of 1,100 shares of $0.50 par treasury stock at $6 per share.

d. Sale of 600 shares of $0.50 par treasury stock for $9 per share. Cost of the treasury stock was $7 per share.

Learning Objective 5

Net Income $122,450

E-F:13-34 Preparing a multi-step income statement

Clix Photographic Supplies, Inc.'s accounting records include the following for 2024:

Loss on Discontinued Operations	30,000	Net Sales	$ 525,000
Cost of Goods Sold	240,000	Operating Expenses	100,000

Assume Clix's income tax rate is 21%. Prepare Clix's multi-step income statement for the year ending December 31, 2024. Omit earnings per share.

Learning Objective 5

Net Income $10.80

E-F:13-35 Computing earnings per share

Faccone Academy Surplus had 60,000 shares of common stock and 9,000 shares of 20%, $15 par value preferred stock outstanding through December 31, 2024. Income from continuing operations for 2024 was $711,000, and loss on discontinued operations (net of income tax saving) was $36,000.

Compute Faccone's earnings per share for 2024, starting with income from continuing operations. Round to the nearest cent.

E-F:13-36 Preparing a statement of retained earnings

Kelly May Bakery, Inc. reported a prior-period adjustment in 2024. An accounting error caused net income of prior years to be overstated by $1,000. Retained Earnings at December 31, 2023, as previously reported, was $48,000. Net income for 2024 was $74,000, and dividends declared were $28,000. Prepare the company's statement of retained earnings for the year ended December 31, 2024.

Learning Objective 6

Retained Earnings Dec. 31, 2024, $93,000

E-F:13-37 Computing earnings per share and price/earnings ratio

Rocket Corp. earned net income of $153,040 and paid the minimum dividend to preferred stockholders for 2024. Assume that there are no changes in common shares outstanding during 2024. Rocket's books include the following figures:

Preferred Stock—6%, $60 par value; 2,000 shares authorized, 1,000 shares issued and outstanding	$ 60,000
Common Stock—$5 par value; 80,000 shares authorized, 48,000 shares issued, 46,700 shares outstanding	240,000
Paid-In Capital in Excess of Par—Common	470,000
Treasury Stock—Common; 1,300 shares at cost	(26,000)

Learning Objective 7

Requirements

1. Compute Rocket's EPS for the year.
2. Assume Rocket's market price of a share of common stock is $12 per share. Compute Rocket's price/earnings ratio.

E-F:13-38 Computing rate of return on common stockholders' equity

LaSalle Exploration Company reported these figures for 2024 and 2023:

Learning Objective 7

	2024	2023
Income Statement—partial:		
Net Income	$ 14,800	$ 19,200
	Dec. 31, 2024	Dec. 31, 2023
Balance Sheet—partial:		
Total Assets	$ 323,000	$ 314,000
Preferred Stock	$ 2,100	$ 2,100
Common Stock	178,000	168,000
Retained Earnings	11,000	7,000
Total Stockholders' Equity	$ 191,100	$ 177,100

Compute rate of return on common stockholders' equity for 2024 assuming no dividends were declared or paid to preferred stockholders.

> Problems Group A

Learning Objectives 1, 2

P-F:13-39A Organizing a corporation and issuing stock

Montel and Jeremy are opening a paint store. There are no competing paint stores in the area. They must decide how to organize the business. They anticipate profits of $350,000 the first year, with the ability to sell franchises in the future. Although they have enough to start the business now as a partnership, cash flow will be an issue as they grow. They feel the corporate form of operation will be best for the long term. They seek your advice.

Requirements

1. What is the main advantage they gain by selecting a corporate form of business now?
2. Would you recommend they initially issue preferred or common stock? Why?
3. If they decide to issue $5 par common stock and anticipate an initial market price of $20 per share, how many shares will they need to issue to raise $2,750,000?

Learning Objectives 1, 2, 4

4. Common stock dividends $402,000

P-F:13-40A Identifying sources of equity, stock issuance, and dividends

Voyage Comfort Specialists, Inc. reported the following stockholders' equity on its balance sheet at June 30, 2024:

Stockholders' Equity	
Paid-In Capital:	
Preferred Stock—7%, ? Par Value; 625,000 shares authorized, 280,000 shares issued and outstanding	$ 1,400,000
Common Stock—$1 Par Value; 3,000,000 shares authorized, 1,340,000 shares issued and outstanding	1,340,000
Paid-In Capital in Excess of Par—Common	2,900,000
Total Paid-In Capital	5,640,000
Retained Earnings	12,000,000
Total Stockholders' Equity	$ 17,640,000

Requirements

1. Identify the different classes of stock that Voyage Comfort Specialists have outstanding.
2. What is the par value per share of Voyage Comfort Specialists' preferred stock?
3. Make two summary journal entries to record issuance of all the Voyage Comfort Specialists' stock for cash. Explanations are not required.
4. No preferred dividends are in arrears. Journalize the declaration of a $500,000 dividend at June 30, 2024, and the payment of the dividend on July 20, 2024. Use separate Dividends Payable accounts for preferred and common stock. An explanation is not required.

P-F:13-41A Journalizing stock issuance and cash dividends and preparing the stockholders' equity section of the balance sheet

Learning Objectives 2, 4

2. Total Stockholders' Equity $454,000

D-Mobile Wireless needed additional capital to expand, so the business incorporated. The charter from the state of Georgia authorizes D-Mobile to issue 50,000 shares of 8%, $50 par value cumulative preferred stock and 160,000 shares of $4 par value common stock. During the first month, D-Mobile completed the following transactions:

Oct. 2	Issued 19,000 shares of common stock for a building with a market value of $240,000.
6	Issued 600 shares of preferred stock for $140 per share.
9	Issued 11,000 shares of common stock for cash of $55,000.
10	Declared a $19,000 cash dividend for stockholders of record on Oct. 20. Use a separate Dividends Payable account for preferred and common stock.
25	Paid the cash dividend.

Requirements

1. Record the transactions in the general journal.
2. Prepare the stockholders' equity section of D-Mobile's balance sheet at October 31, 2024. Assume D-Mobile's net income for the month was $94,000.

P-F:13-42A Journalizing dividends and treasury stock transactions and preparing the stockholders' equity section of the balance sheet

Learning Objectives 3, 4

Nov. 8 Treasury Stock $4,000

Deerborn Manufacturing Co. completed the following transactions during 2024:

Jan. 16	Declared a cash dividend on the 6%, $103 par noncumulative preferred stock (1,050 shares outstanding). Declared a $0.20 per share dividend on the 100,000 shares of $2 par value common stock outstanding. The date of record is January 31, and the payment date is February 15.
Feb. 15	Paid the cash dividends.
Jun. 10	Split common stock 2-for-1.
Jul. 30	Declared a 30% stock dividend on the common stock. The market value of the common stock was $9 per share.
Aug. 15	Distributed the stock dividend.
Oct. 26	Purchased 1,000 shares of treasury stock at $8 per share.
Nov. 8	Sold 500 shares of treasury stock for $10 per share.
30	Sold 300 shares of treasury stock for $4 per share.

Requirements

1. Record the transactions in Deerborn's general journal.
2. Prepare the Deerborn's stockholders' equity section of the balance sheet as of December 31, 2024. Assume that Deerborn was authorized to issue 2,600 shares of preferred stock and 400,000 shares of common stock. Both preferred stock and common stock were issued at par. The ending balance of retained earnings as of December 31, 2024, is $2,060,000.

Learning Objective 5

Net Income $66,000

P-F:13-43A Preparing an income statement

The following information was taken from the records of Chua Motorsports, Inc. at November 30, 2024:

Selling Expenses	$ 110,000	Common Stock, $12 Par Value, 10,000 shares authorized and issued	$ 120,000
Administrative Expenses	115,000		
Income from Discontinued Operations	2,500	Preferred Stock, $7 No-Par Value, 7,000 shares issued	490,000
Cost of Goods Sold	510,000	Income Tax Expense: Continuing Operations	20,000
Treasury Stock—Common (5,000 shares)	75,000		
Net Sales Revenue	819,000	Income Tax Expense: Income from Discontinued Operations	500

Prepare a multi-step income statement for Chua Motorsports for the fiscal year ended November 30, 2024. Include earnings per share.

Learning Objectives 3, 4, 6

2. Retained Earnings Dec. 31, 2024, $126,550

P-F:13-44A Journalizing dividend and treasury stock transactions, preparing a statement of retained earnings, and preparing stockholders' equity

The balance sheet of Goldstein Management Consulting, Inc. at December 31, 2023, reported the following stockholders' equity:

Stockholders' Equity	
Paid-In Capital:	
Common Stock—$10 Par Value; 350,000 shares authorized, 32,000 shares issued and outstanding	$ 320,000
Paid-In Capital in Excess of Par—Common	330,000
Total Paid-In Capital	650,000
Retained Earnings	160,000
Total Stockholders' Equity	$ 810,000

During 2024, Goldstein completed the following selected transactions:

Feb. 6	Declared a 15% stock dividend on common stock. The market value of Goldstein's stock was $25 per share.
15	Distributed the stock dividend.
Jul. 29	Purchased 2,300 shares of treasury stock at $25 per share.
Nov. 27	Declared a $0.10 per share cash dividend on the common stock outstanding.

Requirements

1. Record the transactions in the general journal.
2. Prepare a retained earnings statement for the year ended December 31, 2024. Assume Goldstein's net income for the year was $90,000.
3. Prepare the stockholders' equity section of the balance sheet at December 31, 2024.

P-F:13-45A Computing earnings per share, price/earnings ratio, and rate of return on common stockholders' equity

Bianchi Company reported these figures for 2024 and 2023:

	2024	2023
Income Statement—partial:		
Net Income	$ 34,380	$ 18,000
	Dec. 31, 2024	Dec. 31, 2023
Balance Sheet—partial:		
Total Assets	$ 285,000	$ 280,000
Paid-In Capital:		
Preferred Stock—11%, $9 Par Value; 60,000 shares authorized, 12,000 shares issued and outstanding	$ 108,000	$ 108,000
Common Stock—$2 Par Value; 60,000 shares authorized, 50,000 shares issued and outstanding	100,000	100,000
Paid-In Capital in Excess of Par—Common	14,000	14,000
Retained Earnings	60,500	38,000
Total Stockholders' Equity	$ 282,500	$ 260,000

Requirements

1. Compute Bianchi Company's earnings per share for 2024. Assume the company paid the minimum preferred dividend during 2024. Round to the nearest cent.
2. Compute Bianchi Company's price/earnings ratio for 2024. Assume the company's market price per share of common stock is $9. Round to two decimals.
3. Compute Bianchi Company's rate of return on common stockholders' equity for 2024. Assume the company paid the minimum preferred dividend during 2024. Round to the nearest whole percent.

> Problems Group B

P-F:13-46B Organizing a corporation and issuing stock

Jimmy and Randy are opening a comic store. There are no competing comic stores in the area. They must decide how to organize the business. They anticipate profits of $550,000 the first year, with the ability to sell franchises in the future. Although they have enough to start the business now as a partnership, cash flow will be an issue as they grow. They feel the corporate form of operation will be best for the long term. They seek your advice.

Requirements

1. What is the main advantage they gain by selecting a corporate form of business now?
2. Would you recommend they initially issue preferred or common stock? Why?
3. If they decide to issue $3 par common stock and anticipate an initial market price of $75 per share, how many shares will they need to issue to raise $3,000,000?

Learning Objectives 1, 2, 4

4. Common stock dividends $135,000

P-F:13-47B Identifying sources of equity, stock issuance, and dividends

Tillman Comfort Specialists, Inc. reported the following stockholders' equity on its balance sheet at June 30, 2024:

Stockholders' Equity	
Paid-In Capital:	
Preferred Stock—5%, ? Par Value; 625,000 shares authorized, 325,000 shares issued and outstanding	$ 1,300,000
Common Stock—$1 Par Value; 7,000,000 shares authorized, 1,350,000 shares issued and outstanding	1,350,000
Paid-In Capital in Excess of Par—Common	2,600,000
Total Paid-In Capital	5,250,000
Retained Earnings	11,800,000
Total Stockholders' Equity	$ 17,050,000

Requirements

1. Identify the different classes of stock that Tillman Comfort Specialists has outstanding.
2. What is the par value per share of Tillman Comfort Specialists' preferred stock?
3. Make two summary journal entries to record issuance of all the Tillman Comfort Specialists stock for cash. Explanations are not required.
4. No preferred dividends are in arrears. Journalize the declaration of a $200,000 dividend at June 30, 2024, and the payment of the dividend on July 20, 2024. Use separate Dividends Payable accounts for preferred and common stock. An explanation is not required.

Learning Objectives 2, 4

2. Total Stockholders' Equity $530,000

P-F:13-48B Journalizing stock issuance and cash dividends and preparing the stockholders' equity section of the balance sheet

C-Mobile Wireless needed additional capital to expand, so the business incorporated. The charter from the state of Georgia authorizes C-Mobile to issue 120,000 shares of 9%, $150 par value cumulative preferred stock, and 140,000 shares of $3 par value common stock. During the first month, C-Mobile completed the following transactions:

Oct. 2	Issued 18,000 shares of common stock for a building with a market value of $260,000.
6	Issued 650 shares of preferred stock for $160 per share.
9	Issued 14,000 shares of common stock for cash of $84,000.
10	Declared a $13,000 cash dividend for stockholders of record on Oct. 20. Use a separate Dividends Payable account for preferred and common stock.
25	Paid the cash dividend.

Requirements

1. Record the transactions in the general journal.
2. Prepare the stockholders' equity section of C-Mobile's balance sheet at October 31, 2024. Assume C-Mobile's net income for the month was $95,000.

P-F:13-49B Journalizing dividends and treasury stock transactions and preparing the stockholders' equity section of the balance sheet

Learning Objectives 3, 4

Halborn Manufacturing Co. completed the following transactions during 2024:

1. Nov. 8 Treasury Stock $36,000

Jan. 16	Declared a cash dividend on the 6%, $97 par noncumulative preferred stock (1,150 shares outstanding). Declared a $0.20 per share dividend on the 80,000 shares of $8 par value common stock outstanding. The date of record is January 31, and the payment date is February 15.
Feb. 15	Paid the cash dividends.
Jun. 10	Split common stock 2-for-1.
Jul. 30	Declared a 40% stock dividend on the common stock. The market value of the common stock was $8 per share.
Aug. 15	Distributed the stock dividend.
Oct. 26	Purchased 8,000 shares of treasury stock at $9 per share.
Nov. 8	Sold 4,000 shares of treasury stock for $10 per share.
30	Sold 1,400 shares of treasury stock for $5 per share.

Requirements

1. Record the transactions in Halborn's general journal.
2. Prepare the Halborn's stockholders' equity section of the balance sheet as of December 31, 2024. Assume that Halborn was authorized to issue 2,200 shares of preferred stock and 500,000 shares of common stock. Both preferred stock and common stock were issued at par. The ending balance of retained earnings as of December 31, 2024, is $2,030,000.

P-F:13-50B Preparing an income statement

Learning Objective 5

The following information was taken from the records of Arizona Motorsports, Inc. at November 30, 2024:

Net Income $70,100

Selling Expenses	$ 95,000	Common Stock, $11 Par Value, 13,500 shares authorized and issued	$ 148,500
Administrative Expenses	150,000	Preferred Stock, $2 No-Par Value, 2,000 shares issued	60,000
Income from Discontinued Operations	2,400
Cost of Goods Sold	470,000	Income Tax Expense: Continuing Operations	18,200
Treasury Stock—Common (1,500 shares)	19,500
Net Sales Revenue	801,400	Income Tax Expense: Income from Discontinued Operations	500

Prepare a multi-step income statement for Arizona Motorsports for the fiscal year ended November 30, 2024. Include earnings per share.

Learning Objectives 3, 4, 6

2. Retained Earnings Dec. 31, 2024, $218,280

P-F:13-51B Journalizing dividend and treasury stock transactions, preparing a statement of retained earnings, and preparing stockholders' equity

The balance sheet of Cullins Management Consulting, Inc. at December 31, 2023, reported the following stockholders' equity:

Stockholders' Equity	
Paid-In Capital:	
Common Stock—$10 Par Value; 200,000 shares authorized, 22,000 shares issued and outstanding	$ 220,000
Paid-In Capital in Excess of Par—Common	360,000
Total Paid-In Capital	580,000
Retained Earnings	163,000
Total Stockholders' Equity	$ 743,000

During 2024, Cullins completed the following selected transactions:

Feb. 6	Declared a 5% stock dividend on common stock. The market value of Cullins' stock was $25 per share.
15	Distributed the stock dividend.
Jul. 29	Purchased 2,000 shares of treasury stock at $25 per share.
Nov. 27	Declared a $0.20 per share cash dividend on the common stock outstanding.

Requirements

1. Record the transactions in the general journal.
2. Prepare a retained earnings statement for the year ended December 31, 2024. Assume Cullins' net income for the year was $87,000.
3. Prepare the stockholders' equity section of the balance sheet at December 31, 2024.

Learning Objective 7

P-F:13-52B Computing earnings per share, price/earnings ratio, and rate of return on common stockholders' equity

Gullo Company reported these figures for 2024 and 2023:

	2024	2023
Income Statement—partial:		
Net Income	$ 18,900	$ 24,000
	Dec. 31, 2024	Dec. 31, 2023
Balance Sheet—partial:		
Total Assets	$ 285,000	$ 200,000
Paid-In Capital:		
Preferred Stock—11%, $9 Par Value; 60,000 shares authorized, 10,000 shares issued and outstanding	$ 90,000	$ 90,000
Common Stock—$1 Par Value; 45,000 shares authorized, 30,000 shares issued and outstanding	30,000	30,000
Paid-In Capital in Excess of Par—Common	14,000	14,000
Retained Earnings	51,000	42,000
Total Stockholders' Equity	$ 185,000	$ 176,000

Requirements

1. Compute Gullo Company's earnings per share for 2024. Assume the company paid the minimum preferred dividend during 2024. Round to the nearest cent.
2. Compute Gullo Company's price/earnings ratio for 2024. Assume the company's market price per share of common stock is $9. Round to two decimals.
3. Compute Gullo Company's rate of return on common stockholders' equity for 2024. Assume the company paid the minimum preferred dividend during 2024. Round to the nearest whole percent.

CRITICAL THINKING

> Using Excel

Download Excel problems for this chapter online in MyLab Accounting or at **http://www.pearsonhighered.com/Horngren**.

> Continuing Problem

P-F:13-53 Journalizing stock issuances, cash dividends, and stock dividends; preparing stockholders' equity section of balance sheet

This problem continues the Canyon Canoe Company situation from Chapter F:12. After looking into debt financing through notes, mortgage, and bonds payable, Canyon Canoe Company decides to raise additional capital for the planned business expansion. The company will be able to acquire cash as well as land adjacent to its current business location. Before the following transactions, the balance in Common Stock on January 1, 2027, was $136,000 and included 136,000 shares of common stock issued and outstanding. (There was no Paid-In Capital in Excess of Par—Common.)

Canyon Canoe Company had the following transactions in 2027:

Jan. 1	Issued 50,000 shares of $1 par value common stock for a total of $200,000.
10	Issued 20,000 shares of 4%, $3 par value preferred stock in exchange for land with a market value of $70,000.
Dec. 15	Declared total cash dividends of $15,000.
20	Declared an 8% common stock dividend when the market value of the stock was $4.50 per share.
31	Paid the cash dividends.
31	Distributed the stock dividend.

Requirements

1. Journalize the transactions.
2. Calculate the balance in Retained Earnings on December 31, 2027. Assume the balance on January 1, 2027, was $4,250 and net income for the year was $417,000.
3. Prepare the stockholders' equity section of the balance sheet as of December 31, 2027. There was no preferred stock issued prior to the 2027 transactions.

> Tying It All Together Case F:13-1

Before you begin this assignment, review the Tying It All Together feature in the chapter. It will also be helpful if you review Facebook's 2018 annual report (**https://www.sec.gov/Archives/edgar/data/1326801/000132680119000009/fb-12312018x10k.htm**).

Facebook, Inc. is a mobile application and Web site that enables people to connect, share, discover, and communicate with each other. The company also owns Instagram, Messenger, WhatsApp, and Oculus.

Requirements

1. Review Item 5 (Dividend Policy) of the 2018 annual report. Has Facebook ever paid a cash dividend? Does the company intend to pay cash dividends in the foreseeable future?
2. Review the balance sheet for Facebook. What is the par value of its Class A common shares?
3. Does Facebook have any treasury stock? How do you know?

> Decision Case F:13-1

Lena Kay and Kathy Lauder have a patent on a new line of cosmetics. They need additional capital to market the products, and they plan to incorporate the business. They are considering the capital structure for the corporation. Their primary goal is to raise as much capital as possible without giving up control of the business. Kay and Lauder plan to invest the patent (an intangible asset, which will be transferred to the company's ownership in lieu of cash) in the company and receive 100,000 shares of the corporation's common stock. They have been offered $100,000 for the patent, which provides an indication of the fair market value of the patent.

The corporation's plans for a charter include an authorization to issue 5,000 shares of preferred stock and 500,000 shares of $1 par common stock. Kay and Lauder are uncertain about the most desirable features for the preferred stock. Prior to incorporating, they are discussing their plans with two investment groups. The corporation can obtain capital from outside investors under either of the following plans:

- **Plan 1.** Group 1 will invest $150,000 to acquire 1,500 shares of 6%, $100 par nonvoting, noncumulative preferred stock.
- **Plan 2.** Group 2 will invest $100,000 to acquire 1,000 shares of $5, no-par preferred stock and $70,000 to acquire 70,000 shares of common stock. Each preferred share receives 50 votes on matters that come before the common stockholders.

Requirements

Assume that the corporation has been chartered (approved) by the state.

1. Journalize the issuance of common stock to Kay and Lauder. Explanations are not required.
2. Journalize the issuance of stock to the outsiders under both plans. Explanations are not required.
3. Net income for the first year is $180,000, and total dividends are $30,000. Prepare the stockholders' equity section of the corporation's balance sheet under both plans at the end of the first year.
4. Recommend one of the plans to Kay and Lauder. Give your reasons.

> Financial Statement Case F:13-1

Use **Target Corporation's** financial statements to answer the following questions. Visit **http://www.pearsonhighered.com/Horngren** to view a link to Target Corporation's Fiscal 2018 Annual Report.

Requirements

1. Review the stockholders' equity section of the balance sheet. Did Target have any preferred stock at February 2, 2019?
2. Now examine the notes at the bottom of the balance sheet. Is Target authorized to issue preferred stock? If so, how much?
3. How much of Target Corporation's common stock was outstanding at February 2, 2019? How can you tell?
4. Examine Target Corporation's consolidated statements of cash flows. Did Target pay any cash dividends during the year ending February 2, 2019? If so, how much?
5. Show how Target Corporation computed basic earnings per share of $5.55 for fiscal year 2018. (Ignore diluted earnings per share.)

> Team Project F:13-1

Obtain the annual reports (or annual report data) of five well-known companies. You can get the reports either from the companies' Web sites, from your college library, or by mailing a request directly to the company (allow two weeks for delivery). Or you can go online and search the SEC EDGAR database (**http://www.sec.gov/edgar.shtml**), which includes the financial reports of most well-known companies.

Requirements

1. After selecting five companies, examine their income statements to search for the following items:
   a. Net income or net loss
   b. Earnings per share data
2. Study the companies' balance sheets to answer the following questions:
   a. What classes of stock has each company issued?
   b. Which item carries a larger balance—the Common Stock account or Paid-In Capital in Excess of Par (also labeled Additional Paid-In Capital)?
   c. What percentage of each company's total stockholders' equity is made up of retained earnings?
   d. Do any of the companies have treasury stock? If so, how many shares and how much is the cost?
3. Examine each company's statement of stockholders' equity for evidence of the following:
   a. Cash dividends
   b. Stock dividends
   c. Treasury stock purchases and sales

4. As directed by your instructor, either write a report or present your findings to your class. You may not be able to understand *everything* you find, but neither can the Wall Street analysts! You will be amazed at how much you have learned.

> Communication Activity F:13-1

In 75 words or fewer, explain the difference between stock dividends and stock splits. Include the effect on stock values.

> Quick Check Answers

1. b **2.** d **3.** c **4.** c **5.** d **6.** c **7.** c **8.** b **9.** b **10.** d **11.** c

Long-Term Liabilities   14

Should the Business Take on Additional Debt?

Sophie Animations Studios, Inc. specializes in creating animated feature films for children and young-minded adults. The studio was started by founders Steve Lasseter and Lee Bird and has grown to produce many notable films. The corporation's stock is currently sold on a national stock exchange, and the company is widely respected for its consistent earnings each year.

The corporation plans on expanding its existing operations by building a new studio in Canada that will produce short movies and TV specials. In order to fund this expansion, the corporation is considering several options. One option is for the corporation to issue additional stock to raise the necessary cash. Another option is for the corporation to take on additional debt. As majority stockholders, Steve and Lee have expressed their concern over issuing additional shares of stock. The stockholders are concerned that the additional stock will decrease their ownership percentage in the corporation and also cause the market value of the stock to decrease. Due to these concerns, the corporation has decided that the best option would be to explore ways to secure the cash needed for expansion by taking on additional debt.

Sophie Animations Studios is currently evaluating different types of long-term liability options such as long-term notes payable and mortgages payable. These debts will most likely be secured by the studio building and will offer a reasonable interest rate and time period for repayment. In addition, Sophie Animations Studios is considering a special type of long-term liability, called a *bonds payable*. Bonds payable are issued on a bond market and typically provide a larger cash inflow than notes payable and mortgages payable do. In addition, bonds payable also often provide a longer time period for repayment, some even lasting for as long as 100 years. Each of these long-term liabilities is unique and offers advantages and disadvantages that Sophie Animations Studios needs to consider before it can begin the expansion.

Why Issue a 100-Year Bond Payable?

On July 21, 1993, **The Walt Disney Company** issued a long-term liability, specifically called a *bonds payable*, that would be payable in 100 years! These bonds were issued with an annual interest rate of 7.55%, and the principal of approximately $300 million was scheduled to be repaid in the year 2093. The Walt Disney Company is well known as an international family entertainment and media enterprise that includes broadcast networks, parks and resorts, the Walt Disney studios, consumer products, and interactive technology and games. Why would the Walt Disney Company issue a debt that wouldn't be paid back for 100 years? How are these types of long-term liabilities accounted for and reported on the balance sheet? In this chapter, you learn why companies might issue bonds payable and also how to account for other long-term liabilities, such as long-term notes payable and mortgages payable.

Chapter 14 Learning Objectives

1. Journalize transactions for long-term notes payable and mortgages payable
2. Describe bonds payable
3. Journalize transactions for bonds payable and interest expense using the straight-line amortization method
4. Journalize transactions to retire bonds payable
5. Report liabilities on the balance sheet
6. Use the debt to equity ratio to evaluate business performance
7. Use time value of money to compute present value and future value (Appendix 14A)
8. Journalize transactions for bonds payable and interest expense using the effective-interest amortization method (Appendix 14B)

HOW ARE LONG-TERM NOTES PAYABLE AND MORTGAGES PAYABLE ACCOUNTED FOR?

> **Learning Objective 1**
> Journalize transactions for long-term notes payable and mortgages payable

You have learned that **long-term liabilities** are liabilities that do not need to be paid within one year or within the entity's operating cycle, whichever is longer. Both long-term notes payable and mortgages payable are common long-term liabilities.

Long-term Notes Payable

> **Long-term Liability**
> A liability that does not need to be paid within one year or within the entity's operating cycle, whichever is longer.

Long-term notes payable are typically reported in the long-term liabilities section of the balance sheet. You learned about the current portion of long-term notes payable in a previous chapter. Now, let's focus on the long-term portion of the notes payable and the payments made according to the note contract.

Recall that most long-term notes payable are paid in installments. The *current portion of notes payable* is the principal amount that will be paid within one year—a current liability. The remaining portion is long-term. For example, Smart Touch Learning signed a $20,000 note payable on December 31, 2024. The note will be paid over four years with payments of $5,000 plus 6% interest due each December 31, beginning December 31, 2025. Remember that the current portion of the note, the amount due December 31, 2025, $5,000, is considered a current liability at December 31, 2024. We record the issuance of the note on December 31, 2024, in the following manner:

$$\frac{A\uparrow}{Cash\uparrow} \Big\} = \Big\{ \frac{L\uparrow}{Notes\ Payable\uparrow} + E$$

Date	Accounts and Explanation	Debit	Credit
2024			
Dec. 31	Cash	20,000	
	Notes Payable		20,000
	Received cash in exchange for a 4-year, 6% note.		

> **Amortization Schedule**
> A schedule that details each loan payment's allocation between principal and interest and the beginning and ending loan balances.

On December 31, 2025, Smart Touch Learning will make a $5,000 principal payment plus interest. Exhibit F:14-1 shows an **amortization schedule** for the notes payable. An amortization schedule details each loan payment's allocation between principal and interest and also the beginning and ending balances of the loan. Using the calculation for interest that you have already learned, Smart Touch Learning will calculate interest expense as beginning balance × interest rate × time. The total cash payment is the principal payment plus interest expense. Notice that at the end of the four years, Smart Touch Learning will have paid total interest of $3,000. Also notice that the interest expense decreases each year, as this expense is based on the principal, which is decreasing with each installment payment.

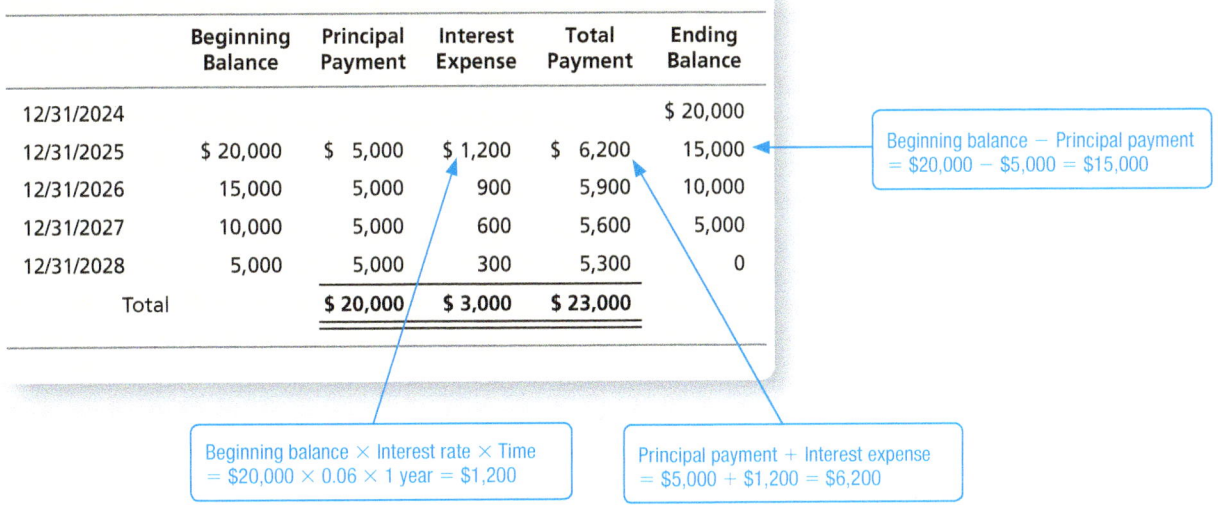

Exhibit F:14-1 | Long-term Notes Payable Amortization Schedule

	Beginning Balance	Principal Payment	Interest Expense	Total Payment	Ending Balance
12/31/2024					$ 20,000
12/31/2025	$ 20,000	$ 5,000	$ 1,200	$ 6,200	15,000
12/31/2026	15,000	5,000	900	5,900	10,000
12/31/2027	10,000	5,000	600	5,600	5,000
12/31/2028	5,000	5,000	300	5,300	0
Total		$ 20,000	$ 3,000	$ 23,000	

Beginning balance − Principal payment = $20,000 − $5,000 = $15,000

Beginning balance × Interest rate × Time = $20,000 × 0.06 × 1 year = $1,200

Principal payment + Interest expense = $5,000 + $1,200 = $6,200

Assume it's now December 31, 2025, and Smart Touch Learning must make its first installment payment of $5,000 principal plus interest on the note. The company's accounting clerk will record the following entry:

Date	Accounts and Explanation	Debit	Credit
2025			
Dec. 31	Notes Payable	5,000	
	Interest Expense	1,200	
	Cash		6,200
	Paid principal and interest payment.		

$$\left.\begin{array}{c} A\downarrow \\ \text{Cash}\downarrow \end{array}\right\} = \left\{\begin{array}{c} L\downarrow \\ \text{Notes} \\ \text{Payable}\downarrow \end{array} + \begin{array}{c} E\downarrow \\ \text{Interest} \\ \text{Expense}\uparrow \end{array}\right.$$

After the December 31, 2025, entry, Smart Touch Learning owes $15,000 ($20,000 original note amount minus the $5,000 principal paid on December 31, 2025). The company will record similar entries for the three remaining payments using the amounts calculated in the amortization schedule.

Mortgages Payable

Mortgages payable include the borrower's promise to transfer the legal title to specific assets if the mortgage isn't paid on schedule. Mortgages payable are a type of long-term notes payable that are secured with specific assets. Like long-term notes payable, the total mortgages payable amount has a portion due within one year (current) and a portion that is due more than one year from the balance sheet date.

Mortgages Payable
Long-term debts that are backed with a security interest in specific property.

14-4 Financial chapter 14

Commonly, mortgages specify a monthly payment of principal and interest to the lender (usually a bank). The most common type of mortgage is on property—for example, a mortgage on your home. Let's review an example.

Assume that on December 31, 2024, Smart Touch Learning purchases a building for $150,000, paying $49,925 in cash and signing a 30-year mortgage for $100,075, taken out at 6% interest that is payable in $600 monthly payments, which includes principal and interest, beginning January 31, 2025. The following entry is used to record this acquisition:

A↑ } = { L↑ } + E
Building↑   Mortgages
Cash↓   Payable↑

Date	Accounts and Explanation	Debit	Credit
2024			
Dec. 31	Building	150,000	
	Mortgages Payable		100,075
	Cash		49,925
	Purchased building with a mortgage payable and cash payment.		

A partial amortization schedule for 2024 and 2025 is shown in Exhibit F:14-2.

Exhibit F:14-2 | **Mortgages Payable Amortization Schedule**

Beginning balance × Interest rate × Time
= $100,075 × 0.06 × 1/12 = $500.38

Total payment − Interest expense
= $600.00 − $500.38 = $99.62

	Beginning Balance	Principal Payment	Interest Expense	Total Payment	Ending Balance
12/31/2024					$ 100,075.00
01/31/2025	$ 100,075.00	$ 99.62	$ 500.38	$ 600.00	99,975.38
02/28/2025	99,975.38	100.12	499.88	600.00	99,875.26
03/31/2025	99,875.26	100.62	499.38	600.00	99,774.64
04/30/2025	99,774.64	101.13	498.87	600.00	99,673.51
05/31/2025	99,673.51	101.63	498.37	600.00	99,571.88
06/30/2025	99,571.88	102.14	497.86	600.00	99,469.74
07/31/2025	99,469.74	102.65	497.35	600.00	99,367.09
08/31/2025	99,367.09	103.16	496.84	600.00	99,263.93
09/30/2025	99,263.93	103.68	496.32	600.00	99,160.25
10/31/2025	99,160.25	104.20	495.80	600.00	99,056.05
11/30/2025	99,056.05	104.72	495.28	600.00	98,951.33
12/31/2025	98,951.33	105.24	494.76	600.00	98,846.09
Total		$ 1,228.91	$ 5,971.09	$ 7,200.00	

Beginning balance − Principal payment
= $100,075.00 − $99.62 = $99,975.38

Notice that as time goes by the portion of the payment applied to principal increases and interest expense decreases.

Long-Term Liabilities Financial 14-5

We can confirm the interest calculations provided in the amortization table. For the first payment, the interest is calculated as $100,075.00 \times 6\% \times 1/12$, or $500.38. The principal of $99.62 is the difference between the monthly payment of $600.00 and the interest expense of $500.38 ($600.00 − $500.38 = $99.62). The $99.62 reduces the mortgages payable from $100,075.00 to $99,975.38 ($100,075.00 − $99.62 = $99,975.38). After reviewing the amortization schedule, Smart Touch Learning records the first mortgage payment as follows:

Date	Accounts and Explanation	Debit	Credit
2025			
Jan. 31	Mortgages Payable	99.62	
	Interest Expense	500.38	
	Cash		600.00
	Paid principal and interest payment.		

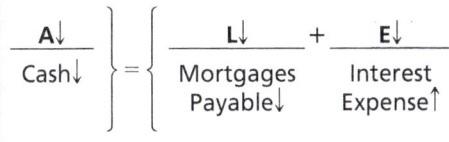

Each mortgage payment will be recorded in a similar journal entry, using the amortization schedule amounts.

Take a moment to review Exhibits F:14-1 and F:14-2. **In Exhibit F:14-1, the principal payment stays the same and the total payment changes. In Exhibit F:14-2, the principal payment varies while the total payment stays the same. Long-term liabilities can be structured either way—with an equal principal payment or equal total payment.** One thing that always changes, though, is the amount of interest expense each period. The amount of interest expense is always calculated on the beginning balance of the loan, and because the beginning balance of the loan is decreasing, the amount of interest expense also decreases.

What is the difference between the mortgages payable amortization schedule and the long-term notes payable amortization schedule?

On January 1, 2024, Fox Corporation signed an $80,000, four-year, 4% note. The loan required Fox to make payments annually on December 31 of $20,000 principal plus interest.

1. Journalize the issuance of the note on January 1, 2024.
2. Journalize the first payment on December 31, 2024.

Check your answers online in MyLab Accounting or at http://www.pearsonhighered.com/Horngren.

For more practice, see Short Exercises S-F:14-1 and S-F:14-2.   MyLab Accounting

WHAT ARE BONDS?

Large companies need large amounts of money to finance their operations. They may take out long-term loans from banks and/or issue bonds payable to the public to raise the money. **Bonds payable** are long-term debts issued to multiple lenders called *bondholders*, usually in increments of $1,000 per bond. For example, a company could borrow $100,000 from one lender (the bank), or it could issue 100 bonds payable, each at $1,000, to 100 different lenders. By issuing bonds payable, companies can borrow millions of dollars from thousands of investors rather than depending on a loan from one single bank or lender. Each investor can buy a specified amount of the company's bonds.

Learning Objective 2
Describe bonds payable

Bond Payable
A long-term debt issued to multiple lenders called *bondholders*, usually in increments of $1,000 per bond.

Each bondholder gets a bond certificate that shows the name of the company that borrowed the money, exactly like a note payable. The certificate states the face value, which is the amount of the bond issue. The bond's face value is also called *maturity value*, *principal*, or *par value*. The company must then pay each bondholder the face value amount at a specific future date, called the *maturity date*.

People buy (invest in) bonds to earn interest. The bond certificate states the interest rate that the company will pay and the dates the interest is due, generally semiannually (twice per year). For example, a five-year, 9% bond issued at a face value of $100,000 on January 1, 2024, will pay 10 semiannual interest payments of $4,500 ($100,000 × 0.09 × 6/12) in addition to the face value payment at the maturity date. The cash flow pattern for this bond is as follows:

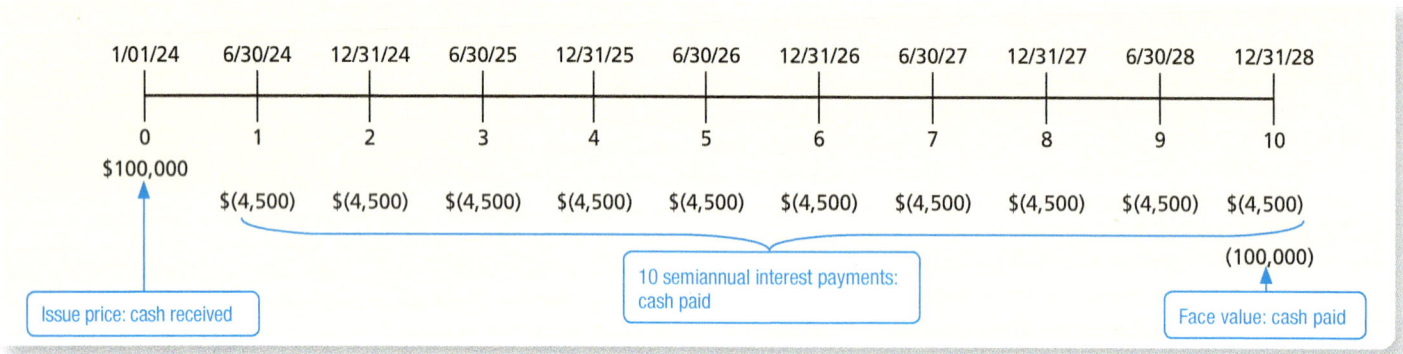

All bond certificates include the following bond fundamentals:

Face Value
The amount a borrower must pay back to the bondholders on the maturity date.

- **Face value**—The amount the borrower must pay back to the bondholders on the maturity date (also called *maturity value*, *principal amount*, or *par value*).
- **Maturity date**—The date on which the borrower must pay the principal amount to the bondholders.
- **Stated interest rate**—The interest rate that determines the amount of cash interest the borrower pays and the investor receives each year (also called *face rate*, *coupon rate*, or *nominal rate*).

Stated Interest Rate
The interest rate that determines the amount of cash interest the borrower pays and the investor receives each year.

Term Bonds
Bonds that all mature at the same time.

Types of Bonds

There are various types of bonds, including the following:

- **Term bonds**—These bonds all mature at the same specified time. For example, $100,000 of term bonds may all mature five years from today.
- **Serial bonds**—Such bonds mature in installments at regular intervals. For example, a $500,000, five-year serial bond may mature in $100,000 annual installments over a five-year period.
- **Secured bonds**—These bonds give the bondholder the right to take specified assets of the issuer if the issuer fails to pay principal or interest.
- **Debentures**—Such bonds are unsecured bonds that are not backed by assets. They are backed only by the creditworthiness of the bond issuer.

Serial Bonds
Bonds that mature in installments at regular intervals.

Secured Bonds
Bonds that give bondholders the right to take specified assets of the issuer if the issuer fails to pay principal or interest.

Debentures
Unsecured bonds backed only by the creditworthiness of the bond issuer.

Long-Term Liabilities Financial 14-7

Bond Prices

A bond can be issued at any price agreed upon by the issuer and the bondholders. A bond can be issued at any of the following:

- **Face value**—Occurs when a bond is issued at face value. Example: A $1,000 bond issued for $1,000.
- **Discount**—A discount on bonds payable occurs when the issue price is less than face value. Example: A $1,000 bond issued for $980. The discount is $20 ($1,000 − $980).
- **Premium**—A premium on bonds payable occurs when the issue price is above face value. Example: A $1,000 bond issued for $1,015. The premium is $15 ($1,015 − $1,000).

> **Discount on Bonds Payable**
> Occurs when a bond's issue price is less than face value.
>
> **Premium on Bonds Payable**
> Occurs when a bond's issue price is more than face value.

The issue price of a bond does not affect the required payment at maturity. In all of the preceding cases, the company must pay the face value of the bonds at the maturity date stated on the face of the bond.

After a bond is issued, investors may buy and sell it through the bond market just as they buy and sell stocks through the stock market. The most well-known bond market is the NYSE Bonds, which lists several thousand bonds.

Bond prices are quoted as a percentage of face value. For example:

- a $1,000 bond quoted at 100 is bought or sold for 100% of face value, $1,000 ($1,000 × 1.00).
- a $1,000 bond quoted at 88.375 is bought or sold for 88.375% of face value, $883.75 ($1,000 × 0.88375).
- a $1,000 bond quoted at 101.5 is bought or sold for 101.5% of face value, $1,015 ($1,000 × 1.015).

The issue price of a bond determines the amount of cash the company receives when it issues the bond. In all cases, the company must pay the bond's face value to retire it at the maturity date.

Exhibit F:14-3 shows example price information for the bonds of Smart Touch Learning. On this particular day, 12 of Smart Touch Learning's 9% bonds maturing in 2027 (indicated by 27) were traded. The bonds' highest price on this day was $795 ($1,000 × 0.795). The lowest price of the day was $784.50 ($1,000 × 0.7845). The closing price (last sale of the day) was $795.

Exhibit F:14-3 | **Bond Price Information**

Bonds	Volume	High	Low	Close
SMT 9% of 27	12	79.5	78.45	79.5

Present Value and Future Value

Money earns interest over time, a fact called the time value of money. Appendix 14A at the end of this chapter covers the time value of money in detail.

Let's see how the time value of money affects bond prices. Assume that a $1,000 bond reaches maturity three years from now and carries no interest. Would you pay $1,000 to purchase this bond? No, because paying $1,000 today to receive $1,000 later yields no interest on your investment. How much would you pay today in order to receive $1,000 in three years? The answer is some amount less than $1,000. Suppose $750 is a fair price. By

> **Time Value of Money**
> Recognition that money earns interest over time.

investing $750 now to receive $1,000 later, you will earn $250 over the three years. The diagram that follows illustrates the relationship between a bond's price (present value) and its maturity amount (future value).

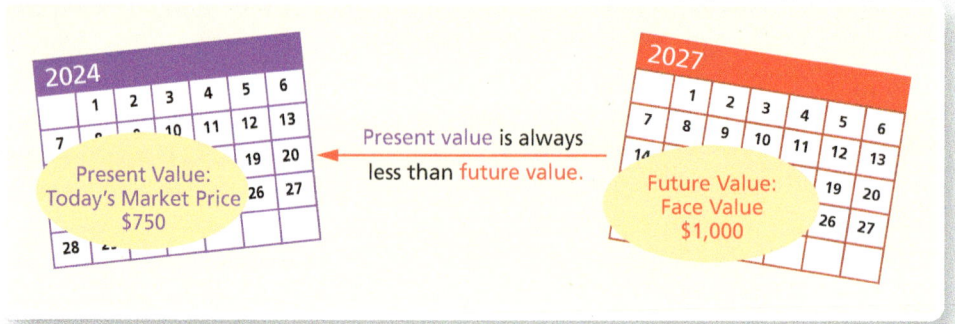

Present Value
The value of an investment today.

The amount that a person would invest *at the present time* is called the **present value**. The present value is the bond's market price. In our example, $750 is the present value (market price of the bond), and the $1,000 face value to be received in three years is the **future value**, the value of the investment at a specific date in the future. We show how to compute the present value and future value in Appendix 14A.

Future Value
The value of an investment at the end of a specific time frame.

Bond Interest Rates

Bonds are sold at their market price (issue price on the date the bonds are first sold), which is the present value of the interest payments the bondholder will receive while holding the bond plus the present value of the bond principal paid at the end of the bond's life. Two interest rates work together to set the price of a bond:

- The stated interest rate determines the amount of cash interest the borrower pays each year. The stated interest rate is printed on the bond certificate and *does not change* from year to year. For example, Smart Touch Learning's 9% bonds payable have a stated interest rate of 9%. Therefore, Smart Touch Learning pays $90 of interest annually on each $1,000 bond. The dollar amount of interest paid is not affected by the issue price of the bond.

Market Interest Rate
The interest rate that investors demand in order to loan their money.

- The **market interest rate** (also known as the *effective interest rate*) is the rate that investors demand to earn for loaning their money. The market interest rate *varies* constantly. A company may issue bonds with a stated interest rate that differs from the market interest rate, due to the time gap between the time the bonds were printed (engraved) showing the stated rate and the actual issuance of the bonds.

Smart Touch Learning may issue its 9% bonds when the market rate has risen to 10%. Will the Smart Touch Learning bonds attract investors in this market? No, because investors can earn 10% on other bonds. Therefore, investors will purchase Smart Touch Learning bonds only at a price *less* than face value. The difference between the lower price and the bonds' face value is a *discount* that will allow the investor to earn 10%, even though Smart Touch Learning's interest checks will be paid at the stated rate of 9%. The difference between what is paid for the bond (less than $1,000) and the bond principal of $1,000 is the interest rate difference between 9% and 10% over the life of the bond.

On the other hand, if the market interest rate is 8%, Smart Touch Learning's 9% bonds will be so attractive that investors will pay more than face value for them because investors will receive more in interest payments than expected. The difference between the higher price and face value is a *premium*. Exhibit F:14-4 shows how the stated interest rate and the market interest rate work together to determine the price of a bond.

Exhibit F:14-4 | Interaction Between Stated Interest Rate, Market Rate, and Price of Bond

Example: Bond with a Stated Interest Rate of 9%

Bond's Stated Interest Rate		Market Interest Rate		Issue Price of Bonds Payable
9%	=	9%	→	Face value of the bond
9%	<	10%	→	Discount (price below face value)
9%	>	8%	→	Premium (price above face value)

Issuing Bonds Versus Issuing Stock

Borrowing by issuing bonds payable carries a risk: The company may be unable to pay off the bonds and the related interest. Why do companies borrow instead of issuing stock? **Debt is a less expensive source of capital than stock, and bonds do not affect the percentage of ownership of the corporation.** Companies face the following decision: How shall we finance a new project—with bonds or with stock?

Suppose Smart Touch Learning has net income of $300,000 and 100,000 shares of common stock outstanding before it begins a new project. Smart Touch Learning needs $500,000 for the project, and the company is considering two plans:

- Plan 1 is to borrow $500,000 at 10% (issue $500,000 of 10% bonds payable).
- Plan 2 is to issue 50,000 shares of common stock for $500,000.

Smart Touch Learning management believes the new cash can be used to increase income before interest and taxes by $200,000 each year. The company estimates income tax expense to be 21%. Exhibit F:14-5 shows the advantage of borrowing as it relates to earnings per share.

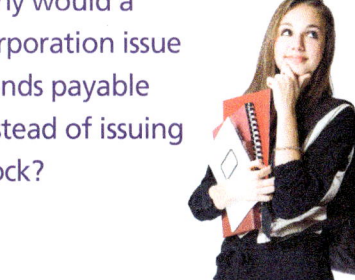

Why would a corporation issue bonds payable instead of issuing stock?

Exhibit F:14-5 | Issuing Bonds Payable Versus Issuing Common Stock

	Plan 1: Issue $500,000 of 10% Bonds Payable		Plan 2: Issue $500,000 of Common Stock	
Net income before new project		$ 300,000		$ 300,000
Expected income on the new project before interest and income tax expenses	$ 200,000		$ 200,000	
Less: Interest expense ($500,000 × 0.10)	50,000		0	
Project income before income tax	150,000		200,000	
Less: Income tax expense (21%)	31,500		42,000	
Project net income		118,500		158,000
Net income with new project		$ 418,500		$ 458,000
Earnings per share with new project:				
Plan 1 ($418,500 / 100,000 shares)		$ 4.19		
Plan 2 ($458,000 / 150,000 shares)				$ 3.05

14-10 Financial  chapter 14

The earnings per share of stock is higher if Smart Touch Learning issues bonds. If all goes well, the company can earn more on the new project ($118,500) than the interest it pays on the bonds ($50,000). Earning more income on borrowed money than the related interest expense is called **financial leverage**. It is widely used to increase earnings per share of common stock. Notice that, even though net income is higher under Plan 2, the earnings per share is lower. Why? Because the earnings must be shared among 50,000 more shares of stock.

Borrowing can increase the earnings per share, but borrowing has its disadvantages. Debts must be paid during unprofitable years as well as profitable years. A company might not have enough cash flow to make the interest payment, thereby defaulting on the debt. Unlike cash dividends, which are optional payments to stockholders, the interest payments on bonds payable are required. Without the cash necessary to make the interest payments, a company could have to declare bankruptcy.

> **Financial Leverage**
> Occurs when a company earns more income on borrowed money than the related interest expense.

Try It!

Determine whether the following bonds payable will be issued at face value, at a premium, or at a discount:

3. A 10% bonds payable is issued when the market interest rate is 8%.
4. A 10% bonds payable is issued when the market interest rate is 10%.
5. A 10% bonds payable is issued when the market interest rate is 12%.

Check your answers online in MyLab Accounting or at http://www.pearsonhighered.com/Horngren.

For more practice, see Short Exercises S-F:14-3 and S-F:14-4. **MyLab Accounting**

HOW ARE BONDS PAYABLE ACCOUNTED FOR USING THE STRAIGHT-LINE AMORTIZATION METHOD?

> **Learning Objective 3**
> Journalize transactions for bonds payable and interest expense using the straight-line amortization method

The basic journal entry to record the issuance of bonds payable debits Cash and credits Bonds Payable. As noted previously, a company may issue bonds, a long-term liability, at *face value*, at a *discount*, or at a *premium*. We begin with the simplest case—issuing bonds payable at face value.

Issuing Bonds Payable at Face Value

Smart Touch Learning has $100,000 of 9% bonds payable that mature in five years. The company issues these bonds at face value on January 1, 2024. The issuance entry is as follows:

$$\frac{A\uparrow}{\text{Cash}\uparrow} \Big\} = \Big\{ \frac{L\uparrow}{\text{Bonds Payable}\uparrow} + E$$

Date	Accounts and Explanation	Debit	Credit
2024			
Jan. 1	Cash	100,000	
	Bonds Payable		100,000
	Issued bonds at face value.		

Long-Term Liabilities Financial 14-11

Smart Touch Learning, the borrower, makes this one-time journal entry to record the receipt of cash and issuance of bonds payable. Semiannual interest payments occur each June 30 and December 31. Smart Touch Learning's first semiannual interest payment is journalized as follows:

Date	Accounts and Explanation	Debit	Credit
2024			
Jun. 30	Interest Expense ($100,000 × 0.09 × 6/12)	4,500	
	Cash		4,500
	Paid semiannual interest on bonds payable.		

$$\frac{A\downarrow}{Cash\downarrow} \bigg\} = \bigg\{ \frac{L}{} + \frac{E\downarrow}{Interest\ Expense\uparrow}$$

Each semiannual interest payment follows this same pattern.

Issuing Bonds Payable at a Discount

Now let's see how to issue bonds payable at a discount. This is one of the most common situations.

We know that market conditions may force a company such as Smart Touch Learning to accept a discounted price for its bonds. Suppose Smart Touch Learning issues $100,000 of its 9%, five-year bonds that pay interest semiannually when the market interest rate is 10%. The market price of the bonds drops to 96.149, which means 96.149% of face value. Smart Touch Learning receives $96,149 ($100,000 × 0.96149) at issuance and makes the following journal entry:

Date	Accounts and Explanation	Debit	Credit
2024			
Jan. 1	Cash	96,149	
	Discount on Bonds Payable ($100,000 − $96,149)	3,851	
	Bonds Payable		100,000
	Issued bonds at a discount.		

$$\frac{A\uparrow}{Cash\uparrow} \bigg\} = \bigg\{ \frac{L\uparrow}{Bonds\ Payable\uparrow\ Discount\ on\ Bonds\ Payable\uparrow} + \frac{E}{}$$

After posting, the bond accounts have the following balances:

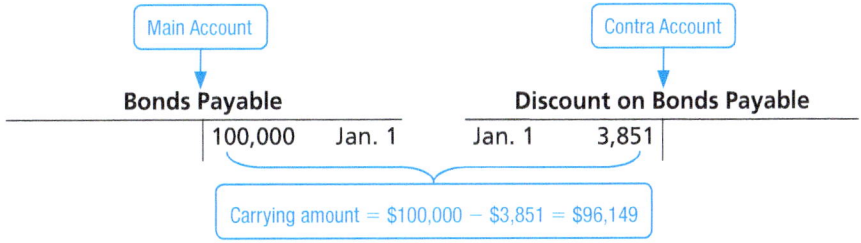

Carrying Amount of Bonds
A bond payable *minus* the discount account current balance or *plus* the premium account current balance.

Discount on Bonds Payable is a contra account to Bonds Payable. Bonds Payable *minus* the discount gives the **carrying amount of bonds** (also known as *carrying value*). Smart Touch Learning would report these bonds payable on the balance sheet as follows immediately after issuance:

Long-term Liabilities:		
Bonds Payable	$100,000	
Less: Discount on Bonds Payable	(3,851)	$96,149

Interest Expense on Bonds Payable Issued at a Discount

In this case, we see that a bond's stated interest rate differs from the market interest rate. The market rate was 10% when Smart Touch Learning issued its 9% bonds. This 1% interest rate difference created the $3,851 discount on the bonds. Smart Touch Learning needed to offer this discount because investors were willing to pay only $96,149 for the $100,000, 9% bonds when they could earn 10% on other bonds.

Smart Touch Learning borrowed $96,149 but still must pay $100,000 when the bonds mature five years later. What happens to the $3,851 discount? The discount is additional interest expense to Smart Touch Learning. The discount raises Smart Touch Learning's true interest expense on the bonds to the market interest rate of 10%. The discount becomes interest expense for Smart Touch Learning through a process called *amortization*, the gradual reduction of an item over time.

Straight-Line Amortization of Bond Discount

Straight-Line Amortization Method
An amortization method that allocates an equal amount of bond discount or premium to each interest period over the life of the bond.

We can amortize a bond discount by dividing it into equal amounts for each interest period. This is called the **straight-line amortization method**. It works very much like the straight-line depreciation method we discussed in the Plant Assets chapter. In our example, the initial discount is $3,851 and there are 10 semiannual interest periods during the bonds' five-year life (5 year life × 2 interest payments per year). Therefore, 1/10 of the $3,851 bond discount ($385) is amortized each interest period. Smart Touch Learning's first semi-annual interest entry is as follows:

$$\frac{A\downarrow}{Cash\downarrow} = \left\{ \frac{L\uparrow}{\text{Discount on Bonds Payable}\downarrow} + \frac{E\downarrow}{\text{Interest Expense}\uparrow} \right.$$

Date	Accounts and Explanation	Debit	Credit
2024			
Jun. 30	Interest Expense ($4,500 + $385)	4,885	
	Discount on Bonds Payable ($3,851 × 1/10)		385
	Cash ($100,000 × 0.09 × 6/12)		4,500
	Paid semiannual interest and amortized discount.		

Interest expense of $4,885 for each six-month period is the sum of the following:

- Stated interest ($4,500, which is paid in cash)
- The amortization of discount, $385

This same entry would be made again on December 31, 2024. The bond discount balance would be $3,081 on December 31, 2024.

Bonds Payable		Discount on Bonds Payable			
	100,000 Jan. 1	Jan. 1	3,851	385	Jun. 30
				385	Dec. 31
		Bal.	3,081		

How would the balance of Bonds Payable be reported on the December 31, 2024 balance sheet?

Long-term Liabilities:		
Bonds Payable	$100,000	
Less: Discount on Bonds Payable	(3,081)	$96,919

Discount on Bonds Payable has a debit balance. Therefore, we credit the Discount on Bonds Payable account to amortize (reduce) its balance. Ten amortization entries will decrease the discount to zero (with rounding). Then the carrying amount of the bonds payable will be $100,000 at maturity—$100,000 in Bonds Payable minus $0 in Discount on Bonds Payable. Exhibit F:14-6 shows the amortization schedule of the bond.

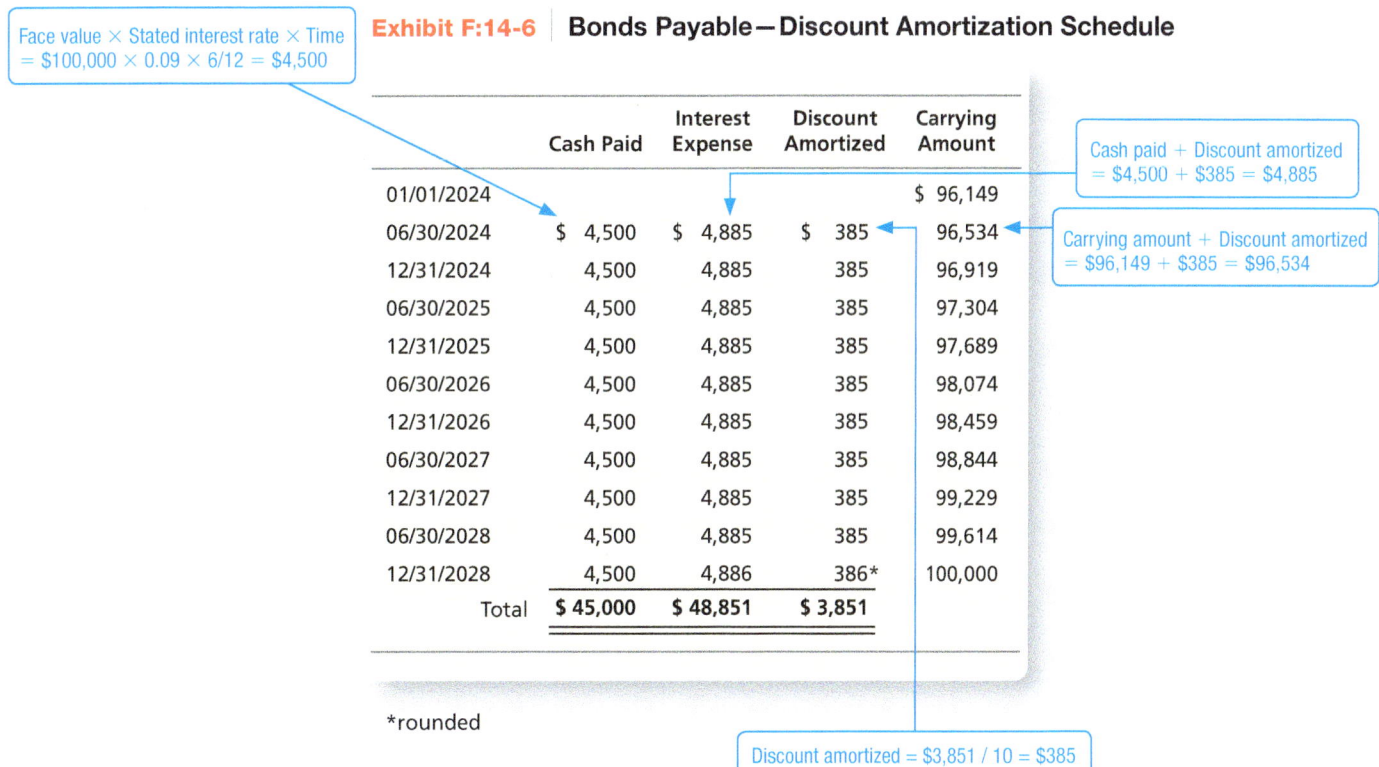

Exhibit F:14-6 | Bonds Payable—Discount Amortization Schedule

	Cash Paid	Interest Expense	Discount Amortized	Carrying Amount
01/01/2024				$ 96,149
06/30/2024	$ 4,500	$ 4,885	$ 385	96,534
12/31/2024	4,500	4,885	385	96,919
06/30/2025	4,500	4,885	385	97,304
12/31/2025	4,500	4,885	385	97,689
06/30/2026	4,500	4,885	385	98,074
12/31/2026	4,500	4,885	385	98,459
06/30/2027	4,500	4,885	385	98,844
12/31/2027	4,500	4,885	385	99,229
06/30/2028	4,500	4,885	385	99,614
12/31/2028	4,500	4,886	386*	100,000
Total	$ 45,000	$ 48,851	$ 3,851	

Face value × Stated interest rate × Time = $100,000 × 0.09 × 6/12 = $4,500

Cash paid + Discount amortized = $4,500 + $385 = $4,885

Carrying amount + Discount amortized = $96,149 + $385 = $96,534

Discount amortized = $3,851 / 10 = $385

*rounded

14-14 Financial chapter 14

Issuing Bonds Payable at a Premium

To illustrate a bond premium, let's change the Smart Touch Learning example. Assume that the market interest rate is 8% when Smart Touch Learning issues its 9%, five-year bonds. These 9% bonds are attractive in an 8% market, and investors will pay a premium to acquire them. Assume the bonds are priced at 104.1 (104.1% of face value). In that case, Smart Touch Learning receives $104,100 cash upon issuance. Smart Touch Learning's entry to borrow money and issue these bonds is as follows:

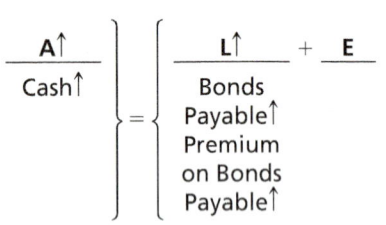

Date	Accounts and Explanation	Debit	Credit
2024			
Jan. 1	Cash	104,100	
	Premium on Bonds Payable ($104,100 − $100,000)		4,100
	Bonds Payable		100,000
	Issued bonds at a premium.		

After posting, the bond accounts have the following balances:

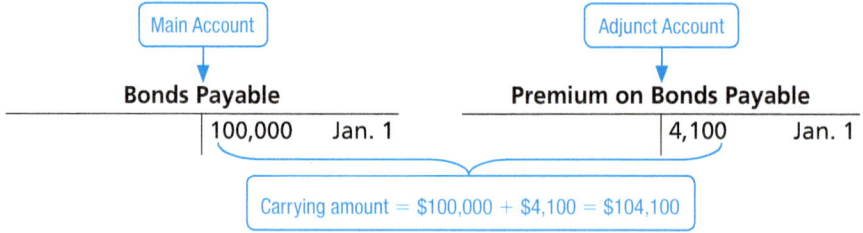

Adjunct Account
An account that is directly related to another account. Adjunct accounts have the same normal balance as the related account and are added to the related account on the balance sheet.

The Bonds Payable account and the Premium on Bonds Payable account each carry a credit balance. The premium is an adjunct account to Bonds Payable. **Adjunct accounts** have the same normal balance as the related account and are added to the related account on the balance sheet. Adjunct accounts work similarly to contra accounts—the only difference is that the adjunct account has the same type of balance as the main account, whereas the contra account has the opposite type of balance of its main account. Therefore, we add the Premium on Bonds Payable to Bonds Payable to determine the bonds' carrying amount. Smart Touch Learning would report these bonds payable on the balance sheet as follows immediately after issuance:

Long-term Liabilities:		
Bonds Payable	$100,000	
Add: Premium on Bonds Payable	4,100	$104,100

Interest Expense on Bonds Payable Issued at a Premium

The 1% difference between the bonds' 9% stated interest rate and the 8% market rate creates the $4,100 premium ($104,100 − $100,000 face value). Smart Touch Learning borrows $104,100 but must pay back only $100,000 at maturity. The premium is like a saving of interest expense to Smart Touch Learning. The premium cuts Smart Touch Learning's cost of borrowing and reduces interest expense to 8%, the market rate. The amortization of bond premium decreases interest expense over the life of the bonds.

Straight-Line Amortization of Bond Premium

In our example, the beginning premium is $4,100 and there are 10 semiannual interest periods during the bonds' five-year life. Therefore, 1/10 of the $4,100 ($410) of bond premium is amortized each interest period. Smart Touch Learning's first semiannual interest entry is as follows:

Date	Accounts and Explanation	Debit	Credit
2024			
Jun. 30	Interest Expense ($4,500 − $410)	4,090	
	Premium on Bonds Payable ($4,100 × 1/10)	410	
	Cash ($100,000 × 0.09 × 6/12)		4,500
	Paid semiannual interest and amortized premium.		

$$A\downarrow \atop Cash\downarrow \Bigg\} = \Bigg\{ {L\downarrow \atop Premium\ on\ Bonds\ Payable\downarrow} + {E\downarrow \atop Interest\ Expense\uparrow}$$

Interest expense of $4,090 is

- Stated interest ($4,500, which is paid in cash)
- *Minus* the amortization of the premium of $410

This same entry would be made again on December 31, 2024. The bond premium balance would be $3,280 on December 31, 2024.

Bonds Payable		Premium on Bonds Payable			
	100,000 Jan. 1	Jun. 30	410	4,100	Jan. 1
		Dec. 31	410		
				3,280	Bal.

At December 31, 2024, immediately after amortizing the bond premium, the bonds have the following carrying amount:

Long-term Liabilities:		
Bonds Payable	$100,000	
Add: Premium on Bonds Payable	3,280	$103,280

At maturity on December 31, 2028, the bond premium will have been fully amortized (it will have a zero balance), and the bonds' carrying amount will be $100,000 (the amount in the Bonds Payable account). Exhibit F:14-7 (on the next page) shows the amortization schedule of the bond.

Exhibit F:14-7 | Bonds Payable—Premium Amortization Schedule

Face value × Stated interest rate × Time
= $100,000 × 0.09 × 6/12 = $4,500

	Cash Paid	Interest Expense	Premium Amortized	Carrying Amount
01/01/2024				$104,100
06/30/2024	$4,500	$4,090	$410	103,690
12/31/2024	4,500	4,090	410	103,280
06/30/2025	4,500	4,090	410	102,870
12/31/2025	4,500	4,090	410	102,460
06/30/2026	4,500	4,090	410	102,050
12/31/2026	4,500	4,090	410	101,640
06/30/2027	4,500	4,090	410	101,230
12/31/2027	4,500	4,090	410	100,820
06/30/2028	4,500	4,090	410	100,410
12/31/2028	4,500	4,090	410	100,000
Total	$45,000	$40,900	$4,100	

Carrying amount − Premium amortized = $104,100 − $410 = $103,690

Cash paid − Premium amortized = $4,500 − $410 = $4,090

Premium amortized = $4,100 / 10 = $410

Schmidt Company issued $100,000, 4%, 10-year bonds payable at 98 on January 1, 2024.

6. Journalize the issuance of the bonds payable on January 1, 2024.
7. Journalize the payment of semiannual interest and amortization of the bond discount or premium (using the straight-line amortization method) on July 1, 2024.
8. Assume the bonds payable was instead issued at 106. Journalize the issuance of the bonds payable and the payment of the first semiannual interest and amortization of the bond discount or premium.

Check your answers online in MyLab Accounting or at http://www.pearsonhighered.com/Horngren.

For more practice, see Short Exercises S-F:14-5 through S-F:14-8. **MyLab Accounting**

HOW IS THE RETIREMENT OF BONDS PAYABLE ACCOUNTED FOR?

Learning Objective 4
Journalize transactions to retire bonds payable

Retirement of bonds payable involves paying the face value of the bond. Bonds can be retired at the maturity date or before.

Retirement of Bonds at Maturity

When the bond is matured, the carrying value always equals the face value. In the case of Smart Touch Learning, with both the discount and premium examples, on December 31, 2028, the carrying amount and face value are $100,000. The entry to retire the bonds, assuming the last interest payment has already been recorded, is as follows:

Date	Accounts and Explanation	Debit	Credit
2028			
Dec. 31	Bonds Payable	100,000	
	Cash		100,000
	Retired bonds payable at maturity.		

$$\left.\begin{array}{c} A\downarrow \\ \text{Cash}\downarrow \end{array}\right\} = \left\{\begin{array}{c} L\downarrow \\ \text{Bonds} \\ \text{Payable}\downarrow \end{array} + E\right.$$

Retirement of Bonds Before Maturity

Normally, companies wait until maturity to pay off, or *retire*, their bonds payable. But companies sometimes retire their bonds prior to maturity. The main reason for retiring bonds early is to relieve the pressure of paying the interest payments.

Some bonds are **callable**, which means the company may *call*, or pay off, the bonds at a specified price. The call price is usually 100 or a few percentage points above face value, perhaps 101 or 102, to provide an incentive to the bondholder. Callable bonds give the issuer the flexibility to pay off the bonds when it benefits the company. The Walt Disney Company 100-year bond, discussed at the beginning of this chapter, is supposed to be paid off in 2093, but Disney can call the bonds any time after 2023. This would allow Disney to pay off the bond earlier, which would reduce the company's long-term liability and reduce the amount paid in interest expense. An alternative to calling the bonds is to purchase any available bonds in the open market at their current market price. Whether the bonds are called or purchased in the open market, the same accounts are used in the journal entry.

Callable Bonds
Bonds that the issuer may call and pay off at a specified price whenever the issuer wants.

Suppose on December 31, 2024, Smart Touch Learning has $100,000 of bonds payable outstanding with a remaining discount balance of $3,081 (the original discount of $3,851 on January 1, 2024 [$100,00 − $96,149], less the straight-line amortization of $385 in June and December of 2024 [$3,851 − $385 − $385]).

Lower interest rates have convinced management to pay off these bonds now. These bonds are callable at 100. If the market price of the bonds is 95, should Smart Touch Learning call the bonds at 100 or purchase them in the open market at 95? The market price is lower than the call price, so Smart Touch Learning should buy the bonds on the open market at their market price. Retiring the bonds on December 31, 2024, at 95 results in a gain of $1,919, computed as follows:

Face value of the bonds being retired	$ 100,000
Less: Discount	(3,081)
Carrying amount of bonds payable	96,919
Less: Market price paid to retire the bonds	(95,000)
Gain on retirement of bonds payable	$ 1,919

14-18 Financial chapter 14

The following entry records retirement of the bonds, immediately after the December 31, 2024, interest payment:

A↓ Cash↓ = L↓ Bonds Payable↓ Discount on Bonds Payable↓ + E↑ Gain on Retirement of Bonds Payable↑

Date	Accounts and Explanation	Debit	Credit
2024			
Dec. 31	Bonds Payable	100,000	
	Discount on Bonds Payable		3,081
	Gain on Retirement of Bonds Payable		1,919
	Cash		95,000
	Retired bonds payable prior to maturity.		

After posting, the bond accounts have zero balances.

Bonds Payable				Discount on Bonds Payable			
		100,000	Jan. 1	Jan. 1	3,851	385	Jun. 30
Dec. 31	100,000					385	Dec. 31
		0	Bal.			3,081	Dec. 31
				Bal.	0		

The journal entry removes the bonds from the books and records a gain on retirement. If the bonds being retired have a premium rather than a discount, any existing premium would be removed with a debit. If Smart Touch Learning retired only half of these bonds, it would remove only half the discount or premium.

When retiring bonds before maturity, follow these steps:

1. Record partial-period amortization of discount or premium and partial-period interest payment if the retirement date does not fall on an interest payment date.
2. Remove the portion of unamortized Discount or Premium that relates to the bonds being retired.
3. Debit Bonds Payable at face value.
4. Credit a gain or debit a loss on retirement.
5. Credit Cash for amount paid to retire the bonds.

9. Herrera Corporation issued a $400,000, 4.5%, 10-year bond payable on January 1, 2024. Journalize the payment of the bond payable at maturity. (Give the date.)

Check your answer online in MyLab Accounting or at http://www.pearsonhighered.com/Horngren.

For more practice, see Short Exercises S-F:14-9 and S-F:14-10. MyLab Accounting

HOW ARE LIABILITIES REPORTED ON THE BALANCE SHEET?

Learning Objective 5
Report liabilities on the balance sheet

At the end of each period, a company reports all of its current and long-term liabilities on the balance sheet. As we have seen throughout the textbook, there are two categories of liabilities: current and long-term. Exhibit F:14-8 shows Smart Touch Learning's liabilities portion of its balance sheet (amounts assumed) that we have discussed up to this point.

Exhibit F:14-8 | Liabilities

SMART TOUCH LEARNING
Balance Sheet (Partial)
December 31, 2024

Liabilities

Current Liabilities:			
Accounts Payable		$ 12,620	
Employee Income Taxes Payable		2,000	
FICA—OASDI Taxes Payable		1,158	
FICA—Medicare Taxes Payable		855	
Employee Health Insurance Payable		180	
United Way Payable		20	
Federal Unemployment Taxes Payable		15	
State Unemployment Taxes Payable		60	
Employee Bonus Payable		1,000	
Vacation Benefits Payable		800	
Income Tax Payable		3,780	
Sales Tax Payable		600	
Estimated Warranty Payable		700	
Notes Payable (short-term)		400	
Current Portion of Mortgage Payable		1,305	
Current Portion of Long-term Notes Payable		5,000	
Total Current Liabilities			$ 30,493
Long-term Liabilities:			
Notes Payable		15,000	
Mortgage Payable		97,541	
Bonds Payable	$ 100,000		
Less: Discount on Bonds Payable	(3,081)	96,919	
Total Long-term Liabilities			209,460
Total Liabilities			**$ 239,953**

TYING IT ALL TOGETHER

The Walt Disney Company is a diversified entertainment company that is comprised of the following different business segments: media networks (cable and broadcast television), parks and resorts (various Walt Disney Resorts), studio entertainment (motion pictures), and consumer products and interactive media (merchandise and multi-platform games). Walt Disney began as a cartoon studio in 1920 and today is known as a leading worldwide entertainment provider. (You can find the Walt Disney Company's 2018 annual report at **https://www.sec.gov/Archives/edgar/data/1001039/000100103918000187/fy2018_q4x10k.htm**)

What are the different types of long-term debt that The Walt Disney Company reports on its balance sheet?

As of September 29, 2018, The Walt Disney Company reports borrowings ($17,084 million), deferred income taxes ($3,109 million), other long-term liabilities ($6,590 million), and redeemable noncontrolling interests ($1,123 million) for total long-term debt of $27,906 million.

In order for a borrowing to be listed as long-term, it must be owed in more than one year. Where do companies, such as Walt Disney, report the current portion of long-term debt?

The current portion of long-term debt should be reported in the current liabilities section of the balance sheet. For example, The Walt Disney Company reports $3,790 million of current portion of long-term borrowings.

14-20 Financial   chapter 14

10. Weaver Corporation includes the following selected accounts in its general ledger at December 31, 2024:

Notes Payable (long-term)	$ 75,000	Interest Payable (due next year)	$ 720
Bonds Payable (long-term)	195,000	Sales Tax Payable	480
Accounts Payable	20,400	Premium on Bonds Payable	5,850
Salaries Payable	1,680	Estimated Warranty Payable	1,080

Prepare the liabilities section of Weaver Corporation's balance sheet at December 31, 2024.

Check your answer online in MyLab Accounting or at http://www.pearsonhighered.com/Horngren.

For more practice, see Short Exercise S-F:14-11. MyLab Accounting

HOW DO WE USE THE DEBT TO EQUITY RATIO TO EVALUATE BUSINESS PERFORMANCE?

Learning Objective 6
Use the debt to equity ratio to evaluate business performance

Debt to Equity Ratio
A ratio that measures the proportion of total liabilities relative to total equity. Total liabilities / Total equity.

The relationship between total liabilities and total equity—called the **debt to equity ratio**—shows the proportion of total liabilities relative to the total equity. Thus, this ratio measures financial leverage. If the debt to equity ratio is greater than 1, then the company is financing more assets with debt than with equity. If the ratio is less than 1, then the company is financing more assets with equity than with debt. The higher the debt to equity ratio, the greater the company's financial risk.

Kohl's Corporation reported total liabilities and total equity (in millions) on its Fiscal 2018 Annual Report as follows:

	February 2, 2019	February 3, 2018
Total liabilities	$ 6,942	$ 7,970
Total equity	5,527	5,419

Kohl's debt to equity ratio as of February 2, 2019 (2018 fiscal year), and February 3, 2018 (2017 fiscal year), can be calculated as follows:

Debt to equity ratio = Total liabilities / Total equity
2018 = $6,942 / $5,527
       = 1.26
2017 = $7,970 / $5,419
       = 1.47

Kohl's debt to equity ratio as of February 2, 2019, is above 1, indicating that the company is financing more assets with debt than with equity. Notice that its debt to equity ratio decreased from 2017 to 2018, when Kohl's had a debt to equity ratio of 1.47. Kohl's debt to equity ratios for both years indicate the company is taking advantage of financial leverage but is at a higher risk of defaulting on its debt and interest payments than a company that finances assets with less debt and more equity.

ETHICS

Should additional debt be issued?

Phillip Mader is president and majority stockholder of Knightly Corporation. Phillip owns 54% of the stock in the corporation. The corporation is in dire need of additional cash inflow in order to maintain operations. Phillip is urging the board of directors to issue additional debt even though he knows that the corporation already has a substantial amount of debt. Phillip is well aware that by issuing additional debt, the corporation's debt to equity ratio will increase significantly. He believes this will negatively affect the corporation's credit rating and will further limit the company's ability to borrow at low interest rates in the future. Phillip, however, believes all of this is offset by his desire to retain control of the corporation. If the corporation doesn't issue additional debt, it will be forced to issue stock in order to obtain the necessary funds. Phillip does not have the ability to purchase any of the additional shares of stock, and he knows that he will lose his majority stockholder status. What should Phillip do? What would you do?

Solution

Phillip's overall ethical responsibility lies with the good of the company over what is best for him. In urging the corporation to issue additional debt, he is putting his needs and desires above the best interests of the corporation and other stockholders. Phillip is aware that by issuing additional debt the corporation will be negatively affected. He should urge the board to issue stock—even though he will not gain personally from the situation. His leadership role as president of the corporation should take precedence over his role as majority stockholder.

11. Payne Corporation has the following accounts as of December 31, 2024:

Total Assets	$ 60,000
Total Liabilities	20,000
Total Equity	40,000

Compute the debt to equity ratio at December 31, 2024.

Check your answer online in MyLab Accounting or at http://www.pearsonhighered.com/Horngren.

For more practice, see Short Exercise S-F:14-12. MyLab Accounting

APPENDIX 14A: The Time Value of Money

WHAT IS THE TIME VALUE OF MONEY, AND HOW ARE PRESENT VALUE AND FUTURE VALUE CALCULATED?

A dollar received today is worth more than a dollar to be received in the future because you can invest today's dollar and earn additional interest so you'll have more cash next year. The fact that invested cash earns interest over time is called the *time value of money*. This concept explains why we would prefer to receive cash sooner rather than later. The time value of money is used to determine the present value of a bond—its market price.

Learning Objective 7

Use time value of money to compute present value and future value

Time Value of Money Concepts

The time value of money depends on these key factors:

1. The principal amount (p)
2. The number of periods (n)
3. The interest rate (i)

Annuity
A stream of equal cash payments made at equal time intervals.

The principal (p) refers to the amount of the investment or borrowing. We state the principal as either a single lump sum or an annuity. For example, if you win the lottery, you have the choice of receiving all the winnings now (a single lump sum) or receiving a series of equal payments for a period of time in the future (an annuity). An **annuity** is a stream of *equal cash payments* made at *equal time intervals*.[1] For example, $100 cash received per month for 12 months is an annuity.

The number of periods (n) is the length of time from the beginning of the investment or borrowing until termination. All else being equal, the shorter the investment or borrowing period, the lower the total amount of interest earned or paid. If you withdraw your savings after four years rather than five years, you will earn less interest. For bonds, the number of periods is the number of interest payments made. For example, if a five-year bond pays interest semiannually, the number of periods will be 10 (5 years × 2 payments per year).

The interest rate (i) is the percentage earned on the investment or paid on the borrowing and can be stated annually or in days, months, or quarters. The interest rate must reflect the number of time periods in the year. A five-year semiannual bond that has an annual market interest rate of 10% will reflect a market interest rate of 5% semiannually (10% per year / 2 periods per year). Interest can be computed as either simple interest or compound interest.

Simple Interest Versus Compound Interest

Simple Interest
Interest calculated only on the principal amount.

Compound Interest
Interest calculated on the principal and on all previously earned interest.

Simple interest means that interest is calculated *only* on the principal amount. **Compound interest** means that interest is calculated on the principal *and* on all previously earned interest. *Compound interest assumes that all interest earned will remain invested and earn additional interest at the same interest rate.* Exhibit F:14A-1 compares simple interest of 6% on a five-year, $10,000 investment with interest compounded yearly (rounded to the nearest dollar). As you can see, the amount of compound interest earned yearly grows as the base on which it is calculated (principal plus cumulative interest to date) grows. Over the life of this investment, the total amount of compound interest is more than the total amount of simple interest. Most investments yield compound interest, so we assume compound interest, rather than simple interest, for this chapter.

Exhibit F:14A-1 | Simple Interest Versus Compound Interest—$10,000 at 6% for 5 Years

Year	Simple Interest Calculation	Simple Interest	Compound Interest Calculation	Compound Interest
1	$10,000 × 6%	$ 600	$10,000 × 6%	$ 600
2	$10,000 × 6%	600	($10,000 + $600) × 6%	636
3	$10,000 × 6%	600	($10,000 + $600 + $636) × 6%	674*
4	$10,000 × 6%	600	($10,000 + $600 + $636 + $674) × 6%	715
5	$10,000 × 6%	600	($10,000 + $600 + $636 + $674 + $715) × 6%	758
	Total interest	$ 3,000	Total interest	$ 3,383

*all calculations rounded to the nearest dollar for the rest of this chapter

---

[1] An *ordinary annuity* is an annuity in which the installments occur at the *end* of each period. An *annuity due* is an annuity in which the installments occur at the beginning of each period. Throughout this chapter, we use ordinary annuities.

Future Value and Present Value Factors

The future value or present value of an investment simply refers to the value of an investment at different points in time. We can calculate the future value or present value of any investment by knowing (or assuming) information about the three factors we listed earlier: (1) the principal amount, (2) number of periods, and (3) the interest rate. For example, in Exhibit F:14A-1, we calculated the interest that would be earned on (1) a $10,000 principal, (2) invested for five years, (3) at 6% interest. The future value of the investment is simply its worth at the end of a specific time frame (for example, five years), or the original principal *plus* the interest earned. In our example, the future value of the investment is as follows:

$$\text{Future value} = \text{Principal} + \text{Interest earned}$$
$$= \$10{,}000 + \$3{,}383$$
$$= \$13{,}383$$

If we invest $10,000 *today*, its *present value* is simply $10,000. Present value is the value of an investment today. So another way of stating the future value is as follows:

$$\text{Future value} = \text{Present value} + \text{Interest earned}$$

If we know the future value and want to find the present value, we can rearrange the equation as follows:

$$\text{Present value} = \text{Future value} - \text{Interest earned}$$
$$\$10{,}000 = \$13{,}383 - \$3{,}383$$

The only difference between present value and future value is the amount of interest that is earned in the intervening time span.

Calculating each period's compound interest, as we did in Exhibit F:14A-1, and then adding it to the present value to determine the future value (or subtracting it from the future value to determine the present value) is tedious. Fortunately, mathematical formulas have been developed that specify future values and present values for unlimited combinations of interest rates (i) and time periods (n). Separate formulas exist for single lump sum investments and annuities.

These formulas are programmed into most business calculators, so the user only needs to correctly enter the principal amount, interest rate, and number of time periods to find present or future values. These formulas are also programmed into spreadsheet functions in Microsoft Excel. Using Excel to calculate present values is illustrated in the Capital Investment Decisions chapter of the Managerial Chapters book. In this chapter, we use present value tables. The present value tables contain the results of the formulas for various interest rate and time period combinations.

The formulas and resulting tables are shown in Appendix A at the end of this book:

1. Present Value of $1 (Appendix A, Table A-1)—used to calculate the value today of one future amount (a lump sum)
2. Present Value of Ordinary Annuity of $1 (Appendix A, Table A-2)—used to calculate the value today of a series of equal future amounts (annuities)
3. Future Value of $1 (Appendix A, Table A-3)—used to calculate the value in the future of one present amount (a lump sum)
4. Future Value of Ordinary Annuity of $1 (Appendix A, Table A-4)—used to calculate the value in the future of a series of equal future amounts (annuities)

Take a moment to look at these tables because we are going to use them throughout the rest of the appendix. Note that the columns are interest rates (*i*) and the rows are periods (*n*).

The numbers in each table, known as present value factors (PV factors) and future value factors (FV factors), are for an investment (or loan) of $1. For example, in Appendix A, Table A-1, the PV factor for interest rate of 6% (*i* = 6%) and 5 periods (*n* = 5) is 0.747. To find the present value of an amount other than $1, multiply the PV factor by the future amount.

The annuity tables are derived from the lump sum tables. For example, the Annuity PV factors (in the Present Value of Ordinary Annuity of $1 table) are the *sums* of the PV factors found in the Present Value of $1 tables for a given number of time periods. The annuity tables allow us to perform one-step calculations rather than separately computing the present value of each annual cash installment and then summing the individual present values or future values.

Present Value of a Lump Sum

The process for calculating present values is often called *discounting future cash flows* because future amounts are discounted (interest removed) to their present value. Let's consider the investment in Exhibit F:14A-1. The future value of the investment is $13,383. So the question is "How much would I have to invest today (in the present time) to have $13,383 five years in the future if I invested at 6%?" Let's calculate the present value using PV factors.

> Present value = Future value × PV factor for *i* = 6%, *n* = 5

We determine the PV factor from the table labeled Present Value of $1 (Appendix A, Table A-1). We use this table for lump sum amounts. We look down the 6% column and across the 5 periods row and find the PV factor is 0.747. We finish our calculation as follows:

> Present value = Future value × PV factor for *i* = 6%, *n* = 5
> = $13,383 × 0.747
> = $9,997

Notice the calculation is off by $3 due to rounding ($10,000 − $9,997). The PV factors are rounded to three decimal places, so the calculations may not be exact. Also, the interest calculations in Exhibit F:14A-1 were rounded to the nearest dollar. Therefore, there are two rounding issues in this exhibit. However, we do have the answer to our question: If approximately $10,000 is invested today at 6% for five years, at the end of five years, the investment will grow to $13,383. Or, conversely, if we expect to receive $13,383 five years from now, its equivalent (discounted) value today is approximately $10,000. In other words, we need to invest approximately $10,000 today at 6% to have $13,383 five years from now.

Present Value of an Annuity

Let's now assume that instead of receiving a lump sum at the end of the five years, you will receive $2,000 at the end of each year. This is a series of equal payments ($2,000) over equal intervals (years), so it is an annuity. How much would you have to invest today to receive these payments, assuming an interest rate of 6%?

We determine the annuity PV factor from the table labeled Present Value of Ordinary Annuity of $1 (Appendix A, Table A-2). We use this table for annuities. We look down the 6% column and across the 5 periods row and find the annuity PV factor is 4.212. We finish our calculation as follows:

> Present value = Amount of each cash inflow × Annuity PV factor for $i = 6\%, n = 5$
> = $2,000 × 4.212
> = $8,424

This means that an investment today of $8,424 at 6% will yield $2,000 per year for the next five years, or total payments of $10,000 over 5 years ($2,000 per year × 5 years). The reason is that interest is being earned on principal that is left invested each year. Let's verify the calculation:

Year	[1] Beginning Balance Previous [4]	[2] Interest [1] × 6%	[3] Withdrawal $2,000	[4] Ending Balance [1] + [2] − [3]
0				$ 8,424
1	$ 8,424	$ 505	$ 2,000	6,929
2	6,929	416	2,000	5,345
3	5,345	321	2,000	3,666
4	3,666	220	2,000	1,886
5	1,886	114*	2,000	0

*rounded up by $1

The chart shows that the initial investment of $8,424 is invested for one year, earning $505 in interest. At the end of that period, the first withdrawal of $2,000 takes place, leaving a balance of $6,929 ($8,424 + $505 − $2,000). At the end of the five years the ending balance is $0, proving that the present value of the $2,000 annuity is $8,424.

Present Value of Bonds Payable

We can use what we have just learned about the present value of a lump sum and present value of an annuity to calculate the present value of bonds payable. The present value of a bond—its market price—is the sum of:

- the present value of the principal amount to be paid at maturity, a single amount (present value of a lump sum)
- *plus* the present value of the future stated interest payments, an annuity because it occurs in equal amounts over equal time periods (present value of an annuity).

Present Value of a Bonds Payable Issued at a Discount

Let's compute the present value of Smart Touch Learning's 9%, five-year bonds. The face value of the bonds is $100,000, and they pay (9% × 6/12) or 4.5% stated interest semiannually. At issuance, the annual market interest rate is 10% (5% semiannually). Therefore, the market interest rate for each of the 10 semiannual periods is 5%. We use 5% to compute the present value (PV) of the maturity value and the present value (PV) of the stated interest. The present value of these bonds is $96,149, computed as shown:

> **Present value of principal:**
> Present value = Future value × PV factor for $i = 5\%$, $n = 10$
>   = \$100,000 × 0.614
>   = \$61,400
>
> **Present value of stated interest:**
> Present value = Amount of each cash flow × Annuity PV factor for $i = 5\%$, $n = 10$
>   = (\$100,000 × 0.09 × 6/12) × 7.722
>   = \$34,749
>
> **Present value of bonds payable:**
> Present value = PV of principal + PV of stated interest
>   = \$61,400 + \$34,749
>   = \$96,149

Notice that the stated interest rate (9% × 6/12 = 4.5%), not the market interest rate (5%), is used to calculate the amount of each cash flow for interest. This is because the bonds payable pay interest based on the rate stated in the contract, not the rate of the market.

Present Value of a Bonds Payable Issued at a Premium

Let's consider a premium price for the Smart Touch Learning bonds. Suppose the market interest rate is 8% at issuance (4% for each of the 10 semiannual periods). We would compute the market price of these bonds as follows:

> **Present value of principal:**
> Present value = Future value × PV factor for $i = 4\%$, $n = 10$
>   = \$100,000 × 0.676
>   = \$67,600
>
> **Present value of stated interest:**
> Present value = Amount of each cash flow × Annuity PV factor for $i = 4\%$, $n = 10$
>   = (\$100,000 × 0.09 × 6/12) × 8.111
>   = \$36,500
>
> **Present value of bonds payable:**
> Present value = PV of principal + PV of stated interest
>   = \$67,600 + \$36,500
>   = \$104,100

Future Value of a Lump Sum

Let's now use the tables to calculate the future value of a lump sum considering the investment in Exhibit F:14A-1. Instead of calculating present value, though, we will change the scenario to evaluate the future value. "If I invested \$10,000 today (in the present time), how much would I have in five years at an interest rate of 6%?" We will calculate the future value using FV factors.

> Future value = Present value × FV factor for $i = 6\%$, $n = 5$

Long-Term Liabilities Financial 14-27

We determine the FV factor from the table labeled Future Value of $1 (Appendix A, Table A-3). We use this table for lump sum amounts. We look down the 6% column and across the 5 periods row and find the FV factor is 1.338. We finish our calculation as follows:

$$\begin{aligned} \text{Future value} &= \text{Present value} \times \text{FV factor for } i = 6\%, n = 5 \\ &= \$10,000 \times 1.338 \\ &= \$13,380 \end{aligned}$$

Notice the calculation is off by $3 due to rounding ($13,380 − $13,383). The FV factors are rounded to three decimal places, so the calculations may not be exact. Also, the interest calculations in Exhibit F:14A-1 were rounded to the nearest dollar. Therefore, there are two rounding issues in this exhibit. However, we do have the answer to our question: If $10,000 is invested today at 6% for five years, at the end of five years, the investment will grow to $13,380.

Future Value of an Annuity

Let's now calculate the future value of an annuity assuming that you will receive $2,000 at the end of each year. This is a series of equal payments ($2,000) over equal intervals (years), so it is an annuity. How much would these payments be worth five years from now, assuming an interest rate of 6%?

We determine the annuity FV factor from the table labeled Future Value of Ordinary Annuity of $1 (Appendix A, Table A-4). We use this table for annuities. We look down the 6% column and across the 5 periods row and find the annuity FV factor is 5.637. We finish our calculation as follows:

$$\begin{aligned} \text{Future value} &= \text{Amount of each cash inflow} \times \text{Annuity FV factor for } i = 6\%, n = 5 \\ &= \$2,000 \times 5.637 \\ &= \$11,274 \end{aligned}$$

This means investing $2,000 per year for five years at 6% will yield $11,274. The reason is that interest is being earned on principal that is left invested each year.

> **12A.** On December 31, 2024, when the market interest rate is 8%, Arnold Corporation issues $200,000 of 6%, 10-year bonds payable. The bonds pay interest semiannually. Determine the present value of the bonds at issuance.
>
> Check your answer online in MyLab Accounting or at http://www.pearsonhighered.com/Horngren.
>
> For more practice, see Short Exercises S-F:14A-13 through S-F:14A-15.   MyLab Accounting

APPENDIX 14B: Effective-Interest Method of Amortization

HOW ARE BONDS PAYABLE ACCOUNTED FOR USING THE EFFECTIVE-INTEREST AMORTIZATION METHOD?

Learning Objective 8

Journalize transactions for bonds payable and interest expense using the effective-interest amortization method

Effective-Interest Amortization Method

An amortization model that calculates interest expense based on the current carrying amount of the bond and the market interest rate at issuance, and then amortizes the difference between the cash interest payment and calculated interest expense as a decrease to the discount or premium.

We began this chapter with straight-line amortization to introduce the concept of amortizing bonds. A more precise way of amortizing bonds used in practice is called the **effective-interest amortization method**. This method calculates interest expense based on the current carrying amount of the bond and the market interest rate at issuance, and then amortizes the difference between the cash interest payment and calculated interest expense as a decrease to the discount or premium. This appendix explains the present value concepts used to amortize bond discounts and premiums using the effective-interest amortization method.

Generally Accepted Accounting Principles require that interest expense be measured using the *effective-interest amortization method* unless the straight-line amounts are similar. In that case, either method is permitted. Total interest expense over the life of the bonds is the same under both methods; however, interest expense each year is different between the two methods. Let's look at how the effective-interest amortization method works.

Effective-Interest Amortization for a Bond Discount

Assume that Smart Touch Learning issues $100,000 of 9% bonds at a time when the market rate of interest is 10%. These bonds mature in five years and pay interest semiannually, so there are 10 semiannual interest payments. As you just saw in Appendix 14A, the issue price of the bonds is $96,149, and the discount on these bonds is $3,851 ($100,000 − $96,149).

When using the effective-interest amortization method, the amount of the interest expense is calculated using the *carrying amount* of the bonds and the *market interest rate*. The interest payment is calculated using the *face value* of the bonds and the *stated interest rate*. The amount of discount amortization is the excess of the calculated interest expense over the interest payment. Exhibit F:14B-1 shows how to calculate interest expense by the effective-interest amortization method.

Exhibit F:14B-1 | Bonds Payable—Discount Amortization Schedule; Effective-Interest Amortization Method

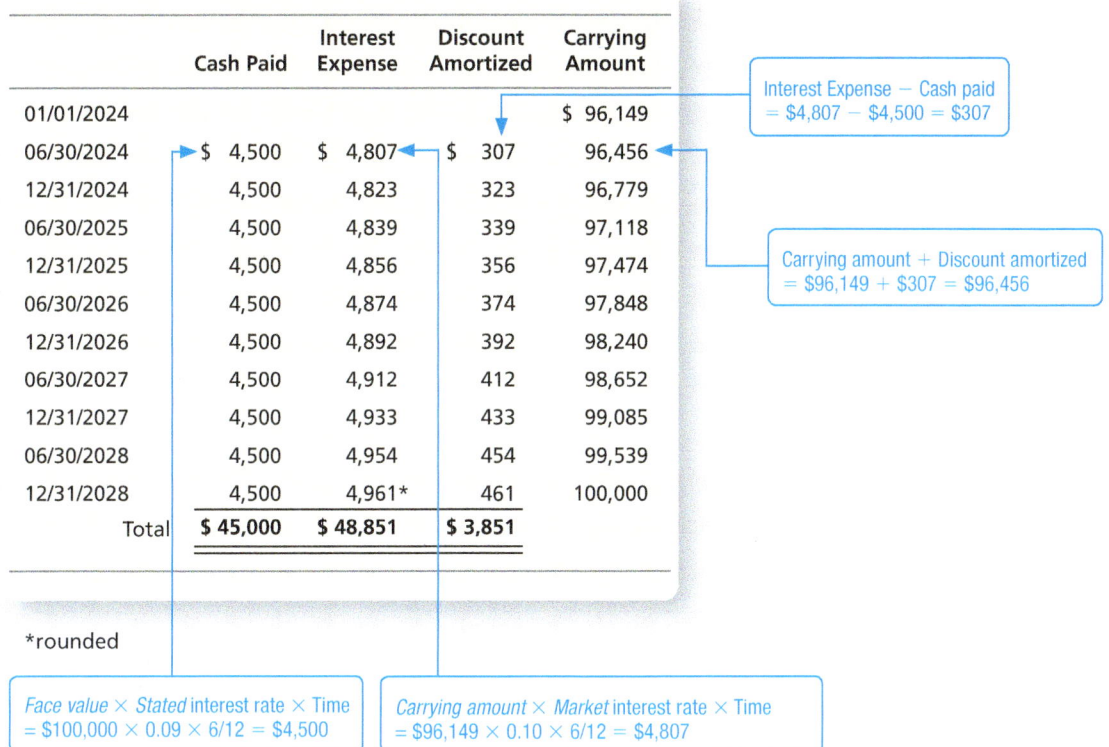

	Cash Paid	Interest Expense	Discount Amortized	Carrying Amount
01/01/2024				$ 96,149
06/30/2024	$ 4,500	$ 4,807	$ 307	96,456
12/31/2024	4,500	4,823	323	96,779
06/30/2025	4,500	4,839	339	97,118
12/31/2025	4,500	4,856	356	97,474
06/30/2026	4,500	4,874	374	97,848
12/31/2026	4,500	4,892	392	98,240
06/30/2027	4,500	4,912	412	98,652
12/31/2027	4,500	4,933	433	99,085
06/30/2028	4,500	4,954	454	99,539
12/31/2028	4,500	4,961*	461	100,000
Total	$ 45,000	$ 48,851	$ 3,851	

*rounded

Interest Expense − Cash paid = $4,807 − $4,500 = $307

Carrying amount + Discount amortized = $96,149 + $307 = $96,456

Face value × Stated interest rate × Time = $100,000 × 0.09 × 6/12 = $4,500

Carrying amount × Market interest rate × Time = $96,149 × 0.10 × 6/12 = $4,807

When recording the interest payment for the bonds payable, the *accounts* debited and credited under the effective-interest amortization method and the straight-line amortization method are the same. Only the *amounts* differ. Smart Touch Learning would record the first interest payment on June 30 as follows:

Date	Accounts and Explanation	Debit	Credit
2024			
Jun. 30	Interest Expense ($96,149 × 0.10 × 6/12)	4,807	
	Discount on Bonds Payable ($4,807 − $4,500)		307
	Cash ($100,000 × 0.09 × 6/12)		4,500
	Paid semiannual interest and amortized discount.		

$\frac{A\downarrow}{Cash\downarrow} = \left\{ \frac{L\uparrow}{\text{Discount on Bonds Payable}\downarrow} + \frac{E\downarrow}{\text{Interest Expense}\uparrow} \right.$

Regardless of which method is used, the *total* amount of cash paid and *total* interest expense is the same. You can verify this by reviewing the totals from Exhibit F:14-6 and Exhibit F:14B-1.

Effective-Interest Amortization of a Bond Premium

Smart Touch Learning may issue its bonds payable at a premium. Assume that Smart Touch Learning issues $100,000 of five-year, 9% bonds when the market interest rate is 8%. The bonds' issue price is $104,100, and the premium is $4,100, as calculated in Appendix 14A. When a bond is issued at a premium, the interest expense calculation using the effective-interest amortization method uses the *carrying amount* of the bonds and the *market interest rate* as shown with a discounted bond. The calculation for the amount of premium amortization is calculated as the difference between the cash paid and the calculated interest expense. Exhibit F:14B-2 provides the amortization schedule using the effective-interest amortization method for Smart Touch Learning.

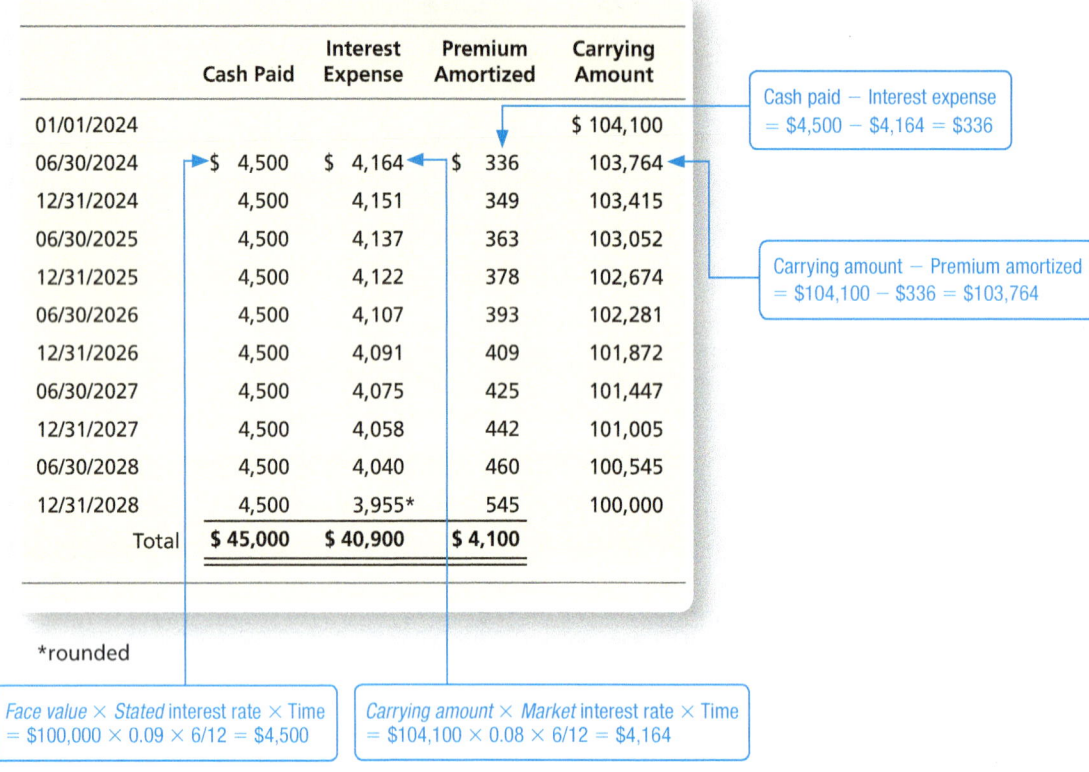

Exhibit F:14B-2 | Bonds Payable—Premium Amortization Schedule; Effective-Interest Amortization Method

	Cash Paid	Interest Expense	Premium Amortized	Carrying Amount
01/01/2024				$ 104,100
06/30/2024	$ 4,500	$ 4,164	$ 336	103,764
12/31/2024	4,500	4,151	349	103,415
06/30/2025	4,500	4,137	363	103,052
12/31/2025	4,500	4,122	378	102,674
06/30/2026	4,500	4,107	393	102,281
12/31/2026	4,500	4,091	409	101,872
06/30/2027	4,500	4,075	425	101,447
12/31/2027	4,500	4,058	442	101,005
06/30/2028	4,500	4,040	460	100,545
12/31/2028	4,500	3,955*	545	100,000
Total	$ 45,000	$ 40,900	$ 4,100	

*rounded

Cash paid − Interest expense = $4,500 − $4,164 = $336

Carrying amount − Premium amortized = $104,100 − $336 = $103,764

Face value × Stated interest rate × Time = $100,000 × 0.09 × 6/12 = $4,500

Carrying amount × Market interest rate × Time = $104,100 × 0.08 × 6/12 = $4,164

Smart Touch Learning will record the first interest payment on June 30 as follows:

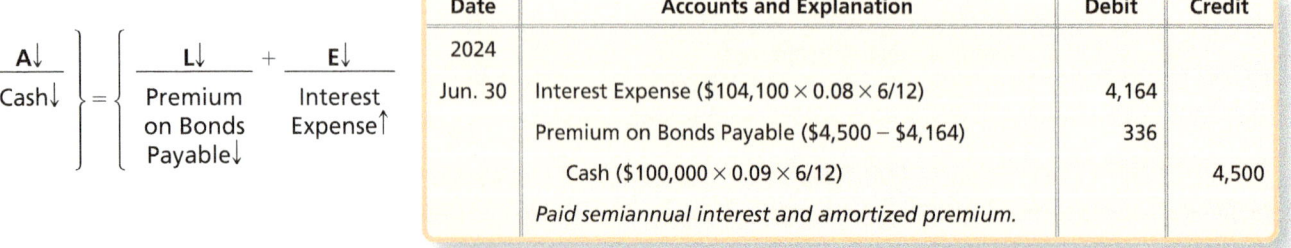

Date	Accounts and Explanation	Debit	Credit
2024			
Jun. 30	Interest Expense ($104,100 × 0.08 × 6/12)	4,164	
	Premium on Bonds Payable ($4,500 − $4,164)	336	
	Cash ($100,000 × 0.09 × 6/12)		4,500
	Paid semiannual interest and amortized premium.		

A↓ / Cash↓ = L↓ / Premium on Bonds Payable↓ + E↓ / Interest Expense↑

Regardless of which method is used, the *total* amount of cash paid and *total* interest expense is the same. You can verify this by reviewing the totals from Exhibit F:14-7 and Exhibit F:14B-2.

13B. On January 1, 2024, when the market interest rate is 6%, Hawkins Corporation issues $200,000 of 8%, five-year bonds payable. The bonds pay interest semiannually. Hawkins Corporation received $217,040 in cash at issuance. Assume interest payment dates are June 30 and December 31.

Prepare an effective-interest amortization method amortization table for the first two semiannual interest periods.

Check your answer online in MyLab Accounting or at http://www.pearsonhighered.com/Horngren.

For more practice, see Short Exercises S-F:14B-16 and S-F:14B-17.   MyLab Accounting

REVIEW

> Things You Should Know

1. How are long-term notes payable and mortgages payable accounted for?

- Long-term notes payable and mortgages payable are reported in the long-term liabilities section of the balance sheet unless there is a portion due within one year. That portion is shown in the current liabilities section of the balance sheet.
- An amortization schedule should be prepared that details each loan payment's allocation between principal and interest and also the beginning and ending balances of the loan.
- Mortgages payable are long-term debts that are backed with a security interest in specific property.

2. What are bonds?

- Bonds payable represent long-term debt issued to multiple lenders called *bondholders*, usually in increments of $1,000 per bond.
- The bond requires a face value payment at maturity and interest payments based on a stated interest rate over the life of the bond.
- A bond can be issued at face value, a discount, or a premium.
  - Face value—Bond is issued at face value. The stated interest rate is equal to the market interest rate.
  - A discount—Bond is issued at less than face value. The stated interest rate is less than the market interest rate.
  - A premium—Bond is issued for more than face value. The stated interest rate is higher than the market interest rate.

3. How are bonds payable accounted for using the straight-line amortization method?

- The basic journal entry to record the issuance of bonds payable debits Cash and credits Bonds Payable.
  - If a bond is issued at a discount, Discount on Bonds Payable, a contra account, will be debited for the difference between the face value and cash received.
  - If a bond is issued at a premium, Premium on Bonds Payable, an adjunct account, will be credited for the difference between the cash received and face value.

- Interest payments must be recorded with a debit to Interest Expense and a credit to Cash.
  - Discount on Bonds Payable and Premium on Bonds Payable must be amortized over the life of the bond.
  - The straight-line amortization method allocates an equal amount of the bond discount or premium to each interest period.

4. How is the retirement of bonds payable accounted for?

- When bonds are retired at maturity, the entry involves a debit to Bonds Payable and a credit to Cash for the face value of the bond.
- Retirement of bonds before maturity involves removing the remaining portion of the discount or premium account and crediting a gain or debiting a loss on retirement.

5. How are liabilities reported on the balance sheet?

- Current and long-term liabilities are reported separately on the balance sheet.
- Bonds payable are shown at the carrying amount.

6. How do we use the debt to equity ratio to evaluate business performance?

- The debt to equity ratio shows the proportion of total liabilities relative to the total equity. The ratio measures financial leverage.
- Total liabilities / Total equity.

7. What is the time value of money, and how are present value and future value calculated? (Appendix 14A)

- The fact that invested money earns interest over time is called the *time value of money*. This concept explains why we would prefer to receive cash sooner rather than later.
- Lump sum payments are one-time cash payments.
- Annuities are streams of equal cash payments made at equal time intervals.
- To calculate the present value of a lump sum:

$$\text{Present value} = \text{Future value} \times \text{PV factor for } i = ?\%, n = ?$$

- To calculate the present value of an annuity:

$$\text{Present value} = \text{Amount of each cash inflow} \times \text{Annuity PV factor for } i = ?\%, n = ?$$

- To calculate the future value of a lump sum:

$$\text{Future value} = \text{Present value} \times \text{FV factor for } i = ?\%, n = ?$$

- To calculate the future value of an annuity:

$$\text{Future value} = \text{Amount of each cash inflow} \times \text{Annuity FV factor for } i = ?\%, n = ?$$

8. **How are bonds payable accounted for using the effective-interest amortization method? (Appendix 14B)**
   - The effective-interest amortization method calculates interest expense based on the current carrying amount of the bond and the market interest rate at issuance and then amortizes the difference between the cash interest payment and calculated interest expense as a decrease to the discount or premium.
   - Using the effective-interest amortization method, the amount of interest expense is calculated using the carrying amount of the bonds and the market interest rate.

> Check Your Understanding

Check your understanding of the chapter by completing this problem and then looking at the solution. Use this practice to help identify which sections of the chapter you need to study more.

West Virginia Power Company has 8%, 10-year bonds payable that mature on June 30, 2034. The bonds are issued on June 30, 2024, and West Virginia Power pays interest each June 30 and December 31.

Requirements

1. Will the bonds be issued at face value, at a premium, or at a discount if the market interest rate on the date of issuance is 7%? If the market interest rate is 10%? (See Learning Objective 2)
2. West Virginia Power issued $100,000 of the bonds at 87.548. Round all calculations to the nearest dollar. (See Learning Objective 2)
   a. Record issuance of the bonds on June 30, 2024.
   b. Record the payment of interest and amortization of the discount on December 31, 2024. Use the straight-line amortization method.
   c. Compute the bonds' carrying amount at December 31, 2024.
   d. Record the payment of interest and amortization of discount on June 30, 2025.

> Solution

Requirement 1

If the market interest rate is 7%, the bonds will be issued at a premium.

If the market interest rate is 10%, the bonds will be issued at a discount.

Requirement 2

Date	Accounts and Explanation	Debit	Credit
2024			
(a) Jun. 30	Cash ($100,000 × 0.87548)	87,548	
	Discount on Bonds Payable ($100,000 − $87,548)	12,452	
	Bonds Payable		100,000
	Issued bonds at a discount.		
(b) Dec. 31	Interest Expense ($4,000 + $623)	4,623	
	Discount on Bonds Payable ($12,452 × 1/20)		623
	Cash ($100,000 × 0.08 × 6/12)		4,000

e. Carrying amount at December 31, 2024

Long-term Liabilities:		
Bonds Payable	$100,000	
Less: Discount on Bonds Payable	(11,829)	$ 88,171

Date	Accounts and Explanation	Debit	Credit
2025			
(d) Jun. 30	Interest Expense ($4,000 + $623)	4,623	
	Discount on Bonds Payable ($12,452 × 1/20)		623
	Cash ($100,000 × 0.08 × 6/12)		4,000

> Key Terms

Adjunct Account (p. 14-14)
Amortization Schedule (p. 14-2)
Annuity (p. 14-22) (Appendix 14A)
Bond Payable (p. 14-5)
Callable Bonds (p. 14-17)
Carrying Amount of Bonds (p. 14-12)
Compound Interest (p. 14-22) (Appendix 14A)
Debentures (p. 14-6)
Debt to Equity Ratio (p. 14-20)

Discount on Bonds Payable (p. 14-7)
Effective-Interest Amortization Method (p. 14-28) (Appendix 14B)
Face Value (p. 14-6)
Financial Leverage (p. 14-10)
Future Value (p. 14-8)
Long-term Liability (p. 14-2)
Market Interest Rate (p. 14-8)
Mortgages Payable (p. 14-3)
Premium on Bonds Payable (p. 14-7)

Present Value (p. 14-8)
Secured Bonds (p. 14-6)
Serial Bonds (p. 14-6)
Simple Interest (p. 14-22) (Appendix 14A)
Stated Interest Rate (p. 14-6)
Straight-Line Amortization Method (p. 14-12)
Term Bonds (p. 14-6)
Time Value of Money (p. 14-7)

> Quick Check

Learning Objective 1

1. Flipco signed a 10-year note payable on January 1, 2024, of $800,000. The note requires annual principal payments each December 31 of $80,000 plus interest at 5%. The entry to record the annual payment on December 31, 2025, includes

    a. a debit to Interest Expense for $36,000.
    b. a debit to Interest Expense for $40,000.
    c. a credit to Notes Payable for $80,000.
    d. a credit to Cash of $120,000.

Learning Objective 2

2. Daniels' bonds payable carry a stated interest rate of 5%, and the market rate of interest is 7%. The issue price of the Daniels' bonds will be at

    a. par value.   c. face value.
    b. a premium.   d. a discount.

Learning Objective 2

3. A bond that matures in installments at regular intervals is a

    a. term bond.   c. periodic bond.
    b. serial bond.   d. terminal bond.

4. Alan Smith Antiques issued its 7%, 20-year bonds payable at a price of $846,720 (face value is $900,000). The company uses the straight-line amortization method for the bond discount or premium. Interest expense for each year is

   a. $65,664.
   b. $60,336.
   c. $63,000.
   d. $59,270.

5. Nicholas Smith Fitness Gym has $700,000 of 20-year bonds payable outstanding. These bonds had a discount of $56,000 at issuance, which was 10 years ago. The company uses the straight-line amortization method. The current carrying amount of these bonds payable is

   a. $672,000.
   b. $644,000.
   c. $700,000.
   d. $728,000.

6. Vasquez issued a $400,000 face value, 8%, 20-year bond at 95. Which of the following is the correct journal entry to record the retirement of the bond at maturity?

Date	Accounts and Explanation	Debit	Credit
a.	Bonds Payable	380,000	
	Cash		380,000
b.	Cash	400,000	
	Bonds Payable		400,000
c.	Bonds Payable	400,000	
	Cash		400,000
d.	Cash	380,000	
	Bonds Payable		380,000

7. Sassy's trial balance shows $200,000 face value of bonds with a discount balance of $2,000. The bonds mature in 10 years. How will the bonds be presented on the balance sheet?

   a. Bonds payable $198,000 (net of $2,000 discount) will be listed as a long-term liability.
   b. Bonds payable $200,000 will be listed as a long-term liability. A $2,000 discount on bonds payable will be listed as a contra current liability.
   c. Bonds payable $200,000 will be listed as a long-term liability.
   d. Bonds payable $200,000 will be listed as a long-term liability. A $2,000 discount on bonds payable will be listed as a current liability.

8. The debt to equity ratio is calculated as

   a. Total assets / Total equity.
   b. Current liabilities / Total equity.
   c. Total liabilities / Total assets.
   d. Total liabilities / Total equity.

9A. Mike Gordon wishes to have $80,000 in five years. If he can earn annual interest of 2%, how much must he invest today?

   a. $42,170
   b. $72,480
   c. $76,080
   d. $88,320

Learning Objective 8
Appendix 14B

10B. Hicks Corporation issued $500,000 of 5%, 10-year bonds payable at a price of 92. The market interest rate at the date of issuance was 6%, and the bonds pay interest semiannually. The journal entry to record the first semiannual interest payment using the effective-interest amortization method is

Date	Accounts and Explanation	Debit	Credit
a.	Interest Expense	14,500	
	Discount on Bonds Payable		2,000
	Cash		12,500
b.	Interest Expense	13,800	
	Discount on Bonds Payable		1,300
	Cash		12,500
c.	Interest Expense	17,000	
	Discount on Bonds Payable		2,000
	Cash		15,000
d.	Interest Expense	16,300	
	Discount on Bonds Payable		1,300
	Cash		15,000

Check your answers at the end of the chapter.

ASSESS YOUR PROGRESS

> Review Questions

1. Where is the current portion of notes payable reported on the balance sheet?
2. What is an amortization schedule?
3. What is a mortgage payable?
4. What is a bond payable?
5. What is the difference between the stated interest rate and the market interest rate?
6. When does a discount on bonds payable occur?
7. When does a premium on bonds payable occur?
8. When a bond is issued, what is its present value?
9. Why would a company choose to issue bonds instead of issuing stock?
10. What is the carrying amount of a bond?
11. In regard to a bond discount or premium, what is the straight-line amortization method?
12. What type of account is Discount on Bonds Payable? What is its normal balance? Is it added to or subtracted from the Bonds Payable account to determine the carrying amount?
13. What type of account is Premium on Bonds Payable? What is its normal balance? Is it added to or subtracted from the Bonds Payable account to determine the carrying amount?

14. What is the journal entry to retire bonds at maturity?
15. What does it mean when a company calls a bond?
16. What are the two categories of liabilities reported on the balance sheet? Provide examples of each.
17. What does the debt to equity ratio show, and how is it calculated?
18A. Explain each of the key factors that the time value of money depends on.
19A. What is an annuity?
20A. How does compound interest differ from simple interest?
21B. In regard to a bond discount or premium, what is the effective-interest amortization method?

> Short Exercises

Assume bonds payable are amortized using the straight-line amortization method unless stated otherwise.

S-F:14-1 Accounting for a long-term note payable

Learning Objective 1

On January 1, 2024, Lakeman-Fay signed a $1,500,000, 15-year, 7% note. The loan required Lakeman-Fay to make annual payments on December 31 of $100,000 principal plus interest.

Requirements

1. Journalize the issuance of the note on January 1, 2024.
2. Journalize the first note payment on December 31, 2024.

S-F:14-2 Accounting for mortgages payable

Learning Objective 1

Ember Company purchased a building with a market value of $280,000 and land with a market value of $55,000 on January 1, 2024. Ember Company paid $15,000 cash and signed a 25-year, 12% mortgage payable for the balance.

Requirements

1. Journalize the January 1, 2024, purchase.
2. Journalize the first monthly payment of $3,370 on January 31, 2024. (Round to the nearest dollar.)

S-F:14-3 Determining bond prices

Learning Objective 2

Bond prices depend on the market rate of interest, stated rate of interest, and time. Determine whether the following bonds payable will be issued at face value, at a premium, or at a discount:

a. The market interest rate is 8%. Idaho issues bonds payable with a stated rate of 7.75%.

b. Austin issued 9% bonds payable when the market interest rate was 8.25%.

c. Cleveland's Cars issued 10% bonds when the market interest rate was 10%.

d. Atlanta's Tourism issued bonds payable that pay the stated interest rate of 8.5%. At issuance, the market interest rate was 10.25%.

Learning Objective 2

S-F:14-4 Pricing bonds

Bond prices depend on the market rate of interest, stated rate of interest, and time.

Requirements

1. Compute the price of the following 8% bonds of Country Telecom.
   - a. $100,000 issued at 75.25
   - b. $100,000 issued at 103.50
   - c. $100,000 issued at 94.50
   - d. $100,000 issued at 103.25
2. Which bond will Country Telecom have to pay the most to retire at maturity? Explain your answer.

Learning Objective 3

S-F:14-5 Determining bond amounts

Savvy Drive-Ins borrowed money by issuing $3,500,000 of 9% bonds payable at 99.5. Interest is paid semiannually.

Requirements

1. How much cash did Savvy receive when it issued the bonds payable?
2. How much must Savvy pay back at maturity?
3. How much cash interest will Savvy pay each six months?

Learning Objective 3

S-F:14-6 Journalizing bond transactions

Power Company issued a $1,000,000, 5%, five-year bond payable at face value on January 1, 2024. Interest is paid semiannually on January 1 and July 1.

Requirements

1. Journalize the issuance of the bond payable on January 1, 2024.
2. Journalize the payment of semiannual interest on July 1, 2024.

Learning Objective 3

S-F:14-7 Journalizing bond transactions

Owen Company issued a $110,000, 11%, 10-year bond payable at 94 on January 1, 2024. Interest is paid semiannually on January 1 and July 1.

Requirements

1. Journalize the issuance of the bond payable on January 1, 2024.
2. Journalize the payment of semiannual interest and amortization of the bond discount or premium on July 1, 2024.

Learning Objective 3

S-F:14-8 Journalizing bond transactions

Wilkes Mutual Insurance Company issued a $100,000, 5%, 10-year bond payable at 111 on January 1, 2024. Interest is paid semiannually on January 1 and July 1.

Requirements

1. Journalize the issuance of the bond payable on January 1, 2024.
2. Journalize the payment of semiannual interest and amortization of the bond discount or premium on July 1, 2024.

S-F:14-9 Journalizing bond transactions including retirement at maturity
Learning Objectives 3, 4

McQueen Company issued a $100,000, 7.5%, 10-year bond payable. Journalize the following transactions for McQueen Company and include an explanation for each entry:

a. Issuance of the bond payable at face value on January 1, 2024.

b. Payment of semiannual cash interest on July 1, 2024.

c. Payment of the bond payable at maturity, assuming the last interest payment had already been recorded. (Give the date.)

S-F:14-10 Retiring bonds payable before maturity
Learning Objectives 3, 4

On January 1, 2024, Powell Company issued $350,000 of 10%, five-year bonds payable at 102. Powell Company has extra cash and wishes to retire the bonds payable on January 1, 2025, immediately after making the second semiannual interest payment. To retire the bonds, Powell Company pays the market price of 98.

Requirements

1. What is Powell Company's carrying amount of the bonds payable on the retirement date?

2. How much cash must Powell Company pay to retire the bonds payable?

3. Compute Powell Company's gain or loss on the retirement of the bonds payable.

S-F:14-11 Preparing the liabilities section of the balance sheet
Learning Objective 5

Luxury Suites Hotels includes the following selected accounts in its general ledger at December 31, 2024:

Notes Payable (long-term)	$ 200,000	Accounts Payable	$ 33,000
Bonds Payable (due 2028)	450,000	Discount on Bonds Payable	13,500
Interest Payable (due next year)	1,000	Salaries Payable	2,600
Estimated Warranty Payable	1,300	Sales Tax Payable	400

Prepare the liabilities section of Luxury Suites' balance sheet at December 31, 2024.

S-F:14-12 Computing the debt to equity ratio
Learning Objective 6

Jackson Corporation has the following amounts as of December 31, 2024.

Total assets	$ 55,250
Total liabilities	22,750
Total equity	32,500

Compute the debt to equity ratio at December 31, 2024.

S-F:14A-13 Determining present value
Learning Objective 7
Appendix 14A

Your grandfather would like to share some of his fortune with you. He offers to give you money under one of the following scenarios (you get to choose):

1. $8,750 per year at the end of each of the next six years

2. $49,650 (lump sum) now

3. $100,450 (lump sum) six years from now

Requirements

1. Calculate the present value of each scenario using a 6% discount rate. Which scenario yields the highest present value? Round to the nearest dollar.
2. Would your preference change if you used a 12% discount rate?

Learning Objective 7
Appendix 14A

S-F:14A-14 Determining the present value of bond at issuance

On December 31, 2024, when the market interest rate is 12%, Benson Realty issues $600,000 of 9.25%, 10-year bonds payable. The bonds pay interest semiannually. Determine the present value of the bonds at issuance.

Learning Objective 7
Appendix 14A

S-F:14A-15 Determining future value

David is entering high school and is determined to save money for college. David feels he can save $5,000 each year for the next four years from his part-time job. If David is able to invest at 6%, how much will he have when he starts college?

Learning Objective 8
Appendix 14B

S-F:14B-16 Using the effective-interest amortization method

On December 31, 2024, when the market interest rate is 8%, Biggs Realty issues $450,000 of 5.25%, 10-year bonds payable. The bonds pay interest semiannually. The present value of the bonds at issuance is $365,732.

Requirements

1. Prepare an amortization table using the effective interest amortization method for the first two semiannual interest periods. (Round to the nearest dollar.)
2. Using the amortization table prepared in Requirement 1, journalize issuance of the bonds and the first two interest payments.

Learning Objective 8
Appendix 14B

S-F:14B-17 Using the effective-interest amortization method

On December 31, 2024, when the market interest rate is 6%, Benson Realty issues $700,000 of 6.25%, 10-year bonds payable. The bonds pay interest semiannually. Benson Realty received $713,234 in cash at issuance.

Requirements

1. Prepare an amortization table using the effective interest amortization method for the first two semiannual interest periods. (Round to the nearest dollar.)
2. Using the amortization table prepared in Requirement 1, journalize issuance of the bonds and the first two interest payments.

> Exercises

Assume bonds payable are amortized using the straight-line amortization method unless stated otherwise.

E-F:14-18 Accounting for long-term notes payable transactions

Learning Objective 1

2. Total Liabilities $65,280

Consider the following note payable transactions of Caleb Video Productions.

2024	
Oct. 1	Purchased equipment costing $80,000 by issuing a five-year, 8% note payable. The note requires annual principal payments of $16,000 plus interest each October 1.
Dec. 31	Accrued interest on the note payable.
2025	
Oct. 1	Paid the first installment on the note.
Dec. 31	Accrued interest on the note payable.

Requirements

1. Journalize the transactions for the company.
2. Considering the given transactions only, what are Caleb Video Productions' total liabilities on December 31, 2025?

E-F:14-19 Preparing an amortization schedule and recording mortgages payable entries

Learning Objective 1

3. Interest Expense $2,750.00

Kellerman Company purchased a building and land with a fair market value of $550,000 (building, $425,000, and land, $125,000) on January 1, 2024. Kellerman signed a 20-year, 6% mortgage payable. Kellerman will make monthly payments of $3,940.37. Round to two decimal places. Explanations are not required for journal entries.

Requirements

1. Journalize the mortgage payable issuance on January 1, 2024.
2. Prepare an amortization schedule for the first two payments.
3. Journalize the first payment on January 31, 2024.
4. Journalize the second payment on February 28, 2024.

E-F:14-20 Analyzing alternative plans to raise money

Learning Objective 2

EPS Plan A $2.06

SB Electronics is considering two plans for raising $4,000,000 to expand operations. Plan A is to issue 9% bonds payable, and plan B is to issue 500,000 shares of common stock. Before any new financing, SB Electronics has net income of $350,000 and 300,000 shares of common stock outstanding. Management believes the company can use the new funds to earn additional income of $700,000 before interest and taxes. The income tax rate is 21%. Analyze the SB Electronics situation to determine which plan will result in higher earnings per share. Use Exhibit F:14-5 as a guide.

E-F:14-21 Determining bond prices and interest expense

Learning Objectives 2, 3

2. Market price $436,100

Jones Company is planning to issue $490,000 of 9%, five-year bonds payable to borrow for a major expansion. The owner, Shane Jones, asks your advice on some related matters.

Requirements

1. Answer the following questions:

   a. At what type of bond price will Jones Company have total interest expense equal to the cash interest payments?

   b. Under which type of bond price will Jones Company's total interest expense be greater than the cash interest payments?

   c. If the market interest rate is 12%, what type of bond price can Jones Company expect for the bonds?

2. Compute the price of the bonds if the bonds are issued at 89.

3. How much will Jones Company pay in interest each year? How much will Jones Company's interest expense be for the first year?

Learning Objective 3

2. Interest Exp. $6,600

E-F:14-22 Journalizing bond issuance and interest payments

On June 30, Parker Company issues 11%, five-year bonds payable with a face value of $120,000. The bonds are issued at face value and pay interest on June 30 and December 31.

Requirements

1. Journalize the issuance of the bonds on June 30.

2. Journalize the semiannual interest payment on December 31.

Learning Objective 3

1. June 30 Discount $18,200

E-F:14-23 Journalizing bond issuance and interest payments

On June 30, Daughtry Limited issues 8%, 20-year bonds payable with a face value of $130,000. The bonds are issued at 86 and pay interest on June 30 and December 31.

Requirements

1. Journalize the issuance of the bonds on June 30.

2. Journalize the semiannual interest payment and amortization of bond discount on December 31.

Learning Objective 3

2. Interest Expense $3,430

E-F:14-24 Journalizing bond transactions

Anderson Company issued $70,000 of 10-year, 9% bonds payable on January 1, 2024. Anderson Company pays interest each January 1 and July 1 and amortizes discount or premium by the straight-line amortization method. The company can issue its bonds payable under various conditions.

Requirements

1. Journalize Anderson Company's issuance of the bonds and first semiannual interest payment assuming the bonds were issued at face value. Explanations are not required.

2. Journalize Anderson Company's issuance of the bonds and first semiannual interest payment assuming the bonds were issued at 92. Explanations are not required.

3. Journalize Anderson Company's issuance of the bonds and first semiannual interest payment assuming the bonds were issued at 103. Explanations are not required.

4. Which bond price results in the most interest expense for Anderson Company? Explain in detail.

E-F:14-25 Journalizing bond issuance and interest payments

Learning Objectives 3, 4

On January 1, 2024, Roberts Unlimited issues 8%, 20-year bonds payable with a face value of $240,000. The bonds are issued at 104 and pay interest on June 30 and December 31.

1. Premium $9,600

Requirements

1. Journalize the issuance of the bonds on January 1, 2024.
2. Journalize the semiannual interest payment and amortization of bond premium on June 30, 2024.
3. Journalize the semiannual interest payment and amortization of bond premium on December 31, 2024.
4. Journalize the retirement of the bond at maturity, assuming the last interest payment has already been recorded. (Give the date.)

E-F:14-26 Retiring bonds payable before maturity

Learning Objective 4

CoastalView Magazine issued $600,000 of 15-year, 5% callable bonds payable on July 31, 2024, at 94. On July 31, 2027, *CoastalView* called the bonds at 101. Assume annual interest payments.

2. Cash $606,000

Requirements

1. Without making journal entries, compute the carrying amount of the bonds payable at July 31, 2027.
2. Assume all amortization has been recorded properly. Journalize the retirement of the bonds on July 31, 2027. No explanation is required.

E-F:14-27 Reporting current and long-term liabilities

Learning Objectives 2, 3, 5

Pediatric Dispensary borrowed $390,000 on January 2, 2024, by issuing a 15% serial bond payable that must be paid in three equal annual installments plus interest for the year. The first payment of principal and interest comes due January 2, 2025. Complete the missing information. Assume the bonds are issued at face value.

	December 31		
	2024	2025	2026
Current Liabilities:			
Bonds Payable	$_____	$_____	$_____
Interest Payable	_____	_____	_____
Long-term Liabilities:			
Bonds Payable	_____	_____	_____

Learning Objectives 2, 3, 5

Total Liabilities $378,000

E-F:14-28 Reporting liabilities

At December 31, MediStat Precision Instruments owes $52,000 on Accounts Payable, Salaries Payable of $12,000, and Income Tax Payable of $10,000. MediStat also has $300,000 of Bonds Payable that were issued at face value that require payment of a $35,000 installment next year and the remainder in later years. The bonds payable require an annual interest payment of $4,000, and MediStat still owes this interest for the current year. Report MediStat's liabilities on its classified balance sheet on December 31, 2024.

Learning Objective 6

E-F:14-29 Computing the debt to equity ratio

Ludwig Corporation has the following data as of December 31, 2024:

Total Current Liabilities	$ 36,210	Total Stockholders' Equity	$?
Total Current Assets	58,200	Other Assets	36,800
Long-term Liabilities	139,630	Property, Plant, and Equipment, Net	206,440

Compute the debt to equity ratio at December 31, 2024.

**Learning Objective 7
Appendix 14A**

2. Present Value $77,594

E-F:14A-30 Determining the present value of bonds payable

Interest rates determine the present value of future amounts. (Round to the nearest dollar.)

Requirements

1. Determine the present value of 10-year bonds payable with face value of $86,000 and stated interest rate of 14%, paid semiannually. The market rate of interest is 14% at issuance.
2. Same bonds payable as in Requirement 1, but the market interest rate is 16%.
3. Same bonds payable as in Requirement 1, but the market interest rate is 12%.

**Learning Objective 8
Appendix 14B**

2. Interest Expense $4,995

E-F:14B-31 Journalizing bond transactions using the effective-interest amortization method

Journalize issuance of the bond and the first semiannual interest payment under each of the following three assumptions. The company amortizes bond premium and discount by the effective-interest amortization method. Explanations are not required.

1. Seven-year bonds payable with face value of $83,000 and stated interest rate of 10%, paid semiannually. The market rate of interest is 10% at issuance. The present value of the bonds at issuance is $83,000.
2. Same bonds payable as in assumption 1, but the market interest rate is 16%. The present value of the bonds at issuance is $62,433.
3. Same bonds payable as in assumption 1, but the market interest rate is 8%. The present value of the bonds at issuance is $91,727.

Problems Group A

P-F:14-32A Journalizing liability transactions and reporting them on the balance sheet

Learning Objectives 1, 5

2. Total Liabilities $653,334

The following transactions of Johnson Pharmacies occurred during 2024 and 2025:

2024

Mar. 1	Borrowed $450,000 from Coconut Creek Bank. The 15-year, 5% note requires payments due annually, on March 1. Each payment consists of $30,000 principal plus one year's interest.
Dec. 1	Mortgaged the warehouse for $250,000 cash with Saputo Bank. The mortgage requires monthly payments of $8,000. The interest rate on the note is 12% and accrues monthly. The first payment is due on January 1, 2025.
31	Recorded interest accrued on the Saputo Bank note.
31	Recorded interest accrued on the Coconut Creek Bank note.

2025

Jan. 1	Paid Saputo Bank monthly mortgage payment.
Feb. 1	Paid Saputo Bank monthly mortgage payment.
Mar. 1	Paid Saputo Bank monthly mortgage payment.
1	Paid first installment on note due to Coconut Creek Bank.

Requirements

1. Journalize the transactions in the Johnson Pharmacies general journal. Round to the nearest dollar. Explanations are not required.
2. Prepare the liabilities section of the balance sheet for Johnson Pharmacies on March 1, 2025, after all the journal entries are recorded.

P-F:14-33A Analyzing, journalizing, and reporting bond transactions

Learning Objectives 2, 3

2. Discount $3,000

Danny's Hamburgers issued 6%, 10-year bonds payable at 90 on December 31, 2024. At December 31, 2026, Danny reported the bonds payable as follows:

Long-term Liabilities:		
Bonds Payable	$ 600,000	
Less: Discount on Bonds Payable	(48,000)	$ 552,000

Danny's pays semiannual interest each June 30 and December 31.

Requirements

1. Answer the following questions about Danny's bonds payable:
   a. What is the maturity value of the bonds?
   b. What is the carrying amount of the bonds at December 31, 2026?
   c. What is the semiannual cash interest payment on the bonds?
   d. How much interest expense should the company record each year?
2. Record the June 30, 2026, semiannual interest payment and amortization of discount.

14-46 Financial chapter 14

Learning Objectives 2, 3, 4

3. June 30, 2024, Interest Expense $25,200

P-F:14-34A Analyzing and journalizing bond transactions

On January 1, 2024, Nurses Credit Union (NCU) issued 8%, 20-year bonds payable with face value of $600,000. The bonds pay interest on June 30 and December 31.

Requirements

1. If the market interest rate is 7% when NCU issues its bonds, will the bonds be priced at face value, at a premium, or at a discount? Explain.
2. If the market interest rate is 9% when NCU issues its bonds, will the bonds be priced at face value, at a premium, or at a discount? Explain.
3. The issue price of the bonds is 92. Journalize the following bond transactions:
    a. Issuance of the bonds on January 1, 2024.
    b. Payment of interest and amortization on June 30, 2024.
    c. Payment of interest and amortization on December 31, 2024.
    d. Retirement of the bond at maturity on December 31, 2043, assuming the last interest payment has already been recorded.

Learning Objectives 2, 3, 4

June 30, 2024, Interest Expense $37,750

P-F:14-35A Analyzing and journalizing bond transactions

On January 1, 2024, Educators Credit Union (ECU) issued 8%, 20-year bonds payable with face value of $1,000,000. These bonds pay interest on June 30 and December 31. The issue price of the bonds is 109.

Journalize the following bond transactions:

a. Issuance of the bonds on January 1, 2024.
b. Payment of interest and amortization on June 30, 2024.
c. Payment of interest and amortization on December 31, 2024.
d. Retirement of the bond at maturity on December 31, 2043, assuming the last interest payment has already been recorded.

Learning Objectives 5, 6

1. Total Liabilities $276,200

P-F:14-36A Reporting liabilities on the balance sheet and computing debt to equity ratio

The accounting records of Pack Leader Wireless include the following as of December 31, 2024:

Accounts Payable	$ 77,000	Salaries Payable	$ 7,500
Mortgages Payable (long-term)	73,000	Bonds Payable (current portion)	25,000
Interest Payable	18,000	Premium on Bonds Payable	10,000
Bonds Payable (long-term)	63,000	Unearned Revenue (short-term)	2,700
Total Stockholders' Equity	140,000		

Requirements

1. Report these liabilities on the Pack Leader Wireless balance sheet, including headings and totals for current liabilities and long-term liabilities.
2. Compute Pack Leader Wireless's debt to equity ratio at December 31, 2024.

Learning Objectives 7, 8 Appendixes 14A, 14B

3. Jan. 1, 2024, Cash $629,634

P-F:14AB-37A Determining the present value of bonds payable and journalizing using the effective-interest amortization method

Brad Nelson, Inc. issued $600,000 of 7%, six-year bonds payable on January 1, 2024. The market interest rate at the date of issuance was 6%, and the bonds pay interest semiannually.

Requirements

1. How much cash did the company receive upon issuance of the bonds payable? (Round to the nearest dollar.)
2. Prepare an amortization table for the bond using the effective-interest method, through the first two interest payments. (Round to the nearest dollar.)
3. Journalize the issuance of the bonds on January 1, 2024, and the first and second payments of the semiannual interest amount and amortization of the bonds on June 30, 2024, and December 31, 2024. Explanations are not required.

P-F:14AB-38A Determining the present value of bonds payable and journalizing using the effective-interest amortization method

Learning Objectives 7, 8
Appendixes 14A, 14B

Relaxation, Inc. is authorized to issue 7%, 10-year bonds payable. On January 1, 2024, when the market interest rate is 12%, the company issues $300,000 of the bonds. The bonds pay interest semiannually.

3. Jan. 1, 2024, Cash $214,035

Requirements

1. How much cash did the company receive upon issuance of the bonds payable? (Round to the nearest dollar.)
2. Prepare an amortization table for the bond using the effective-interest method, through the first two interest payments. (Round to the nearest dollar.)
3. Journalize the issuance of the bonds on January 1, 2024, and the first and second payments of the semiannual interest amount and amortization of the bonds on June 30, 2024, and December 31, 2024. Explanations are not required.

> Problems Group B

P-F:14-39B Journalizing liability transactions and reporting them on the balance sheet

Learning Objectives 1, 5

The following transactions of Great Value Pharmacies occurred during 2024 and 2025:

2. Total Liabilities $661,776

2024

Mar. 1		Borrowed $390,000 from Bartow Bank. The six-year, 13% note requires payments due annually, on March 1. Each payment consists of $65,000 principal plus one year's interest.
Dec. 1		Mortgaged the warehouse for $350,000 cash with Saylor Bank. The mortgage requires monthly payments of $7,000. The interest rate on the note is 9% and accrues monthly. The first payment is due on January 1, 2025.
31		Recorded interest accrued on the Saylor Bank note.
31		Recorded interest accrued on the Bartow Bank note.

2025

Jan. 1		Paid Saylor Bank monthly mortgage payment.
Feb. 1		Paid Saylor Bank monthly mortgage payment.
Mar. 1		Paid Saylor Bank monthly mortgage payment.
1		Paid first installment on note due to Bartow Bank.

Requirements

1. Journalize the transactions in the Great Value Pharmacies general journal. Round to the nearest dollar. Explanations are not required.
2. Prepare the liabilities section of the balance sheet for Great Value Pharmacies on March 1, 2025, after all the journal entries are recorded.

Learning Objectives 2, 3

2. Discount $2,250

P-F:14-40B Analyzing, journalizing, and reporting bond transactions

Johnny's Hamburgers issued 8%, 10-year bonds payable at 85 on December 31, 2024. At December 31, 2026, Johnny reported the bonds payable as follows:

Long-term Liabilities:		
Bonds Payable	$ 300,000	
Less: Discount on Bonds Payable	(36,000)	$ 264,000

Johnny pays semiannual interest each June 30 and December 31.

Requirements

1. Answer the following questions about Johnny's bonds payable:
   a. What is the maturity value of the bonds?
   b. What is the carrying amount of the bonds at December 31, 2026?
   c. What is the semiannual cash interest payment on the bonds?
   d. How much interest expense should the company record each year?
2. Record the June 30, 2026, semiannual interest payment and amortization of discount.

Learning Objectives 2, 3, 4

3. June 30 Interest Expense $7,350

P-F:14-41B Analyzing and journalizing bond transactions

On January 1, 2024, Doctors Credit Union (DCU) issued 7%, 20-year bonds payable with face value of $200,000. The bonds pay interest on June 30 and December 31.

Requirements

1. If the market interest rate is 5% when DCU issues its bonds, will the bonds be priced at face value, at a premium, or at a discount? Explain.
2. If the market interest rate is 8% when DCU issues its bonds, will the bonds be priced at face value, at a premium, or at a discount? Explain.
3. The issue price of the bonds is 93. Journalize the following bond transactions:
   a. Issuance of the bonds on January 1, 2024.
   b. Payment of interest and amortization on June 30, 2024.
   c. Payment of interest and amortization on December 31, 2024.
   d. Retirement of the bond at maturity on December 31, 2043, assuming the last interest payment has already been recorded.

Learning Objectives 2, 3, 4

June 30 Interest Expense $15,600

P-F:14-42B Analyzing and journalizing bond transactions

On January 1, 2024, Electricians Credit Union (ECU) issued 8%, 20-year bonds payable with face value of $400,000. The bonds pay interest on June 30 and December 31. The issue price of the bonds is 104.

Journalize the following bond transactions:

a. Issuance of the bonds on January 1, 2024.
b. Payment of interest and amortization on June 30, 2024.
c. Payment of interest and amortization on December 31, 2024.
d. Retirement of the bond at maturity on December 31, 2043, assuming the last interest payment has already been recorded.

P-F:14-43B Reporting liabilities on the balance sheet and computing debt to equity ratio

Learning Objectives 5, 6

The accounting records of Compass Wireless include the following as of December 31, 2024:

1. Total Liabilities $286,200

Accounts Payable	$ 74,000	Salaries Payable	$ 7,500
Mortgages Payable (long-term)	80,000	Bonds Payable (current portion)	25,000
Interest Payable	21,000	Premium on Bonds Payable	13,000
Bonds Payable (long-term)	63,000	Unearned Revenue (short-term)	2,700
Total Stockholders' Equity	145,000		

Requirements

1. Report these liabilities on the Compass Wireless balance sheet, including headings and totals for current liabilities and long-term liabilities.
2. Compute Compass Wireless's debt to equity ratio at December 31, 2024.

P-F:14AB-44B Determining the present value of bonds payable and journalizing using the effective-interest amortization method

Learning Objectives 7, 8
Appendixes 14A, 14B

Ari Goldstein issued $300,000 of 11%, five-year bonds payable on January 1, 2024. The market interest rate at the date of issuance was 10%, and the bonds pay interest semiannually.

3. Jan. 1, 2024, Cash $311,613

Requirements

1. How much cash did the company receive upon issuance of the bonds payable? (Round to the nearest dollar.)
2. Prepare an amortization table for the bond using the effective-interest method, through the first two interest payments. (Round to the nearest dollar.)
3. Journalize the issuance of the bonds on January 1, 2024, and the first and second payments of the semiannual interest amount and amortization of the bonds on June 30, 2024, and December 31, 2024. Explanations are not required.

P14AB-45B Determining the present value of bonds payable and journalizing using the effective-interest amortization method

Learning Objectives 7, 8
Appendixes 14A, 14B

Sleep Well, Inc. is authorized to issue 9%, 10-year bonds payable. On January 1, 2024, when the market interest rate is 10%, the company issues $500,000 of the bonds. The bonds pay interest semiannually.

3. Jan. 1, 2024, Cash $468,895

Requirements

1. How much cash did the company receive upon issuance of the bonds payable? (Round to the nearest dollar.)
2. Prepare an amortization table for the bond using the effective-interest method, through the first two interest payments. (Round to the nearest dollar.)
3. Journalize the issuance of the bonds on January 1, 2024, and the first and second payments of the semiannual interest amount and amortization of the bonds on June 30, 2024, and December 31, 2024. Explanations are not required.

CRITICAL THINKING

> Using Excel

Download Excel problems for this chapter online in MyLab Accounting or at **http://www.pearsonhighered.com/Horngren**.

> Continuing Problem

P-F:14-46 Describing bonds, journalizing transactions for bonds payable using the straight-line amortization method, and journalizing transactions for a mortgage payable

This problem continues the Canyon Canoe Company situation from Chapter F:13. Canyon Canoe Company is considering raising additional capital for further expansion. The company wants to finance a new business venture into guided trips down the Amazon River in South America. Additionally, the company wants to add another building on their land to offer more services for local customers.

Canyon Canoe Company plans to raise the capital by issuing $210,000 of 7.5%, six-year bonds on January 2, 2026. The bonds pay interest semiannually on June 30 and December 31. The company receives $208,476 when the bonds are issued.

The company also issues a mortgage payable for $450,000 on January 2, 2026. The proceeds from the mortgage will be used to construct the new building. The mortgage requires annual payments of $45,000 plus interest for ten years, payable on December 31. The mortgage interest rate is 8%.

Requirements

1. Will the bonds issue at face value, a premium, or a discount?
2. Record the following transactions. Include dates and round to the nearest dollar. Omit explanations.
   a. Cash received from the bond issue.
   b. Cash received from the mortgage payable.
   c. Semiannual bond interest payments for 2026. Amortize the premium or discount using the straight-line amortization method.
   d. Payment on the mortgage payable for 2026.
5. Calculate the total interest expense incurred in 2026.

COMPREHENSIVE PROBLEM

> Comprehensive Problem for Chapters F:11, F:13, and F:14

The Tusquittee Company is a retail company that began operations on October 1, 2024, when it incorporated in the state of North Carolina. The Tusquittee Company is authorized to issue 100,000 shares of $1 par value common stock and 50,000 shares of 5%, $50 par value preferred stock. The company sells a product that includes a one-year warranty and records estimated warranty payable each month. Customers are charged a 6% state sales tax. The company uses a perpetual inventory system. There are three employees who are paid a monthly salary on the last day of the month.

Following is the chart of accounts for The Tusquittee Company. As a new business, all beginning balances are $0.

The Tusquittee Company
Chart of Accounts

Cash	Dividends Payable—Common
Merchandise Inventory	Notes Payable
Land	Mortgages Payable
Building	Common Stock—$1 Par Value
Store Fixtures	Paid-In Capital in Excess of Par—Common
Accumulated Depreciation	Paid-In Capital from Treasury Stock Transactions
Accounts Payable	Retained Earnings
Employee Income Taxes Payable	Treasury Stock—Common
FICA—OASDI Taxes Payable	Cash Dividends
FICA—Medicare Taxes Payable	Sales Revenue
Employee Health Insurance Payable	Cost of Goods Sold
Federal Unemployment Taxes Payable	Salaries Expense
State Unemployment Taxes Payable	Payroll Tax Expense
Income Tax Payable	Utilities Expense
Sales Tax Payable	Depreciation Expense
Estimated Warranty Payable	Warranty Expense
Interest Payable	Income Tax Expense
	Interest Expense

The Tusquittee Company completed the following transactions during the last quarter of 2024, its first year of operations:

Oct. 1		Issued 25,000 shares of $1 par value common stock for cash of $10 per share.
	1	Issued a $200,000, 10-year, 8% mortgage payable for land with an existing store building. Mortgage payments of $2,425 are due on the first day of each month, beginning November 1. The assets had the following market values: Land, $40,000; Building, $160,000.
	1	Issued a one-year, 10% note payable for $10,000 for store fixtures. The principal and interest are due October 1, 2025.
	3	Purchased merchandise inventory on account from Top Rate for $125,000, terms n/30.
	15	Paid $160 for utilities.
	31	Recorded cash sales for the month of $185,000 plus sales tax of 6%. The cost of the goods sold was $110,000 and estimated warranty payable was 8%.
	31	Recorded October payroll and paid employees.
	31	Accrued employer payroll taxes for October.
Nov. 1		Paid the first mortgage payment.
	3	Paid Top Rate for the merchandise inventory purchased on October 3.
	10	Purchased merchandise inventory on account from Top Rate for $150,000, terms n/30.
	12	Purchased 500 shares of treasury stock for $15 per share.
	15	Paid all liabilities associated with the October 31 payroll.
	15	Remitted (paid) sales tax from October sales to the state of North Carolina.
	16	Paid $6,000 to satisfy warranty claims.
	17	Declared cash dividends of $1 per outstanding share of common stock.
	18	Paid $245 for utilities.
	27	Paid the cash dividends.
	30	Recorded cash sales for the month of $140,000 plus sales tax of 6%. The cost of the goods sold was $84,000 and estimated warranty payable was 8%.
	30	Recorded November payroll and paid employees.
	30	Accrued employer payroll taxes for November.
Dec. 1		Paid the second mortgage payment.
	10	Paid Top Rate for the merchandise inventory purchased on November 10.
	12	Paid $7,500 to satisfy warranty claims.
	15	Sold 300 shares of treasury stock for $20 per share.
	15	Paid all liabilities associated with the November 30 payroll.
	15	Remitted (paid) sales tax from November sales to the state of North Carolina.
	18	Paid $220 for utilities.
	19	Purchased merchandise inventory on account from Top Rate for $90,000, terms n/30.
	31	Recorded cash sales for the month of $210,000 plus sales tax of 6%. The cost of the goods sold was $126,000 and estimated warranty payable was 8%.
	31	Recorded December payroll and paid employees.
	31	Accrued employer payroll taxes for December.

Requirements

1. In preparation for recording the transactions, prepare:
   a. An amortization schedule for the first three months of the mortgage payable issued on October 1. Round interest calculations to the nearest dollar.
   b. Payroll registers for October, November, and December. All employees worked October 1 through December 31 and are subject to the following FICA taxes: OASDI: 6.2% on first $132,900 earned; Medicare: 1.45% up to $200,000, 2.35% on earnings above $200,000. Additional payroll information includes:

Employee	Monthly Salary	Federal Income Tax	Health Insurance
Kate Jones	$ 6,000	$ 1,800	$ 300
Mary Smith	5,000	1,000	300
Sherry Martin	3,000	450	300

   c. Calculations for employer payroll taxes liabilities for October, November, and December: OASDI: 6.2% on first $132,900 earned; Medicare: 1.45%; SUTA: 5.4% on first $7,000 earned; FUTA: 0.6% on first $7,000 earned.

2. Record the transactions in the general journal. Omit explanations.
3. Post to the general ledger.
4. Record adjusting entries for the three-month period ended December 31, 2024:
   a. Depreciation on the Building, straight-line, 40 years, no residual value.
   b. Store Fixtures, straight-line, 20 years, no residual value.
   c. Accrued interest expense on the note payable for the store fixtures.
   d. Accrued interest expense on the mortgage payable.
   e. Accrued income tax expense of $36,000.
5. Post adjusting entries and prepare an adjusted trial balance.
6. Prepare a multi-step income statement and statement of retained earnings for the quarter ended December 31, 2024. Prepare a classified balance sheet as of December 31, 2024. Assume that $13,840 of the mortgage payable is due within the next year.
7. Evaluate the company's success for the first quarter of operations by calculating the following ratios. The market price of the common stock is $25 on December 31, 2024. Round to two decimal places.
   a. Times interest earned
   b. Debt to equity
   c. Earnings per share
   d. Price/earnings ratio
   e. Rate of return on common stock

8. The Tusquittee Company wants to expand and is considering options for raising additional cash. The company estimates net income before the expansion of $250,000 in 2025 and that the expansion will provide additional operating income of $75,000 in 2025. The company intends to sell the shares of treasury stock, so use issued shares for the analysis rather than current shares outstanding. Compare these options, assuming a 21% income tax rate:

   Plan 1: Issue 10,000 additional shares of common stock for $20 per share

   Plan 2: Issue $200,000 in 20-year, 12% bonds payable.

   Which option will contribute more net income in 2025? Which option provides the highest EPS?

> Tying It All Together Case F:14-1

Before you begin this assignment, review the Tying It All Together feature in the chapter. It will also be helpful if you review The Walt Disney Company's 2018 annual report (**https://www.sec.gov/Archives/edgar/data/1001039/000100103918000187/fy2018_q4x10k.htm**).

The Walt Disney Company is a diversified entertainment company that is comprised of several different business segments. Walt Disney began as a cartoon studio in 1920 and today is known as a leading worldwide entertainment provider.

Requirements

1. On The Walt Disney Company's balance sheet dated September 29, 2018, the company reports borrowings of $17,084 million. Review Note 8 (Borrowings) of the company's annual report. What are the different types of borrowings the company holds?
2. Perform a Web search for the terms commercial paper and medium-term notes. What do each of these terms mean?
3. Review the information included in Note 8. What are the maturity dates for The Walt Disney Company's U.S. medium-term notes?

> Decision Case F:14-1

The following questions are not related.

Requirements

1. Duncan Brooks needs to borrow $500,000 to open new stores. Brooks can borrow $500,000 by issuing 5%, 10-year bonds at 96. How much will Brooks actually receive in cash under this arrangement? How much must Brooks pay back at maturity? How will Brooks account for the difference between the cash received on the issue date and the amount paid back?
2. Brooks prefers to borrow for longer periods when interest rates are low and for shorter periods when interest rates are high. Why is this a good business strategy?

> Ethical Issue F:14-1

Raffie's Kids, a nonprofit organization that provides aid to victims of domestic violence, low-income families, and special-needs children, has a 30-year, 5% mortgage on the existing building. The mortgage requires monthly payments of $3,000. Raffie's bookkeeper is preparing financial statements for the board and, in doing so, lists the mortgage balance of $287,000 under current liabilities because the board hopes to be able to pay the mortgage off in full next year. Of the mortgage principal, $20,000 will be paid next year if Raffie's pays according to the mortgage agreement. The board members call you, their trusted CPA, to advise them on how Raffie's Kids should report the mortgage on its balance sheet. What is the ethical issue? Provide and discuss the reason for your recommendation.

> Fraud Case F:14-1

Bill and Edna had been married for two years and had just reached the point where they had enough savings to start investing. Bill's uncle Dave told them that he had recently inherited some very rare railroad bonds from his grandmother's estate. He wanted to help Bill and Edna get a start in the world and would sell them 50 of the bonds at $100 each. The bonds were dated 1873, beautifully engraved, showing a face value of $1,000 each. Uncle Dave pointed out that "United States of America" was printed prominently at the top and that the U.S. government had established a sinking fund to retire the old railroad bonds. A sinking fund is a fund established for the purpose of repaying the debt. It allows the organization (the U.S. government, in this example) to set aside money over time to retire the bonds. All Bill and Edna needed to do was hold on to them until the government contacted them, and they would eventually get the full $1,000 for each bond. Bill and Edna were overjoyed—until a year later when they saw the exact same bonds for sale at a coin and stamp shop priced as "collectors' items" for $9.95 each!

Requirements

1. If a company goes bankrupt, what happens to the bonds it issued and the investors who bought the bonds?
2. When investing in bonds, how can you tell whether the bond issue is a legitimate transaction?
3. Is there a way to determine the relative risk of corporate bonds?

> Financial Statement Case F:14-1

Use the **Target Corporation** financial statements to answer the following questions. Visit **http://www.pearsonhighered.com/Horngren** to view a link to Target Corporation's Fiscal 2018 Annual Report.

Requirements

1. How much was Target Corporation's long-term debt at February 2, 2019?
2. Compute Target Corporation's debt to equity ratio at February 2, 2019. How does it compare to **Kohl's Corporation's** ratio?

> Quick Check Answers

1. a   2. d   3. b   4. a   5. a   6. c   7. a   8. d   9A. b   10B. b

Investments 15

How Should the Business Invest Its Excess Cash?

Donavon Gill, portfolio manager for GMP Investors, had just finished a meeting with his newest client, Sarah Miller. Sarah is the CEO of Miller Construction, a profitable construction firm with offices throughout the United States. Sarah had requested a meeting with Donavon to discuss an investment plan for the business. Miller Construction was interested in investing its excess cash and, as CEO, Sarah had come to Donavon with a number of questions.

During the meeting, Donavon had shared with Sarah a variety of different investment options that the business could consider. One option might be for Miller Construction to invest in other corporations' stocks (called *equity securities*). Another option for the business might be investing in bonds (called *debt securities*). He also talked to Sarah about why the business might want to invest in each type of security. Donavon knew that it was his responsibility to provide a custom solution for Miller Construction so that Sarah's business would meet its earnings needs.

Sarah was also interested in how Miller Construction would report these investments on its financial statements. She knew that investments in debt and equity securities were reported as assets on the balance sheet, but she was concerned that there might be some additional reporting requirements. Donavon was glad that Sarah was considering these issues and was happy to help her. He shared with her that the type of security (debt or equity) and the length of time the security was held (short-term versus long-term) determined how it was reported on the financial statements. Donavon also suggested that she talk to her company's accountant before deciding on the business's investment plan. He knew that there were a lot of issues to consider when choosing how to invest excess cash.

Why Would a Company Invest?

Many of you are familiar with the famous businessman Warren Buffett, but you might not know that he is the primary stockholder and CEO of **Berkshire Hathaway, Inc**. Berkshire Hathaway is a holding company that owns a large number of other businesses (called *subsidiaries*), including the popular automobile insurer GEICO and the railroad system operator Burlington Northern Santa Fe. In addition to owning subsidiaries, Berkshire Hathaway also invests cash in other corporations' stock, such as The Coca-Cola Company (9.4% ownership), Southwest Airlines Co. (8.7% ownership), and Apple Inc. (5.4% ownership). Investing excess cash in corporations' stocks and bonds is a common practice; many businesses (and individuals) do this. In this chapter, you learn why companies might invest in securities and how these investments are reported on the financial statements.

15-2 Financial  chapter 15

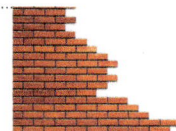

Chapter 15 Learning Objectives

1. Identify why companies invest in debt and equity securities and classify investments
2. Account for investments in debt securities
3. Account for investments in equity securities
4. Describe and illustrate how debt and equity securities are reported
5. Use the rate of return on total assets to evaluate business performance

WHY DO COMPANIES INVEST?

Learning Objective 1
Identify why companies invest in debt and equity securities and classify investments

Just as individuals invest in a variety of companies' stocks and bonds, the same is true for businesses. Investments in stocks or bonds can range from a few securities to the acquisition of an entire company. In this chapter, we examine debt (bonds) and equity (stock) accounting for the investor who buys them.

Debt Securities Versus Equity Securities

Investor
The owner of a bond or stock of a corporation.

Investee
The corporation that issued the bond or stock to the investor.

Security
A share or interest representing financial value.

Debt Security
Investment in notes or bonds payable issued by another company.

Equity Security
Investment in stock ownership in another company that sometimes pays cash dividends or issues stock dividends.

The owner of a bond or stock of a corporation is referred to as the **investor**. The corporation that issued the bond or stock is referred to as the **investee**. For example, if you own shares of Smart Touch Learning's stock, you are the investor and Smart Touch Learning is the investee.

Investors can invest in either debt securities or equity securities. A **security** is a share or interest representing financial value. Securities are represented by a certificate (such as a stock certificate) and are commonly traded on an exchange (such as the New York Stock Exchange). A **debt security** is an investment in notes or bonds payable issued by another company. Debt securities represent a credit relationship with another company or governmental entity, and typically pay interest for a fixed period and a final payment of face value at the end of the term. Debt securities include U.S. government securities (Treasury bills), municipal bonds, and corporate bonds. An **equity security** is an investment in stock ownership in another company and sometimes pays cash dividends or issues stock dividends. Equity securities include common and preferred stock.

Reasons to Invest

Why would a company invest in debt or equity securities? Let's look at two common reasons:

1. The company may have short-term, excess cash that it doesn't need for normal operations. This excess cash could be the result of temporary or seasonal business fluctuations, or it could be cash available for a longer term. The company wants to make the best use of its excess cash, so it invests in debt or equity securities to generate investment income. This investment income may come from interest earned from debt investments, dividends earned from stock investments, and/or increases in the market value of the security.
2. The company may invest in debt or equity securities of other companies to pursue a certain business strategy. For example, a company may invest in a key vendor's debt or equity securities to further enhance a business relationship with that vendor. Doing so might strengthen the relationship between the investing company and the vendor.

Investments  Financial 15-3

Of course, there are other reasons a company may want to invest in other companies' debt or equity securities, but the reasons we identified above are the most common. Now, let's turn to a few basics of investing in debt or equity securities.

ETHICS

It's just a tip, isn't it?

Arlene Barry had just left the most recent board meeting of Panda Toy Manufacturing. Arlene served as chairman of the board and was also a majority stockholder in the business. Panda Toy Manufacturing had just learned that the company was being sued by a multinational retail toy store for failure to use flame-retardant filling in its stuffed panda bears. Arlene knew that the business had been cutting costs and had intentionally used filling that was not up to appropriate standards. She was sure that Panda Toy would lose the lawsuit and knew that the value of her stock would drop considerably. Arlene was considering quickly selling her stock before the lawsuit became public knowledge. What should Arlene do? What would you do?

Solution

If Arlene sells her investment in Panda Toy Manufacturing, she could be found guilty of illegal insider trading. Insider trading occurs when a corporate officer, director, or employee buys or sells stock after learning information obtained during the performance of the individual's duties that is considered to be non-public information about a company. If Arlene wants to sell her shares of Panda Toy, she should wait until after the information has become public. This type of sale would be considered legal insider trading and would need to be reported to the U.S. Securities and Exchange Commission (SEC) to notify the public of a change in ownership of the manufacturer's stock.

Classification and Reporting of Investments

Investments are first classified based on the length of time the investor intends to hold the investment. The two classifications are similar to the balance sheet classifications you learned previously.

- **Short-term investments** are investments in debt and equity securities that the investor intends to sell in one year or less. Short-term investments are reported as current assets.
- **Long-term investments** are all investments that are not short-term. Long-term investments include debt and equity securities that the investor expects to hold longer than one year or debt or equity securities that are not readily marketable—for instance, a stock investment in a small or privately held company that is not traded on any stock exchange.

Debt Securities

Debt securities can be further classified into three specific types based on how long the investor intends to hold the investment.

- **Trading debt investments**[1] are debt securities the investor intends to sell in the very near future—days, weeks, or only a few months—with the intent of generating a profit on a quick sale. Trading debt investments are categorized as current assets.
- **Held-to-maturity (HTM) debt investments** are debt securities the investor intends to hold and has the ability to hold until they mature. Held-to-maturity debt investments are categorized as current assets or long-term assets on the balance sheet, depending on the maturity date.

Short-term Investment
An investment in debt and equity securities that the investor intends to sell in one year or less.

Long-term Investment
An investment in debt and equity securities that the investor intends to hold for longer than one year.

Trading Debt Investment
A debt security that the investor plans to sell in the very near future.

Held-to-Maturity (HTM) Debt Investment
A debt security the investor intends to hold and has the ability to hold until it matures.

---

[1] In January 2016, FASB issued new guidance on financial instruments, *Financial Instruments—Overall*. Under this new guidance, the designation of trading investments (equity) and available-for-sale investments (equity) will be eliminated. Trading investments (debt) and available-for-sale investments (debt) will remain. This new guidance goes into effect for fiscal years after December 15, 2017, and early adoption is not permitted. The applicable sections of the text have been updated for this new guidance.

Available-for-Sale (AFS) Debt Investment
A debt security that isn't a trading debt investment or a held-to-maturity debt investment.

- **Available-for-sale (AFS) debt investments** include all debt securities that aren't trading debt investments or held-to-maturity debt investments. Available-for-sale debt investments are reported either as current assets or long-term assets on the balance sheet. AFS debt investments are reported as current assets if the business expects to sell them within one year. All other AFS debt investments that are planned to be held longer than a year are reported as long-term assets.

Equity Securities

Equity securities can also be classified into three specific types based on the investor's level of influence over the investee company.

- **No significant influence.** Investments in which the investor lacks the ability to participate in the decisions of the investee company are treated as **no significant influence equity investments**. Generally, the investor owns less than 20% of the investee's voting stock. These equity investments are reported as either current assets or long-term assets on the balance sheet depending on how long the investor intends to hold the security.

No Significant Influence Equity Investment
An equity security in which the investor lacks the ability to participate in the decisions of the investee company.

- **Significant influence.** **Significant influence equity investments** are equity securities in which the investor has the ability to exert influence over operating and financial decisions of the investee company. Generally, the investor owns from 20% to 50% of the investee's voting stock. Significant influence equity investments are reported as long-term assets on the balance sheet.

Significant Influence Equity Investment
An equity security in which the investor has the ability to exert influence over operating and financial decisions of the investee company.

- **Controlling interest.** **Controlling interest equity investments** are equity securities in which the investor owns more than 50% of the investee's voting stock. Controlling interest investments are consolidated into the investor's financial statements and are discussed in more advanced accounting courses.

Controlling Interest Equity Investment
An equity security in which the investor owns more than 50% of the investee's voting stock.

Exhibit F:15-1 summarizes the different types of investments.

Exhibit F:15-1 | Types of Investments

Types of Investments	Definition
Debt securities—*Classified by how long the investor intends to hold the investment*	
Trading debt investment	A debt security that the investor plans to sell in the very near future.
Held-to-maturity (HTM) debt investment	A debt security the investor intends to hold and has the ability to hold until it matures.
Available-for-sale (AFS) debt investment	A debt security that isn't a trading debt investment or a held-to-maturity debt investment.
Equity securities—*Classified by the investor's level of influence over the investee company*	
No significant influence equity investment	An equity security in which the investor lacks the ability to participate in the decisions of the investee company.
Significant influence equity investment	An equity security in which the investor has the ability to exert influence over operating and financial decisions of the investee company.
Controlling interest equity investment	An equity security in which the investor owns more than 50% of the investee's voting stock.

Try It!

Match the key term to the scenario.

1. Available-for-sale debt investments
2. Controlling interest equity investments
3. Trading debt investments
4. Held-to-maturity debt investments
5. Significant influence equity investments
6. No significant influence equity investments

a. Jane owns 53% of Richard's Roses' voting stock.
b. Joe owns a debt security in Bones, Inc. and intends to hold it until maturity.
c. Jeannie owns a debt security in Cricket, Inc. and plans on selling the debt after one year.
d. Jimenez owns 5% of Delgado, Inc.'s voting stock but does not have the ability to participate in the decisions of Delgado, Inc.
e. Jacob owns 24% of Pay, Inc.'s voting stock and has the ability to exert influence over Pay, Inc.
f. Jim owns a debt security in Tag, Inc.'s and plans on holding the debt for only a week.

Check your answers online in MyLab Accounting or at http://www.pearsonhighered.com/Horngren.

For more practice, see Short Exercise S-F:15-1. **MyLab Accounting**

HOW ARE INVESTMENTS IN DEBT SECURITIES ACCOUNTED FOR?

Let's begin by discussing how debt securities are accounted for, including the purchase, interest revenue earned, and disposition of the securities.

Learning Objective 2

Account for investments in debt securities

Purchase of Debt Securities

Assume Smart Touch Learning has excess cash to invest and pays $100,000 to buy $100,000 face value, 9%, five-year Neon Company bonds on July 1, 2024. The bonds are issued on July 1, 2024. The bonds pay interest on June 30 and December 31. Smart Touch Learning intends to hold the bonds to maturity and will, therefore, record them as held-to-maturity debt investments. Smart Touch Learning's accounting clerk will record the investment in debt securities at cost, including any brokerage fees paid, with the following entry:

Date	Accounts and Explanation	Debit	Credit
2024			
Jul. 1	Held-to-Maturity Debt Investments	100,000	
	Cash		100,000
	Purchased investment in bonds.		

$\dfrac{A\updownarrow}{\text{HTM Debt Investments}\uparrow}{\text{Cash}\downarrow} = \{ \underline{\quad L \quad} + \underline{\quad E \quad}$

Interest Revenue

On December 31, 2024, Smart Touch Learning would receive the first interest payment on the bond investment. Smart Touch Learning's entry to record the receipt of interest on December 31, 2024, is as follows:

A↑ } = { L + E↑
Cash↑   Interest
              Revenue↑

Date	Accounts and Explanation	Debit	Credit
2024			
Dec. 31	Cash	4,500	
	Interest Revenue ($100,000 × 0.09 × 6/12)		4,500
	Received cash interest.		

Smart Touch Learning would repeat this entry every six months for the five years—each time interest payments are received.

Disposition at Maturity

When Smart Touch Learning disposes of the bonds at maturity (June 30, 2029), it will receive the face value of the bond and record the following entry, assuming the last interest payment has already been recorded:

A↕ } = { L + E
Cash↑
HTM Debt
Investments↓

Date	Accounts and Explanation	Debit	Credit
2029			
Jun. 30	Cash	100,000	
	Held-to-Maturity Debt Investments		100,000
	Disposed of bond at maturity.		

Other Accounting Issues for Debt Investments

In this example, we illustrated the accounting for held-to-maturity debt investments. Debt securities can also be trading debt investments and available-for-sale debt investments. The accounting for these is the same as illustrated above. The only difference is the use of a different account name for the investment. In addition, debt securities can be purchased at face value, at a discount, or at a premium. In our example, we purchased the debt securities at face value. If a debt security is purchased at a discount or at a premium, the discount/premium must be amortized when the interest revenue is earned. This amortization can be done using either the straight-line amortization method or the effective-interest amortization method and is similar to recording the amortization of discount or premium on bonds payable covered in a later chapter.

7. On January 1, 2024, the College Corporation decides to invest in Small Town bonds. The bonds mature on December 31, 2028, and pay interest of 4% on June 30 and December 31. The market rate of interest was 4% on January 1, 2024, so the $20,000 maturity-value bonds sold for face value. College Corporation intends to hold the bonds until maturity. Journalize the transactions related to College Corporation's investment in Small Town bonds during 2024.

Check your answers online in MyLab Accounting or at http://www.pearsonhighered.com/Horngren.

For more practice, see Short Exercise S-F:15-2. **MyLab Accounting**

HOW ARE INVESTMENTS IN EQUITY SECURITIES ACCOUNTED FOR?

The accounting for equity securities must be separated into three categories based on the investor's level of influence over the investee company.

> **Learning Objective 3**
> Account for investments in equity securities

Equity Securities with No Significant Influence (Fair Value Method)

Equity securities in which the investor lacks the ability to participate in the decisions of the investee company are initially accounted for at cost and then adjusted for fair value at the end of each period (covered in learning objective 4).

Purchase

Assume Smart Touch Learning has excess cash to invest and buys 1,000 shares of stock in Yellow Corporation for $26.16 per share on March 1, 2024. Smart Touch Learning does not have the ability to participate in the decisions of Yellow Corporation because it owns a small percentage of the total shares of Yellow Corporation. Smart Touch Learning records the purchase as follows:

Date	Accounts and Explanation	Debit	Credit
2024			
Mar. 1	Equity Investments ($26.16 per share × 1,000 shares)	26,160	
	Cash		26,160
	Purchased investment in stock.		

$$\underline{A \uparrow \downarrow} \left.\begin{array}{l} \\ \text{Equity} \\ \text{Investments} \uparrow \\ \text{Cash} \downarrow \end{array}\right\} = \left\{\begin{array}{l} \underline{L} + \underline{E} \\ \\ \\ \end{array}\right.$$

Dividend Revenue

Yellow Corporation declares and pays a cash dividend of $0.16 per share on June 9, 2024. Smart Touch Learning will receive the cash dividend on June 9 and record the entry as follows:

Date	Accounts and Explanation	Debit	Credit
2024			
Jun. 9	Cash	160	
	Dividend Revenue ($0.16 per share × 1,000 shares)		160
	Received cash dividend.		

$$\underline{A \uparrow} \left.\begin{array}{l} \\ \text{Cash} \uparrow \end{array}\right\} = \left\{\begin{array}{l} \underline{L} + \underline{E \uparrow} \\ \\ \text{Dividend} \\ \text{Revenue} \uparrow \end{array}\right.$$

Disposition

Assume on July 15, 2024, Smart Touch Learning sells 800 shares of Yellow Stock for $25,000. Smart Touch Learning compares the cash received with the cost of the stock disposed of and determines the amount of gain or loss as follows:

Cash received	$ 25,000
Less: Cost of stock disposed of (800 shares × $26.16)	20,928
Gain or (Loss)	$ 4,072

15-8 Financial chapter 15

Smart Touch Learning will then record the following journal entry:

Date	Accounts and Explanation	Debit	Credit
2024			
Jul. 15	Cash	25,000	
	Equity Investments		20,928
	Gain on Disposal		4,072
	Disposed of investment in stock.		

A↑ Cash↑ / Equity Investments↓ } = { L + E↑ Gain on Disposal↑

Remember that Gain on Disposal is a temporary equity account and is reported in the Other Income and (Expenses) section of the income statement. If the company had sold the stock at a loss, the account Loss on Disposal would be recorded as a debit and also reported in the Other Income and (Expenses) section of the income statement.

Equity Securities with Significant Influence (Equity Method)

When a company invests in equity securities with 20% to 50% ownership in the investee's voting stock, the investor can *significantly influence* the investee's decisions. This influence may be helpful if the investee's and investor's businesses are somehow related. These types of investments must be accounted for using the equity method.

Purchase

Investments accounted for by the equity method are recorded at cost at the time of purchase. Suppose Smart Touch Learning pays $400,000 to purchase 40% of the common stock of Kline, Inc. Smart Touch Learning then refers to Kline as an *affiliated company*. Smart Touch Learning's entry to record the purchase of this investment on January 6, 2024, follows. Notice that the investor includes the name of the investee on the account to signify that Smart Touch Learning has significant influence over Kline, Inc.

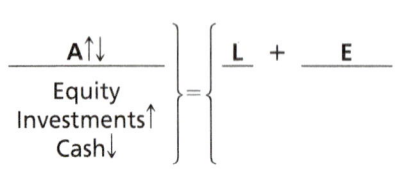

Date	Accounts and Explanation	Debit	Credit
2024			
Jan. 6	Equity Investments—Kline, Inc.	400,000	
	Cash		400,000
	Purchased investment in stock (equity method).		

Dividends Received and Share of Net Income

When Smart Touch Learning receives cash dividends from Kline, it records its proportionate part of the cash dividends. Suppose that Kline declares and pays a cash dividend of $50,000 on June 30, 2024. Because Smart Touch Learning owns 40% of the stock, it receives 40%, or $20,000, of the dividend. Smart Touch Learning receives this dividend and makes the following journal entry:

Date	Accounts and Explanation	Debit	Credit
2024			
Jun. 30	Cash ($50,000 × 0.40)	20,000	
	Equity Investments—Kline, Inc.		20,000
	Received cash dividend (equity method).		

A↑↓ } = { L + E
Cash↑
Equity Investments↓

The Equity Investments account is credited for the receipt of a dividend because it decreases the investor's investment. In other words, the dividends are treated as if they were a return of capital rather than as earnings.

Under the equity method, the investor also must record annually its share of the investee's net income. The investor debits the Equity Investments account and credits Revenue from Investments when the investee reports income. As Smart Touch Learning's equity in Kline increases, so does the Equity Investments account on the investor's books.

Suppose Kline reported net income of $125,000 for 2024. Smart Touch Learning would record 40% of this amount as an increase in the investment account, as follows:

> In using the equity method, when a dividend is received, why is the Equity Investments account credited instead of Dividend Revenue?

Date	Accounts and Explanation	Debit	Credit
2024			
Dec. 31	Equity Investments—Kline, Inc.	50,000	
	Revenue from Investments ($125,000 × 0.40)		50,000
	Recorded revenue earned from investment (equity method).		

A↑ } = { L + E↑
Equity Investments↑   Revenue from Investments↑

After the preceding entries are posted, Smart Touch Learning's Equity Investments T-account shows its equity in the net assets of Kline as follows:

```
         Equity Investments—Kline, Inc.
Jan. 6       400,000  |  20,000   Jun. 30
Dec. 31       50,000  |
Bal.         430,000  |
```

Smart Touch Learning would report the equity investments on the balance sheet and the revenue from investments on the income statement.

Disposition

When Smart Touch Learning decides to sell its investment in Kline, Inc. it will need to determine whether there is a gain or loss. Suppose Smart Touch Learning sells 10% of the Kline common stock for $40,000 on January 1, 2025. Smart Touch Learning will calculate the gain or loss as follows and record the following journal entry:

Cash received	$ 40,000
Less: Book value on date of disposal ($430,000 × 0.10)	43,000
Gain or (Loss)	$ (3,000)

15-10 Financial chapter 15

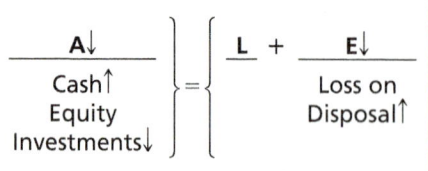

Date	Accounts and Explanation	Debit	Credit
2025			
Jan. 1	Cash	40,000	
	Loss on Disposal	3,000	
	Equity Investments—Kline, Inc.		43,000
	Disposed of part of investment in stock (equity method).		

Equity Securities with Controlling Interest (Consolidation Method)

Parent Company
A company that owns a controlling interest in another company.

Subsidiary Company
A company that is controlled by another corporation.

Consolidation Accounting
The way to combine the financial statements of two or more companies that have the same owners.

Consolidated Statements
Financial statements that combine the balance sheets, income statements, and statements of cash flow of the parent company with those of its controlling interest affiliates.

Many large corporations own controlling interests in other companies. An investor owns a controlling interest when the investor has legal control over the investee company and generally owns more than 50% of the investee's voting stock. This type of investment enables the investor to elect a majority of the board of directors and thereby control the investee. The corporation that controls the other company is called the **parent company**, and the company that is controlled by another corporation is called the **subsidiary company**.

In equity securities with more than 50% ownership, the parent usually prepares consolidated financial statements. **Consolidation accounting** is the way to combine the financial statements of two or more companies that have the same owners. Many published financial reports include consolidated statements. **Consolidated statements** combine the financial statements (such as the balance sheets, income statements, and statements of cash flow) of the parent company with those of its controlling interest affiliates. The final outcome is a single set of statements, as if the parent and its subsidiaries were the same entity. This topic is covered in advanced accounting courses.

8. On May 15, 2024, Mayer Co. invests $8,000 in John, Inc. stock. John pays Mayer a $200 dividend on November 15, 2024. Mayer sells the John stock on December 10, 2024, for $7,500. Assume the Mayer Co. does not have significant influence over John, Inc. Journalize the 2024 transactions related to Mayer's investment in John stock.

Check your answers online in MyLab Accounting or at http://www.pearsonhighered.com/Horngren.

For more practice, see Short Exercises S-F:15-3 and S-F:15-4. MyLab Accounting

HOW ARE DEBT AND EQUITY SECURITIES REPORTED?

Learning Objective 4
Describe and illustrate how debt and equity securities are reported

Corporations' debt and equity securities are reported on the balance sheet in either the current or the long-term asset section. How they are reported, though, depends upon the type of investment.

Trading Debt Investments (Fair Value Method)

Fair Value
The price that would be used if the investments were sold on the market.

Trading debt investments, those that the investor plans to sell in the very near future, are initially recorded at cost. At the end of each period, though, trading debt securities must be adjusted and reported at fair value. **Fair value** is the price that would be used if the company

Investments Financial 15-11

were to sell the investments on the market. The company will make a year-end adjustment of the trading debt investment to bring the account to market value. This adjustment is recorded as an unrealized holding gain or loss and is reported in the Other Income and (Expenses) section of the income statement.

> *It's important to note the distinction between unrealized and realized gains or losses. Unrealized gains or losses occur when a company adjusts an asset to fair value but has not yet disposed of the asset. Realized gains or losses occur when a company disposes of an asset and represents the difference between the cash received at time of disposal and the basis of the asset.*

Suppose that on December 31, 2024, Smart Touch Learning reported trading debt investments of $26,160. After careful evaluation, Smart Touch Learning concluded that the market value of the trading debt investments had decreased to $24,000. The company has an unrealized loss of $2,160 on the investments ($24,000 − $26,160). At year-end, Smart Touch Learning would record the following adjusting entry:

Date	Accounts and Explanation	Debit	Credit
2024			
Dec. 31	Unrealized Holding Loss—Trading	2,160	
	Fair Value Adjustment—Trading		2,160
	Adjusted trading debt investments to market value.		

A↓ = L + E↓
Fair Value Adjustment↓ = Unrealized Holding Loss↑

After the adjustment, the investment T-accounts would appear as follows:

Trading Debt Investments		Fair Value Adjustment—Trading	
Bal. 26,160			2,160 Dec. 31

$26,160 − $2,160 = $24,000

> *In this case, the Fair Value Adjustment account has a credit balance, and it is considered a contra account and is subtracted from the Trading Debt Investments account to determine carrying value. If the account has a debit balance, it is considered an adjunct account and is added to the Trading Debt Investments account to determine carrying value.*

The combined T-accounts show the $24,000 balance for trading debt investments. Smart Touch Learning would report its trading debt investments on the balance sheet at $24,000 at December 31, 2024, and the $2,160 unrealized holding loss on the trading debt investments on the 2024 income statement as follows:

SMART TOUCH LEARNING
Balance Sheet (Partial)
December 31, 2024

Current Assets:	
Trading Debt Investments (at fair value; cost $26,160)	$ 24,000

SMART TOUCH LEARNING
Income Statement (Partial)
For the Year Ended December 31, 2024

Other Income and (Expenses):	
Unrealized Holding Loss—Trading	$ (2,160)

Disposition

When a trading debt security is disposed, the fair value adjustment is ignored in determining the calculation of the gain or loss. The disposition is handled as we have shown earlier in the chapter. The amount of gain or loss is calculated as the difference between the cash received and the cost of the stock disposed. At the end of the year, the company would evaluate its remaining trading debt securities and make a year-end adjustment to current market value.

Available-for-Sale Debt Investments (Fair Value Method)

Available-for-sale (AFS) debt investments are reported as *current assets* on the balance sheet if the business expects to sell them within one year. All other AFS debt investments that are planned to be held longer than a year are reported as *long-term assets* on the balance sheet. The fair value method is also used to account for AFS debt investments.

AFS debt investments are reported on the balance sheet at current market value. This requires a year-end adjustment of the AFS debt investment to current market value, much like the treatment of trading debt investments. However, the unrealized holding gains and losses on AFS debt investments are not reported on the income statement. They are recorded as an adjustment to the Unrealized Holding Gain—Available-for-Sale account or Unrealized Holding Loss—Available-for-Sale account, which is included in Other Comprehensive Income on the Statement of Comprehensive Income and as a component of Accumulated Other Comprehensive Income in the stockholders' equity section of the balance sheet.

Assume on December 31, 2024, Smart Touch Learning reported long-term available-for-sale debt investments of $60,000. After careful review, the company determines the market value of the AFS debt investments has increased to $64,000. Smart Touch Learning has an unrealized holding gain of $4,000 on the investment ($64,000 market value minus $60,000 purchase price). At year-end, Smart Touch Learning would make the following adjustment:

Date	Accounts and Explanation	Debit	Credit
2024			
Dec. 31	Fair Value Adjustment—Available-for-Sale	4,000	
	Unrealized Holding Gain—Available-for-Sale		4,000
	Adjusted available-for-sale debt investments to market value.		

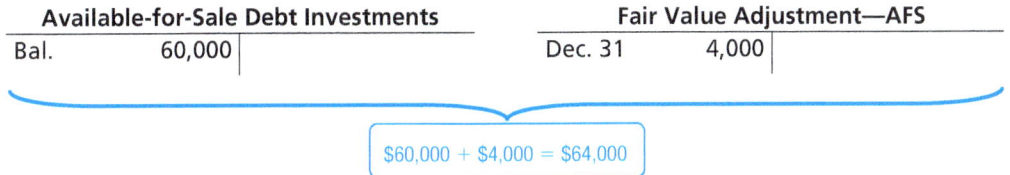

After posting the December 31, 2024, adjustment, the investment T-accounts would appear as follows:

Available-for-Sale Debt Investments		Fair Value Adjustment—AFS	
Bal. 60,000		Dec. 31 4,000	

$60,000 + $4,000 = $64,000

The combined T-accounts show the $64,000 balance for the AFS debt investments. Smart Touch Learning would report the investment on the balance sheet at $64,000 at December 31, 2024. The $4,000 Unrealized Holding Gain—Available-for-Sale would be reported in the stockholders' equity section of the balance sheet as Accumulated Other Comprehensive Income as shown here:

SMART TOUCH LEARNING
Balance Sheet (Partial)
December 31, 2024

Assets
Long-term Assets:
  Available-for-Sale Debt Investments (at fair value; cost $60,000) $ 64,000

Stockholders' Equity
Accumulated Other Comprehensive Income:
  Unrealized Holding Gain—AFS $ 4,000

It's important to remember that unrealized holding gains or losses on available-for-sale debt investments are not included in net income. Instead, they are included as other comprehensive income, which are adjustments to net income to determine comprehensive income. **Comprehensive income** is the company's change in total stockholders' equity from all sources other than owners' investments and dividends. Comprehensive income includes net income plus some specific gains and losses, as follows:

- Unrealized holding gains or losses on *available-for-sale debt investments*
- Foreign currency translation adjustments
- Gains or losses from post-retirement benefit plans
- Deferred gains or losses from derivatives

Comprehensive Income
A company's change in total stockholders' equity from all sources other than owners' investments and dividends.

The calculation of these items is explained in advanced accounting courses. For now, you need to know that these items do not enter into the determination of net income but, instead, are reported as other comprehensive income.

Comprehensive income can be reported one of two ways: as a second income statement or combined with a traditional income statement into a combined statement of comprehensive income. An example of how comprehensive income can be reported is shown in Exhibit F:15-2.

Exhibit F:15-2 | **Comprehensive Income**

SMART TOUCH LEARNING Comprehensive Income Statement For the Year Ended December 31, 2024	
Net Income	$ 100,000
Other Comprehensive Income:	
Unrealized Holding Gain—AFS	4,000
Comprehensive Income	$ 104,000

Disposition

It is important to note that disposition of available-for-sale debt investments is handled in the same manner as trading debt investments. Any prior period fair value adjustment is ignored when calculating the amount of the gain or loss. The gain or loss is determined as the difference between the amount received and the cost of the investment. At the end of the year, the company would evaluate their remaining available-for-sale debt investments and make a year-end adjustment to current market value.

Held-to-Maturity Debt Investments (Amortized Cost)

Held-to-maturity (HTM) debt investments are normally reported at amortized cost, which is explained in advanced accounting courses. Depending on the maturity date, the HTM debt investment will be reported as a current asset or a long-term asset on the balance sheet. When the maturity date is within one year of the balance sheet date, the HTM debt investment is reported as a current asset; otherwise, the asset is reported as long-term. Interest revenue earned on HTM debt investments is reported on the income statement in the Other Income and (Expenses) section.

Equity Investments with No Significant Influence (Fair Value Method)

Equity investments with no significant influence must also be adjusted at the end of the year and reported at fair value. Similar to trading debt investments, the company will make a year-end adjustment of the equity investment to bring the account to market value. The adjustment is recorded as an unrealized holding gain or loss and is reported in the Other Income and (Expenses) section of the income statement.

Exhibit F:15-3 summarizes the accounting methods for debt and equity securities and also the financial statement effects.

Investments Financial 15-15

Exhibit F:15-3 | **Debt and Equity Securities—Accounting Methods and Financial Statement Effects**

Types of Investments	Accounting Methods	Financial Statement Effects — Balance Sheet	Financial Statement Effects — Income Statement
Trading Debt Investments	Fair Value: Unrealized Holding Gain or Loss is included in net income.	The investment is reported as a current asset on the balance sheet.	Interest revenue is reported on the income statement.
Held-to-Maturity Debt Investments	Amortized Cost	Depending on the maturity date, the investment is reported as a current or long-term asset on the balance sheet.	Interest revenue is reported on the income statement.
Available-for-Sale Debt Investments	Fair Value: Unrealized Holding Gain or Loss is included in Other Comprehensive Income and reported as a separate component of stockholders' equity.	The investment is reported as a current or long-term asset on the balance sheet depending on management's intent.	Interest revenue is reported on the income statement.
No Significant Influence Equity Investments	Fair Value: Unrealized Holding Gain or Loss is included in net income.	The investment is reported as a current or long-term asset on the balance sheet depending on management's intent.	Dividend revenue is reported on the income statement.
Significant Influence Equity Investments	Equity	The investment is reported as a long-term asset on the balance sheet.	A percentage share of investee's net income is reported on the income statement.
Controlling Interest Equity Investments	Consolidation	The balance sheets of the parent and subsidiary are combined.	The income statements of the parent and subsidiary are combined.

TYING IT ALL TOGETHER

Berkshire Hathaway, Inc. is a holding company owning subsidiaries that engage in a variety of different business activities including insurance, freight rail transportation, utilities and energy, manufacturing, services, and retail. Companies such as GEICO, Burlington Northern Santa Fe, Benjamin Moore, and See's Candies are included in the list of Berkshire Hathaway's subsidiaries. (You can find Berkshire Hathaway, Inc.'s 2018 annual report at **https://www.sec.gov/Archives/edgar/data/1067983/000119312519048926/d678758d10k.htm**)

What type of investments does Berkshire Hathaway report on its balance sheet?

Berkshire Hathaway reports both debt and equity securities on its balance sheet. The company classifies the investments as fixed maturity securities (debt investments), equity securities, and equity securities with significant influence.

How are Berkshire Hathaway's investments classified?

The company, in the notes to the financial statements, reports that held-to-maturity investments are carried at amortized cost and trading securities are acquired with the intent to sell in the near term and are carried at fair value. All other securities are classified as available-for-sale and are carried at fair value. The equity method is used for equity investments in which the company has the ability to exercise significant influence but not control.

15-16　Financial chapter 15

9. On August 20, 2024, Mraz Co. decides to invest excess cash of $2,500 by purchasing Virginia, Inc. bonds. At year-end, December 31, 2024, the market price of the bonds was $2,000. The investment is categorized as available-for-sale debt. Journalize the adjusting entry needed at December 31, 2024.

Check your answer online in MyLab Accounting or at http://www.pearsonhighered.com/Horngren.

For more practice, see Short Exercises S-F:15-5 and S-F:15-6. **MyLab Accounting**

HOW DO WE USE THE RATE OF RETURN ON TOTAL ASSETS TO EVALUATE BUSINESS PERFORMANCE?

Learning Objective 5
Use the rate of return on total assets to evaluate business performance

Rate of Return on Total Assets
A ratio that measures the success a company has in using its assets to earn income. (Net income + Interest expense) / Average total assets.

The **rate of return on total assets**, or simply *return on assets*, measures a company's success in using assets to earn a profit. There are two ways that a company can finance its assets:

- Debt—A company can borrow money from creditors to purchase assets. Creditors earn interest on the money that is loaned.
- Equity—A company may receive cash or other assets from stockholders. Stockholders invest in the company and hope to receive a return on their investment.

Rate of return on total assets is calculated by adding interest expense to net income and dividing by average total assets. Interest expense is added back to net income to determine the real return on the assets regardless of the corporation's financing choices (debt or equity).

Using **Kohl's Corporation's** Fiscal 2018 Annual Report, for the year ended February 2, 2019, we can determine its rate of return on total assets. Visit **http://www.pearsonhighered.com/Horngren** to view a link to Kohl's Corporation's annual report. Net income and interest expense are taken from the company's income statement, and total assets is taken from the balance sheet as follows (in millions):

Total Assets, February 2, 2019	$ 12,469
Total Assets, February 3, 2018	13,389
For Year Ended February 2, 2019:	
Interest Expense	256
Net Income	801

The rate of return on total assets is calculated as:

> Rate of return on total assets = (Net income + Interest expense) / Average total assets
> = ($801 + $256) / [$12,469 + $13,389) / 2]
> = 0.082 = 8.2%

Kohl's Corporation has a rate of return on total assets of 8.2%, which means that for each $1.00 invested in the company's average assets, the company earned $0.08 in profits before considering interest expense. What is a good rate of return on total assets? There is no single answer because rates of return vary widely by industry. Suppose that for the department stores industry, a 12% rate of return on total assets is considered good. In that case, Kohl's Corporation's 8.2% return on assets would be considered very low compared to the industry average.

Investments Financial 15-17

10. Lee Co. reported the following items on its 2024 financial statements:

Total Assets, December 31, 2024	$ 10,000
Total Assets, December 31, 2023	15,000
For Year Ended December 31, 2024:	
Interest Expense	150
Net Income	850

Determine Lee's rate of return on total assets for 2024.

Check your answer online in MyLab Accounting or at http://www.pearsonhighered.com/Horngren.

For more practice, see Short Exercise S-F:15-7. **MyLab Accounting**

REVIEW

> Things You Should Know

1. Why do companies invest?

- Companies invest in debt or equity securities to generate investment income or to pursue a certain business strategy.
- A debt security is an investment in notes or bonds payable issued by another company.
- An equity security is an investment in stock ownership in another company that sometimes pays cash dividends or issues stock dividends.
- Investments are classified as either short-term or long-term investments.
- Debt securities can be classified into three categories:
    - Trading debt investments—debt securities the investor intends to sell in the very near future
    - Held-to-maturity (HTM) debt investments—debt securities the investor intends to hold and has the ability to hold until they mature
    - Available-for-sale (AFS) debt investments—debt securities that aren't trading debt investments or held-to-maturity debt investments
- Equity securities can be classified into three categories:
    - No significant influence equity investments—equity securities in which the investor lacks the ability to participate in the decisions of the investee company
    - Significant influence equity investments—equity securities in which the investor has the ability to exert influence over operating and financial decisions of the investee company. Generally the investor owns 20% to 50% of the investee's voting stock.
    - Controlling interest equity investments—equity securities in which the investor owns more than 50% of the investee's voting stock

2. How are investments in debt securities accounted for?

- Investments in debt securities are recorded at cost, including any brokerage fees paid.
- The receipt of interest revenue is recorded with a debit to Cash and a credit to Interest Revenue.
- Debt securities disposed of at maturity are recorded with a debit to Cash and a credit to the Debt Investments account.

3. How are investments in equity securities accounted for?

- Equity securities with no significant influence
  - The purchase is recorded at cost, including any brokerage fees paid.
  - The receipt of dividend revenue is recorded with a debit to Cash and a credit to Dividend Revenue.
  - Disposition could involve either a gain or loss on disposal.
- Equity securities with significant influence
  - The purchase is recorded at cost.
  - Dividends declared and received are recorded with a debit to Cash and a credit to Equity Investments. A dividend reduces the investor's investment.
  - The investor's share of net income is recorded as a debit to Equity Investments and a credit to Revenue from Investments. Net income increases the investor's investment.
  - Disposition could involve either a gain or loss on disposal.
- Equity securities with controlling interest are recorded using the consolidation method, which involves the parent company preparing consolidated financial statements.

4. How are debt and equity securities reported?

- Trading debt investments, available-for-sale debt investments, and equity investments with no significant influence are reported at fair value on the balance sheet.
  - The unrealized holding gain or loss incurred on trading debt investments and equity investments are reported on the income statement as Other Income and (Expenses).
  - The unrealized holding gain or loss incurred on available-for-sale debt investments is not included in net income. It is, instead, reported as part of accumulated other comprehensive income included in stockholders' equity on the balance sheet.
- Held-to-maturity debt investments are reported at amortized cost on the balance sheet.

5. How do we use the rate of return on total assets to evaluate business performance?

- The rate of return on total assets measures a company's success in using its assets to earn a profit.
- (Net income + Interest expense) / Average total assets.

> Check Your Understanding

Check your understanding of the chapter by completing this problem and then looking at the solution. Use this practice to help identify which sections of the chapter you need to study more.

Requirements

1. Identify the appropriate accounting method for each of the following situations (See Learning Objective 1):
   a. Investment in 25% of the investee company's stock of which the investor has significant influence
   b. Available-for-sale debt investment
   c. Investment in more than 50% of the investee company's stock
   d. Bond investment that matures in four years. The investor plans to hold the bond for the full four years.

2. At what amount should the following trading debt investment portfolio be reported on the December 31, 2024, balance sheet? (See Learning Objective 4)

Bond	Investment Cost	Current Market Value
Purple	$ 5,000	$ 5,500
Yellow	61,200	53,000
Black	3,680	6,230
Totals	$ 69,880	$ 64,730

   Journalize any adjusting entry required on December 31.

3. An investor paid $67,900 on January 1, 2024, to acquire 40% of Finn-Girl, Inc.'s outstanding common stock. The investor had significant influence of Finn-Girl, Inc. For the year ending December 31, 2024, Finn-Girl's net income was $80,000, and on June 14, the company declared and paid cash dividends of $55,000 to all stockholders. Journalize the investor's transactions related to the Finn-Girl investment: (a) purchase of the investment, (b) receipt of dividends, (c) investor's share of net income, and (d) sale of Finn-Girl stock for $80,100 on January 3, 2025. (See Learning Objective 3)

> Solutions

Requirement 1

a. Equity   b. Fair value   c. Consolidation   d. Amortized cost

Requirement 2

The trading debt investments should be reported at market value, $64,730, on the balance sheet. The adjusting entry required to report the investments at fair value is as follows:

Date	Accounts and Explanation	Debit	Credit
2024			
Dec. 31	Unrealized Holding Loss—Trading ($64,730 − $69,880)	5,150	
	Fair Value Adjustment—Trading		5,150
	Adjusted trading debt investments to market value.		

The Unrealized Holding Loss—Trading would be reported as an Other Income and (Expenses) item on the income statement.

Requirement 3

Date	Accounts and Explanation	Debit	Credit
2024			
(a) Jan. 1	Equity Investments—Finn-Girl, Inc.	67,900	
	Cash		67,900
	Purchased investment in stock (equity method).		
(b) Jun. 14	Cash	22,000	
	Equity Investments—Finn-Girl, Inc. ($55,000 × 0.40)		22,000
	Received cash dividends (equity method).		
(c) Dec. 31	Equity Investments—Finn-Girl, Inc.	32,000	
	Revenue from Investments ($80,000 × 0.40)		32,000
	Recorded revenue earned from investment (equity method).		
2025			
(d) Jan. 3	Cash	80,100	
	Equity Investments—Finn-Girl, Inc.		77,900
	Gain on Disposal		2,200
	Disposed of investment in stock (equity method).		

Calculations for disposal:

Equity Investments—Finn-Girl, Inc.

Jan. 1	67,900	22,000	Jun. 14
Dec. 31	32,000		
Bal.	77,900		

Cash received	$ 80,100
Less: Book value of stock disposed of	77,900
Gain or (Loss)	$ 2,200

> Key Terms

Available-for-Sale (AFS) Debt Investment (p. 15-4)
Comprehensive Income (p. 15-13)
Consolidated Statements (p. 15-10)
Consolidation Accounting (p. 15-10)
Controlling Interest Equity Investment (p. 15-4)
Debt Security (p. 15-2)
Equity Security (p. 15-2)
Fair Value (p. 15-10)
Held-to-Maturity (HTM) Debt Investment (p. 15-3)
Investee (p. 15-2)
Investor (p. 15-2)
Long-term Investment (p. 15-3)
No Significant Influence Equity Investment (p. 15-4)
Parent Company (p. 15-10)
Rate of Return on Total Assets (p. 15-16)
Security (p. 15-2)
Short-term Investment (p. 15-3)
Significant Influence Equity Investment (p. 15-4)
Subsidiary Company (p. 15-10)
Trading Debt Investment (p. 15-3)

> Quick Check

1. Assume Intervale Railway is considering investing in Pale Co. stock for three months. The investment will represent 5% of the voting stock of Pale Co. How would the investment be classified?

    Learning Objective 1

    a. Significant influence equity investment
    b. No significant influence equity investment
    c. Held-to-maturity debt investment
    d. Controlling interest equity investment

2. Which of the following investments is most likely classified as a held-to-maturity debt investment?

    Learning Objective 1

    a. 80% stock ownership in a subsidiary
    b. 100% ownership in voting stock of a supplier
    c. 10-year bonds
    d. None of the above

3. If Intervale Railway invests $100,000 in 5% bonds at face value that the company intends to hold until the bond maturity date, the interest revenue recognized when each semiannual interest payment is received would be recorded as a

    Learning Objective 2

    a. credit to Cash, $2,500.
    b. credit to Interest Revenue, $2,500.
    c. debit to Held-to-Maturity Debt Investments, $2,500.
    d. debit to Dividend Revenue, $2,500.

4. A company invested $45,000 in Yale Co. stock. The investment represented 5% of the voting stock of Yale Co. If the Yale Co. stock investment paid dividends, what account would be credited?

    Learning Objective 3

    a. Equity Investments
    b. Interest Revenue
    c. Dividend Revenue
    d. Cash

5. If a company owns 25% of the voting stock of Pink Co. and can exercise significant influence, dividends received will be

    Learning Objective 3

    a. credited to Equity Investments—Pink Co.
    b. credited to Dividend Revenue.
    c. debited to Equity Investments—Pink Co.
    d. credited to Cash.

6. Best Appliances owns 90% of the voting stock of Wratchet, Inc. Which of the following is true?

    Learning Objective 3

    a. The financial statements of Best would be consolidated into Wratchet.
    b. Wratchet would be considered the parent entity.
    c. Best would be considered the parent entity.
    d. Both a and c are correct.

7. Yale Co. purchased a bond on October 4 of the current year for $45,000 and classified it as available-for-sale. The market value of the investment at year-end is $42,000. What value will be reported in net income for the adjustment, if any?

    Learning Objective 4

    a. $42,000
    b. $0
    c. $(3,000)
    d. Not enough information is given to determine the amount included in net income.

15-22 Financial chapter 15

Learning Objective 4

8. Harvard Co. purchased a bond on December 1 of the current year for $30,000 and classified the investment as trading. The market value of the investment at year-end is $36,000. What value will be reported in net income for the adjustment?

   a. $36,000   b. $(6,000)   c. $6,000   d. $30,000

Learning Objective 4

9. Bendi Corp. purchased 1,000 shares of Kala Corp. for $16 per share. The investment represents 5% ownership, and Bendi does not have significant influence. The fair value at year-end is $15 per share. Assuming no other transactions occurred, where would the $1 per share difference be reported on the year-end financial statements?

   a. Other Income and (Expense)   c. Operating Income
   b. Other Comprehensive Income   d. None of the above

Learning Objective 5

10. Panjab Company reported the following information on its financial statements:

Total Assets, December 31, 2024	$ 400,000
Total Assets, December 31, 2025	440,000
For Year Ended December 31, 2025:	
Interest Expense	2,000
Net Income	40,000

What is Panjab's rate of return on total assets?

   a. 10.0%   c. 10.5%
   b. 9.5%   d. None of the above

Check your answers at the end of the chapter.

ASSESS YOUR PROGRESS

> Review Questions

1. What is a debt security?
2. What is an equity security?
3. Why would a company invest in debt or equity securities?
4. Briefly describe the specific types of debt and equity securities.
5. How is the purchase of a held-to-maturity debt security at face value recorded?
6. When disposing of an available-for-sale debt investment, where is the gain or loss on disposal reported in the financial statements?
7. What method is used for investments in equity securities when the investor has significant influence and typically 20% to 50% ownership? Briefly describe how dividends declared and received and share of net income are reported.
8. What method is used for investments in equity securities with more than 50% ownership? Briefly describe this method.
9. What adjustment must be made at the end of the period for trading debt investments and available-for-sale debt investments?
10. Where on the financial statements is an unrealized holding gain or loss on trading debt investments reported?

11. Where on the financial statements is an unrealized holding gain or loss on available-for-sale debt investments reported?
12. What is comprehensive income, and what does it include?
13. How are held-to-maturity debt investments reported on the financial statements?
14. What does the rate of return on total assets measure, and how is it calculated?

> Short Exercises

S-F:15-1 Identifying why companies invest and classifying investments
Learning Objective 1

Garden Haven has excess cash of $15,000 at the end of the harvesting season. Garden Haven will need this cash in four months for normal operations.

Requirements
1. What are some reasons why Garden Haven may choose to invest in debt or equity securities?
2. What type of classification would Garden Haven's investment fall within—short-term or long-term? Why?

S-F:15-2 Accounting for debt investments
Learning Objective 2

On January 1, 2024, Chaucer's Restaurant decides to invest in Lake Turner bonds. The bonds mature on December 31, 2029, and pay interest on June 30 and December 31 at 4% annually. The market rate of interest was 4% on January 1, 2024, so the $90,000 maturity value bonds sold for face value. Chaucer's intends to hold the bonds until December 31, 2029.

Requirements
1. Journalize the transactions related to Chaucer's investment in Lake Turner bonds during 2024.
2. In what category would Chaucer's report the investment on the December 31, 2024, balance sheet?

S-F:15-3 Accounting for equity investments
Learning Objective 3

On January 1, 2024, Bark Company invests $10,000 in Roots, Inc. stock. Roots pays Bark a $400 dividend on August 1, 2024. Bark sells the Roots' stock on August 31, 2024, for $10,450. Assume the investment is categorized as a short-term equity investment and Bark Company does not have significant influence over Roots, Inc.

Requirements
1. Journalize the transactions for Bark's investment in Roots' stock.
2. What was the net effect of the investment on Bark's net income for the year ended December 31, 2024?

S-F:15-4 Accounting for equity investments
Learning Objective 3

On January 1, 2024, Bryant, Inc. decides to invest in 3,750 shares of Farrier stock when the stock is selling for $16 per share. On August 1, 2024, Farrier paid a $0.70 per share cash dividend to stockholders. On December 31, 2024, Farrier reports net income of $50,000 for 2024. Assume Farrier has 15,000 shares of voting stock outstanding during 2024 and Bryant has significant influence over Farrier.

Requirements

1. Identify what type of investment the Farrier stock is for Bryant.
2. Journalize the transactions related to Bryant's investment in the Farrier stock during 2024.
3. In what category and at what value would Bryant's report the investment on the December 31, 2024, balance sheet?

Learning Objectives 3, 4

S-F:15-5 Accounting for debt investments

On February 1, 2024, Bell Co. decides to invest excess cash of $16,800 by purchasing a Grant, Inc. bond at face value. At year-end, December 31, 2024, the fair value of the Grant bond was $19,600. The investment is categorized as a trading debt investment.

Requirements

1. Journalize the transactions for Bell's investment in Grant, Inc. for 2024.
2. In what category and at what value would Bell report the asset on the December 31, 2024, balance sheet? In what account would the market price change in Grant's bond be reported, if at all?
3. What was the net effect of the investment on Bell's net income for the year ended December 31, 2024?

Learning Objectives 3, 4

S-F:15-6 Accounting for debt investments

On June 1, 2024, Josh's Restaurant decides to invest excess cash of $54,400 from the tourist season by purchasing a Jackrabbit, Inc. bond at face value. At year-end, December 31, 2024, Jackrabbit's bond had a market value of $51,200. The investment is categorized as an available-for-sale debt investment and will be held for the short-term.

Requirements

1. Journalize the transactions for Josh's investment in Jackrabbit, Inc. for 2024.
2. In what category and at what value would Josh report the asset on the December 31, 2024, balance sheet? In what account would the market price change in Jackrabbit's stock be reported, if at all?
3. What was the net effect of the investment on Josh's net income for the year ended December 31, 2024?

Learning Objective 5

S-F:15-7 Computing rate of return on total assets

Barot's 2024 financial statements reported the following items—with 2023 figures given for comparison:

BAROT, INC.
Balance Sheet
As of December 31, 2024 and 2023

	2024	2023
Total Assets	$ 32,978	$ 30,660
Total Liabilities	19,400	11,560
Total Stockholders' Equity (all common)	13,578	19,100
Total Liabilities and Stockholders' Equity	$ 32,978	$ 30,660

Net income for 2024 was $3,910, and interest expense was $240. Compute Barot's rate of return on total assets for 2024. (Round to the nearest percent.)

> Exercises

E-F:15-8 Accounting for debt investments
Learning Objective 2

Griffin purchased a bond on January 1, 2024, for $140,000. The bond has a face value of $140,000 and matures in 10 years. The bond pays interest on June 30 and December 31 at a 3% annual rate. Griffin plans on holding the investment until maturity.

Requirements
1. Journalize the 2024 transactions related to Griffin's bond investment. Explanations are not required.
2. Journalize the transaction related to Griffin's disposition of the bond at maturity on December 31, 2033. (Assume the last interest payment has already been recorded.) Explanations are not required.

E-F:15-9 Accounting for debt investments
Learning Objective 2

Advance & Co. owns vast amounts of corporate bonds. Suppose Advance buys $1,100,000 of FermaCo bonds at face value on January 2, 2024. The FermaCo bonds pay interest at the annual rate of 3% on June 30 and December 31 and mature on December 31, 2033. Advance intends to hold the investment until maturity.

Requirements
1. Journalize any required 2024 entries for the bond investment.
2. How much cash interest will Advance receive each year from FermaCo?
3. How much interest revenue will Advance report during 2024 on this bond investment?

E-F:15-10 Accounting for debt investments
Learning Objective 2

2a. Int. Rev. CR $36,000

League Up & Co. owns vast amounts of corporate bonds. Suppose League Up buys $900,000 of CocoCorp bonds at face value on January 2, 2024. The CocoCorp bonds pay interest at the annual rate of 8% on June 30 and December 31 and mature on December 31, 2028. League Up intends to hold the investment until maturity.

Requirements
1. How would the bond investment be classified on League Up's December 31, 2024, balance sheet?
2. Journalize the following on League Up's books:
   a. Receipt of final interest payment on December 31, 2028.
   b. Disposition of the investment at maturity on December 31, 2028.

E-F:15-11 Accounting for debt investments
Learning Objectives 2, 4

Peyton Investments completed the following investment transactions during 2024:

2024		
Jan. 5		Purchased Vedder Company's $400,000 bond at face value. Peyton classified the investment as available-for-sale. The Vedder bond pays interest at the annual rate of 4% on June 30 and December 31 and matures on December 31, 2030. Management's intent is to keep the bonds for several years.
Jun. 30		Received an interest payment from Vedder.
Dec. 31		Received an interest payment from Vedder.
	31	Adjusted the investment to its current market value of $396,000.

15-26 Financial chapter 15

Requirements

1. Journalize Peyton's investment transactions. Explanations are not required.
2. Prepare a partial balance sheet for Peyton's Vedder investment as of December 31, 2024.
3. Prepare a comprehensive income statement for Peyton Investments for year ended December 31, 2024. Assume net income was $200,000.

Learning Objectives 3, 4

E-F:15-12 Accounting for equity investments

Strategic Investments completed the following investment transactions during 2024:

Jan. 14	Purchased 800 shares of Phyflexon stock, paying $50 per share. The investment represents 4% ownership in Phyflexon's voting stock. Strategic does not have significant influence over Phyflexon. Strategic intends to hold the investment for the indefinite future.
Aug. 22	Received a cash dividend of $0.24 per share on the Phyflexon stock.
Dec. 31	Adjusted the investment to its current market value of $45 per share.
31	Phyflexon reported net income of $330,000 for the year ended 2024.

Requirements

1. Journalize Strategic's investment transactions. Explanations are not required.
2. Classify and prepare a partial balance sheet for Strategic's Phyflexon investment as of December 31, 2024.
3. Prepare a partial income statement for Strategic Investments for year ended December 31, 2024.

Learning Objectives 3, 4

E-F:15-13 Accounting for equity investments

Captain Investments completed the following investment transactions during 2024:

Jan. 14	Purchased 200 shares of Velcon stock, paying $53 per share. The investment represents 4% ownership in Velcon's voting stock. Captain does not have significant influence over Velcon. Captain intends to hold the investment for the indefinite future.
Aug. 22	Received a cash dividend of $0.28 per share on the Velcon stock.
Dec. 31	Adjusted the Velcon investment to its current market value of $58.

Requirements

1. Journalize the entries for 2024. Explanations are not required.
2. What account(s) and amount(s), if any, would be reported on Captain's income statement for the year ended December 31, 2024?

Learning Objective 3

E-F:15-14 Accounting for equity investments

1. Revenue from Investments CR $45,000

Money Man Investments completed the following transactions during 2024:

Jan. 14	Purchased 400 shares of Technomite stock, paying $56 per share. The investment represents 25% ownership in Technomite's voting stock and Money Man has significant influence over Technomite. Money Man intends to hold the investment for the indefinite future.
Aug. 22	Received a cash dividend of $0.27 per share on the Technomite stock.
Dec. 31	Technomite's current market value is $51 per share.
31	Technomite reported net income of $180,000 for the year ended 2024.

Requirements

1. Journalize Money Man's transactions. Explanations are not required.
2. Classify and prepare partial financial statements for Money Man's 25% Technomite investment for the year ended December 31, 2024.

E-F:15-15 Accounting for equity investments

Learning Objective 3

Suppose that on January 6, 2024, East Coast Motors paid $280,000,000 for its 35% investment in Boxcar Motors. East Coast has significant influence over Boxcar after the purchase. Assume Boxcar earned net income of $90,000,000 and paid cash dividends of $45,000,000 to all outstanding stockholders during 2024. (Assume all outstanding stock is voting stock.)

3. $295,750,000 Bal.

Requirements

1. What method should East Coast Motors use to account for the investment in Boxcar Motors? Give your reasoning.
2. Journalize all required 2024 transactions related to East Coast Motors's Boxcar investment. Include an explanation for each entry.
3. Post all 2024 transactions to the investment T-account. What is its balance after all the transactions are posted? How would this balance be classified on the balance sheet dated December 31, 2024?

E-F:15-16 Classifying and accounting for equity investments

Learning Objectives 1, 3, 4

Boston Today Publishers completed the following investment transactions during 2024 and 2025:

1. Dec. 31 Fair Value Adjustment—Equity Investments CR $32,500

2024		
Dec. 6	Purchased 2,500 shares of Loveable stock at a price of $24.00 per share, intending to sell the investment next month. Boston did not have significant influence over Loveable.	
23	Received a cash dividend of $1.50 per share on the Loveable stock.	
31	Adjusted the investment to its market value of $11.00 per share.	
2025		
Jan. 27	Sold the Loveable stock for $18.20 per share.	

Requirements

1. Journalize Boston Today's investment transactions. Explanations are not required.
2. On December 31, 2024, how would the Loveable stock be classified, and at what value would it be reported on the balance sheet?

E-F:15-17 Computing rate of return on total assets

Learning Objective 5

Montane Exploration Company reported these figures for 2024 and 2023:

Avg. total assets $284,000,000

Income Statement—partial:	2024	2023
Interest Expense	$ 16,700,000	$ 16,500,000
Net Income	16,900,000	20,200,000
Balance Sheet—partial:	Dec. 31, 2024	Dec. 31, 2023
Total Assets	$ 316,000,000	$ 420,000,000

Compute the rate of return on total assets for 2024. (Round to two decimals.)

> Problems Group A

Learning Objective 2

1. Dec. 31 Int. Rev. CR $15,000

P-F:15-18A Accounting for debt investments

Suppose Solomon Brothers purchases $500,000 of 6% bonds of Morin Corporation at face value on January 1, 2024. These bonds pay interest on June 30 and December 31 each year. They mature on December 31, 2028. Solomon intends to hold the Morin bond investment until maturity.

Requirements

1. Journalize Solomon Brothers' transactions related to the bonds for 2024.
2. Journalize the entry required on the Morin bonds maturity date. (Assume the last interest payment has already been recorded.)

Learning Objectives 1, 2, 3, 4

2. Sep. 16 Gain on Disposal CR $5,880

P-F:15-19A Classifying and accounting for debt and equity investments

Jetway Corporation generated excess cash and invested in securities as follows:

2024	
Jul. 2	Purchased 4,200 shares of Pogo, Inc. common stock at $12.00 per share. Jetway plans to sell the stock within three months, when the company will need the cash for normal operations. Jetway does not have significant influence over Pogo.
Aug. 21	Received a cash dividend of $0.80 per share on the Pogo stock investment.
Sep. 16	Sold the Pogo stock for $13.40 per share.
Oct. 1	Purchased a Violet bond for $20,000 at face value. Jetway classifies the investment as trading and short-term.
Dec. 31	Received a $100 interest payment from Violet.
31	Adjusted the Violet bond to its market value of $22,000.

Requirements

1. Classify each of the investments made during 2024. (Assume the equity investments represent less than 20% of ownership of outstanding voting stock.)
2. Journalize the 2024 transactions. Explanations are not required.
3. Prepare T-accounts for the investment assets and show how to report the investments on Jetway's balance sheet at December 31, 2024.
4. Where is the unrealized holding gain or loss associated with the trading debt investment reported?

Learning Objectives 3, 4

1. Dec. 31 Fair Value Adjustment—Equity Investments DR $4,000

P-F:15-20A Accounting for equity investments

The beginning balance sheet of Waterfall Source Co. included a $400,000 investment in Evan stock (20% ownership, Waterfall has significant influence over Evan). During the year, Waterfall Source completed the following investment transactions:

Mar. 3	Purchased 4,000 shares at $11 per share of Lili Software common stock as a long-term equity investment, representing 7% ownership, no significant influence.
May 15	Received a cash dividend of $0.61 per share on the Lili investment.
Dec. 15	Received a cash dividend of $70,000 from Evan investment.
31	Received Evan's annual report showing $300,000 of net income.
31	Received Lili's annual report showing $120,000 of net income for the year.
31	Evan's stock fair value at year-end was $390,000.
31	Lili's common stock fair value at year-end was $12 per share.

Requirements

1. Journalize the transactions for the year of Waterfall Source.
2. Post transactions to T-accounts to determine the December 31, 2024, balances related to the investment and investment income accounts.
3. Prepare Waterfall Source's partial balance sheet at December 31, 2024, from your answers in Requirement 2.
4. Where is the unrealized holding gain or loss associated with the Lili stock reported?

> Problems Group B

P-F:15-21B Accounting for debt investments

Suppose Hale and Sons purchases $800,000 of 3.5% bonds of Tyson Way Corporation at face value on January 1, 2024. These bonds pay interest on June 30 and December 31 each year. They mature on December 31, 2033. Hale and Sons intends to hold the Tyson Way bond investment until maturity.

Learning Objective 2

1. Dec. 31 Int. Rev. CR $14,000

Requirements

1. Journalize Hale and Sons' transactions related to the bonds for 2024.
2. Journalize the entry required on the Tyson Way bonds maturity date. (Assume the last interest payment has already been recorded.)

P-F:15-22B Classifying and accounting for debt and equity investments

Captain Transfer Corporation generated excess cash and invested in securities as follows:

Learning Objectives 1, 2, 3, 4

2. Sep. 16 Gain on Disposal CR $2,940

2024		
Jul. 2	Purchased 4,200 shares of Naradon, Inc. common stock at $13.00 per share. Captain Transfer plans to sell the stock within three months, when the company will need the cash for normal operations. Captain Transfer does not have significant influence over Naradon.	
Aug. 21	Received a cash dividend of $0.40 per share on the Naradon stock investment.	
Sep. 16	Sold the Naradon stock for $13.70 per share.	
Oct. 1	Purchased a Purple bond for $40,000 at face value. Captain Transfer classifies the investment as trading and short-term.	
Dec. 31	Received a $600 interest payment from Purple.	
31	Adjusted the Purple bond to its market value of $44,000.	

Requirements

1. Classify each of the investments made during 2024. (Assume the equity investments represent less than 20% of ownership of outstanding voting stock.)
2. Journalize the 2024 transactions. Explanations are not required.
3. Prepare T-accounts for the investment assets and show how to report the investments on Captain Transfer's balance sheet at December 31, 2024.
4. Where is the unrealized holding gain or loss associated with the trading debt investment reported?

15-30 Financial chapter 15

Learning Objectives 3, 4

1. Dec. 31 Fair Value Adjustment—Equity Investments DR $5,000

P-F:15-23B Accounting for equity investments

The beginning balance sheet of Text Source Co. included a $700,000 investment in Taylor stock (20% ownership).

During the year, Text Source completed the following investment transactions:

Mar. 3	Purchased 5,000 shares at $13 per share of Josh Software common stock as a long-term equity investment, representing 3% ownership, no significant influence.
May 15	Received a cash dividend of $0.69 per share on the Josh investment.
Dec. 15	Received a cash dividend of $100,000 from Taylor investment.
31	Received Taylor's annual report showing $100,000 of net income.
31	Received Josh's annual report showing $620,000 of net income for the year.
31	Taylor's stock fair value at year-end was $620,000.
31	Josh's common stock fair value at year-end was $14 per share.

Requirements

1. Journalize the transactions for the year of Text Source.
2. Post transactions to T-accounts to determine the December 31, 2024, balances related to the investment and investment income accounts.
3. Prepare Text Source's partial balance sheet at December 31, 2024, from your answers in Requirement 2.
4. Where is the unrealized holding gain or loss associated with the Josh stock reported?

CRITICAL THINKING

> Using Excel

Download Excel problems for this chapter online in MyLab Accounting or at http://www.pearsonhighered.com/Horngren.

> Continuing Problem

P-F:15-24 Accounting for debt and equity investments

This problem continues the Canyon Canoe Company situation from Chapter F:14. Amber and Zack Wilson are pleased with the growth of their business and have decided to invest its temporary excess cash in a brokerage account. The company had the following securities transactions in 2025.

Jul. 1	Purchased 8,000 shares in Adobe Outdoor Adventure Company for $3 per share. Canyon Canoe does not have significant influence over Adobe.
7	Purchased 35% of the stock of Bison Backpacks consisting of 43,750 shares of stock (out of a total of 125,000 shares) for $5 per share. Canyon Canoe does have significant influence over Bison.
10	Purchased a bond from Camelot Canoes with a face value of $80,000. Canyon Canoe intends to hold the bond to maturity. The bond pays interest semiannually on June 30 and December 31.
Sep. 30	Received dividends of $0.15 per share from Adobe.
Nov. 1	Received dividends of $0.30 per share from Bison.
Dec. 31	Received an interest payment of $3,200 from Camelot Canoes.
31	Bison Backpacks reported net income of $30,000 for the year. Canyon Canoe Company's share of the net income is $5,250.
31	Adjusted the Adobe stock for a market value of $2.98 per share.

Requirements

1. Journalize the transactions including any entries, if required, at December 31, 2025.
2. Determine the effect on Canyon Canoe Company's net income for the year for each of the three investments.

> Tying It All Together Case F:15-1

Before you begin this assignment, review the Tying It All Together feature in the chapter. It will also be helpful if you review Berkshire Hathaway, Inc.'s 2018 annual report (**https://www.sec.gov/Archives/edgar/data/1067983/000119312519048926/d678758d10k.htm**).

Berkshire Hathaway, Inc. is a holding company owning subsidiaries that engage in a variety of different business activities including insurance, freight rail transportation, utilities and energy, manufacturing, services and retail.

Requirements

With a partner or group, lead your class in a discussion of the following questions or write a report as directed by your instructor.

1. Review Note 3 (Investments in fixed maturity securities). At December 31, 2018, what type of investments in securities with fixed maturities did the company hold?
2. Review Note 4 (Investments in equity securities). At December 31, 2018, what type of investments in equity securities did the company hold?
3. Review Note 1(d) (Investments in fixed maturity securities) and Note 1(e) (Investments in equity securities). How, if at all, does the company use fair value measurements in regards to its investments?

> Decision Case F:15-1

Rock Designs, Inc. is a jewelry store located in Miramar Beach, Florida. After Valentine's Day, the store often has excess cash to get it through the three-month slow season. The primary stockholder, Hardy Rock, wants to make this seasonal cash work for the business.

Requirements

1. Identify which investment class options are available to Rock Designs, Inc.
2. The company identifies that it wants to invest in the technology sector and has narrowed its choices to three companies: Apple, Inc., Google, Inc., and Microsoft Corporation. Prepare a brief analysis comparing the three companies and recommend one of the three based on your analysis.

> Ethical Issue F:15-1

As a result of the recent mortgage crisis, many banks reported record losses to their mortgage receivables and other assets based on the decline in these assets' fair values.

Requirements

1. What would the effect be to stakeholders if such losses were not reported in a timely way?

2. If a business chooses not to report these losses, is there an ethical issue involved? Who is hurt?

> Fraud Case F:15-1

Wild Adventure conducts tours of wildlife reserves around the world. The company recently purchased a lodge in Adelaide, Australia, securing a 4% mortgage from First Bank. In addition to monthly payments, Wild Adventure must provide annual reports to the bank showing that the company has a current ratio of 1.2 or better.

After reviewing the annual reports, the CEO, N. O. Scrooge, approached Carl Hauptfleisch, the CFO, and stated, "We've decided we are going to move all our long-term debt investments into our brokerage account so we can sell them soon. Carl, go ahead and make the adjusting entries as of the current year-end."

Carl made the adjustments even though he doesn't think the company will actually go ahead with the planned sale of the long-term debt investments. The subsequent year, the economy turned, and the company's travel revenues dropped more than 60%. Wild Adventure eventually defaulted on the First Bank loan.

Requirements

1. What effect did the adjustments have on the financial statements? What effect did the adjustments have on the current ratio?

2. What type of information in the financial reports would have helped the bank detect this reclassification?

3. Has a fraud occurred? If so, what is the fraud?

> Financial Statement Case F:15-1

Details about a company's investments appear in a number of places in the annual report. Use **Target Corporation's** Fiscal 2018 annual report to answer the following questions. Visit **http://www.pearsonhighered.com/Horngren** to view a link to Target Corporation's Fiscal 2018 annual report.

Requirements

1. Calculate the rate of return on total assets for Target Corporation for the year ended February 2, 2019.

2. Compare Target Corporation's rate of return on total assets to **Kohl's Corporation's** ratio. Discuss the differences.

> ## Communication Activity F:15-1

In 150 words or fewer, explain the difference between trading debt investments and available-for-sale debt investments.

> # Quick Check Answers

1. b **2.** c **3.** b **4.** c **5.** a **6.** c **7.** b **8.** c **9.** a **10.** a

The Statement of Cash Flows

16

Why Doesn't the Business Have Any Cash?

David National reviewed his company's income statement with a confused look on his face. The statement reported a net profit of $20,000 for the past quarter. David knew that sales had been increasing in his small sporting equipment retail shop, and he expected this trend to continue through the end of the year. But David didn't understand why the income statement showed a profit. The company's payroll clerk had called him earlier in the day and told him that there wasn't enough cash in the bank to pay the employees' monthly salaries.

It didn't make sense to David that the company could report a $20,000 profit on the income statement but not have enough cash to pay the payroll. He figured that the newly hired accountant, Mark Maloney, must have made a mistake.

David picked up the phone to call Mark. He had several questions to ask him. Why didn't the company have any cash in the bank? How was the company using its cash? How could the company report a $20,000 profit but not have that much cash in the bank? Where did the cash received from customers go?

After speaking with his accountant, David learned that the profit reported on the income statement didn't represent cash and that it was important that he review the company's statement of cash flows. The statement of cash flows, Mark told him, reports the cash receipts and cash payments of the business. It shows the sources and uses of cash and helps answer the question "Where did the cash go?"

Why Is Cash So Important?

You can probably answer that question from your own experience. It takes cash to pay bills and to generate future income for a business. Businesses, such as **Amazon.com, Inc.,** a retail Web site that sells everything from sporting equipment to household goods, closely monitors cash. Amazon.com is interested in where its cash came from (receipts) and how its cash is spent (payments). One way for Amazon.com to monitor its cash receipts and payments is by preparing a statement of cash flows. For example, on Amazon.com's 2018 statement of cash flows, the corporation reported that it paid $13.4 million purchasing property and equipment and that it paid $1,184 million cash for income taxes (net of refunds). It also reported that from 2017 to 2018 the corporation had an increase in cash of $10,317 million. In this chapter, you learn what a statement of cash flows is and why it is useful to a business. In addition, you learn how to prepare the statement and understand why companies and investors carefully monitor the statement of cash flows.

16-2 Financial chapter 16

Chapter 16 Learning Objectives

1. Identify the purposes of the statement of cash flows and distinguish among operating, investing, and financing cash flows
2. Prepare the statement of cash flows by the indirect method
3. Use free cash flow to evaluate business performance
4. Prepare the statement of cash flows by the direct method (Appendix 16A)
5. Prepare the statement of cash flows by the indirect method using a spreadsheet (Appendix 16B)

WHAT IS THE STATEMENT OF CASH FLOWS?

Learning Objective 1
Identify the purposes of the statement of cash flows and distinguish among operating, investing, and financing cash flows

Up to this point, you have learned about three financial statements—the income statement, the statement of retained earnings, and the balance sheet. Each of these financial statements reports specific items about a company. The income statement reports net income or net loss for the time period. The statement of retained earnings reports the changes in retained earnings during the time period, and the balance sheet reports a company's financial position. None of these statements reports specifically on the changes in cash.

When a comparative balance sheet for two periods is presented, it shows whether cash increased or decreased. But the balance sheet does not show *why* cash increased or decreased. We need the statement of cash flows for that. The **statement of cash flows** reports on a business's cash receipts and cash payments for a specific period. This statement does the following:

Statement of Cash Flows
Reports on a business's cash receipts and cash payments for a specific period.

Cash Flows
Cash receipts and cash payments of a business.

- Reports on the **cash flows** of a business—where cash came from (receipts) and how cash was spent (payments).
- Reports why cash increased or decreased during the period.
- Covers a span of time and is dated the same as the income statement—"Year Ended December 31, 2024," for example.

Purpose of the Statement of Cash Flows

The statement of cash flows explains why net income as reported on the income statement does not equal the change in the cash balance. In essence, the statement of cash flows is the link between the accrual-based income statement and the cash reported on the balance sheet.

How do people use cash flow information? The statement of cash flows helps do the following:

- **Predict future cash flows.** Past cash receipts and payments help predict future cash flows.
- **Evaluate management.** Wise investment decisions help the business prosper, while unwise decisions cause the business to have problems. Investors and creditors use cash flow information to evaluate managers' decisions.
- **Predict ability to pay debts and dividends.** Lenders want to know whether they will collect on their loans. Stockholders want dividends on their investments. The statement of cash flows helps make these predictions.

Classification of Cash Flows

There are three basic types of cash flow activities, and the statement of cash flows has a section for each:

- Operating activities
- Investing activities
- Financing activities

Each section reports cash inflows (cash receipts coming into the company) and cash outflows (cash payments going out of the company) based on these three classifications.

Operating Activities

Operating activities is the first section on the statement of cash flows and is often the most important category. The operating activities section reports on activities that create revenue or expense in the entity's business. It reflects the day-to-day operations of the business such as cash receipts (cash inflows) from customers for the sales of merchandise inventory and services and the cash payments (cash outflows) for purchases of merchandise inventory or for operating expenses. The operating activities section also includes cash receipts (cash inflows) for interest revenue and dividend income and cash payments (cash outflows) for interest expense and income tax expense.

Operating Activities
Activities that create revenue or expense in the entity's business; a section of the statement of cash flows.

Investing Activities

Investing activities is the second category listed on the statement of cash flows. This section reports cash receipts and cash payments that increase or decrease long-term assets such as property, plant, equipment, notes receivable, and investments. It includes the cash inflow from selling and the cash outflow for the purchase of these long-term assets. In addition, it includes the lending (cash outflow) and collection (cash inflow) of long-term notes receivable.

Investing Activities
Activities that increase or decrease long-term assets; a section of the statement of cash flows.

Financing Activities

The last category on the statement of cash flows is financing activities. Financing activities include cash inflows and outflows involved in long-term liabilities and equity. This includes issuing stock, paying dividends, and buying and selling treasury stock. It also includes borrowing money and paying off long-term liabilities such as notes payable, bonds payable, and mortgages payable.

Each section of the statement of cash flows affects a different part of the balance sheet. The operating activities section reports on how cash flows affect the current accounts—current assets and current liabilities. Investing activities affect the long-term assets. And the financing activities affect long-term liabilities and equity. Exhibit F:16-1 shows the relationship between operating, investing, and financing cash flows and the various parts of the balance sheet.

Financing Activities
Activities that increase or decrease long-term liabilities and equity; a section of the statement of cash flows.

IFRS
Under IFRS, interest revenue and dividend income may be reported either as an operating activity or as an investing activity. Interest expense and dividends paid may be reported either as an operating activity or as a financing activity.

Exhibit F:16-1 | **Operating, Investing, and Financing Cash Flows and the Balance Sheet Accounts**

Non-cash Investing and Financing Activities

Investing and financing activities that do not involve cash.

Non-cash Investing and Financing Activities

The three sections of the statement of cash flows report only activities that involve cash. Companies do make investments that do not require cash. They also obtain financing that does not involve cash. Such transactions are called **non-cash investing and financing activities**. Examples of these activities include the purchase of equipment financed by a long-term note payable or the contribution of equipment by a stockholder in exchange for common stock. These activities are not included in the statement of cash flows. Instead, they appear either as a separate schedule at the bottom of the statement or in the notes to the financial statements.

Exhibit F:16-2 summarizes the different sections on the statement of cash flows.

Exhibit F:16-2 | Sections of the Statement of Cash Flows

Operating Activities	Cash Inflows: • From customers for the sales of merchandise inventory and services • For interest revenue and dividend income Cash Outflows: • For the purchase of merchandise inventory and payment of operating expenses • For interest expense and income tax expense
Investing Activities	Cash Inflows: • From the sale of property, plant, equipment, and investments • From the collection of long-term notes receivable Cash Outflows: • To purchase property, plant, equipment, and investments • For loans made to borrowers
Financing Activities	Cash Inflows: • From issuance of stock and selling treasury stock • From receipt of borrowing money Cash Outflows: • For payment of dividends and buying treasury stock • For repayments of loans
Non-cash Investing and Financing Activities	A separate schedule that includes investing and financing activities that *do not* include cash

The statement of cash flows reports only activities that involve either the receipt of cash or the payment of cash. If a transaction does not involve cash, it will not be included in the operating, investing, or financing sections of the statement of cash flows.

Two Formats for Operating Activities

There are two ways to format the operating activities section of the statement of cash flows:

- The **indirect method** starts with net income and adjusts it to net cash provided by operating activities.
- The **direct method** restates the income statement in terms of cash. The direct method shows all the cash receipts and all the cash payments from operating activities.

The indirect and direct methods use different computations but produce the same amount of net cash flow from operating activities. Both methods present investing activities and financing activities in exactly the same format. Only the *operating activities* section is presented differently between the two methods.

We begin with the indirect method because most companies use it. To focus on the direct method, review Appendix 16A, located at the end of this chapter.

Indirect Method
A format of the operating activities section of the statement of cash flows; starts with net income and reconciles to net cash provided by operating activities.

Direct Method
A format of the operating activities section of the statement of cash flows; lists the operating cash receipts and cash payments.

IFRS
IFRS permits the use of either the direct or indirect method.

Identify each item as operating (O), investing (I), financing (F), or non-cash (N).

1. Cash receipt from the sale of equipment
2. Cash payment for salaries
3. Cash receipt from the collection of long-term notes receivable
4. Purchase of equipment in exchange for notes payable
5. Cash receipt from the issuance of common stock

Check your answers online in MyLab Accounting or at http://www.pearsonhighered.com/Horngren.

For more practice, see Short Exercises S-F:16-1 and S-F:16-2.   MyLab Accounting

HOW IS THE STATEMENT OF CASH FLOWS PREPARED USING THE INDIRECT METHOD?

To prepare the statement of cash flows, you need the income statement for the current year, as well as the balance sheets from the current and prior years. In addition, you need to review the transactions for some additional information. For illustrative purposes, we will use ShopMart, Inc., a fictitious retail store that sells electronics, home furnishings, home

Learning Objective 2
Prepare the statement of cash flows by the indirect method

supplies, and more. ShopMart's comparative balance sheet is shown in Exhibit F:16-3, and its income statement is shown in Exhibit F:16-4. Additional information provided by ShopMart includes the following:

- Purchased $310,000 in plant assets by paying cash.
- Sold plant assets with a cost of $55,000 and accumulated depreciation of $15,000, yielding a gain of $10,000.
- Received $90,000 cash from issuance of notes payable.
- Paid $10,000 cash to retire notes payable.
- Received $120,000 cash from issuing shares of common stock.
- Paid $20,000 cash for purchase of shares of treasury stock.

Exhibit F:16-3 | **Comparative Balance Sheet**

SHOPMART, INC.
Comparative Balance Sheet
December 31, 2024 and 2023

	2024	2023	Increase (Decrease)
Assets			
Current Assets:			
Cash	$ 22,000	$ 42,000	$ (20,000)
Accounts Receivable	90,000	73,000	17,000
Merchandise Inventory	143,000	145,000	(2,000)
Long-term Assets:			
Plant Assets	507,000	252,000	255,000
Accumulated Depreciation—Plant Assets	(47,000)	(42,000)	(5,000)
Total Assets	$715,000	$470,000	$245,000
Liabilities			
Current Liabilities:			
Accounts Payable	$ 90,000	$ 50,000	$ 40,000
Accrued Liabilities	5,000	10,000	(5,000)
Long-term Liabilities:			
Notes Payable	160,000	80,000	80,000
Total Liabilities	255,000	140,000	115,000
Stockholders' Equity			
Common Stock, no par	370,000	250,000	120,000
Retained Earnings	110,000	80,000	30,000
Treasury Stock	(20,000)	0	(20,000)
Total Stockholders' Equity	460,000	330,000	130,000
Total Liabilities and Stockholders' Equity	$715,000	$470,000	$245,000

Exhibit F:16-4 | Income Statement

SHOPMART, INC.
Income Statement
Year Ended December 31, 2024

Net Sales Revenue		$ 286,000
Cost of Goods Sold		156,000
Gross Profit		130,000
Operating Expenses:		
Salaries and Wages Expense	$ 56,000	
Depreciation Expense—Plant Assets	20,000	
Other Operating Expense	16,000	
Total Operating Expenses		92,000
Operating Income		38,000
Other Income and (Expenses):		
Interest Revenue	12,000	
Dividend Revenue	9,000	
Gain on Disposal of Plant Assets	10,000	
Interest Expense	(15,000)	
Total Other Income and (Expenses)		16,000
Income Before Income Taxes		54,000
Income Tax Expense		14,000
Net Income		$ 40,000

To prepare the statement of cash flows by the indirect method, we follow Steps 1–5:

Step 1: Complete the cash flows from operating activities section using net income and adjusting for increases or decreases in current assets (other than cash) and current liabilities. Also adjust for gains or losses from long-term assets and non-cash expenses such as depreciation expense.

Step 2: Complete the cash flows from investing activities section by reviewing the long-term assets section of the balance sheet.

Step 3: Complete the cash flows from financing activities section by reviewing the long-term liabilities and equity sections of the balance sheet.

Step 4: Compute the net increase or decrease in cash during the year. The change in cash is the key reconciling figure for the statement of cash flows and must match the change in cash reported on the comparative balance sheet.

Step 5: Prepare a separate schedule reporting any non-cash investing and financing activities.

16-8 Financial  chapter 16

Let's apply these steps to show the operating activities of ShopMart. Exhibit F:16-5 presents the completed statement of cash flows.

Exhibit F:16-5 | Statement of Cash Flows—Indirect Method

SHOPMART, INC.
Statement of Cash Flows
Year Ended December 31, 2024

Cash Flows from Operating Activities:			
Net Income			$ 40,000
Adjustments to Reconcile Net Income to Net Cash Provided by Operating Activities:			
Depreciation Expense—Plant Assets		$ 20,000	
Gain on Disposal of Plant Assets		(10,000)	
Increase in Accounts Receivable		(17,000)	
Decrease in Merchandise Inventory		2,000	
Increase in Accounts Payable		40,000	
Decrease in Accrued Liabilities		(5,000)	30,000
Net Cash Provided by Operating Activities			70,000
Cash Flows from Investing Activities:			
Cash Payment for Acquisition of Plant Assets		(310,000)	
Cash Receipt from Disposal of Plant Assets		50,000	
Net Cash Used for Investing Activities			(260,000)
Cash Flows from Financing Activities:			
Cash Receipt from Issuance of Notes Payable		90,000	
Cash Payment of Notes Payable		(10,000)	
Cash Receipt from Issuance of Common Stock		120,000	
Cash Payment for Purchase of Treasury Stock		(20,000)	
Cash Payment of Dividends		(10,000)	
Net Cash Provided by Financing Activities			170,000
Net Increase (Decrease) in Cash			(20,000)
Cash Balance, December 31, 2023			42,000
Cash Balance, December 31, 2024			$ 22,000

Step 1: Operating Activities
Step 2: Investing Activities
Step 3: Financing Activities
Step 4: Net Increase (Decrease) in Cash

Cash Flows from Operating Activities

When using the indirect method, the statement of cash flows operating activities section begins with net income (or net loss) because revenues and expenses, which affect net income, produce cash receipts and cash payments. Revenues bring in cash receipts, and expenses must be paid. But net income as shown on the income statement is accrual-based, and the cash flows (cash basis net income) do not always equal the accrual basis revenues and expenses. For example, sales *on account* generate revenues that increase net income, but the company has not yet collected cash from those sales. Accrued expenses decrease net income, but the company has not paid cash *if the expenses are accrued.*

To go from net income to net cash flow from operating activities, we must make some adjustments to net income on the statement of cash flows. These additions and subtractions follow net income and are labeled *Adjustments to Reconcile Net Income to Net Cash Provided by Operating Activities.*

Depreciation, Depletion, and Amortization Expenses

These adjustments include adding back non-cash expenses such as depreciation, depletion, and amortization expenses. These expenses are added back to net income to reconcile net income to net cash flow from operating activities. Let's see why this occurs. Depreciation is recorded as follows:

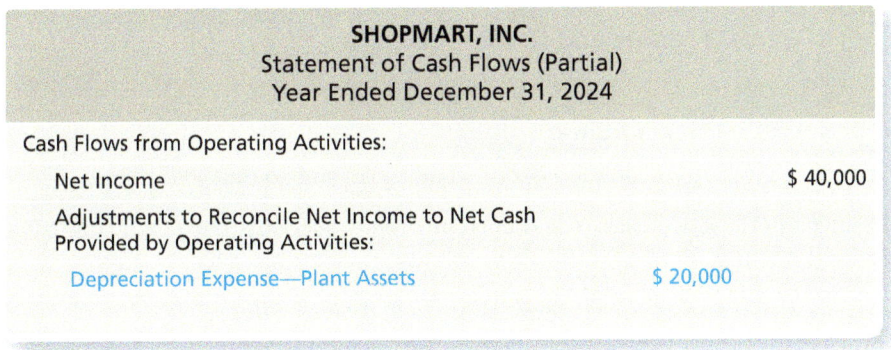

You can see that depreciation does not affect cash as there is no Cash account in the journal entry. Depreciation is a non-cash expense. The cash outflow related to depreciation occurred when the asset was purchased, not as it is depreciated. However, depreciation, like all the other expenses, decreases net income. Therefore, to go from net income to net cash flows, we must remove depreciation by adding it back to net income.

SHOPMART, INC.
Statement of Cash Flows (Partial)
Year Ended December 31, 2024

Cash Flows from Operating Activities:	
Net Income	$ 40,000
Adjustments to Reconcile Net Income to Net Cash Provided by Operating Activities:	
Depreciation Expense—Plant Assets	$ 20,000

Suppose you had only two transactions during the period:

- Cash sale of $60,000
- Depreciation expense of $20,000

Accrual basis net income is $40,000 ($60,000 − $20,000), but net cash flow from operations is $60,000. To reconcile from net income, depreciation of $20,000 must be added to net income, $40,000, to determine net cash flow from operations, $60,000. We would also add back any depletion and amortization expenses because they are non-cash expenses, similar to depreciation.

Gains and Losses from Non-operating Activities

Gains and losses from non-operating activities, such as the disposal of long-term assets (investing activity), sale of investments (investing activity), or retirement of bonds (financing activity), are included in net income. However, since these are non-operating activities, the gains and losses must be removed from net income on the statement of cash flows so the total cash receipts can be shown in the investing or financing sections.

Exhibit F:16-4, ShopMart's income statement, includes a gain on disposal of plant assets. During 2024, ShopMart sold equipment, and there was a gain of $10,000 on the sale. The gain was included in the calculation of net income on the income statement, so the gain must be removed from operating cash flows. The gain increased net income, so it is subtracted in the operating activities section.

16-10   Financial   chapter 16

SHOPMART, INC.
Statement of Cash Flows (Partial)
Year Ended December 31, 2024

Cash Flows from Operating Activities:		
Net Income		$ 40,000
Adjustments to Reconcile Net Income to Net Cash Provided by Operating Activities:		
Depreciation Expense—Plant Assets	$ 20,000	
Gain on Disposal of Plant Assets	(10,000)	

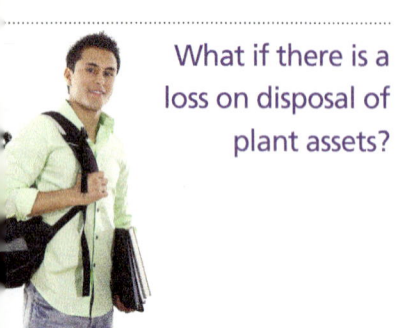

What if there is a loss on disposal of plant assets?

On the other hand, **a loss on the disposal of plant assets would decrease net income on the income statement, so the amount of the loss would be reversed to determine the net cash provided by operating activities on the statement of cash flows.** For example, a $5,000 loss on disposal of plant assets would be a $5,000 addition to net income on the statement of cash flows to determine net cash provided by operating activities.

Changes in Current Assets and Current Liabilities

Most current assets and current liabilities result from operating activities. For example:

- Accounts receivable result from sales.
- Merchandise inventory relates to cost of goods sold, and so on.

Changes in the current asset and current liability accounts create adjustments to net income on the statement of cash flows, as follows:

- **An increase in a current asset other than cash causes a decrease adjustment to net income.** If Accounts Receivable, Merchandise Inventory, or Prepaid Expenses increases, then the adjustment to net income is a decrease. For example, ShopMart's balance sheet in Exhibit F:16-3 shows that Accounts Receivable increased by $17,000. Accounts Receivable is increased when the company makes sales on account and decreases when the company collects cash from customers. Therefore, there were more sales on account (revenue earned and reported on the income statement) than cash collections, the amount we want to reflect on the statement of cash flows. Because the indirect method of accounting for operating activities begins with net income, subtract the $17,000 increase in the current asset Accounts Receivable to adjust accrual-based net income to net cash flows provided by operating activities.

- **A decrease in a current asset other than cash causes an increase adjustment to net income.** Decreases in current assets will have the opposite effect as illustrated above. ShopMart's Merchandise Inventory decreased by $2,000. What caused the decrease? ShopMart must have sold more merchandise inventory than it purchased. Therefore, we add the decrease in Merchandise Inventory of $2,000 to net income on the statement of cash flows.

- **An increase in a current liability causes an increase adjustment to net income.** ShopMart's Accounts Payable increased by $40,000. This means there were more purchases on account than cash paid for the purchases, resulting in an increase to the liability. Accordingly, even though net income was reduced by the expense, cash was not reduced as much. Therefore, an increase in a current liability is *added* to net income in the statement of cash flows.

- **A decrease in a current liability causes a decrease adjustment to net income.** Decreases in current liabilities have the opposite effect of increases. The payments of the current liabilities were more than the accrual of the expenses. Therefore, we subtract decreases in current liabilities from net income to get net cash flow from operating activities. ShopMart's Accrued Liabilities decreased by $5,000. That change shows up as a $5,000 decrease adjustment to net income.

SHOPMART, INC.
Statement of Cash Flows (Partial)
Year Ended December 31, 2024

Cash Flows from Operating Activities:		
Net Income		$ 40,000
Adjustments to Reconcile Net Income to Net Cash Provided by Operating Activities:		
Depreciation Expense—Plant Assets	$ 20,000	
Gain on Disposal of Plant Assets	(10,000)	
Increase in Accounts Receivable	(17,000)	
Decrease in Merchandise Inventory	2,000	
Increase in Accounts Payable	40,000	
Decrease in Accrued Liabilities	(5,000)	30,000

DECISIONS

What can be done to create a positive cash flow?

Meggie Mohamed, CEO, knew that the bank would carefully review her company's most recent statement of cash flows before determining if it would approve the loan needed for expansion. The bank loan officer had told her that it is important that the business show strong operating cash flows. Meggie knows that her company's operating cash flow for this past quarter will most likely be negative. Although the company recorded significant revenue, most of the revenue was recorded as receivables. Meggie expects that the cash will come in soon, but not in time to report a positive operating cash flow. What should Meggie do? What would you do?

Solution

Meggie could explain to the bank officer that her company is expecting to collect a significant amount of cash in the near future on outstanding receivables. She could provide detailed collection information including the estimated time frame of collection and the amount expected. Meggie also has another option. She could look into selling the receivables to another business, often called a *factor*. By selling the receivables, the company will be able to decrease its accounts receivable balance, increase its cash balance, and report a positive balance in operating cash flows.

Evaluating Cash Flows from Operating Activities

During 2024, ShopMart's operating activities provided a net cash inflow of $70,000 ($40,000 + $30,000), so the amount is labeled Net Cash *Provided by* Operating Activities. If this amount were a net cash outflow, ShopMart would report Net Cash *Used for* Operating Activities.

SHOPMART, INC.
Statement of Cash Flows (Partial)
Year Ended December 31, 2024

Cash Flows from Operating Activities:		
Net Income		$ 40,000
Adjustments to Reconcile Net Income to Net Cash Provided by Operating Activities:		
Depreciation Expense—Plant Assets	$ 20,000	
Gain on Disposal of Plant Assets	(10,000)	
Increase in Accounts Receivable	(17,000)	
Decrease in Merchandise Inventory	2,000	
Increase in Accounts Payable	40,000	
Decrease in Accrued Liabilities	(5,000)	30,000
Net Cash Provided by Operating Activities		70,000

The operating activities section (indirect method) always starts with accrual basis net income. Adjustments are then made to determine the cash basis net income. Exhibit F:16-6 summarizes the adjustments made to reconcile net income to net cash provided by operating activities.

Exhibit F:16-6 | Adjustments Made to Reconcile Net Income to Net Cash Provided by Operating Activities

Item	Adjustment to Net Income on Statement of Cash Flows
Depreciation, Depletion, and Amortization Expense	Increase
Gains on Non-operating Activities	Decrease
Losses on Non-operating Activities	Increase
Increases in Current Assets other than Cash	Decrease
Decreases in Current Assets other than Cash	Increase
Increases in Current Liabilities	Increase
Decreases in Current Liabilities	Decrease

Cash Flows from Investing Activities

Investing activities affect long-term assets, such as Plant Assets, Investments, and Notes Receivable. These are shown on ShopMart's balance sheet (Exhibit F:16-3). Now, let's see how to compute the investing cash flows.

When computing investing cash flows, it is helpful to evaluate the T-accounts for each long-term asset. The T-account will show if there was an acquisition or disposal that happened during the year. Let's look at the Plant Assets and Accumulated Depreciation accounts for ShopMart.

Plant Assets			
12/31/2023	252,000		
Acquisitions	310,000	55,000	Disposals
12/31/2024	507,000		

Accumulated Depreciation—Plant Assets			
		42,000	12/31/2023
Disposals	15,000	20,000	Depr. Exp.
		47,000	12/31/2024

Depreciation Expense is from the income statement.

The beginning and ending balances for each account are taken directly from the comparative balance sheet. Depreciation expense has been included in the Accumulated Depreciation account, and this was taken from the income statement. The acquisition and disposal information came from the additional information provided when we introduced the example:

- Purchased $310,000 in plant assets by paying cash.
- Sold plant assets with a cost of $55,000 and accumulated depreciation of $15,000, yielding a gain of $10,000.

We now know that ShopMart paid $310,000 cash to purchase plant assets. This item is listed first in the investing activities section and shown as an outflow of cash, as indicated by the parentheses.

Next we need to determine the amount of cash received for the disposal of plant assets. Using the information provided, we can recreate the journal entry for the disposal and solve for the missing cash amount.

Date	Accounts and Explanation	Debit	Credit
	Cash	?	
	Accumulated Depreciation—Plant Assets	15,000	
	Gain on Disposal of Plant Assets		10,000
	Plant Assets		55,000

$A\uparrow$ Cash↑ Accumulated Depreciation↓ Plant Assets↓ = L + $E\uparrow$ Gain on Disposal↑

We compute the cash receipt from the disposal as follows:

Cash received = Cost − Accumulated Depreciation + Gain − Loss
= $55,000 − $15,000 + $10,000
= $50,000

The cash receipt from the sale of plant assets of $50,000 is shown next in the investing activities section. As there are no other changes to long-term assets, the net cash from investing activities is determined. Notice that this is a net cash outflow, as indicated by the parentheses, and is reported as Net Cash *Used for* Investing Activities.

16-14 Financial chapter 16

In this partial statement, we are showing only the investing activities section of the statement of cash flows. Remember that the investing activities section is reported after the operating activities section.

SHOPMART, INC.
Statement of Cash Flows (Partial)
Year Ended December 31, 2024

Cash Flows from Investing Activities:		
Cash Payment for Acquisition of Plant Assets	(310,000)	
Cash Receipt from Disposal of Plant Assets	50,000	
Net Cash Used for Investing Activities		(260,000)

Cash Flows from Financing Activities

Financing activities affect the long-term liability and equity accounts, such as Long-term Notes Payable, Bonds Payable, Common Stock, and Retained Earnings. To determine the cash flows from financing activities, we need to review each of these account types.

Long-term Liabilities

The T-account for ShopMart's Notes Payable is shown below. Additional information concerning notes payable is also provided by the company as follows:

- Received $90,000 cash from issuance of notes payable.
- Paid $10,000 cash to retire notes payable.

	Notes Payable		
		80,000	12/31/2023
Payment	10,000	90,000	Issuance
		160,000	12/31/2024

The beginning and ending balances of Notes Payable are taken from the comparative balance sheet. For ShopMart, a new issuance of notes payable is known to be a $90,000 cash receipt and is shown by the following journal entry:

$$\frac{A\uparrow}{Cash\uparrow} \Big\} = \Big\{ \frac{L\uparrow}{Notes\ Payable\uparrow} + E$$

Date	Accounts and Explanation	Debit	Credit
	Cash	90,000	
	Notes Payable		90,000

In addition, ShopMart paid $10,000 cash to retire notes payable.

$$\frac{A\downarrow}{Cash\downarrow} \Big\} = \Big\{ \frac{L\downarrow}{Notes\ Payable\downarrow} + E$$

Date	Accounts and Explanation	Debit	Credit
	Notes Payable	10,000	
	Cash		10,000

The Statement of Cash Flows Financial 16-15

The cash inflow and cash outflow associated with these notes payable are listed first in the cash flows from financing activities section.

SHOPMART, INC.
Statement of Cash Flows (Partial)
Year Ended December 31, 2024

Cash Flows from Financing Activities:
Cash Receipt from Issuance of Notes Payable   90,000
Cash Payment of Notes Payable   (10,000)

Common Stock and Treasury Stock

Cash flows for financing activities are also determined by analyzing the stock accounts. For example, the amount of new issuances of stock is determined by analyzing the stock accounts and reviewing the additional information provided:

- Received $120,000 cash from issuing shares of common stock.
- Paid $20,000 cash for purchase of shares of treasury stock.

ShopMart's stock T-accounts are as follows:

Common Stock

		250,000	12/31/2023
Retirement	0	120,000	Issuance
		370,000	12/31/2024

Treasury Stock

12/31/2023	0		
Purchase	20,000	0	Disposal
12/31/2024	20,000		

The common stock account shows a new stock issuance of $120,000 and would be recorded by the following journal entry:

Date	Accounts and Explanation	Debit	Credit
	Cash	120,000	
	Common Stock		120,000

$\frac{A\uparrow}{Cash\uparrow} \Big\} = \Big\{ \frac{L}{} + \frac{E\uparrow}{Common\ Stock\uparrow}$

This is shown as $120,000 cash inflow in the financing activities section of the statement.

Treasury stock also changed on ShopMart's balance sheet. The T-account is showing an acquisition of treasury stock that would be recorded as follows:

Date	Accounts and Explanation	Debit	Credit
	Treasury Stock	20,000	
	Cash		20,000

$\frac{A\downarrow}{Cash\downarrow} \Big\} = \Big\{ \frac{L}{} + \frac{E\downarrow}{Treasury\ Stock\uparrow}$

The $20,000 is shown as a cash outflow in the financing section of the statement of cash flows for the purchase of treasury stock.

SHOPMART, INC.
Statement of Cash Flows (Partial)
Year Ended December 31, 2024

Cash Flows from Financing Activities:	
Cash Receipt from Issuance of Notes Payable	90,000
Cash Payment of Notes Payable	(10,000)
Cash Receipt from Issuance of Common Stock	120,000
Cash Payment for Purchase of Treasury Stock	(20,000)

Dividend Payments

The amount of dividend payments can be computed by analyzing the Retained Earnings account. First, we input the balances from the balance sheet:

Retained Earnings

		80,000	12/31/2023
Net Loss	?	?	Net Income
Dividends	?		
		110,000	12/31/2024

Retained Earnings increases when companies earn net income. Retained Earnings decreases when companies have a net loss and when they declare dividends. We know that ShopMart earned net income of $40,000 from the income statement in Exhibit F:16-4.

Retained Earnings

		80,000	12/31/2023
Net Loss	?	40,000	Net Income
Dividends	?		
		110,000	12/31/2024

Net Income is from the income statement.

ShopMart can't have both net income and net loss for the same period; therefore, the missing value must be the amount of dividends ShopMart declared. Solving for the dividends follows:

Ending Retained Earnings = Beginning Retained Earnings + Net Income − Net loss − Dividends
$110,000 = $80,000 + $40,000 − $0 − Dividends
Dividends = $80,000 + $40,000 − $0 − $110,000
Dividends = $10,000

So our final Retained Earnings T-account shows the following:

Retained Earnings

		80,000	12/31/2023
		40,000	Net Income
Dividends	10,000		
		110,000	12/31/2024

In order for the cash dividends to be reported on the statement of cash flows, the company must have paid the dividends. In this case, we know the cash dividends are paid because there are no dividends payable reported on ShopMart's balance sheet. Companies can also distribute stock dividends. A stock dividend has *no* effect on Cash and is *not* reported in the financing activities section of the statement of cash flows. ShopMart had no stock dividends, only cash dividends, which will be shown as an outflow in the financing activities section of the statement of cash flows.

SHOPMART, INC.
Statement of Cash Flows (Partial)
Year Ended December 31, 2024

Cash Flows from Financing Activities:		
Cash Receipt from Issuance of Notes Payable	$ 90,000	
Cash Payment of Notes Payable	(10,000)	
Cash Receipt from Issuance of Common Stock	120,000	
Cash Payment for Purchase of Treasury Stock	(20,000)	
Cash Payment of Dividends	(10,000)	
Net Cash Provided by Financing Activities		170,000

TYING IT ALL TOGETHER

Amazon.com, Inc. opened its virtual doors on the internet in July 1995 and completed an initial public offering in May 1997. The company serves customers through its retail Web sites selling millions of unique products. In addition, the company manufactures and sells electronic devices including Kindle e-readers and Fire tablets. Amazon.com also offers Amazon Prime, a membership program that includes unlimited free shipping on items and access to un-limited streaming of movies and TV episodes. (You can find Amazon.com, Inc.'s annual report at **https://www.sec.gov/Archives/edgar/data/1018724/000101872419000004/amzn-20181231x10k.htm**)

What format does Amazon.com, Inc. use for its statement of cash flows?

Amazon.com, Inc. uses an indirect method statement of cash flows. This method starts with net income and adjusts net income to net cash provided by operating activities.

On Amazon.com, Inc.'s statement of cash flows, the company reports cash provided by operating activities for the year ended December 31, 2018, of $30,723 million. What were the operating cash flows a result of?

Cash flows from operating activities reports on activities that create revenue or expense in the company's business. This section reflects the day-to-day operations. Amazon.com reports that the company's operating cash flows result primarily from cash received from customers and advertisers. The cash inflows are offset by cash payments for products and services, employee compensation, and interest payments on long-term obligations.

Did Amazon.com, Inc. pay a cash dividend in 2018? How would an investor know?

Amazon.com did not pay a cash dividend in 2018. An investor could easily tell if a company paid a cash dividend by reviewing the financing activities section of the statement of cash flows. This section reports cash inflows and outflows associated with long-term liabilities and equity, including the payment of cash dividends.

Net Change in Cash and Cash Balances

To complete the statement of cash flows, the net change in cash and its effect on the beginning cash balance must be shown. This represents the total change in cash for the period and reconciles the statement of cash flows. First, the net increase or decrease in cash is computed by combining the cash provided by or used for operating, investing, and financing activities. In the case of ShopMart, there is a net decrease in the cash balance of $20,000 for the year and is calculated as follows:

> Net increase (decrease) in cash = Net cash provided by operating activities − Net cash used for investing activities + Net cash provided by financing activities
> = $70,000 − $260,000 + $170,000
> = $(20,000)

Next, the beginning cash from December 31, 2023, is listed at $42,000, as shown on the comparative balance sheet. The net decrease of $20,000 is subtracted from beginning cash of $42,000, which equals the ending cash balance on December 31, 2024, of $22,000. This is the key to the statement of cash flows—it explains why the cash balance for ShopMart decreased by $20,000, even though the company reported net income for the year.

SHOPMART, INC.
Statement of Cash Flows (Partial)
Year Ended December 31, 2024

Net Cash Provided by Operating Activities	$ 70,000
Net Cash Used for Investing Activities	(260,000)
Net Cash Provided by Financing Activities	170,000
Net Increase (Decrease) in Cash	(20,000)
Cash Balance, December 31, 2023	42,000
Cash Balance, December 31, 2024	$ 22,000

Before moving on, take a moment to review the completed Statement of Cash Flows shown earlier in Exhibit F:16-5.

Non-cash Investing and Financing Activities

The last step in preparing the statement of cash flows is to prepare the non-cash investing and financing activities section. This section typically appears at the bottom of the statement of cash flows or in the notes to the financial statements. Our ShopMart example did not include transactions of this type because the company did not have any non-cash transactions during the year. So, to illustrate them, let's consider three non-cash transactions for another fictitious company, The Outdoors, Inc. How would they be reported? First, we gather the non-cash activities for the company:

1. Acquired $300,000 building by issuing common stock.
2. Acquired $70,000 land by issuing notes payable.
3. Retired $100,000 notes payable by issuing common stock.

Now, we consider each transaction individually.

1. The Outdoors issued common stock of $300,000 to acquire a building. The journal entry to record the purchase would be as follows:

Date	Accounts and Explanation	Debit	Credit
	Building	300,000	
	Common Stock		300,000

$$\frac{A\uparrow}{\text{Building}\uparrow} \Big\} = \Big\{ \frac{L}{} + \frac{E\uparrow}{\text{Common Stock}\uparrow}$$

This transaction would not be reported on the statement of cash flows because no cash was paid or received. But the building and the common stock are important. The purchase of the building is an investing activity. The issuance of common stock is a financing activity. Taken together, this transaction is a *non-cash investing and financing activity*.

2. The second transaction listed indicates that The Outdoors acquired $70,000 of land by issuing a note. The journal entry to record the purchase would be as follows:

Date	Accounts and Explanation	Debit	Credit
	Land	70,000	
	Notes Payable		70,000

$$\frac{A\uparrow}{\text{Land}\uparrow} \Big\} = \Big\{ \frac{L\uparrow}{\text{Notes Payable}\uparrow} + \frac{E}{}$$

This transaction would not be reported on the statement of cash flows because no cash was paid or received. But the land and the notes payable are important. The purchase of the land is an investing activity. The issuance of the note is a financing activity. Taken together, this transaction is a *non-cash investing and financing activity*.

3. The third transaction listed indicates that The Outdoors retired $100,000 of debt by issuing common stock. The journal entry to record the transaction would be as follows:

Date	Accounts and Explanation	Debit	Credit
	Notes Payable	100,000	
	Common Stock		100,000

$$\frac{A}{} \Big\} = \Big\{ \frac{L\downarrow}{\text{Notes Payable}\downarrow} + \frac{E\uparrow}{\text{Common Stock}\uparrow}$$

This transaction would not be reported on the statement of cash flows because no cash was paid or received. But the notes payable and the stock issuance are important. The retirement of the note and the issuance of the common stock are both financing activities. Taken together, this transaction, even though it is two financing transactions, is reported in the *non-cash investing and financing activities*.

Non-cash investing and financing activities are reported in a separate part of the statement of cash flows. Exhibit F:16-7 (on the next page) illustrates non-cash investing and financing activities for The Outdoors. This information is either reported at the bottom of the statement of cash flows or can be disclosed in a note.

16-20　Financial chapter 16

Exhibit F:16-7 | Non-cash Investing and Financing Activities

THE OUTDOORS, INC.
Statement of Cash Flows (Partial)
Year Ended December 31, 2024

Non-cash Investing and Financing Activities:	
Acquisition of building by issuing common stock	$ 300,000
Acquisition of land by issuing notes payable	70,000
Retirement of notes payable by issuing common stock	100,000
Total Non-cash Investing and Financing Activities	$ 470,000

Try It!

6. Owl, Inc.'s accountants have assembled the following data for the year ended December 31, 2024:

Cash receipt from sale of equipment	$ 20,000
Depreciation expense	12,000
Cash payment of dividends	4,000
Cash receipt from issuance of common stock	12,000
Net income	30,000
Cash purchase of land	25,000
Increase in current liabilities	10,000
Decrease in current assets other than cash	8,000

Prepare Owl's statement of cash flows using the indirect method for the year ended December 31, 2024. Assume beginning and ending Cash are $12,000 and $75,000 respectively.

Check your answer online in MyLab Accounting or at http://www.pearsonhighered.com/Horngren.

For more practice, see Short Exercises S-F:16-3 through S-F:16-9.   **MyLab Accounting**

HOW DO WE USE FREE CASH FLOW TO EVALUATE BUSINESS PERFORMANCE?

Learning Objective 3
Use free cash flow to evaluate business performance

Free Cash Flow
The amount of cash available from operating activities after paying for planned investments in long-term assets and after paying dividends to shareholders. Net cash provided by operating activities − Cash payments planned for investments in long-term assets − Cash dividends.

Throughout this chapter, we have focused on cash flows from operating, investing, and financing activities. Some investors want to know how much cash a company can "free up" for new opportunities. **Free cash flow** is the amount of cash available from operating activities after paying for planned investments in long-term assets and after paying cash dividends to shareholders. Free cash flow can be computed as follows:

> Free cash flow = Net cash provided by operating activities − Cash payments planned for investments in long-term assets − Cash dividends

The Statement of Cash Flows Financial 16-21

Many companies use free cash flow to estimate the amount of cash that would be available for unexpected opportunities. Suppose ShopMart expects net cash provided by operations of $200,000. Assume the company plans to spend $160,000 to modernize its retail facilities and pays $15,000 in cash dividends. In this case, ShopMart's free cash flow would be $25,000 ($200,000 − $160,000 − $15,000). If a good investment opportunity comes along, the company should have $25,000 cash available to invest.

Data Analytics in Accounting

Cash flow statements, like other financial statements, are historically focused. The statements present information related to past transactions and information. Companies, though, need the ability to quickly monitor their free cash flow and identify cash available for unexpected opportunities and threats. Data analytics software, such as Tableau and Microsoft PowerBI, allows companies to capture financial data from multiple sources (bank statements, credit cards, and investment activity) in real time. For example, Tableau has partnered with SWIFT, a financial messaging network, to provide companies with daily or near-time views of cash balances and transactions. Companies can use dashboards, a tool that visually tracks, analyzes, and displays key data, to identify trends and patterns and build stronger financial forecasts. This enables companies to have a clear understanding of their free cash flow and where they are headed financially.

7. Kalapono Company expects the following for 2024:

- Net cash provided by operating activities of $100,000.
- Net cash provided by financing activities of $10,000.
- Net cash used for investing activities of $20,000 (no sales of long-term assets).
- Cash dividends paid to stockholders was $2,000.

How much free cash flow does Kalapono expect for 2024?

Check your answer online in MyLab Accounting or at http://www.pearsonhighered.com/Horngren.

For more practice, see Short Exercise S-F:16-10. MyLab Accounting

APPENDIX 16A: Preparing the Statement of Cash Flows by the Direct Method

HOW IS THE STATEMENT OF CASH FLOWS PREPARED USING THE DIRECT METHOD?

The Financial Accounting Standards Board (FASB) prefers the direct method of reporting cash flows from operating activities. The direct method provides clearer information about the sources and uses of cash than does the indirect method. However, very few non-public companies use the direct method because it takes more computations than the indirect method. Investing and financing cash flows are presented identically under both direct and indirect methods. Because only the preparation of the operating activities section differs, it is all we discuss in this appendix.

Learning Objective 4
Prepare the statement of cash flows by the direct method

Cash Flows from Operating Activities

In the indirect method, we start with accrual basis net income and then adjust it to cash basis through a series of adjusting items. When using the direct method, we take each line item of the income statement and convert it from accrual to cash basis. So, in essence, the operating activities section of the direct-method cash flows statement is really just a cash-basis income statement. Now let's apply this information to ShopMart.

Cash Collections from Customers

The first item on the income statement shown in Exhibit F:16-4 is Net Sales Revenue. Net Sales Revenue represents the total of all sales, whether for cash or on account. The balance sheet account related to Net Sales Revenue is Accounts Receivable. Accounts Receivable went from $73,000 at December 31, 2023, to $90,000 at December 31, 2024, an increase of $17,000 indicating the company had more sales than cash receipts. Net Sales Revenue can be converted to cash receipts from customers as follows:

Cash receipts from customers = Net Sales Revenue + Beginning Accounts Receivable − Ending Accounts Receivable
= $286,000 + $73,000 − $90,000
= $269,000

Accounts Receivable			
12/31/2023	73,000		
Sales	286,000	269,000	Cash receipts
12/31/2024	90,000		

Sales Revenue	
	286,000

This is the amount of cash receipts from customers related to Net Sales Revenue.

So, the cash ShopMart received from customers is $269,000. This is the first item in the operating activities section of the direct-method statement of cash flows.

SHOPMART, INC.
Statement of Cash Flows (Partial)
Year Ended December 31, 2024

Cash Flows from Operating Activities:
　Receipts:
　　Collections from Customers　　　　　　　　　　$ 269,000

Had ShopMart had a decrease in Accounts Receivable, the amount of cash collections from customers would be higher than Net Sales Revenue.

The Statement of Cash Flows

Cash Receipts of Interest Revenue

The income statement reports interest revenue of $12,000. The balance sheet account related to Interest Revenue is Interest Receivable. Because there is no Interest Receivable account on the balance sheet, the interest revenue must have all been received in cash. So, the statement of cash flows shows interest received of $12,000.

SHOPMART, INC.
Statement of Cash Flows (Partial)
Year Ended December 31, 2024

Cash Flows from Operating Activities:	
Receipts:	
Collections from Customers	$ 269,000
Interest Revenue Received	12,000

Cash Receipts of Dividend Revenue

The income statement reports dividend revenue of $9,000. The balance sheet account related to Dividend Revenue is Dividends Receivable. As with the interest, there is no Dividends Receivable account on the balance sheet. Therefore, the dividend revenue must have all been received in cash. So, the statement of cash flows shows cash received from dividends of $9,000.

SHOPMART, INC.
Statement of Cash Flows (Partial)
Year Ended December 31, 2024

Cash Flows from Operating Activities:		
Receipts:		
Collections from Customers	$ 269,000	
Interest Revenue Received	12,000	
Dividends Received on Investments	9,000	
Total Cash Receipts		$ 290,000

Payments to Suppliers

Payments to suppliers include all payments for the following:

- Merchandise inventory
- Operating expenses except employee compensation, interest, and income taxes

Suppliers, also called *vendors*, are those entities that provide the business with its merchandise inventory and essential services. The accounts related to supplier payments for merchandise inventory are Cost of Goods Sold, Merchandise Inventory, and Accounts Payable. Cost of Goods Sold on the income statement was $156,000. Merchandise Inventory decreased from $145,000 at December 31, 2023, to $143,000 at December 31, 2024. Accounts Payable increased from $50,000 at December 31, 2023, to $90,000 at December 31, 2024. We can calculate the cash paid for inventory as follows:

Cash paid for merchandise inventory = Cost of Goods Sold − Beginning Merchandise Inventory + Ending Merchandise Inventory
+ Beginning Accounts Payable − Ending Accounts Payable
= $156,000 − $145,000 + $143,000 + $50,000 − $90,000
= $114,000

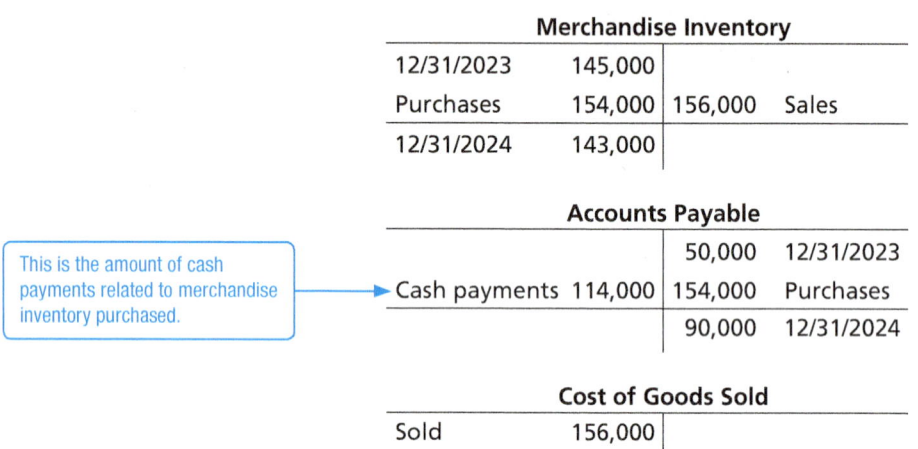

The accounts related to supplier payments for operating expenses are Other Operating Expense and Accrued Liabilities. Other operating expenses on the income statement were $16,000. Accrued Liabilities decreased from $10,000 at December 31, 2023, to $5,000 at December 31, 2024. Cash paid for operating expenses can be calculated as follows:

Cash paid for other operating expenses = Other Operating Expense + Beginning Accrued Liabilities − Ending Accrued Liabilities
= $16,000 + $10,000 − $5,000
= $21,000

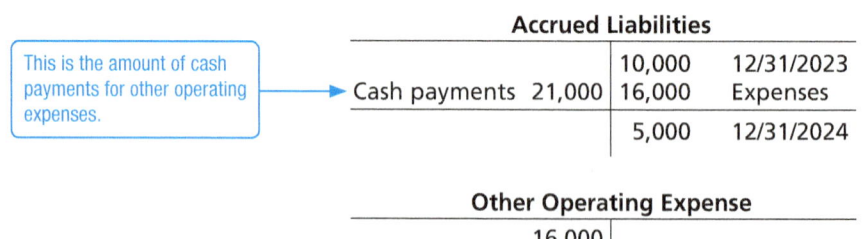

Adding the cash paid for merchandise inventory and the cash paid for other operating expenses together, we get total cash paid to suppliers of $135,000 ($114,000 + $21,000).

SHOPMART, INC.
Statement of Cash Flows (Partial)
Year Ended December 31, 2024

Cash Flows from Operating Activities:		
Receipts:		
Collections from Customers	$ 269,000	
Interest Revenue Received	12,000	
Dividends Received on Investments	9,000	
Total Cash Receipts		$ 290,000
Payments:		
To Suppliers	(135,000)	

Payments to Employees

This category includes payments for salaries, wages, and other forms of employee compensation. Accrued amounts are not cash flows because they have not yet been paid. The accounts related to employee payments are Salaries and Wages Expense from the income statement and Salaries and Wages Payable from the balance sheet. Because there is not a Salaries and Wages Payable account on the balance sheet, the Salaries and Wages Expense account must represent all amounts paid in cash to employees. So, the statement of cash flows shows cash payments to employees of $56,000.

SHOPMART, INC.
Statement of Cash Flows (Partial)
Year Ended December 31, 2024

Cash Flows from Operating Activities:		
Receipts:		
Collections from Customers	$ 269,000	
Interest Revenue Received	12,000	
Dividends Received on Investments	9,000	
Total Cash Receipts		$ 290,000
Payments:		
To Suppliers	(135,000)	
To Employees	(56,000)	

Payments for Interest Expense and Income Tax Expense

These cash payments are reported separately from the other expenses. The accounts related to interest payments are Interest Expense from the income statement and Interest Payable from the balance sheet. Because there is no Interest Payable account on the balance sheet, the Interest Expense account from the income statement must represent all amounts paid in cash for interest. So, the statement of cash flows shows cash payments for interest of $15,000.

The accounts related to income tax payments are Income Tax Expense from the income statement and Income Tax Payable from the balance sheet. Because there is no Income Tax Payable account on the balance sheet, the Income Tax Expense account from the income statement must represent all amounts paid in cash for income tax. So, the statement of cash flows shows cash payments for income tax of $14,000.

SHOPMART, INC.
Statement of Cash Flows (Partial)
Year Ended December 31, 2024

Cash Flows from Operating Activities:		
Receipts:		
Collections from Customers	$ 269,000	
Interest Revenue Received	12,000	
Dividends Received on Investments	9,000	
Total Cash Receipts		$ 290,000
Payments:		
To Suppliers	(135,000)	
To Employees	(56,000)	
For Interest	(15,000)	
For Income Tax	(14,000)	
Total Cash Payments		(220,000)

Are depreciation expense and gain or loss on non-operating activities included in the operating activities section when using the direct method?

Non-cash Expenses and Gains or Losses on Non-operating Activities

Non-cash expenses and gains or losses on non-operating activities are reported on the income statement but are not included in the operating activities when using the direct method. Non-cash expenses are not reported because these items do not affect cash. The cash received from the disposal of long-term assets or sale of investments is reported in the investing activities section. Cash paid to retire bonds is reported in the financing section.

Net Cash Provided by Operating Activities

To calculate net cash provided by operating activities using the direct method, we add all the cash receipts and cash payments described previously and find the difference. For Shop-Mart, total cash receipts were $290,000. Total cash payments were $220,000. So, net cash provided by operating activities is $70,000. If you refer back to the indirect method statement of cash flows shown in Exhibit F:16-5, you will find that it showed the same $70,000 for net cash provided by operating activities. The amount is the same, only the method by which it was calculated was different.

The remainder of ShopMart's statement of cash flows is exactly the same as what we calculated using the indirect method. Exhibit F:16A-1 shows the completed statement of cash flows using the direct method for operating activities.

Exhibit F:16A-1 | **Statement of Cash Flows—Direct Method**

SHOPMART, INC.
Statement of Cash Flows
Year Ended December 31, 2024

Cash Flows from Operating Activities:		
Receipts:		
Collections from Customers	$ 269,000	
Interest Revenue Received	12,000	
Dividends Received on Investments	9,000	
Total Cash Receipts		$ 290,000
Payments:		
To Suppliers	(135,000)	
To Employees	(56,000)	
For Interest	(15,000)	
For Income Tax	(14,000)	
Total Cash Payments		(220,000)
Net Cash Provided by Operating Activities		70,000
Cash Flows from Investing Activities:		
Cash Payment for Acquisition of Plant Assets	(310,000)	
Cash Receipt from Disposal of Plant Assets	50,000	
Net Cash Used for Investing Activities		(260,000)
Cash Flows from Financing Activities:		
Cash Receipt from Issuance of Notes Payable	90,000	
Cash Payment of Notes Payable	(10,000)	
Cash Receipt from Issuance of Common Stock	120,000	
Cash Payment for Purchase of Treasury Stock	(20,000)	
Cash Payment of Dividends	(10,000)	
Net Cash Provided by Financing Activities		170,000
Net Increase (Decrease) in Cash		(20,000)
Cash Balance, December 31, 2023		42,000
Cash Balance, December 31, 2024		$ 22,000

16-28 Financial  chapter 16

Try It!

8A. Big Island, Inc. began 2024 with cash of $40,000. During the year, Big Island earned revenue of $200,000 and collected $120,000 from customers. Expenses for the year totaled $160,000, of which Big Island paid $65,000 in cash to suppliers and $80,000 in cash to employees. The company received $2,000 cash for interest revenue and paid $10,000 for income taxes. Big Island also paid $35,000 to purchase equipment and a cash dividend of $15,000 to its stockholders during 2024. Prepare the company's operating activities section of the statement of cash flows for the year ended December 31, 2024. Use the direct method.

Check your answer online in MyLab Accounting or at http://www.pearsonhighered.com/Horngren.

For more practice, see Short Exercises S-F:16A-11 through S-F:16A-14. **MyLab Accounting**

APPENDIX 16B: Preparing the Statement of Cash Flows Using the Indirect Method and a Spreadsheet

HOW IS THE STATEMENT OF CASH FLOWS PREPARED USING THE INDIRECT METHOD AND A SPREADSHEET?

Learning Objective 5
Prepare the statement of cash flows by the indirect method using a spreadsheet

This chapter discussed the uses of the statement of cash flows in decision making and showed how to prepare the statement using T-accounts. The T-account approach works well as a learning device. In practice, however, most companies face complex situations. In these cases, a spreadsheet can help in preparing the statement of cash flows.

The spreadsheet starts with the beginning balance sheet and concludes with the ending balance sheet. Two middle columns—one for debit amounts and the other for credit amounts—complete the spreadsheet. These columns, labeled "Transaction Analysis," hold the data for the statement of cash flows. Accountants can prepare the statement directly from the lower part of the spreadsheet. This appendix is based on the ShopMart data used in this chapter. We illustrate this approach only with the indirect method for operating activities. This method could be used for the direct method as well.

The *indirect* method reconciles accrual basis net income to net cash provided by operating activities. Exhibit F:16B-1 is the spreadsheet for preparing the statement of cash flows by the *indirect* method. Panel A shows the transaction analysis, and Panel B gives the information to prepare the statement of cash flows.

The Statement of Cash Flows Financial 16-29

Exhibit F:16B-1 | Spreadsheet for Statement of Cash Flows—Indirect Method

SHOPMART, INC.
Spreadsheet for Statement of Cash Flows
Year Ended December 31, 2024

Panel A—Balance Sheet:

	Balance 12/31/2023	Transaction Analysis DEBIT	Transaction Analysis CREDIT	Balance 12/31/2024
Cash	$ 42,000		20,000 (n)	$ 22,000
Accounts Receivable	73,000	(d) 17,000		90,000
Merchandise Inventory	145,000		2,000 (e)	143,000
Plant Assets	252,000	(h) 310,000	55,000 (c)	507,000
Accumulated Depreciation—Plant Assets	(42,000)	(c) 15,000	20,000 (b)	(47,000)
Total Assets	$ 470,000			$ 715,000
Accounts Payable	50,000		40,000 (f)	90,000
Accrued Liabilities	10,000	(g) 5,000		5,000
Notes Payable	80,000	(j) 10,000	90,000 (i)	160,000
Total Liabilities	140,000			255,000
Common Stock, no par	250,000		120,000 (k)	370,000
Retained Earnings	80,000	(m) 10,000	40,000 (a)	110,000
Treasury Stock	0	(l) 20,000		(20,000)
Total Liabilities and Stockholders' Equity	$ 470,000	$ 387,000	$ 387,000	$ 715,000

Panel B—Statement of Cash Flows:

		DEBIT	CREDIT	
Cash Flows from Operating Activities:				
Net Income		(a) 40,000		
Adjustments to Reconcile Net Income to Net Cash Provided by Operating Activities:				
Depreciation Expense—Plant Assets		(b) 20,000		
Gain on Disposal of Plant Assets			10,000 (c)	
Increase in Accounts Receivable			17,000 (d)	
Decrease in Merchandise Inventory		(e) 2,000		
Increase in Accounts Payable		(f) 40,000		
Decrease in Accrued Liabilities			5,000 (g)	
Net Cash Provided by Operating Activities				
Cash Flows from Investing Activities:				
Cash Payment for Acquisition of Plant Assets			310,000 (h)	
Cash Receipt from Disposal of Plant Assets		(c) 50,000		
Net Cash Used for Investing Activities				
Cash Flows from Financing Activities:				
Cash Receipt from Issuance of Notes Payable		(i) 90,000		
Cash Payment of Notes Payable			10,000 (j)	
Cash Receipt from Issuance of Common Stock		(k) 120,000		
Cash Payment for Purchase of Treasury Stock			20,000 (l)	
Cash Payment of Dividends			10,000 (m)	
Net Cash Provided by Financing Activities				
Net Increase (Decrease) in Cash		(n) 20,000		
Total		$ 382,000	$ 382,000	

APPENDIX 16B

The following is a listing of the transaction analysis provided on the spreadsheet using the indirect method:

a. Net income of $40,000 is the first operating cash inflow. Net income is entered on the spreadsheet (Panel B) as a debit to Net Income under Cash Flows from Operating Activities and as a credit to Retained Earnings on the balance sheet (Panel A).

b. Next come the adjustments to net income, starting with depreciation of $20,000—transaction (b)—which is debited to Depreciation Expense—Plant Assets and credited to Accumulated Depreciation—Plant Assets.

c. This transaction is the sale of plant assets. The $10,000 gain on the sale is entered as a credit to Gain on Disposal of Plant Assets—a subtraction from net income—under operating cash flows. This credit removes the $10,000 gain from operating activities because the cash proceeds from the sale were $50,000, not $10,000. The $50,000 sale amount is then entered on the spreadsheet under investing activities. Entry (c) is completed by crediting the plant assets' cost of $55,000 to the Plant Assets account and debiting Accumulated Depreciation—Plant Assets for $15,000.

d. Entry (d) debits Accounts Receivable for its $17,000 increase during the year. This amount is credited to Increase in Accounts Receivable under operating cash flows.

e. This entry credits Merchandise Inventory for its $2,000 decrease during the year. This amount is debited to Decrease in Merchandise Inventory under operating cash flows.

f. This entry credits Accounts Payable for its $40,000 increase during the year. Then it is debited to show as Increase in Accounts Payable under operating cash flows.

g. This entry debits Accrued Liabilities for its $5,000 decrease during the year. Then it is credited to show as Decrease in Accrued Liabilities under operating cash flows.

h. This entry debits Plant Assets for the purchase of $310,000 and credits Cash Payment for Acquisition of Plant Assets under investing cash flows.

i. This entry is represented by a credit to Notes Payable and a debit under cash flows from financing activities of $90,000 (Cash Receipt from Issuance of Notes Payable).

j. This entry is the opposite of (i). It is represented by a debit (reduction) of $10,000 to Notes Payable and a credit under Cash Flows from Financing Activities for Cash Payment of Notes Payable.

k. This entry debits Cash Receipts from Issuance of Common Stock of $120,000 under financing cash flows. The offsetting credit is to Common Stock.

l. The purchase of treasury stock debited the Treasury Stock account on the balance sheet $20,000. The corresponding cash flow entry Cash Payment for Purchase of Treasury Stock credits $20,000 to reduce cash flow.

m. The $10,000 reduction (debit) to the Retained Earnings account is the result of dividends declared and paid by the company. So, we show Cash Payment of Dividends as a credit in the financing section.

n. The final item in Exhibit F:16B-1 is the Net Increase (Decrease) in Cash. It is shown as a credit to Cash and a debit to Net Increase (Decrease) in Cash of $20,000.

In Panel B of Exhibit F:16B-1, the debits represent increases (or inflows) of cash and the credits represent decreases (or outflows). This is because debits increase Cash and credits decrease Cash.

9B. Muench, Inc.'s accountant has partially completed the spreadsheet for the statement of cash flows. Fill in the remaining missing information.

MUENCH, INC.
Spreadsheet for Statement of Cash Flows
Year Ended December 31, 2024

Panel A—Balance Sheet:	Balance 12/31/2023	Transaction Analysis DEBIT	Transaction Analysis CREDIT	Balance 12/31/2024
Cash	$ 16,000			$ 20,000
Accounts Receivable	3,250			5,000
Plant Assets	14,000	1,000		15,000
Accumulated Depreciation	(100)		100	(200)
Total Assets	$ 33,150			$ 39,800
Accounts Payable	5,000			3,500
Common Stock, no par	24,150		5,850	30,000
Retained Earnings	4,000	5,700		6,300
Total Liabilities and Stockholders' Equity	$ 33,150			$ 39,800

Panel B—Statement of Cash Flows:				
Cash Flows from Operating Activities:				
Net Income				
Adjustments to Reconcile Net Income to Net Cash Provided by Operating Activities:				
Depreciation Expense—Plant Assets		100		
Increase in Accounts Receivable				
Decrease in Accounts Payable				
Net Cash Provided by Operating Activities				
Cash Flows from Investing Activities:				
Cash Payment for Acquisition of Plant Assets			1,000	
Net Cash Used for Investing Activities				
Cash Flows from Financing Activities:				
Cash Receipt from Issuance of Common Stock		5,850		
Cash Payment of Dividends			5,700	
Net Cash Provided by Financing Activities				
Net Increase (Decrease) in Cash				

Check your answer online in MyLab Accounting or at http://www.pearsonhighered.com/Horngren.

For more practice, see Short Exercise S-F:16B-15. **MyLab Accounting**

REVIEW

> Things You Should Know

1. **What is the statement of cash flows?**

    - The statement of cash flows reports on a business's cash receipts and cash payments for a specific period.
    - There are three basic types of cash flow activities:
        - Operating activities—Reports on activities that create revenue or expense in the entity's business.
        - Investing activities—Reports cash receipts and cash payments that increase or decrease long-term assets.
        - Financing activities—Includes cash receipts and cash payments involved in long-term liabilities and equity.
    - Non-cash investing and financing activities are not included in the statement of cash flows but appear either as a separate schedule at the bottom of the statement or in the notes to the financial statements.
    - There are two ways to format operating activities on the statement of cash flows:
        - Indirect method—Starts with net income and adjusts it to net cash provided by operating activities.
        - Direct method—Restates the income statement in terms of cash.

2. **How is the statement of cash flows prepared using the indirect method?**

    - **Step 1:** Complete the cash flows from operating activities section using net income and adjusting for increases or decreases in current assets (other than cash) and current liabilities. Also adjust for gains or losses on long-term assets and non-cash expenses.
    - **Step 2:** Complete the cash flows from investing activities section by reviewing the long-term assets section of the balance sheet.
    - **Step 3:** Complete the cash flows from financing activities section by reviewing the long-term liabilities and equity sections of the balance sheet.
    - **Step 4:** Compute the net increase or decrease in cash during the year.
    - **Step 5:** Prepare a separate schedule reporting any non-cash investing and financing activities.

3. **How do we use free cash flow to evaluate business performance?**

    - Free cash flow is the amount of cash available from operating activities after paying for planned investments in long-term assets and after paying cash dividends to shareholders.
    - Free cash flow = Net cash provided by operating activities − Cash payments planned for investments in long-term assets − Cash dividends.

4. **How is the statement of cash flows prepared using the direct method? (Appendix 16A)**

    - The operating activities section is the only section that differs between the direct and indirect methods.
    - When using the direct method, each line item on the income statement is converted from accrual basis to cash basis.

5. **How is the statement of cash flows prepared using the indirect method and a spreadsheet? (Appendix 16B)**
   - A spreadsheet can be used to help in preparing the statement of cash flows.
   - The spreadsheet helps accountants analyze the changes in balance sheet accounts.

> Check Your Understanding

Check your understanding of the chapter by completing this problem and then looking at the solution. Use this practice to help identify which sections of the chapter you need to study more.

The Adams Corporation reported the following income statement for 2024 and comparative balance sheet for 2024 and 2023, along with transaction data for 2024:

ADAMS CORPORATION
Comparative Balance Sheet
December 31, 2024 and 2023

	2024	2023	Increase (Decrease)
Assets			
Current Assets:			
Cash	$ 29,200	$ 3,000	$ 26,200
Accounts Receivable	22,000	23,000	(1,000)
Merchandise Inventory	35,000	34,000	1,000
Long-term Assets:			
Plants Assets	153,200	97,200	56,000
Accumulated Depreciation—Plant Assets	(27,200)	(25,200)	(2,000)
Total Assets	$ 212,200	$ 132,000	$ 80,200
Liabilities			
Current Liabilities:			
Accounts Payable	$ 35,000	$ 26,000	$ 9,000
Accrued Liabilities	7,000	9,000	(2,000)
Income Tax Payable	10,000	10,000	0
Long-term Liabilities:			
Bonds Payable	84,000	53,000	31,000
Total Liabilities	136,000	98,000	38,000
Stockholders' Equity			
Common Stock, no par	52,000	20,000	32,000
Retained Earnings	34,200	19,000	15,200
Treasury Stock	(10,000)	(5,000)	(5,000)
Total Stockholders' Equity	76,200	34,000	42,200
Total Liabilities and Stockholders' Equity	$ 212,200	$ 132,000	$ 80,200

ADAMS CORPORATION
Income Statement
Year Ended December 31, 2024

Net Sales Revenue		$ 662,000
Cost of Goods Sold		560,000
Gross Profit		102,000
Operating Expenses:		
Salaries and Wages Expense	$ 46,000	
Depreciation Expense—Plant Assets	10,000	
Rent Expense	2,000	
Total Operating Expenses		58,000
Operating Income		44,000
Other Income and (Expenses):		
Loss on Disposal of Plant Assets	(2,000)	
Total Other Income and (Expenses)		(2,000)
Net Income Before Income Taxes		42,000
Income Tax Expense		8,800
Net Income		$ 33,200

Transaction data for 2024

Cash paid for purchase of equipment	$140,000
Cash payment of dividends	18,000
Issuance of common stock to retire bonds payable	13,000
Issuance of bonds payable to borrow cash	44,000
Cash receipt from issuance of common stock	19,000
Cash receipt from sale of equipment (Cost, $84,000; Accumulated Depreciation, $8,000)	74,000
Cash paid for purchase of treasury stock	5,000

Prepare Adams Corporation's statement of cash flows for the year ended December 31, 2024. Format cash flows from operating activities by the indirect method. (See Learning Objective 2)

> Solution

ADAMS CORPORATION
Statement of Cash Flows
Year Ended December 31, 2024

Cash Flows from Operating Activities:		
Net Income		$ 33,200
Adjustments to Reconcile Net Income to Net Cash Provided by Operating Activities:		
Depreciation Expense—Plant Assets	$ 10,000	
Loss on Disposal of Plant Assets	2,000	
Decrease in Accounts Receivable	1,000	
Increase in Merchandise Inventory	(1,000)	
Increase in Accounts Payable	9,000	
Decrease in Accrued Liabilities	(2,000)	19,000
Net Cash Provided by Operating Activities		52,200
Cash Flows from Investing Activities:		
Cash Payment for Acquisition of Plant Assets	(140,000)	
Cash Receipt from Disposal of Plant Assets	74,000	
Net Cash Used for Investing Activities		(66,000)
Cash Flows from Financing Activities:		
Cash Receipt from Issuance of Bonds Payable	44,000	
Cash Receipt from Issuance of Common Stock	19,000	
Cash Payment for Purchase of Treasury Stock	(5,000)	
Cash Payment of Dividends	(18,000)	
Net Cash Provided by Financing Activities		40,000
Net Increase (Decrease) in Cash		26,200
Cash Balance, December 31, 2023		3,000
Cash Balance, December 31, 2024		$ 29,200
Non-cash Investing and Financing Activities:		
Issuance of Common Stock to Retire Bonds Payable		$ 13,000
Total Non-cash Investing and Financing Activities		$ 13,000

Relevant T-accounts:

Plant Assets

12/31/2023	97,200		
Acquisitions	140,000	84,000	Disposals
12/31/2024	153,200		

Accumulated Depreciation—Plant Assets

		25,200	12/31/2023
Disposals	8,000	10,000	Depr. Exp.
		27,200	12/31/2024

Bonds Payable

		53,000	12/31/2023
Retirement	13,000	44,000	Issuance
		84,000	12/31/2024

Common Stock

		20,000	12/31/2023
Retirement	0	13,000	Issuance
		19,000	Issuance
		52,000	12/31/2024

Treasury Stock

12/31/2023	5,000		
Purchase	5,000	0	Disposal
12/31/2024	10,000		

Retained Earnings

		19,000	12/31/2023
		33,200	Net Income
Dividends	18,000		
		34,200	12/31/2024

> Key Terms

Cash Flows (p. 16-2)
Direct Method (p. 16-5)
Financing Activities (p. 16-3)
Free Cash Flow (p. 16-20)
Indirect Method (p. 16-5)
Investing Activities (p. 16-3)
Non-cash Investing and Financing Activities (p. 16-4)
Operating Activities (p. 16-3)
Statement of Cash Flows (p. 16-2)

> Quick Check

1. The purposes of the statement of cash flows are to
   a. evaluate management decisions.
   b. determine ability to pay debts and dividends.
   c. predict future cash flows.
   d. All of the above

   Learning Objective 1

2. The main categories of cash flow activities on the statement of cash flows are
   a. direct and indirect.
   b. current and long-term.
   c. non-cash investing and financing.
   d. operating, investing, and financing.

   Learning Objective 1

3. Operating activities are most closely related to
   a. long-term assets.
   b. current assets and current liabilities.
   c. long-term liabilities and stockholders' equity.
   d. dividends and treasury stock.

   Learning Objective 1

4. Which item does *not* appear on a statement of cash flows prepared by the indirect method?
   a. Collections from customers
   b. Depreciation expense
   c. Net income
   d. Gain on sale of land

   Learning Objective 2

5. Leather Shop earned net income of $57,000 after deducting depreciation of $5,000 and all other expenses. Current assets decreased by $4,000, and current liabilities increased by $8,000. How much was Leather Shop's net cash provided by operating activities (indirect method)?
   a. $40,000
   b. $66,000
   c. $48,000
   d. $74,000

   Learning Objective 2

6. The Plant Assets account and Accumulated Depreciation—Plant Assets account of Star Media show the following:

   Learning Objective 2

   Plant Assets

12/31/2023	100,000		
Acquisitions	428,000	52,500	Disposals
12/31/2024	475,500		

   Accumulated Depreciation—Plant Assets

		20,000	12/31/2023
Disposals	10,500	34,000	Depr. Exp.
		43,500	12/31/2024

   Star Media sold plant assets at an $11,000 loss. Where on the statement of cash flows should Star Media report the sale of plant assets? How much should the business report for the sale?
   a. Financing cash flows—cash receipt of $42,000
   b. Investing cash flows—cash receipt of $53,000
   c. Investing cash flows—cash receipt of $31,000
   d. Investing cash flows—cash receipt of $42,000

Learning Objective 2

7. Mountain Water Corp. issued common stock of $28,000 to pay off long-term notes payable of $28,000. In what section(s) would these transactions be recorded?

   a. Financing activities payment of note, $(28,000)
   b. Financing activities cash receipt, $28,000
   c. Non-cash investing and financing activities, $28,000
   d. Both a and b are correct.

Learning Objective 3

8. Holmes, Inc. expects net cash flow from operating activities to be $160,000, and the company plans purchases of equipment of $83,000 and repurchases of stock of $24,000. What is Holmes's free cash flow?

   a. $53,000
   b. $160,000
   c. $77,000
   d. $83,000

Learning Objective 4
Appendix 16A

9A. Maxwell Furniture Center had accounts receivable of $20,000 at the beginning of the year and $54,000 at year-end. Revenue for the year totaled $116,000. How much cash did the business collect from customers?

   a. $150,000
   b. $62,000
   c. $116,000
   d. $82,000

Learning Objective 5
Appendix 16B

10B. If accrued liabilities increased during the year, which of the following is correct when using a spreadsheet to complete the statement of cash flows (indirect method)?

   a. Increase in Accrued Liabilities would be debited
   b. Increase in Accrued Liabilities would be credited
   c. Accrued Liabilities would be debited
   d. None of the above is correct.

Check your answers at the end of the chapter.

ASSESS YOUR PROGRESS

> Review Questions

1. What does the statement of cash flows report?
2. How does the statement of cash flows help users of financial statements?
3. Describe the three basic types of cash flow activities.
4. What types of transactions are reported in the non-cash investing and financing activities section of the statement of cash flows?
5. Describe the two formats for reporting operating activities on the statement of cash flows.
6. Describe the five steps used to prepare the statement of cash flows by the indirect method.
7. Explain why depreciation expense, depletion expense, and amortization expense are added to net income in the operating activities section of the statement of cash flows when using the indirect method.
8. If a company experienced a loss on disposal of long-term assets, how would this be reported in the operating activities section of the statement of cash flows when using the indirect method? Why?

9. If current assets other than cash increase, what is the effect on cash? What about a decrease in current assets other than cash?
10. If current liabilities increase, what is the effect on cash? What about a decrease in current liabilities?
11. What accounts on the balance sheet must be evaluated when completing the investing activities section of the statement of cash flows?
12. What accounts on the balance sheet must be evaluated when completing the financing activities section of the statement of cash flows?
13. What should the net change in cash section of the statement of cash flows always reconcile with?
14. What is free cash flow, and how is it calculated?
15A. How does the direct method differ from the indirect method when preparing the operating activities section of the statement of cash flows?
16B. Why might a spreadsheet be helpful when completing the statement of cash flows?

> Short Exercises

S-F:16-1 Describing the purposes of the statement of cash flows

Learning Objective 1

Financial statements all have a goal. The statement of cash flows does as well. Describe how the statement of cash flows helps investors and creditors perform each of the following functions:

a. Predict future cash flows.
b. Evaluate management decisions.
c. Predict the ability to make debt payments to lenders and pay dividends to stockholders.

S-F:16-2 Classifying items on the statement of cash flows

Learning Objective 1

Cash flow items must be categorized into one of four categories. Identify each item as operating (O), investing (I), financing (F), or non-cash (N).

a. Cash purchase of merchandise inventory
b. Cash payment of dividends
c. Cash receipt from the collection of long-term notes receivable
d. Cash payment for income taxes
e. Purchase of equipment in exchange for notes payable
f. Cash receipt from the sale of land
g. Cash received from borrowing money
h. Cash receipt for interest income
i. Cash receipt from the issuance of common stock
j. Cash payment of salaries

Learning Objectives 1, 2 **S-F:16-3 Classifying items on the indirect statement of cash flows**

Destiny Corporation is preparing its statement of cash flows by the *indirect* method. Destiny has the following items for you to consider in preparing the statement:

a. Increase in accounts payable
b. Payment of dividends
c. Decrease in accrued liabilities
d. Issuance of common stock
e. Gain on sale of building
f. Loss on sale of land
g. Depreciation expense
h. Increase in merchandise inventory
i. Decrease in accounts receivable
j. Purchase of equipment

Identify each item as a(n):

- Operating activity—addition to net income (O+) or subtraction from net income (O−)
- Investing activity—cash inflow (I+) or cash outflow (I−)
- Financing activity—cash inflow (F+) or cash outflow (F−)
- Activity that is not used to prepare the indirect statement of cash flows (N)

Learning Objective 2 **S-F:16-4 Computing cash flows from operating activities—indirect method**

DVR Equipment, Inc. reported the following data for 2024:

Income Statement:	
Net Income	$ 43,000
Depreciation Expense	6,000
Balance Sheet:	
Increase in Accounts Receivable	6,000
Decrease in Accounts Payable	2,000

Compute DVR's net cash provided by operating activities—indirect method.

Learning Objective 2 **S-F:16-5 Computing cash flows from operating activities—indirect method**

Winding Road Cellular accountants have assembled the following data for the year ended April 30, 2024:

Cash receipt from sale of land	$ 27,000	Net income	$ 55,000
Depreciation expense	2,000	Cash purchase of equipment	44,000
Cash payment of dividends	5,800	Decrease in current liabilities	20,000
Cash receipt from issuance of common stock	17,000	Increase in current assets other than cash	27,000

Prepare the *operating* activities section using the indirect method for Winding Road Cellular's statement of cash flows for the year ended April 30, 2024.

Note: Short Exercise S-F:16-5 must be completed before attempting Short Exercise S-F:16-6.

Learning Objective 2 **S-F:16-6 Computing cash flows from investing and financing activities**

Use the data in Short Exercise S-F:16-5 to complete this exercise. Prepare Winding Road Cellular's statement of cash flows using the indirect method for the year ended April 30, 2024. Assume beginning and ending Cash are $48,000 and $52,200, respectively.

S-F:16-7 Computing investing and financing cash flows

Learning Objective 2

Preston Media Corporation had the following income statement and balance sheet for 2024:

PRESTON MEDIA CORPORATION
Income Statement
Year Ended December 31, 2024

Sales Revenue	$ 80,000
Depreciation Expense—Plant Assets	11,000
Other Expenses	50,000
Net Income	$ 19,000

PRESTON MEDIA CORPORATION
Comparative Balance Sheet
December 31, 2024 and 2023

	2024	2023
Assets		
Current Assets:		
Cash	$ 5,000	$ 3,900
Accounts Receivable	9,600	5,100
Long-term Assets:		
Plants Assets	105,350	84,350
Accumulated Depreciation—Plant Assets	(29,350)	(18,350)
Total Assets	$ 90,600	$ 75,000
Liabilities		
Current Liabilities:		
Accounts Payable	$ 8,000	$ 4,500
Long-term Liabilities:		
Notes Payable	9,000	12,000
Total Liabilities	17,000	16,500
Stockholders' Equity		
Common Stock, no par	27,000	23,000
Retained Earnings	46,600	35,500
Total Stockholders' Equity	73,600	58,500
Total Liabilities and Stockholders' Equity	$ 90,600	$ 75,000

Requirements

1. Compute the acquisition of plant assets for Preston Media Corporation during 2024. The business sold no plant assets during the year. Assume the company paid cash for the acquisition of plant assets.

2. Compute the payment of a long-term note payable. During the year, the business issued a $4,400 note payable.

Learning Objective 2

Note: Short Exercise S-F:16-7 must be completed before attempting Short Exercise S-F:16-8.

S-F:16-8 Preparing the statement of cash flows—indirect method

Use the Preston Media Corporation data in Short Exercise S-F:16-7 and the results you calculated from the requirements. Prepare Preston Media's statement of cash flows—indirect method—for the year ended December 31, 2024.

Learning Objective 2

S-F:16-9 Computing the change in cash; identifying non-cash transactions

Jennifer's Wedding Shops earned net income of $27,000, which included depreciation of $16,000. Jennifer's acquired a $119,000 building by borrowing $119,000 on a long-term note payable.

Requirements

1. How much did Jennifer's cash balance increase or decrease during the year?
2. Were there any non-cash transactions for the company? If so, show how they would be reported in the statement of cash flows.

Learning Objective 3

S-F:16-10 Computing free cash flow

Julie Lopez Company expects the following for 2024:

- Net cash provided by operating activities of $148,000.
- Net cash provided by financing activities of $56,000.
- Net cash used for investing activities of $77,000 (no sales of long-term assets).
- Cash dividends paid to stockholders of $7,000.

How much free cash flow does Lopez expect for 2024?

Learning Objective 4
Appendix 16A

S-F:16A-11 Preparing a statement of cash flows using the direct method

Jelly Bean, Inc. began 2024 with cash of $58,000. During the year, Jelly Bean earned revenue of $595,000 and collected $614,000 from customers. Expenses for the year totaled $427,000, of which Jelly Bean paid $212,000 in cash to suppliers and $205,000 in cash to employees. Jelly Bean also paid $148,000 to purchase equipment and a cash dividend of $57,000 to its stockholders during 2024. Prepare the company's statement of cash flows for the year ended December 31, 2024. Format operating activities by the direct method.

Learning Objective 4
Appendix 16A

S-F:16A-12 Preparing operating activities using the direct method

Amy's Learning Center has assembled the following data for the year ended June 30, 2024:

Payments to suppliers	$ 115,000
Cash payment for purchase of equipment	39,000
Payments to employees	66,000
Payment of notes payable	34,000
Payment of dividends	7,500
Cash receipt from issuance of stock	22,000
Collections from customers	188,000
Cash receipt from sale of land	58,000
Cash balance, June 30, 2023	41,000

Prepare the *operating* activities section of the business's statement of cash flows for the year ended June 30, 2024, using the direct method.

Note: Short Exercise S-F:16A-12 must be completed before attempting Short Exercise S-F:16A-13.

S-F:16A-13 Preparing the direct method statement of cash flows

Learning Objective 4
Appendix 16A

Use the data in Short Exercise S-F:16A-12 and your results. Prepare the business's complete statement of cash flows for the year ended June 30, 2024, using the *direct* method for operating activities.

S-F:16A-14 Preparing the direct method statement of cash flows

Learning Objective 4
Appendix 16A

Red Toy Company reported the following comparative balance sheet:

RED TOY COMPANY
Comparative Balance Sheet
December 31, 2024 and 2023

	2024	2023
Assets		
Current Assets:		
Cash	$ 21,000	$ 17,000
Accounts Receivable	53,000	42,000
Merchandise Inventory	76,000	88,000
Prepaid Expenses	3,100	2,100
Long-term Assets:		
Plants Assets, Net	221,000	185,000
Investments	77,000	91,000
Total Assets	$ 451,100	$ 425,100
Liabilities		
Current Liabilities:		
Accounts Payable	$ 42,000	$ 38,000
Salaries Payable	25,000	20,000
Accrued Liabilities	7,000	16,000
Long-term Liabilities:		
Notes Payable	61,000	69,000
Total Liabilities	135,000	143,000
Stockholders' Equity		
Common Stock, no par	45,000	40,000
Retained Earnings	271,100	242,100
Total Stockholders' Equity	316,100	282,100
Total Liabilities and Stockholders' Equity	$ 451,100	$ 425,100

Requirements

1. Compute the collections from customers during 2024 for Red Toy Company. Sales Revenue totaled $134,000.

2. Compute the payments for inventory during 2024. Cost of Goods Sold was $79,000.

Learning Objective 5
Appendix 16B

S-F:16B-15 Using a spreadsheet to complete the statement of cash flows—indirect method

Companies can use a spreadsheet to complete the statement of cash flows. Each item that follows is recorded in the transaction analysis columns of the spreadsheet.

a. Net income
b. Increases in current assets (other than Cash)
c. Decreases in current liabilities
d. Cash payment for acquisition of plant assets
e. Cash receipt from issuance of common stock
f. Depreciation expense

Identify each as being recorded by a Debit or Credit in the *statement of cash flows* section of the spreadsheet.

> Exercises

Learning Objective 1

E-F:16-16 Classifying cash flow items

Consider the following transactions:

a. Purchased equipment for $130,000 cash.
b. Issued $14 par preferred stock for cash.
c. Cash received from sales to customers of $35,000.
d. Cash paid to vendors, $17,000.
e. Sold building for $19,000 gain for cash.
f. Purchased treasury stock for $28,000.
g. Retired a notes payable with 1,250 shares of the company's common stock.

Identify the category of the statement of cash flows in which each transaction would be reported.

E-F:16-17 Classifying transactions on the statement of cash flows—indirect method

Consider the following transactions:

Date	Accounts and Explanation	Debit	Credit
a.	Cash	72,000	
	Common Stock		72,000
b.	Treasury Stock	16,500	
	Cash		16,500
c.	Cash	88,000	
	Sales Revenue		88,000
d.	Land	103,000	
	Cash		103,000
e.	Depreciation Expense—Equipment	6,800	
	Accumulated Depreciation—Equipment		6,800
f.	Dividends Payable	19,500	
	Cash		19,500
g.	Land	22,000	
	Notes Payable		22,000
h.	Cash	9,600	
	Equipment		9,600
i.	Bonds Payable	51,000	
	Cash		51,000
j.	Building	137,000	
	Notes Payable		137,000
k.	Loss on Disposal of Equipment	1,800	
	Accumulated Depreciation—Equipment	200	
	Equipment		2,000

Identify the category of the statement of cash flows, indirect method, in which each transaction would be reported.

E-F:16-18 Classifying items on the indirect statement of cash flows

The statement of cash flows categorizes like transactions for optimal reporting.

Identify each item as a(n):

- Operating activity—addition to net income (O+) or subtraction from net income (O−)
- Investing activity—cash inflow (I+) or cash outflow (I−)
- Financing activity—cash inflow (F+) or cash outflow (F−)
- Non-cash investing and financing activity (NIF)
- Activity that is not used to prepare the indirect statement of cash flows (N)

The *indirect* method is used to report cash flows from operating activities.

a. Loss on sale of land.
b. Acquisition of equipment by issuance of note payable.
c. Payment of long-term debt.
d. Acquisition of building by issuance of common stock.
e. Increase in Salaries Payable.
f. Decrease in Merchandise Inventory.
g. Increase in Prepaid Expenses.
h. Decrease in Accrued Liabilities.
i. Cash sale of land (no gain or loss).
j. Issuance of long-term note payable to borrow cash.
k. Depreciation Expense.
l. Purchase of treasury stock.
m. Issuance of common stock.
n. Increase in Accounts Payable.
o. Net income.
p. Payment of cash dividend.

Learning Objective 2

Net Cash Prov. by Op. Act. $16,000

E-F:16-19 Computing operating activities cash flow—indirect method

The records of Vintage Color Engraving reveal the following:

Net income	$ 36,000	Depreciation expense	$ 5,000
Sales revenue	53,000	Decrease in current liabilities	19,000
Loss on sale of land	4,000	Increase in current assets other than cash	10,000
Acquisition of land	35,000		

Compute cash flows from operating activities by the indirect method for year ended December 31, 2024.

Learning Objective 2

Net Cash Prov. by Op. Act. $49,500

E-F:16-20 Computing operating activities cash flow—indirect method

The accounting records of CD Sales, Inc. include the following accounts:

Account	Beginning Balance	Ending Balance
Cash	$ 7,500	$ 6,500
Accounts Receivable	21,000	17,500
Merchandise Inventory	20,000	30,000
Accounts Payable	15,000	19,000

Accumulated Depreciation—Equipment

	56,000 Jul. 1
	2,000 Depr. Exp.
	58,000 Jul. 31

Retained Earnings

	63,000 Jul. 1
Dividends 15,000	50,000 Net Inc.
	98,000 Jul. 31

Compute CD's net cash provided by (used for) operating activities during July 2024. Use the indirect method.

E-F:16-21 Preparing the statement of cash flows—indirect method

The income statement of Boost Plus, Inc. follows:

Learning Objective 2

Net Cash Prov. by Op. Act. $89,000

BOOST PLUS, INC.
Income Statement
Year Ended September 30, 2024

Net Sales Revenue		$ 231,000
Cost of Goods Sold		94,000
Gross Profit		137,000
Operating Expenses:		
Salaries Expense	$ 54,000	
Depreciation Expense—Plant Assets	27,000	
Total Operating Expenses		81,000
Net Income Before Income Taxes		56,000
Income Tax Expense		12,000
Net Income		$ 44,000

Additional data follow:

a. Acquisition of plant assets is $124,000. Of this amount, $108,000 is paid in cash and $16,000 by signing a note payable.

b. Cash receipt from sale of land totals $20,000. There was no gain or loss.

c. Cash receipts from issuance of common stock total $36,000.

d. Payment of notes payable is $15,000.

e. Payment of dividends is $5,000.

f. From the balance sheet:

	September 30	
	2024	2023
Cash	$ 30,000	$ 13,000
Accounts Receivable	46,000	61,000
Merchandise Inventory	94,000	88,000
Land	82,000	102,000
Plant Assets	214,000	90,000
Accumulated Depreciation	(61,000)	(34,000)
Accounts Payable	32,000	15,000
Accrued Liabilities	12,000	20,000
Notes Payable (long-term)	16,000	15,000
Common Stock, no par	40,000	4,000
Retained Earnings	305,000	266,000

Prepare Boost Plus's statement of cash flows for the year ended September 30, 2024, using the indirect method. Include a separate section for non-cash investing and financing activities.

Learning Objective 2

2. Book Value on Plant Assets Sold $7,000

E-F:16-22 Computing cash flows for investing and financing activities

Consider the following facts for Java Jolt:

a. Beginning and ending Retained Earnings are $45,000 and $70,000, respectively. Net income for the period is $60,000.

b. Beginning and ending Plant Assets are $124,500 and $134,500, respectively.

c. Beginning and ending Accumulated Depreciation—Plant Assets are $21,500 and $26,500, respectively.

d. Depreciation Expense for the period is $17,000, and acquisitions of new plant assets total $29,000. Plant assets were sold at a $5,000 gain.

Requirements

1. How much are cash dividends?
2. What was the amount of the cash receipt from the sale of plant assets?

Learning Objective 2

2. Payment: $8,000
4. Dividends $47,000

E-F:16-23 Computing the cash effect

Rouse Exercise Equipment, Inc. reported the following financial statements for 2024:

ROUSE EXERCISE EQUIPMENT, INC. Income Statement Year Ended December 31, 2024		
Net Sales Revenue		$ 713,000
Cost of Goods Sold		342,000
Gross Profit		371,000
Operating Expenses:		
Depreciation Expense	$ 54,000	
Other Operating Expenses	210,000	
Total Operating Expenses		264,000
Net Income		$ 107,000

ROUSE EXERCISE EQUIPMENT, INC.
Comparative Balance Sheet
December 31, 2024 and 2023

	2024	2023
Assets		
Current Assets:		
Cash	$ 17,000	$ 16,000
Accounts Receivable	57,000	46,000
Merchandise Inventory	79,000	90,000
Long-term Assets:		
Plants Assets	260,500	216,400
Accumulated Depreciation—Plant Assets	(38,500)	(32,400)
Investments	96,000	73,000
Total Assets	$ 471,000	$ 409,000
Liabilities		
Current Liabilities:		
Accounts Payable	$ 72,000	$ 71,000
Salaries Payable	3,000	5,000
Long-term Liabilities:		
Notes Payable	61,000	69,000
Total Liabilities	136,000	145,000
Stockholders' Equity		
Common Stock, no par	45,000	34,000
Retained Earnings	290,000	230,000
Total Stockholders' Equity	335,000	264,000
Total Liabilities and Stockholders' Equity	$ 471,000	$ 409,000

Requirements

1. Compute the amount of Rouse Exercise's acquisition of plant assets. Assume the acquisition was for cash. Rouse Exercise disposed of plant assets at book value. The cost and accumulated depreciation of the disposed asset was $47,900. No cash was received upon disposal.

2. Compute new borrowing or payment of long-term notes payable, with Rouse Exercise having only one long-term notes payable transaction during the year.

3. Compute the issuance of common stock with Rouse Exercise having only one common stock transaction during the year.

4. Compute the payment of cash dividends.

Note: Exercise E-F:16-23 must be completed before attempting Exercise E-F:16-24.

E-F:16-24 Preparing the statement of cash flows—indirect method

Use the Rouse Exercise Equipment data in Exercise E-F:16-23. Prepare the company's statement of cash flows—indirect method—for the year ended December 31, 2024. Assume investments are purchased with cash.

Learning Objective 2

Net Cash Prov. by Op. Act. $160,000

Learning Objective 2

Total Non-cash Inv. and Fin. Act. $153,000

E-F:16-25 Identifying and reporting non-cash transactions

Dirtbikes, Inc. identified the following selected transactions that occurred during the year ended December 31, 2024:

a. Issued 750 shares of $3 par common stock for cash of $17,000.

b. Issued 5,100 shares of $3 par common stock for a building with a fair market value of $96,000.

c. Purchased new truck with a fair market value of $29,000. Financed it 100% with a long-term note.

d. Retired short-term notes of $28,000 by issuing 1,900 shares of $3 par common stock.

e. Paid long-term note of $10,500 to Bank of Tallahassee. Issued new long-term note of $23,000 to Bank of Trust.

Identify any non-cash transactions that occurred during the year and show how they would be reported in the non-cash investing and financing activities section of the statement of cash flows.

Learning Objective 3

E-F:16-26 Analyzing free cash flow

Use the Rouse Exercise Equipment data in Exercises E-F:16-23 and E-F:16-24. Rouse plans to purchase a truck for $23,000 and a forklift for $125,000 next year. In addition, it plans to pay cash dividends of $3,500. Assuming Rouse plans similar activity for 2025, what would be the amount of free cash flow?

Learning Objective 4
Appendix 16A

Net Cash Prov. by Op. Act. $3,000

E-F:16A-27 Preparing operating activities cash flow—direct method

The accounting records of Four Seasons Parts reveal the following:

Payment of salaries and wages	$ 34,000	Net income	$ 21,000
Depreciation expense	10,000	Payment of income tax	16,000
Payment of interest	17,000	Collection of dividend revenue	5,000
Payment of dividends	5,000	Payment to suppliers	51,000
Collections from customers	116,000		

Compute cash flows from operating activities using the *direct* method for the year ended December 31, 2024.

E-F:16A-28 Preparing the statement of cash flows—direct method

The income statement and additional data of Value Corporation follow:

VALUE CORPORATION
Income Statement
Year Ended June 30, 2024

Net Sales Revenue		$ 233,000
Cost of Goods Sold		104,000
Gross Profit		129,000
Operating Expenses:		
Salaries Expense	$ 48,000	
Depreciation Expense—Plant Assets	21,000	
Advertising Expense	12,000	
Total Operating Expenses		81,000
Operating Income		48,000
Other Income and (Expenses):		
Dividend Revenue	7,000	
Interest Expense	(2,500)	
Total Other Income and (Expenses)		4,500
Net Income Before Income Taxes		52,500
Income Tax Expense		7,500
Net Income		$ 45,000

Learning Objective 4
Appendix 16A

Net Cash Prov. by Op. Act. $76,000

a. Collections from customers are $13,000 more than sales.
b. Dividend revenue, interest expense, and income tax expense equal their cash amounts.
c. Payments to suppliers are the sum of cost of goods sold plus advertising expense.
d. Payments to employees are $3,000 more than salaries expense.
e. Cash payment for the acquisition of plant assets is $102,000.
f. Cash receipts from sale of land total $29,000.
g. Cash receipts from issuance of common stock total $38,000.
h. Payment of long-term notes payable is $10,000.
i. Payment of dividends is $9,000.
j. Cash balance at June 30, 2023, was $21,000; at June 30, 2024, it was $43,000.

Prepare Value Corporation's statement of cash flows for the year ended June 30, 2024. Use the *direct* method.

E-F:16A-29 Computing cash flow items—direct method

Consider the following facts:

a. Beginning and ending Accounts Receivable are $24,000 and $20,000, respectively. Credit sales for the period total $68,000.
b. Cost of goods sold is $77,000.

Learning Objective 4
Appendix 16A

1. Cash Receipts from Cust. $72,000

c. Beginning Merchandise Inventory balance is $29,000, and ending Merchandise Inventory balance is $26,000.

d. Beginning and ending Accounts Payable are $12,000 and $16,000, respectively.

Requirements

1. Compute cash collections from customers.
2. Compute cash payments for merchandise inventory.

**Learning Objective 4
Appendix 16A**

2. Cash Paid for Merchandise Inventory $18,542
7. Dividends $374

E-F:16A-30 Computing cash flow items—direct method

A-One Mobile Homes reported the following in its financial statements for the year ended December 31, 2024:

	2024	2023
Income Statement		
Net Sales Revenue	$ 25,118	$ 21,893
Cost of Goods Sold	18,074	15,501
Depreciation Expense	271	234
Other Operating Expenses	4,632	4,277
Income Tax Expense	530	482
Net Income	$ 1,611	$ 1,399
Balance Sheet		
Cash	$ 21	$ 19
Accounts Receivable	798	615
Merchandise Inventory	3,483	2,832
Property, Plant, and Equipment, net	4,351	3,437
Accounts Payable	1,547	1,364
Accrued Liabilities	938	851
Long-term Liabilities	477	461
Common Stock, no par	670	443
Retained Earnings	5,021	3,784

Requirements

1. Compute the collections from customers.
2. Compute payments for merchandise inventory.
3. Compute payments of other operating expenses.
4. Compute the acquisitions of property, plant, and equipment (no sales of property during 2024).
5. Compute the amount of borrowing, with A-One paying no long-term liabilities.
6. Compute the cash receipt from issuance of common stock.
7. Compute the payment of cash dividends.

**Learning Objective 5
Appendix 16B**

E-F:16B-31 Using a spreadsheet to prepare the statement of cash flows—indirect method

Use the Boost Plus, Inc. data in Exercise E-F:16-21 to prepare the spreadsheet for the 2024 statement of cash flows. Format cash flows from operating activities by the indirect method.

> Problems Group A

P-F:16-32A Identifying the purpose and preparing the statement of cash flows—indirect method

Learning Objectives 1, 2

American Rare Coins (ARC) was formed on January 1, 2024. Additional data for the year follow:

2. Net Income $266,400
4. Net Cash Used by Op. Act. $(48,000)

a. On January 1, 2024, ARC issued no par common stock for $450,000.

b. Early in January, ARC made the following cash payments:
   1. For store fixtures, $53,000
   2. For merchandise inventory, $340,000
   3. For rent expense on a store building, $20,000

c. Later in the year, ARC purchased merchandise inventory on account for $239,000. Before year-end, ARC paid $139,000 of this accounts payable.

d. During 2024, ARC sold 2,400 units of merchandise inventory for $275 each. Before year-end, the company collected 85% of this amount. Cost of goods sold for the year was $250,000, and ending merchandise inventory totaled $329,000.

e. The store employs three people. The combined annual payroll is $96,000, of which ARC still owes $3,000 at year-end.

f. At the end of the year, ARC paid income tax of $17,000. There are no income taxes payable.

g. Late in 2024, ARC paid cash dividends of $44,000.

h. For store fixtures, ARC uses the straight-line depreciation method, over five years, with zero residual value.

Requirements

1. What is the purpose of the statement of cash flows?
2. Prepare ARC's income statement for the year ended December 31, 2024. Use the single-step format, with all revenues listed together and all expenses listed together.
3. Prepare ARC's balance sheet at December 31, 2024.
4. Prepare ARC's statement of cash flows using the indirect method for the year ended December 31, 2024.

P-F:16-33A Preparing the statement of cash flows—indirect method

Learning Objective 2

Accountants for Morganson, Inc. have assembled the following data for the year ended December 31, 2024:

Net Cash Used for Inv. Act. $(15,500)

	2024	2023
Current Assets:		
Cash	$ 99,400	$ 25,000
Accounts Receivable	64,100	69,700
Merchandise Inventory	83,000	75,000
Current Liabilities:		
Accounts Payable	57,600	55,200
Income Tax Payable	14,800	16,800

Transaction Data for 2024:

Issuance of common stock for cash	$ 38,000	Payment of notes payable	$ 46,100
Depreciation expense	24,000	Payment of cash dividends	50,000
Purchase of equipment with cash	74,000	Issuance of notes payable to borrow cash	62,000
Acquisition of land by issuing long-term notes payable	119,000	Gain on sale of building	4,500
Book value of building sold	54,000	Net income	68,500

Prepare Morganson's statement of cash flows using the indirect method. Include an accompanying schedule of non-cash investing and financing activities.

Learning Objective 2

P-F:16-34A Preparing the statement of cash flows—indirect method with non-cash transactions

Net Cash Prov. by Op. Act. $125,100

The 2024 income statement and comparative balance sheet of Rolling Hills, Inc. follow:

ROLLING HILLS, INC.
Income Statement
Year Ended December 31, 2024

Net Sales Revenue		$ 440,000
Cost of Goods Sold		209,200
Gross Profit		230,800
Operating Expenses:		
Salaries Expense	$ 77,400	
Depreciation Expense—Plant Assets	14,400	
Other Operating Expenses	10,200	
Total Operating Expenses		102,000
Operating Income		128,800
Other Income and (Expenses):		
Interest Revenue	8,700	
Interest Expense	(21,100)	
Total Other Income and (Expenses)		(12,400)
Net Income Before Income Taxes		116,400
Income Tax Expense		20,000
Net Income		$ 96,400

ROLLING HILLS, INC.
Comparative Balance Sheet
December 31, 2024 and 2023

	2024	2023
Assets		
Current Assets:		
Cash	$ 26,900	$ 15,700
Accounts Receivable	26,500	25,400
Merchandise Inventory	79,800	91,500
Long-term Assets:		
Land	35,100	14,000
Plant Assets	124,840	114,650
Accumulated Depreciation—Plant Assets	(18,940)	(17,950)
Total Assets	$ 274,200	$ 243,300
Liabilities		
Current Liabilities:		
Accounts Payable	$ 35,700	$ 30,400
Accrued Liabilities	28,700	30,300
Long-term Liabilities:		
Notes Payable	79,000	108,000
Total Liabilities	143,400	168,700
Stockholders' Equity		
Common Stock, no par	88,900	64,500
Retained Earnings	41,900	10,100
Total Stockholders' Equity	130,800	74,600
Total Liabilities and Stockholders' Equity	$ 274,200	$ 243,300

Additionally, Rolling Hills purchased land of $21,100 by financing it 100% with long-term notes payable during 2024. During the year, there were no sales of land, no retirements of stock, and no treasury stock transactions. A plant asset was disposed of for $0. The cost and the accumulated depreciation of the disposed asset was $13,410. The plant acquisition was for cash.

Requirements

1. Prepare the 2024 statement of cash flows, formatting operating activities by the *indirect* method.
2. How will what you learned in this problem help you evaluate an investment?

Learning Objectives 2, 3

1. Net Cash Used for Inv. Act. $(152,700)

P-F:16-35A Preparing the statement of cash flows—indirect method, evaluating cash flows, and measuring free cash flows

The comparative balance sheet of Jackson Educational Supply at December 31, 2024, reported the following:

	2024	2023
Current Assets:		
Cash	$ 87,700	$ 23,500
Accounts Receivable	15,300	22,000
Merchandise Inventory	62,600	60,400
Current Liabilities:		
Accounts Payable	28,100	26,100
Accrued Liabilities	10,600	11,300

Jackson's transactions during 2024 included the following:

Payment of cash dividends	$ 16,200	Depreciation expense	$ 16,700
Purchase of equipment with cash	54,700	Purchase of building with cash	98,000
Issuance of long-term notes payable to borrow cash	48,000	Net income	57,600
Issuance of common stock for cash	105,000		

Requirements

1. Prepare the statement of cash flows of Jackson Educational Supply for the year ended December 31, 2024. Use the indirect method to report cash flows from operating activities.
2. Evaluate Jackson's cash flows for the year. Mention all three categories of cash flows and give the reason for your evaluation.
3. If Jackson plans similar activity for 2025, what is its expected free cash flow?

Learning Objective 4
Appendix 16A

2. Total Assets $1,051,400
3. Net Cash Prov. by Op. Act. $308,500

P-F:16A-36A Preparing the statement of cash flows—direct method

Boundary Rare Coins (BRC) was formed on January 1, 2024. Additional data for the year follow:

a. On January 1, 2024, BRC issued no par common stock for $475,000.
b. Early in January, BRC made the following cash payments:
   1. For store fixtures, $53,000
   2. For merchandise inventory, $260,000
   3. For rent expense on the store building, $13,000
c. Later in the year, BRC purchased merchandise inventory on account for $240,000. Before year-end, BRC paid $160,000 of this accounts payable.
d. During 2024, BRC sold 2,200 units of merchandise inventory for $450 each. Before year-end, the company collected 85% of this amount. Cost of goods sold for the year was $330,000, and ending merchandise inventory totaled $170,000.
e. The store employs three people. The combined annual payroll is $80,000, of which BRC still owes $4,000 at year-end.
f. At the end of the year, BRC paid income tax of $24,000. There are no income taxes payable.

g. Late in 2024, BRC paid cash dividends of $40,000.

h. For store fixtures, BRC uses the straight-line depreciation method, over five years, with zero residual value.

Requirements

1. Prepare BRC's income statement for the year ended December 31, 2024. Use the single-step format, with all revenues listed together and all expenses listed together.

2. Prepare BRC's balance sheet at December 31, 2024.

3. Prepare BRC's statement of cash flows for the year ended December 31, 2024. Format cash flows from operating activities by the *direct* method.

P-F:16A-37A Preparing the statement of cash flows—direct method

Use the Rolling Hills, Inc. data from Problem P-F:16-34A.

Requirements

1. Prepare the 2024 statement of cash flows by the direct method.

2. How will what you learned in this problem help you evaluate an investment?

P-F:16B-38A Using a spreadsheet to prepare the statement of cash flows—indirect method

The 2024 comparative balance sheet and income statement of Appleton Group, Inc. follow. Appleton disposed of a plant asset at book value during 2024.

Learning Objective 4
Appendix 16A

1. Net Cash Prov. by Op. Act. $125,100
Collections from Cust. $438,900

Learning Objective 5
Appendix 16B

Cash Pmt. of Div. $28,300
Cash Pmt. for Acq. of Land $25,200

APPLETON GROUP, INC.
Income Statement
Year Ended December 31, 2024

Net Sales Revenue		$ 443,000
Cost of Goods Sold		205,800
Gross Profit		237,200
Operating Expenses:		
Salaries Expense	$ 76,800	
Depreciation Expense—Plant Assets	15,400	
Other Operating Expenses	49,300	
Total Operating Expenses		141,500
Operating Income		95,700
Other Income and (Expenses):		
Interest Revenue	11,600	
Interest Expense	(24,400)	
Total Other Income and (Expenses)		(12,800)
Net Income Before Income Taxes		82,900
Income Tax Expense		16,200
Net Income		$ 66,700

APPLETON GROUP, INC.
Comparative Balance Sheet
December 31, 2024 and 2023

	2024	2023
Assets		
Current Assets:		
Cash	$ 14,700	$ 15,900
Accounts Receivable	42,200	43,900
Merchandise Inventory	97,600	93,900
Long-term Assets:		
Land	42,200	17,000
Plant Assets	121,950	110,750
Accumulated Depreciation—Plant Assets	(20,250)	(16,450)
Total Assets	$ 298,400	$ 265,000
Liabilities		
Current Liabilities:		
Accounts Payable	$ 25,900	$ 26,900
Accrued Liabilities	24,500	22,700
Long-term Liabilities:		
Notes Payable	51,000	65,000
Total Liabilities	101,400	114,600
Stockholders' Equity		
Common Stock, no par	138,900	130,700
Retained Earnings	58,100	19,700
Total Stockholders' Equity	197,000	150,400
Total Liabilities and Stockholders' Equity	$ 298,400	$ 265,000

Prepare the spreadsheet for the 2024 statement of cash flows. Format cash flows from operating activities by the indirect method. A plant asset was disposed of for $0. The cost and accumulated depreciation of the disposed asset was $11,600. There were no sales of land, no retirement of common stock, and no treasury stock transactions. Assume plant asset and land acquisitions were for cash.

> Problems Group B

Learning Objectives 1, 2

2. Net Income $492,800
4. Net Cash Prov. by Op. Act. $359,500

P-F:16-39B Identifying the purpose and preparing the statement of cash flows—indirect method

Classic Rare Coins (CRC) was formed on January 1, 2024. Additional data for the year follow:

a. On January 1, 2024, CRC issued no par common stock for $525,000.

b. Early in January, CRC made the following cash payments:

   1. For store fixtures, $51,000
   2. For merchandise inventory, $240,000
   3. For rent expense on a store building, $18,000

c. Later in the year, CRC purchased merchandise inventory on account for $243,000. Before year-end, CRC paid $153,000 of this accounts payable.

d. During 2024, CRC sold 2,800 units of merchandise inventory for $325 each. Before year-end, the company collected 95% of this amount. Cost of goods sold for the year was $290,000, and ending merchandise inventory totaled $193,000.

e. The store employs three people. The combined annual payroll is $82,000, of which CRC still owes $5,000 at year-end.

f. At the end of the year, CRC paid income tax of $17,000. There was no income taxes payable.

g. Late in 2024, CRC paid cash dividends of $38,000.

h. For store fixtures, CRC uses the straight-line depreciation method, over five years, with zero residual value.

Requirements

1. What is the purpose of the statement of cash flows?
2. Prepare CRC's income statement for the year ended December 31, 2024. Use the single-step format, with all revenues listed together and all expenses listed together.
3. Prepare CRC's balance sheet at December 31, 2024.
4. Prepare CRC's statement of cash flows using the indirect method for the year ended December 31, 2024.

P-F:16-40B Preparing the statement of cash flows—indirect method

Learning Objective 2

Accountants for Benson, Inc. have assembled the following data for the year ended December 31, 2024:

Net Cash Prov. by Op. Act. $85,700

	2024	2023
Current Assets:		
Cash	$ 105,100	$ 18,000
Accounts Receivable	64,400	68,900
Merchandise Inventory	86,000	82,000
Current Liabilities:		
Accounts Payable	58,000	56,100
Income Tax Payable	14,700	16,900

Transaction Data for 2024:

Issuance of common stock for cash	$ 37,000	Payment of notes payable	$ 47,100
Depreciation expense	24,000	Payment of cash dividends	53,000
Purchase of equipment with cash	69,000	Issuance of notes payable to borrow cash	68,000
Acquisition of land by issuing long-term notes payable	123,000	Gain on sale of building	4,500
Book value of building sold	61,000	Net income	66,000

Prepare Benson's statement of cash flows using the indirect method. Include an accompanying schedule of non-cash investing and financing activities.

Learning Objective 2

1. Net Cash Prov. by Op. Act. $136,300

P-F:16-41B Preparing the statement of cash flows—indirect method with non-cash transactions

The 2024 income statement and comparative balance sheet of Sweet Valley, Inc. follow:

SWEET VALLEY, INC.
Income Statement
Year Ended December 31, 2024

Net Sales Revenue		$ 445,000
Cost of Goods Sold		203,200
Gross Profit		241,800
Operating Expenses:		
Salaries Expense	$ 77,400	
Depreciation Expense—Plant Assets	14,500	
Other Operating Expenses	10,100	
Total Operating Expenses		102,000
Operating Income		139,800
Other Income and (Expenses):		
Interest Revenue	8,200	
Interest Expense	(21,100)	
Total Other Income and (Expenses)		(12,900)
Net Income Before Income Taxes		126,900
Income Tax Expense		19,400
Net Income		$ 107,500

SWEET VALLEY, INC.
Comparative Balance Sheet
December 31, 2024 and 2023

	2024	2023
Assets		
Current Assets:		
Cash	$ 26,300	$ 15,400
Accounts Receivable	26,400	25,100
Merchandise Inventory	79,300	91,300
Long-term Assets:		
Land	34,900	14,000
Plant Assets	115,790	108,330
Accumulated Depreciation—Plant Assets	(19,890)	(18,630)
Total Assets	$ 262,800	$ 235,500
Liabilities		
Current Liabilities:		
Accounts Payable	$ 35,600	$ 30,100
Accrued Liabilities	28,900	30,800
Long-term Liabilities:		
Notes Payable	78,000	105,000
Total Liabilities	142,500	165,900
Stockholders' Equity		
Common Stock, no par	88,200	64,800
Retained Earnings	32,100	4,800
Total Stockholders' Equity	120,300	69,600
Total Liabilities and Stockholders' Equity	$ 262,800	$ 235,500

Additionally, Sweet Valley purchased land of $20,900 by financing it 100% with long-term notes payable during 2024. During the year, there were no sales of land, no retirements of stock, and no treasury stock transactions. A plant asset was disposed of for $0. The cost and the accumulated depreciation of the disposed asset was $13,240. Plant asset was acquired for cash.

Requirements

1. Prepare the 2024 statement of cash flows, formatting operating activities by the *indirect* method.
2. How will what you learned in this problem help you evaluate an investment?

16-62 Financial chapter 16

Learning Objectives 2, 3

1. Net Cash Used for Inv. Act. $(157,400)

P-F:16-42B Preparing the statement of cash flows—indirect method, evaluating cash flows, and measuring free cash flows

The comparative balance sheet of Robeson Educational Supply at December 31, 2024, reported the following:

	2024	2023
Current Assets:		
Cash	$ 83,900	$ 20,500
Accounts Receivable	14,500	21,800
Merchandise Inventory	61,800	60,400
Current Liabilities:		
Accounts Payable	29,600	28,100
Accrued Liabilities	10,500	11,900

Robeson's transactions during 2024 included the following:

Payment of cash dividends	$ 21,200	Depreciation expense	$ 17,400
Purchase of equipment with cash	54,400	Purchase of building with cash	103,000
Issuance of long-term notes payable to borrow cash	44,000	Net income	63,600
Issuance of common stock for cash	111,000		

Requirements

1. Prepare the statement of cash flows of Robeson Educational Supply for the year ended December 31, 2024. Use the indirect method to report cash flows from operating activities.
2. Evaluate Robeson's cash flows for the year. Mention all three categories of cash flows and give the reason for your evaluation.
3. If Robeson plans similar activity for 2024, what is its expected free cash flow?

Learning Objective 4
Appendix 16A

2. Total Assets $1,118,800
3. Collections from Cust. $918,000

P-F:16A-43B Preparing the statement of cash flows—direct method

Diversion Rare Coins (DRC) was formed on January 1, 2024. Additional data for the year follow:

a. On January 1, 2024, DRC issued no par common stock for $450,000.
b. Early in January, DRC made the following cash payments:
   1. For store fixtures, $46,000
   2. For merchandise inventory, $310,000
   3. For rent expense on a store building, $18,000
c. Later in the year, DRC purchased merchandise inventory on account for $238,000. Before year-end, DRC paid $138,000 of this accounts payable.
d. During 2024, DRC sold 2,700 units of merchandise inventory for $400 each. Before year-end, the company collected 85% of this amount. Cost of goods sold for the year was $340,000, and ending merchandise inventory totaled $208,000.
e. The store employs three people. The combined annual payroll is $97,000, of which DRC still owes $6,000 at year-end.

f. At the end of the year, DRC paid income tax of $18,000. There was no income taxes payable.

g. Late in 2024, DRC paid cash dividends of $35,000.

h. For store fixtures, DRC uses the straight-line depreciation method, over five years, with zero residual value.

Requirements

1. Prepare DRC's income statement for the year ended December 31, 2024. Use the single-step format, with all revenues listed together and all expenses listed together.
2. Prepare DRC's balance sheet at December 31, 2024.
3. Prepare DRC's statement of cash flows for the year ended December 31, 2024. Format cash flows from operating activities by the direct method.

P-F:16A-44B Preparing the statement of cash flows—direct method

Use the Sweet Valley data from Problem P-F:16-41B.

Learning Objective 4
Appendix 16A

Requirements

1. Prepare the 2024 statement of cash flows by the direct method.
2. How will what you learned in this problem help you evaluate an investment?

1. Net Cash Prov. by Op. Act. $136,300
Collections from Cust. $443,700

P-F:16B-45B Using a spreadsheet to prepare the statement of cash flows—indirect method

The 2024 comparative balance sheet and income statement of Attleboro Group, Inc. follow. Attleboro disposed of a plant asset at book value in 2024.

Learning Objective 5
Appendix 16B

Cash Pmt. of Div. $28,200
Cash Pmt. of N/P $13,000

ATTLEBORO GROUP, INC.
Income Statement
Year Ended December 31, 2024

Net Sales Revenue		$ 441,000
Cost of Goods Sold		205,400
Gross Profit		235,600
Operating Expenses:		
Salaries Expense	$ 76,300	
Depreciation Expense	15,300	
Other Operating Expenses	49,600	
Total Operating Expenses		141,200
Operating Income		94,400
Other Income and (Expenses):		
Interest Revenue	11,500	
Interest Expense	(24,400)	
Total Other Income and (Expenses)		(12,900)
Net Income Before Income Taxes		81,500
Income Tax Expense		16,200
Net Income		$ 65,300

ATTLEBORO GROUP, INC.
Comparative Balance Sheet
December 31, 2024 and 2023

	2024	2023
Assets		
Current Assets:		
Cash	$ 14,000	$ 15,500
Accounts Receivable	42,000	43,700
Merchandise Inventory	96,800	93,300
Long-term Assets:		
Land	36,400	11,000
Plant Assets	121,250	112,850
Accumulated Depreciation—Plant Assets	(20,350)	(18,650)
Total Assets	$ 290,100	$ 257,700
Liabilities		
Current Liabilities:		
Accounts Payable	$ 24,500	$ 26,000
Accrued Liabilities	23,900	22,600
Long-term Liabilities:		
Notes Payable	56,000	69,000
Total Liabilities	104,400	117,600
Stockholders' Equity		
Common Stock, no par	129,500	121,000
Retained Earnings	56,200	19,100
Total Stockholders' Equity	185,700	140,100
Total Liabilities and Stockholders' Equity	$ 290,100	$ 257,700

Prepare the spreadsheet for the 2024 statement of cash flows. Format cash flows from operating activities by the indirect method. A plant asset was disposed of for $0. The cost and accumulated depreciation of the disposed asset was $13,600. There were no sales of land, no retirement of common stock, and no treasury stock transactions. Assume plant asset and land acquisitions were for cash.

CRITICAL THINKING

> Using Excel

Download Excel problems for this chapter online in MyLab Accounting or at **http://www.pearsonhighered.com/Horngren**.

> Continuing Problem

P-F:16-46 Preparing the statement of cash flows—indirect method

This problem continues the Canyon Canoe Company situation from Chapter F:15. Canyon Canoe Company's comparative balance sheet is shown below. 2025 amounts are assumed, but include several transactions from prior chapters.

CANYON CANOE COMPANY
Comparative Balance Sheet
December 31, 2025 and 2024

	2025	2024
Assets		
Current Assets:		
Cash	$ 523,693	$ 12,125
Short-term Investments, net	23,840	0
Accounts Receivable, net	2,422	7,600
Merchandise Inventory	355	0
Office Supplies	60	165
Prepaid Rent	0	2,000
Property, Plant, and Equipment:		
Land	155,000	85,000
Building	610,000	35,000
Canoes	12,000	12,000
Office Furniture and Equipment	150,000	0
Accumulated Depreciation—PP&E	(35,180)	(850)
Total Assets	**$ 1,442,190**	**$ 153,040**
Liabilities		
Current Liabilities:		
Accounts Payable	$ 5,195	$ 3,050
Utilities Payable	745	295
Telephone Payable	700	325
Wages Payable	4,250	1,250
Notes Payable	15,000	0
Interest Payable	350	50
Unearned Revenue	500	350
Long-term Liabilities:		
Notes Payable	7,200	7,200
Mortgage Payable	405,000	0
Bonds Payable	210,000	0
Discount on Bonds Payable	(1,270)	0
Total Liabilities	647,670	12,520
Stockholders' Equity		
Paid-In Capital:		
Preferred Stock	60,000	0
Paid-In Capital in Excess of Par—Preferred	10,000	0
Common Stock	186,000	136,000
Paid-In Capital in Excess of Par—Common	150,000	0
Retained Earnings	388,520	4,520
Total Stockholders' Equity	794,520	140,520
Total Liabilities and Stockholders' Equity	**$ 1,442,190**	**$ 153,040**

16-66 Financial chapter 16

Additional data follow:

1. The income statement for 2025 included the following items:
   a. Net income, $417,000.
   b. Depreciation expense for the year, $34,330.
   c. Amortization on the bonds payable, $254.
2. There were no disposals of property, plant and equipment during the year. All acquisitions of PP&E were for cash except the land, which was acquired by issuing preferred stock.
3. The company issued bonds payable with a face value of $210,000, receiving cash of $208,476.
4. The company distributed 4,000 shares of common stock in a stock dividend when the market value was $4.50 per share. All other dividends were paid in cash.
5. The common stock, except for the stock dividend, was issued for cash.
6. The cash receipt from the notes payable in 2025 is considered a financing activity because it does not relate to operations.

Requirement

Prepare the statement of cash flows for the year ended December 31, 2025, using the indirect method.

> Tying It All Together Case F:16-1

Before you begin this assignment, review the Tying It All Together feature in the chapter. It will also be helpful if you review Amazon.com, Inc.'s 2018 annual report (**https://www.sec.gov/Archives/edgar/data/1018724/000101872419000004/amzn-20181231x10k.htm**).

Amazon.com, Inc. serves its customers through its retail Web sites, selling millions of unique products. In addition, the company manufactures and sells electronic devices including Kindle e-readers and Fire tablets. Amazon.com also offers Amazon Prime, a membership program that includes unlimited free shipping on items and access to unlimited streaming of movies and TV episodes.

Requirements

1. Review Item 7 (Management's Discussion and Analysis of Financial Condition and Results of Operations) included in the 2018 Annual Report. What does Amazon.com, Inc. state is the company's financial focus? What are free cash flows and how does Amazon.com plan to increase its free cash flows?
2. Review the statement of cash flows for Amazon.com, Inc. What type of noncash adjustments to net income did Amazon.com report in 2018?
3. Review the 2018 statement of cash flows for Amazon.com, Inc. What was the net cash provided (used) for investing activities? What were the cash inflows and outflows related to this section?
4. Review the 2018 statement of cash flows for Amazon.com, Inc. What was the net cash provided (used) for financing activities? What were the cash inflows and outflows related to this section?

> Decision Case F:16-1

Theater by Design and Show Cinemas are asking you to recommend their stock to your clients. Because Theater by Design and Show Cinemas earn about the same net income and have similar financial positions, your decision depends on their statement of cash flows, summarized as follows:

	Theater by Design		Show Cinemas	
Net Cash Provided by Operating Activities		$ 30,000		$ 70,000
Cash Provided by (Used for) Investing Activities:				
Purchase of Plant Assets	$ (20,000)		$ (100,000)	
Sale of Plant Assets	40,000	20,000	10,000	(90,000)
Cash Provided by (Used for) Financing Activities:				
Issuance of Common Stock		0		30,000
Payment of Long-term Debt		(40,000)		0
Net Increase (Decrease) in Cash		$ 10,000		$ 10,000

Based on their cash flows, which company looks better? Give your reasons.

> Ethical Issue F:16-1

Moss Exports is having a bad year. Net income is only $60,000. Also, two important overseas customers are falling behind in their payments to Moss, and Moss's accounts receivable are ballooning. The company desperately needs a loan. The Moss Exports Board of Directors is considering ways to put the best face on the company's financial statements. Moss's bank closely examines cash flow from operating activities. Daniel Peavey, Moss's controller, suggests reclassifying the receivables from the slow-paying clients as long-term. He explains to the board that removing the $80,000 increase in accounts receivable from current assets will increase net cash provided by operations. This approach may help Moss get the loan.

Requirements

1. Using only the amounts given, compute net cash provided by operations, both without and with the reclassification of the receivables. Which reporting makes Moss look better?

2. Under what condition would the reclassification of the receivables be ethical? Unethical?

> Financial Statement Case F:16-1

Details about a company's cash flows appear in a number of places in the annual report. Use **Target Corporation's** Fiscal 2018 Annual Report to answer the following questions. Visit **http://www.pearsonhighered.com/Horngren** to view a link to Target Corporation's Fiscal 2018 Annual Report.

Requirements

1. Which method does Target use to report net cash flows from *operating* activities? How can you tell?
2. Target earned net income during 2018. Did operations *provide* cash or *use* cash during 2018? Give the amount. How did net cash provided by (used for) operations during 2018 compare with net income in 2018?
3. For the year ended February 2, 2019 (fiscal year 2018), did Target pay cash dividends? If so, how much?
4. For the year ended February 2, 2019, did Target use cash to purchase property, plant, and equipment? If so, how much?

> Quick Check Answers

1. d **2.** d **3.** b **4.** a **5.** d **6.** c **7.** c **8.** c **9A.** d **10B.** a

Financial Statement Analysis 17

What Companies Should I Invest In?

Clara Wu misses her mom, Sylvia, a lot these days. Her mom always knew just the right words to say when Clara came to visit after a long, hard day at work, and her mom's chocolate cookies always worked magic in making her feel better. Since her mom passed away six months ago, Clara has had to make a lot of decisions on her own. As executor of her mom's estate, she was responsible for helping the accountant and attorney finalize the financial details and the estate paperwork. Clara knew that once the estate was settled, she would be receiving a large amount of cash. She knew that deciding what to do with the cash would be a very important decision.

When Clara met with her financial planner, she shared her goals of paying off her student loans and other personal debt and then saving toward her retirement. She wanted to take the cash remaining after paying off her debts and invest it in the stock market. Clara was worried, though. She tried to stay current on the financial markets by reading the business section of the newspaper and listening to the financial news, but she wasn't sure how to decide which companies would be the best investment choices. Clara's financial planner advised her that there are a number of tools that she could use to evaluate companies and determine which company is more profitable. Other tools will be helpful in helping her determine trends across a period of time. Clara knew that with help from her financial planner and these tools she could make sense out of companies' financial statements and invest with a confidence that would make her mom proud.

What Are the Tools That Help Users Analyze a Business?

In this chapter, you learn about tools that allow users to see beyond the pure numbers on the financial statements and translate them into meaningful analysis. So far you have learned some of what it takes to prepare financial statements; now you will learn how to use financial statements to help manage a company effectively, make wise investments, and compare one company to another. Certified financial planners who work for companies, such as **Raymond James Financial, Inc.,** a financial services holding company that operates a full-service brokerage and investment firm headquartered in Florida, analyze financial statements to compare a company's performance across several periods of time. This comparison helps investors determine how a company is performing over time. In addition, financial planners use another tool, called *ratio analysis*, to measure one company against other companies in the same industry. Whether you will be an investor, an employee, or a manager of a company, knowing how to evaluate a company's performance accurately will help you make smart business decisions.

17-2 Financial  chapter 17

Chapter 17 Learning Objectives

1 Explain how financial statements are used to analyze a business
2 Perform a horizontal analysis of financial statements
3 Perform a vertical analysis of financial statements
4 Compute and evaluate the standard financial ratios

HOW ARE FINANCIAL STATEMENTS USED TO ANALYZE A BUSINESS?

Learning Objective 1
Explain how financial statements are used to analyze a business

In this chapter, we use what you have learned about financial statements to analyze Smart Touch Learning. We will determine if it was profitable, as well as its overall financial health.

Purpose of Analysis

Investors and creditors cannot evaluate a company by examining only one year's data. That is why most financial statements cover at least two periods. In fact, most financial analyses cover trends over three to five years. This chapter shows you how to use some of the analytical tools for charting a company's progress through time. These tools can be used by small business owners to measure performance, by financial analysts to analyze stock investments, by auditors to obtain an overall sense of a company's financial health, by creditors to determine credit risk, or by any other person wanting to compare financial data in relevant terms.

To accurately determine the financial performance of a company, such as Smart Touch Learning, we need to compare its performance in the following ways:

- from year to year
- with a competing company
- with the same industry as a whole

After this comparison, we will have a better idea of how to judge the company's present situation and predict what might happen in the near future.

Tools of Analysis

There are three main ways to analyze financial statements:

- Horizontal analysis provides a year-to-year comparison of a company's performance in different periods.
- Vertical analysis provides a way to compare different companies.
- Ratio analysis can be used to provide information about a company's performance. It is used most effectively to measure a company against other companies in the same industry and to denote trends within the company.

Corporate Financial Reports

Before we discuss the different tools available for financial statement analysis, let's review corporate financial reports.

Financial Statement Analysis  Financial 17-3

Publicly traded corporations have their stock listed on public stock exchanges, such as the New York Stock Exchange or the NASDAQ. They are required by the Securities and Exchange Commission (SEC) to file annual and quarterly reports (also called a *Form 10-K* and *Form 10-Q*). An **annual report** provides information about a company's financial condition. These reports help investors make informed investment decisions.

Annual Report
Provides information about a company's financial condition.

Business Overview

A typical annual report begins with an overview of the business—including the industry the company is in, its growth strategy, and an overview of the company's brands. It also often discusses the company's competitors and the risks related to the company's business.

Management's Discussion and Analysis of Financial Condition and Results of Operations

Another part of the annual report is **management's discussion and analysis of financial condition and results of operations (MD&A)**. This section of the annual report is intended to help investors understand the results of operations and the financial condition of the company. It is important to realize that this section is written by the company and could present a biased view of the company's financial condition and results. This section of the report is the company's attempt to explain its financial statements and to discuss its performance.

The MD&A section is of interest to investors, though, because it often contains information that is not found in the financial data. Such information might include how a company is planning to spend its cash during the next year for property, plant, and equipment or whether significant changes are expected to occur that would cause revenue or expenses to increase or decrease in the future. This section often provides forward-looking information that can be useful to investors who are trying to estimate what future earnings will be for the company.

Management's Discussion and Analysis of Financial Condition and Results of Operations (MD&A)
The section of the annual report that is intended to help investors understand the results of operations and the financial condition of the company.

Report of Independent Registered Public Accounting Firm

A report of the independent registered public accounting firm (often referred to as the *auditor's report*) is included in an annual report. The audit report attests to the fairness of the presentation of the financial statements and states whether the financial statements are presented in accordance with Generally Accepted Accounting Principles (GAAP). This report is prepared by an independent external auditor who has performed an audit on the financial statements. In addition, the external auditor is responsible for assessing the effectiveness of the company's internal controls.

Most audit reports have *unqualified opinions*, which means that the financial statements are presented fairly, in all material respects. A *qualified opinion* might be issued if the financial statements include a departure from GAAP. If the auditor finds that the financial statements are not represented fairly, an *adverse opinion* would be given.

DECISIONS

Should an unqualified opinion be issued?

Patty Schneider was performing the independent audit for Drake Storage, Inc. Patty was reviewing the work that her staff auditors had completed, and she had several concerns about the company's financial statements. Patty's staff had determined that Drake had underreported its cost of goods sold in order to overstate net income. Patty had spoken to Drake Storage's audit committee and discussed her concerns. The audit committee disagreed with the accounting firm's findings. What should Patty do?

Solution

Patty's accounting firm should issue either a qualified opinion or an adverse opinion. To issue an unqualified opinion stating that the financial statements are presented fairly in all material respects would be misleading to investors and creditors. As an independent auditor, Patty's primary responsibility is to report on the fairness of the financial statements and assure the public that the financial statements are presented in accordance with GAAP. If they are not, her firm has a responsibility to issue either a qualified or adverse opinion.

17-4 Financial  chapter 17

Financial Statements

An annual report contains the four basic financial statements you have learned in this textbook: the balance sheet (sometimes referred to as *statement of financial position*), the income statement (or *statement of operations*), the statement of stockholders' equity, and the statement of cash flows. Corporations are required to report multiple-period information for all financial statements. For example, the **Kohl's Corporation** 2018 Annual Report presents financial data for the past three fiscal periods (2018, 2017, and 2016).

Notes to Financial Statements

Immediately following the financial statements are the notes to the financial statements. These notes include a summary of significant accounting policies and explanations of specific items on the financial statements. These notes are an important part of the financial statements and are often referred to by investors to understand the information included in the financial statements.

Match the different parts of the annual report with the appropriate description.

1. Includes the income statement, balance sheet, statement of stockholders' equity, and statement of cash flows.
2. Attests to the fairness of the presentation of the financial statements.
3. Includes a summary of significant accounting policies and explanations of specific items on the financial statements.
4. Is written by the company to help investors understand the results of operations and the financial condition of the company.

a. Notes to financial statements
b. Report of independent registered public accounting firm
c. Management's discussion and analysis of financial condition and results of operations (MD&A)
d. Financial statements

Check your answers online in MyLab Accounting or at http://www.pearsonhighered.com/Horngren.

For more practice, see Short Exercise S-F:17-1.   MyLab Accounting

HOW DO WE USE HORIZONTAL ANALYSIS TO ANALYZE A BUSINESS?

Learning Objective 2
Perform a horizontal analysis of financial statements

Many decisions hinge on whether the numbers—sales, expenses, and net income, for example—are increasing or decreasing. For example, have sales and other revenues risen from last year? By how much?

Sales may have increased, but considered in isolation, this fact is not very helpful. The *percentage change* in sales over time is more relative and, therefore, more helpful. For example, if a company had sales of $100,000 one year and sales increased by $50,000 the next year, that would be a significant increase. However, if the company had sales of $1 billion and sales increased by $50,000, that would not be significant. Therefore, it is often more relevant to know the percentage increase than the dollar increase.

Financial Statement Analysis

The study of percentage changes in line items from comparative financial statements is called **horizontal analysis**. Horizontal analysis compares the change in each financial statement item from one year to the next. Computing a percentage change in comparative statements requires two steps:

1. Compute the dollar amount of the change in a line item from the earlier period to the later period.
2. Divide the dollar amount of change by the earlier period amount and multiply by 100. We call the earlier period the *base period*.

Horizontal Analysis
The study of percentage changes in line items from comparative financial statements. (Dollar amount of change / Base period amount) × 100.

Horizontal analysis is illustrated for Smart Touch Learning as:

	2026	2025	Increase (Decrease) Amount	Percentage
Net Sales Revenue	$858,000	$803,000	$55,000	6.8%

Smart Touch Learning's net sales revenue increased by 6.8% during 2026, computed as follows:

Step 1: Compute the dollar amount of change in sales from 2025 to 2026:

> Dollar amount of change = Later period amount − Earlier period amount
> = $858,000 − $803,000
> = $55,000

Step 2: Divide the dollar amount of change by the base period amount and multiply by 100. This computes the percentage change for the period:

> Horizontal analysis % = (Dollar amount of change / Base period amount) × 100
> = ($55,000 / $803,000) × 100
> = 6.8%*

*All percentage calculations are rounded to the nearest tenth for the rest of this chapter.

Horizontal Analysis of the Income Statement

The horizontal analysis of Smart Touch Learning's income statement is shown in Exhibit F:17-1 (on the next page). This comparative income statement reveals a significant amount of growth during 2026. Net sales revenue increased by 6.8% while Cost of Goods Sold increased by only 0.8%, resulting in a 17.3% increase in gross profit. Additionally, Smart Touch Learning was able to control its operating expenses, creating a 77.2% growth in operating income.

Two items on Smart Touch Learning's income statement with the slowest growth rates are Cost of Goods Sold and Administrative Expenses. Cost of Goods Sold increased by only 0.8%, and administrative expenses decreased by 4.1%. On the bottom line, net income grew by an incredible 88.2%. That is real progress!

Exhibit F:17-1 | Comparative Income Statement—Horizontal Analysis

SMART TOUCH LEARNING
Income Statement
Years Ended December 31, 2026 and 2025

	2026	2025	Increase (Decrease) Amount	Percentage
Net Sales Revenue	$ 858,000	$ 803,000	$ 55,000	6.8%
Cost of Goods Sold	513,000	509,000	4,000	0.8
Gross Profit	345,000	294,000	51,000	17.3
Operating Expenses:				
Selling Expenses	126,000	114,000	12,000	10.5
Administrative Expenses	118,000	123,000	(5,000)	(4.1)
Total Operating Expenses	244,000	237,000	7,000	3.0
Operating Income	101,000	57,000	44,000	77.2
Other Income and (Expenses):				
Interest Revenue	4,000	0	4,000	—
Interest Expense	(24,000)	(14,000)	10,000	71.4
Total Other Income and (Expenses)	(20,000)	(14,000)	6,000	42.9
Income Before Income Taxes	81,000	43,000	38,000	88.4
Income Tax Expense	17,000	9,000	8,000	88.9
Net Income	$ 64,000	$ 34,000	$ 30,000	88.2%

Horizontal Analysis of the Balance Sheet

Horizontal analysis of Smart Touch Learning's comparative balance sheet is shown in Exhibit F:17-2. This analysis also shows growth in assets, with total assets increasing by 22.2%. Notice that both Cash and Cash Equivalents and Prepaid Expenses decreased during the year, but these decreases were offset by increases in other assets.

    Smart Touch Learning's total liabilities also grew. Total liabilities increased by 33.0%. This is another indicator of positive growth for Smart Touch Learning because it implies the corporation is using debt to grow the company. While total liabilities increased, one type of liability, Accrued Liabilities, actually decreased, as indicated by the liability figures in parentheses.

Financial Statement Analysis  Financial 17-7

Exhibit F:17-2 | Comparative Balance Sheet—Horizontal Analysis

SMART TOUCH LEARNING
Balance Sheet
December 31, 2026 and 2025

	2026	2025	Increase (Decrease) Amount	Percentage
Assets				
Current Assets:				
Cash and Cash Equivalents	$ 29,000	$ 32,000	$ (3,000)	(9.4)%
Accounts Receivable, Net	114,000	85,000	29,000	34.1
Merchandise Inventory	113,000	111,000	2,000	1.8
Prepaid Expenses	6,000	8,000	(2,000)	(25.0)
Total Current Assets	262,000	236,000	26,000	11.0
Property, Plant, and Equipment, Net	507,000	399,000	108,000	27.1
Long-term Investments	18,000	9,000	9,000	100.0
Total Assets	$ 787,000	$ 644,000	$ 143,000	22.2%
Liabilities				
Current Liabilities:				
Accounts Payable	$ 73,000	$ 68,000	$ 5,000	7.4%
Accrued Liabilities	27,000	31,000	(4,000)	(12.9)
Notes Payable	42,000	27,000	15,000	55.6
Total Current Liabilities	142,000	126,000	16,000	12.7
Long-term Liabilities	289,000	198,000	91,000	46.0
Total Liabilities	431,000	324,000	107,000	33.0
Stockholders' Equity				
Common Stock, no par	186,000	186,000	0	0.0
Retained Earnings	170,000	134,000	36,000	26.9
Total Stockholders' Equity	356,000	320,000	36,000	11.3
Total Liabilities and Stockholders' Equity	$ 787,000	$ 644,000	$ 143,000	22.2%

Trend Analysis

Trend analysis is a form of horizontal analysis. Trend percentages indicate the direction a business is taking. For example, how have sales changed over a five-year period? What trend does net income show? These questions can be answered by trend analysis over a period, such as three to five years.

Trend analysis percentages are computed by selecting a base period (for example, the earliest year). The base period amounts are set equal to 100%. The amounts for each subsequent year are expressed as a percentage of the base amount. To compute trend analysis percentages, we divide each item for the following years by the base period amount and multiply by 100.

> **Trend Analysis**
> A form of horizontal analysis in which percentages are computed by selecting a base period as 100% and expressing amounts for following periods as a percentage of the base period amount. (Any period amount / Base period amount) × 100.

$$\text{Trend \%} = (\text{Any period amount} / \text{Base period amount}) \times 100$$

17-8 Financial   chapter 17

Assume Smart Touch Learning's Net Sales Revenue were $750,000 in 2022 and rose to $858,000 in 2026. To illustrate trend analysis, review the trend of net sales revenue during 2022–2026. The base year is 2022, the earliest year, so that year's percentage is set equal to 100.

	2026	2025	2024	2023	2022
Net Sales Revenue	$ 858,000	$ 803,000	$ 780,000	$ 748,000	$ 750,000
Trend Percentages	114.4%	107.1%	104.0%	99.7%	100.0%

We want percentages for the five-year period 2022–2026. We compute these by dividing each year's net sales revenue amount by the 2022 net sales revenue amount and multiply by 100. For example, the trend percentage for 2023 is calculated as follows:

$$\text{Trend \%} = (\text{Any period amount} / \text{Base period amount}) \times 100$$
$$= (\$748,000 / \$750,000) \times 100$$
$$= 99.7\%$$

What is the difference between horizontal analysis and trend analysis?

Notice that net sales revenue decreased slightly in 2023, indicated by a percentage less than 100%, and then the rate of growth increased from 2024–2026. You can perform a trend analysis on any one or multiple item(s) you consider important. Trend analysis is widely used to predict the future health of a company.

Trend analysis and horizontal analysis are very similar, but they can be used to indicate different things for a company. **Horizontal analysis allows a company to see the percentage change from one year to the next. Trend analysis shows the percentage change from a base year forward to determine whether the trend in net sales revenue, for example, is positive or negative over a longer period of time.**

Try It!

5. Freedom Corp. reported the following on its comparative income statement:

(In millions)	2025	2024
Net Sales Revenue	$ 10,000	$ 8,000
Cost of Goods Sold	4,500	3,000

Prepare a horizontal analysis of net sales revenue, cost of goods sold, and gross profit—both in dollar amounts and in percentages.

Check your answers online in MyLab Accounting or at http://www.pearsonhighered.com/Horngren.

For more practice, see Short Exercises S-F:17-2 and S-F:17-3. MyLab Accounting

HOW DO WE USE VERTICAL ANALYSIS TO ANALYZE A BUSINESS?

Learning Objective 3
Perform a vertical analysis of financial statements

As you have seen, horizontal analysis and trend analysis percentages highlight changes in an item from year to year, or over *time*. But no single technique gives a complete picture of a business, so we also need vertical analysis.

Vertical analysis of a financial statement shows the relationship of each item to its base amount, which is the 100% figure. Every other item on the statement is then reported as a percentage of that base. For the income statement, net sales revenue is the base. For the balance sheet, total assets is the base.

> Vertical analysis % = (Specific item / Base amount) × 100

Vertical Analysis
An analysis of a financial statement that reveals the relationship of each statement item to its base amount, which is the 100% figure. (Specific item / Base amount) × 100.

Vertical Analysis of the Income Statement

Exhibit F:17-3 shows the completed vertical analysis of Smart Touch Learning's 2026 and 2025 comparative income statement.

Exhibit F:17-3 | **Comparative Income Statement—Vertical Analysis**

SMART TOUCH LEARNING
Income Statement
Years Ended December 31, 2026 and 2025

	2026	Percent of Total	2025	Percent of Total
Net Sales Revenue	$ 858,000	100.0%	$ 803,000	100.0%
Cost of Goods Sold	513,000	59.8	509,000	63.4
Gross Profit	345,000	40.2	294,000	36.6
Operating Expenses:				
Selling Expenses	126,000	14.7	114,000	14.2
Administrative Expenses	118,000	13.8	123,000	15.3
Total Operating Expenses	244,000	28.4	237,000	29.5
Operating Income	101,000	11.8	57,000	7.1
Other Income and (Expenses):				
Interest Revenue	4,000	0.5	0	0.0
Interest Expense	(24,000)	(2.8)	(14,000)	(1.7)
Total Other Income and (Expenses)	(20,000)	(2.3)	(14,000)	(1.7)
Income Before Income Taxes	81,000	9.4	43,000	5.4
Income Tax Expense	17,000	2.0	9,000	1.1
Net Income	$ 64,000	7.5%	$ 34,000	4.2%

The vertical analysis percentage for Smart Touch Learning's cost of goods sold is 59.8% of net sales revenue (($513,000 / $858,000) × 100 = 59.8%) in 2026 and 63.4% (($509,000 / $803,000) × 100 = 63.4%) in 2025. This means that for every $1 in net sales revenue, almost $0.60 in 2026 and approximately $0.63 in 2025 is spent on cost of goods sold. This percentage decrease in cost of goods sold helps explain the percentage increase in gross profit as calculated in the horizontal analysis in Exhibit F:17-1. Smart Touch Learning was able to decrease the cost of goods sold by more than $0.03 for every $1 of net sales revenue.

Smart Touch Learning's net income is 7.5% of net sales revenue in 2026 and 4.2% of net sales revenue in 2025. That improvement from 2025 to 2026 is extremely good. Suppose under normal conditions a company's net income is 10% of revenues. A drop to 4% may cause the investors to be alarmed and sell their stock.

Vertical Analysis of the Balance Sheet

Exhibit F:17-4 depicts the vertical analysis of Smart Touch Learning's balance sheet. The base amount (100%) is total assets. The base amount is also total liabilities and stockholders' equity because they are exactly the same number (remember the accounting equation); in 2026, that's $787,000.

Exhibit F:17-4 | Comparative Balance Sheet—Vertical Analysis

SMART TOUCH LEARNING
Balance Sheet
December 31, 2026 and 2025

	2026	Percent of Total	2025	Percent of Total
Assets				
Current Assets:				
Cash and Cash Equivalents	$ 29,000	3.7%	$ 32,000	5.0%
Accounts Receivable, Net	114,000	14.5	85,000	13.2
Merchandise Inventory	113,000	14.4	111,000	17.2
Prepaid Expenses	6,000	0.8	8,000	1.2
Total Current Assets	262,000	33.3	236,000	36.6
Property, Plant, and Equipment, Net	507,000	64.4	399,000	62.0
Long-term Investments	18,000	2.3	9,000	1.4
Total Assets	$ 787,000	100.0%	$ 644,000	100.0%
Liabilities				
Current Liabilities:				
Accounts Payable	$ 73,000	9.3%	$ 68,000	10.6%
Accrued Liabilities	27,000	3.4	31,000	4.8
Notes Payable	42,000	5.3	27,000	4.2
Total Current Liabilities	142,000	18.0	126,000	19.6
Long-term Liabilities	289,000	36.7	198,000	30.7
Total Liabilities	431,000	54.8	324,000	50.3
Stockholders' Equity				
Common Stock, no par	186,000	23.6	186,000	28.9
Retained Earnings	170,000	21.6	134,000	20.8
Total Stockholders' Equity	356,000	45.2	320,000	49.7
Total Liabilities and Stockholders' Equity	$ 787,000	100.0%	$ 644,000	100.0%

The vertical analysis of Smart Touch Learning's balance sheet reveals several interesting things:

- Current assets make up 33.3% of total assets in 2026 and 36.6% of total assets in 2025. This is typical for most companies with current assets representing close to 30% of total assets.
- Total liabilities are 54.8% of total assets in 2026, increasing slightly from 2025, 50.3%.
- Stockholders' equity makes up 45.2% of total assets in 2026 and 49.7% of total assets in 2025. The percentage share of total assets was nearly equally distributed between total liabilities and total equity for both years.

Common-Size Statements

Horizontal analysis and vertical analysis provide much useful data about a company. As we have seen, Smart Touch Learning's percentages depict a very successful company. But the data apply only to one business.

To compare Smart Touch Learning to another company, we can use a common-size statement. A **common-size statement** reports only percentages—the same percentages that appear in a vertical analysis. By only reporting percentages, it removes dollar value bias when comparing one company to another company. **Dollar value bias** is the bias one sees from comparing numbers in absolute (dollars) rather than relative (percentage) terms. For us, $1 million seems like a large number. For some large companies, it is immaterial.

We could prepare common-size statements for Smart Touch Learning from year to year; however, we will start by preparing common-size income statements for Smart Touch Learning and Learning School, another fictitious company, both of which compete in the same industry. Which company earns a higher percentage of revenues as profits for its shareholders? Exhibit F:17-5 gives both companies' common-size income statements for 2026 so that we can compare them on a relative, not absolute, basis.

Common-Size Statement
A financial statement that reports only percentages (no dollar amounts).

Dollar Value Bias
The bias one sees from comparing numbers in absolute (dollars) rather than relative (percentage) terms.

Exhibit F:17-5 | Common-Size Income Statement—Smart Touch Learning Versus Learning School

SMART TOUCH LEARNING Versus LEARNING SCHOOL
Common-Size Income Statement
Year Ended December 31, 2026

	Smart Touch Learning	Learning School
Net Sales Revenue	100.0%	100.0%
Cost of Goods Sold	59.8	36.3
Gross Profit	40.2	63.7
Operating Expenses:		
Selling Expenses	14.7	21.8
Administrative Expenses	13.8	7.3
Total Operating Expenses	28.4	29.1
Operating Income	11.8	34.6
Other Income and (Expenses):		
Interest Revenue	0.5	11.5
Interest Expense	(2.8)	(10.3)
Total Other Income and (Expenses)	(2.3)	1.2
Income Before Income Taxes	9.4	35.8
Income Tax Expense	2.0	7.2
Net Income	7.5%	28.6%

Exhibit F:17-5 shows that Learning School was more profitable than Smart Touch Learning in 2026. Learning School's gross profit percentage is 63.7%, compared with Smart Touch Learning's 40.2%. This means that Learning School is earning more gross profit from every dollar of revenue than Smart Touch Learning is earning. And, most importantly, Learning School's percentage of net income to revenues is 28.6%. That means more than one-fourth of Learning School's revenues result in profits for the company's stockholders. Smart Touch

Learning's percentage of net income to revenues, on the other hand, is 7.5%, significantly lower than Learning School's. Smart Touch Learning's lower net income is directly attributable to its larger percentage of cost of goods sold to net sales revenue. Smart Touch Learning's cost of goods sold represents 59.8% of net sales revenue, whereas Learning School's cost of goods sold is only 36.3%.

Benchmarking

Benchmarking is the practice of comparing a company's performance with best practices from other companies. It often uses the common-size percentages in a graphical manner to highlight differences. There are two main types of benchmarks in financial statement analysis: benchmarking against a key competitor and benchmarking against the industry average.

> **Benchmarking**
> The practice of comparing a company's performance with best practices from other companies.

Benchmarking Against a Key Competitor

Exhibit F:17-5 uses a key competitor, Learning School, to compare Smart Touch Learning's profitability. The two companies compete in the same industry, so Learning School serves as an ideal benchmark for Smart Touch Learning. The charts in Exhibit F:17-6 highlight the profitability difference between the companies. Focus on the segments of the graphs showing cost of goods sold and net income. Learning School is clearly more profitable than Smart Touch Learning, primarily because its cost of goods sold is significantly lower.

Exhibit F:17-6 | **Graphical Analysis of Common-Size Income Statement—Smart Touch Learning Versus Learning School**

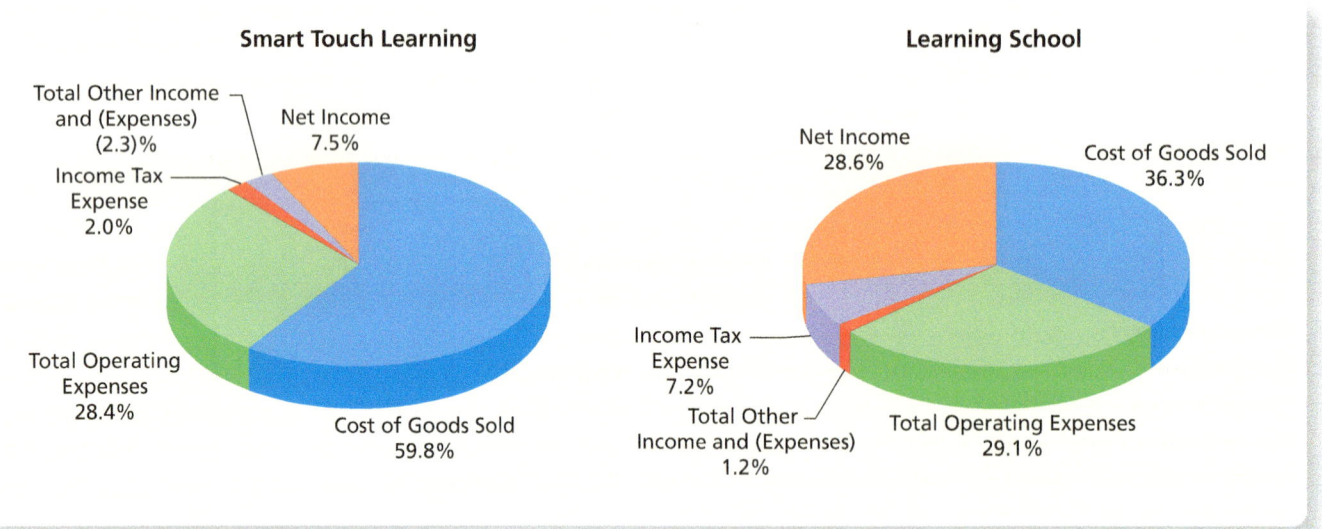

Benchmarking Against the Industry Average

The industry average can also serve as a very useful benchmark for evaluating a company. An industry comparison would show how Smart Touch Learning is performing alongside the average for the e-learning industry. *Annual Statement Studies*, published by the Risk Management Association, provides common-size statements for most industries. To compare Smart Touch Learning to the industry average, we would simply insert the industry-average common-size income statement in place of Learning School in Exhibit F:17-5.

> As you are taking classes toward your degree, how do you know how quickly you can complete your studies? If you knew the average credit hours taken each semester was 12 credit hours, then 12 credit hours would be your benchmark. Comparing the number of classes you take to the average of 12 credit hours a semester is the same concept as benchmarking. Maybe you are taking 15 credit hours a semester. Then you'd be completing your degree faster than the average student. Maybe you take only three credit hours in the spring so you can work a part-time job. Then you'd be completing classes at a slower pace than average.

Try It!

6. Monroe Corp. reported the following amounts on its balance sheet at December 31, 2024 and 2023:

	2024	2023
Cash and Receivables	$ 35,000	$ 40,000
Merchandise Inventory	20,000	15,000
Property, Plant, and Equipment, Net	80,000	60,000
Total Assets	$ 135,000	$ 115,000

Prepare a vertical analysis of Monroe Corp. for 2024 and 2023.

Check your answers online in MyLab Accounting or at http://www.pearsonhighered.com/Horngren.

For more practice, see Short Exercises S-F:17-4 and S-F:17-5. **MyLab Accounting**

HOW DO WE USE RATIOS TO ANALYZE A BUSINESS?

Online financial databases, such as LexisNexis and the Dow Jones, provide data on thousands of companies. Suppose you want to compare some companies' recent earnings histories. You might want to compare companies' returns on stockholders' equity. You could use a computer to search the databases and give you the names of the 20 companies with the highest return on equity. You can use any ratio to search for information that is relevant to a particular decision.

Remember, however, that no single ratio tells the whole picture of any company's performance. Different ratios explain different aspects of a company. The ratios we discuss in this chapter may be classified and used for the following purposes:

- Evaluating the ability to pay current liabilities
- Evaluating the ability to sell merchandise inventory and collect receivables
- Evaluating the ability to pay long-term debt
- Evaluating profitability
- Evaluating stock as an investment

Learning Objective 4
Compute and evaluate the standard financial ratios

We will use the comparative income statement and balance sheet of Smart Touch Learning, shown in Exhibit F:17-7 (on the next page), to discuss the ratios that can be used to evaluate a company. Let's begin by discussing ratios that can be used to evaluate a company's ability to pay its current liabilities.

Exhibit F:17-7 | Comparative Financial Statements

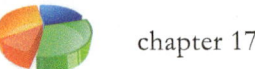

SMART TOUCH LEARNING
Balance Sheet
December 31, 2026 and 2025

	2026	2025
Assets		
Current Assets:		
Cash and Cash Equivalents	$ 29,000	$ 32,000
Accounts Receivable, Net	114,000	85,000
Merchandise Inventory	113,000	111,000
Prepaid Expenses	6,000	8,000
Total Current Assets	262,000	236,000
Property, Plant, and Equipment, Net	507,000	399,000
Long-term Investments	18,000	9,000
Total Assets	$ 787,000	$ 644,000
Liabilities		
Current Liabilities:		
Accounts Payable	$ 73,000	$ 68,000
Accrued Liabilities	27,000	31,000
Notes Payable	42,000	27,000
Total Current Liabilities	142,000	126,000
Long-term Liabilities	289,000	198,000
Total Liabilities	431,000	324,000
Stockholders' Equity		
Common Stock, no par	186,000	186,000
Retained Earnings	170,000	134,000
Total Stockholders' Equity	356,000	320,000
Total Liabilities and Stockholders' Equity	$ 787,000	$ 644,000

SMART TOUCH LEARNING
Income Statement
Years Ended December 31, 2026 and 2025

	2026	2025
Net Sales Revenue	$ 858,000	$ 803,000
Cost of Goods Sold	513,000	509,000
Gross Profit	345,000	294,000
Operating Expenses:		
Selling Expenses	126,000	114,000
Administrative Expenses	118,000	123,000
Total Operating Expenses	244,000	237,000
Operating Income	101,000	57,000
Other Income and (Expenses):		
Interest Revenue	4,000	0
Interest Expense	(24,000)	(14,000)
Total Other Income and (Expenses)	(20,000)	(14,000)
Income Before Income Taxes	81,000	43,000
Income Tax Expense	17,000	9,000
Net Income	$ 64,000	$ 34,000

Evaluating the Ability to Pay Current Liabilities

In this section, we discuss one equation and three ratios that measure a company's ability to pay current liabilities.

Working Capital

Working Capital
A measure of a business's ability to meet its short-term obligations with its current assets. Current assets − Current liabilities.

Determining a company's working capital is a good starting place to evaluate a company's ability to pay its current liabilities. **Working capital** measures the ability to meet short-term obligations with current assets. Working capital is defined as follows:

> Working capital = Current assets − Current liabilities

Smart Touch Learning's working capital at December 31, 2026 and 2025 is calculated as follows:

> Working capital = Current assets − Current liabilities
> 2026: $262,000 − $142,000 = $120,000
> 2025: $236,000 − $126,000 = $110,000

Financial Statement Analysis  Financial 17-15

Smart Touch Learning's working capital is positive, indicating that the company has more current assets than current liabilities, but additional information would be helpful. Three additional decision tools based on working capital are the cash ratio, acid-test ratio, and current ratio.

Cash Ratio

Cash is an important part of every business. Without an adequate supply of available cash, businesses cannot continue to operate. Businesses, therefore, monitor cash very carefully. One measure that can be used to calculate a company's liquidity is the cash ratio. The **cash ratio** helps to determine a company's ability to meet its short-term obligations and is calculated as cash plus cash equivalents divided by total current liabilities.

Notice that the cash ratio includes cash and cash equivalents. As a reminder, cash equivalents are highly liquid investments that can be converted into cash in three months or less. Examples of cash equivalents are money-market accounts and investments in U.S. government securities.

The cash ratios of Smart Touch Learning, at December 31, 2026 and 2025, along with the average for the industry, are as follows:

Cash Ratio
A measure of a company's ability to pay current liabilities from cash and cash equivalents: (Cash + Cash equivalents) / Total current liabilities.

$$\text{Cash ratio} = \frac{\text{Cash + Cash equivalents}}{\text{Total current liabilities}}$$

$$2026: \frac{\$29,000}{\$142,000} = 0.20$$

$$2025: \frac{\$32,000}{\$126,000} = 0.25$$

$$\text{Industry average} = 0.40$$

The cash ratio has decreased slightly from 2025 to 2026 due to a decrease in available cash and cash equivalents and an increase in total current liabilities. This ratio is the most conservative valuation of liquidity because it looks at only cash and cash equivalents, leaving out other current assets such as merchandise inventory and accounts receivable. Notice that for both years, the cash ratio was below 1.0. Having a cash ratio below 1.0 is a good thing. A cash ratio above 1.0 might signify that the company has an unnecessarily large amount of cash supply. This cash could be used to generate higher profits or be distributed as dividends to stockholders. However, a very low ratio doesn't send a strong message to investors and creditors that the company has the ability to repay its short-term debt.

Acid-Test (or Quick) Ratio

The **acid-test ratio** (sometimes called the *quick ratio*) tells us whether a company could pay all its current liabilities if they came due immediately. That is, could the company pass the acid test? The acid-test ratio is not as stringent as the cash ratio because it includes more assets in the calculation.

To compute the acid-test ratio, we add cash and cash equivalents, short-term investments (those that may be sold in the next 12 months or the business operating cycle, whichever is longer), and net current receivables (accounts receivable and notes receivable, net of allowances) and divide this sum by total current liabilities. Merchandise inventory and prepaid expenses are *not* included in the acid-test ratio because they are the least-liquid current assets. Smart Touch Learning's acid-test ratios for 2026 and 2025 are shown on the next page:

Acid-Test Ratio
The ratio of the sum of cash, cash equivalents, short-term investments, and net current receivables to total current liabilities. The ratio tells whether the entity could pay all its current liabilities if they came due immediately. (Cash including cash equivalents + Short-term investments + Net current receivables) / Total current liabilities.

$$\text{Acid-test ratio} = \frac{\text{Cash including cash equivalents} + \text{Short-term investments} + \text{Net current receivables}}{\text{Total current liabilities}}$$

$$2026: \frac{\$29{,}000 + \$0 + \$114{,}000}{\$142{,}000} = 1.01$$

$$2025: \frac{\$32{,}000 + \$0 + \$85{,}000}{\$126{,}000} = 0.93$$

$$\text{Industry average} = 0.46$$

The company's acid-test ratio improved during 2026 and is significantly better than the industry average. The norm for the acid-test ratio ranges from 0.20 for shoe retailers to 1.20 for manufacturers of equipment, as reported by the Risk Management Association. An acid-test ratio of 0.90 to 1.00 is acceptable in most industries.

Current Ratio

> **Current Ratio**
> Measures the company's ability to pay current liabilities from current assets. Total current assets / Total current liabilities.

The most widely used ratio is the **current ratio**, which is calculated as the total current assets divided by total current liabilities. The current ratio measures a company's ability to pay its current liabilities with its current assets. It is less stringent than the acid-test ratio and the cash ratio because it includes all current assets in the calculation.

The current ratios of Smart Touch Learning, at December 31, 2026 and 2025, along with the average for the industry, are as follows:

$$\text{Current ratio} = \frac{\text{Total current assets}}{\text{Total current liabilities}}$$

$$2026: \frac{\$262{,}000}{\$142{,}000} = 1.85$$

$$2025: \frac{\$236{,}000}{\$126{,}000} = 1.87$$

$$\text{Industry average} = 0.60$$

A high current ratio indicates that the business has sufficient current assets to maintain normal business operations. Compare Smart Touch Learning's current ratio of 1.85 for 2026 with the industry average of 0.60.

What is an acceptable current ratio? The answer depends on the industry. The norm for companies in most industries is around 1.50, as reported by the Risk Management Association. Smart Touch Learning's current ratio of 1.85 is strong. Keep in mind that we would not want to see a current ratio that is too high, say 2.5. This would indicate that the company is too liquid and, therefore, is not using its current assets effectively. For example, the company may need to reduce merchandise inventory levels so as not to tie up available resources.

ETHICS

Should the debt be reclassified?

Victor Brannon, senior accountant for Moose Corporation, was preparing the latest financial ratios. He knew that the ratios were watched carefully by Moose Corporation's lenders due to strict loan agreements that required the corporation to maintain a minimum current ratio of 1.5. Victor knew that the past quarter's financial ratios would not meet the lenders' requirements. His boss, Cara Romano, suggested that Victor classify a note payable due in 11 months as a long-term liability. What should Victor do? What would you do?

Solution

Liabilities are classified as current if they will be settled within one year or the operating cycle, whichever is longer. The classification between current and long-term is clear. Victor should not classify the note payable as a long-term liability. It should be classified as current even though the corporation will not meet the lenders' requirements.

Financial Statement Analysis  Financial 17-17

Evaluating the Ability to Sell Merchandise Inventory and Collect Receivables

In this section, we discuss five ratios that measure a company's ability to sell merchandise inventory and collect receivables.

Inventory Turnover

The **inventory turnover** ratio measures the number of times a company sells its average level of merchandise inventory during a year. A high rate of turnover indicates ease in selling merchandise inventory; a low rate indicates difficulty. A value of 4 means that the company sold its average level of merchandise inventory four times—once every three months—during the year.

To compute inventory turnover, we divide cost of goods sold by the average merchandise inventory for the period. We use the cost of goods sold—not sales—because both cost of goods sold and inventory are stated *at cost*. Sales at *sales price* are not comparable with merchandise inventory *at cost*.

Smart Touch Learning's inventory turnover for 2026 is as follows:

$$\text{Inventory turnover} = \frac{\text{Cost of goods sold}}{\text{Average merchandise inventory}}$$

$$2026: \frac{\$513,000}{[(\$111,000 + \$113,000)/2]} = 4.58$$

$$\text{Industry average} = 27.70$$

Inventory Turnover
Measures the number of times a company sells its average level of merchandise inventory during a period. Cost of goods sold / Average merchandise inventory.

Cost of goods sold comes from the income statement (Exhibit F:17-7). Average merchandise inventory is figured by adding the beginning merchandise inventory of $111,000 to the ending inventory of $113,000 and dividing by 2. (See the balance sheet, Exhibit F:17-7. Remember that 2025's ending balances become 2026's beginning balances.)

Inventory turnover varies widely with the nature of the business. For example, most manufacturers of farm machinery have an inventory turnover close to three times a year. In contrast, companies that remove natural gas from the ground hold their merchandise inventory for a very short period of time and have an average turnover of 30. Smart Touch Learning's turnover of 4.58 times a year means, on average, the company has enough inventory to handle sales for almost 80 days (365 / 4.58 times). The inventory turnover is very low for this industry, which has an average turnover of 27.70 times per year. This ratio has identified an area in which Smart Touch Learning needs to improve.

Days' Sales in Inventory

Another key measure is the **days' sales in inventory** ratio. This measures the average number of days merchandise inventory is held by the company. Smart Touch Learning's days' sales in inventory for 2026 is as follows:

$$\text{Days' sales in inventory} = \frac{365 \text{ days}}{\text{Inventory turnover}}$$

$$2026: \frac{365 \text{ days}}{4.58} = 79.7 \text{ days}$$

$$\text{Industry average} = 13 \text{ days}$$

Days' Sales in Inventory
Measures the average number of days that inventory is held by a company. 365 days / Inventory turnover.

Days' sales in inventory is a way of expressing inventory turnover in different terms, namely in days per year rather than times per year. The inventory turnover for 2026 was 4.58 times per year, which is the equivalent of every 79.7 days. Companies strive to have a high inventory turnover and a low days' sales in inventory.

17-18 Financial  chapter 17

Days' sales in inventory varies widely, depending on the business. Smart Touch Learning's days' sales in inventory of 79.7 days is too high for its industry, which has an average days' sales in inventory ratio of only 13 days. This ratio has identified an area in which Smart Touch Learning needs to improve. Smart Touch Learning should focus on reducing average merchandise inventory held. By decreasing average merchandise inventory, the company can increase inventory turnover and lower the average days' sales in merchandise inventory. Smart Touch Learning will also be able to reduce its merchandise inventory storage and insurance costs as well as reduce the risk of holding obsolete merchandise inventory.

Gross Profit Percentage

> **Gross Profit Percentage**
> Measures the profitability of each sales dollar above the cost of goods sold. Gross profit / Net sales revenue.

Gross profit (sometimes called *gross margin*) is net sales revenue minus the cost of goods sold. Merchandisers strive to increase the **gross profit percentage** (also called the *gross margin percentage*). This ratio measures the profitability of each net sales dollar above the cost of goods sold and is computed as gross profit divided by net sales revenue.

The gross profit percentage is one of the most carefully watched measures of profitability. It reflects a business's ability to earn a profit on the merchandise inventory. The gross profit earned on merchandise inventory must be high enough to cover the remaining operating expenses and to earn net income. A small increase in the gross profit percentage from last year to this year may signal an important rise in income. Conversely, a small decrease from last year to this year may signal trouble.

Smart Touch Learning's gross profit percentage for 2026 is as follows:

$$\text{Gross profit percentage} = \frac{\text{Gross profit}}{\text{Net sales revenue}}$$

$$2026: \frac{\$345,000}{\$858,000} = 0.402 = 40.2\%$$

Industry average = 43%

Gross profit percentage varies widely, depending on the business. Smart Touch Learning's gross profit percentage is 40.2%, which is slightly lower than the industry average of 43%. This ratio has identified an area in which Smart Touch Learning needs to improve. To increase gross profit percentage, Smart Touch Learning needs to decrease the cost of the merchandise inventory and/or increase revenue (sales price). Additionally, addressing Smart Touch Learning's inventory turnover issues will probably help Smart Touch Learning to increase its gross profit percentage.

Accounts Receivable Turnover Ratio

> **Accounts Receivable Turnover Ratio**
> A ratio that measures the number of times the company collects the average accounts receivable balance in a year. Net credit sales / Average net accounts receivable.

The **accounts receivable turnover ratio** measures the number of times the company collects the average receivables balance in a year. The higher the ratio, the faster the cash collections. However, a receivable turnover that is too high may indicate that credit is too tight, causing the loss of sales to good customers. To compute accounts receivable turnover, we divide net credit sales (assuming all Smart Touch Learning's sales from Exhibit F:17-7 are on account) by average net accounts receivable.

Smart Touch Learning's accounts receivable turnover ratio for 2026 is computed as follows:

$$\text{Accounts receivable turnover ratio} = \frac{\text{Net credit sales}}{\text{Average net accounts receivable}}$$

$$2026: \frac{\$85,000}{[(\$85,000 + \$114,000) / 2]} = 8.6$$

Industry average = 29.1

Net credit sales, assumed to equal net sales, comes from the income statement (Exhibit F:17-7). Average net accounts receivable is figured by adding the beginning Accounts Receivable of $85,000 to the ending Accounts Receivable of $114,000 and dividing by 2. (See the balance sheet, Exhibit F:17-7.)

Smart Touch Learning's accounts receivable turnover ratio of 8.6 times per year is much slower than the industry average of 29.1. Why the difference? Smart Touch Learning is a fairly new business that sells to established people who pay their accounts over time. Further, this turnover coincides with the lower-than-average inventory turnover. So, Smart Touch Learning may achieve a higher accounts receivable turnover by increasing its inventory turnover ratio.

Days' Sales in Receivables

Days' sales in receivables, also called the *collection period*, indicates how many days it takes to collect the average level of receivables and is computed as 365 days divided by the accounts receivable turnover ratio. The number of days in average accounts receivable should be close to the number of days customers are allowed to make payment. The shorter the collection period, the more quickly the organization can use its cash. The longer the collection period, the less cash is available for operations.

To compute this ratio for Smart Touch Learning for 2026, we divide 365 days by the accounts receivable turnover ratio we previously calculated:

$$\text{Days' sales in receivables} = \frac{365 \text{ days}}{\text{Accounts receivable turnover ratio}}$$

$$2026: \frac{365 \text{ days}}{8.6} = 42.4 \text{ days}$$

$$\text{Industry average} = 25 \text{ days}$$

> **Days' Sales in Receivables**
> The ratio of average net accounts receivable to one day's sales. The ratio tells how many days it takes to collect the average level of accounts receivable. 365 days / Accounts receivable turnover ratio.

The ratios to evaluate receivables are similar to the inventory ratios. We are stating the same information in different terms. The accounts receivable turnover ratio expresses the result in the number of times per year receivables are collected, and the days' sales in receivables expresses the result in the number of days per year that it takes to collect the receivables.

Smart Touch Learning's ratio tells us that 42.4 average days' sales remain in Accounts Receivable and need to be collected. The company's days' sales in receivables ratio is much higher (worse) than the industry average of 25 days. We need to determine the company's credit terms to assess this ratio. Smart Touch Learning might give its customers a longer time to pay, such as 45 days versus 30 days. Alternatively, Smart Touch Learning's credit department may need to review the criteria it uses to evaluate individual customers' credit. Without the customers' good paying habits, the company's cash flow would suffer.

Evaluating the Ability to Pay Long-term Debt

The ratios discussed so far yield insight into current assets and current liabilities. They help us measure ability to sell merchandise inventory, collect receivables, and pay current liabilities. Most businesses also have long-term debt. Three key indicators of a business's ability to pay long-term liabilities are the debt ratio, the debt to equity ratio, and the times-interest-earned ratio.

Debt Ratio

The relationship between total liabilities and total assets—called the **debt ratio**—shows the proportion of assets financed with debt and is calculated by dividing total liabilities by total assets. If the debt ratio is 100%, then all the assets are financed with debt. A debt ratio of 50% means that half the assets are financed with debt, and the other half are financed by the owners of the business. The higher the debt ratio, the higher the company's financial risk. The debt ratio can be used to evaluate a business's ability to pay its debts.

> **Debt Ratio**
> Shows the proportion of assets financed with debt. Total liabilities / Total assets.

The debt ratios for Smart Touch Learning at the end of 2026 and 2025 follow:

$$\text{Debt ratio} = \frac{\text{Total liabilities}}{\text{Total assets}}$$

$$2026: \frac{\$431,000}{\$787,000} = 0.548 = 54.8\%$$

$$2025: \frac{\$324,000}{\$644,000} = 0.503 = 50.3\%$$

Industry average = 69%

Both total liabilities and total asset amounts are from the balance sheet, presented in Exhibit F:17-7. Smart Touch Learning's debt ratio in 2026 of 54.8% is not very high. The Risk Management Association reports that the average debt ratio for most companies ranges from 57% to 67%, with relatively little variation from company to company. Smart Touch Learning's debt ratio indicates a fairly low-risk position compared with the industry average debt ratio of 69%.

Debt to Equity Ratio

Debt to Equity Ratio
A ratio that measures the proportion of total liabilities relative to total equity. Total liabilities / Total equity.

The relationship between total liabilities and total equity—called the **debt to equity ratio**—shows the proportion of total liabilities relative to total equity. Thus, this ratio measures financial leverage. If the debt to equity ratio is greater than 1, then the company is financing more assets with debt than with equity. If the ratio is less than 1, then the company is financing more assets with equity than with debt. The higher the debt to equity ratio, the greater the company's financial risk.

The debt to equity ratios for Smart Touch Learning at the end of 2026 and 2025 follow:

$$\text{Debt to equity ratio} = \frac{\text{Total liabilities}}{\text{Total equity}}$$

$$2026: \frac{\$431,000}{\$356,000} = 1.21$$

$$2025: \frac{\$324,000}{\$320,000} = 1.01$$

Industry average = 2.23

Smart Touch Learning's debt to equity ratio in 2026 of 1.21 is not very high. Smart Touch Learning's debt to equity ratio indicates a fairly low-risk position compared with the industry average debt to equity ratio of 2.23.

Times-Interest-Earned Ratio

Times-Interest-Earned Ratio
Evaluates a business's ability to pay interest expense. (Net income + Income tax expense + Interest expense) / Interest expense.

The debt ratio and debt to equity ratio say nothing about the ability to pay interest expense. Analysts and investors use the **times-interest-earned ratio** to evaluate a business's ability to pay interest expense. This ratio measures the number of times earnings before interest and taxes (EBIT) can cover (pay) interest expense. This ratio is also called the *interest-coverage ratio*. A high times-interest-earned ratio indicates a business's ease in paying interest expense; a low ratio suggests difficulty. The times-interest-earned ratio is calculated as EBIT (Net income + Income tax expense + Interest expense) divided by interest expense.

Financial Statement Analysis  Financial 17-21

Calculation of Smart Touch Learning's times-interest-earned ratio follows:

$$\text{Times-interest-earned ratio} = \frac{\text{Net income} + \text{Income tax expense} + \text{Interest expense}}{\text{Interest expense}}$$

$$2026: \frac{\$64,000 + \$17,000 + \$24,000}{\$24,000} = 4.38$$

$$2025: \frac{\$34,000 + \$9,000 + \$14,000}{\$14,000} = 4.07$$

$$\text{Industry average} = 7.80$$

The company's times-interest-earned ratios of 4.38 for 2026 and 4.07 for 2025 are significantly lower than the industry average of 7.80 times, but they are slightly better than the ratio for the average U.S. business. The norm for U.S. business, as reported by the Risk Management Association, falls in the range of 2.0 to 3.0. When you consider Smart Touch Learning's debt ratio and its times-interest-earned ratio, Smart Touch Learning appears to have little difficulty paying its long-term liabilities.

Evaluating Profitability

The fundamental goal of business is to earn a profit. Ratios that measure profitability often are reported in the business press. Let's examine five profitability measures.

Profit Margin Ratio

The **profit margin ratio** shows the percentage of each net sales dollar earned as net income. In other words, the profit margin ratio shows how much net income a business earns on every $1.00 of sales. This ratio focuses on the profitability of a business and is calculated as net income divided by net sales revenue.

Smart Touch Learning's profit margin ratio follows:

$$\text{Profit margin ratio} = \frac{\text{Net income}}{\text{Net sales revenue}}$$

$$2026: \frac{\$64,000}{\$858,000} = 0.075 = 7.5\%$$

$$2025: \frac{\$34,000}{\$803,000} = 0.042 = 4.2\%$$

$$\text{Industry average} = 1.7\%$$

> **Profit Margin Ratio**
> A profitability measure that shows how much net income is earned on every dollar of net sales. Net income / Net sales revenue.

Both net income and net sales revenue amounts are from the income statement presented in Exhibit F:17-7. Companies strive for a high profit margin. The higher the profit margin, the more sales dollars end up as profit. The increase in Smart Touch Learning's profit margin ratio from 2025 to 2026 is significant and identifies the company as more successful than the average e-learning providers, whose profit margin ratio is 1.7%.

Rate of Return on Total Assets

The **rate of return on total assets** measures a company's success in using its assets to earn a profit. There are two ways that a company can finance its assets:

- **Debt**—A company can borrow cash from creditors to purchase assets. Creditors earn interest on the money that is loaned.
- **Equity**—A company receives cash or other assets from stockholders. Stockholders invest in the company and hope to receive a return on their investment.

> **Rate of Return on Total Assets**
> A ratio that measures the success a company has in using its assets to earn income. (Net income + Interest expense) / Average total assets.

Rate of return on total assets is calculated by adding interest expense to net income and dividing by average total assets. Interest expense is added back to net income to determine the real return on the assets regardless of the corporation's financing choices (debt or equity).

Computation of the rate of return on total assets ratio for Smart Touch Learning follows:

$$\text{Rate of return on total assets} = \frac{\text{Net income} + \text{Interest expense}}{\text{Average total assets}}$$

$$2026: \frac{\$64,000 + \$24,000}{[(\$644,000 + \$787,000) / 2]} = 0.123 = 12.3\%$$

$$\text{Industry average} = 6.0\%$$

Net income and interest expense come from the income statement (Exhibit F:17-7). Average total assets is figured by adding the beginning total assets of $644,000 to the ending total assets of $787,000 and dividing by 2. (See the balance sheet, Exhibit F:17-7.) Smart Touch Learning's rate of return on total assets ratio of 12.3% is much better than the industry average of 6.0%.

Asset Turnover Ratio

Asset Turnover Ratio
Measures how efficiently a business uses its average total assets to generate sales. Net sales revenue / Average total assets.

The **asset turnover ratio** measures the amount of net sales revenue generated for each average dollar of total assets invested. This ratio measures how well a company is using its assets to generate sales revenues. To compute this ratio, we divide net sales revenue by average total assets.

Smart Touch Learning's 2026 asset turnover ratio is as follows:

$$\text{Asset turnover ratio} = \frac{\text{Net sales revenue}}{\text{Average total assets}}$$

$$2026: \frac{\$858,000}{[(\$644,000 + \$787,000) / 2]} = 1.20 \text{ times}$$

$$\text{Industry average} = 3.52 \text{ times}$$

Smart Touch Learning's asset turnover ratio of 1.20 is much lower than the industry average of 3.52 times, indicating that Smart Touch Learning is generating less net sales revenue for each average dollar of total assets invested. Recall that Smart Touch Learning's gross profit percentage was lower than the industry's also. Normally, companies with high gross profit percentages will have low asset turnover. Companies with low gross profit percentages will have high asset turnover ratios. This is another area in which Smart Touch Learning's management must consider options to increase sales and decrease its average total assets to improve this ratio.

Rate of Return on Common Stockholders' Equity

Rate of Return on Common Stockholders' Equity
Shows the relationship between net income available to common stockholders and their average common equity invested in the company. (Net income − Preferred dividends) / Average common stockholders' equity.

A popular measure of profitability is **rate of return on common stockholders' equity**, often shortened to *return on equity*. This ratio shows the relationship between net income available to common stockholders and their average common equity invested in the company. The rate of return on common stockholders' equity shows how much income is earned for each $1 invested by the common shareholders.

To compute this ratio, we first subtract preferred dividends from net income to get net income available to the common stockholders. (Smart Touch Learning does not have any preferred stock issued, so preferred dividends are zero.) Then we divide net income available to common stockholders by average common stockholders' equity during the year.

Financial Statement Analysis

Common equity is total stockholders' equity minus preferred equity. Average common stockholders' equity is the average of the beginning and ending common stockholders' equity balances.

The 2026 rate of return on common stockholders' equity for Smart Touch Learning follows:

$$\text{Rate of return on common stockholders' equity} = \frac{\text{Net income} - \text{Preferred dividends}}{\text{Average common stockholders' equity}}$$

$$2026: \frac{\$64,000 - \$0}{[(\$320,000 + \$356,000)/2]} = 0.189 = 18.9\%$$

$$\text{Industry average} = 10.5\%$$

Smart Touch Learning's rate of return on common stockholders' equity of 18.9% is higher than its rate of return on total assets of 10.1%. This difference results from borrowing at one rate—say, 8%—and investing the money to earn a higher rate, such as the firm's 18.9% return on equity. This practice is called **trading on the equity**, or using *leverage*. It is directly related to the debt ratio. The higher the debt ratio, the higher the leverage. Companies that finance operations with debt are said to *leverage* their positions.

During good times, leverage increases profitability. But leverage can have a negative impact on profitability as well. Therefore, leverage is a double-edged sword, increasing profits during good times but compounding losses during bad times. Compare Smart Touch Learning's rate of return on common stockholders' equity with the industry average of 10.5%. Once again, Smart Touch Learning is performing much better than the average company in its industry. A rate of return on common stockholders' equity of 15% to 20% year after year is considered good in most industries. At 18.9%, Smart Touch Learning is doing well.

Trading on the Equity
Earning more income on borrowed money than the related interest expense, thereby increasing the earnings for the owners of the business.

Earnings per Share (EPS)

Earnings per share (EPS) is perhaps the most widely quoted of all financial statistics. EPS is the only ratio that must appear on the financial statements. Earnings per share reports the amount of net income (loss) for each share of the company's *outstanding common stock*. Earnings per share is calculated as net income minus preferred dividends divided by the weighted average number of common shares outstanding. Preferred dividends are subtracted from net income because the preferred stockholders have the first claim to dividends. The computation for the weighted average number of common shares outstanding is covered in advanced accounting courses. For simplicity, we will determine earnings per share on the average number of shares outstanding, calculated as the beginning balance plus ending balance divided by two.

FASB requires that earnings per share appear on the income statement. Corporations report a separate EPS figure for each element of income, which was shown in more detail in the stockholders' equity chapter.

Smart Touch Learning's EPS for 2026 and 2025 follow. (Note that Smart Touch Learning had 10,000 shares of common stock outstanding throughout both years.)

Earnings per Share (EPS)
Amount of a company's net income (loss) for each share of its outstanding common stock. (Net income − Preferred dividends) / Weighted average number of common shares outstanding.

$$\text{Earnings per share} = \frac{\text{Net income} - \text{Preferred dividends}}{\text{Weighted average number of common shares outstanding}}$$

$$2026: \frac{\$64,000 - \$0}{10,000 \text{ shares}} = \$6.40 \text{ per share}$$

$$2025: \frac{\$34,000 - \$0}{10,000 \text{ shares}} = \$3.40 \text{ per share}$$

$$\text{Industry average} = \$9.76 \text{ per share}$$

Smart Touch Learning's EPS increased significantly in 2026 (by 88%). Its stockholders should not expect this big a boost in EPS every year. Most companies strive to increase EPS by 10% to 15% annually, and leading companies do so. But even the most successful companies have an occasional bad year. EPS for the industry at $9.76 is significantly more than Smart Touch Learning's 2026 EPS. Therefore, Smart Touch Learning needs to work on continuing to increase EPS by increasing its net income so that it is more competitive with other companies in its industry.

Evaluating Stock as an Investment

Investors purchase stock to earn a return on their investment. This return consists of two parts: (1) gains (or losses) from selling the stock at a price above (or below) purchase price and (2) dividends. The ratios we examine in this section help analysts evaluate stock investments.

Price/Earnings Ratio

> **Price/Earnings Ratio**
> The ratio of the market price of a share of common stock to the company's earnings per share. Measures the value that the stock market places on $1 of a company's earnings. Market price per share of common stock / Earnings per share.

The **price/earnings ratio** is the ratio of the market price of a share of common stock to the company's earnings per share. The price/earnings ratio shows the market price of $1 of earnings. This ratio, abbreviated P/E, appears in many print or online stock listings and measures the value that the stock market places on a company's earnings.

Calculations for the P/E ratios of Smart Touch Learning follow. The market prices of common stock for real companies can be obtained from a financial Web site, a stockbroker, or the company's Web site. The market price for Smart Touch Learning's common stock was $60 at the end of 2026 and $35 at the end of 2025. The earnings per share values were calculated immediately before the P/E ratio.

$$\text{Price / earnings ratio} = \frac{\text{Market price per share of common stock}}{\text{Earnings per share}}$$

$$2026: \frac{\$60 \text{ per share}}{\$6.40 \text{ per share}} = 9.38$$

$$2025: \frac{\$35 \text{ per share}}{\$3.40 \text{ per share}} = 10.29$$

$$\text{Industry average} = 17.79$$

Smart Touch Learning's P/E ratio for 2026 of 9.38 means that the company's stock is selling at 9.38 times one year's earnings per share. Smart Touch Learning would like to see this ratio increase in future years in order to be more in line with the industry average P/E of 17.79.

Dividend Yield

> **Dividend Yield**
> Ratio of annual dividends per share of stock to the stock's market price per share. Measures the percentage of a stock's market value that is returned annually as dividends to stockholders. Annual dividend per share / Market price per share.

Dividend yield is the ratio of annual dividends per share to the stock's market price per share. This ratio measures the percentage of a stock's market value that is returned annually as dividends to shareholders. *Preferred* stockholders, who invest primarily to receive dividends, pay special attention to dividend yield.

Assume Smart Touch Learning paid annual cash dividends of $1.20 per share of common stock in 2026 and $1.00 in 2025. As noted previously, market prices of the company's common stock were $60 in 2026 and $35 in 2025. The firm's dividend yields on common stock follow:

$$\text{Dividend yield} = \frac{\text{Annual dividend per share}}{\text{Market price per share}}$$

2026: $\dfrac{\$1.20 \text{ per share}}{\$60 \text{ per share}} = 0.020 = 2.0\%$

2025: $\dfrac{\$1.00 \text{ per share}}{\$35 \text{ per share}} = 0.029 = 2.9\%$

Industry average = 3.6%

In this calculation, we are determining the dividend yield for common stock. Dividend yield can also be calculated for preferred stock.

An investor who buys Smart Touch Learning's common stock for $60 can expect to receive 2.0% of the investment annually in the form of cash dividends. The industry, however, is paying out 3.6% annually. An investor might be willing to accept lower dividends (cash now) if the stock's market price is growing (cash later when the stock is sold).

Dividend Payout

Dividend payout is the ratio of annual dividends declared per common share relative to the earnings per share of the company. This ratio measures the percentage of earnings paid annually to common shareholders as cash dividends.

Recall that Smart Touch Learning paid annual cash dividends of $1.20 per share of common stock in 2026 and $1.00 in 2025. Earnings per share were calculated as $6.40 per share for 2026 and $3.40 for 2025. So, Smart Touch Learning's dividend payout yields are as follows:

$$\text{Dividend payout} = \frac{\text{Annual dividend per share}}{\text{Earnings per share}}$$

2026: $\dfrac{\$1.20 \text{ per share}}{\$6.40 \text{ per share}} = 0.19 = 19\%$

2025: $\dfrac{\$1.00 \text{ per share}}{\$3.40 \text{ per share}} = 0.29 = 29\%$

Industry average = 63%

Dividend Payout
The ratio of dividends declared per common share relative to the earnings per share of the company. Annual dividend per share / Earnings per share.

Smart Touch Learning's dividend payout ratios of 19% in 2026 and 29% in 2025 are less than the industry average of 63%. Smart Touch Learning, being a fairly new company, might be retaining more of its earnings for growth and expansion. An investor who buys Smart Touch Learning's common stock may predict annual cash dividends to be about 19% of earnings, based on the 2026 dividend payout ratio. This investor would want to see higher market prices and higher asset turnover for Smart Touch Learning in the future for Smart Touch Learning to stay competitive.

Red Flags in Financial Statement Analyses

Analysts look for *red flags* in financial statements that may signal financial trouble. Recent accounting scandals highlight the importance of these red flags. The following conditions may reveal that the company is too risky:

- **Movement of sales, merchandise inventory, and receivables.** Sales, merchandise inventory, and receivables generally move together. Increased sales lead to higher receivables and may require more merchandise inventory (or higher inventory turnover) to meet demand. Unexpected or inconsistent movements among sales, merchandise inventory, and receivables make the financial statements look suspect.
- **Earnings problems.** Has net income decreased significantly for several years in a row? Did the company report net income in previous years but now is reporting a net loss? Most companies cannot survive losses year after year.
- **Decreased cash flow.** Cash flow validates net income. Is net cash flow from operating activities consistently lower than net income? If so, the company is in trouble. Are the sales of plant assets a major source of cash? If so, the company may face a cash shortage.
- **Too much debt.** How does the company's debt ratio compare to that of major competitors? If the debt ratio is too high, the company may be unable to pay its debts.
- **Inability to collect receivables.** Are days' sales in receivables growing faster than for competitors? If so, a cash shortage may be looming.
- **Buildup of merchandise inventories.** Is inventory turnover too slow? If so, the company may be unable to sell goods, or it may be overstating merchandise inventory.

Do any of these red flags apply to Smart Touch Learning from the analyses we did in the chapter? Although the financial statements depict a strong and growing company, the analysis pointed out several areas of weakness for Smart Touch Learning that include low inventory turnover, low accounts receivable turnover, low gross profit margin, low times interest earned, low asset turnover, and low earnings per share. Smart Touch Learning should continue to carefully monitor its financial statements as it continues to grow. Exhibit F:17-8 summarizes the financial ratios that you have learned in this chapter.

Exhibit F:17-8 | Using Ratios in Financial Statement Analysis

Ratio	Computation	Information Provided
Evaluating the ability to pay current liabilities:		
Working capital	Current assets − Current liabilities	A business's ability to meet its short-term obligations with its current assets.
Cash ratio	$\dfrac{\text{Cash + Cash equivalents}}{\text{Total current liabilities}}$	The company's ability to pay current liabilities from cash and cash equivalents.
Acid-test ratio	$\dfrac{\text{Cash including cash equivalents + Short-term investments + Net current receivables}}{\text{Total current liabilities}}$	The company's ability to pay all its current liabilities if they came due immediately.
Current ratio	$\dfrac{\text{Total current assets}}{\text{Total current liabilities}}$	The company's ability to pay current liabilities from current assets.

Financial Statement Analysis  Financial 17-27

Exhibit F:17-8 | **Using Ratios in Financial Statement Analysis (Continued)**

Ratio	Computation	Information Provided
Evaluating the ability to sell merchandise inventory and collect receivables:		
Inventory turnover	$\dfrac{\text{Cost of goods sold}}{\text{Average merchandise inventory}}$	The number of times a company sells its average level of merchandise inventory during a period.
Days' sales in inventory	$\dfrac{365 \text{ days}}{\text{Inventory turnover}}$	The average number of days that inventory is held by a company.
Gross profit percentage	$\dfrac{\text{Gross profit}}{\text{Net sales revenue}}$	The profitability of each sales dollar above the cost of goods sold.
Accounts receivable turnover ratio	$\dfrac{\text{Net credit sales}}{\text{Average net accounts receivable}}$	The number of times the company collects the average receivables balance in a year.
Days' sales in receivables	$\dfrac{365 \text{ days}}{\text{Accounts receivable turnover ratio}}$	The number of days it takes to collect the average level of receivables.
Evaluating the ability to pay long-term debt:		
Debt ratio	$\dfrac{\text{Total liabilities}}{\text{Total assets}}$	The proportion of assets financed with debt.
Debt to equity ratio	$\dfrac{\text{Total liabilities}}{\text{Total equity}}$	The proportion of total liabilities relative to total equity.
Times-interest-earned ratio	$\dfrac{\text{Net income + Income tax expense + Interest expense}}{\text{Interest expense}}$	A business's ability to pay interest expense.
Evaluating profitability:		
Profit margin ratio	$\dfrac{\text{Net income}}{\text{Net sales revenue}}$	How much net income is earned on every dollar of net sales revenue.
Rate of return on total assets	$\dfrac{\text{Net income + Interest expense}}{\text{Average total assets}}$	The success a company has in using its assets to earn income.
Asset turnover ratio	$\dfrac{\text{Net sales revenue}}{\text{Average total assets}}$	How efficiently a business uses its average total assets to generate sales.
Rate of return on common stockholders' equity	$\dfrac{\text{Net income − Preferred dividends}}{\text{Average common stockholders' equity}}$	The relationship between net income available to common stockholders and their average common equity invested in the company.
Earnings per share	$\dfrac{\text{Net income − Preferred dividends}}{\text{Weighted average number of common shares outstanding}}$	Amount of a company's net income (loss) for each share of its outstanding common stock.
Evaluating stock as an investment:		
Price/earnings ratio	$\dfrac{\text{Market price per share of common stock}}{\text{Earnings per share}}$	The value the stock market places on $1 of a company's earnings.
Dividend yield	$\dfrac{\text{Annual dividend per share}}{\text{Market price per share}}$	The percentage of a stock's market value that is returned annually as dividends to stockholders.
Dividend payout	$\dfrac{\text{Annual dividend per share}}{\text{Earnings per share}}$	Ratio of dividends declared per common share relative to the earnings per share of the company.

Try It!

The financial statements of Ion Corporation include the following items:

	Current Year	Preceding Year
Balance Sheet:		
Cash	$ 6,000	$ 8,000
Short-term Investments	4,400	10,700
Net Accounts Receivable	21,600	29,200
Merchandise Inventory	30,800	27,600
Prepaid Expenses	6,000	3,600
Total Current Assets	68,800	79,100
Total Current Liabilities	53,200	37,200
Income Statement:		
Net Sales Revenue	$ 184,800	
Cost of Goods Sold	126,000	

Compute the following ratios for the current year:

7. Current ratio
8. Acid-test ratio
9. Inventory turnover
10. Gross profit percentage

Check your answers online in MyLab Accounting or at http://www.pearsonhighered.com/Horngren.

For more practice, see Short Exercises S-F:17-6 through S-F:17-12.   MyLab Accounting

REVIEW

> Things You Should Know

1. **How are financial statements used to analyze a business?**
   - There are three main ways to analyze financial statements:
     - Horizontal analysis
     - Vertical analysis
     - Ratio analysis
   - Annual reports provide information about a company's financial condition and include the following:
     - Business overview
     - Management's discussion and analysis of financial condition and results of operations (MD&A)

- Report of independent registered public accounting firm
- Financial statements
- Notes to the financial statements

2. How do we use horizontal analysis to analyze a business?

- Horizontal analysis is the study of percentage changes in line items from comparative financial statements. It compares one year to the next. (Dollar amount of change / Base period amount) × 100.
- Trend analysis is a form of horizontal analysis in which percentages are computed by selecting a base year as 100% and expressing the amounts for following periods as a percentage of the base period amount. (Any period amount / Base period amount) × 100.

3. How do we use vertical analysis to analyze a business?

- Vertical analysis reveals the relationship of each statement item to its base amount, which is the 100% figure. (Specific item / Base amount) × 100.
  - For the income statement, net sales revenue is the base.
  - For the balance sheet, total assets is the base.
- Common-size statements are financial statements that report only percentages—the same percentages that appear in vertical analysis.
- Benchmarking is the practice of comparing a company's performance with its prior performance or with best practices from other companies.

4. How do we use ratios to analyze a business?

- Ratios can be used to evaluate a company's:
  - ability to pay current liabilities
  - ability to sell merchandise inventory and collect receivables
  - ability to pay long-term debt
  - profitability
  - stock as an investment
- Exhibit F:17-8 summarizes common ratios that can be used to analyze a business.

> Check Your Understanding F:17-1

Check your understanding of the chapter by completing this problem and then looking at the solution. Use this practice to help identify which sections of the chapter you need to study more.

Kimball Corporation makes cell phone covers and has the following comparative income statement for the years ended December 31, 2025 and 2024:

KIMBALL CORPORATION
Income Statement
Years Ended December 31, 2025 and 2024

	2025	2024
Revenues:		
Net Sales Revenue	$ 300,000	$ 250,000
Other Revenues	0	1,000
Total Revenues	300,000	251,000
Expenses:		
Cost of Goods Sold	214,200	170,000
Engineering, Selling, and Administrative Expenses	54,000	48,000
Interest Expense	6,000	5,000
Income Tax Expense	4,000	3,000
Other Expenses	2,700	0
Total Expenses	280,900	226,000
Net Income	$ 19,100	$ 25,000

Requirement

Perform a horizontal analysis and a vertical analysis of Kimball Corporation. State whether 2025 was a good year or a bad year, and give your reasons. (See Learning Objectives 2 and 3)

> Solution

KIMBALL CORPORATION
Income Statement
Years Ended December 31, 2025 and 2024

			Increase (Decrease)	
	2025	2024	Amount	Percentage
Revenues:				
Net Sales Revenue	$ 300,000	$ 250,000	$ 50,000	20.0%
Other Revenues	0	1,000	(1,000)	—
Total Revenues	300,000	251,000	49,000	19.5
Expenses:				
Cost of Goods Sold	214,200	170,000	44,200	26.0
Engineering, Selling, and Administrative Expenses	54,000	48,000	6,000	12.5
Interest Expense	6,000	5,000	1,000	20.0
Income Tax Expense	4,000	3,000	1,000	33.3
Other Expenses	2,700	0	2,700	—
Total Expenses	280,900	226,000	54,900	24.3
Net Income	$ 19,100	$ 25,000	$ (5,900)	(23.6)%

The horizontal analysis shows that net sales revenue increased 20.0%. Total expenses increased by 26.5%, and net income decreased 23.6%. So, even though Kimball's net sales revenue increased, the company's expenses increased by a larger percentage, netting an overall 23.6% reduction in net income between the years. That indicates that 2025 was a bad year in comparison to 2024. This analysis identifies areas in which management should review more data. For example, cost of goods sold increased 26.0%. Managers would want to know why this increase occurred to determine whether the company can implement cost-saving strategies (such as purchasing from other, lower-cost vendors).

KIMBALL CORPORATION
Income Statement
Years Ended December 31, 2025 and 2024

	2025	Percent	2024	Percent
Revenues:				
Net Sales Revenue	$ 300,000	100.0%	$ 250,000	100.0%
Other Revenues	0	0.0	1,000	0.4
Total Revenues	300,000	100.0	251,000	100.4
Expenses:				
Cost of Goods Sold	214,200	71.4	170,000	68.0
Engineering, Selling, and Administrative Expenses	54,000	18.0	48,000	19.2
Interest Expense	6,000	2.0	5,000	2.0
Income Tax Expense	4,000	1.3	3,000	1.2
Other Expenses	2,700	0.9	0	0
Total Expenses	280,900	93.6	226,000	90.4
Net Income	$ 19,100	6.4%	$ 25,000	10.0%

The vertical analysis shows changes in the line items as percentages of net sales revenue. A few notable items are:

- Cost of Goods Sold increased from 68.0% to 71.4%;
- Engineering, Selling, and Administrative Expenses decreased from 19.2% to 18.0%.

These two items are Kimball's largest dollar expenses, so their percentage changes are important. This indicates that cost controls need to be improved, especially for COGS.

The 2025 net income declined to 6.4% of sales, compared with 10.0% the preceding year. Kimball's increase in cost of goods sold is the biggest factor in the overall decrease in net income as a percentage of sales.

> ## Check Your Understanding F:17-2

Check your understanding of the chapter by completing this problem and then looking at the solution. Use this practice to help identify which sections of the chapter you need to study more.

JAVA, INC.
Four-Year Selected Financial Data
Years Ended January 31, 2025–2022

Operating Results:	2025	2024	2023	2022
Net Sales Revenue	$ 13,848	$ 13,673	$ 11,635	$ 9,054
Cost of Goods Sold	9,704	8,599	6,775	5,318
Interest Expense	109	75	45	46
Income from Operations	338	1,455	1,817	1,333
Income Tax Expense	100	263	338	247
Net Income (Net Loss)	(8)	877	1,127	824
Cash Dividends on Common Stock	76	75	76	77
Financial Position:				
Merchandise Inventory	1,677	1,904	1,462	1,056
Total Assets	7,591	7,012	5,189	3,963
Current Ratio	1.48	0.95	1.25	1.20
Stockholders' Equity	3,010	2,928	2,630	1,574
Average Number of Shares of Common Stock Outstanding	860	879	895	576

Requirements

Using the financial data presented above, compute the following ratios and evaluate Java's results for 2025–2023 (See Learning Objective 4):

1. Profit margin ratio
2. Earnings per share
3. Inventory turnover
4. Times-interest-earned ratio
5. Rate of return on common stockholders' equity
6. Gross profit percentage

> Solution

	2025	2024	2023
1. Profit margin ratio	$\dfrac{\$(8)}{\$13,848} = (0.06\%)$	$\dfrac{\$877}{\$13,673} = 6.4\%$	$\dfrac{\$1,127}{\$11,635} = 9.7\%$
2. Earnings per share	$\dfrac{\$(8)}{860 \text{ shares}} = \$(0.01)$ per share	$\dfrac{\$877}{879 \text{ shares}} = \$1.00$ per share	$\dfrac{\$1,127}{895 \text{ shares}} = \$1.26$ per share
3. Inventory turnover	$\dfrac{\$9,704}{(\$1,904 + \$1,677)/2} = 5.4$ times	$\dfrac{\$8,599}{(\$1,462 + \$1,904)/2} = 5.1$ times	$\dfrac{\$6,775}{(\$1,056 + \$1,462)/2} = 5.4$ times
4. Times-interest-earned ratio	$\dfrac{[\$(8) + \$100 + \$109]}{\$109} = 1.8$ times	$\dfrac{(\$877 + \$263 + \$75)}{\$75} = 16.2$ times	$\dfrac{(\$1,127 + \$338 + \$45)}{\$45} = 33.6$ times
5. Rate of return on common stockholders' equity	$\dfrac{\$(8)}{(\$2,928 + \$3,010)/2} = (0.3\%)$	$\dfrac{\$877}{(\$2,630 + \$2,928)/2} = 31.6\%$	$\dfrac{\$1,127}{(\$1,574 + \$2,630)/2} = 53.6\%$
6. Gross profit percentage	$\dfrac{(\$13,848 - \$9,704)}{\$13,848} = 29.9\%$	$\dfrac{(\$13,673 - \$8,599)}{\$13,673} = 37.1\%$	$\dfrac{(\$11,635 - \$6,775)}{\$11,635} = 41.8\%$

Evaluation: During this period, Java's operating results deteriorated on all these measures except inventory turnover. The times-interest-earned ratio and rate of return on common stockholders' equity percentages are down sharply. From these data, it is clear that Java could sell its coffee, but not at the markups the company enjoyed in the past. The final result, in 2025, was a net loss for the year.

> Key Terms

Accounts Receivable Turnover Ratio (p. 17-18)
Acid-Test Ratio (p. 17-15)
Annual Report (p. 17-3)
Asset Turnover Ratio (p. 17-22)
Benchmarking (p. 17-12)
Cash Ratio (p. 17-15)
Common-Size Statement (p. 17-11)
Current Ratio (p. 17-16)
Days' Sales in Inventory (p. 17-17)
Days' Sales in Receivables (p. 17-19)
Debt Ratio (p. 17-19)

Debt to Equity Ratio (p. 17-20)
Dividend Payout (p. 17-25)
Dividend Yield (p. 17-24)
Dollar Value Bias (p. 17-11)
Earnings per Share (EPS) (p. 17-23)
Gross Profit Percentage (p. 17-18)
Horizontal Analysis (p. 17-5)
Inventory Turnover (p. 17-17)
Management's Discussion and Analysis of Financial Condition and Results of Operations (MD&A) (p. 17-3)

Price/Earnings Ratio (p. 17-24)
Profit Margin Ratio (p. 17-21)
Rate of Return on Common Stockholders' Equity (p. 17-22)
Rate of Return on Total Assets (p. 17-21)
Times-Interest-Earned Ratio (p. 17-20)
Trading on the Equity (p. 17-23)
Trend Analysis (p. 17-7)
Vertical Analysis (p. 17-9)
Working Capital (p. 17-14)

> Quick Check

Liberty Corporation reported the following financial statements:

LIBERTY CORPORATION
Comparative Balance Sheet
December 31, 2025 and 2024

	2025	2024
Assets		
Current Assets:		
Cash and Cash Equivalents	$ 2,450	$ 2,094
Accounts Receivable	1,813	1,611
Merchandise Inventory	1,324	1,060
Prepaid Expenses	1,709	2,120
Total Current Assets	7,296	6,885
Other Assets	18,500	15,737
Total Assets	$ 25,796	$ 22,622
Liabilities		
Current Liabilities	$ 7,230	$ 8,467
Long-term Liabilities	4,798	3,792
Total Liabilities	12,028	12,259
Stockholders' Equity		
Common Stock, no par	6,568	4,363
Retained Earnings	7,200	6,000
Total Stockholders' Equity	13,768	10,363
Total Liabilities and Stockholders' Equity	$ 25,796	$ 22,622

LIBERTY CORPORATION
Income Statement
Year Ended December 31, 2025

Net Sales Revenue	$ 20,941
Cost of Goods Sold	7,055
Gross Profit	13,886
Operating Expenses	7,065
Operating Income	6,821
Interest Expense	210
Income Before Income Taxes	6,611
Income Tax Expense	2,563
Net Income	$ 4,048

1. What part of the Liberty's annual report is written by the company and could present a biased view of financial conditions and results?

   a. Balance Sheet
   b. Management's Discussion and Analysis of Financial Condition and Results of Operations (MD&A)
   c. Auditor's Report
   d. Income Statement

   Learning Objective 1

2. Horizontal analysis of Liberty's balance sheet for 2025 would report

   a. Cash as 9.50% of total assets.
   b. a 17% increase in Cash and Cash Equivalents.
   c. a current ratio of 1.01.
   d. inventory turnover of 6 times.

   Learning Objective 2

3. Vertical analysis of Liberty's balance sheet for 2025 would report

   a. Cash as 9.50% of total assets.
   b. inventory turnover of 6 times.
   c. a current ratio of 1.01.
   d. a 17% increase in Cash.

   Learning Objective 3

4. Which statement best describes Liberty's acid-test ratio for 2025?

   a. Greater than 1
   b. Equal to 1
   c. Less than 1
   d. None of the above

   Learning Objective 4

5. Liberty's inventory turnover during 2025 was (amounts rounded)

   a. 6 times.
   b. 7 times.
   c. 8 times.
   d. not determinable from the data given.

   Learning Objective 4

6. Assume all sales are on credit. During 2025, Liberty's days' sales in receivables ratio was (amounts rounded)

   a. 34 days.
   b. 30 days.
   c. 32 days.
   d. 28 days.

   Learning Objective 4

7. Which measure expresses Liberty's times-interest-earned ratio? (amounts rounded)

   a. 54.7%
   b. 19 times
   c. 34.5%
   d. 32 times

   Learning Objective 4

8. Liberty's rate of return on common stockholders' equity can be described as

   a. weak.
   b. normal.
   c. strong.
   d. average.

   Learning Objective 4

9. The company has 2,500 shares of common stock outstanding. What is Liberty's earnings per share?

   a. $1.62
   b. $1.75
   c. $2.73
   d. 2.63 times

   Learning Objective 4

10. The company has 2,500 shares of common stock outstanding and the market price is $20 per share. What is Liberty's price/earnings ratio?

    a. 0.08
    b. $0.08
    c. 12.35
    d. 12.35 times

    Learning Objective 4

Check your answers at the end of the chapter.

ASSESS YOUR PROGRESS

> Review Questions

1. What are the three main ways to analyze financial statements?
2. What is an annual report? Briefly describe the key parts of the annual report.
3. What is horizontal analysis, and how is a percentage change computed?
4. What is trend analysis, and how does it differ from horizontal analysis?
5. What is vertical analysis? What item is used as the base for the income statement? What item is used as the base for the balance sheet?
6. Describe a common-size statement and how it might be helpful in evaluating a company.
7. What is benchmarking, and what are the two main types of benchmarks in financial statement analysis?
8. Briefly describe the ratios that can be used to evaluate a company's ability to pay current liabilities.
9. Briefly describe the ratios that can be used to evaluate a company's ability to sell merchandise inventory and collect receivables.
10. Briefly describe the ratios that can be used to evaluate a company's ability to pay long-term debt.
11. Briefly describe the ratios that can be used to evaluate a company's profitability.
12. Briefly describe the ratios that can be used to evaluate a company's stock as an investment.
13. What are some common red flags in financial statement analysis?

> Short Exercises

Learning Objective 1

S-F:17-1 Explaining financial statements

Caleb King is interested in investing in Orange Corporation. What types of tools should Caleb use to evaluate the company?

Learning Objective 2

S-F:17-2 Performing horizontal analysis

Verifine Corp. reported the following on its comparative income statement:

(In millions)	2025	2024
Revenue	$ 9,890	$ 9,690
Cost of Goods Sold	6,250	6,000

Prepare a horizontal analysis of revenues and gross profit—both in dollar amounts and in percentages—for 2025.

Learning Objective 2

S-F:17-3 Calculating trend analysis

Muscateer Corp. reported the following revenues and net income amounts:

(In millions)	2025	2024	2023	2022
Revenue	$ 9,610	$ 9,355	$ 9,050	$ 8,950
Net Income	7,290	6,790	5,020	4,300

Requirements

1. Calculate Muscateer's trend analysis for revenues and net income. Use 2022 as the base year and round to the nearest percent.
2. Which measure increased at a higher rate during 2023–2025?

S-F:17-4 Performing vertical analysis

Learning Objective 3

Great Value Optical Company reported the following amounts on its balance sheet at December 31, 2024 and 2023:

	2024	2023
Cash and Receivables	$ 80,640	$ 80,575
Merchandise Inventory	56,840	54,450
Property, Plant, and Equipment, Net	142,520	139,975
Total Assets	$ 280,000	$ 275,000

Prepare a vertical analysis of Great Value's assets for 2024 and 2023.

S-F:17-5 Preparing common-size income statement

Learning Objective 3

Data for Connor, Inc. and Alto Corp. follow:

	Connor	Alto
Net Sales Revenue	$ 13,000	$ 22,000
Cost of Goods Sold	7,917	15,730
Other Expenses	4,342	5,170
Net Income	$ 741	$ 1,100

Requirements

1. Prepare common-size income statements.
2. Which company earns more net income?
3. Which company's net income is a higher percentage of its net sales revenue?

Use the following information for Short Exercises S-F:17-6 through S-F:17-10.

Accel's Companies, a home improvement store chain, reported the following summarized figures:

ACCEL'S COMPANIES
Income Statement
Years Ended May 31, 2024 and 2023

	2024	2023
Net Sales Revenue	$ 40,600	$ 40,500
Cost of Goods Sold	28,400	30,600
Interest Expense	600	570
All Other Expenses	4,300	8,200
Net Income	$ 7,300	$ 1,130

ACCEL'S COMPANIES
Balance Sheet
May 31, 2024 and 2023

Assets	2024	2023	Liabilities	2024	2023
Cash	$ 2,400	$ 900	Total Current Liabilities	$ 28,000	$ 13,200
Short-term Investments	28,000	9,000	Long-term Liabilities	13,900	10,300
Accounts Receivable	7,500	5,200	Total Liabilities	41,900	23,500
Merchandise Inventory	6,900	8,600	**Stockholders' Equity**		
Other Current Assets	8,000	1,500	Common Stock	11,000	11,000
Total Current Assets	52,800	25,200	Retained Earnings	29,900	19,700
All Other Assets	30,000	29,000	Total Equity	40,900	30,700
Total Assets	**$ 82,800**	**$ 54,200**	Total Liabilities and Equity	**$ 82,800**	**$ 54,200**

Accel's has 10,000 common shares outstanding during 2024.

Learning Objective 4 — **S-F:17-6 Evaluating current ratio**

Requirements

1. Compute Accel's Companies' current ratio at May 31, 2024 and 2023.
2. Did Accel's Companies' current ratio improve, deteriorate, or hold steady during 2024?

Learning Objective 4 — **S-F:17-7 Computing inventory, gross profit, and receivables ratios**

Requirements

1. Compute the inventory turnover, days' sales in inventory, and gross profit percentage for Accel's Companies for 2024.
2. Compute days' sales in receivables during 2024. Round intermediate calculations to three decimal places. Assume all sales were on account.
3. What do these ratios say about Accel's Companies' ability to sell inventory and collect receivables?

Learning Objective 4 — **S-F:17-8 Measuring ability to pay liabilities**

Requirements

1. Compute the debt ratio and the debt to equity ratio at May 31, 2024, for Accel's Companies.
2. Is Accel's ability to pay its liabilities strong or weak? Explain your reasoning.

Learning Objective 4 — **S-F:17-9 Measuring profitability**

Requirements

1. Compute the profit margin ratio for Accel's Companies for 2024.
2. Compute the rate of return on total assets for 2024.
3. Compute the asset turnover ratio for 2024.
4. Compute the rate of return on common stockholders' equity for 2024.
5. Are these rates of return strong or weak? Explain your reasoning.

S-F:17-10 Computing EPS and P/E ratio

Requirements

1. Compute earnings per share (EPS) for 2024 for Accel's. Round to the nearest cent.
2. Compute Accel's Companies' price/earnings ratio for 2024. The market price per share of Accel's stock is $12.50.
3. What do these results mean when evaluating Accel's Companies' profitability?

S-F:17-11 Using ratios to reconstruct an income statement

Old Mills' income statement appears as follows (amounts in thousands):

OLD MILLS Income Statement Year Ended December 31, 2024	
Net Sales Revenue	$ 6,900
Cost of Goods Sold	(a)
Selling and Administrative Expenses	1,710
Interest Expense	(b)
Other Expenses	120
Income Before Income Taxes	1,150
Income Tax Expense	(c)
Net Income	(d)

Use the following ratio data to complete Old Mills' income statement:

1. Inventory turnover is 3.70 (beginning Merchandise Inventory was $810; ending Merchandise Inventory was $770).
2. Profit margin ratio is 14%.

S-F:17-12 Using ratios to reconstruct a balance sheet

Traditional Mills' balance sheet appears as follows (amounts in thousands):

TRADITIONAL MILLS Balance Sheet December 31, 2024			
Assets		**Liabilities**	
Cash	$ 45	Total Current Liabilities	$ 2,500
Accounts Receivables	(a)	Long-term Note Payable	(e)
Merchandise Inventory	800	Other Long-term Liabilities	760
Prepaid Expenses	(b)	Total Liabilities	(f)
Total Current Assets	(c)		
Plant Assets, Net	(d)	**Stockholders' Equity**	
Other Assets	2,490	Stockholders' Equity	2,450
Total Assets	$ 7,000	Total Liabilities and Stockholders' Equity	$ (g)

Use the following ratio data to complete Traditional Mills' balance sheet.
1. Current ratio is 0.72.
2. Acid-test ratio is 0.36.

> Exercises

Learning Objective 2

1. Net Income 34.7%

E-F:17-13 Performing horizontal analysis—income statement

Data for Mulberry Designs, Inc. follow:

MULBERRY DESIGNS, INC.
Comparative Income Statement
Years Ended December 31, 2024 and 2023

	2024	2023
Net Sales Revenue	$ 431,000	$ 372,350
Expenses:		
Cost of Goods Sold	203,850	186,000
Selling and Administrative Expenses	99,000	93,250
Other Expenses	9,000	4,650
Total Expenses	311,850	283,900
Net Income	$ 119,150	$ 88,450

Requirements

1. Prepare a horizontal analysis of the comparative income statement of Mulberry Designs, Inc. Round percentage changes to one decimal place.
2. Why did 2024 net income increase by a higher percentage than net sales revenue?

Learning Objective 2

1. 2025 Net Income 153%

E-F:17-14 Computing trend analysis

Grand Oaks Realty's net revenue and net income for the following five-year period, using 2021 as the base year, follow:

	2025	2024	2023	2022	2021
Net Revenue	$ 1,360,000	$ 1,180,000	$ 1,147,000	$ 1,008,000	$ 1,044,000
Net Income	127,000	120,000	87,000	75,000	83,000

Requirements

1. Compute a trend analysis for net revenue and net income. Round to the nearest full percent.
2. Which grew faster during the period, net revenue or net income?

E-F:17-15 Performing vertical analysis of a balance sheet

Theta Designs, Inc. has the following data:

THETA DESIGNS, INC.
Comparative Balance Sheet
December 31, 2024 and 2023

	2024	2023
Assets		
Total Current Assets	$ 25,000	$ 73,440
Property, Plant, and Equipment, Net	153,600	168,300
Other Assets	21,400	64,260
Total Assets	$ 200,000	$ 306,000
Liabilities		
Total Current Liabilities	$ 27,600	$ 49,266
Long-term Debt	72,400	208,998
Total Liabilities	100,000	258,264
Stockholders' Equity		
Total Stockholders' Equity	100,000	47,736
Total Liabilities and Stockholders' Equity	$ 200,000	$ 306,000

Learning Objective 3

2024 Current Assets: 12.5%

Perform a vertical analysis of Theta Designs' balance sheet for each year.

E-F:17-16 Preparing common-size income statements

Refer to the data presented for Mulberry Designs, Inc. in Exercise E-F:17-13.

Requirements

1. Prepare a comparative common-size income statement for Mulberry Designs, Inc. using the 2024 and 2023 data. Round percentages to one-tenth percent (three decimal places).
2. To an investor, how does 2024 compare with 2023? Explain your reasoning.

Learning Objective 3

1. 2024 Net Income 27.6%

E-F:17-17 Computing working capital changes

Data for Research Enterprises follows:

	2025	2024	2023
Total Current Assets	$ 490,000	$ 320,000	$ 230,000
Total Current Liabilities	235,000	160,000	115,000

Compute the dollar amount of change and the percentage of change in Research Enterprises' working capital each year during 2025 and 2024. What do the calculated changes indicate?

Learning Objective 4

2025 Working Capital $255,000

Learning Objective 4

e. 89 days

E-F:17-18 Computing key ratios

The financial statements of Valerie's Natural Foods include the following items:

	Current Year	Preceding Year
Balance Sheet:		
Cash	$ 16,000	$ 26,000
Short-term Investments	19,000	28,000
Net Accounts Receivable	60,000	92,000
Merchandise Inventory	78,000	74,000
Prepaid Expenses	17,000	6,000
Total Current Assets	190,000	226,000
Total Current Liabilities	136,000	82,000
Income Statement:		
Net Credit Sales	$ 476,000	
Cost of Goods Sold	312,000	

Compute the following ratios for the current year:

a. Current ratio
b. Cash ratio
c. Acid-test ratio
d. Inventory turnover
e. Days' sales in inventory
f. Days' sales in receivables
g. Gross profit percentage

Learning Objective 4

d. 2024: 61.9%

E-F:17-19 Analyzing the ability to pay liabilities

Big Beautiful Photo Shop has asked you to determine whether the company's ability to pay current liabilities and total liabilities improved or deteriorated during 2024. To answer this question, you gather the following data:

	2024	2023
Cash	$ 58,000	$ 47,000
Short-term Investments	34,000	0
Net Accounts Receivable	140,000	124,000
Merchandise Inventory	217,000	272,000
Total Assets	530,000	565,000
Total Current Liabilities	288,000	205,000
Long-term Notes Payable	40,000	50,000
Income from Operations	165,000	158,000
Interest Expense	55,000	41,000

Compute the following ratios for 2024 and 2023 and evaluate the company's ability to pay its current liabilities and total liabilities:

a. Current ratio
b. Cash ratio
c. Acid-test ratio
d. Debt ratio
e. Debt to equity ratio

E-F:17-20 Analyzing profitability

Learning Objective 4

1. 2025: 15.2%

Micatin, Inc.'s comparative income statement follows. The 2023 data are given as needed.

MICATIN INC.
Comparative Income Statement
Years Ended December 31, 2025 and 2024

	2025	2024	2023
Net Sales Revenue	$ 181,000	$ 160,000	
Cost of Goods Sold	93,500	86,500	
Selling and Administrative Expenses	45,000	40,500	
Interest Expense	8,000	12,000	
Income Tax Expense	7,000	4,400	
Net Income	$ 27,500	$ 16,600	

Additional data:

	2025	2024	2023
Total Assets	$ 209,000	$ 187,000	$ 167,000
Common Stockholders' Equity	96,000	91,500	80,500
Preferred Dividends	2,000	2,000	0
Common Shares Outstanding During the Year	15,000	15,000	10,000

Requirements

1. Calculate the profit margin ratio for 2025 and 2024.
2. Calculate the rate of return on total assets for 2025 and 2024.
3. Calculate the asset turnover ratio for 2025 and 2024.
4. Calculate the rate of return on common stockholders' equity for 2025 and 2024.
5. Calculate the earnings per share for 2025 and 2024.
6. Calculate the 2025 dividend payout on common stock. Assume dividends per share for common stock are equal to $1.13 per share.
7. Did the company's operating performance improve or deteriorate during 2025?

E-F:17-21 Evaluating a stock as an investment

Learning Objective 4

Dividend Yield 2024: 1.4%

Data for Oxford State Bank follow:

	2024	2023
Net Income	$ 71,900	$ 64,300
Dividends—Common	22,000	22,000
Dividends—Preferred	16,800	16,800
Total Stockholders' Equity at Year-End (includes 95,000 shares of common stock)	770,000	610,000
Preferred Stock	200,000	200,000
Market Price per Share of Common Stock	$ 16.50	$ 10.00

Evaluate the common stock of Oxford State Bank as an investment. Specifically, use the three stock ratios to determine whether the common stock has increased or decreased in attractiveness during the past year. Round to two decimal places.

Learning Objective 4

Total Assets $2,800,000

E-F:17-22 Using ratios to reconstruct a balance sheet

The following data are adapted from the financial statements of Bridget's Shops, Inc.:

Total Current Assets	$ 1,216,000
Accumulated Depreciation	2,000,000
Total Liabilities	1,540,000
Preferred Stock	0
Debt Ratio	55%
Current Ratio	1.60

Prepare Bridget's condensed balance sheet as of December 31, 2024.

> Problems Group A

Learning Objectives 2, 4

2. 2025: 16.7%

P-F:17-23A Computing trend analysis and rate of return on common stockholders' equity

Net sales revenue, net income, and common stockholders' equity for Eyesight Mission Corporation, a manufacturer of contact lenses, follow for a four-year period.

	2025	2024	2023	2022
Net Sales Revenue	$ 766,000	$ 708,000	$ 644,000	$ 664,000
Net Income	60,000	38,000	36,000	44,000
Ending Common Stockholders' Equity	368,000	352,000	326,000	296,000

Requirements

1. Compute trend analyses for each item for 2023–2025. Use 2022 as the base year and round to the nearest whole percent.
2. Compute the rate of return on common stockholders' equity for 2023–2025, rounding to three decimal places.

Learning Objective 3

1. Net Income 11.3%

P-F:17-24A Performing vertical analysis

The Klein Department Stores, Inc. chief executive officer (CEO) has asked you to compare the company's profit performance and financial position with the averages for the industry. The CEO has given you the company's income statement and balance sheet as well as the industry average data for retailers.

KLEIN DEPARTMENT STORES, INC.
Income Statement Compared with Industry Average
Year Ended December 31, 2024

	Klein	Industry Average
Net Sales Revenue	$ 778,000	100.0%
Cost of Goods Sold	524,372	65.8
Gross Profit	253,628	34.2
Operating Expenses	159,490	19.7
Operating Income	94,138	14.5
Other Expenses	6,224	0.4
Net Income	$ 87,914	14.1%

KLEIN DEPARTMENT STORES, INC.
Balance Sheet Compared with Industry Average
December 31, 2024

	Klein	Industry Average
Current Assets	$ 339,000	70.9%
Property, Plant, and Equipment, Net	130,000	23.6
Intangible Assets, Net	7,000	0.8
Other Assets	24,000	4.7
Total Assets	$ 500,000	100.0%
Current Liabilities	$ 232,000	48.1%
Long-term Liabilities	111,000	16.6
Total Liabilities	343,000	64.7
Stockholders' Equity	157,000	35.3
Total Liabilities and Stockholders' Equity	$ 500,000	100.0%

Requirements

1. Prepare a vertical analysis for Klein for both its income statement and balance sheet.
2. Compare the company's profit performance and financial position with the average for the industry.

Note: Problem P-F:17-24A must be completed before attempting Problem P-F:17-25A.

P-F:17-25A Preparing common-size statements, analysis of profitability and financial position, comparison with the industry, and using ratios to evaluate a company

Learning Objectives 3, 4

2. Gross Profit Percentage 32.6%

Consider the data for Klein Department Stores presented in Problem P-F:17-24A.

Requirements

1. Prepare a common-size income statement and balance sheet for Klein. The first column of each statement should present Klein's common-size statement, and the second column, the industry averages.
2. For the profitability analysis, compute Klein's (a) gross profit percentage and (b) profit margin ratio. Compare these figures with the industry averages. Is Klein's profit performance better or worse than the industry average?
3. For the analysis of financial position, compute Klein's (a) current ratio and (b) debt to equity ratio. Compare these ratios with the industry averages. Assume the current ratio industry average is 1.47, and the debt to equity industry average is 1.83. Is Klein's financial position better or worse than the industry averages?

P-F:17-26A Determining the effects of business transactions on selected ratios

Learning Objective 4

Financial statement data of *Style Traveler Magazine* include the following items:

1. Current Ratio 1.55

Cash	$ 23,000
Accounts Receivable, Net	81,000
Merchandise Inventory	185,000
Total Assets	635,000
Accounts Payable	99,000
Accrued Liabilities	37,000
Short-term Notes Payable	51,000
Long-term Liabilities	224,000
Net Income	68,000
Common Shares Outstanding	20,000 shares

Requirements

1. Compute *Style Traveler*'s current ratio, debt ratio, and earnings per share. Round all ratios to two decimal places, and use the following format for your answer:

Current Ratio	Debt Ratio	Earnings per Share

2. Compute the three ratios after evaluating the effect of each transaction that follows. Consider each transaction *separately*.

   a. Purchased merchandise inventory of $49,000 on account.

   b. Borrowed $127,000 on a long-term note payable.

c. Issued 2,000 shares of common stock, receiving cash of $107,000.

d. Received cash on account, $5,000.

Learning Objective 4 **P-F:17-27A** Using ratios to evaluate a stock investment

Comparative financial statement data of Sanfield, Inc. follow:

1. 2024: e. 48.9%

SANFIELD, INC.
Comparative Income Statement
Years Ended December 31, 2024 and 2023

	2024	2023
Net Sales Revenue	$ 462,000	$ 430,000
Cost of Goods Sold	236,000	213,000
Gross Profit	226,000	217,000
Operating Expenses	135,000	133,000
Income from Operations	91,000	84,000
Interest Expense	8,000	12,000
Income Before Income Tax	83,000	72,000
Income Tax Expense	18,000	22,000
Net Income	$ 65,000	$ 50,000

SANFIELD, INC.
Comparative Balance Sheet
December 31, 2024 and 2023

	2024	2023	2022*
Assets			
Current Assets:			
Cash	$ 99,000	$ 97,000	
Accounts Receivable, Net	109,000	117,000	$ 100,000
Merchandise Inventory	142,000	164,000	207,000
Prepaid Expenses	15,000	5,000	
Total Current Assets	365,000	383,000	
Property, Plant, and Equipment, Net	215,000	177,000	
Total Assets	$ 580,000	$ 560,000	$ 599,000
Liabilities			
Total Current Liabilities	$ 222,000	$ 244,000	
Long-term Liabilities	113,000	92,000	
Total Liabilities	335,000	336,000	
Stockholders' Equity			
Preferred Stock, 4%	92,000	92,000	
Common Stockholders' Equity, no par	153,000	132,000	85,000
Total Liabilities and Stockholders' Equity	$ 580,000	$ 560,000	

* Selected 2022 amounts

1. Market price of Sanfield's common stock: $51.48 at December 31, 2024, and $37.08 at December 31, 2023.

2. Common shares outstanding: 16,000 on December 31, 2024, and 15,000 on December 31, 2023 and 2022.

3. All sales are on credit.

Requirements

1. Compute the following ratios for 2024 and 2023:
    a. Current ratio
    b. Cash ratio
    c. Times-interest-earned ratio
    d. Inventory turnover
    e. Gross profit percentage
    f. Debt to equity ratio
    g. Rate of return on common stockholders' equity
    h. Earnings per share of common stock
    i. Price/earnings ratio

2. Decide (a) whether Sanfield's ability to pay debts and to sell inventory improved or deteriorated during 2024 and (b) whether the investment attractiveness of its common stock appears to have increased or decreased.

P-F:17-28A Using ratios to decide between two stock investments

Learning Objective 4

Assume that you are purchasing an investment and have decided to invest in a company in the digital phone business. You have narrowed the choice to Digitalized Corp. and Every Zone, Inc. and have assembled the following data.

1. Digitalized e. $4.25

Selected income statement data for the current year:

	Digitalized	Every Zone
Net Sales Revenue (all on credit)	$ 423,035	$ 493,845
Cost of Goods Sold	210,000	260,000
Interest Expense	0	19,000
Net Income	51,000	72,000

Selected balance sheet and market price data at the *end* of the current year:

	Digitalized	Every Zone
Current Assets:		
Cash	$ 24,000	$ 17,000
Short-term Investments	40,000	14,000
Accounts Receivable, Net	40,000	48,000
Merchandise Inventory	66,000	97,000
Prepaid Expenses	23,000	12,000
Total Current Assets	**$ 193,000**	**$ 188,000**
Total Assets	$ 266,000	$ 323,000
Total Current Liabilities	105,000	96,000
Total Liabilities	105,000	128,000
Common Stock:		
$1 par (12,000 shares)	12,000	
$1 par (17,000 shares)		17,000
Total Stockholders' Equity	161,000	195,000
Market Price per Share of Common Stock	76.50	114.48
Dividends Paid per Common Share	1.10	1.00

Selected balance sheet data at the *beginning* of the current year:

	Digitalized	Every Zone
Balance Sheet:		
Accounts Receivable, Net	$ 41,000	$ 54,000
Merchandise Inventory	81,000	87,000
Total Assets	261,000	272,000
Common Stock:		
$1 par (12,000 shares)	12,000	
$1 par (17,000 shares)		17,000

Your strategy is to invest in companies that have low price/earnings ratios but appear to be in good shape financially. Assume that you have analyzed all other factors and that your decision depends on the results of ratio analysis.

Requirements

1. Compute the following ratios for both companies for the current year:
   a. Acid-test ratio
   b. Inventory turnover
   c. Days' sales in receivables
   d. Debt ratio
   e. Earnings per share of common stock
   f. Price/earnings ratio
   g. Dividend payout
2. Decide which company's stock better fits your investment strategy.

Learning Objectives 2, 4

P-F:17-29A Completing a comprehensive financial statement analysis

3. 2024: Inventory turnover 8.04

In its annual report, ABC Athletic Supply, Inc. includes the following five-year financial summary:

ABC ATHLETIC SUPPLY, INC.
Five-Year Financial Summary (Partial; adapted)

(Dollar amounts in thousands except per share data)	2024	2023	2022	2021	2020	2019
Net Sales Revenue	$ 250,000	$ 216,000	$ 191,000	$ 161,000	$ 134,000	
Net Sales Revenue Increase	16%	13%	19%	20%	17%	
Domestic Comparative Store Sales Increase	5%	6%	4%	7%	9%	
Other Income—Net	2,110	1,840	1,760	1,690	1,330	
Cost of Goods Sold	189,250	164,592	148,216	126,385	106,396	
Selling and Administrative Expenses	41,210	36,330	31,620	27,440	22,540	
Interest:						
Interest Expense	(1,080)	(1,380)	(1,400)	(1,020)	(830)	
Interest Income	125	165	155	235	190	
Income Tax Expense	4,470	3,900	3,700	3,320	2,700	
Net Income	16,225	11,803	7,979	4,760	3,054	
Per Share of Common Stock:						
Net Income	1.60	1.30	1.20	1.00	0.78	
Dividends	0.40	0.38	0.34	0.30	0.26	
Financial Position						
Current Assets, Excluding Merchandise Inventory	$ 30,700	$ 27,200	$ 26,700	$ 24,400	$ 21,500	
Merchandise Inventory	24,500	22,600	21,700	19,000	17,500	$ 16,700
Property, Plant, and Equipment, Net	51,400	45,200	40,000	35,100	25,600	
Total Assets	106,600	95,000	88,400	78,500	64,600	
Current Liabilities	32,300	28,000	28,300	25,000	16,500	
Long-term Debt	23,000	21,500	17,600	19,100	12,000	
Stockholders' Equity	51,300	45,500	42,500	34,400	36,100	
Financial Ratios						
Acid-Test Ratio	1.0	1.0	0.9	1.0	1.3	
Rate of Return on Total Assets	17.2%	14.4%	11.2%	8.1%	7.1%	
Rate of Return on Common Stockholders' Equity	33.5%	26.8%	20.8%	13.5%	13.0%	

Requirements

Analyze the company's financial summary for the fiscal years 2020–2024 to decide whether to invest in the common stock of ABC. Include the following sections in your analysis.

1. Trend analysis for net sales revenue and net income (use 2020 as the base year).
2. Profitability analysis.
3. Evaluation of the ability to sell merchandise inventory.
4. Evaluation of the ability to pay debts.
5. Evaluation of dividends.
6. Should you invest in the common stock of ABC Athletic Supply, Inc.? Fully explain your final decision.

> Problems Group B

P-F:17-30B Computing trend analysis and rate of return on stockholders' common equity

Learning Objectives 2, 4

2. 2024: 11.9%

Net sales revenue, net income, and common stockholders' equity for Azbel Mission Corporation, a manufacturer of contact lenses, follow for a four-year period.

	2025	2024	2023	2022
Net Sales Revenue	$ 758,000	$ 701,000	$ 639,000	$ 659,000
Net Income	59,000	40,000	39,000	42,000
Ending Common Stockholders' Equity	360,000	346,000	324,000	302,000

Requirements

1. Compute trend analyses for each item for 2023–2025. Use 2022 as the base year and round to the nearest whole percent.
2. Compute the rate of return on common stockholders' equity for 2023–2025, rounding to three decimal places.

P-F:17-31B Performing vertical analysis

Learning Objective 3

1. Net Income 10.9%

The Randall Department Stores, Inc. chief executive officer (CEO) has asked you to compare the company's profit performance and financial position with the averages for the industry. The CEO has given you the company's income statement and balance sheet as well as the industry average data for retailers.

RANDALL DEPARTMENT STORES, INC.
Income Statement Compared with Industry Average
Year Ended December 31, 2024

	Randall	Industry Average
Net Sales Revenue	$ 783,000	100.0%
Cost of Goods Sold	527,742	65.8
Gross Profit	255,258	34.2
Operating Expenses	163,647	19.7
Operating Income	91,611	14.5
Other Expenses	6,264	0.4
Net Income	$ 85,347	14.1%

RANDALL DEPARTMENT STORES, INC.
Balance Sheet Compared with Industry Average
December 31, 2024

	Randall	Industry Average
Current Assets	$ 310,040	70.9%
Property, Plant, and Equipment, Net	119,600	23.6
Intangible Assets, Net	7,360	0.8
Other Assets	23,000	4.7
Total Assets	$ 460,000	100.0%
Current Liabilities	$ 210,680	48.1%
Long-term Liabilities	103,960	16.6
Total Liabilities	314,640	64.7
Stockholders' Equity	145,360	35.3
Total Liabilities and Stockholders' Equity	$ 460,000	100.0%

Requirements

1. Prepare a vertical analysis for Randall for both its income statement and balance sheet.
2. Compare the company's profit performance and financial position with the average for the industry.

Note: Problem P-F:17-31B must be completed before attempting Problem P-F:17-32B.

Learning Objectives 3, 4

1. Current Assets 67.4%

P-F:17-32B Preparing common-size statements, analysis of profitability and financial position, comparison with the industry, and using ratios to evaluate a company

Consider the data for Randall Department Stores presented in Problem P-F:17-31B.

Requirements

1. Prepare a common-size income statement and balance sheet for Randall. The first column of each statement should present Randall's common-size statement, and the second column, the industry averages.
2. For the profitability analysis, compute Randall's (a) gross profit percentage and (b) profit margin ratio. Compare these figures with the industry averages. Is Randall's profit performance better or worse than the industry average?
3. For the analysis of financial position, compute Randall's (a) current ratio and (b) debt to equity ratio. Compare these ratios with the industry averages. Assume the current ratio industry average is 1.47, and the debt to equity industry average is 1.83. Is Randall's financial position better or worse than the industry averages?

Learning Objective 4

1. Earnings per Share $1.38

P-F:17-33B Determining the effects of business transactions on selected ratios

Financial statement data of *Modern Traveler's Magazine* include the following items:

Cash	$ 19,000
Accounts Receivable, Net	82,000
Merchandise Inventory	183,000
Total Assets	638,000
Accounts Payable	102,000
Accrued Liabilities	35,000
Short-term Notes Payable	50,000
Long-term Liabilities	221,000
Net Income	69,000
Common Shares Outstanding	50,000 shares

Requirements

1. Compute *Modern Traveler's* current ratio, debt ratio, and earnings per share. Round all ratios to two decimal places and use the following format for your answer:

Current Ratio	Debt Ratio	Earnings per Share

2. Compute the three ratios after evaluating the effect of each transaction that follows. Consider each transaction *separately*.

    a. Purchased merchandise inventory of $42,000 on account.
    b. Borrowed $121,000 on a long-term note payable.
    c. Issued 5,000 shares of common stock, receiving cash of $103,000.
    d. Received cash on account, $5,000.

P-F:17-34B Using ratios to evaluate a stock investment

Comparative financial statement data of Garfield, Inc. follow:

Learning Objective 4

1. 2023: e. 50.2%

GARFIELD, INC.
Comparative Income Statement
Years Ended December 31, 2024 and 2023

	2024	2023
Net Sales Revenue	$ 461,000	$ 424,000
Cost of Goods Sold	241,000	211,000
Gross Profit	220,000	213,000
Operating Expenses	137,000	135,000
Income from Operations	83,000	78,000
Interest Expense	9,000	13,000
Income Before Income Tax	74,000	65,000
Income Tax Expense	18,000	24,000
Net Income	$ 56,000	$ 41,000

GARFIELD, INC.
Comparative Balance Sheet
December 31, 2024 and 2023

	2024	2023	2022*
Assets			
Current Assets:			
Cash	$ 99,000	$ 98,000	
Accounts Receivable, Net	108,000	114,000	$ 107,000
Merchandise Inventory	146,000	164,000	202,000
Prepaid Expenses	20,000	9,000	
Total Current Assets	373,000	385,000	
Property, Plant, and Equipment, Net	211,000	181,000	
Total Assets	$ 584,000	$ 566,000	$ 602,000
Liabilities			
Total Current Liabilities	$ 227,000	$ 246,000	
Long-term Liabilities	117,000	100,000	
Total Liabilities	344,000	346,000	
Stockholders' Equity			
Preferred Stock, 3%	98,000	98,000	
Common Stockholders' Equity, no par	142,000	122,000	89,000
Total Liabilities and Stockholders' Equity	$ 584,000	$ 566,000	

* Selected 2022 amounts

1. Market price of Garfield's common stock: $69.36 at December 31, 2024, and $38.04 at December 31, 2023.
2. Common shares outstanding: 14,000 on December 31, 2024, and 12,000 on December 31, 2023 and 2022.
3. All sales are on credit.

Requirements

1. Compute the following ratios for 2024 and 2023:
   a. Current ratio
   b. Cash ratio
   c. Times-interest-earned ratio
   d. Inventory turnover
   e. Gross profit percentage
   f. Debt to equity ratio
   g. Rate of return on common stockholders' equity
   h. Earnings per share of common stock
   i. Price/earnings ratio

2. Decide (a) whether Garfield's ability to pay debts and to sell inventory improved or deteriorated during 2024 and (b) whether the investment attractiveness of its common stock appears to have increased or decreased.

Learning Objective 4

1c. Green Zone 38 days

P-F:17-35B Using ratios to decide between two stock investments

Assume that you are purchasing an investment and have decided to invest in a company in the digital phone business. You have narrowed the choice to All Digital Corp. and Green Zone, Inc. and have assembled the following data.

Selected income statement data for the current year:

	All Digital	Green Zone
Net Sales Revenue (all on credit)	$ 417,925	$ 493,115
Cost of Goods Sold	209,000	258,000
Interest Expense	0	14,000
Net Income	58,000	72,000

Selected balance sheet and market price data at the *end* of the current year:

	All Digital	Green Zone
Current Assets:		
Cash	$ 23,000	$ 18,000
Short-term Investments	37,000	17,000
Accounts Receivable, Net	39,000	49,000
Merchandise Inventory	64,000	102,000
Prepaid Expenses	21,000	17,000
Total Current Assets	$ 184,000	$ 203,000
Total Assets	$ 263,000	$ 326,000
Total Current Liabilities	105,000	99,000
Total Liabilities	105,000	134,000
Common Stock:		
$1 par (10,000 shares)	10,000	
$2 par (14,000 shares)		28,000
Total Stockholders' Equity	158,000	192,000
Market Price per Share of Common Stock	92.80	128.50
Dividends Paid per Common Share	1.20	0.90

Selected balance sheet data at the *beginning* of the current year:

	All Digital	Green Zone
Balance Sheet:		
Accounts Receivable, Net	$ 41,000	$ 54 000
Merchandise Inventory	81,000	89,000
Total Assets	258,000	277,000
Common Stock:		
$1 par (10,000 shares)	10,000	
$2 par (14,000 shares)		28,000

Your strategy is to invest in companies that have low price/earnings ratios but appear to be in good shape financially. Assume that you have analyzed all other factors and that your decision depends on the results of ratio analysis.

Requirements

1. Compute the following ratios for both companies for the current year:
    a. Acid-test ratio
    b. Inventory turnover
    c. Days' sales in receivables
    d. Debt ratio
    e. Earnings per share of common stock
    f. Price/earnings ratio
    g. Dividend payout
2. Decide which company's stock better fits your investment strategy.

Learning Objectives 2, 4

3. 2024: Inventory turnover 8.86

P-F:17-36B Completing a comprehensive financial statement analysis

In its annual report, XYZ Athletic Supply, Inc. includes the following five-year financial summary:

XYZ ATHLETIC SUPPLY, INC.
Five-Year Financial Summary (Partial; adapted)

(Dollar amounts in thousands except per share data)	2024	2023	2022	2021	2020	2019
Net Sales Revenue	$ 275,000	$ 222,000	$ 199,000	$ 171,000	$ 131,000	
Net Sales Revenue Increase	24%	12%	16%	31%	17%	
Domestic Comparative Store Sales Increase	6%	6%	5%	8%	10%	
Other Income—Net	2,090	1,780	1,770	1,700	1,310	
Cost of Goods Sold	208,725	169,386	154,822	134,235	103,883	
Selling and Administrative Expenses	41,280	36,340	31,670	27,450	22,540	
Interest:						
Interest Expense	(1,070)	(1,370)	(1,330)	(1,100)	(800)	
Interest Income	140	155	150	230	140	
Income Tax Expense	4,420	3,900	3,610	3,390	2,730	
Net Income	21,735	12,939	9,488	6,755	2,497	
Per Share of Common Stock:						
Net Income	1.10	0.80	0.70	0.50	0.28	
Dividends	0.45	0.43	0.39	0.35	0.31	
Financial Position						
Current Assets, Excluding Merchandise Inventory	$ 30,900	$ 27,200	$ 26,800	$ 24,400	$ 21,800	
Merchandise Inventory	24,700	22,400	21,600	19,300	17,000	$ 16,800
Property, Plant, and Equipment, Net	51,600	46,200	40,500	35,000	25,200	
Total Assets	107,200	95,800	88,900	78,700	64,000	
Current Liabilities	32,600	27,800	28,800	25,600	17,000	
Long-term Debt	23,000	21,200	16,800	18,600	12,900	
Stockholders' Equity	51,600	46,800	43,300	35,500	34,100	
Financial Ratios						
Acid-Test Ratio	0.9	1.0	0.9	1.0	1.3	
Rate of Return on Total Assets	22.5%	15.5%	12.8%	10.9%	9.9%	
Rate of Return on Common Stockholders' Equity	44.2%	28.7%	24.1%	19.4%	18.9%	

Requirements

Analyze the company's financial summary for the fiscal years 2020–2024 to decide whether to invest in the common stock of XYZ. Include the following sections in your analysis.

1. Trend analysis for net sales revenue and net income (use 2020 as the base year).
2. Profitability analysis.
3. Evaluation of the ability to sell merchandise inventory.
4. Evaluation of the ability to pay debts.
5. Evaluation of dividends.
6. Should you invest in the common stock of XYZ Athletic Supply, Inc.? Fully explain your final decision.

CRITICAL THINKING

> Using Excel

Download Excel problems for this chapter online in MyLab Accounting or at http://www.pearsonhighered.com/Horngren.

> Continuing Problem

P-F:17-37 Using ratios to evaluate a stock investment

This problem continues the Canyon Canoe Company situation from Chapter F:16. The company wants to invest some of its excess cash in trading securities and is considering two investments, The Paddle Company (PC) and Recreational Life Vests (RLV). The income statement, balance sheet, and other data for both companies follow for 2025 and 2024, as well as selected data for 2023:

	THE PADDLE COMPANY Comparative Financial Statements Years Ended December 31			RECREATIONAL LIFE VESTS Comparative Financial Statements Years Ended December 31		
Income Statement	2025	2024	2023	2025	2024	2023
Net Sales Revenue	$ 430,489	$ 425,410		$ 410,570	$ 383,870	
Cost of Goods Sold	258,756	256,797		299,110	280,190	
Gross Profit	171,733	168,613		111,460	103,680	
Operating Expenses	153,880	151,922		78,290	70,830	
Operating Income	17,853	16,691		33,170	32,850	
Interest Expense	865	788		2,780	2,980	
Income before Income Tax	16,988	15,903		30,390	29,870	
Income Tax Expense	5,137	4,809		8,780	8,630	
Net Income	$ 11,851	$ 11,094		$ 21,610	$ 21,240	
Balance Sheet						
Assets						
Cash & Cash Equivalents	$ 69,159	$ 70,793		$ 65,730	$ 55,270	
Accounts Receivable	44,798	44,452	$ 44,104	39,810	38,650	$ 36,460
Merchandise Inventory	79,919	66,341	76,363	68,500	65,230	59,930
Other Current Assets	15,494	16,264		24,450	37,630	
Total Current Assets	209,370	197,850		198,490	196,780	
Long-term Assets	89,834	90,776		116,760	116,270	
Total Assets	$ 299,204	$ 288,626	$ 276,482	$ 315,250	$ 313,050	$ 310,640
Liabilities						
Current Liabilities	$ 69,554	$ 60,232		$ 90,810	$ 90,010	
Long-term Liabilities	31,682	29,936		96,310	105,890	
Total Liabilities	101,236	90,168		187,120	195,900	

	THE PADDLE COMPANY Comparative Financial Statements Years Ended December 31			RECREATIONAL LIFE VESTS Comparative Financial Statements Years Ended December 31		
Balance Sheet (continued)	2025	2024	2023	2025	2024	2023
Stockholders' Equity						
Common Stock	72,795	80,885		111,530	102,480	
Retained Earnings	125,173	117,573		16,600	14,670	
Total Stockholders' Equity	197,968	198,458	197,668	128,130	117,150	103,840
Total Liabilities and Stockholders' Equity	$ 299,204	$ 288,626		$ 315,250	$ 313,050	
Other Data						
Market price per share	$ 21.38	$ 33.82		$ 46.37	$ 51.64	
Annual dividend per share	0.32	0.30		0.53	0.45	
Weighted average number of shares outstanding	9,000	8,000		9,000	8,000	

Requirements

1. Using the financial statements given, compute the following ratios for both companies for 2025 and 2024. Assume all sales are credit sales. Round all ratios to two decimal places.

   a. Current ratio
   b. Cash ratio
   c. Inventory turnover
   d. Accounts receivable turnover
   e. Gross profit percentage
   f. Debt ratio
   g. Debt to equity ratio
   h. Profit margin ratio
   i. Asset turnover ratio
   j. Rate of return on common stockholders' equity
   k. Earnings per share
   l. Price/earnings ratio
   m. Dividend yield
   n. Dividend payout

2. Compare the companies' performance for 2025 and 2024. Make a recommendation to Canyon Canoe Company about investing in these companies. Which company would be a better investment, The Paddle Company or Recreational Life Vests? Base your answer on ability to pay current liabilities, ability to sell merchandise and collect receivables, ability to pay long-term debt, profitability, and attractiveness as an investment.

> Decision Case F:17-1

Lance Berkman is the controller of Saturn, a dance club whose year-end is December 31. Berkman prepares checks for suppliers in December, makes the proper journal entries, and posts them to the appropriate accounts in that month. However, he holds onto the checks and mails them to the suppliers in January.

Requirements

1. What financial ratio(s) is(are) most affected by the action to hold onto the checks until January?
2. What is Berkman's purpose in undertaking this activity?

> Ethical Issue F:17-1

Ross's Lipstick Company's long-term debt agreements make certain demands on the business. For example, Ross may not purchase treasury stock in excess of the balance of retained earnings. Also, long-term debt may not exceed stockholders' equity, and the current ratio may not fall below 1.50. If Ross fails to meet any of these requirements, the company's lenders have the authority to take over management of the company.

Changes in consumer demand have made it hard for Ross to attract customers. Current liabilities have mounted faster than current assets, causing the current ratio to fall to 1.47. Before releasing financial statements, Ross's management is scrambling to improve the current ratio. The controller points out that an investment can be classified as either long-term or short-term, depending on management's intention. By deciding to convert an investment to cash within one year, Ross can classify the investment as short-term—a current asset. On the controller's recommendation, Ross's board of directors votes to reclassify long-term investments as short-term.

Requirements

1. What effect will reclassifying the investments have on the current ratio? Is Ross's true financial position stronger as a result of reclassifying the investments?
2. Shortly after the financial statements are released, sales improve; so, too, does the current ratio. As a result, Ross's management decides not to sell the investments it had reclassified as short-term. Accordingly, the company reclassifies the investments as long-term. Has management behaved unethically? Give the reasoning underlying your answer.

> Financial Statement Case F:17-1

Use **Target Corporation's** Fiscal 2018 Annual Report to answer the following questions. Visit **http://www.pearsonhighered.com/Horngren** to view a link to the Target Corporation Annual Report.

Requirements

1. Compute trend analyses for Sales and Net earnings/(loss). Use fiscal year 2016 as the base year. What is the most notable aspect of these data?
2. Perform a vertical analysis for Target Corporation's balance sheet as of February 2, 2019 (fiscal year 2018), and February 3, 2018 (fiscal year 2017). Include only these main categories:

Assets:
　Total current assets
　Property and equipment, net
　Operating lease assets
　Other noncurrent assets
　Total assets

Liabilities and shareholders' investment:
　Total current liabilities
　Total noncurrent liabilities
　Total shareholders' investment
　Total liabilities and shareholders' investment

> Team Projects

Team Project F:17-1

Select an industry you are interested in and pick any company in that industry to use as the benchmark. Then select two other companies in the same industry. For each category of ratios, compute all the ratios for the three companies. Write a two-page report that compares the two companies with the benchmark company.

Team Project F:17-2

Select a company and obtain its financial statements. Convert the income statement and the balance sheet to common size and compare the company you selected to the industry average. The Risk Management Association's *Annual Statement Studies* and Dun & Bradstreet's *Industry Norms & Key Business Ratios* publish common-size statements for most industries.

> Quick Check Answers

1. b **2.** b **3.** a **4.** c **5.** a **6.** b **7.** d **8.** c **9.** a **10.** c

Appendix A

Present Value Tables

Table A-1 Present Value of $1

Present Value

Periods	1%	2%	3%	4%	5%	6%	7%	8%	9%	10%	12%	14%	15%	16%	18%	20%
1	0.990	0.980	0.971	0.962	0.952	0.943	0.935	0.926	0.917	0.909	0.893	0.877	0.870	0.862	0.847	0.833
2	0.980	0.961	0.943	0.925	0.907	0.890	0.873	0.857	0.842	0.826	0.797	0.769	0.756	0.743	0.718	0.694
3	0.971	0.942	0.915	0.889	0.864	0.840	0.816	0.794	0.772	0.751	0.712	0.675	0.658	0.641	0.609	0.579
4	0.961	0.924	0.888	0.855	0.823	0.792	0.763	0.735	0.708	0.683	0.636	0.592	0.572	0.552	0.516	0.482
5	0.951	0.906	0.863	0.822	0.784	0.747	0.713	0.681	0.650	0.621	0.567	0.519	0.497	0.476	0.437	0.402
6	0.942	0.888	0.837	0.790	0.746	0.705	0.666	0.630	0.596	0.564	0.507	0.456	0.432	0.410	0.370	0.335
7	0.933	0.871	0.813	0.760	0.711	0.665	0.623	0.583	0.547	0.513	0.452	0.400	0.376	0.354	0.314	0.279
8	0.923	0.853	0.789	0.731	0.677	0.627	0.582	0.540	0.502	0.467	0.404	0.351	0.327	0.305	0.266	0.233
9	0.914	0.837	0.766	0.703	0.645	0.592	0.544	0.500	0.460	0.424	0.361	0.308	0.284	0.263	0.225	0.194
10	0.905	0.820	0.744	0.676	0.614	0.558	0.508	0.463	0.422	0.386	0.322	0.270	0.247	0.227	0.191	0.162
11	0.896	0.804	0.722	0.650	0.585	0.527	0.475	0.429	0.388	0.350	0.287	0.237	0.215	0.195	0.162	0.135
12	0.887	0.788	0.701	0.625	0.557	0.497	0.444	0.397	0.356	0.319	0.257	0.208	0.187	0.168	0.137	0.112
13	0.879	0.773	0.681	0.601	0.530	0.469	0.415	0.368	0.326	0.290	0.229	0.182	0.163	0.145	0.116	0.093
14	0.870	0.758	0.661	0.577	0.505	0.442	0.388	0.340	0.299	0.263	0.205	0.160	0.141	0.125	0.099	0.078
15	0.861	0.743	0.642	0.555	0.481	0.417	0.362	0.315	0.275	0.239	0.183	0.140	0.123	0.108	0.084	0.065
16	0.853	0.728	0.623	0.534	0.458	0.394	0.339	0.292	0.252	0.218	0.163	0.123	0.107	0.093	0.071	0.054
17	0.844	0.714	0.605	0.513	0.436	0.371	0.317	0.270	0.231	0.198	0.146	0.108	0.093	0.080	0.060	0.045
18	0.836	0.700	0.587	0.494	0.416	0.350	0.296	0.250	0.212	0.180	0.130	0.095	0.081	0.069	0.051	0.038
19	0.828	0.686	0.570	0.475	0.396	0.331	0.277	0.232	0.194	0.164	0.116	0.083	0.070	0.060	0.043	0.031
20	0.820	0.673	0.554	0.456	0.377	0.312	0.258	0.215	0.178	0.149	0.104	0.073	0.061	0.051	0.037	0.026
21	0.811	0.660	0.538	0.439	0.359	0.294	0.242	0.199	0.164	0.135	0.093	0.064	0.053	0.044	0.031	0.022
22	0.803	0.647	0.522	0.422	0.342	0.278	0.226	0.184	0.150	0.123	0.083	0.056	0.046	0.038	0.026	0.018
23	0.795	0.634	0.507	0.406	0.326	0.262	0.211	0.170	0.138	0.112	0.074	0.049	0.040	0.033	0.022	0.015
24	0.788	0.622	0.492	0.390	0.310	0.247	0.197	0.158	0.126	0.102	0.066	0.043	0.035	0.028	0.019	0.013
25	0.780	0.610	0.478	0.375	0.295	0.233	0.184	0.146	0.116	0.092	0.059	0.038	0.030	0.024	0.016	0.010
26	0.772	0.598	0.464	0.361	0.281	0.220	0.172	0.135	0.106	0.084	0.053	0.033	0.026	0.021	0.014	0.009
27	0.764	0.586	0.450	0.347	0.268	0.207	0.161	0.125	0.098	0.076	0.047	0.029	0.023	0.018	0.011	0.007
28	0.757	0.574	0.437	0.333	0.255	0.196	0.150	0.116	0.090	0.069	0.042	0.026	0.020	0.016	0.010	0.006
29	0.749	0.563	0.424	0.321	0.243	0.185	0.141	0.107	0.082	0.063	0.037	0.022	0.017	0.014	0.008	0.005
30	0.742	0.552	0.412	0.308	0.231	0.174	0.131	0.099	0.075	0.057	0.033	0.020	0.015	0.012	0.007	0.004
40	0.672	0.453	0.307	0.208	0.142	0.097	0.067	0.046	0.032	0.022	0.011	0.005	0.004	0.003	0.001	0.001
50	0.608	0.372	0.228	0.141	0.087	0.054	0.034	0.021	0.013	0.009	0.003	0.001	0.001	0.001		

Table A-2 Present Value of Ordinary Annuity of $1

Present Value

Periods	1%	2%	3%	4%	5%	6%	7%	8%	9%	10%	12%	14%	15%	16%	18%	20%
1	0.990	0.980	0.971	0.962	0.952	0.943	0.935	0.926	0.917	0.909	0.893	0.877	0.870	0.862	0.847	0.833
2	1.970	1.942	1.913	1.886	1.859	1.833	1.808	1.783	1.759	1.736	1.690	1.647	1.626	1.605	1.566	1.528
3	2.941	2.884	2.829	2.775	2.723	2.673	2.624	2.577	2.531	2.487	2.402	2.322	2.283	2.246	2.174	2.106
4	3.902	3.808	3.717	3.630	3.546	3.465	3.387	3.312	3.240	3.170	3.037	2.914	2.855	2.798	2.690	2.589
5	4.853	4.713	4.580	4.452	4.329	4.212	4.100	3.993	3.890	3.791	3.605	3.433	3.352	3.274	3.127	2.991
6	5.795	5.601	5.417	5.242	5.076	4.917	4.767	4.623	4.486	4.355	4.111	3.889	3.784	3.685	3.498	3.326
7	6.728	6.472	6.230	6.002	5.786	5.582	5.389	5.206	5.033	4.868	4.564	4.288	4.160	4.039	3.812	3.605
8	7.652	7.325	7.020	6.733	6.463	6.210	5.971	5.747	5.535	5.335	4.968	4.639	4.487	4.344	4.078	3.837
9	8.566	8.162	7.786	7.435	7.108	6.802	6.515	6.247	5.995	5.759	5.328	4.946	4.772	4.607	4.303	4.031
10	9.471	8.983	8.530	8.111	7.722	7.360	7.024	6.710	6.418	6.145	5.650	5.216	5.019	4.833	4.494	4.192
11	10.368	9.787	9.253	8.760	8.306	7.887	7.499	7.139	6.805	6.495	5.938	5.453	5.234	5.029	4.656	4.327
12	11.255	10.575	9.954	9.385	8.863	8.384	7.943	7.536	7.161	6.814	6.194	5.660	5.421	5.197	4.793	4.439
13	12.134	11.348	10.635	9.986	9.394	8.853	8.358	7.904	7.487	7.103	6.424	5.842	5.583	5.342	4.910	4.533
14	13.004	12.106	11.296	10.563	9.899	9.295	8.745	8.244	7.786	7.367	6.628	6.002	5.724	5.468	5.008	4.611
15	13.865	12.849	11.938	11.118	10.380	9.712	9.108	8.559	8.061	7.606	6.811	6.142	5.847	5.575	5.092	4.675
16	14.718	13.578	12.561	11.652	10.838	10.106	9.447	8.851	8.313	7.824	6.974	6.265	5.954	5.669	5.162	4.730
17	15.562	14.292	13.166	12.166	11.274	10.477	9.763	9.122	8.544	8.022	7.120	6.373	6.047	5.749	5.222	4.775
18	16.398	14.992	13.754	12.659	11.690	10.828	10.059	9.372	8.756	8.201	7.250	6.467	6.128	5.818	5.273	4.812
19	17.226	15.678	14.324	13.134	12.085	11.158	10.336	9.604	8.950	8.365	7.366	6.550	6.198	5.877	5.316	4.844
20	18.046	16.351	14.877	13.590	12.462	11.470	10.594	9.818	9.129	8.514	7.469	6.623	6.259	5.929	5.353	4.870
21	18.857	17.011	15.415	14.029	12.821	11.764	10.836	10.017	9.292	8.649	7.562	6.687	6.312	5.973	5.384	4.891
22	19.660	17.658	15.937	14.451	13.163	12.042	11.061	10.201	9.442	8.772	7.645	6.743	6.359	6.011	5.410	4.909
23	20.456	18.292	16.444	14.857	13.489	12.303	11.272	10.371	9.580	8.883	7.718	6.792	6.399	6.044	5.432	4.925
24	21.243	18.914	16.936	15.247	13.799	12.550	11.469	10.529	9.707	8.985	7.784	6.835	6.434	6.073	5.451	4.937
25	22.023	19.523	17.413	15.622	14.094	12.783	11.654	10.675	9.823	9.077	7.843	6.873	6.464	6.097	5.467	4.948
26	22.795	20.121	17.877	15.983	14.375	13.003	11.826	10.810	9.929	9.161	7.896	6.906	6.491	6.118	5.480	4.956
27	23.560	20.707	18.327	16.330	14.643	13.211	11.987	10.935	10.027	9.237	7.943	6.935	6.514	6.136	5.492	4.964
28	24.316	21.281	18.764	16.663	14.898	13.406	12.137	11.051	10.116	9.307	7.984	6.961	6.534	6.152	5.502	4.970
29	25.066	21.844	19.188	16.984	15.141	13.591	12.278	11.158	10.198	9.370	8.022	6.983	6.551	6.166	5.510	4.975
30	25.808	22.396	19.600	17.292	15.372	13.765	12.409	11.258	10.274	9.427	8.055	7.003	6.566	6.177	5.517	4.979
40	32.835	27.355	23.115	19.793	17.159	15.046	13.332	11.925	10.757	9.779	8.244	7.105	6.642	6.234	5.548	4.997
50	39.196	31.424	25.730	21.482	18.256	15.762	13.801	12.233	10.962	9.915	8.304	7.133	6.661	6.246	5.554	4.999

Future Value Tables

Table A-3 — Future Value of $1

Future Value

Periods	1%	2%	3%	4%	5%	6%	7%	8%	9%	10%	12%	14%	15%
1	1.010	1.020	1.030	1.040	1.050	1.060	1.070	1.080	1.090	1.100	1.120	1.140	1.150
2	1.020	1.040	1.061	1.082	1.103	1.124	1.145	1.166	1.188	1.210	1.254	1.300	1.323
3	1.030	1.061	1.093	1.125	1.158	1.191	1.225	1.260	1.295	1.331	1.405	1.482	1.521
4	1.041	1.082	1.126	1.170	1.216	1.262	1.311	1.360	1.412	1.464	1.574	1.689	1.749
5	1.051	1.104	1.159	1.217	1.276	1.338	1.403	1.469	1.539	1.611	1.762	1.925	2.011
6	1.062	1.126	1.194	1.265	1.340	1.419	1.501	1.587	1.677	1.772	1.974	2.195	2.313
7	1.072	1.149	1.230	1.316	1.407	1.504	1.606	1.714	1.828	1.949	2.211	2.502	2.660
8	1.083	1.172	1.267	1.369	1.477	1.594	1.718	1.851	1.993	2.144	2.476	2.853	3.059
9	1.094	1.195	1.305	1.423	1.551	1.689	1.838	1.999	2.172	2.358	2.773	3.252	3.518
10	1.105	1.219	1.344	1.480	1.629	1.791	1.967	2.159	2.367	2.594	3.106	3.707	4.046
11	1.116	1.243	1.384	1.539	1.710	1.898	2.105	2.332	2.580	2.853	3.479	4.226	4.652
12	1.127	1.268	1.426	1.601	1.796	2.012	2.252	2.518	2.813	3.138	3.896	4.818	5.350
13	1.138	1.294	1.469	1.665	1.886	2.133	2.410	2.720	3.066	3.452	4.363	5.492	6.153
14	1.149	1.319	1.513	1.732	1.980	2.261	2.579	2.937	3.342	3.798	4.887	6.261	7.076
15	1.161	1.346	1.558	1.801	2.079	2.397	2.759	3.172	3.642	4.177	5.474	7.138	8.137
16	1.173	1.373	1.605	1.873	2.183	2.540	2.952	3.426	3.970	4.595	6.130	8.137	9.358
17	1.184	1.400	1.653	1.948	2.292	2.693	3.159	3.700	4.328	5.054	6.866	9.276	10.76
18	1.196	1.428	1.702	2.026	2.407	2.854	3.380	3.996	4.717	5.560	7.690	10.58	12.38
19	1.208	1.457	1.754	2.107	2.527	3.026	3.617	4.316	5.142	6.116	8.613	12.06	14.23
20	1.220	1.486	1.806	2.191	2.653	3.207	3.870	4.661	5.604	6.728	9.646	13.74	16.37
21	1.232	1.516	1.860	2.279	2.786	3.400	4.141	5.034	6.109	7.400	10.80	15.67	18.82
22	1.245	1.546	1.916	2.370	2.925	3.604	4.430	5.437	6.659	8.140	12.10	17.86	21.64
23	1.257	1.577	1.974	2.465	3.072	3.820	4.741	5.871	7.258	8.954	13.55	20.36	24.89
24	1.270	1.608	2.033	2.563	3.225	4.049	5.072	6.341	7.911	9.850	15.18	23.21	28.63
25	1.282	1.641	2.094	2.666	3.386	4.292	5.427	6.848	8.623	10.83	17.00	26.46	32.92
26	1.295	1.673	2.157	2.772	3.556	4.549	5.807	7.396	9.399	11.92	19.04	30.17	37.86
27	1.308	1.707	2.221	2.883	3.733	4.822	6.214	7.988	10.25	13.11	21.32	34.39	43.54
28	1.321	1.741	2.288	2.999	3.920	5.112	6.649	8.627	11.17	14.42	23.88	39.20	50.07
29	1.335	1.776	2.357	3.119	4.116	5.418	7.114	9.317	12.17	15.86	26.75	44.69	57.58
30	1.348	1.811	2.427	3.243	4.322	5.743	7.612	10.06	13.27	17.45	29.96	50.95	66.21
40	1.489	2.208	3.262	4.801	7.040	10.29	14.97	21.72	31.41	45.26	93.05	188.9	267.9
50	1.645	2.692	4.384	7.107	11.47	18.42	29.46	46.90	74.36	117.4	289.0	700.2	1,084

Appendix A A-3

Table A-4 | Future Value of Ordinary Annuity of $1

Future Value

Periods	1%	2%	3%	4%	5%	6%	7%	8%	9%	10%	12%	14%	15%
1	1.000	1.000	1.000	1.000	1.000	1.000	1.000	1.000	1.000	1.000	1.000	1.000	1.000
2	2.010	2.020	2.030	2.040	2.050	2.060	2.070	2.080	2.090	2.100	2.120	2.140	2.150
3	3.030	3.060	3.091	3.122	3.153	3.184	3.215	3.246	3.278	3.310	3.374	3.440	3.473
4	4.060	4.122	4.184	4.246	4.310	4.375	4.440	4.506	4.573	4.641	4.779	4.921	4.993
5	5.101	5.204	5.309	5.416	5.526	5.637	5.751	5.867	5.985	6.105	6.353	6.610	6.742
6	6.152	6.308	6.468	6.633	6.802	6.975	7.153	7.336	7.523	7.716	8.115	8.536	8.754
7	7.214	7.434	7.662	7.898	8.142	8.394	8.654	8.923	9.200	9.487	10.09	10.73	11.07
8	8.286	8.583	8.892	9.214	9.549	9.897	10.26	10.64	11.03	11.44	12.30	13.23	13.73
9	9.369	9.755	10.16	10.58	11.03	11.49	11.98	12.49	13.02	13.58	14.78	16.09	16.79
10	10.46	10.95	11.46	12.01	12.58	13.18	13.82	14.49	15.19	15.94	17.55	19.34	20.30
11	11.57	12.17	12.81	13.49	14.21	14.97	15.78	16.65	17.56	18.53	20.65	23.04	24.35
12	12.68	13.41	14.19	15.03	15.92	16.87	17.89	18.98	20.14	21.38	24.13	27.27	29.00
13	13.81	14.68	15.62	16.63	17.71	18.88	20.14	21.50	22.95	24.52	28.03	32.09	34.35
14	14.95	15.97	17.09	18.29	19.60	21.02	22.55	24.21	26.02	27.98	32.39	37.58	40.50
15	16.10	17.29	18.60	20.02	21.58	23.28	25.13	27.15	29.36	31.77	37.28	43.84	47.58
16	17.26	18.64	20.16	21.82	23.66	25.67	27.89	30.32	33.00	35.95	42.75	50.98	55.72
17	18.43	20.01	21.76	23.70	25.84	28.21	30.84	33.75	36.97	40.54	48.88	59.12	65.08
18	19.61	21.41	23.41	25.65	28.13	30.91	34.00	37.45	41.30	45.60	55.75	68.39	75.84
19	20.81	22.84	25.12	27.67	30.54	33.76	37.38	41.45	46.02	51.16	63.44	78.97	88.21
20	22.02	24.30	26.87	29.78	33.07	36.79	41.00	45.76	51.16	57.28	72.05	91.02	102.4
21	23.24	25.78	28.68	31.97	35.72	39.99	44.87	50.42	56.76	64.00	81.70	104.8	118.8
22	24.47	27.30	30.54	34.25	38.51	43.39	49.01	55.46	62.87	71.40	92.50	120.4	137.6
23	25.72	28.85	32.45	36.62	41.43	47.00	53.44	60.89	69.53	79.54	104.6	138.3	159.3
24	26.97	30.42	34.43	39.08	44.50	50.82	58.18	66.76	76.79	88.50	118.2	158.7	184.2
25	28.24	32.03	36.46	41.65	47.73	54.86	63.25	73.11	84.70	98.35	133.3	181.9	212.8
26	29.53	33.67	38.55	44.31	51.11	59.16	68.68	79.95	93.32	109.2	150.3	208.3	245.7
27	30.82	35.34	40.71	47.08	54.67	63.71	74.48	87.35	102.7	121.1	169.4	238.5	283.6
28	32.13	37.05	42.93	49.97	58.40	68.53	80.70	95.34	113.0	134.2	190.7	272.9	327.1
29	33.45	38.79	45.22	52.97	62.32	73.64	87.35	104.0	124.1	148.6	214.6	312.1	377.2
30	34.78	40.57	47.58	56.08	66.44	79.06	94.46	113.3	136.3	164.5	241.3	356.8	434.7
40	48.89	60.40	75.40	95.03	120.8	154.8	199.6	259.1	337.9	442.6	767.1	1,342	1,779
50	64.46	84.58	112.8	152.7	209.3	290.3	406.5	573.8	815.1	1,164	2,400	4,995	7,218

Glossary

Accelerated Depreciation Method A depreciation method that expenses more of the asset's cost near the start of its useful life and less at the end of its useful life. (p. 10-11)

Account A detailed record of all increases and decreases that have occurred in an individual asset, liability, or equity during a specific period. (p. 2-2)

Account Number On a check, the number that identifies the account upon which the payment is drawn. (p. 8-18)

Accounting The information system that measures business activities, processes the information into reports, and communicates the results to decision makers. (p. 1-2)

Accounting Cycle The process by which companies produce their financial statements for a specific period. (p. 4-17)

Accounting Equation The basic tool of accounting, measuring the resources of the business (what the business owns or has control of) and the claims to those resources (what the business owes to creditors and to the owners): Assets = Liabilities + Equity. (p. 1-10)

Accounting Information System (AIS) A system that collects, records, stores, and processes accounting data to produce information that is useful for decision makers. (p. 7-2)

Accounts Payable A short-term liability that will be paid in the future. (p. 1-13)

Accounts Payable Subsidiary Ledger A subsidiary ledger that includes an accounts payable account for each vendor that contains detailed information such as the amount purchased, paid, and owed. (p. 7-7)

Accounts Receivable The right to receive cash in the future from customers for goods sold or for services performed. (pp. 1-14, 9-2)

Accounts Receivable Subsidiary Ledger A subsidiary ledger that includes an accounts receivable account for each customer that contains detailed information such as the amount sold, received, and owed. (p. 7-6)

Accounts Receivable Turnover Ratio A ratio that measures the number of times the company collects the average accounts receivable balance in a year. Net credit sales / Average net accounts receivable. (pp. 9-26, 17-18)

Accrual Basis Accounting Accounting method that records revenues when earned and expenses when incurred. (p. 3-2)

Accrued Expense An expense that the business has incurred but has not yet paid. (p. 3-14)

Accrued Liability A liability for which the business knows the amount owed, but the bill has not been paid. (p. 2-3)

Accrued Revenue A revenue that has been earned but for which the cash has not yet been collected. (p. 3-18)

Accumulated Depreciation The sum of all the depreciation expense recorded to date for a depreciable asset. (p. 3-11)

Acid-Test Ratio The ratio of the sum of cash, cash equivalents, short-term investments, and net current receivables to total current liabilities. The ratio tells whether the entity could pay all its current liabilities if they came due immediately. (Cash including cash equivalents + Short-term investments + Net current receivables) / Total current liabilities. (pp. 9-25, 17-15)

Adjunct Account An account that is directly related to another account. Adjunct accounts have the same normal balance as the related account and are added to the related account on the balance sheet. (p. 14-14)

Adjusted Trial Balance A list of all the accounts with their adjusted balances. (p. 3-22)

Adjusting Entry An entry made at the end of the accounting period that is used to record revenues to the period in which they are earned and expenses to the period in which they occur. (p. 3-7)

Administrative Expenses Operating expenses incurred that are not related to marketing the company's goods and services. (p. 5-26)

Aging-of-Receivables Method A method of estimating uncollectible receivables by determining the balance of the Allowance for Bad Debts account based on the age of individual accounts receivable. (p. 9-16)

Allowance for Bad Debts A contra asset account, related to accounts receivable, that holds the estimated amount of uncollectible accounts. (p. 9-8)

Allowance Method A method of accounting for uncollectible receivables in which the company estimates bad debts expense instead of waiting to see which customers the company will not collect from. (p. 9-8)

Amortization The process by which businesses spread the allocation of an intangible asset's cost over its useful life. (p. 10-25)

Amortization Schedule A schedule that details each loan payment's allocation between principal and interest and the beginning and ending loan balances. (p. 14-2)

Annual Report Provides information about a company's financial condition. (p. 17-3)

Annuity A stream of equal cash payments made at equal time intervals. (p. 14-22)

Appropriation of Retained Earnings Restriction of a portion of retained earnings that is recorded by a journal entry. (p. 13-26)

Asset Turnover Ratio Measures how efficiently a business uses its average total assets to generate sales. Net sales revenue / Average total assets. (pp. 10-29, 17-22)

Assets Economic resources that are expected to benefit the business in the future and something the business owns or has control of. (p. 1-10)

Audit An examination of a company's financial statements and records. (p. 1-9)

Authorized Stock The maximum number of shares of stock that the corporate charter allows the corporation to issue. (p. 13-3)

Available-for-Sale (AFS) Debt Investment A debt security that isn't a trading debt investment or a held-to-maturity debt investment. (p. 15-4)

Bad Debts Expense The cost to the seller of extending credit. It arises from the failure to collect from some credit customers. (p. 9-6)

Balance Sheet Reports on the assets, liabilities, and owner's equity of the business as of a specific date. (p. 1-19)

Bank Reconciliation A document explaining the reasons for the difference between a depositor's cash records and the depositor's cash balance in its bank account. (p. 8-19)

Bank Statement A document from the bank that reports the activity in the customer's account. It shows the bank account's beginning and ending balances and lists the month's cash transactions conducted through the bank account. (p. 8-18)

Benchmarking The practice of comparing a company's performance with best practices from other companies. (p. 17-12)

Bond Payable A long-term debt issued to multiple lenders called *bondholders*, usually in increments of $1,000 per bond. (p. 14-5)

Book Value A depreciable asset's cost minus accumulated depreciation. (pp. 3-12, 10-10)

Callable Bonds Bonds that the issuer may call and pay off at a specified price whenever the issuer wants. (p. 14-17)

Canceled Checks Physical or scanned copies of the maker's cashed (paid) checks. (p. 8-18)

Capital Deficiency A partnership's claim against a partner. Occurs when a partner's capital account has a debit balance. (p. 12-24)

Capital Expenditure An expenditure that increases the capacity or efficiency of a plant asset or extends its useful life. Capital expenditures are debited to an asset account. (p. 10-6)

Capital Stock Represents the individual's ownership of the corporation's capital. (p. 13-3)

Capitalize Recording the acquisition of land, building, or other assets by debiting (increasing) an asset account. (p. 10-4)

G-1

G-2 Glossary

Carrying Amount of Bonds A bond payable *minus* the discount account current balance or *plus* the premium account current balance. (p. 14-12)

Cash Basis Accounting Accounting method that records revenues only when cash is received and expenses only when cash is paid. (p. 3-2)

Cash Equivalent A highly liquid investment that can be converted into cash in three months or less. (p. 8-24)

Cash Flows Cash receipts and cash payments of a business. (p. 16-2)

Cash Payments Journal Special journal used to record cash payments by check and currency. (p. 7-16)

Cash Ratio A measure of a company's ability to pay current liabilities from cash and cash equivalents: (Cash + Cash equivalents) / Total current liabilities. (pp. 8-24, 17-15)

Cash Receipts Journal Special journal used to record cash receipts. (p. 7-10)

Certified Financial Planner (CFP) Certified professional who specializes in budgeting, planning for retirement, and managing finances. (p. 1-5)

Certified Management Accountants (CMAs) Professional accountants who specialize in accounting and financial management knowledge. (p. 1-4)

Certified Public Accountants (CPAs) Licensed professional accountants who serve the general public. (p. 1-4)

Chart of Accounts A list of all of a company's accounts with their account numbers. (p. 2-4)

Chartered Global Management Accountant (CGMA) Professional accountant with advanced knowledge in finance, operations, strategy, and management. (p. 1-4)

Check A document that instructs a bank to pay the designated person or business a specified amount of money. (p. 8-17)

Classified Balance Sheet A balance sheet that places each asset and each liability into a specific category. (p. 4-4)

Closing Entries Entries that transfer the revenues, expenses, and Owner, Withdrawals balances to the Owner, Capital account to prepare the company's books for the next period. (p. 4-10)

Closing Process A step in the accounting cycle that occurs at the end of the period. The closing process consists of journalizing and posting the closing entries to set the balances of the revenues, expenses, Income Summary, and Owner, Withdrawals accounts to zero for the next period. (p. 4-9)

Cloud Computing Software and data are stored on a third-party server instead of by the business and can be accessed by employees via the Internet. (p. 7-21)

Collusion Two or more people working together to circumvent internal controls and defraud a company. (p. 8-6)

Commercial Substance A characteristic of a transaction that causes a change in future cash flows. (p. 10-30)

Committee of Sponsoring Organizations (COSO) A committee that provides thought leadership related to enterprise risk management, internal control, and fraud deterrence. (p. 8-2)

Common Stock Represents the basic ownership of a corporation. (p. 13-5)

Common-Size Statement A financial statement that reports only percentages (no dollar amounts). (p. 17-11)

Compound Interest Interest calculated on the principal and on all previously earned interest. (p. 14-22)

Compound Journal Entry A journal entry that is characterized by having multiple debits and/or multiple credits. (p. 2-15)

Comprehensive Income A company's change in total stockholders' equity from all sources other than owners' investments and dividends. (p. 15-13)

Conservatism A business should report the least favorable figures in the financial statements when two or more possible options are presented. (p. 6-3)

Consistency Principle A business should use the same accounting methods and procedures from period to period. (p. 6-2)

Consolidated Statements Financial statements that combine the balance sheets, income statements, and statements of cash flow of the parent company with those of its controlling interest affiliates. (p. 15-10)

Consolidation Accounting The way to combine the financial statements of two or more companies that have the same owners. (p. 15-10)

Contingent Liability A potential liability that depends on some future event. (p. 11-17)

Contra Account An account that is paired with, and is listed immediately after, its related account in the chart of accounts and associated financial statement and whose normal balance is the opposite of the normal balance of the related account. (p. 3-11)

Control Account An account whose balance equals the sum of the balances in a group of related accounts in a subsidiary ledger. (p. 7-7)

Controlling Interest Equity Investment An equity security in which the investor owns more than 50% of the investee's voting stock. (p. 15-4)

Copyright Exclusive right to reproduce and sell a book, musical composition, film, other work of art, or intellectual property. (p. 10-26)

Corporation A business organized under state law that is a separate legal entity. (pp. 1-7, 13-2)

Cost of Goods Available for Sale The total cost spent on inventory that was available to be sold during a period. (p. 6-8)

Cost of Goods Sold (COGS) The cost of the merchandise inventory that the business has sold to customers. (p. 5-3)

Cost Principle A principle that states that acquired assets and services should be recorded at their actual cost. (pp. 1-8, 10-3)

Credit The right side of a T-account. (p. 2-6)

Credit Memorandum An increase in a bank account. (p. 8-20)

Credit Terms The payment terms of purchase or sale as stated on the invoice. (p. 5-8)

Creditor Any person or business to whom a business owes money. (p. 1-4)

Cumulative Preferred Stock Preferred stock whose owners must receive all dividends in arrears plus the current year dividend before the corporation pays dividends to the common stockholders. (p. 13-17)

Current Asset An asset that is expected to be converted to cash, sold, or used up during the next 12 months or within the business's normal operating cycle if the cycle is longer than a year. (p. 4-5)

Current Liability A liability that must be paid with cash, or with goods and services, within one year or within the entity's operating cycle if the cycle is longer than a year. (pp. 4-5, 11-2)

Current Portion of Notes Payable The amount of the principal that is payable within one year of the balance sheet date. (p. 11-5)

Current Ratio Measures the company's ability to pay current liabilities from current assets. Total current assets / Total current liabilities. (pp. 4-19, 17-16)

Days' Sales in Inventory Measures the average number of days that inventory is held by a company. 365 days / Inventory turnover. (pp. 6-22, 17-17)

Days' Sales in Receivables The ratio of average net accounts receivable to one day's sales. The ratio tells how many days it takes to collect the average level of accounts receivable. 365 days / Accounts receivable turnover ratio. (pp. 9-26, 17-19)

Debentures Unsecured bonds backed only by the creditworthiness of the bond issuer. (p. 14-6)

Debit The left side of a T-account. (p. 2-6)

Debit Memorandum A decrease in a bank account. (p. 8-20)

Debt Ratio Shows the proportion of assets financed with debt. Total liabilities / Total assets. (pp. 2-26, 17-19)

Debt Security Investment in notes or bonds payable issued by another company. (p. 15-2)

Debt to Equity Ratio A ratio that measures the proportion of total liabilities relative to total equity. Total liabilities / Total equity. (pp. 14-20, 17-20)

Debtor The party to a credit transaction who takes on an obligation/payable. (p. 9-2)

Deferred Expense An asset created when a business makes advance payments of future expenses. (p. 3-7)

Deferred Revenue A liability created when a business collects cash from customers in advance of completing a service or delivering a product. (p. 3-13)

Deficit Debit balance in the Retained Earnings account. (p. 13-25)

Depletion The process by which businesses spread the allocation of a natural resource's cost over its usage. (p. 10-24)

Deposit in Transit A deposit recorded by the company but not yet by its bank. (p. 8-19)

Deposit Ticket A bank form that is completed by the customer and shows the amount of each deposit. (p. 8-17)

Depreciable Cost The cost of a plant asset minus its estimated residual value. (p. 10-9)

Depreciation The process by which businesses spread the allocation of a plant asset's cost over its useful life. (pp. 3-9, 10-2)

Direct Method A format of the operating activities section of the statement of cash flows; lists the operating cash receipts and cash payments. (p. 16-5)

Direct Write-off Method A method of accounting for uncollectible receivables in which the company records bad debts expense when a customer's account receivable is uncollectible. (p. 9-6)

Disclosure Principle A business's financial statements must report enough information for outsiders to make knowledgeable decisions about the company. (p. 6-2)

Discount on Bonds Payable Occurs when a bond's issue price is less than face value. (p. 14-7)

Dishonor a Note Failure of a note's maker to pay a note receivable at maturity. (p. 9-23)

Dissolution Ending of a partnership. (p. 12-3)

Dividend A distribution of a corporation's earnings to stockholders. (p. 13-5)

Dividend in Arrears A preferred stock dividend is in arrears if the dividend has not been paid for the year and the preferred stock is cumulative. (p. 13-17)

Dividend Payout The ratio of dividends declared per common share relative to the earnings per share of the company. Annual dividend per share / Earnings per share. (p. 17-25)

Dividend Yield Ratio of annual dividends per share of stock to the stock's market price per share. Measures the percentage of a stock's market value that is returned annually as dividends to stockholders. Annual dividend per share / Market price per share. (p. 17-24)

Dollar Value Bias The bias one sees from comparing numbers in absolute (dollars) rather than relative (percentage) terms. (p. 17-11)

Double-Declining-Balance Method An accelerated depreciation method that computes annual depreciation by multiplying the depreciable asset's decreasing book value by a constant percent that is two times the straight-line depreciation rate. (p. 10-11)

Double-Entry System A system of accounting in which every transaction affects at least two accounts. (p. 2-6)

Earnings per Share (EPS) Amount of a company's net income (loss) for each share of its outstanding common stock. (Net income − Preferred dividends) / Weighted average number of common shares outstanding. (pp. 13-24, 17-23)

Economic Entity Assumption An organization that stands apart as a separate economic unit. (p. 1-7)

Effective-Interest Amortization Method An amortization model that calculates interest expense based on the current carrying amount of the bond and the market interest rate at issuance, and then amortizes the difference between the cash interest payment and calculated interest expense as a decrease to the discount or premium. (p. 14-28)

Electronic Data Interchange (EDI) A streamlined process that bypasses paper documents altogether. Computers of customers communicate directly with the computers of suppliers to automate routine business transactions. (p. 8-11)

Electronic Funds Transfer (EFT) A system that transfers cash by electronic communication rather than by paper documents. (p. 8-18)

Encryption Rearranging plain-text messages by a mathematical process—the primary method of achieving security in e-commerce. (p. 8-5)

Enterprise Resource Planning (ERP) Software system that can integrate all of a company's functions, departments, and data into a single system. (p. 7-21)

Equity The owners' claims to the assets of the business. (p. 1-10)

Equity Security Investment in stock ownership in another company that sometimes pays cash dividends or issues stock dividends. (p. 15-2)

Estimated Returns Inventory An asset account used to estimate the cost of merchandise inventory a company will receive in returns. (p. 5-15)

Evaluated Receipts Settlement (ERS) A procedure that compresses the payment approval process into a single step by comparing the receiving report to the purchase order. (p. 8-11)

Expenses The costs of selling goods or services. (p. 1-11)

External Auditor An outside accountant, completely independent of the business, who evaluates the controls to ensure that the financial statements are presented fairly, in accordance with GAAP. (p. 8-4)

Extraordinary Repair Repair work that generates a capital expenditure because it extends the asset's life past the normal expected life. (p. 10-6)

Face Value The amount a borrower must pay back to the bondholders on the maturity date. (p. 14-6)

Fair Value The price that would be used if the investments were sold on the market. (p. 15-10)

Faithful Representation Providing information that is complete, neutral, and free from error. (p. 1-7)

Federal Insurance Contributions Act (FICA) The federal act that created the Social Security tax that provides retirement, disability, and medical benefits. (p. 11-8)

Financial Accounting The field of accounting that focuses on providing information for external decision makers. (p. 1-3)

Financial Accounting Standards Board (FASB) The private organization that oversees the creation and governance of accounting standards in the United States. (p. 1-6)

Financial Leverage Occurs when a company earns more income on borrowed money than the related interest expense. (p. 14-10)

Financial Statements Business documents that are used to communicate information needed to make business decisions. (p. 1-17)

Financing Activities Activities that increase or decrease long-term liabilities and equity; a section of the statement of cash flows. (p. 16-3)

Firewall A device that enables members of a local network to access the network, while keeping nonmembers out of the network. (p. 8-5)

First-In, First-Out (FIFO) Method An inventory costing method in which the first costs into inventory are the first costs out to cost of goods sold. Ending inventory is based on the costs of the most recent purchases. (p. 6-7)

Fiscal Year An accounting year of any 12 consecutive months that may or may not coincide with the calendar year. (p. 3-4)

FOB Destination Situation in which the buyer takes ownership (title) to the goods at the delivery destination point and the seller typically pays the freight. (p. 5-10)

FOB Shipping Point Situation in which the buyer takes ownership (title) to the goods when the goods leave the seller's place of business (shipping point) and the buyer typically pays the freight. (p. 5-10)

Franchise Privilege granted by a business to sell a product or service under specified conditions. (p. 10-27)

Free Cash Flow The amount of cash available from operating activities after paying for planned investments in long-term assets and after paying dividends to shareholders. Net cash provided by operating activities − Cash payments planned for investments in long-term assets − Cash dividends. (p. 16-20)

Freight In The transportation cost to ship goods to the purchaser's warehouse; therefore, it is freight on purchased goods. (p. 5-10)

Freight Out The transportation cost to ship goods out of the seller's warehouse; therefore, it is freight on goods sold to a customer. (p. 5-10)

Future Value The value of an investment at the end of a specific time frame. (p. 14-8)

General Partner A partner who has unlimited personal liability in the partnership. (p. 12-4)

General Partnership A form of partnership in which each partner is a co-owner of the business, with all the privileges and risks of ownership. (p. 12-4)

Generally Accepted Accounting Principles (GAAP) Accounting guidelines, currently formulated by the Financial Accounting Standards Board (FASB); the main U.S. accounting rule book. (p. 1-6)

Going Concern Assumption Assumes that the entity will remain in operation for the foreseeable future. (p. 1-8)

Goodwill Excess of the cost of an acquired company over the sum of the market values of its net assets (assets minus liabilities). (p. 10-27)

Gross Pay The total amount of salary, wages, commissions, and any other employee compensation before taxes and other deductions. (p. 11-7)

Gross Profit Excess of Net Sales Revenue over Cost of Goods Sold. (p. 5-4)

Gross Profit Percentage Measures the profitability of each sales dollar above the cost of goods sold. Gross profit / Net sales revenue. (pp. 5-27, 17-18)

Hardware Electronic equipment that includes computers, monitors, printers, and the network that connects them. (p. 7-21)

Held-to-Maturity (HTM) Debt Investment A debt security the investor intends to hold and has the ability to hold until it matures. (p. 15-3)

Horizontal Analysis The study of percentage changes in line items from comparative financial statements. (Dollar amount of change / Base period amount) × 100. (p. 17-5)

Impairment A permanent decline in asset value. (p. 10-25)

Imprest System A way to account for petty cash by maintaining a constant balance in the petty cash account. At any time, cash plus petty cash tickets must total the amount allocated to the petty cash fund. (p. 8-12)

Income Statement Reports the *net income* or *net loss* of the business for a specific period. (p. 1-18)

Income Summary A temporary account into which revenues and expenses are transferred prior to their final transfer into the Owner, Capital account. Summarizes net income (or net loss) for the period. (p. 4-10)

Income Tax Expense Expense incurred by a corporation related to federal and state income taxes. (p. 13-23)

Income Tax Withholding Income tax deducted from an employee's gross pay. (p. 11-7)

Indirect Method A format of the operating activities section of the statement of cash flows; starts with net income and reconciles to net cash provided by operating activities. (p. 16-5)

Intangible Asset An asset with no physical form that is valuable because of the special rights it carries. (pp. 4-5, 10-25)

Interest The revenue to the payee for loaning money—the expense to the debtor. (p. 9-18)

Interest Period The period of time during which interest is computed. It extends from the original date of the note to the maturity date. (p. 9-19)

Interest Rate The percentage rate of interest specified by the note. (p. 9-19)

Internal Auditor An employee of the business who ensures the company's employees are following company policies, that the company meets all legal requirements, and that operations are running efficiently. (p. 8-4)

Internal Control The organizational plan and all the related measures adopted by an entity to safeguard assets, encourage employees to follow company policies, promote operational efficiency, and ensure accurate and reliable accounting records. (p. 8-2)

Internal Control Report A report by management describing its responsibility for and the adequacy of internal controls over financial reporting. (p. 8-3)

International Accounting Standards Board (IASB) The private organization that oversees the creation and governance of International Financial Reporting Standards (IFRS). (p. 1-8)

International Financial Reporting Standards (IFRS) A set of global accounting guidelines, formulated by the International Accounting Standards Board (IASB). (p. 1-8)

Inventory Costing Method A method of approximating the flow of inventory costs in a business that is used to determine the amount of cost of goods sold and ending merchandise inventory. (p. 6-6)

Inventory Shrinkage The loss of inventory that occurs because of theft and damage. (p. 5-19)

Inventory Turnover Measures the number of times a company sells its average level of merchandise inventory during a period. Cost of goods sold / Average merchandise inventory. (pp. 6-22, 17-17)

Investee The corporation that issued the bond or stock to the investor. (p. 15-2)

Investing Activities Activities that increase or decrease long-term assets; a section of the statement of cash flows. (p. 16-3)

Investor The owner of a bond or stock of a corporation. (p. 15-2)

Invoice A seller's request for payment from the purchaser. (p. 5-5)

Issue Price The amount that the corporation receives from issuing stock. (p. 13-7)

Issued Stock Stock that has been issued but may or may not be held by stockholders. (p. 13-3)

Journal A record of transactions in date order. (p. 2-10)

Land Improvement A depreciable improvement to land, such as fencing, sprinklers, paving, signs, and lighting. (p. 10-3)

Large Stock Dividend A stock dividend greater than 20% to 25% of the issued and outstanding stock. (p. 13-19)

Last-In, First-Out (LIFO) Method An inventory costing method in which the last costs into inventory are the first costs out to cost of goods sold. The method leaves the oldest costs—those of beginning inventory and the earliest purchases of the period—in ending inventory. (p. 6-9)

Ledger The record holding all the accounts of a business, the changes in those accounts, and their balances. (p. 2-5)

Legal Capital The portion of stockholders' equity that cannot be used for dividends. (p. 13-15)

Liabilities Debts that are owed to creditors. (pp. 1-10, 11-2)

License Privilege granted by a government to use public property in performing services. (p. 10-27)

Limited Liability Company (LLC) A form of business organization that is neither a partnership nor a corporation but combines the advantages of both. (pp. 1-7, 12-5)

Limited Liability Partnership (LLP) A form of partnership in which each partner is protected from the malpractice or negligence of the other partners. (p. 12-5)

Limited Partner A partner who has limited personal liability in the partnership. (p. 12-5)

Limited Partnership (LP) A partnership with at least two classes of partners: one or more general partners and one or more limited partners. (p. 12-4)

Liquidation The process of going out of business by selling the entity's assets, paying its liabilities, and distributing any remaining cash to the partners based on their equity balances. (p. 12-20)

Liquidity A measure of how quickly an item can be converted to cash. (p. 4-5)

Lock-Box System A system in which customers send their checks to a post office box that belongs to a bank. A bank employee empties the box daily and records the deposits into the company's bank account. (p. 8-9)

Long-term Asset An asset that will not be converted to cash or used up within the business's operating cycle or one year, whichever is greater. (p. 4-5)

Long-term Investment An investment in debt and equity securities that the investor intends to hold for longer than one year. (pp. 4-5, 15-3)

Long-term Liability A liability that does not need to be paid within one year or within the entity's operating cycle, whichever is longer. (pp. 4-5, 11-2, 14-2)

Lower-of-Cost-or-Market (LCM) Rule Rule that merchandise inventory should be reported in the financial statements at whichever is lower—its historical cost or its market value. (p. 6-17)

Maker The party who issues the check. (p. 8-17)

Management's Discussion and Analysis of Financial Condition and Results of Operations (MD&A) The section of the annual report that is intended to help investors understand the results of operations and the financial condition of the company. (p. 17-3)

Managerial Accounting The field of accounting that focuses on providing information for internal decision makers. (p. 1-3)

Market Interest Rate The interest rate that investors demand in order to loan their money. (p. 14-8)

Matching Principle Guides accounting for expenses, ensures that all expenses are recorded when they are incurred during the period, and matches those expenses against the revenues of the period. (p. 3-5)

Materiality Concept A company must perform strictly proper accounting only for items that are significant to the business's financial situation. (p. 6-3)

Maturity Date The date when a note is due. (p. 9-2)

Maturity Value The sum of the principal plus interest due at maturity. (p. 9-19)

Memorandum Entry An entry in the journal that notes a significant event, but has no debit or credit amount. (p. 13-22)

Merchandise Inventory The merchandise that a business sells to customers. (p. 5-2)

Merchandiser A business that sells merchandise, or goods, to customers. (p. 5-2)

Modified Accelerated Cost Recovery System (MACRS) A depreciation method that is used for tax purposes. (p. 10-14)

Monetary Unit Assumption The assumption that requires the items on the financial statements to be measured in terms of a monetary unit. (p. 1-8)

Mortgages Payable Long-term debts that are backed with a security interest in specific property. (p. 14-3)

Multi-Step Income Statement Income statement format that contains subtotals to highlight significant relationships. In addition to net income, it reports gross profit and operating income. (p. 5-24)

Mutual Agency Every partner can bind the business to a contract within the scope of the partnership's regular business operations. (p. 12-3)

Natural Resource An asset that comes from the earth and is consumed. (p. 10-24)

Net Income The result of operations that occurs when total revenues are greater than total expenses. (p. 1-11)

Net Loss The result of operations that occurs when total expenses are greater than total revenues. (p. 1-11)

Net Pay Gross pay minus all deductions. The amount of compensation that the employee actually takes home. (p. 11-7)

Net Realizable Value The net value a company expects to collect from its accounts receivable. Accounts Receivable less Allowance for Bad Debts. (p. 9-8)

Network The system of electronic linkages that allows different computers to share the same information. (p. 7-21)

No Significant Influence Equity Investment An equity security in which the investor lacks the ability to participate in the decisions of the investee company. (p. 15-4)

No-Par Stock Stock that has no amount (par) assigned to it. (p. 13-5)

Non-cash Investing and Financing Activities Investing and financing activities that do not involve cash. (p. 16-4)

Noncumulative Preferred Stock Preferred stock whose owners do not receive passed dividends. (p. 13-17)

Nonsufficient Funds (NSF) Check A check for which the maker's bank account has insufficient money to pay the check. (p. 8-20)

Normal Balance The balance that appears on the increase side of an account. (p. 2-7)

Notes Payable A *written* promise made by the business to pay a debt, usually involving *interest*, in the future. (p. 2-3)

Notes Receivable A written promise that a customer will pay a fixed amount of principal plus interest by a certain date in the future. (pp. 2-3, 9-2)

Obsolete An asset is considered obsolete when a newer asset can perform the job more efficiently. (p. 10-8)

Operating Activities Activities that create revenue or expense in the entity's business; a section of the statement of cash flows. (p. 16-3)

Operating Cycle The time span during which cash is paid for goods and services, which are then sold to customers and cash is collected. (p. 4-5)

Operating Expenses Expenses, other than Cost of Goods Sold, that are incurred in the entity's major ongoing operations. (p. 5-4)

Operating Income Measures the results of the entity's major ongoing activities. Gross profit minus operating expenses. (p. 5-26)

Other Income and Expenses Revenues or expenses that are outside the normal, day-to-day operations of a business, such as a gain or loss on the sale of plant assets or interest expense. (p. 5-26)

Outstanding Check A check issued by a company and recorded on its books but not yet paid by its bank. (p. 8-19)

Outstanding Stock Issued stock in the hands of stockholders. (p. 13-4)

Owner's Capital Owner contributions to a business. (p. 1-10)

Owner's Withdrawals Payments of equity to the owner. (p. 1-11)

Paid-In Capital Represents amounts received from the stockholders of a corporation in exchange for stock. (p. 13-6)

Paid-In Capital in Excess of Par Represents amounts received from stockholders in excess of par value. (p. 13-7)

Par Value An amount assigned by a company to a share of its stock. (p. 13-5)

Parent Company A company that owns a controlling interest in another company. (p. 15-10)

Partnership A business with two or more owners and not organized as a corporation. (pp. 1-7, 12-2)

Partnership Agreement The contract between partners that specifies such items as the name, location, and nature of the business; the name, capital contribution, and duties of each partner; and the method of sharing profits and losses among the partners. (p. 12-2)

Patent An intangible asset that is a federal government grant conveying an exclusive 20-year right to produce and sell a process, product, or formula. (p. 10-25)

Payee The individual or business to whom the check is paid. (p. 8-17)

Payroll Register A schedule that summarizes the earnings, withholdings, and net pay for each employee. (p. 11-9)

Pension Plan A plan that provides benefits to retired employees. (p. 11-15)

Percent-of-Receivables Method A method of estimating uncollectible receivables by determining the balance of the Allowance for Bad Debts account based on a percentage of accounts receivable. (p. 9-13)

Percent-of-Sales Method A method of estimating uncollectible receivables that calculates bad debts expense based on a percentage of net credit sales. (p. 9-12)

Periodic Inventory System An inventory system that requires businesses to obtain a physical count of inventory to determine quantities on hand. (p. 5-4)

Permanent Account An account that is *not* closed at the end of the period—the asset, liability, and Owner, Capital accounts. (p. 4-9)

Perpetual Inventory System An inventory system that keeps a running computerized record of merchandise inventory. (p. 5-4)

Petty Cash A fund containing a small amount of cash that is used to pay for minor expenditures. (p. 8-11)

Post-Closing Trial Balance A list of the accounts and their balances at the end of the period after journalizing and posting the closing entries. It should include only permanent accounts. (p. 4-16)

Posting Transferring data from the journal to the ledger. (p. 2-10)

Preemptive Right Stockholder's right to maintain his or her proportionate ownership in the corporation. (p. 13-5)

Preferred Stock Stock that gives its owners certain advantages over common stockholders, such as the right to receive dividends before the common stockholders and the right to receive assets before the common stockholders if the corporation liquidates. (p. 13-5)

Premium The amount above par at which a stock is issued. (p. 13-7)

Premium on Bonds Payable Occurs when a bond's issue price is more than face value. (p. 14-7)

Prepaid Expense A payment of an expense in advance. (p. 2-3)

Present Value The value of an investment today. (p. 14-8)

Price/Earnings Ratio The ratio of the market price of a share of common stock to the company's earnings per share. Measures the value that the stock market places on $1 of a company's earnings. Market price per share of common stock / Earnings per share. (pp. 13-28, 17-24)

Principal The amount loaned by the payee and borrowed by the maker of the note. (p. 9-18)

Prior-Period Adjustment A correction to Retained Earnings for an error of an earlier period. (p. 13-26)

Profit Margin Ratio A profitability measure that shows how much net income is earned on every dollar of net sales. Net income / Net sales revenue. (p. 17-21)

Property, Plant, and Equipment (PP&E) Long-lived, tangible assets, such as land, buildings, and equipment, used in the operation of a business. (pp. 3-9, 4-5, 10-2)

Public Company A company that sells its stock to the general public. (p. 8-2)

Public Company Accounting Oversight Board (PCAOB) Monitors the work of independent accountants who audit public companies. (p. 1-9)

Purchase Allowance An amount granted to the purchaser as an incentive to keep goods that are not "as ordered." (p. 5-7)

Purchase Discount A discount that businesses offer to purchasers as an incentive for early payment. (p. 5-8)

Purchase Return A situation in which sellers allow purchasers to return merchandise that is defective, damaged, or otherwise unsuitable. (p. 5-7)

Purchases Journal Special journal used to record all purchases of merchandise inventory, office supplies, and other assets on account. (p. 7-14)

Rate of Return on Common Stockholders' Equity Shows the relationship between net income available to common stockholders and their average common equity invested in the company. (Net income − Preferred dividends) / Average common stockholders' equity. (pp. 13-28, 17-22)

Rate of Return on Total Assets A ratio that measures the success a company has in using its assets to earn income. (Net income + Interest expense) / Average total assets. (pp. 15-16, 17-21)

Receivable A monetary claim against a business or an individual. (p. 9-2)

Refunds Payable A liability account used to estimate the amount of refunds that will be paid to customers in the future. (p. 5-15)

Relative-Market-Value Method A method of allocating the total cost (100%) of multiple assets purchased at one time. Total cost is divided among the assets according to their relative market values. (p. 10-5)

Remittance Advice An optional attachment to a check that tells the business the reason for the payment. (p. 8-8)

Residual Value The expected value of a depreciable asset at the end of its useful life. (pp. 3-10, 10-9)

Retailer A type of merchandiser who buys merchandise either from a manufacturer or a wholesaler and then sells those goods to consumers. (p. 5-2)

Retained Earnings Equity earned by profitable operations of a corporation that is not distributed to stockholders. (p. 13-6)

Return on Assets (ROA) Measures how profitably a company uses its assets. Net income / Average total assets. (p. 1-22)

Revenue Expenditure An expenditure that does not increase the capacity or efficiency of an asset or extend its useful life. Revenue expenditures are debited to an expense account. (p. 10-6)

Revenue Recognition Principle Requires companies to record revenue when (or as) the entity satisfies each performance obligation. (p. 3-4)

Revenues Amounts earned from delivering goods or services to customers. (p. 1-10)

Reversing Entry A special journal entry that eases the burden of accounting for transactions in the next period. Such entries are the exact opposite of a prior adjusting entry. (p. 4-22)

Routing Number On a check, the 9-digit number that identifies the bank upon which the payment is drawn. (p. 8-18)

S Corporation A corporation with 100 or fewer stockholders that can elect to be taxed in the same way as a partnership. (p. 12-6)

Sales Allowance A reduction in the amount owed by a customer that does not involve the return of merchandise inventory. (p. 5-16)

Sales Discounts Reduction in the amount of revenue earned on sales for early payment. (p. 5-16)

Sales Journal Special journal used to record credit sales. (p. 7-7)

Sales Return A reduction in the amount owed by a customer due to the return of merchandise. (p. 5-14)

Sales Revenue The amount that a merchandiser earns from selling its inventory. (p. 5-12)

Sarbanes-Oxley Act (SOX) Requires management to review internal control and take responsibility for the accuracy and completeness of their financial reports. (pp. 1-9, 8-3)

Secured Bonds Bonds that give bondholders the right to take specified assets of the issuer if the issuer fails to pay principal or interest. (p. 14-6)

Securities and Exchange Commission (SEC) U.S. governmental agency that oversees the U.S. financial markets. (p. 1-6)

Security A share or interest representing financial value. (p. 15-2)

Selling Expenses Operating expenses related to marketing and selling the company's goods and services. (p. 5-25)

Separation of Duties Dividing responsibilities between two or more people to limit fraud and promote the accuracy of accounting records. (p. 8-4)

Serial Bonds Bonds that mature in installments at regular intervals. (p. 14-6)

Server The main computer where data are stored, which can be accessed from many different computers. (p. 7-4)

Short-term Investment An investment in debt and equity securities that the investor intends to sell in one year or less. (p. 15-3)

Short-term Note Payable A written promise made by the business to pay a debt, usually involving interest, within one year or less. (p. 11-4)

Signature Card A card that shows each authorized person's signature for a bank account. (p. 8-17)

Significant Influence Equity Investment An equity security in which the investor has the ability to exert influence over operating and financial decisions of the investee company. (p. 15-4)

Simple Interest Interest calculated only on the principal amount. (p. 14-22)

Single-Step Income Statement Income statement format that groups all revenues together and then lists and deducts all expenses together without calculating any subtotals. (p. 5-23)

Small Stock Dividend A stock dividend of less than 20% to 25% of the issued and outstanding stock. (p. 13-19)

Social Security (FICA) Tax Federal Insurance Contributions Act (FICA) tax, which is withheld from employees' pay and matched by the employer. (p. 11-8)

Software Set of programs or instructions that drives the computer to perform the work desired. (p. 7-21)

Sole Proprietorship A business with a single owner. (p. 1-7)

Source Document Provides the evidence and data for accounting transactions. (pp. 2-9, 7-3)

Special Journal An accounting journal designed to record one specific type of transaction. (p. 7-5)

Specific Identification Method An inventory costing method based on the specific cost of particular units of inventory. (p. 6-6)

Stated Interest Rate The interest rate that determines the amount of cash interest the borrower pays and the investor receives each year. (p. 14-6)

Stated Value Stock No-par stock that has been assigned an amount similar to par value. (p. 13-5)

Statement of Cash Flows Reports on a business's cash receipts and cash payments for a specific period. (pp. 1-20, 16-2)

Statement of Owner's Equity Shows the changes in the owner's capital account for a specific period. (p. 1-18)

Statement of Partners' Equity Summary of the changes in each partner's capital account for a specific period of time. (p. 12-8)

Stock Certificate Paper evidence of ownership in a corporation. (p. 13-3)

Stock Dividend A distribution by a corporation of its own stock to its stockholders. (p. 13-18)

Stock Split An increase in the number of issued and outstanding shares of stock coupled with a proportionate reduction in the par value of the stock. (p. 13-22)

Stockholders' Equity A corporation's equity that includes paid-in capital and retained earnings. (p. 13-6)

Straight-Line Amortization Method An amortization method that allocates an equal amount of bond discount or premium to each interest period over the life of the bond. (p. 14-12)

Straight-Line Method A depreciation method that allocates an equal amount of depreciation each year. (Cost − Residual value) / Useful life. (pp. 3-10, 10-9)

Subsidiary Company A company that is controlled by another corporation. (p. 15-10)

Subsidiary Ledger Record of accounts that provides supporting details on individual balances, the total of which appears in a general ledger account. (p. 7-6)

T-Account A summary device that is shaped like a capital T with debits posted on the left side of the vertical line and credits on the right side of the vertical line. (p. 2-6)

Temporary Account An account that relates to a particular accounting period and is closed at the end of that period—the revenues, expenses, Income Summary, and Owner, Withdrawals accounts. (p. 4-9)

Term Bonds Bonds that all mature at the same time. (p. 14-6)

Time Period Concept Assumes that a business's activities can be sliced into small time segments and that financial statements can be prepared for specific periods, such as a month, quarter, or year. (p. 3-4)

Time Value of Money Recognition that money earns interest over time. (p. 14-7)

Times-Interest-Earned Ratio Evaluates a business's ability to pay interest expense. (Net income + Income tax expense + Interest expense) / Interest expense. (pp. 11-19, 17-20)

Timing Difference Difference that arises between the balance on the bank statement and the balance on the company's books because of a time lag in recording transactions. (p. 8-19)

Trademark An asset that represents distinctive identifications of a product or service. (p. 10-27)

Trading Debt Investment A debt security that the investor plans to sell in the very near future. (p. 15-3)

Trading on the Equity Earning more income on borrowed money than the related interest expense, thereby increasing the earnings for the owners of the business. (p. 17-23)

Transaction An event that affects the financial position of the business and can be measured with faithful representation. (p. 1-12)

Treasury Stock A corporation's own stock that it has previously issued and later reacquired. (p. 13-11)

Trend Analysis A form of horizontal analysis in which percentages are computed by selecting a base period as 100% and expressing amounts for following periods as a percentage of the base period amount. (Any period amount / Base period amount) × 100. (p. 17-7)

Trial Balance A list of all ledger accounts with their balances at a point in time. (p. 2-24)

Underwriter A firm that handles the issuance of a company's stock to the public, usually assuming some of the risk by agreeing to buy the stock if the firm cannot sell all of the stock to its clients. (p. 13-7)

Unearned Revenue A liability created when a business collects cash from customers in advance of providing services or delivering goods. (p. 2-3)

Unemployment Compensation Taxes Payroll tax paid by employers to the government, which uses the cash to pay unemployment benefits to people who are out of work. (p. 11-11)

Units-of-Production Method A depreciation method that allocates a varying amount of depreciation each year based on an asset's usage. (p. 10-10)

Unlimited Personal Liability When a partnership (or a sole proprietorship) cannot pay its debts with business assets, the partners (or the proprietor) must use personal assets to meet the debt. (p. 12-3)

Useful Life Length of the service period expected from an asset. May be expressed in time or usage. (p. 10-8)

Vendor The individual or business from whom a company purchases goods. (p. 5-3)

Vertical Analysis An analysis of a financial statement that reveals the relationship of each statement item to its base amount, which is the 100% figure. (Specific item / Base amount) × 100. (p. 17-9)

Warranty An agreement that guarantees a company's product against defects. (p. 11-15)

Weighted-Average Method An inventory costing method based on the weighted-average cost per unit of inventory that is calculated after each purchase. Weighted-average cost per unit is determined by dividing the cost of goods available for sale by the number of units available. (p. 6-11)

Wholesaler A type of merchandiser who buys goods from manufacturers and then sells them to retailers. (p. 5-2)

Working Capital A measure of a business's ability to meet its short-term obligations with its current assets. Current assets − Current liabilities. (p. 17-14)

Worksheet An internal document that helps summarize data for the preparation of financial statements. (p. 3-26)

Subject Index

A

Account form, 4-7
Account numbers, 8-18
Accounting
    careers in, 1-5
    governance of, 1-6–1-11
    reasons to study, 1-1
    users of, 1-3–1-4
    uses of, 1-2–1-5
Accounting cycle, 4-17–4-18
Accounting equation, 1-10–1-11, 2-2
Accounting information systems (AISs), 7-1–7-54
    components of, 7-3–7-4
    computerized, 7-3, 7-4, 7-21–7-25
    effective, 7-2–7-3
    purchases, cash payments, and other transactions in, 7-14–7-20
    sales and cash receipts in, 7-5–7-14
Accounting software, for small businesses, 7-21
Accounts, 2-2–2-6. *See also* Bank accounts; T-account
    adjunct, 14-14
    asset, 2-3
    capital, of partners, 12-4
    contra, 3-11
    control, 7-7
    four-column, 2-22–2-23
    liability, 2-3
    permanent, 4-9
    temporary, 4-9, 4-10–4-14
    uncollectible. *See* Uncollectible accounts
Accounts payable, 11-2
Accounts Payable, 1-13
Accounts payable subsidiary ledger, 7-6–7-7, 7-16, 7-18
Accounts receivable, 9-2, 10-2
Accounts Receivable, 1-14
Accounts receivable subsidiary ledger, 7-6–7-7, 7-10, 7-13
Accounts receivable turnover ratio, 9-26, 10-26, 17-18–17-19, 17-27
Accrual basis accounting, 3-2–3-5
    concepts and principles applying to, 3-4–3-5
Accrued expenses
    adjusting entries for, 3-14–3-17
    impact on financial statements, 3-26
Accrued Liability, 2-3
Accrued revenues, 3-18–3-21
    adjusting entries for, 3-18–3-21
    impact on financial statements, 3-26
Accumulated Depreciation, 3-11
Acid-test ratio, 9-25–9-26, 10-25–10-26, 17-15–17-16, 17-26
Actual cost, 1-8
Additional paid-in capital, 13-7–13-8
Adjunct accounts, 14-14
Adjusted trial balance, 3-22–3-24
    worksheet and, 3-26–3-28

Adjusting entries, 3-2, 3-6–3-22
    impact on financial statements, 3-24–3-26
    for merchandising businesses, 5-19–5-20
    in periodic inventory system, 5-33–5-36
    worksheet and, 3-26–3-28
Adjusting the books, 3-1
Administrative expenses, 5-26
Admission of a partner, 12-14–12-17
    by contributing to partnership, 12-15–12-17
    by purchasing existing partner's interest, 12-14–12-15
Adverse opinions, 17-3
Aging-of-receivables method, 9-16–9-17, 9-18, 10-16–10-17, 10-18
Allowance for Bad Debts, 9-8, 10-8
Allowance for Doubtful Accounts, 9-8, 10-8
Allowance for Uncollectible Accounts, 9-8, 10-8
Allowance method, 9-8–9-18, 10-8–10-18
    direct write-off method compared with, 9-11, 10-11
    estimating and recording bad debts expense using, 9-12–9-17, 10-12–10-17
    income statement approach vs. balance sheet approach with, 9-17–9-18, 10-17–10-18
    recording bad debts expense using, 9-8–9-9, 10-8–10-9
    recovery of accounts previously written off using, 9-10–9-11, 10-10–10-11
    writing off uncollectible accounts using, 9-9–9-10, 10-9–10-10
American Institute of Certified Public Accountants (AICPA), 1-4
Amortization
    effective-interest method for, 14-28–14-31
    in statement of cash flows, 16-9
Amortization schedules, 14-2–14-3, 14-4–14-5
Amortized cost, 15-14
Annual reports, 17-3–17-4
Annual Statement Studies, 17-12
Annuities, 14-22
    future value of, 14-27, A-4
    present value of, 14-24–14-25, A-2
Appropriations of retained earnings, 13-26
Articles of partnership, 12-2
Asset accounts, 2-3
Asset turnover ratio, 17-22, 17-27
Assets, 1-11, 2-2
    current, 4-5, 15-12, 16-10–16-11
    fixed. *See* Property, plant, and equipment
    intangible, 4-5
    long-term, 4-5, 15-12
    other than cash, issuing stock for, 13-9
    partner withdrawal of, 12-12–12-13
    plant. *See* Property, plant, and equipment
    return on, 1-22–1-23, 15-16–15-17
    sale of, liquidation of a partnership and, 12-23–12-25
    total, rate of return on, 7-21–7-22, 7-27, 15-16–15-17
Auditors, 8-4
Auditor's report, 17-3
Audits, 1-9, 8-5

I-1

Subject Index

Authorized stock, 13-3
Available-for-sale (AFS) debt investments, 15-4, 15-12–15-14, 15-15

B

Bad checks, 8-20, 8-22
Bad debts expense, 9-6, 10-6
Balance, normal, 2-7–2-8
Balance sheet, 1-17, 1-19, 4-2
   account form of, 4-7
   classified, 4-4–4-7
   horizontal analysis of, 17-6–17-7
   income costing methods and, 6-15–6-16
   liabilities on, 14-18–14-20
   of merchandising businesses, 5-26
   report form of, 4-7
   vertical analysis of, 17-10
   worksheets and, 4-7
Balance sheet approaches, for estimating and recording bad debts expense, 9-13–9-18, 10-13–10-18
Bank accounts, as control devices, 8-17–8-24
Bank checks, 2-10
Bank collections, 8-20
Bank errors, 8-20
Bank reconciliations, 8-19–8-22
   journalizing transactions from, 8-23–8-24
Bank statements, 8-18
Base period, 17-5
Benchmarking, 17-12–17-13
Benefits, 11-6
Bills, 5-5
Bondholders, 14-5
Bonds, 14-5–14-18. *See also* Debt securities
   callable, 14-17
   carrying amount (value) of, 14-12, 14-30
   debentures as, 14-6
   interest rates on, 14-8–14-9
   issuance of, stock issuance vs., 14-9–14-10
   prices of, 14-7
   secured, 14-6
   serial, 14-6
   term, 14-6
Bonds payable, 14-1, 14-5
   discount on, 14-7
   effective-interest amortization method and, 14-28–14-31
   issued at a discount, 14-11–14-13
   issued at a premium, 14-14–14-16
   issued at face value, 14-10–14-11
   premium on, 14-7
   present value of, 14-25–14-26
   retirement of, 14-16–14-18
   straight-line amortization method for, 14-10–14-16
Bonus plans, 11-14–11-15
Bonuses
   as employee compensation, 11-6
   withdrawal of a partner and. *See* Withdrawal of a partner

Book errors, 8-21
Book value, 3-12
Businesses. *See also* Corporations; Partnerships
   evaluating performance of. *See* Evaluating business performance
   small, accounting software for, 7-21
   types of, compared, 1-7, 12-6
   as users of accounting information, 1-3

C

Callable bonds, 14-17
Canceled checks, 8-18
Capital, 1-8
   legal, 13-15
   owner's, 1-10
   paid-in (contributed), 13-6
   working, 17-14–17-15, 17-26
Capital accounts, of partners, 12-4
Capital balances, allocation of profits and losses based on, 12-10–12-12
Capital deficiency, sale of assets at a loss with, liquidation of a partnership and, 12-23–12-25
Capital stock, 13-3, 13-5
Carrying amount (value) of bonds, 14-12, 14-30
Cash
   net, provided by operating activities, 16-26
   net change in, in statement of cash flows, 16-18
   partner withdrawal of, 12-12–12-13
   petty, 8-11–8-14
Cash balances, net change in, in statement of cash flows, 16-18
Cash basis accounting, 3-2–3-3
Cash collections, from customers, 16-22
Cash disbursements journal, 7-16
Cash equivalents, 8-24
Cash flows, 16-2. *See also* Statement of cash flows
   classification of, 16-3–16-4
   from financing activities, 16-14–16-17
   free, 16-20–16-21
   future, discounting, 14-24
   from investing activities, 16-12–16-14
   from operating activities, 16-8–16-12, 16-22–16-27
   positive, creating, 16-11
Cash payments
   internal control procedures for, 8-9–8-11
   recording in cash payments journal, 7-18
Cash payments journal, 7-5, 7-6, 7-16–7-19
Cash ratio, 8-24–8-25, 17-15
Cash receipts
   of dividend revenue, 16-23
   of interest revenue, 16-23
   internal control procedures for, 8-7–8-9
   in manual accounting information systems, 7-5–7-14
   recording in cash receipts journal, 7-12–7-13
Cash receipts journal, 7-5, 7-6, 7-10–7-14
   posting from, 7-13–7-14
   recording cash receipts in, 7-12–7-13

Cash sales, in perpetual inventory system, 5-12–5-13
Certified Financial Planners (CFPs), 1-5
Certified fraud examiner (CFE), 2-1
Certified Management Accountants (CMAs), 1-4
Certified Public Accountants (CPAs), 1-4
Chart of accounts, 2-4–2-5
Chartered Global Management Accountant (CGMA) designation, 1-4
Check register, 7-16
Checks, 8-17–8-18
   canceled, 8-18
   cash payments by, 8-9–8-11
   nonsufficient funds (hot or bad), 8-20, 8-22
   outstanding, 8-19–8-20, 8-22
Classified balance sheet, 4-4–4-7
Closing entries, 4-10
   in periodic inventory system, 5-33–5-36
Closing process, 4-9–4-15
   for merchandising businesses, 5-20–5-22
Cloud computing, 7-21
Collection period, 9-26, 10-26, 17-19, 17-27
   decreasing, 9-4–9-5, 10-4–10-5
Collusion, 8-6–8-7
Commissions, 11-6
Committee of Sponsoring Organizations (COSO), 8-2
Common-size statements, 17-11–17-12
Common stock, 13-5
   declaring and paying dividends on, 13-16
   earnings per share of, 13-24–13-25
   issuance of. *See* Stock issuance
   in statement of cash flows, 16-15
Compatibility of accounting information systems, 7-3
Compound interest, 14-22
Compound journal entries, 2-15
Comprehensive income, 15-13–15-14
Computerized accounting information systems, 7-3, 7-4, 7-21–7-25
Conservatism, merchandise inventory and, 6-3
Consistency principle, merchandise inventory and, 6-2
Consolidated statements, 15-10
Consolidation accounting, 15-10
Contingent liabilities, 11-17–11-18
Continuing operations, on corporate income statement, 13-24
Contra accounts, 3-11
Contributed capital, 13-6
Control. *See also* Internal control
   in accounting information systems, 7-3
   over merchandise inventory, 6-3–6-4
Control accounts, 7-7
Control procedures, 8-3
Controller, 8-4
Controlling interest equity investments, 15-4, 15-15
Corporations, 1-7, 13-1–13-58
   advantages and disadvantages of, 13-3
   annual reports of, 17-3–17-4
   bonds issued by. *See* Bonds; Bonds payable; Debt securities
   characteristics of, 13-2–13-3
   evaluating performance of, 13-27–13-29

   financial reports of, 17-2–17-4
   income statement of, 13-23–13-25
   privately held, 13-2
   public, 13-2
   S corporations, 12-6
   statement of retained earnings of, 13-25–13-26
   statement of stockholders' equity of, 13-26–13-27
   stock of. *See* Dividends; Equity securities; Stock; Stock issuance; Stock splits; Treasury stock
   stockholders' equity and. *See* Stockholders' equity
   stockholders of. *See* Stockholders
Cost of goods available for sale, 6-8
Cost of Goods Sold (COGS), 5-3
Cost of Sales, 5-3
Cost principle, 1-8
Costs
   amortized, 15-14
   historical, 1-8
   of merchandise inventory, 6-1
   net, of inventory purchased, in perpetual inventory system, 5-11–5-12
Credit, 2-6–2-8
Credit card sales, 9-5, 10-5
   internal controls for, 8-14–8-16
   in perpetual inventory system, 5-12–5-13
Credit memoranda, 8-20
Credit terms, 5-8
Creditors, 9-2, 9-18, 10-2, 10-18
   as users of accounting information, 1-4
Cryptocurrencies, 8-6
Cumulative preferred stock, 13-17
Current assets, 4-5, 15-12
   changes in, in statement of cash flows, 16-10–16-11
Current liabilities, 4-5, 11-1–11-6
   accounts payable as, 11-2
   changes in, in statement of cash flows, 16-10–16-11
   current portion of long-term notes payable as, 11-5
   estimated, 11-14–11-17
   evaluating ability to pay, 17-14–17-16, 17-26
   sales tax payable as, 11-3–11-4
   short-term notes payable as, 11-4–11-5
   unearned revenue as, 11-3–11-4
Current maturity, 11-5
Current ratio, 4-19–4-20, 17-16, 17-26
Customers, 7-7

D

Data analytics, 1-6
   chart of accounts and, 2-5
   cryptocurrencies and, 8-6
   free cash flow and, 16-21
   merchandise inventory and, 6-4
Date of record, 13-15
Days' sales in inventory, 6-22–6-23, 17-17–17-18, 17-27
Days' sales in receivables, 9-26, 10-26, 17-19, 17-27

Debentures, 14-6
Debit, 2-6–2-8
Debit card sales, 9-5, 10-5
    internal controls for, 8-14–8-16
Debit memoranda, 8-20
Debt, purchases with, 2-27
Debt ratio, 17-19–17-20, 17-27
    evaluating business performance using, 2-26–2-27
Debt securities, 15-1, 15-5–15-6
    classification of, 15-3–15-4
    disposition at maturity, 15-6
    equity securities vs., 15-2
    interest revenue and, 15-6
    purchase of, 15-5
    reporting of, 15-10–15-14
    trading, 15-3, 15-4, 15-10–15-12, 15-15
Debt to equity ratio, 14-20–14-21, 17-20, 17-27
Debtors, 9-2, 9-18, 10-2, 10-18
Declaration date, 13-15
Defaulting on a note, 9-23, 10-23
Deferred expenses
    adjusting entries for, 3-7–3-13
    alternative method of recording, 3-28–3-29
    impact on financial statements, 3-26
Deferred revenue, 2-3, 3-13–3-14, 11-3–11-4
    adjusting entries for, 3-13–3-14
    alternative method of recording, 3-30–3-31
    dividend, cash receipts of, 16-23
    impact on financial statements, 3-26
Deficits, 13-25
Depletion, in statement of cash flows, 16-9
Deposit tickets, 8-17
Deposits in transit, 8-19, 8-22
Depreciation, 3-9–3-13
    in statement of cash flows, 16-9
Direct method for statement of cash flows, 16-5, 16-21–16-28
Direct write-off method, 9-6–9-7, 10-6–10-7
    allowance method compared with, 9-11, 10-11
    limitation of, 9-7, 10-7
    recording and writing off uncollectible accounts using, 9-6, 10-6
    recovery of accounts previously written off using, 9-6–9-7, 10-6–10-7
Disclosure principle, merchandise inventory and, 6-2–6-3
Discontinued operations, on corporate income statement, 13-24
Discount on bonds payable, 14-7, 14-8, 14-11–14-13
    effective-interest amortization method for, 14-28–14-29
    present value of bonds issued at a discount and, 14-25–14-26
Discounting future cash flows, 14-24
Dishonoring notes, 9-23, 10-23
Disposition
    of debt securities, 15-6, 15-12
    of equity securities, 15-7–15-8, 15-9–15-10
Dissolution, of a partnership, 12-3
Dividend payout, 17-25, 17-27
Dividend revenue, cash receipts of, 16-23
Dividend yield, 17-24–17-25, 17-27

Dividends, 13-2, 13-3, 13-5
    cash, 13-15–13-18, 13-22, 16-23
    on common stock, declaring and paying, 13-16
    on equity securities, 15-7, 15-8–15-9
    payments of, in statement of cash flows, 16-16–16-17
    on preferred stock, declaring and paying, 13-16–13-18
    stock, 13-18–13-22
Dividends in arrears, 13-17
Documents, 8-5
    source, 7-3–7-4
Dollar value bias, 17-11
Double-entry system, 2-6–2-9
    T-account and, 2-6–2-9
Doubtful accounts expense, 9-6, 10-6
Drawings, 1-11
Due date, 9-19, 10-19

E

E-commerce, 8-5, 8-6
Earnings per share (EPS), 13-27–13-28, 17-23–17-24, 17-27
    on corporate income statement, 13-24–13-25
Economic entity assumption, 1-7–1-8
Effective-interest amortization method, 14-28–14-31
    for bond discount, 14-28–14-29
    for bond premium, 14-29–14-30
Effective interest rate, 14-8–14-9
Electronic data interchange (EDI), 8-11
Electronic devices, 8-5
Electronic funds transfers (EFTs), 8-18, 8-20, 8-22
Employee compensation. See Payroll
Employee payroll withholding deductions, 11-7–11-10
    for income tax, 11-7–11-8
    optional, 11-7, 11-9
    payment of, 11-13
    required, 11-7
    for Social Security (FICA) tax, 11-8–11-9
Employer payroll taxes, 11-11–11-12
    payment of, 11-13
Encryption, 8-5
Enterprise resource planning (ERP) systems, 7-21
Environment, internal controls and, 8-4
Equity, 1-10–1-11, 2-4, 4-6
    stockholders'. See Stockholders' equity
    trading on, 17-23
Equity method, 15-8–15-10
Equity securities, 15-1, 15-7–15-10. See also Stock
    classification of, 15-4
    with controlling interest, consolidation method for, 15-10
    debt securities vs., 15-2
    disposition of, 15-7–15-8, 15-9–15-10
    dividend revenue and, 15-7, 15-8–15-9
    with no significant influence, fair value method for, 15-7–15-8, 15-14
    purchase of, 15-7, 15-8
    share of net income and, 15-8–15-9
    with significant influence, equity method for, 15-8–15-10

Errors
    bank, 8-20
    book, 8-21
    correcting, 7-22
    merchandise inventory, financial statements and, 6-19–6-21
    slide, 2-26
    transposition, 2-26
    in trial balance, correcting, 2-25–2-26
Estimated current liabilities, 11-14–11-17
Estimated Returns Inventory, 5-15
Estimation, of bad debts expense, with allowance method, 9-12–9-17, 10-12–10-17
Ethics, 1-9
    debt classification and, 17-16
    debt issuance and, 14-21
    error correction and, 7-22
    gifts from vendors and, 5-9
    merchandise inventory and, 6-21
    partners' purchases and, 12-3
    receipts and, 2-10
    recording revenue early and, 4-20
    stock tips and, 15-3
    timing of recording accrued expenses and, 3-17
    uncollectible accounts estimates and, 9-9, 10-9
    valuation of a building and, 13-9
Evaluated receipts settlement (ERS), 8-11
Evaluating business performance
    accounts receivable turnover ratio for, 9-26, 10-26, 17-18–17-19
    acid-test ratio for, 9-25–9-26, 10-25–10-26, 17-15–17-16
    asset turnover ratio for, 17-22
    cash ratio for, 8-24–8-25, 17-15
    current ratio for, 4-19–4-20, 17-16
    days' sales in inventory for, 6-21–6-23, 17-17–17-18
    days' sales in receivables for, 9-26, 10-26, 17-19
    debt ratio for, 2-26–2-27, 17-19–17-20
    debt to equity ratio for, 14-20–14-21, 17-20
    dividend payout for, 17-25
    dividend yield for, 17-24–17-25
    earnings per share for, 13-27–13-28, 17-23–17-24
    financial statements for, 1-22–1-23
    free cash flow for, 16-20–16-21
    gross profit percentage for, 5-27–5-28, 17-18
    horizontal analysis for, 17-4–17-8
    inventory turnover for, 6-21–6-23, 17-17
    price/earnings ratio for, 13-28, 17-24
    profit margin ratio for, 17-21
    rate of return on common stockholders' equity for, 13-28–13-29, 17-22–17-23
    rate of return on total assets for, 15-16–15-17, 17-21–17-22
    times-interest-earned ratio for, 11-19, 17-20–17-21
    trend analysis for, 17-7–17-8
    vertical analysis for, 17-8–17-10
    working capital and, 17-14–17-15
Expense recognition principle, 3-5
Expenses, 1-11
    accrued. *See* Accrued expenses
    administrative, 5-26
    bad debts, 9-6
    deferred. *See* Deferred expenses
    doubtful accounts, 9-6, 10-6
    income tax, 13-23, 16-25–16-26
    interest. *See* Interest expense
    non-cash, 16-26
    operating, 5-4
    other, 5-26
    selling, 5-25
    uncollectible accounts (bad debts, doubtful accounts), 9-6, 10-6
External auditors, 8-4

F

Face value
    of a bond, 14-6
    issuing bonds payable at, 14-10–14-11
Factors, 9-5, 10-5
Fair value, 15-10–15-11
Fair value method, 15-7–15-8
    for available-for-sale debt investments, 15-12–15-14
    for equity investments with no significant influence, 15-14
    for trading debt investments, 15-10–15-12
Faithful representation, 1-7
Federal Insurance Contributions Act (FICA), withholding for, 11-8–11-9
Federal Unemployment Tax Act (FUTA), 11-11–11-12
Financial accounting, managerial accounting vs., 1-3
Financial Accounting Standards Board (FASB), 1-6
Financial leverage, 14-10
Financial statement analysis, 17-1–17-13
    corporate financial reports and, 17-2–17-4
    horizontal, 17-4–17-8
    purpose of, 17-2
    red flags in, 17-26–17-27
    tools of, 17-2
    trend, 17-7–17-8
    vertical, 17-8–17-10
Financial statements, 1-17–1-21. *See also specific financial statements*
    analysis of. *See* Financial statement analysis
    in annual report, 17-4
    common-size, 17-11–17-12
    corporate, 13-23–13-27
    debt and equity securities and, 15-15
    evaluating business performance using, 1-22–1-23
    impact of adjusting entries on, 3-24–3-26
    merchandise inventory errors and, 6-19–6-21
    of merchandising businesses, 5-23–5-26
    notes to, 17-4
    order of preparing, 4-2
    of partnerships, 12-8
    in periodic inventory system, 5-33
    preparing from trial balance, 2-24–2-25
    relationships among, 4-3–4-4
    viewing in QuickBooks, 7-24
    worksheets and, 4-7–4-9

Financing activities, 1-20, 16-3
  cash flows from, 16-14–16-17
  non-cash, 16-4, 16-18–16-20
Firewalls, 8-5
First-in, first-out (FIFO) method, 6-7–6-9
  periodic inventory system and, 6-25
  perpetual inventory system and, 6-7–6-9
Fiscal year, 3-4
Fixed assets. *See* Property, plant, and equipment
Flexibility, of accounting information systems, 7-3
FOB destination, 5-10
FOB shipping point, 5-10
Footing, 7-10
Form 10-K, 17-3
Form 10-Q, 17-3
Four-column accounts, 2-22–2-23
Free cash flow, 16-20–16-21
Freight in, 5-10, 5-11
  within discount period, 5-11
Freight out, 5-10
  in perpetual inventory system, 5-16–5-17
Future value, 14-8, 14-23–14-24
  of an annuity, 14-27
  of a lump sum, 14-26–14-27
  tables of, A-3–A-4

G

Gains, from non-operating activities, 16-9–16-10, 16-26
General journal, 7-5, 7-6, 7-19
General ledger
  posting from cash payments journal to, 7-19
  posting from cash receipts journal to, 7-10, 7-13
  posting from purchases journal to, 7-16
  posting from sales journal to, 7-10
General partners, 12-4
General partnerships, 12-4
Generally Accepted Accounting Principles (GAAP), 1-6–1-7, 1-8
Gifts, from vendors, 5-9
Going concern assumption, 1-8
Gross margin (gross profit), 5-4, 17-18, 17-27
Gross pay, 11-7
Gross profit (gross margin), 5-4, 17-18, 17-27
Gross profit percentage, 15-27, 17-18
  for evaluating business performance, 5-27–5-28

H

Hardware, 7-21
Health benefits, 11-15
Held-to-maturity (HTM) debt investments, 15-3, 15-4, 15-14, 15-15
Historical cost, 1-8
Horizontal analysis, 15-4–15-8
  of balance sheet, 15-6–15-7
  of income statement, 15-5–15-6
  trend analysis as, 15-7–15-8
Hot checks, 8-20, 8-22

I

Imprest system, 8-12
Income
  comprehensive, 15-13–15-14
  net. *See* Net income
  operating (from operations), 5-26
  other, 5-26
Income statement, 1-17, 1-18, 4-2
  common-size, 15-11–15-12
  corporate, 13-23–13-25
  horizontal analysis of, 15-5–15-6
  income costing methods and, 6-14–6-15
  of merchandising businesses, 5-23–5-26
  multi-step, 5-24–5-26
  single-step, 5-23–5-24
  vertical analysis of, 15-9
  worksheets and, 4-7
Income statement approach, for estimating and recording bad debts expense, 9-12–9-13, 9-17–9-18, 10-12–10-13, 10-17–10-18
Income Summary, 4-10
Income tax expense
  corporate income statement and, 13-23
  payments for, 16-25–16-26
Income tax withholding, 11-7–11-8
Income taxes
  of corporations, 13-2–13-3
  partnerships and, 12-4
Indirect method, for statement of cash flows, 16-5–16-20, 16-28–16-31
Individuals, as users of accounting information, 1-3
Industry average, benchmarking against, 15-12
Inflation, 1-8
Information systems, 8-3–8-4
Input devices, in accounting information systems, 7-3
Insider trading, 15-3
Institute of Management Accountants (IMA), 1-4
Intangible assets, 4-5
Interest
  on checking accounts, 8-20, 8-22
  on notes receivable, 9-18, 9-20–9-23, 10-18, 10-20–10-23
  simple vs. compound, 14-22
Interest-coverage ratio, 11-19, 15-20–15-21, 15-27
Interest expense
  on bonds issued at a discount, 14-12
  on bonds issued at a premium, 14-14
  payments for, 16-25–16-26
Interest period, of notes receivable, 9-19, 10-19
Interest rates
  on bonds, 14-6, 14-8–14-9
  market (effective), 14-8–14-9, 14-30
  on notes receivable, 9-19, 10-19
  stated, 14-6
Interest revenue
  cash receipts of, 16-23
  debt securities and, 15-6

Internal auditors, 8-4
Internal control, 8-1–8-53
  bank accounts as control devices and, 8-17–8-24
  for cash payments, 8-9–8-11
  for cash receipts, 8-7–8-9
  components of, 8-3–8-4
  for debit and credit card sales, 8-14–8-16
  limitations of, 8-6–8-7
  over payroll, 11-13
  over receivables, 9-3, 10-3
  for petty cash, 8-11–8-14
  procedures for, 8-4–8-6
  Sarbanes-Oxley Act and, 8-2–8-3
Internal control reports, 8-3
International Accounting Standards Board (IASB), 1-8
International Financial Reporting Standards (IFRS), 1-3, 1-8
  cash flow activities and, 16-3, 16-5
  financial statements and, 4-2
  on internal controls, 8-3
  inventory costing and, 6-10
  receivable recognition and reporting and, 9-9, 10-9
Inventory. *See* Merchandise inventory
Inventory costing methods, 6-6–6-14
  financial statements and, 6-14–6-17
  first-in, first-out method as, 6-7–6-9
  last-in, first-out method as, 6-9–6-11
  specific identification method as, 6-6–6-7
  weighted-average method as, 6-11–6-14
Inventory shrinkage, adjusting for, 5-20
Inventory turnover, 6-22–6-23, 15-17, 15-27
Investees, 15-2
Investing activities, 1-20, 16-3
  cash flows from, 16-12–16-14
  non-cash, 16-4, 16-18–16-20
Investments, 15-1–15-33. *See also* Bonds; Debt securities; Equity securities; Stock
  classification and reporting of, 15-3–15-4
  evaluating stock as, 15-24–15-25, 15-27
  long-term, 4-5, 15-3
  reasons for making, 15-1, 15-2–15-3
  short-term, 15-3
Investors, 15-2
  as users of accounting information, 1-4
Invoices, 5-5
Issue price, 13-7
Issued stock, 13-3

J

Journal entries
  for accrued expenses, 3-14–3-17
  for accrued revenues, 3-18–3-21
  adjusting. *See* Adjusting entries
  for bank reconciliations, 8-23–8-24
  closing. *See* Closing entries
  compound, 2-15
  for deferred expenses, 3-7–3-13
  for deferred revenues, 3-13–3-14
  under first-in, first-out method, 6-9
  under last-in, first-out method, 6-10–6-11
  for payroll, 11-10–11-11
  reversing, 4-21–4-24
  under weighted-average method, 6-13
Journalizing, 2-10–2-20
Journals, 2-10
  special, 7-5–7-6

K

Key competitors, benchmarking against, 15-12

L

Large stock dividends, 13-19, 13-21–13-22
Last-in, first-out (LIFO) method, 6-9–6-11
  periodic inventory system and, 6-26
  perpetual inventory system and, 6-9–6-11
Ledgers, 2-5
  general. *See* General ledger
  subsidiary, 7-6–7-7
Legal capital, 13-15
Leverage, 15-23
Liabilities, 1-11, 2-2, 11-2
  accrued, 2-3
  on balance sheet, 14-18–14-20
  contingent, 11-17–11-18
  current. *See* Current liabilities
  long-term. *See* Long-term liabilities
Liability, unlimited, of partners, 12-3
Liability accounts, 2-3
Limited liability companies (LLCs), 1-7, 12-5–12-6
Limited liability partnerships (LLPs), 12-5
Limited life, of a partnership, 12-3
Limited partners, 12-5
Limited partnerships (LPs), 12-4–12-5
Liquidation of a corporation, 13-5
Liquidation of a partnership, 12-20–12-26
  sale of assets at a gain and, 12-20–12-22
  sale of assets at a loss with capital deficiency and, 12-23–12-25
Liquidity, 4-5
Lock-box systems, 8-8
Long-term assets, 4-5, 15-12
Long-term debt, evaluating ability to pay, 15-19–15-21, 15-27
Long-term investments, 4-5, 15-3
Long-term liabilities, 4-5, 11-2, 14-1–14-52
  on balance sheet, 14-18–14-20
  bonds payable as. *See* Bonds payable
  mortgages payable as, 14-3–14-5
  notes payable as, 14-2–14-3
  in statement of cash flows, 16-14–16-15
Long-term notes payable, current portion of, 11-5

Losses
    net. *See* Net losses
    from non-operating activities, 16-9–16-10, 16-26
    of partnerships, allocation of, 12-8–12-14
Lower-of-cost-or-market (LCM) rule, 6-17–6-18
    adjusting entry for merchandise inventory and, 6-17–6-18
    computing the lower-of-cost-or-market and, 6-17
Lump sum
    future value of, 14-26–14-27
    present value of, 14-24

M

Maker
    of a check, 8-17
    of notes receivable, 9-18, 10-18
Management's discussion and analysis of financial condition and results of operations (MD&A), 15-3
Managerial accounting, financial accounting vs., 1-3
Market interest rate, 14-8–14-9, 14-30
Matching principle, 3-5
Materiality concept, merchandise inventory and, 6-3
Maturity date, 11-5
    of bonds, 14-6
    of notes receivable, 9-2, 9-19–9-20, 10-2, 10-19–10-20
Maturity value
    of bonds, 14-6
    of notes receivable, 9-19, 10-19
Medicare, withholding for, 11-8
Memorandum entries, 13-22
Merchandise inventory, 5-1, 5-2, 6-1–6-55
    accounting principles related to, 6-2–6-3
    adjusting for estimated sales returns, 5-20–5-21
    control over, 6-3–6-4
    cost of, 6-1
    costing methods for. *See* Inventory costing methods
    data analytics in, 6-4
    errors in, financial statements and, 6-19–6-21
    evaluating ability to sell, 15-17–15-19, 15-27
    inventory systems for. *See* Periodic inventory system; Perpetual inventory system
    lower-of-cost-or-market rule and, 6-17–6-18
    monitoring levels of, 6-21–6-23
    periodic inventory system and, 6-23–6-27
    perpetual inventory system and, 6-5–6-14
    shrinkage of, adjusting for, 5-20
Merchandisers, 5-1–5-80
    adjusting entries for, 5-10–5-20
    closing accounts of, 5-20–5-22
    closing entries for, 5-20–5-22
    financial statements for, 5-23–5-26
    inventory and. *See* Merchandise inventory
    multiple performance obligations and, 5-28–5-29
    operating cycle of, 5-2–5-4
Monetary unit assumption, 1-8
Money, time value of, 14-7–14-8
Monitoring of controls, 8-4
Mortgages payable, 14-3–14-5
Moving-average method, 6-11–6-14
Multi-step income statement, 5-24–5-26
Multiple performance obligations, in perpetual inventory system, 5-28–5-29
Mutual agency, 12-3

N

Net cash, provided by operating activities, 16-26
Net cost, of inventory purchased
    in periodic inventory system, 5-32
    in perpetual inventory system, 5-11–5-12
Net income, 1-11
    closing temporary accounts and, 4-10–4-12
    determining, 4-8
    share of, equity securities and, 15-8–15-9
Net losses, 1-11
    closing temporary accounts and, 4-13
    determining, 4-8
Net pay, 11-7
Net realizable value, 9-8, 10-8
Networks, 7-21
No-par stock, 13-5
    issuing, 13-8
No significant influence equity investments, 15-4, 15-15
Nominal accounts. *See* Temporary accounts
Non-cash expenses, 16-26
Non-cash investing and financing activities, 16-4
    in statement of cash flows, 16-18–16-20
Non-operating activities, gains and losses from, 16-9–16-10, 16-26
Noncumulative preferred stock, 13-17
Nonsufficient funds (NSF) checks, 8-20, 8-22
Normal balance, 2-7–2-8
Note term, 9-19, 10-19
Notes payable
    current portion of, 14-2
    long-term, current portion of, 11-5, 14-2–14-3
    short-term, 11-4–11-5
Notes Payable, 2-3
Notes receivable, 9-2–9-3, 9-18–9-24, 10-2–10-3, 10-18–10-24
    dishonored, recording, 9-23, 10-23
    honored, recording, 9-21–9-23, 10-21–10-23
    interest on, 9-18, 9-20–9-23, 10-18, 10-20–10-23
    maturity date of, 9-2, 9-19–9-20, 10-2, 10-19–10-20
Notes Receivable, 2-3

O

OASDI, withholding for, 11-8
Operating activities, 1-20, 16-3
    cash flows from, 16-8–16-12, 16-22–16-27
    evaluating cash flows from, 16-11–16-12
    formats for, 16-5

Operating cycle, 4-5
  of a merchandising business, 5-2–5-3
Operating expenses, 5-4
Operating income, 5-26
Operational assets. *See* Property, plant, and equipment
Other income and expenses, 5-26
Other receivables, 9-3, 10-3
Outstanding checks, 8-19–8-20, 8-22
Outstanding stock, 13-4
Overtime, 11-6
Owner's capital, 1-10
Owner's equity, 1-10, 1-10–1-11, 2-4, 4-6
Owner's withdrawals, 1-11

P

Paid-in capital, 13-6
Paid-in Capital in Excess of Par, 13-7–13-8
Par value, 13-5
  of a bond, 14-6
Parent company, 15-10
Partnership agreement, 12-2
Partnerships, 1-7, 12-1–12-52
  admission of a partner, 12-14–12-17
  advantages and disadvantages of, 12-4
  allocation of profits and losses of, 12-8–12-14
  characteristics of, 12-2–12-4
  financial statements of, 12-8
  general, 12-4
  limited, 12-4–12-5
  liquidation of. *See* Liquidation of a partnership
  start-up of, 12-7
  withdrawal of a partner, 12-17–12-19
Pathways Vision Model, 1-2–1-3
Payables, 2-2
Payees
  of checks, 8-17
  of notes receivable, 9-18, 10-18
Payment date, 13-15
Payment terms, 5-8
Payments
  to employees, 16-25
  for interest expense and income tax expense, 16-25–16-26
  to suppliers, 16-23–16-25
Payroll, 11-6–11-14
  employee withholding deductions and, 11-7–11-10
  employer payroll taxes and, 11-11–11-12
  gross pay and net (take-home) pay and, 11-7
  internal control over, 11-13
  journalizing, 11-10–11-11
  payment of employee payroll withholding deductions and, 11-13
  payment of employer payroll taxes and, 11-13
Payroll register, 11-9–11-10
Pension plans, 11-15

Percent-of-receivables method, for estimating and recording bad debts expense, 9-13–9-16, 9-18, 10-13–10-16, 10-18
Percent-of-sales method, 9-12–9-13, 10-12–10-13
Periodic inventory system, 5-4, 5-30–5-36, 6-23–6-27
  adjusting entries in, 5-33–5-36
  closing entries in, 5-33–5-36
  financial statements in, 5-33
  first-in, first-out method and, 6-25
  last-in, first-out method and, 6-26
  net cost of inventory purchased in, 5-32
  purchase discounts in, 5-31
  purchase returns and allowances in, 5-30–5-31
  purchases in, 5-30
  sales in, 5-32
  transportation costs in, 5-32
  weighted-average method and, 6-26
Permanent accounts, 4-9
Perpetual inventory system, 5-4–5-18, 6-5–6-14
  cash and credit card sales in, 5-12–5-13
  first-in, first-out method and, 6-7–6-9
  last-in, first-out method and, 6-9–6-11
  multiple performance obligations in, 5-28–5-29
  net cost of inventory purchased in, 5-11–5-12
  purchase allowances in, 5-7
  purchase discounts in, 5-8–5-9
  purchase returns in, 5-7
  purchases in, 5-6–5-7
  sales on account with discount in, 5-16–5-17
  sales on account with no discount in, 5-13–5-14
  sales returns and allowances in, 5-14–5-16
  specific identification method and, 6-6–6-7
  transportation costs in, 5-10–5-11, 5-18
  weighted-average method and, 6-11–6-14
Petty cash, 8-11
  internal control procedures for, 8-11–8-14
Petty cash fund, 8-12
  changing the amount of, 8-14
  replenishing, 8-12–8-14
Plant assets. *See* Property, plant, and equipment
Post-closing trial balance, 4-16–4-17
Posting, 2-10–2-20
  from cash payments journal, 7-18–7-19
  from cash receipts journal, 7-13–7-14
  ledger accounts after, 2-20–2-22
  from purchases journal, 7-16
  from sales journal, 7-10
Preemptive rights, 13-5
Preferred stock, 13-5
  cumulative, 13-17
  declaring and paying dividends on, 13-16–13-18
  issuing, 13-10
  noncumulative, 13-17
Premium, issuing common stock at, 13-7–13-8
Premium on bonds payable, 14-7, 14-8, 14-14–14-16
  effective-interest amortization method for, 14-29–14-30
  present value of bonds issued at a premium and, 14-26

Prepaid Expense, 2-3
Prepaid expenses. *See* Deferred expenses
Present value, 14-8, 14-23–14-24
    of an annuity, 14-24–14-25, A-2
    of bonds payable, 14-25–14-26
    of a lump sum, 14-24
    tables of, A-1–A-2
Price/earnings ratio, 13-28, 15-24, 15-27
Prices, of bonds, 14-7
Principal, of notes receivable, 9-18, 10-18
Principal of a bond, 14-6
Prior-period adjustments, 13-26
Privately held corporations, 13-2
Profit margin ratio, 15-21, 15-27
Profitability, evaluating, 15-21–15-24, 15-27
Profits, of partnerships, allocation of, 12-8–12-14
Promissory notes, 9-18, 10-18, 11-5. *See also* Notes receivable
Property, plant, and equipment, 3-9, 4-5
    depreciation of, 3-9–3-13, 16-9
Public accounting firms, reports of, 15-3
Public companies, 8-2
Public Company Accounting Oversight Board (PCAOB), 1-9
Public corporations, 13-2
Purchase allowances
    in periodic inventory system, 5-30–5-31
    in perpetual inventory system, 5-7
Purchase discounts
    in periodic inventory system, 5-31
    in perpetual inventory system, 5-8–5-9
Purchase invoices, 2-10, 5-5
Purchase returns
    in periodic inventory system, 5-30–5-31
    in perpetual inventory system, 5-7
Purchases
    on account, recording in purchases journal, 7-16
    with debt, 2-27
    of debt securities, 15-5
    of equity securities, 15-7, 15-8
    in periodic inventory system, 5-30
    in perpetual inventory system, 5-6–5-7
    of treasury stock, 13-11
Purchases journal, 7-5, 7-6, 7-14–7-16

Q

Qualified opinions, 15-3
Quick ratio, 9-25–9-26, 10-25–10-26, 15-15–15-16, 15-26
QuickBooks, 7-21, 7-22–7-24
    creating a sales invoice in, 7-22–7-23
    entering bills in, 7-23–7-24
    viewing financial statements in, 7-24

R

Rate of return on common stockholders' equity, 13-28–13-29, 15-22–15-23, 15-27

Rate of return on total assets, 15-16–15-17, 15-21–15-22, 15-27
Ratio analysis, 15-13–15-25
    of ability to pay current liabilities, 15-14–15-16
    of ability to pay long-term debt, 15-19–15-21
    of ability to sell merchandise inventory and collect receivables, 15-17–15-19
    of profitability, 15-21–15-24
Receivables, 2-2, 9-1–9-56, 10-1–10-56. *See also* Notes receivable
    decreasing collection time and credit risk and, 9-4–9-5, 10-4–10-5
    evaluating ability to collect, 15-17–15-19, 15-27
    factoring and pledging, 9-5, 10-5
    internal control over, 9-3, 10-3
    recording sales on credit and, 9-3–9-4, 10-3–10-4
    types of, 9-2–9-3, 10-2–10-3
    uncollectibles and. *See* Uncollectible accounts
Record date, 13-15
Recording transactions, 2-9–2-23
    four-column account and, 2-22–2-23
    journalizing and, 2-10–2-20
    ledger accounts after posting and, 2-20–2-22
    posting and, 2-10–2-20
    source documents and, 2-9–2-10
Refunds Payable, 5-15
Relevance, in accounting information systems, 7-3
Remittance advice, 8-7
Report form, 4-7
Residual value, 3-10
Retailers, 5-2
Retained earnings, 13-6. *See also* Statement of retained earnings
    appropriations of, 13-26
Retirement of bonds, 14-16–14-18
    at maturity, 14-16–14-17
    before maturity, 14-17–14-18
Return on assets (ROA), 1-22–1-23, 15-16–15-17
Revenue recognition principle, 3-4–3-5
Revenues, 1-10
    accrued. *See* Accrued revenues
    deferred. *See* Deferred revenue
    dividend, cash receipts of, 16-23
    earned, calculation of, 3-1
    interest, cash receipts of, 16-23
    interest, debt securities and, 15-6
    recording early, 4-20
    sales, adjusting for estimated sales returns, 5-20–5-21
    unearned. *See* Deferred revenue
Reversing entries, 4-21–4-24
Risk assessment, 8-3
Routing numbers, 8-18

S

S corporations, 12-6
Sage 50 Accounting, 7-21
Salaries, 11-6
Sales
    in manual accounting information systems, 7-5–7-14

Subject Index **I-11**

in periodic inventory system, 5-32
of treasury stock, 13-11–13-14
Sales allowances, in perpetual inventory system, 5-16
Sales discounts, in perpetual inventory system, 5-16–5-17
Sales invoices, 2-10, 5-5
Sales journal, 7-5, 7-6, 7-7–7-10
   posting from, 7-10
Sales on account
   decreasing collection time and credit risk on, 9-4–9-5, 10-4–10-5
   in perpetual inventory account, 5-13–5-14, 5-16–5-17
   in perpetual inventory system, 5-16–5-17
   recording, 7-7–7-10, 9-3–9-4, 10-3–10-4
Sales Return, 5-14
Sales returns
   estimated, adjusting for, 5-20-5-21
   in perpetual inventory account, 5-14–5-15
Sales revenue, adjusting for estimated sales returns, 5-20–5-21
Sales Revenue (Sales), 5-3, 5-12–5-13
Sales tax payable, 11-3
Sarbanes-Oxley Act (SOX), 1-9, 8-2–8-3
Secured bonds, 14-6
Securities, 15-2. *See also* Bonds; Debt securities; Equity securities; Investments; Stock
Securities and Exchange Commission (SEC), 1-6
Selling expenses, 5-25
Separation of duties, 8-4
Serial bonds, 14-6
Servers, 7-4
Service charges, 8-20, 8-22
Service Revenue, 5-3
Services, allocation of profits and losses based on, 12-10–12-12
Shareholders. *See* Stockholders
Short-term investments, 15-3
Short-term notes payable, 11-4–11-5
Signature cards, 8-17
Significant influence equity investments, 15-4, 15-15
Simple interest, 14-22
Single-step income statement, 5-23–5-24
Slide errors, 2-26
Small stock dividends, 13-19–13-21
Social Security (FICA) tax
   employer's contribution for, 11-11
   withholding for employee's contribution to, 11-8–11-9
Software, 7-21
Sole proprietorships, 1-7
Source documents, 2-9–2-10, 7-3–7-4
Special journals, 7-5–7-6
Specific identification method, 6-6–6-7
Spreadsheets, for statement of cash flows, 16-28–16-31
State Unemployment Tax Act (SUTA), 11-11–11-12
Stated interest rate, 14-6
Stated ratios, allocation of profits and losses based on, 12-9–12-12
Stated value stock, 13-5
   issuing, 13-9

Statement of cash flows, 1-17, 1-20–1-21, 16-1–16-68. *See also* Cash flows
   direct method for, 16-5, 16-21–16-28
   indirect method for, 16-5–16-20
   purpose of, 16-2
Statement of earnings. *See* Income statement
Statement of financial position. *See* Balance sheet
Statement of operations. *See* Income statement
Statement of owner's equity, 1-17, 1-18–1-19, 4-2
   of merchandising businesses, 5-26
Statement of partners' equity (statement of partners' capital), 12-8, 12-13
Statement of retained earnings, 13-25–13-26
Statement of stockholders' equity, 13-26–13-27
Stock. *See also* Equity securities
   authorized, 13-3
   capital, 13-3, 13-5
   common. *See* Common stock
   decisions regarding investment in, 1-22
   dividends on. *See* Dividends
   earnings per share of, 7-23–7-24, 7-27
   as investment, evaluating, 15-24–15-25, 15-27
   issuance of. *See* Stock issuance
   issued, 13-3
   no-par, 13-5, 13-8
   outstanding, 13-4
   par value, 13-5
   preferred. *See* Preferred stock
   of public companies, 8-2–8-3
   stated value, 13-5, 13-9
   treasury. *See* Treasury stock
Stock certificates, 13-3
Stock dividends, 13-18–13-22
   reasons to issue, 13-19
   recording, 13-19–13-22
Stock issuance, 13-6–13-10
   bond issuance vs., 14-9–14-10
   of common stock at a premium, 13-7–13-8
   of common stock at par value, 13-7
   of common stock for assets other than cash, 13-9
   of no-par common stock, 13-8
   of preferred stock, 13-10
   of stated value common stock, 13-9
Stock splits, 13-22
Stockholders, 13-2
Stockholders' equity, 13-3–13-6
   capital stock and, 13-5
   common, rate of return on, 13-28–13-29
   stockholders' rights and, 13-4–13-5
Stockouts, 6-4
Straight-line amortization method, 14-12
   bond discount and, 14-12–14-13
   bond premium and, 14-15–14-16
Straight-line method, 3-10
Straight time, 11-6

Subsidiary accounts, 9-4, 10-4
Subsidiary company, 15-10
Subsidiary ledgers, 7-6–7-7

T

T-account, 2-6–2-9
   determining balance of, 2-9
   increases and decreases in, 2-6–2-7
   normal balance of, 2-7–2-8
Take-home pay, 11-7
Taxes. *See* Employee payroll withholding deductions; Employer payroll taxes; Income tax expense; Income taxes
Taxing authorities, as users of accounting information, 1-4
Temporary accounts, 4-9
   closing, 4-10–4-14
Term bonds, 14-6
Time-and-a-half, 11-6
Time period concept, 3-4
Time value of money, 14-7–14-8, 14-21–14-27. *See also* Future value; Present value
Times-interest-earned ratio, 11-19, 15-20–15-21, 15-27
Timing differences, 8-19
Total assets, rate of return on, 15-16–15-17
Trade receivables. *See* Accounts receivable
Trading debt securities, 15-3, 15-4, 15-10–15-12, 15-15
Trading on the equity, 15-23
Transactions, 1-11–1-12
   analysis of, 1-12–1-16
   recording. *See* Recording transactions
Transportation costs
   in periodic inventory system, 5-32
   in perpetual inventory system, 5-10–5-11
Transpositions, 2-26
Treasurer, 8-4
Treasury stock, 13-11–13-15
   purchase of, 13-11
   retirement of, 13-15
   sale of, 13-11–13-14
   in statement of cash flows, 16-15–16-16
Trend analysis, 15-7–15-8
Trial balance, 2-24–2-26
   adjusted, 3-22–3-24
   correcting errors in, 2-25–2-26
   post-closing, 4-16–4-17
   preparing financial statements from, 2-24–2-25
   unadjusted, 3-6

U

Unadjusted trial balance, 3-6
Uncollectible accounts, 9-6–9-18, 10-6–10-18
   allowance method for, 9-8–9-18, 10-8–10-18
   direct write-off method for, 9-6–9-7, 10-6–10-7
Uncollectible accounts expense, 9-6, 10-6
Underwriters, 13-7
Unearned revenue. *See* Deferred revenue
Unemployment compensation taxes, 11-11–11-12
Unlimited personal liability, of partners, 12-3
Unqualified opinions, 15-3

V

Vacation benefits, 11-15
Vendors, 7-7
   gifts from, 5-9
Vertical analysis, 15-8–15-10
   of balance sheet, 15-10
   of income statement, 15-9

W

Wages, 11-6
Warranties, 11-15–11-16
Weighted-average method, 6-11–6-14
   periodic inventory system and, 6-26
   perpetual inventory system and, 6-11–6-14
Wholesalers, 5-2
Withdrawal of a partner, 12-17–12-19
   bonus to existing partners and, 12-18–12-19
   bonus to withdrawing partner and, 12-19
   at book value, 12-18
   death of a partner and, 12-19
Withholding allowances, 11-7
Withholding deductions. *See* Employee payroll withholding deductions
Working capital, 15-14–15-15, 15-26
Worksheets, 3-26–3-28
   financial statement preparation and, 4-7–4-9
Write-offs, 9-1, 10-1

Company Index

A
Amazon.com, Inc., 9-1, 9-12, 9-25, 9-54, 16-1, 16-17, 16-66

B
Berkshire Hathaway, Inc., 15-1, 15-15, 15-31

C
Cedar Fair, L.P., 12-1, 12-5, 12-50
Chipotle Mexican Grill, Inc., 8-1, 8-16, 8-52

D
Dick's Sporting Goods, Inc., 6-1, 6-18, 6-54

F
Facebook, Inc., 13-1, 13-6, 13-56
Fry's Electronics, 2-20, 2-61

H
Hyatt Hotels Corporation, 4-1, 4-15

I
iHeartMedia, Inc., 3-1, 3-25, 3-63

K
Kohl's Corporation, 1-22, 2-27, 4-19, 5-27, 6-3, 6-22–6-23, 8-24–8-25, 8-53, 10-29–10-30, 10-56, 11-19, 13-28, 14-20, 14-52, 15-15, 15-32, 17-4

M
Macy's, Inc., 5-1, 5-10, 5-78
McDonald's Corporation, 10-1, 10-29, 10-55

R
Raymond James Financial, Inc., 17-1

S
Starbucks Corporation, 1-1, 1-20, 1-51

T
Target Corporation, 1-23, 1-53, 3-65, 6-55, 8-53, 10-56, 13-57, 14-52, 15-32, 16-68

U
UnitedHealth Group Incorporated, 11-1, 11-16

W
The Walt Disney Company, 14-1, 14-19, 14-50

Photo Credits

Front Matter
Page iii: (top) Bill Woodhull; (bottom) Richard Smith

Chapter 1
Page 1-1: (top) Bragin Alexey/Shutterstock; (middle right) Barbara Tripp/Shutterstock; (bottom left) lightwavemedia/Shutterstock; page 1-2: (top right) Fotolia; page 1-4: Monkey Business Images/Shutterstock; page 1-15: (top) Iodrakon/Shutterstock; (bottom right) michaeljung/Shutterstock; page 1-19: Rido/Shutterstock; page 1-20: Mike Flippo/Shutterstock

Chapter 2
Page 2-1: (top) Djordje Radivojevic/Shutterstock; (middle right) amasterphotographer/Shutterstock; (bottom left) pikselstock/Shutterstock; page 2-2: (top left) allstars/Shutterstock; (middle right) Djordje Radivojevic/Shutterstock; (bottom left) lithian/Shutterstock; page 2-5: Monkey Business Images/Shutterstock; page 2-7: Iodrakon/Shutterstock; page 2-15: michaeljung/Shutterstock

Chapter 3
Page 3-1: (top) Ragnarocks/Fotolia; (middle right) Brand X Pictures/Stockbyte/Getty Images; (bottom left) Yuri Arcurs/Fotolia; page 3-2: (top right) Illustrart/Fotolia; (bottom left) Lisa F. Young/Shutterstock; page 3-11: Rido/Shutterstock

Chapter 4
Page 4-1: (top) Dimedrol68/Shutterstock; (middle right) njaj/Shutterstock; (bottom left) mountainpix/Shutterstock; page 4-2: (top right) Andrew Buckin/Shutterstock; page 4-8: Mike Flippo/Shutterstock; page 4-13: lithian/Shutterstock

Chapter 5
Page 5-1: (top) wasanajai/Shutterstock; (middle right) Gino Santa Maria/Shutterstock; (bottom left) Pavelbendov/Fotolia; page 5-2: (top left) Eimantas Buzas/Shutterstock; (middle right) Diana Taliun/Shutterstock; page 5-4: Monkey Business Images/Shutterstock; page 5-9: iodrakon/Shutterstock; page 5-13: Lisa F. Young/Shutterstock

Chapter 6
Page 6-1: (top) Ari N/Shutterstock; (middle right) Luisa Leal Photography/Shutterstock (bottom left) Blend Images/Alamy Stock Photo; p. 6-2: (top left) Tritooth/Fotolia; (middle right) yevgeniy11/Shutterstock; page 6-15: michaeljung/Shutterstock

Chapter 7
Page 7-1: (top) Zhukov Oleg/Shutterstock; (middle right) Stefan/Fotolia; (bottom left) NatUlrich/Shutterstock; page 7-2: (top right) djama/Fotolia

Chapter 8
Page 8-1: (top) Todd Taulman Photography/Shutterstock; (middle right) Eric Gevaert/Shutterstock; (bottom left) michaeljung/Shutterstock; page 8-2: (middle right) krungchingpixs/Shutterstock; page 8-13: Rido/Shutterstock

Chapter 9
Page 9-1: (top) Jmiks/Shutterstock; (middle right) Josep Suria/Shutterstock; (bottom left) ESB Professional/Shutterstock; page 9-2: (top right) Photobac/Shutterstock; page 9-9: Mike Flippo/Shutterstock; page 9-15: lithian/Shutterstock

Chapter 10
Page 10-1: (top) J. Helgason/Shutterstock; (middle right) Kjpargeter/Shutterstock; (bottom left) Dmitry Kalinovsky/Shutterstock; page 10-2: (middle right) JPL Designs/Shutterstock; page 10-14: Monkey Business Images/Shutterstock; page 10-26: iodrakon/Shutterstock; page 10-28: (bottom right) Mim Friday/Alamy Stock Photo

Chapter 11
Page 11-1: (top) Y H Lim/Alamy Stock Photo; (middle right) Elisanth/Shutterstock; (bottom left) Carlo Dapino/Shutterstock; page 11-2: (top right) Pan Xunbin/Shutterstock; page 11-9: michaeljung/Shutterstock

Chapter 12
Page 12-1: (top) Flipser/Shutterstock; (middle right) kartouchken/123RF; (bottom left) Guenter Fischer/Getty Images; page 12-2: (middle right) kartouchken/Fotolia; page 12-14: Lisa F. Young/Shutterstock

Chapter 13
Page 13-1: (top) AG-PHOTOS/Shutterstock; (middle right) Nuttapong/Shutterstock; (bottom left) StockLite Shutterstock; page 13-2: (top right) David C. Dominici/Shutterstock; page 13-5: Rido/Shutterstock

Chapter 14
Page 14-1: (top) Albachiaraa/Fotolia; (middle right) Arkadiusz Fajer/Fotolia; (bottom left) PeopleImages/Getty; page 14-2: (top left) Shutterstock; (middle right) Alex Staroseltsev/Shutterstock; page 14-5: Mike Flippo/Shutterstock; page 14-9: lithian/Shutterstock

Chapter 15
Page 15-1: (top) Iodrakon/Shutterstock; (middle right) Bambuh/Shutterstock; (bottom left) MinDof/Shutterstock; page 15-2: (top right) Ievgenii Meyer/Shutterstock; page 15-9: Monkey Business Images/Shutterstock

Chapter 16
Page 16-1: (top) Nielskliim/Shutterstock; (middle right) kongsky/Shutterstock; (bottom left) HomeArt/Shutterstock; page 16-2: (top left) Aaron Amat/Shutterstock; (middle right) untitled/Shutterstock; page 16-10: iodrakon/Shutterstock; page 16-26: michaeljung/Shutterstock

Chapter 17
Page 17-1: (top) get4net/Fotolia; (middle right) rangizzz/Fotolia; (bottom left) IMAGEMORE Co. Ltd./Alamy Stock Photo; page 17-2: (middle right) Pokomeda/Shutterstock; page 17-8: Lisa F. Young/Shutterstock